SOURCEBOOK ON LAW OF TRUSTS

Second Edition

Cavendish Publishing Limited

London • Sydney

SOURCEBOOK ON LAW OF TRUSTS

Second Edition

Mohamed Ramjohn, LLB, LLM, ATII, JP
Barrister, Principal Lecturer in Law
Thames Valley University

Cavendish Publishing Limited

London • Sydney

First published in 1998 by Cavendish Publishing Limited, The Glass House, Wharton Street, London WC1X 9PX, United Kingdom
Telephone: +44 (0) 171 278 8000 Facsimile: +44 (0) 171 278 8080
E-mail: info@cavendishpublishing.com
Visit our Home Page on http://www.cavendishpublishing.com

First edition 1995
Second edition 1998

British Library Cataloguing in Publication Data.

Ramjohn, M
Sourcebook on Law of Trusts – 2nd ed
1. Trusts and trustees– England – Digests
2. Trusts and trustees – Wales – Digests
I. Title
346.4′2′2059

ISBN 1 85941 186 X

Printed and bound in Great Britain by
Biddles Ltd, Guildford and King's Lynn

To C, F and N

PREFACE TO THE FIRST EDITION

The law of trusts has developed over the centuries as essentially a case law subject tempered occasionally by statutory intervention. Indeed, trust law continues to develop in modern society as new situations arise. Such developments are best traced by considering the exposition of judges and the precise words used in statutes. The principal objectives of writing this book are to present the relevant principles of law in an intelligible and simplified form and, at the same time, to provide easy access to a collection of primary source materials in an effort to facilitate understanding of the law and stimulate critical thought. In my experience, the initial perception of the difficulty of the subject is grossly exaggerated. Trusts law is adaptable and stimulating with the right chemical balance of challenge and interest!

This collection of primary source materials is intended to be suitable for university law students and those reading trusts for professional examinations.

The facts of the more important cases and statutory materials are stated in the text and are not relegated to footnotes. The book does not attempt to cover all the topics that are sometimes included in an equity course. The equitable doctrines of conversion, reconversion, satisfaction, performance, election and assignment have been omitted. It is the author's view that these topics may be more conventionally studied in a succession or probate law textbook. In addition, the equitable remedies of specific performance, injunctions, rectification and rescission have been omitted from this work. It would not have been possible to do justice to these topics within the constraints appropriate to a book of this kind. Many informative books on these topics are readily available on the market.

I would like to thank the members of staff at Cavendish Publishing who have assisted me in the preparation of this book. I am especially grateful to Jo Reddy and Sonny Leong, without whose support and encouragement this work would not have been possible. My thanks are also due to Professor Paul Dobson and Mr George Webster, both of Thames Valley University, who, despite not having a direct connection with the production of this book, have rendered invaluable indirect assistance and encouragement.

M Ramjohn
December 1994

PREFACE TO THE SECOND EDITION

The four years which have passed since the publication of the first edition of this book have been a period of rapid development in the law of trusts. This has necessitated extensive revision of the text. As far as statutory material is concerned, the Trusts of Land and Appointment of Trustees Act 1996 has had a pervasive effect on the subject. This involved major rewriting of Chapters 10, 18 and 19.

In view of the vast array of case law on the subject, the uninitiated may be tempted to conclude that it is possible to argue any proposition, either way, with equal legal justification. But devotees of the subject will recognise that it is generally the more recent decisions which can be regarded as being the more authoritative. Some of the recent case law developments include: *Royal Brunei Airlines Sdn Bhd v Tan Ming* [1995] 3 WLR 64 (dishonest third party liable as a constructive trustee for assisting the trustee to commit a breach of trust); *Target Holdings Ltd v Redferns* [1995] 3 All ER 785 (no causal connection between breach of trust and loss); *Boscawen v Bajwa* [1995] All ER 769 (the extent to which a building society was entitled to trace its funds); *Tribe v Tribe* [1996] Ch 107 (rebuttal of the presumption of advancement regarding a transfer intended for an attempted unlawful purpose); *Neville v Wilson* [1996] 3 All ER 171 (whether a constructive trust within s 53(2) of the Law of Property Act 1925 exempts a disponer from the requirements of s 53(1)(c) of the same Act); *Trustees of FC Jones v Jones* [1996] 3 WLR 703 (tracing investment profits in an action for money had and received); *Westdeutsche Landesbank Girozentrale v Islington BC* [1996] 2 All ER 961 (whether compound interest is payable on sums received by a local authority under an *ultra vires* agreement); *Goulding v James* [1997] 2 All ER 239 (whether a testator's intention is relevant in deciding to approve a scheme of variation); *Kershaw v Wallis (No 2)* (1997) *The Times*, 10 February (claim in equity not statute-barred); *Foskett v McKeown* [1997] 3 All ER 392 (trust beneficiaries' right to trace trust funds); *Armitage v Nurse* [1997] 3 WLR 1046 (the effect of an exclusion clause designed to limit the liability of trustees); *Swindle v Harrison* [1997] 4 All ER 705 (whether loss to the trust flowed from breach of fiduciary duties); and *AG v Blake* [1998] 1 All ER 833 (whether the profits earned from the memoirs of a secret agent are payable to the Crown). There are still many areas of uncertainty and confusion which are a source of great complexity and in respect of which only time and further decisions may provide solutions.

The publishers and I were particularly anxious to ensure that this book is accessible to, and the contents are easily digestible by, undergraduates and other students reading trusts law. I have approached this task and included appropriate materials with this objective in mind. The structure and layout of the text and materials were designed to produce a book with the flow, coherence and direction of a textbook and to provide the reader with a substantial amount of material, from a variety of sources, to be absorbed.

I would like to thank all those who reviewed the first edition. Many of the suggestions made for the book's improvement have been taken on board.

Innovations include guidance within the text from a small selection of articles. I have endeavoured to compile a list of articles for supplementary reading at the end of each chapter. As a result partly of this new material, and partly of further reflection on presenting the materials, the size of the book has increased by over 150 pages. Indeed, very few pages have escaped entirely without change.

I wish to thank my colleagues at Thames Valley University for their enormous patience and support while this edition was being prepared. Those who deserve specific mention include Sodi Kakouris, Kwame Akuffo, Sue Collier, Diana Iller, Margaret Britt and Hilary Panford. I am extremely grateful to Jo Reddy and the editorial staff of Cavendish Publishing for their assistance in producing this edition.

I have tried to explain and summarise the law of trusts up to June 1998. As ever, the responsibility for all errors and omissions rests with me.

M Ramjohn

June 1998

ACKNOWLEDGMENTS

The author and publishers are most grateful and would like to thank the following for permission to reproduce copyright material:

Blackwell Publishers for extracts from the Modern Law Review.

Butterworths for extracts from the All England Law Reports.

The Incorporated Council for Law Reporting for England and Wales: for extracts from the Law Reports and Weekly Law Reports.

Jordan Publishing for extracts from the Family Law Reports.

Sweet and Maxwell for extracts from the Property, Planning and Compensation Reports, the Conveyancer and the Law Quarterly Review.

Tolley Publishing for extracts from Trust Law International.

Blackstone Press for extracts from the Web Journal of Current Legal Issues.

CONTENTS

TABLE OF CASES

TABLE OF STATUTES

TABLE OF ABBREVIATIONS

All England Law Reports	All ER
Ambler	Amb
American Journal of International Law	AJIL
Appeal Cases	AC
Appeal Cases	App Cas
Australian Law Reports	ALR
Atkyns	Atk
Bankruptcy and Commercial Law Cases	BCLC
Beaven	Beav
Bligh's New Series	Bli (NS)
Brown	Bro
Brown's Reports of Cases in Chancery	Bro CC
British Tax Review	BTR
Calthrop's Customs and Liberties of London	Cal
Cambridge Law Journal	CLJ
Cases in Chancery	Ch Cas
Chancery Division	Ch D
Chancery Division	Ch
Clerk and Finnelly	Cl & Fin
Common Law Reports	CLR
Commonwealth Law Reports	Com LR
Current Law Yearbook	CLY
Cowper	Cowp
Conveyancer and Property Lawyer	Conv
Cox Equity	Cox Eq
Cray and Phillips	Cr & Ph
De Gex and Smale	De G & Sm
De Gex, Fisher and Jones	De GF & J
Dickens	Dick
De Gex, Jones and Smith	DJ & S
Douglas	Dougl
Ellis and Ellis	E & E
Estates Gazette	EG
Exchequer Division	Ex D
Equity Cases	Eq
Espinasse	Esp
Family Law Reports	FLR
House of Lords' Cases	HL Cas
Irish Reports	IR
Journal of Business Law	JBL
Johnson and Hemming	J & H

King's Bench Law Reports	KB
Law Journal, Chancery	LJ Ch
Law Journal, King's Bench	LJKB
Law Reports, Scotch and Divorce Appeals	LR Sc & Div
Law Recorder, Ireland	LRIR
Law Times, New Series	LT
Law Times Reports	LTOS
MacNaghten and Gordon	Mac & G
Merivale	MER
Myline and Craig	My & Cr
Myline and Keen	My & K
Modern Law Review	MLR
Northern Ireland Law Reports	NI
New South Wales Law Reports	NSWLR
Law Report, Probate Division	P
Property and Compensation Reports	P & CR
Phillips	Ph
Peere Williams	P Wms
Queen's Bench Law Reports	QB/QBD
Reports in Chancery	Rep Ch
Reports of Patents, Design and Trade Marks Cases	RPC
Russell	Russ
Select Cases	Sel Ca
Simons	Sim
Simon's Tax Cases	STC
Solicitor's Journal	SJ
Trusts and Trustees International Asset Management	T & T
Tax Cases	TC
Times Law Reports	TLR
Trust Law International	Tru LI
Vesey	Ves
Vesey Junior	Ves Jun
Victoria Law Reports	VLR
Weekly Law Reports	WLR
Weekly Notes	WN

CHAPTER 1

HISTORICAL OUTLINES OF EQUITY

> Equity is the branch of law, which, before the Judicature Acts 1873–75 was applied and administered by the Court of Chancery. [Maitland, I, *Lectures on Equity*, 1969, Cambridge: CUP.]

Originally, the expressions 'equity' or 'rules of equity' were synonymous with rules of justice and conscience. Individual Lord Chancellors did not consciously set out to develop a system of rules, but attempted in individual cases to achieve fairness and justice *ad hoc*.

Today, it would not be accurate to correlate 'equity' with 'justice' for rules of equity have become settled in much the same way as the common law.

PETITIONS TO THE LORD CHANCELLOR

In the 13th century, the available writs covered a narrow ground – even if a claim came within the scope of an existing writ, the plaintiff may not achieve justice before a common law court, for example, in an action commenced by the writs of debt and detinue, the defendant was entitled to wage his law. In addition, a great deal of unnecessary intricacies were attendant on the pleadings. The pleadings were drafted by experts and the rule in those days was that an incorrect pleading invariably led to the loss of the claim. Moreover, only damages was available as a remedy at law. There were numerous occasions when this remedy proved inadequate.

An aggrieved plaintiff was entitled to petition the King in Council praying for relief. These petitions were dealt with by the King's Prime Minister – the Lord Chancellor who was an ecclesiastic well versed in the law. Later on, the petitions were addressed directly to the Lord Chancellor who personally dealt with the more important cases. Eventually the Chancellor and staff formed a court called the Court of Chancery.

Procedure in Chancery

The petition was presented by way of a bill filed by the plaintiff. Since proceedings were not commenced by writ as in the common law courts there was never any strict procedure to be followed. The intervention by the Lord Chancellor (creating new rights and remedies) did not need validation by the pretence adopted by the common law courts of declaring the law from time immemorial, but the Chancellor did not abandon his responsibility in deciding on the justice and merits of individual cases.

A *subpoena* in appropriate cases would be served on the defendant to compel his appearance to attend and answer the petition. The defendant was required to draft his answers on oath called 'interrogatories'.

Usually the evidence was given on affidavit so that proceedings were confined to hearing legal arguments on both sides, but occasionally when the testimony of a witness (including the parties) is required to be received in the court, the witness would testify on oath and be subject to cross-examination by the Chancellor and the opposing party.

The relevant decree of the court was issued in the name of the Chancellor and acted *in personam* on the defendant.

CONTENTS OF EQUITY

One of the most important contributions of equity was in the field of the use or trust.

Use

There were a variety of reasons for the creation of a use in the 13th and 14th centuries.

Crusades

A landowner who went on the crusades and fearing for his life and the consequences of a succession of his wealth may convey land to another (B) during the crusade. Before the Wills Act 1540, wills were not recognised at common law.

Ownership by Franciscan monks

As a result of their vow as to poverty, a community of Franciscan monks may transfer land to B, C and D to their use.

Avoidance of feudal incidents

By far the most important reason for the creation of a use was to avoid the feudal incidents inherent in land ownership such as wardship and *escheat* (no heir). These burdens were avoided if the land was vested in a number of *feoffees to use* (trustees). The feoffees were unlikely to die together or without heir. Those who died could be replaced. The feoffees to use were required to hold the land for the benefit of the *cestui que* trust (or beneficiary).

Position of feoffee

At law, the feoffee was regarded as the absolute owner of the property and liable to the incidents of tenure, that is, the common law did not recognise the interest of the *cestui que* trust. But in Chancery, the feoffee was compelled to carry out their obligations created by the use, that is, to recognise the interest and act for the benefit of the *cestui que* trust. Moreover, the Chancery developed the rule that any third parties who took the land from the feoffee with knowledge of the existence of the use, was bound by the use. Hence the rule which subsists today that the use (or trust) is valid against the world except a *bona fide* transferee of the legal estate for value without notice.

Position of the *cestui que* use

This individual's interest was not recognised at law but was granted recognition in equity and thus acquired an equitable interest. He was entitled to petition the Court of Chancery to have his interest and rights protected against the feoffee and the world.

Statute of Uses 1535

The principal objection to the use was the loss to the King of revenue that arose from the incidents of tenure. The King needed all the revenue he could muster during the 16th century and the growth of the use hindered this process. Ultimately, the Statute of Uses 1535 was passed to reduce the scope of the use.

The statute provided that:

> ... where any person(s) shall be seised of any lands or other hereditaments to the use, confidence or trust of any person(s), in every such case such person(s) that shall have any such use, confidence or trust in fee simple, fee tail, term of life or for years or otherwise shall stand and be seised, deemed and adjudged in lawful seisin, estate and possession of and in the same lands in such like estates as they had or shall have in the use.

The statute did not suppress all uses. It only applied where the *feoffee was seised to the use of another* – if the feoffee held only for a term of years he would not be seised and the statute would not apply. In addition, where the feoffee had active duties to perform the statute did not apply because the *cestui que* use acquired property only after the feoffee had collected the rents and profits or performed his duties. In any event the Act did not execute uses in respect of personal property.

Use upon a use

The effect of the Statute of Uses was not to abolish uses *per se* but executed the use, whereby the *cestui que* use became the legal owner and the feudal dues were collected from him.

For example, A (feoffee) holds land to the use of B (*cestui que* use). Under the Act, B became the legal owner (and beneficial owner).

A technique was adopted in order to create 'a use upon a use' in the hope that the first use would be executed and the second use rendered effective, that is, 'to A to the use of B to the use of C'. The effect of this technique was that B held the property to the use of C.

This device did not find favour with the courts at law. The method adopted for defeating this avoidance practice was to treat the second use as repugnant to the first use and thus void. In *Jane Tyrrel's Case*,[1] JT settled land in favour of herself for life, remainder to her son with a gift over ('to the use of JT for life remainder to her son with a gift over to the heirs of JT'). The court held that the second use was repugnant and void and the son took absolutely.

The Court of Chancery at first did not disagree with this result even though B was never intended to be the beneficial owner. By the 17th century the decline in the value of money led to the feudal dues becoming of little consequence. This factor motivated the Chancellor to give effect to the intention of the creator of the use (settlor). All that was necessary was to add a second use and make the conveyance run 'to the use of B upon trust for C'. The effect was that B was called a trustee, who held the legal title and C, a beneficiary or *cestui que* trust, who held the equitable title.

Struggle over injunctions

The Court of Chancery adopted the strategy of issuing a 'common injunction' against the litigant who had obtained a common law remedy unjustly or indeed to prevent him resorting to the common law to obtain a remedy. The use of the common injunction had the effect of sterilising the common law order and was viewed with great dissatisfaction by common law judges. In the *Earl of Oxford* case,[2] an action was brought in respect of a lease. Judgment in default was entered in favour of the original plaintiff at common law. The defendant (petitioner) instituted a suit in the Chancery Court. A common injunction was issued against the original plaintiff, and he was served with a *subpoena* to appear in the Chancery Court.

The Court of Chancery held that the defendant was entitled to relief.

1 (1557) Dyer 155.
2 (1615) 1 Rep Ch 1.

> **Lord Ellesmere LC:** The office of the Chancellor is to correct man's consciences for frauds, breach of trusts, wrongs and oppressions of whatsoever nature and to soften and mollify the extremity of the law ... When judgment is obtained by oppression, wrong and a hard conscience, the Chancellor will frustrate and set it aside, not for any error or defect in the judgment but for the hard conscience of the party.

The controversy was eventually resolved by James I in the 17th century. He referred the matter to Bacon, the Attorney General and others learned in the law. They decided in favour of the Court of Chancery. Thereafter, by and large, the principles of common law and equity were treated as parts of a complete body of law. This prompted Maitland to write 'Equity came not to destroy the law but to fulfil it' (Maitland, I, *Lectures on Equity*, 1969, Cambridge: CUP).

CONTRIBUTIONS OF EQUITY

The contributions of equity in the development of the law may be classified into three categories:

(a) exclusive jurisdiction (new rights). This category refers to the rights which the Court of Chancery had created and which the common law courts failed to enforce, for example, trusts, mortgages, partnerships, administration of estates, bankruptcy company law, etc;

(b) concurrent jurisdiction (new remedies). Equity developed a wide range of remedies for the enforcement of rights both at law and in equity. They are all discretionary. Examples are:

  (i) specific performance – an order to force the defendant to fulfil his bargain;

  (ii) injunctions – an order to restrain a party from committing a wrong;

  (iii) rectification – an order of the court requiring the defendant to modify a document to reflect the agreement made with the plaintiff;

  (iv) account – an order requiring a party who has control of money belonging to the plaintiff, to report on the way in which the funds have been spent;

(c) auxiliary jurisdiction (new procedures). Procedural rules created by the Court of Chancery are discovery of documents, testimony on oath, *subpoena* of witnesses and interrogatories.

Court of Appeal in Chancery

The 18th and 19th centuries witnessed great strides forward in the development of equity. However, the personnel in the Court of Chancery proved to be corrupt. Frequently such personnel were bribed in order to issue the common injunction. In addition, the court became overloaded with petitions which resulted in delays. Until 1813, there were only two judges in the Court of Chancery, namely, the Lord Chancellor and the Master of the Rolls. They were unhurried in arriving at their decisions.

In 1813, a Vice Chancellor was appointed. In 1841, two more Vice Chancellors were appointed. In 1851, two Lord Justices of Appeal in Chancery were appointed. By the early 19th century, the Lord Chancellor had ceased to hear petitions at first instance. In 1851, the Court of Appeal in Chancery was created to hear appeals from decisions of Vice Chancellors and the Master of the Rolls. This court consisted of the Lord Chancellor and two Lords Justices of Appeal. There was a further appeal to the House of Lords.

Nineteenth century reforms

Before Parliament intervened, the Court of Chancery was capable of granting only equitable remedies. Likewise, common law courts could have granted only the legal remedy of damages. This inconvenience was overcome by two statutory provisions:

(1) the Common Law Procedure Act 1854. This Act permitted the common law courts to grant equitable remedies;

(2) the Chancery Amendment Act 1858 (Lord Cairns' Act). This Act gave the Court of Chancery power to award damages in addition to or in substitution for an injunction or specific performance.

But, what was needed was a more radical change which fused the administration of law and equity. It was an unnecessary waste of time and resources to require claimants entitled to common law and equitable rights or remedies to go to the respective court to redress their wrongs.

This change was effected by the Judicature Acts 1873–1975 which adopted the following policies:

(1) the abolition of the separate courts of Queen's Bench, Exchequer, Common Pleas, Chancery, Probate, the Divorce Court and the Court of Admiralty. Instead, the Supreme Court of the Judicature was created. The High Court was divided into divisions known as the Queen's Bench, Chancery and the Probate, Divorce and Admiralty. (The latter was renamed the Family Division, the Admiralty jurisdiction was transferred to the Queen's Bench Division and the probate business was transferred to the Chancery Division under the Administration of Justice Act 1970.);

(2) each division of the High Court exercises both legal and equitable jurisdiction. Thus, any point of law or equity may be raised in and determined by any division;

(3) it was foreseen that a court which applied rules of common law and equity would face a conflict where the common law rules produce one result and equity rules another, for example, s 4 of the Statute of Frauds 1677 (now repealed) enacted that contracts for the sale or other disposition of land must be evidenced in writing. The strict common law rule was rigidly adhered to whether this produced unjust results or not. Equity adopted a notion of part performance which entitled the court to intervene in order to prevent fraud even though all the terms of the contract were not in writing.

Section 25(11) of the Judicature Act 1873 provides:

> Generally, in all matters not hereinbefore mentioned in which there is any conflict or variance between the rules of equity and the rules of common law with reference to the same matter, the rules of equity shall prevail.

The effect of the Acts is therefore procedural in the sense that the administration of law and equity has been fused as distinct from the fusion of the rules of law and equity.

Maxims of equity

The intervention of the court of equity over the centuries may be reduced into a number of maxims. The importance of the maxims ought not to be overstated. They are far from being rigid principles but exist as terse sentences which only illustrate the policy underlying specific principles.

Equity will not suffer a wrong to be without a remedy

This maxim illustrates the intervention of the Court of Chancery to provide a remedy if none was obtainable at common law. At the same time it must not be supposed that every infringement of a right was capable of being remedied. The 'wrongs' which equity was prepared to invent new remedies to redress were those subject to judicial enforcement in the first place.

Equity follows the law

The view originally taken by the court of equity was that deliberate and carefully considered rules of common law would be followed. Equity only intervened when some important factor became ignored by the law.

Where there is equal equity, the law prevails

Equity did not intervene when, according to equitable principles, no injustice results in adopting the solution imposed by law.

Thus, the *bona fide* purchaser of the legal estate for value without notice is capable of acquiring an equitable interest both at law and in equity.

Where the equities are equal, the first in time prevails

Where two persons have conflicting interests in the same property the rule is that the first in time has priority at law and in equity, *qui prior est tempore potior est jure*.

He who seeks equity must do equity

A party who claims equitable relief is required to act fairly towards his opponent, for example, a tracing order would not be obtained in equity if the effect would be to promote injustice.

He who comes to equity must come with clean hands

The assumption here is that the plaintiff or party claiming an equitable relief must demonstrate that he has not acted with impropriety in respect of the claim.

Delay defeats equity (equity aids the vigilant and not the indolent)

Where a party has slept on his rights and has given the defendant the impression that he has waived his rights, a court of equity may refuse its assistance to the plaintiff. This is known as the doctrine of laches.

Equality is equity

Where two or more parties have an interest in the same property but their respective interests have not been quantified, equity as a last resort may divide the interest equally.

Equity looks at the intent rather than the form

The court looks at the substance of an arrangement rather than its appearance in order to ascertain the intention of the parties, for example, a deed is not treated in equity as a substitute for consideration.

Equity imputes an intention to fulfil an obligation

The principle here is based on the premise that if a party is under an obligation to perform an act and he performs an alternative but similar act, equity assumes that the second act was done with the intention of fulfilling the obligation.

Equity regards as done that which ought to be done

If a person is under an obligation to perform an act which is specifically enforceable, the parties acquire the same rights and liabilities in equity as though the act had been performed.

Equity acts in personam

Originally, equitable orders were enforced against the person of the defendant with the ultimate sanction of imprisonment. A later equitable invention permitted an order to be attached to the defendant's property, that is, *in rem*. Today this maxim has lost much of its importance.

SUPPLEMENTARY READING

Winder, W, 'Precedent in equity' (1941) 57 LQR 245

Mason, A, 'The place of equity and equitable remedies in contemporary society' (1994) 110 LQR 238

Gardner, S, 'Two maxims of equity' (1995) 54 CLJ 60

Pettit, P, 'He who comes into equity must come with clean hands' [1990] Conv 416

CHAPTER 2

INTRODUCTION TO TRUSTS

DEFINITION

There are a variety of definitions of trusts which have been used from time to time. It is not an easy task to offer a precise definition of a trust for the concept has been developed piecemeal over a number of centuries.

Underhill's definition

> A trust is an equitable obligation binding a person (called a trustee) to deal with property over which he has control (called the trust property) for the benefit of persons (called beneficiaries or *cestui que* trust) of whom he himself may be one and any of whom may enforce the obligation. [Underhill, A and Hayton, D, *Law of Trusts and Trustees*, 14th edn, 1987, London: Butterworths, p 1.]

It should be noted that, although this is a fairly comprehensive definition, charitable trusts such as the RSPCA and the NSPCC (enforceable by the Attorney General) and, exceptionally, valid private purpose trusts (not enforceable by the beneficiaries) are excluded from the definition. However, Underhill's definition highlights a number of features inherent in trust law such as the obligatory nature of trusts, the notion that control is vested in the trustees on behalf of beneficiaries who are entitled to protect their interests and enforce the trust duties.

In essence, the mechanism of the trust is an equitable device by which property is controlled by trustees for the benefit of others, called beneficiaries. For a variety of reasons it may be prudent to prevent the entire ownership of property (both legal and equitable) being vested and enjoyed by one person. A trust may be set up in order to advance such objective.

By origin, the trust was the exclusive product of the now defunct Court of Chancery, but since the Judicature Acts 1873 and 1875 trusts may be enforced in any court of law.

Article 2 of the Recognition of Trusts Act 1987

Enacting the terms of the Hague Convention on the Recognition of Trusts:

> For the purposes of this Convention, the term 'trust' refers to the legal relationship created – *inter vivos* or on death – by a person, the settlor, when assets have been placed under the control of a trustee for the benefit of a beneficiary or for a specified purpose.

> A trust has the following characteristics:
>
> (a) the assets constitute a separate fund and are not a part of the trustee's own estate;
>
> (b) title to the trust assets stands in the name of another person on behalf of the trustee;
>
> (c) the trustee has the power and the duty, in respect of which he is accountable, to manage, employ or dispose of the assets in accordance with the terms of the trust and the special duties imposed upon him by law.
>
> The reservation by the settlor of certain rights and powers and the fact that the trustee may himself have rights as a beneficiary, are not necessarily inconsistent with the existence of a trust.

This definition has been formulated by reference to the characteristics of a trust.

Characteristics of a trust

The following list sets out some of the main features of a trust:

Mandatory

A trust (unlike a power of distribution) is obligatory. The trustees have no choice as to whether or not they may fulfil the intention of the settlor. The trustees are required to fulfil the terms of the trust as stipulated in the trust instrument and implied by rules of law. The trustees have a number of duties imposed on them in order to maintain a balance between the trustees and the beneficiaries, for example, trustees are not allowed to derive a benefit from acting as trustees unless authorised. The beneficiaries are given a *locus standi* to ensure that the trustees carry out their duties. (But, note the anomalous nature of private purpose trusts, see below, p 534.)

Separation of the legal and equitable titles

The legal title to property is a representation to the world that the legal owner has the right to retain and control the property. The equitable title is the right to enjoy the property. Such right may be enforced against anyone interfering with the interest except a *bona fide* transferee of the legal estate for value without notice. The equitable owner under a 'bare trust' (that is, a trust under which the trustees have no active duties to perform) is incapable of asserting his rights to the assets as against a *bona fide* purchaser of the legal interest from the trustee.

***MCC Proceeds Inc v Lehman Brothers International (Europe)* (1998) *The Times*, January 14, CA**

Macmillan Incorporated, a Delaware company, was taken over in 1988 by Maxwell Communications Corporation plc (MCC) and became controlled by

Robert Maxwell and members of his family. Macmillan Inc placed shares in a wholly owned subsidiary (Berlitz International Inc) together with the relevant share certificates, in the name of Bishopsgate Investment Trust plc (a nominee company controlled by Mr Maxwell). An agreement was entered into declaring that Bishopsgate held the legal title to the shares as nominees for Macmillan, who retained the beneficial interest in the shares. The agreement specified that, on Macmillan's written demand, Bishopsgate would immediately transfer the shares to Macmillan. Without Macmillan's knowledge or consent, Bishopsgate pledged the certificates with the defendants as collateral under a stock lending scheme. The defendants, who were ignorant of Macmillan's interest in the shares and certificates, subsequently arranged for the cancellation of the certificates on transfer of the shares into a central depository paperless system in New York. The defendants subsequently sold the shares to an associated company, Shearson Lehman Bros Holdings plc. The plaintiffs, who were Macmillan's successors and assignees, instituted proceedings against the defendants in conversion. The claim was based on the ground that Macmillan had a beneficial interest in the shares and certificates and was entitled to an immediate right to possession. Such interest, the plaintiffs claimed, was sufficient to maintain an action in conversion and that the defendants' lack of knowledge of Bishopsgate's wrongdoing or of Macmillan's interest was no defence to the conversion claim. The judge granted an application to the defendants to strike out the plaintiffs' claim for conversion on the ground that no reasonable cause of action was disclosed on the facts. The plaintiffs appealed to the Court of Appeal.

The Court of Appeal dismissed the appeal on the following grounds:

(a) the defendants, who were *bona fide* purchasers of the legal interest in the shares without notice of any breach of trust by Bishopsgate or of any claim by Macmillan, acquired good title to the shares and certificates, free from any adverse claims. Thus, the plaintiffs' claim was extinguished. The plaintiffs enjoyed an equitable interest in the shares and certificates and, in the circumstances, their interest was overreached;

(b) a claim for conversion of goods was not maintainable by a person who had only an equitable interest in the property. Conversion was a common law cause of action and the common law did not recognise the equitable interests of beneficiaries under a trust. Accordingly, the common law recognised only the title of the trustee as a person normally entitled to immediate possession of the trust property. The plaintiffs' claim in conversion could not be maintained as its predecessor in title, Macmillan, had only an equitable interest in the shares and certificates. This rule of substantive law was not altered by the Judicature Acts 1873–75, which merely fused the administration of law and equity.

When the two titles are united in the hands of one person to such an extent that there is no separation of interest (not even a nominal separation), no trust exists. It would follow that such a person, with both legal and equitable interests, has not only the right to control the property but also the right to benefit and enjoy the same.

For example, A buys a computer from his own funds for his sole use. A has both the legal and equitable interests (referred to as the absolute entitlement or title to the property). No trust exists. But if A and B purchase the computer for their joint benefit so that the legal and equitable interests are divided, a trust is created even though the same persons are both trustees and beneficiaries.

One of the key issues in understanding trust law is to appreciate that the two titles (legal and equitable) may be separated. When this is the case a trust is created. The legal title is acquired by the trustee but the beneficial interest or equitable title is acquired by the equitable owner.

The settlor's position

The settlor is the creator of an express trust. He decides the form which the trust property may take, the interests of the beneficiaries, the identity of the beneficiaries, the persons who will be appointed trustees. Indeed, he may appoint himself one of the trustees or the sole trustee. In short, the settlor is the author of the trust.

For example, S, a settlor, purchases land which is conveyed in the names of T and T(1) (trustees) on trust for the sole benefit of B (beneficiary). An express trust is created. Indeed, in this example, S is capable of being one of the trustees and at the same time one of the beneficiaries. S may even be the sole beneficiary under the trust. Once there is a separation of the legal interest from the equitable title (which may be established through more than one owners) a trust is created.

Once the trust is created, the settlor *qua* settlor loses all control or interest in the trust property. Unless he has reserved an interest for himself, he is not entitled to derive a benefit from the trust property nor is he allowed to control the conduct of the trustees. In other words, following the creation of a trust, the settlor in his capacity as settlor is treated as a stranger in respect of the trust.

In *Re Bowden*,[1] the settlor, before becoming a nun and in order to undertake the vows of poverty, chastity and obedience, transferred property to trustees on trust for specified beneficiaries. Later, she changed her mind when she left the convent and attempted to reclaim the property for her benefit. The court held that, since the trust was created, the claimant as a settlor, lost all interest in the property and therefore could not recover the property.

> **Bennett J:** ... the persons appointed trustees under the settlement received the settlor's interest ... and, immediately after it had been received by them, as a

1 [1936] Ch 71.

> result of her own act and her own declaration ... it became impressed with the trusts contained in the settlement.

The trustees' position

The trustees bear the responsibility of controlling and managing the trust property solely for the benefit of the beneficiaries.

They are the representatives of the trust. Owing to the opportunities to take advantage of their position as controllers of the property, rules of equity were formulated to impose a collection of strict and rigorous duties on the trustees. Indeed, the trustees' duties are so onerous that (subject to authority in the trust instrument) the trustees are not even entitled to invest trust moneys as they might do with their own funds, but are required to invest in authorised investments.

Trustees are liable in their personal capacity for mismanaging the trust funds and in extreme cases may be made bankrupt, should they neglect their duties.

The beneficiary's position

The beneficiaries (as the owners of the equitable interest) are given the power to compel the due administration of the trust. They are entitled to sue the trustees and any third party for damages (joining the trustees in the action as co-defendants). In addition, the beneficiaries may trace the trust property in the hands of third parties with the exception of *bona fide* transferees of the legal estate for value without notice. The beneficiaries are given an interest in the trust property and are entitled to assign the whole or part of such interest to others. The beneficiaries are entitled to terminate the trust by directing the trustees to transfer the legal title to them provided that they have attained the age of majority, and are *compos mentis* and absolutely entitled to the trust property. See *Saunders v Vautier* (1841) 4 Beav 115 (below, p 837).

Trust property

Any property which is capable of being transferred may be the subject matter of the trust. Thus, land (real property), chattels (tangible moveable property such as computers), chattel real (leases) or intangible personal property (such as shares in a company, intellectual property, loans, etc) may be the subject matter of a trust.

Inter vivos *or will*

Trusts may be created either *inter vivos* (during the lifetime of the settlor) or on death, by will or on an intestacy (under the Administration of Estates Act 1925 as amended).

Classification of trusts

There are many ways of classifying trusts. The simplest classification is into express, implied and statutory trusts.

Express trusts

An express trust is one created in accordance with the express intention of the settlor. The settlor is required to transfer the relevant property to third party trustees subject to the terms of the trust manifested in favour of the beneficiaries, see *Re Bowden* (above, p 14). Alternatively, the settlor may expressly declare himself a trustee for the benefit of the objects (that is, self-declaration of trust). For example, S, the holder of 900 shares in British Gas plc declares that the shares are held on trust for his son, B, absolutely. S will become the trustee for the benefit of his son.

Express trusts may be sub-classified into 'private' and 'charitable' trusts. Private trusts exist for the benefit of persons or benefit a narrow section of the public. For example, a gift on trust for the education of the children of the settlor. There are a number of anomalous trusts in respect of which the beneficiaries are private purposes. These beneficiaries are obviously incapable of enforcing such trusts, for example, a trust for the benefit of the testator's pets or a trust for the execution and maintenance of a monument in memory of the testator. These are called 'hybrid' trusts or trusts for imperfect obligations. Charitable trusts are public trusts which benefit the public as a whole in a number of specified ways such as the relief of poverty, the advancement of education the propagation of religion and other purposes which are beneficial to society within the spirit and intendment of the preamble to the Charitable Uses Act 1601.

Express trusts may be classified into 'fixed' and 'discretionary' trusts. A fixed trust is one where the beneficiaries and their interests are identified by the settlor. The trustees have no duty to select the beneficiaries or to quantify their interest. The settlor has declared the interests that may be enjoyed by the beneficiaries.

For example, on trust for A for life remainder to B absolutely. A enjoys the interest or income for as long as he lives whereas, B has a vested interest in the capital or the entire property subject to A's interest.

A discretionary trust is one whereby the trustees are given a duty to exercise their discretion in order to distribute the property in favour of a selected group of persons. The objects, individually considered, do not have an interest in the property but have only a hope (*spes*) of acquiring an interest in the property, prior to the exercise of the discretion by the trustees.

For example, £50,000 is transferred to T and T(1) as trustees in order to distribute the property to such of the settlor's relations as the trustees may decide in their absolute discretion. All the settlor's relations are not beneficiaries *simpliciter* but form a class from whom the trustees are required to select and distribute to the appropriate beneficiaries.

For example, for a period of 21 years from the date of the transfer to hold on trust to apply the income to such of the settlor's children as the trustees may decide in their absolute discretion.

Discretionary trusts may be 'exhaustive' or 'non-exhaustive'.

An 'exhaustive' discretionary trust is one where the trustees are required to distribute the income and/or capital to the objects. The trustees are given a discretion as to which objects may benefit and the 'quantum' of the benefit.

A 'non-exhaustive' discretionary trust is one where the trustees are not required to distribute the entirety of the income and/or capital but may retain or accumulate the relevant property at their discretion (see below, p 146).

Implied trusts

There are two types of implied trusts, namely, 'resulting' and 'constructive' trusts.

Resulting trusts

These are trusts which spring back in favour of the settlor in accordance with his presumed intention. The trust may be created in order to fill a gap in ownership or a surplus of trust funds are left over after the trust purpose has been fulfilled. In *Davis v Richards & Wallington Industries*,[2] the question in issue concerned the ownership of surplus funds held by group pension schemes following the appointment of receivers and managers. It was established that the surplus derived from overpayments by the employers. The court decided that the surplus was held on resulting trust for the employer contributors. Similarly, a resulting trust will be set up when a transfer of property is subject to a condition precedent which fails. In *Barclays Bank v Quistclose Investments*,[3] Rolls Razor Ltd negotiated a loan from Quistclose Investments for the specific purpose of paying a dividend on its shares. The sum was paid into a separate account with Barclays Bank. Before the dividend was paid Rolls Razors went into liquidation. On a claim by the bank to be entitled to use the funds to pay off Rolls Razor's debts, the court held that Quistclose was entitled to the return of the funds by way of a resulting trust.

In addition, a 'resulting trust' may be created by the courts in accordance with the presumed intention of the settlor. The settlor or his estate is presumed to be the equitable owner. An occasion giving rise to this presumption is the purchase of property in the name of another.

2 [1991] 1 WLR 1511.

3 [1970] AC 567.

For example, B purchases shares and directs the vendor to transfer the legal title to the shares in the name of T. T is presumed to hold the shares on trust for B.

Constructive trusts

A constructive trust is created by the court in an effort to do justice and conscience to the parties. On occasions when a trustee abuses the confidence reposed in him by realising an unauthorised profit derived from the trust property, or becomes unjustly enriched at another's expense, the court may impose a constructive trust on the party who acted with impropriety. These are occasions when the courts feel that it is inappropriate for a person to retain the equitable interest for his own benefit. In *Boardman v Phipps*,[4] a solicitor acting on behalf of the trust obtained confidential information and acquired for himself shares in a company in which the trustees were part owners. The company prospered and the shareholders made substantial profits through the efforts of the solicitor. The court held that the solicitor as a constructive trustee was accountable to the trust for the profits made.

Statutory trusts

Statutory trusts are trusts created by Parliament.

Section 33 of the Administration of Estates Act 1925 declares that the personal representatives of an intestate are required to hold all the deceased's property upon trust with power to postpone the sale.

Section 33(1) of the Administration of Estates Act 1925, as amended by Trusts of Land and Appointment of Trustees Act 1996 (TLATA), provides:

> On the death of a person intestate as to any real or personal estate, that estate shall be held by his personal representatives with a power to sell it.

Section 34(2) of the Law of Property Act 1925 enacts that where land is conveyed to persons in undivided shares it will vest in the first four named persons upon trust for all the grantees beneficially as tenants in common.

Section 34(2) of the Law of Property Act, as amended by TLATA 1996, provides:

> Where ... land is expressed to be conveyed to any persons in undivided shares and those persons are of full age, the conveyance shall (notwithstanding anything to the contrary in this Act) operate as if the land had been expressed to be conveyed to the grantees, or if there are more than four grantees, to the four first named in the conveyance, as joint tenants in trust for the persons interested in the land.

4 [1967] 2 AC 46.

Section 36(1) of the Law of Property Act 1925 provides that where land is conveyed to joint tenants, it vests in the first four named persons on trust for sale for all the grantees as joint tenants.

Section 36(1) of the Law of Property Act, as amended by TLATA 1996, provides:

> Where a legal estate (not being settled land) is beneficially limited to or held in trust for any persons as joint tenants, the same shall be held in trust, in like manner as if the persons beneficially entitled were tenants in common, but not so as to sever their joint tenancy in equity.

Reasons for creation of trusts

The trust concept is a flexible institution which may be created for a variety of reasons.

Tax avoidance

One of the most popular reasons for the creation of a trust is to avoid or mitigate the settlor's liability to tax. There are many ways in which this objective may be achieved. Subject to statutory provisions to the contrary, the settlor, having exhausted his personal relief from income tax may alienate his income by way of a trust in favour of another who may use his relief to reduce the amount of tax payable, for example, a settlor may transfer 50,000 shares in Moneybags Ltd to trustees for the benefit of his impecunious nephew, N Trustees pay income tax at the basic rate of tax. On distributing the income, the beneficiary, N is entitled to set off his personal relief against the income liable to income tax.

To protect spendthrift beneficiaries

The settlor may believe that an outright transfer of property to a donee may result in the dissipation of the fund by the donee. To avoid this the settlor may create a protective trust under s 33 of the Trustee Act 1925 in favour of the child. The protective trust is a determinable life interest in favour of the beneficiary which terminates on the happening of any course of events which is capable of prejudicing the interest of the beneficiary. On termination of the life interest a discretionary trust is set up and the life tenant becomes an object of the discretionary trust. The terms of the trust laid out in s 33 may be adapted to suit the needs of any settlor.

To avoid adverse publicity from a published will

On death, a testator's will is published and transfers as well as the identity of the beneficiaries may become public. In order to avoid adverse publicity, a testator may create a fully secret trust by transferring property under his will to a person (say a legatee) whose identity is not a source of embarrassment. Before his death the testator will make a bargain with the legatee to the effect that following the receipt of the legacy he wil be required to hold the property on trust for the secret beneficiary (say, his illegitimate child). Thus, the existence of the trust and the identity of the beneficiary will be concealed on the face of the will.

To protect purchasers entering into commercial transactions

A customer who makes an advance payment for goods may be entitled to utilise the trust concept in order to secure the return of the purchase money in the event of the company going into liquidation. In *Re Kayford*,[5] customers made advance payments to a mail order company when ordering goods. Following advice, the company paid these sums into a separate account. The company treated funds in this account as belonging to customers until the goods were delivered in accordance with the order. On the liquidation of the company the court held that the funds were impressed with a trust in favour of the customers who failed to receive their goods.

Clubs and unincorporated associations

Unincorporated associations have no separate legal existence. Such bodies are not entitled to own funds separately for their members. The funds are owned by the members and the club is treated as the collective 'alter ego' of the members. The members may elect or appoint officers of the club. The officers may hold the club's assets and income as trustees for the purposes declared in the constitution of the association.

SUPPLEMENTARY READING

Bartlett, R, 'When is a trust not a trust? The National Health Service' [1996] 60 Conv 186

Goodhart, W, 'Trust law for the 21st century' (1996) 10(2) Tru LI 38

Hayton, D, 'Developing the law of trusts for the 21st century' (1990) 106 LQR 87

Hayton, D, 'Trust law and occupational pension schemes' [1993] 57 Conv 283

Millett, P, 'Equity – the road ahead' (1995) 9(2) Tru LI 35

Milner, M, 'Pension trust : a new trust forum' [1997] Conv 89

Moffatt, G, 'Pension funds: a fragmentation of trust law' (1993) 56 MLR 471

Nobles, R, 'Pensions Act 1995' (1996) 59 MLR 241

5 [1975] 1 WLR 279.

CHAPTER 3

EXPRESS PRIVATE TRUSTS

THE REQUIREMENTS

Capacity to create the trust

On the assumption that the settlor is the owner of the relevant property, the general principles concerning the capacity or authority to dispose of property apply with equal force to determine whether or not the settlor has the capacity to create a trust.

Mental incapacity

Under the Mental Health Act 1983, a mental patient, who is incapable of managing his affairs and in respect of whom a receiver has been appointed does not have the capacity to create a trust. Any purported disposition by him including the attempted creation of a trust will be void on the ground that the appointment of a receiver has the effect of suspending the patient's right to manage his affairs.

If a receiver has not been appointed, a gratuitous transfer may be set aside only if it is established that the transferor was incapable of managing his affairs owing to mental disorder. On the other hand, a disposition for valuable consideration will not be set aside on the ground of mental incapacity if at the time of the disposition the transferee was unaware of the incapacity.

Minors

A settlement made by a minor or infant (person under the age of 18) is voidable in the sense that it is binding and effective on the minor unless he repudiates it during his minority or within a reasonable time after attaining the age of majority. This is a question of fact. Moreover, by virtue of s 1(6) of the Law of Property 1925, an infant does not have the capacity to hold the legal estate in land, although such individual may enjoy the equitable interest in land.

Modes of creating an express trust

A trust is perfectly created when the trust property is 'at home', that is, the trustees have acquired the property subject to the terms of the trust as declared by the settlor. There are two modes of creating an express trust:

(a) The settlor may transfer property to third party trustees subject to the terms of the trust as declared by the settlor. Thus, the settlor will be required to effect the trust in two stages. One stage imposes on the settlor the obligation to transfer the property to the trustees and the settlor fulfils his obligations. The other stage requires the settlor to declare the terms of the trust, that is, to comply with the three certainties test (see below). The settlor may be one of the trustees and/or one of the beneficiaries. As the author of the trust he is required to identify the trustees and beneficiaries. It must follow that both these requirements or stages are complementary. A transfer of property to another without a declaration of trust, will be construed as nothing more than a gift in favour of the transferee, and a declaration of trust executed with the intention of making a third party a trustee for another will be of no effect if the third party has not acquired the property.

    For example, S, the legal and equitable owner of land wishes to make T1 and T2 trustees of the property for the benefit of B, his nephew. S will have to transfer the legal title to T1 and T2 and declare the terms of the trust in favour of B. On completion of these requirements B will acquire an equitable interest in the land.

(b) The other mode of creating an express trust requires the settlor to declare that the relevant property retained by him is held as a trustee subject to the terms of the trust, that is, a self declaration of trust. This mode has the advantage of requiring the settlor to execute one transaction, namely, the declaration of trust. No third party trustee is involved in the arrangement. Although there is no physical transfer of property to the trustees, the declaration of trust has the effect of altering the nature of ownership of the settlor from beneficial entitlement to that of trusteeship. In other words, the settlor's interest will be converted from absolute entitlement to partial ownership as trustee for the beneficiaries as declared. For example, S, the legal and equitable owner of shares wishes to declare himself a trustee for B, absolutely. S is required to declare himself a trustee for B absolutely. On completion of this requirement S will become the bare legal owner and B will become the sole equitable owner.

    The same type of trust may be effected by S, who may be both a trustee and a beneficiary. This will be the case where a partial transfer of the equitable interest is made in favour of B with S retaining the legal title and part of the equitable interest. This will be the position if S retains a life interest but transfers the equitable remainder interest to B. Note that since there are no formal requirements in respect of such transactions (see below) the declaration may be made orally, but for the sake of convenience the terms ought to be reduced into writing.

The significance of this issue is that the beneficiaries will acquire equitable interests in the property which they may protect, even though they are 'volunteers' (that is, they have not provided consideration). This is called a perfect trust. Conversely, an imperfect trust is one where the settlor has not fully complied with either of these two modes of creation. An imperfect trust exists as an agreement to create a trust which is enforceable only by those who have furnished consideration. Two equitable maxims summarise the general rule, 'equity will not assist a volunteer' and 'equity will not perfect an imperfect gift'.

The classical statement concerning the various modes of creating a trust was enunciated by Turner LJ.

Milroy v Lord (1862) 31 LJ Ch 798, HC

> **Turner LJ:** ... in order to render a voluntary settlement valid and effectual, the settlor must have done everything which, according to the nature of the property comprised in the settlement, was necessary to be done in order to transfer the property and render the settlement binding upon him. He may, of course, do this ... if he transfers the property to a trustee for the purposes of the settlement, or declares that he himself holds it in trust for those purposes ... but, in order to render the settlement binding, one or other of these modes must ... be resorted to, for there is no equity in this court to perfect an imperfect gift. The cases go further to this extent, that if the settlement is intended to be effectuated by one of the modes to which I have referred, the court will not give effect to it by applying another of those modes. If it is intended to take effect by transfer, the court will not hold the intended transfer to operate as a declaration of trust, for then every imperfect instrument would be made effectual by being converted into a perfect trust.

Thus, in order to create an express trust, the settlor is required to fulfil two conditions, namely:

(i) transfer the property to the trustees; and

(ii) declare the terms of the trust.

Transfer of the property to the trustees

The settlor is required to convey or vest the property in the hands of the trustees. No trust may be created unless the trustees have the relevant property under their control and management.

The transfer may be effected by way of a gift or a contract. The correct mode of transfer is required to be followed in order to vest the property in the hands of the trustees. The requirements concerning the mode of transfer of property vary with the nature of the property and the type of interest (whether legal or equitable) which the settlor intends to transfer. Thus, the transfer of the legal title to land requires a conveyance. Tangible moveable property (chattel) requires delivery with the intention of transferring the property. The assignment of a legal chose in action (for example, a debt) requires writing and notice to the debtor. The transfer of the legal title to shares requires an appropriate entry in the company's register made in pursuance of a proper instrument of transfer.

In appropriate circumstances, the transfer may be effective in equity despite the failure of the transferor to complete the transfer of the legal title. This would be the position when the settlor has done all in his power to give the trustee the legal title and the only hurdle to the complete transfer of the legal title lies outside the settlor's control. This difficulty is frequently experienced in respect of shares where the transfer is required to be executed in accordance with the company's articles of association followed by registration in the company's share register (ss 182 and 183 of the Companies Act 1985). The articles of association of most private companies give the directors an absolute discretion to refuse to register a transfer of shares without stating reasons (notification of refusal is required to be made within two months of the instrument of transfer being lodged with the company – s 183 of the Companies Act 1985). A transferor who has executed the appropriate documents of transfer of shares and has delivered the same to the company in the expectation that the transfer of the legal title will be complete, will have done everything that is required of him to transfer the shares. The directors may or may not refuse to register the shares. This is a matter which is beyond the transferor's control. In this event, the transfer of the equitable title to the shares will be complete. The transferor will hold the legal title to the shares on constructive trust for the transferee. Accordingly, voting powers are required to be exercised in favour of the beneficiaries. Likewise, dividends declared are held in trust for the beneficiaries. A transfer, for estate duty (and inheritance tax) purposes, will be recognised on the earlier date of the transfer of the equitable interest.

Re Rose [1952] Ch 499, CA

On 30 March 1943, the settlor executed a transfer of 20,000 shares to his wife. The transfers were in the form required by the company's articles of association. The transfers were registered in the company's books on 30 June 1943. On the date of death of the settlor, it was necessary to know the precise date of the transfer for estate duty purposes. If the transfer had taken place before 10 April 1943, no estate duty was payable. The Revenue claimed that duty was payable on the ground that the transfer was not complete until 30 June 1943.

The Court of Appeal held that as the settlor had done everything in his power to transfer the shares the gifts were complete on 30 March 1943.

Lord Evershed MR: I agree that if a man purporting to transfer property executes documents which are not apt to effect that purpose, the court cannot then extract from those documents some quite different transaction and say that they were intended merely to operate as a declaration of trust which *ex facie* they were not; but if a document is apt and proper to transfer the property – is, in truth, the appropriate way in which the property must be transferred – then it does not seem to me to follow from the statement of Turner LJ that, as a result, either during some limited period or otherwise, a trust may not arise, for the purpose of giving effect to the transfer. The simplest case will, perhaps, provide an illustration. If a man executes a document transferring all his equitable interest, say, in shares, that document, operating and intended to operate as a transfer, will give rise to and take effect as a trust, for the assignor will then be a trustee of the legal estate in the shares for the person in whose favour he has made an assignment of his beneficial interest. And for my part I do not think that *Milroy v Lord* is an authority which compels this court to hold that in this case, where, in the terms of Turner LJ's judgment, the settlor did everything which, according to the nature of the property comprised in the settlement, was necessary to be done by him in order to transfer the property, the result necessarily negatives the conclusion that, pending registration, the settlor was a trustee of the legal interest for the transferee.

I think the matter might be put, perhaps, in a somewhat different fashion though it reaches the same end. Whatever might be the position during the period between the execution of this document and the registration of the shares, the transfers were, on 30 June 1943, registered. After registration, the title of Mrs Rose was beyond doubt complete in every respect, and if Mr Rose had received a dividend between execution and registration and Mrs Rose had claimed to have that dividend handed to her, what would Mr Rose's answer have been? It could no longer be that the purported gift was imperfect; it had been made perfect. I am not suggesting that the perfection was retroactive. But what else could he say? How could he, in the face of his own statement under seal, deny the proposition that he had, on 30 March 1943, transferred the shares to his wife? By the phrase 'transfer the shares' surely must be meant transfer to her 'the shares and all my right, title and interest thereunder.' Nothing else could sensibly have been meant. Nor can he, I think, make much of the fact that this was a voluntary settlement on his part.

Contrast *Milroy v Lord*.

Milroy v Lord [1862] 31 LJ Ch 798, HC

A settlor attempted to transfer to Lord 50 shares in the Louisiana Bank upon trust for the benefit of the plaintiffs. The legal title to the shares was transferable by entry on the books of the bank. Lord held a power of attorney, executed by the settlor, entitling him to transfer the shares. The settlor gave the share certificates to Lord and directed him to effect the registration of the shares in his (Lord's) name but Lord failed to exercise the power and paid dividends to the plaintiffs during the settlor's lifetime. On the settlor's death, Lord gave the share certificates to the settlor's executors and the question arose whether the shares were held upon trust for the plaintiffs.

The court held that there was no gift of the shares to the objects nor was there a transfer of the shares to the intended trustee. Having failed to transfer the shares to the trustee, the court will not infer that the settlor is a trustee for the plaintiffs.

> **Turner LJ:** ... there is not here any transfer either of the class of shares or of the other to the objects of the settlement, and the question therefore must be whether a valid and effectual trust in favour of those objects was created in the defendant Samuel Lord or in the settlor himself as to all or any of these shares. Now it is plain that it was not the purpose of this settlement, or the intention of the settlor, to constitute himself a trustee of the bank shares. The intention was that the trust should be vested in the defendant Samuel Lord, and I think therefore that we should not be justified in holding that by the settlement, or by any parol declaration made by the settlor, he himself became a trustee of these shares for the purposes of the settlement. By doing so we should be converting the settlement or the parol declaration to a purpose wholly different from that which was intended to be effected by it and, as I have said, creating a perfect trust out of an imperfect transaction ...
>
> The more difficult question is, whether the defendant Samuel Lord did not become a trustee of these shares? Upon this question I have felt considerable doubt; but in the result, I have come to the conclusion that no perfect trust was ever created in him. The shares, it is clear, were never legally vested in him; and the only ground on which he can be held to have become a trustee of them is that he held a power of attorney under which he might have transferred them into his own name; but he held that power of attorney as the agent of the settlor; and if he had been sued by the plaintiffs as trustee of the settlement for an account under the trust, and to compel him to transfer the shares into his own name as trustee, I think he might well have said: 'These shares are not vested in me; I have no power over them except as the agent of the settlor, and without his express directions I cannot be justified in making the proposed transfer, in converting an intended into an actual settlement.' A court of equity could not, I think, decree the agent of the settlor to make the transfer, unless is could decree the settlor himself to do so, and it is plain that no such decree could have been made against the settlor. In my opinion, therefore, this decree cannot be maintained as to the fifty Louisiana Bank shares ...

Contrast *Re Fry* (1946) (where the transferor failed to fulfil all his duties. The transfer of the equitable interest was a nullity).

Re Fry, Chase National Executors and Trustees Corporation Ltd v Fry and Others [1946] Ch 312, HC

In 1940, the testator, who was resident in the US, intended to make an *inter vivos* gift to his son, Sydney Fry. The subject matter of the intended transfer was shares held in an English company. Such transfers were subject to the Defence (Finance) Regulations 1939 which prohibited the transfer of any securities by a person resident outside the sterling area unless Treasury permission and licence were obtained. The testator executed a transfer and sent it to the company for registration. The company notified the testator of the need to complete Treasury licence forms. After such forms were completed, but before the licence was granted, the testator died. The question in issue was whether Sydney Fry was entitled to force the testator's personal representatives to complete the transfer.

It was held that, since the gift was incomplete, the son was not entitled to call on the personal representatives to obtain for him the legal and beneficial interests in the shares.

> **Romer J:** Sydney Fry and the Cavendish Trust clearly had not acquired, at the date of the testator's death, the legal title to the shares which they now claim, because the transfers had not been registered by Liverpool Borax Ltd. Had they, however, arrived at the position which entitled them, as against that company, to be put on the register of members? Had everything been done which was necessary to put the transferees into the position of the transferor? If these questions, could be answered affirmatively, the transferees would have had more than an inchoate title; they would have had it in their own hands to require registration of the transfers. Having regard, however, to the Defence (Finance) Regulations, 1939, it is impossible, in my judgment, to answer the questions other than in the negative. The requisite consent of the Treasury to the transactions had not been obtained, and, in the absence of it, the company was prohibited from registering the transfers. In my opinion, accordingly, it is not possible to hold that, at the date of the testator's death, the transferees had either acquired a legal title to the shares in question, or the right, as against all other persons (including Liverpool Borax Ltd) to be clothed with such legal title.
>
> Moreover, the Treasury might in any case have required further information of the kind referred to in the questionnaire which was submitted to him, or answers supplemental to those which he had given in reply to it; and, if so approached, he might have refused to concern himself with the matter further, in which case I do not know how anyone could have compelled him to do so. Apart, however, from considerations of this kind, it appears to me that the Defence (Finance) Regulations, 1939, reg 3A, prevents me from giving effect to the argument, however formulated, that at the time of the testator's death a complete equitable assignment had been effected. The interest in the shares so acquired by the assignees would indubitably be an 'interest in securities,' within the meaning of reg 3A; and, inasmuch as they are prohibited from acquiring such an interest except with permission granted by the Treasury, this court cannot recognise a claim to such an interest where the consent of the Treasury was never given to its acquisition. The assignment and acceptance of the interest would both be equally incapable of recognition in the absence of Treasury sanction, and that sanction was never in fact obtained; it might indeed (although the probabilities are certainly otherwise) never have been forthcoming at all.
>
> In the result, I have arrived at the conclusion (with regret, as I frankly confess) that there is no principle which enables me to hold that Sydney Fry and the Cavendish Trust are entitled to the shares which the testator undoubtedly desired them to have.

The same principle applies to registered land following the execution of the relevant documents and pending registration of the transferee (see *Mascall v Mascall*).[1]

If the settlor's property consists solely of an equitable interest, he, the settlor, is required to do everything in his power to effect the transfer. An omission on the part of the intended transferor to fulfil one or more of his duties concerning the assignment of the interest will result in an ineffective transfer (see *Re McCardle*).[2]

Section 53(1)(c) of the Law of Property Act 1925

In addition, if the settlor (transferor) owns the equitable interest in property subsisting under a trust and wishes to transfer this interest to another as trustee or beneficiary, he is required to transfer the interest in writing in order to comply with s 53(1)(c) of the Law of Property Act 1925. In other words, a beneficiary under a trust who wishes to assign his equitable interest may only accomplish his aim by reducing the transfer in writing. If T1 and T2 hold the legal title concerning property upon trust for B, a beneficiary. A transfer of B's equitable title must be in writing. It makes no difference whether the equitable interest exists in realty or personalty. Section 53(1)(c) of the Law of Property Act 1925 states:

> A disposition of an equitable interest or trust subsisting at the time of the disposition, must be in writing signed by the person disposing of the same, or by his agent thereunto lawfully authorised in writing or by will.

The policy of enacting this sub-section was to prevent fraud by nullifying oral 'hidden' transfers in respect of either real or personal properties. The effect of the provision is that writing, executed by the intended transferor of the equitable interest, is mandatory. A purported oral disposition is void. The signature of the transferor or his agent lawfully appointed in writing will be sufficient compliance with the requirements of the sub-section.

The various modes of disposing of a subsisting equitable interest were summarised by Romer LJ in *Timpson's Executors v Yerbury*.

***Timpson's Executors v Yerbury (HM Inspector of Taxes)* [1936] 1 KB 645, CA**

Mrs Timpson was a beneficiary under a New York trust which gave the beneficiary a right to resort to the English Court of Equity in order to compel the trustees to discharge their duties. Mrs Timpson directed the trustees from time to time to pay certain sums to her children. These sums were remitted to England and paid to or on behalf of the children. On Mrs Timpson's death the question arose whether her estate was liable to income tax in respect of the

1 (1985) 49 P & CR 119.

2 [1951] Ch 668.

sums paid to the children. In other words the issue was whether Mrs Timpson had alienated such part of her interest in favour of her children.

Held in favour of the Revenue, Mrs Timpson's estate was correctly assessed to income tax.

> **Romer LJ:** The only question, therefore, that falls to be determined on this appeal is whether the sums paid to each of the children of Mrs Timpson in pursuance of the requests made by her to the American trustees were paid out of her income, or whether they were paid out of the income of that child.
>
> It becomes, therefore, necessary to ascertain whether the letters which were addressed by Mrs Timpson to her trustees operated to vest in the children respectively an equitable interest in the net income in the hands of the trustees to the extent mentioned in those letters. If they did, the remittances made by the trustees to each of the children in this country in pursuance of the letters formed part of the income of that child. If they did not, the remittances never ceased to be income of Mrs Timpson. For she alone could dispose of her equitable interest in the income – the trustees had no power to do so – and it is not suggested that except by the letters she herself ever made any such disposition.
>
> Now the equitable interest in property in the hands of a trustee can be disposed of by the person entitled to it in favour of a third party in any one of four different ways. The person entitled to it:
>
> (1) can assign it to the third party directly;
>
> (2) can direct the trustees to hold the property in trust for the third party;
>
> (3) can contract for valuable consideration to assign the equitable interest to him; or
>
> (4) can declare himself to be a trustee for him of such interest.
>
> In the present case, the last two methods may be disregarded. For if the letters could possibly be regarded as constituting a contract between Mrs Timpson and the children mentioned in them – and obviously they cannot – there was no consideration for such contract. Nor is it possible to maintain that Mrs Timpson by the letters constituted herself a trustee of any part of her income for any of her children. 'For a man to make himself a trustee,' said Sir George Jessel MR in *Richards v Delbridge*, 'there must be an expression of intention to become a trustee'. 'It is true,' he had said in an earlier part of his judgment, 'he need not use the words, "I declare myself a trustee", but he must do something which is equivalent to it, and use expressions which have that meaning'.
>
> Unless, therefore, the letters constituted an assignment to the children respectively of the equitable interest of Mrs Timpson in the net income to the extent therein mentioned, by one of the first two methods to which I have referred, no equitable interest in the income ever passed to them.

It is true that, in order to effect an assignment of an equitable interest, no particular form of words is necessary so long as the intention to assign is made clear. In *William Brandt's Sons & Co v Dunlop Rubber Co*,[3] Lord

3 [1905] AC 454.

MacNaghten, after stating that an equitable assignment does not always purport to be an assignment or use the language of an assignment, said in relation to the equitable assignment of a debt:

> It may be addressed to the debtor. It may be couched in the language of command. It may be a courteous request. It may assume the form of mere permission. The language is immaterial if the meaning is plain. All that is necessary is that the debtor should be given to understand that the debt has been made over by the creditor to some third person. If the debtor ignores such a notice, he does so at his peril. If the assignment be for valuable consideration and communicated to the third person, it cannot be revoked by the creditor.
>
> But no document can effect an assignment of an equitable interest unless it results in a vesting of the interest in the assignee, so that after notice of it is given to the trustee, the latter becomes a trustee of the interest for the assignee. I regard the letters as no more than revocable mandates given to the trustees, and conferring no rights whatsoever upon Mrs Timpson's children. There was no valuable consideration given by the children nor were the letters ever communicated to them by anybody. The mandates were, therefore, revocable at all times material to the present case.

But, s 53(1)(c) has no application to the original creation of a trust. The sub-section is only applicable when a beneficiary (under a subsisting trust) wishes to dispose of his equitable interest to another. Thus, s 53(1)(c) is not applicable where S, the settlor, with both legal and equitable interests in property, wishes to transfer the equitable interest to B, a beneficiary. The sub-section is applicable where the equitable owner under a subsisting trust wishes to dispose of his interest to another, for example, B, a beneficiary under a trust wishes to transfer his interest to C. This transfer must be in writing otherwise the purported transfer is void. See *Grey v IRC*.[4] The issue here was whether an equitable owner of personalty subsisting under a trust, through a verbal direction to the trustees to hold the property upon trust for a third party, succeeded in disposing of his interest, despite the clear wording of s 53(1)(c) of the Law of Property Act 1925.

Grey v Inland Revenue Commissioners [1960] AC 1, HL

In 1949, Mr Hunter (the settlor) transferred shares of a nominal sum to trustees upon trust for his six grandchildren. In 1955, the settlor transferred 18,000 £1 shares to the same trustees upon trust for himself. In an attempt to avoid *ad valorem* stamp duty (payable on instruments which transfer any property or interest in property), the settlor verbally instructed the trustees to hold the shares upon trust for the grandchildren. The trustees subsequently executed confirmatory documents affirming the oral instructions. The Revenue assessed the documents to *ad valorem* stamp duty.

4 [1960] AC 1.

The House of Lords held that the oral instructions were ineffective for non-compliance with s 53(1)(c), but the documents effectively transferred the equitable interest and were stampable.

> **Lord Radcliffe:** My Lords, there is nothing more in this appeal than the short question whether the oral direction that Mr Hunter gave to his trustees on 18 February 1955, amounted in any ordinary sense of the words to a 'disposition of an equitable interest or trust subsisting at the time of the disposition', I do not feel any doubt as to my answer. I think that it did. Whether we describe what happened in technical or in more general terms, the full equitable interest in the eighteen thousand shares concerned, which at that time was his, was (subject to any statutory invalidity) diverted by his direction from this ownership into the beneficial ownership of the various equitable owners, present and future, entitled under his six existing settlements.
>
> In my opinion, it is a very nice question whether a parol declaration of trust of this kind was or was not within the mischief of s 9 of the Statute of Frauds. The point has never, I believe, been decided and perhaps it never will be. Certainly, it was long established as law that while a declaration of trust respecting land or any interest therein required writing to be effective a declaration of trust respecting personalty did not. Moreover, there is warrant for saying that a direction to his trustee by the equitable owner of trust property prescribing new trusts of that property was a declaration of trust. But it does not necessarily follow from that that such a direction, if the effect of it was to determine completely or *pro tanto* the subsisting equitable interest of the maker of the direction, was not also a grant or assignment for the purposes of s 9 and therefore required writing for its validity. Something had to happen to that equitable interest in order to displace it in favour of the new interests created by the direction: and it would be at any rate logical to treat the direction as being an assignment of the subsisting interest to the new beneficiary or beneficiaries or, in other cases, a release or surrender of it to the trustee.
>
> I do not think, however, that that question has to be answered for the purposes of this appeal. It can only be relevant if s 53(1) of the Law of Property Act 1925 is treated as a true consolidation of the three sections of the Statute of Frauds concerned and as governed, therefore, by the general principle, with which I am entirely in agreement, that a consolidating Act is not to be read as effecting changes in the existing law unless the words it employs are too clear in their effect to admit of any other construction. But, in my opinion, it is impossible to regard s 53 of the Law of Property Act 1925 as a consolidating enactment in this sense.
>
> The Law of Property Act 1925 itself was, no doubt, strictly a consolidating statute. But what it consolidated was not merely the Law of Property Act 1922, a statute which had itself effected massive changes in the law relating to real property and conveyancing, but also the later Law of Property (Amendment) Act 1924. The Statute of Frauds sections had not been touched by the Act of 1922, but they were, in effect, repealed and re-enacted in altered form by the operation of s 3 of the Act of 1924. This new wording is what is carried into s 53 of the Act of 1925.

For these reasons I think that there is no direct link between s 53(1)(c) of the Act of 1925 and s 9 of the Statute of Frauds. The link was broken by the changes introduced by the amendment Act of 1924, and it was those changes that s 53 must be taken as consolidating. If so, it is inadmissible to allow the construction of the word 'disposition' in the new Act to be limited or controlled by any meaning attributed to the words 'grant' or 'assignment' in s 9 of the old Act.

Appeal dismissed.

However, s 53(1)(c) has no application where the equitable owner effectively terminates the trust by directing the trustees to transfer their legal title to a third party and, in the same transaction, assigns the equitable interest to the third party. The rationale behind this principle, as stated by the Law Lords in *Vandervell v IRC*, is that the unification of the legal and equitable interests is outside of the mischief of s 53(1)(c). Thus, the beneficiary under a subsisting trust may avoid the rigour of s 53(1)(c) by effecting the transfer of both the legal and equitable interests to a third party (see *Vandervell v IRC*).

***Vandervell v Inland Revenue Commissioners* [1967] 2 AC 291, HL (Lords Pearce, Upjohn and Wilberforce; Lords Reid and Donovan dissenting on the subsistence of the resulting trust that attracted surtax in Mr Vandervell's hands)**

In 1958, Mr Vandervell decided to donate £150,000 to the Royal College of Surgeons to found a chair of pharmacology. He decided to achieve this purpose by transferring 100,000 ordinary shares in Vandervell Products Limited (a private company controlled by Mr Vandervell) to the college subject to an option (vested in a separate company, Vandervell Trustee Company) to re-purchase the shares for £5,000. In pursuance of this scheme, Mr Vandervell orally directed the National Provincial Bank (which held the legal title to the shares on behalf of Mr Vandervell) to transfer the shares to the college, subject to the option exercisable by the Trustee company. The bank complied with the directions. During the tax years 1958–59 and 1959–60, dividends on the shares amounting to £162,500 and £87,500 respectively were paid to the college. In October 1961, the trustee company exercised the option and paid the college £5,000 and recovered the shares. The Inland Revenue assessed Mr Vandervell to surtax in respect of the dividends on the grounds that Mr Vandervell had not absolutely divested himself from the shares so that the dividends fell to be treated as his income within s 415 of the Income Tax Act 1952. In addition, Mr Vandervell had not transferred his equitable interest in the shares to the college for failure to comply with s 53(1)(c) of the Law of Property Act 1925.

Held:

(i) in favour of the Revenue on the ground that Mr Vandervell had retained an equitable interest in the shares by way of a resulting trust. This trust had been created by reference to the incomplete disposal of the equitable interest in the option (Lords Reid and Donovan dissenting);

(ii) in favour of Mr Vandervell on the ground that s 53(1)(c) was inapplicable when the equitable owner in a composite transaction transfers the equitable interest to a third party and directs the trustees to transfer the legal title to the same third party, namely the college.

Lord Upjohn: The question is whether notwithstanding the plainly expressed intention of the appellant by himself or his agents the absence of writing prevented any equitable or beneficial interest in the shares passing to the college so that contrary to his wishes and understanding they remained bare trustees for him. This depends entirely upon the true construction of s 53(1)(c) of the Law of Property Act 1925, which the Crown maintain makes writing necessary to pass the beneficial interest. This section was generally thought to re-enact s 9 of the Statute of Frauds and that section had never been applied to a trust of an equitable interest of pure personalty. Before the cases of *Grey v IRC* (1960) and *Oughtred v IRC* (1960), both in your Lordships' House, this argument would have been quite untenable.

It was shown in those cases that the Law of Property Act 1925 was not re-enacting s 9 but that it had been amended by the Law of Property Act 1924. The relevant words of s 53 are:

> ... a disposition of an equitable interest or trust subsisting at the time of the disposition, must be in writing signed by the person disposing of the same ...

Those words were applied in *Grey* and *Oughtred* to cases where the legal estate remained outstanding in a trustee and the beneficial owner was dealing and dealing only with the equitable estate. That is understandable; the object of the section, as was the object of the old Statute of Frauds, is to prevent hidden oral transactions in equitable interests in fraud of those truly entitled, and making it difficult, if not impossible, for the trustees to ascertain who are in truth his beneficiaries. But when the beneficial owner owns the whole beneficial estate and is in a position to give directions to his bare trustee with regard to the legal as well as the equitable estate there can be no possible ground for invoking the section where the beneficial owner wants to deal with the legal estate as well as the equitable estate.

I cannot agree with Diplock LJ [in the Court of Appeal] that *prima facie* a transfer of the legal estate carries with it the absolute beneficial interest in the property transferred; this plainly is not so, for example, the transfer may be on a change of trustee; it is a matter of intention in each case. But if the intention of the beneficial owner in directing the trustee to transfer the legal estate to X is that X should be the beneficial owner I can see no reason for any further document or further words in the document assigning the legal estate also expressly transferring the beneficial interest; the greater includes the less. X may be wise to secure some evidence that the beneficial owner intended him to take the beneficial interest in case his beneficial title is challenged at a later date but it certainly cannot, in my opinion, be a statutory requirement that to effect its passing there must be some writing under s 53(1)(c).

Counsel for the Crown admitted that where the legal and beneficial estate was vested in the legal owner and he desired to transfer the whole legal and beneficial estate to another he did not have to do more than transfer the legal estate and he did not have to comply with s 53(1)(c); and I can see no relevant difference between that case and this.

As I have said, that section is, in my opinion, directed to cases where dealings with the equitable estate are divorced from the legal estate and I do not think any of their Lordships in *Grey* and *Oughtred* had in mind the case before your Lordships. To hold the contrary would make assignments unnecessarily complicated; if there had to be assignments in express terms of both legal and equitable interests that would make the section more productive of injustice than the supposed evils it was intended to prevent.

I turn, then, to the second point.

Where A transfers, or directs a trustee for him to transfer, the legal estate in property to B otherwise than for valuable consideration it is a question of the intention of A in making the transfer whether B was to take beneficially or on trust and, if the latter, on what trusts. If, as a matter of construction of the document transferring the legal estate, it is possible to discern A's intentions, that is an end of the matter and no extraneous evidence is admissible to correct and qualify his intentions so ascertained.

But if, as in this case (a common form share transfer), the document is silent, then there is said to arise a resulting trust in favour of A. But this is only a presumption and is easily rebutted. All the relevant facts and circumstances can be considered in order to ascertain A's intentions with a view to rebutting this presumption.

As Lindley LJ said in *Standing v Bowring*:[5]

> Trusts are neither created nor implied by law to defeat the intentions of donors or settlors; they are created or implied or are held to result in favour of donors or settlors in order to carry out and give effect to their true intentions, expressed or implied.

The law was well stated by Mellish LJ in *Fowkes v Pascoe*:[6]

> Now, the Master of the Rolls appears to have thought that because the presumption that it was a trust and not a gift must prevail if there was no evidence to rebut the presumption, therefore when there was evidence to rebut the presumption he ought not to consider the probability or improbability of the circumstances of the case, and whether the presumption was really true or not, but ought to decide the case on the ground that the evidence of Pascoe and his wife taken alone was not satisfactory. But, in my opinion, when there is once evidence to rebut the

5 (1885) 31 Ch D 282.

6 (1875) 10 Ch App 343.

> presumption, the court is put in the same position as a jury would be, and then we cannot give such influence to the presumption in point of law as to disregard the circumstances of the investment, and to say that neither the circumstances nor the evidence are sufficient to rebut the presumption.

James LJ in the same case also pointed out in effect that it was really a jury matter, on the basis, I may add, of weighing the evidence on the balance of probabilities.

But the doctrine of resulting trust plays another very important part in our law and, in my opinion, is decisive of this case.

If A intends to give away all his beneficial interest in a piece of property and thinks he has done so but, by some mistake or accident or failure to comply with the requirements of the law, he has failed to do so, either wholly or partially, there will, by operation of law, be a resulting trust for him of the beneficial interest of which he had failed effectually to dispose. If the beneficial interest was in A and he fails to give it away effectively to another or others or on charitable trusts it must remain in him. Early references to equity, like Nature, abhorring a vacuum, are delightful but unnecessary. Let me give an example close to this case.

A, the beneficial owner, informs his trustees that he wants forthwith to get rid of his interest in the property and instructs him to hold the property forthwith upon such trusts as he will hereafter direct; that beneficial interest, notwithstanding the expressed intention and belief of A that he has thereby parted with his whole beneficial interest in the property, will inevitably remain in him for he has not given the property away effectively to or for the benefit of others. As Plowman J said: 'As I see it, a man does not cease to own property simply by saying "I don't want it". If he tries to give it away the question must always be, has he succeeded in doing so or not?'

The grant of an option to purchase is very different from a grant of a legal estate in some real or personal property without consideration to a person nominated by the beneficial owner.

The grantee of an option has not, in reality, an estate in the property. Of course, he has an interest in it which can be measured by saying that he can obtain an injunction preventing the grantor from parting with the property except subject to the option and in this case having regard to the express terms of clause 2 from parting with the property at all; and that he can enforce the option against all subsequent owners except purchasers for value without notice. Essentially, however, an option confers no more than a contractual right to acquire property on payment of a consideration, and that seems to me a very different thing from the ordinary case where the doctrine of a resulting trust has been applied. However, it is a question of intention whether the appellant and the trustee company intended that the option should be held by the trustee company beneficially or as a trustee and, if the latter, upon what trusts. As the option deed is itself quite silent upon this point all the relevant facts and circumstances must be looked at to solve this question. As I think the facts and circumstances are sufficient for this purpose without resort to this long stop presumption, it is unnecessary finally to decide whether the doctrine of resulting trust does apply to an option.

While the Court of Appeal assumed that there was a resulting trust of the option for the appellant – they did not decide it upon that ground alone. Diplock LJ said: 'It is next contended that the trustee company took the option beneficially. This also seems to me to fly in the face of the evidence' – which he then examined in some detail.

Wilmer LJ in the next judgment said: 'Later – prompted, I suspect, by certain observations made by members of this court – the argument was developed that the trustee company should be regarded as taking the option beneficially.'

He also examined the evidence and came to the conclusion that there was no intention to give any beneficial interest to the trustee company. Harman LJ came to the same conclusion.

My Lords, this question is really one of inference from primary facts, but having regard to the way in which the matter has developed I should be reluctant to differ from the courts below, and I do not think that the question whether the doctrine of resulting trust applies to options, on the facts of this case in the least degree invalidates the reasoning of the Court of Appeal or its conclusions upon this point.

I agree with the conclusions of the Court of Appeal and Plowman J that the intention was that the trustee company should hold on such trusts as might thereafter be declared by the trustee company or the appellant and so in the event for the appellant.

That is sufficient to dispose of the appeal, but one question was debated in the Court of Appeal, though not before your Lordships, and that is whether the option was held by the trustee company upon such trusts as the trustee company in its discretion should declare or as the appellant should declare. Once it is established that the trustee company held solely as trustee that, as the Court of Appeal held, matters not. The appellant could at any time revoke that discretion if he had vested it in the trustee company.

For the reasons I have given earlier, it follows that until these trusts should be declared there was a resulting trust for the appellant. This is fatal to his case, and I would dismiss the appeal.

Lord Donovan: ... If, owning the entire estate, legal and beneficial, in a piece of property, and desiring to transfer that entire estate to another, I do so by means of a disposition which *ex facie* deals only with the legal estate, it would be ridiculous to argue that s 53(1)(c) has not been complied with, and that therefore the legal estate alone had passed. The present case, it is true, is different in its facts in that the legal and equitable estates in the shares were in separate ownership; but when the taxpayer, being competent to do so, instructed the bank to transfer the shares to the college, and made it abundantly clear that he wanted to pass, by means of that transfer, his own beneficial or equitable interest, plus the bank's legal interest, he achieved the same result as if there had been no separation of the interests. The transfer thus made, pursuant to his intentions and instructions, was a disposition, not of the equitable interest alone, but of the entire estate in the shares. In such a case, I see no room for the operation of s 53(1)(c) ...

> **Lord Wilberforce:** There remains the alternative point taken by the Crown that, in any event, by virtue of s 53(1)(c) of the Law of Property Act 1925, the appellant never effectively disposed of the beneficial interest in the shares to the Royal College of Surgeons. This argument I cannot accept. Section 53(1)(c), a successor to the dormant s 9 of the Statute of Frauds, has recently received a new lease of life as an instrument in the hands of the Revenue. The sub-section, which has twice recently brought litigants to this House (*Grey v IRC*; *Oughtred v IRC*), is certainly not easy to apply to the varied transactions in equitable interests which now occur. However, in this case no problem arises.
>
> The shares in question, the 100,000 'A' shares in Vandervell Products Ltd, were, prior to 14 November 1958, registered in the name of the National Provincial Bank Ltd upon trust for the appellant absolutely. On 14 November 1958, the appellant's solicitor received from the bank a blank transfer of the shares, executed by the bank, and the share certificate. So at this stage the appellant was the absolute master of the shares and only needed to insert his name as transferee in the transfer and to register it to become the full legal owner. He was also the owner in equity. On 19 November 1958, the solicitor (or Mr Robins – the case is ambiguous) on behalf of Mr Vandervell, who intended to make a gift, handed the transfer to the college which, in due course, sealed it and obtained registration of the shares in the college's name. The case should then be regarded as one in which the appellant himself has, with the intention to make a gift, put the college in a position to become the legal owner of the shares, which the college in fact became. If the appellant had died before the college had obtained registration, it is clear, on the principle of *Re Rose*, that the gift would have been complete, on the basis that he had done everything in his power to transfer the legal interest, with an intention to give, to the college. No separate transfer, therefore, of the equitable interest ever came to or needed to be made and there is no room for the operation of the sub-section. What the position would have been had there simply been an oral direction to the legal owner (viz, the bank) to transfer the shares to the College, followed by such a transfer, but without any document in writing signed by Mr Vandervell as equitable owner, is not a matter which calls for consideration here. The Crown's argument on this point fails but, for the reasons earlier given, I would dismiss the appeal.

A controversial issue, which has yet to be resolved, is whether a declaration of trust by an equitable owner of a part of his interest under a subsisting trust is required to be in writing. The view seems to be that if the equitable owner declares a trust in respect of his entire interest so that he drops out of the picture, writing is required. But if he declares a trust in respect of a part of his interest so that a new trust is created in respect of a part of his original interest, imposing active duties on him to perform, writing is not essential. For example, if T1 and T2 hold the legal title on trust for B, a beneficiary, absolutely, and B declares himself a trustee of the shares for B for life with remainder to C absolutely, this declaration may not be within s 53(1)(c). The transfer of the remainder interest to C concerns a new trust and s 53(1)(c) is not applicable to the creation of trusts (see *Re Lashmar*).[7] This view has been challenged by Brian Green[8] (see below, p 54).

Section 53(2) of the Law of Property Act 1925 enacts that 'this section does not affect the creation or operation of resulting, implied or constructive trusts'.

The effect of s 53(2) is to dispense with writing in respect of implied, resulting and constructive trusts. Controversy surrounds the extent to which s 53(1)(c) may be restricted by the operation of the constructive and resulting trusts. On the one hand, a number of Law Lords have declined to recognise the constructive trust as relieving the transferor from the full rigour of s 53(1)(c) (see the opinions of Lords Cohen and Denning in *Oughtred v IRC*).[9] On the other hand, a constructive trust exception to an all pervasive s 53(1)(c) would appear to be consistent with policy and common sense. After all, a constructive trust is created by the courts in order to satisfy the demands of justice and conscience. If the circumstances surrounding a transaction demand the imposition of a constructive trust by the courts in order to maintain a balance between the trustees and the beneficiaries, the requirement of writing under s 53(1)(c) ought not to impede this process (see the opinion of Lord Radcliffe in *Oughtred v IRC* and Megarry VC in *Re Holt's Settlement*[10] and the compromise adopted by Lord Denning MR in *Re Vandervell's Trust (No 2)*.[11]

Oughtred v Inland Revenue Commissioners [1960] AC 206, HL (Lords Jenkins, Keith and Denning; Lords Radcliffe and Cohen dissenting)

Mrs Oughtred was the tenant for life under a settlement which comprised 200,000 shares in a company. The remainder interest in the shares was held on trust for her son, Peter, absolutely. Mrs Oughtred was also the absolute owner of 72,700 shares in the same company. As part of an estate duty scheme, Mrs Oughtred and Peter orally agreed on 18 June 1956 to transfer her absolute interest in 72,700 shares to Peter in exchange for Peter's remainder interest in 200,000 shares. The oral agreement was followed by the execution of three documents, all dated 26 June 1956.

(1) Mrs Oughtred executed a simple transfer to nominees for Peter of her 72,700 shares 'in consideration of 10 s';

(2) a deed of release expressed to be made between Mrs Oughtred of the first part, Peter of the second part and the trustees of the settlement of the third part, the parties confirmed that the trustees held the 200,000 shares upon trust for Mrs Oughtred absolutely;

7 [1891] 1 Ch 258.

8 (1984) 37 MLR 385.

9 [1960] AC 206.

10 [1969] Ch 100.

11 [1974] Ch 269.

(3) by a simple transfer, the trustees transferred the 200,000 shares to Mrs Oughtred 'in consideration of 10 s'.

The Inland Revenue claimed that the transfer of the 200,000 shares attracted *ad valorem* stamp duty on 'the amount or value of the consideration for the sale'. Section 54 of the Stamp Act 1891 declares that 'a conveyance on sale includes every instrument ... whereby any property, or any estate or interest is transferred to or vested in a purchaser upon the sale thereof' (for a recent application of this principle, see *Parinhy (Hatfield) Ltd v IRC* [1997] NPC 179). The Commissioners of Inland Revenue upheld the claim, but on appeal to the High Court, Upjohn J allowed the appeal and dismissed the claim. His decision was reversed by the Court of Appeal on the grounds that the transfer of the legal interest was 'a conveyance on sale'. The constructive trust doctrine did not replace the transfer for there still remained something which could be conveyed as part of the bargain namely, Peter's reversionary interest. The transfer of this reversionary interest attracted *ad valorem* stamp duty. On appeal to the House of Lords:

Held (3:2 majority), affirming the decision of the Court of Appeal that *ad valorem* stamp duty was payable on the transfer of Peter's reversionary interest in 200,000 shares:

> **Lord Radcliffe** (dissenting): The whole point of the present appeal seems to me to turn on the question whether it is open to a court of law to deduce from the documents of this case that Mrs Oughtred's title to her son's equitable reversionary interest rested upon anything more than the oral agreement which admittedly took place.
>
> My Lords, on this short point my opinion is that such a deduction is not open to a court of law. The materials that would support it are simply not there. I think that the judgment of Upjohn J in the High Court, which was in favour of Mrs Oughtred, was correct, and I agree with his reasons. I am afraid that I do not agree with the judgment of the Court of Appeal, which was in favour of the commissioners, or with the conclusion which, as I understand, commends itself to a majority of your Lordships.
>
> The reasoning of the whole matter, as I see it, is as follows: On 18 June 1956, the son owned an equitable reversionary interest in the settled shares: by his oral agreement of that date he created in his mother an equitable interest in her reversion, since the subject matter of the agreement was property of which specific performance would normally be decreed by the court. He thus became a trustee for her of that interest *sub modo*: having regard to sub-s (2) of s 53 of the Law of Property Act, 1925, sub-s (1) of that section did not operate to prevent that trusteeship arising by operation of law. On 26 June, Mrs Oughtred transferred to her son the shares which were the consideration for her acquisition of his equitable interest: upon this transfer he became in a full sense and without more a trustee of his interest for her. She was the effective owner of all outstanding equitable interests. It was thus correct to recite in the deed of release to the trustees of the settlement, which was to wind up their trust, that the trust fund was by then held upon trust for her absolutely. There was, in

fact, no equity to the shares that could be asserted against her, and it was open to her, if she so wished, to let the matter rest without calling for a written assignment from her son. Given that the trustees were apprised of the making of the oral agreement and of Mrs Oughtred's satisfaction of the consideration to be given by her, the trustees had no more to do than to transfer their legal title to her or as she might direct. This and no more is what they did.

It follows that, in my view, this transfer cannot be treated as a conveyance of the son's equitable reversion at all. The trustees had not got it: he never transferred or released it to them: how then could they convey it? With all respect to those who think otherwise, it is incorrect to say that the trustees' transfer was made either with his authority or at his direction. If the recital as to Mrs Oughtred's rights was correct, as I think that it was, he had no remaining authority to give or direction to issue. A release is, after all, the normal instrument for winding up a trust when all the equitable rights are vested and the legal estate is called for from the trustees who hold it. What the release gave the trustees from him was acquittance for the trust administration and accounts to date, and the fact that he gave it in consideration of the legal interest in the shares being vested in his mother adds nothing on this point. Nor does it, with respect, advance the matter to say, correctly, that at the end of the day Mrs Oughtred was the absolute owner of the shares, legal and equitable.

Lastly, I ought perhaps to say that I do not myself see any analogy between the operations embraced by the oral agreement and documents and the common case of a sale of shares by an owner for whom they are held by a nominee or bare trustee. What is sold there is the shares themselves, not the owner's equitable interest. What is passed by the transfer executed by his nominee is the shares, according to the contract, without any incumbrance on the title, equitable or legal.

Lord Cohen (dissenting): Upjohn J [in the High Court] rejected the respondents' argument. He held that sub-s (2) afforded a complete answer to it, saying:

> This was an oral agreement for value, and accordingly, on the making thereof, Peter, the vendor, became a constructive trustee of his equitable reversionary interest in the trust funds for the appellant. No writing to achieve that result was necessary, for an agreement of sale and purchase of an equitable interest in personalty (other than chattels real) may be made orally, and s 53 has no application to a trust arising by construction of law.

The Court of Appeal did not accept Upjohn J's conclusion as to the effect of sub-s (2) but did not find it necessary to express a concluded opinion as to the effect of s 53.

Before your Lordships Mr Wilberforce was prepared to agree that on the making of the oral agreement Peter became a constructive trustee of his equitable reversionary interest in the settled funds for the appellant, but he submitted that nonetheless s 53(1)(c) applied and accordingly Peter could not assign that equitable interest to the appellant except by a disposition in writing. My Lords, with that I agree, but it does not follow that the transfer was a conveyance of that equitable interest on which *ad valorem* stamp duty was payable under the Stamp Act 1891. It might well be that there has been no document transferring the equitable interest. The appellant may have been content to rely on getting in the legal interest by the transfer and on the fact that it would be impossible for Peter to put forward successfully a claim to an equitable interest in the settled shares once the consideration shares had been transferred to him or his nominees by the appellant.

My Lords, The Stamp Act 1891, imposes stamp duty on documents, not transactions. The transfer does not attract *ad valorem* duty unless, to use the language of s 54 of the Act, it is an 'instrument ... whereby any property, or any estate or interest in any property, upon the sale thereof is transferred to or vested in a purchaser'. The words 'upon the sale thereof' must, in relation to this case, mean 'on the sale of Peter's equitable interest'. It is, as the Court of Appeal recognises, impossible to say that the transfer had the effect of transferring the equitable interest since the transferors never had that interest to transfer, nor, in my opinion, can it be said that by the transfer Peter's equitable interest was vested in the appellant. The appellant as a result of what was done on June 26 was, as the release recognised, absolutely entitled to the settled shares, but that was not because the equitable interest was transferred to or vested in her by the transfer but because Peter, having become a constructive trustee for her of his equitable interest, could not, after his nominees had received the consideration shares, as they did on 26 June 1956, dispute the appellant's title to the settled shares.

Lord Denning: Was this transfer 'a conveyance or transfer on sale, of any property' such as to attract stamp duty on the value of the consideration? I have no doubt it was. Peter had agreed to sell his reversionary interest in the 200,000 shares to his mother for a stated consideration (the 72,700 shares). He did not convey this reversionary interest direct to her, nor did he convey it to the trustees of the settlement. But he authorised the trustees to convey it to her – not in the shape of a reversionary interest as such – but by way of enlarging her life interest into absolute ownership. It is clear to me that, by the transfer so made by his authority, she acquired his reversionary interest as effectively as if he had conveyed it direct to her. And that is quite enough to attract stamp duty. In my opinion, every conveyance or transfer by which an agreement for sale is implemented is liable to stamp duty on the value of the consideration. It is not necessary for the instrument of implementation to be between the same parties as the agreement for sale, nor for it to relate to the self- same property as the agreement for sale. Suffice it that the instrument is the means by which the parties choose to implement the bargain they have made. It is then a 'conveyance or transfer 'on sale' of any property – which I take to mean a conveyance or transfer consequent upon the sale of the property and in implementation of it. Thus, when an equitable owner of shares (registered in the name of a nominee) agrees to sell them to a purchaser, and it is implemented by a transfer by the nominee to the purchaser, the transfer is a conveyance upon sale of any property – although, of course, the parties to the agreement are different from the parties to the transfer. And when two people are equitable co-owners of shares – and one of them agrees to sell his interest to the other – and it is implemented by a transfer of the shares by the trustees (with the authority of the one) to the other, the transfer is a conveyance upon sale of any property – although, of course, the property which is transferred is different from the property in the agreement.

I do not think it necessary to embark upon a disquisition on constructive trusts: because I take the view that, even if the oral agreement of 18 June 1956, was effective to transfer Peter's reversionary interest to his mother, nevertheless, when that oral agreement was subsequently implemented by the transfer, then the transfer became liable to stamp duty. But I may say that I do not think the oral agreement was effective to transfer Peter's reversionary interest to his mother. I should have thought that the wording of s 53(1)(c) of the Law of Property Act 1925, clearly made a writing necessary to effect a transfer: and s 53(2) does not do away with that necessity.

Lord Jenkins (with whom Lord Keith concurred): The question, then, is whether upon the true construction of s 54 of the Act of 1891, and having regard to the terms and effect of the oral agreement and the nature of the interests with respect to which that agreement was made, the disputed transfer was an instrument whereby property in the shape of the settled shares or any estate or interest in that property was transferred 'upon the sale thereof' to a purchaser in the person of the appellant.

It is not open to doubt that the oral agreement amounted to an agreement for the sale by Peter, for a purchase consideration consisting of the free shares, of his reversionary interest in the settled shares to the appellant. It is also plain that the parties intended that the sale should have the effect of enlarging the appellant's life interest in the settled shares into absolute ownership thereof and should accordingly be completed on 26 June by an immediate out-and-out transfer of the settled shares by the trustees to the appellant for her own absolute use and benefit, again the satisfaction by her of the consideration due to Peter in the shape of the free shares. The expressed intention of the parties that the appellant's life interest should be enlarged into absolute ownership appears to me to be indistinguishable in its effect from an intention that the appellant's life interest should merge in the reversionary interest, so as to convert that interest into an immediate absolute interest in possession, discharged from the life interest.

It is said, and said truly, that stamp duty is imposed on instruments, not transactions, and that a transaction of sale carried out without bringing into existence an instrument which has the effect of transferring to or vesting in the purchaser the property sold attracts no duty: see *per* Lord Esher in *IRC v Angus*[12] where he said: 'The first thing to be noticed is that the thing which is made liable to the duty is an "instrument".'

It is said that, inasmuch as the oral agreement was an agreement of sale and purchase, it gave rise ... to a constructive trust of the reversionary interest in favour of the appellant, subject to performance by her of her obligation to transfer to Peter the free shares forming the consideration for the sale. It is said that this trust, being constructive, was untouched by s 53(1)(c) in view of the exemption afforded by s 53(2), and that the appellant's primary argument still holds good.

12 (1889) 23 QB 579.

I find it unnecessary to decide whether s 53(2) has the effect of excluding the present transaction from the operation of s 53(1)(c), for, assuming in the appellant's favour that the oral contract did have the effect in equity of raising a constructive trust of the settled shares for her untouched by s 53(1)(c), I am unable to accept the conclusion that the disputed transfer was prevented from being a transfer of the shares to the appellant on sale because the entire beneficial interest in the settled shares was already vested in the appellant under the constructive trust, and there was accordingly nothing left for the disputed transfer to pass to the appellant except the bare legal estate. The constructive trust in favour of a purchaser which arises on the conclusion of a contract for sale is founded upon the purchaser's right to enforce the contract in proceedings for specific performance. In other words, he is treated in equity as entitled by virtue of the contract to the property which the vendor is bound under the contract to convey to him. This interest under the contract is no doubt a proprietary interest of a sort, which arises, so to speak, in anticipation of the execution of the transfer for which the purchaser is entitled to call. But its existence has never (so far as I know) been held to prevent a subsequent transfer, in performance of the contract, of the property contracted to be sold from constituting for stamp duty purposes a transfer on sale of the property in question. Take the simple case of a contract for the sale of land. In such a case a constructive trust in favour of the purchaser arises on the conclusion of the contract for sale, but (so far as I know) it has never been held on this account that a conveyance subsequently executed in performance of the contract is not stampable *ad valorem* as a transfer on sale. Similarly, in a case like the present one, but uncomplicated by the existence of successive interests, a transfer to a purchaser of the investments comprised in a trust fund could not, in my judgment, be prevented from constituting a transfer on sale for the purposes of stamp duty by reason of the fact that the actual transfer had been preceded by an oral agreement for sale.

In truth, the title secured by a purchaser by means of an actual transfer is different in kind from, and may well be far superior to, the special form of proprietary interest which equity confers on a purchaser in anticipation of such transfer.

This difference is of particular importance in the case of property such as shares in a limited company. Under the contract the purchaser is no doubt entitled in equity as between himself and the vendor to the beneficial interest in the shares, and (subject to due payment of the purchase consideration) to call for a transfer of them from the vendor as trustee for him. But it is only on the execution of the actual transfer that he becomes entitled to be registered as a member, to attend and vote at meetings, to effect transfers on the register, or to receive dividends otherwise than through the vendor as his trustee.

The parties to a transaction of sale and purchase may no doubt choose to let the matter rest in contract. But if the subject matter of a sale is such that the full title to it can only be transferred by an instrument, then any instrument they execute by way of transfer of the property sold ranks for stamp duty purposes as a conveyance on sale notwithstanding the constructive trust in favour of the purchaser which arose on the conclusion of the contract.

In the context of a variation of the terms of a trust under the Variation of Trusts Act 1958 (see below, p 858), Megarry VC, in *Re Holt's Settlement*, adopted Lord Radcliffe's reasoning in *Oughtred v IRC*, despite the fact that the latter's judgment was a minority opinion.

Re Holt's Settlement [1969] 1 Ch 100, HC

> **Megarry VC:** Mr Millett for the tenant for life, provided ... [a] means of escape from s 53(1)(c) in his helpful reply: 'Where, as here, the arrangement consists of an agreement made for valuable consideration, and that agreement is specifically enforceable, then the beneficial interests pass to the respective purchasers on the making of the agreement. Those interests pass by virtue of the species of constructive trust made familiar by contracts for the sale of land, whereunder the vendor becomes a constructive trustee for the purchaser as soon as the contract is made ...' Section 53(2), he continued, provides that: 'This section does not affect the creation or operation of resulting, implied or constructive trusts.'
>
> Accordingly, because the trust was constructive, s 53(1)(c) was excluded. He supported this contention by the House of Lords' decision in *Oughtred v IRC*. He relied in particular upon passages in the speeches of Lord Radcliffe and Lord Cohen, albeit that they were dissenting on the main point for decision. He pointed out that although Lord Jenkins (with whom Lord Keith concurred) had not decided the point, he had assumed for the purposes of his speech that it was correct, and that the rejection of the contention by Lord Denning was in a very brief passage. 'Mr Millett accepts that if there were to be some subsequent deed of family arrangement which would carry out the bargain, then this deed might well be caught by s 53(1)(c); but that, he said, cannot affect the "arrangement" and the parties might well be willing to let matters rest on that.' It seems to me that there is considerable force in this argument in cases where the agreement is specifically enforceable, and in its essentials I accept it ... For this and the other reasons I have given, though with some hesitation, I accordingly hold this to be the case.

The case, *Neville v Wilson* (see below, p 45), is a landmark decision, representing the first decision since the High Court case of *Re Holt's Settlement* [1969] 1 Ch 100 to consider rationally the relationship between ss 53(1)(c) and 53(2) of the Law of Property Act 1925. Incidentally, Megarry VC in *Re Holt* followed the dissenting opinion of Lord Radcliffe in *Oughtred v IRC* [1960] AC 206.

In *Oughtred v IRC,* three Law Lords (Lords Denning, Cohen and Radcliffe) considered the relationship between the two sub-sections of the Law of Property Act. Lord Denning sided with the majority opinions (on the issue of stamp duty) delivered by Lord Jenkins, with whom Lord Keith concurred. Lord Denning, in an uncharacteristically short speech, decided that the wording of s 53(2) was not intended to limit s 53(1)(c). This view was delivered without explanation. Lord Cohen dissented on the question of the imposition of stamp duty, but to a large extent agreed with Lord Denning on the relationship between the two sub-sections. Lord Cohen expressed the view that the transferor became a constructive trustee of his equitable interest for the transferee, but that, nonetheless, s 53(1)(c) applied. At the same time, the transferor could not rely on the non-compliance with s 53(1)(c) in order to defeat the transferee's interest, for he is treated as a constructive trustee. This view appears to be synonymous with an estoppel. Lord Radcliffe was the only Law Lord who gave a sound rational analysis of the relationship between the two sub-sections. His view was that the constructive trust (and, likewise, the resulting trust) was exempt from the formal requirements of s 53(1)(c). This was consistent with the wording of s 53(2) and settled principles. Thus, comparing the above three opinions of the Law Lords, it would appear that Lord Radcliffe's view represented, in more than one sense, a minority view incorporating a more realistic and rational analysis of the relationship between the two sub-sections. Above all, a constructive trust is created by the courts to satisfy the demands of justice and conscience. If the circumstances surrounding a transaction demand the imposition of a constructive trust by the courts in order to maintain a balance between the trustees and the beneficiaries, the formal requirement of writing under s 53(1)(c) ought not impede this process. It was against this background that Megarry VC in *Re Holt* decided to endorse Lord Radcliffe's opinion.

Lord Denning in *Re Vandervell's Trust (No2)* [1974] Ch 269 (see below, p 48) proceeded on a different platform when he decided that equitable estoppel prevented Mr Vandervell – and, after his death, his executors – from relying on the formal requirements of s 53(1)(c).

In *Neville v Wilson,* Nourse LJ, after analysing the speeches of the Law Lords, decided that the effect of the agreement in 1969 constituted each shareholder a constructive trustee for the other shareholders. On this basis there was no convincing reason to restrict the effect of the general words enacted in s 53(2).

Neville v Wilson [1996] 3 WLR 460, CA

JE Neville Ltd (J Ltd), a small family company, was the registered owner of all the issued share capital in another company, Universal Engineering Co Ltd (U Ltd), save for 120 ordinary shares, which were registered in the names of two directors of U Ltd as nominees for J Ltd. In 1965, the directors of U Ltd resolved that U Ltd shares registered in the name of J Ltd be transferred to the shareholders of J Ltd in proportions corresponding to their shareholdings in J Ltd. The transfers were executed within two weeks of the resolution. Neither the resolution of the directors nor the subsequent transfers extended to the 120 shares registered in the names of the directors of U Ltd. By 1970, J Ltd, although not formally liquidated, was treated by all concerned as being defunct. In July 1970, it was struck off the register and dissolved with the consequence that any assets owned beneficially by J Ltd passed to the Crown as *bona vacantia*. The question in issue concerned the beneficial ownership of the remaining 120 shares registered in the names of U Ltd directors. The plaintiffs claimed that J Ltd intended to distribute all its shares in U Ltd including the 120 shares in dispute. Thus, the plaintiffs argued that the shares were held on constructive trust for the shareholders in J Ltd. This, the plaintiffs claimed, was a true interpretation of the 1965 resolution. The judge dismissed the plaintiffs' claim and decided that no such distribution was intended. The plaintiffs appealed and raised an alternative argument to the effect that an agreement was entered into between the shareholders of J Ltd for the informal liquidation of J Ltd which had the effect of disposing not only the assets but also its equitable interest in the remaining 120 shares in U Ltd. In other words, the shareholders of J Ltd agreed to a process whereby J Ltd's debts and liabilities were discharged and the balance of its assets, whether ascertained or not, were distributed to its shareholders rateably according to their shareholdings, *in specie* or in cash. The questions in issue were:

(i) whether there was an oral agreement for the informal liquidation of the company and, if so;

(ii) whether it had the effect of disposing of the company's equitable interest in the shares of another company within s 53(1)(c) of the Law of Property Act 1925.

The Court of Appeal decided in favour of the plaintiffs. It was an undisputed fact that after 1969, J Ltd was treated by all concerned as being defunct. From that it was reasonable to infer that its shareholders, in making their agreement, intended that it should not be left with any assets. In other words, it was reasonable to infer that the shareholders intended their agreement to apply to all assets, whether known or unknown.

The effect of the agreement was to create a constructive trust within s 53(2) of the Law of Property Act 1925 which dispensed with the requirement for writing under s 53(1)(c).

> **Nourse LJ:** This is a dispute between the shareholders of a small family company. The substantial questions now in issue are whether there was an agreement for the informal liquidation of the company and, if so, whether it had the effect of disposing of the company's equitable interest in the shares of another company. The latter question involves a consideration of s 53(1)(c) and (2) of the Law of Property Act 1925 and a point left open by the House of Lords in *Oughtred v IRC* [1960] AC 206.
>
> It is an undisputed fact that after 1969 JEN was treated by all concerned as being defunct. From that it is reasonable to infer that its shareholders, in making their agreement, intended that it should not be left with any assets. To put it in another way, it is reasonable to infer that they would have given an affirmative answer to the question whether they intended their agreement to apply to all assets whether known or unknown. Moreover, the parts of Mr Hyde's evidence on which Mr Barker relied can be explained as being what he perceived to have been the practical consequences of the agreement. They

do not restrict the scope of the agreement itself. We should add that, whatever Mr Hyde's state of knowledge may have been at any earlier time or times, we accept that in 1969 he was very likely unaware that the equitable interest in the 120 shares was vested in JEN. But that is by no means decisive of the effect of the agreement.

We are therefore of the opinion that in about April 1969 the shareholders of JEN entered into an agreement with one another for the informal liquidation of JEN as contended for by Mr Jacob and thus, as part of it, for the division of JEN's equitable interest in the 120 ordinary shares in UEC registered in the names of the widow and Mr Wilson amongst themselves, as Mr Hyde put it, 'on a shareholding basis', in other words, in proportions corresponding to their existing shareholdings.

The effect of the agreement, more closely analysed, was that each shareholder agreed to assign his interest in the other shares of JEN's equitable interest in exchange for the assignment by the other shareholders of their interests in his own aliquot share. Each individual agreement having been a disposition of a subsisting equitable interest not made in writing, there then arises the question whether it was rendered ineffectual by s 53 of the Law of Property Act 1925.

Those provisions have been considered in a number of authoritative decisions starting with *Grey v IRC* [1960] AC 1 and *Oughtred v IRC* [1960] AC 206. Mr Jacob relied on *Re Vandervell's Trusts (No 2)* [1974] Ch 269; *Oughtred v IRC* [1960] AC 206 and *Vandervell v IRC* [1967] 2 AC 291. In the *Vandervell* cases the facts were materially different and neither is of assistance here. The question depends on the correct view of a point left open in *Oughtred v IRC* [1960] AC 206.

The simple view of the present case is that the effect of each individual agreement was to constitute the shareholder an implied or constructive trustee for the other shareholders, so that the requirement for writing contained in sub-s (1)(c) of s 53 was dispensed with by sub-s (2). That was the view taken by Upjohn J [1958] Ch 383 at first instance and by Lord Radcliffe in the House of Lords in *Oughtred v Inland Revenue Commissioners* [1960] AC 206.

[His Lordship considered the views of the Law Lords in *Oughtred*'s case and continued:] The views of their Lordships as to the effect of s 53 can be summarised as follows: Lord Radcliffe, agreeing with Upjohn J, thought that sub-s (2) applied. He gave reasons for that view. Lord Cohen and Lord Denning thought that it did not. Although neither of them gave reasons, they may be taken to have accepted the submissions of Mr Wilberforce at pp 220–22. Lord Keith and Lord Jenkins expressed no view either way. We should add that, when the case was in this court, Lord Evershed MR, in delivering the judgment of himself, Morris and Ormerod LJJ, said [1958] Ch 678, p 687:

> In this court the case for the Crown has, we think, been somewhat differently presented, and in the end of all, the question under s 53 of the Law of Property Act 1925, does not, in our judgment, strictly call for a decision. We are not, however, with all respect to the judge, prepared to accept, as we understand it, his conclusion upon the effect of s 53 of the Law of Property Act 1925.

> The basis of this court's decision was the same as that adopted by the majority of the House of Lords.
>
> We do not think that there is anything in the speeches in the House of Lords which prevents us from holding that the effect of each individual agreement was to constitute the shareholder an implied or constructive trustee for the other shareholders. In this respect we are of the opinion that the analysis of Lord Radcliffe, based on the proposition that a specifically enforceable agreement to assign an interest in property creates an equitable interest in the assignee, was unquestionably correct; cf *London and South Western Railway Co v Gomm* (1882) 20 Ch D 562, p 581, *per* Sir George Jessel MR. A greater difficulty is caused by Lord Denning's outright rejection of the application of s 53(2), with which Lord Cohen appears to have agreed.
>
> So far as it is material to the present case, what sub-s (2) says is that sub-s (1)(c) does not affect the creation or operation of implied or constructive trusts. Just as in *Oughtred v IRC* [1960] AC 206, the son's oral agreement created a constructive trust in favour of the mother, so here each shareholder's oral or implied agreement created an implied or constructive trust in favour of the other shareholders. Why then should sub-s (2) not apply? No convincing reason was suggested in argument and none has occurred to us since. Moreover, to deny its application in this case would be to restrict the effect of general words when no restriction is called for, and to lay the ground for fine distinctions in the future. With all the respect which is due to those who have thought to the contrary, we hold that sub-s (2) applies to an agreement such as we have in this case.
>
> For these reasons we have come to the conclusion that the agreement entered into by the shareholders of JEN in about April 1969 was not rendered ineffectual by s 53 of the Act of 1925.

In *Re Vandervell's Trusts (No 2)*, Lord Denning MR in the Court of Appeal conceded that equitable estoppel provides an exception to the rigid requirements enacted in s 53(1)(c). Stephenson LJ (in the same case) although expressing some hesitation about the decision, supported the other Lord Justices of Appeal.

Re Vandervell's Trusts (No 2) [1974] Ch 269, CA

This was a sequel to *Vandervell v IRC* (see above, p 32). In October 1961, V directed the trustee company to exercise the option. The trustee company complied with this instruction, taking £5,000 from the children's settlement in order to re-purchase the shares from the college. In 1965, V received a surtax assessment from the Revenue in respect of the dividends from the shares. Such dividends were paid to the trustee company. The assessment was made on the basis that the equitable title to the shares, like the option, was held on resulting trust for V. Following this assessment, V executed a deed which transferred all interest, if any, which he may have retained in the shares in favour of the children's settlement. In 1967, V died. V's executors claimed the dividends from the trustee company.

The Court of Appeal held in favour of the trustee company on the ground that the resulting trust of the option in favour of V terminated on the date of the exercise of the option. A declaration of trust in favour of the children's settlement was effectively made by reference to three items of evidence. First, the exercise of the option was funded from the children's settlement. Secondly, the dividends were paid to the trustee company for the benefit of the children's settlement. Thirdly, the trustee company had informed the Revenue that the option was exercised and the shares were held upon the trusts of the children's settlement.

[After detailing the facts his Lordship continued:]

Lord Denning MR: During his lifetime Mr Vandervell was a very successful engineer. He had his own private company – Vandervell Products Ltd – 'the products company', as I will call it – in which he owned virtually all the shares. It was in his power to declare dividends as and when he pleased. In 1949 he set up a trust for his children. He did it by forming Vandervell Trustees Ltd – 'the trustee company', as I will call it. He put three of his friends and advisers in control of it. They were the sole shareholders and directors of the trustee company. Two were chartered accountants. The other was his solicitor. He transferred money and shares to the trustee company to be held in trust for the children. Such was the position at the opening of the first period.

Summary of the claims

The root cause of all the litigation is the claim of the Revenue authorities.

The first period – 1958–61: The Revenue authorities claimed that Mr Vandervell was the beneficial owner of the option and was liable for surtax on the dividends declared from 1958–61. This came to £250,000. The claim of the Revenue was upheld by the House of Lords (see *Vandervell v IRC*).

The second period – 1961–65: The Revenue authorities claimed that Mr Vandervell was the beneficial owner of the shares. They assessed him for surtax in respect of the dividends from 11 October 1961, to 19 January 1965, amounting to £628,229. The executors dispute the claim of the Revenue. They appealed against the assessments. But the appeal was, by agreement, stood over pending the case now before us. The executors have brought this action against the trustee company. They seek a declaration that, during the second period, the dividends belonged to Mr Vandervell himself, and they ask for an account of them. The Revenue asked to be joined as parties to the action. This court did join them (see *Vandervell Trustees Ltd v White*) but the House of Lords reversed the decision. So this action has continued – without the presence of the Revenue – whose claim to £628,229 has caused all the trouble.

The third period – 1965–67: The Revenue agreed that they have no claim against the estate for this period.

The law for this first period

The first period was considered by the House of Lords in *Vandervell v IRC*. They held, by a majority of 3:2, that during this period the trustee company held the option as a trustee. The terms of the trust were stated in two ways. Lord Upjohn (with the agreement of Lord Pearce) said that the proper inference was that:

> ... the trustee company should hold as trustee on such trusts as [Mr Vandervell] or the trustee company should from time to time declare.

Lord Wilberforce said that 'the option was held [by the trustee company] on trusts not at the time determined, but to be decided on a later date'.

The trouble about the trust so stated was that it was too uncertain. The trusts were not declared or defined with sufficient precision for the trustees to ascertain who the beneficiaries were. It is clear law that a trust (other than a charitable trust) must be for ascertainable beneficiaries: see *Re Gulbenkian's Settlement Trusts per* Lord Upjohn. Seeing that there were no ascertainable beneficiaries, there was a resulting trust for Mr Vandervell. But if and when Mr Vandervell should declare any defined trusts, the resulting trust would come to an end. As Lord Upjohn said 'until these trusts should be declared there was a resulting trust for [Mr Vandervell]'.

During the first period, however, Mr Vandervell did not declare any defined trusts. The option was, therefore, held on a resulting trust for him. He had not divested himself absolutely of the shares. He was, therefore, liable to pay surtax on the dividends.

The law for the second period

In October and November 1961 the trustee company exercised the option. It paid £5,000 out of the children's settlement. The Royal College of Surgeons transferred the legal estate in the 100,000 'A' shares to the trustee company. Thereupon the trustee company became the legal owner of the shares. This was a different kind of property altogether. Whereas previously the trustee company had only a chose in action of one kind – an option – it now had a chose in action of a different kind – the actual shares. This trust property was not held by the trustee company beneficially. It was held by the company on trust. On this occasion a valid trust was created at the time of the transfer. It was manifested in clear and unmistakable fashion. It was precisely defined. The shares were to be held on the trusts of the children's settlement. The evidence of intention is indisputable:

(i) the trustee company used the children's money – £5,000 – with which to acquire the shares; this would be a breach of trust unless they intended the shares to be an addition to the children's settlement;

(ii) the trustee company wrote to the Revenue authorities the letter of 2 November 1961, declaring expressly that the shares 'will henceforth be held by them upon the trusts of the children's settlement';

(iii) thenceforward, all the dividends received by the trustee company were paid by it to the children's settlement and treated as part of the funds of the settlement. This was all done with the full assent of Mr Vandervell.

> Such being the intention, clear and manifest, at the time when the shares were conveyed to the trustee company, it is sufficient to create a trust.

Counsel for the executors admitted that the intention of Mr Vandervell and the trustee company was that the shares should be held on trust for the children's settlement. But he said that this intention was of no avail. He said that during the first period Mr Vandervell had an equitable interest in the property, namely, a resulting trust; that he never disposed of this equitable interest (because he never knew he had it); and that in any case it was the disposition of an equitable interest which, under s 53 of the Law of Property Act 1925, had to be in writing, signed by him or his agent, lawfully authorised by him in writing (and there was no such writing produced). He cited *Grey v IRC* and *Oughtred v IRC*.

There is a complete fallacy in that argument. A resulting trust for the settlor is born and dies without any writing at all. It comes into existence wherever there is a gap in the beneficial ownership. It ceases to exist whenever that gap is filled by someone becoming beneficially entitled. As soon as the gap is filled by the creation or declaration of a valid trust, the resulting trust comes to an end. In this case, before the option was exercised, there was a gap in the beneficial ownership. So there was a resulting trust for Mr Vandervell. But, as the option was exercised and the shares registered in the trustees' name there was created a valid trust of the shares in favour of the children's settlement. Not being a trust of land, it could be created without any writing. A trust of personalty can be created without writing. Both Mr Vandervell and the trustee company had done everything which needed to be done to make the settlement of these shares binding on them. So there was a valid trust (see *Milroy v Lord, per* Turner LJ).

The law as to third period

The executors admit that from 19 January 1965, Mr Vandervell had no interest whatsoever in the shares. The deed of that date operated so as to transfer all his interest thenceforward to the trustee company to be held by them on trust for the children. I asked counsel for the executors: what is the difference between the events of October and November 1961 and the event of 19 January 1965? He said that it lay in the writing. In 1965 Mr Vandervell disposed of his equitable interest in writing, whereas in 1961 there was no writing. There was only conduct or word of mouth. That was insufficient. And, therefore, his executors were not bound by it.

The answer to this argument is what I have said. Mr Vandervell did not dispose in 1961 of any equitable interest. All that happened was that his resulting trust came to an end – because there was created a new valid trust of the shares for the children's settlement.

Estoppel

Even if counsel for the executors were right in saying that Mr Vandervell retained an equitable interest in the shares, after the exercise of the option, the question arises whether Mr Vandervell can in the circumstances be heard to assert the claim against his children. Just see what happened. He himself arranged for the option to be exercised. He himself agreed to the shares being transferred to the trustee company. He himself procured his products company to declare dividends on the shares and to pay them to the trustee company for the benefit of the children. Thenceforward, the trustee company invested the money and treated it as part of the children's settlement. If he himself had lived, and not died, he could not have claimed it back. He could not be heard to say that he did not intend the children's trust to have it. Even a court of equity would not allow him to do anything so inequitable and unjust. Now that he has died, his executors are in no better position. If authority were needed, it is to be found in *Milroy v Lord*. In that case Thomas Medley assigned to Samuel Lord 50 shares in the Bank of Louisiana on trust for his niece; but the shares were not formally transferred into the name of Samuel Lord. The bank, however, paid the dividends to Samuel Lord. He paid them to the niece, and then, at Thomas Medley's suggestion, the niece used those dividends to buy shares in a fire insurance company – taking them in the name of Thomas Medley. After Thomas Medley's death, his executors claimed that the bank shares belonged to them as representing him, and also the fire insurance shares. Knight-Bruce and Turner LJJ held that the executors were entitled to the bank shares, because 'there is no equity in this court to perfect an imperfect gift'. But the executors were not entitled to the fire insurance shares. Turner LJ said:

> ... the settlor made a perfect gift to [the niece] of the dividends upon these shares, so far as they were handed over or treated by him as belonging to her, and these insurance shares were purchased with dividends which were so handed over or treated.

So here Mr Vandervell made a perfect gift to the trustee company of the dividends on the shares, so far as they were handed over or treated by him as belonging to the trustee company for the benefit of the children. Alternatively, there was an equitable estoppel. His conduct was such that it would be quite inequitable for him to be allowed to enforce his strict rights (under a resulting trust) having regard to the dealings which had taken place between the parties (see *Hughes v Metropolitan Railway Co* (1877) 2 App Cas 439).

I would allow the appeal and dismiss the claim of the executors.

Stephenson LJ: I have had more doubt than my brethren whether we can overturn the judgment of Megarry J [at first instance] in what I have not found an easy case. Indeed, treading a (to me) dark and unfamiliar path, I had parted from both my fellow travellers and, following the windings of counsel for the executors' argument, had nearly reached a different terminus before the light which they threw on the journey enabled me to join them at the same conclusion.

To expound my doubts would serve no useful purpose; to state them shortly may do no harm. The cause of all the trouble is what the judge called 'the ill-fated option' and its incorporation in a deed which was 'too short and simple' to rid Mr Vandervell of the beneficial interest in the disputed shares, as a bare majority of the House of Lords held, not without fluctuation of mind on the part of one of them (Lord Upjohn), in *Vandervell v IRC*. The operation of law or equity kept for Mr Vandervell or gave him back an equitable interest which he did not want and would have thought he had disposed of if he had ever known it existed. It is therefore difficult to infer that he intended to dispose or ever did dispose of something he did not know he had until the judgment of Plowman J in *Vandervell v IRC*, which led to the deed of 1965, enlightened him, or to find a disposition of it in the exercise by the trustee company in 1961 of its option to purchase the shares. And even if he had disposed of his interest, he did not dispose of it by any writing sufficient to comply with s 53(1)(c) of the Law of Property Act 1925.

But Lord Denning MR and Lawton LJ are able to hold that no disposition is needed because: (1) the option was held on such trusts as might thereafter be declared by the trustee company or Mr Vandervell himself; and (2) the trustee company has declared that it holds the shares in the children's settlement. I do not doubt the first, because it was apparently the view of the majority of the House of Lords in *Vandervell v IRC*. I should be more confident of the second if it had been pleaded or argued either here or below and we had had the benefit of the learned judge's views on it. I see, as perhaps did counsel, difficulties in the way of a limited company declaring a trust by parol or conduct and without a resolution of the board of directors, and difficulties also in the way of finding any declaration of trust by Mr Vandervell himself in October or November 1961, or any conduct then or later which would in law or equity estop him from denying that he made one.

However, Lord Denning MR and Lawton LJ are of the opinion that these difficulties, if not imaginary, are not insuperable and that these shares went into the children's settlement in 1961 in accordance with the intention of Mr Vandervell and the trustee company – a result with which I am happy to agree as it seems to me to be in accordance with the justice and the reality of the case.

Lawton LJ began with the point that it was the late Mr Vandervell's intention that the trustee company should hold the option on such trusts as might thereafter be declared by the trustee company or Mr Vandervell himself and held that the trustee company declared trusts for the children in 1961. He also held that Mr Vandervell was estopped from denying the existence of a beneficial interest for his children.

He went on to create a most unlawyerlike distinction between the option held on a resulting trust and the shares acquired upon exercising the option: he took the view that after the option had been exercised it had been extinguished, so no old equitable interest existed to be capable of assignment, so that only new equitable interests could be created! However, the option is not distinct from the shares but merely a limited right created out of the larger bundle of rights inherent in the ownership of the shares. For this very reason the House of Lords in *Vandervell v IRC* had held that Vandervell, the original beneficial owner of the shares, who had remained beneficial owner under a resulting trust of the option relating to the shares, had failed to divest himself absolutely of the shares which the option governed. If the right to the shares under the option was held by the trustee company under a resulting trust for Vandervell then any shares actually acquired by exercising the right should surely be similarly held under a resulting trust.

Although a conscious and intentional transfer of a subsisting equitable interest must be in writing, it seems that when an equitable owner intends to disclaim an equitable interest the disclaimer is not required to be in writing. The reason being that no one may be compelled to retain an equitable interest. The manifestation of an intention to disown an interest will be sufficient to disclaim that interest. The effect is that on a disclaimer by an equitable owner, a resulting trust will be created in favour of the settlor or his estate in the absence of provisions to the contrary.

In *Re Paradise Motor Co*, one of the questions in issue was whether a disclaimer of an equitable interest in shares operated by way of a 'disposition' within s 53(1)(c).

Re Paradise Motor Co [1968] 1 WLR 1125, CA

> **Dankwerts LJ:** We think that the short answer to this is that a disclaimer operates by way of avoidance and not by way of disposition. For the general aspects of disclaimer we refer briefly to the discussion in *Re Stratton's Disclaimer* [1958] Ch 42.

In addition, nominations by pension fund holders of the persons who will become entitled to benefits under a pension fund after the deaths of the pension fund holders are not 'dispositions' within s 53(1)(c). Accordingly, such nominations are not required to be in writing. (See *Re Danish Bacon Co Staff Pension Fund*.)

Re Danish Bacon Co Staff Pension Fund [1971] 1 WLR 248, HC

> **Megarry J:** What I am concerned with is a transaction whereby the deceased dealt with something which *ex hypothesi* could never be his. He was not disposing of his pension, nor of his right to the contributions and interest if he left the company's service. He was dealing merely with a state of affairs that would arise if he died while in the company's pensionable service, or after he had left it without becoming entitled to a pension. If he did this, then the contributions and interest would, by force of the rules, go either to his nominee, if he had made a valid nomination, or to his personal representatives, if he had not. If he made a nomination, it was revocable at any time before his death.
>
> The question is thus whether an instrument with this elective, contingent and defeasible quality, which takes effect only on the death of the person signing it, can fairly be said to be a 'a disposition of an equitable interest or trust subsisting at the time of the disposition'. Mr Ferris put much emphasis on the word 'subsisting': however wide the word 'disposition' might be in its meaning, there was no disposition of a subsisting equity, he said, I should hesitate to describe an instrument which has a mere possibility of becoming a 'disposition' as being in itself a disposition *ab initio*; and I agree that the word, 'subsisting' also seems to point against the nomination falling within s 53(1)(c) ... I very much doubt whether the nomination falls within s 53(1)(c); but as I have indicated, I do not have to decide that point, and I do not do so.

Brian Green, in '*Grey, Oughtred and Vandervell*: a contextual reappraisal' [1984] 47 MLR 385, subjected the four decisions (including *Re Vandervell's Trusts (No*

2)) to a searching analysis. The focus of attention was to ascertain the ambit of s 53(1)(c) of the Law of Property Act 1925. He asserts that the policy of enacting s 53(1)(c), like s 9 of the Statute of Frauds 1677, was: '(i) to prevent hidden oral transactions in equitable interests in fraud of those truly entitled; and (ii) to enable trustees to know where the equitable interests behind their trusts reside at any particular time.' Moreover, the sub-section draws no distinction between dealings with equitable interests carrying beneficial rights on the one hand and, on the other hand, dealings with equitable interests shorn of beneficial rights, that is, valuable and valueless equitable interests. Green contends that both types of interests fall within the ambit of s 53(1)(c).

He states:

> ... it is said that a declaration of trust over a subsisting equitable interest, with beneficial entitlement annexed thereto, is not within the sub-section since it merely entails a disposition of beneficial interest, and not of the subsisting equitable interest itself, which continues to exist in its original proprietor despite the declaration having taken place. If this is right then s 53(1)(c) is seen to operate in a somewhat arbitrary fashion, permitting the oral declaration of trust which shifts the valuable beneficial rights out of a subsisting equitable interest, but requiring written assignment if, at a later stage, the declarant decided to part with the valueless equitable interest retained by him ... at most, a declaration of trust over a subsisting equitable interest involves a disposition 'out of' that interest, not a disposition of the interest itself – and it is to dispositions of subsisting equitable interests, not to dispositions 'out of' such interests, that the literal words of s 53(1)(c) are addressed.
>
> [Professor Hayton] expressed the view that, in deciding whether a 'declaration of trust' over a subsisting equitable interest falls within s 53(1)(c), it is necessary to distinguish between declarations under which the declarant purports to reserve to himself an active role as trustee of the derivative equitable interest established by him, and declarations whereby the declarant renders himself a bare trustee for others. The former case is said to fall outside s 53(1)(c), whilst the latter is said to be within it on the basis that the declarant having no further role to play simply 'drops out of the picture' from the moment of declaration onwards. Three 19th century cases are cited in support of this view, *Onslow v Wallis* (1849) 1 Mac & G 506; *Re Lashmar* [1891] 1 Ch 258; *Grainge v Wilberforce* (1889) 5 TLR 436.

Mr Green examines these cases and concludes:

> ... this somewhat inelegant distinction between declarations within s 53(1)(c) and declarations outside it, whatever its intuitive appeal, is certainly not justified by the 19th century authorities marshalled in its support, and is inconsistent with the view adopted by the House of Lords in *Oughtred v IRC* (1960) in relation to a constructive bare trustee of an equitable interest who most definitely remained 'in the picture' until the execution of a 'completion document' deliberately removed him from it.

Battersby, G, in 'Formalities for the disposition of equitable interests under a trust' [1979] Conv 17, examined, in detail, five important cases concerning s 53(1)(c) of the Law of Property Act 1925. These cases are: *Grey v IRC* [1960]

AC 1; *Oughtred v IRC* [1960] AC 206; *Vandervell v IRC* [1967] 2 AC 291; *Re Holt's Settlement* [1969] 1 Ch 100; *Re Vandervell's Trust (No 2)* [1974] Ch 269. After carefully analysing the bases of these decisions, Mr Battersby tabulates his conclusion as follows:

(1) the beneficiary (B) assigns his beneficial interest directly to a third party (X). This is clearly within s 53(1)(c) and must be in writing;

(2) B assigns his interest to new trustees to hold on trust for X. The assignment to the trustees must be in writing, but there is also a declaration of trust, which requires written evidence if the trust property is land. The assignment itself need not contain any particulars of the new trusts, see *Re Tyler's Fund Trusts* [1967] 3 All ER 389;

(3) B directs the original trustees to hold his interest for X. This is a disposition within s 53(1)(c), see *Grey v IRC*, but, it is submitted, is not at the same time a declaration of trust;

(4) B, the absolute beneficial owner, directs the trustees to convey the legal title to X, with the intention that X shall hold beneficially, and the trustees execute the conveyance. X takes beneficially, and there is no need for any separate written assignment by X, see *Vandervell v IRC*;

(5) B contracts for value to assign to X. If the contract is specifically enforceable it creates a constructive trust in favour of X. The original trustees will hold directly for X, so that the transaction resembles an assignment by B to X; nevertheless, it is submitted that, as a constructive trust, the transaction is exempted by s 53(2) from the requirements of writing, see *Oughtred v IRC; Re Holt; per* Lord Wilberforce in *Vandervell v IRC*;

(6) B contracts for value to assign to new trustees to hold on trust for X. The result is the same as in transaction (5) above, but in addition there is an express declaration of trust which, if it relates to land, must be evidenced in writing;

(7) B declares himself a trustee in favour of X. It is submitted that B will drop out of the picture, unless he has active duties to perform as a trustee. In the latter case, the transaction is a declaration of trust, and must be evidenced in writing if it relates to land. In the former case, the original trustees hold for X directly, the transaction is in truth an assignment and must be in writing, see *Grainge v Wilberforce* (1889) 5 TLR 436; *Re Lashmar* [1891] 1 Ch 258;

(8) B, the absolute beneficial owner, declares himself a trustee in favour of X for life, then for Y absolutely. B has active duties to perform as a trustee, since otherwise the duties of the original trustees would be enlarged; the transaction is therefore a declaration of trust, and must be evidenced in writing if it relates to land. B can call for the legal title, see *Onslow v Wallis* (1849) 1 Mac & G 506;

(9) B is the legal and beneficial owner of personal property which he conveys to persons as trustees but without declaring any beneficial interests. B therefore is beneficially entitled under a resulting trust. B then declares that the trustees shall hold for X. Despite the exemption of a resulting trust

from the requirement of writing, it is submitted that B's declaration is a disposition to X which must be in writing, unless the declaration is made by a person other than B under a power reserved to that person by the original conveyance to the trustees, and therefore having priority to the resulting trust, see *Re Vandervell's Trusts (No 2)*.

The declaration of trust

The additional requirement imposed on the settlor in order to perfect a trust is the declaration of the terms of the trust such as, the identity of the trustees and beneficiaries, the ascertainment of the trust property and the nature of the beneficial interest. The expression 'declaration of trust' is a phrase which reflects the settlor's intention to create a trust including the terms of the trust.

Generally, no formalities are required to be complied with for, 'equity looks at the intent rather than the form'. Thus, the declaration of trust may be made orally or by conduct or in writing. Exceptionally, Parliament may impose formal requirements for the creation of a trust.

Law of Property Act 1925

Section 53(1)(b) provides that:

> ... a declaration of trust respecting any land or any interest therein must be manifested and proved by some writing signed by some person who is able to declare such trust or by his will.

The predecessor to this sub-section was enacted in the Statute of Frauds 1677 which was passed for the purpose of preventing fraud by requiring evidence of the terms of the trust in writing.

Under Sched 1 of the Interpretation Act 1978,' 'land' includes buildings and other structures, land covered with water, and any estate, interest, easement, servitude or right in or over land'.

By virtue of s 205(1)(ix) of the Law of Property Act 1925:

> (ix) 'land' includes land of any tenure, and mines and minerals, whether or not held apart from the surface, buildings or parts of buildings (whether the division is horizontal, vertical or made in any other way) and other corporeal hereditaments; also a manor, an advowson, and a rent and other incorporeal hereditaments, and an easement, right, privilege, or benefit in, over, or derived from land; but *not an undivided share in land*; and 'mines and minerals' include any strata or seam of minerals or substances in or under the land, and powers of working and getting the same but not an undivided share thereof; and 'manor' includes a lordship, and reputed manor or lordship; and 'hereditament' means any real property which on an intestacy occurring before the commencement of this Act might have devolved upon an heir;
>
> (x) 'legal estates' mean the estates, interests and charges, in or over land (subsisting or created in law) which are by this Act authorised to subsist or to be created as legal estates; 'equitable interests' mean all the other

> interests and charges in or over land or in the proceeds of sale thereof; and equitable interest 'capable of subsisting as a legal estate' means such as could validly subsist or be created as a legal estate under this Act.

Under the Trusts of Land and Appointment of Trustees Act 1996 (which came into force on 1 January 1997), an all pervasive concept known as a 'trust of land' has been created. This term is applicable to all trusts – express, resulting, constructive or statutory – which include land (s 1). The dual concepts of strict settlements and trusts for sale, which existed prior to the introduction of the 1996 Act, are now treated as trusts of land. Express trusts for sale may still be created after the 1996 Act, but these take effect as trusts of land. A power to postpone the sale is implied into every trust for sale, which is capable of being postponed indefinitely in the exercise of the discretion of the trustees. This power to postpone the sale is incapable of being excluded by the settlor.

Section 3 of the Act abolishes the doctrine of conversion. The effect is that land held upon trust for sale is treated as realty and the interests of the beneficiaries under the trust are treated as interests in land, for example, If S, a settlor, transfers land to trustees, T1 and T2, to hold upon trust for sale for A and B equally, the beneficiaries are treated as enjoying interests in land. A declaration of trust by A and/or B of his or their interests falls within s 53(1)(b) of the Law of Property Act 1925.

Writing for these purposes may be taken to mean any permanent form of representation. In this respect, regard may be had to s 13(1) of the Civil Evidence Act 1995. For the purpose of the documentary evidence rule in civil cases under the Act, a document means:

> ... anything in which information of any description is recorded ...
>
> ... a statement means any representation of fact or opinion, however made.

The document is required to incorporate all the terms of the trust, signed by the person declaring the trust (settlor). If, however, there is a series of documents, each incorporating a material term of the trust, each document may be joined together to form a complete memorandum, provided that a subsequent document is referred to in the earlier document, and each document or one of the composite documents is signed by the settlor. The signature of agents of the settlor is not permitted. The settlor's signature may constitute any form of endorsement of the terms of the document, such as initials, thumbprint, etc. Reference may be made to the expression 'sign' in s 1(4) of the Law of Property (Miscellaneous Provisions) Act 1989 which states that, for the purposes of s 1 of the Act, '"sign", in relation to an instrument, includes making one's mark on the instrument and "signature" is to be construed accordingly'.

The effect of s 53(1)(b) is that a declaration of trust in respect of real property is required to be evidenced in writing. Non-compliance with this formal requirement renders the declaration of trust unenforceable. In other words, the trust is not rendered void, but instead, no one is entitled to enforce the trust for failure to satisfy s 53(1)(b). If evidence of the terms of the trust in writing is adduced subsequent to the declaration, the trust will be enforced not from the date of the execution of the document, but from the earlier date of the parol declaration of trust, for example, on day one, S, a settlor, orally declares himself a trustee of his real property, Blackacre, in favour of B, a beneficiary. This trust is unenforceable for non-compliance with s 53(1)(b). On day two, S executes a signed document containing the terms of the trust. The trust is now enforceable retrospectively from day one.

Section 53(2) enacts that 'this section shall not affect the creation or operation of implied, resulting and constructive trusts'.

In other words, a plaintiff who claims an equitable interest in land without being able to establish the terms of the trust in writing, is entitled to prove that his interest arises by way of a resulting or constructive trust. (These are implied trusts created by the courts, see below, Chapters 8 and 9.)

Hodgson v Marks [1971] Ch 892, CA

In this case, Mrs H transferred the legal title to her house in favour of her lodger (Evans) on the oral understanding that the property would continue to be hers. Evans then attempted to sell the house to Marks who had notice of the agreement but claimed that Mrs H's interest was unenforceable. Mrs H relied on s 53(2). The court held that Mrs H retained her equitable interest by way of a resulting trust which exempted her from the formal requirements under s 53(1)(b).

> **Russell LJ:** ... the evidence is clear that transfer [to Mr Evans] was not intended to operate as a gift, and, in those circumstances, I do not see why there was not a resulting trust of the beneficial interest to the plaintiff, which would not, of course, be affected by s 53(1). It was argued that a resulting trust is based upon implied intention, and that where there is an express trust for the transferor intended and declared – albeit ineffectively – there is no room for such an implication. I do not accept that. If an attempted express trust fails, that seems to me just the occasion for implication of a resulting trust, whether the failure be due to uncertainty, or perpetuity, or lack of form. It would be a strange outcome if the plaintiff were to lose her beneficial interest because her evidence had not been confined to negativing a gift but had additionally moved into a field forbidden by s 53(1) for lack of writing. I remark in this connection that we are not concerned with the debatable question whether on a voluntary transfer of land by A to stranger B there is a presumption of a resulting trust. The accepted evidence is that this was not intended as a gift, notwithstanding the reference to love and affection in the transfer, and s 53(1) does not exclude that evidence.

Section 2 of the Law of Property (Miscellaneous Provisions) Act 1989 provides:

> (1) A contract for the sale or other disposition of an interest in land can only be made in writing and only by incorporating all the terms which the parties have expressly agreed in one document or, where contracts are exchanged, in each.

(2) The terms may be incorporated in a document either by being set out in it or by reference to some other document.

(3) The document incorporating the terms or, where contracts are exchanged, one of the documents incorporating them (but not necessarily the same one must be signed by or on behalf of each party to the contract.

(4) ...

(5) This section does not apply in relation to:

(a) ...

(b) ...

(c) ...

and nothing in this section affects the creation or operation of resulting, implied or constructive trusts.

(6) In this section:

'disposition' has the same meaning as in the Law of Property Act 1925;

'interest in land' means any estate, interest or charge in or over land or in or over the proceeds of sale of land'.

Unlike s 53(1)(b) of the Law of Property Act 1925, non-compliance with the 1989 Act renders the purported transfer void. But both provisions are subject to the existence of a resulting or constructive trust.

The declaration of trust may take two forms – either:

(1) a direction to the trustees to hold the property subject to the terms set out by the settlor (a third party declaration); or

(2) an acknowledgment by the settlor as to his new status as trustee in respect of property retained by him (a self-declaration). Accordingly, the settlor, as the original owner of both the legal and equitable interests in property, may transfer the legal title to a trustee subject to the terms of the trust or the settlor may retain the legal title but declare himself a trustee of the property for the benefit of another or others. In either case, the test is whether the settlor intended to impose a trust in respect of the relevant property and whether he had set out the minimum set of terms. This is a question which varies with the facts of each case.

THE THREE CERTAINTIES

The 'three certainties' test exists as a means of ascertaining whether the settlor has validly declared the terms of the trust. This test was laid down by Lord Langdale MR in *Knight v Knight*[13] as:

(a) certainty of intention;

13 (1840) 3 Beav 148.

(b) certainty of subject matter; and

(c) certainty of objects.

Per Lord Langdale MR in *Knight v Knight*:

> ... the recommendation, entreaty, or wish shall be held to create a trust.
>
> First, if the words were so used, that upon the whole, they ought to be construed as imperative; secondly, if the subject of the recommendation or wish be certain; and thirdly, if the objects or persons intended to have the benefit of the recommendation or wish be also certain.
>
> On the other hand, if the giver (donor) accompanies his expression of wish, or request by other words, from which it is to be collected, that he did not intend the wish to be imperative: or if it appears from the context that the first taker was intended to have a discretionary power to withdraw any part of the subject from the object of the wish or request; or if the objects are not such as may be ascertained with sufficient certainty, it has been held that no trust is created.

Certainty of intention

This test requires the court to consider the words used by the settlor and all the surrounding circumstances, including the settlor's conduct, in order to ascertain whether the settlor intended to impose the obligations of trusteeship in respect of property for the benefit of the beneficiaries. This narrow requirement is materially different from an intention merely to benefit another. There are many different ways of benefiting another, but the narrow issue here is whether the settlor has gone further and declared his intention to impose an equitable obligation on the trustees in respect of the property. The question is simply whether the settlor manifested an intention to create a trust. This is a question of fact and degree. Although desirable, the settlor need not use the expression 'trust', but substitute expressions used by the settlor must have this effect in order to create a trust, for 'equity looks at the intent rather than the form'.

Jones v Lock (1865) LR 1 Ch App 25, CA

Robert Jones placed a cheque for £900 into the hand of his nine month old baby, saying 'I give this to baby and I am going to put it away for him'. He then took the cheque from the child and told his nanny: 'I am going to put this away for my son.' He put the cheque in his safe. A few days later, he told his solicitor: 'I shall come to your office on Monday to alter my will, that I may take care of my son.' He died the same day. The question in issue was whether the cheque belonged to the child or the residuary legatees under Robert Jones' will. The court held that the cheque belonged to the residuary legatees. The transfer to the child was imperfect and Jones had not declared a trust of the cheque.

> **Lord Cranworth LC:** I cannot bring myself to think that, either on principle or on authority, there has been any gift or any valid declaration of trust. No doubt a gift may be made by any person *sui juris* and *compos mentis*, by conveyance of a real estate or by delivery of a chattel; and there is no doubt also that, by some decisions, unfortunate I must think them, a parol declaration of trust of personalty may be perfectly valid even when voluntary. If I give any chattel that, of course, passes by delivery, and if I say, expressly or impliedly, that I constitute myself a trustee of personalty, that is a trust executed, and capable of being enforced without consideration. I do not think it necessary to go into any of the authorities cited before me; they all turn upon the question, whether what has been said was a declaration of trust or an imperfect gift. In the latter case the parties would receive no aid from a court of equity if they claimed as volunteers. But when there has been a declaration of trust, then it will be enforced, whether there has been consideration or not. Therefore, the question in each case is one of fact; has there been a gift or not, or has there been a declaration of trust or not? I should have every inclination to sustain this gift, but unfortunately I am unable to do; the case turns on the very short question whether Jones intended to make a declaration that he held the property in trust for the child; and I cannot come to any other conclusion than that he did not. I think it would be a very dangerous example if loose conversations of this sort, in important transactions of this kind, should have the effect of declarations of trust.

Contrast *Paul v Constance*.

Paul v Constance [1977] 1 WLR 527, CA

Mrs Paul and Mr Constance lived together as man and wife. Mr C received £950 compensation for an industrial injury and both parties agreed to put the money in a deposit account in Mr C's name. On numerous occasions, both before and after the opening of the account, Mr C told Mrs P that the money was as much hers as his. After Mr C's death, Mrs P claimed the fund from Mrs C, the administrator. The court held in favour of Mrs P as Mr C, by his words and deeds, declared himself a trustee for himself and Mrs P of the damages.

> **Scarman LJ:** The only point taken by the defendant on her appeal to this court goes to the question whether or not there was, in the circumstances of this case, an express declaration of trust. It is conceded that if there was the trust would be enforceable.
>
> Counsel for the defendant drew the attention of the court to the so called three certainties that have to be established before the court can infer the creation of a trust. He referred us to *Snell's Principles of Equity*, in which the three certainties are set out. We are concerned only with one of the three certainties, and it is this:
>
> > The words [that is the words of the declaration relied on] must be so used that on the whole they ought to be construed as imperative. [A little later on the learned author says:] No particular form of expression is necessary for the creation of a trust, if on the whole it can be gathered that a trust was

> intended ... A trust may well be created, although there may be an absence of any expression in terms imposing confidence ... A trust may thus be created without using the word 'trust', for what the court regards is the substance and effect of the words used.

Counsel for the defendant has taken the court through the detailed evidence and submits that one cannot find anywhere in the history of events a declaration of trust in the sense of finding the deceased man, Mr Constance, saying: 'I am now disposing of my interest in this fund so that you, Mrs Paul, now have a beneficial interest in it.' Of course, the words which I have just used are stilted lawyers' language, and counsel for the plaintiff was right to remind the court that we are dealing with simple people, unaware of the subtleties of equity, but understanding very well indeed their own domestic situation. It is right that one should consider the various things that were said and done by the plaintiff and Mr Constance during their time together against their own background and in their own circumstances.

Counsel for the defendant drew our attention to two cases, and he relies on them as showing that, though a man may say in clear and unmistakable terms that he intends to make a gift to some other person, for instance his child or some other member of his family, yet that does not necessarily disclose a declaration of trust; and, indeed, in the two cases to which we have been referred the court held that, though there was a plain intention to make a gift, it was not right to infer any intention to create a trust.

The first of the two cases is *Jones v Lock* (1865). *Jones v Lock* was a classic case where the intention to make a gift failed because the gift was imperfect. So an attempt was made to say: 'Well, since the gift was imperfect, nevertheless, one can infer the existence of a trust.' But Lord Cranworth LC would have none of it.

In the other case to which counsel for the defendant referred us, *Richards v Delbridge*,[14] the facts were that a Mr Richards, who employed a member of his family in his business, was minded to give the business to the young man. He evidenced his intention to make this gift by endorsing on the lease of the business premises a short memorandum to the effect that:

> This deed [ie, the deed of leasehold] and all thereto belonging I give to Edward ... [ie, the boy] from this time forth with all stock in trade.

Jessel MR who decided the case, said that there was in that case the intention to make a gift, but the gift failed because it was imperfect; and he refused from the circumstances of the imperfect gift to draw the inference of the existence of a declaration of trust or the intention to create one. The *ratio decidendi* appears clearly from the report. It is a short passage, and because of its importance I quote it:

> In *Milroy v Lord* Lord Justice Turner, after referring to the two modes of making a voluntary settlement valid and effectual, adds these words: 'The cases, I think, go further, to this extent, that if the settlement is intended to be effectuated by one of the modes to which I have referred, the court will

14 (1874) LR 18 Eq 11.

> not give effect to it by applying another of those modes. If it is intended to take effect by transfer, the court will not hold the intended transfer to operate as a declaration of trust, for then every imperfect instrument would be made effectual by being converted into a perfect trust.' It appears to me that that sentence contains the whole law on the subject.

There is no suggestion of a gift by transfer in this case. The facts of those cases do not, therefore, very much help the submission of counsel for the defendant, but he was able to extract from them this principle: that there must be a clear declaration of trust, and that means there must be clear evidence from what is said or done of an intention to create a trust, or as counsel for the defendant put it, 'an intention to dispose of a property or a fund so that somebody else to the exclusion of the disponet acquires the beneficial interest in it. He submitted that there was no such evidence'.

When one looks to the detailed evidence to see whether it goes as far as that – and I think that the evidence does have to go as far as that – one finds that from the time that Mr Constance received his damages right up to his death he was saying, on occasions, that the money was as much the plaintiff's as his. When they discussed the damages, how to invest them or what to do with them, when they discussed the bank account, he would say to her: 'The money is as much yours as mine.' The judge, rightly treating the basic problem in the case as a question of fact, reached this conclusion. He said:

> I have read through my notes, and I am quite satisfied that it was the intention of [the plaintiff] and Mr Constance to create a trust in which both of them were interested.

In this court the issue becomes: was there sufficient evidence to justify the judge reaching that conclusion of fact? In submitting that there was, counsel for the plaintiff draws attention first and foremost to the words used. When one bears in mind the unsophisticated character of Mr Constance and his relationship with the plaintiff during the last few years of his life, counsel for the plaintiff submits that the words that he did use on more than one occasion namely: 'This money is as much yours as mine,' convey clearly a present declaration that the existing fund was as much the plaintiff's as his own. The judge accepted that conclusion. I think he was well justified in doing so and, indeed, I think he was right to do. There are, as counsel for the plaintiff reminded us, other features in the history of the relationship between the plaintiff and Mr Constance which support the interpretation of those words as an express declaration of trust. I have already described the interview with the bank manager when the account was opened. I have mentioned also the putting of the 'bingo' winnings into the account, and the one withdrawal for the benefit of both of them.

It might, however, be thought that this was a borderline case, since it is not easy to pinpoint a specific moment of declaration, and one must exclude from one's mind any case built on the existence of an implied or constructive trust; for this case was put forward at the trial and is now argued by the plaintiff as one of express declaration of trust. It was so pleaded, and it is only as such that it may be considered in this court. The question, therefore, is whether in all the circumstances the use of those words on numerous occasions as between Mr

Constance and the plaintiff constituted an express declaration of trust. The judge found that they did. For myself, I think he was right so to find. I therefore would dismiss the appeal.

Re Kayford Ltd [1975] 1 All ER 604, CA

A mail order company received advice from accountants as to the method of protecting advance payments of the purchase price or deposits for goods ordered by customers. The company was advised to open a separate bank account to be called 'Customer Trust Deposit Account' into which future sums of money received for goods not yet delivered to customers were to be paid. The company accepted the advice and its managing director gave oral instructions to the company's bank, but instead of opening a new account, a dormant deposit account in the company's name was used for this purpose. A few weeks later the company was put into liquidation. The question in issue was whether the sums paid into the bank account were held upon trust for customers who had paid wholly or partly for goods which were not delivered or whether they formed part of the general assets of the company.

Held that a valid trust had been created in favour of the relevant customers in accordance with the intention of the company and the arrangements effected. The position remained the same even though payment was not made into a separate banking account.

Megarry J: The question for me is whether the money in the bank account (apart from the dormant amount of £47.80 and interest on it), is held on trust for those who paid it, or whether it forms part of the general assets of the company. Counsel for the joint liquidators, one of whom is in fact Mr Wainwright, has contended that there is no trust, so that the money forms part of the general assets of the company and so will be available for the creditors generally. On the other hand, there is a Mr Joels, who on 12 December paid the company £32.20 for goods which have not been delivered; and counsel for him seeks a representation order on behalf of all others whose moneys have been paid into the bank account, some 700 or 800 in number. I make that order. Counsel for the representative beneficiary, of course, argued for the existence of an effective trust. I may say at the outset that on the facts of the case counsel for the joint liquidators was unable to contend that any question of a fraudulent preference arose. If one leaves on one side any case in which an insolvent company seeks to declare a trust in favour of creditors, one is concerned here with the question not of preferring creditors but of preventing those who pay money from becoming creditors, by making them beneficiaries under a trust.

Now there are clearly some loose ends in the case. Mr Kay, advised to establish a 'Customers' Trust Deposit Account', seems to have thought that it did not matter what the account was called so long as there was a separate account; and so the dormant deposit account suggested by the bank manager was used. The bank statement for this account is before me, and on the first page, for which the title is simply 'Deposit Account Kayford Ltd', nearly £26,000 is credited. The second and third pages have the words 'Customer Trust Deposit account' added after the previous title of the account; and Mr Joel's payment was made after these words had been added. Mr Kay also left matters resting on a telephone conversation with the bank manager until he wrote his letter of 12 December to the bank. That letter reads: 'We confirm our instructions regarding the opening of the Deposit account for customer deposits for new orders'; and he then makes some mention of other accounts with the bank. The letter goes on: 'Please ensure the re-opened deposit account is titled "Customer Trust Deposit Account".'

I feel no doubt that the intention was that there should be a trust. There are no formal difficulties. The property concerned is pure personalty, and so writing, though desirable, is not an essential. There is no doubt about the so called 'three certainties' of a trust. The subject matter to be held on trust is clear, and so are the beneficial interests therein, as well as the beneficiaries. As for the requisite certainty of words, it is well settled that a trust can be created without using the words 'trust' or 'confidence' or the like: the question is whether in substance a sufficient intention to create a trust has been manifested.

In *Re Nanwa Gold Mines Ltd*[15] the money was sent on the faith of a promise to keep it in a separate account, but there is nothing in that case or in any other authority that I know of to suggest that this is essential. I feel no doubt that here a trust was created. From the outset the advice (which was accepted) was to establish a trust account at the bank. The whole purpose of what was done was to ensure that the moneys remained in the beneficial ownership of those who sent them, and a trust is the obvious means of achieving this. No doubt the general rule is that if you send money to a company for goods which are not delivered, you are merely a creditor of the company unless a trust has been created. The sender may create a trust by using appropriate words when he sends the money (though I wonder how many do this, even if they are equity lawyers), or the company may do it by taking suitable steps on or before receiving the money. If either is done, the obligations in respect of the money are transformed from contract to property, from debt to trust. Payment into a separate bank account is useful (though by no means conclusive) indication of an intention to create a trust, but of course there is nothing to prevent the company from binding itself by a trust even if there are no effective banking arrangements.

Accordingly, of the alternative declarations sought by the summons, the second, to the effect that the money is held in trust for those who paid it, is in my judgment the declaration that should be made.

I should, however, add one thing. Different considerations may perhaps arise in relation to trade creditors; but here I am concerned only with members of the public, some of whom can ill afford to exchange their money for a claim to a dividend in the liquidation, and all of whom are likely to be anxious to avoid this. In cases concerning the public, it seems to me that where money in advance is being paid to a company in return for the future supply of goods or services, it is an entirely proper and honourable thing for a company to do what this company did, on skilled advice, namely, to start to pay the money

15 [1955] 1 WLR 1080.

> into a trust account as soon as there begin to be doubts as to the company's ability to fulfil its obligations to deliver the goods or provide the services. I wish that, sitting in this court, I had heard of this occurring more frequently; and I can only hope that I shall hear more of it in the future.

In *Don King Productions Inc v Warren*, the court decided that, where an attempted assignment of rights under a contract supported by consideration was ineffective in law, because the contract involved the provision of personal services, or a clause in the contract prohibited such assignment, it is still open to the parties to create a trust of the benefit of the obligations under the contract. Whether the terms of the contract prohibit such a declaration of trust depends on the facts of each case. But a contractual term prohibiting an assignment *prima facie* does not extend to declarations of trust of the benefits of the contract. Accordingly, the parties retained their freedom to create a trust of benefits under the contract.

***Don King Productions Inc v Warren and Others* [1998] 2 All ER 608, HC**

The plaintiff, Don King Productions Inc (DKP), a company owned by Mr Don King, is the leading boxing promoter in the USA. The first defendant, Mr Frank Warren (W), is the leading boxing promoter in the UK. The other defendants are Mr Warren's business associates. In 1994, the plaintiff and defendants agreed to extend their business relationship and entered into two partnership agreements for the purpose of the promotion and management of boxing in Europe. In the first agreement, W purported to assign to the partnership all benefits and burdens of his existing promotion and management agreements with boxers. In the second agreement it was provided that the partners would hold all promotion and management agreements for the benefit of the partnership absolutely. It transpired that some of the promotion agreements and all of the management agreements contained express provisions prohibiting assignments. Thereafter, W entered into fresh agreements, including a 'multi-fight agreement' for the broadcasting of certain fights in the USA. A dispute arose between the parties as to W's entitlement to enter into the 'multi-fight agreement' and the partnership was terminated. The plaintiff commenced proceedings against the defendants.

The issue before the court was whether the benefit of the promotion and management agreements was capable of being the subject matter of a trust, despite the express clause prohibiting assignment.

The court held in favour of the plaintiff. In accordance with the intention of the parties, the promotion and management agreements were held by the partners as trustees for the partnership. Accordingly, W's entry into the 'multi-fight agreement' intended for his benefit was in breach of the duties owed to the plaintiff.

Lightman J:

(1) Declaration of trust

The defendants sought to discourage me from finding the existence of any trust in this case, and they invoked for this purpose the long established principle restated in *Westdeutsche Landesbank Girozentrale v Islington London BC* [1996] AC 669, pp 704–05, that the wholesale importation into commercial law of equitable principles would be inconsistent with the certainty and speed which are the essential requirements for the orderly conduct of business affairs. There can however be no sustainable objection on these grounds to recognition of a trust if the parties have manifested their intention to create it, *a fortiori*, when this is necessary to achieve justice between the parties. Justice does so require its recognition when the 'trustee' has already received the full agreed consideration for the beneficial interest in the subject matter of the trust. For this purpose it makes no difference that the subject matter is a chose in action. 'The scope of the trusts recognised in equity is unlimited. There can be a trust of a chattel or of a chose in action, or of a right or obligation under an ordinary legal contract, just as much as a trust of land,' see *Lord Strathcona Steamship Co Ltd v Dominion Coal Co Ltd* [1926] AC 108, p 124, *per* Lord Shaw.

The *Westdeutsche* case is also authority for the proposition (contrary to previous thinking), that the fact that the legal ownership is vested in one person and the beneficial ownership is vested in another does not necessarily involve the relationship of trustee and beneficiary. This proposition (counsel has suggested), supports a possible view that the contractual rights may be vested in Mr Warren and the beneficial ownership of those rights may be vested in the partners without the creation of any trust or trust relationship. I do not, however, think that this is a possibility in this case. The reasoning of the House of Lords was that the existence of an obligation binding the conscience of the person vested with the legal ownership is the hallmark of a trust. Only if, and so long as, the exceptional circumstances exist where separation of the legal and equitable ownership does not give rise to or co-exist with such an obligation, will a trust relationship not come into being. If and so long as legal ownership of the PM & A (promotion, management and associated) agreements remained in one or other partner and the beneficial ownership was in the partnership, the necessary fiduciary obligation coexisted and so did a trust.

As a matter of general principle it is, I think, quite clear that a trust may exist of a contract, and this may extend, not merely to the benefit of the rights conferred, but also the benefit of being a contracting party. This will occur when. for example, a trustee or partner enters into a contract as such or a trustee or partner or other fiduciary becomes a constructive trustee of the contract. It is important to recognise that a trust of the benefit of the contract (and in particular of the benefit of being a contracting party), may be more beneficial to the beneficiaries than the mere assignment to them of the benefit of the covenants contained in it. For according to established principles the trustee will hold any benefit arising from his trusteeship (and in particular his being a contracting party), such as renewals of the contract, on trust for the beneficiaries whether or not the renewal would have been granted to anyone other than the trustee or was assignable: see, for example, *Pathirana v Pathirana* [1967] 1 AC 233 and *Thompson's Trustee-in-Bankruptcy v Heaton* [1974] 1 All ER 1239; [1974] 1 WLR 605.

There can be no doubt that the partnership in this case could have validly entered into management and promotion contracts with boxers: the partners in such a case would hold the contract as a partnership asset. The issue raised is whether one of the partners who has entered into such an agreement in his own name alone can subsequently hold such a contract as a partnership asset. The defendants contend that this is not possible without the consent of the other parties to the management and promotion contracts (ie, the boxers) because the contracts involve the rendering of personal services and by their terms are not assignable.

(2) Assignment of rights

It is clear that a purported assignment of a contract or the rights arising under a contract may be ineffective as such because the contract involves the rendering of personal services or prohibits their assignment. The question arises whether a purported assignment for valuable consideration, ineffective as an assignment for the above reasons, may be effective as a declaration of trust or as imposing fiduciary duties on the assignor. The defendants contend that it cannot be so effective.

General principles

The applicable principles emerging from the authorities in a field still undeveloped are as follows:

(1) It is not possible (save pursuant to statutory authority), without a novation, to transfer the burden of a contract to a third party.

(2) In the case of contractual obligation, where the obligation is such that the identity of the person who performs it is a matter of indifference to the contracting party for whose benefit the obligation is imposed (the obligee) (for example, the payment of a sum of money or the delivery of a fungible), the other contracting party (the obligor) may delegate to a third party the performance of the obligation: see *British Waggon Co v Lea & Co* (1880) 5 QBD 149; [1874–80] All ER 135. But otherwise no such delegation is possible. Thus, in the absence of a contractual provision to the contrary, in the case of a publishing contract, the author cannot delegate to someone the performance of the duty of writing the book and the publisher cannot delegate to someone else the performance of the duty of publishing it.

(3) The only assignment in respect of a contract which is legally possible is an assignment of the benefit of the contract (ie, the rights thereby created) or some benefit (for example, the profits) derived by the assignor from the contract. The distinction is between the assignment of rights under the contract and of what is referred to as 'the fruits'. A provision for the assignment of a contract is to be construed as the assignment of the benefit of the contract: see *Linden Gardens Trust Ltd v Lenesta Sludge Disposals Ltd* [1993] 3 All ER 417, p 427; [1994] 1 AC 85, p 103. The assignment may expressly or by implication require the assignor to perform outstanding obligations on his part under the agreement, so as to enable the assignee to obtain the full benefit intended (subject, if necessary, to the assignee

indemnifying the assignor against the cost); and to hold the benefit of being the contracting party (and accordingly, for example, the opportunity to obtain a renewal) as trustee for the assignee.

(4) Whether or not the benefit can be assigned depends primarily upon the terms of the contract and secondarily upon the character of the obligations. The benefit of some obligations of a party under one contract may be assignable, whilst, at the same time, others under the same contract may not: assignability is not a matter of all obligations arising under a contract or none at all.

(5) The contract may expressly or impliedly permit assignment of rights not otherwise so assignable: see *Devefi Pty Ltd v Mateffy Pearl Nagy Pty Ltd* [1993] RPC 493, p 503. The contract may likewise prohibit assignment of rights otherwise *prima facie* assignable. Such contractual provisions are legally effective. The purpose of the non-assignment clause is the genuine commercial interest of a party of ensuring that contractual relations are only with the person he has selected as the other party to the contract and no one else. This is particularly important in areas such as building contracts which are 'pregnant with disputes': see *Linden Gardens Trust Ltd v Lenesta Sludge Disposals Ltd* [1993] 3 All ER 417, pp 431–32; [1994] 1 AC 85, pp 107–08. Such a clause avoids the possibility of a third party being enabled to raise issues of set-off not available to the other contracting party. Unless specially drafted to draw such a distinction, the prohibition attaches equally to the assignment of the right to future performance of the contract and the right to receive benefits accrued under the contract ... The clause also preserves the parties' rights of set-off against each other and saves them having any concern whether there has or has not been, or preserving any record of, any assignment of the benefit of the contract by the other party.

(6) Unless the contract expressly or impliedly otherwise provides, the character of an obligation precludes assignment of the benefit of the obligation if the identity of the obligee is material to the obligor: see *Tolhurst v Associated Portland Cement Manufacturers (1900) Ltd* [1902] 2 KB 660, p 668, *per* Collins MR. For the effect of such an assignment can alter the substance of the obligation. For this reason an employer cannot assign the benefit of an obligation of the employee to serve him, for the choice of employer is material to the employee: and the employer cannot, without his consent, transform a contract to serve him into a contract to serve anyone else. Accordingly, any purported assignment or contract to assign will have no effect at law or in equity: see *per* Lord Atkin in *Nokes v Doncaster Amalgamated Collieries Ltd* [1940] 3 All ER 549, p 561; [1940] AC 1014, p 1033. Again, for the same reason, neither an author nor his publisher may assign the right to performance of the other's obligations under a publishing agreement: see the case of *Devefi*. But the benefit of any obligation of the employer to pay his salary, or of a publisher to pay royalties to an author, is (in default of a term of the contract to the contrary) assignable, since the identity of the recipient is a matter of indifference to the employer or publisher: consider *Linden Gardens Trust Ltd v Lenesta Sludge Disposals Ltd* [1993] 3 All ER 417, p 428; [1994] 1 AC 85, p 105 and *Devefi Pty Ltd v Mateffy Pearl Nagy Pty* [1993] RPC 493, p 505.

(7) A declaration of trust in favour of a third party of the benefit of obligations or the profits obtained from a contract is different in character from an assignment of the benefit of the contract to that third party: see *Devefi Pty Ltd v Mateffy Pearl Nagy Pty* ... Whether the contract contains a provision prohibiting such a declaration of trust must be determined as a matter of construction of the contract. Such a limitation upon the freedom of the party is not lightly to be inferred and a clause prohibiting assignments is, *prima facie*, restricted to assignments of the benefit of the obligation and does not extend to declarations of trust of the benefit: consider *Pincott v Moorstons Ltd* [1937] 1 All ER 513, p 516. In the words of Lord Browne-Wilkinson, in *Linden Gardens Trust Ltd v Lenesta Sludge Disposals Ltd* [1993] 3 All ER 417, p 431; [1994] 1 AC 85, p 108):

> ... a prohibition on assignment normally only invalidates the assignment as against the other party to the contract so as to prevent the transfer of the chose in action: in the absence of the clearest words it cannot operate to invalidate the contract as between the assignor and assignee and even then it may be ineffective on the grounds of public policy.

Application of principles

The application of these principles to this case produces the situation that neither the first nor the second agreement could effectively vest the PM & A agreements in, or assign the benefit of them to, the partnership, but none of the PM & A agreements (so far as I have been able to ascertain) contained any provision purporting to prohibit or having the effect of prohibiting the partners declaring themselves trustees of the PM & A agreements entered into in their own names for the partnership. It is necessary, however, to turn to the question raised by the defendants: whether the nature of the PM & A agreements was nonetheless such as to preclude such a declaration of trust.

[Counsel for the defendant] has submitted that a party cannot, without the consent of the other parties to the contract, make himself or become a trustee in respect of a contract which involves personal skill and confidence and which prohibits assignments.

(1) Personal skill and confidence

[Counsel for the defendant] submits that the assumption of trusteeship by a party to such a contract would involve him in creating a conflict between the duties owed to the other party to the contract and those duties owed to the beneficiaries under the trust. He drew the distinction between the case where the other parties to the contract deliberately contract with trustees as such (for example, as partners in a partnership) and accordingly consent to such a conflict, and the case where, by a subsequent declaration of trust by the other party to the contract, such a conflict is foisted on them without their consent. This contention fails for (amongst others) the following reasons: (a) there is in neither of these situations any objectionable conflict of duty. It is a matter of everyday experience that the same persons owe fiduciary duties to one set of people (for example, one partner to the other partners in a solicitors' firm or a director to the company that employs him) and at the same time fiduciary duties to another (for example, to the solicitors' or company's clients). The reason that there is no problem of conflict is that one set of these duties (namely, the duties assumed to the client) is paramount. The fiduciary owes to the client in the performance of the duties owed to the client a duty of undivided loyalty; and (b) a party to a contract involving fiduciary duties who declares himself a trustee of the contract has the paramount duty to perform his obligations under the contract and to fulfil his duty of undivided loyalty to the other contracting party. Indeed, this accords with the recognition by equity that the first duty of a trustee is to preserve the trust property (in this case the contract itself).

(2) Non-assignable contracts

[Counsel for the defendant] further submitted that, where a contract contains a provision prohibiting assignment, a party cannot, by a declaration of trust or otherwise, make himself the trustee of the benefit of that contract, because this would defeat the whole purpose of the non-assignment obligation which is to ensure that the other contracting party alone, and no one else, can enforce the obligations contained in the contract against him; and that if a trust is created and if the trustee refuses to enforce an obligation, the beneficiary may sue for enforcement, joining the trustee as a defendant: see *Vandepitte v Preferred Accident Insurance Corp of New York* [1933] AC 70, p 79; [1932] All ER 527, p 532.

This contention likewise fails for (amongst others) the following reasons: (a) if one party wishes to protect himself against the other party declaring himself a trustee, and not merely against an assignment, he should expressly so provide. That has not been done in this case; (b) the applicable principles of trust law in this situation are the basic principles and those (and only those) whose rationale have application in this commercial context (see *Target Holdings Ltd v Redferns (A Firm)* [1995] 3 All ER 785, pp 795–96; [1996] AC 421, p 436). The courts will accordingly be astute to disallow use of the procedural shortcut sanctioned in *Vandepitte*'s case in a commercial context where it has no proper place. A beneficiary cannot be allowed to abrogate the fullest protection that the parties to the contract have secured for themselves, under the terms of the contract, from intrusion into their contractual relations by third parties; (c) a declaration of trust cannot prejudice the rights of the obligor. If the contract requires any judgment to be exercised, whether by the obligor or the obligee, an assignment cannot alter who is to exercise it, or how that judgment is to be exercised, or vest the right to make that judgment in the court; (d) the rule in *Saunders v Vautier* (1841) 4 Beav 115; [1835–42] All ER 58 (which enables the sole beneficiary or beneficiaries to give directions to the trustee) only applies if the beneficiary is entitled to wind up the trust and require the trustee to assign to him the subject matter of the trust. If the trust cannot be determined because the trustee has, under the contract, held as a trust asset outstanding obligations and has no power to transfer the trust asset to the beneficiary or his order, the rule does not apply: see *Re Brockbank (Decd), Ward v Baker* [1948] 1 All ER 287; [1948] Ch 206. Accordingly, in a case where the subject matter of the trust is a non-assignable contract and there are outstanding obligations to be performed by the trustee, the beneficiary under the trust cannot interfere.

> Accordingly, in principle, I can see no objection to a party to contracts involving skill and confidence or containing non-assignment provisions from becoming trustee of the benefit of being the contracting party as well as the benefit of the rights conferred. I can see no reason why the law should limit the parties' freedom of contract to creating trusts of the fruits of such contracts received by the assignor or to creating an accounting relationship between the parties in respect of the fruits. The broader approach, which I favour, appears to be in accord with the authorities, so far as they go. The leading authority is *Re Turcan* (1888) 40 Ch D 5. The Vice Chancellor of the County Palatine of Lancaster (Bristowe VC) in that case held that an agreement to assign a non-assignable policy constituted the assignor a trustee of the policy for the assignee. The Court of Appeal upheld the validity of the trusteeship of these assets, and Lord Browne-Wilkinson in *Linden Gardens Trust Ltd v Lenesta Sludge Disposals Ltd* [1993] 3 All ER 417, p 428; [1994] 1 AC 85, p 104, referred to *Re Turcan* as authority for the proposition that a party to a contract may agree with a third party to account for him for the fruits he receives from the other contracting party. No doubt was cast by the Court of Appeal in *Re Turcan* or by the House of Lords in the *Linden Gardens* case on the decision of Bristowe VC. As Lord Browne-Wilkinson said in the *Linden Gardens* case [1993] 3 All ER 417, pp 430–31; [1994] 1 AC 85, p 107) the House of Lords only had to consider the validity of the restriction of an assignment which would have the effect of bringing the assignee into direct contractual relations with the other party to the contract. The view of Bristowe VC finds some support in *Devefi Pty Ltd v Mateffy Pearl Nagy Pty Ltd* [1993] RPC 493, pp 555–56 and *Williams v Commissioner of Inland Revenue* [1965] NZLR 395, p 401. But most importantly this view accords with common sense and justice and achieves the commercial objective of the parties.
>
> **Result**
>
> I accordingly hold that the clear intent of the parties, manifested in the first and second agreements, was that the PM & A agreements should be held by the partnership or by the partners for the benefit of the partnership absolutely, and that this intent should be given fullest possible effect. The agreements have accordingly at all times been held by the partners as trustees for the partnership. Accordingly, the ordinary equitable principles apply (including the rule in *Keech v Sandford*) and the partnership assets include all renewal and replacement agreements obtained by any partner during the partnership and over the period between dissolution and the completion of winding up.

Precatory words

The same principle applies to testamentary dispositions. Words of entreaty, prayer, confidence, expectation or hope, known as 'precatory' words, may or may not create a trust. Such ambiguous words are required to be construed by the courts in order to ascertain the intention of the testator.

Re Adams and the Kensington Vestry (1884) 27 Ch D 394, CA

A testator left property, by his will, subject to the following clause: 'unto and to the absolute use of my wife, Harriet, in full confidence that she will do what is right as to the disposal thereof between my children either in her lifetime or by will after her decease.' The question in issue was whether a trust in favour of the children was created. The court held that no trust was created and the wife acquired the property beneficially.

> **Cotton LJ:** Undoubtedly, to my mind, in the later cases, especially *Lambe v Eames*[16] and *Re Hutchinson and Tenant*,[17] both the Court of Appeal and the late Master of the Rolls shewed a desire really to find out what, upon the true construction, was the meaning of the testator, rather than to lay hold of certain words which in other wills had been held to create a trust, although on the will before them they were satisfied that that was not the intention. I have no hesitation in saying myself, that I think some of the older authorities went a great deal too far in holding that some particular words appearing in a will were sufficient to create a trust. Undoubtedly confidence, if the rest of the context shews that a trust is intended, may make a trust, but what we have to look at is the whole of the will which we have to construe, and if the confidence is that she will do what is right as regards the disposal of the property, I cannot say that that is, on the true construction of the will, a trust imposed upon her. Having regard to the later decisions, we must not extend the old cases in any way, or rely upon the mere use of any particular words, but, considering all the words which are used, we have to see what is their true effect, and what was the intention of the testator as expressed in his will. In my opinion, here he has expressed his will in such a way as not to shew an intention of imposing a trust on the wife, but on the contrary, in my opinion, he has shewn an intention to leave the property, as he says he does, to her absolutely.

Contrast this case with *Comiskey v Bowring-Hanbury*.

Comiskey and Others v Bowring-Hanbury and Another [1905] AC 84, HL

Mr Hanbury, the testator, transferred his property by his will to his widow:

> ... in full confidence that she will make such use of it as I should have made myself and that at her death she will devise it to such one or more of my nieces as she may think fit and in default of any disposition by her thereof by her will. I hereby direct that all my estate and property acquired by her under this my will shall at her death be equally divided among the surviving said nieces.

The widow having acquired the property took out an originating summons to determine whether on construction of the will she took the property absolutely or subject to a trust in favour of the nieces.

16 (1871) 6 Ch App 597.

17 (1878) 8 Ch D 540.

Held that, on construction of the will, the intention of the testator was to transfer the property absolutely to his widow for life and after her death, one or more of his nieces was or were entitled to benefit subject to a selection by his widow. Failing such selection, the nieces were entitled equally.

> **Lord Davey:** Reading this will without paying any attention to legal rules, and for the purpose only of seeking the testator's intention and the meaning of the words he used, it is obvious that he did not intend that his wife should have an absolute power to dispose of the estate in her lifetime or otherwise than by her will.
>
> I do not myself attach any great importance to the use of the word 'absolutely'. Reading it as qualifying or expressing the estate which the wife had to take, it does not seem to me to do more than to give here a fee simple. It is now admitted that she has a fee simple, and the question is whether there is a good executory limitation capable of taking effect upon her death. The use of the word 'absolutely', as defining the amount of the estate which is given to the wife, must of course be subject to any executory limitation or any other valid limitation or exception which you find engrafted on that estate in fee simple; therefore I attach no importance, or very little importance, to the use of the word 'absolutely'.
>
> My Lords, in my opinion the question really is this: Do those words, 'in default of any disposition by her thereof by her will or testament', mean any disposition in favour either of the nieces or anybody else, or are they, as Mr Warmington contended, to be construed as relating to such a disposition as that which he has expressed his confidence that his wife would make? I come to the conclusion that the testator is speaking only of a default of any such disposition as he had expressed his confidence that his wife would make, and, if so, I am of opinion that there is a good executory limitation.
>
> Therefore, even if you treat the words 'in confidence' as only expressing a hope or belief, the will would run thus: 'I hope and believe that she will give the estate to one or more of my nieces, but if she does not do so, then I direct that it shall be equally divided between them.' I think that is a perfectly good limitation. The true antithesis I think is between the words 'such one or more of my nieces as she may think fit' and the words 'equally divided between my surviving said nieces'.

Re Steele's Will Trusts, National Provincial Bank Ltd v Steele [1948] Ch 603, HC

The testatrix, Mrs Adelaide Steele, who died on 19 November 1929, by her will provided as follows:

> I give my diamond necklace to my son, Charles, to go and be held as an heirloom by him and by his eldest son on his decease and to go and descend to the eldest son of such eldest son and so to the eldest son of his descendants as far as the rules of law and equity will permit (and I request my said son to do all in his power by his will or otherwise to give effect to this my wish).

Charles died in April 1945 having made a will declaring: 'I give my diamond necklace to my trustees upon trust for my son, Ronald, during his life and after his death for his eldest son absolutely.'

It was clear that the provision in Adelaide's will bore a striking similarity to a clause included in the testatrix's will in *Shelley v Shelley* (1868). In that case, the court decided that a trust was imposed on the eldest son of the settlor for life with remainder to his eldest son for life and continuing, subject to the perpetuities rule, in trust for the eldest son.

The question in issue was whether Charles took the necklace absolutely or whether there was a trust for a succession of the eldest sons of eldest sons, subject to the perpetuity rule.

Held that, on construction of the will, a trust was created.

Wynn-Parry J: The question which arises is whether on the true construction of the passage in clause 2 of the will of the testatrix which I have read, the necklace became vested in the testatrix's son, Charles Steele, absolutely, or, whether it was held on trust for Charles Steele for his life and after his death for his son, Charles Ronald Steele, for his life, and after his death for David Steele for his life, and after the death of the survivor on trust for the eldest son or grandson of the third plaintiff, David Steele, and otherwise in the manner decided in *Shelley v Shelley*, including the ultimate trust (in default of any male issue of David Steele who takes an absolutely vested interest) in favour of Charles Steele absolutely. In *Shelley v Shelley* the testatrix by her will made the following bequest ((1868) LR 6 Eq 540):

> I give my best long string of pearl earrings, bracelets with diamond snaps, and my pearl necklace and earrings, and all my rings with pearls, diamonds and emeralds mixed, and all the rest of my pearls and emeralds [and other jewels] to my nephew, John Shelley, to go and be held as heirlooms by him, and by his eldest son on his decease, and to go and descend to the eldest son of such eldest son, and so on, to the eldest son of his descendants, as far as the rules of law or equity will permit. And I request my said nephew to do all in his power, by his will or otherwise, to give effect to this my wish as to these things so directed to go as heirlooms as aforesaid.

With the exception of the latter words, 'as to these things so directed to go as heirlooms as aforesaid', the relevant provision in the will which I have to construe in terms *mutatis mutandis* exactly corresponds with those in the will which fell to be construed in *Shelley v Shelley*. In that case it was held that on the true construction of that provision a valid executory trust was created for John Shelley for life with remainder to his eldest son for his life and on the death of that eldest son in trust for his eldest son to be a vested interest in him when he should attain 21, but if he should die in his father's lifetime or after his death without having attained 21, leaving an eldest son born before his father's death, in trust for such last mentioned eldest son to be a vested interest when he should attain 21, and, subject to these limitations, the jewels vested in John Shelley absolutely and passed by his will. The basis of the decision was this. Sir W Page Wood VC, held that the words of the gift to John Shelley 'to go and be held as heirlooms by him and by his eldest son on his decease' if they stood alone, would have been a gift to the first taker for life and on his death would have gone to the next taker absolutely.

The Vice Chancellor held that the addition of those words prevented the first taker from receiving the gift absolutely. The order in *Shelley v Shelley* was:

> ... that a good executory trust was created by the will and codicil of the testatrix, Helen Parker, of the jewels and jewellery thereby respectively bequeathed as heirlooms, and that such trust ought to have been executed by the late John Shelley, the nephew of the said testatrix, and that defendant Elizabeth Shelley, the widow and executrix of the said John Shelley, is now bound to execute such trust ... that under such trust the said John Shelley was entitled to the enjoyment of such jewels and jewellery during his life, and that plaintiff Edward Shelley, the eldest son of the said John Shelley is entitled to the enjoyment thereof during his life, and that upon the death of the said plaintiff the same will be held in trust for the eldest son of the said Edward Shelley, if living at the decease of the said Edward Shelley, the same to become a vested interest in such son when he shall attain the age of 21 years, but if he shall die in the lifetime of the said plaintiff Edward Shelley, or after him under the age of 21 years, leaving an eldest son born before the plaintiff's decease, then in trust for such last mentioned eldest son, to be a vested interest when he shall attain the age of 21 years; and in case the said jewels shall not become absolutely vested in any person under the limitations aforesaid, then (subject to the life interest of the said Edward Shelley) in trust for the said John Shelley absolutely.

It is, therefore, clear that, if *Shelley v Shelley* governs the present case, there is complete machinery for working out the trust on which this necklace ought to be held. The attack is made on the basis that, in view of the modern trend of decisions as regards precatory trusts, *Shelley v Shelley* should not be followed. I do not propose to embark on a detailed review of the authorities, but will content myself with observing that it appears to me from a review of the later authorities to which I was referred – *Re Hamilton (Decd)*,[18] *Re Williams (Decd)*[19]and *Re Hill (Decd)*[20] – that there is no ground for regarding the authority of *Shelley v Shelley* as being no longer binding.

Shelley v Shelley has stood for eighty years and I have before me a will which, as I have already observed, is, as regards the relevant passage, couched in the same language *mutatis mutandis* as that which was considered by Wood VC, in *Shelley v Shelley*. That appears to me to afford the strongest indication that the testatrix by this will, which appears clearly on the face of it to have been prepared with professional aid, intended that the diamond necklace in question should devolve in the same manner as the jewellery in *Shelley v Shelley* was directed to devolve by the order made therein. Having regard to the nature of this indication of intention and to the circumstances, I cannot see any good reason why, notwithstanding the admitted trend of modern decisions, I should treat *Shelley v Shelley* as wrongly decided, and, therefore, a case which I ought not to follow.

18 [1895] 2 Ch 370.

19 [1897] 2 Ch 12.

20 [1897] 1 QB 483.

> I come to the conclusion that I must declare that, on the true construction of the will of the testatrix, the diamond necklace should have been held on trust for Charles Steele for his life, and after his death for the second plaintiff, Charles Ronald Steele, for his life, and after his death for David Steele, the third plaintiff, for his life, and after the death of the survivor of them on trust for the eldest son or grandson of the third plaintiff, David Steele, and otherwise in the manner decided in *Shelley v Shelley* including the ultimate trust (in default of any male issue of David Steele who take an absolutely vested interest) in favour of Charles Steele absolutely and that the order in this case will follow *mutatis mutandis* the minutes which appear in the case of *Shelley v Shelley*. If the courts decide that the transferor did not manifest an intention to create a trust, the assignee or transferee takes the property beneficially. This is treated as a gift to the assignee.

An alternative approach is to the effect that where the donor has created a general gift in favour of A, subject to a specific intended gift in favour of B and the specific gift fails, then the court will treat the gift to A as absolute or unconditional, unhindered by any limitation in favour of B. In the case of wills, A's estate is entitled to retain the property.

See *Hancock v Watson*[21] (sometimes known as the rule in *Lassence v Tierney*).[22]

Hancock v Watson [1902] AC 14, HL

In this case, a testator gave his residuary estate to trustees on trust for his widow for life and after her death to be divided into five portions. Two portions were donated to a friend, Susan Drake for life and after her death upon trust for her children, but in default of issue in favour of the children of the testator's brother, Charles, on condition that they attain the age of 21 or earlier marriage. Susan died without issue. At the time of her death Charles' children had attained the age of 21 or married. The questions in issue were (a) whether Charles' children took the property in accordance with the testator's will, (b) alternatively, on Susan's death whether the estate of the original testator was entitled to the property.

The House of Lords held that the intended gift in favour of Charles' children was void for infringing the perpetuity rule. On construction, the testator created an absolute gift in favour of Susan subject to trusts which failed. In these circumstances, the absolute gift took effect to the exclusion of the testator. Thus, Susan was entitled to dispose of the property in any way she liked.

> **Lord Davey:** The appellants second point is that the two fifths allotted to Susan Drake on failure of the gift over goes to the next of kin of the testator, and not to Susan's representatives. I confess to some surprise at hearing this point treated as arguable. For, in my opinion, it is settled law that if you find an

21 [1902] AC 14.

22 (1849) 1 Mac & G 551.

> absolute gift to a legatee in the first instance, and trusts are engrafted or imposed on that absolute interest which fail, either from lapse or invalidity or any other reason, then the absolute gift takes effect so far as the trusts have failed to the exclusion of the residuary legatee or next of kin (of the original testator) as the case may be. Of course, as Lord Cottenham pointed out in *Lassence v Tierney* (1849), if the terms of the gift are ambiguous, you may seek assistance in construing it – in saying whether it is expressed as an absolute gift or not – from the other parts of the will, including the language of the engrafted trusts. But when the court has once determined that the first gift is in terms absolute, then if it is a share of the residue (as in the present case) the next of kin are excluded in any event.

Certainty of subject matter

The subject matter may take a variety of forms such as land, shares, chattels, etc, but whatever form it takes the trust property is required to be specified with sufficient clarity to enable the court to identify the same. When the property subject to an intended trust is uncertain the intended express trust fails. This is because it would be unclear which property is allegedly subject to the trust and the transferee may take the property beneficially unburdened by a trust. In effect this issue may be interconnected with certainty of intention.

Sprange v Barnard (1789) 2 Bro CC 585, CA

A testatrix provided as follows:

> This is my last will and testament at my death, for my husband Thomas Sprange, to bewill to him the sum of £300, which is now in the joint stock annuities, for his sole use; and, at his death, *the remaining part of what is left, that he does not want for his own wants and use*, to be divided between my brother John Crapps, my sister Wickenden, and my sister Bauden, to be equally divided between them.

The stock being vested in trustees, Thomas Sprange applied to them for payment, but they refused; whereupon he filed this bill.

> **Lord Arden MR:** It is contended, for the persons to whom it is given in remainder, that he shall only have it for his life, and that the words are strictly mandatory on him to dispose of it in a certain way; but it is only to dispose of what he has no occasion for: therefore the question is whether he may not call for the whole; and it seems to be perfectly clear on all the authorities that he may. I agree with the doctrine in *Pierson v Garnet*[23] following the cases *Harland v Trigg*[24] and *Wynne v Hawkins*[25] *that the property, and the person to whom it is to be given, must be certain* in order to raise a trust. Now here the property is wasting, as it is only what shall remain at this death ... It is contended that the

23 (1787) 2 Bas CC 225.

24 (1782) 1 Bas CC 142.

25 (1782) 1 Bas CC 179.

court ought to impound the property; but it appears to me to be a trust which would be impossible to be executed. I must, therefore, declare him to be absolutely entitled to the £300, and decree it to be transferred to him.

Palmer v Simmonds (1854) 2 Drew 221, HC

A testatrix by her will disposed of the residue of her estate to Thomas Harrison subject to the following stipulation: 'that if he should die without lawful issue he will, after providing for his widow during her life, leave the bulk of my said residuary estate unto' four named persons equally. The court held that no trust was intended for there was no property capable of being subject to a trust.

> **Kindersley VC:** What is the meaning then of bulk? The appropriate meaning, according to its derivation, is something which bulges out. [His Honour referred to *Todd's Johnson and Richardson's Dictionary* for the different meanings and etymology of the word.] Its popular meaning we all know. When a person is said to have given the bulk of his property, what is meant is not the whole but the greater part, and that is in fact consistent with its classical meaning. When, therefore, the testatrix uses that term, can I say she has used a term expressing a definite, clear, certain part of her estate, or the whole of her estate? I am bound to say she has not designated the subject as to which she expresses her confidence; and I am therefore of the opinion that there is no trust created; that Harrison took absolutely, and those claiming under him now take.

The test is whether the subject matter of the trust is identified or capable of being identified with sufficient precision to enable a court to attach an order to such property.

The purchase of a specific quantity of goods from a supplier, who fails to identify and appropriate stock in pursuance of the sale, will not transfer property in the goods to the purchaser. Moreover, the supplier will not, without more, be treated as a trustee for the purchaser. The property may be too imprecise for the court to attach an order.

Re London Wine Company (Shippers) Ltd 1986 PCC 121, HC

The company had substantial stocks of wine in a number of warehouses. Large quantities were sold but in many instances remained warehoused with the company. There was no appropriation from the bulk of any wine to answer particular contracts, but the customer received from the company a 'certificate of title' describing the wine for which he had paid. He was charged storage and insurance periodically.

When receivers were appointed, there were sufficient stocks to satisfy all claims. The court considered three types of transaction: (a) a single purchaser of the total stock of a particular wine; (b) a number of purchasers whose combined purchases exhausted the total stock of a particular wine; (c) a number of purchasers whose combined purchases did not exhaust the relevant stock.

Oliver J held that legal title had not passed in any case. There was no ascertainment. Orders could have been fulfilled from any source, not necessarily existing stocks. There was no undivided interest.

There was no trust for there was no certainty of subject matter. No proprietary right arose from the payment of purchase money. The existence of a right to specific performance does not necessarily imply a proprietary interest in the subject matter. Hence, the claims wholly failed.

> **Oliver J:** A farmer could, by appropriate words, declare himself to be a trustee of a specified proportion of his whole flock and thus create an equitable tenancy in common between himself and the named beneficiary, so that a proprietary interest would arise in the beneficiary in an undivided share of all the flock and its produce. But the mere declaration that a given number of animals would be held upon trust could not, I should have thought, without very clear words pointing to such an intention, result in the creation of an interest in common in the proportion which that number bears to the number of the whole at the time of the declaration. And where the mass from which the numerical interest is to take effect is not itself ascertainable at the date of the declaration, such a conclusion becomes impossible.

It would appear that, notwithstanding property in the goods passing to the purchaser, the suppliers who retain possession of the goods are not automatically treated as trustees for the purchasers.

Re Staplyton [1994] 1 WLR 1181, HC

Wines kept by companies in warehouses for customers but not marked with customers' names were treated as 'ascertained' for the purpose of s 16 of the Sale of Goods Act 1979. But such contracts for the sale of goods did not *per se* create equitable interests in favour of customers.

> **Judge Baker QC:** We next come to the decision of the Court of Appeal in *Re Wait* [1927] 1 Ch 606. W bought 1,000 tons of wheat to be shipped from Oregon. He sub-sold 500 tons to the claimants, who paid in full. It was shipped but before it arrived W went bankrupt. His trustee claimed to receive the whole of the 1,000 tons, leaving the claimants to their rights in damages. The majority held that the 500 tons due to the claimants had not been appropriated and so this was not specific or ascertained goods in respect of which specific performance could be ordered under s 52 of the Act of 1893. The interest of the case lies in the acute division of opinion in the court. Sargant LJ would have held that the claimants had an equitable assignment of part enforceable against the whole. The view of the majority can best be taken from the following passages in the judgment of Atkin LJ, at pp 629–30, 636:
>
>> In any case, however, I am of opinion that the claimants fail, and that to grant the relief claimed would violate well established principles of common law and equity. It would also appear to embarrass to a most serious degree the ordinary operations of buying and selling goods, and the banking operations which attend them ... The rules for transfer of property as between seller and buyer, performance of the contract, rights

> of the unpaid seller against the goods, unpaid seller's lien, remedies of the seller, remedies of the buyer, appear to be complete and exclusive statements of the legal relations both in law and equity. They have, of course, no relevance when one is considering rights, legal or equitable, which may come into existence dehors the contract for sale. A seller or a purchaser may, of course, create any equity he pleases by way of charge, equitable assignment or any other dealing with, or disposition of, goods, the subject matter of sale; and he may, of course, create such an equity as one of the terms expressed in the contract of sale. But the mere sale or agreement to sell, or the acts in pursuance of such a contract mentioned in the code, will only produce the legal effects which the code states.

> This landmark decision demonstrates that, normally, a contract for the sale of goods takes effect at law, and gives rise to no equitable interest in favour of the buyer.
>
> In the present case we are concerned with the buying and selling of consumables. I am bound by the decision in *Re Wait* [1927] 1 Ch 606 to hold that a contract for the sale of goods does not, of itself, create equitable rights. Furthermore, as Gault J himself commented in *Liggett v Kensington* [1993] 1 NZLR 257, p 279: 'A contractual obligation to store the goods of another does not give rise to a trust.' The respective rights and obligations of the parties are governed exclusively by the terms of the two contracts.

Specific property may be delineated as trust property such as a pecuniary legacy or identified paintings, etc. But equally effective would be property which is subject to a clear criterion which is capable of identifying the property from a group of assets, such as the residue of the testator's estate. In respect of a declaration of trust of part of a holding of shares, it appears to be unnecessary to identify the shares which are subject to the trust by reference to the numbers stated in the certificates. It would be sufficient if the settlor qualifies the shares to such an extent that the court is entitled to ascertain the shares which are subject to the trust.

Hunter v Moss [1993] 1 WLR 934, HC

In this case, the defendant declared himself a trustee for the benefit of the plaintiff in respect of a 5% holding in the issued share capital of a company (1,000 issued shares). The defendant was the registered holder 950 shares. The judge held that a trust was created in respect of 50 of the defendant's 950 shares. The defendant applied by motion to set aside the judgment on the ground that the purported trust failed for uncertainty of subject matter. The defendant argued that his failure to appropriate the relevant shares resulted in the subject matter of the intended trust being unascertainable. The High Court held in favour of the plaintiff on the ground that the test for certainty of subject matter did not necessarily require segregation or appropriation of the trust property. The test is satisfied if immediately after the declaration of trust the court could have made an order for the execution of the trust. Since the shares were of the same category and thus equally capable of fulfilling the trust obligation, the quantification of the intended trust holding was sufficient to satisfy the test for certainty of subject matter.

> **Colin Rimer QC** (sitting as a deputy High Court judge, reasoned thus): Approaching the matter as one of principle, I therefore take the view that the subject matter of the trust which the defendant declared was sufficiently certain and that in consequence the trust was a valid one.
>
> Although I have been referred to no English authority dealing specifically with the point, it was, however, the subject of a decision of the Supreme Court of Missouri in *Rollestone v National Bank of Commerce in St Louis*.[26] In that case the court found that a Mr Milliken had purported to declare himself trustee for the plaintiff, Mr Rollestone, of 10,000 shares with a par value of $1 each in a mining company, such shares forming part of a larger holding held by Mr Milliken. The 10,000 shares were not specifically identified.
>
> With regard to the argument that this rendered the trust void for uncertainty as to its subject matter Ragland J said, at p 398:
>
>> It is next contended that, as the evidence does not show that any particular portion of the stock was set apart for Rollestone and a certificate issued therefor, the alleged trust must fail for lack of a definitely ascertained subject. But it clearly appears from Milliken's statements that he was carrying Rollestone for 10,000 shares of the capital stock of the Golden Cycle Mining Company. Now Milliken at that time had more than 1,000,000 shares standing in his name on the corporation's books, all of which were exactly alike in kind and value. There was no earmark by which any one of them could be distinguished from the others, so as to give it additional value or importance. They were like grain of a uniform quality, where one bushel is of the same kind and value as another: *Caswell v Putnam*.[27] The words '10,000 shares of capital stock' embodied, therefore, an accurate description of definite property rights in the corporation. A certificate of the same number of shares would have evidenced nothing more: *Richardson v Shaw*.[28] Appellants' contention under this head is disallowed.
>
> Save that, with respect, I do not wholly agree that it was appropriate to answer the question there in point by analogy with tangible assets such as bushels of grain, I find those observations persuasive and convincing, and I agree with them. They appear to me to be directly in point in the present case.
>
> A similar point potentially arose for decision in the Californian District Court of Appeal in the later case of *Busch v Truitt*.[29] In that case Mr Busch sought to establish a trust of shares in the Dried Food Products Company on the basis of a letter from Mr Truitt, the alleged trustee, stating that 'My records now show that I owe you 1,380 shares of escrowed stock which is made up of advances to me from time to time as follows' and then referring to, *inter alia*, various

26 (1923) 252 SW 394.

27 120 NY 153, p 157; 24 NE 287.

28 (1908) 209 US 365; 28 Sup Ct 512; 52 L Ed 835; 14 Ann Case 981.

29 (1945) 160 P 2d 925.

payments made by Mr Busch. Mr Truitt held 17,145 shares in the company in his own name, but there was no evidence that his holding had increased in consequence of his various transactions with Mr Busch. Moore J, with whose judgment Wood and McComb JJ both concurred, held first that there was no express trust, saying, at p 928:

> It could not have been an express trust, for there is no evidence that decedent ever declared that he held any shares of stock belonging to the respondent or that he held certain corporate stock in which Busch had an ownership to the extent of 1,380 shares or in any amount.

He also rejected the argument that there was a resulting trust and then went on to say, at p 928:

> Before one who claims to be the beneficiary of a trust can realise upon his claim, he must identify the specific property to which he has title or which was acquired with funds furnished by him. *Holland v Bank of Italy;*[30] *Roncelli v Fugazi;*[31] *Lathrop v Bampton;*[32] *Byrne v Byrne.*[33] He who claims to be the beneficiary of an alleged trust must be able to identify the trust fund or follow it through its mutations. Failing to do so, he is no more than a general creditor.

There was a suggestion that that statement is inconsistent with the view expressed in the earlier *Rollestone* case,[34] which I have quoted above. I do not, for my part, accept that it is. The statement is a general one, with the essence of which I do not in any way disagree. In the context in which it appears in the judgment I do not, however, read it as also making the narrower point that a trust declared in respect of part of a larger holding of shares will only be valid if particular shares are identified as being subject to the trust. The various cases referred to are not authorities which purport to decide that particular point and they do not justify the passage being so interpreted. If, however, the statement is to be so regarded, then I prefer the different view expressed in the *Rollestone* case.

Finally, the point raised by Mr Hartman was also referred to in the decision of Gummow J in *Herdegen v Federal Commissioner of Taxation* (1988) 84 ALR 271. The question there was whether or not Mr and Mrs Herdegen had validly constituted themselves trustees for themselves and others of shares forming parts of larger holdings which each of them held in a particular company, Mr and Mrs Herdegen being respectively the holders of 59 and 41 shares. Gummow J found on the facts that no such trusts as were alleged were established. He then said, at p 279:

> I should add that with respect to the 38 shares allegedly held on trust by Mr Herdegen, no attempt was made to indicate how they were selected from among the parcel of 59 shares numbered one to 10 and 52 to 100. The

30 115 Cal App 472; 1 P 2d 1031.

31 44 Cal App 249; 186 P 373.

32 31 Cal 17; 89 Am Dec 141.

33 113 Cal 294; 45 P 536.

34 (1923) 252 SW 394.

> same is true of Mrs Herdegen's shares. As to whether such specific identification was essential to establish certainty of subject matter, or whether the shares might be treated as fungible for this purpose, the authorities appear to be unsettled: *Rollestone v National Bank of Commerce*;[35] *Busch v Truitt*.[36]
>
> Gummow J accordingly appears to have regarded the point as less than clearly established and, being able to decide the case on other grounds, he left the point open.
>
> In this case I cannot leave the point open. In my judgment the decision in *Rollestone v National Bank of Commerce in St Louis*,[37] reflected the correct principle and I approach the present case in the same way. In the result I conclude that the trust which I have found the defendant to have declared was not void for lack of certainty as to its subject matter, and I do not accept Mr Hartman's submissions to the contrary.'

In *Re Harvard Securities Ltd (In Liquidation), Holland v Newbury and Another* (1997) *The Times*, 18 July, the High Court decided that although there could not, in English law, be a valid equitable assignment of an unappropriated interest in chattels, there could be such an equitable assignment of shares.

Harvard, a licensed dealer in securities, had acquired and sold to clients various registered Australian and USA shares. The clients were told in writing that their non-numbered shares were held in nominee names on their behalf. The question in issue was whether there was certainty of subject matter in order to create an express trust. The leading authorities considered by the court were:

(1) *Re Wait* [1927] 1 Ch 606, where a majority of the Court of Appeal had held that sub-purchasers of 500 tons of wheat, out of a cargo of '1,000 tons *ex Challenger*', who had paid for that 500, but not taken delivery before the purchaser went bankrupt, had no beneficial interest;

(2) *Re London Wine Company (Shippers) Ltd* 1986 PCC 121, where Mr Justice Oliver had held, similarly, that purchasers out of the company's substantial stocks of wine, who had been given certificates of title as sole and beneficial owners, got no beneficial interest, even when purchasing the total stock of a particular wine;

(3) *Re Goldcorp Exchange Ltd* [1995] 1 AC 74, where the Privy Council, approving both the previous cases, ruled similarly in respect to claims by customers to whom Goldcorp had sold bullion which it then purported to store for them;

35 (1923) 252 SW 394, p 398.

36 (1945) 160 P 2d 925, p 928; affirmed 163 P 2d 739.

37 (1923) 252 SW 394.

(4) *Hunter v Moss* [1994] 1 WLR 452, the Court of Appeal decided that a trust was declared, where a registered holder of 950 shares in a company with 1,000 shares issued capital, orally agreed that he would hold 5% of the issued shares in trust for Hunter. Dillon LJ distinguished *London Wine* as being concerned with the appropriations of chattels and when the property in chattels passed.

Underhill and Hayton's *Law Relating to Trusts and Trustees*, 15th edn, 1995, boldly submitted that *Hunter v Moss* was wrong because 'there is no sound reasoning for distinguishing trusts of goods from trusts of intangibles'.

The High Court felt bound by *Hunter v Moss* and distinguished the other authorities on the ground that those were concerned with chattels. Therefore, in the present case, the holders of rights to shares were held to have beneficial interests in them.

Re Golay Morris v Bridgewater and Others [1965] 2 All ER 660, HC

A testator by his will directed his executors to let Tossy enjoy one of his flats during her lifetime and 'to receive a reasonable income from my other properties'.

The question in issue was whether the direction was void for uncertainty.

Held that the direction was valid. The words 'reasonable income' imported an objective enquiry as to the amount of income.

> **Ungoed-Thomas J:** Another question that arises is whether this gift of reasonable income fails for uncertainty. There are two classes of cases with which I am concerned in interpreting this particular provision in the will: the first is where a discretion is given to specified persons to quantify the amount; the other class of case is where no such discretion is expressly conferred on any specified person. It is common ground that in this case the trustees are not given that discretion, so that, if 'reasonable income' does not fail for uncertainty, then it would be open to a beneficiary to go to court to ascertain whether any amount quantified by the trustees was a 'reasonable' amount in accordance with the provisions of the will.
>
> Does this gift of a 'reasonable income', without specifying any person to quantify it, fail for uncertainty?
>
> It is, however, submitted that what the court is concerned with in the interpretation of this will is not to ascertain what is 'reasonable income' in the opinion of the court but to ascertain the testator's intention in using the words 'reasonable income'. The question therefore comes to this: whether the testator by the words 'reasonable income' has given a sufficient indication of his intention to provide an effective determinant of what he intends, so that the court, in applying that determinant, can give effect to the testator's intention.
>
> Whether the yardstick of 'reasonable income' was applied by trustees under a discretion given to them by a testator or applied by a court in the course of interpreting and applying the words 'reasonable income' in a will, the yardstick sought to be applied by the trustees in the one case and the court in

the other case would be identical. The trustees might be other than the original trustees named by the testator and the trustees could even surrender their discretion to the court. It would seem to me to be drawing too fine a distinction to conclude that an objective yardstick which different persons sought to apply would be too uncertain, not because of uncertainty in the yardstick but as between those who seek to apply it.

In this case, however, the yardstick indicated by the testator is not what he or any other specified person subjectively considers to be reasonable but what he identifies objectively as 'reasonable income'. The court is constantly involved in making such objective assessments of what is reasonable and it is not to be deterred from doing so because subjective influences can never be wholly excluded. In my view the testator intended by 'reasonable income' the yardstick which the court could and would apply in quantifying the amount so that the direction in the will is not in my view defeated by uncertainty.'

Contrast *Re Kolb's Will Trusts.*

Re Kolb's Will Trusts, Lloyds Bank Ltd v Ullmann and Others [1961] 3 All ER 811, HC

By his will, a testator who died in May 1959 directed his trustees *inter alia* to invest the proceeds of sale of trust property in such stocks, shares and/or convertible debentures in the 'blue chip' category as his trustees should think fit. The question in issue was whether the expression 'blue chip' category was void for uncertainty.

Held that the direction was void for uncertainty. On construction of the will, the testator had not empowered the trustees to decide independently the issue but the testator intended to adopt a purely subjective standard (which was unclear) for identifying the type of investments.

Cross J: Who is to say whether the shares of any given company are in the 'blue chip' class or whether any given investment trust is of high class standing? As a matter of construction of the clause it is, I think, clear that the opinion of the trustees whether any investment is or is not a 'blue chip' is not to be decisive. The testator evidently considered 'blue chip' investments to be a class of investments existing independently of the judgment of the trustees among which his trustees were to have a power of selection.

Mr John Arnold Ellert, who has been a member of the Stock Exchange, London, for nearly thirty years, has made an affidavit in which he deals with the meaning of the expression 'blue chip'. He says that this term is commonly applied by members of the Stock Exchange and financial journalists to the ordinary stocks and shares of industrial or commercial companies of the highest standing from an investor's point of view, but that there is no strict definition of the term and the opinions of different stockbrokers and others differ as to what stocks and shares can properly be called 'blue chips' at any given time. He goes on as follows:

> I myself am of opinion that the following essential conditions should be satisfied before an investment can be regarded as in the 'blue chip' class:

(a) the company should have a paid-up capital of not less than £1,000,000;

(b) the company should have a dividend record over at least 10 years showing a progressive increase, either unbroken or broken only by a decreased dividend in one or two years easily explicable by reference to external conditions (such as a credit squeeze or period of dear money) and followed by resumed progress;

(c) The dividend currently paid should be covered by profits of at least double the amount.

I should not regard an investment as a 'blue chip', even though fulfilling the above mentioned conditions, if its price has for the time being been pushed, in my opinion, too high so as to over-discount the company's future prospects. Many conservative stockbrokers would restrict the term 'blue chip' to the ordinary stocks and shares of companies dealing in the necessaries of life or other highly protected trades (for example, Cerebos Ltd or Reckitt & Coleman Holdings Ltd), but I personally feel that this is too narrow a view.

The conclusion which I draw is that, while there are, no doubt, many investments which all persons competent to judge of such matters would call 'blue chips' and many others which no person competent to judge would call 'blue chips', there are a number of investments which some stockbrokers would class as 'blue chips' but which other stockbrokers equally competent would not class as 'blue chips'. It was argued that this fact does not affect the validity of the clause. A first class investment is, it was said, a clear enough conception and in case of dispute the court would have to decide on the evidence of stockbrokers whether or not any given investment was or was not first class, just as it has to decide on the evidence of surveyors whether or not a house is in good tenantable repair. The fact that the evidence of the experts might and probably would be conflicting is, it was said, just as irrelevant in the one case as in the other. The question whether some word or phrase in a legal document can be said to have an objective meaning so that the court can decide on evidence whether or not a particular state of facts falls within it, or whether on the other hand its meaning depends essentially on the views of the man who uses it, often comes before the court. Thus, to take recent examples, one may contrast the decision of Harman J, in *Re Gresham's Settlement, Lloyds Bank Ltd v Sayer* where the phrase in question was 'by or with whom [he] may ... be ... residing', with the decision of Upjohn J, in *Re Sayer Trust, MacGregor v Sayer*[38] where the word in question was 'dependants'.

In this case I feel no doubt on which side of the line the phrase in question falls. Whether or not an investment is 'first class' or 'blue chip' depends essentially on the standards applied by the speaker and cannot be regarded as an objective quality of the investment. The testator might have made his trustees the judges; but, as he has not done so, that part of the clause is, in my judgment, void for uncertainty. It follows from this, I think, that the prohibition against investment in trustee or fixed interest investments is also

38 [1957] Ch 423.

> ineffective. That prohibition only has a meaning on the footing that the provision for investment in 'blue chips' is effective. If that were not so, the result would be that the trustees would have no powers of investment at all.

If the trust property is certain but the interest intended for the beneficiary is uncertain then, although the purported express trust fails, a resulting trust may be set up for the benefit of the settlor or his estate.

In *Boyce v Boyce*,[39] the trust property consisted of two houses to be taken by each of two beneficiaries. One of the named beneficiaries was required to make a selection from the two houses and the house not selected was required to be held on trust for the other named beneficiary. The beneficiary failed to make the selection with the effect that the express trust failed for uncertainty of beneficial interest and both houses were held on resulting trust for the testator's estate.

It must be stressed that this was an exceptional case and the harshness of the result stemmed from the preliminary ruling by the judge to the effect that a personal obligation was created in order to identify the beneficial interest.

Certainty of objects (beneficiaries)

It is obvious that no express trust may stand when it is unclear in whose favour the trust has been created. The settlor has a duty to identify the beneficiaries with a sufficient degree of precision. The effect of uncertainty of objects (assuming certainty of intention and property) is that the intended express trust fails and a resulting trust is set up for the benefit of the settlor or his estate. The test for certainty of objects varies with the type of trust intended. The courts have drawn a distinction between 'fixed' (non-discretionary) and discretionary trusts.

Fixed trusts

These are trusts in which the number of beneficiaries and the extent of their interests are specified in the trust instrument. The test for certainty of objects is whether the objects are ascertained or capable of being ascertained. In other words, at the time of the creation of the trust the trustees are required to draw up a comprehensive list of all the beneficiaries. Failure to achieve this would result in the failure of the express trust, for example, £50,000 is transferred to trustees T1 and T2 to distribute equally between all my friends.

See *IRC v Broadway Cottages Trust*[40] (below, p 165).

39 (1849) 16 Sim 476.

40 [1955] Ch 20.

Discretionary trusts

A discretionary trust is one whereby the objects are not given an interest in the property but the trustees are invested with a duty to select, in their discretion, the beneficiaries and/or their interests from amongst a class of objects. In short, the trustees are required to decide on the identity of the beneficiaries from a class of objects and the corresponding interests which they may acquire.

For example, 'on trust, for 21 years, to distribute the dividends from my shareholding in Marks & Spencer plc to such of my dependants and relatives as my trustees will decide in their absolute discretion'. The trustees are required to decide not only who will benefit, but also the quantum of the interest of the beneficiaries from within the class of objects, namely, the settlor's dependants and relatives.

The test for certainty of objects is whether the trustees may say with certainty that a given postulant (individual) is or is not a member of a class of objects. Thus, the test is whether the qualifying class or classes of objects is or are capable of being defined and it is unnecessary to draw up a list of all the objects.

See *McPhail v Doulton*[41] (below, p 165).

SUPPLEMENTARY READING

Clarke, P, 'Mr Vandervell again' (1974) 38 Conv 405

Goodhart, W and Jones, G, 'The infiltration of equitable doctrine into English commercial law' (1980) 43 MLR 489

Grubb, A, ' Powers, trusts and classes of objects' [1982] Conv 432

Harpum, C, 'Administrative unworkability and purpose trusts' [1986] CLJ 391

Hayton, D, 'Certainty of objects – what is heresy?' [1984] Conv 307

Hill, G, 'Section 2 of the Law of Property (Miscellaneous Provisions) Act 1989' (1990) 106 LQR 396

Howell, J, 'Informal conveyances and s 2 of the Law of Property (Miscellaneous Provisions) Act 1989' [1990] Conv 441

Jones, A, 'Creating a trust over an unascertained part of a homogeneous whole' [1993] Conv 466

41 [1971] AC 424.

Martin, J, 'Certainty of objects – what is heresy?' [1984] Conv 304

Martin, J, 'Validity of trust of unidentified shares' [1996] Conv 223

Nolan, R, 'The triumph of technicalities' (1996) 55 CLJ 436

Pettit, P, 'Farewell s 40' [1989] Conv 431

Thompson, M, 'Disposition of equitable interests' [1996] Conv 368

Youdan, T, 'Formalities for trusts of land and the doctrine in *Rochefoucauld v Boustead*' [1984] CLJ 306

CHAPTER 4

CONSTITUTION AND EFFECT OF AN EXPRESS TRUST

CONSTITUTION OF A TRUST

It was stated earlier (see above, p 22) that an express trust may be created in one of two ways, namely, the transfer of the property to third party trustees subject to a declaration of trust or the retention of the property by the settlor subject to the terms of the trust. See *Milroy v Lord* (above, p 23). If either mode of creation has been fully implemented by the settlor, the trust is treated as perfect or completely constituted. The issue about to be discussed examines the scope of these two requirements.

If the settlor adopts an improper mode of creating a trust, the intention of the settlor will not be construed as sufficient to create a perfect trust by implying a different mode of creation, for otherwise all imperfect gifts will be construed as perfect. Thus, if the settlor intended to create a trust by way of a transfer of property to (third party) trustees subject to a declaration of trust, but failed to effect the transfer, the retention of the property by the settlor will not be construed as retention by him as a trustee. The trust will not become perfect by implying the second mode of creation, for there is a vital distinction between an intention to transfer property to trustees and an intention to retain property in the capacity as trustee. Likewise, an ineffectual gift will not be sufficient to imply an intention to make the intended donor a trustee for the intended donee. Since the gift is imperfect, trust principles will not be implied to perfect the imperfect gift. 'Equity will not perfect an imperfect gift.'

Richards v Delbridge (1874) LR 18 Eq 11, CA

A settlor attempted to assign a lease of business premises to his grandson by endorsing the lease and signing a memorandum: 'This deed and all thereto I give to R from this time henceforth with all stock in trade.' He gave the lease to R's mother to hold on his behalf. On the death of the settlor it was ascertained that his will made no reference to the business premises. The question in issue was whether the lease belonged to the grandson or the residuary beneficiaries under the testator's will.

The court held that there was an imperfect gift *inter vivos* as the assignment not being under seal was ineffectual to transfer the lease. Further, no trust had been created as the grandfather did not declare himself a trustee of the lease for the grandson. The court will not construe an ineffectual transfer as a valid declaration of trust.

> **Sir George Jessel MR:** The principle is a very simple one. A man may transfer his property, without valuable consideration, in one of two ways: he may either do such acts as amount in law to a conveyance or assignment of the property, and thus completely divest himself of the legal ownership, in which case the person who by those acts acquires the property takes it beneficially, or on trust, as the case may be; or the legal owner of the property may, by one or other of the modes recognised as amounting to a valid declaration of trust, constitute himself a trustee, and, without an actual transfer of the legal title, may so deal with the property as to deprive himself of its beneficial ownership, and declare that he will hold it from that time forward on trust for the other person. It is true he need not use the words, 'I declare myself a trustee', but he must do something which is equivalent to it, and use expressions which have that meaning; for, however anxious the court may be to carry out a man's intention, it is not at liberty to construe words otherwise than according to their proper meaning ...
>
> The true distinction appears to me to be plain, and beyond dispute: for a man to make himself a trustee there must be an expression of intention to become a trustee, whereas words of present gift show an intention to give over property to another, and not retain it in the donor's own hands for any purpose, fiduciary or otherwise.
>
> In *Milroy v Lord* (1862), Lord Justice Turner, after referring to the two modes of making a voluntary settlement valid and effectual, adds these words:
>
>> The cases, I think, go further, to this extent, that if the settlement is intended to be effectuated by one of the modes to which I have referred, the Court will not give effect to it by applying another of those modes. If it is intended to take effect by transfer, the Court will not hold the intended transfer to operate as a declaration of trust, for then every imperfect instrument would be made effectual by being converted into a perfect trust.

But the settlor may incorporate both modes of creating a trust, namely, declaring that he will retain the property as trustee pending the transfer to third party, trustees. Once the (third party) trustees ultimately acquire the relevant property during the lifetime of the settlor, the trust becomes perfect. It is immaterial how the trustees acquire the property provided that their acquisition was not improper. It is essential that the settlor expressly declares himself a trustee pending the transfer for the court will not imply this requirement.

Re Ralli's Will Trusts [1964] Ch 288, HC

In 1899, a testator died leaving the residue of his estate upon trust for his wife for life with remainder to his two children, Helen and Irene absolutely. In 1924, Helen covenanted in her marriage settlement and under clause 7 to settle all her 'existing and after acquired property' upon trusts which failed and ultimately on trust for the children of Irene. The settlement declared that all the property comprised within the terms of the covenant will under clause

8 'become subject in equity to the settlement hereby covenanted to be made'. Irene's husband was appointed on of the trustees of the settlement. In 1946, Irene's husband was also appointed a trustee of the 1899 settlement. In 1956, Helen died and, in 1961, the widow died. Irene's husband became the sole surviving trustee of both the 1899 settlement and Helen's settlement. The question in issue was whether Helen's property from the 1899 settlement was held upon trust subject to Helen's marriage settlement or subject to Helen's personal estate. The court held that, by virtue of the declaration in Helen's settlement in 1924, Helen, and since her death, her personal representative (Irene's husband), held her share of the 1899 settlement subject to the trust of Helen's settlement. This was the position even though the vesting of the property in Irene's husband came to him in his other capacity as trustee of the 1899 settlement. The same result was reached by virtue of the *Strong v Bird* principle.

> **Buckley J** (held that the vested reversionary interest, being existing property of Helen at the time she made what he construed as an independent declaration of trust pending assignment to the trustees of her marriage settlement, was held on the trusts of the marriage settlement. He then continued): In my judgment the circumstances that the plaintiff holds the fund because he was appointed a trustee of the will is irrelevant. He is at law the owner of the fund and the means by which he became so have no effect on the quality of his legal ownership. The question is: for whom, if any one, does he hold the fund in equity? In other words, who can successfully assert an equity against him disentitling him to stand on his legal right? It seems to me to be indisputable that Helen, if she were alive, could not do so, for she has solemnly covenanted under seal to assign the fund to the plaintiff and the defendants can stand in no better position. It is, of course, true that the object of the covenant was not that the plaintiff should retain the property for his own benefit, but that he should hold it on the trusts of the settlement. It is also true that, if it were necessary to enforce performance of the covenant, equity would not assist the beneficiaries under the settlement, because they are mere volunteers; and that for the same reason the plaintiff, as trustee of the settlement, would not be bound to enforce the covenant and would not be constrained by the court to do so, and indeed, it seems, might be constrained by the court not to do so. As matters stand, however, there is no occasion to invoke the assistance of equity to enforce the performance of the covenant. It is for the defendants to invoke the assistance of equity to make good their claim to the fund. To do so successfully they must show that the plaintiff cannot conscientiously withhold it from them. When they seek to do this, he can point to the covenant which, in my judgment, relieves him from any fiduciary obligation that he would otherwise owe to the defendants as Helen's representatives. In so doing the plaintiff is not seeking to enforce an equitable remedy against the defendants on behalf of persons who could not enforce such a remedy themselves: he is relying on the combined effect of his legal ownership of the fund and his legal right to enforce the covenant. That an action on the covenant might be statute-barred is irrelevant, for there is no occasion for such an action.

> Had someone other than the plaintiff been the trustee of the will and held the fund, the result of this part of the case would, in my judgment, have been different; and it may seem strange that the rights of the parties should depend on the appointment of the plaintiff as a trustee of the will in 1946, which for present purposes may have been a quite fortuitous event. The result, however, in my judgment, flows – and flows, I think, quite rationally – from the consideration that the rules of equity derive from the tenderness of a court of equity for the consciences of the parties. There would have been nothing unconscientious in Helen or her personal representatives asserting her equitable interests under trusts of the will against a trustee who was not a covenantee under clause 7 of the settlement, and it would have been unconscientious for such a trustee to disregard those interests. Having obtained a transfer of the fund, it would not have been unconscientious in Helen to refuse to honour her covenant, because the beneficiaries under her settlement were mere volunteers: nor seemingly would the court have regarded it as unconscientious in the plaintiff to have abstained from enforcing the covenant either specifically or in damages, for the reason, apparently, that he would have been under no obligation to obtain for the volunteers indirectly what they could not obtain directly. In such circumstances Helen or her personal representatives could have got and retained the fund. In the circumstances of the present case, on the other hand, it is not unconscientious in the plaintiff to withhold from Helen's estate the fund which Helen covenanted that he should receive: on the contrary, it would have been unconscientious in Helen to seek to deprive the plaintiff of that fund, and her personal representatives can be in no better position. The inadequacy of the volunteers' equity against Helen and her estate consequently is irrelevant, for that equity does not come into play; but they have a good equity as against the plaintiff, because it would be unconscientious of him to retain as against them any property which he holds in consequence of the provisions of the settlement.
>
> For these reasons I am of opinion that in the events which have happened the plaintiff now holds the fund in question on the trusts of the marriage settlement, and I will so declare.

A trust may only be created in respect of existing property. Accordingly, a trust cannot be created in respect of an expectancy or future property such as an anticipated interest under a will during the lifetime of the testator. The reason being that there is no property which is capable of being subject to the protection of equity.

Re Ellenborough [1903] 1 Ch 697, HC

Emily Law was entitled to property under the will of her brother, Lord Ellenborough. Before his death, Emily voluntarily covenanted to convey her anticipated inheritance to trustees upon trust. On his death, the covenantor changed her mind and declined to transfer the property to the covenantees who brought an action claiming a declaration as to whether Emily may be forced to perform the agreement.

The court held against the covenantees. No trust was created by the covenant and the agreement was not enforceable.

Buckley J: The question is whether a volunteer can enforce a contract made by deed to dispose of an expectancy. It cannot be and is not disputed that if the deed had been for value the trustees could have enforced it. If value be given, it is immaterial what is the form of assurance by which the disposition is made, or whether the subject of the disposition is capable of being thereby disposed of or not. An assignment for value binds the conscience of the assignor. A court of equity against him will compel him to do that which *ex hypothesi* he has not yet effectually done. Future property, possibilities, and expectancies are all assignable in equity for value: *Tailby v Official Receiver.*[1] But when the assurance is not for value, a court of equity will not assist a volunteer. In *Meek v Kettlewell,*[2] affirmed by Lord Lyndhurst,[3] the exact point arose which I have here to decide, and it was held that a voluntary assignment of an expectancy, even though under seal, would not be enforced by a court of equity. 'The assignment of an expectancy', says Lord Lyndhurst,[4] 'such as this is, cannot be supported unless made for a valuable consideration'. It is however suggested that that decision was overruled or affected by the decision of the Court of Appeal in *Kekewich v Manning,*[5] and a passage in White and Tudor's *Leading Cases in Equity*, 7th edn, Vol ii, p 851, was referred to upon the point. In my opinion *Kekewich v Manning* has no bearing upon that which was decided in *Meek v Kettlewell.* The assignment in *Kekewich v Manning* was not of an expectancy, but of property. 'It is non legal and equitable principles', said Knight-Bruce LJ, 'we apprehend, clear that a person *sui juris*, acting freely, fairly, and with sufficient knowledge, ought to have and has it in his power to make, in a binding and effectual manner, a voluntary gift of any part of his property, whether capable or incapable of manual delivery, whether in possession or reversionary, and however circumstanced.' The important words there are 'of his property'. The point of *Meek v Kettlewell* and of the case before me is that the assignment was not of property, but of a mere expectancy. On 22 December 1893, that with which the grantor was dealing was not her property in any sense. She had nothing more than an expectancy. In *Re Tilt*[6] there was again a voluntary assignment of an expectancy, and the point was not regarded as arguable. 'It was rightly admitted,' said Chitty J, 'that as, when this plaintiff executed the deed of 1880, she had no interest whatever in the fund in question, which was a mere expectancy, the deed was wholly inoperative both at law and in equity, being entirely voluntary'. By 'wholly inoperative' there the learned judge of course did not mean that if the voluntary settlor had handed over the funds the trustees would not have held them upon the trusts, but that the grantees under the deed could not enforce it as against the settlor

1 (1888) 13 App Cas 523.
2 (1842) 1 Hare 464.
3 (1843) 1 Ph 342.
4 *Ibid*, p 347.
5 (1851) 1 De GM & G 176, p 187.
6 (1896) 74 LT 163.

in a court of equity or elsewhere. In my judgment the interest of the plaintiff as sole heiress-at-law and next of kin of the late Lord Ellenborough was not effectually assigned to the trustees by the deed, and the trustees cannot call upon her to grant, assign, transfer, or pay over to them his residuary real and personal estate.

Re Brooks' Settlement Trusts [1939] 1 Ch 993, HC

Under a marriage settlement, the income of the settled fund was payable to the wife for life with remainder to such of her issue as she might by deed or will appoint and, in default of appointment, on trust in favour of all of her children in equal shares. In 1929, T, one of her sons executed a voluntary settlement whereby he assigned his share, whether vested or contingent, in the trust property to Lloyds Bank Ltd as trustees. In 1939, his mother exercised the power of appointment in his favour in respect of £3,517. Thereupon, Lloyds Bank Ltd applied to the court to determine whether it should pay T the £3,517.

The court decided that the sum ought to be paid to T for, prior to an appointment by his mother, T had an interest which was subject to defeasance and was defeasible by a valid appointment executed by his mother. T, therefore, was only entitled to assign this defeasible interest in 1929. The mother's appointment in 1939 defeated the original interest enjoyed by T (as an object entitled in default of appointment) and, at the same time, transferred an interest in the sum of £3,517 to T.

Farwell J: The legal position in the case of a special power of appointment is not in any doubt at all. Referring to *Farwell on Powers*, 3rd edn, 1916, p 310, 'The exercise of a power of appointment divests (either wholly or partially according to the terms of the appointment) the estates limited in default of appointment and creates a new estate, and that, too, whether the property be real or personal'. Then there is a reference to a decision in the *Duke of Northumberland v IRC*,[7] where this statement was adopted by Hamilton J, as he then was. The effect of this is that in the case of a special power the property is vested in the persons who take in default of appointment, subject, of course, to any prior life interest, but liable to be divested at any time by a valid exercise of the power, and the effect of such an exercise of the power is to defeat wholly or *pro tanto* the interests which up to then were vested in the persons entitled in default of appointment and to create new estates in those persons in whose favour the appointment had been made. That being so, it is, in my judgment, impossible to say that until an appointment has been made in favour of this son, the son had any interest under his mother's settlement, other than an interest as one of the people entitled in default of appointment; he had an interest in that; but that interest was liable to be divested, and, if an appointment was made (as in fact it was made) in favour of the son, then to that extent the persons entitled in default were defeated and he was given an

7 [1911] 2 KB 343.

> interest in the funds which he had never had before and which came into being for the first time when the power was exercised. No doubt it is quite true to say that the appointment has to be read into the marriage settlement, but, in my judgment, that it is not sufficient ground for saying that at the time when this voluntary settlement was made the son had any interest at all in the fund other than this vested interest in default of appointment; for the rest, he had nothing more than a mere expectancy, the hope that at some date his mother might think fit to exercise the power of appointment in his favour, but, until she did so choose, he had nothing other than his interest in default of appointment to which he could point and say: 'that is a fund to which I shall become entitled in future or to which I am contingently entitled'. Apart from this he was not contingently entitled at all; he had no interest whatever in the fund until the appointment had been executed.
>
> If that be the true view, as I believe it to be, the result must be that, whatever the language of the settlement may be, the settlor under the voluntary settlement was purporting to assign to the trustees something to which he might in certain circumstances become entitled in the future, but to which he was not then entitled in any sense at all, and if that be so, then it is plain on the authorities that the son cannot be compelled to hand over or to permit the trustees to retain this sum that he is himself entitled to call upon them to pay it over to him.
>
> Notwithstanding the fact that the language of this voluntary settlement as a matter of construction is wide enough to comprise this interest, the principle of law which I have stated makes it impossible to enforce the settlement to that extent and prevents the settlor from being compelled by this court to transfer or permit the trustees to retain this money as part of the funds subject thereto.
>
> ... I feel compelled by the principles to which I have referred to hold that the answer to the summons must be that the trustees ought to pay to the defendant the sum in question on the footing that that settlement does not operate as a valid assignment or declaration of trust in respect thereof. I make that declaration accordingly.

A settlor may create a trust of the benefit of a deed provided that the property is in existence at the time of the creation. The approach here is based on the notion that the trust property may take the form of the benefit under a deed to transfer money (that is, a chose in action). Such benefit may be assigned to the trustees. On the date of the execution of the deed, the covenantees, trustees, will acquire the benefit of the deed. The declaration of trust will have the effect of transferring the equitable interest to the beneficiaries. In short, the deed will have the effect of creating the trust property (chose in action), assigning the benefit of the chose in action to the beneficiaries and declaring the trust.

For example, S, a settlor, and T, a trustee, execute a deed whereby S agrees to transfer the right to £20,000 to T on trust for B absolutely. S fails to transfer the sum to T. Nevertheless, the trust may be perfect, for the benefit of the deed may have been transferred to T in accordance with S's intention on the date of the execution of the deed.

Fletcher v Fletcher (1844) 4 Hare 67, HC

Ellis Fletcher covenanted (for himself, his heirs, executors and administrators) with trustees (their heirs, executors, administrators and assigns) to the effect that if either or both of his natural issue, Jacob and John survive him and attain the age of 21, Ellis' executors would pay to the covenantees (or heirs, etc) £60,000 within 12 months of his death to be held on trust for the relevant natural issue. In the circumstances, Jacob alone survived the settlor and attained the age of 21. The surviving trustees declined to act in respect of the trust unless the court ordered otherwise. Jacob brought an action directly against the executors claiming that he become solely entitled to the property.

Held in favour of Jacob. A trust of the covenant was created in favour of the plaintiff, who was entitled to enforce it as a beneficiary.

Wigram VC: The first proposition relied upon against the claim in equity was, that equity will not interfere in favour of a volunteer. A court of equity, for example, will not, in favour of a volunteer, enforce the performance of a contract *in specie*. That it will, however, sometimes act in favour of a volunteer is proved by the common case of a volunteer on a bond who may prove his bond against the assets. Again, where the relation of trustee and *cestui que* trust is constituted, as where property is transferred from the author of the trust into the name of a trustee, so that he has lost all power of disposition over it, and the transaction is complete as regards him, the trustee, having accepted the trust, cannot say he holds it, except for the purposes of the trust; if it is not already perfect. This covenant, however, is already perfect. The covenantor is liable at law, and the court is not called upon to do any act to perfect it. One question made in argument has been whether there can be a trust of a covenant the benefit of which shall belong to a third party; but I cannot think there is any difficulty in that. Suppose, in a case of a personal covenant to pay a certain annual sum for the benefit of a third person, the trustee were to bring an action against the covenantor; would he be afterwards allowed to say he was not a trustee? If he cannot do so after once acknowledging the trust, then there is a case in which there is a trust of a covenant for another ... The proposition, therefore, that in no case can there be a trust of a covenant is clearly too large, and the real question is whether the relation of trustee and *cestui que* trust is established in the present case.

I think the proposition insisted upon, that because the covenant was voluntary therefore the plaintiff could not recover in equity, was too broadly stated. I referred to the case of a volunteer by specialty claiming payment out of assets, and to the case of one claiming under a voluntary trust, where a third has been transferred. The rule against relief to volunteers cannot, I conceive, in a case like that before me, be stated higher than this, that a court of equity will not, in favour of a volunteer, give to a deed any effect beyond what the law will give to it. But if the author of the deed has subjected himself to a liability at law, and the legal liability comes regularly to be enforced in equity ... the observation that the claimant is a volunteer is of no value in favour of those who represent the author of the deed. If, therefore, the plaintiff himself were the covenantee so that he could bring the action in his own name, it follows, from what I have

> said, that in my opinion he might enforce payment out of the assets of the covenantor in this case. Then, does the interposition of the trustee of this covenant make any difference? I think it does not.
>
> The testator has bound himself absolutely. There is a debt created and existing. I give no assistance against the testator. I only deal with him as he has dealt by himself, and, if in such a case the trustee will not sue without the sanction of the court, I think it is right to allow the *cestui que* trust to sue for himself, in the name of the trustee, either at law, or in this court, as the case may require. The rights of the parties cannot depend upon mere accident and caprice.

But, this principle, by its nature, is restricted to debts enforceable at law which are in existence at the time of the declaration.

Re Cook's Settlement Trust [1965] Ch 902, HC

Settled property in the nature of paintings were transferred to Sir Francis Cook by his father. At the same time, Sir Francis covenanted with the trustees to the effect that if any of the paintings were sold during his lifetime the net proceeds of sale would be paid to the trustees to be held by them upon trusts in favour of Sir Francis' children. Sir Francis gave one of the paintings to his wife who wished to sell it. The trustees issued a summons to ascertain whether on the sale of the painting, the trustees would be obliged to enforce the covenant for the benefit of the children.

The court held that, since Sir Francis' children were volunteers, they could not enforce the covenant. Accordingly, the trustees were directed not to enforce the covenant. Further, the trust was not perfect within the *Fletcher v Fletcher* principle.

> **Buckley J:** The covenant with which I am concerned did not, in my opinion, create a debt enforceable at law, that is to say, a property right, which, although to bear fruit only in the future and on a contingency, was capable of being made the subject of an immediate trust, as was held to be the case in *Fletcher v Fletcher*. Nor is this covenant associated with property which was the subject of an immediate trust, as in *Williamson v Codrington*.[8] Nor did the covenant relate to property which then belonged to the covenantor, as in *Re Cavendish Browne's Settlement Trusts*.[9] In contrast to all these cases, this covenant on its true construction is, in my opinion, an executory contract to settle a particular fund or particular funds of money which at the date of the covenant did not exist and which might never come into existence. It is analogous to a covenant to settle an expectation or to settle after acquired property. The case, in my judgment, involves the law of contract, not the law of trusts ...

8 (1750) 1 Ves Sen 511.

9 (1916) 61 SJ 27.

> Accordingly, the second and third defendants are not in my judgment entitled to require the trustees to take proceedings to enforce the covenant, even if it is capable of being construed in a manner favourable to them.

EFFECT OF A PERFECT TRUST

Once the trust is constituted, the beneficiaries are given a recognisable interest in the property. They are entitled to protect their interest against anyone, with the exception of a *bona fide* transferee of the legal estate for value without notice. See *MCC Proceeds Inc v Lehman* (above, p 12). The beneficiaries are entitled to sue directly for either a common law remedy or in appropriate cases, an equitable remedy irrespective of whether or not they have provided consideration (*Fletcher v Fletcher*). In any event, the trustees (as representatives of the trust) are entitled to sue or be sued on behalf of the trust. This is the position even though the beneficiaries are volunteers.

Paul v Paul (1882) 20 Ch D 742, CA

Under a marriage settlement, property was settled on the wife for life, with remainder to the husband for life if he should survive her, with remainder to the issue of the marriage and failing issue, on trust for the next of kin (the wife's father). There were no children from the marriage. The husband and wife sought to have the fund paid to them claiming that the next of kin was a volunteer and unable to enforce the trust. The court held in favour of the next of kin. Since the trust was completely constituted, the beneficiaries, including the next of kin were entitled to enforce it. It was therefore immaterial that the next of kin was a volunteer.

A volunteer is one who has not provided valuable consideration. Valuable consideration is treated as either common law consideration in money or money's worth or marriage consideration. Common law consideration is the price promised by each party to an agreement. Marriage consideration has been judicially described as 'the most valuable consideration imaginable'. It takes the form of a settlement made before and in consideration of marriage, that is, an ante-nuptial settlement or a post-nuptial settlement made in pursuance of an ante-nuptial agreement. An ante-nuptial agreement is one made on condition that the marriage takes place, on the occasion of the marriage and for the purpose of facilitating the marriage. See *Re Park (Decd) (No 2)*.[10] The persons who are treated as providing marriage consideration are the parties to the marriage and the issue of the marriage, including remoter issue. Any other children connected with the parties to the marriage are

10 [1972] Ch 385.

volunteers. Thus, illegitimate, legitimated and adopted children as well as children of a subsequent marriage are volunteers. But exceptionally, the interest of such volunteer children may be intertwined with the interest of the non-volunteers to such an extent that the non-volunteers are required to acknowledge the interest of the volunteers. In this event, the volunteers may obtain incidental benefits, ancillary to the interest of the non-volunteer, see *AG v Jacob-Smith*.[11]

EFFECT OF AN IMPERFECT TRUST

The significance of identifying volunteers is that, unless they are beneficiaries under an express trust, they are not entitled to equitable assistance under an imperfect trust. In other words, the imperfect trust operates as an agreement to create a trust and in accordance with contractual principles, a party is only entitled to sue for a breach of contract if he has provided valuable consideration for the promise. 'Equity will not assist a volunteer' and 'equity will not perfect an imperfect gift'. Accordingly, a non-volunteer may compel the covenantee (intended trustee) to bring an action in law for damages for breach of a contract to create a trust, or the non-volunteer may claim an equitable remedy of specific performance forcing the covenantor to transfer the property to the intended trustee. The effect would be equivalent to the imperfect trust being treated as perfect. In other words, the plaintiff (non-volunteer) in respect of an imperfect trust is placed in the same position as a beneficiary under a perfect trust and is entitled to such equitable assistance as is appropriate in the circumstances.

Jefferys v Jefferys (1841) Cr & Ph 138, HC

A father voluntarily conveyed freehold property to the trustees upon trust for the benefit of his daughters. He also covenanted with the trustees to surrender copyhold properties to the trustees subject to the same trust. He died without surrendering the copyholds and by his will devised parts of both the freehold and copyhold to his widow. After his death, the daughters sought to have the trusts of the deed carried into effect and to compel the widow to surrender the copyhold property.

The court held that, in respect of the freehold, the trust was completely constituted and the daughter's interest was complete. However, in respect of the copyhold, the trust was incompletely constituted and since the daughters were volunteers, they had no right to compel the widow to part with the legal interest, which she had legitimately acquired.

11 [1895] 2 QB 341.

Pullan v Koe [1913] 1 Ch 9, HC

By a marriage settlement made in 1859, a wife covenanted to settle after-acquired property of £100 and over. In 1879, she received a gift of £285 but did not transfer the relevant sum to the trustees. Instead, the money was paid into her husband's bank account and he later invested it in bonds which remained in his estate at the time of his death in 1909. The trustees of the marriage settlement claimed the securities from the husband's executors on behalf of the children of the marriage. The executors pleaded the Statute of Limitations as a defence.

Held in favour of the trustees, who were entitled to trace the intended trust assets in favour of the non-volunteers.

> **Swinfen Eady J:** It was contended that the bonds never in fact became trust property, as both the wife and husband were only liable in damages for breach of covenant, and that the case was different from cases where property which has once admittedly become subject to the trusts of an instrument has been improperly dealt with, and is sought to be recovered. In my opinion as soon as the £285 was paid to the wife it became in equity bound by and subject to the trusts of the settlement. The trustees could have claimed that particular sum, could have obtained at once the appointment of a receiver of it, if they could have shewn a case of jeopardy, and, if it had been invested and the investment could be traced, could have followed the money and claimed the investment.
>
> This point was dealt with by Jessel MR in *Smith v Lucas*,[12] where he said:
>
>> What is the effect of such a covenant in equity? It has been said that the effect in equity of the covenant of the wife, as far as she is concerned, is that it does not affect her personally, but that it binds the property: that is to say, it binds the property under the doctrine of equity that that is to be considered as done which ought to be done. That is in the nature of specific performance of the contract no doubt. If, therefore, this is a covenant to settle the future-acquired property of the wife, and nothing more is done by her, the covenant will bind the property.
>
> Again in *Collyer v Issacs*,[13] Jessel MR said:
>
>> A man can contract to assign property which is to come into existence in the future, and when it has come into existence, equity, treating as done that which ought to be done, fastens upon that property, and the contract to assign thus becomes a complete assignment. If a person contracts for value, for example, in his marriage settlement, to settle all such real estate as his father shall leave him by will, or purports actually to convey by the deed all such real estate the effect is the same. It is a contract for value which will bind the property if the father leaves any property to his son.

12 (1881) 18 Ch D 531, p 543.

13 (1881) 19 Ch D 342, p 351.

> The property being thus bound, these bonds became trust property, and can be followed by the trustees and claimed from a volunteer.
>
> Again the trustees are entitled to come into a court of equity to enforce a contract to create a trust, contained in a marriage settlement, for the benefit of the wife and the issue of the marriage, all of whom are within the marriage consideration. The husband covenanted that he and his heirs, executors, and administrators, should, as soon as circumstances would admit, convey, assign, and surrender to the trustees the real or personal property to which his wife should become beneficially entitled. The trustees are entitled to have the covenant specifically enforced by a court of equity. In *Re D'Angibau*[14] and in *Re Plumptre's Marriage Settlement*[15] it was held that the court would not interfere in favour of volunteers, not within the marriage consideration, but here the plaintiffs are the contracting parties and the object of the proceeding is to benefit the wife and issue of the marriage.

In effect, a completely constituted trust, in terms of enforcement, is similar to an incompletely constituted trust in favour of someone who has furnished consideration.

On the other hand, a volunteer is not entitled to maintain an action in equity, directly or indirectly, in order to force the settlor to perfect an imperfect gift.

In Re Plumptre's Marriage Settlement, Underhill v Plumptre [1910] 1 Ch 609, HC

A marriage settlement, dated 7 October 1878, made between Alice of the first part (the wife), Reginald of the second part (the husband) and the trustees of the third part contained a covenant to settle the wife's after acquired property which exceeded £500 upon trust to pay the income to the wife during the joint lives of herself and husband and following the death of either of them to the survivor for life with remainder as to capital and income for the issue of the marriage and in default of issue upon trust for the wife's statutory next of kin. In August 1884, the husband bought stock in the wife's name for £1,018. In May 1887, she sold this stock for £1,125 and purchased Grand Trunk Railway of Canada stock which remained in her name at the date of her death intestate and without issue on 2 February 1909. The husband took out letters of administration to her estate on 21 August 1909. In November 1909, the trustees issued an originating summons requiring the determination of the court as to whether they were bound to take any steps on behalf of the next of kin to enforce the covenant.

Held that the claim was statute-barred but, in any event, the next of kin, as a volunteer and stranger to the marriage consideration, was not entitled to enforce the covenant.

14 (1880) 15 Ch D 228, p 242.

15 [1910] 1 Ch 609.

Eve J: Mr Clayton, on behalf of the next of kin, contends that they are not necessarily volunteers thereunder for the purpose of enforcing the covenant against the husband, and further that, even assuming the facts to be as stated in the question, the Court is not concerned to consider whether his clients could obtain the performance of the covenant by proceedings in equity inasmuch as the applicants, parties to the contract, are trustees of the covenant for all their *cestuis que* trust, and can and ought to enforce it by action at law, that is to say, by an action to recover as damages for breach of the covenant a sum equal to the value of the property which would have been vested in them had the covenant been complied with. I will deal with this latter contention first. Could such an action at law be successfully maintained today? I do not think it could. The covenant is an executory covenant, of which there was a clear breach in 1884, and although it is a continuing breach in the sense that it still exists, the cause of action arose in, or shortly after, August of that year. The result, therefore, is that the next of kin, if they are entitled to any relief, must resort to this Court to obtain it.

Now what is their position here? They are not in my opinion *cestuis que* trust under the settlement, for nothing therein amounts to a declaration of trust, or to anything more than an executory contract on the part of the husband and wife; it is, so far as the next of kin are concerned, what Cotton J calls a voluntary contract to create a trust as distinguished from a complete voluntary trust such as existed in the case of *Fletcher v Fletcher*, on which Mr Clayton so strongly relied. The collaterals are not parties to the contract; they are not within the marriage consideration and cannot be considered otherwise than as volunteers, and in these respects it makes no difference that the covenant sought to be enforced is the husband's and that the property sought to be brought within it comes from the wife. For each of the foregoing propositions authority is to be found in the judgment of the Court of Appeal in *Re D'Angibau;* and in the same judgment is to be found this further statement – that where, as in this case, the husband has acquired a legal title as administrator of his wife to property which was subject to the contract to settle, volunteers are not entitled to enforce against that legal title the contract to create a trust contained in the settlement. I think that judgment really disposes of the second question upon this summons, but before answering it, as I propose to do, in the negative, I ought perhaps to add that the argument founded on the rule that equity looks on that as done which ought to be done is, in my opinion, met and disposed of by what Lindley LJ says in *Re Anstis.*[16] After stating the rule he adds:

> But this rule, although usually expressed in general terms, is by no means universally true. Where the obligation to do what ought to be done is not an absolute duty, but only an obligation arising from contract, that which ought to be done is only treated as done in favour of some person entitled to enforce the contract as against the person liable to perform it.

I therefore answer the second question by saying that the applicants are not bound to take any steps.

16 (1886) 31 Ch D 596.

See also *Re McCardle* (1951).[17]

A testator (who died in 1935) left his residuary estate upon trust for his widow for life with remainder to his five children equally. Part of the estate consisted of a bungalow which was occupied in 1943 by M (one of the testator's sons) and his wife. During their occupation, certain repairs, valued at £488, were carried out to the bungalow and were paid for by Mrs M. Two years later (1945), the five children signed a document declaring: 'In consideration of your carrying out certain alterations to the property ... we, the beneficiaries under the will hereby agree that the executors shall repay you from the said estate when so distributed the said sum of £488 in settlement of such improvements.' In 1948, the widow died. In 1950, Mrs M claimed payment of £488 from the executors. The children (other than M) objected to the sum being paid.

The court held in favour of the defendants on the following grounds:

(i) the document, on construction, did not constitute an immediate assignment by the beneficiaries of their equitable interest to Mrs M, but instead, purported to create a contract whereby the executors shall, at a future date (when the estate was distributed) pay £488;

(ii) since the repairs and agreement to to remunerate constituted two separate transactions, the consideration was past.

IMPERFECT TRUSTS BY DEEDS

Section 1 of the Law of Property (Miscellaneous Provisions) Act 1989 abolishes the requirement of affixing a seal on a document in order to create a deed (originally called a covenant or specialty contract).

Section 1 of the Law of Property (Miscellaneous Provisions) Act 1989 provides:

> (1) Any rule of law which:
>
> (a) restricts the substances on which a deed may be written;
>
> (b) requires a seal for the valid execution of an instrument as a deed by an individual; or
>
> (c) requires authority by one person to another to deliver an instrument as a deed on his behalf to be given by deed, is abolished.

A deed is any document intended and executed as a deed which is signed and delivered by the parties in the presence of attesting witnesses.

Section 1(2) of the Law of Property (Miscellaneous Provisions) Act 1989 enacts:

17 [1951] 1 All ER 905, CA.

> An instrument shall not be a deed unless:
>
> (a) it makes it clear on its face that it is intended to be a deed by the person making it or, as the case may be, by the parties to it (whether by describing itself as a deed or expressing itself to be or signed as a deed or otherwise); and
>
> (b) it is validly executed as a deed by that person or, as the case may be, one or more of those parties.

Section 1(3) declares that:

> An instrument is validly executed as a deed by an individual if, and only if:
>
> (a) it is signed:
>
> (i) by him in the presence of a witness who attests the signature; or
>
> (ii) at his discretion and in his presence and the presence of two witnesses who each attest the signature; and
>
> (b) it is delivered as a deed by him or a person authorised to do so on his behalf.

The consequence of executing a deed is that it constitutes an agreement enforceable at common law, notwithstanding the absence of consideration. A claim may exist for damages for breach of contract even though the plaintiff (party to the deed) did not furnish consideration for the promise.

Equity, on the other hand, adopts a different approach to deeds and refuses to recognise the special nature of such agreements. Courts of equity require the plaintiffs to establish the existence of consideration before becoming entitled to its assistance by claiming the equitable remedy of specific performance or any other equitable remedy. 'Equity would not assist a volunteer.' See *Re Plumptre's Settlement* (above, p 105).

Moreover, a party to a deed (the covenantee or intended trustee) may not be compelled by a volunteer to bring an action for damages against the covenantor for breach of a deed to create a trust. The volunteer, not being a party to the deed, requires equitable assistance to claim an interest under the deed. But the court will not assist the volunteer by such circuitous device. The reason being that a volunteer should not be placed in a position where he may obtain by indirect means, a remedy which he may not enjoy by direct procedure.

For example, S, by deed agrees with T, an intended trustee, that future property to be acquired by S will be transferred to T to hold on trust for B, a beneficiary (volunteer), absolutely. S acquires property but fails to transfer the same to T. It is clear that B may not directly claim damages for he is not a party to the contract. B may not directly claim an equitable remedy for he is a volunteer. In addition, B may not force T to sue S for damages on his behalf because he is a volunteer. Hence, B may not obtain a remedy indirectly by enlisting equitable support.

Re Pryce, Nevill v Pryce [1917] 1 Ch 234, HC

In 1887, a marriage settlement contained a covenant to settle the wife's after acquired property upon trust as to income for the wife for life with remainder to her husband for life if he should survive her, with an ultimate remainder as to capital and income or trust for the issue of the marriage but failing issue on trust for the wife's next of kin. In 1916, the husband gave his wife £4,700. The husband died in 1907 and there was no issue of the marriage. The trustees issued a summons for the court to determine whether the trustees ought to take any steps to enforce the covenant.

Held that the trustees ought not to take any steps to enforce the covenant. The trust was imperfect. The wife's next of kin were volunteers who could not maintain an action to enforce the covenant. Likewise, the next of kin may not obtain a remedy indirectly, namely damages through the directions of the court requiring the trustees to enforce the covenant.

> **Eve J:** The question I have to decide is whether the plaintiffs as trustees of the marriage settlement ought to take steps to obtain transfer and payment to them of these promises.
>
> Although the court would probably compel fulfilment of the contract to settle at the instance of any persons within the marriage consideration (see *per* Cotton LJ in *Re D'Angibau*), and in their favour will treat the outstanding property as subjected to an enforceable trust (*Pullan v Koe*), 'volunteers have no right whatever to obtain specific performance of a mere covenant which has remained as a covenant and has never been performed', see *per* James LJ in *Re D'Angibau*. Nor could damages be awarded either in this court, or, I apprehend, at law, where, since the Judicature Act, the same defences would be available to the defendant as would be raised in an action brought in this court for specific performance or damages.
>
> In these circumstances, seeing that the next of kin could neither maintain an action to enforce the covenant nor for damages for breach of it, and that the settlement is not a declaration of trust constituting the relationship of trustee and *cestui que* trust between the defendant and the next of kin, in which case effect could be given to the trusts even in favour of volunteers, but is a mere voluntary contract to create a trust, ought the court now for the sole benefit of these volunteers to direct the trustees to take proceedings to enforce the defendant's covenant? I think it ought not; to do so would be to give the next of kin by indirect means relief they cannot obtain by any direct procedure, and would in effect be enforcing the settlement as against the defendant's legal right to payment and transfer from the trustees of the parents' marriage settlement. The circumstances are not unlike those which existed in the case of *Re D'Angibau*, and I think the position here is covered by the judgments of the Lords Justices in that case.
>
> Accordingly, I declare that the trustees ought not to take any steps to compel the transfer or payment to them of the premises assured to the wife by the deed of 12 December 1904.

This principle has been extended even further in order to prevent T, by his own volition, from pursuing his common law remedy for damages for breach of contract. The assumption is that the damages which would have been awarded to the plaintiff (T) may be held on trust for the volunteer (B) thus allowing the volunteer indirect access to the courts.

Re Kay's Settlement [1939] 1 All ER 245, HC

A young spinster voluntarily covenanted to settle after acquiring property upon trust *inter alia* for any children she may have. (This covenant was not an ante-nuptial agreement.) She subsequently married and had three children. Later still, she became entitled to property but failed to settle the same. The trustees instituted proceedings in order to force the covenantor to settle the property in accordance with the agreement.

The court held that since the children were volunteers they could not claim the benefit of the agreement. Accordingly, the trustees were directed not to take proceedings to enforce the covenant.

> **Simonds J:** The trustees have issued this summons, making as parties to it, first, the settlor herself and, secondly, her infant children, who are beneficiaries under the settlement. But, be it observed, though beneficiaries, her children are, for the purpose of this settlement, to be regarded as volunteers, there being no marriage consideration, which would have entitled them to sue, though they are parties to his application. The trustees ask whether, in the event which has happened of the settlor having become entitled to certain property, they should take proceedings against her to compel performance of the covenant or to recover damages on her failure to implement it ... The settlor has appeared by Mr Evershed and has contended, as she was entitled to contend, that the only question before the court was whether the trustees ought to be directed to take such proceedings; that is to say, she contended that the only question before the court was precisely that question which Eve J had to deal with in *Re Pryce*.[18] She has said that the question before me is not primarily whether, if she were sued, such an action would succeed (as to which she might have a defence, I know not what), but whether, in the circumstances as they are stated to the court, the trustees ought to be directed to take proceedings against her.
>
> As to that, the argument before me has been, on behalf of the children of the marriage, beneficiaries under the settlement, that, although it is conceded that the trustees could not successfully take proceedings for specific performance of the agreements contained in the settlement, yet they could successfully, and ought to be directed to, take proceedings at law to recover damages for the non-observance of the agreements contained in the settlement ... In the circumstances I must say that I felt considerable sympathy for the argument which was put before me by Mr Winterbotham on behalf of the children, that there was, at any rate, on the evidence before the court today, no reason why

18 [1917] 1 Ch 234.

the trustees should not be directed to take proceedings to recover what damages might be recoverable at law for breach of the agreements entered into by the settlor in her settlement. But on a consideration of *Re Pryce* it seemed to me that so far as this court was concerned the matter was concluded and that I ought not to give any directions to the trustees to take the suggested proceedings.

In *Re Pryce* the circumstances appear to me to have been in no wise different from those which obtain in the case which I have to consider.

[His Lordship considered the facts in *Re Pryce* and continued:]

That is the exact point which has been urged on me with great insistence by Mr Winterbotham. Whatever sympathy I might feel for his argument, I am not justified in departing in any way from this decision, which is now 21 years old. The learned judge, Eve J, in *Re Pryce* went on:

> In these circumstances, seeing that the next of kin could neither maintain an action to enforce the covenant nor for damages for breach of it, and that the settlement is to a declaration of trust constituting the relationship of trustee and *cestui que* trust between the defendant and the next of kin, in which case effect could be given to the trusts even in favour of volunteers, but is a mere voluntary contract to create a trust, ought the court now for the sole benefit of these volunteers to direct the trustees to take proceedings to enforce the defendant's covenant? I think it ought not; to do so would be to give the next of kin by indirect means relief they cannot obtain by any direct procedure, and would in effect be enforcing the settlement as against the defendant's legal right to payment and transfer from the trustees of the parents' marriage settlement.

It is true that in those last words the learned judge does not specifically refer to an action for damages, but it is clear that he has in his mind directions both with regard to an action for specific performance and an action to recover damages at law or, now, in this court.

In those circumstances it appears to me that I must follow the learned judge's decision and I must direct the trustees not to take any steps either to compel performance of the covenant or to recover damages through her failure to implement it.

Re Cavendish Browne's Settlement Trusts, Horner v Rawle [1916] WN 341, HC

By a voluntary covenant, dated 19 September 1911, made between the settlor and the trustees, the settlor covenanted that she will transfer to the trustees property to which she was entitled under the will of two others. The transfer was expressed to be subject to the terms of a trust. The covenant included a power of revocation.

The settlor died on 24 December 1914 intestate without having exercised the power of revocation. Her administrators applied by summons to determine whether damages were payable for breach of the covenant.

Held that the trustees were entitled to recover substantial damages from the administrators for breach of covenant. The measure of such damages was the value of the property which would have come into the hands of the trustees if the covenant had been duly performed.

A possible reconciliation with *Re Pryce* and *Re Kay* is that in *Re Cavendish Browne,* the property covenanted to be transferred was in existence on the date of the covenant.

If, however, the volunteer is a party to the deed, he will be entitled to bring an action at law for damages for breach of the agreement and equity will not interfere with his power to bring such action. In this situation, the plaintiff will be seeking to give effect directly to his common law rights by bringing an action for damages. His rights will not be dependent on a third party taking proceedings to represent his interest.

Cannon v Hartley [1949] Ch 213, HC

By a deed of separation executed on 23 January 1941 between the defendant (H) of the first part, his wife (W) of the second part and the plaintiff, their daughter, of the third part – H covenanted *inter alia* as follows:

> If and whenever during the lifetime of W or daughter, H shall become entitled to any money or property exceeding £1,000 he will forthwith settle one half of such money upon trust for himself for life, then to W for life with remainder to the daughter absolutely.

In 1944, H became entitled to £12,500. W died in 1946. H refused to execute the settlement in accordance with the covenant. The daughter brought an action claiming damages for breach of covenant.

The court held that the plaintiff was entitled to succeed.

> **Romer J:** It has been argued on behalf of the defendant that the plaintiff, not having given any consideration for this covenant by her father, is not only unable to apply to a court of equity for the enforcement of the covenant by way of specific performance, but that she is also disqualified from suing at common law for damages for breach of the covenant.
>
> It is, of course, well established that in such a case as this a volunteer cannot come to a court of equity and ask for relief which is peculiar to the jurisdiction of equity, viz, specific performance; but for my part I thought it was reasonably clear that, the document being under seal, the covenantee's claim for damages could be entertained, and that is still my belief ...
>
> But the defendant relies (and this appears to be the foundation of his defence) upon some observations made by Eve J in *Re Pryce*, and on the subsequent decision of Simonds J in in *Re Kay's Settlement.*
>
> [The learned judge then considered the judgments of Eve J in *Re Pryce* and Simonds J in *Re Kay* and continued:]
>
> Now it appears to me that neither *Re Pryce* nor *Re Kay's Settlement* is any authority for the proposition which has been submitted to me on behalf of the

> defendant. In neither case were the claimants parties to the settlement in question, nor were they within the consideration of the deed. When volunteers were referred to in *Re Pryce* it seems to me that what Eve J intended to say was that they were not within the class of non-parties, if I may use that expression, to whom Cotton LJ recognised in *Re D'Angibau* that the court would afford assistance. In the present case the plaintiff, although a volunteer, is not only a party to the deed of separation but is also a direct covenantee under the very covenant upon which she is suing. She does not require the assistance of the court to enforce the covenant for she has a legal right herself to enforce it. She is not asking for equitable relief for damages at common law for breach of covenant.
>
> For my part, I am quite unable to regard *Re Pryce*, which was a different case dealing with totally different circumstances, or anything which Eve J said therein, as amounting to an authority negativing the plaintiff's right to sue in the present case. I think that what Eve J was pointing out in *Re Pryce* was that the next of kin who were seeking to get an indirect benefit had no right to come to a court of equity because they were not parties to the deed and were not within the consideration of the deed and, similarly, they would have no right to proceed at common law by an action for damages, as the court of common law would not entertain a suit at the instance of volunteers who were not parties to the deed which was sought to be enforced, any more than the court of equity would entertain such a suit.
>
> It was suggested to me in argument that in such a case as the present, where the covenant is to bring in after-acquired property, an action for damages for breach of that covenant is in effect the same as a suit for specific performance of a covenant to settle. I myself think that the short answer to that is that the two things are not the same at all. The plaintiff here is invoking no equitable relief; she is merely asking for monetary compensation for a breach of covenant.
>
> I shall accordingly direct an inquiry as to the damages sustained by the plaintiff for breach by the defendant of the covenant with the plaintiff contained in clause 7 of the deed of separation.

Furthermore, a non-volunteer may bring an action at law or in equity against the other party to the deed. This claim may be brought for his own benefit (see *Pullan v Koe*) or apparently for the benefit of others, including volunteers. This appears to represent the view taken by the Law Lords in *Beswick v Beswick*.[19]

Beswick v Beswick [1968] AC 58, HL

Peter Beswick was assisted in his business as a coal merchant by his nephew, the defendant. Peter entered into a contract, by deed, with the defendant for the transfer of the business. The material terms were that Peter will assign the business to the defendant in consideration of the defendant employing him as

19 [1968] AC 58.

a consultant for the remainder of his life at £6, 10 s a week and paying an annuity of £5 a week to his widow after his death. Peter subsequently died. The defendant paid the widow the first £5 but thereafter refused to pay any more. The widow sued the defendant as administratrix of her husband's estate and in her personal capacity for arrears of the annuity and for specific performance of the agreement. The High Court dismissed the action. The Court of Appeal allowed her appeal on the ground that, as administratrix, the plaintiff was entitled to specific performance. The defendant appealed to the House of Lords. It was not argued that the plaintiff was entitled to pursue her claim in her personal capacity.

Held, by the House of Lords, that the plaintiff was entitled, as administratrix of her husband's estate, to specific performance of the agreement. In short, her deceased husband could have enforced the agreement on behalf of his volunteer wife and since an award of damages was an inadequate remedy the rights under the agreement were adequately protected by an order of specific performance.

> **Lord Reid:** The respondent's [plaintiff's] second argument is that she is entitled in her capacity of administratrix of her deceased husband's estate to enforce the provision of the agreement for the benefit of herself in her personal capacity, and that a proper way of enforcing that provision is to order specific performance. That would produce a just result, and, unless there is some technical objection, I am of the opinion that specific performance ought to be ordered.
>
> **Lord Pearce:** My Lords, if the annuity had been payable to a third party in the lifetime of Beswick senior and there had been default, he could have sued in respect of the breach. His administratrix is now entitled to stand in his shoes and to sue in respect of the breach which has occurred since his death. It is argued that the estate can recover only nominal damages and that no other remedy is open, either to the estate or to the personal plaintiff. Such a result would be wholly repugnant to justice and common sense. And if the argument were right it would show a very serious defect in the law.
>
> In the first place, I do not accept the view that damages must be nominal. Lush LJ in *Lloyd's v Harper* (1880) 16 Ch D 290, said:
>
>> Then the next question which, no doubt, is a very important and substantial one, is that Lloyd's, having sustained no damage themselves, could not recover for the losses sustained by the third parties by reason of the default of Robert Harper as an underwriter. That, to my mind, is a startling and alarming doctrine, and a novelty, because I consider it to be an established rule of law that where a contract is made with A for the benefit of B, A can sue on the contract for the benefit of B, and recover all that B could have recovered if the contract had been made with B himself.
>
> In the present case I think that the damages, if assessed, must be substantial. It is not necessary, however, to consider the amount of damages more closely since this is a case in which, as the Court of Appeal rightly decided, the more appropriate remedy is that of specific performance.

> What, then, is the obstacle to granting specific performance? It is argued that since the widow personally had no rights which she personally could enforce the court will not make an order which will have the effect of enforcing those rights. I can find no principle to this effect. The condition as to payment of an annuity to the widow personally was valid. The estate (though not the widow personally) can enforce it. Why should the estate be barred from exercising its full contractual rights merely because in doing so it secures justice for the widow who, by a mechanical defect of our law, is unable to assert her own rights? Such a principle would be repugnant to justice and fulfil no other object than that of aiding the wrongdoer. I can find no ground on which such a principle should exist.
>
> In *Hohler v Aston* [1920] 2 Ch 420 Sargant J enforced a contract relating to the purchase of a house for the benefit of third parties. The third parties were joined as plaintiffs, but the relief was given to the plaintiff who had made the contract for their benefit:
>
>> The third parties, of course, cannot themselves enforce a contract made for their benefit, but the person with whom the contract is made is entitled to enforce the contract.
>
> In *Keenan v Handley* (1864) 12 WR 930, the court enforced an agreement providing the benefit of an annuity in favour of a mother who was a party to the agreement and, after her death, to her child, who was not a party to it.
>
> In my opinion, the plaintiff as administratrix is entitled to a decree of specific performance.

See also *Coulls v Bagot's Executor and Trustee Co Ltd* [1967] ALR 385; *Jackson v Horizon Holidays Ltd* [1975] 1 WLR 1468, CA; *Jarvis v Swan Tours Ltd* [1973] QB 233.

In an article entitled, 'The power of trustees to enforce covenants in favour of volunteers' (1960) 76 LQR 100, Professor Elliott considers the extent to which a volunteer covenantee (B) is prohibited from suing the covenantor (A) for damages for breach of contract to create a trust for the benefit of a volunteer non-covenantee (C). Simonds J, in *Re Kay* (1939), prohibited B from bringing such an action relying on the reasoning of Eve J in *Re Pryce* (1917). Professor Elliott believes that the reasoning in *Re Pryce* (as distinct from the decision) was incorrect. Eve J relied on the decision in *Re D'Angibau* (1880), but this case was quite distinct from the issue as to whether the trustee-covenantee may sue for damages for the benefit of the volunteer non-covenantee. More importantly, Eve J's reasoning in *Re Pryce* is flawed in that he adopted the principle that in an action for damages in a court of equity, the same defences may be open to the defendant as were available in an action for an equitable remedy. This is doubtful because *Cox v Barnard* (1850) 8 Hare 310 decided that a court of equity has the ability to award damages in order to avoid a circuity of actions, 'The court will not make two suits out of one'. The view in *Cox v Barnard* being the correct approach that should have been adopted in *Re Pryce*, it followed that *Re Kay* which relied on *Re Pryce* was equally misdirected. The execution of a covenant at law is an alternative to consideration. Substantial damages ought to be recoverable which represents the measure of loss suffered by the covenantee, provided that he is willing to sue at law. In *Lloyd's v Harper* (1880) 16 Ch D 290, the Court of Appeal made it clear that, if B contracts with A as trustee for C, he can recover substantial damages for breach of contract. These damages ought to be held upon trust for the intended beneficiary.

Elliott concludes thus:

> ... contrary to what Eve J suggests, an action at law by the covenantee would be successful and would be rewarded by substantial damages, unless of course it was statute-barred or there was some other legal or equitable defence available. The fact that the proposed beneficiary, C, could not himself maintain an action is both self-evident and irrelevant in an action by B, the covenantee. It is only relevant if C comes crying to equity asking for assistance in obliging B to lend his name to an action against A. In such a case, one would agree with Eve J that the court should not direct B to take proceedings; not because that would be to give C, by indirect means, relief which he cannot obtain by any direct procedure; but because he requires the assistance of the court to constitute him *cestui que trust* and as a volunteer he shall not have that assistance.
>
> It is hoped that it has been demonstrated that the alleged power of the court to prevent a covenantee suing at law on a covenant for the benefit of a volunteer rests on a misapprehension of equity's relations with volunteers.
>
> In truth, the interposition of a trustee-covenantee cannot make any material difference to the volunteer, provided that the trustee is willing to sue at law; yet if *Re Pryce* and *Re Kay's Settlement* are right, even a willing trustee will be directed not to sue. Since there is no discernable difference between the volunteer-covenantee who is willing to help him, the conclusion must be that these cases are wrong on this point.

In 'The public policy of *Re Cook's Settlement*' (1969) 85 LQR 213, WA Lee, in defence of *Re Pryce* and *Re Kay*, contends that these cases relate to the law of contract and not to the law of trust. These cases concerned covenants to settle unascertained after-acquired property which did not generate choses in action. Thus, the promises did not form the subject matter of trusts. Even if a chose in action was vested in the covenantee and he sues on the covenant and obtains judgment for damages, the monetary award in Lee's view ought to be held on resulting or constructive trust for the covenantor. Lee submits that there is no justification for identifying damages awarded at law as the property contracted to be settled, so as thereby to render the trust completely constituted. It is up to the settlor to take the ultimate and irrevocable step of transferring the property upon trust, save for cases within the *Strong v Bird* or *Re Ralli* principle.

MW Friend, in 'Trusts of voluntary covenants: an alternative approach' [1982] Conv 280, examines third party rights under voluntary, but unfulfilled, covenants. A enters into a voluntary covenant with B to settle property upon trust for C but A fails to transfer the property to B. Friend, in his article, examines the nature of C's remedy (if any) against A. If A agrees to settle a sum of money on B in trust for C, this arrangement may create a debt (chose in action) in favour of B. B is entitled to sue A and recover substantial damages which he is required to hold in trust for C, see *Fletcher v Fletcher* (1844):

> Because B has covenanted with A as a trustee for C, he automatically holds his right to sue for the debt on trust for C; there is thus a completely constituted trust of the benefit of the covenant. Thus, C may either request B to sue A, or he may join B as a co-defendant in the action if B refuses to act.

Friend emphasises the vital distinction between contracts supported by consideration and voluntary covenants. Specific performance may be decreed in respect of the former, but not the latter type of contract and such a decree has the effect of completely constituting the trust. This would be the position if the covenantee (B) has suffered loss or where the promise creates a debt enforceable at law.

Friend also examines the rights of the parties under covenants to settle existing property, other than money and covenants to settle after-acquired property, and concludes thus:

> (1) Unless B is the agent of C, or unless B or C has suffered financial loss (in which case any damages recovered by B will be held in trust for C), C can only succeed against A if there is a completely constituted trust of the benefit of the covenant. The question is therefore to determine the circumstances in which such a trust will be inferred. It is suggested that this will in turn depend upon the nature of the property covenanted to be settled.
>
> (2) A voluntary covenant to settle money creates a debt. Where it is clear that B has covenanted as a trustee for C, there will be a completely constituted trust of the chose in action generated by the covenant, so that C can recover.
>
> (3) A voluntary covenant to settle specific and presently existing property other than money may create a debt, in which case the above principles apply. Otherwise, then, unless there is clear evidence of an intention on the part of B to constitute himself a trustee for C of the benefit of the covenant, or unless C falls within the notional 'meritorious consideration', he will be without a remedy.
>
> (4) A voluntary covenant to settle after-acquired property probably generates a proprietary chose in action as soon as the promise is made. Although there is no theoretical reason why such a chose in action should not be capable of being held in trust, such a view is not supported by authority. Thus, in such a case C will be without a remedy.
>
> (5) Where consideration has been furnished, the availability of specific performance and the application of the maxim, 'Equity looks on that as done which ought to be done', allows the inference of a trust of the benefit

> of the contract to be made. In such a case C can recover damages to compensate him for his own loss.

David Goddard, in 'Equity, volunteers and ducks' [1988] Conv 19, examines third parties' rights under contracts. In respect of a voluntary promise under seal to create a trust for a third party, for example, A covenants with B to transfer property to him to hold on trust for C, the issue is whether B may sue A for damages for breach of contract. It was decided in *Re Kay* that B will be prevented from suing A for damages, despite having a common law right to bring an action for damages for breach of contract. Moreover, it has been suggested that B has suffered no loss and therefore cannot obtain substantial damages. Goddard questions this rule and suggests as follows:

> Actions for damages, popularly so called, can be divided into the true action for damages, where a loss which is not too remote, arising from a breach, is recovered; and the action for an agreed sum – an example of which is an action for the price. In an action for an agreed sum, all one need prove is that a legally actionable promise to pay the sum was made, payment is due, and that it has not been paid. The court will then award to the promisee that sum, neither more or less regardless of the loss suffered.

Goddard also examines the argument that B acquires a chose in action, that is, the promise with A makes B the legal owner of the promise. On this basis, the issue arises as to the identity of the beneficial owner of the promise. The suggestion was made that as no trust of the promise was declared and no consideration was given for it, the promise is held on resulting trust for A. Goddard considers this result absurd and suggests that by a process of elimination, the beneficial interest in the promise must be vested in C.

SUPPLEMENTARY READING

Barton, J, 'Trusts and covenants' (1975) 91 LQR 236

Hornby, J, 'Covenants in favour of volunteers' (1962) 78 LQR 228

Jaconelli, J, 'Privity: the trust exception examined' [1998] Conv 88

Jones, G, 'The enforcement of settlements in equity by volunteers' [1965] CLJ 46

Matheson, D, 'The enforceability of a covenant to create a trust' (1966) 29 MLR 397

Meagher, R and Lehane, L, 'Trusts of voluntary covenants' (1976) 92 LQR 425

Williams, G, 'Contracts for the benefit of third parties' (1943) 7 MLR 123

CHAPTER 5

EXCEPTIONS TO THE RULE THAT EQUITY WILL NOT PERFECT AN IMPERFECT GIFT

In limited circumstances, equity developed a number of exceptions to the general rule that, 'equity will not perfect an imperfect gift' and 'equity will not assist a volunteer'. The effect of these exceptions is to permit a volunteer to perfect an imperfect gift or gain assistance from a court of equity despite being classified as a volunteer.

THE RULE IN *STRONG V BIRD*

A perfect gift of property requires the donor to transfer the property to the donee with the intention of gifting the property to the donee. The rule in *Strong v Bird* is that if an *inter vivos* gift is imperfect by reason only of the transfer to the donee being incomplete, the gift will become perfect when the donee acquires the property in the capacity of executor of the donor's estate. In probate law, the deceased's estate devolves on his executor, who, after payment of all the debts of the testator is required to distribute the estate in accordance with the testator's will. The donee/executor will take the property beneficially in accordance with the intention of the donor, even though he acquires the asset in the capacity of executor of the donor's estate.

Strong v Bird (1874) LR 18 Eq 315, CA

The defendant's stepmother lived with him and his wife, paying for board and lodging. He had borrowed £1,000 from her and it was agreed that the debt should be repaid by deductions of £100 from each quarter's rent. Deductions were made for two quarters and on the third quarter the stepmother refused to hold the defendant to the agreement and paid the full rent until her death. This arrangement by conduct, did not discharge the debt at law since there was no consideration for the release. The defendant became the sole executor of his stepmother's estate. The next of kin now attempted to recover the money from the defendant.

The court held that the transfer of the relevant sum had been perfected and the debt extinguished by the appointment of the defendant as executor. The stepmother's donative intention had continued until her death.

> **Sir George Jessel MR:** The law requires nothing more than this, that in a case where the thing which is the subject of donation is transferable or releasable at law, the legal transfer or release shall take place. Allowing this rule to operate to its full extent, what occurred was this. The donor, or the alleged donor, had

> made her will, and by that will had appointed Mr Bird, the alleged donee, executor. After her death he proved the will, and the legal effect of that was to release the debt in law, and therefore the condition which is required, namely, that the release shall be perfect at law, was complied with by the testatrix making him executor. It is not necessary that the legal change shall knowingly be made by the donor with a view to carry out the gift. It may be made for another purpose; but if the gift is clear, and there is to be no recall of the gift, and no intention to recall it, so that the person who executes the legal instrument does not intend to invest the person taking upon himself the legal ownership with any other character, there is no reason why the legal instrument should not have its legal effect.
>
> For instance, suppose it occurred that the person made a memorandum on the title deeds of an estate to this effect: 'I give Blackacre to AB', and afterwards conveyed that estate to AB by a general description, not intending in any way to change the previous gift, would there be any equity to make the person who had so obtained the legal estate a trustee for the donor? The answer would be that there is no resulting trust: this is rebutted by shewing that the person who conveyed did not intend the person taking the conveyance to be a trustee, and although the person conveying actually thought that there was not one of the estates conveyed, because that person thought that he had not given the estate before, still the estate would pass at law, notwithstanding that idea, and there being no intention to revoke the gift, surely it would get rid of any resulting trust. On the same principle, when a testator makes his debtor executor, and thereby releases the debt at law, he is no longer liable at law. It is said that he would be liable in this court: and so he would, unless he could shew some reason for not being made liable. Then what does he shew here? Where he proves to the satisfaction of the court a continuing intention to give; and it appears to me that there being the continuing intention to give, and there being a legal act which transferred the ownership or released the obligation – for it is the same thing – the transaction is perfected, and he does not want the aid of a court of equity to carry it out, or to make it complete, because it is complete already, and there is no equity against him to take the property away from him. On that ground I shall hold that this gentleman had a perfect title to the £900.

The donor's intention is of paramount importance. It is the donor's intention which entitles the court to perfect the gift at the instance of the volunteer, executor. The donor is required to manifest a present, continuing intention to make an *inter vivos* gift. Thus, the rule will not be satisfied if the donor declares an intention to transfer property to the donee in the future, see *Re Freeland.*[1]

1 [1952] Ch 110.

Re Freeland [1952] Ch 110, CA

The plaintiff claimed that the testatrix had given her a Hillman motor car in March 1949, but that since it was not in a roadworthy condition, it was not delivered to her, but remained in the testatrix's garage. The plaintiff further alleged that, in May 1949, the defendant borrowed the car from the testatrix after the latter had repaired it. The defendant retained possession of the car until the testatrix's death. The testatrix appointed the plaintiff and defendant to be her executors. The plaintiff claimed a declaration that she was the owner of the car under the *Strong v Bird* rule.

It was held, by the Court of Appeal, that the *Strong v Bird* rule was not applicable because there was no continuing intention to make an immediate out and out gift to the plaintiff. The rule could not be extended to future gifts.

> **Sir Raymond Evershed MR:** The loan of the motor car by the testatrix to the defendant was fatal to the plaintiff's claim that there was a continuing intention on the part of the testatrix to make an immediate gift. The principle in *Strong v Bird* was directed to perfecting gifts complete in all respects except as regards the legal formalities necessary for the proper transfer of title to the particular property in question. It was confined to cases where nothing remained to be done but the mere formality of transfer in order to perfect what was intended to be an immediate gift *inter vivos*. There was no room for the application of the principle where there was an intention to give which was not completed because the intended donor desired first to apply the subject matter of the gift to some other purpose. In such a case the intended donee when appointed executor could not say that nothing remained to complete his gift but the transfer, because, had he asked the donor to transfer the property, the donor's answer would have been that it was his intention to give the property to the donee after he had used it for a prior purpose.

Similarly, it must be established that the testator's intention to gift the asset to his executor was unbroken in the sense that from the time of the declaration of intention to the date of his death the donor had not changed his mind. Accordingly, the rule is not satisfied if the donor once had the relevant intention to give away the asset, but had forgotten about the purported gift and treated the property as his own up to the date of his death. See *Re Wale*.

Re Wale (Decd) [1956] 1 WLR 1346, HC

Elizabeth Wale was the absolute owner of certain 'A' shares, registered in her name. She was also entitled to certain 'B' investments under her husband's will. These investments were registered in the names of her husband's executors (Elizabeth therefore had an equitable interest in the 'B' investments). In 1939, Elizabeth voluntarily agreed in writing to transfer both sets of shares to trustees upon trust for her daughter, but failed to take steps to transfer the shares to the trustees. For the remainder of her life she showed no indication of remembering the covenant with the trustees. By her will she left her property to her two sons. Her two sons and daughter were appointed executors. On her death in 1953, the family solicitor produced the 1939 settlement. The question in issue concerned entitlement to the shares, whether the daughter was entitled under the settlement or the sons under the will.

The court held that:

(i) as regards the 'A' shares, the settlor held the legal title which she failed to transfer to the trustees. The daughter as a volunteer and non party to the covenant was not entitled to assistance either in equity or at law to perfect the imperfect trust. The rule in *Strong v Bird* was not applicable because the donor's intention to make the gift did not continue until her death. These shares passed to the sons under the will;

(ii) in relation to the 'B' shares, since Elizabeth had only an equitable interest in these investments, the covenant operated as a valid assignment of her interest (in compliance with s 53(1)(c) of the Law of Property Act 1925) to the trustees upon trust for her daughter.

The rule has been extended to perfect an imperfect trust where the trustee/executor acquires the property under the will of the donor. In other words, the capacity in which the property is acquired is immaterial for the purpose of ascertaining whether the trust is perfect, provided that the transferee/executor was appointed a trustee. Thus, in *Re Ralli* (see above, p 94), when Irene's husband became a trustee of the 1899 settlement, he acquired *inter alia* Helen's property as executor and since he was also appointed a trustee of Helen's intended marriage settlement in 1924, he had therefore acquired the trust property and was required to hold the same on trust for the beneficiaries under the 1924 settlement.

Moreover, the simple rule in *Strong v Bird* was unjustifiably extended in *Re James*[2] to transfers made to the administrator on an intestacy. But, Walton J, in *Re Gonin*, severely criticised this unwarranted extension and expressed serious doubts as to the validity of the decision.

Re Gonin (Decd) [1979] Ch 16, HC

A mother who wanted to make a gift of her house to her daughter, erroneously believed that she could not do so because the daughter was illegitimate. As an alternative, the mother wrote out a cheque for £33,000 in her daughter's favour. This cheque was found after her mother's death. At this point the cheque could not be cashed because on the mother's death the funds in her account became frozen. The daughter became administratrix of her mother's estate and claimed the house under the *Strong v Bird* rule.

2 [1935] 1 Ch 449.

The court held against the claimant on the ground that there was no continuing intention to give the house to the daughter.

> **Walton J:** I start from the simple proposition that if the defendant in *Strong v Bird* itself had been an administrator instead of an executor the case would have been decided the other way, since it distinctly proceeded on the basis that at law the appointment of the person as an executor effected a release of any debt due from the executor to the testator, a doctrine which was never applied to an administrator. One can see why this should be so: by appointing the executor, the testator has by his own act made it impossible for the debtor to sue himself. And, indeed, so far has the rule been taken, that although it will no longer apply if the person appointed executor has renounced probate, yet it will still apply if power to prove has been reserved to him.
>
> The appointment of an administrator is not the act of the deceased but of law. It is often a matter of pure chance which of many persons equally entitled to a grant of letters of administration finally takes them out. Why, then, should any special tenderness be shown to a person so selected by law and not the will of the testator. It would seem an astonishing doctrine of equity that if the person who wishes to take the benefit of the rule in *Strong v Bird* manages to be the person to obtain a grant then he will be able to do so, but if a person equally entitled manages to obtain a prior grant, then he will not be able to do so. This appears to treat what ought to be a simple rule of equity as something in the nature of a lottery.

Gilbert Kodilinye, in 'A fresh look at the rule in *Strong v Bird*' [1982] Conv 14, examines the basis of the rule in *Strong v Bird*. He concludes that the criticisms by Walton J in *Re Gonin* of the principle in *Re James* were unfounded. The administrator of the deceased's estate is in the same position as the executor for the purposes of the *Strong v Bird* rule. Both fiduciaries acquire the deceased's property. As an administrator, the deceased's property is acquired by the next of kin by operation of law. Whereas the executor obtains the testator's estate by the conscious and positive act of naming the executor in his will. For the purpose of the rule, it is immaterial how the legal estate vests in the personal representative. There is no requirement that the vesting of the estate in the donee must come about through the voluntary act of the donor.

In addition, Kodilinye contends that the application of the *Strong v Bird* rule to *Re Ralli* marks an unjustified extension of the principle for the following reasons:

> (i) the plaintiff [in *Re Ralli*] was trustee of a third party's, not the donor's, will;
>
> (ii) [in *Re Ralli*] there was no attempted immediate gift of any property but only a promise to settle property in the future;
>
> (iii) it is doubtful whether *Strong v Bird* applies where the executor appointed is not the intended donee of the beneficial interest but a trustee of such interest for the donee;

(iv) it was central to Buckley J's reasoning in *Re Ralli* that the settlor had bound herself by covenant to assign the property to the trustees of the marriage settlement, and he expressly limited his decision to such a case;

(v) Buckley J did not expressly base his decision on *Strong v Bird*.

DONATIO MORTIS CAUSA (DEATH BED GIFTS)

A *donatio mortis causa* (DMC) is the *inter vivos* delivery of property by a person contemplating death, subject to the intention that the gift shall take effect only on the donor's death. The effect is that on the donor's death the gift becomes unconditional and the donee is entitled to retain the property, or, if the gift is still imperfect, the donee (volunteer) may compel the personal representatives to perfect the transfer of the property to him. The donee under a DMC takes the asset in preference to beneficiaries under the will or an intestacy.

For example, T made his will disposing of all his property to A and on his death bed delivers to B, his watch and building society passbook showing a credit balance of £100. On T's death, the gift of the watch becomes complete. The transfer of the building society funds is incomplete but B will be entitled to compel T's personal representatives to perfect the gift.

Duffield v Elwes (1827) Cr & Ph 138, CA

> **Eldon LJ:** Nothing can be more clear than that a DMC must be a gift made by a donor in contemplation of the conceived approach of death – that the title is not complete until he is actually dead, and that the question therefore can never be what the donor can be compelled to do, but what the donee in the case of a DMC can call upon the representatives, real or personal, of the donor to do; the question is this, whether the act of the donor being, as far as the act of the donor itself is to be viewed, complete. The persons who represent that donor are not bound to complete that which, as far as the act of the donor is concerned was incomplete; in other words, after the death of the donor, the executor is not to be considered a trustee for the donee. I apprehend that really the question does not turn at all upon what the donor could do, or what the donor could not do; but if it was a good DMC, what the donee of that donor could call upon the representatives of the donor to do after the death of that donor.

A DMC is distinct from an absolute *inter vivos* gift because the transfer of the asset is conditional on death and during the lifetime of the donor the transfer of the property is incomplete. On the other hand, a DMC is different from a testamentary gift for the conditional transfer of property *inter vivos* is not made by will. Thus, the formalities under the Wills Act 1837 are not required to be complied with.

Re Beaumont [1902] 1 Ch 889, CA

> **Buckley J** (p 892): A DMC is a singular form of gift. It may be said to be of an amphibious nature, being a gift which is neither entirely *inter vivos* nor testamentary. It is an act *inter vivos* by which the donee is to have absolute title to the gift not at once but if the donor dies. If the donor dies the title becomes absolute not under the will but as against the executor. In order to make the gift valid it must be made so as to take complete effect on the donor's death.

Re Craven's Estate (No 1) [1937] 1 Ch 423, HC

> **Farwell J:** Generally speaking, it is not permissible by the law of this country for a person to dispose of his or her property after his or her death except by an instrument executed in accordance with the provisions of the Wills Act 1837. One exception to the general rule is the case of a *donatio mortis causa*, but in order that it may be valid certain conditions must be exactly complied with; otherwise the attempted *donatio* is not effected and the property remains part of the property of the testatrix at her death passing under her will. The conditions which are essential to a *donatio mortis causa* are firstly, a clear intention to give, but to give only if the donor dies, whereas if the donor does not die then the gift is not to take effect and the donor is to have back the subject matter of the gift. Secondly, the gift must be made in contemplation of death, by which is meant not the possibility of death at some time or other, but death within the near future, what may be called death for some reason believed to be impending. Thirdly, the donor must part with dominion over the subject matter of the *donatio* ...

Thus, there are three conditions to be satisfied in order to create a valid DMC:

(1) the gift is made in contemplation of death;

(2) it is conditional on death; and

(3) dominion over the property is transferred to the donee.

Gift made in contemplation of death

It is necessary for the donor to contemplate death more specifically than by reflecting that we must all die some day. The test here is subjective and the court may decide this question by having regard to the surrounding circumstances such as the injuries or illness of the donor, or the fact that the donor was a patient in a hospital, etc. Indeed, the condition will be satisfied if the donor contemplated death from one cause but dies from another cause.

Wilkes v Allington [1931] 2 Ch 104, HC

The donor was suffering from an incurable disease (cancer) and made the gift knowing that he did not have long to live. As things turned, he lived for an even shorter time than he thought, because he died two months later from pneumonia. The court held that the gift was valid.

Transfer *inter vivos* but conditional on death

This requirement distinguishes a DMC from an absolute *inter vivos* gift. The intention must be that the gift will automatically become complete on death but subject to the condition that it may be revoked by the donor expressly and will automatically be revoked if he recovers from his illness within a reasonable period of time. The court is required to consider all the circumstances in deciding whether this requirement is satisfied.

Express revocation may take the form of the donor resuming dominion over the property. This would depend on the intention of the donor. Recovery of the property for safe custody will not have this effect. It is impossible for the donor to revoke a DMC by will, for the will takes effect after death and on death the gift becomes perfect. It follows that if the donee predeceases the donor the gift will fail, for the donee's title is conditional on the death of the donor, and on the donee's death title reverts back to the donor.

Parting with dominion

Re Craven's Estate (No 1) [1937] Ch 423, HC

> **Farwell J:** I have considered what the reason for imposing as a condition of a valid *donatio* that the donor must part with dominion over the subject matter thereof and the answer seems to me to be that the subject matter of the *donatio* must be some definite property, and, to ensure that, the donor must put it out of his power between the date of the donation and the date of the death to alter the subject matter of the gift and substitute other chattels of the gift remained in the dominion of the donor, the donor might at any time between the *donatio* and the gift deal with it as he or she pleased. Take for instance the case of a box. The donor says to the donee: 'This box contains certain valuables which are to be yours in the event of my death from the operation which I am going to undergo in a few days, but I propose to retain the box and the key of the box.' If that was the position it would be open to the donor at any time to take out of the box whatever was in it replacing it with other valuables, and in my view it is in order that that should parted with dominion so that whatever the original subject matter of the *donatio* was it should remain the subject matter in the event of the death of the donor. In the case of the box it is not necessary to hand over the box if the key is handed over because it is assumed that the key which unlocks the box being in the possession of the donee the donor cannot have access to the contents so as to deal with them in any way.

The basic rule is that the property to be disposed of must be actually handed over to the donee or to someone else as trustee for the donee. This transfer must be accompanied by the necessary intent to part with dominion or control over the property during the lifetime of the donor. No difficulty arises with small articles in respect of which possession may be transferred by the physical delivery to the donee, for example, jewellery, books, paintings, etc. But it is a question of degree as to whether the intention to transfer dominion over the property has been manifested. Delivery of the property for safe custody would be insufficient evidence.

In *Reddell v Dobree*,[3] the donor gave a locked cash box to the intended donee, telling her that it contained money for her to use after his death, and that on his death she should obtain the key from his son. The donor required the intended donee to produce the box to him at three monthly intervals for the remainder of his life. The production was done on two occasions and after inspection by the donor the box was returned to the donee. The donor kept the key to the box during his lifetime. The question in issue was whether there was a valid DMC of the box and its contents. The court held that there was no valid DMC because the donor had retained full power over the property throughout his lifetime.

When the article is too bulky to be physically handed over, it is sufficient for the donor to hand over the means whereby the donee may take possession and control, provided that at the same time the donor is deprived of the power of dealing with the property, for example, delivery of a key to a trunk or safe has been regarded as an effective delivery of the property in the trunk or safe.

The retention of a duplicate set of keys by the donor may be construed as evidence of the retention of dominion over the chattel provided that there was a conscious decision on the part of the donor to retain control.

Re Craven's Estate (No 1) [1937] 1 Ch 423, HC

> **Farwell J:** I know of no decided cases in which the question has arisen whether the handing over of a box and one key, it being proved that there was another key retained by the donor, would be sufficient [to transfer dominion] ... it would probably be held not to be sufficient parting with dominion because the donor would have retained dominion over the box and the contents of the box by retaining the power to open it although it might be in the possession of the donee.

More recently, the Court of Appeal considered that the effect of the retention of a spare set of keys by the donor would vary with the facts of each case. The reason for the retention will be considered by the courts. If the purpose of the retention of the keys is to retain control over the property then, obviously, dominion would not be transferred. On the other hand, if the retention of the key is not a deliberate and conscious decision taken by the donor this, in itself, may not be inconsistent with the transfer of dominion. The question is determined by having regard to the donor's intention.

3 (1839) 10 Sim 244.

Woodard v Woodard (1991) *The Times*, 18 March, CA

The plaintiff, sole beneficiary and personal representative of her late husband's estate, brought an action against her son claiming the proceeds of sale of a car which was sold by the defendant shortly after his father's death. The defendant claimed that the car was the subject matter of an outright gift in accordance with his father's intention. Possession of the car was obtained or retained during the period of his father's hospitalisation while suffering from the condition, leukaemia (from which he failed to recover). Witnesses testified that the donor said, at various times a few days before his death, that the defendant may keep the car ('You may keep the key'). The trial judge decided that there was an outright gift of the car to the defendant.

On appeal, the Court of Appeal held that the circumstances did not create an outright gift but a valid DMC was constituted. On the facts, the court decided that an inference could be drawn that the father's intention was conditional on death. On the question of whether dominion over the car was transferred, the court adopted a common sense approach and decided that since the defendant already had possession of the car, the declaration of intention by the father was sufficient to transfer dominion over the car. It was unnecessary for the father to re-acquire possession of the car from the son as a preliminary to transferring dominion or control to the defendant. The significance of the retention of a spare set of keys was considered by the court and a practical solution was offered. The motive or purpose of retention by the donor was to be judged by having regard to the facts of each case. If the purpose of retention of a spare set of keys by the donor was to retain control over the property, then a DMC would not be established. But if the evidence shows that the retention of the additional key was not a deliberate and conscious effort by the donor, control or dominion may be transferred.

Reliance was placed on the judgment of Lawrence J in *Re Stoneham*. In this case, the claimant, who was in possession of old oak furniture, arms and armour belonging to the testator, alleged that a perfect *inter vivos* gift was made to him in accordance with the intention of the donor. It was unnecessary for the claimant to release possession of the chattels to the donor and re-acquire the same. Accordingly, the testator could not dispose of the same under his will. The court held in favour of the claimant.

> **Lawrence J:** In my judgment the foundation of the rule affirmed by the Court of Appeal in *Cochrane v Moore*,[4] is that in order to constitute a perfect gift by word of mouth of chattels capable of delivery the donee must have had the chattels delivered into his possession by the donor or by someone on his behalf. In principle, I can see no distinction between a delivery antecedent to the gift and a delivery concurrent with or subsequent to the gift. Nor can I see

4 [1890] 25 QBD 57.

> any reason in principle why the rule should not apply to a case where chattels have been delivered to the donee before the gift as bailee or in any other capacity, so long as they are actually in his possession at the time of the gift to the knowledge of the donor. The donor if he wanted to recover the chattels would have to bring an action against the donee whether he had delivered the chattels prior to the gift or the delivery had accompanied or followed the gift, and the donee in such an action could plead the gift as a defence whenever the chattels had been delivered to him and, in the case of a prior delivery, in whatever capacity he had originally received them. As showing that all that the law requires in the case of a verbal gift of chattels is that the property in and the possession of the chattels should unite in the recipient ...
>
> In *Cain v Moon*[5] it was held that antecedent delivery to the donee to hold in a different capacity was a sufficient delivery to satisfy the rule requiring delivery in parol gifts of chattels. This case would have been a direct authority in favour of the claimant's contention but for the fact that it was a case of a *donatio mortis causa* and not a case of gift *inter vivos*. It will be observed that the court decided the case on the footing that as regards delivery a *donatio mortis causa* stood on precisely the same footing as a gift *inter vivos*, a view, which if taken in its literal sense, would seem to be inaccurate. See *Re Wasserberg*.[6] Both the learned judges who decided *Cain v Moon*, however, were of opinion that in a parol gift of chattels *inter vivos* any further delivery was unnecessary where the chattels were already in the possession of the intended donee, and Wills J gives the following illustration:
>
>> Suppose a man lent a book to a friend who expressed himself pleased with the book, whereupon the lender, finding he had a second copy, told his friend that he need not return the copy he had lent him; it would be very strange if in such a case there were no complete gift, the book being in the possession of the intended donee.
>
> In the result, after having examined all the authorities to which my attention has been called, I have come to the conclusion that there is no decision which prevents my giving effect to the claimant's contention. I therefore hold that the old oak furniture, arms and armour in question were effectually given by the testator to the claimant in the Spring of 1913, and did not belong to the testator at the date of his death.

LORD EVERSHED MR IN *BIRCH V TREASURY SOLICITOR*

Choses in action (bank accounts, etc) are incapable of physical delivery. The question in issue is whether the donee can adduce sufficient evidence to compel the personal representatives to complete the gift by transferring the

5 [1896] 2 QB 283.

6 [1915] 1 Ch 105.

legal title to the chose. The test is whether the donor has delivered a document of title to the donee, that is, a document which is essential evidence of title to the chose.

> The real test is whether the instrument amounts to a transfer as being the essential *indicia* or evidence of title, possession or production of which entitles the possessor to the money or property purported to be given.

Birch v Treasury Solicitor [1951] 1 Ch 298, CA

Mrs Birch, shortly before her death in hospital on 29 March 1948, expressed her wish that the plaintiff, her nephew and his wife, be paid the funds within three joint stock bank accounts and a Post Office Savings account in the event of her death. Mrs Birch delivered to the plaintiffs the passbooks to the various bank accounts and the Post Office Savings book, reiterating her wish. On the death of Mrs Birch, the Treasury Solicitor took out letters of administration. The plaintiffs commenced proceedings claiming the funds in the various accounts by way of *donationes mortis causa*.

Held that the circumstances established valid *donationes mortis causa*. The bank and Post Office Savings book were *indicia* or evidence of title as the books contained a stipulation that they were required to be produced in order to withdraw funds.

> **Lord Evershed MR:** The question raised on this appeal is whether on the evidence there was a valid *donatio mortis causa* of certain bank accounts to the two plaintiffs, who are husband and wife. The trial judge has held that there was not.
>
> If we are right in concluding that the evidence supports in other respects a valid *donatio mortis causa*, there remains the more difficult question whether any and, if so, which of the sums of money specified in para 6 of the statement of claim are from their nature, and in the light of the evidence given on the defendants' behalf, capable of being the subject matter of a *donatio*. Upon this point the judge was of opinion that the sum of £3,328, 9 s, 6 d standing to the deceased's credit in the Post Office Savings Bank was so capable. In this respect he followed the decision of Byrne J in *Re Weston*.[7]
>
> There remain accordingly the three sums to the credit of the deceased, namely:
>
> (1) £55 with the London Trustee Savings Bank;
>
> (2) £646, 11 s, 2 d with Barclays Bank Ltd; and
>
> (3) £1,353, 1 s, 8 d with Westminster Bank Ltd.
>
> In considering these three cases the judge applied the test stated by Luxmoore LJ sitting as an additional judge of the Chancery Division, in *Delgoffe v Fader*.[8]

7 [1902] 1 Ch 680.

8 [1939] Ch 922.

'The test,' he said, 'whether the delivery of the document constitutes a good *donatio mortis causa* of a chose in action depends on the answer to the question whether the document expresses the terms of which the subject matter of the chose in action is held by the donor, or the terms under which the chose in action came into existence'.

We have examined numerous authorities relating to this difficult subject matter. But, although it seems clearly established that there may be a valid *donatio mortis causa* of property other than such only as is capable of manual delivery, it must be confessed that there was, at any rate before *Delgoffe v Fader*, no clear or precise statement of the limiting conditions applicable in such cases.

The English law in regard to *donationes mortis causa* must be taken largely to rest upon the well known judgment of Hardwicke LC, in *Ward v Turner*[9] and as appears from Lord Hardwicke's judgment, the English law (derived at least in part from the civil law) is in many respects anomalous. It was indeed questioned at one time whether the old decisions supporting *donationes mortis causa* were consistent with the Wills Act 1837, on the ground that they are in a sense testamentary in that full effect is not given to them until the donor's death. Being before that date incomplete, the gifts are then (unlike other gifts or trusts) rendered perfect and complete by the law.

The question then is where actual transfer does not or cannot take place, what will 'amount to that'? As a matter of principle the *indicia* of title, as distinct from mere evidence of title, the document or thing the possession or production of which entitles the possessor to the money or property purported to be given, should satisfy Lord Hardwicke's condition. On this ground, in our judgment, the validity of a donation of money standing to the donor's credit in a Post Office Savings Bank deposit, or a mortgage debt, should be sustained; and it appears to us irrelevant in such cases whether all the terms of the contract out of which a chose in action arises are stated in the document of title.

It is true that, in *Re Weston*, Byrne J founded himself on the view that the document, that is, the deposit book, expresses the terms on which (the money) is held and shows what the contract between the parties is, and cited *Moore v Darton*[10] and *Re Dillon*.[11] 'An examination of the savings bank book in the present case,' he said, 'appears to me to show a fulfilment of the test; and although every rule regulating the contract is not set out in the book itself, all the essential rules are'. The judge, however, went on to state that the deposit book was not a mere receipt but that 'it must, as stated on the fact of it, be produced whenever any money is deposited or withdrawn'.

In our judgment, and having regard to the circumstances of the case, Cotton LJ, cannot be taken as laying down that in a case of alleged *donatio* of a chose in action such as a sum of money on deposit with a bank, the deposit note or book must contain all, or all the material terms of the contract. Neither Lindley LJ, nor Lopes LJ, gives any support in his judgment for that proposition. Both

9 (1752) 2 Ves Sen 431.

10 (1851) 4 D & G and Sen 517.

11 (1890) 44 Ch D 76.

> those judges confined themselves to disposing of the argument based on the endorsed form of cheque, and, having disposed of that argument, treated the deposit note as having been established by authority as a good subject matter of donation.
>
> In our judgment, accordingly, Byrne J, in *Re Weston*, and Luxmoore LJ, in *Delgoffe v Fader*, went further than was necessary in stating that a record of all the essential terms of the contract in the document handed over was a condition or test of the validity of the donation. For reasons which we have attempted to give, we think that the real test is whether the instrument 'amounts to a transfer' as being the essential *indicia* or evidence of title, possession or production of which entitles the possessor to the money or property purported to be given.
>
> What, then, is the evidence in this case as to the necessity for production of the books upon any withdrawal – for this, in the view we take, is the essential matter? In each case upon the face of the deposit book such production was beyond doubt made a term or condition of the deposit. But, as we have said, Mr Buckley has contended that, whatever the strict contractual terms, as a matter of practice, at least in the case of the two joint stock banks, such production was not required; and it is perhaps a matter of common knowledge (as we found to be the fact in *Delgoffe v Fader*), that a so called deposit account may by arrangement between banker and customer be operated much as a current account so that the deposit book is no more than an ordinary bank pass book.
>
> What, then, is the evidence here? In the case of the London Trustee Savings Bank, Mr Buckley did not, and could not, press the point far; for, according to the local actuary: 'Really, we always insist on the production of the passbook except in exceptional circumstances where hardship may be caused, for instance, with a lost passbook.' The requirements of the two joint stock banks, Barclays and Westminster, are no doubt less stringent.
>
> We think, accordingly, that in the case of both banks the condition stated on the face of the deposit books must be taken to have remained operative, ie, that the book was, and is, the essential *indicia* of title and that delivery of the book 'amounted to transfer' of the chose in action.
>
> The result is that, in our judgment, the plaintiffs are entitled to succeed as to the deposits in all three cases, the London Savings Bank, Barclays Bank and Westminster Bank. And we think the result satisfactory, for it avoids, as it seems to us desirable to avoid, fine distinctions between moneys on deposit with the Post Office Savings Bank on the one hand and with trustee savings banks and joint stock banks on the other, where in the latter cases the deposit account is a true deposit account as distinct from an ordinary current account.

Similarly, the title deeds to unregistered land are essential *indicia* or evidence of title. The transfer of the title deeds accompanied by the relevant donative intent is capable of constituting a DMC.

Sen v Headley [1991] 2 WLR 1308, CA

The plaintiff had been a close friend of the deceased (Mr Hewett). They lived together as man and wife for many years. During the final months of his life, the plaintiff visited him regularly in hospital. On his deathbed, Mr Hewett told the plaintiff that the house and contents were hers. The deeds to the house were in a steel box and the sole key was given to her. The plaintiff also had a set of keys to the house. Mr Hewett had retained his own set of house keys. After his death, intestate, the plaintiff claimed the house as a DMC. No claim had been made in respect of the contents. The next of kin, a sister, nephew and a niece of Mr Hewett defended the claim. The trial judge (Mummery J) held in favour of the next of kin, applying the principle in *Duffield v Elwes* to the effect that land cannot be the subject matter of a DMC. In addition, he decided that Mr Hewett had retained dominion over the house. The plaintiff appealed to the Court of Appeal.

The court held in favour of the plaintiff. Owing to the modern development of the law the transfer of the title deeds to unregistered land were sufficient to transfer (and did transfer) dominion over the house. The court acknowledged that a DMC has the effect of circumventing the formal requirements (such as s 9 of the Wills Act 1837), but recognised that the doctrine is capable of amounting to a constructive trust. The retention of the house keys by Mr Hewett was, in the circumstances, insufficient evidence of retention of ownership.

> **Nourse LJ:** *Donationes mortis causa* may be said to have been an anomaly in our law, both for their immunity to the Statute of Frauds[12] and the Wills Act[13] and as exceptions to the rule that there is no equity to perfect an imperfect gift. But both Lord Hardwicke and Lord Eldon, while making to regret the doctrine, established extensions of it beyond a simple gift of a chattel by its delivery; the former to a gift of money secured by a bond, by delivery of the bond; the latter to a gift of money secured by a mortgage of land, by delivery of the mortgage deed. Later decisions have included gifts of other choses in action by delivery of the essential *indicia* of title. What has never before been directly decided in England is whether the doctrine applies to a gift of land by delivery of the title deeds. Lord Eldon undoubtedly thought that it did not, a view which has generally been assumed to be correct. Now, Mummery J (at first instance) has given a decision in line with that assumption and we have to say whether we agree with him or not.
>
> It cannot be doubted that title deeds are the essential *indicia* of title to unregistered land. Moreover, on the facts found by the judge, there was here a constructive delivery of the title deeds of 56 Gordon Road equivalent to an actual handing of them by Mr Hewett to Mrs Sen. And it could not be suggested that Mr Hewett did not part with dominion over the deeds. The two

12 1677 (29 Cha 2, c 3).

13 1837 (7 Will 4 & 1 Vict, c 26).

questions which remain to be decided are: first, whether Mr Hewett parted with dominion over the house; secondly, if he did, whether land is capable of passing by way of a *donatio mortis causa*. We have traced the need for there to be a parting with dominion over the subject matter of the gift, that is, with the ability to control it, to the judgment of Lord Kenyon CJ in *Hawkins v Blewitt*,[14] where he said:

> In the case of a *donatio mortis causa*, possession must be immediately given. That has been done here; a delivery has taken place; but it is also necessary that by parting with the possession, the deceased should also part with the dominion over it. That has not been done here.

A similar view was taken in *Reddell v Dobree*[15] and in *Re Johnson*.[16] In each of those three cases the alleged donor delivered a locked box to the alleged donee and either retained or took back the key to it; in *Reddel v Dobree* he also reserved and exercised a right to take back the box. In each of them it was held that the alleged donor had retained dominion over the box and that there had been no *donatio mortis causa*.

It appears therefore that the need for there to be a parting with dominion was first identified in cases where the subject matter of the gift was a locked box and its contents. In *Birch v Treasury Solicitor*,[17] as we have seen, a similar need was recognised where the subject matter of the gift was a chose in action. Without in any way questioning that need, we think it appropriate to observe that a parting with dominion over an intangible thing such as a chose in action is necessarily different from a parting with dominion over a tangible thing such as a locked box and its contents. We think that in the former case a parting with dominion over the essential *indicia* of title will *ex hypothesi* usually be enough. Mummery J found great difficulty in seeing how the delivery of the title deeds could ever amount to a parting with dominion over the land to the extent that the donor 'has put it out of his power to alter the subject matter of the gift between the date of the gift and the date of his death'. We respectfully think that that test, which was taken from the judgment of Farwell J in *Re Craven's Estate*,[18] was misunderstood by the judge. Having pointed out that Mr Hewett retained until his death the entire legal and equitable interest in the house, he continued:[19]

> Without taking any action against Mrs Sen to recover the title deeds from her, he was fully empowered as absolute owner to make a declaration of trust in respect of the house in favour of another person or to enter into a binding contract with another person for the sale of the house. The beneficiary under such a declaration of trust and the purchaser under such a contract would be entitled to an equitable interest in the house which would take priority over any claim that Mrs Sen would have by way of donatio mortis causa on Mr Hewett's death.

14 (1798) 2 Esp 663.

15 (1839) 10 Sim 244.

16 (1905) 92 LT 357.

17 [1951] Ch 298.

18 [1937] Ch 423, p 427.

19 [1990] Ch 728, pp 742–43.

To that it must be answered that the same objection could be taken in the case of a chose in action. A donor of money secured by a bond or a mortgage who had delivered the bond or the mortgage deed to the donee could in like manner constitute himself a trustee of the benefit of his security for some third party or he could assign it for value. But it has never been suggested that the donor's continuing ability to take either of those steps amounts to a retention of dominion over the chose in action. We therefore respectfully disagree with the judge's view, if such it was, that a delivery of title deeds can never amount to a parting with dominion over the land. As appears from *Birch v Treasury Solicitor*,[20] the question is one to be decided on the facts of the individual case.

We do not suggest that there might never be a state of facts where there was a parting with dominion over the essential *indicia* of title to a chose in action but nevertheless a retention of dominion over the chose itself. And it is just possible to conceive of someone, who, in contemplation of impending death, had parted with dominion over the title deeds of his house to an alleged donee, nevertheless granting a tenancy of it to a third party; for which purpose proof of the title to the freehold by production of the deeds is not usually necessary. On facts such as those there might be a case for saying that the alleged donor had not parted with dominion over the house. But nothing comparable happened here. It is true that in the eyes of the law Mr Hewett, by keeping his own set of keys to the house, retained possession of it. But the benefits which thereby accrued to him were wholly theoretical. He uttered the words of gift, without reservation, two days after his readmission to hospital, when he knew that he did not have long to live and when there could have been no practical possibility of his ever returning home. He had parted with dominion over the title deeds. Mrs Sen had her own set of keys to the house and was in effective control of it. In all the circumstances of the case, we do not believe that the law requires us to hold that Mr Hewett did not part with dominion over the house. We hold that he did.

Having now decided that the third of the general requirements for a *donatio mortis causa* was satisfied in this case, we come to the more general question whether land is capable of passing by way of such a gift. For this purpose we must return to *Duffield v Elwes*.[21] While that decision was supported by pronouncements from both Lord Hardwicke and Lord Mansfield, we believe that it was, for its times, creative, if not quite revolutionary.

Let it be agreed that the doctrine is anomalous. Anomalies do not justify anomalous exceptions. If due account is taken of the present state of the law in regard to mortgages and choses in action, it is apparent that to make a distinction in the case of land would be to make just such an exception. A *donatio mortis causa* of land is neither more nor less anomalous than any other. Every such gift is a circumvention of the Wills Act 1837. Why should the additional statutory formalities (such as the requirements of s 53(1)(b) of the Law of Property Act 1925 and s 2 of the Law of Property (Miscellaneous) Act 1989 for the creation and transmission of interests in land be regarded as some

20 [1951] Ch 298.

21 (1827) 1 Bli (NS) 497.

larger obstacle. The only step which has to be taken is to extend the application of the implied or constructive trust arising on the donor's death from the conditional to the absolute estate. Admittedly, that is a step which the House of Lords would not have taken in *Duffield v Elwes*,[22] and, if the point had been a subject of decision, we would have loyally followed it in this court. But we cannot decide a case in 1991 as the House of Lords would have decided it, but did not decide it, in 1827. We must decide it according to the law as it stands today. Has any sound reason been advanced for not making the necessary extension? Having carefully considered the reasons put forward by Mummery J as elaborated in the argument of Mr Leeming for the defendant, we do not think that there has. While we fully understand the judge's view that there was a special need for judicial caution at his level of decision, it is notable that the two previous authorities in this court, *Re Dillon*[23] and *Birch v Treasury Solicitor*,[24] have extended rather than restricted the application of the doctrine. Indeed, we think that the latter decision may have put others of the earlier authorities on choses in action in some doubt. Moreover, certainty of precedent, while in general most desirable, is not of as great an importance in relation to a doctrine which is as infrequently invoked as this. Finally, while we certainly agree that the policy of the law in regard to the formalities for the creation and transmission of interests in land should be upheld, we have to acknowledge that that policy has been substantially modified by the development to which we have referred.

Mummery J also considered the Commonwealth authorities and the views expressed in the texts which have dealt with the question. We agree with him that the two Canadian cases do not really assist us. As for the two Australian decisions at first instance, *Watts v Public Trustee*[25] and *Bayliss v Public Trustee*,[26] we observe that in neither of them does it appear that the arguments covered the full extent of the ground which has been covered in the present case. In particular, it seems that in neither was the inner significance of Lord Eldon's speech in *Duffield v Elwes*[27] brought to the court's attention. Moreover, of the views expressed in the texts, none is based on anything more than the briefest discussion of the question. Most, although not quite all, subscribe to the assumption which has generally been made since Lord Eldon's time. There used to be, no doubt there still is, a maxim *communis error facit jus*. But the error referred to is one of decision, not of assumption. Here we would say *communis sumptio non facit jus*.

We hold that land is capable of passing by way of a *donatio mortis causa* and that the three general requirements for such a gift were satisfied in this case. We therefore allow Mrs Sen's appeal.

22 (1827) 1 Bli (NS) 497.

23 (1890) 44 Ch D 76.

24 [1951] 1 Ch 298.

25 (1949) 50 SR (NSW) 130.

26 (1988) 12 NSWLR 540.

27 (1827) 1 Bli (NS) 497.

TYPES OF PROPERTY WHICH ARE INCAPABLE OF BEING THE SUBJECT MATTER OF A DMC

Cheques

The donor's cheque is a revocable order to the bank to pay the person in whose favour the cheque is drawn and is incapable of being the subject matter of a DMC. Payment of the cheque may be revoked during the lifetime of the donor and is revoked on death.

Re Beaumont [1902] 1 Ch 889, HC

> **Buckley J:** If, prior to the donor's death, the cheque is presented and paid there is no question of a DMC of the cheque, although there may be a question whether the money has been received on the terms that it shall only be retained in case of the donor's death. If the cheque is not presented in the donor's lifetime, the gift is ineffectual, it is revoked by the donor's death.

In this case, Mr Beaumont, who was very ill and in fear of impending death, on 19 February 1901 drew a cheque for £300 in favour of Mrs Ewbank, to whom it was delivered. Mrs E endorsed the cheque and on 23 February it was presented for payment at Mr B's bank, where his account was overdrawn. The bank manager refused payment, stating that Mr B's alleged signature was unlike his ordinary signature and required confirmation of the genuineness of the signature. The court found as a fact that the manager was willing to lend the money if he was satisfied that the signature was genuine. Mr B died on 25 February 1901 without the cheque having been cashed. Mrs E claimed that Mr B's personal representatives ought to be compelled to complete her title on the ground of a valid DMC.

The court held that the cheque was a revocable mandate which was not a proper subject matter of a DMC.

> **Buckley J:** The cheque is only a revocable mandate, which may be stopped in the donor's lifetime and is revoked at his death. If, before the donor's death, the cheque is presented and paid, there is no question of a [DMC] of the cheque, although there may be a question whether the money has been received on the terms that it shall only be retained in case of the donor's death.
>
> If the cheque is not presented in the donor's lifetime, the gift is ineffectual; the cheque is a revocable order which is revoked by the donor's death.

Land

At one stage, it was perceived that land was incapable of being the subject matter of a DMC. In *Duffield v Elwes*,[28] Lord Eldon, in an *obiter* pronouncement, laid down this rule. However, in *Sen v Headley*, the Court of Appeal decided that delivery of the title deeds to unregistered land was capable of constituting a valid DMC. It would appear that the *Duffield v Elwes* principle is restricted to interests in registered land.

Shares

In *Staniland v Willot*,[29] it was decided that shares in a public company were capable of being the subject matter of a DMC. Whereas in *Moore v Moore*,[30] and *Re Weston*,[31] it was decided that railway stock and building society shares were not capable of being comprised in a DMC. The position today remains far from clear. It is submitted that the better view is the approach adopted in *Re Weston*, for share certificates are not documents of title.

PROPRIETARY ESTOPPEL

Propietary estoppel is a right given to a volunteer whenever a landowner stands by and permits a volunteer to improve his property by incurring expenditure on the assumption that there will be a transfer of an interest to him. The landowner and his successors in title will be estopped from denying the estate acquired by the volunteer.

In *Dillwyn v Llewellyn*,[32] a father, wishing his son to live nearby, offered him a farm so that he could build a house on the land. The son accepted the offer, spent £14,000 building a house on the land with the knowledge and approval of the father. No conveyance of the legal estate was ever made. After the father's death the son claimed that the land ought to be conveyed to him. The court held that the father's actions entitled the son to claim the legal estate from the father. Likewise, the father's personal representatives were obliged to convey the fee simple to the claimant.

> **Lord Westbury:** A voluntary agreement will not be completed or assisted by a court of equity, in cases of mere gift. If anything be wanting to complete the title of the donee, a court of equity will not assist him in obtaining it; for a mere

28 (1827) 1 Bli (NS) 497.

29 (1852) 3 Mac & G 664.

30 (1874) LR 18 Eq 474.

31 [1902] 1 Ch 680.

32 (1862) 4 De GF & J 517.

> donee can have no right to claim more than he has received. But the subsequent acts of the donor may give the donee the right or ground of claim which he did not acquire from the original gift. If A puts B in possession of a piece of land and tells him 'I give it to you that you may build a house on it', and B, on the strength of that promise, with the knowledge of A expends a large sum of money in building a house, I cannot doubt that the donee acquires a right from the subsequent transaction to call on the donor to perform that contract and complete the imperfect donation which was made.
>
> The equity of the donee and the estate to be claimed by virtue of it depend on the transaction, that is, on the acts done, and not on the language of the memorandum, except as that shows the purpose and intent of the gift. The estate was given as the site of a dwelling to be erected by the son. The ownership of the dwelling house and the ownership of the estate must be considered as intended to be co-extensive and co-equal. No one builds a house for his own life only, and it is absurd to suppose that it was intended by either party that the house, at the death of the son, should become the property of the father.

The starting point is *Ramsden v Dyson*,[33] where a tenant at will built on the land in the belief that he would be entitled to demand a long lease. The majority in the House of Lords held that he would not succeed in the claim. Lord Kingsdon dissented on the facts and stated the principle of law thus:

> **Lord Kingsdon:** The rule of law applicable to the case appears to me to be this: if a man, under a verbal agreement with a landlord for a certain interest in the land, or, what amounts to the same thing, under an expectation, created or encouraged by the landlord, that he shall have a certain interest, takes possession of such land, with the consent of the landlord, and upon the faith of such promise or expectation, with the knowledge of the landlord, and without objection by him, lays out money upon the land, a court of equity will compel the landlord to give effect to such promise or expectation.

Since this decision, the ingredients of the claim were set out in more detail by Fry J in *Willmot v Barber*.[34] These were called the five probanda.

> **Fry J:** A man is not to be deprived of his legal rights unless he has acted in such a way as would make it fraudulent for him to set up those rights. What then are the elements necessary to constitute fraud? In the first place, the plaintiff must have made a mistake as to his legal rights. Secondly, the plaintiff must have expended some money or must have done some act (not necessarily upon the defendant's land) on the faith of his mistaken belief. Thirdly, the defendant, the possessor of the legal right must know of the existence of his own right which is inconsistent with the right claimed by the plaintiff. Fourthly, the defendant must know of the plaintiff's mistaken belief of his rights ... Lastly, the defendant must have encouraged the plaintiff in his expenditure of money or in the other acts which he has done, either directly or by abstaining from

33 (1866) LR 1 HL 129.

34 (1880) 15 Ch D 96.

> asserting his legal right. Where all these elements exists, there is fraud of such a nature as will entitle the court to restrain the possessor of the legal right from exercising it, but nothing short of this will do.

Further refinements of the principle of law indicate that, if the landowner makes assurances to the promisee which were relied on by the latter, the volunteer promisee may acquire an interest in the land which the court considers just and equitable. In this respect, a presumption will arise that the volunteer, promisee, has relied on the promise and although a lot of cases of proprietary estoppel involve expenditure or a detriment undertaken by the promisee, this appears to be unnecessary. This extremely broad basis of proprietary estoppel was laid down by the Court of Appeal in *Greasley and Others v Cooke*.

Greasley and Others v Cooke [1980] 3 All ER 710, CA

The plaintiff had given assurances to the defendant, a maid, to the effect that she was entitled to remain in the house for as long as she wished. The defendant remained in the house, caring for the family (including a mentally retarded child), without payment. In possession proceedings brought against her, it was held that an equity in the defendant's favour was raised and an order was made entitling her to occupy the house rent free for as long as she wished to stay there.

> **Lord Denning MR:** The statements to the defendant were calculated to influence her, so as to put her mind at rest, so that she should not worry about being turned out ... There is a presumption that [she remained in the house] relying on assurances given to her ... The burden is not on her but on them to prove that she did not rely on their assurances. They did not prove it, nor did their representatives. So she is presumed to have relied on them ... It so happens that in many of these cases of proprietary estoppel there has been expenditure of money. But that is not a necessary element. I see that in *Snell's on Equity* it is said that A must have incurred expenditure or otherwise have prejudiced himself. But I do not think that that is necessary. It is sufficient if the party, to whom the assurance is given, acts on the faith of it, in such circumstances that it would be unjust and inequitable for the party making the assurance to go back on it.

More recently, the principle was restated on a much more flexible basis. The test is whether it would be unconscionable for the defendant to deny the interest of the plaintiff, volunteer and promisee. In other words, the equity in favour of the promisee arises if, having regard to all the circumstances of the case, it would be unconscionable to deny the promisee an interest or right in the land.

Taylor Fashions Ltd v Liverpool Victoria Trustees [1981] 1 All ER 897, HC

> **Oliver J:** The more recent cases indicate that the application of the *Ramsden v Dyson* principle ... requires a very much broader approach which is directed

> rather at ascertaining whether it would be unconscionable for a party to be permitted to deny that which, knowingly or unknowingly, he has allowed or encouraged another to assume to his detriment than to inquiring whether the circumstances can be fitted within the confines of some preconceived formula serving as a universal yardstick for every form of unconscionable behaviour. So regarded, knowledge of the true position by the party alleged to be estopped becomes merely one of the relevant factors (it may even be a determining factor in certain cases) in the overall inquiry. This approach, so it seems to me, appears very clearly from the authorities.

The precise nature of the estate that may be acquired by the volunteer is left to the discretion of the court and varies with the circumstances of the case. In particular, the interest that may be acquired would depend on the nature of the promise made, the degree of expenditure if any, incurred, the events which have taken place since the promise was made and the appropriate method of granting relief, for example, the plaintiff may acquire the freehold estate, a license, a life interest, etc.

Voyce v Voyce [1991] 62 P & R 290, CA

> **Nicholls LJ:** The extent to which the landowner is precluded or estopped depends on all the circumstances. Regard must be had to the subject matter of the dispute, what was said and done by the parties at the time and what has happened since.

In this case, the defendant, shortly after his marriage in 1958 was allowed to move into a cottage known as Coles Cottage, which was part of the Coles Farm property owned by the defendant's mother. The mother told the defendant that he would be entitled to take the cottage provided that it was renovated to her satisfaction. It was agreed that this condition was satisfied at great expense to the defendant. No deed of gift was executed in favour of the defendant. In 1964, the mother made a gift of the farm and the cottage, duly executed by deed of gift, to the plaintiff (her younger son). The plaintiff was aware that the defendant was living in the cottage. The mother subsequently died. In 1984, the plaintiff claimed an order requiring the defendant to vacate the cottage. The judge held in favour of the defendant and made an order requiring the freehold of the cottage and specified garden to be transferred to the defendant absolutely. The plaintiff appealed against that decision on the ground that the judge had wrongly exercised his discretion since the defendant's equity could have been satisfied by a narrower order granting the defendant, at best, a right of occupation during his life.

The Court of Appeal dismissed the appeal and held that, in view of the promise made by the mother, the substantial expenditure incurred by the defendant, the knowledge and status of the plaintiff, the defendant was entitled to the conveyance of the freehold cottage and garden.

Inwards v Baker [1965] 2 QB 29, CA

A father suggested to his son, who was interested in a plot of land on which to build a bungalow, that he (the son) should build the bungalow on a portion of his land. The son acceded to the father's request, looked no further for a site and built a bungalow on the father's land. The father made no contractual arrangement or promise as to the terms on which the son should occupy the land or for how long he should remain in occupation, but the son believed that he would be allowed to remain there for his lifetime or for so long as he wished. The father died 20 years later and by his will, made nearly 10 years before his original promise to his son, vested the property in trustees for the benefit of persons other than the son. The trustees now claimed possession of the bungalow.

The court held that since the son expended money on the land to the knowledge of his father and in the expectation that he would be allowed to remain in occupation for as long as he wished, an equity was created in favour of the son. An order was made permitting the son to remain in the bungalow for as long as he wished.

> **Lord Denning MR:** Even though there is no binding contract to grant any particular interest to the licensee, nevertheless, the court can look at the circumstances and see whether there is an equity arising out of the expenditure of money. All that is necessary is that the licensee should, at the request or with the encouragement of the landlord, have spent the money in the expectation of being allowed to stay there. If so, the court will not allow that expectation to be defeated where it would be inequitable to do so.

Pascoe v Turner [1979] 1 WLR 431, CA

The Court of Appeal decided that in view of the special facts of this case a conveyance of the legal estate was an appropriate remedy to give effect to the equity which was created in favour of the defendant. In this case, the plaintiff, having lived with the defendant as man and wife in the plaintiff's house had told the defendant repeatedly that the house was hers to keep. In reliance on this promise, the defendant used her own money to effect repairs and improvements to the house. The plaintiff left the defendant for another woman and moved out of the house. The defendant, stayed in the house but was served with a notice to determine her licence. The court decided in favour of the defendant. A licence to live in the house for her lifetime would not have offered her sufficient protection, instead, the court awarded a conveyance of the house.

> **Cummings-Bruce LJ:** The court must grant a remedy effective to protect her against future manifestations of his ruthlessness. It was conceded that if she is granted a licence, such a licence cannot be registered as a land charge, so that she may find herself ousted by a purchaser for value without notice. If she has in the future to do further and more expensive repairs she may only be able to finance them by a loan, but as a licensee she cannot charge the house. The

plaintiff as legal owner may well find excuse for entry in order to do what may plausibly represent as necessary works and so contrive to derogate from her enjoyment of the licence in ways that make it difficult or impossible for the court to give her effective protection. Weighing such considerations, this court concludes that the equity to which the facts in this case give rise can only be satisfied by compelling the plaintiff to give effect to his promise and her expectations. He has so acted that he must now perfect the gift.

***Griffiths v Williams* (1977) 248 EG 947, CA**

A daughter looked after her mother in her latter years and expended her own money on repairs and improvements to the house. She did so for two reasons, primarily for the care of the mother but also in the belief that she would be entitled to the house for the remainder of her life. The mother left the house by will to another relative. The Court of Appeal decided that the most appropriate way to give effect to her equity in the house was to grant her a non-assignable lease, at a nominal rent, determinable on death.

SUPPLEMENTARY READING

Baker, P, 'Land as a *donatio mortis causa*' (1993) 109 LQR 19

Barlow, A, 'Gifts *inter vivos* of a chose in possession by delivery of a key' (1956) 19 MLR 394

Davis, C, 'Proprietary estoppel: future interests and future property' [1996] Conv 193

Martin, J, 'Casenotes on *Sen v Headley* and *Woodward v Woodward*' [1992] Conv 53

Milne, P, 'Proprietary estoppel in a procrustean bed' (1995) 58 MLR 413

Pawlowski, M, 'Death bed gifts' (1994) 144 NLJ 48

Samuels, A, '*Donatio mortis causa* of a share certificate' (1966) 30 Conv 189

Thompson, M, 'From representation to explanation – estoppel as a cause of action' [1983] CLJ 257

Thompson, M, 'The widow's plight – *Lloyds Bank plc v Carrick*' [1996] Conv 295

CHAPTER 6

DISCRETIONARY TRUSTS

MERE POWERS AND DISCRETIONARY TRUSTS

The concept of a 'discretionary trust' in trust law is a generic description of duties and powers of trustees in respect of a class of objects and the property subject to a trust. In tax law, 'trusts without an interest in possession' is adopted as a substitute. In its broadest sense, a discretionary trust is a trust in respect of which the trustees are given a discretion to pay or apply the income or capital or both, to or for the benefit of all or anyone of a group or class of objects on such terms and conditions as the trustees may see fit.

For example, S, a settlor, transfers a cash fund of £100,000 to trustees on trust to pay or apply the income and capital (including accumulations of income) to or for the benefit of any or all of the settlor's children, A, B and C as the trustees may decide in their absolute discretion.

In this example, a discretionary trust is created in respect of both income and capital. The trustees are required to decide in whose favour the property (income and capital) may be distributed. In year 1, the trustees may distribute the entire income to A. In year 2, the trustees may distribute the income and a portion of the capital to B and in year 3 the income may be distributed equally to A, B and C and the entire capital distributed to C.

Fixed/discretionary trusts

The antithesis of a discretionary trust is a 'fixed' trust or trust with an interest in possession, that is, on the date of the creation of the trust the settlor has defined the interest acquired by each beneficiary with relative precision and ownership of such interest is vested in each beneficiary. Since the income and capital are acquired by each beneficiary, he or she is entitled to sell, exchange or gift away his or her interest subject to provisions to the contrary as detailed in the trust instrument. Whereas, under a discretionary trust, the individual members of the class of objects have only a hope or *spes* of acquiring a benefit under the trust. In other words, under a discretionary trust, the members of the class of objects, prior to the exercise of the trustees' discretion, do not enjoy an interest in the trust property but are treated as potential beneficiaries and are incapable of disposing of their potential interests by way of a trust.

For example, trustees hold on trust for the children of the settlor, D, E and F in equal shares absolutely. This is a fixed trust, for the trustees have no discretion to decide the extent of the beneficial interest which the objects may enjoy. The settlor has quantified their interest. On the date of the creation of the trust, each beneficiary has a fixed one third share of the fund which he or she may sell, exchange or give away as he or she likes.

Combination of fixed and discretionary trusts

Moreover, the settlor may create a combination of discretionary and fixed trusts. In this event, it would be necessary to know the precise scope of the discretionary trust, that is, whether the trustees' discretion extends to income only or to capital including accumulations of income. The fixed trust will take effect in respect of property not subject to the discretionary trust.

For example, property is held for a period not exceeding 21 years from the date of creation on trust to apply the income as it arises to or for the benefit of any or all of the settlor's children, G, H and I as the trustees may decide in their absolute discretion and, subject thereto, to apply the capital on trust for the survivors of my said children in equal shares. The discretionary trust exists for 21 years in respect of the income of the trust fund, but the capital is held on fixed trust for the surviving children in equal shares at the end of the period of the discretionary trust.

A discretionary trust may be either 'exhaustive' or 'non-exhaustive' in accordance with the intention of the settlor.

Exhaustive discretionary trusts

An exhaustive discretionary trust is one where during the trust period, the trustees are required to distribute the income or capital or both, but retain a discretion as to the mode of distribution and the persons to whom the distribution may be made. Thus, in the above example, an exhaustive discretionary trust of the income from the trust is created in favour of the class of objects, G, H and I. The trustees are required to distribute the income each year as it arises, but have a discretion as to the persons who may actually benefit.

Non-exhaustive discretionary trusts

A non-exhaustive discretionary trust is one where the trustees are given a discretion as to whether or not to distribute the property (either income or capital). A non-exhaustive discretionary trust of income exists where the trustees may legitimately decide not to distribute the income and the settlor has specified the effect of non-distribution, for example, the undistributed income will be accumulated or paid to another. In short, a non-exhaustive discretionary trust of the income is a trust for distribution of the income coupled with a power to accumulate or otherwise dispose of the undistributed income.

For example, on trust to apply the income to the settlor's children, J, K and L as the trustees may decide in their absolute discretion and subject thereto, to distribute the capital and any accumulated income in favour of X, Y and Z equally.

Similarly, a non-exhaustive discretionary trust of capital exists where the trustees are not obliged to distribute all the capital during the trust period. In this event, the settlor will normally specify in whose favour the undistributed capital shall be taken, otherwise it is held on resulting trust for the settlor.

It is not possible to create a non-exhaustive discretionary trust of both income and capital for this would lack an obligation to distribute income or capital which is the hallmark of a trust. In such a case if the trustees are given a discretion as to whether to distribute both the income and capital the settlor would have created a mere power of appointment in favour of a fiduciary (see below, p 152).

It follows that the distinction between an exhaustive and non-exhaustive discretionary trust is based on the ability of the trustees to fail to distribute the property which is subject to the discretion. In the ordinary course of events, the trustees will be required to accumulate the income that has not been distributed. The accumulated income is treated as capitalised income or capital in both trust law and tax law.

Inland Revenue Commissioners v Blackwell Minor's Trustees (1925) 10 TC 235, HC

A testator, by his will, gave property on trust for his eldest son on attaining the age of majority, with gifts over. He also gave the trustees the power to apply any part of the income to which the child shall become absolutely or contingently entitled, towards his maintenance and education and any unapplied income was directed to be accumulated and added to capital. The question in issue was whether income which was accumulated by the trustees during the child's minority formed part of the child's income for income tax purposes.

The court held that the accumulated income did not form part of the child's income but became converted into capital.

> **Rowlatt J:** The first point which Mr Latter makes is this. He says it does not matter whether the interest of the eldest son under the will is vested or contingent, because even assuming that this specific request is vested in the eldest son ... the part of the income which is accumulated is not income of the infant. It is a very important point, but I have come to the conclusion that he is right. It is perfectly true to say, as Mr Harman did, that in a case of that kind the income must come to the infant in the end if his interest is vested; but in my judgment it does not come to him as income; it comes to him in the future

in the form of capital. The trustees are directed to accumulate it, and accumulate it they must. It is income which is in trust for him in the sense that he will ultimately get it, but it is not in trust for him in the sense that the trustees have to pay the income to him year by year while he is an infant; all he can get while he is an infant is such amount as they allow for his maintenance. I think it is quite different if the infant has the right to the money now but where the money remains in the hands of his trustees not because of any directions in the will which directed it to be accumulated, but because he is an infant and cannot receive the money and give a receipt for it, and it therefore remains in the hands of the trustees being invested but lying ready for him waiting for the time when the infant can give a good receipt for it; I think that is quite different. I think in that case it would be his income now, although he could not touch it and he could not give a receipt for it. But where the will expressly provides that the surplus income shall be accumulated and only lets the trustees spend a certain amount on his maintenance, it seems to me that it is not the income of the minor yet.

Period of accumulation

Parliament has restricted the maximum period in which a settlor may permit an accumulation of income under a trust.

Section 164 of the Law of Property Act 1925 (as amended by s 13 of the Perpetuities and Accumulations Act 1964) provides:

(1) No person may by any instrument or otherwise settle or dispose of any property in such manner that the income thereof shall, save as hereinafter mentioned, be wholly or partially accumulated for any longer period than one of the following, namely:

(a) the life of the grantor or settlor; or

(b) a term of 21 years from the death of the grantor, settlor or testator; or

(c) the duration of the minority or respective minorities only of any person or persons who under the limitations of the instrument directing the accumulations would, for the time being, if of full age, be entitled to the income directed to be accumulated.

In every case where any accumulation is directed otherwise than as aforesaid, the direction shall (save as hereinafter mentioned) be void; and the income of the property directed to be accumulated shall, so long as the same is directed to be accumulated contrary to this section, go to and be received by the person or persons who would have been entitled thereto if such accumulation had not been directed.

(2) This section does not extend to any provision:

(i) for payment of the debts of any grantor, settlor, testator or other person;

(ii) for raising portions for:

(a) any child, children or remoter issue of any grantor, settlor or testator; or

(b) any child, children or remoter issue of a person taking any interest under any settlement or other disposition directing the accumulations or to whom any interest is thereby limited;

(iii) ...

(3) ...

Section 13 of the Perpetuities and Accumulations Act 1964 enacts:

(1) The periods for which accumulations of income under a settlement or other disposition are permitted by s 164 of the Law of Property Act 1925 shall include:

(a) a term of 21 years from the date of the making of the disposition; and

(b) the duration of the minority or respective minorities of any person or persons in being at that date.

(2) It is hereby declared that the restrictions imposed by the said s 164 apply in relation to a power to accumulate income whether or not there is a duty to exercise that power, and that they apply whether or not the power to accumulate extends to income produced by the investment of income previously accumulated.

The combined effect of s 164 of the Law of Property Act 1925 and s 13 of the Perpetuities and Accumulation Act 1964 is that the settlor is entitled to select any one (but only one) of the following periods as the maximum period during which the trustees may accumulate the income. These periods are (s 164 of the Law of Property Act 1925):

(1) the life of the settlor;

(2) a term of 21 years from the death of the settlor or testator;

(3) the minority or respective minorities of any person or persons living or *en ventre sa mère* at the death of the settlor or testator;

(4) the minority or respective minorities only of any person or persons who, under the limitations of the instrument directing the accumulations, would for the time being, if of full age, be entitled to the income directed to be accumulated; Section 13 of the Perpetuities and Accumulation Act 1964;

(5) a term of 21 years from the date of the making of the disposition;

(6) the minority or respective minorities of any person or persons in being at that date.

A direction to accumulate which exceeds the periods mentioned above, but which is otherwise valid will be void only in so far as it exceeds the appropriate statutory period. In short, the excess period alone is void, for example, if the accumulation is ordered for the life of a person other than the settlor (which is not one of the stated periods) the power to accumulate will be valid for 21 years.

Reasons for creating discretionary trusts

Flexibility

The settlor has a choice of creating either a 'fixed' or 'discretionary' trust. If he can foresee with relative precision the circumstances governing the object of his bounty, he may decide to create a fixed trust, for example, the settlor may wish his wife to enjoy a life interest in his estate and both of his children to take an equal share in remainder. On the creation of such trust the beneficiaries acquire a quantified or quantifiable interest in the trust property. Even though the beneficiaries' circumstances may subsequently change the interests of the beneficiaries will remain the same as on the date of the creation of the trust. Thus, if one of his children becomes a millionaire and the other suffers a severe disability and is in need of greater financial resources from the trust than his half share in the capital, the trustees, without more, are not entitled to provide additional assistance from the trust.

On the other hand, where the settlor is uncertain as to future events and wishes the trustees to react to changed circumstances and the needs of the potential beneficiaries, he may create a discretionary trust. This would require the trustees to take into consideration the circumstances, including fiscal factors surrounding individual members of the class of objects. The trustees may well take into account that the distribution of income will be more tax efficient if paid to objects with lower income and transfers of capital may be more beneficial to those with larger incomes. The effect is that the discretionary trust has the advantage of flexibility. Indeed, the settlor may be one of the trustees, and even if he is not, he may still be entitled to exercise some influence over the trustees.

Protection of objects from creditors

Since an object under a discretionary trust is not entitled to an interest in the trust property, prior to the exercise of the discretion in his favour, but is merely entitled to a hope of acquiring a benefit, the bankruptcy of such an object does not entitle the trustee in bankruptcy to a share of the trust fund. The trustee in bankruptcy is only entitled to funds paid to the object in the exercise of the discretion of the trustees. Moreover, the trustee in bankruptcy is not entitled to claim funds paid to third parties (such as tradesmen and hoteliers) in discharge of obligations *bona fide* undertaken by the potential beneficiaries.

Administrative discretion

Virtually all trusts (fixed and discretionary) involve the exercise of powers and discretions on the part of trustees. Thus, the trustees may have a power or discretion over the type of investments which may be made by the trust, whether to appoint agents on behalf of the trust, whether to apply income for the maintenance of infant beneficiaries, whether to make an advancement on behalf of a beneficiary, whether to appoint additional trustees, etc. But, these powers and discretions are of an administrative nature, and do not affect the beneficial entitlement of the objects. Accordingly, the existence of such administrative powers do not create discretionary trusts but are consistent with both fixed and discretionary trusts.

Mere powers and trust powers

The settlor may authorise another or others to distribute property to a class of objects but without imposing an obligation to distribute the same. This is called a mere power of appointment (or bare power or power collateral).

For example, S may transfer property by will to his widow, W, for life with the remainder to such of his children A, B and C as W may appoint by will. W is referred to as a donee of the power and A, B and C as the objects of the power. They are not beneficiaries but, like the objects of a discretionary trust, are potential beneficiaries or have a *spes* of enjoying a benefit prior to the exercise of the power in their favour. If W makes a valid appointment in favour of the objects, they become beneficiaries in respect of the amount of property distributed in their favour. On the other hand, if the donee of the power fails to make an appointment, the property may be held on resulting trust for the settlor or his estate.

In order to dispense with the resulting trust, it is customary for the settlor to insert an 'express gift over in default of appointment' in the trust instrument. If this clause is inserted, the objects under the 'gift over' take the property unless the donee of the power validly exercises the power. Indeed, *prima facie* the individuals entitled on a gift over in default of appointment are entitled to the property subject to such interest being defeated on a valid exercise of the power.

The donee of the power may be granted a 'personal' or a 'fiduciary' power of appointment in favour of the objects. A 'personal' or non-fiduciary power is a power of appointment granted to a donee of the power in his capacity as an individual such as the testator's widow in the above example. There is no duty to consider exercising the authority, nor is there a duty to distribute the property in favour of the objects. In short, the donee of the power is given almost complete freedom in exercising his discretion. Indeed, the donee of the power may release the power even if this would mean that he will benefit from the release. On the assumption that the donee of the power wishes to exercise the authority, the only obligation imposed on him is to distribute the property *bona fide* in favour of the specified objects.

Re Hay's Settlement Trusts [1982] 1 WLR 202, HC

> **Megarry VC** (described the scope of the authority given to a non-fiduciary donee of the power thus): If he does exercise the power, he must, of course confine himself to what is authorised, and not go beyond it ... A person who is not in a fiduciary position is free to exercise the power in any way he wishes unhampered by any fiduciary duties ...

A 'fiduciary' power, unlike a personal power, is a power of appointment granted to an individual *virtute officio*, such as a trustee. The fiduciary power is similar to a personal power in only one respect in that there is no obligation to distribute the property. But unlike a personal power, the trustees are required to deal with the discretion in a responsible manner. Accordingly, a number of duties are imposed on the trustees which have been summarised by Megarry VC in *Re Hay's Settlement Trust*, thus:

> ... the duties of a trustee which are specific to a mere power seem to be threefold. Apart from the obvious duty of obeying the trust instrument, and in particular of making no appointment that is not authorised by it, the trustee must, first, consider periodically whether or not he should exercise the power; second, consider the range of objects of the power; and third, consider the appropriateness of individual appointments. I do not assert that this list is exhaustive; but as the authorities stand it seems to me to include the essentials, so far as relevant to the case before me.

Re Manisty's Settlement [1973] 3 WLR 341, HC

> **Templeman J:** If a person within the ambit of the power is aware of its existence he can require the trustees to consider exercising the power and in particular to consider a request on his part for the power to be exercised in his favour. The trustees must consider this request, and if they decline to do so or can be proved to have omitted to do so, then the aggrieved person may apply to the court which may remove the trustees and appoint others in their place. This, as I understand it, is the only right and only remedy of any object of the power ... The court may also be persuaded to intervene by removing the trustees if the trustees act 'capriciously', that is to say, act for reasons which I apprehend could be said to be irrational, perverse or irrelevant to any sensible expectation of the settlor; for example, if they chose a beneficiary by height or complexion or by the irrelevant fact that he was a resident of Greater London.

Trust powers

By way of contrast, the settlor may create a 'trust power' or a 'power in the nature of a trust'. This gift is like a chameleon. On the face of the trust instrument, the gift looks like a mere power but on a true construction of the instrument the courts decide that a trust is imposed on the trustees to distribute the relevant property amongst the objects. In substance, a trust power is a discretionary trust in that the trustees are required to distribute the subject matter of their discretion, whether this be income or capital. Thus, the trustees may not release their discretion and if they refuse to exercise their discretion the court will intervene. If the wording of the settlement is unclear, the court will be called on to decide whether a power or a trust power was intended by the settlor.

Per Lord Eldon in *Brown v Higgs*:[1]

> There are not only a mere trust and a mere power, but there is also known to this court a power, which the party to whom it is given, is entrusted and required to execute; and with regard to that species of power the court considers it as partaking so much of the nature and qualities of a trust, that if the person who has that duty imposed on him does not discharge it, the court will, to a certain extent, discharge the duty in his room and place ...

The effect is that whether a mere power of appointment (albeit a fiduciary power) or a trust power is created is a highly speculative question. The court is required to place itself in the position of the testator or settlor and consider whether the author of the will or trust intended to 'authorise' (mere power) or 'compel' (trust power) the trustees to distribute the fund. This is a question of degree.

In *Burrough v Philcox*,[2] the testator transferred property on trust for his two children for life, with remainder to his issue and declared that if they should die without issue, the survivor should have the power to dispose by will 'among my nieces and nephews, or their children, either all to one or to as many of them as my surviving child shall think fit'. The testator's children died without issue and without any appointment having been made by the survivor. It was held that a trust was created in favour of the testator's nieces and nephews and their children. The trust was subject to a power of selection in the surviving child.

Per Lord Cottenham:

> Where there appears a general intention in favour of a class, and a particular intention in favour of individuals of a class to be selected by another person, and the particular intention fails from that selection not having been made, the court will carry into effect the general intention in favour of the class.

Contrast *Re Weekes' Settlement*.

Re Weekes' Settlement [1897] 1 Ch 289, HC

By her will, a testatrix transferred property to her husband for life with a 'power to dispose of all such property by will amongst our children'. There was no express gift over in default of appointment. The husband died intestate without exercising the power in favour of the children. The surviving

1 (1803) 8 Ves 561.
2 (1840) 5 My & Gr 72.

children claimed that an implied gift over in default of appointment was created in their favour and thus were entitled in equal shares.

The court rejected this claim and decided that, on construction of the instrument, a mere power of appointment was created by the testatrix. There was no clear indication in the will that the testatrix intended the power to be regarded in the nature of a trust. The property was held on resulting trust for the heir of the testatrix.

> **Romer J:** ... The husband did not exercise the power of appointment, and the question is whether the children take in default of appointment.
>
> Now, apart from the authorities, I should gather from the terms of the will that it was a mere power that was conferred on the husband, and not one coupled with a trust that he was bound to exercise. I see no words in the will to justify me in holding that the testatrix intended that the children should take if her husband did not execute the power.
>
> This is not a case of a gift to the children with power to the husband to select, or to such of the children as the husband should select by exercising the power.
>
> If in this case the testatrix really intended to give a life interest to her husband and a mere power to appoint if he chose, and intended if he did not think fit to appoint that the property should go as in default of appointment according to the settlement, why should she be bound to say more than she has said in this will?
>
> I come to the conclusion on the words of this will that the testatrix only intended to give a life interest and a power to her husband – certainly she has not said more than that.
>
> Am I then bound by the authorities to hold otherwise? I think I am not.

A brief survey of the cases illustrate how unpredictable the question whether a 'mere power of appointment' or a 'trust power' is created is likely to be. However, there are two pieces of evidence which determine the issue conclusively in favour of a mere power of appointment, namely:

(a) The existence of an express gift over in default of appointment is inconsistent with a trust. An express alternative gift in the event of the donee of the power failing to exercise the power is treated as an express gift over in default of appointment. The testator or settlor has implicitly condoned the non-exercise of the power by declaring in whose favour the beneficial interest will be transferred, for example, 'upon trust to distribute in favour of such of the objects, A, B and C as the trustees may decide in their discretion, but failing to distribute the property, I hereby declare that D shall be entitled to the property'. In this example, D is the object entitled on the gift over and is treated as the primary object with an interest subject to defeasance.

Re Mills, Mills v Lawrence [1930] 1 Ch 654, CA

A testator by his will set up a trust and directed that all statutory accumulations of income were to be held upon such trusts for the benefit of all or any of the children and remoter issue of the testator's father who, in the opinion of the testator's brother, one of the trustees of the will, should evidence an ability and desire to maintain the family fortune by replacing the sums of which it had been depleted by death duties and other taxation, as the testator's brother should by deed revocable or irrevocable appoint, and in default of such appoint in trust for such brother absolutely. The brother entitled in default of appointment (one of the trustees) wanted to release the power in order to trigger off the gift over in favour of himself. This was only possible if the will created a mere power of appointment as opposed to a trust power.

The Court of Appeal held that the will created a power appendant or appurtenant to, and not a power coupled with, a trust or a duty in the nature of a trust and, accordingly, the power could be validly released.

> **Lord Hanworth MR:** If there is a fiduciary duty connected with the power, the power, being in the nature of a trust, cannot be released, because a breach of trust must not be committed ... I find it impossible to treat the power in this case as so connected with a duty that it is a power in the nature of a trust, which cannot be released by the donee. There is a gift over to the donee himself, and this takes the case out of the rule in *Farwell on Powers*, 3rd edn, 1916, p 528.
>
> If there is a power to appoint, among certain objects, but no express gift to those objects, and no gift over in default of appointment, the court implies a trust for or a gift to those objects equally, if the power be not exercised. Here there is a gift over to the donee in default of appointment and a gift to him until appointment, and, therefore, it is not, to my mind, possible to construe this clause as one in which there is a gift to the possible objects of the power – namely, the children or remoter issue of the first Lord Hillingdon. It follows that it is not a power which is coupled with or embedded in a trust.

(b) A general power of appointment is by definition incapable of being a trust power for the courts are incapable of exercising such power. A general power of appointment is one which entitles the donee of the power to appoint in favour of anyone, including himself. Thus, there are no limits to the objects of such a power of appointment. Anyone is a potential beneficiary. But owing to the principle that all property is required to be owned, the donee of the power is treated as being entitled to the property until he disposes of it in favour of another.

Similarly, a hybrid or intermediate power of appointment is incapable of being a trust power. A hybrid power is similar in appearance to a general power save for the disqualification from benefiting an excluded class of objects, for example, 'on trust for X to appoint in favour of anyone except the settlor and his spouse'.

Blausten v Inland Revenue Commissioners [1972] Ch 256, HC

In this case, the settlement gave the trustees the power to introduce any person other than the settlor as a member of a class of objects, but subject to the written consent of the settlor. It was held that a hybrid power of appointment was created.

Re Manisty's Settlement [1973] 3 WLR 341, HC

Here, the trustees were given a power to add objects to a class of potential beneficiaries which excluded the settlor, his wife and certain named persons. It was held that a valid hybrid power of appointment was created.

> **Templeman J**: The power to add beneficiaries and to benefit the persons so added is exercisable in favour of anyone in the world except the settlor, his wife, the other members of the excepted class for the time being and the trustees ... This is not a general power exercisable in favour of a class, but an intermediate power exercisable in favour of anyone, with certain exceptions ... The argument based on the principle of non-delegation stems from the proposition that a testator must not delegate to other persons the right to make a will for him. It is however, established by authority that a testator and *a fortiori* a settlor, may create powers of disposition exercisable by individuals or by trustees without thereby infringing any rule against delegation ... In *Re Park* Clauson J held valid an intermediate power conferred by a testator on an individual to appoint to anyone in the world, except the donee of the power ... in *Re Abrahams' Will Trust,* Cross J held valid an intermediate power conferred by a testator on trustees to appoint to anyone in the world except the trustees, and he expressly rejected the argument based on the principle of non-delegation. I conclude that the settlor in the present case was not precluded by the doctrine of non-delegation from conferring an intermediate power on his trustees.

Moreover, a testator may create a hybrid power of appointment by will, authorising his executors or trustees to distribute the property after his death. If the power would have been valid had it been created *inter vivos,* the mere fact that it was created by will does not invalidate it. Such disposition does not amount to a delegation of testamentary freedom and does not contravene the Wills Act 1837.

Re Beatty (Decd) Hinves and Others v Brooke and Others [1990] 1 WLR 1503, HC

The testatrix died in 1986, leaving an estate valued at £32 m, and by will made the following dispositions:

> **Clause 3(a):**
>
> I bequeath all my personal chattels ... to my trustees who shall at any time or times (but nevertheless within the period of two years following my death or such shorter period as they my trustees in writing decide) allocate divide or make over all or any such personal chattels to or among such person or persons (whether individual or corporate) as they think fit and any of my said personal chattels not so allocated divided or made over shall fall into and become part of my residuary estate ...

Clause 4(a):

> I bequeath a legacy of £1.5 m to my trustees' subject to similar terms as included in clause 3(a) above.

Subject to these gifts, Mrs Beatty left the residue of her estate in three equal shares, subject to certain trusts and gifts over to her daughter and grandchildren.

During the two years following the death, the trustees distributed £150,000 worth of the chattels and £1.2 m of the money in accordance with the testatrix's wishes. The testatrix's residuary beneficiaries challenged the distributions. The executors and trustees applied to the court to determine the validity of clauses 3 and 4 of the will.

Hoffman J decided that both clauses were valid. The clauses created hybrid powers of appointment which conferred fiduciary duties on the executors and trustees.

> **Hoffman J:** The powers, being fiduciary, are not general powers in the sense of the traditional classification which equates such a power with an outright beneficial disposition to the donee himself. Nor are they special powers in the traditional sense. The objects of the powers can hardly be described as a class. They are intermediate or hybrid powers of the kind considered in *Re Park*.[3]
>
> Mr Price (counsel for the residuary beneficiaries) conceded that if clauses 3 and 4 had appeared in a settlement (*inter vivos*), they would have been valid powers. But he said that as part of a will they were invalidated by the rule that a testator cannot delegate the making of his will. This, he said, was a rule of common law distinct from the equitable rules concerning the certainty requirements for trusts and powers. The common law rule reflected the view that the right to make a will was a personal privilege, to be exercised with care and circumspection and not lightly delegated to others. The formalities of the Wills Act 1837 would have little point if the will was a mere enabling document, leaving the real choice of the beneficiaries to be made by the executors. In support of the existence of such a rule, Mr Price cited a number of statements by eminent judges in the House of Lords. Two passages from *Chichester Diocesan Fund and Board of Finance (Incorporated) v Simpson*[4] are sufficiently typical to make further citation unnecessary. Lord Simonds said, at p 371:
>
>> It is a cardinal rule, common to English and to Scots law, that a man may not delegate his testamentary power. To him the law gives the right to dispose of his estate in favour of ascertained or ascertainable persons. He does not exercise that right if in effect he empowers his executors to say what person or objects are to be his beneficiaries. To this salutary rule there is a single exception. A testator may validly leave it to his executors to determine what charitable objects shall benefit, so long as charitable and no other objects may benefit.

3 [1932] 1 Ch 580.

4 [1944] AC 341.

Lord Macmillan said, at p 349:

> The choice of beneficiaries must be the testator's own choice. He cannot leave the disposal of his estate to others. The only latitude permitted is that, if he designates with sufficient precision a class of persons or objects to be benefited, he may delegate to his trustees the selection of individual persons or objects within the defined class. The class must not be described in terms so vague and indeterminate that the trustees are afforded no effective guidance as to the ambit of their power of selection.

If these remarks are divorced from their context, they can cause considerable difficulty. Lord Simonds, as we have seen, emphasised that there was only a single exception to his rule against delegation, namely, that a testator could allow his trustee to choose the specific recipients of a general gift to charity. But Lord Simonds must also have known, as Lord Macmillan expressly acknowledged, that for centuries testators had been creating special powers of appointment. Furthermore, they had also been creating general powers of appointment. It could be said of the latter that because they were equivalent to gifts to the donee beneficially, no delegation was involved: the exercise of the power was a disposal of the donee's property rather than that of the testator. This would be consistent with the way such powers were treated for the purposes of the rule against perpetuities. But Lord Simonds would almost certainly also have known that in *Re Park*[5] Clauson J had upheld the validity of a power to appoint to anyone but the donee, which is not susceptible of a similar explanation.

I find it hard to imagine that Lord Simonds, in the *Chichester Diocesan Fund* case,[6] regarded his remarks as casting doubt on the validity of testamentary powers of appointment, whether special, general or intermediate. The context in which he spoke was the consideration of a gift for purposes ('charitable or benevolent') which was expressed in language so conceptually vague that it would be impossible for the court to say whether any specific application was within the terms of the will or not. If an application of money in accordance with such a gift were to be upheld, it would not be giving effect to the will of the testator because that, *ex hypothesi*, was incapable of being enforced. It would be giving effect to the autonomous act of the executor. In this sense, it would be truly a delegation of the testamentary power. But the execution of an otherwise valid general, special, or intermediate power is giving effect to the testator's will and not making a will for a testator who has failed to do so himself. The reason why Lord Simonds said that charitable gifts were the only exception to this rule was because they are, indeed, the only case in which the courts will uphold a gift in terms which would otherwise be regarded as too vague. Thus, it seems to me that Lord Simonds, like other judges in earlier cases concerning gifts void for uncertainty, was intending to do no more than to state in forceful and dramatic terms the rule that a gift which is expressed in language too vague to be enforced cannot be rescued by giving the executor a

5 [1932] 1 Ch 580.

6 [1944] AC 341, p 371.

power of choice. Lord Simonds would, I think, have been astonished to learn that he had just outlawed the use of widely expressed powers, or perhaps even any powers at all, in wills. No such thoughts seem to have been entertained at the time in Lincoln's Inn. In *Re Jones*,[7] which was decided some six months after Lord Simonds had delivered his speech, Vaisey J followed *Re Park*[8] and upheld the validity of a broad intermediate power in a will.

It seems to me, however, that a common law rule against testamentary delegation, in the sense of a restriction on the scope of testamentary powers, is a chimera, a shadow cast by the rule of certainty, having no independent existence. This was in effect the view taken by Cross J in *Re Abrahams' Will Trusts*,[9] where he was specifically invited to say that cases like *Re Park*[10] and *Re Jones*[11] were inconsistent with the supposed rule against delegation as stated in the cases in the House of Lords to which I have referred. Cross J refused to do so and upheld the validity of a testamentary power which, although dealing with fairly remote trusts, was expressed in the broadest possible terms. Mr Price invited me not to follow *Re Abrahams' Will Trusts*[12] and the two earlier cases, saying that they were only *ex tempore* judgments by judges of first instance. I am afraid I have now added another to the list, though, probably, after the benefit of fuller argument than my predecessors heard. Nevertheless, I respectfully think that Cross J was right.

The result is that once it is conceded that clauses 3 and 4 qualify as powers which would be valid if created by deed, there is in my judgment no rule of law to invalidate them because they happen to be in a will. Nor can I think of any good reason why such a distinction should exist. The solemn nature of a will, the interests of the next of kin in default and the provisions of the Wills Act 1837, seem to me insufficient grounds for introducing one. Furthermore, the invalidation of wide testamentary powers of appointment would involve considerable injustice to the beneficiaries of testators who, relying on cases like *Re Park*[13] which have stood without adverse criticism for nearly 60 years, have conferred such powers on their trustees. For example, as Mr Parker, for the trustees in this case, pointed out, *Williams on Wills*,[14] contains a precedent in the widest possible terms for a testamentary power to take advantage of the inheritance tax relief obtainable under s 144 of the Inheritance Tax Act 1984 on a rearrangement of the beneficial interests within two years of the death. There is no warning in the book that such a power might be invalid and, in my judgment, no reason why there should have been. So I shall accordingly declare that clauses 3 and 4 of the will are valid.

7 [1945] Ch 105.
8 [1932] 1 Ch 580.
9 [1969] 1 Ch 463.
10 [1932] 1 Ch 580.
11 [1945] Ch 105.
12 [1969] 1 Ch 463.
13 [1932] 1 Ch 580.
14 6th edn, 1987, London: Butterworths, Vol 2, p 1474.

However, a special power of appointment may or may not create a trust power. A special power of appointment confers on the trustee an authority or a duty to distribute the fund in favour of a specific class of objects, such as the children of the settlor. If there is no express gift over in default of appointment, it is extremely difficult to predict whether a special power of appointment creates a trust power or a mere power. The court ultimately decides this question in accordance with the intention of the testator or settlor. But there is no rule of construction to the effect that the absence of a gift over in default of appointment automatically interprets the settlor's intention as pointing in the direction of a trust power. Indeed, the absence of an express gift over in default of appointment is nothing more than an argument that the settlor intended to create a trust. The weight of such an argument will vary with the facts of each case.

Re Weekes' Settlement [1897] 1 Ch 289, HC

> **Romer J:** The authorities do not show, in my opinion, that there is a hard-and-fast rule that a gift to A for life with a power to A to appoint among a class and nothing more must, if there is no gift over in the will, be held a gift by implication to the class in default of the power being exercised. In my opinion the cases show ... that you must find in the will an indication that the testatrix did intend the class or some of the class to take – intended in fact that the power should be regarded in the nature of a trust, only a power of selection being given, as, for example, a gift to A for life with a gift over to such of a class as A shall appoint ...

In *Re Gestetner's Settlement* (1953) (below, p 161), Harman J categorised the various types of powers in the following summary:

> It seems to be law, at any rate in this court, that a power may be a general power (which has often been called the equivalent of property because the donee can exercise it in his own favour), or it can be a special power, namely, a power to benefit a known and defined class of persons, or it can be something betwixt and between.

THE GIVEN POSTULANT TEST

Test for certainty of objects

The test for certainty of objects varies with the nature of the transfer effected by the settlor. The position today is that if the settlor creates on the one hand a mere power of appointment or trust power the test for certainty of objects is the 'given postulant' criterion. On the other hand, if the settlor creates a fixed trust the test for certainty of objects is the 'list test'.

Mere powers

The test for powers has always been whether the donee of the power may say with certainty that a given individual (postulant) is or is not a member of a class of objects. This test was laid down by Harman J in *Re Gestetner's Settlement*:[15]

> The trustees as I see it, have a duty to consider whether or not they are to distribute any and, if so, what part of the fund and if so, to whom they should distribute it ... if therefore, there be no duty to distribute, but only a duty to consider, there is no difficulty in ascertaining whether any given postulant is a member of the specified class. Of course, it can be easily postulated whether John Doe or Richard Roe is or is not eligible to receive the settlor's bounty. It is not necessary that the trustees worry their heads to survey the world from China to Peru when there are perfectly good objects of the class in England.

In essence, the 'given postulant test' will be satisfied if the boundaries concerning the identification of the classes of objects are clearly drawn and it is unnecessary to name each member of the class of objects, for example, if a power of distribution is given in favour of the relatives of the settlor. The gift will be valid if the expression 'relatives' is capable of a legal definition so that the trustees may be able to distinguish the objects from the non-objects. It is unnecessary for the trustees to identify each object.

Re Gestetner's Settlement, Barnett and Others v Blumka and Others [1953] 1 Ch 672, HC

By an *inter vivos* settlement, a capital fund was held upon trust for members of a specified class of objects as the trustees might appoint, with a gift over in default of appointment. The specified class included:

(a) four named individuals;

(b) descendants of the settlor's father, David Gestetner or his uncle, Jacob;

(c) any spouse, widow or widower of any such person as aforesaid;

(d) five specified charitable bodies;

(e) any former employees of the settlor or his wife.

The settlor, his spouse and the trustees were excluded from the class. The Inland Revenue claimed that the express trust was void and a resulting trust was created in favour of the settlor. The trustees applied to the court for directions.

The court held that the power of appointment was valid. Although the trustees did not have a duty to select the beneficiaries from the class of objects, there was a duty to consider distributing the fund.

15 [1953] 1 Ch 672.

> **Harman J:** ... If a power be a power collateral, or a power appurtenant, or any of those powers which do not impose a trust upon the conscience of the donee, then I do not think that it can be the law that it is necessary to know of all the objects in order to appoint to one of them. If that were so, many appointments which are made every day would be bad. It must often be uncertain whether there will be further objects coming into existence. It may often be uncertain what objects are in existence; but, in an ordinary family settlement, the fact that a father did not know whether one of his sons had married and had children or not could not possibly invalidate the exercise by him of a power of appointment in favour of those grandchildren of whom he did not know ...
>
> The document on its face shows that there is no obligation on the trustees to do more than consider – from time to time, I suppose – the merits of such persons of the specified class as are known to them and, if they think fit, to give them something ...
>
> If, therefore, there be no duty to distribute, but only a duty to consider, it does not seem to me that there is any authority binding on me to say that this whole trust is bad. In fact, there is no difficulty, as has been admitted, in ascertaining whether any given postulant is a member of the specified class. Of course, if that could not be ascertained the matter would be quite different, but of John Doe or Richard Roe it can be postulated easily enough whether he is or is not eligible to receive the settlor's bounty. There being no uncertainty in that sense, I am reluctant to introduce a notion of uncertainty in the other sense, by saying that the trustees must worry their heads to survey the world from China to Peru, when there are perfectly good objects of the class in England ... There is no uncertainty in so far as it is quite certain whether particular individuals are objects of the power. What is not certain is how many objects there are; and it does not seem to me that such an uncertainty will invalidate a trust worded in this way.

Prior to the House of Lords' decision in *Re Gulbenkian's Settlement*,[16] the courts adopted a diluted approach to the given postulant test, namely, whether at least one person fell within the class of objects, even though it may not be possible to say whether others come within the class or fall outside of it. The House of Lords in *Re Gulbenkian's Settlement* overruled this approach and reiterated the strict given postulant test. In this case, a special power of appointment was granted to trustees to appoint in favour of Nubar Gulbenkian, 'any wife and his children or remoter issue ... and any person ... in whose house or apartment or in whose company or under whose care and control or by or with whom he may from time to time be employed or residing' subject to a gift over in default of appointment. The House of Lords held that the gift created a valid power of appointment within the *Gestetner* test and overruled the diluted approach to the test adopted by the Court of Appeal.

16 [1970] AC 508.

Lord Upjohn: My Lords ... Lord Denning MR [in the Court of Appeal], propounded a test in the case of powers collateral, namely that if you can say of one particular person meaning thereby, apparently, any one person only that he is clearly within the category the whole power is good though it may be difficult to say in other cases whether a person is or is not within the category, and he supported that view by reference to authority. Winn LJ said that where there was not a complete failure by reason of ambiguity and uncertainty, the court would give effect to the power as valid, rather than hold it defeated, since it will not have wholly failed, which put – though more broadly – the view expressed by Lord Denning MR. Counsel for the respondents, in his second line of argument, relied on these observations as a matter of principle, but he candidly admitted that he could not rely on any authority. Moreover, Lord Denning MR expressed the view that the different doctrine with regard to trust powers should be brought into line with the rule with regard to conditions precedent and powers collateral. So I propose to make some general observations on this matter.

If a donor (be he a settlor or testator) directs trustees to make some specified provision for 'John Smith', then to give effect to that provision it must be possible to identify 'John Smith'. If the donor knows three John Smiths then by the most elementary principles of law neither the trustees nor the court in their place can give effect to that provision; neither the trustees nor the court can guess at it. It must fail for uncertainty unless of course admissible evidence is available to point to a particular John Smith as the object of the donor's bounty.

Then, taking it one stage further, suppose the donor directs that a fund, or the income of a fund, should be equally divided between members of a class. That class must be as defined as the individual; the court cannot guess at it. Suppose the donor directs that a fund be divided equally between 'my old friends', then unless there is some admissible evidence that the donor has given some special 'dictionary' meaning to that phrase which enables the trustee to identify the class with sufficient certainty, it is plainly bad as being too uncertain. Suppose that there appeared before the trustees (or the court) two or three individuals who plainly satisfied the test of being among 'my old friends' the trustees could not consistently with the donor's intentions accept them as claiming the whole or any defined part of the fund. They cannot claim the whole fund for they can show no title to it unless they prove they are the only members of the class which of course they cannot do, and so, too, by parity of reasoning they cannot claim any defined part of the fund and there is no authority in the trustees or the court to make any distribution among a smaller class than that pointed out by the donor. The principle is, in my opinion, that the donor must make his intentions sufficiently plain as to the object of his trust and the court cannot give effect to it by misinterpreting his intentions by dividing the fund merely among those present. Secondly, and perhaps it is the most hallowed principle, the Court of Chancery, which acts in default of trustees, must know with sufficient certainty the objects of the beneficence of the donor so as to execute the trust. Then, suppose the donor does not direct an equal division of his property among the class but gives a power of selection to his trustees among the class; exactly the same principles must apply. The trustees have a duty to select the donees of the donor's bounty from among the class designated by the donor; he has not entrusted them with any power to select the donees merely from among known claimants who are within the class, for that is constituting a narrower class and the donor has given them no power to do this.

So if the class is insufficiently defined the donor's intentions must in such cases fail for uncertainty. Perhaps I should mention here that it is clear that the question of certainty must be determined as of the date of the document declaring the donor's intention (in the case of a will, his death). Normally the question of certainty will arise because of the ambiguity of definition of the class by reason of the language employed by the donor, but occasionally owing to some of the curious settlements executed in recent years it may be quite impossible to construct even with all the available evidence anything like a class capable of definition (*Re Sayer's Trust*), though difficulty in doing so will not defeat the donor's intentions (*Re Hain's Settlement*). But I should add this: if the class is sufficiently defined by the donor the fact that it may be difficult to ascertain the whereabouts or continued existence of some of its members at the relevant time matters not. The trustees can apply to the court for directions to pay a share into court.

But when mere or bare powers are conferred on donees of the power (whether trustees or others) the matter is quite different. As I have already pointed out, the trustees have no duty to exercise it in the sense that they cannot be controlled in any way. If they fail to exercise it then those entitled in default of its exercise are entitled to the fund. Perhaps the contrast may be put forcibly in this way: in the first case it is a mere power to distribute with a gift over in default; in the second case it is a trust to distribute among the class defined by the donor with merely a power of selection within that class. The result is in the first case even if the class of appointees among whom the donees of the power may appoint is clear and ascertained and they are all of full age and *sui juris*, nevertheless they cannot compel the donees of the power to exercise it in their collective favour. If, however, it is a trust power, then those entitled are entitled (if they are of full age and *sui juris*) to compel the trustees to pay the fund over to them, unless the fund is income and the trustees have power to accumulate for the future.

Again, the basic difference between a mere power and a trust power is that in the first case trustees owe no duty to exercise it and the relevant fund or income falls to be dealt with in accordance with the trusts in default of its exercise whereas in the second case the trustees must exercise the power and in default the court will.

So, with all respect to the contrary view, I cannot myself see how consistently with principle, it is possible to apply to the execution of a trust power the principles applicable to the permissible exercise by the donees, even if the trustees of mere powers; that would defeat the intention of donors completely.

But with respect to mere powers, while the court cannot compel the trustees to exercise their powers, yet those entitled to the fund in default must clearly be entitled to restrain the trustees from exercising it save among those within the power. So the trustees, or the court, must be able to say with certainty who is within and who is without the power. It is for this reason that I find myself unable to accept the broader position advanced by Lord Denning MR and Winn LJ, mentioned earlier, and agree with the proposition as enunciated in *Re Gestetner* and the later cases.

Fixed and discretionary trusts

Prior to the House of Lords' decision in *McPhail v Doulton (sub nom Re Baden),* the test for certainty of objects, applicable to all express private trusts, was whether the beneficiaries (or objects) were ascertained or ascertainable, ie,whether the trustees were capable of drawing up a comprehensive list of all the beneficiaries (or objects). This was known as the 'list test' or the 'Broadway Cottages test'. If the trustees were unable to draw up such a list the trust was void for uncertainty of objects. This test was applicable to both fixed and discretionary trusts but was considered too restrictive only in respect of discretionary trusts.

In *IRC v Broadway Cottages Trust,*[17] a settlement was created whereby trustees held property upon trust to apply the income for the benefit of all or any of a class of objects including, *inter alia,* the settlor's wife, specific relations of the settlor and the Broadway Cottages Trust, a charitable institution. The trustees paid income to the Broadway Cottages Trust and claimed exemption from income tax in respect of this. It was not possible to ascertain all the objects who might fall within the class of objects but it was possible to determine with certainty whether a particular person was a member of the class. The question in issue was whether the trust was valid or void. The Court of Appeal held that the trust was void for uncertainty of objects and the claim for a repayment of income tax failed.

The test continues to be applicable to fixed trusts but in respect of discretionary trusts what was needed was a much broader test than the list test. This change in the test concerning objects was adopted by the House of Lords in *McPhail v Doulton.*

McPhail v Doulton [1971] AC 424, HL

In this case, Mr Bertram Baden executed a settlement and under clause 9(a) empowered the trustees to apply the net income in their absolute discretion 'to or for the benefit of any of the officers and employees or ex-officers or ex-employees of the company or to any relatives or dependants of any such persons in such amounts at such times and on such conditions (if any) as they think fit ...'. The trustees were under no obligation to exhaust the income in any one year. They were also entitled to realise capital if the income was insufficient. The issue was whether a mere power or a trust power was created and whether the gift was valid. The High Court and the Court of

17 [1955] Ch 20.

Appeal decided that a mere power of appointment was created which was valid as satisfying the *Gulbenkian* test. Had a trust power been created, this would have been void as not satisfying the restrictive *Broadway Cottages* test. The House of Lords decided that a trust power was intended by the settlor, rejected the *Broadway Cottages* test in respect of discretionary trusts and extended the *Gulbenkian* test to discretionary trusts.

> **Lord Wilberforce:** My Lords, this appeal is concerned with the validity of a trust deed dated 17 July 1941, by which Mr Bertram Baden established a fund for the benefit, broadly, of the staff of the respondent company Matthew Hall & Co Ltd.
>
> In this House, the appellants contended that the provisions of clause 9(a) constitute a trust and not a power. If that is held to be the correct result both sides agree that the case must return to the Chancery Division for consideration, on this footing, whether this trust is valid. But here comes a complication. In the present state of authority, the decision as to validity would turn on the question whether a complete list (or on another view a list complete for practical purposes) can be drawn up of all possible beneficiaries. This follows from the Court of Appeal's decision in *IRC v Broadway Cottages Trust* as applied in later cases by which, unless this House decides otherwise, the Court of Chancery would be bound. The respondents invite your Lordships to review this decision and challenge its correctness. So the second issue which arises, if clause 9(a) amounts to a trust, is whether the existing test for its validity is right in law and if not, what the test ought to be.
>
> Before dealing with these two questions some general observations, or reflections, may be permissible. It is striking how narrow and in a sense artificial is the distinction, in cases such as the present, between trusts or as the particular type of trust is called, trust powers, and powers. It is only necessary to read the learned judgments in the Court of Appeal to see that what to one mind may appear as a power of distribution coupled with a trust to dispose of the undistributed surplus, by accumulation or otherwise, may to another appear as a trust for distribution coupled with a power to withhold a portion and accumulate or otherwise dispose of it. A layman and, I suspect, also a logician, would find it hard to understand what difference there is.
>
> It does not seem satisfactory that the entire validity of a disposition should depend on such delicate shading. And if one considers how in practice reasonable and competent trustees would act, and ought to act, in the two cases, surely a matter very relevant to the question of validity, the distinction appears even less significant. To say that there is no obligation to exercise a mere power and that no court will intervene to compel it, whereas a trust is mandatory and its execution must be compelled, may be legally correct enough, but the proposition does not contain an exhaustive comparison of the duties of persons who are trustees in the two cases. A trustee of an employees' benefit fund, whether given a power or a trust power, is still a trustee and he would surely consider in either case that he has a fiduciary duty; he is most likely to have been selected as a suitable person to administer it from his knowledge and experience, and would consider he has a responsibility to do so according to its purpose. It would be a complete misdescription of his

position to say that, if what he has is a power unaccompanied by an imperative trust to distribute, he cannot be controlled by the court if he exercised it capriciously, or outside the field permitted by the trust (cf *Farwell on Powers*). Any trustee would surely make it his duty to know what is the permissible area of selection and then consider responsibly, in individual cases, whether a contemplated beneficiary was within the power and whether, in relation to other possible claimants, a particular grant was appropriate.

Correspondingly, a trustee with a duty to distribute, particularly among a potentially very large class, would surely never require the preparation of a complete list of names, which anyhow would tell him little that he needs to know. He would examine the field, by class and category; might indeed make diligent and careful enquiries, depending on how much money he had to give away and the means at his disposal, as to the composition and needs of particular categories and of individuals within them; decide on certain priorities or proportions, and then select individuals according to their needs or qualifications. If he acts in this manner, can it really be said that he is not carrying out the trust?

Differences there certainly are between trusts (trust powers) and powers, but as regards validity should they be so great as that in one case complete, or practically complete ascertainment is needed, but not in the other? Such distinction as there is would seem to lie in the extent of the survey which the trustee is required to carry out; if he has to distribute the whole of a fund's income, he must necessarily make a wider and more systematic survey than if his duty is expressed in terms of a power to make grants. But just as, in the case of a power, it is possible to underestimate the fiduciary obligation of the trustee to whom it is given, so, in the case of a trust (trust power), the danger lies in overstating what the trustee requires to know or to enquire into before he can properly execute his trust. The difference may be one of degree rather than of principle; in the well known words of Sir George Farwell (*Farwell on Powers*) trusts and powers are often blended, and the mixture may vary in its ingredients.

With this background I now consider whether the provisions of clause 9(a) constitute a trust or a power. Naturally read, the intention of the deed seems to me clear: clause 9(a), whose language is mandatory ('shall'), creates, together with a power of selection, a trust for distribution of the income ... I therefore agree with Russell LJ and would ... allow the appeal, declare that the provisions of clause 9(a) constitute a trust and remit the case to the Chancery Division for determination whether on this basis clause 9 is (subject to the effects of s 164 of the Law of Property Act 1925) valid or void for uncertainty.

This makes it necessary to consider whether, in so doing, the court should proceed on the basis that the relevant test is that laid down in the *Broadway Cottages* case or some other test. That decision gave the authority of the Court of Appeal to the distinction between cases where trustees are given a power of selection and those where they are bound by a trust for selection. In the former case the position, as decided by this House, is that the power is valid if it can be said with certainty whether any given individual is or is not a member of the class and does not fail simply because it is impossible to ascertain every member of the class (the *Gulbenkian* case). But in the latter case it is said to be necessary, for the trust to be valid, that the whole range of objects (I use, the language of the Court of Appeal) should be ascertained or capable of ascertainment.

The respondents invited your Lordships to assimilate the validity test for trusts to that which applies to powers. Alternatively, they contended that in any event the test laid down in the *Broadway Cottages* case was too rigid, and that a trust should be upheld if there is sufficient practical certainty in its definition for it to be carried out, if necessary with the administrative assistance of the court, according to the expressed intention of the settlor. I would agree with this, but this does not dispense from examination of the wider argument. The basis for the *Broadway Cottages* case principle is stated to be that a trust cannot be valid unless, if need be, it can be executed by the court, and (though it is not quite clear from the judgment where argument ends and decision begins) that the court can only execute it by ordering an equal distribution in which every beneficiary shares. So it is necessary to examine the authority and reason for this supposed rule as to the execution of trusts by the court.

Assuming, as I am prepared to do for present purposes, that the test of validity is whether the trust can be executed by the court, it does not follow that execution is impossible unless there can be equal division. As a matter of reason, to hold that a principle of equal division applied to trusts such as the present is certainly paradoxical. Equal division is surely the last thing the settlor ever intended; equal division among all may, probably would, produce a result beneficial to none. Why suppose that the court would lend itself to a whimsical execution? And as regards authority, I do not find that the nature of the trust, and of the court's powers over trusts, calls for any such rigid rule. Equal division may be sensible and has been decreed, in cases of family trusts for a limited class, here there is life in the maxim 'equality is equity', but the cases provide numerous examples where this has not been so, and a different type of execution has been ordered, appropriate to the circumstances.

So I came to *IRC v Broadway Cottages Trust*. This was certainly a case of trust, and it proceeded on the basis of an admission, in the words of the judgment, 'that the class of 'beneficiaries' is incapable of 'ascertainment''. In addition to the discretionary trust of income, there was a trust of capital for all the beneficiaries living or existing at the terminal date.

This necessarily involved equal division and it seems to have been accepted that it was void for uncertainty since there cannot be equal division among a class unless all the members of the class are known. The Court of Appeal applied this proposition to the discretionary trust of income, on the basis that execution by the court was only possible on the same basis of equal division. They rejected the argument that the trust could be executed by changing the trusteeship, and found the relations cases of no assistance as being in a class by themselves. The court could not create an arbitrarily restricted trust to take effect in default of distribution by the trustees. Finally, they rejected the submission that the trust could take effect as a power, a valid power could not be spelt out of an invalid trust.

> So I think we are free to review the *Broadway Cottages* case. The conclusion which I would reach, implicit in the previous discussion, is that the wide distinction between the validity test for powers and that for trust powers, is unfortunate and wrong, that the rule recently fastened on the courts by the *Broadway Cottages* case ought to be discarded, and that the test for the validity of trust powers ought to be similar to that accepted by this House in *Re Gulbenkian's Settlement Trusts* for powers, namely that the trust is valid if it can be said with certainty that any given individual is or is not a member of the class.
>
> Assimilation of the validity test does not involve the complete assimilation of trust powers with powers. As to powers, I agree with my noble and learned friend Lord Upjohn in *Re Gulbenkian's Settlement* that although the trustees may, and normally will, be under a fiduciary duty to consider whether or in what way they should exercise their power, the court will not normally compel its exercise. It will intervene if the trustees exceed their powers, and possibly if they are proved to have exercised it capriciously. But in the case of a trust power, if the trustees do not exercise it, the court will; I respectfully adopt as to this the statement in Lord Upjohn's opinion. I would venture to amplify this by saying that the court, if called on to execute the trust power, will do so in the manner best calculated to give effect to the settlor's or testator's intentions. It may do so by appointing new trustees, or authorising or directing representative persons of the classes of beneficiaries to prepare a scheme of distribution, or even, should the proper basis for distribution appear, by itself directing the trustees so to distribute. The books give many instances where this has been done and I see no reason in principle why they should not do so in the modern field of discretionary trusts (see *Brunsden v Woolredge; Supple v Lowson; Liley v Hey* and *Lewin on Trusts*). Then, as to the trustees' duty of enquiry or ascertainment, in each case the trustees ought to make such a survey of the range of objects or possible beneficiaries as will enable them to carry out their fiduciary duty (cf *Liley v Hey*). A wider and more comprehensive range of enquiry is called for in the case of trust powers than in the case of powers.

Moreover, Lord Wilberforce laid down three limitations in respect of the 'given postulant test', thus:

> Two final points: first, as to the question of certainty, I desire to emphasise the distinction clearly made and explained by Lord Upjohn (in *Re Gulbenkian*) between linguistic or semantic uncertainty which, if unresolved by the court, renders the gift void, and the difficulty of ascertaining the existence or whereabouts of members of the class, a matter with which the court can appropriately deal on an application for directions. There may be a third case where the meaning of the words used is clear but the definition of beneficiaries is so hopelessly wide as not to form 'anything like a class' so that the trust is administratively unworkable or in Lord Eldon LC's words one that cannot be executed (*Morice v Bishop of Durham*). I hesitate to give examples for they may prejudice future cases, but perhaps 'all the residents of Greater London' will serve. I do not think that a discretionary trust for 'relatives' even of a living person falls within this category ...

Semantic or linguistic uncertainty

This proviso is applicable to both powers and trusts. If the gift suffers from such uncertainty, it is void. This involves uncertainty or vagueness in defining the class or classes of individuals in respect of whom the trustees are entitled or required to exercise their discretion, for example, a distribution by the trustees, in their discretion in favour of anyone in respect of whom the trustees may consider has a moral claim on the settlor.

Evidential uncertainty

This principle applies to both powers and trusts but does not invalidate either. This limitation concerns uncertainty in ascertaining the existence or whereabouts of objects. In this event, the trustees may apply to the courts for directions and the courts may make such order as is appropriate in the circumstances.

Administrative unworkability

This involves situations where the testator or settlor expressed the class of objects so broadly that it becomes difficult for the court to ascertain any sensible exercise of the discretion. In the event of the trustees failing to exercise their discretion the court may find it difficult to exercise the discretion in a rational manner, for example, a duty to distribute a fund in favour of such of the residents of Greater London as the trustees may decide in their absolute discretion. This type of uncertainty does not affect the validity of powers of appointment. See *Re Manisty's Settlement* but has the effect of invalidating trusts.

Re Manisty's Settlement [1973] 3 WLR 341, HC

> **Templeman J:** It is said that if a power is too wide the trustees cannot perform the duty reiterated in *Gulbenkian* and *McPhail v Doulton* of considering from time to time whether and how to exercise the power and the court cannot determine whether or not the trustees are in breach of their duty. In my judgment, however, the mere width of a power cannot make it impossible for trustees to perform their duty nor prevent the court from determining whether the trustees are in breach ... I conclude from *Gestetner, Gulbenkian; McPhail v Doulton* and *Baden (No 2)* that a power cannot be uncertain merely because it is wide in ambit.

The effect of vagueness of objects in respect of a trust power was considered in *R v District Auditors ex p West Yorkshire County Council* ('any or all of the inhabitants of West Yorkshire').

R v District Auditor ex p West Yorkshire Metropolitan County Council (1986) 26 RVR 24, DC

The council, threatened with abolition by the Government, settled £400,000 on trust to spend the capital and income within two years from the transfer for the purposes of benefiting, 'any or all or some of the inhabitants' of West Yorkshire (about 2.5 m) by:

(a) assisting their economic development within the county;

(b) providing assistance for youth, ethnic and minority groups; and

(c) informing interested persons or bodies of the consequences of the proposed abolition of the Metropolitan County Councils.

The question in issue was whether the gift was valid or void for uncertainty.

The court held that the purported gift was void, for on construction, a trust was intended which was administratively unworkable.

> **Lloyd LJ:** I am prepared to assume in favour of the council, without deciding that the class is defined with sufficient clarity. I do not decide the point because it might, as it seems to me, be open to argument what is meant by 'an inhabitant' of the county of West Yorkshire. But I put that difficulty on one side. For there is, to my mind, a more fundamental difficulty. A trust with as many as two and a half million potential beneficiaries is, in my judgment, quite simply unworkable. The class is far too large. In *Re Gulbenkian's Settlements*[18] Lord Reid said at p 518:
>
>> It may be that there is a class of case where, although the description of a class of beneficiaries is clear enough, any attempt to apply it to the facts would lead to such administrative difficulties that it would for that reason be held to be invalid.
>
> It seems to me that the present trust comes within the third case to which Lord Wilberforce refers. I hope I am not guilty of being prejudiced by the example which he gave. But it could hardly be more apt, or fit the facts of the present case more precisely.
>
> Lord Wilberforce's *dictum* has also been the subject of a good deal of academic comment and criticism, noticeably by L McKay.[19] I should have welcomed further argument on these matters, but through no fault of counsel for the County Council this was not possible. So I have to do the best I can.
>
> My conclusion is that the *dictum* of Lord Wilberforce remains of high persuasive authority, despite *Re Manisty*. *Manisty*'s case was concerned with a power, where a function of the court is more restricted. In the case of a trust, the court may have to execute the trust. Not so in the case of a power. That there may still be a distinction between trusts and powers in this connection was recognised by Templeman J himself in the sentence immediately following his quotation of Lord Wilberforce's *dictum*, when he said:

18 [1970] AC 508.

19 McKay, L, '*Re Baden* and the third class of certainty' (1974) 38 Conv 269; and Emery, CT, 'The most hallowed principle – certainty of beneficiaries in trusts and powers of appointment' (1982) 98 LQR 551.

> In these guarded terms, Lord Wilberforce appears to refer to trusts which may have to be executed and administered by the court and not to powers where the court has a very much more limited function.
>
> There can be no doubt that the declaration of trust in the present case created a trust and not a power. Following Lord Wilberforce's *dictum*, I would hold that the definition of the beneficiaries of the trust is 'so hopelessly wide, as to be incapable of forming 'anything like a class'. I would therefore reject counsel for the County Council's argument that the declaration of trust can take effect as an express private trust.
>
> Since, as I have already said, it was not argued that the trust can take effect as a valid charitable trust, it follows that the declaration of trust is ineffective. What we have here, in a nutshell, is a non-charitable purpose trust. It is clear law that, subject to certain exceptions, such trusts are void: see *Lewin on Trusts*, pp 17–19. The present case does not come within any of the established exceptions. Nor can it be brought within the scope of such recent decisions as *Re Denley's Trust Deed*,[21] and *Re Lipinski's Will Trusts*,[22] since there are, for the reasons I have given, no ascertained or ascertainable beneficiaries.

Following the decision of the House of Lords in *McPhail v Doulton* the case was remitted to the High Court to decide whether the new test for certainty of objects in respect of trust powers was satisfied. The High Court decided in favour of validity. This decision was affirmed by the Court of Appeal in *Re Baden's Deed Trusts (No 2)*.[23] The question in issue was whether the expressions, 'relatives' and 'dependants' were linguistically certain.

The Court of Appeal held that the test was satisfied (although Stamp LJ was prepared to give a narrower definition of 'relatives' than the other Lords Justices of Appeal). The expression, 'relatives', was taken to mean anyone who may establish a common ancestry with the settlor and the term, 'dependants', was defined as a person who is wholly or partly dependent on the means of another.

Each Lord Justice of Appeal adopted a different approach to the *Gestetner* test.

Hardcastle, IM, in 'Administrative unworkability: a reassessment of an abiding problem' [1990] Conv 24, reviews the arguments advanced for and against the workability criterion. The author examines the basis of the 'unworkability' criterion, propounded by Lord Wilberforce in *McPhail v Doulton*, as a method of invalidating a discretionary trust and suggests that it is an extension of the 'evidential uncertainty' criterion. He questions whether the mere size of a class of objects alone is sufficient to invalidate a trust and submits that the idea is based on a potentially innumerable class of

20 16th edn, 1950, London: Sweet & Maxwell.

21 [1969] 1 Ch 373.

22 [1976] Ch 235.

23 [1973] Ch 9.

beneficiaries coupled with a lack of provable definitional criteria. Unlike Emery (see [1982] 98 LQR 551), Hardcastle takes the view that administrative unworkability is extended to fixed trusts. He also considers whether the same notion is extended to powers of appointment.

Hardcastle writes:

> A trust must be one which the courts can control. Where judicial execution has been undertaken, there have normally been 'metes and bounds' within which the trusts have been defined; parameters that act as 'pointers or guides' to enable the court to substitute its own discretion for that of the trustees. In the course of so doing, the paramount objective of the court has been to execute the trust in a practical way; one best calculated to realise the settlor's intentions. The court has several options at its disposal, and the problem lies in determining when barriers to judicial execution are such that all such options are otiose.
>
> The incertitude stemming from immeasurably wide classes makes a nonsense of judicial supervision of the trustees' duties, since who is to say that a given selection of a beneficiary is wrong, and according to what criteria? ... Perhaps the unworkability criteria should only be employed where the trustees are unable to devise even a preliminary strategy, and where the court is similarly 'none the wiser'.

Controversy in applying the given postulant test

The judges have enunciated differing views in respect of the approach to the given postulant test. Some judges have expressed a lax approach to the test while others have adhered to the strict test. There seems to be five approaches to the test.

The question of fact approach

This approach is based on the assumption that the gift is conceptually certain (that is, linguistically certain). It then becomes a question of evidence or fact as to whether an individual proves to be within the class. Failure to discharge this burden of proof means that he is outside the class. In this respect it makes no difference whether the class is small or large. It is submitted that this approach concerns the practicalities of exercising the discretion as opposed to a test of validity of the gift. This mode of applying the test was laid down by Sachs LJ in *Re Baden (No 2)* thus:

> **Sachs LJ:** Once the class of persons to be benefited is conceptually certain it then becomes a question of fact to be determined on evidence whether any postulant has on enquiry been proved to be within it; if he is not so proved then he is not in it. That position remains the same whether the class to be benefited happens to be small (such as 'first cousins') or large (such as 'members of the X Trade Union' or 'those who have served in the Royal Navy'). The suggestion that such trusts could be invalid because it might be impossible to prove of a given individual that he was not in the relevant class is wholly fallacious.

Applying this approach to the facts in *Re Baden (No 2)*, it would appear that it would be up to the trustees to be convinced that a given individual is a relative or dependant of an officer or ex-officer, etc, of the specified company. Failure to convince the trustees means that the individual is not within the class.

The substantial number approach

This approach advocated by Megaw LJ in *Re Baden (No 2)* is to the effect that in terms of validity of the gift the test for certainty of objects is whether a substantial number of objects are within the class of objects and it is immaterial whether it is not possible to say with certainty that other objects are within or outside the class of objects. What is a substantial number of objects is for the courts to decide. Accordingly, the given postulant test is diluted to a substantial number of objects test.

> **Megaw LJ:** The main argument of counsel for the defendant executors was founded on a strict and literal interpretation of the words in which the decision of the House of Lords in *Re Gulbenkian's Settlement Trust* was expressed. That decision laid down the test for the validity of powers of selection. It is relevant for the present case, because in the previous excursion of this case to the House of Lords it was held that there is no relevant difference in the test of validity, whether the trustees are given a power of selection or, as was held by their Lordships to be the case in this trust deed, a trust for selection. The test in either case is what may be called the *Gulbenkian* test. The *Gulbenkian* test, as expressed by Lord Wilberforce (and again in almost identical words in a later passage) is this:
>
> > ... the power is valid if it can be said with certainty whether any given individual is or is not a member of the class and does not fail simply because it is impossible to ascertain every member of the class.
>
> The executors' argument concentrates on the words 'or is not' in the first of the two limbs of the sentence quoted above: 'if it can be said with certainty whether any given individual *is or is not a* member of the class'. It is said that those words have been used deliberately, and have only one possible meaning; and that, however startling or drastic or unsatisfactory the result may be – and counsel for the defendant executors does not shrink from saying that the consequence is drastic – this court is bound to give effect to the words used in the House of Lords' definition of the test. It would be quite impracticable for the trustees to ascertain in many cases whether a particular person was not a relative of an employee. The most that could be said is: 'There is no proof that he is a relative.' But there would still be no 'certainty' that such a person was not a relative. Hence, so it is said, the test laid down by the House of Lords is satisfied, and the trust is void. For it cannot be said with certainty, in relation to any individual, that he is not a relative.
>
> In my judgment, much too great emphasis is placed in the executors' argument on the words 'or is not'. To my mind, the test is satisfied if, as regards at least a substantial number of objects, it can be said with certainty that they fall within the trust; even though, as regards a substantial number of other persons, if

> they ever for some fanciful reason fell to be considered, the answer would have to be, not 'they are outside the trusts', but 'it is not proven whether they are in or out'. What is a 'substantial number' may well be a question of common sense and of degree in relation to the particular trust: particularly where, as here, it would be fantasy, to use a mild word, to suggest that any practical difficulty would arise in the fair, proper and sensible administration of this trust in respect of relatives and dependants.

The advantage of this approach is that the gift remains valid despite the fact that the classes of objects are incapable of definition. To a limited extent the broad objective of the settlor will be fulfilled. But this approach attracts a number of objections such as the striking similarity with the now defunct 'one person approach' which had been overruled by the House of Lords in *Re Gulbenkian*. The substantial number test seems to be a variant of the outdated approach. In addition, this diluted approach to the given postulant test creates a class within a class. The class as laid down by the settlor is varied to include only a substantial number of objects. It is questionable whether such an approach accords with the intention of the settlor. *Per* Lord Upjohn in *Re Gulbenkian*:

> The trustees have a duty to select the donees from among the class designated by the donor; he has not entrusted them with any power to select the donees merely from among known claimants who are within the class, for that is constituting a narrower class and the donor has given them no power to do this.

The strict approach

Stamp LJ subscribed to the view that the 'any given postulant test' requires the trustees to say of any individual that he either is clearly within or outside the class of objects. Accordingly, everyone is classified as being within or outside the class of objects. This requires clarity and precision in defining the qualifying class or classes of objects without listing the objects who fall within the class or classes. If such precise definitions are not forthcoming the gift is void.

> **Stamp LJ** (in *Re Baden (No 2)*): Counsel for the defendant executors, fastening on those words, 'if it can be said with certainty that any given individual is or is not a member of the class', submitted in this court that a trust for distribution among officers and employees or ex-officers or ex-employees or any of their relatives or dependants does not satisfy the test. You may say with certainty that any given individual is or is not an officer, employee, ex-officer or ex-employee. You may say with certainty that a very large number of given individuals are relatives of one of them; but, so the argument runs, you will never be able to say with certainty of many given individuals that they are not. I am bound to say that I had thought at one stage of counsel's able argument that this was no more than an exercise in semantics and that the phrase on which he relies indicated no more than that the trust was valid if there was such certainty in the definition of membership of the class that you could say

with certainty that some individuals were members of it; that it was sufficient that you should be satisfied that a given individual presenting himself has or has not passed the test and that it matters not that having failed to establish his membership – here his relationship – you may, perhaps wrongly, reject him. There are, however, in my judgment serious difficulties in the way of a rejection of counsel's submission.

The first difficulty, as I see it, is that the rejection of counsel's submission holding that the trust is good if there are individuals – or even one – of whom you can say with certainty that he is a member of the class. That was the test adopted by and the decision of the Court of Appeal in the *Gulbenkian* case, where what was under consideration was a power of distribution among a class conferred on trustees as distinct from a trust for distribution: but when the *Gulbenkian* case came before the House of Lords that test was decisively rejected and the more stringent test on which counsel for the defendant executors insists was adopted. Clearly, Lord Wilberforce in expressing the view that the test of validity of a discretionary trust ought to be similar to that accepted by the House of Lords in the *Gulbenkian* case did not take the view that it was sufficient that you could find individuals who were clearly members of the class; for he himself remarked, towards the end of his speech as to the trustees' duty of enquiring or ascertaining, that in each case the trustees ought to make such a survey of the range of objects or possible beneficiaries as will enable them to carry out their fiduciary duty. It is not enough that trustees should do nothing but distribute the fund among those objects of the trust who happen to be at hand or present themselves. I have already called attention to Lord Wilberforce's opinion that the trustees ought to make such a survey of the range of objects or possible beneficiaries as will enable them to carry out their fiduciary duty, and I ought perhaps to add that he indicated that a wider and more comprehensive range of enquiry is called for in the case of what I have called discretionary trusts than in the case of fiduciary powers. But, as I understand it, having made the appropriate survey, it matters not that it is not complete or fails to yield a result enabling you to lay out a list or particulars of every single beneficiary. Having done the best they can, the trustees may proceed on the basis similar to that adopted by the court where all the beneficiaries cannot be ascertained and distribute on the footing that they have been: see, for example, *Re Benjamin*. What was referred to as 'the complete ascertainment test' laid down by this court in the *Broadway Cottages* case is rejected. So also is the test laid down by this court the *Gulbenkian* case. Validity or invalidity is to depend on whether you can say of *any* individual and the accent must be on that word 'any', for it is not simply the individual whose claim you are considering who is spoken of – that he 'is or is not a member of the class', for only thus can you make a survey of the range of objects or possible beneficiaries.

If the matter rested there, it would in my judgment follow that, treating the word 'relatives' as meaning descendants from a common ancestor, a trust for distribution such as is here in question would not be valid. Any 'survey of the range of objects or possible beneficiaries' would certainly be incomplete, and I am able to discern no principle on which such a survey could be conducted or where it should start or finish. The most you could do, so far as regards

> relatives, would be to find individuals who are clearly members of the class – the test which was accepted in the Court of Appeal, but rejected in the House of Lords, in the *Gulbenkian* case. The matter does not however, rest there ... *Harding v Glyn* is authority endorsed by the decision of the House that a discretionary trust for 'relations' was a valid trust to be executed by the court by distribution to the next of kin. The class of beneficiaries thus becomes a clearly defined class and there is no difficulty in determining whether a given individual is within it or without it.
>
> Does it then make any difference that here the discretionary trust for relations was a reference not to the relations of a deceased person but of one who was living? I think not. The next of kin of a living person are as readily ascertainable at any given time as the next of kin of one who is dead.

The dictionary approach

The dictionary approach is based on the notion that the settlor may adopt a definition of the class or classes of objects specifically in a clause in the trust instrument. The effect is that there is likely to be little doubt as to the category of objects intended to benefit, for example, the settlor may give the trustees a discretion to distribute in favour of such of my 'old friends' as they may decide. He may then define the expression 'old friends' in any way he considers appropriate. In this way the class of objects which would otherwise have failed may be rescued by the settlor. A variation on this theme entitles the settlor to appoint a third person (or trustee) as sole arbiter of the definition of the class of objects and perhaps all issues incidental to the exercise or non-exercise of the discretion. This approach was sanctioned by the Court of Appeal in *Re Tuck's Settlement Trusts.*

***Re Tuck's Settlement Trusts* (1978) Ch 49, HC**

In this case, Sir Adolf Tuck, the first baronet, made a settlement in 1912 with the intention of ensuring that each baronet in succession would marry an 'approved wife'. The settlement provided for the payment of income to the baronet for the time being so long as he should be of the Jewish faith and married and living with an 'approved wife'. An 'approved wife' was identified in the settlement as 'a wife of Jewish blood by one or both of her parents and who has been brought up in and has never departed from and at the date of her marriage continues to worship according to the Jewish faith.' The settlor then added an arbitration clause to the effect that '... the decision of Chief Rabbi in London ... shall be conclusive'. Sir Adolf died in 1926. He was succeeded by his eldest son, Sir William Tuck, who married an approved wife. Sir William died 1954 and was succeeded by his eldest son, Sir Bruce Tuck. Sir Bruce first married an approved wife but was divorced in 1964. In 1968, he married a lady who was not an approved wife. The question in issue was whether the limitation was valid or void.

The Court of Appeal held that the limitation was not void on the grounds that the restriction created a condition precedent which was not wholly uncertain, and the Chief Rabbi clause constituted a valid delegation of decision making power on the relevant questions of fact, in the event of a dispute. The clause was similar to an arbitration clause in contract law.

> **Lord Denning MR:** In making his submissions, Mr Dillon used two phrases which have begun to fascinate Chancery lawyers. They are 'conceptual uncertainty' and 'evidential uncertainty'. After a little probing, I began to understand a little about them. 'Conceptual uncertainty' arises where a testator or settlor makes a bequest or gift upon a condition in which he has not expressed himself clearly enough. He has used words which are too vague and indistinct for a court to apply. They are not sufficiently precise. So the court discards the condition as meaningless. It makes it of no effect, at any rate when it is a condition subsequent.
>
> 'Evidential uncertainty' arises where the testator or settlor, in making the condition, has expressed himself clearly enough. The words are sufficiently precise. But the court has difficulty in applying them in any given situation because of the uncertainty of the facts. It has to resort to extrinsic evidence to discover the facts, for instance, to ascertain those whom the testator or settlor intended to benefit and those whom he did not. Evidential uncertainty never renders the condition meaningless. The court never discards it on that account. It applies the condition as best it can on the evidence available.
>
> The dichotomy between 'conceptual' and 'evidential' uncertainty was adumbrated by Jenkins J in *Re Coxen*.[24] It is implicit in Lord Upjohn's speech in *Re Gulbenkian's Settlement* [1970] AC 508 and accepted by Lord Wilberforce in *Re Baden's Deed Trusts (McPhail v Doulton)*.[25] I must confess that I find the dichotomy most unfortunate. It has led the courts to discordant decisions. I will give some relevant instances. On the one hand, a condition that a person shall 'not be of Jewish parentage' has been held by the House of Lords to be void for conceptual uncertainty, at any rate in a condition subsequent: see *Clayton v Ramsden*,[26] and a condition that a person shall be 'of the Jewish race' was held by Danckwerts J to be void for conceptual uncertainty, even in a condition precedent: see *Re Tarnpolsk* (1958). The reason in each case being that the testator had given no information or clue as to what percentage or proportion of Jewish blood would satisfy the requirement. Is it to be 100%, or will 75%, or 50% be sufficient? The words do not enable any definite answer to be given.
>
> On this reasoning the condition in the Tuck settlement that an 'approved wife' should be of 'Jewish blood' would seem to be afflicted with conceptual uncertainty.
>
> On the other hand, a condition that a person shall be 'of the Jewish faith' has produced diverse views. Four out of the five Law Lords thought that it was void for conceptual uncertainty, at any rate in a condition subsequent: see *Clayton v Ramsden* (1943), but Lord Wright thought it was sufficiently clear and

24 [1948] Ch 747.

25 [1971] AC 424.

26 [1943] AC 320.

distinct to be able to be applied: see *Clayton v Ramsden*. Lord Cross afterwards agreed with him: see *Blathwayt v Baron Cawley*.[27] So also did Buckley J at any rate in a condition precedent: see *Re Selby's Will Trust* (1966). I should range myself with Lord Wright. His view is supported by reference to the cases on other religions. Thus a condition that a person should be or not be 'of the Roman Catholic faith' is not open to objection on the ground of uncertainty, either in a condition precedent or a condition subsequent: see *Blathwayt v Baron Cawley*, by Lord Wilberforce: nor a condition that he shall or shall not be an 'adherent of the doctrine of the Church of England', at any rate in a condition precedent: see *Re Allen* [1953] Ch 810, nor a condition that he shall be 'of the Lutheran religion': see *Patton (WR) v Toronto General Trusts Corporation* (1930). The reason being in each case that evidence can be given of the tenets of that religion or faith so as to see if the person is or is not an adherent of it.

On this reasoning the condition in the Tuck settlement about 'Jewish Faith' would seem to be valid and not avoided for conceptual uncertainty.

In addition to those troubles, there is another distinction to be found in the cases. It is between conditions precedent and conditions subsequent. Conceptual uncertainty may avoid a condition subsequent, but not a condition precedent. I fail to see the logic of this distinction. Treating the problem as one of construction of words, there is no sense in it. If the words are conceptually uncertain – so as to avoid a condition subsequent – they are just as conceptually uncertain in a condition precedent – and should avoid it also. But it is a distinction authorised by this court in *Re Allen* and acknowledged by Lord Wilberforce in *Blathwayt v Baron Cawley*.

I deplore both these dichotomies, for a simple reason and a good reason. They serve in every case to defeat the intention of the testator or settlor. The courts say: 'We are not going to give effect to his intentions – because he has not expressed himself with sufficient distinctness or clearness.'

How is any testator or settlor to overcome these legal difficulties? Sir Adolf Tuck in this settlement said: 'Let any dispute or doubt be decided by the Chief Rabbi.' That seemed to him a good solution, and it seems a good solution. The Chief Rabbi should be able to decide – better than anyone else – whether a wife was 'of Jewish blood' and had been brought up 'according to the Jewish faith' ... I see no reason why a testator or settlor should not provide that any dispute or doubt should be resolved by his executors or trustees, or even a third person. To prove this, I will first state the law in regard to contracts. Here the general principle is that whenever persons agree together to refer a matter to a third person for decision, and further agree that his decision is to be final and binding upon them, then, so long as he arrives at his decision honestly and in good faith, the two parties are bound by it. They cannot reopen it for mistakes or errors on his part, either in fact or law, or for any reason other than fraud or collusion ... Such an agreement (to abide by the decision of a third person) does not oust the jurisdiction of the courts. It only offends when the parties go further and seek by their agreement to take the law out of the hands of the

27 [1976] AC 397.

> courts and put it into the hands of a private tribunal without recourse to the courts in case of error of law ... If the appointed person should find difficulty in the actual wording of the will or settlement, the executors or trustees can always apply to the court for directions so as to assist in the interpretation of it. But if the appointed person is ready and willing to resolve the doubt or difficulty, I see no reason why he should not do so. So long as he does not misconduct himself or come to a decision which is wholly unreasonable, I think his decision should stand ... But still the testator may even today think that the courts of law are not really the most suitable means of deciding the dispute or doubt. He would be quite right. As this very case shows, the courts may get bogged down in distinctions between conceptual uncertainty and evidential uncertainty: and between conditions subsequent and conditions precedent. The testator may want to cut out all that cackle, and let someone decide it who really will understand what the testator is talking about: and thus save an expensive journey to the lawyers and the courts. For my part, I would not blame him. I would give effect to his intentions ... So it comes to this: if there is any conceptual uncertainty in the provisions of this settlement, it is cured by the Chief Rabbi clause.

This approach is objectionable on the ground that the relevant clause is arbitrary in effect. There is a limit to the extent to which a settlor or testator may 'rescue' a class of objects. If the class of objects is incapable of definition, no arbitrator would be capable of applying a rational definition of the class. Moreover, it is not open to the testator or settlor to adopt the trustees' opinion as the criterion to determine the objects of the mere power or trust power without clear guidance in the first place as to the class or classes of objects.

Re Coxen, McCallum v Coxen [1948] 1 Ch 747, HC

A testator devised a dwelling house to his trustees subject to a direction to permit his widow to 'reside therein during her life, or so long as she shall desire to reside therein' and specified that 'if in the opinion of the trustees she permanently ceases to reside therein' the house would form part of the residuary estate. The question in issue was whether the limitation was valid or void.

The court held that the restriction was clear and valid.

> **Jenkins J:** It seems to me that so far as definition goes the double event involved in the condition ... is prescribed with sufficient certainty and precision. I see no reason why a judge of fact should not on any given state of facts be perfectly capable of deciding whether it has or has not happened ... The circumstance that it may be difficult in this or that state of facts to determine whether the double event has happened or not does not, in my judgment, make the condition bad ...
>
> I have so far treated the condition as if it was simply in the terms 'if she shall have ceased permanently to reside' whereas its actual terms are 'if in the opinion of my trustees she shall have ceased permanently to reside'. That I think makes a material difference. The opinion of the trustees that the double

> event has happened, and not simply the happening of the double event, is what brings about the cesser of Lady Coxen's interest. If the testator had insufficiently defined the state of affairs on which the trustees were to form their opinion, he would not I think have saved the condition from invalidity on the ground of uncertainty merely by making their opinion the criterion ... but as I have already indicated, I think the relevant double event is sufficiently defined to make it perfectly possible for the trustees (as the judges of fact for this purpose) to decide whether it has happened or not, and in my view the testator by making the trustees' opinion the criterion has removed the difficulties which might otherwise have ensued.

In addition, a dictionary clause has the tendency to oust the jurisdiction of the courts except in cases where the arbitrator has acted in bad faith. Generally, 'ouster clauses' are void on public policy grounds, see *Re Raven*.

Re Raven [1915] 1 Ch 673, HC

The testator by his will dated 29 September 1911, bequeathed a charitable legacy of £1,000 to the 'National Association for the Prevention of Consumption' and directed in his will that 'if any doubt shall arise in any case as to the identity of the institution intended to benefit, the question shall be decided by my trustees whose decision shall be final and binding on the parties'. There was no society of that name but there was a society incorporated in 1899 whose full name was 'The National Association for the Prevention of Consumption and other Forms of Tuberculosis'. This association had power to constitute branches, and amongst other branches there was an unincorporated branch whose full name was 'The Leicester Branch of the National Association for the Prevention of Consumption and other Forms of Tuberculosis'. The testator had been a subscriber to the Leicester branch for some years prior to his death, but had not subscribed to the National Association itself. The legacy was claimed by each of the charities which for this purpose were independent institutions. The trustees of the will and the Leicester branch were keen to allow the trustees to decide the question of the identity of the beneficiary. The National Association, on the other hand, insisted that the court should decide the question.

The High Court held that the arbitration clause in the will was void on grounds of repugnancy and public policy, for it purported to oust the jurisdiction of the Courts. In addition, the legacy was payable to the National Association for extrinsic evidence was not admissible in the circumstances.

> **Warrington J:** It is said that in this case a doubt has arisen whether the legacy in question ought to be given to one institution or another. The trustees desire to decide the question finally if they have power so to do. Of the two institutions between whom it is said that a doubt exists, one desires that the trustees should decide and the other desires and this is the important point – to have the question determined by the law of the land, that is to say, by the King's courts administering the law ... In my opinion it is not competent for a testator to

confer certain legal rights by giving legacies and at the same time to say that the question whether that legal right is or is not to be enjoyed is not to be determined by the ordinary tribunal – in other words, it is not competent for him to deprive the person to whom that legal right is given of one of the incidents of that legal right; and if necessary I should be prepared to rest my decision upon the ground that the attempt to do so is an attempt to do two inconsistent things. In my opinion the gift of a legacy to a legatee, even if it be of doubtful construction, is in fact a gift to the person who shall be determined to be the legatee according to legal principles, and to give effect to a provision such as the provision which the testator has inserted in his will in the present case is in fact to assert the direct contrary and to say that the gift is not to the person who shall be determined to be the legatee by the courts which administer the legal principles to which I have referred, but to the person who shall be decided to be the legatee by the trustees, who by the will are unfettered and may make their decision upon such grounds as they think fit ... I think therefore that I can safely decide the point on that ground alone; but I also think that I may and ought to decide it on wider grounds, namely, that it is contrary to public policy to attempt to deprive persons of their right of resorting to ordinary tribunals for the purpose of establishing their legal rights ... In the present case, certain rights are claimed, namely, the right to be treated as a legatee, the existence of which does not depend upon the fulfilment of any condition precedent or upon anything to be ascertained by a prescribed method. It has been attempted to say that the gift is equivalent to a gift to such institution as the trustees shall select. In my opinion that is not the effect of this gift. The gift of this legacy is to a particular institution, and that institution, if it proves its right, is entitled to the legacy and is not in the position of having to fulfil any condition precedent; nor does the right depend on ascertainment by any prescribed method; the right is ascertained by the gift itself. That being so, it seems to me impossible for the testator to qualify that gift by providing that the right to the legacy, the subject of the gift, shall be determined by some tribunal other than that of the country ...

It is plain that the testator has in terms given the legacy to the National Association itself and not to a branch of the association. Then it is urged that there is such a latent ambiguity in the testator's language that I ought to admit evidence of actual intention outside the will altogether, and that, if that evidence is admitted, it is quite clear that the testator meant to give the legacy to the branch and not the association. In my opinion extrinsic evidence of intention ... can only be admitted where there is a description applying indifferently to more than one person or society, while in the present case the description does not in my opinion apply indifferently to more than one society, but applies only to the National Association; and, if I were to admit such evidence of intention as is suggested, I should in fact be allowing the testator to make a will by word of mouth.

Gifts subject to conditions precedent and subsequent

The approach here is based on the property law distinction between gifts subject to conditions precedent and subsequent. In the case of gifts subject to conditions precedent, the requirement of certainty is less strict as opposed to gifts subject to conditions subsequent (see *Blathwayt v Baron Cawley*).[28] A gift subject to a condition precedent is one where the donee does not acquire an interest in the property until he satisfies the relevant condition for example, a gift of £500 to A provided that he passes his year one LLB examinations. A does not obtain the property until he passes the relevant examination. On the other hand, a gift subject to a condition subsequent is one which vests in the donee but terminates on the occasion when the relevant condition is satisfied, for example, an endowment to B until he passes his year one LLB examinations. Here, B obtains a vested interest which is determined when he passes the relevant examinations.

***Re Allen (Decd), Faith v Allen* [1953] 1 Ch 810, CA**

A testator devised his dwelling house and another property, subject to life interests, to the eldest son of his nephew, Francis, subject to the qualification that he shall be 'a member of the Church of England and an adherent to the doctrine of that Church'. The question in issue was whether the qualification was valid or void.

The Court of Appeal held that the qualification created a condition precedent and, to satisfy it, it was not necessary that the condition be capable of exact definition. The claimant was required to prove that he, at least, satisfied the limitation.

> **Sir Raymond Evershed MR:** The judge was, in my opinion, plainly right in his view that the formula here in question is not a condition subsequent. In my judgment the effect of such a formula as part of a condition subsequent differs from its effect in a condition precedent or as part of a qualification or limitation ...
>
> A condition subsequent operates to divest or determine a gift or estate previously or otherwise vested; so that if the condition be void the gift or estate remains. It has long been established that the courts (which are inclined against the divesting of gifts or estates already vested) will hold a condition subsequent void if its terms are such that (apart from mere difficulties of construction of the language or of the ascertainment of the facts) it cannot clearly be known in advance or from the beginning what are the circumstances the happening of which will cause the divesting or determination of the gift or estate. The strictness of the special rule as to conditions subsequent was the basis of all the opinions of the noble Lords in *Clayton v Ramsden* [Lord Evershed then referred to the judgment of Lord Russell of Killowen]. I feel

28 [1976] AC 397.

therefore, no doubt that if the present formula constituted a condition subsequent it would ... be held to be void – its second part falls clearly, I think, within the reasoning and language of Lord Russell and Lord Romer in *Clayton v Ramsden* to which I shall later again refer

... In the present case, if the formula constitutes a condition precedent, I will assume that failure to satisfy the condition will involve failure to take the benefit of the devise. And the same result is equally (if not more) clear if the formula is not a condition at all but part of the description of the devisee (as though it were to the eldest son who should have red hair); in other words, is a limitation or qualification, as I think it is ...

In any case, and whether the formula be a condition precedent or a qualification, it seems to me that no such general or academic test is called for as a condition subsequent requires. All that the claiming devisee has to do is at the relevant date to establish, if he can, that he satisfies the condition or qualification whatever be the appropriate test. If the formula is such as to involve questions of degree (as, *prima facie*, is implicit in any requirement of 'adherence' or 'attachment' to a particular faith or creed), the uncertainty of the test contemplated may well invalidate the formula as a condition subsequent but will not, in my judgment, necessarily do so in the case of a condition precedent; for if the claimant be able to satisfy any, or at least any reasonable test, is he disentitled to the benefit of the gift? ... A condition subsequent divesting an estate vested in A if A at some relevant date should not be a tall man would, as it seems to me, be held void for uncertainty. For tallness being a matter of degree, by what standard is it, for the supposed purposes, to be judged? If 'tallness' is achieved by being above the 'average' height, then what average is contemplated? The average of A's town or neighbourhood, the average of Englishmen, the average of all mankind? And would a man in height above the average, say of all Englishmen, by however small a fraction of an inch, be called 'tall' in any ordinary sense? But questions of this kind, which might be fatal to the supposed formula as a condition subsequent, might have no application in the case of a condition precedent or qualification; for a claimant who was 6 ft 6 inches tall might fairly say that he satisfied the testator's requirement judged by any reasonable standard.

It may well be that, in a case such as I have supposed, very difficult questions might arise, for example, if the claimant proved that he was a man very slightly above the average height of Englishmen. The court would then have to decide on the facts and on the construction of the bequest (for example, that by 'tall' the testator had meant 'lofty') whether the claimant satisfied the requirements of the testator and had established his claim to the gift. But I am not persuaded that where a formula constitutes a condition precedent or a qualification it is right for the court to declare the condition or qualification void for uncertainty so as thereby to defeat all possible claimants to the gift unless the terms of the condition or qualification are such that it is impossible to give them any meaning at all, or such that they involve repugnancies or inconsistencies in the possible tests which they postulate, as distinct, for example, from mere problems of degree.

If I have stated the relevant principles I will now try to apply them to the formula here in question. And as regards the qualification of membership of the Church of England, it seems to me that, notwithstanding the differences in degree which the language contemplates, they do not suffice to render void for uncertainty this part of a formula regarded as a qualification. Thus, if it so happened that the eldest of the sons of Francis Allen was at the relevant date (whatever that date may be) a prelate or dignitary of the Church, he would fairly claim to satisfy any reasonable test implicit in the words – the contrary view might at least, to my mind be said to shock common sense ...

The second part of the formula is, however, in my view very much more difficult. The testator clearly intended that the devisee should not only outwardly 'belong to' the Church of England, but that his membership should be in some sense conscientious as well. So much it is easy to state. But the reference to 'adherence' and to the 'doctrine' of the Church raise inevitably the problems of uncertainty and degree to which Lord Russell and Lord Romer drew attention in their opinions in *Clayton v Ramsden* already cited ... which would clearly, in my view, be fatal in any event to the validity of the formula if it were part of the terms of a condition subsequent. But are the words when used as part of a qualification so uncertain as necessarily to vitiate the gift? With considerable hesitation I have come to the conclusion that they are not. On the evidence so far before the court it does not seem to me that the words are shown to involve any insoluble inconsistency, or that they are incapable of any reasonably clear meaning or any sensible definition at all – as might, for example, be the case if the devisee were required to be 'a pure blooded Englishman'. If the supposition again be made that the eldest of the sons of Francis Allen were a prelate or a dignitary of the Church of England, it seems to me liable to offend against common sense if the court were compelled to say that he was none the less incapable of taking because he was incapable of qualifying as 'an adherent of the doctrine ' of the Church.

... I have already stated my view that the principles applicable to a condition precedent differ from those applicable to a condition subsequent. Moreover, on the facts of the case the result was the same if the condition was void for uncertainty whether it was a condition subsequent or a condition precedent; for if the former, the grandson took free from the condition, and if the latter, he took as the testatrix's sole next of kin ...

I think that it follows from what I have said that had the language of the condition in *Clayton v Ramsden* relating to the Jewish faith formed part of a qualification or condition precedent, it is probable (at least) that the decision of the House of Lords would have been in a sense opposite to that in the case which was decided. It follows also, I think, that the principles applicable to a condition precedent must be taken materially to differ from those applicable to a condition subsequent (and it is not always easy to determine whether a condition is of one kind or the other). Right or wrong, I accept these consequences. And I am unable to do so with somewhat less misgiving for these reasons: first, because, on the matter of principle, I think that Vaisey J was also of that opinion; second, because in the case of a will it is in general the function and duty of a court to construe the testator's language with reasonable liberality and to try, if it can, to give sensible effect to the intention he has expressed. To this general rule conditions subsequent seem to me to be an exception.

Clayton v Ramsden [1943] AC 320, HL (Lords Atkin, Thankerton, Russell of Killowen and Romer; Lord Wright dissenting)

By his will, a testator bequeathed a legacy and a share of the residue of his estate upon trust for his daughter, Edna for life with remainder on trust for her issue equally. The gift was subject to forfeiture (expressly inserted by the testator), if she should marry a person 'not of Jewish parentage and of the Jewish faith'. Edna married the appellant, Harold Clayton, who was an English Wesleyan who was admittedly not of Jewish parentage. The question in issue was whether the forfeiture clause was valid or void.

The House of Lords held that on construction the clause created a composite set of conditions subsequent which were void for uncertainty. The majority decided that both limbs of the disqualification clause were void.

> **Lord Russell of Killowen:** My Lords, for the reasons which I will indicate I am of the opinion that your Lordships should hold this condition of defeasance to be void, and allow this appeal. The courts have always insisted that conditions of defeasance, in order to be valid, should be so framed that the persons affected (or the court, if they seek its guidance) can from the outset know with certainty the exact event on the happening of which their interests are to be divested. The principle was enunciated many years ago by Lord Cranworth in *Clavering v Ellison* in the following words: 'Where a vested estate is to be defeated by a condition on a contingency that is to happen afterwards, that condition must be such that the court can see from the beginning, precisely and distinctly, upon the happening of what event it was that the preceding vested estate was to determine.' In all such cases that is the test which has to be applied to the particular condition which the testator has chosen to impose ...
>
> Let me now apply the principle to this condition. The crucial words are 'who is not of Jewish parentage and of the Jewish faith'. A preliminary question was raised. Is this one condition, or do the words impose alternative conditions on the happening of either of which a forfeiture occurs. This is a question of construction, separate from the main question. The testator has insisted on his daughter's husband having both the qualifications which he has mentioned. It was suggested that, if there was no uncertainty as to one of the qualifications, and the husband did not possess it, the forfeiture clause would operate. I cannot agree with this view, for its corollary would be that marriage with a husband not of Jewish parentage (whatever those words mean) but who before the wedding became a convert to the Jewish faith (whatever those words mean) would not bring about a forfeiture, a result quite inconsistent with the intention of the testator as disclosed by the language which he has used. I am of the opinion that there is here only one condition of forfeiture, and that the whole of the contingency on the happening of which the forfeiture is to take place must be certain.
>
> I now turn to consider the words 'of Jewish parentage'. The first doubt which is obviously inherent in them is whether they refer to race or religion or to both ... It may very well be that if, on the true construction of the words, they did refer to race, they might be too vague. It might be said that in the absence of any intimation of the percentage of Hebrew blood which the testator had in

> mind, it would be impossible to determine whether or not a given person fell within the language used. I express no opinion on that matter ...
>
> In my opinion, on construction, the words 'of Jewish parentage' refer to race. Other elements of doubt surrounds the words. Must both parents be of the Jewish race, or would one alone, and which, suffice? I confess myself unable to find any context which provides an answer, but the answer may well be that, in the absence of a context to the contrary, the true construction is that both parents must be of the Jewish race. But at this point the real difficulty begins, namely, the question of degree. The testator has given no information or clue as to what percentage or proportion of Jewish blood in the husband will satisfy the requirement that he should be of Jewish parentage. The daughter could never, before marrying the man of her choice, be certain that he came up to requisite standard of Jewish parentage, nor could a court enlighten her beforehand. The standard is unknown, and incapable of ascertainment. It is this uncertainty of degree which prevents the divesting event from being seen precisely and distinctly from the beginning, and uncertainty attaching to the requirement of Jewish parentage avoids the whole condition subsequent, with the result that no defeasance takes place.
>
> In these circumstances it is unnecessary to express an opinion on the certainty of the words 'of Jewish faith', but, had it been necessary, I should have felt a difficulty in holding that their meaning was clear or certain. It seems to me that ... the testator has given no indication of the degree of attachment or adherence to the faith which he requires on the part of his daughter's husband. The requirement that a person shall be of Jewish faith seems to me too vague to enable it to be said with certainty that a particular individual complies with the requirement.

The approach adopted by the High Court in *Re Barlow's Will Trust*[29] was more or less a practical approach towards the validity of the gift but based on two assumptions, first, that the quantum of the gift did not vary with the extent of the class of objects. In other words the property and paintings, were to be acquired at an undervalue. This privilege did not vary with the extent of the class of objects as opposed to a gift of £1,000 to be divided equally between 'my old friends'. Second, the gift was subject to a condition precedent which entitled the court to adopt a more liberal application of the test of certainty.

Re Barlow's Will Trusts [1979] 1 All ER 296, HC

A testatrix died in 1975 leaving a valuable collection of paintings. Her immediate survivors were eight nephews and nieces, 24 great nephews and nieces and 14 great great nephews and nieces.

By her will, the testatrix directed her executor to sell the remainder of her collection subject to the provision that 'any member of my family and any friends of mine' be allowed to purchase any of the paintings at a catalogue

29 [1979] 1 All ER 296; [1979] 1 WLR 278.

price compiled in 1970 which was substantially below their market value on the date of death.

The executors applied to the court to ascertain whether the direction was void for uncertainty and guidance as to the appropriate method for identifying members of the testatrix's family.

The court held that the direction as to 'friends' was valid, for the properties were to be distributed *in specie* to persons answering the description 'friend'. The court also gave guidelines on the identification of friends namely:

(a) the relationship with the testatrix was of long standing;

(b) the relationship must have been social as opposed to a business or professional relationship;

(c) when circumstances permitted they met frequently. The expression 'family' meant a blood relationship with the testatrix.

> **Browne-Wilkinson J:** The main questions which arise for my decision are:
>
> (a) whether the direction to allow members of the family and friends to purchase the pictures is void for uncertainty since the meaning of the word 'friends' is too vague to be given legal effect; and
>
> (b) what persons are to be treated as being members of the testatrix's family.
>
> I will deal first with the question of uncertainty.
>
> Those arguing against the validity of the gift in favour of the friends contend that, in the absence of any guidance from the testatrix, the question, 'who were her friends?', is incapable of being answered. The word is said to be 'conceptually uncertain' since there are so many different degrees of friendship and it is impossible to say which degree the testatrix had in mind. In support of this argument they rely on Lord Upjohn's remarks in *Re Gulbenkian's Settlement Trusts, Whishaw v Stephens* and the decision of the House of Lords in *McPhail v Doulton* (on appeal from *Re Baden's Deed Trusts*) to the effect that it must be possible to say who is within and who is without the class of friends. They say that since the testatrix intended all her friends to have the opportunity to acquire a picture it is necessary to be able to ascertain with certainty all the members of that class.
>
> Counsel for the fourth defendant, who argued in favour of the validity of the gift, contended that the tests laid down in the *Gulbenkian* case, and *McPhail v Doulton* were not applicable in this case. The test, he says, is that laid down by the Court of Appeal in *Re Allen* as appropriate in cases where the validity of a condition precedent or description is in issue, namely that the gift is valid if it is possible to say of one or more persons that he or they undoubtedly qualify even though it may be difficult to say of others whether or not they qualify.
>
> The distinction between the *Gulbenkian* test and the *Re Allen* test is, in my judgment, well exemplified by the word 'friends'. The word has a great range of meanings; indeed, its exact meaning probably varies slightly from person to person. Some would include only those with whom they had been on intimate terms over a long period; others would include acquaintances whom they

liked. Some would include people with whom their relationship was primarily business; others would not. Indeed, many people, if asked to draw up a complete list of their friends, would probably have some difficulty in deciding whether certain of the people they knew were really 'friends' as opposed to 'acquaintances'. Therefore, if the nature of the gift was such that it was legally necessary to draw up a complete list of 'friends' of the testatrix or to be able to say of any person that 'he is not a friend', the whole gift would probably fail even as to those who, by any conceivable test, were friends. But in the case of a gift of a kind which does not require one to establish all the members of the class (for example, 'a gift of £10 to each of my friends'), it may be possible to say of some people that, on any test, they qualify. Thus, in *Re Allen*, Evershed MR took the example of a gift to X 'if he is a tall man'; a man 6 ft 6 inches tall could be said on any reasonable basis to satisfy the test, although it might be impossible to say whether a man, say 5 ft 10 inches high satisfied the requirement.

So in this case, in my judgment, there are acquaintances of a kind so close that, on any reasonable basis, anyone would treat them as being 'friends'. Therefore, by allowing the disposition to take effect in their favour, one would certainly be giving effect to part of the testatrix's intention even though as the others it is impossible to say whether or not they satisfy the test.

In my judgment, it is clear that Lord Upjohn in *Re Gulbenkian* was considering only cases where it was necessary to establish all the members of the class. He made it clear that the reason for the rule is that in a gift which requires one to establish all the members of the class (for example, 'a gift to my friends in equal shares') you cannot hold the gift good in part, since the quantum of each friend's share depends on how many friends there are. So all persons intended to benefit by the donor must be ascertained if any effect is to be given to the gift. In my judgment, the adoption of Lord Upjohn's test by the House of Lords in *McPhail v Doulton* is based on the same reasoning, even though in that case the House of Lords held that it was only necessary to be able to survey the class of objects of a power of appointment and not to establish who all the members were. But such reasoning has no application to a case where there is a condition or description attached to one or more individual gifts; in such cases, uncertainty as to some other persons who may have been intended to take does not in any way affect the quantum of the gift to persons who undoubtedly possess the qualification. Hence, in my judgment, the different test laid down in *Re Allen*. The recent decision of the Court of Appeal in *Re Tuck's Settlement Trust* establishes that the test in *Re Allen* is still the appropriate test in considering such gifts, notwithstanding the *Gulbenkian* and *McPhail v Doulton* decisions.

Accordingly, in my judgment, the proper result in this case depends on whether the disposition in clause 5(a) is properly to be regarded as a series of individual gifts to persons answering the description 'friend' (in which case it will be valid), or a gift which requires the whole class of friends to be established (in which case it will probably fail).

The effect of clause 5(a) is to confer on friends of the testatrix a series of options to purchase. Although it is obviously desirable as a practical matter that steps should be taken to inform those entitled to the options of their rights, it is common ground that there is no legal necessity to do so. Therefore, each person coming forward to exercise the option has to prove that he is a friend; it is not legally necessary, in my judgment, to discover who all the friends are. In order to decide whether an individual is entitled to purchase, all that is required is that the executors should be able to say of that individual whether he has proved that he is a friend. The word 'friend' therefore is description or qualification of the option holder.

It was suggested that by allowing undoubted friends to take I would be altering the testatrix's intentions. It is said that she intended all her friends to have a chance to buy any given picture, and since some people she might have regarded as friends will not be able to apply, the number of competitors for that picture will be reduced. This may be so, but I cannot regard this factor making it legally necessary to establish the whole class of friends. The testatrix's intention was that a friend should acquire a picture. My decision gives effect to that intention.

I therefore hold, that the disposition does not fail for uncertainty, but that anyone who can prove that by any reasonable test he or she must have been a friend of the testatrix is entitled to exercise the option. Without seeking to lay down any exhaustive definition of such test, it may be helpful if I indicate certain minimum requirements:

(a) the relationship must have been a long standing one;

(b) the relationship must have been a social relationship as opposed to a business or professional relationship;

(c) although there may have been long periods when circumstances prevented the testatrix and applicant from meeting, when circumstances did permit they must have met frequently. If in any case the executors entertain any real doubt whether an applicant qualifies, they can apply to the court to decide the issue.

Finally, on this aspect of the case I should notice two further cases to which I was referred. The first is *Re Gibbard*,[30] in which Plowman J upheld the validity of a power to appoint to 'any of my old friends'. It is not necessary for me to decide whether that decision is still good law, in that it applied the *Re Allen* test to powers of appointment. But it does show that, if the *Re Allen* test is the correct test, the word 'friends' is not too uncertain to be given effect. Secondly, in *Re Lloyd's Trust Instruments* (unreported but extracts from which are to be found in *Brown v Gould* [1972] Ch 53) Megarry J stated:

> If there is a trust for 'my old friends', all concerned are faced with uncertainty as to the concept or idea enshrined in those words. It may not be difficult to resolve that 'old' means not 'aged' but 'of long-standing'; but then there is the question of how long is 'long'. Friendship, too, is a concept with almost infinite shades of meaning. Where the concept is uncertain, the gift is void. Where the concept is certain, then mere difficulty in tracing and discovering those who are entitled normally does not invalidate the gift.

30 [1967] 1 WLR 42.

> The extract that I have read itself shows that the judge was considering a trust for 'my old friends' (which required the whole class to be ascertained) and not such a case as I have to deal with. In my judgment, that *dictum* was not intended to apply to such a case as I have before me.
>
> I turn now to the question, who are to be treated as 'members of my family'? It is not suggested that this class is too uncertain. The contest is between those who say that only the next of kin of the testatrix are entitled and those who say that everyone related by blood to the testatrix is included ...
>
> In the absence of issue, the *prima facie* meaning of 'family' means 'relations', that is to say those related by blood. The context of the will may show that the testatrix had a special class in mind, but I can find no sufficient context in this will to find that the testatrix meant any narrower class to take. However, there is a rule of construction that limits gifts to relations to the statutory next of kin of the testator. The authorities clearly establish that the reason for this rule is that, unless such a limitation is introduced, the gift would fail for uncertainty, it being impossible to establish all the persons who are related by blood, however remotely ... That this is the reason for the rule is made abundantly clear by Jenkins LJ in *Re Gansloser's Will Trust* where he describes this need for limiting the class to the next of kin as 'justification for imputing a wholly conventional and artificial intention to the testator'.
>
> In the case of a gift to 'my relations in equal shares', such an artificial construction is necessary to save the gift from failing for uncertainty. But for the same reasons as I have sought to give in dealing with the word 'friends', in this particular case the option to the members of the family would not in any event fail for uncertainty even if it included all the testatrix's blood relations; anyone seeking to exercise the option would have to prove simply that he had a blood relationship.
>
> There being, therefore, no reason to give the words in this will an artificially limited meaning, I decline to do so. The fact that in this will the testatrix described a beneficiary as her great niece strongly suggests that she regarded that beneficiary as a member of her family. Yet that great niece is not one of next of kin. Accordingly, the artificially limited construction would defeat the testatrix's intention. There being no need so to construe the clause in order to validate it, I hold that the word has its ordinary meaning and includes all persons related by blood to the testatrix.

But, in *Re Tepper's Will Trusts*, the court admitted extrinsic evidence in order to clarify the definition of the class of objects in the context of a gift subject to a condition subsequent.

Re Tepper's Will Trusts, Kramer and Another v Ruda and Others [1987] Ch 358, HC

By his will made in 1953, a testator (a devout Jew), who died in 1959, left his residuary estate upon trust, *inter alia*, for his grandchildren living at the date of his death 'provided that they attain the age of 25 years and shall not marry outside the Jewish faith'. The testator had six grandchildren, four of whom married persons of the Jewish faith and two married persons outside the

Jewish faith. The question in issue was whether the restrictive clause was valid or void.

The court held that the clause created a condition subsequent which was *prima facie* void for uncertainty, but extrinsic evidence, if available, was admissible to clarify the meaning of the expression 'of Jewish faith' in a way which was consistent with the notion which the testator had in mind. The proceedings were adjourned pending inquiries concerning the availability of such evidence.

> **Scott J:** But lack of certainty as to the meaning of 'the Jewish faith' does seem to me to be bound to be the case where every testator and every will are concerned. I have already remarked that the contents of Nathan Tepper's will, read as a whole, show him to have been a devout Jew and I think, a practicing Jew. He practised his religion according to some tenets and in some community of Jewry; I do not know which and I do not know in what manner: there is no evidence of that. But a will falls to be construed, it is sometimes said, from the testator's armchair. The question is what the testator, sitting in his armchair, meant by 'the Jewish faith'. Direct evidence of his intention is not admissible; but I would have regarded as admissible extrinsic of the Jewish faith as practised by the testator and his family. It would, in my view, be well arguable that when the testator in his will referred to 'the Jewish faith' he meant the Jewish faith in accordance with which he practised his religion. I would have regarded it as possible and, indeed, likely that objective evidence might be available as to what was the Jewish faith in accordance with which he practised his religion. If evidence of that character were adduced it might well, in my view, be possible to attribute to the expression 'the Jewish faith' a meaning sufficiently certain to enable the *Clayton v Ramsden* test to be satisfied. This approach to construction is, in my view, supported by that of the Court of Appeal in *Re Tuck's Settlement Trusts* ...
>
> A question of construction of a will depends on the language of the particular will construed with the aid of admissible evidence of relevant surrounding circumstances. A decision by another court, even a court as august as the House of Lords, is not binding on the question whether in Nathan Tepper's will a sufficiently certain meaning can be attributed to the expression 'the Jewish faith' so as to enable the conditions of defeasance to be upheld. Counsel for the defendants, in the event that I should decide against them on the condition precedent or condition of defeasance point, and I have done so, have asked for the opportunity to adduce extrinsic evidence of surrounding circumstances in order to elucidate the meaning of the expression 'the Jewish faith' as used by the testator in his will. I think I should give them an opportunity to do so.
>
> If there is no more evidence than that which is before me now, it seems to me inevitable that the proviso must be declared void for uncertainty. The case would, in the event, be on all fours with *Clayton v Ramsden*. But, as I have said, that state of affairs does not seem to me to be inevitable.

Lindsay McKay, in '*Re Barlow* and the certainty of objects rule' [1980] Conv 263, examined the validity of the test laid down in *Re Barlow* and suggested that it is an unjustified extension of the test overruled by the House of Lords in *Re Gulbenkian*. McKay contends:

> A variety of conflicting tests were proffered by lower courts as being the 'proper' criteria by which certainty issues were to be resolved. One which surfaced briefly is the Court of Appeal decision in *Re Gulbenkian* [1968] Ch 126, in respect of trust powers, [which] was a test adopted by an earlier Court of Appeal [*Re Allen* [1953] 1 Ch 810] in relation to conditions precedent, namely, whether it could be said of any *one* individual that he satisfied the beneficiary-defining words. Without discussing its propriety as the test of certainty of conditions precedent, the House of Lords [in *Re Gulbenkian*] at once rejected it in the context of both trust powers and discretionary trusts. It did not surface in the *Baden* litigation.
>
> The decision of Browne-Wilkinson J in *Re Barlow's Will Trusts* has, however, brought the test into contention once again. The thrust of that decision is that the test is not limited to issues of certainty of conditions precedent but is in some circumstances the appropriate criterion for assessing the validity of the beneficiary-defining language of a broader class of settlement. This approach invites an analysis of the propriety of the extension of the test beyond the area of conditions precedent. But it does more than that. It also raises the broader issue, not resolved in *Re Gulbenkian*, of whether even in that narrow context the test can be regarded as good law following the *Baden* and *Gulbenkian* decisions.
>
> ... the test of certainty laid down in *Re Allen* is inadequate ... it is defined, seemingly deliberately, in such a way as to ensure compliance with it in virtually every case. It is indeed difficult to conceive of any language in respect of which it will not be satisfied, other than that which would be capricious in any event. Certainly, those trusts most frequently used as illustrations of post-*McPhail v Doulton* 'semantic uncertainty' – trusts for 'those with a moral claim upon me' for instance – will have no difficulty in satisfying it. That its avoiding potential is virtually non-existent is, of course, no bad thing in itself. But what is objectionable, in terms of the policy considerations, is that it provides no basis for filtering out those trusts which are manifestly inadequate in terms of the control and supervision to which the trustee will be subject.
>
> At first glance there seems little in common between either the fact situation of *Re Allen* and that of *McPhail v Doulton* or the respective issues of certainty thrown up by those fact situations. Nor, also at the superficial level, does the test of certainty articulated by Lord Wilberforce in the latter decision seem broadly appropriate to a resolution of issues such as that before the Court of Appeal in the earlier case. On an impressionistic basis, the indications point the other way. The *McPhail v Doulton* test was laid down in respect of discretionary trusts. In condition precedent cases, such as that in *Re Allen*, there is seldom a discretion in the trustee. It is usually only a matter of determining whether the applicant before the trustees with an (otherwise) unqualified entitlement to the fund fulfils the last remaining condition. On this basis the emphasis in *Re Allen* on an individual claimant rather than upon each and every potential beneficiary might seem 'proper'. In respect of discretionary trusts on the other hand, the prevailing fact situation is quite different. No individual has a fixed entitlement. The exercise of a discretion, rather than the fulfilment of a qualifying condition, stands between each potential beneficiary

> and payment. There is typically a range of persons among whom the discretion is to be exercised. Most significantly, the trustees have obligations to survey and consider the range of possible beneficiaries prior to making any payment. In these circumstances, the *McPhail v Doulton* emphasis upon an ability to determine of *any* individual whether he is or is not a member of the class might seem, again impressionistically, a 'proper' emphasis. Browne-Wilkinson J may have had this general distinction in mind in *Re Barlow*, when he refused to categorise the trust before him as one for 'a class' but rather as one conferring a series of individual gifts to persons answering the description 'friend'.

McKay concludes by saying:

> The view forwarded in this note is that the test [laid down in *Re Allen*] is both wrong in principle and must be regarded as being inconsistent with those later decisions [*Re Gulbenkian* and *McPhail v Doulton*], that it should not have been adopted by Browne-Wilkinson J, and that the decision in *Re Barlow* is on that account incorrect.

FIDUCIARY DUTIES

Duties imposed on trustees of a fiduciary power and discretionary trust

The duties imposed on the trustees in respect of a fiduciary power are similar to the duties imposed on discretionary trustees. The main difference between the two gifts is that in the former, there is no obligation imposed on the trustees to exercise their discretion but in the context of a discretionary trust the trustees are required to exercise their discretion. A discretionary trust is mandatory in nature. Thus, under a fiduciary power, the trustees are required to act responsibly and *bona fide* consider, from time to time, whether to exercise their discretion, but having done so, they may legitimately fail to exercise their discretion (see *Re Hay's Settlement*, above, p 152). In this event, the gift over in default of appointment will take effect. Whereas, under a discretionary trust if the discretionary trustees fail to exercise their discretion the courts will intervene and repair the omission by the trustees.

Per Lord Upjohn in *Re Gulbenkian* (1970):

> The basic difference between a mere power and a trust power is that in the first case trustees owe no duty to exercise it and the relevant fund or income falls to be dealt with in accordance with the trusts in default of its exercise, whereas in the second case the trustees must exercise the trust and in default the court will.

If the trustees exercise their discretion under a fiduciary power of appointment, the trustees are required to comply with the same duties imposed on discretionary trustees. There would no longer be a distinction between the fiduciary power and the trust but this would only be the case in the event of an exercise of the discretion.

There are two kinds of discretionary trusts – exhaustive and non-exhaustive (see above, p 146). In an exhaustive discretionary trust, the trustees are required to distribute the relevant property (income or capital) within a reasonable period of time. On the other hand, an non-exhaustive discretionary trust is one where the trustees may legitimately fail to distribute the property. In this event the property is retained by the trustees, for example, in the case of a non-exhaustive discretionary trust of income on a failure to distribute the income within a reasonable time the income will be accumulated and becomes capitalised income (or capital). Thus, in such a case the discretion may be exercised by a decision to accumulate the income.

Whether the trust is exhaustive or not, the trustees are under a duty to refrain from acting capriciously, but is under a duty to act in a responsible manner, surveying the range of objects both in terms of the categories of objects and the qualifications of individual objects with a view to distribution.

Per Lord Wilberforce in *McPhail v Doulton*:

> A trustee with a duty to distribute, particularly among a potentially very large class, would surely never require the preparation of a complete list of names, which anyhow would tell him little that he needs to know. He would examine the field, by class and category; might indeed make diligent and careful enquiries, depending on how much money he had to give away and the means at his disposal, as to the composition and needs of particular categories and of individuals within them; decide on certain priorities or proportions and then select individuals according to their needs and qualifications.

If the trustees act in good faith and with due care and attention confirming the exercise of their discretion within the terms authorised by the settlor, the courts will not interfere with the trustees' discretion.

The distinction between an exhaustive and a non-exhaustive discretionary trust becomes significant when the trustees fail to exercise their discretion. This will be evident if the trustees fail to distribute the relevant property (exhaustive) or fail to take relevant factors into consideration (non-exhaustive). In these circumstances, the court will intervene and execute the unfulfilled duty of the trustees. The court has a variety of options available to it in order to execute the trust, but whichever course is adopted its objective would be to give effect to the intentions of the settlor or testator. The court is entitled to appoint new trustees, able and willing to exercise the discretion or direct the trustees to distribute the fund. Alternatively, the court may direct representatives of the classes of objects to prepare a scheme of distribution or in appropriate cases the court may order an equal division of the funds in favour of the objects. This last course of action would be appropriate in cases of family trusts of a limited class. Moreover, in the case of an exhaustive discretionary trust where the trustees have failed to distribute the income and subsequently declare an intention to repair their omission by distributing undistributed income, the court is entitled to permit the trustees to make the distribution.

Re Locker's Settlement, Meachem and Others v Sachs and Others [1978] 1 All ER 216, HC

By a settlement made in December 1963, a discretionary trust was set up to apply the income of the trust fund among a class of objects including individuals and charitable institutions. The trustees accumulated all of the income until 5 April 1968. From this date the trustees dealt with the trust income in exercise of their discretion. But they retained a substantial fund representing income which was accumulated until 1968. The trustees applied to the court for directions regarding the accumulated income.

The court held that, since the trustees had wished to repair their breach by distributing the accumulated income, the court would permit the trustees to do so. But, the discretion may only be exercised in favour of the objects which were available at the time that the discretion ought to have been exercised.

> **Goulding J:** It is common ground that it was the duty of the trustees to distribute the trust income within a reasonable time after it came into their hands: compare *Re Gourju's Will Trusts* (1943). It is also common ground that subject to one point arising on clause 10 of the settlement ... the court itself can execute such a discretionary trust as is here in question if the trustees fail to do so. Lord Wilberforce in *McPhail v Doulton* (1971) (better known as *Re Baden's Deed Trusts*) explained how the court can act in such a matter. He said:
>
> > ... the court, if called upon to execute the trust power, will do so in the manner best calculated to give effect to the settlor's or testator's intentions. It may do so by appointing new trustees, or by authorising or directing representative persons of the classes of beneficiaries to prepare a scheme of distribution, or even, should the proper basis for distribution appear by itself directing the trustees so to distribute.
>
> A court of equity, where trustees have failed to discharge their duty of prompt discretionary distribution of income, is concerned to make them as owners of the trust assets at law, dispose of them in accordance with the requirements of conscience; that is, to give benefits to the *cestuis que* trust in accordance with the confidence that the settlor reposed in them, the trustees. In a case such as the present, where the trustees desire to repair their breach of duty, and to make restitution by doing late what they ought to have done early, and where they are in no way disabled from doing so, the court should, in my judgment, permit and encourage them to take that course. A tardy distribution at the discretion of the trustees is, after all, nearer to prompt distribution at the discretion of the trustees, which is what the settlor intended, than a tardy distribution by the trustees at the discretion of someone else. There are, no doubt, cases where a manifestation of obstinacy or bias on the part of the trustees, or of hostility and suspicion (even unjustified hostility and suspicion) on the part of the potential *cestuis que* trust, or some other circumstance, must make such a solution of the problem inadvisable. The court may readily listen to the misgivings of potential beneficiaries who have been unable to get the trustees to exercise their discretion after repeated requests and are hoping themselves, if they have the *locus standi* to do so, to invoke the court's jurisdiction ...

> It has been argued by Mr Blackburne, on behalf of some of the objects of the trust, that once a reasonable time for the distribution of a particular item of income has elapsed, the trustees' discretion over that income is extinguished and either cannot be revived, or ought not to be revived, by the court. That submission is founded on *Re Allen-Meyrick's Will Trust* (1966) and *Re Gulbenkian's Settlements (No 2)* (1970). They, however, concerned permissive, as distinct from obligatory, discretionary powers, and in each case the trust instrument contained a subsisting trust to take effect in default of exercise of the power. The discretion of the trustees ought to be exercised promptly, if at all, where its exercise is optional, just as it ought to be exercised promptly in every case where its exercise is obligatory. But the consequences of non-exercise are to my mind quite different in the two situations ...
>
> I will declare that the discretion of the plaintiffs, or the trustees for the time being of the settlement, is exercisable as regards the money and investments mentioned in the answer to the first question, only in favour of such objects or of some or one of them as would have been objects of the said discretion had it been exercised within a reasonable time after receipt of the income respectively represented thereby.

Interest of objects under a discretionary trust

Under a fixed trust, the beneficiaries are given quantified or quantifiable interests in the trust property as of right which each may enjoy, sell, exchange or give away as they please. Each beneficiary is entitled to the protection of a court of equity and is empowered to pursue actions in order to enforce such rights, for example, a gift to the trustees on trust for A for life, remainder to B absolutely. A has a vested interest in possession and is entitled to the income as of right from the trust fund for life. B has a vested interest in the capital of the fund as of right and would acquire an absolute interest on A's death.

Individual interest

In respect of a discretionary trust, the trustees are given a discretion to decide what interest, if any, may be distributed to the objects. The objects are dependent on the trustees exercising their discretion in their favour. No object is entitled to a quantifiable interest in the property. Prior to the exercise of the discretion, the objects, individually considered, have an expectation or hope of acquiring a benefit. Each object does not have a right to the income of the fund but merely a right to require the trustees to consider whether they will distribute any property to the object. If the trustees decide to distribute property to an object, he gets it not by reason of having the right to have his case considered, but only because the trustees have decided to distribute the property to him. See *Gartside v IRC* (below, p 198). This is the position whether the discretionary trust is exhaustive or non-exhaustive.

***Gartside and Another v Inland Revenue Commissioners* [1968] AC 553, HL**

By his will, the testator who died in January 1941 transferred one quarter share of his estate upon trust for the benefit of his son, John and family. The settlement provided that during John's lifetime the trustees were given an unfettered discretion to provide the income from the trust fund 'for or towards the maintenance, support or otherwise for the benefit of John or his wife or children (if any) ... and shall accumulate the surplus of the said income ...' (non-exhaustive discretionary trust). The accumulations of income were to be added to the trust fund and the trustees were given a discretion to apply the same for the maintenance, support and benefit of the same class of discretionary objects during John's lifetime, and after his death the capital was to be held on trust for such of his children as shall attain 21 or, if daughters, marry. John married in 1942 and had twin sons born in 1945. The trustees accumulated all of the income until 1960. In 1961, they paid out income of £786 to John and £50 to his wife and accumulated the balance. In 1962 the trustees advanced accumulated income to the twins. John died in 1963. It was conceded that estate duty was payable on the remainder of the trust funds by virtue of John's death, but in addition, the Revenue claimed duty on the sums advanced to the twins in 1962 on the ground that the advancement amounted to a termination of an interest in possession.

The House of Lords held in favour of the trustees on the ground that the class of discretionary beneficiaries did not have, individually or collectively, an interest in possession prior to the exercise of the trustees' discretion in their favour. Accordingly, the advancement in 1962 did not amount to a termination of an interest in possession.

> **Lord Reid:** The argument for the Crown was that the duty of the trustees to exercise that discretion from time to time gave to each of John, his wife and his two sons an interest in the fund, that that interest extended to the whole fund because the trustees could at any time have given the whole of the income from it to any of them, and that these interests were interests in possession. They say that it is immaterial whether or not the trustees ever at any time in fact gave to any of these beneficiaries any sum or other benefit: they each had interests in possession of the whole fund even if none of them ever received anything from it.
>
> The trustees argued that a person's right to require trustees of a discretionary trust to consider from time to time whether or not to apply the whole or some part of the income of the trust funds for the benefit is not an interest, and in any event is not an interest in possession, in the whole fund or in any part of it.
>
> The word 'interest', as an ordinary word of English language, is capable of having many meanings, and it is equally clear that in these provisions its meaning cannot be limited by any technicality of English law ... A person who has a contingent right to some benefit from a trust fund in some future event, has a present right to prevent the trustees from dissipating the fund; but that right is not an interest in possession separate from and in addition to his contingent interest ...

Next comes the question of what is meant by an interest 'extending' to the whole or a part of the income of certain property. Normally that must mean that the owner of the interest is entitled to receive that income. In that case ... on the cesser of that interest, someone else will become entitled to receive the income accruing from and after the cesser. So the right to receive income will change hands ...

Where a number of persons are members of a company or other corporation which has a separate legal personality, the incorporation can of course have a single right different from the rights of any of its members. Otherwise two or more persons cannot have a single right, unless they hold it jointly or in common. Clearly, objects of a discretionary trust do not have that: they each have individual rights; they are in competition with each other and what the trustees give to one is his alone.

I think that this idea of a group or class right must have arisen in this way. Where the trustees are bound to distribute the whole income among the discretionary beneficiaries and have no power to retain any part of it or use any part of it for any other purposes, you cannot tell what anyone of the beneficiaries will receive until the trustees have exercised their discretion. But you can say with absolute certainty that the individual rights of the beneficiaries when added up or taken together will extend to the whole income. You can have an equation $x + y + z = 100$, although you do not yet know the value of x or y or z. And that may lead to important results where the trust is of that character. But that is not this case.

In my judgment an examination of the relevant provisions of this legislation leads to the clear conclusion that objects of a discretionary trust do not have interests extending to the whole or any part of the income of the trust fund ... *a fortiori* they do not have interests in possession ... To have an interest in possession does not merely mean that you possess the interest. You also possess an interest in expectancy for you may be able to assign it and you can rely on it to prevent the trustees from dissipating the trust fund. 'In possession' must mean that your interest enables you to claim now whatever may be the subject of the interest. For instance, if it is the current income from a certain fund your claim may yield nothing if there is no income, but your claim is a valid claim, and if there is any income you are entitled to get it; but a right to require trustees to consider whether they will pay you something does not enable you to claim anything. If the trustees do decide to pay you something, you do not get it by reason of having the right to have your case considered: you get it only because the trustees have decided to give it to you. Even if I had thought that objects of discretionary trusts have interests, I would not find any good reason for holding that they have interests in possession.

Lord Wilberforce: The obligation to distribute the whole income does not entitle any object to the whole or any definable part of the income, and, therefore, the object cannot have a quantifiable interest in the fund. The only right which any object has in an exhaustive, as in a non-exhaustive, trust is to have the trustees exercise their discretion and to be protected by the court in that right.

***Pearson v Inland Revenue Commissioners* [1981] AC 753, HL**

By a settlement made in November 1964, capital and income were transferred to trustees for the benefit of the settlor's three daughters, Fiona, Serena and Julia in equal shares. The settlement also gave the trustees an overriding power to appoint the whole or part of the fund to the same objects or to accumulate so much of the income as they may think fit.

On 20 March 1976 the trustees appointed a sum of £16,000 (part of the capital) to Fiona. The Inland Revenue assessed the trustees to capital transfer tax on a capital distribution. The assessment was based on the assumption that, prior to the appointment, Fiona did not enjoy an interest in possession because the trustees were under a duty to consider whether the income should be paid to the objects in equal shares or be accumulated. The appointment however, gave Fiona an interest in possession with the consequence that capital transfer tax under Sched 5, para 6(2) of the Finance Act 1975 became payable.

The trustees argued that an 'interest in possession' meant a right to present enjoyment of the property (even subject to defeasance) and the existence of a prior power (of appointment or accumulation) to deal with the income does not, by itself, convert an interest which would otherwise be in possession into one not in possession.

The House of Lords held in favour of the Inland Revenue.

Viscount Dilhorne: My Lords, the only question to be decided in this appeal is whether Fiona Pilkington and her two sisters, Serena and Julia, were after they were 21 and before 27 March 1974 entitled to interests in possession in settled property. The trustees say that they were and the Crown says that they were not.

The Finance Act 1975 introduced capital transfer tax under which tax is charged 'on the value transferred by a chargeable transfer'. Subject to certain exceptions, a transfer of value is any disposition made by a person as a result of which the value of his estate immediately after the disposition is less than it would be but for the disposition, and a chargeable transfer is any transfer of value made by an individual after 26 March 1974.

Schedule 5 to the Act has effect with regard to settled property. This Schedule draws a distinction between what may be called fixed interest trusts and discretionary trusts. A person entitled to an interest in possession in settled property is in general treated as if he was beneficially entitled to the property in which his interest subsists. If during his life, his interest in possession comes to an end, there is a charge to tax as if he had himself made a transfer of value and the value transferred had been equal to the value of the property in which his interest subsisted. If he dies and is then entitled to an interest in possession, tax is charged as if immediately before his death he had made a transfer of value equal to the value of his estate of which his interest in possession formed part. On the other hand, if he becomes absolutely entitled to the property in which he had an interest in possession there is no charge to tax; nor is there if his interest in possession comes to an end but on the same occasion he becomes entitled to another interest in possession in the property.

It follows that if Fiona had an interest in possession in the 13,333 shares settled by her father, she would not have become liable to capital transfer tax on the appointment to her of the £16,000. On the other hand, if there was no interest in possession of the settled property when the appointment was made, the position is very different ...

If Fiona became entitled to the £16,000 at a time when no interest in possession subsisted in that, a capital distribution of £16,000 has to be treated as having been made. Further, every 10 years from the date of the relevant transfer occurring after 1 April 1980 tax is charged at the rate of 30% of the rate which would otherwise be chargeable on the value of the property in the settlement in which no interest in possession subsists.

The meaning to be given to the words 'interest in possession in settled property' is thus of vital importance in ascertaining liability to capital transfer tax.

No attempt is made in the Finance Act 1975 to define 'interest in possession' apart from the definition in Sched 5, para 11(10) and the definition for the purpose of applying the Schedule to Scotland. What then should be the approach to construing those words in the Act? In my view one should first seek to determine the ordinary and natural meaning of those words and then consider whether there is anything in the context in which they are used to lead to the conclusion that the proper interpretation of them involves a departure from the ordinary and natural meaning. In Preston's *Elementary Treatise on Estates*[31] an estate in possession is stated to be one which gives 'a present right of present enjoyment'. This was contrasted with an estate in remainder which it was said gave 'a right of future enjoyment'. In Fearne's *Contingent Remainders*[32] it was said that an estate is vested when there is an immediate fixed right of present or future enjoyment, that an estate is vested in possession when there exists a right of present enjoyment, that an estate is vested in interest when there is a present fixed right of future enjoyment and that an estate is contingent when a right of enjoyment is to accrue on an event which is dubious and uncertain.

In the light of these statements, it appears that in the 19th century the words 'an interest in possession' would have been interpreted as ordinarily meaning the possession of a right to the present enjoyment of something. The Crown in its case contends that 'a beneficiary only has an interest in possession if his interest enables him to claim the whole or an ascertainable part of the net income, if any, of the property at the moment at which it is in the hands of the trustees'. The trustees in their case contend that the phrase 'interest in possession' simply denotes an interest which is not in reversion a present right of present enjoyment.

31 2nd edn, 1820, p 89.

32 10th edn, 1844, Vol 1, p 2.

So the parties agree that for there to be an interest in possession, there must be a present right to the present enjoyment of something, the Crown contending that it must be to the enjoyment of the whole or part of the net income of the settled property.

The difficulty lies in its application to the facts of the present case. It is said by both parties to be one of fundamental importance. Whether or not that is the case, all we have to decide is whether on reaching 21, Fiona and her sisters acquired interests in possession in settled property. In other words had they then a present right of present enjoyment of anything?

As to that, there are, it seems to me, two possible conclusions. The first is that the power of appointment under clause 2 not having been exercised, the three sisters on reaching that age acquired interests in possession, defeasible, should the trustees decide to exercise their power to accumulate income. They were then entitled absolutely to the capital and income of the trust fund in equal shares subject to the exercise of that power. The second is that they never secured an interest in possession for they never acquired, on reaching that age, the right to the enjoyment of anything. Their enjoyment of any income from the trust fund depended on the trustees' decision as to the accumulation of income. They would only have a right to any income from the trust fund if the trustees decided it should not be accumulated or if they failed to agree that it should be or if they delayed a decision on this matter for so long that a decision then to accumulate and withhold income from the sisters, would have been unreasonable.

In *Gartside v IRC*, an estate duty case, Lord Reid said:[33]

> 'In possession' must mean that your interest enables you to claim now whatever may be the subject of the interest. For instance, if it is the current income from a certain fund, your claim may yield nothing if there is no income, but your claim is a valid claim, and if there is any income you are entitled to get it; but a right to require trustees to consider whether they will pay you something does not enable you to claim anything. If the trustees do decide to pay you something, you do not get it by reason of having the right to have your case considered; you get it only because the trustees have decided to give it to you.

That case concerned a discretionary trust where payment was made to the beneficiaries at the discretion of the trustees. Here the three sisters' entitlement to income was subject to the trustees' power of accumulate. On reaching 21 they had no valid claim to anything. If there was any income from the settled property, they were not entitled to it. Their right to anything depended on what the trustees did or did not do and the receipt of income by them appears to me to have been just as much at the discretion of the trustees as was the receipt of income by the beneficiaries in the *Gartside* case.

It was recognised by the trustees that, if clause 3 had created a trust to accumulate subject to which the trust fund was to be held in trust for the three sisters absolutely on their attaining 21, they would not have secured an interest

33 [1968] AC 553, p 607; [1968] 1 All ER 121, p 128.

> in possession on reaching that age. It makes all the difference, so it was said, that the trustees were not under a duty to accumulate but only had power to do so if they thought fit. I am not able to accept this for in neither case can it, in my opinion, be said that the sisters on attaining that age secured the right to the present enjoyment of anything.
>
> A distinction has in my opinion to be drawn between the exercise of a power to terminate a present right to present enjoyment and the exercise of a power which prevents a present right of present enjoyment arising. If in this case the power of appointment under clause 2 had been exercised before the sisters became 21, it could not be said that they then got an interest in possession.
>
> The Crown, while contending that it made no difference in this case that the sisters' entitlement was subject to a power to accumulate as distinct from being subject to a trust to do so, contended that a distinction was to be drawn between what may be called the administrative and the dispositive powers in a trust deed ... and in my opinion there is a very real distinction. A life tenant has an interest in possession but his interest only extends to the net income of the property, that is to say, after deduction from the gross income or expenses, etc, properly incurred in the management of the trust by the trustees in the exercise of their powers. A dispositive power is a power to dispose of the net income. Sometimes the line between an administrative and a dispositive power may be difficult to draw but that does not mean that there is not a valid distinction. In the present case the Crown contended that the power given by clause 21 to apply income towards the payment of duties, taxes, etc, which, but for the provisions of the clause, would be payable out of or charged on capital was a dispositive power and that this clause alone would prevent the sisters having an interest in possession on reaching 21. I do not think that this is so. I think this clause falls on the administrative side of the line and merely elucidates the meaning to be given to clause 14.
>
> In my opinion the words 'interest in possession' in Sched 5 should be given their ordinary natural meaning which I take to be present right of present enjoyment and as in my view the sisters on attaining 21 did not obtain that this appeal should succeed.

Indeed, a sole member of a class of discretionary objects is not entitled as of right to claim the income from the trust while there remains a possibility that other members might come into existence.

Re Trafford's Settlement [1984] 1 All ER 1108, HC

By a settlement made in June 1951, Mr John Trafford created a settlement. Clause 2(a) declared as follows:

> The trustees shall hold the income of the Trust Funds during the life of the Settlor upon protective trusts and shall pay or apply the same to or for the benefit of the settlor and of any wife whom he may marry and the child or children of the settlor by any wife whom he may marry or any of them as the trustees shall in their absolute discretion think fit.

By clause 2(b), the settlor declared that after his death, the trustees shall hold so much of the income of the trust funds as he (the settlor) would by deed or will appoint upon protective trusts for the benefit of any surviving wife during her life, or for any lesser period. The settlor remained unmarried and did not have children. He died in June 1978. In 1983, the Revenue assessed the trustees to capital transfer tax on the value of the settlement funds on the grounds that:

(i) the settlor enjoyed a determinable life interest within s 33 of the Trustee Act 1925, that is, an interest in possession which was subject to defeasance;

(ii) alternatively, the settlor was entitled as of right to the income as it accrued to the trustees.

The trustees argued that a protective life interest within s 33 was not created by clause 2(a) and the words 'upon protective trusts' within clause 2(a) were merely descriptive. The intention of the settlor was to create a discretionary trust, for on bankruptcy, a protective trust in favour of the settlor would be void against the trustee in bankruptcy. In addition, clause 2(a) did not state a principal beneficiary. Moreover, the settlor did not have an interest in possession under the discretionary trust despite being the only member of the class of objects. The reason being that the class of objects was not closed, and once there was a possibility that another or other members was or were capable of being included in the class, no one member was entitled to claim the income as of right.

The court held in favour of the trustees on both grounds.

Peter Gibson J: Two issues have been debated before me. First, on the true construction of clause 2(a) of the settlement, (a) did the settlor have a determinable life interest which was never determined until his death, as counsel for the Crown contends, or (b) was the settlor only interested as an object of the discretionary trust of income contained in clause 2(a), as counsel for the trustees contends. If the answer is in sense (a), counsel for the trustees accepts that the settlor had an interest in possession and the Crown succeeds. But, second, if the answer is in sense (b), did the settlor nevertheless have an interest in possession by virtue of being the only object of the discretionary trust of income? Counsel for the Crown contends that he had such an interest; counsel for the trustees argue for the contrary.

In summary, I am left in no doubt that it is impossible to read into clause 2(a) the words for which counsel for the Crown contends. I accept that the reference to protective trusts in that clause is a description of the trust intended to protect the settlor in relation to the income of the property settled by him during the lifetime of the settlor. Consequently, in my judgment the trust in clause 2(a) took effect as an immediate discretionary trust and subsisted as such until the settlor's death.

When income is received by the trustees of a discretionary trust of income, the sole object of the class which is not yet closed cannot in my judgment claim an immediate entitlement to that income. It is always possible that before a

> reasonable time for the distribution of that income has elapsed another object will come into existence or be ascertained and have a claim to be considered as a potential recipient of the benefit of that income. So long as that possibility exists, the sole object's entitlement is subject to the possibility that the income will be properly diverted by the trustees to the future object once he comes into existence or is ascertained. Indeed, in strictness the entitlement of the sole object is only an entitlement that the trustees should consider whether to pay income to him. In respect of income already received it may be possible to say that such an entitlement has arisen, but for present purposes I must consider the position immediately before the death of the settlor not in relation to income previously received by the trustees but in relation to the settlor's rights to income then or thereafter accruing. Such income as it accrued was subject to the possibility that it could properly be withheld by the trustees from the settlor and diverted to a future beneficiary, unlikely though the possibility of such beneficiary coming into existence or being ascertained undoubtedly was in the present case. On that footing the settlor did not immediately before his death have an interest in possession.

It follows that if an object assigns his rights under a discretionary trust to a third party or becomes bankrupt, the assignee or trustee-in-bankruptcy can be in no better position than the object. Accordingly, the assignee or trustee-in-bankruptcy obtains property at the discretion of the trustees and have no right to demand the income as it arises.

Re Coleman, Henry v Strong (1888) 39 Ch D 443, CA

A testator by his will directed his trustees to pay the income, after the death of his widow, for the maintenance, education and advancement of his children 'in such manner as they shall deem most expedient until the youngest of the children attains the age of 21 years'. At the time of the death of the widow, there were four children, two of whom had attained the age of 21 but the youngest was aged seven years. The trustees shortly afterwards paid each of the adult children one quarter of the income. The eldest son made an absolute assignment for consideration of all his interest under the will to Henry. The trustees declined to pay any funds to Henry who applied to the court for an order requiring the trustees to pay him. He argued that the assignor acquired an interest in possession.

It was held that Henry was entitled to no interest in the income except such sums as were paid to the beneficiary and reduced into possession.

> **Cotton LJ:** I am of the opinion that no child has a right to any share of the income. The trustees have a discretion to apply the income for the maintenance of the children in such manner as they think fit. This excludes the notion of the children being entitled to aliquot shares ... Here no property is given to JS Coleman, but only a discretion to the trustees to apply such part as they think fit of the income for his benefit ...

However, following an assignment of rights to third parties, any income actually paid to the assignor may be claimed by the assignee or trustee-in-bankruptcy in the capacity as a representative of the assignor vis à vis the trust. But a payment in a non-traceable form by the trustees to another, on behalf of the object of the trust, may not be claimed by the assignee or trustee-in-bankruptcy.

Per Cotton LJ in *Re Coleman*:

> Does the assignment include every benefit which the trustees give to JS Coleman out of income? I think not. If the trustees were to pay an hotel-keeper to give him a dinner he would get nothing but the right to eat a dinner, and that is not property which could pass by assignment or bankruptcy, but if they pay or deliver money or goods to him, or appropriate money or goods to be paid or delivered to him, the money or goods would pass by the assignment.

Of course, income legitimately paid to an object in the exercise of the discretion of the trustees becomes the property of the beneficiary as and when the trustees exercise their discretion in his favour. Moreover, it is not true to say that individual objects under a discretionary trust do not have rights under the trust. Each object has the right to be considered to be entitled to the property in the exercise of the discretion of the trustees. In addition, each object has the right to require the trustees to exercise their discretion *bona fide* in a responsible manner and within the limits as laid down by the settlor.

Per Lord Wilberforce in *Gartside v IRC* (1968):

> No doubt in a certain sense a beneficiary under a discretionary trust has an 'interest': the nature of it may, sufficiently for the purpose, be spelt out by saying that he has a right to be considered as a potential recipient of benefit by the trustees and a right to have his interest protected by a court of equity.

Group interest

In respect of the collective interest of the totality of objects under a discretionary trust, there seems to exist a discrepancy regarding their interest in trust law and estate duty law (inheritance tax law). In trust law, if all the objects entitled to both income and capital act in unison and if they are of full age and sound mind, they are entitled to terminate the discretionary trust and acquire the property for their own benefit. This principle is applicable to both exhaustive and non-exhaustive trusts. For example, if trustees hold property on discretionary trust to distribute the income in favour of all or any of a closed group of persons, A, B and C for 21 years and subject thereto the capital is held on trust for D. Provided A, B, C and D are of full age and sound mind and are in agreement, they may terminate the trust.

Similarly, the objects collectively are entitled to assign their interests to a third party. In these circumstances, the third party is entitled to demand the fund from the trustee.

Re Smith, Public Trustee v Aspinall [1928] Ch 915, HC

In this case, a testator gave one quarter of the residue of his estate to trustees on trust to pay, at their absolute discretion, the income for the maintenance of Mrs Aspinall for life and/or all or any of her children. On the death of Mrs Aspinall, the trustees were required to pay both income and capital, including capitalised income, to the children in equal shares. Mrs Aspinall joined with her two surviving children and the personal representative of her deceased child in executing an assignment of their interest in favour of Legal and General Assurance Company in order to secure a mortgage. The question in issue was whether the trustees were required to pay the income as it arose to the company until the discharge of the mortgage or whether they were at liberty to pay the income at their discretion to Mrs Aspinall. It was held that the income was payable to the company because the sole objects of the trust were entitled to dispose of the entire income.

> **Romer J:** What is to happen where the trustees have a discretion whether they will apply the whole or only a portion of the fund for the benefit of one person, but are obliged to apply the rest of the fund, so far as not applied for the benefit of the first named person, to or for the benefit of a second named person? There, two people together are the sole objects of the discretionary trust and, between them, are entitled to have the whole fund applied to them or for their benefit ... you treat all the people put together just as though they formed one person, for whose benefit the trustees were directed to apply the whole of a particular fund.

In estate duty law (the same applies in inheritance tax law), all the objects acting collectively are not treated as owning the trust property. Indeed, the objects are treated as owning individual rights which are in competition with each other as distinct from property rights held jointly or in common.

Per Lord Reid in *Gartside v IRC*:

> Two or more persons cannot have a single right unless they hold it jointly or in common. But clearly objects of a discretionary trust do not have that: they each have individual rights: they are in competition with each other and what the trustees give to one is his alone.

The above statement was made in the context of a non-exhaustive discretionary trust. The same view was echoed in the context of an exhaustive discretionary trust.

Cross J, in *Re Weir's Settlement Trust*, said:

> The objects of a discretionary trust – together, if there is a power of accumulation, with those interested in capital – may no doubt be said to be collectively the persons interested in the income as it accrues before the trustees have decided how to deal with it. But they do not have concurrent interests in the income. They have separate interests in it which are individually unquantifiable though added together they cover the whole ... Even if the trust is exhaustive and there is no power to withhold income, the objects have individual competing interests, not concurrent interests in the income.

Distribution of surplus assets under a pension scheme

A fiduciary power which is exercisable in respect of a pension fund, is sometimes treated as a unique power which cannot be released. The trustees of the pension scheme are required to have regard to the interests of the employees, who are treated as members of the scheme. If the discretionary power is vested in the employer, but which is in liquidation or receivership, the court is required to exercise the power. The reason being that the pension funds are not treated as the assets of the company and, in any event, the liquidator or receiver owes his duties to the creditors.

Mettoy Pension Trustees Ltd v Evans [1990] 1 WLR 1587, HC

Mettoy Co plc launched an occupational pension scheme on 1 January 1968. The plaintiff, a wholly owned subsidiary of Mettoy, became the sole trustee of the scheme. In 1980, with the introduction of new legislation new scheme rules were made. Rule 13(5) provided as follows:

> Any surplus of the trust fund remaining after securing all the aforesaid liabilities in full may, at the absolute discretion of the employer be applied to secure further benefits within the limits stated in the rules, and any further balance thereafter remaining shall be properly apportioned amongst the principal employer and each participating employer.

Mettoy experienced financial difficulties and receivers were appointed in 1983. The company was wound up in 1984. As a consequence, the scheme was required to be liquidated. The plaintiff asked the court for directions in respect of a surplus of funds.

Warner J held that r 13(5) created a fiduciary power which could not be released or exercised by a receiver or liquidator. Accordingly, the court was required to decide what method of exercise would be appropriate.

> **Warner J:** The beneficiaries under a pension scheme such as this are not volunteers. Their rights have contractual and commercial origins. They are derived from the contracts of employment of the members. The benefits provided under the scheme have been earned by the service of the members under those contracts and, where the scheme is contributory, *pro tanto* by their contributions.
>
> It would be inappropriate and indeed perverse to construe such documents so strictly as to undermine their effectiveness or their effectiveness for their purpose. I do not think that, in saying that, I am saying anything different from, what was said by Lord Upjohn when in *In Re Gulbenkian's Settlements*,[34] he referred, in the context of a private settlement, to 'the duty of the court by the exercise of its judicial knowledge and experience in the relevant matter, innate common sense and desire to make sense of the settlor's or parties' expressed intentions, however obscure and ambiguous the language that may

34 [1970] AC 508, p 522.

have been used, to give a reasonable meaning to that language it if can do so without doing complete violence to it.

What the court has to do here is to perform that duty in the comparatively novel and different context of pension scheme trusts. The most important and difficult, though by no means the only, question in this case is as to the validity of the conferment on the employer, by the last paragraph of r 13(5) of the 1983 rules, of the discretion to augment benefits out of surplus.

I turn to para (2) of the originating summons which raises questions about the discretion conferred on the employer by the last paragraph of r 13(5) of the 1983 rules. Logically (though not as the originating summons happens to be framed) the first of those questions is whether that discretion is a fiduciary power. As Mr Walker pointed out, so to express the question is, in a way, to oversimplify it, because there are different kinds of fiduciary power. Mr Walker, in an impartial and helpful way, afforded me a wide-ranging and illuminating discussion of the law about fiduciary powers as it has so far been developed in the context of trusts. It is not necessary for me, for the purpose of deciding this case, to express a view on all the points that Mr Walker made in the course of that discussion.

I am attracted by his submission that the classification of powers into powers simply collateral, powers in gross, and powers appendant or appurtenant, which was set out by Sir George Jessel MR in *Re D'Angibau*,[35] is now of antiquarian interest only. That seems to be the view also of the authors of Megarry and Wade on *The Law of Real Property*.[36] I accept at all events that that classification is of no assistance in deciding the present case. Mr Walker suggested a more pertinent classification, which I accept, of fiduciary discretions into four categories. In this classification, category 1 comprises any power given to a person to determine the destination of trust property without that person being under any obligation to exercise the power or to preserve it. Typical of powers in this category is a special power of appointment given to an individual where there is a trust in default of appointment. In such a case the donee of the power owes a duty to the beneficiaries under that trust not to misuse the power, but he owes no duty to the objects of the power. He may therefore release the power but he may not enter into any transaction that would amount to a fraud on the power, a fraud on the power being a wrong committed against the beneficiaries under the trust in default of appointment: see *Re Mills*[37] and *Re Greaves*.[38] It seems to me to follow that, where the donee of the power is the only person entitled under the trust in default of appointment, the power is not a fiduciary power at all, because then the donee owes no duty to anyone. That was the position in *Re Mills*[39] and will be the position here if the discretion in the last paragraph of r 13(5) of the 1983 rules is in category 1.

35 (1879) 15 Ch D 228, p 232.

36 5th edn, 1984, London: Sweet & Maxwell, p 489.

37 [1930] 1 Ch 654.

38 [1954] Ch 434.

39 [1930] 1 Ch 654.

Category 2 comprises any power conferred on the trustees of the property or on any other person as a trustee of the power itself: *per* Romer LJ, at p 669. I will, as Chitty J did in *Re Somes*,[40] call a power in this category 'a fiduciary power in the full sense'. Mr Walker suggested as an example of such powers vested in persons other than the trustees of the property the powers of the managers of a unit trust. A power in this category cannot be released; the donee of it owes a duty to the objects of the power to consider, as and when may be appropriate, whether and if so how he ought to exercise it; and he is to some extent subject to the control of the courts in relation to its exercise: see, for instance, *Re Abrahams' Will Trusts*;[41] *Re Manisty's Settlement*;[42] and *Re Hay's Settlement Trusts*.[43]

Category 3 comprises any discretion which is really a duty to form a judgment as to the existence or otherwise of particular circumstances giving rise to particular consequences. Into this category fall the discretions that were in question in such cases as *Weller v Ker*;[44] *Dundee General Hospitals Board of Management v Walker*[45] and the two cases reported by LEXIS that I have already mentioned, namely, *Kerr v British Leyland (Staff) Trustees Ltd*[46] and *Mihlenstedt v Barclays Bank International Ltd*.[47]

Category 4 comprises discretionary trusts, that is to say, cases where someone, usually but not necessarily the trustees, is under a duty to select from among a class of beneficiaries those who are to receive, and the proportions in which they are to receive, income or capital of the trust property. Mr Walker urged me to eschew the phrases 'trust power', 'power coupled with a duty', 'power coupled with a trust' and 'power in the nature of a trust', which, as he demonstrated by means of an impressive survey of reported cases, have been variously used to describe discretions in categories 2, 3 and 4.

In the present case the question is whether the discretion given to the employer by the last paragraph of r 13(5) of the 1983 rules is in category 1 or category 2. That depends on whether the words by which that discretion is expressed to be conferred on the employer mean in effect no more than that the employer is free to make gifts out of property of which it is the absolute beneficial owner or whether those words import that the employer is under a duty to the objects of the discretion to consider whether and if so how the discretion ought to be exercised. That is a question of construction of the deed of 1983 in the light of the surrounding circumstances.

40 [1896] 1 Ch 250, p 255.

41 [1969] 1 Ch 463,p 474, *per* Cross J.

42 [1974] Ch 17, p 24, *per* Templeman J.

43 [1982] 1 WLR 202, p 210, *per* Sir Robert Megarry VC.

44 (1866) LR 1 Sc & Div 11.

45 [1952] 1 All ER 896.

46 [1989] IRLR 522.

47 (1989) *The Times*, 18 August; Court of Appeal (Civil Division) Transcript No 817 of 1989.

Mr Nugee placed some reliance on the judgment of Buckley J in *Re Wills' Trust Deeds*.[48] As Mr Walker pointed out, the actual decision in that case probably cannot stand with the later decision of the Court of Appeal in *Muir v IRC*.[49] Mr Walker also criticised Buckley J's reasoning on a number of grounds. I do not find it necessary in this case to express a view on those criticisms. Mr Nugee relied on two passages in Buckley J's judgment. The first was the passage at pp 227–29 where Buckley J suggested that powers fell broadly into two classes, which he termed respectively 'beneficial' and 'vicarious' powers, and pointed to factors that might indicate whether a particular power was in one class or the other. I do not think that that classification is relevant in the present case because it depends essentially on the existence of a settlor and on the ascertainment of his intention in conferring a power on another person: whether his intention was 'to confer a benefit of a kind on the donee' or 'that the donee shall in the exercise of the power act on the settlor's behalf to achieve an end desired by the settlor in respect of which he placed his confidence in the donee of the power'.

Here there is no settlor in the sense in which that expression was used by Buckley J or if, on the dubious ground that the 1986 pension scheme was a 'balance of cost scheme' one treats the employer as the settlor, there is no distinct donee on whom that settlor could have wished to confer a benefit by means of the power or in whom that settlor could have placed its confidence to act on its behalf. On this view the settlor and the donee are the same person. The other passage relied on by Mr Nugee was at pp 236–37, where Buckley J set out the propositions which he considered to be established by the authorities he had cited.

The fifth of those propositions was:

> ... where a power is conferred on someone who is not a trustee of the property to which the power relates or, if he be such a trustee, is not conferred on him in that capacity, then in the absence of a trust in favour of the objects of the power in default of appointment, the donee is, at any rate *prima facie*, not under any duty recognisable by the court to exercise a power such as to disenable him from releasing the power.

Mr Nugee submitted that that proposition applied here. In my view it affords but slender guidance, because I doubt if Buckley J had a case of the present kind in mind and because of his use of the words 'at any rate *prima facie*'.

I have come to the conclusion that the discretion conferred on the employer by the last paragraph of r 13(5) of the 1983 rules is a fiduciary power in the full sense. The considerations that have led me to that conclusion are these. If that discretion is not such a fiduciary power it is, from the point of view of the beneficiaries under the scheme, illusory. As I have pointed out, the words conferring the power mean no more, on that construction of them, than that the employer is free to make gifts to those beneficiaries out of property of which it is the absolute beneficial owner, so that at best those words amount to

48 [1964] Ch 219.

49 [1966] 1 WLR 1269.

what Hutchison J in *El Awadi v Bank of Credit and Commerce International SA Ltd*,[50] called 'a true but pointless assertion'. The *Courage Group* case[51] illustrates one possible consequence of the discretion being of that nature. If the employer were acquired by a takeover raider (to use Millett J's expression in that case) there would be nothing whatever to prevent that raider from rendering itself entitled to the entire surplus ... If, as has happened in this case, the employer should become insolvent, the discretion would inevitably not be exercised, because it would become exercisable on behalf of the employer by someone, be he receiver or liquidator, whose duties to creditors required him to refrain from exercising it. This brings me to consider, parenthetically, the submissions that were made to me on the subsidiary questions raised by para (2) of the originating summons, viz, whether in the events that have happened the discretion is exercisable by the receivers, by the liquidator or by neither.

The exercise of a fiduciary power in the full sense vested in the company cannot be necessary for distributing its assets. Whether it may be necessary for winding up the affairs of the company is less clear. However the liquidator in this case would, as Mr Inglis-Jones submitted, be precluded from exercising the power because, if he did so, he would be in a position where his duties conflicted. As trustee of the power he would be under a duty to hold the balance between the interests of the beneficiaries under the pension scheme and the interests of the persons entitled to share in the assets of the company, namely its creditors and possibly its contributories. As liquidator his duty would be to have regard primarily, if not exclusively, to the interests of the creditors and contributories. His position in that respect would differ from that of the directors of the company while it was a going concern, for they would be able to pay proper regard to the interests of the beneficiaries under the pension scheme and would be concerned to do so if only for the sake of the company's reputation as an employer.

The question then arises, if the discretion is a fiduciary power which cannot be exercised either by the receivers or by the liquidator, who is to exercise it? I heard submissions on that point. The discretion cannot be exercised by the directors of the company, because on the appointment of the liquidator all the powers of the directors ceased. I was referred to a number of authorities on the circumstances in which the court may interfere with or give directions as to the exercise of discretions vested in trustees, namely, *Gisborne v Gisborne*;[52] *Re Hodges*;[53] *Tabor v Brooks*;[54] *Klug v Klug*;[55] *Re Allen-Meyrick's Will Trusts*;[56] *Re Baden's Deed Trusts*;[57] *Re Manisty's Settlement*[58] and *Re Locker's Settlement*.[59]

50 [1990] 1 QB 606, p 617.
51 [1987] 1 WLR 495.
52 (1877) 2 App Cas 300.
53 (1878) 7 Ch D 754.
54 (1878) 10 Ch D 273.
55 [1918] 2 Ch 67.
56 [1966] 1 WLR 499.
57 [1971] AC 424.
58 [1974] Ch 17, pp 25–26.
59 [1977] 1 WLR 1323.

None of those cases deal directly with a situation in which a fiduciary power is left with no one to exercise it. They point however to the conclusion that in that situation the court must step in. Mr Inglis-Jones and Mr Walker urged me to say that in this case the court should step in by giving directions to the trustees as to the distribution of the surplus in the pension fund. They relied in particular on the passage in *Re Baden's Deed Trusts*,[60] where Lord Wilberforce said:

> As to powers, I agree with my noble and learned friend Lord Upjohn in *Re Gulbenkian's Settlements*[61] that although the trustees may, and normally will, be under a fiduciary duty to consider whether or in what way they should exercise their power, the court will not normally compel its exercise. It will intervene if the trustees exceed their powers, and possibly if they are proved to have exercised it capriciously. But in the case of a trust power, if the trustees do not exercise it, the court will: I respectfully adopt as to this, the statement in Lord Upjohn's opinion (p 525). I would venture to amplify this by saying that the court, if called upon to execute the trust power, will do so in the manner best calculated to give effect to the settlor's or testator's intentions. It may do so by appointing new trustees, or by authorising or directing representative persons of the classes of beneficiaries to prepare a scheme of distribution, or even, should the proper basis for distribution appear by itself directing the trustees so to distribute. The books give many instances where this has been done, and I see no reason in principle why they should not do so in the modern field of discretionary trust.

Clearly, in the first two sentences of that passage, Lord Wilberforce was referring to a discretion in category 2 and in the following part of it to a discretion in category 4. In that latter part he was indicating how the court might give effect to a discretionary trust when called on to execute it. It seems to me, however, that the methods he indicated could be equally appropriate in a case where the court was called on to intervene in the exercise of a discretion in category 2. In saying that, I do not overlook that, in *Re Manisty's Settlement*,[62] Templeman J expressed the view that the only right and the only remedy of an object of the power who was aggrieved by the trustees' conduct would be to apply to the court to remove the trustees and appoint others in their place. However, the earlier authorities to which I was referred, such as *Re Hodges*[63] and *Klug v Klug*,[64] had not been cited to Templeman J. I conclude that, in a situation such as this, it is open to the court to adopt whichever of the methods indicated by Lord Wilberforce appears most appropriate in the circumstances.

60 [1971] AC 424, pp 456, 457.

61 [1970] AC 508.

62 [1974] Ch 17, p 25.

63 (1878) 7 Ch D 754.

64 [1918] 2 Ch 67.

SUPPLEMENTARY READING

Emery, C, 'The most hallowed principle – certainty of beneficiaries in trusts and powers of appointment' (1982) 98 LQR 551

Gardner, S, 'Fiduciary powers in Toytown' (1991) 107 LQR 214

Grbich, Y, '*Baden*: awakening the conceptually moribund trust' (1974) 37 MLR 643

Grubb, A, 'Powers, trusts and classes of objects – *Re Hay's Settlement*' [1982] Conv 432

Harris, J, 'Trust, power and duty' (1971) 87 LQR 31

Martin, J, 'Casenote on *Mettoy v Pension Trustees Ltd*' [1991] Conv 364

Sheridan, L, 'Discretionary trusts' (1957) 21 Conv 55

CHAPTER 7

PROTECTIVE TRUSTS

It is self-evident that an incident of the trust relationship is that the beneficiary becomes the owner of the equitable interest. Subject to provisions to the contrary this equitable interest is subject to the vicissitudes of the beneficiary which may result in a misapplication of the interest and, should the beneficiary become bankrupt, the interest may be subject to the claims of the creditors.

For example, S, a settlor transfers 2,000 shares to T(1) and T(2) to hold on trust for B, aged 20, absolutely. B may sell or otherwise dispose of his interest and dissipate the proceeds of sale or may incur debts to such an extent that the trust property will be available for distribution to creditors.

In order to safeguard the trust property from a prodigal beneficiary, the settlor has a variety of options available to him. He may create the following:

(1) a discretionary trust in favour of a class of objects including the intended beneficiary;

(2) a determinable interest in favour of the beneficiary;

(3) a protective trust under s 33 of the Trustee Act 1925 in favour of the intended beneficiary.

DISCRETIONARY TRUST

This topic was examined earlier (see above, p 145), but pertinent issues in this context are the nature of the interest of an object under a discretionary trust, the fiduciary nature of the trustees' discretion, the creation of a non-exhaustive discretionary trust, the effect of an assignment of rights under a discretionary trust and the consequence of being a sole object of a discretionary trust.

Determinable interest

A determinable interest is an estate which *prima facie* is treated as an estate less than an absolute interest in property and denotes the event or events which will determine the interest. On the occurrence of the determining event, the interest ceases or becomes void automatically. There is no need for the settlor or any other person to take steps to enforce the limitation. If no gift over is specified by the draftsman, the settlor would become entitled to the interest by way of a resulting trust but it is customary for the settlor to indicate in whose favour the gift over will take effect.

For example, S may settle a fund on B for life until he attempts to alienate the interest or becomes bankrupt, with remainder to C absolutely. In this case, a determinable life interest is created in favour of B with a gift over for the benefit of C. If B attempts to alienate his interest, his right of enjoyment terminates automatically and C acquires the absolute interest. Likewise, if B becomes bankrupt, his trustees in bankruptcy acquire nothing in respect of the trust property because B's interest terminates immediately and the gift over takes effect.

The settlor ought to be wary about creating an interest subject to a condition subsequent as opposed to a determinable interest. The distinction is subtle but significant. A conditional interest is *prima facie* an absolute interest which is reduced by an event (or events) that has (or have) the effect of terminating the interest. When the relevant condition(s) is (are) satisfied, the interest becomes voidable (as opposed to a determinable interest) and positive steps are required to avoid the interest. Another distinction between a conditional and a determinable interest is that, if the limitation specified in a conditional interest is void (such as being contrary to public policy), the interest takes effect as if the limitation had not been imposed. Thus, the beneficiary may acquire an absolute life interest. Whereas if the limitation imposed on a determinable interest is treated as void, the interest or estate fails altogether. The intended beneficiary would not acquire an interest. Expressions such as 'on condition that' and provided that' have been construed as creating a conditional interest but words like 'until', 'so long as', 'whilst' or 'during' create determinable interests.

Brandon v Robinson (1811) 18 Ves 429, HL

> **Lord Eldon:** There is no doubt that property may be given to a man until he shall become bankrupt. It is equally clear, generally speaking, that if property is given to a man for his life, the donor cannot take away the incidents to a life estate; and as I have observed, a disposition to a man, until he shall become bankrupt, and after his bankruptcy over, is quite different from an attempt to give to him for his life, with a proviso that he shall not sell or alienate it. If that condition is so expressed as to amount to a limitation, reducing the interest short of a life interest, neither the man nor his assignees can have it beyond the period limited.

In *Brandon v Robinson*, a testator transferred property by will on trust for sale for his children in equal shares. He directed that the share of his son, Thomas, be invested and the income paid to him 'provided that' the income shall not be grantable, assignable or otherwise transferable with a remainder on such occasion. Thomas subsequently became bankrupt. The assignee in bankruptcy claimed the interest on the grounds that a conditional interest was created and the condition was void as against the trustee-in-bankruptcy. The effect was that the interest became absolute and the creditors were entitled. The court held in favour of the trustee in bankruptcy.

Contrast *Rochford v Hackman*.

Rochford v Hackman (1852) 21 LJ Ch 511, HC

In this case, the testator had bequeathed property to trustees to pay the income to the testator's wife for life, with remainder on trust to pay a fourth share of the income to his eldest son for life with remainder to that son's children subject to the direction 'that in case my said wife or any of my said children shall in any manner sell, assign or transfer his or their share in the said dividends, the bequest shall cease as if the same had not been mentioned and as if such person or persons were dead. After the testator's wife's death, the eldest son became bankrupt. The trustee-in-bankruptcy claimed the son's share. It was held that a determinable interest was created with a valid gift over. The direction in the will operated to determine the son's life interest automatically on his insolvency. The gift over took effect with the result that the trustee-in-bankruptcy became entitled to nothing because the eldest son's share was transferred to his two children.

> **Turner VC:** The court has to collect the intention of the testator from the whole will, looking at the primary disposition for the purpose of seeing to what extent the interest is given and to the ulterior disposition for the purpose of seeing to what extent and in what events the primary disposition is defeated. If there is a limitation over and it meets the events which have occurred, it is plain that the testator did not intend the life interest to continue in that event and it ceases accordingly, but if the limitation over does not meet the events which have occurred, the life interest continues in that event. I am of the opinion that the testator has been made a valid gift over on a determinable event.

Although a determinable limitation may be imposed in the event of a beneficiary becoming bankrupt, a settlor is not entitled to create a determinable interest for himself for life until bankruptcy *simpliciter* with a remainder over on such occasion. Such a clause is not void *ab initio* but is voidable against the trustee-in-bankruptcy. Accordingly, if the settlor purports to create such an interest and becomes bankrupt his interest will vest in his trustee-in-bankruptcy and will accrue for the benefit of his creditors.

Re Burroughs-Fowler [1916] 2 Ch 251, HC

In this case, a settlor created an ante-nuptial settlement under which be received the income from the trust property for life or until bankruptcy or had suffered to do anything whereby the income or any part of it became payable to another with a gift over to his wife for life. He was later adjudicated bankrupt. It was held that, although a determinable interest had been created, the determining limitation was void as against the trustee-in-bankruptcy. Accordingly, the settlor's life interest became vested in the trustee-in-bankruptcy.

But, if the circumstances were such that a determinable event other than bankruptcy occurs allowing the gift over to take effect prior to the bankruptcy of the settlor (beneficiary), the interest will vest in the persons entitled in remainder. The result will be that the trustee-in-bankruptcy is excluded *Re Detmold*.[1]

***Re Detmold* (1889) 40 Ch D 585, HC**

In this case, a settlor created a marriage settlement, dated 24 August 1881, under which he transferred a quantity of shares on trust to pay the income to himself 'during his life or until he shall become bankrupt or assign or charge the said income or shall do something whereby the same or some part thereof, would, through his act, default or by operation of law become vested in or payable to some other person or persons' with a gift over on trust to pay the income to his wife during her life. On 19 July 1988, a creditor of the husband obtained an order appointing himself 'receiver' of the income arising under the settlement. On a subsequent date, the settlor was declared bankrupt. It was held that on the appointment the settlor had done an act (involuntarily) which, by operation of law, had the effect of attempting to alienate his interest. The result was that since the determining event occurred the gift over took effect and the income became payable to the wife of the settlor. The subsequent bankruptcy of the settlor came later in time, accordingly, the trustee in bankruptcy was not entitled to the income from the trust.

> **North J:** Under the trusts of this settlement, the wife is clearly entitled to the income, if the prior life interest given to the husband has legally come to an end. In my opinion, the appointment of a receiver by the order of 19 July established that the husband had done something whereby the income of the trust fund or part thereof, would, through his act, default or operation of law become vested in or payable to some other person. The trustee-in-bankruptcy is also bound by that order. Before the date of the bankruptcy the husband has done an act by which the right to receive the income had become vested in another person and therefore the gift over in favour of the wife had taken effect.

Protective trust under s 33 of the Trustee Act 1925

A protective trust under s 33 involves a determinable life interest in favour of the principal beneficiary and, in the event of a termination or forfeiture of the interest taking place, the establishment of a discretionary trust of the income in favour of a class of objects including the principal beneficiary, his or her spouse and issue. But, if the principal beneficiary has no spouse or issue, the capital and income will be held on discretionary trust in favour of the

1 (1889) 40 Ch D 585.

principal beneficiary and his or her next of kin. This 'ready made' protective trust exists as a device to obviate the risk to the settlor of inadvertently creating a conditional interest instead of a determinable interest. It is unnecessary for the settlor to set out the details of the trust. All that is required is that the settlor manifest an intention to create a protective trust. The model trust under s 33 will be adopted, see *Re Wittke*.[2] In this case, a testatrix directed that specified property be held on 'protective trust' for the benefit of his sister. The court decided that this reference was sufficient to incorporate the protective trust under s 33 of the Trustee Act 1925.

In any event, the settlor is entitled to set up his express protective trust incorporating as much detail as he considers appropriate. Furthermore, s 33(2) entitles the settlor to adopt any variation of the structure of the protective trust as laid down in s 33(1).

For example, the settlor may incorporate the s 33 trust, but exclude the discretionary trust that arises when the forfeiture event takes place and substitute a remainder interest of both capital and income in favour of the principal beneficiary's issue, or failing issue his next of kin.

Section 33(3) enacts what would have been implied in any event, namely, that s 33 does not validate any provision which would be liable to be set aside. Accordingly a determinable life interest in favour of the settlor is void as against his trustee-in-bankruptcy. See *Re Burroughs-Fowler* (1916) (above, p 217).

Determining events (forfeiture)

Section 33(1)(i) adopts a broad formula for ascertaining the time when the life interest will be determined, namely:

> when the principal beneficiary does or attempts to do or suffers any act or thing, or until any event happens, other than an advance under any statutory or express power, whereby, if the said income were payable during the trust period to the principal beneficiary ... he would be deprived of the right to receive the same on any part thereof ...

It is to be noted that an advancement under an express or statutory power (s 32 of the Trustee Act 1925) is excluded from the forfeiting events. An advancement involves the provision of an enduring benefit on behalf of a beneficiary such as the provision of a house or the setting up of a business.

The burden of proving a forfeiture lies on any party who claims that a determining event has taken place. In this respect, the principal beneficiary may rely on a presumption that the forfeiting event has not taken place until the contrary is proved to the satisfaction of the court.

The formula not only includes the acts or omissions of the principal beneficiary but also circumstances outside his control which deprive him of

2 [1944] Ch 166.

the right to receive the income under the trust. Accordingly, the purported sale, gift or other disposition by the principal beneficiary of his interest, as well as his bankruptcy have the effect of activating the determining event. In addition an involuntary transfer of the life interest to another may cause a forfeiture of the beneficial interest see *Re Gourju's Will Trust*.[3] In this case, a testator instructed his trustees by his will to hold the income of his residuary estate under a s 33 protective trust for his widow for life. The widow, an English national, became marooned in German occupied Nice and France and was regarded as an 'enemy' under the provisions of the Trading With the Enemy Act 1939 and orders made thereunder. The effect was that income which was payable to an 'enemy' became payable to the Custodian of Enemy Property and the initial payee lost all rights to that money. The question in issue was whether this event amounted to a forfeiture of the principal beneficiary's interest. The court held that an event had happened which deprived the widow of the right to receive the income and determined her life interest. Thus, the income which had accrued before the event but remained unpaid to the widow became payable to the Custodian of Enemy Property, but the income which accrued after the event was to be held on a discretionary trust for the benefit of the specified objects.

The court came to a different conclusion in *Re Hall*[4] where under an express protective trust, La Comtesse de Prahas was bequeathed an annuity which was liable to forfeiture if she alienated her annuity or became bankrupt or suffered any act whereby the annuity became payable to another. The Countess was a French national who lived in France but was regarded as an 'enemy' under the 1939 Act.

The court held that no forfeiture had occurred because on construction of the clause positive acts done by the annuitant were capable in the circumstances of causing the forfeiting event to take place. The annuitant had simply lived in France which was the natural thing for a French national to do. The fact that she remained there when the war had started was not an event contemplated by the clause. The decision would have been different had she been a British national who remained in France at the relevant time.

Other examples of forfeiting events are:

Re Balfour's Settlement[5] – the impounding by trustees of part of the income of the principal beneficiary in order to repair a breach of trust instigated by the beneficiary prior to the date of bankruptcy of the beneficiary.

3 [1943] Ch 24.

4 [1944] Ch 46.

5 [1938] Ch 928.

Re Baring's Settlement Trust[6] – a sequestration order against the beneficiary following her failure to obey a court order to return her infant children to the jurisdiction of the court.

Re Dennis's Settlement Trusts[7] – the execution of a deed of variation releasing the principal beneficiary's right to part of the income. It seems that there is forfeiture if a representative of the principal beneficiary is appointed in order to look after the beneficiary's interests as opposed to a transfer of property to a representative for the benefit of another *Re Oppenheim's Will Trusts*[8] – the appointment of a receiver to handle the affairs of the beneficiary who was certified as a person of unsound mind did not cause a forfeiture.

> **Harman J:** It seems to me that the forfeiture was not intended to operate in a case of this kind where no one else will be entitled to the benefit of the income in the event which has happened. It was intended to prevent the income from getting into other hands.

Likewise, fees paid to the receiver who was appointed in order to represent the interests of a person of unsound mind did not cause a forfeiture. See *Re Westby's Settlement*.[9]

Section 57 of the Trustee Act 1925 and forfeiture

Section 57 of the Trustee Act 1925 empowers the court to authorise the trustees to perform any act connected with the management and administration of the trust which is not authorised by the trust instrument (such as any sale, lease, mortgage, surrender, release or other disposition, or any purchase, investment, acquisition, expenditure or other transaction) if the court considers it expedient to do so. In the exercise of its power the court is required to have regard to the interests of all the beneficiaries under the trust as opposed to any individual beneficiary.

The section has been considered by the courts as though it has been inserted into every trust with the effect that if the court orders the trustees to mortgage the principal beneficiary's interest in order to discharge certain pressing liabilities, this event by itself would not cause a forfeiture. See *Re Mair*[10] *per* Farwell J:

> If and when the court sanctions an arrangement or transaction under s 57, it must be taken to have done it as though the power which is being put into operation had been inserted in the trust instrument as an overriding power ... the forfeiture clause remains attached to the income which is payable to the tenant for life from time to time.

6 [1940] Ch 737.

7 [1942] Ch 283.

8 [1950] Ch 633.

9 [1950] Ch 296.

10 [1935] Ch 562.

On the other hand, if a scheme is sanctioned by the court and the principal beneficiary fails to comply with the scheme this omission, by itself, will amount to a forfeiture of the life tenant's interest. See *Re Salting*.[11]

Series of protective trusts

In order to avoid condemning a beneficiary to a discretionary class of objects for the rest of his life because of an indiscretion during his youth, it is possible to create a series of protective trusts at various stages in the beneficiary's life, for example, one set until the beneficiary is 25, another from 25 to 35, a third from 35 to 45 and another for the rest of his life. The effect would be that an indiscretion would not irretrievably condemn the beneficiary to an expectation under a discretionary trust for the rest of his life but would give him a fresh start on the date of the next protective trust. This policy was adopted in *Re Richardson's Will Trusts*.

Re Richardson's Will Trusts [1958] Ch 504, HC

In this case, a testator bequeathed £2,000 to trustees to hold the income on a s 33 protective trust for the benefit of his grandson, Douglas William Evans until he reached the age of 35. If, on attaining that age, the grandson had not attempted to do or suffer any act or thing whereby he became deprived of the right to receive all or part of the income or capital, he would become entitled to the capital absolutely. If, on the other hand, he had made such attempt or sufferance or such event had happened then he was to receive the income on protective trusts for the rest of his life. Before the grandson attained 35, he became divorced from his wife and an order was made by the court charging his interest with an annual payment of £50 for the benefit of his ex-wife. The grandson reached the age of 35 and 10 months later was adjudicated bankrupt. The trustee-in-bankruptcy claimed the income from the trust fund. The court held that: (a) the maintenance order caused a forfeiture of the beneficiary's interest; (b) as a consequence of the forfeiture the trustees held the income on the second set of protective trust. Accordingly, the act of bankruptcy created a second forfeiture of the income with the result that the discretionary trust was set up. The trustee-in-bankruptcy received nothing from the trust.

> **Danckwerts J:** It seems to me that the effect of the order was to create, or attempt to create, an equitable charge on his interest under the testator's will. When this order was made, if he had been absolutely entitled, he would have been deprived of the right to receive part of the income, because part of the income was to be payable to his former wife to the extent of £50 a year. Consequently, it seems to me that there was a forfeiture at that date; but in any

11 [1932] 2 Ch 57.

> case under the express terms of the will he never succeeded in attaining his absolute interest, and the protective trusts which were to take effect during the rest of his life in accordance with s 33 Trustee Act 1925 came into effect because the direction was, if such event had happened, that the protective trusts were to come into effect. Consequently, I have come to the conclusion that, in the events which have happened in this case, by the time that Douglas William Evans became bankrupt his interest under the will had been forfeited, and a discretionary trust had come into effect. Consequently, the trustee-in-bankruptcy cannot take anything under the testator's will.

However, in the subsequent case, *General Accident Fire and Life Assurance Corporation v IRC*,[12] the Court of Appeal decided that a matrimonial order diverting part of the income belonging to the principal beneficiary in favour of his divorced wife did not cause a forfeiture because such trusts are deemed to be subject to the order of the court. Although the *General Accident* case has cast some doubt on the *ratio* of *Re Richardson*, it seems that the technique adopted in the latter case is sound and may be explored by draftsmen.

Consequences of forfeiture

Under s 33 of the Trustee Act 1925 on the occasion of the forfeiture of the principal beneficiary's interest, a discretionary trust is set up in favour of the principal beneficiary and spouse and issue. If there is no spouse or issue, the class will include the beneficiary's next of kin. It appears that the discretionary trust is of an exhaustive nature, that is, the trustees are required to distribute the income in favour of the objects. Thus, the trustees have no power to accumulate the income. See *Re Gourju's Will Trust*. But, the trustees are not required to distribute the income in favour of the principal beneficiary although they may in the exercise of their discretion distribute to any one or more of the objects. If the trustees distribute income in favour of the principal beneficiary, such funds (*Re Coleman*)[13] or the surplus, beyond that which is needed for his support (*Re Ashby*)[14] may be claimed by the trustee-in-bankruptcy.

Moreover, all the objects of the discretionary trust if they are *sui juris* and absolutely entitled to the trust property may get together and terminate the trust or assign the trust property to another. See *Re Smith, Public Trustee v Aspinall*.[15]

12 [1963] 1 WLR 1207.
13 (1888) 39 Ch D 433.
14 [1892] 1 QB 872.
15 [1928] Ch 915.

VOIDABLE TRUSTS

A voidable trust is one which may be set aside in limited circumstances. In this context, a number of provisions have been enacted which have the effect of upsetting trusts, that is, frustrating the attempts of settlors transferring property beyond the reach of claimants.

But, for special provisions to the contrary, a settlor who was about to undertake some hazardous venture would have been entitled to transfer property to his wife and/or children in order to prevent his property being claimed by creditors.

There are a number of provisions which have the effect of making such trusts voidable.

Bankruptcy provisions: ss 339–42 of the Insolvency Act 1986

The policy of these provisions is to empower the trustee in bankruptcy of a settlor to recover trust property on behalf of the creditors.

Transactions at an undervalue

Section 339 of the Insolvency Act 1986 enables the trustee in bankruptcy to apply to the court for relief where a person is adjudicated bankrupt, but during the five years before the presentation of the petition he had entered into a transaction at an undervalue.

A transaction is at an undervalue if:

(a) it is a gift by the bankrupt; or

(b) the bankrupt received no consideration; or

(c) the bankrupt entered into the transaction in consideration of marriage; or

(d) the bankrupt received consideration which, in money or money's worth, was significantly less in value than that provided by the bankrupt.

Thus, the creation of a trust (by way of a gratuitous transfer of property to trustees) in favour of the settlor's children within one year of the presentation of a petition of bankruptcy, may be set aside by the trustee in bankruptcy.

The mental state of the bankrupt need not be proved.

Preference of creditors: s 340 of the Insolvency Act 1986

Where an individual is adjudicated bankrupt but has given a preference to a creditor, surety or guarantor within specified time limits, the trustee-in-bankruptcy may apply to the court for relief.

A transaction is a preference if a debtor:

(a) does anything or suffers anything to be done that has the effect of putting a creditor, surety or guarantor for any of the debts or liabilities into a position which, in the event of his bankruptcy, will be better than if that thing had not been done or suffered; and

(b) was insolvent at the time; and

(c) was influenced by a desire to produce the effect of putting such creditor, etc, into a better position.

A person is insolvent if he cannot from his own resources meet his debts and liabilities as they fall due or if the value of his assets is less than the amount of his liabilities taking into account protective and contingent liabilities (s 341(3)).

A preferential transaction in favour of an associate of the bankrupt is presumed to be influenced by a desire of putting such creditor into a better position until the contrary is proved (s 340(5)).

An associate is exhaustively defined in s 435 and includes relatives of the bankrupt or spouse, as well as partners, employers, employees and related companies.

The time limits are defined in s 341 – in the case of a preference with a non-associate and not at an undervalue the period is six months. But, in the case of a preference in favour of an associate, the period is two years before the petition of bankruptcy.

For example, if an insolvent debtor arranges with a creditor to give effect to a judgment debt in order to give the creditor the benefit of a charge over the debtor's assets conferred by enforcement proceedings, the transaction is capable of being construed as an actionable preference.

In respect of proceedings under ss 339 and 340, the court may make such order as it thinks fit for restoring the position to what it would have been if the bankrupt had not entered the transaction. But, the court's power of redress does not affect two categories of third parties, namely:

(i) any *bona fide* transferee for value without notice of the relevant circumstances who acquires the property from another but who in turn acquired such property as a party to the undervalue or preference; and

(ii) any person receiving a benefit in good faith for value without notice of the relevant circumstances.

Transactions defrauding creditors: ss 423–25 of the Insolvency Act 1986

The policy of these sections is designed to upset transactions at an undervalue for the purpose:

(a) of putting assets beyond the reach of a person who is making, or may at some time make, a claim against him; or

(b) of otherwise prejudicing the interests of such a person in relation to the claim which he is making or may make.

The section is wider than s 339 in the sense that there is no time limit (such as five years before the presentation of the bankruptcy petition) attaching to the transactions which may be upset. In addition the claim for relief is not dependent on the solvency of the party entering into the impugned transaction. But, s 423 is subject to the limitation that the transaction entered into must have been at an undervalue. Thus, the court has no jurisdiction if the transaction was entered into for valuable and adequate consideration even if the transferee is aware that it was entered into with the intention of prejudicing the interest of creditors.

The court is entitled to make such order as it thinks fit for:

(i) restoring the position to what it would have been if the transaction had not been entered into; and

(ii) protecting the interests of persons who are victims of the transaction.

The creation of a tenancy of a farm in favour of the wife of the transferor in order to defeat the claims of creditors, will be set aside at the instance of the creditors.

Agricultural Mortgage Corporation plc v Woodward and Another (1994) *The Times*, 30 May, CA

The first defendant was a farmer who borrowed £700,000 from the plaintiff on the security of his farm. When the first defendant fell into arrears, the plaintiff gave him a deadline for the arrears to be cleared. Shortly before the deadline expired, the farmer signed a tenancy agreement with his wife, the second defendant. The effect of the agreement was that the farmer made his wife a tenant of the mortgaged farm at an annual rent of £37,250. The plaintiff claimed that this agreement ought to be set aside by the court for it was a transaction within s 423 of the Insolvency Act 1986. This section relates to

(1) ... transactions entered into at an undervalue; and a person enters into such a transaction with another person if:

  (a) ...

  (b) ...

  (c) he enters into a transaction with the other for a consideration the value of which, in money or money's worth, is significantly less than the value, in money or money's worth, of the consideration provided by himself.

(2) Where a person has entered into such transaction, the court may ... make such order as it thinks fit for:

(a) restoring the position to what it would have been if the transaction had not been entered into; and

(b) protecting the interests of persons who are victims of the transaction.

(3) In the case of a person entering into such a transaction, an order shall only be made if the court is satisfied that it was entered into by him for the purpose:

(a) of putting assets beyond the reach of a person who is making, or may at some time make, a claim against him; or

(b) of otherwise prejudicing the interests of such a person in relation to the claim which he is making or may make.

Section 436 of the 1986 Act defines a 'transaction' as 'including a gift, agreement or arrangement ...'.

The plaintiff alleged that, taking the transactions as a whole, the annual rent payable by the second defendant under the tenancy agreement was significantly less than the market rent. The tenancy, if effective, gave the wife three valuable benefits, namely: (i) safeguarding the family home; (ii) enabling her to acquire and carry on the family farming business; and (iii) a surrender value in respect of the farm. In its proper context, the transaction plainly conferred, and was intended to confer, on her significant enhanced benefits beyond the rights granted by the tenancy agreement itself, for which enhanced benefits she did not pay.

The defendants argued that the annual rent, considered in isolation, represented the full market rent. The alleged threefold benefits relied on by the plaintiff were irrelevant. These would all be available to any person who took a tenancy of the farm.

The Court of Appeal allowed the appeal, decided in favour of the plaintiff and set aside the agreement under s 423(1)(c). The tenancy agreement could not be considered in blinkers. When the transactions were viewed as a whole, the benefits which the farmer attempted to confer on his wife were significantly greater in value, in money or money's worth, than the value of the consideration provided by her. To hold otherwise would fly in the face of reality and common sense.

SUPPLEMENTARY READING

Furey, N, 'Bankruptcy and the family – the effect of the Insolvency Act 1986' (1987) 17 Family Law 316

Potterton, R and Cullen, S, 'Transactions at an undervalue' (1994) 138 SJ 710

Williams, G, 'The doctrine of repugnancy – conditions in gifts' (1943) 59 LQR 343

CHAPTER 8

RESULTING TRUSTS

AXIOMATIC

An express trust arises out of the settlor's or testator's express intention. As we have seen, subject to any formalities imposed by statute, this intention may be expressed wholly or partly, orally or by conduct or in writing. In order to ascertain the terms of the trust (such as the beneficiaries and their interests, the trust property and the trustees) the court is required to construe the evidence which manifests the intention of the creator of the trust.

By way of contrast, a resulting trust is implied by equity in favour of the settlor or his estate, if he is dead. Such trust arises by virtue of the unexpressed or implied intention of the settlor or testator. The settlor or his estate becomes the beneficial owner under the resulting trust. It is as though the settlor had retained a residual interest in the property, albeit implied or created by the courts. The expression, 'resulting trust', derives from the Latin verb, *resultare* meaning to spring back (in effect, to the original owner). Examples are the transfer of property subject to a condition precedent which cannot be achieved, or the creation of an express trust which becomes void. In these circumstances the legal owner or transferee holds the property on trust for the settlor or his estate. See *Vandervell v IRC*.

Re Vandervell's Trusts (No 2) [1974] 1 All ER 47, HC

Megarry J classified resulting trusts into two categories, namely, 'automatic' and 'presumed' (although his decision was reversed by the Court of Appeal). Automatic resulting trusts arise where the beneficial interest under an express trust remains undisposed of. Such trusts arise in order to fill a gap of ownership. The equitable or beneficial interest cannot exist in the air and ought to remain with the settlor. The 'presumed' resulting trust arises, in the absence of evidence to the contrary, when property is purchased in the name of another, or property is voluntarily transferred to another, for example, A purchases property which is conveyed in the name of B, or A transfers property to B. In these circumstances, B *prima facie* holds the property on trust for A.

> **Megarry J:** It seems to me that the relevant points on resulting trusts may be put in a series of propositions ... The propositions are the broadest generalisations, and do not purport to cover the exceptions and qualifications that doubtless exist. Nevertheless, these generalisations at least provide a

starting point for the classification of a corner of equity which might benefit from some attempt at classification. The propositions are as follows:

(1) if a transaction fails to make any effective disposition of any interest it does nothing. This is so at law and in equity, and has nothing to do with resulting trusts;

(2) normally the mere existence of some unexpressed intention in the breast of the owner of the property does nothing: there must at least be some expression of that intention before it can effect any result. To yearn is not to transfer;

(3) before any doctrine of resulting trust can come into play, there must at least be some effective transaction which transfers or creates some interest in property;

(4) where A effectually transfers to B (or creates in his favour) any interest in any property, whether legal or equitable, a resulting trust for A may arise in two distinct classes of case. For simplicity, I shall confine my statement to cases in which the transfer or creation is made without B providing any valuable consideration, and where no presumption of advancement can arise; and I shall state the position for transfers without specific mention of new interests:

   (a) the first class of case is where the transfer to B is not made on any trust. If, of course, it appears from the transfer that B is intended to hold on certain trusts, that will be decisive, and the case is not within this category; and similarly if it appears that B is intended to take beneficially. But in other cases there is a rebuttable presumption that B holds on a resulting for A. The question is not one of the automatic consequences of a dispositive failure by A, but one of presumption: the property has been carried to B, and from the absence of consideration and any presumption of advancement, B is presumed not only to hold the entire interest on trust, but also to hold the beneficial interest for A absolutely. The presumption thus establishes both that B is to take on trust and also what that trust is. Such resulting trust may be called 'presumed resulting trusts';

   (b) the second class of case is where the transfer to B is made on trusts which some or all of the beneficial interest undisposed of. Here B automatically holds on resulting trust for A to the extent that the beneficial interest has not been carried to him or others. The resulting trust here does not depend on any intentions or presumptions, but is the automatic consequence of A's failure to dispose of what is vested in him. Since *ex hypothesi* the transfer is on trust, the resulting trust does not establish the trust but merely carries back to A the beneficial interest that has not been disposed of. Such resulting trusts may be called 'automatic resulting trusts';

(5) where trustees hold property in trust for A, and it is they who, at A's direction, make the transfer to B, similar principles apply, even though on the face of the transaction the transferor appears to be the trustee and not A. If the transfer to B is on trust, B will hold any beneficial interest that has

> not been effectually disposed of on an automatic resulting trust for the true transferor, A. If the transfer to B is not on trust, there will be a rebuttable presumption that B holds on a resulting trust for A.

AUTOMATIC RESULTING TRUSTS

The policy which underpins this type of resulting trust involves the destination of the beneficial interest when the instrument creating the trust is silent as to the application of the equitable interest. The resulting trust arises in a variety of situations such as the failure of an express trust, or the transfer of property to trustees without specifying the terms of the trust, or the transfer of property is made subject to a condition precedent which is incapable of being fulfilled, or where the trust exhausts only some of the trust property. Indeed, it may be possible to classify the occasions which give rise to an automatic resulting trust into two categories, namely:

(a) failure of an express trust; and

(b) the destination of a surplus of trust funds.

Failure of an express trust

Where the transfer of property is made subject to a condition precedent which has not been achieved, the transferee is required to re-transfer the property back to the original owner. This result is based on the assumption that the foundation on which the transfer or trust was made, did not materialise. The transferee is treated as a trustee on behalf of the original transferor or his estate.

Re Ames' Settlement [1946] Ch 217, HC

In this case, a settlor transferred £10,000 to trustees in consideration of the marriage of his son on trust for the parties to the marriage for life with remainder to the issue of the marriage absolutely. The marriage ceremony was a nullity for the son was already validly married. The court held that a resulting trust for the settlor's estate had arisen.

> **Vaisey J:** It seems to me that the claim of the executors of the settlor must succeed. I think that the case is, having regard to the wording of the settlement, a simple case of money paid on a consideration which failed. I do not think that that hypothetical class of next of kin (who were only brought in, so to speak, and given an interest in the fund on the basis and footing that there was going to be a valid marriage between John Ames and Miss Hamilton) have really any merits in equity, and I do not see how they can claim under the express terms of a document which, so far as regards the persons with whom the marriage consideration was concerned, has utterly and completely failed. If

their claim be good, it is difficult to see at what precise period of time their interest became an interest in possession. But I hold that their claim is not good, and that they have not been able to establish it.

Similarly, where funds are paid to a borrower in order to advance a specific purpose, to such an extent that the funds do not become the general property of the borrower, and the object of the loan has not been achieved, the funds become subject to a resulting trust in favour of the lender. Accordingly, the borrower's trustee-in-bankruptcy or assignee of the debtor, with notice of the stipulated purpose, take the property subject to the trust.

Barclays Bank Ltd v Quistclose Investments Ltd [1970] AC 56, HL

The defendant, Quistclose Ltd, loaned £209,719 to Rolls Razors Ltd on the agreed condition that the latter would use the money to pay a dividend to its shareholders. Q Ltd's cheque for the relevant sum was sent to R Ltd with a covering letter dated 15 July 1964 which reiterated the purpose of the loan thus, 'We would like to confirm the agreement reached with you this morning that this amount will only be used to meet the dividend due'. Q Ltd's cheque was paid into a separate account opened specifically for this purpose with Barclays Bank Ltd which knew of the purpose of the loan.

Before the dividend was paid, R Ltd went into voluntary liquidation and Barclays Ltd claimed to use the amount to set off against the overdrafts of Rolls Ltd's other account at the bank.

The House of Lords held that the terms of the loan were such as to impress on the money a trust in favour of Q Ltd in the event of the dividend not being paid and since Barclays had notice of the nature of the loan it was not entitled to set off the amount against R Ltd's overdraft.

Lord Wilberforce: Two questions arise, both of which must be answered favourably to the respondents if they are to recover the money from the appellants. The first is whether, as between the respondents and Rolls Razor Ltd, the terms on which the loan was made were such as to impress on the sum of £209,719 a trust in their favour in the event of the dividend not being paid. The second is whether, in that event, the appellants had such notice of the trust or of the circumstances giving rise to it as to make the trust binding on them.

It is not difficult to establish precisely on what terms the money was advanced by the respondents to Rolls Razor Ltd. There is no doubt that the loan was made specifically in order to enable Rolls Razor Ltd to pay the dividend. There is equally, in my opinion, no doubt that the loan was made only so as to enable Rolls Razor Ltd to pay the dividend and for no other purpose. This follows quite clearly from the terms of the letter of Rolls Razor Ltd to the appellants of 15 July 1964, which letter, before transmission to the appellants, was sent to the respondents under open cover in order that the cheque might be (as it was enclosed in it). The mutual intention of the respondents and of Rolls Razor Ltd and the essence of the bargain, was that the sum advanced should not become part of the assets of Rolls Razor Ltd but should be used exclusively for payment of a particular class of its creditors, namely, those entitled to the dividend. A necessary consequence from this, by process simply of interpretation, must be that if, for any reason, the dividend could not be paid, the money was to be returned to the respondents: the word 'only' or 'exclusively' can have no other meaning or effect.

That arrangements of this character for the payment of a person's creditors by a third person, give rise to a relationship of a fiduciary character or trust, in favour, as a primary trust, of the creditors, and secondarily, if the primary trust fails, of the third person, has been recognised in a series of decisions over some 150 years.

[His Lordship then reviewed some of the authorities on the point such as *Toovey v Milne*;[1] *Edwards v Glynn*;[2] *Re Rogers ex p Holland and Hannen*;[3] *Re Drucker (No 1) ex p Basden*;[4] and *Re Hooley ex p Trustees*;[5] and continued:] These cases have the support of longevity, authority, consistency and, I would add, good sense. But they are not binding on your Lordships and it is necessary to consider such arguments as have been put why they should be departed from or distinguished.

It is said, first, that the line of authorities mentioned above stands on its own and is consistent with other, more modern, decisions. Those are cases in which money has been paid to a company for the purpose of obtaining an allotment of shares (see *Moseley v Cressey's Co*;[6] *Stewart v Austin*;[7] *Re Nanwa Gold Mines Ltd, Ballantyne v Nanwa Gold Mines Ltd*).[8] I do not think it necessary to examine these cases in detail, nor to comment on them, for I am satisfied that they do not affect the principle on which this appeal should be decided. They are merely examples which show that, in the absence of some special arrangement creating a trust (as was shown to exist in *Re Nanwa Gold Mines Ltd*), payments of this kind are made on the basis that they are to be included in the company's assets. They do not negative the proposition that a trust may exist where the mutual intention is that they should not be included.

The second, and main, argument for the appellants was of a more sophisticated character. The transaction, it was said, between the respondents and Rolls Razor Ltd, was one of loan, giving rise to a legal action of debt. This necessarily excluded the implication of any trust, enforceable in equity, in the respondents' favour: a transaction may attract one action or the other, it could not admit of both.

---

1 (1819) 2 B & Ald 683.
2 (1859) 2 E & E 29.
3 (1891) 8 Morr 243.
4 [1902] 2 KB 237.
5 (1915) 84 LJKB 181.
6 (1865) LR 1 Eq 405.
7 (1866) LR 3 Eq 299.
8 [1955] 3 All ER 219.

My Lords, I must say that I find this argument unattractive. Let us see what it involves. It means that the law does not permit an arrangement to be made by which one person agrees to advance money to another, on terms that the money is to be used exclusively to pay debts of the latter, and if, and so far as not so used, rather than becoming a general asset of the latter available to his creditors at large, is to be returned to the lender. The lender is obliged, in such a case, because he is a lender, to accept, whatever the mutual wishes of lender and borrower may be, that the money he was willing to make available for one purpose only shall be freely available for others of the borrower's creditors for whom he has not the slightest desire to provide.

There is surely no difficulty in recognising the co-existence in one transaction of legal and equitable rights and remedies: when the money is advanced, the lender acquires an equitable right to see that it is applied for the primary designated purpose ... when the purpose has been carried out (ie, the debt paid) the lender has his remedy against the borrower in debt: if the primary purpose cannot be carried out, the question arises if a secondary purpose (ie, repayment to the lender) has been agreed, expressly or by implication: if it has, the remedies of equity may be invoked to give effect to it, if it has not (and the money is intended to fall within the general fund of the debtor's assets) then there is the appropriate remedy for recovery of the loan. I can appreciate no reason why the flexible interplay of law and equity cannot let these practical arrangements, and other variations if desired: it would be to the discredit of both systems if they could not. In the present case the intention to create a secondary trust for the benefit of the lender, to arise if the primary trust, to pay the dividend, could not be carried out, is clear and I can find no reason why the law should not give effect to it ...

I pass to the second question, that of notice ... It is common ground, and I think right, that a mere request to put the money into a separate account is not sufficient to constitute notice. But on 15 July 1964, the appellants, when they received the cheque, also received the covering letter of that date ... Previously there had been a telephone conversation between Mr Goldbart and Mr Parker, to which I have also referred. From these there is no doubt that the appellants were told that the money had been provided on loan by a third person and was to be used only for the purpose of paying the dividend. This was sufficient to give them notice that it was trust money and not assets of Rolls Razor Ltd: the fact, if it be so, that they were unaware of the lenders' identity (though the respondents' name as drawers was on the cheque) is of no significance.

Carreras Rothmans Ltd v Freeman Matthews Treasure Ltd [1984] 3 WLR 1016, HC

Carreras Rothmans Ltd (CR), a cigarettes and tobacco manufacturer, contracted Freeman Matthews Treasure Ltd (FMT), an advertising agency, to manage the advertising side of its business. CR paid FMT on a monthly basis. Such fees were paid not only in respect of FMT's services but also in discharge of FMT's liabilities to media creditors. In 1983, FMT found itself in financial difficulties. CR, fearing the adverse implications on its business dealings if

FMT were to collapse, made a special agreement with FMT to pay the latter's monthly invoices. In July 1983, CR agreed with FMT that a special bank account should be established in FMT's name, to be used 'only for the purposes of meeting the accounts of the media and production fees of third parties directly attributable to CR's involvement with the agency'. The bank was aware of this agreement. On 26 July 1983, CR paid £597,128 into the special account. On 3 August 1983, FMT went into liquidation. The media creditors called upon CR to meet FMT's liabilities in full. CR complied with their demands and took assignments from the media creditors of their rights against FMT. The liquidator of FMT refused to pay any moneys out of the special account. CR claimed a declaration that the moneys in the special account were held on trust for the sole purpose of paying FMT's fees and media creditors ought to be repaid to CR.

The court (Peter Gibson J) held in favour of CR. The moneys in the special account were subject to a trust in favour of CR.

> **Peter Gibson J:** The July agreement was plainly intended to vary the contractual position of the parties as to how, as the contract letter put it, payments made by the plaintiff to the defendant for purely onwards transmission, in effect, to the third parties creditors, would be dealt with. If one looks objectively at the genesis of the variation, the plaintiff was concerned about the adverse effect on it if the defendant, which the plaintiff knew to have financial problems, ceased trading and the third party creditors of the defendant were not paid at a time when the defendant had been put in funds by the plaintiff. The objective was accurately described by Mr Higgs in his informal letter of 19 July as to protect the interests of the plaintiff and the third parties. For this purpose a special account was to be set up with a special designation. The moneys payable by the plaintiff were to be paid not to the defendant beneficially but directly into that account so that the defendant was never free to deal as it pleased with the moneys so paid. The moneys were to be used only for the specific purpose of paying the third parties and as the cheque letter indicated, the amount paid matched the specific invoices presented by the defendant to the plaintiff. The account was intended to be little more than a conduit pipe, but the intention was plain that whilst in the conduit pipe the moneys should be protected. There was even a provision covering the possibility (though what actual situation it was intended to meet it is hard to conceive) that there might be a balance left after payment and in that event the balance was to be paid to the plaintiff and not kept by the defendant. It was thus clearly intended that the moneys once paid would never become the property of the defendant. That was the last thing the plaintiff wanted in view of its concern about the defendant's financial position. As a further precaution the bank was to be put on notice of the conditions and purpose of the account. I infer that this was to prevent the bank attempting to exercise any rights of set off against the moneys in the account.
>
> Mr Potts submitted that there was no recognition in the *Quistclose* case that anyone else had an enforceable right and that in particular a person in the position of the plaintiff discharging a debt had no right to enforce any trust. It

> is of course true that there are factual differences between the *Quistclose* case and the present case. The transaction there was one of loan with no contractual obligation on the part of the lender to make payment prior to the agreement for the loan. In the present case there is no loan but there is an antecedent debt owed by the plaintiff.
>
> I doubt if it is helpful to analyse the *Quistclose* type of case in terms of the constituent parts of a conventional settlement, though it may of course be crucial to ascertain in whose favour the secondary trust operates (as in the *Quistclose* case itself) and who has an enforceable right. In my judgment the principle in all these cases is that equity fastens on the conscience of the person who receives from another property transferred for a specific purpose only and not therefore for the recipient's own purposes, so that such person will not be permitted to treat the property as his own or to use it for other than the stated purpose. Most of the cases in this line are cases where there has been an agreement for consideration so that in one sense each party has contributed to providing the property. But if the common intention is that property is transferred for a specific purpose and not so as to become the property of the transferee, the transferee cannot keep the property if for any reason that purpose cannot be fulfilled. I am left in no doubt that the provider of the moneys in the present case was the plaintiff. True it is that its own witnesses said that if the defendant had not agreed to the terms of the contract letter, the plaintiff would not have broken its contract but would have paid its debt to the defendant, but the fact remains that the plaintiff made its payment on the terms of that letter and the defendant received the moneys only for the stipulated purpose. That purpose was expressed to relate only to the moneys in the account. In my judgment therefore the plaintiff can be equated with the lender in *Quistclose* as having an enforceable right to compel the carrying out of the primary trust.

In addition, an automatic resulting trust will arise where an intended express trust fails *ab initio* for any reason whatsoever. In this event, the trustees have no option but to hold the property on resulting trust for the settlor.

Chichester Diocesan Fund v Simpson [1944] AC 341, HL

The House of Lords held that a bequest for 'charitable or benevolent objects' failed as a charitable gift and the funds distributed to various charities would be held on resulting trust for the testator's next of kin.

Likewise, where the settlor earmarks trust property and transfers the same to trustees but fails to declare the terms of the trust the trustees hold on resulting trust for the settlor. This is so, even though the retention of an interest may not accord with the intention of the settlor.

Vandervell v Inland Revenue Commissioners [1967] 2 AC 291, HL

In 1958, Mr Vandervell wished to give £150,000 to the Royal College of Surgeons to found a chair of pharmacology. He decided to do this by transferring 100,000 shares in his private company, Vandervell Products Ltd, to the college and subsequently declare dividends. He instructed a bank, the National Provincial Bank, which held shares as nominee for Mr Vandervell, to transfer the relevant shares to the College. This transfer was subject to an option, vested in a different company, Vandervell Trustees Ltd to re-purchase the shares for £5,000. Dividends of £266,000 were declared and in 1961 Mr Vandervell requested the trustee company to exercise the option. The trustees duly obliged, exercised the option with £5,000 of trust funds and acquired the relevant shares. The Inland Revenue claimed that the dividends were subject to surtax under s 415(2) of the Income Tax Act 1952 (now s 683 of the Income and Corporation Taxes Act 1988) as Mr V had not 'absolutely divested himself of all interest' in the shares since Mr V held the equitable interest in the option (and consequently the shares) by way of a resulting trust.

The House of Lords held that Mr V had retained an interest in the shares through an interest in the option by way of a resulting trust.

> **Lord Upjohn:** If A intends to give away all his beneficial interest in a piece of property and thinks that he has done so, but by some mistake or accident or failure to comply with the requirements of the law he has failed to do so ... there will, by operation of law, be a resulting trust of the beneficial interest which he has failed effectively to dispose of. If the beneficial interest was in A and he fails to give it away, it remains in him.

Acceleration as opposed to resulting trust

The doctrine of an acceleration of a postponed interest is based on the notion that if a prior interest under a trust fails so that the reason for postponement disappears, a subsequent interest may be brought forward and be enjoyed immediately. The gap in ownership may be filled by an acceleration of a subsequent interest. There is no room for a resulting trust in order to delay the enjoyment of the subsequent interest, for instance, the life tenant who disclaims his life interest may accelerate the remainder interest. Such complications often happen where a draftsman of a trust or will fails to foresee a contingency which has in fact taken place. The court will construe the trust instrument or will in order to ascertain whether there is a gap in ownership and whether the doctrine of acceleration is capable of filling that gap. This will vary with the facts of each case. An example where there was no room for an acceleration of an interest is *Re Cochrane*.[9]

Re Cochrane's Settlement Trusts, Shaw v Cochrane and Others [1955] 1 All ER 222, HC

By a post-nuptial settlement dated 17 August 1898, assets were vested in trustees on trust to pay the income to the wife for life, 'so long as she shall

9 [1955] Ch 309.

continue to reside with the said, WJB Cochrane' and after her death or prior determination of the trust in her favour, to the husband for life and after the death of the survivor, on trust for their issue in equal shares. The survivor of the husband and wife was given a power of appointment to distribute the fund to the issue of the marriage and in default of such appointment in favour of the children equally. The wife, during the subsistence of the marriage, ceased to reside with her husband. Her interest therefore ceased. The husband enjoyed a life interest in the fund until his death in January 1953, his wife survived him. The question in issue was whether the children's interest could be accelerated on the death of their father.

Held that despite the clear omission by the draftsman there was no room to read into the settlement a term accelerating the interests of the children. The wife continued to retain a power of appointment in favour of the children. Accordingly, during the remainder of her life a resulting trust was set up.

> **Harman J:** The question I have to determine is, what happens to the trust fund, or the income thereof on the death of the husband? The settlement is silent on income thereof on the death of the husband?
>
> *Re Akeroyd's Settlement*.[10] In that case there was a marriage settlement in which the income was limited to the wife for life with remainder to her husband until he should become bankrupt with a limitation over to their issue after the decease of the survivor. The husband became bankrupt and his wife predeceased him. The question was: Was there a gap? It was held that the limitation over had taken effect, and that the income of the trust fund between the death of the wife and the death of the husband belonged to the children. Lindley LJ, after reciting the limitations for the husband and wife, said (at p 366):
>
>> That is intelligible enough. Then there is a trust in remainder which does not fit all the events upon which his interest, [that is, the husband's interest] is to cease. The gift over is confined to his death, and after the decease of the survivor of the husband and wife ... then to the children. Then there are clauses of advancement by the trustee with the consent of the husband. I confess that, without knowing anything at all about the events which have happened, about the date of his liquidation, the circumstances of his discharge, and when these interests fell into possession, but looking only at the recitals and at the operative part of the deed, it does appear to me to be as plain as can be, that the real intention of the parties was that this property was to go to the children upon the determination of the life interest of their parents. I cannot doubt that for a moment. I do not call that guessing. The intention is plain; but by a piece of bad drafting the draftsman has failed to give full effect to that plain intention, because in the gift over he has confined it to one of the events instead of putting in some general words which would cover the whole;

10 [1893] 3 Ch 363.

> but that particular kind of flaw does not require a suit to rectify the instrument. The mistake can be corrected by construction provided the intention is clear and plain from the document itself.

Is it clear here not only that something has been left out but also what it is that ought to be supplied? The second is much the more difficult matter to decide. One can see that the limitations over do not marry with the prior trusts, and that it should have been obvious to the draftsman that the event which in fact has happened might happen. But is it clear that the gift over should, so to speak, be accelerated? I do not think it is clear on this particular settlement, and I base my decision on this, that I cannot see clearly what it is that would have been written in. There is a power for the spouses jointly to appoint to issue and there is a power for the survivor to appoint. It is clear and conceded that the fourth defendant, notwithstanding that she forfeited her interest in her husband's lifetime, still has for the rest of her life, following her husband's death, power to dispose of the fund as the survivor of the two, either by deed or by will. That power clearly did not cease with the cesser of her interest, so that she could alter the beneficial interests by appointing not to the children but in favour of grandchildren or by making an unequal division between her daughters, and it seems to me in the face of that that it is impossible to say that the interest vested in the children at the date of the cesser of the husband's interest. It was in fact admitted before me that the fund could not be distributed so long as the power of appointment in the survivor of the two spouses was outstanding, and that alone seems to me to show that it is not true to say that the remainder should vest until the event has happened which is stated to be the event in the deed, viz, the death of the survivor of the husband and wife.

The result is that the draftsman has failed to provide for the event which has happened. Though this is the last resort to which the law has recourse when the draftsman has failed to dispose of that which he has set out to dispose of, yet here, I think, there is a resulting trust of the income of the fund until the death of the survivor of the spouses. The income will be divisible according to the proportion one part bears to the other or if the parts have become intermixed then in proportion to their respective values as recited in the settlement.

Resulting trust of the surplus of trust funds

Where express trusts or specific gifts of property have utilised only a part of the funds so that there remains a surplus of assets, the destination of this moiety of funds varies with the surrounding circumstances of each case. The following solutions have been adopted by the courts:

(1) The surplus is held on resulting trust for the settlor or the donor on the ground that he had parted with the funds for a specific purpose and by implication had retained an interest in the remainder where the specific purpose remained unfulfilled.

Re The Trusts of the Abbott Fund [1900] 2 Ch 326, HC

Funds were collected for the relief of two sisters who were dumb and deaf. In 1891, an appeal was made to invite subscriptions to enable the ladies to reside in lodgings in Cambridge and to provide for their 'very moderate wants'. Considerable sums were received leaving a large surplus outstanding on the death of the ladies in 1899. The question in issue was whether the personal representatives of the ladies or the subscribers to the fund were entitled to the surplus.

It was held that, since there was no intention that the fund would ever be the absolute property of the ladies but merely that the trustees should have a discretion as to the method of making payments for the ladies' benefit, there was a resulting trust for the subscribers.

> **Stirling J:** The ladies are both dead, and the question is whether so far as this fund has not been applied for their benefit, there is a resulting trust of it for the subscribers. I cannot believe that it was ever intended to become the absolute property of the ladies so that they should be in a position to demand a transfer of it to themselves, or so that if they became bankrupt the trustee in the bankruptcy should be able to claim it. I believe it was intended that it should be administered by Mr Smith, or the trustees who had been nominated in pursuance of the circular. I do not think the ladies ever became absolute owners of this fund. I think that the trustee or trustees were intended to have a wide discretion as to whether any, and if any what, part of the fund should be applied for the benefit of the ladies and how the application should be made. That view would not deprive them of all right in the fund, because if the trustees had not done their duty – if they either failed to exercise their discretion or exercised it improperly – the ladies might successfully have applied to the court to have the fund administered according to the terms of the circular. In the result, therefore, there must be a declaration that there is a resulting trust of the moneys remaining unapplied for the benefit of the subscribers to the Abbott fund.
>
> If a testator has given the whole of a fund, whether of capital or income, to a beneficiary, whether directly or through the medium of a trustee, he is regarded, in the absence of any contraindication, as having manifested an intention to benefit that person to the full extent of the subject matter, notwithstanding that he may have expressly stated that the gift is made for a particular purpose, which may prove to be impossible of performance or which may not exhaust the subject matter. This is because the testator has given the whole fund; he has not given so much of the fund as a trustee or anyone else should determine, but the whole fund. This must be reconciled with the testator's having specified the purpose for which the gift is made. This reconciliation is achieved by treating the reference to the purpose as merely a statement of the testator's motive in making the gift. Any other interpretation of the gift would frustrate the testator's expressed intention that the whole subject matter shall be applied for the benefit of the beneficiary.

The same solution was adopted where a collection was raised by means of anonymous donors in the case of *Re Gillingham Bus Disaster Fund*.

Re Gillingham Bus Disaster Fund [1958] Ch 300, HC

Funds were raised by means of collecting boxes following a disaster where marine cadets were maimed or killed by a bus. The collection was to be used for funeral expenses, caring for the disabled and 'for worthy causes' in memory of the dead boys (non-charitable purposes). A surplus of funds remained after the bus company admitted liability and paid substantial sums for similar purposes. The court was asked to determine the destination of the surplus.

It was held that having regard to the circumstances, the donors did not part 'out and out' with their contributions but only for the specific purposes as stated in the appeal. In this respect, it was immaterial that the donors contributed anonymously. Accordingly, the surplus amount was held on resulting trust for the donors. The sum was paid into court to await claimants.

> **Harman J:** The general principle must be that where money is held upon trust and the trusts declared do not exhaust the fund it will revert to the donor or settlor under what is called a resulting trust. The reasoning behind this is that the settlor or donor did not part with his money absolutely out and out but only *sub modo* to the extent that his wishes as declared by the declaration of trust should be carried into effect. When, therefore, this has been done any surplus still belongs to him. This doctrine does not, in my judgment, rest on any evidence of the state of mind of the settlor, for in the vast majority of cases no doubt he does not expect to see his money back: he has created a trust which so far as he can see will absorb the whole of it. The resulting trust arises where that expectation is for some unforeseen reason cheated of fruition, and is an inference of law based on after-knowledge of the event.
>
> In my judgment the Crown has failed to show that this case should not follow the ordinary rule merely because there was a number of donors who, I will assume, are unascertainable. I see no reason myself to suppose that the small giver who is anonymous has any wider intention than the large giver who can be named. They all give for the one object. If they can be found by inquiry the resulting trust can be executed in their favour. If they cannot I do not see how the money could then ... change its destination and become *bona vacantia*. It will be merely money held upon a trust for which no beneficiary can be found. Such cases are common and where it is known that there are beneficiaries the fact that they cannot be ascertained does not entitle the Crown to come in and claim. The trustees must pay the money into court like any other trustee who cannot find his beneficiary. I conclude, therefore, that there must be an inquiry for the subscribers to this fund.

(2) The surplus is retained by the transferee or beneficiary. On construction of the circumstances, the court may decide that the ulterior purpose of the settlor may be fulfilled by permitting the transferee or beneficiary to retain the property even though the specific or primary intention of the settlor or donor has become frustrated. This solution may be adopted when the donee or beneficiary is still capable of deriving a benefit from the property. In this event, there is no room for the resulting trust solution for, in a sense, the overriding objective is still capable of being achieved.

Re Andrew's Trust, Carter v Andrew [1905] 2 Ch 48, HC

In 1881, money was donated 'for or towards' the education of the infant children of a deceased clergyman. By 1899, the children had completed their formal education with only part of the fund. The court was asked to determine the destination of the fund.

It was held (distinguishing *Re Abbott* on the ground that, in the present case, the beneficiaries were still alive whereas, in the earlier case, the ladies had died) that the surplus was taken by the children in equal shares. There was no resulting trust for, in the circumstances, the intentions of the subscribers were to benefit the children and education was merely one method of providing that benefit.

> **Kekewich J:** I have been referred by counsel for the applicants to *Re Trust of the Abbott Fund*,[11] but it is absolutely different from the case now before the court. It seems to me that the guiding principle is to be found in several authorities examined by Wood VC in In *Re Sanderson's Trust*,[12] and the judgment of the Vice Chancellor in that case. One passage may be usefully cited:
>
> > There are two classes of cases between which the general distinction is sufficiently clear, although the precise line of demarcation is occasionally somewhat difficult to obtain. If a gross sum be given, or if the whole income of the property be given, and a special purpose be assigned for that gift, this court always regards the gift as absolute, and the purpose merely as the motive of the gift, and therefore holds that the gift takes effect as to the whole sum or the whole income, as the case may be.
>
> Here the only specified object was the education of the children. But I deem myself to construe 'education' in the broadest possible sense, and not to consider the purpose exhausted because the children have attained such ages that education in the vulgar sense is no longer necessary. Even if it be construed in the narrower sense it is, in Wood VC's language, merely the motive of the gift, and the intention must be taken to have been to provide for the children in the manner (they all being then infants) most useful.
>
> Therefore ... I am prepared to hold that the shares and accumulated dividends belong to the children, and the only remaining question is in what proportions do they take. The letter states that the fund was not subscribed for equal division, but was intended to defray the expenses of all as deemed necessary, and apparently the trustees of the fund exercised their discretion in dividing the money so far as it was divided at all. But there is no longer room for discretion, and I think the only safe course is to hold that the children are entitled to what remains in equal shares.

A similar result was reached by the Court of Appeal in *Re Osoba*.

11 [1900] 2 Ch 326.

12 (1857) 3 K & J 497.

Re Osoba [1979] 1 WLR 247, CA

In this case, a gift was made by will to the testator's widow 'for her maintenance and for the training of my daughter up to university grade'. The widow died and the daughter completed her formal education. It was held that the widow and daughter took as joint tenants and on the death of the widow the daughter succeeded to the entire fund. The references to maintenance and education in the will were merely declarations of the testator's motive for the gift.

> **Buckley LJ:** If a testator has given the whole of a fund, whether of capital or income, to a beneficiary ... he is regarded, in the absence of any contraindication, as having manifested an intention to benefit that person to the full extent of the subject matter ... This is because the testator has given the whole fund; he has not given so much of the fund as the trustee or anyone else should determine, but the whole fund. This must be reconciled with the testator having specified the purpose for which the gift is made. This reconciliation is achieved by treating the reference to the purpose as merely a statement of the testator's motive in making the gift. Any other interpretation of the gift would frustrate the testator's expressed intention that the whole subject matter should be applied for the benefit of the beneficiary. These considerations have, I think, added force where the subject matter is the testator's residue, so that any failure of the gift would result in intestacy. The specified purpose is regarded as of less significance than the dispositive act of the testator.

DISSOLUTION OF UNINCORPORATED ASSOCIATION

An unincorporated association is a group of individuals joined together to promote a common purpose or purposes, such as a cricket or golf and trade union activities. Such associations vary in size and objectives, some may be long standing or exist with a view to making profits and have open or restricted membership. They differ from incorporated associations in that they lack a legal personality – separate and distinct from its members. The association is regulated by its rules which have the effect of imposing an implied contract between all the members *inter se*. Thus, all the members are collectively joined together by the rules of the association. Its affairs are normally handled by a committee and its assets may be held on trust for the association in order to ensure that the association's property is kept separate from its members.

The rules of the association usually provide the procedure and ownership rights in respect of a distribution of the assets of the society on a dissolution.

Conservative and Unionist Central Office v Burrell [1982] 1 WLR 522, CA

Lawton LJ laid down the following definition of an unincorporated association which was referred to, but not defined, in the Taxes Act 1988.

> **Lawton LJ:** I infer that by 'unincorporated association' in this context Parliament meant two or more persons bound together for one or more common purposes, not being business purposes, by mutual undertakings, each having mutual duties and obligations, in an organisation which has rules which identify in whom control of it and its funds rests and upon what terms and which can be joined or left at will. The bond of union between the members of an unincorporated association has to be contractual.

The issue to be considered in this context concerns the occasions when the rules are silent as to the destination of assets following a dissolution of an unincorporated association. In effect, there are a number of issues involved, namely, whether the members of the association (and, if so, whether only members on the date of dissolution or all members, past and present) are entitled to the assets on a distribution or should the Crown be entitled as *bona vacantia*? If the members are entitled, how much ought they to claim? In short, the question is on what basis should a distribution of assets of a society be made?

So far the courts have adopted the following three approaches to this question.

The resulting trust

This was the original remedy adopted and represents, in theory, a solution to the problem, although the more recent cases have considered this basis of distribution with disfavour. This approach was adopted in *Re Printers and Transferrers Society*.

Re Printers and Transferrers Society [1899] 2 Ch 84, HC

In this case, a trade union society was founded by weekly subscriptions to raise funds for strikes and other benefits for its members. The scale of benefits varied with the duration of membership. The rules of the society were silent as to the mode of distribution of assets on a dissolution. There were assets of £1,000 and the society consisted of 201 subsisting members. The court held that a resulting trust was set up in favour of subsisting members on the date of dissolution and the assets were divisible in proportion to their contributions over the years (for example, a member of 10 years' standing received 10 times more of the funds than a member for one year only) irrespective of benefits received over the years.

> **Byrne J:** Immediately prior to the dissolution, who was interested in the funds of the association? The then members of the association, and no one else; and so long as the society should continue it would be the existing members for the time being who would have the interest; the interest being in the nature of a

> contingent benefit for such of the members as required payments to be made to them under the rules, or as were entitled to payments under the rules. There is this observation to make about *Cunnack v Edwards*:[13] there were at the time of the application no existing members of the association, and the argument really was whether the property in question belonged to the Crown as *bona vacantia*, or was to be distributed among the representatives of the persons who had contributed the fund. That state of circumstances does not exist in the present case; here there are existing members. Now, a careful reading of the judgment of the Court of Appeal in *Cunnack v Edwards* points to this as the leading ground of the decision: that, on the true construction of the rules in that case, it was held that each member on making a payment had finally and forever parted with the whole of his interest in the money he so subscribed in favour of third parties. That does not exist in the present case. The funds provided here are for the benefit of members for the time being; it is true they would not all necessarily take the same amount – some of them might and perhaps did get nothing, some did get a good deal under the rules; but they were all alike entitled to a contingent benefit on the happening of certain events, though the different classes on becoming entitled would receive at different rates.
>
> The present case also differs from *Cunnack v Edwards* in another respect. The advisors of the Crown were by my direction communicated with, and disclaim any interest in this fund, and do not claim it as *bona vacantia*. Therefore, what I have to consider is, to whom does this fund belong, and how ought it properly to be distributed? I think that the members of the association at the time of the passing of the resolution for dissolution were among them the only persons who can establish a claim to this fund.
>
> Then, the next question I have to consider is, ought that fund to be divided among them equally, or ought it to be divided among them in proportion either to payments respectively made by them to the society, or, as it is put on behalf of others, in proportion to the contingent benefits to which they were entitled, that is to say, in the proportion of one and two, or in any other manner? I think practically it reduces itself to this: I must decide that it is divisible among them equally, or divisible among them, as put by Mr Farwell on behalf of the class whom he represents, in proportion to their contribution to the funds of the society. Now, the true principle I think is to be found in this – that there is a resulting trust in favour of those who have contributed to these funds, and I think that the proper and legitimate way of dividing therefore, will be in accordance with the amounts contributed by the existing members at the time of the passing of the resolution.

This approach was followed with some variations in *Re Hobourn Aero Components Air Raid Distress Fund*.[14] In this case, the surplus funds were held on resulting trust for everyone who contributed, past and present, in proportion to their contributions but with a reduction for any benefits received from the fund.

13 [1895] 1 Ch 489.

14 [1946] Ch 194.

Re Hobourn Aero Components Ltd's Air Raid Distress Fund, Ryan v Forrest [1946] Ch 144, HC

The facts were as follows. During the war years from 1940 to the end of 1944, collections were made weekly from the employees of a company operating three munitions factories. The moneys were initially expended on comforts or money payments for servicemen abroad or on leave, who were ex-employees or dependants of employees of the company. After September 1940, the collected funds were also used to relieve cases of employees who had suffered damage and distress from air raids. On the closing down of the fund, a claim was made for the determination of the surplus moneys.

Cohen J:

(a) While the relief of distress caused by air raids was a charitable purpose under the fourth heading of Lord MacNaghten's classification in Pemsel's case, but the beneficiaries of the present fund (the employees of a company) did not constitute a sufficient section of society to be treated as charity;

(b) the contributors (past and present) were therefore entitled to a return of a due proportion of their contributions subject to deductions to be made for any moneys or value received.

[Having decided that the gift failed as a charity, the learned judge continued:]

I therefore turn to the second question raised by the summons. The Crown does not claim the fund as *bona vacantia*, and the question is as to how it ought to be distributed amongst the contributories thereto. The form of the question suggests that persons who had ceased to contribute before 9 September 1944, the date on which contributions ceased, might be excluded but counsel whose interest it was to support this argument admitted that there was no valid ground for any such limitation. In my opinion, he was right in making this admission, since the basis on which the contributions are returned is that each donor retained an interest in the amount of his contributions except so far as they are applied for the purposes for which they were subscribed. Moreover, the rule in *Clayton's Case*,[15] is not applicable in such a case (see *Re British Red Cross Balkan Fund*).[16] The question was also raised whether a subscriber who received benefit from the fund was bound to bring the amount of that benefit into hotchpot for the purposes of the distribution. My attention was called to two cases in which orders had been made for distribution of the fund without regard to such contributions. (See *Re Printers and Transferrers Amalgamated Trades Protection Society*,[17] and *Re Lead Company's Workmen's Fund Society*.)[18] But in both those cases the decision to this effect was based on the difficulty and the expense involved in ascertaining the amount of the respective benefits and the persons to whom they were paid. In the present case I was told by Mr

15 (1816) 1 Mer 572.

16 [1914] 2 Ch 419.

17 [1899] 2 Ch 184.

18 [1904] 2 Ch 196.

> Dinham, the company's accountant, that while considerable labour would be involved, there would be no difficulty in ascertaining the amounts of the benefits or the recipients, and I have come to the conclusion that I should not be justified in deviating from the general principle, that a person seeking to participate in the distribution of a fund must bring into hotchpot anything he has already received therefrom. Accordingly, I propose to declare that the fund now available for distribution ought to be distributed amongst all the persons who during their employment by Hobourn Aero Components Ltd, contributed to the fund at any time after 12 December 1940, in proportion to the total amount contributed by them respectively to the fund, each such person bringing into hotchpot any amount received by him by way of benefit out of the fund.

The courts have repeatedly stressed that the resulting trust is unsuitable in this context for the members paid their subscriptions on a contractual basis. The distribution of assets ought to be effected on a contractual basis.

Bona vacantia

A second solution adopted by the courts is that the members of a society who make their contributions have received, or are receiving, or expect to receive benefits from the funds of the society during its continuance. On the date of liquidation, such members do not expect the return of their subscriptions or assets of the society for the members had parted 'out and out' with their subscriptions. Accordingly, the assets of the society may be taken by the Crown as *bona vacantia*. This doctrine means that where property has no apparent owner it will pass to the Crown. This solution is adopted only as a last resort when the settlor, beneficiary and no one else is entitled to claim the property. The property being ownerless, the Crown steps in to fill the gap.

Cunnack v Edwards [1896] 2 Ch 679, CA

A society was formed to raise funds by subscriptions, fines, etc, from its members in order to provide annuities for the widows of deceased members. By 1879, all the members had died and by 1892 the last widow died. There was a surplus of funds of £1,250. The personal representatives of the last widow claimed the fund.

The Court of Appeal held that the Crown took the fund as *bona vacantia*. There was no room for a resulting trust in favour of past members for each member on paying his contribution parted with all interest in his subscription subject to one reservation, that if he left a widow she was to be provided for during widowhood.

> **Smith LJ:** As the member paid his money to the society, so he divested himself of all interest in this money for ever, with this one reservation, that if the member left a widow she was to be provided for during her widowhood. Except as to this he abandoned and gave up the money forever.

A similar result was achieved in *Re West Sussex Constabulary's Widows, Children and Benevolent Fund Trusts.*[19]

Re West Sussex Constabulary's Widows, Children and Benevolent Fund Trusts [1971] Ch 1, HC

A fund was established for providing payments to widows of deceased members of the West Sussex Constabulary. Clause (10) of the Rules provided that, with exceptions, a member who resigned would forfeit all claims to the fund. Receipts were derived from four classes of contributors, namely:

(a) identifiable donations and legacies;

(b) members subscriptions;

(c) collecting boxes; and

(d) proceeds of entertainment, sweepstakes and raffles.

On 1 January 1968, the Constabulary was amalgamated with other police forces and the fund came to an end. The question in issue concerned the distribution of the fund.

It was held by the court that with the exception of contributors in category (a) (such donations were made for a specific purpose which failed, hence a resulting trust was set up for these contributors), the balance of the fund passed to the Crown as *bona vacantia*. The contributors within category (b) had got what they bargained for, following *Cunnack v Edwards* (see above, p 247). In any event, members' contributions were received by way of contract and not trust.

The contributors in category (c) were treated as parting with their moneys 'out and out'. The court refused to follow *Re Gillingham* (see above, p 241) on the ground that that solution was 'absurd and inconceivable'. In respect of contributors in category (d), they received what they were contractually entitled to, indeed, it was conceivable that they did not contribute directly to the fund.

> **Goff J**: First, it was submitted that the fund belongs exclusively and in equal shares to all those persons now living who were members on 31 December 1967, and the personal representatives of all the then members since deceased, to all of whom I will refer collectively as 'the surviving members'. That argument is based on the analogy of the members' club cases, and the decisions in *Re Printers and Transferrers Amalgamated Trades Protection Society;*[20] *Re Lead Company's Workmen's Fund Society;*[21] and the Irish case of *Tierney v Tough.*[22] The *ratio decidendi* of the first two of those cases was that there was a

19 [1971] Ch 1.

20 [1899] 2 Ch 184.

21 [1904] 2 Ch 196.

22 [1914] 1 IR 142.

resulting trust, but that would not give the whole fund to the surviving members, unless rule 10 of the fund's rules could somehow be made to carry to them the contributions of the former members despite the failure of the purposes of the fund (as was pointed out by O'Connor MR in *Tierney v Tough* at p 155), and unless indeed the moneys raised from outside sources also could somehow be made to accrue to the surviving members. I agree with Ungoed-Thomas J that the *ratio decidendi* of *Tierney v Tough* is to be preferred: see *Re St Andrew's Allotment Association*.[23]

This brings one back to the principle of the members' clubs, and I cannot accept that as applicable for three reasons. First, it simply does not look like it; this was nothing but a pensions or dependent relatives' fund not at all akin to a club; secondly, in all the cases where the surviving members have taken, with the sole exception of *Tierney v Tough,* the club society or organisation existed for the benefit of the members for the time being exclusively, whereas in the present case, as in *Cunnack v Edwards*,[24] only third parties could benefit. Moreover, in *Tierney v Tough* the exception was minimal and discretionary and can, I think, fairly be disregarded. Finally, this very argument was advanced and rejected by Chitty J in *Cunnack v Edwards* at first instance,[25] and was abandoned on the hearing of the appeal. That judgment also disposes of the further argument that the surviving members of the fund had power to amend the rules under rule 14 and could therefore have reduced the fund into possession, and so ought to be treated as the owners of it or the persons for whose benefit it existed at the crucial moment. They had the power but they did not exercise it, and it is now too late.

Then it was argued that there is a resulting trust, with several possible consequences. If this be the right view there must be a primary division of the fund into three parts, one representing contributions from former members, another contributions from the surviving members, and the third moneys raised from outside sources.

In my judgment the doctrine of resulting trust is clearly inapplicable to the contributions of both classes. Those persons who remained members until their deaths are in any event excluded because they have had all they contracted for, either because their widows and dependants have received or are in receipt of the prescribed benefits, or because they did not have a widow or dependants. In my view that is inherent in all the speeches in the Court of Appeal in *Cunnack v Edwards*.[26] Further, whatever the effect of the fund's rule 10 may be upon the contributions of those members who left prematurely, they and the surviving members alike are also in my judgment unable to claim under a resulting trust because they put up their money on a contractual basis and not one of trust: see *per* Harman J in *Re Gillingham Bus Disaster Fund*.[27] The

23 [1969] 1 WLR 229, p 238.

24 [1896] 2 Ch 679.

25 [1895] 1 Ch 489.

26 [1896] 2 Ch 679.

27 [1958] Ch 300, p 314.

only case which has given me difficulty on this aspect of the matter is *Re Hobourn Aero Components Ltd's Air Raid Distress Fund*,[28] where in somewhat similar circumstances it was held there was a resulting trust. The argument postulated, I think, the distinction between contract and trust but in another connection, namely, whether the fund was charitable. There was in that case a resolution to wind up but that was not, at all events as expressed, the *ratio decidendi*: see *per* Cohen J at p 97, but, as Cohen J observed, there was no argument for *bona vacantia*. Moreover, no rules or regulations were ever made and although in fact £1 per month was paid or saved for each member serving with the forces, there were no prescribed contractual benefits. In my judgment that case is therefore distinguishable.

Accordingly, in my judgment all the contributions of both classes are *bona vacantia*, but I must make a reservation with respect to possible contractual rights. In *Cunnack v Edwards*[29] and *Braithwaite v AG*[30] all the members had received, or provision had been made for, all the contractual benefits. Here the matter has been cut short. Those persons who died whilst still in membership cannot, I conceive, have any rights because in their case the contract has been fully worked out, and on a contractual basis I would think that members who retired would be precluded from making any claim by rule 10, although that is perhaps more arguable. The surviving members, on the other hand, may well have a right in contract on the ground of frustration or total failure of consideration, and that right may embrace contributions made by past members, though I do not see how it could apply to moneys raised from outside sources. I have not, however, heard any argument based on contract and therefore the declarations I propose to make will be subject to the reservation which I will later formulate. This will not prevent those parts of the fund which are *bona vacantia* from being paid over to the Crown as it has offered to give a full indemnity to the trustees.

I must now turn to the moneys raised from outside sources. Counsel for the Treasury Solicitor made an overriding general submission that there cannot be a resulting trust of any of the outside moneys because in the circumstances it is impossible to identify the trust property; no doubt something could be achieved by complicated accounting, but this, he submitted, would not be identification but notional reconstruction. I cannot accept that argument. In my judgment, in a case like the present, equity will cut the Gordian knot by simply dividing the ultimate surplus in proportion to the sources from which it has arisen. There may be cases of tolerable simplicity where the court will be more refined, but in general, where a fund has been raised from mixed sources, interest has been earned over the years and income – and possibly capital – expenditure has been made indiscriminately out of the fund as an entirety, and then the venture comes to an end prematurely or otherwise, the court will not find itself baffled but will cut the Gordian knot as I have said.

28 [1946] Ch 86.

29 [1895] 1 Ch 489.

30 [1909] 1 Ch 510.

Then counsel divided the outside moneys into three categories, first, the proceeds of entertainments, raffles and sweepstakes; secondly, the proceeds of collecting boxes; and, thirdly, donations, including legacies if any, and he took particular objections to each.

I agree that there cannot be any resulting trust with respect to the first category. I am not certain whether Harman J in *Re Gillingham Bus Disaster Fund*,[31] meant to decide otherwise. It appears to me to be impossible to apply the doctrine of resulting trust to the proceeds of entertainments and sweepstakes and such-like money raising operations for two reasons: first, the relationship is one of contract and not of trust; the purchaser of a ticket may have the motive of aiding the cause or he may not; he may purchase a ticket merely because he wishes to attend the particular entertainment or to try for the prize, but whichever it be, he pays his money as the price of what is offered and what he receives; secondly, there is in such cases no direct contribution to the fund at all; it is only the profit, if any, which is ultimately received and there may even be none.

In any event, the first category cannot be any more susceptible to the doctrine than the second to which I now turn. Here one starts with the well known dictum of PO Lawrence J in *Re Welsh Hospital (Netley) Fund*[32] where he said:

> So far as regards the contributors to entertainments, street collections, etc, I have no hesitation in holding that they must be taken to have parted with their money out and out. It is inconceivable that any person paying for a concert ticket or placing a coin in a collecting box presented to him in the street should have intended that any part of the money so contributed should be returned to him when the immediate object for which the concert was given or the collection made had come to an end. To draw such an inference would be absurd on the face of it.

This was adopted by Upjohn J in *Re Hillier's Trusts*,[33] where the point was actually decided.

The analysis of Upjohn J was approved by Denning LJ in the Court of Appeal,[34] although it is true he went on to say that the law makes a presumption of charity. I quote from p 714:

> Let me first state the law as I understand it in regard to money collected for a specific charity by means of a church collection, a flag day, a whist drive, a dance, or some such activity. When a man gives money on such an occasion, he gives it, I think, beyond recall. He parts with the money out and out ...

In *Re Ulverston and District New Hospital Building Trusts*,[35] Jenkins LJ threw out a suggestion that there might be a distinction in the case of a person who could prove that he put a specified sum in a collecting box, and, in the *Gillingham*

31 [1958] Ch 300.

32 [1921] 1 Ch 655, p 660.

33 [1954] 1 WLR 9.

34 [1954] 1 WLR 700.

35 [1956] Ch 622, p 633.

case,[36] Harman J after noting this, decided that there was a resulting trust with respect to the proceeds of collections.

It will be observed that Harman J considered that *Re Welsh Hospital (Netley) Fund*,[37] *Re Hillier's Trusts* and *Re Ulverston and District New Hospitality Building Trusts* did not help him greatly because they were charity cases. It is true that they were, and, as will presently appear, that is in my view very significant in relation to the third category, but I do not think it was a valid objection with respect to the second, and for my part I cannot reconcile the decision of Upjohn J in *Re Hillier's Trusts* with that of Harman J in the *Gillingham* case. As I see it, therefore, I have to choose between them. On the one hand it may be said that Harman J had the advantage, which Upjohn J had not, of considering the suggestion made by Jenkins LJ. On the other hand, that suggestion with all respect, seems to me somewhat fanciful and unreal. I agree that all who put their money into collecting boxes should be taken to have the same intention, but why should they not all be regarded as intending to part with their money out and out absolutely in all circumstances? I observe that PO Lawrence J in *Re Welsh Hospital*[38] used very strong words. He said any other view was inconceivable and absurd on the face of it. That commends itself to my humble judgment, and I therefore prefer and follow the judgment of Upjohn J in *Re Hillier's Trusts* ... Therefore, where, as in the present case, the object was neither equivocal nor charitable, I can see no justification for infecting the third category with the weaknesses of the first and second, and I cannot distinguish this part of the case from *Re Abbott Fund Trusts*.[39]

In general I direct two inquiries: (1) What donations of specific amounts other than through collecting-boxes but including legacies were at any time given to the fund and by whom, and whether any living donors have since died and, if so, who are their personal representatives, and who are the personal representatives of any testators by whom such legacies were bequeathed? (2) What is the total amount of: (a) the contributions made by the members since the inception of the fund; (b) the proceeds of entertainments, sweepstakes, collections and any similar money raising activities; and (c) such donations including legacies? I then direct the total net assets after payment of costs to be divided between these three portions *pro rata*.

And I make the following declarations: first, that the portion attributable to donations and legacies is held on a resulting trust for the donors or their estates of the respective testators; secondly, that the remainder of the fund is *bona vacantia*.

These declarations are, however, without prejudice to: (1) any claim which may be made in contract by any person or the personal representatives of any person who was at any time a member; and (2) any right or claim of the trustees to be indemnified against any such claim out of the whole fund including the portion attributable to donations and legacies.

36 [1958] Ch 300.

37 [1921] 1 Ch 655.

38 *Ibid*, p 661.

39 [1900] 2 Ch 326.

Contractual basis

The courts in *Cunnack v Edwards* and *Re West Sussex* adopted the notion that members contributed to the society on a contractual basis but decided on the facts that such contributions were taken by the Crown as *bona vacantia*. In more recent cases, the courts have decided that subsisting members of the association are entitled to participate in the distribution of the society's funds. Their contributions were made as an accretion to the funds of the association by reference to the contract made *inter se* in accordance with the rules of the society. The members control the association subject to the constitution of the society. Equally, the subsisting members alone ought to be entitled to the surplus funds on a dissolution, in the absence of any agreement between members to the contrary. In *Re Sick and Funeral Society of St John's Sunday School, Golcar*,[40] the court decided that since the rules of the society differentiated between the two categories of members, the distribution of the assets to the subsisting members would likewise be conducted on the basis of this inequality. Subject to this qualification, all the subsisting members were treated alike.

Re Sick and Funeral Society of St John's Sunday School, Golcar [1973] Ch 51, HC

In 1866, a society was formed at a Sunday school to provide for sickness and death benefits for its members. Teachers and children were entitled to join and subscriptions were based on a sliding scale according to age; those under 13 paying half of one old pence per week (rule 9) and those over 12 paying one old pence. The benefits for those paying the full subscription were twice those of the smaller subscribers (rules 12 and 14).

On 12 December 1966, a meeting unanimously decided to wind up the Society as from 31 December. No further subscriptions were paid. There was some £4,000 of surplus assets.

Before the assets were distributed among the current members, four ex-members, who had been excluded from membership for failure to pay subscriptions since 1963 (rules 9 and 17), claimed to pay up their arrears and to participate. A further meeting was held in September 1968 in which it was again resolved to wind up the Society and to distribute the assets among the persons who were members on 31 December 1966 and the personal representatives of such members who had subsequently died.

It was held that the distribution would be made with full shares for full members and half shares for the children. The ex-members were excluded.

> **Megarry J:** In my judgment the substantive rights of all concerned crystallised on 31 December 1966, when, in accordance with the resolution of 12 December

40 [1973] Ch 51.

1966, the society ceased all its activities ... Accordingly, in my judgment the personal representatives of each deceased member are entitled to the share to which that member would have been entitled had he lived ...

I turn to question 2. This relates to the basis of distribution. Is each member entitled to an equal share, or is there to be a division into full shares and half-shares, with those paying one half a week entitled only to a half-share, and those paying 1 d a week a full share? Or is the basis of distribution to be proportionate to the amounts respectively contributed by each member? The first step, in my view, is to decide between the first two contentions on the one hand and the third on the other: is the proper basis that of division per capita, whether in full or half shares, or that of division in proportion to the amounts contributed? In discussing this, I speak, of course, in general terms, and subject to any other basis for division that is to be discerned in the rules or any other source.

The authorities are in a curious state. In *Re Printers and Transferrers Amalgamated Trades Protection Society*[41] [see above, p 244], Byrne J applied the amounts contributed basis to a trade union, putting matters on the footing of a resulting trust, and directing division on that basis among the members existing at the time of the resolution for dissolution. In *Re Lead Company's Workmen's Fund Society*,[42] Warrington J followed this decision in the case of an unregistered friendly society. In these cases payments for forfeitures, fines, sick benefits and so on, were disregarded. In *Tierney v Tough*,[43] another case of an unregistered friendly society, O'Connor MR was critical of the application of the law relating to resulting trusts to such cases. Despite his criticism, however, he directed division on the basis of the amounts contributed. On the other hand, in the case of clubs, *Brown v Dale*[44] supports the per capita basis, though it is so shortly reported as to provoke more questions than it answers. *Feeney and Shannon v MacManus*,[45] another club case, also supports the same basis. The case is a little remarkable in that the headnote proclaims that *Tierney v Tough*[46] was 'applied'; and it appears that the basis of the decision was not so much that equal division was right, but that equality was necessary because ascertaining the proportionate contributions was an impossibility. Finally, in *Re St Andrew's Allotment Association*,[47] concerning an allotment association, Ungoed-Thomas J considered these cases together with *Re Blue Albion Cattle Society*[48] (1966) *The Guardian*, 28 May, where Cross J had applied the per capita basis to a cattle-breeding society. In the *St Andrew's* case Ungoed-Thomas J said at p 238; at p 154:

41 [1899] 2 Ch 184.

42 [1904] 2 Ch 196.

43 [1914] 1 IR 142.

44 (1878) 9 Ch D 78.

45 [1937] IR 23.

46 [1914] 1 IR 142.

47 [1969] 1 WLR 229; [1969] 1 All ER 147.

48 [1966] CLY 1274.

> If the true principle is that laid down in *Tierney v Tough*[49] and that principle certainly seems to me preferable to the principle of the resulting trust adopted in *Re Printers and Transferrers Amalgamated Trades Protection Society*,[50] then it would seem to me that *prima facie* the assets are distributable between members at the relevant date *per capita*. It is conceivable that a basis for distinguishing the friendly and mutual benefit society cases may be that, whereas in the club cases enjoyment *ab initio* and equality are contemplated, yet in the friendly and mutual benefit society cases what are contemplated are advantages related contributions.

The reference to the principle laid down in *Tierney v Tough* must, I think, be to the comments of O'Connor MR which rejected the concept of resulting trust, rather than to the actual decision, which was on the basis of the proportionate contributions that flow from the concept of resulting trust.

It seems to me, with all respect, that much of the difficulty arises from confusing property with contract. A resulting trust is essentially a property concept: any property that a man does not effectually dispose of remains his own. If, then, there is a true resulting trust in respect of an unexpended balance of payments made to some club or association, there will be a resulting trust in respect of that unexpended balance, and the beneficiaries under that trust will be those who made the payments. If any are dead, the trusts will be for their estates; death does not deprive a man of his beneficial interest. Yet, in what I may call 'the resulting trust cases', the beneficiaries who were held to be entitled were the members living at the time of the dissolution to the exclusion of those who had died or otherwise ceased to be members. If, then, there was any resulting trust, it must be a trust modified in some way, perhaps by some unexplained implied term, that distinguishes between the quick and the dead. It cannot be merely an ordinary resulting trust.

On the other hand, membership of a club or association is primarily a matter of contract. The members make their payments, and in return they become entitled to the benefits of membership in accordance with the rules. The sums they pay cease to be their individual property, and so cease to be subject to any concept of resulting trust. Instead, they become the property, through the trustees of the club or association, of all the members for the time being, including themselves. A member who, by death or otherwise, ceases to be a member thereby ceases to be the part owner of any of the club's property: those who remain continue owners. If, then, dissolution ensues, there must be a division of the property of the club or association among those alone who are owners of that property, to the exclusion of former members. In that division, I cannot see what relevance there can be in the respective amounts of the contributions. The newest member, who has made a single payment when he joined only a year ago, is as much a part owner of the property of the club or association as a member who has been making payments for 50 years. Each has had what he has paid for: the newest member has had the benefits of

49 [1914] 1 IR 142.

50 [1899] 2 Ch 184.

> membership for a year or so and the oldest member for 50 years. Why should the latter, who for his money has had the benefits of membership for 50 times as long as the former, get the further benefit of receiving 50 times as much in the winding up?
>
> I have, of course, been speaking in the broadest of outlines; but I must say that the view taken on principle by O'Connor MR in *Tierney v Tough*[51] and by Ungoed-Thomas J in *Re St Andrew's Allotment Association*[52] seem to me to be preferable to the other view, despite certain difficulties in the basis of distinction between the club cases and the others tentatively suggested by Ungoed-Thomas J in the passage that I have read: at p 238; at p 154. Accordingly, I reject the basis of proportionate division in favour of equality, or division *per capita*. But then the second question arises, namely, whether the principle of equality prevails not only when there is no more than one class of members but when there are two or more classes. Is the proposed division into shares and half shares sound, or ought it to be rejected in favour of equality throughout?
>
> On the footing that the rules of a club or association form the basis of the contract between all the members, I must look at the rules of the society to see whether they indicate any basis other than that of equality. It seems to me that they do. Those aged from five to 12 years old pay contributions at half the rate (rule 9), and correspondingly their allowances (rule 12) and death benefit (rule 14) are also paid at half the rate. Where the rules have written into them the basis of inequality this ought also to be applied to the surplus property of the society. A distinction between classes of members is quite different from a distinction between individual members of the same class based on the amounts contributed by each member. At any given moment one can say that the rights and liabilities of all the members of one class differ in the same way from the rights and liabilities of all the members of the other class, irrespective of the length of membership or anything else. It was indeed suggested that the words 'two classes of subscribers' in rule 9 did not mean that there were two classes of members, the word 'subscribers' being in contrast with the word 'member' used in the next sentence. But the rules are too ill drafted for any such inferences to be drawn; and rule 5, providing for special meetings of the committee when requested by three 'subscribers', and a general meeting if required by 20 of the 'members', strongly suggests that the terms are used interchangeably. At any rate, I have heard no sensible explanations of the distinction.

The court came to a similar conclusion (excluding any claim of the Crown as *bona vacantia*) in *Re Bucks Constabulary Widows' and Orphans' Fund Friendly Society (No 2)*.

51 [1914] 1 IR 142.

52 [1969] 1 WLR 229; [1969] 1 All ER 147.

Re Bucks Constabulary Widows' and Orphans' Fund Friendly Society (No 2) [1979] 1 WLR 936, HC

The objects of a friendly society included the relief of widows and orphans of deceased members of Bucks Constabulary. In April 1968, the Bucks Constabulary was amalgamated with others to form the Thames Valley Constabulary. The question in issue concerned whether the assets should be distributed among the subsisting members on the date of dissolution or whether they shall pass to the Crown as *bona vacantia*.

The court held that the fund belonged to the subsisting members on the date of dissolution and they took the fund in equal shares (per capita).

Walton J: Before considering the relevant legislation, it is I think desirable to view the question of the property of unincorporated associations in the round. If a number of persons associate together, for whatever purpose, if that purpose is one which involves the acquisition of cash or property of any magnitude, then, for practical purposes, some one or more persons have to act in the capacity of treasurers or holders of the property. In any sophisticated association there will accordingly be one or more trustees in whom the property which is acquired by the association will be vested. These trustees will of course not hold such property on their own behalf. Usually there will be a committee of some description which will run the affairs of the association; though, of course, in a small association the committee may well comprise all the members; and the normal course of events will be that the trustee, if there is a formal trustee, will declare that he holds the property of the association in his hands on trust to deal with it as directed by the committee. If the trust deed is a shade more sophisticated it may add that the trustee holds the assets on trust for the members in accordance with the rules of the association. Now in all such cases it appears to me quite clear that, unless under the rules governing the association the property thereof has been wholly devoted to charity, or unless and to the extent to which the other trusts have validly been declared of such property, the persons, and the only persons, interested therein are the members. Save by way of a valid declaration of trust in their favour, there is no scope for any other person acquiring any rights in the property of the association, although of course it may well be that third parties may obtain contractual or proprietary rights, such as a mortgage, over those assets as the result of a valid contract with the trustees or members of the committee as representing the association.

I can see no reason for thinking that this analysis is any different whether the purpose for which the members of the association associate are a social club, a sporting club, to establish a widows' and orphans' fund, to obtain a separate Parliament for Cornwall, or to further the advance of alchemy. It matters not. All the assets of the association are held in trust for its members (of course subject to the contractual claims of anybody having a valid contract with the association) save and except to the extent to which valid trusts have otherwise been declared of its property. I would adopt the analysis made by Brightman J in *Re Recher's Will Trusts* [see below, p 545].

All this doubtless seems quite elementary, but it appears to me to have been lost sight of to some extent in some of the decisions which I shall hereafter have to consider in detail in relation to the destination on dissolution of the funds of unincorporated associations.

Now, in the present case, I am dealing with a society which was registered under the Friendly Societies Act 1896. This does not have any effect at all on the unincorporated nature of the society. The fact is made very explicit by the provisions of s 49(1) of the 1896 Act which reads as follows:

> All property belonging to a registered society, whether acquired before or after the society is registered, shall vest in the trustees for the time being of the society, for the use and benefit of the society and the members thereof, and of all persons claiming through the members according to the rules of the society.

There can be no doubt, therefore, that in the present case the whole of the property of the society is vested in the trustees for the use and benefit of the society and the members thereof and of all persons claiming through the members according to the rules of the society. I do not think I need go through the rules in detail. They are precisely what one would expect in the case of an association whose main purpose in life was to enable members to make provision for widows and orphans. Members paid a contribution in exchange for which in the event of their deaths their widows and children would receive various benefits. There is indeed no rule which says what is to happen to surplus assets of the society on a dissolution. But in view of s 49(1) there is no need. The assets must continue to be held, the society having been dissolved, and the widows and orphans being out of the way, simply for the use and benefit of the members of the society, albeit they will all now be former members.

This indeed appears to be obvious that in a work of great authority on all matters connected with friendly societies, Baden Fuller, the learned author says this:

> If the rules provide for the termination of the society they usually also provide for the distribution of the funds in that event, but if on the termination of a society no provision has been made by the rules for the distribution of its funds, such funds are divisible among the existing members at the time of the termination or dissolution in proportion to the amount contributed by each member for entrance fees and subscriptions, and irrespective of fines or payments made to members in accordance with the rules.

Solicitors to the funds as *bona vacantia* are unsuitable in the present case. I say 'in the present case' because there are undoubtedly cases where the assets of an unincorporated association do become *bona vacantia*. To quote Baden Fuller again:

> A society may sometimes become defunct or moribund by its members either all dying or becoming so reduced in numbers that it is impossible either to continue the society or to dissolve it by instrument; in such cases the surplus funds, after all existing claims (if any) under the rules have been satisfied or provided for, are not divisible among the surviving

> members ... or the last survivor ... or the representative of the last survivor ... nor is there any resulting trust in favour of the personal representatives of the members of the society ... not even in favour of honorary members in respect of donations by them ... but a society which, though moribund, had at a testator's death one member and three annuitant beneficiaries, was held to be existing so as to prevent the lapse of a legacy bequeathed to it by the testator ... In these circumstances two cases seem to occur: if the purposes of the society are charitable, the surplus will be applicable *cy-près* ... but if the society is not a charity, the surplus belongs to the Crown as *bona vacantia*.

Before I turn to a consideration of the authorities, it is I think pertinent to observe that all unincorporated societies rest in contract to this extent, that there is an implied contract between all of the members *inter se* governed by the rules of the society. In default of any rule to the contrary, and it will seldom if ever be that there is such a rule, when a member ceases to be a member of the association he *ipso facto* ceases to have any interest in its funds. Once again, so far as friendly societies are concerned, this is made very clear by s 49(1), that it is the members, the present members, who, alone, have any right in the assets. As membership always ceases on death, past members or the estates of deceased members therefore have no interest in the assets. Further, unless expressly so provided by the rules, unincorporated societies are not really tontine societies, intended to provide benefits for the longest liver of the members. Therefore, although it is difficult to say in any given case precisely when a society becomes moribund, it is quite clear that if a society is reduced to a single member neither he, still less his personal representatives on his behalf, can say he is or was the society and therefore entitled solely to its fund. It may be that it will be sufficient for the society's continued existence if there are two members, but if there is only one the society as such must cease to exist. There is no association, since one can hardly associate with oneself or enjoy one's own society. And so indeed the assets have become ownerless.

Finally, there comes a case which gives me great concern, *Re West Sussex Constabulary's Widows, Children and Benevolent (1930) Fund Trusts*[53] (see above, p 248). The case is indeed easily distinguishable from the present case in that what was there under consideration was a simple unincorporated association and not a friendly society, so that the provisions of s 49(1) of the 1896 Act do not apply. Otherwise the facts in that case present remarkable parallels to the facts in the present case.

[The learned judge, after referring to Goff J's judgment in *Re West Sussex Constabulary Fund*, continued:]

It will be observed that the first reason given by the judge for his decision is that he could not accept the principle of the members' clubs as applicable. This is a very interesting reason, because it is flatly contrary to the successful argument of Mr Ingle Joyce who appeared for the Attorney General in the case. Goff J purported to follow *Cunnack v Edwards*. His argument was as follows:

53 [1971] Ch 1.

> This society was nothing more than a club, in which the members had no transmissible interest: *Re St James' Club*.[54] Whatever the members, or even the surviving member, might have done while alive, when they died their interest in the assets of the club died with them.

And in the Court of Appeal,[55] he used the arguments he had used below. If all that Goff J meant was that the purposes of the fund before him were totally different from those of a members' club then of course one must agree, but if he meant to imply that there was some totally different principle of law applicable one must ask why that should be. His second reason is that in all the cases where the surviving members had taken, the organisation existed for the benefit of the members for the time being exclusively. This may be so, so far as actual decisions go, but what is the principle? Why are the members not in control, complete control, save as to any existing contractual rights, of the assets belonging to their organisation? One could understand the position being different if valid trusts had been declared of the assets in favour of third parties, for example charities, but that this was emphatically not the case was demonstrated by the fact that Goff J recognised that the members could have altered the rules prior to dissolution and put the assets into their own pockets. If there was no obstacle to their doing this, it shows in my judgment quite clearly that the money was theirs all the time. Finally, he purports to follow *Cunnack v Edwards* and it will be seen from the analysis which I have already made of that case that it was extremely special in its facts, resting on a curious provision of the 1829 Act which is no longer applicable. As I have already indicated, in the light of s 49(1) of the 1896 Act the case before Goff J is readily distinguishable, but I regret that, quite apart from that, I am wholly unable to square it with the relevant principles of law applicable.

The conclusion therefore is that, as on dissolution there were members of the society here in question in existence, its assets are held on trust for such members to the total exclusion of any claim on behalf of the Crown. The remaining question under this head which falls now to be argued is, of course, whether they are simply held *per capita*, or, as suggested in some of the cases, in proportion to the contributions made by each.

I think that there is no doubt that, as a result of modern cases springing basically from the decision of O'Connor MR in *Tierney v Tough*, judicial opinion has been hardening and is now firmly set along the lines that the interests and rights of persons who are members of any type of unincorporated association are governed exclusively by contract, that is to say the rights between themselves and their rights to any surplus assets. I say that to make it perfectly clear that I have not overlooked the fact that the assets of the society are usually vested in trustees on trust for the members. But that is quite a separate and distinct trust bearing no relation to the claims of the members *inter se* on the surplus funds so held on trust for their benefit.

54 (1852) 2 De GM & G 383.

55 [1896] 2 Ch 679.

That being the case, *prima facie* there can be no doubt at all but that the distribution is on the basis of equality, because, as between a number of people contractually interested in a fund, there is no other method of distribution if no other method is provided by the terms of the contract, and it is not for one moment suggested here that there is any other method of distribution provided by the contract. We are, of course, dealing here with a friendly society, but that really makes no difference to the principle. The Friendly Societies Acts do not incorporate the friendly society in any way and the only effect that it has is, as I pointed out in my previous judgment in this case, that there is a section which makes it crystal clear in the Friendly Societies Act 1896 that the assets are indeed held on trust for the members.

Now the fact that the *prima facie* rule is a matter of equality has been recently laid down, not of course for the first time, in two cases to which I need do no more than refer, *Re St Andrew's Allotment Association's Trusts*,[56] a decision of the late Ungoed-Thomas J, and *Re Sick and Funeral Society of St John's Sunday School, Golcar*,[57] a decision of Megarry J. Neither of those cases was, however, the case of a friendly society, and there are a number of previous decisions in connection with friendly societies, and, indeed, *Tierney v Tough*[58] itself is such a case, where the basis of distribution according to the subscriptions paid by the persons among whom the fund is to be distributed has been applied, and it has been suggested that perhaps those decisions are to be explained along the lines that a friendly society, or similar society, is thinking more of benefits to members, and that, thinking naturally of benefits to members, you think, on the other side of the coin, of subscriptions paid by members. But in my judgment that is not a satisfactory distinction of any description, because one is now dealing with what happens at the end of the life of the association; there are surplus funds, funds which have not been required to carry out the purposes of the association, and it does not seem to me it is a suitable method of distribution to say that one then looks to see what the purposes of the society were while the society was a going concern.

An ingenious argument has been put by counsel for the third and fifth defendants: the members of the society are entitled in equity to the surplus funds which are distributable among them, therefore they are to be distributed among them according to equitable principles and those principles should, like all equitable principles, be moulded to fit the circumstances of the case, and in one case it would therefore be equitable to distribute in equal shares, in another case it might be equitable to distribute in proportion to the subscription that they have paid, and I suppose that in another case it might be equitable to distribute according to the length of their respective feet, following a very well known equitable precedent. Well, I completely deny the basic premise. The members are not entitled in equity to the fund; they are entitled at law. It is a matter, so far as the members are concerned, of pure contract, and, being a matter of pure contract, it is, in my judgment, as far as distribution

56 [1969] 1 WLR 229.

57 [1973] Ch 51.

58 [1914] IR 142.

> is concerned, completely divorced from all questions of equitable doctrines. It is a matter of simple entitlement, and that entitlement must be, and can only be, in equal shares.

The courts apply similar principles as above in respect of the surplus funds on the winding up of pension schemes. The terms of the scheme are required to be construed and are treated as of paramount importance. The contractual basis of creating rights under the scheme is treated as highly relevant to, but not conclusive of, the question whether the resulting trust ought to be imposed. Thus, in *Davis v Richards and Wallington Industries Ltd*, the court decided that in respect of a pension fund surplus, the employer's contributions were subject to a resulting trust, but the employees' contributions were payable to the Crown as *bona vacantia*.

Davis v Richards and Wallington [1990] 1 WLR 1511, HC

In 1975, a group of companies established, by way of trust, a pension scheme to replace a previous scheme originally set up in 1968. The contributions were derived from three sources namely, employers' contributions, employees' contributions and the transferred funds. In 1982, the companies terminated the scheme due to financial difficulties. The question in issue *inter alia* was whether the surplus funds (£3 m) were held on resulting trust for the contributors or were taken by the Crown as *bona vacantia*.

The court held that the employers' contributions were held on resulting trust. The employees' contributions were taken by the Crown. The portion of the surplus attributable to the transferred funds, were taken by the Crown as *bona vacantia*.

> **Scott J:** I am satisfied that it is possible for a disposition of property to be made on terms which make it plain that the transferor affirmatively desires to exclude all possibility of a resulting trust in his favour. The presumption of law is against this and such an expression needs to be clear and unambiguous more especially as the likely result is that the property concerned, if there is such a failure as would normally give rise to a resulting trust, will pass as *bona vacantia* and that is a result which should not lightly be imputed to any transferor.'
>
> The provision in a trust deed necessary to exclude a resulting trust need not, in my opinion, be express. In the absence of an express provision it would, I think, often be very difficult for a sufficiently clear intention to exclude a resulting trust to be established. But, in general, any term that can be expressed can also, in suitable circumstances, be implied. In my opinion, a resulting trust will be excluded not only by an express provision but also if its exclusion is to be implied. If the intention of a contributor that a resulting trust should not apply is the proper conclusion, it would not be right, in my opinion, for the law to contradict that intention. In my judgment, therefore, the fact that a payment to a fund has been made under contract and that the payer has obtained all that he or she bargained for under the contract is not necessarily a decisive argument against resulting trust.

I must apply these principles to the surplus in the present case. The fund was, as I have said, fed from three sources: employees' contributions, transfers from other pension schemes and employers' contributions. The employees' contributions were made under contract. Employees were obliged to contribute 5% of salary. They were entitled, in return, to the specified pension and other benefits. The funds from other pension schemes, too, were transferred under contract. There would have been three parties to all these contracts, namely, the trustees of the transferor scheme, the trustees of the 1975 scheme and the transferring members themselves. Perhaps the employer company would have been a party as well. The transfer would certainly have been made with its consent. Under these contracts, by implication if not expressly, the transferor trustees would have been discharged from liability in respect of the transferred funds, whether liability to the transferring employee members or liability to the employer company

Finally, there are the employers. They, too, made their contributions under contract; they made them under the contracts of employment between themselves and their employees. But there is a very important difference between the contractual obligation of the employees and that of the employers. The employees' contractual obligation was specific in amount – 5% of salary. The employers' contractual obligation was conceptually certain but the amount was inherently uncertain. The obligation was to pay whatever was necessary to fund the scheme. The terms of rule 3 of Part II of the 1975 rules describe accurately, in my opinion, the contractual obligation of the employers:

> The employer will pay to the trustees such amounts as may from time to time be necessary to enable the trustees to maintain the benefits ...

In practice, the amount of the employers' contributions in respect of each employee was actuarially calculated. The calculations were based on assumptions as to the time when the benefits would become payable and as to the amount of the employee's final salary at that time. If the scheme should terminate before that time, the amount paid would be bound to have been more than needed to have been paid in order to fund the employee's benefits as at the date of termination.

Two separate questions seem to me to require to be answered. First, to what extent should the surplus, the £3 m odd, be regarded as derived from each of these three sources? One possible answer is that there should be a calculation of the total amount of employees' contributions, the total amount of funds transferred from other companies' pension schemes and the total amount of employers' contributions, and that the surplus should be regarded as derived from these three sources in the same proportions as the three totals bear to one another. I do not accept that this is right. It ignores the different bases on which these contributions were paid. Since the employers' obligation was to pay whatever was from time to time necessary to fund the various scheme benefits and since the employees' 5% contributions and the amount of the transferred funds constituted the base from which the amount of the employers' contributions would from time to time have to be assessed, it is logical, in my judgment, to treat the scheme benefits as funded first by the employees' contributions and the transferred funds, and only secondarily by the employers' contributions, and, correspondingly, to treat the surplus as provided first by the employers' contributions and only secondarily by the employees' contributions and the transferred funds.

There are two possible factual situations to be considered. It is possible (although, I think, very unlikely) that the employees' contributions and the funds transferred from the pension schemes of other companies would, without there having been any contribution at all from the employers, have been sufficient to provide in full for all the scheme benefits and, perhaps, still to have left some surplus. If that is the position, it would follow that, with the advantage of hindsight, the employers need not have made any contributions at all in order to have funded the benefits. This situation would, in my judgment, require that that surplus (which would be bound, I think, to be very small) should be regarded as derived from the employees' contributions and the transferred funds and that the balance of the surplus should be regarded as derived from the employers' contributions.

The much more likely situation is that some contribution at least was required from the employers in order to produce assets sufficient to provide all the scheme benefits to which employees became entitled on 31 July 1982. In that event the whole of the surplus, in my judgment, should be regarded as derived from the employers' contributions. This conclusion is, to my mind, in accordance both with logic and with equity. The actuarial calculations on which the employers' actual contributions were based were themselves based upon a series of assumptions. The termination of the scheme invalidated the assumptions. The employers had, in the event, made payments exceeding the amount necessary to discharge their obligation to fund the benefits to which the employees eventually became entitled. There is a well established equity that enables accounts drawn up under a mistake to be reopened. See Goff and Jones, *The Law of Restitution*, 3rd edn, 1986, p 199. In cases such as the present there was no mistake at the time the contributions were assessed and paid. The actuarial calculations were, I am sure, impeccable. But subsequent events having invalidated some of the assumptions underlying the calculations, the case is, in my opinion, strongly analogous to that of an account drawn up under a mistake. In my opinion, equity should treat the employers as entitled to claim the surplus, or so much of it as derived from the overpayments.

The second question is whether a resulting trust applies to the surplus, or to so much of the surplus as was derived from each of the three sources to which I have referred. As to the surplus derived from the employers' contributions, I can see no basis on which the resulting trust can be excluded. The equity to which I referred in the previous paragraph demands, in my judgment, the conclusion that the trustees hold the surplus derived from the employers' contributions upon trust for the employers. There is no express provision excluding a resulting trust and no circumstances from which, in my opinion, an implication to that effect could be drawn. On the other hand, in my judgment, the circumstances of the case seem to me to point firmly and clearly to the conclusion that a resulting trust in favour of the employees is excluded.

The circumstances are these:

(i) Each employee paid his or her contributions in return for specific financial benefits from the fund. The value of these benefits would be different for each employee, depending on how long he had served, how old he was when he joined and how old he was when he left. Two employees might have paid identical sums in contributions but have become entitled to benefits of a very different value. The point is particularly striking in respect of the employees (and there were several of them) who exercised their option to a refund of contributions. How can a resulting trust work as between the various employees *inter se*? I do not think it can and I do not see why equity should impute to them an intention that would lead to an unworkable result.

(ii) The scheme was established to take advantage of the legislation relevant to an exempt approved scheme and a contracted out scheme. The legislative requirements placed a maximum on the financial return from the fund to which each employee would become entitled. The proposed rules would have preserved the statutory requirements. A resulting trust cannot do so. In my judgment, the relevant legislative requirements prevent imputing to the employees an intention that the surplus of the fund derived from their contributions should be returned to them under a resulting trust. In my judgment, therefore, there is no resulting trust for the employees.

Finally, there are the transferred funds. The intention, in my judgment, appears sufficiently clear from the documents by which the transfers were effected and from the surrounding circumstances that the trustees of the transferred schemes were divesting themselves once and for all of the transferred funds. So far as the employee members of the transferee schemes were concerned there could not, for the same reasons as those I have already given, be a resulting trust in favour of them. So far as the employer contributors to those funds were concerned, ie, the companies whose shares had been taken over, they were not all in the same position *vis à vis* the transferred funds. Some of the transferor schemes expressly excluded any refund of assets to the employer contributors. Those employers could not, therefore, assert any resulting trust. As to the others, it is possible to regard the transferred funds as being subject to some contingent resulting trust of surplus in favour of employer contributors. But, as I understand the evidence, it would be virtually impossible now to identify the part of the £3 m odd surplus that represented the surplus (if there was one) inherent in any of the transferred funds. In my judgment, it is reasonable in the circumstances to regard the employer contributors to the transferred funds, as well as the employee contributors, as intending that the funds should vest in the 1975 scheme trustees to the entire exclusion of any claim under the transferor scheme, whether under the rules thereof or by way of resulting trust. Here again, I do not think equity should impute to the parties an impracticable and unworkable intention.

Accordingly, in my judgment, if any part of the surplus has derived from employees' contributions or from the funds transferred from the pension schemes of other companies, that part of the surplus devolves as *bona vacantia*. Subject thereto, the surplus is, in my judgment, held upon trust for the employer contributors.

Date of dissolution

In the ordinary course of events, the date of the dissolution of an association will not be in dispute. This will be the date when a formal resolution is passed to wind up the association. But, exceptionally, an association may become inactive for an exceptionally long period of time, the formal resolution to wind up the body may not, in itself, reflect the true state of affairs concerning the date of termination. In these circumstances, the extraordinarily prolonged period of inactivity may offer strong evidence of spontaneous dissolution. The court will decide, on the facts, the precise date of dissolution. The subsisting members of the association will then be entitled to participate in the distribution of the assets. But mere inactivity, by itself, is insufficient to constitute spontaneous dissolution. The association may be treated as going through a dormant period.

In re GKN Bolts & Nuts Ltd (Automotive Division), Birmingham Works Sports And Social Club, Leek v Donkersley [1982] 1 WLR 774, HC

In 1946, the trustees of a social club established for the benefit of company employees bought a sports ground. By 1969, the club was in financial difficulties and the sports ground was no longer in use. In January 1975, membership cards ceased to be issued. In February 1975, the last general meeting was held. No further annual accounts were prepared. In April 1975, the club ceased to be registered for VAT. In September 1975, the stocks of the club were sold. On 18 December 1975, a special meeting of the club was convened to consider an offer which was made to buy the sports ground and the members voted unanimously to sell the property. The sale did not take place but in May 1978, planning permission was granted for development of the site. On 21 July 1978, the trustees entered into a conditional contract to sell the club. This sale became unconditional on 4 August 1978, completion of the sale took place on 18 August 1978. The issues before the court were:

(a) whether the club ceased to exist and if so, when?

(b) as from which date were the assets distributable to the members?

Held, by Megarry VC:

(a) that the club ceased to exist on 18 December 1975, the date of the resolution to sell the sports ground. On this date, it was clear that the club accepted that it could no longer carry out its objects;

(b) that, applying the principle in the *Golcar* and *Re Bucks Constabulary* cases, the distribution of the assets would be on the basis of equality among members (ordinary or full) irrespective of the length of membership or amount of subscriptions paid.

> **Megarry VC:** The starting point is to consider whether there was a dissolution of the club on 18 December 1975, the date of the resolution to sell. The rules of the club do not help, for they are all directed to the operation of the club as a

going concern. It is plain that there never was an agreement by the entire membership that the club should be dissolved, and of course there has been no exercise by the court of its inherent jurisdiction to order a dissolution. The question therefore is whether there has been what was called in argument a spontaneous dissolution of the club.

As a matter of principle I would hold that it is perfectly possible for a club to be dissolved spontaneously. I do not think that mere inactivity is enough: a club may do little or nothing for a long period, and yet continue in existence. A cataleptic trance may look like death without being death. But inactivity may be so prolonged or so circumstanced that the only reasonable inference is that the club has become dissolved. In such cases there may be difficulty in determining the *punctum temporis* of dissolution: the less activity there is, the greater the difficulty of fastening upon one date rather than another as the moment of dissolution. In such cases the court must do the best it can by picking a reasonable date somewhere between the time when the club could still be said to exist, and the time when its existence had clearly come to an end.

I think that some such doctrine is supported by authority. In *Abbatt v Treasury Solicitor*,[59] a British Legion Club ceased to function, and in 1954 a meeting of the members of the club resolved to change the club into a working men's club, though without specifying any details. Some five months later the change-over took place; and Pennycuick J held that at the date of the change-over the former club ceased to exist and its property became distributable among those who were then members. The members of a club, he said were, by an implied term in the contract of membership, precluded from obtaining the realisation and distribution of the property of the club so long as the club functioned; but 'once the club ceases to function the reason for this disappears and the right of the existing members must, I think, crystallise once and for all': see p 567. At pp 568, 569 he made it clear that no resolution or order of the court was needed to bring about this result. This decision was reversed on appeal,[60] but on different grounds which did not affect this point; and I think counsel were right to concede that the decision on spontaneous dissolution was part of the ratio and was not affected by the appeal.

In *Re William Denby & Sons Ltd Sick and Benevolent Fund*,[61] Brightman J classified four categories of cases in which an unregistered friendly society or benevolent fund should be regarded as having been dissolved or terminated so that its assets became distributable. The first three categories of dissolution or termination were: (1) in accordance with the rules; (2) by agreement of all persons interested; and (3) by order of the court in the exercise of its inherent jurisdiction. The fourth category was when the substratum on which the society or fund was founded had gone, so that the society or fund no longer had any effective purpose, and the assets became distributable without any order of the court. On the facts of the case, it was held that the substratum had not gone, so that the fund was not distributable; but the judgment considered a

59 [1969] 1 WLR 561.

60 [1969] 1 WLR 1575.

61 [1971] 1 WLR 973.

number of the authorities, and plainly supports the view that there may be a spontaneous dissolution of a society. The judgment does not mention the *Abbatt* case,[62] though it was cited in argument; but I think the two cases have much in common as supporting a doctrine of spontaneous dissolution. Brightman J[63] expressed grave doubts whether mere inactivity of the officers of the society or the fund would suffice and in this I would respectfully concur. Mere inactivity is equivocal: suspended animation may be continued life, not death; and the mere cessation of function that was mentioned in the *Abbatt* case would not, I think, suffice *per se*. But inactivity coupled with other circumstances may demonstrate that all concerned regard the society as having ceased to have any purpose or function, and so as no longer existing. I think that short inactivity coupled with strong circumstances, or long inactivity coupled with weaker circumstances may equally suffice. The question is whether, put together, the facts carry sufficient conviction that the society is at an end and not merely dormant. For myself, I would hesitate a little about the use of the phrase 'substratum has gone' in this context. It has a beguiling sound; but it has strong overtones of the Companies Court. There, it may form the basis of a winding up order, but it does not by itself initiate or complete the termination of the existence of the company. It therefore seems not altogether appropriate for establishing that there has been a spontaneous dissolution. I also hesitate to use the term 'frustration', with all its contractual overtones. However, this is a mere matter of nomenclature, and does not affect the principle. The question is whether on the facts of the present case the society ceased to exist on 18 December 1975. On that date, the position was that the club had ceased to operate as a club for several months. The picture was not one of mere inactivity alone; there were positive acts towards the winding up of the club. The sale of the club's stock of drinks was one instance, and others were the ending of the registration for VAT, and the dismissal of the steward. The cessation of any club activities, the ending of the use of the sports ground and the abandonment of preparing accounts or issuing membership cards were all in one sense examples of inactivity; but I think that there was in all probability some element of deliberation in these matters, and not a mere inertia. In Mr Sher's phrase, there was a systematic dismantling of the club and its activities.

However that may be, the resolution to sell the sports ground seems to me to conclude the matter. Having taken all steps, active or passive, required to terminate the activities of the club, short of passing a formal resolution to wind it up or dissolve it, the general meeting of the club resolved to sell the club's last asset.

The cessation of all club activities, the general knowledge of attempts to get planning permission in order to sell the sports ground, and then the holding of a general meeting to discuss a sale, even with (on this assumption) inadequate notice, seem to me to mark an acceptance by all concerned that the club was a club no more but merely a collection of individuals with expectations of dividing the proceeds of sale of the one remaining asset of the club. Whether it

62 [1969] 1 WLR 561.

63 [1971] 1 WLR 973, pp 981–82.

is put in terms of the club ceasing to function, or whether it is expressed as being a case where the substratum has gone or whether it is said that the club had become inactive and the surrounding circumstances sufficiently indicated that those concerned regarded the club as having ceased to have any purpose or function, and so as no longer existing, the answer in each case is the same. The rules of 1974 stated that the objects of the club were 'to promote the different games of sport, to provide facilities for recreation and to encourage good fellowship among all members'; and all must have recognised that the club had become incapable of carrying out any of its objects. If the resolution to sell the sports ground is valid, as I think it is, that merely reinforces my conclusion that the club ceased to exist as such on 18 December 1975.

I turn to the question of the shares in which those who were members on 18 December 1975, are to divide the assets of the club.

For the reasons that I gave in *Re Sick and Funeral Society of St John's Sunday School, Golcar*[64] (a case which was applied by Walton J in *Re Bucks Constabulary Widows' and Orphans' Fund Friendly Society (No 2))*,[65] I think that where, as here, there is nothing in the rules or anything else to indicate a different basis, the distribution should be on a basis of equality, irrespective of the length of membership or the amount of the subscriptions paid. That seems to me to be particularly appropriate where, as here, the amount of the subscription is so small and the acquisition of the last remaining asset of the club occurred so long ago.

I have not so far differentiated between the different classes of members. Rule 2 of the rules of 1974 begins by providing that the club should consist of 'ordinary and honorary members and, in special cases, of temporary members as hereinafter provided'. The rule then turns to deal with 'full members', 'honorary members', 'associates', 'temporary members' and the spouses of members and their children up to 18 years old who are 'entitled to membership without voting rights'. There is nothing to explain any difference between 'ordinary members' and 'full members', and I think that they are merely different names for the same thing: see, for example, rules 2.6, 2.7 and 7.4. Only full members or ordinary members had voting rights at general meetings, but I must consider whether any other categories of membership are entitled to share in the assets of the club. I do not think that they are.

'Associates' are 'employees who are members of a group company club having similar objects' (rule 2.4). They have to write their names in a book, with the names of their clubs, and that gives them 'the same rights and privileges' as ordinary members, and makes them 'subject to the same rules', save that they may not vote at a meeting of the club or take away intoxicating liquor for consumption off the premises. 'Temporary members' (rule 2.5) are those invited by the committee to participate in the sporting and other amenities of the club; and this is limited to the day of the sporting or social event. The spouses and minor children of members, who are merely 'entitled to membership without voting rights' (rule 2.2), seem to me to fall within much

64 [1973] Ch 51.

65 [1979] 1 WLR 936.

> the same category as associates and temporary members. The object in each case seems to me to confer the right to use the club premises and facilities without imposing the powers and responsibilities of full members, for whom alone do the rules provide for the payment of subscriptions. The position of honorary members is more complex; and I am not at all sure that there are in fact any. By rule 8 of the rules of 1962, each employee was able to nominate one person for free honorary membership until the following 31 December. Honorary membership was also open to those whom the club wished to honour, to persons temporarily engaged in the company's organisation to whom the club wished to extend its activities, and to 'other persons sponsored by employee members who shall pay a subscription at the rate of 10 shillings per annum'. Rule 9 provided that honorary members should 'have no voting powers or interest in the club's assets', so that even those who paid their 10 shillings a year had no property rights.
>
> If there were no honorary members left, whether life members or subscribing, there is nothing to decide on this point. If there were any such members, I would hold that, as matters stand, they are not entitled to share in the club's assets. I say that partly because of rule 9 of the rules of 1962, partly because of what is generally understood by the term 'honorary member', and partly because of the general background for honorary membership of this club. I therefore hold that no members except those who are properly called 'full members' or 'ordinary members' are entitled to any interest in the assets of the club.

Brian Green, in 'The dissolution of unincorporated non-profit associations' (1980) 45 MLR 626, examines the modes of dissolution of unincorporated associations and the judicial methods of distributing the funds. On the latter issue, Mr Green highlights four solutions, namely, equal division, tenancy in common, proportionate division based on a resulting trust and *bona vacantia*.

The equal division of the funds appears to be the court's *prima facie* response, save when the society's rules indicate that a different method of distribution is appropriate, see *Re Sick and Funeral Society, Golcar*:

> As a conclusion of last resort, the maxim, 'Equality is equity' produces certainty and fairness between parties, and was the context in which it was adopted in the early cases: *Brown v Dale* (1878) 9 Ch 51 and *Feeny and Shannon v MacManus* [1937] IR 23. The more modern cases represent an unnecessary and illegitimate departure from the past authorities by elevating a maxim of last resort to the status of a *prima facie* presumption.

Megarry J in *Golcar* decided that past contributions of present members did not entitle them to join in the distribution of the society's assets because they had enjoyed the benefits of membership. Green attacks this reasoning as false logic:

> The initial claim is a narrow contractual one, the alleged conclusion is a quite separate proposition of property law. The question, 'Who is entitled to share in the benefits which the society exists to provide?', does not even provide an automatic answer to the question, 'Who is entitled to share in the society's

> property when it is dissolved?' let alone to the further question: 'How should the property be divided between those who are entitled to share it?

Green contends that the tenancy in common provides the guiding principle which should be adopted by the courts on a distribution on dissolution. In the majority of cases the surplus assets of a society may comprise contributions from a variety of sources – the abandoned property of past members, donations from non-members and members. Green submits: 'this property should be divided on the same proportionate basis ...'

The resulting trust solution is appropriate where a member's subscription is construed as having been handed over on a primary trust which fails when the association is dissolved. The existence of the primary trust would depend on all the circumstances surrounding membership of a society, and it may be that the association's charter would be thought particularly important in this context. This solution was adopted in *Re Printers and Transferrers Society*, but the decision was criticised on the ground that resulting trust principles could not account for the exclusion of the rights of past members.

Green lists five reasons why the co-ownership principles ought to be given preference over the resulting trust solution. First, the co-ownership rule is applicable to all cases, whereas the resulting trust rule is applicable where a primary purpose can be ascertained. Secondly, the common ownership rule will be exhaustive of the society's surplus assets but the resulting trust is strictly limited to returning members' contributions. Thirdly, the tenancy in common solution will not lead to priority of members over the society's general creditors in the event of a liquidation or bankruptcy. Fourthly, the primary trust attendant on the resulting trust solution requires someone in whose favour the court may decree performance in the event of default by the trustees of the society's purposes. Fifthly, a resulting trust claim may be void if it fails to vest within the perpetuity period.

Finally, Green, after examining the cases which adopted the *bona vacantia* solution, concludes that:

> ... members will only be unable to claim an interest in their association's funds in the rare case where an express or externally imposed regulation prevents them doing so. Aside of these limited occasions, *bona vacantia* is an improper conclusion in these cases.

PRESUMED RESULTING TRUST

On the creation of an express trust, the declaration of the settlor's intention would be decisive as to the ownership of the beneficial interest. Similarly, on the creation of a gift the donor transfers the beneficial interest to the donee. However, in a presumed resulting trust, the destination of the beneficial interest is unclear on the face of the instrument effecting the transfer. In an effort to reduce the element of doubt concerning the beneficial interest, the court implies or presumes a trust in favour of the transferor. The rationale behind this principle is that equity is inclined to lean against a gift.

A presumed resulting trust is a *prima facie* rule of evidence which is capable of being rebutted. When there is no definitive evidence in the first place concerning the transferor's real intention, but merely a purchase of property or the voluntary transfer of property in the name of another, equity *prima facie* considers the transferee as a trustee for the transferor. In short, the transferor is presumed to have retained the equitable title. The transferee is presumed to obtain a nominal interest in the property. The rule is arbitrary but the presumption has the advantage of determining the ownership of the beneficial interest, subject to evidence to the contrary.

There are two occasions when the presumption arises, namely:

(i) a purchase of property in the name of another; and

(ii) a voluntary conveyance of property in the name of another.

Purchase in the name of another

The rule is that where a purchaser contracts with a vendor to acquire real or personal property, but directs the vendor to transfer the property in the name of another, the transferee is presumed to hold the property on trust for the purchaser. Parol evidence is admissible in order to identify the purchaser.

Thus, if A purchases shares in the name of B (that is, B becomes the legal owner), the latter is presumed to hold the shares on trust for A. B is a mere nominee for A until he rebuts the presumption.

Similarly, where A and B jointly purchase a house and have it conveyed in the name of B so that B becomes the legal owner of the house, B is presumed to hold the house on trust for both A and B in proportion to the contribution made by each of them. If A provides four fifths and B, one fifth of the purchase monies, B is presumed to hold the house for himself beneficially as to one fifth and the remainder on trust for A.

Bull v Bull [1955] 1 QB 234, CA

In 1949, the plaintiff and his mother, the defendant, jointly purchased a freehold house. The plaintiff contributed a greater part of the purchase price than the defendant. The house was conveyed in the sole name of the plaintiff. The plaintiff and defendant lived together in the house. In April 1953, on the marriage of the plaintiff, it was agreed that the defendant should occupy two rooms and the plaintiff and his wife should occupy the rest of the house. Differences arose between the parties and the plaintiff brought an action for possession of the house.

Held, by the Court of Appeal, in favour of the defendant. The plaintiff was not allowed to recover possession of the house. The intention of the parties at the time of the purchase was that they became tenants in common. The plaintiff held the property as trustee on trust for sale for both of them. The defendant, as a tenant in common was entitled to remain in the house until it was sold.

> **Denning LJ:** The son, is of course, the legal owner of the house, but the mother and son are, I think, equitable tenants in common. Each is entitled in equity to an undivided share in the house, the share of each being in proportion to his or her respective contribution. Each of them is entitled to the possession of the land and to the use and enjoyment of it in a proper manner. Neither can turn out the other; but, if one of them should take more than his proper share, the injured party can bring an action for an account. If one of them should go so far as to oust the other, he is guilty of trespass.
>
> Since 1925 there has been no such thing as a legal tenancy in common. All tenancies in common now are equitable only and they take effect behind a [trust of land] (s 36(4) of the Settled Land Act 1925). Nevertheless, until a sale takes place, these equitable tenants in common have the same right to enjoy the land as legal tenants used to have ...
>
> My conclusion, therefore, is that when there are two equitable tenants in common, then, until the place is sold, each of them is entitled concurrently with the other to the possession of the land and to the use and enjoyment of it in a proper manner: and that neither of them is entitled to turn out the other.

The permutations of circumstances giving rise to the presumption are abundant. If the subject matter of the purchase is not vested in the name(s) of the purchaser(s), the *prima facie* rule is that the person(s) in whose name(s) the property is conveyed, is (are) presumed to hold on trust in favour of the individual(s) who provided the purchase monies. Accordingly, the burden of rebutting the presumption lies on the party against whom the presumption operates.

Dyer v Dyer (1788) 2 Cox Eq 92, HC

> **Eyre CB:** The clear result of all the cases, without a single exception is that the trust of a legal estate, whether taken in the names of the purchasers and others jointly, or in the names of others without that of the purchaser, whether in one name or several; whether jointly or successive – results to the man who advances the purchase money. It is the established doctrine of a court of equity that this resulting trust may be rebutted by circumstances in evidence.

In this respect, rent payable under a flat sharing arrangement is not treated as a purchase, for the tenants merely acquire the right to occupy the premises. Accordingly, such arrangement does not involve the presumption. Hence, if A and B share a flat as tenants which is taken in A's name and the parties contribute to the outgoings, this arrangement does not involve a resulting trust. Moreover, if A purchases the flat from his own resources and has it conveyed in his name, B is not entitled to claim an interest in the property.

Savage v Dunningham [1973] 3 WLR 471, HC

The plaintiffs and defendant shared a flat but the agreement was taken in the defendant's name. The rent and other expenses were shared equally between the plaintiffs and defendant. The defendant purchased the flat from his own resources. The plaintiffs claimed an interest by way of a resulting trust.

The court held in favour of the defendant. The payment of rent could not be equated with purchase moneys.

> **Plowman J:** Rent, unlike purchase money, is not paid for the acquisition of a capital asset, but for the use of the property during the term.

Likewise, a general loan (whether secured or not) which is used to purchase property but which is treated as a transaction separate from the purchase, so that the borrower is entitled to use the funds as he wishes, does not give rise to the presumption of resulting trust. The lender, undoubtedly, retains his right to have the loan repaid but enjoys no beneficial interest in the property purchased. Thus, if B lends a sum of money to A who uses the amount to purchase a house taken in A's name, B, the creditor, is not entitled to claim an interest in the house by way of a presumed resulting trust. B's remedy is to bring an action for the recovery of the money loaned. If the loan was secured on the house purchased by A by way of a mortgage, B may, in appropriate circumstances, enforce his rights as mortgagee but, subject to these rights, B has no interest in the property, simply because he made no contribution to the purchase of the property.

Hoare v Hoare (1982) *The Times*, 9 November, HC

Mr Guy Hoare's son, Derrick, had become engaged to Zoe at Christmas 1969. The couple lived with Mr and Mrs Hoare in a public house in Redhill. Derrick and Zoe were married in April 1973 and moved into their new home in July 1973. As the total earnings of Derrick and Zoe were insufficient to obtain a mortgage, Mr Hoare and Derrick took out a joint mortgage with the Abbey National Building Society. The property was transferred into the joint names of Mr Hoare and Derrick. The purchase price was £12,500. The mortgage amount was £10,000 repayable by means of an endowment policy effected on Derrick's life. Mr Hoare paid a deposit of £2,047 towards the purchase price of the house but was repaid £950 by Derrick and Zoe, leaving a balance of £1,097. Mr Hoare had also made monthly, mortgage payments to the building society amounting in total to £4,014. With tax reliefs of £1,355 and repayments by Derrick and Zoe to Mr Hoare, the latter had contributed only £444 more than Derrick and Zoe. By August 1976, the joint incomes of Derrick and Zoe had increased considerably and Derrick wanted the mortgage transferred into his sole name. On 27 August 1976, he filled in the appropriate forms and returned them to the building society for their consideration. Sadly, on 10 September 1976, before the transfer was completed, Derrick died intestate in an air disaster over Yugoslavia. The effect was that the legal title in the house became vested in Mr Hoare. The insurance monies were more than enough to pay off the mortgage (which was done) and produced a surplus of £5,620.

Zoe now claimed a declaration that she was entitled to the entire beneficial interest in the house, subject to the payment of £1,097 to Mr Hoare as repayment of an interest free loan. Mr Hoare claimed to be entitled to a half share in the house.

Held, by Foster J, in favour of Zoe, on the ground that the intention of the defendant was to facilitate Derrick and Zoe in obtaining the matrimonial home by means of an interest free loan. There was never an understanding that Mr Hoare would acquire an interest in the house.

Voluntary transfer in the name of another

Another state of affairs which gives rise to a presumed resulting trust is the occasion of a voluntary transfer of personal property in the name of another. No consideration is provided by the person in whose favour the transfer is made.

For example, if A transfers the legal title to shares in the name of B, a resulting trust is presumed in favour of A.

Re Vinogradoff [1935] WN 68, HC

In this case, a grandmother voluntarily transferred £800 worth of War Loan stock into the joint names of herself and granddaughter, then aged four. By her will, the grandmother transferred her interest in the stock to another. Following the grandmother's death, the executors brought an action to determine what interest, if any, the granddaughter held in the stock. It was decided that the transfer created a resulting trust in favour of the grandmother. Accordingly, the granddaughter was required to hold the stock on trust for her grandmother's estate.

On the other hand, where real property is voluntarily conveyed in the name of another, a presumption of resulting trust does not automatically arise in accordance with s 60(3) of the Law of Property Act 1925 which provides:

> In a voluntary conveyance a resulting trust for the grantor shall not be implied merely by reason that the property is not expressed to be conveyed for the use or benefit of the grantee.

However, a resulting trust may still arise in accordance with the intention of the grantor, despite a voluntary conveyance in the name of the grantee. See *Hodgson v Marks*[66] (above, p 59).

66 [1971] Ch 892.

It is unclear whether s 60(3) is applicable if the property is voluntarily conveyed in the joint names of the grantor and grantee. A case could be made out that s 60(3) is not applicable and a resulting trust will be presumed in favour of the grantor in accordance with the general rule.

Presumption of advancement

A presumption of advancement, unlike a presumption of a resulting trust, is a presumption of a gift in favour of the transferee. Where there is a special relationship between the transferor and transferee, a purchase of property in the name of another or the voluntary transfer of real or personal property in another's name gives rise to a presumption of a gift. Thus, the transferor is presumed to lose his beneficial interest in the property. This presumption, like the presumption of a resulting trust, may be rebutted by evidence of the intention of the transferor.

Bennet v Bennet (1879) 10 Ch D 474, CA

> **Sir George Jessel MR:** The doctrine of equity as regards presumption of gifts is this, that where one person stands in such a relation to another that there is an obligation on that person to make a provision for the other, and we find either a purchase or investment in the name of the other, or in the joint names of the person and the other, of an amount which could constitute a provision for the other, the presumption arises of an intention on the part of the person to discharge the obligation to the other; and therefore, in the absence of evidence to the contrary, that purchase or investment is held to be in itself evidence of a gift. In other words, the presumption of gift arises from the moral obligation to give.
>
> That reconciles all the cases upon the subject but one, because nothing is better established than this, that as regards a child, a person, not the father of the child, may put himself in the position of one *in loco parentis* to the child, and so incur the obligation to make provision for the child ...
>
> But the father is under that obligation from the mere fact of his being the father, and therefore no evidence is necessary to show the obligation to provide for his child, because that is part of his duty. In the case of a father, you have only to prove the fact that he is the father, and when you have done that the obligation at once arises; but in the case of a person *in loco parentis* you must prove that he took upon himself the obligation.

The special relationships with the transferees which give rise to the presumption of advancement are occasions which the courts have recognised in the past as involving a moral obligation on the part of the transferor to benefit the transferee. These are:

(a) the transferee is the wife of the transferor;

(b) a transfer by a father to his legitimate child;

(c) occasions when the transferor stand *in loco parentis patris* to the child.

Husband and wife

The strength of this presumption as a means of ascertaining ownership of family assets has been reduced since the mid-1940s. See *Pettitt v Pettitt*[67] (below, p 367). The principle applicable to the family home will be discussed later under constructive trusts.

The presumption operates when the husband transfers property in the name of his wife. The presumption of resulting trust applies if the wife transfers property in the name of the husband. The essential point is that the wife (transferee) is required to be the lawful wife of the transferor so that the presumption of advancement will not, of course, arise in favour of a mistress or similar relationships.

Father and child

'Child' refers to the legitimate child of the transferor. If the father transfers property or purchases property in the name of his legitimate child, the presumption of a gift arises. This presumption is not displaced by slight evidence, see *Shephard v Cartwright*.[68]

On the other hand, if the mother transfers property in the name of her legitimate child, the presumption of a resulting trust arises (see the summary of the principle stated by Jessel MR in *Bennet v Bennet*, above, p 276).

Persons standing in loco parentis patris

This category of presumed gifts is applicable to persons who undertake the duties of fatherhood in respect of the child. These duties, apparently, cannot be undertaken by a female donor.

Bennet v Bennet (1879) 10 Ch D 474, CA

> **Jessel MR:** A person *in loco parentis* means a person taking upon himself the duty of a father of a child to make provision for that child. It is clear that the presumption can only arise from that obligation, and therefore the doctrine can only have reference to the obligation of a father to provide for his child, and nothing else.

Whether the donor stands *in loco parentis* to the donee is a question of degree. The essential issue is whether the male donor has placed himself in the position of a father to that child, that is, treating the child as his own, maintaining and providing care and attention for the child.

67 [1970] AC 777.

68 [1955] AC 431.

Re Paradise Motor Company [1968] 1 WLR 1125, CA

In 1948, F, the stepfather of S executed a transfer of 350 shares in favour of S, whom he treated in the same way as his three other sons. S's name appeared in the company's register of members. In 1954, F, having fallen out with S, wished to claim back 300 of the shares. In pursuance of this objective, F procured a transfer to himself of 300 shares which appeared to bear S's signature (this was not authorised). The company's register of members was accordingly altered. In 1964, the company was wound up and £12,000 was available for distribution. The liquidator informed S that he was the registered holder of 50 shares only. S told his half brother and the liquidator that he laid no claim to the shares. Later, he changed his mind and claimed to be entitled to 350 shares in the company.

Held, in favour of F, on the following grounds:

(a) the relationship between F and S was such as to give rise to the presumption of advancement in favour of S. *Prima facie*, in 1948, F was treated as having made a gift of 350 shares to S;

(b) S's statement to his half brother and the liquidator manifested an intention to disclaim his interest in the holding of 350 shares;

(c) this disclaimer *inter vivos* (was outside the province of s 53(1)(c) of the Law of Property Act 1925, because it operates by way of 'avoidance' rather than 'disposition') could not, in the circumstances, be withdrawn and amounted to a rebuttal of the presumption of advancement. F was therefore entitled to claim the benefit of 350 shares.

Rebuttal of the presumptions

The presumptions of resulting trust and advancement are, in a sense, artificial rules for deciding the intention of the transferor or purchaser and may give way to the real intention of the parties.

Although the weight of the presumptions will vary with the circumstances of each case, the courts will consider all the surrounding facts and decide whether the presumption has been rebutted or not. The quality of the rebutting evidence varies from case to case.

Fowkes v Pascoe (1875) LR 10 Ch App 343, CA

> **Mellish LJ:** ... the presumption must ... be of very different weight in different cases. In some cases it would be very strong indeed. If, for instance, a man invested a sum of stock in the name of himself and his solicitor, the inference would be very strong indeed that it was intended solely for the purpose of a trust, and the court would require very strong evidence on the part of the solicitor to prove that it was intended as a gift; and certainly his own evidence would not be sufficient. On the other hand, a man may make an investment of stock in the name of himself and some person, although not a child or wife, yet

> in such a position to him as to make it extremely probable that the investment was intended as a gift. In such a case, although the rule of law, if there is no evidence at all, would compel the court to say that the presumption of trust must prevail, even if the court might not believe that the fact was in accordance with the presumption, yet, if there is evidence to rebut the presumption, then the court must go into the actual facts.

In this case, Mrs Baker purchased stock in the joint names of herself and John Pascoe, the son of Mrs Baker's daughter in law. By her will, Mrs Baker gave her residuary estate to her daughter in law for life with remainder to John Pascoe and his sister in equal shares. After Mrs Baker's death, John Pascoe claimed to be entitled to the dividends due before and after her death as well as the stock capital after her death.

Held that the claimant was entitled to the dividends and the stock capital after Mrs Baker's death. The resulting trust in favour of Mrs Baker which arose on the date of purchase was rebutted, but only after her death. Thus, she was entitled to the income during her lifetime.

> **Mellish LJ** (continued): It appears to me utterly impossible, as the Lord Justice has said, to come to any other conclusion than that the first investment was made for the purpose of gift and not for the purpose of trust. It was either for the purpose of trust or else for the purpose of gift; and therefore any evidence which shews it was not for the purpose of trust is evidence to shew that it was for the purpose of gift. We find a lady of considerable fortune, having no nearer connections than Mr Pascoe, who was then a young man living in her house, and for whom she was providing. We find her, manifestly out of her savings, buying a sum of £250 stock in the joint names of herself and him, and at the same time buying another sum of £250 stock, on the very same day, in the joint names of herself and a lady who was living with her as a companion. Then, applying one's common sense to that transaction, what inference is it possible to draw, except that the purchases were intended for the purpose of gifts? If they were intended for the purpose of trusts, what possible reason was there why the two sums were not invested in the same names? Besides, at the very same time the lady had a large sum of stock in her own name, and could anything be more absurd than to suppose that a lady with £4,000 or £5,000 in her own name at that time in the same stock, and having a sum of £500 to invest out of her savings, should go and invest £250 in the name of herself and a young gentleman who was living in her house, and another £250 in the name of herself and her companion, and yet intend the whole to be for herself? I cannot come to any other conclusion than that it must have been intended by way of a present after her death.
>
> Then, when we have once arrived at the conclusion that the first investment was intended as a gift (and the second was exactly similar), and when we find that the account was opened for the purpose of gift, those facts appear to me to rebut the presumption altogether, because when an account is once found to be opened for the purpose of gift there is very strong reason to suppose that everything added to that account was intended for the purpose of gift also. Assuming the testatrix to know that she had made a gift, and had invested a

sum of money in stock in the joint names of herself and Pascoe for the purpose of making a present to him, it would certainly be a very extraordinary thing that she should go and add other large sums to that account, not for the purpose of making a present to him, but for the purpose of his being a trustee. I cannot help coming to the conclusion that, as a matter of fact, these investments were intended for the purpose of gift.

Lord Grey v Lady Grey (1677) 2 Swan 594, HC

The court held that a conveyance of real property from a father to his adult son created the presumption of advancement and the presumption was not rebutted when the son allowed the father to receive the rents from the land. Such conduct was an 'act of reverence and good manners'.

If an infant acts in accordance with the directions of his father, this evidence may be insufficient to rebut the presumption of advancement for the infant may not have been capable of exercising an independent judgment.

Shephard v Cartwright [1955] AC 431, HL

> **Viscount Simonds:** It appears to me to be an indispensable condition of such conduct being admissible that it should be performed with knowledge of the material facts. In the present case, the undisputed fact that the appellants under their father's guidance did what they were told without inquiry or knowledge precludes the admission in evidence of their conduct and, if it were admitted would deprive it of all probative value.

In this case, the court laid down the test of admissibility of evidence, namely, evidence of matters arising after the transaction, so as to be independent from the purchase, may only be admissible against the party who performed the act or made the declaration; whereas, acts and declarations occurring before such transaction, are admissible for or against the party.

In the present case, the dispute arose in respect of the following facts. In 1929, the plaintiffs' father promoted several private companies and had the shares allotted to to his three children. In a series of subsequent transactions, these shares were sold and a large portion of the proceeds of sale dissipated. In 1934, the children signed documents at the request of their father without understanding the effect of what they were doing. The result was that the shares were sold by the father and the proceeds of sale paid into their accounts. In 1935, the father obtained the children's signatures to documents authorising him to withdraw moneys from their accounts. By 1936, the father had withdrawn all the money from the accounts, some of it he used for the benefit of the children but a large part of it remained unaccounted for at the time of his death in 1949.

The children brought an action against their father's executors claiming an account of the money due to them.

Held, by the House of Lords, in favour of the children, on the following grounds:

(a) the registration of the shares in the children's names created a presumption of advancement;

(b) the events which took place after the allotment (signatures of the children) were capable of being evidence against the children in that the evidence could be construed as 'admissions' against their interest. But, such evidence was not admissible against the children because they signed the documents under the guidance and control of their father. They did what they were told without inquiry or knowledge;

(c) accordingly, the presumption of advancement was not rebutted.

Viscount Simonds: My Lords, I do not distinguish between the purchase of shares and the acquisition of shares upon allotment, and I think that the law is clear that on the one hand where a man purchases shares and they are registered in the name of a stranger there is a resulting trust in favour of the purchaser; on the other hand, if they are registered in the name of a child or one to whom the purchaser then stood *in loco parentis*, there is no such resulting trust but a presumption of advancement. Equally, it is clear that the presumption may be rebutted but should not, as Lord Eldon said, give way to slight circumstances: *Finch v Finch*.[69]

It must then be asked by what evidence can the presumption be rebutted, and it would, I think, be very unfortunate if any doubt were cast (as I think it has been by certain passages in the judgments under review) upon the well settled law on this subject. It is, I think, correctly stated in substantially the same terms in every textbook that I have consulted and supported by authority extending over a long period of time. I will take, as an example, a passage from *Snell's Equity*, 24th edn, 1954, p 153, which is as follows:

> The acts and declarations of the parties before or at the time of the purchase, or so immediately after it as to constitute a part of the transaction, are admissible in evidence either for or against the party who did the act or made the declaration ... But subsequent declarations are admissible as evidence only against the party who made them, and not in his favour.

I do not think it necessary to review the numerous cases of high authority upon which this statement is founded. It is possible to find in some earlier judgments reference to 'subsequent' events without the qualifications contained in the textbook statement: it may even be possible to wonder in some cases how in the narration of facts certain events were admitted to consideration. But the burden of authority in favour of the broad proposition as stated in the passage I have cited is overwhelming and should not be disturbed.

But although the applicable law is not in doubt, the application of it is not always easy. There must often be room for argument whether a subsequent act is part of the same transaction as the original purchase of transfer, and equally whether subsequent acts which it is sought to adduce in evidence ought to be

69 (1975) 119 SJ 793.

regarded as admissions by the party so acting, and if they are so admitted, further facts should be admitted by way of qualification of those admissions ...

The first question, then, is whether any subsequent events are admissible as part of the original transaction to prove that the deceased had not in 1929 the intention of advancement which the law presumes. My Lords, for nearly five years nothing happened which could by any means be regarded as throwing light upon his original intention, but an event did happen which would amply explain a change in that intention. For within a short time of their promotion the businesses of the six companies were prosperous beyond all expectation. In the year 1931, their combined profits were £57,780, in 1932, £128,525 and in 1933, £344,671. It is not surprising that in the light of this great success the deceased and his co-adventurer, Meyer, should form a public company to acquire all the shares of all the six companies. This they did.

My Lords, at the outset of this opinion I said that there must often be room for argument whether subsequent events can be regarded as forming part of the original transaction so as to be admissible evidence of intention and in this case it has certainly been vigorously argued that they can. But, though I know of no universal criterion by which a link can for this purpose be established between one event and another, here I see insuperable difficulty in finding any link at all. The time factor alone of nearly five years is almost decisive, but, apart from that, the events of 1934 and 1935, whether taken singly or in their sum, appear to me to be wholly independent of the original transaction. It is in fact fair to say that, so far from flowing naturally and inevitably from it, they probably never would have happened but for the phenomenal success of the enterprise. Nor can I give any weight to the argument much pressed upon us that the deceased was an honourable man and therefore could not have acted as he did, if he had in 1929 intended to give the shares outright to his children.

If, then, these events cannot be admitted in evidence as part of the original transaction, can they be admitted to rebut the presumption on the ground that they are admissions by the appellants against interest? I conceive it possible, and this view is supported by authority, that there might be such a course of conduct by a child after a presumed advancement as to constitute an admission by him of his parent's original intention, though such evidence should be regarded jealousy. But it appears to me to be an indispensable condition of such conduct being admissible that it should be performed with knowledge of the material facts. In the present case the undisputed fact that the appellants under their father's guidance did what they were told without inquiry or knowledge precludes the admission in evidence of their conduct and, if it were admitted, would deprive it of all probative value. It is otherwise however, with the conduct of the deceased. I have already made it clear that the respondents have failed to discharge the burden which rests on them of rebutting the presumption of advancement. The appellants, therefore, in my opinion, need no reinforcement from subsequent events. But, since inevitably in a complex case like this, either upon the footing of being examined *de benesse* or because they have been admitted for some other purpose than the proof of intention, all the facts relevant or irrelevant have been reviewed, I do not hesitate to say that the only conclusion which I can form about the deceased's original intention is that he meant the provision he then made for his children to be for their permanent advancement. He may well have changed his mind at a later date, but it was too late. He may have thought that, having made an absolute gift, he could yet revoke it. This is something that no one will ever know. The presumption which the law makes is not to be thus rebutted. If it were my duty to speculate upon these matters, my final question would be why the deceased should have put these several parcels of shares in six different companies into the names of his wife and three children unless he meant to make provision for them, and since counsel have not been able to suggest any, much less any plausible, reason why he should have done so, I shall conclude that the intention which the law imputes to him was in fact his intention. The reasoning which made so strong an appeal to Mellish LJ in *Fowkes v Pascoe*[70] has in this case also particular weight.

Re Gooch (1890) 62 LT 384, HC

The presumption of advancement was rebutted. A father bought shares in the name of his son to enable him (the son) to qualify as a director of a company. The son consistently paid the dividends over to his father and later delivered the share certificates to him.

Re Paradise Motor Co Ltd [1968] 1 WLR 1125, CA

The presumption of advancement was rebutted by a disclaimer. A stepfather, who stood *in loco parentis* to his stepson, transferred a block of shares in his name. After an argument with his stepfather, the stepson told his half brother and the liquidator of the company that he was no longer interested in the relevant shares. This had the effect of disclaiming his interest and rebutting the presumption of advancement.

Warren v Guerney [1944] 2 All ER 472, CA

The retention of the title deeds, coupled with a statement made by a father at the time of the conveyance of a house in the name of his daughter, were sufficient evidence to rebut the presumption of advancement.

In this case, a father purchased a house for £300 in 1929 and had it conveyed in the name of his daughter. At same time, he declared orally, that his wish after his death was that the house should be used for the benefit of his three daughters equally. The father retained the title deeds. In 1943, the father signed a document headed 'my wish' in which he repeated his earlier oral declaration. He died in 1944, the title deeds were still in his possession at the time of his death. The executors of the father's will contended that the daughter became a trustee of the property for her father's estate.

Held, by the Court of Appeal, in favour of the executors, on the following grounds:

70 (1875) 10 Ch App 343.

(a) the document headed, 'my wish' was not admissible in evidence as it was a subsequent declaration by the donor, but did not operate against the donor's interest;

(b) but, the retention of the title deeds by the father coupled with his contemporaneous declaration at the time of the purchase were sufficient evidence in rebuttal of the presumption.

Thus, the daughter held the house as trustee for her father's estate.

> **Morton LJ:** It is well established that when a parent buys a property and has it conveyed into the name of his child, there arises a presumption that the parent intended to make a gift or advancement to the child of that property. Of course, that is a presumption which can be rebutted by evidence that that was not the father's intention. The father retained the title deeds of the property and he still had them in his possession when he died in the year 1944.
>
> Three points were taken by counsel for the appellant. First of all, he contended that the judge was wrong in admitting as evidence a document headed 'my wish', which he held was signed by Elijah Gurney, which was dated 6 September 1943. In my view counsel's contention under that heading was quite correct. The document headed 'my wish' was not admissible in evidence. It was in the nature of a subsequent declaration by the alleged donor, which was not against his own interest, and it is clearly established that subsequent declarations by the alleged donor are only admissible if they are against his interest. The reason for that is quite obvious. If the rule were otherwise, it would be extremely easy for persons to manufacture evidence, even although at the time when they made the purchase they in fact intended the child to have the gift of the property.
>
> The second contention put forward by counsel for the appellants was that, on the admissible evidence, the judge was not justified in coming to the conclusion that the defendants had rebutted the presumption of advancement. In my view, there was ample evidence to justify that conclusion of the judge. In the first place, there is the fact that the father retained the title deeds from the time of purchase to the time of his death. I think that is a very significant fact, because title deeds, as it was said in *Coke on Littleton*, are 'sinews of the land'. One would have expected the father to have handed them over, either to the plaintiff or her husband, if he had intended the gift. It is to be noted that the judge accepted the evidence given by the plaintiff's mother, Mary Ann Gurney, and by her brother, Meyrick George Gurney, and rejected the evidence of Denis Warren, the plaintiff's husband, where it conflicted with that given by those two witnesses.
>
> I do not intend to travel all through the evidence given before the county court judge, but I wish to read one portion of it only, which, it seems to me, is of the utmost importance. Meyrick George Gurney gave evidence as follows:
>
>> I am the son of Elijah Gurney and his executor. In 1929 father said he had thought of buying one of the properties for plaintiff: asked me which I thought best.

> Pausing there, the words 'for plaintiff' might, if they had stood alone, seem to indicate that a gift was intended, but that possible meaning is displaced by what follows:
>
> > I said 'Fairview'. Father said he had been talking to Warren. Father said Warren had said if father bought the house he would pay for the house as he could. I went with father to Wadeson, the solicitor. Father required property made in my sister's name, so that there could be no trouble at a later date, as Warren had to pay for it at a later date. Father said he should keep the deeds as security.
>
> There are other passages of importance in the evidence. There are passages in the evidence of Mary Ann Gurney, containing statements as to contemporaneous declarations by the testator. There are certain statements made by the plaintiff herself against her own interest: for instance, the statement that she had not enough money to pay any rent. But I need not go further into the evidence. It seems to me, on the passages which I have referred to alone, the county court judge was fully justified in coming to his conclusion. The passage I have read from the evidence of Meyrick Gurney is a passage of the evidence of a witness whom the judge believed, and it seems to me that those contemporaneous declarations are quite sufficient to rebut the presumption even if they stood alone.
>
> It is quite clear that contemporaneous declarations by the alleged donor are admissible in evidence. I am satisfied that there was ample evidence upon which the judge could found his conclusion, and, indeed, it is difficult to see how, on the evidence which he believed, he could have reached any other conclusion.
>
> [The third contention raised by counsel for the appellants was not related to the beneficial ownership of the house.]

In *McGrath v Wallis* (see below), the Court of Appeal decided that a house acquired for joint occupation by a father and son, but conveyed in the sole name of the son, gave rise to the equitable presumption of advancement, which was rebutted by comparatively slight evidence. The court reiterated Lord Upjohn's view in *Pettitt v Pettitt* [1970] AC 777, to the effect that the presumptions of advancement and resulting trust, when properly understood and applied to circumstances of today, remained as useful as ever in solving questions of title, but are readily rebutted by comparatively slight evidence. Although *Pettitt v Pettitt* was a case between husband and wife, the same principle applies to transactions between father and child.

McGrath v Wallis (1995) *The Times*, 13 April, CA

In 1959, the father of the plaintiff (daughter) and the defendant (the plaintiff's brother) acquired a house in Luton which was placed in the sole name of the father and remained the family home for many years. The plaintiff lived there until she married in 1974. The defendant lived there until his mother died in 1985. In 1986, the father decided to sell the house and move elsewhere. To acquire the second house (Talbot Road) an additional amount was required to be raised by way of a mortgage. The father was not employed at the time, but a mortgage offer was made by a building society to the defendant and, in due course, the house was conveyed into his sole name. The father instructed his solicitors to draw up a deed which was intended to have been a declaration of trust. The deed declared that the Talbot Road house was to be held by the defendant upon trust for his father and himself in unequal shares of 80% and 20% respectively. The deed was never sent to the father by the solicitors but was found unsigned in their files. The father died intestate in 1990 and the plaintiff claimed to be entitled to a share of the Talbot Road property. The defendant denied that she had any such interest. The trial judge decided in favour of the defendant, on the ground that the presumption of advancement arose in favour of the defendant and the plaintiff had failed to discharge the burden of proof cast on her. The plaintiff appealed to the Court of Appeal.

The court allowed the appeal. In the circumstances, the presumption of advancement was rebutted by evidence in accordance with the intention of the parties. This was reflected in the sharing of the beneficial interest between the father and son on an 80:20% basis. The decisive factors were:

(a) the defendant alone was acceptable as a mortgagor of the property;

(b) the father had never told the defendant that he had instructed the solicitors not to proceed with the declaration of trust;

(c) no reason had been suggested for the father wishing to divest himself of all interest in the house.

It would appear that this rule, concerning the admissibility of evidence, has been overtaken by the Civil Evidence Act 1995 which admits the relevant evidence, even evidence of subsequent acts or declarations, either for or against the actor or declarant. Section 2 is an extremely broad provision which admits both hearsay and narrative assertions made orally or in a document or otherwise and irrespective of whether the maker of the statement is a witness or not. In this context, no cases have been decided. The document which was excluded in *Warren v Guerney* would now be admissible under s 1 of the 1995 Act. The weight to be attached to the evidence will vary with the facts of each case. Section 4 of the Act declares that the court is required to consider all the circumstances in which the statement was made, including the question whether the statement was made contemporaneously with the occurrence with the event or not.

Section 1 of the Civil Evidence Act 1995: admissibility of hearsay evidence

(1) In civil proceedings evidence shall not be excluded on the ground that it is hearsay.

Section 4 of the Civil Evidence Act 1995: considerations relevant to weighing of hearsay evidence

(1) In estimating the weight (if any) to be given to hearsay evidence in civil proceedings the court shall have regard to any circumstances from which any inference can reasonably be drawn as to the reliability or otherwise of the evidence.

(2) Regard may be had, in particular, to the following:

  (a) whether it would have been reasonable and practicable for the party to whom the evidence was adduced to have produced the maker of the original statement as a witness;

  (b) whether the original statement was made contemporaneously with the occurrence or existence of the matters stated;

  (c) whether the evidence involves multiple hearsay;

  (d) whether any person involved had any motive to conceal or misrepresent matters;

  (e) whether the original statement was an edited account, or was made in collaboration with another or for a particular purpose;

  (f) whether the circumstances in which the evidence is adduced as hearsay are such as to suggest an attempt to prevent proper evaluation of its weight:

    (i) where before that person is called the court allows evidence of the making of the statement to be given on behalf of that party by some other person; or

    (ii) in so far as the court allows the person by whom the statement was made to narrate it in the course of his examination-in-chief on the ground that to prevent him from doing so would adversely affect the intelligibility of his evidence.

(3) Where in any civil proceedings a statement which was made otherwise than in a document is admissible by virtue of this section, no evidence other than direct oral evidence by the person who made the statement or by any person who heard or otherwise perceived it being made shall be admissible for the purpose of proving it, provided that if the statement in question was made by a person while giving oral evidence in some other legal proceedings (whether civil or criminal), it may be proved in any manner authorised by the court.

Originally, the court did not allow a party to rebut the presumption of advancement by adducing evidence of his own attempted illegality or fraudulent purpose, on public policy grounds (but see *Tribe v Tribe*, below, p 302). If the transfer is made in order to avoid creditors and the transferor becomes insolvent, then, by virtue of the Insolvency Act 1986, the conveyance may be set aside by the court. The situation that we are now considering is in respect of a transfer in order to put the property out of reach of the creditors. The precaution taken by the transferor proves unnecessary because he (the transferor) does not become insolvent, but wishes to put the clock back to what it was before the transfer. In short, the claim is made by the transferor to recover the property from the transferee. The court has applied the following maxim, 'He who comes to Equity, must come with clean hands'.

Gascoigne v Gascoigne [1918] 1 KB 223, CA

In this case a husband, who was heavily in debt, took a lease of land. In order to protect his property from his creditors, he arranged for the lease to be taken in his wife's name. The wife was also aware of the purpose for the husband's action. He then built a bungalow on the land with his own money. Later, when the marriage had broken down, the husband claimed that the wife held the lease as trustee for him and called on her to assign it to him. The wife contended that the presumption of advancement existed in her favour and this presumption could not be rebutted by evidence of her husband's impropriety.

Held, by Lush LJ, reversing the decision of the county court judge, the presumption of advancement could not be rebutted by evidence of the husband's fraudulent conduct, despite the wife being a party to the transaction.

> **Lush LJ:** Now, assuming that there was evidence to support the finding that the defendant was a party to the scheme which the plaintiff admitted, but without deciding it, what the learned judge has done is this: he has permitted the plaintiff to rebut the presumption which the law raises by setting up his own illegality and fraud, and to obtain relief in equity because he has succeeded in proving it. The plaintiff cannot do this; and, whether the point was taken or not in the county court this court cannot allow a judgment to stand which has given relief under such circumstances as that.

Re Emery's Investments Trust [1959] Ch 410, HC

A husband, who transferred shares in the name of his wife in order to evade the tax laws of a foreign country, was not allowed to adduce evidence of the purpose of the transfer.

This principle was approved by the Court of Appeal in *Tinker v Tinker*[71] where a husband acting honestly, on the advice of his solicitors, conveyed the matrimonial home (bought solely by him) into the name of his wife as a precaution to avoid his creditors, in the event of his business failing. In the circumstances his business did not fail. On a breakdown of the marriage, the husband claimed to be entitled to the property.

The court held that the presumption of advancement was not rebutted for the husband was not allowed to adduce evidence of his improper motives for the conveyance.

71 [1970] 1 All ER 540.

Tinker v Tinker [1970] 1 All ER 540, CA

The facts appear in the judgment of Lord Denning MR.

Lord Denning MR: In this case, the husband and wife were married on September 23, 1955. They have two children, daughters, who are now aged eleven and seven years. There are divorce proceedings between them. We are concerned today with the beneficial ownership of a house in Cornwall. The parties originally had their home in Cheshire. It was in the husband's name alone. In 1967, the husband was minded to move with the whole family to Cornwall. He bought a garage business near Bodmin in his own name. It cost some £32,500. He also entered into negotiations to purchase a desirable residence for himself and his family. It is called Halgavor House. At first he thought of having it put into his own name. But, on consulting his solicitor, he decided that it should be put into his wife's name. The reason was so that, in case his garage business was not a success, his creditors should not be able to take it. The contract was drawn up on 11 November 1967. It was in the wife's name. So was the conveyance.

A few weeks later the marriage broke up. The wife stayed in Cheshire. The husband in Cornwall. The wife first claimed the house in Cheshire as hers. The findings of the registrar negatived that claim. Counsel for the wife did not press the appeal as to it. It was clearly unsustainable. The wife next claimed the house near Bodmin as hers. Because it was put into her name. The registrar dismissed her claim to it. He found that the husband was an honest businessman intending and able to honour his financial commitments; that he intended this house to belong to him beneficially; and accordingly that the wife held the house in trust for her husband absolutely. The wife appeals to this court.

The evidence shows clearly that the husband put the house into his wife's name so that it should not be taken by his creditors. In his evidence he said:

> In October 1967 not true that I gave the Halgavor House to my wife. Reason put in wife's name was because I had never previously been in a garage business – lack of experience is always a risk. I was advised that should the business fail the house would be taken as part of the assets of the business. Recommended therefore house should be put in wife's name. This was explained to my wife by Mr Chisholm [that is, the solicitor] in his office.

If further evidence is needed, it is in his own affidavit, where he states:

> The only reason that Halgavor House was put into the [wife's] name was as a matter of caution in case the business venture should wholly fail and it should be taken that this house was part of the business assets; we were both advised about this.

After the differences arose, the husband's solicitors wrote and said: '... we have learnt today that [the wife] is the owner of a residence in Cornwall.'

So it is plain that the husband had the house put into his wife's name so as to avoid any risk of it being taken by his creditors in case his business was not a success. What is the result in law? In *Gascoigne v Gascoigne* (1918) [see above, p 288], it was held that, when a husband put a house in his wife's name so as to avoid it being taken by his creditors, the house belonged to the wife. The husband could not be heard to say that it belonged to him, because he could not be allowed to take advantage of his own dishonesty. That case was applied in *Re Emery's Investments' Trusts, Emery v Emery* (1959) [see above, p 288], and also in *McEvoy v Belfast Banking Co Ltd*.[72] We were invited by counsel for the husband to overrule those decisions. But in my opinion they are good law.

Then counsel for the husband said that *Gascoigne v Gascoigne* is distinguishable, because there the husband was dishonest, whereas here the registrar has found that the husband was honest. Counsel relied in this regard on *Davies v Otty*.[73] There a man's wife had left him ten years ago. He justifiably believed that she was dead and married another woman. Then he was told that his first wife was still alive. Being fearful that he might be charged with bigamy, he conveyed property to the defendant on the distinct understanding that it was to be done away with when the unpleasantness was over. He was, of course, quite innocent of bigamy. The court ordered the defendant to reconvey the property to him. In that case it is obvious that the defendant was trustee for the plaintiff who throughout was acting quite honestly and quite consistently.

Accepting that in the present case the husband was honest – he acted, he said, on the advice of his solicitor – nevertheless, I do not think that he can claim that the house belongs to him. The solicitor did not give evidence. But the only proper advice that he could give was: 'In order to avoid the house being taken by your creditors, you can put it into your wife's name; but remember that, if you do, it is your wife's and you cannot go back on it.'

But, whether the solicitor gave that advice or not, I am quite clear that the husband cannot have it both ways. So he is on the horns of a dilemma. He cannot say that the house is his own and, at one and the same time, say that it is his wife's. As against his wife, he wants to say that it belongs to him. As against his creditors, that it belongs to her. That simply will not do. Either it was conveyed to her for her own use absolutely; or it was conveyed to her as trustee for her husband. It must be one or other. The presumption is that it was conveyed to her as trustee for her husband. It must be one or other. The presumption is that it was conveyed to her for her own use; and he does not rebut that presumption by saying that he only did it to defeat his creditors. I think that it belongs to her.

Salmon LJ: The wife did not put up a penny. The contract to purchase, however, was in her name and the house was conveyed into her name. The burden of displacing the presumption of advancement is therefore on the husband. This burden can in many cases be displaced without much effort. It seems to me, however, that in his case the husband's evidence, far from displacing the presumption, has done much to reinforce it.

72 [1934] NI 67.

73 (1865) 35 Beav 208.

***Rowan v Dann* (1992) 64 P & CR 202, CA**

The court adopted a different approach to the issue. If the transfer creates a resulting trust in favour of the transferor, so that *prima facie* he retains the equitable interest and he does not rely on his own improper conduct in order to recover the property, the court may allow him to do so. It is immaterial that the defendant raises the issue that the transferor does not have 'clean hands'.

In this case, Rowan was the owner of farmland. He granted tenancies to Dann in order to prevent the assets falling into the hands of his creditors, should he become bankrupt, and also in pursuance of an intended joint business venture. No rent was actually paid although such payment was stipulated in the agreement. Rowan claimed that the land should revert to him under a resulting trust as the purpose of the transfer (a joint business venture) had failed to materialise. Dann claimed that Rowan could not rely on the resulting trust as he did not have 'clean hands', having created sham tenancies in order to defeat his creditors.

Held, by the Court of Appeal, in favour of Rowan. A resulting trust existed in favour of Rowan by reason of the failure of the joint business venture. The improper, underlying purpose of the transfer was common to both sides. The creditors were not disadvantaged and Rowan did not have to rely on the unlawful purpose to support his claim.

> **Scott LJ** (after considering *Gascoigne v Gascoigne* (see above, p 288) and *Tinker v Tinker* (see above, p 289) continued): In each of these cases the plaintiff could not succeed without rebutting the presumption of advancement. The present case is quite different. There is a resulting trust in favour of Mr Rowan by reason of the failure of the joint business venture. This conclusion of a proprietary equitable interest in favour of Mr Rowan is consistent with a long line of authorities of which *Quistclose Investments v Rolls Razor Ltd* [see above, p 232] is a well known example.
>
> Mr Rowan did not have anything to rebut. He did not have to rely on his dishonest intention to defeat his creditors in order to establish the equitable interest under the resulting trust. In my judgment there is nothing in the principles established by the *Gascoigne v Gascoigne* line of cases that assist the appellants in the present case ...

If a transaction is entered into for an improper purpose, such as to defeat creditors, but the purpose is not carried out, a party thereto may be entitled to resile from the transaction to the extent that it is still executory and to recover anything paid or transferred under it. See *Chitty on Contracts*.[74] A good example of this is *Taylor v Bowers*,[75] where the plaintiff had transferred his stock-in-trade to another in order to prevent his creditors getting hold of the goods. Later he brought an action to recover the goods. He succeeded.

74 26th edn, 1989, London: Sweet & Maxwell, Vol 1, para 1275.

75 (1876) 1 QBD 291.

Mellish LJ: ... if the illegal transaction had been carried out, the plaintiff himself, in my judgment, could not afterwards have recovered the goods. But the illegal transaction was not carried out; it wholly came to an end. To hold that the plaintiff is enabled to recover does not carry out the illegal transaction, but the effect is to put everybody in the same situation as they were before the illegal transaction was determined upon, and before the parties took any steps to carry it out. That, I apprehend, is the true distinction in point of law. If money is paid or goods delivered for an illegal purpose, the person who had so paid the money or delivered the goods may recover them back before the illegal purpose is carried out; but if he waits till the illegal purpose is carried out, or if he seeks to enforce the illegal transaction, in neither case can he maintain an action; the law will not allow that to be done.

In *Chettiar v Chettiar*[76] Lord Denning said: 'If the fraudulent purpose had not been carried out, there might well have been room for repentance and the father might have been allowed to have the land retransferred to him.'

Mr Rowan is *prima facie* entitled to the benefit of the resulting trust in his favour that came into existence on the collapse of the joint venture project. He cannot be deprived of that proprietary interest unless circumstances are brought to the attention of the court that justify that consequence. I would answer Mr Picarda's point (counsel for the defendant) by repeating remarks made by James LJ in *Haigh v Kaye*, and cited with approval by Lord Denning in *Chettiar v Chettiar*:

> If a defendant means to say that he claims to hold property given to him for an immoral purpose, in violation of all honour and honesty, he must say so in plain terms, and must clearly put forward his own scoundrelism, if he means to reap the benefit of it.

I take this passage to mean that at least it is for the defendant to put forward the circumstances on which reliance is to be placed in support of an illegality defence. In the present case, there is no evidence that the scheme to defeat creditors was put into effect. There is no evidence that any creditor was persuaded to hold his hand in the belief that Mr Rowan's land was encumbered by the tenancies and the option. In my opinion, the present case is on its facts covered by the principle expressed in *Taylor v Bowers*.

Tinsley v Milligan [1993] 3 WLR 126, HL (Lords Jauncey of Tullichettle, Lowry and Browne-Wilkinson; Lords Keith of Kinkel and Goff of Chieveley dissenting)

The House of Lords reviewed the authorities and adopted the approach laid down in *Rowan v Dann*. There is no inflexible or rigid rule to the effect that evidence of a fraudulent or unlawful purpose for a conveyance is sufficient to prevent an equitable owner recovering his property, if he does not rely on this purpose to support his claim.

76 [1962] AC 294.

The plaintiff and defendant jointly purchased a house which was conveyed in the name of the plaintiff. Over a period of years, the defendant, with the knowledge and assent of the plaintiff made false claims on the Department of Social Security. Having the property in the sole name of the plaintiff assisted in the fraud. A very small amount of the proceeds of fraud was put into the house by the defendant. The plaintiff also made fraudulent claims on the DSS but was convicted, fined and ordered to make repayments. The parties had an argument. This led to the plaintiff serving a notice to quit on the defendant. The defendant counterclaimed for a declaration that the property was held on trust for sale for both parties in equal shares.

Held, by the House of Lords, in favour of the claimant (the defendant), affirming the decision of the Court of Appeal, but on different grounds.

Prima facie, the claimant had an equitable interest in the property equivalent to the contribution she made to its purchase. Since she was not relying on her own illegality in order to maintain her interest, the court would not prevent her establishing her claim.

> **Lord Browne-Wilkinson:** Neither at law nor in equity will the court enforce an illegal contract which has been partially, but not fully, performed. However, it does not follow that all acts done under a partially performed contract are of no effect. In particular it is now clearly established that at law (as opposed to in equity), property in goods or land can pass under, or pursuant to, such a contract. If so, the rights of the owner of the legal title thereby acquired will be enforced, provided that the plaintiff can establish such title without pleading or leading evidence of the illegality. It is said that the property lies where it falls, even though legal title to the property was acquired as a result of the property passing under the illegal contract itself. [His Lordship reviewed the following common law cases: *Bowmakers Ltd v Barnet Instruments Ltd*;[77] *Ferret v Hill*;[78] *Taylor v Chester*;[79] *Alexander v Rayson*[80] and concluded:]
>
> From these authorities the following propositions emerge:
>
> (1) property in chattels and land can pass under a contract which is illegal and therefore would have been unenforceable as a contract;
>
> (2) a plaintiff can at law enforce property rights so acquired provided that he does not need to rely on the illegal contract for any purpose other than providing the basis of his claim to a property right;
>
> (3) it is irrelevant that the illegality of the underlying agreement was either pleaded or emerged in evidence: if the plaintiff has acquired legal title under the illegal contract that is enough.
>
> I have stressed the common law rules as to the impact of illegality on the acquisition and enforcement of property rights because it is the appellant's

77 [1945] KB 65.

78 (1854) 15 CB 207.

79 (1869) LR 4 QB 309.

80 [1936] 1 KB 169.

contention that different principles apply in equity. In particular it is said that equity will not aid Miss Milligan to assert, establish or enforce an equitable, as opposed to a legal, proprietary interest since she was a party to the fraud on the DSS. The house was put in the name of Miss Tinsley alone (instead of joint names) to facilitate the fraud. Therefore, it is said, Miss Milligan does not come to equity with clean hands: consequently, equity will not aid her. Most authorities to which we were referred deal with enforcing proprietary rights under a trust: I will deal with them in due course. But before turning to them, I must point out that if Miss Tinsley's argument is correct, the results would be far reaching and, I suggest, very surprising. There are many proprietary rights, apart from trusts, which are only enforceable in equity. For example, an agreement for a lease under which the tenant has entered is normally said to be as good as a lease, since under such an agreement equity treats the lease as having been granted and the 'lessee' as having a proprietary interest enforceable against the whole world except the *bona fide* purchaser for value without notice. Would the result in *Ferret v Hill*[81] have been different if there had only been an agreement for a lease? Say that in *Taylor v Chester*[82] the plaintiff had deposited by way of security share certificates instead of half a bank note (thereby producing only an equitable security): would the outcome have been different? Similarly, if the plaintiff were relying on an assignment of a chose in action would he succeed if the assignment was a legal assignment but fail if it were equitable?

In my judgment to draw such distinctions between property rights enforceable at law and those which require the intervention of equity would be surprising. More than 100 years has elapsed since law and equity became fused. The reality of the matter is that, in 1993, English law has one single law of property made up of legal and equitable interests. Although for historical reasons legal estates and equitable estates have differing incidents, the person owning either type of estate has a right of property, a right *in rem* not merely a right *in personam*. If the law is that a party is entitled to enforce a property right acquired under an illegal transaction, in my judgment the same rule ought to apply to any property right so acquired, whether such right is legal or equitable.

In the present case, Miss Milligan claims under a resulting or implied trust. The court below have found, and it is not now disputed, that apart from the question of illegality Miss Milligan would have been entitled in equity to a half share in the house in accordance with the principles exemplified in *Gissing v Gissing*;[83] *Grant v Edwards*[84] and *Lloyds Bank plc v Rosset*.[85] The creation of such an equitable interest does not depend upon a contractual obligation but on a common intention acted upon by the parties to their detriment. It is a development of the old law of resulting trust under which, where two parties have provided the purchase money to buy a property which is conveyed into the name of one of them alone, the latter is presumed to hold the property on a

81 (1854) 15 CB 207.

82 (1869) LR 4 QB 309.

83 [1971] 1 AC 886.

84 [1986] Ch 638.

85 [1991] AC 107.

resulting trust for both parties in shares proportionate to their contributions to the purchase price. In arguments, no distinction was drawn between strict resulting trusts and a *Gissing v Gissing* type of trust.

A presumption of resulting trust also arises in equity when A transfers personalty or money to B: see *Snell's Equity*;[86] *Standing v Bowring*;[87] *Dewar v Dewar*.[88] Before 1925, there was also a presumption of resulting trust when land was voluntarily transferred by A to B: it is arguable, however, that the position has been altered by the 1925 property legislation: see *Snell's Equity*.[89] The presumption of a resulting trust is, in my view, crucial in considering the authorities. On that presumption (and on the contrary presumption of advancement) hinges the answer to the crucial question 'does a plaintiff claiming under a resulting trust have to rely on the underlying illegality?' Where the presumption of resulting trust applies, the plaintiff does not have to rely on the illegality. If he proves that the property is vested in the defendant alone but that the plaintiff provided part of the purchase money, or voluntarily transferred the property to the defendant, the plaintiff establishes his claim under a resulting trust unless either the contrary presumption of advancement displaces the presumption of resulting trust or the defendant leads evidence to rebut the presumption of resulting trust. Therefore, in cases where the presumption of advancement does not apply, a plaintiff can establish his equitable interest in the property without relying in any way on the underlying illegal transaction. In this case Miss Milligan as defendant simply pleaded the common intention that the property should belong to both of them and that she contributed to the purchase price: she claimed that in consequence the property belonged to them equally. To the same effect was her evidence in chief. Therefore, Miss Milligan was not forced to rely on the illegality to prove her equitable interest. Only in the reply and the course of Miss Milligan's cross-examination did such illegality emerge: it was Miss Tinsley who had to rely on that illegality.

Although the presumption of advancement does not directly arise for consideration in this case, it is important when considering the decided cases to understand its operation. On a transfer from a man to his wife, children or others to whom he stands *in loco parentis*, equity presumes an intention to make a gift. Therefore, in such a case, unlike the case where the presumption of resulting trust applies, in order to establish any claim the plaintiff has himself to lead evidence sufficient to rebut the presumption of gift and in so doing will normally have to plead, and give evidence of, the underlying illegal purpose.

Against this background, I turn to consider the authorities dealing with the position in equity where A transferred property to B for an illegal purpose.

86 29th edn, 1990, London: Sweet & Maxwell, pp 183–84.

87 (1885) 31 Ch D 282, p 287, *per* Cotton LJ.

88 [1975] 1 WLR 1532, p 1537.

89 *Ibid*, fn 86, p 182.

[His Lordship considered the following earlier cases: *Cottington v Fletcher*;[90] and *Muckleston v Brown*[91] and continued:]

In *Curtis v Perry*,[92] Nantes and Chiswell (who was a Member of Parliament) were partners. Ships had been purchased by Nantes out of partnership assets but registered in the sole name of Nantes. When Chiswell discovered the position, the ships were shown in the partnership books as being partnership property. However, with Chiswell's connivance the ships remained registered in the sole name of Nantes so as to evade a statutory prohibition against the ships being used for government contracts if owned by a Member of Parliament. In a dispute between the partnership creditors and Nantes' separate creditors, Lord Eldon held in favour of the latter. He said, at p 746:

> The moment the purpose to defeat the policy of the law by fraudulently concealing that this was his property is admitted, it is very clear he ought not to be heard in this court to say, that is his property. In the case of a bill filed to have a reconveyance of a qualification given by the plaintiff to his son to enable him to sit in Parliament, the purpose being answered, the bill was very properly dismissed by Lord Kenyon with costs.

The law was developing in another direction during the 19th century. There was originally a difference of view as to whether a transaction entered into for an illegal purpose would be enforced at law or in equity if the party had repented of his illegal purpose before it had been put into operation, ie, the doctrine of *locus poenitentiae*. It was eventually recognised both at law and in equity that if the plaintiff had repented before the illegal purpose was carried through, he could recover his property: see *Taylor v Bowers*;[93] *Symes v Hughes*.[94] The principle of *locus poenitentiae* is in my judgment irreconcilable with any rule that where property is transferred for an illegal purpose no equitable proprietary right exists. The equitable right, if any, must arise at the time at which the property was voluntarily transferred to the third party or purchased in the name of the third party. The existence of the equitable interest cannot depend upon events occurring after that date. Therefore, if, under the principle of *locus poenitentiae*, the courts recognise that an equitable interest did arise out of the underlying transaction, the same must be true where the illegal purpose was carried through. The carrying out of the illegal purpose cannot, by itself, destroy the pre-existing equitable interest. The doctrine of *locus poenitentiae* therefore demonstrates that the effect of illegality is not to prevent a proprietary interest in equity from arising or to produce a forfeiture of such right: the effect is to render the equitable interest unenforceable in certain circumstances. The effect of illegality is not substantive but procedural. The question therefore is: 'in what circumstances will equity refuse to enforce equitable rights which undoubtedly exist?'

90 (1740) 2 Atk 155.

91 (1806) 6 Ves 52.

92 (1802) 6 Ves 739.

93 (1876) 1 QBD 291.

94 (1875) LR 9 Eq 475.

It is against this background that one has to assess the more recent law. Although in the cases decided during the last 100 years there are frequent references to Lord Eldon's wide principle, with one exception (*Cantor v Cox*)[95] none of the English decisions are decided by simply applying that principle. They are all cases where the unsuccessful party was held to be precluded from leading evidence of an illegal situation in order to rebut the presumption of advancement. Lord Eldon's rule would have provided a complete answer whether the transfer was made to a wife or child (where the presumption of advancement would apply) or to a stranger. Yet with one exception none of the cases in this century has been decided on that simple basis. The majority of cases have been those in which the presumption of advancement applied: in those authorities the rule has been stated as being that a plaintiff cannot rely on evidence of his own illegality to rebut the presumption applicable in such cases that the plaintiff intended to make a gift of the property to the transferee. Thus in *Gascoigne v Gascoigne*;[96] *McEvoy v Belfast Banking Co Ltd*;[97] *Re Emery's Investments Trusts*;[98] *Palaniappa Chettiar v Arunasalam Chettiar*;[99] and *Tinker v Tinker*[100] the crucial point was said to be the inability of the plaintiff to lead evidence rebutting the presumption of advancement. In each case the plaintiff was claiming to recover property voluntarily transferred to, or purchased in the name of, a wife or child, for an illegal purpose. Although reference was made to Lord Eldon's principle, none of those cases was decided on the simple ground (if it were good law) that equity would not in any circumstances enforce a resulting trust in such circumstances. On the contrary, in each case the rule was stated to be that the plaintiff could not recover because he had to rely on the illegality to rebut the presumption of advancement.

In my judgment, the explanation for this departure from Lord Eldon's absolute rule is that the fusion of law and equity has led the courts to adopt a single rule (application both at law and in equity) as to the circumstances in which the court will enforce property interests acquired in pursuance of an illegal transaction, viz, the *Bowmakers* rule.[101] A party to an illegality can recover by virtue of a legal or equitable property interest if, but only if, he can establish his title without relying on his own illegality. In cases where the presumption of advancement applies, the plaintiff is faced with the presumption of gift and therefore cannot claim under a resulting trust unless and until he has rebutted that presumption of gift: for those purposes the plaintiff does have to rely on the underlying illegality and therefore fails.

The position is well illustrated by two decisions in the Privy Council. In the first, *Singh v Ali*,[102] a plaintiff who had acquired legal title to a lorry under an

95 (1976) 239 EG 121.

96 [1918] 1 KB 223.

97 [1934] NI 67.

98 [1959] Ch 410.

99 [1962] AC 294.

100 [1970] P 136, pp 141h, 142c.

101 [1945] KB 65.

102 [1960] AC 167.

illegal transaction was held entitled to succeed against the other party to the illegality in detinue and trespass. The Board approved the *Bowmakers* test. Two years later, in *Palaniappa Chettiar v Arunasalam Chettiar*,[103] the Board had to consider the case where a father, who had transferred land to his son for an illegal purpose, sought to recover it under a resulting trust. It was held that he could not, since he had to rely on his illegal purpose in order to rebut the presumption of advancement. The Board distinguished, at p 301, the decision in *Haigh v Kaye*[104] on the following grounds:

> It appears to their Lordships, however, that there is a clear distinction between *Haigh v Kaye* and the present case. In *Haigh v Kaye* the plaintiff conveyed a freehold estate to the defendant. In the conveyance it was stated that a sum of £850 had been paid by the defendant for it. The plaintiff proved that no such sum was paid and claimed that the defendant was a trustee for him. Now in that case the plaintiff had no reason to disclose any illegality and did not do so. It was the defendant who suggested that the transaction was entered into for a fraudulent purpose. He sought to drag it in without pleading it distinctly and he was not allowed to do so. But in the present case the plaintiff had of necessity to disclose his own illegality to the court and for this reason he had not only to get over the fact that the transfer stated that the son paid £7,000 for the land. He had also to get over the presumption of advancement, for, whenever a father transfers property to his son, there is a presumption that he intended it as a gift to his son; and if he wishes to rebut that presumption and to say that his son took as trustee for him, he must prove the trust clearly and distinctly, by evidence properly admissible for the purposes, and not leave it to be inferred from slight circumstances: see *Shepherd v Cartwright*.[105]

Further, the Board distinguished *Singh v Ali*.[106] It was pointed out that in *Singh v Ali* the plaintiff founded his claim on a right of property in the lorry and his possession of it. The Board continued:[107]

> [The plaintiff] did not have to found his cause of action on an immoral or illegal act. He was held entitled to recover. But in the present case the father has of necessity to put forward, and indeed, assert, his own fraudulent purpose, which he has fully achieved. He is met therefore by the principle stated long ago by Lord Mansfield 'No court will lend its aid to a man who founds his cause of action upon an immoral or an illegal act', see *Holman v Johnson*.[108]

103 [1962] AC 294.
104 (1872) LR 7 Ch 469.
105 [1955] AC 431, p 445.
106 [1960] AC 167.
107 [1962] AC 294, p 303.
108 (1775) 1 Cowp 341, p 343.

In my judgment these two cases show that the Privy Council was applying exactly the same principle in both cases although in one case the plaintiff's claim rested on a legal title and in the other on an equitable title. The claim based on the equitable title did not fail simply because the plaintiff was a party to the illegal transaction; it only failed because the plaintiff was bound to disclose and rely upon his own illegal purpose in order to rebut the presumption of advancement. The Privy Council was plainly treating the principle applicable both at law and in equity as being that a man can recover property provided that he is not forced to rely on his own illegality.

I therefore reach the conclusion that, although there is no case overruling the wide principle stated by Lord Eldon, as the law has developed the equitable principle has become elided into the common law rule. In my judgment the time has come to decide clearly that the rule is the same whether a plaintiff founds himself on a legal or equitable title: he is entitled to recover if he is not forced to plead or rely on the illegality, even if it emerges that the title on which he relied was acquired in the course of carrying through an illegal transaction.

As applied in the present case, that principle would operate as follows. Miss Milligan established a resulting trust by showing that she had contributed to the purchase price of the house and that there was common understanding between her and Miss Tinsley that they owned the house equally. She had no need to allege or prove why the house was conveyed into the name of Miss Tinsley alone, since that fact was irrelevant to her claim: it was enough to show that the house was in fact vested in Miss Tinsley alone. The illegality only emerged at all because Miss Tinsley sought to raise it. Having proved these facts, Miss Milligan had raised a presumption of resulting trust. There was no evidence to rebut that presumption. Therefore Miss Milligan should succeed. This is exactly the process of reasoning adopted by the Ontario Court of Appeal in *Gorog v Kiss*[109] which in my judgment was rightly decided.

Finally, I should mention a further point which was relied on by Miss Tinsley. It is said that once the illegality of the transaction emerges, the court must refuse to enforce the transaction and all claims under it whether pleaded or not: see *Scott v Brown, Doering, McNab & Co.*[110] Therefore, it is said, it does not matter whether a plaintiff relies on or gives evidence of the illegality: the court will not enforce the plaintiff's rights. In my judgment, this submission is plainly ill founded. There are many cases where a plaintiff has succeeded, notwithstanding that the illegality of the transaction under which she acquired the property has emerged: see, for example, *Bowmakers Ltd v Barnet Instruments Ltd*[111] and *Singh v Ali.*[112] In my judgment the court is only entitled and bound to dismiss a claim on the basis that it is founded on an illegality in those cases where the illegality is of a kind which would have provided a good defence if

109 (1977) 78 DLR (3d) 690.

110 [1892] 2 QB 724.

111 [1945] KB 65

112 [1960] AC 167.

raised by the defendant. In a case where the plaintiff is not seeking to enforce an unlawful contract but founds his case on collateral rights acquired under the contract (such as a right of property) the court is neither bound nor entitled to reject the claim unless the illegality of necessity forms part of the plaintiff's case.

I would, therefore, dismiss the appeal.

Likewise, in *Silverwood v Silverwood*, despite the unlawful nature of the transaction, the plaintiff (claimant) did not have to rely on evidence of illegality in order to establish a claim based on a resulting trust. This was presumed in his favour. Moreover, in order to rebut a defence that the transfer was intended as a gift, the plaintiff is entitled to lead evidence of the unlawful nature of the transaction. It would be 'absurd as well as unjust' to prevent the plaintiff adducing such evidence.

Silverwood v Silverwood (1997) 74 P & CR 453, CA

The plaintiff (Geoffrey) was appointed sole executor of the will of his mother, Daisy. In February 1991, when Daisy was aged 88, the sum of £21,278 was withdrawn from her account and deposited in equal shares in the names of her two grandchildren, Gillian and Andrew. An application was made on Daisy's behalf for Income Support. On the application form no reference was made to the monies transferred to the grandchildren. The DSS commenced paying income support to, or on behalf of, Daisy. Under Daisy's will, Geoffrey and another brother, Arnold, were made the only beneficiaries. After Daisy's death, the plaintiff obtained probate of the will and commenced proceedings against the defendants, seeking recovery of the monies paid in 1991. The defendants contended that the monies paid to them were by way of a gift. The judge decided in favour of the plaintiff, applying the principle in *Tinsley v Milligan*. The defendants appealed.

The Court of Appeal dismissed the appeal and affirmed the decision of the judge on the ground that the resulting trust in favour of the plaintiff was not rebutted. The defence, that the donor intended to make a gift, was rejected. The plaintiff was entitled to lead rebutting evidence of the unlawful nature of the transaction to show that no gift was intended.

Peter Gibson LJ (referred to Lord Browne-Wilkinson's judgment in *Tinsley v Milligan* and continued): The test is whether, of necessity, reliance is placed by the claimant on the illegality in proving his claim. Whether there is reliance such as would disentitle the claimant to succeed depends on the particular circumstances of the particular case, and it is of importance in this regard to look at the pleadings. Thus, as Lord Browne-Wilkinson pointed out, Miss Milligan as defendant simply pleaded the common intention that the property should belong to both her and Miss Tinsley and that she, Miss Milligan, contributed to the purchase price, and she claimed that, in consequence, the property belonged to them equally. Lord Browne-Wilkinson

> went on to say that to the same effect was Miss Milligan's evidence-in-chief, and only in the reply of Miss Tinsley and, in the course of the cross-examination of Miss Milligan, did such illegality emerge.
>
> There is, therefore, a factual difference between *Tinsley v Milligan* and the present case, in that in our case *the defendants did not plead the illegality and some evidence of the illegality was led by Geoffrey*. Mr Carswell (counsel for the defendants) said that Geoffrey led in-chief, enthusiastically and at length, evidence by witness statements which were supplemented by live testimony, asserting that the transfer of money out of Mrs Silverwood's account was made in fraud of the DSS, so that Mrs Silverwood would qualify for income support. In this regard, Mr Carswell referred to the witness statements of Geoffrey and of two of his witnesses, Mr Ellis and Gillian's ex-husband, Mr Whiteley, and to parts of their oral evidence. Having read all the evidence, I think Mr Carswell's description of what Geoffrey did is somewhat overstated. But the only relevance of that evidence was to rebut the defence that the transfer to Andrew and Gillian was a gift, a defence which the judge found to have been concocted.
>
> It would be absurd as well as unjust if a claimant, claiming a resulting trust, could not lead evidence of fraud in order to disprove a spurious defence. Consistently with the statement of principle by Lord Browne-Wilkinson, I do not regard the leading of that evidence as of crucial importance. To claim title under the resulting trust, Geoffrey had no need to allege or prove why the money was transferred to Andrew and Gillian, and for that purpose he did not rely on the illegality, which did not, of necessity, form part of Geoffrey's case. He did not plead the illegality: he simply pleaded the transfer to Andrew and Gillian and the consequent resulting trust. Accordingly, the test laid down by the majority in *Tinsley v Milligan*, namely, whether, of necessity, reliance is placed by the claimant on the illegality in pursuing his claim, is not satisfied.
>
> I would add that, in my view, it would be a travesty of justice if Miss Milligan, who undoubtedly was an active participant in the fraud earned out in that case, could succeed under a resulting trust in her favour, but Mrs Silverwood, who on no footing was a protagonist in the fraud carried out by Arnold, could not. The judge, in my judgment, was right to hold that, in accordance with *Tinsley v Milligan*, Geoffrey was entitled to succeed.

The Court of Appeal in *Tribe v Tribe* (see below, p 302) decided that, where the presumption of advancement is created by a transfer of property intended to promote an unlawful purpose, but which had not been carried into effect, the transferor is entitled to adduce evidence of the unlawful purpose in order to rebut the presumption of advancement. *Gascoigne v Gascoigne* was distinguished on the ground that, in that case, there was sufficient evidence that the husband intended to transfer the beneficial interest in the house to his wife. Moreover, *Tinker v Tinker* was regarded as a case where the husband's evidence confirmed the presumption of advancement as distinct from rebutting it.

Tribe v Tribe **[1995] 3 WLR 913, CA**

A father voluntarily transferred shares to his son. The purpose of the transfer was to deceive creditors by creating the appearance that the father no longer owned the shares in the company. The father never carried the illegal purpose into effect, in that he had no cause to rely on the transfer as against any creditor. The father now claimed the return of the shares from the son. The judge at first instance allowed the father to lead evidence of the illegal purpose in order to rebut the presumption of advancement on the ground that the illegal purpose had not been carried into effect. Having admitted the evidence the judge held that the father's claim succeeded. The son appealed to the Court of Appeal.

The court dismissed the appeal and ruled that the prohibition against a claimant founding his action on an illegal act had led to seemingly unjust results. The courts had made exceptions to this rule. In *Tinsley v Milligan*, the House of Lords decided that where the legal interest in property is transferred to another in order to promote an illegal purpose and the presumption of a resulting trust operated in favour of the transferor, the latter was entitled to recover the property on the ground that he was not forced to rely on the illegality but only on the resulting trust that arose in his favour on the transfer. In this case, the Court of Appeal expressed the view that the Law Lords in *Tinsley v Milligan* did not decide that a claimant was not entitled to restitution where the illegal purpose had not been carried into effect. In order to rebut the presumption of advancement in respect of a transfer for an intended illegal purpose, it was necessary for the claimant to show:

(i) that the illegal purpose had not been carried out;

(ii) that he intended to retain a beneficial interest in the property based on compelling circumstantial evidence; and

(iii) that he concealed this interest from his creditors.

> **Millett LJ:** Ordinarily, a man who makes a gratuitous transfer of property to another for an illegal purpose, is not allowed to rely on his purpose in making the transfer in order to rebut the presumption of advancement: see *Tinsley v Milligan* [1994] 1 AC 340, p 375, where Lord Browne-Wilkinson said:
>
> > In cases where the presumption of advancement applies, the plaintiff is faced with the presumption of gift and therefore cannot claim under a resulting trust unless and until he has rebutted that presumption of gift: for those purposes the plaintiff does have to rely on the underlying illegality and therefore fails.
>
> The question in the present case is whether there is an exception to this principle where the transferor withdraws from the transaction before any part of the illegal purpose has been carried into effect. Unless that exception applies, the plaintiff's claim to recover his own shares from the defendant whom he trusted to hold them as his nominee must fail.

There are, in my opinion, two questions of some importance which fall for decision in the present case. The first is whether, once property has been transferred to a transferee for an illegal purpose in circumstances which give rise to the presumption of advancement, it is still open to the transferor to withdraw from the transaction before the purpose has been carried out and, having done so, give evidence of the illegal purpose in order to rebut the presumption of advancement. The second is whether, if so, it is sufficient for him to withdraw from the transaction, because it is no longer necessary, and without repenting of his illegal purpose. I shall deal with these two questions in turn.

The presumption of advancement and the *locus poenitentiae*

In *Tinsley v Milligan* [1994] 1 AC 340, p 370 Lord Browne-Wilkinson summarised the common law rules which govern the effect of illegality on the acquisition and enforcement of property rights in three propositions:

(1) property in chattels and land can pass under a contract which is illegal and therefore would have been unenforceable as a contract;

(2) a plaintiff can, at law, enforce property rights so acquired provided that he does not need to rely on the illegal contract for any purpose other than providing the basis of his claim to a property right;

(3) it is irrelevant that the illegality of the underlying agreement was either pleaded or emerged in evidence: if the plaintiff has acquired legal title under the illegal contract that is enough.

The decision of the majority of their Lordships in that case was that the same principles applied in equity. It is, therefore, now settled that neither at law nor in equity may a party rely on his own fraud or illegality in order to found a claim or rebut a presumption, but that the common law and equity alike will assist him to protect and enforce his property rights if he can do so without relying on the fraud or illegality. This is the primary rule.

It is, however, also settled both at law and in equity that a person who has transferred property for an illegal purpose can nevertheless recover his property provided that he withdraws from the transaction before the illegal purpose has been wholly or partly performed. This is the doctrine of the *locus poenitentiae* and it applies in equity as well as at law: see *Symes v Hughes* (1870) LR 9 Eq 475 for the former, and *Taylor v Bowers* (1876) 1 QBD 291 for the latter. The availability of the doctrine in a restitutionary context was expressly confirmed by Lord Browne-Wilkinson in *Tinsley v Milligan* [1994] 1 AC 340, p 374.

While both principles are well established, the nature of the relationship between them is unclear. Is the doctrine of the *locus poenitentiae* co-extensive with, and by way of general exception to, the primary rule? The question in the present case is whether a plaintiff who has made a gratuitous transfer of property to a person in whose favour the presumption of advancement arises, can withdraw from the transaction before the illegal purpose has been carried into effect and then recover the property by leading evidence of his illegal purpose in order to rebut the presumption. Closely connected with this question is its converse: is a plaintiff who has made such a transfer in circumstances which give rise to a resulting trust so that he has no need to rely on the illegal purpose, as in *Tinsley v Milligan* itself, barred from recovering if the illegal purpose has been carried out? If both questions are answered in the negative, then either the *locus poenitentiae* is a common law doctrine which has no counterpart in equity or it is a contractual doctrine which has no place in the law of restitution.

It is convenient to consider first the position at common law. It is important to bear in mind that the common law starts from the opposite premise from that on which equity bases the presumption of resulting trust. In an action for money had and received, for example, whatever the relationship between the parties, the burden lies on the plaintiff to prove that the money was not paid by way of gift or pursuant to an enforceable contract. Absence of consideration is not of itself a ground of restitution: it is for the transferor to show that no gift was intended.

The leading cases on illegality and resulting trusts prior to *Tinsley v Milligan* are *Curtis v Perry* (1802) 6 Ves 739; *Ex p Yallop* (1808) 15 Ves 60; *Groves v Groves* (1829) 3 Y & J 163; *Coultwas v Swan* (1870) 18 WR 746; *Symes v Hughes* (1875) LR 9 Eq 475; *Re Great Berlin Steamboat Co* (1884) 26 Ch D 616; *Petherpermal Chetty v Muniandi Servai* (1908) LR 35 Ind App 98; and *Rowan v Dann* (1992) 64 P & CR 202.

[His Lordship reviewed these authorities and continued:]

Prior to *Tinsley v Milligan*, no transferor had ever succeeded in recovering his property by enforcing a resulting trust where he had transferred the property for an illegal purpose and that purpose had been carried out. In *Re Great Berlin Steamboat Co*, the transferor failed to recover for this very reason; in other cases where the transferor has succeeded he did so only because the illegal purpose had not been carried out.

A resulting trust, like the presumption of advancement, rests on a presumption which is rebuttable by evidence: see *Standing v Bowring* (1885) 31 Ch D 282, p 287. The transferor does not need to allege or prove the purpose for which property was transferred into the name of the transferee; in equity he can rely on the presumption that no gift was intended. But the transferee cannot be prevented from rebutting the presumption by leading evidence of the transferor's subsequent conduct to show that it was inconsistent with any intention to retain a beneficial interest. Suppose, for example, that a man transfers property to his nephew in order to conceal it from his creditors, and suppose that he afterwards settles with his creditors on the footing that he has no interest in the property. Is it seriously suggested that he can recover the property? I think not. The transferor's own conduct would be inconsistent with the retention of any beneficial interest in the property. I can see no reason why the nephew should not give evidence of the transferor's dealings with his creditors to rebut the presumption of a resulting trust and show that a gift was intended. He would not be relying on any illegal arrangement, but implicitly denying it. The transferor would have to give positive evidence of his intention to retain a beneficial interest and dishonestly conceal it from his creditors, evidence which he would not be allowed to give once the illegal purpose had been carried out.

This analysis is not, in my view, inconsistent with a passage in Lord Browne-Wilkinson's speech [1994] 1 AC 340, p 374, where he said:

> The equitable right, if any, must arise at the time at which the property was voluntarily transferred to the third party or purchased in the name of the third party. The existence of the equitable interest cannot depend upon events occurring after that date. Therefore if, under the principle of *locus poenitentiae*, the courts recognise that an equitable interest did arise out of the underlying transaction, the same must be true where the illegal purpose was carried through. The carrying out of the illegal purpose cannot, by itself, destroy the pre-existing equitable interest.

But it does not follow that subsequent conduct is necessarily irrelevant. Where the existence of an equitable interest depends upon a rebuttable presumption or inference of the transferor's intention, evidence may be given of his subsequent conduct in order to rebut the presumption or inference which would otherwise be drawn.

Tinsley v Milligan is, in my opinion, not authority for the proposition that a party who transfers property for an illegal purpose in circumstances which give rise to a resulting trust can invariably enforce the trust and recover the property, even though the illegal purpose has been carried into effect. I do not accept the suggestion that cases such as *Re Great Berlin Steamboat Co* have been impliedly overruled or that the dicta in the many cases, including *Taylor v Bowers* (1876) 1 QBD 291 and *Singh v Ali* [1960] AC 167, indicating that the result would have been otherwise if the illegal purpose had or had not been carried out must be taken to have been overruled.

The question in the present case is the converse: whether the transferor can rebut the presumption of advancement by giving evidence of his illegal purpose so long as the illegal purpose has not been carried into effect. The leading cases on illegality and the presumption of advancement are *Childers v Childers* (1857) 3 K & J 310; *Crichton v Crichton* (1895) 13 R 770; *Perpetual Executors and Trustees Association of Australia Ltd v Wright* (1917) 23 CLR 185; *Gascoigne v Gascoigne* [1918] 1 KB 223; *McEvoy v Belfast Banking Co Ltd* [1935] AC 24; *Re Emery's Investments Trusts* [1959] Ch 410; *Palaniappa Chettiar v Arunasalam Chettiar* [1962] AC 294; and *Tinker v Tinker* [1970] P 136.

[His Lordship considered these authorities and continued:] The question whether a transferor can repudiate his fraudulent scheme before it is carried into effect and then give evidence of his dishonest intention in order to rebut the presumption of advancement did not fall for consideration in either of those cases. It was not considered in *Gascoigne v Gascoigne*, where it was arguably too late for him to do so; and it did not arise in *Tinker v Tinker*, where he was found to have had no dishonest intention.

In my opinion, the weight of the authorities supports the view that a person who seeks to recover property transferred by him for an illegal purpose can lead evidence of his dishonest intention whenever it is necessary for him to do so provided that he has withdrawn from the transaction before the illegal purpose has been carried out. It is not necessary, if he can rely on an express or resulting trust in his favour; but it is necessary (i) if he brings an action at law, and (ii) if he brings proceedings in equity and needs to rebut the presumption of advancement. The availability of the *locus poenitentiae* is well documented in the former case. I would not willingly adopt a rule which differentiated between the rule of the common law and that of equity in a restitutionary context.

It is, of course, true that equity judges are fond of saying that a party 'cannot be heard to say' that his purpose was dishonest, and that this approach represents a mainspring of equitable jurisprudence. A man who puts himself in a position where his interest conflicts with his duty, for example, 'cannot be heard to say' that he acted in accordance with his interest; he is treated as having acted in accordance with his duty: see, for example, *Re Biss* [1903] 2 Ch 40, p 45 and *AG for Hong Kong v Reid* [1994] 1 AC 324. But this is a substantive rule of equity, not a merely procedural rule, as the primary rule appears to be, and it does not preclude the court from taking cognisance of an uneffectuated intention from which the party in question has resiled.

At heart the question for decision in the present case is one of legal policy. The primary rule which precludes the court from lending its assistance to a man who founds his cause of action on an illegal or immoral act often leads to a denial of justice. The justification for this is that the rule is not a principle of justice but a principle of policy: see the much quoted statement of Lord Mansfield CJ in *Holman v Johnson* (1775) 1 Cowp 341, p 343. The doctrine of the *locus poenitentiae* is an exception which operates to mitigate the harshness of the primary rule. It enables the court to do justice between the parties even though, in order to do so, it must allow a plaintiff to give evidence of his own dishonest intent. But he must have withdrawn from the transaction while his dishonesty still lay in intention only. The law draws the line once the intention has been wholly or partly carried into effect.

Seen in this light, the doctrine of the *locus poenitentiae*, although an exception to the primary rule, is not inconsistent with the policy which underlies it. It is, of course, artificial to think that anyone would be dissuaded by the primary rule from entering into a proposed fraud, if only because such a person would be unlikely to be a studious reader of the law reports or to seek advice from a lawyer whom he has taken fully into his confidence. But, if the policy which underlies the primary rule is to discourage fraud, the policy which underlies the exception must be taken to be to encourage withdrawal from a proposed fraud before it is implemented, an end which is no less desirable. And, if the former objective is of such overriding importance that the primary rule must be given effect, even where it leads to a denial of justice, then in my opinion the latter objective justifies the adoption of the exception where this enables justice to be done.

To my mind these considerations are even more compelling since the decision in *Tinsley v Milligan*. One might hesitate before allowing a novel exception to a rule of legal policy, particularly a rule based on moral principles. But the primary rule, as it has emerged from that decision, does not conform to any discernible moral principle. It is procedural in nature and depends on the adventitious location of the burden of proof in any given case. Had the plaintiff transferred the shares to a stranger or distant relative whom he trusted, albeit for the same dishonest purpose, it cannot be doubted that he would have succeeded in his claim. He would also have succeeded if he had given them to the defendant and procured him to sign a declaration of trust in his favour. But he chose to transfer them to a son whom he trusted to the extent of dispensing with the precaution of obtaining a declaration of trust. If that is fatal to his claim, then the greater the betrayal, the less the power of equity to give a remedy.

In my opinion the following propositions represent the present state of the law:

(1) title to property passes both at law and in equity even if the transfer is made for an illegal purpose. The fact that title has passed to the transferee does not preclude the transferor from bringing an action for restitution;

(2) the transferor's action will fail if it would be illegal for him to retain any interest in the property;

(3) subject to (2), the transferor can recover the property if he can do so without relying on the illegal purpose. This will normally be the case where the property was transferred without consideration in circumstances where the transferor can rely on an express declaration of trust or a resulting trust in his favour;

(4) it will almost invariably be so where the illegal purpose has not been carried out. It may be otherwise where the illegal purpose has been carried out and the transferee can rely on the transferor's conduct as inconsistent with his retention of a beneficial interest;

(5) the transferor can lead evidence of the illegal purpose whenever it is necessary for him to do so provided that he has withdrawn from the transaction before the illegal purpose has been wholly or partly carried into effect. It will be necessary for him to do so:

   (i) if he brings an action at law; or

   (ii) if he brings proceedings in equity and needs to rebut the presumption of advancement;

(6) the only way in which a man can protect his property from his creditors is by divesting himself of all beneficial interest in it. Evidence that he transferred the property in order to protect it from his creditors, therefore, does nothing by itself to rebut the presumption of advancement; it reinforces it. To rebut the presumption it is necessary to show that he intended to retain a beneficial interest and conceal it from his creditors;

(7) the court should not conclude that this was his intention without compelling circumstantial evidence to this effect. The identity of the transferee and the circumstances in which the transfer was made would be highly relevant. It is unlikely that the court would reach such a conclusion where the transfer was made in the absence of an imminent and perceived threat from known creditors.

I would dismiss this appeal.

SUPPLEMENTARY READING

Creighton, P, 'The recovery of property transferred for illegal purposes' (1997) 60 MLR 102

Cullity, M, ' Joint bank accounts with volunteers' (1969) 84 LQR 530

Dowling, A, 'The presumption of advancement between mother and child' [1996] Conv 274

Euonchong, N, 'Title clauses and illegal transactions' (1995) 111 LQR 135

Hayton, D, 'Note on *Hussey v Palmer*' (1973) 37 Conv 65

Kenny, A, 'Trust clauses for lawyers and their clients' (1995) 139 SJ 826

Kodilinye, G, 'Resulting trusts, advancements and fraudulent transfers – *Sekhon v Alissa*' [1990] Conv 213

Millett, P, 'The *Quistclose* trust: who can enforce it?' (1985) 101 LQR 269

Pettit, P, 'Illegality and repentance' (1996) 10 Tru LI 51

Rickett, C, 'Unincorporated associations and their dissolution' [1980] CLJ 88

Rose, F, 'Gratuitous transfers and illegal purposes' (1996) 112 LQR 386

Smart, P, 'Holding property for non-charitable purposes: mandates, conditions and estoppels' [1987] Conv 415

Swadling, W, 'A new role for resulting trusts' (1996) 16 LS 110

CHAPTER 9

CONSTRUCTIVE TRUSTS: CONFLICT OF DUTY AND INTEREST

A constructive trust as distinct from express and resulting trusts, is not created in accordance with the express or implied intention of the settlor. It is a device created by the courts in the interests of justice and good conscience. The rationale for the creation of such trusts is the prevention of unjust enrichment at the expense of an innocent party. The constructive trust forms a residual category of trusts which is called into play whenever the court desires to impose a trust and no other category of trusts is suitable. The courts reserve to themselves the power to interpret a transaction as giving rise to a constructive trust. The court will have regard to all the circumstances surrounding a transaction and in particular, the conduct of the relevant parties in order to decide whether in the interest of justice a trust ought to be imposed.

For example, T1 and T2 hold property on trust but, in breach of trust, purport to sell the property to X, a third party, who has knowledge of the breach of trust. Although T1 and T2 are already express trustees they will become constructive trustees of any unauthorised profit made from their office as trustee, such as the proceeds of sale received from X. By virtue of X's participation in the breach with knowledge of the facts he will be treated as a constructive trustee of the property in favour of the innocent beneficiary.

Thus, the constructive trust may be imposed on express trustees and other fiduciaries in respect of any unauthorised benefits received by them. In addition, strangers or third parties who have misconducted themselves with knowledge that their actions constitute an unwarranted interference with the interest of the beneficiary will become constructive trustees.

The effect of a constructive trust is similar in many ways to any other type of trust in that the beneficiary retains a proprietary interest in the subject matter of the trust. In the event of the constructive trustee becoming bankrupt, the trust property is granted priority over his creditors in favour of the beneficiaries. If the trustee has disposed of the property the beneficiary is entitled to 'trace' his funds in the hands of a third party, not being a *bona fide* transferee of the legal estate for value without notice. See *MCC Proceeds v Lehman Bros Inc* (above, p 12). However, an express trust differs from a constructive trust in that the settlor is the creator of an express trust, whereas, a constructive trust is created by the court. In addition, the express trust is more likely to continue for a duration determined by the settlor but the constructive trust may take the form of a court order requiring a fiduciary or third party to transfer property to a beneficiary and will end when this event is achieved. Moreover, an express trustee may be entitled to exercise a variety of powers such as the power to appoint agents and other trustees, the power to maintain infant beneficiaries, the power to make advancements of capital, the power to invest trust funds, etc. A constructive trustee has no such powers but is only required to comply with the order of the court.

In English law, although the boundaries surrounding a constructive trust cannot be precisely drawn, for the circumstances that may give rise to a constructive trust are inexhaustible, a number of general categories may be posited as to when the trust may be imposed. On the other hand, in the US, the constructive trust is defined in a relatively precise manner from the point of view of 'unjust enrichment', a constructive trust arises 'where a person holding title to property is subject to an equitable duty to convey it to another on the ground that he would be unjustly enriched if he were permitted to retain it' (American Restatement on Restitution). In other words, in the US, the constructive trust institution is used as a remedy to rectify certain wrongs.

Carl Zeiss Stiftung v Herbert Smith & Co and Another (No 2) [1969] 2 Ch 276, CA

> **Edmund-Davies LJ:** English law provides no clear and all-embracing definition of a constructive trust. Its boundaries have been left perhaps deliberately vague, so as not to restrict the court by technicalities in deciding what the justice of a particular case may demand. But it appears that in this country unjust enrichment or other personal advantage is not a *sine qua non*. Thus, in *Nelson v Larholt*,[1] it was not suggested that the defendant was himself one penny better off by changing an executor's cheques; yet, as he ought to have known of the executor's want of authority to draw them, he was held liable to refund the estate, both on the basis that he was a constructive trustee for the beneficiaries and on a claim for money had and received to their use. Nevertheless, the concept of unjust enrichment has its value as providing one example among many of what, for lack of a better phrase, I would call 'want of probity', a feature which recurs through and seems to connect all those cases drawn to the court's attention where a constructive trust has been held to exist. *Snell's Principles of Equity* expresses the same idea by saying,[2] that:
>
> > A possible definition is that a constructive trust is a trust which is imposed by equity in order to satisfy the demands of justice and good conscience, without reference to any express or presumed intention of the parties.
>
> It may be objected that, even assuming the correctness of the foregoing, it provides no assistance, inasmuch as reference to 'unjust enrichment', 'want of probity' and 'the demands of justice and good conscience' merely introduces vague concepts which are in turn incapable of definition and which therefore provide no yardstick. I do not agree. Concepts may defy definition and yet the presence in or absence from a situation of that which they denote may be beyond doubt. The concept of 'want of probity' appears to provide a useful touchstone in considering circumstances said to give rise to constructive trusts,

1 [1948] 1 KB 339.

2 26th edn, 1966, London: Sweet & Maxwell, p 201.

> and I have not found it misleading when applying it to the many authorities cited to this court. It is because of such a concept that evidence as to 'good faith', 'knowledge' and 'notice' plays so important a part in the reported decisions.

In the UK, remedies exist in quasi-contract which are based on unjust enrichment so the use of the constructive trust to provide a remedy is not justifiable. More so, it is equally unwarranted to equate a constructive trust with a resulting trust.

Hussey v Palmer [1972] 1 WLR 1286, CA

> **Lord Denning MR:** Although the plaintiff alleged that there was a resulting trust, I should have thought that the trust in this case, if there was one, was more in the nature of a constructive trust: but this is more a matter of words than anything else. The two run together. By whatever name it is described, it is a trust imposed by law whenever justice and good conscience require it. It is a liberal process, founded upon large principles of equity, to be applied in cases where the legal owner cannot conscientiously keep the property for himself alone, but ought to allow another to have the property or the benefit of it or a share in it. The trust may arise at the outset when the property is acquired, or later on, as the circumstances may require. It is an equitable remedy by which the court can enable an aggrieved party to obtain restitution. It is comparable to the legal remedy of money had and received which, as Lord Mansfield said, is 'very beneficial and therefore much encouraged' [*Moses v Macferlan*].[3] Thus, we have repeatedly held that, when one person contributes towards the purchase price of a house, the owner holds it on a constructive trust for him, proportionate to his contribution, even though there is no agreement between them, and no declaration of trust to be found, and no evidence of any intention to create a trust. Instances are numerous where a wife has contributed money to the initial purchase of a house or property; or later on to the payment of mortgage instalments; or has helped in a business: see *Falconer v Falconer*;[4] *Heseltine v Heseltine*;[5] *Re Cummins (Decd)*.[6] Similarly when a mistress has contributed money, or money's worth, to the building of a house: *Cooke v Head*.[7] Very recently we held that a purchaser who bought a cottage subject to the rights of the occupier held it on trust for her benefit: *Binions v Evans*.[8] In all those cases it would have been quite inequitable for the legal owner to take the property for himself and exclude the other from it. So the law imputed or imposed a trust for his or her benefit.

In this case, the plaintiff paid £607 in providing an extension to the house of her daughter and son in law. The extension was built to accommodate the

3 (1760) 2 Burr 1005, p 1012.

4 [1970] 1 WLR 1333.

5 [1971] 1 WLR 342.

6 [1972] Ch 62.

7 [1972] 1 WLR 518.

8 [1972] Ch 359.

plaintiff who, at that time was living with the defendants. A dispute arose between the parties and the plaintiff left the house. She now claimed an interest in the house. The Court of Appeal decided by a majority that a trust was created in her favour in respect of her contribution in providing the extension (Denning MR decided that a constructive trust was created in favour of the plaintiff, Phillimore LJ decided the case on the basis of a resulting trust in favour of the plaintiff and Cairns LJ decided that no trust was created but the plaintiff loaned the amount to the defendants).

Hussey v Palmer [1972] 1 WLR 1286, CA

Lord Denning MR: The present case is well within the principles of those cases. Just as a person who pays part of the purchase price acquires an equitable interest in the house, so also he does when he pays for an extension to be added to it.

In the present case Mrs Hussey paid £607 to a builder for the erection of this extension. It may well be, as the defendant says, that there was no contract to repay it at all. It was not a loan to the son in law. She could not sue him for repayment. He could not have turned her out. If she had stayed there until she died, the extension would undoubtedly have belonged beneficially to the son in law. If, during her lifetime, he had sold the house, together with the extension, she would be entitled to be repaid the £607 out of the proceeds. He admits this himself. But he has not sold the house. She has left, and the son in law has the extension for his own benefit and could sell the whole if he so desired. It seems to me to be entirely against conscience that he should retain the whole house and not allow Mrs Hussey any interest in it, or any charge upon it. The court should, and will, impose or impute a trust by which Mr Palmer is to hold the property on terms under which, in the circumstances that have happened, she has an interest in the property proportionate to the £607 which she put into it. She is quite content if he repays her the £607. If he does not repay the £607, she can apply for an order for sale, so that the sum can be paid to her. But the simplest way for him would be to raise the £607 on mortgage and pay it to her. But, on the legal point raised, I have no doubt there was a resulting trust, or more accurately, a constructive trust, for her, and I would so declare. I would allow the appeal accordingly.

Phillimore LJ: I agree. It is common ground that Mrs Hussey paid £607 to enable her son in law to have an extension made to his house in which she was going to live. It is quite clear that she did not intend to make him a gift of the money. She herself said she regarded it as a loan. It is true that the son in law in his defence said that he assumed the money was paid by her as a gift to him; but in a later amended defence he said that she was to be repaid if the house was sold at an early date. That clearly does not fit with a gift: it goes a long way to confirm her case that it was not a gift. Here is an example of what so often happens. This mother in law advanced money to improve the property of her son in law. She did not intend to make a gift of the money. She could not afford to do that. No terms of repayment were agreed except perhaps in the event of the house being sold at an early date. She has described it as a loan, and that might be true. I do not for myself think that it would be inconsistent

> with the transaction also being or involving a resulting trust. In all the circumstances here, in the absence of clear arrangements for repayment and in circumstances where repayment on demand might be very difficult for the son in law, I should have thought it was more appropriate to regard it as an example of a resulting trust; and I would accordingly entirely agree with Lord Denning MR that she has an interest in this house proportionate to the £607 which she paid. It follows that this appeal should be allowed.
>
> **Cairns LJ** (dissenting): It must be a common thing indeed for a parent or a parent in law to make a loan of money to a son or daughter or a son in law which both of them know is a loan, as to which it is obvious that there is no immediate prospect of repayment, but which in law is a loan repayable on demand. In my view that is the position here. As it was a loan, I think it is quite inconsistent with that to say that it could create a resulting trust at the same time. I accept as a correct statement of law the short passage in Underhill's *Law of Trusts and Trustees*,[9] in these words:
>
>> Where the purchase money is provided by a third party at the request of and by way of loan to the person to whom the property is conveyed there is no resulting trust in favour of the third party, for the lender did not advance the purchase money as purchaser ... but merely as lender.
>
> And it seems to me that that proposition is equally applicable where it is not a matter of the property being purchased, but a matter of a builder being paid for an extension to a property which already belongs to the borrower of the money. For these reasons I consider that the plaintiff was certainly not entitled to succeed on the evidence which she had given.

It ought to be pointed out that Lord Denning's view that the constructive trust is an equitable remedy does not represent the traditional view of English courts. The constructive trust creates a property right in favour of the claimant. The plaintiff then adopts the most appropriate remedy in order to give effect to such right.

Re Sharpe [1980] 1 All ER 198, HC

> **Browne-Wilkinson J:** Even if it be right to say that the courts can impose a constructive trust as a remedy in certain cases (which to my mind is a novel concept in English law), in order to provide a remedy the court must first find a right which has been infringed ... The introduction of an interest under a constructive trust is an essential ingredient if the plaintiff has any right at all. Therefore ... it cannot be that the interest in property arises for the first time when the court declares it to exist. The right must have arisen at the time of the transaction in order for the plaintiff to have any right the breach of which can be remedied ...

The courts have adopted a pragmatic, broad based approach towards constructive trusts which, although classifiable into various categories, remain subject to extension and development.

9 12th edn, 1970, London: Sweet & Maxwell, p 210.

Carl Zeiss Stiftung v Herbert Smith & Co **[1969] 2 Ch 276, CA**

> **Edmund-Davies LJ:** English law provides no clear and all-embracing definition of a constructive trust. Its boundaries have been left perhaps deliberately vague, so as not to restrict the court by technicalities in deciding what the justice of a particular case may demand.

CATEGORIES OF CONSTRUCTIVE TRUSTS

Trustee or fiduciary making an unauthorised profit

The rule is that a person occupying a position of confidence (such as a trustee or fiduciary) is prohibited from deriving any personal benefit by availing himself of his position in the absence of authority from the beneficiaries, trust instrument or the court. In other words, the trustee or fiduciary should not place himself in position where his duty may conflict with his personal interest. If such a conflict occurs and the trustee obtains a benefit or profit, the advantage is held on constructive trust for the beneficiary.

Keech v Sandford **[1726] Sel Cas Ch 61, HL**

The defendant, a trustee, held the profits of a lease of Romford market on trust for a minor. Before the expiration of the lease, the defendant requested a renewal of the lease in favour of the beneficiary personally, but this was refused. The trustee than attempted to renew the lease in his capacity as trustee for the infant but this was also refused. The lessor agreed to renew the lease in favour of the trustee personally and this was done. In an action on behalf of the beneficiaries, the court held that the profits of the renewed lease were held on constructive trust in favour of the beneficiaries.

> **Lord King LC:** I must consider this as a trust for the infant, for I very well see, if a trustee, on the refusal to renew, might have a lease to himself, few trust estates would be renewed to the *cestui que* use. Though I do not say there is fraud in this case, yet he should rather have let it run out than to have had the lease to himself. It may seem hard that the trustee is the only person of all mankind who might not have the benefit of the lease; but it is very proper that the rule should be strictly pursued and not in the least relaxed; for it is very obvious what would be the consequences of letting trustees have the lease, on refusal to renew to the *cestui que* trust.

Perhaps the reason for this harsh rule is that the courts are reluctant to run the risk of finding it difficult in many cases to ascertain accurately whether or not an unfair advantage has been taken by the trustee or not. Unfairness to the trustee is not the major concern but the primary consideration of the courts is to ensure that there is no possibility of injustice to the beneficiaries.

Bray v Ford [1896] AC 44, HL

> **Lord Herschell:** It is an inflexible rule of a court of equity that a person in a fiduciary position ... is not, unless otherwise expressly provided, entitled to make a profit; he is not allowed to put himself in a position where his interest and his duty conflict. It does not appear to me that this rule is ... founded upon principles of morality. I regard it rather as based on the consideration that human nature being what it is, there is a danger, in such circumstances, of the person holding a fiduciary interest being swayed by interest rather than duty, and thus prejudicing those he is bound to protect. It has, therefore, been deemed expedient to lay down this positive rule.

The doctrine in *Keech v Sandford* (as it is sometimes called) has been extended to other fiduciary relationships such as agents on behalf of principals; directors in favour of companies; partners vis à vis co-partners; solicitors in respect of clients. A fiduciary is an individual who is aware that his judgment and confidence is being relied on, and has been relied on, by the plaintiff.

Apart from the traditional categories of fiduciaries, the existence of such relationship is a question for the court to decide. In such cases, the plaintiff is required to establish the following three propositions:

(1) the defendant holds a fiduciary position towards the plaintiff; and

(2) the defendant obtained a benefit; and

(3) there is a causal connection between the relationship and the benefit.

Failure to establish all of these conditions would lead to a failure in the proceedings.

Re Biss [1903] Ch 40, CA (Collins MR, Romer and Cozens-Hardy LJJ)

The lessee of a house in Westminster carried on a profitable business as a lodgings-housekeeper, but died intestate. His widow took out letters of administration and with her two adult children continued to carry on the business under the existing lease. On the expiration of the original lease, the widow applied to the lessor for a new lease for the benefit of the estate. The lessor refused, but granted a new lease to one of the sons personally. The widow applied to the court to have the new lease treated as held on behalf of the estate.

The Court of Appeal held that the son was entitled to the lease beneficially on the ground that he did not stand in a fiduciary relationship to the others interested in the estate.

> **Collins MR:** The appellant (son) is simply one of the next of kin of the former tenant and had, as such, a possible interest in the term. He is not, as such, trustee for the others interested, nor is he in possession. The administratrix represented the estate and alone had the right to renew incident thereon, and unquestionably could renew only for the benefit of the estate. But is the appellant in the same category? Or is he entitled to go into the facts to shew that he had not, in point of fact, abused his position, or in any sense intercepted an advantage coming by way of accretion to the estate. He did not take under a

> will or a settlement with interests coming after his own, but simply got a possible share upon an intestacy in case there was a surplus of assets over debts. It seems to me that this obligation cannot be put higher than that of any other tenant in common against whom it would have to be established, not as a presumption of law but as an inference of fact, that he had abused his position. If he is not under a personal incapacity to take a benefit, he is entitled to shew that the renewal was not in fact an accretion to the original term, and that it was not until there had been an absolute refusal on the part of the lessor and after full opportunity to the administratrix to procure it for the estate if she could, that he accepted a proposal of renewal made to him by the lessor. These questions cannot be considered or discussed when the party is by his position debarred from keeping a personal advantage derived directly or indirectly out of his fiduciary or quasi-fiduciary position, but when he is not so debarred I think it becomes a question of fact whether that which he has received was in his hands an accretion to the interest of the deceased, or whether the connection between the estate and the renewal had not been wholly severed by the action of the lessor before the appellant accepted a new lease. This consideration seems to get rid of any difficulty that one of the next of kin was an infant. The right or hope of renewal incident to the estate was determined before the appellant intervened.

In this case, the application by the widow was under the rule against 'self-dealing' (a phrase coined by Megarry VC, in *Tito v Waddell (No 2)* [1977] Ch 106). This rule is a derivative of the *Keech v Sandford* principle. See *Ex p Lacey* and *Ex p James* (below, p 318). An impugned purchase by the trustee or trustees of trust property is treated as a voidable transaction at the instance of the beneficiaries, even though the purchase may have the appearance of being fair. This rule cannot be evaded by transfers to nominees with the ultimate aim of benefiting the trustee (or trustees), for such nominees, with knowledge of the circumstances, cannot acquire a better title than the trustee. Alternatively, if the trustee has resold the property and realised a profit, the beneficiaries may adopt the sale and require the trustee to account for the profit. Another occasion when the plaintiff failed in his attempt to set aside the transaction is *Holder v Holder* (see below, p 317).

A related principle is the rule of 'fair dealing' (referred to by Megarry VC in *Tito v Waddell (No 2)*). This concerns the trustee purchasing the beneficiary's interest. The approach of the courts in this context is less stringent as compared with the 'self dealing' rule. The issue is whether the trustee can discharge the onus of proving that he has made full disclosure of the material facts to the beneficiary, to such an extent that the latter is able to exercise an independent judgment as to the nature and extent of the sale.

Lord Eldon in *Coles v Trecothick* (1804) 9 Ves 234, said:

> ... a trustee may buy from the *cestui que* trust, provided there is a distinct and clear contract, ascertained to be such after a jealous and scrupulous examination of all the circumstances, proving that the *cestui que* trust intended the trustee should buy; and there is no fraud, no concealment, no advantage taken, by the trustee of information, acquired by him in the character of trustee.

The rule against 'self-dealing' is applicable to executors (as fiduciaries), but on the special facts in *Holder v Holder*, the Court of Appeal decided that the sale to Victor was valid.

Holder v Holder [1968] Ch 353, CA (Harman, Danckwerts and Sellers LJJ)

The testator appointed his widow, daughter and one of his sons, Victor, to be his executors and trustees. Victor at first took a few minor steps in connection with the administration of the estate (signing cheques, etc) but then abstained from taking any further part in the administration. One of the assets of the estate included a farm. Victor had acquired no special knowledge of the farm in his capacity as executor and all the knowledge about the farm was acquired as a tenant of that farm. The farm was then offered for sale at an auction subject to Victor's tenancy. At the auction, Victor made a successful bid for the farm. Another son applied to the court for the sale to be set aside.

The Court of Appeal held that, owing to the special circumstances of this case, the sale ought not be set aside for the following reasons:

(a) Victor had not instructed the valuer nor had he arranged the auction;

(b) Victor had never assumed the duties of executor, for he had done virtually nothing in the administration of the estate, nor had Victor any influence on the two other executors in respect of the sale;

(c) in any case, Victor had made no secret of his intention to buy the farm and had paid a good price for the property;

(d) Victor was not relied upon by other beneficiaries to protect their interests.

> **Harman LJ:** It was admitted at the bar in the court below that the acts of Victor were enough to constitute intermeddling with the estate and that his renunciation was ineffective. On this footing, he remained a personal representative, even after probate had been granted to his co-executors, and could have been obliged by the creditor or a beneficiary to re-assume the duties of the executor. The judge decided in favour of the plaintiff on this point because Victor at the time of the sale was himself still in a fiduciary position and like any other trustee could not purchase the trust property. I feel the force of this argument, but doubt its validity in the very special circumstances of this case. The reason for this rule is that a man may not be both vendor and purchaser; but Victor was never in that position here. He took no part in instructing the valuer who fixed the reserves or in the preparations for the auction. Everyone in the family knew that he was not a seller but a buyer. In this case Victor never assumed the duties of an executor. It is true that he concurred in signing a few cheques for trivial sums and endorsing a few insurance policies, but he never, so far as appears, interfered in any way with the administration of the estate. It is true he managed the farms, but he did that as tenant and not as executor. He acquired no special knowledge as executor. What he knew he knew as tenant of the farms.
>
> Another reason lying behind the rule is that there must never be a conflict of duty and interest, but in fact there was none here in the case of Victor, who

> made no secret throughout that he intended to buy. There is of course ample authority that a trustee cannot purchase [the trust property]. The leading cases are decisions of Lord Eldon – *Ex p Lacey*[10] and *Ex p James*.[11] In the former case the Lord Chancellor expressed himself thus:
>
>> The rule I take to be this; not, that a trustee cannot buy from his *cestui que* trust, but, that he shall not buy from himself. If a trustee will so deal with his *cestui que* trust, that the amount of the transaction shakes off the obligation, that attaches upon him as trustee, then he may buy. If that case is rightly understood, it cannot lead to much mistake. The true interpretation of what is there reported does not break in upon the law as to trustees. The rule is this. A trustee, who is entrusted to sell and manage for others, undertakes in the same moment in which he becomes a trustee, not to manage for the benefit and advantage of himself.
>
> In *Ex p James*, the same Lord Chancellor said:
>
>> This doctrine as to purchases by trustees, assignees and persons having a confidential character, stands much more upon general principle than upon the circumstances of any individual case. It rests upon this; that the purchase is not permitted in any case, however honest the circumstances; the general interests of justice requiring it to be destroyed in every instance.
>
> These are no doubt strong words, but it is to be observed that Lord Eldon was dealing with cases where the purchaser was at the time of sale acting for the vendors. In this case Victor was not so acting; his interference with the administration of the estate was of a minimal character and the last cheque he signed was in August before he executed the deed of renunciation. He took no part in the instructions for probate, nor in the valuations or fixing of the reserves. Everyone concerned knew of the renunciation and of the reason for it, namely, that he wished to be a purchaser. Equally, everyone, including the three firms of solicitors engaged, assumed that the renunciation was effective and entitled Victor to bid. I feel great doubt whether the admission made at the bar was correct, as did the judge, but assuming it was right, the acts were only technically acts of intermeddling and I find no case where the circumstances are parallel. Of course, I feel the force of the judge's reasoning that if Victor remained an executor he is within the rule, but in a case where the reasons behind the rule do not exist I do not feel bound to apply it. My reasons are that the beneficiaries never looked to Victor to protect their interests. They all knew he was in the market as purchaser; that the price paid was a good one and probably higher than anyone, not a sitting tenant, would give. Further, the first two defendants alone acted as executors and sellers: they alone could convey: they were not influenced by Victor in connection with the sales.
>
> I hold, therefore, that the rule does not apply in order to disentitle Victor to bid at the auction, as he did ...

On the other hand, a fiduciary relationship had existed in:

---

10 (1802) 6 Ves 625.

11 (1803) 8 Ves 337.

English v Dedham Vale Properties [1978] 1 WLR 93, HC

In this case, during negotiations for the purchase of land, the purchasers in the name of and purportedly acting for the vendors, sought and obtained planning permission for the land. The vendors did not consent to this application but had they been aware this would have influenced the purchase price.

It was held that a fiduciary relationship had been established between the parties. The purchasers were liable to account to the vendors for the profits which accrued as a result of the grant of planning permission.

> **Slade J:** If a person, without any preceding authority, purports to enter into a contract with a third party for and on behalf of an alleged named principal and the named principal later ratifies and adopts the contract, the relationship of principal and agent will usually be treated as arising between the two parties concerned with all the normal consequences attaching to such relationship: See *Bowstead on Agency*.[12] In the present case, however, the defendant cannot be said to be a self-appointed agent of the plaintiffs in respect of any contract entered on their behalf.
>
> In my judgment, in the end the question of the liability, if any, of the defendant to account must depend on the view which the court takes as to the nature of the relationship subsisting between the defendant and the plaintiffs at the date when the planning application was made. The liability to account would, in my judgment, arise if, though only if the relationship was in the eyes of equity a fiduciary one in the sense that it imposed relevant fiduciary duties on the defendant towards the plaintiffs. In this context, I regard one point as being of great significance. As I have indicated, if the plaintiffs had learned of the application which had been made in their names and in respect of their property before contracts had been exchanged, they would have been entitled to say to the defendant and Mr Mead: 'We ratify and adopt this application, which has been made in our names, as our own application and neither of you are to have anything more to do with it.' Furthermore, this is, I think effectively the course which the plaintiffs would have actually adopted, unless a more favourable form of contract had then been offered to them. This being so, I do not think that a court of equity should or will allow the defendant to be in a better position than that in which it would have found itself if, before exchange of contracts, the defendant, or Mr Mead had told the plaintiffs of the application which had been made in their names, as I think it or he should have told them. I do not think that the categories of fiduciary relationships which give rise to a constructive trusteeship should be regarded as falling into a limited number of straitjackets or as being necessarily closed. They are, after all, no more than formulae for equitable relief. As Ungoed-Thomas J said in *Selangor United Rubber Estates Ltd v Cradock (No 3)*:[13]
>
> > The court of equity says that the defendant shall be liable in equity, as though he were a trustee. He is made liable in equity as trustee by the

12 14th edn, 1976, London: Sweet & Maxwell, pp 37 *et seq*.

13 [1968] 1 WLR 1555, p 1582.

> imposition or construction of the court of equity. This is done because in accordance with equitable principles applied by the court of equity it is equitable that he should be held liable as though he were a trustee. Trusteeship and constructive trusteeship are equitable conceptions.

It has not been submitted that, but for the making of the planning permission, any fiduciary relationship could be said to have arisen between Mrs English and the defendant or Mr Harrington before the exchange of contracts. Mr Joseph in effect submitted that the mere making of a planning application could not by itself have given rise to any such relationship, when none would have otherwise existed. I see the force of this submission but am not in the end convinced by it. My reasons may be put in the form of two general propositions:

(1) where during the course of negotiations for a contract for the sale and purchase of property, the proposed purchaser, in the name of and purportedly as agent on behalf of the vendor, but without the consent or authority of the vendor, takes some action in regard to the property (whether it be the making of a planning application, a contract for the sale of the property, or anything else) which, if disclosed to the vendor, might reasonably be supposed to be likely to influence him in deciding whether or not to conclude the contract, a fiduciary relationship in my judgment arises between the two parties;

(2) such fiduciary relationship gives rise to the consequences that there is a duty on the proposed purchaser to disclose to the vendor before the conclusion of the contract what he has done as the vendor's purported agent, and correspondingly, in the event of non-disclosure, there is a duty on him to account to him for any profit made in the course of the purported agency, unless the vendor consents to his retaining it. In such circumstances, the person who, for his own private purposes, uses the vendor's name and purports to act as his agent cannot reasonably complain if the law subjects him to the same consequences vis à vis his alleged principal as if he had actually had the authority which he purported to have.

On my analysis of the facts of the present case, the plaintiffs never consented to the defendant or Mr Harrington, or Mr Mead purporting to make the planning application as their agent before contract; the fact that this had been done was never disclosed to them before the exchange of contracts; and they never consented to the defendant's retaining the profit ultimately received by it as a result of the making of the planning application. In these circumstances, the defendant is in my judgment accountable for such profit.

Similarly, an individual becomes a fiduciary if he purports to act on behalf of a trust without authority, and obtains confidential information as a result of being an apparent representative of the trust. In this event, any profits obtained by the fiduciary in connection with the use of such confidential information is subject to the trust. Indeed, the confidential information obtained in such circumstances may be treated as trust property.

Boardman and Another v Phipps [1967] 2 AC 46, HL (Lords Cohen, Hodson and Guest; Viscount Dilhorne and Lord Upjohn dissenting)

In this case, the trust property consisted of shares in a company. One of the beneficiaries and Mr Boardman, the solicitor to the trust, were dissatisfied with the way the company's business was organised and obtained control of the company on behalf of the trust by acting on privileged information available only to the trust. The company was re-organised and substantial profits accrued to the trust. Mr Boardman at all material times, had acted honestly but wrongly believed that he had the full approval of the trustees and beneficiaries. John Phipps, a beneficiary, claimed that Mr Boardman and his accomplice were required to account to the trust for their profits as constructive trustees.

The House of Lords held that the appellants were fiduciaries and were liable to account for their profits. But the court awarded them generous remuneration for their efforts.

> **Lord Hodson:** The proposition of law involved in this case is that no person standing in a fiduciary position, when a demand is made upon him by the person to whom he stands in the fiduciary relationship to account for profits acquired by him by reason of the opportunity and the knowledge, or either, resulting from it, is entitled to defeat the claim upon any ground save that he made profits with the knowledge and assent of the other person.
>
> It is obviously of importance to maintain the proposition in all cases and to do nothing to whittle away its scope or the absolute responsibility which it imposes.
>
> The person concerned in this case, namely, Mr Thomas Boardman and Mr Tom Phipps, are not trustees in the strict sense but are said to be constructive trustees by reason of the fiduciary position in which they stood. As Lord Selborne pointed out in *Barnes v Addy*:[14]
>
> > That responsibility [viz, that of trustees] may no doubt be extended in equity to others who are not properly trustees, if they are found either making themselves trustees *de son tort*, or actually participating in any fraudulent conduct of the trustee to the injury of the *cestui que* trust. But, on the other hand, strangers are not to be made constructive trustees merely because they act as the agents of trustees in transactions within their legal powers, transactions, perhaps of which a court of equity may disapprove, unless those agents receive and become chargeable with some part of the trust property, or unless they assist with knowledge in a dishonest and fraudulent design on the part of the trustee.
>
> There is no question of fraud in this case; it has never been suggested that the appellants acted in any other than an open and honourable manner.

14 (1874) 9 Ch App 244.

If, however, they are in a fiduciary position they are as trustees bound by duty, succinctly stated by Lord Cranworth LC in *Aberdeen Railway Co v Blaikie Brothers*:[15]

> And it is a rule of universal application, that no one, having such duties to discharge, shall be allowed to enter into engagements in which he has, or can have, a personal interest conflicting, or which possibly may conflict, with the interests of those whom he is bound to protect.

So far as Mr Tom Phipps is concerned, he was not placed in a fiduciary position by reason of his being a beneficiary under his father's will. He was acting as agent for trustees with Mr Boardman before any question of acting with him for his own benefit arose. He has not, however, sought to be treated in a different way from Mr Boardman upon whom the conduct of the whole matter depended and with whom he has acted throughout as a co-adventurer; he does not claim that he should succeed in this appeal if Mr Boardman fails.

Mr Boardman's fiduciary position arose from the facts that he was at all material times solicitor to the trustees of the will of Mr Phipps senior. This is admitted, although counsel for the appellants has argued, and argued correctly, that there is no such post as solicitor to trustees. The trustees either employ a solicitor or they do not in a particular case and there is no suggestion that they were under any contractual or other duty to employ Mr Boardman or his firm. Nevertheless, as an historical fact they did employ him and look to him for advice at all material times and this is admitted. It was as solicitor to the trustees that he obtained the information ... This information enabled him to acquire knowledge of a most extensive and valuable character which was the foundation upon which a decision could, and was taken to buy the shares in Lester & Harris Ltd.

This information was obtained on behalf of the trustees, most of it at a time during the history of the negotiations when the proposition was to divide the assets of the company between two groups of shareholders. This object could not have been effected without a reconstruction of the company and Mr Boardman used the strong minority shareholding which the trustees held, that is to say, 8,000 shares in the company, wielding this holding as a weapon to enable him to obtain the information of which he subsequently made use.

As to this it is said on behalf of the appellants that information as such is not necessarily property and it is only trust property which is relevant. I agree, but it is nothing to the point to say that in these times corporate trustees, for example, the public trustee and others, necessarily acquire a mass of information in their capacity of trustees for a particular trust and cannot be held liable to account if knowledge so acquired enables them to operate to their own advantage, or to that of other trusts. Each case must depend on its own facts and I dissent from the view that information is of its nature something which is not properly to be described as property. We are aware that what is called 'know how' in the commercial sense is property which may be very valuable as an asset. I agree with the learned judge and with the Court

15 (1854) 1 Macq 461, HL.

of Appeal that the confidential information acquired in this case which was capable of being and was turned to account can be properly regarded as the property of the trust. It was obtained by Mr Boardman by reason of the opportunity which he was given as solicitor acting for the trustee in the negotiations with the chairman of the company, as the correspondence demonstrates. The end result was that out of the special position in which they were standing in the course of the negotiations the appellants got the opportunity to make a profit and the knowledge that it was there to be made.

The appellants argue that this is not enough, and in support of the contention rely on the authority of *Aas v Benham*.[16] This case was concerned with a partnership of shipbrokers, and the defendant carried on the business of ship builder, using knowledge acquired in partnership business. A claim against him to account to the partnership for the profits of his business as ship builder failed. Lindley LJ said that it is not the source of information but the use to which it is put which is important:

> To hold that a partner [or trustee] can never derive any personal benefit from information which he obtains as a partner would be manifestly absurd.

It was held that the defendant was not liable to account because the profit was made outside the scope of the partnership and that in no sense was the defendant acting as the agent of the partners. Similarly the appellants contend that the purchase of the shares in question was outside the scope of the fiduciary relationship existing between them and the trustees.

The case of partnership is special in the sense that a partner is the principal as well as the agent of the other partners and works in a defined area of business so that it can normally be determined whether the particular transaction is within or without the scope of the partnership.

It is otherwise in the case of a general trusteeship or fiduciary position such as was occupied by Mr Boardman, the limits of which are not readily defined, and I cannot find that the decision in the case of *Aas v Benham* assists the appellants, although the purchase of the share was an independent purchase financed by themselves. *Aas v Benham* was a case pending on the alleged relationship of principal and agent as it exists between one partner and another. There was no such relationship here but the position of an agent is relevant and the expression, 'self-appointed agent' used by the learned judge is a convenient way to describe someone who, assuming to act as agent for another, receives property belonging to that other so that the property is held by the self-constituted agent as trustee for such other. Such a case was *Lyell v Kennedy*.[17] Thus, the learned judge found that the appellants were in the same position as if they had been agents for the trustees in the technical sense for the purpose of using the trust shareholding to extract knowledge of the affairs of the company and ultimately to improve the company's profit-earning capacity.

16 [1891] 2 Ch 244.

17 (1889) 14 App Cas 437.

Keech v Sandford[18] was a case in which it was impossible for the *cestui que* trust to obtain the renewal of a lease, nevertheless the trustee was held accountable for renewal obtained by him. Similarly, in *Regal (Hastings) Ltd v Gulliver*, from which some of your Lordships have cited passages, the directors of Regal were held accountable to the company for the profit they made in acquiring shares when the opportunity fell to them as directors of the company, notwithstanding the fact that it was impossible for Regal to take the shares owing to lack of funds.

Regal (Hastings) Ltd v Gulliver differs from this case mainly in that the directors took up shares and made a profit thereby, it having been originally intended that the company should buy these shares. Here there was no such intention on the part of the trustees. There is no indication that they either had the money or would have been ready to apply to the court for sanction enabling them to do so. On the contrary, Mr Fox, the active trustee and an accountant who concerned himself with the details of the trust property, was not prepared to agree to the trustee buying the shares and encouraged the appellants to make the purchase. This does not affect the position. As *Keech v Sandford* shows, the inability of the trust to purchase makes no difference to the liability of the appellants, if liability otherwise exists. The distinction on the facts as to intention to purchase shares between this case and *Regal (Hastings) Ltd v Gulliver* is not relevant. The company (Regal) had not the money to apply for the shares upon which the profit was made. The directors took the opportunity which they had presented to them to buy the shares with their own money and were held accountable. Mr Fox's refusal as one of the trustees to take any part in the matter on behalf of the trust, so far as he was concerned, can make no difference. Nothing short of fully informed consent which the learned judge found not to have been obtained could enable the appellants in the position which they occupied having taken the opportunity provided by that position to make a profit for themselves.

Likewise it is no answer to the respondent's claim that there was no contract of agency and that the appellants were at all times acting for themselves without concealment and indeed with the encouragement of one of the trustees, namely, Mr Fox.

If they received confidential information from Lester & Harris in their capacity as representing the trustees it matters not whether or not there was a true agency. I refer again to the passage from Lord Wright's judgment in *Regal (Hastings) Ltd v Gulliver* when he speaks of 'an agent, a director, a trustee or other person in an analogous fiduciary position' and, as an illustration, says that the most usual and typical case of this nature is that of principal and agent.

The relevant information is not any information but special information which I think must include that confidential information given to the appellants which is so fully detailed in the judgment of Wilberforce J. There is a passage

18 (1726) Sel Cas Ch 437.

in *Aas v Benham* in the judgment of Bowen LJ which I think is of assistance, although the learned Lord Justice was dealing with partnership, not trusteeship: he was explaining some observation of Cotton LJ in *Dean v MacDowell*.[19] These were:

> Again, if he [that is, a partner] makes any profit by the use of any property of the partnership, including, I may say, information which the partnership is entitled to, there the profit is made out of the partnership property.

Bowen LJ commented:

> He is speaking of information which a partnership is entitled to in such a sense that it is information which is the property, or is to be included in the property of the partnership – that is to say, information the use of which is valuable to them as a partnership, and to the use of which they have a vested interest. But you cannot bring the information obtained in this case within that definition.

Aas v Benham is an important case as showing that a partner may make a profit from information obtained in the course of the partnership business where he does so in another firm which is outside the scope of the partnership business. In that case the partnership business was shipbroking and the profit made was in a business which had no connection with that of the partnership.

This shows the limitation which must be kept in mind in considering the sense in which each partner is the agent of the partnership, but does not assist the appellant. Mr Boardman continued to be in a fiduciary position up to and including the time when the shares were purchased (March 1959), and the scope of the trust concerning which his fiduciary relationship exist was not limited in the same way as a partnership carrying on a particular business.

It cannot, in my opinion, be said that the purchase of shares in Lester & Harris was outside the scope of the fiduciary relationship in which Mr Boardman stood to the trust.

The confidential information which the appellants obtained at a time when Mr Boardman was admittedly holding himself out as solicitor for the trustees was obtained by him as representing the trustees, the holders of 8,000 shares of Lester & Harris. As Russell LJ put it:

> The substantial trust shareholding was an asset of which one aspect was its potential use as a means of acquiring knowledge of the company's affairs, or of negotiating allocations of the company's assets, or of including other shareholders to part with their shares.

Whether this aspect is properly to be regarded as part of the trust assets is, in my judgment, immaterial. The appellants obtained knowledge by reason of their fiduciary position and they cannot escape liability by saying that they were acting for themselves and not as agents of the trustees. Whether or not the trust or the beneficiaries in their stead could have taken advantage of the information is immaterial, as the authorities clearly show. No doubt it was but

19 (1877) 8 Ch D 345.

> a remote possibility that Mr Boardman would ever be asked by the trustees to advise on the desirability of an application to the court in order that the trustees might avail themselves of the information obtained. Nevertheless, even if the possibility of conflict is present between personal interest and the fiduciary position the rule of equity must be applied. This appears from the observation of Lord Cranworth LC in *Aberdeen Railway Co v Blaikie.*
>
> It is said that the appellants never had the necessary facts pleaded against them to raise the question of conflict of interest so that they did not have the opportunity of dealing with allegations which would be relevant thereto: I cannot see what further facts were relevant to be raised other than those to which reference has been made in the judgment in the court below and in the speeches of your Lordships. The question whether or not there was a fiduciary relationship at the relevant time must be a question of law and the question of conflict of interest directly emerges from the facts pleaded, otherwise no question of entitlement to a profit would fall to be considered. No positive wrongdoing is proved or alleged against the appellants but they cannot escape from the consequence of the acts involving liability to the respondent unless they can prove consent. This they endeavoured without success to do, for, although they gave the respondent some information, that which they gave was held by the learned judge to be insufficient and there is no appeal against his decision on this point.
>
> I agree with the decision of the learned judge and with that of the Court of Appeal which, in my opinion, involves a finding that there was a potential conflict between Boardman's position as solicitors to the trustees and his own interest in applying for the shares. He was in a fiduciary position vis à vis the trustees and through them vis à vis the beneficiaries. For these reasons in my opinion the appeal should be dismissed; but I should add that I am in agreement with the learned judge that payment should be allowed on a liberal scale in respect of the work and skill employed in obtaining the shares and the profits therefrom.

In accordance with the rule in *Keech v Sandford*, a trustee is not entitled to receive any remuneration or benefit for his services as trustee, except that he may be reimbursed in respect of expenditure properly incurred in connection with his trusteeship (s 30(2) of the Trustee Act 1925).

Williams v Barton [1927] 2 Ch 9, HC

Barton, one of two trustees under a will, was employed as a stockbroker's clerk and in this capacity was entitled to commission on business introduced to his firm. He persuaded his co-trustee to use his firm to value the trust property. Barton took no part in the work of valuation. The trustees paid the fees charged by the firm and Barton received his commission. The co-trustee now claimed to recover the commission on behalf of the trust.

The court held that, despite the valuation was quite proper in the circumstances, Barton was required to account for the commission because the opportunity to earn the reward derived from his position as trustee.

> **Russell J:** It is a well established and salutary rule of equity that a trustee may not make a profit out of his trust. A person who has the management of property as a trustee is not permitted to gain any profit by availing himself of his position, and will be a constructive trustee of any such profit for the benefit of the persons equitably entitled to the property.
>
> It was argued on behalf of the defendant that the case was altogether outside that rule of equity, because the sums received by the defendant were merely parts of his salary paid to him by his employers under the contract of service and were not of a character for which he is liable to account.
>
> The point is not an easy one and there is little, if any, authority to assist in its determination. The situation is an unusual one and the contract of service presents the following peculiar features. The remuneration has no relation to the services, which the defendant has to render to his employers. The defendant, while bound to render the services, might get no remuneration at all if he introduced no work, or introduced none which was acceptable to his employers. The amount of his remuneration depends (subject to his employers' acceptance orders) upon his own efforts, but upon efforts not in relation to the work which he is engaged to do. Any increase of his remuneration rests with him.
>
> From this it seems to me evident that the case falls within the mischief which is sought to be prevented by this rule. The case is clearly one where his duty as trustee and his interest in an increased remuneration are in direct conflict. As a trustee, it is his duty to give the estate the benefit of his unfettered advice in choosing the stockbrokers to act for the estate; as the recipient of half the fees to be earned by George Burnand & Co on work introduced by him his obvious interest is to choose or recommend them for the job.
>
> In the event that has happened they have been chosen, and chosen because the defendant was a trustee, with the result that half of what the estate pays must necessarily pass through them to the defendant as part of his remuneration for other services rendered, but as an addition to the remuneration which he would otherwise have received for those self-same services. The services rendered remain unchanged, but the remuneration for them has been increased. He has increased his remuneration by virtue of his trusteeship. In my opinion this increase of remuneration is profit made by the defendant out of and by reason of his trusteeship, which he would not have made but for his position as trustee.

The logical effect of this rule is that if a trustee legitimately appoints an agent to do trust work that agent may be paid, but if the trustee himself performs the relevant duties he may not be paid.

In *Box v Barclays Bank plc*, the High Court refused to impose a constructive trust on the defendant, despite the unlawful receipt of funds by an unlicensed deposit-taking business conducted by a party which banked with the defendant. The court decided that under the Banking Act 1987, the plaintiff's contractual remedies were expressly preserved. It was therefore unnecessary and inappropriate to provide an alternative remedy based in equity.

Box and Others v Barclays Bank plc [1998] 1 All ER 108, HC

Each of the three plaintiffs, Mrs Box, Mrs Brown and Mrs Jacobs, invested funds with a deposit-taking business run by Sylcon Finance Ltd (Sylcon). Sylcon paid the funds into an account at Barclays Bank plc (the defendant). At all material times the account was overdrawn, although none of the plaintiffs were aware of this. In October 1992, the Bank of England commenced proceedings against Sylcon, on the ground that the latter company was carrying on a deposit-taking business without being authorised under Pt 1 of the Banking Act 1987. Section 3(1) of the Banking Act 1987 declares: '... no person shall ... accept a deposit in the course of carrying on a deposit-taking business unless that person ... is authorised by the Bank ...' Section 3(3) of the Act provides as follows: 'The fact that a deposit has been taken in contravention of this section shall not affect any civil liability arising in respect of the deposit.' An order was made freezing the assets of Sylcon and subsequently the business was liquidated. The plaintiffs proved as creditors and received a distribution of only 12 p in the pound in respect of the amounts claimed. The plaintiffs claimed to recover their losses on the ground that the business of Sylcon was tainted by illegality under s 3(1) of the Banking Act 1987, and therefore the deposits were held on constructive trust and could be recovered from the defendant.

The court held that the unlicensed deposit-taking business of Sylcon constituted a special form of illegality in respect of which s 3(3) of the 1987 Act preserved the ordinary contractual remedies of the depositors. Thus, it was unnecessary to create an alternative remedy in equity. Indeed, to do so would have been contrary to the express provisions of s 3(3) of the Act.

> **Ferris J:** Mr Browne-Wilkinson [counsel for the plaintiffs] argued that the contracts of deposit were affected by illegality, and that, on authority, equity would impose a constructive trust so as to enable the plaintiffs to recover their money. He said that there is a principle under which, where money passes under an illegal transaction in relation to which the recipient of the money is at fault to a greater degree than the payer, equity will give the payer a right to recover his money. This right, being equitable, will bind successors in title to the original recipient unless they take in good faith and for value and without notice of it.
>
> In support of this argument Mr Browne-Wilkinson referred me to four decisions of Lord Mansfield in the 18th century. These were *Moses v Macferlan* [1760] 2 Burr 1005; *Clarke v Shee* [1774] 2 Cowp 197; *Browning v Morris* [1778] 2 Cowp 790; and *Smith v Bromley*, reported as part of the decision in another case at (1778) 2 Dougl 696. I do not think that I need to do more in relation to these authorities than to cite from the judgment of Lord Mansfield in *Moses v Macferlan*, when he said (at p 1012):
>
>> This kind of equitable action, to recover back money, which ought not in justice to be kept, is very beneficial, and therefore much encouraged. It lies only for money which, *ex aequo et bono*, the defendant ought to refund: it

> does not lie for money paid by the plaintiff, which is claimed of him as payable in point of honour and honesty, although it could not have been recovered from him by any course of law; as in payment of a debt barred by the Statute of Limitations, or contracted during his infancy, or to the extent of principal and legal interest upon an usurious contract, or for money fairly lost at play; because in all these cases, the defendant may retain it with a safe conscience, though by positive law he was barred from recovering. But it lies for money paid by mistake; or upon a consideration which happens to fail: or for money got through imposition (express or implied); or extortion; or oppression: or an undue advantage taken of the plaintiff's situation, contrary to laws made for the protection of persons under those circumstances.
>
> In one word, the gist of this kind of action is, that the defendant, upon the circumstances of the case, is obliged by the ties of natural justice and equity to refund the money.

That principle was applied by Parker J in *Lodge v National Union* [1907] 1 Ch 300, where a borrower who had given security to an unregistered money lender was held to be entitled to recover that security, but only on terms that he repaid the money which he had borrowed.

It is notable, however, that in all of the 18th century cases, the plaintiff either had no right to recover without resort to the principle declared by Lord Mansfield, or was in a position where any contract on which he might have sued was tainted by illegality and, unless the principle be applied, unenforceable.

In the cases with which I am concerned, however, it is clear that the illegal taking of deposits by Sylcon does not vitiate the contracts between depositor and Sylcon. This is the result of s 3(3) of the Banking Act, under which this fact is 'not to affect any civil liability arising in respect of the deposit or the money deposited'. Mr Browne-Wilkinson argued that the effect of s 3(3) is neutral so far as his trust claim is concerned. He admitted that the section neutralises a possible defence of illegality in respect of a claim in contract, but it leaves untouched the alternative claim in equity.

I cannot accept this argument. In my view illegality consisting of the taking of deposits by a person who conducts an unlicensed deposit-taking business constitutes a special form of illegality which does not bring in its train the ordinary consequences of illegality at common law. This is achieved by means of s 3(3). That sub-section leaves the ordinary contractual remedies of the depositor intact. It is unnecessary in these circumstances to seek an alternative remedy in equity. Indeed, to do so would go against the very terms of s 3(3). It is not suggested that there would be a remedy in equity were it not for the illegality consisting of the contravention of s 3(1). But if that contravention gives rise to an equitable remedy where none would otherwise exist this would 'affect' the civil liability arising in respect of the deposit by giving the new remedy. Section 3(3) expressly negatives this.

This view accords with the decision of the Court of Appeal in *SCF Finance Ltd v Masri* [1987] 1 QB 1002. While that was a decision on the provisions of the Banking Act 1979, which in some respects are very different from those of the

> Banking Act 1987 with which I am concerned, those provisions included (in s 1(1)) a prohibition similar in substance to that imposed by s 3(1) of the 1987 Act and (in s 1(8)) a provision which is indistinguishable from s 3(3) of the 1987 Act. The Court of Appeal had no difficulty in construing s 1(8) literally.
>
> I therefore reject the argument that Sylcon held the money placed with it by the plaintiffs on a trust arising from the fact, which I accept, that Sylcon accepted that money in the course of carrying on an illegal deposit-taking business.

In *AG v Blake* (see below, p 331), the Court of Appeal decided that a former member of the Secret Intelligence Service was no longer a fiduciary in respect of information which was no longer confidential. However, in the special circumstances of this case, the profits earned by a former member of the security services from writing his autobiography *were* capable of being confiscated by an injunction instituted at the instance of the Attorney General. There were three issues for consideration by the court. First, whether the Attorney General was the appropriate party to institute the claim. Secondly, whether the defendant had committed a breach of duty, criminal or otherwise, by publishing his memoirs. Thirdly, on the assumption that there was a breach of a duty, whether an appropriate remedy was available to deal with the breach. The court decided that the Attorney General's role as guardian of the public interest entitled him to invoke the aid of the civil courts in order to lend support to the criminal law. In *Gouriet v Union of Post Office Workers* [1978] AC 435, the House of Lords decided that the Attorney General had such *locus standi*. This power of the Attorney General is not only exercisable when a statute provides an inadequate remedy or when the criminal courts are not able to act in sufficient time, but may be exercised to prevent the criminal law being flouted, and thereby being brought into disrepute.

With regard to the issue of whether there was a breach of duty, the Court of Appeal affirmed the decision of the High Court. A fiduciary duty did not continue, notwithstanding the termination of the contract which gave rise to it. Irrespective of the origin of the duty of confidentiality, it goes no further than is reasonably necessary for the protection of the interests of the service. The courts will not condone or impose a duty that represented an unreasonable restraint of trade, for example, an ex-member of the security service could not be prevented from going into business as an adviser on security matters. Similarly, the duty imposed by the law would not prevent the publication of originally secret information that had already become public knowledge. However, the defendant was guilty of a serious criminal offence, a breach of s 1(1) of the Official Secrets Act 1989, an offence for which he would never be tried and punished, but from which he hoped to derive financial benefits. If he were to succeed in this venture his conduct would have been tantamount to bringing the criminal law into disrepute.

In the interest of public policy, the remedy of an injunction would have the effect of preserving the relevant assets, pending a claim to confiscate the sums payable as royalties. The jurisdiction of the court was not limited to granting an injunction in order to restrain the commission or repeated commission of an offence. In the exceptional circumstances that existed on the facts, where the offence had already been committed, an injunction to restrain Mr Blake from receiving further benefits from his delict had the effect of satisfying the demands of the public interest and was not disproportionate.

***Attorney General v Blake (Jonathan Cape Ltd, Third Party)* [1998] 1 All ER 833, CA**

The defendant, George Blake, was a member of the Secret Intelligence Service (SIS) from 1944 to 1961. In 1951, he became an agent for the Soviet Union. From that time until his arrest in 1960, he disclosed secret information and documents to the Soviet Union. In 1961, he was convicted of an offence under the Official Secrets Act 1911 and was sentenced to 42 years' imprisonment. In 1966, he escaped from Wormwood Scrubbs and made his way to Moscow, where he lived. In 1989, Mr Blake wrote his autobiography detailing his activities as a member of the SIS. He received £50,000 advance royalties, £50,000 on delivery of the final manuscript and £50,000 on publication of the book. The book, *No Other Choice*, was published in 1990. Mr Blake was entitled to receive royalties from future sales of the book. The Crown, suing through the Attorney General, claimed the financial benefits obtained from the publication of the book, in addition to future royalties. The claim was based on the ground that, in writing the book, the defendant acted in breach of his duty of confidentiality owed to the Crown as an ex-member of the SIS. It was claimed that the Crown was the beneficial owner of the copyright in the book and the defendant was accountable to the Crown for all sums received in respect of the publication. It was not contended that in writing the book the defendant had committed any breach of his duty of confidence. Moreover, it was conceded by the Crown that the information contained in the book relating to the SIS was no longer confidential. The High Court dismissed the claim on the ground that an ex-member of the SIS did not owe the Crown a continuing duty not to use any information imparted to him in that capacity in order to generate a profit or benefit himself. On the facts, the Crown had not established any abuse by the defendant of his position as a former member of the SIS. The Attorney General appealed to the Court of Appeal on a different ground namely, to prevent George Blake, a criminal, retaining the profits directly derived from the commission of his crime. The Crown claimed an injunction seeking to restrain the offender from receiving, or authorising anyone to receive on his behalf, payments or other benefits connected with the book.

Held, allowing the appeal and granting the injunction in order to uphold the public policy of denying a criminal the profits of his crime: it is an offence under s 1(1) of the Official Secrets Act 1989 for a former member of the SIS to disclose official information without lawful authority, whether or not the information was secret or confidential and whether or not its disclosure would be damaging to the national interest. Originally, the Crown had not sought an injunction to prevent publication and, thus, could not now establish loss. But an injunction restraining the defendant from receiving any further payments from the publishers ensured that the criminal law was not flouted and thereby brought into disrepute.

> **Lord Woolf MR:** The issues which this appeal raises are of considerable importance. They involve consideration of whether Her Majesty's Attorney General is entitled to any remedy in: (a) private; or (b) public law, to prevent a former member of the Secret Intelligence Service (SIS) receiving substantial royalties for the publication of a book, when the submission of the manuscript of the book for publication was in breach of contract and a criminal offence and when certain information contained in the manuscript had been, but was no longer, secret or confidential.
>
> **(1) The private law claim**
>
> **(A) Breach of fiduciary duty**
>
> Before us, the Crown has repeated and amplified what is essentially the same submission as it advanced before Sir Richard Scott VC. Its reasoning is as follows:
>
> (1) The respondent was formerly a servant of the Crown.
>
> (2) He was therefore in a fiduciary relationship with the Crown.
>
> (3) This fiduciary relationship gave rise to a fiduciary duty to use the Crown's property, including confidential information, only for the benefit of the Crown or for purposes authorised by the Crown.
>
> (4) The fiduciary duty continued after the respondent's service with the Crown was terminated. Were it to cease when he left the service of the Crown the duty would be emasculated.
>
> (5) Since the duty is based on the fiduciary relationship which exists between employer and employee, and not on the confidential nature of the information in question, it continued after the information ceased to be confidential.
>
> We are unable to accept the last two propositions, which are dependent upon each other. We do not recognise the concept of a fiduciary obligation which continues notwithstanding the determination of the particular relationship which gives rise to it. Equity does not demand a duty of undivided loyalty from a former employee to his former employer, and it does not impose a duty to maintain the confidentiality of information which has ceased to be confidential. The Crown's attempt to derive a fiduciary duty from a combination of two fiduciary relationships which have both come to an end is extremely misconceived.
>
> In the present case, the respondent was bound by contract not to disclose official information without clearance, but he was bound in equity by a different obligation, not to disclose information which was still confidential. By submitting the manuscript for publication without obtaining clearance, the

respondent was in breach of contract; but he was not in breach of fiduciary duty. Not every breach of duty by a fiduciary is a breach of fiduciary duty, and a fiduciary may commit a breach of contract without committing a breach of fiduciary duty: see *Bristol and West Building Society v Mothew* [1996] 4 All ER 698. *A fortiori*, a former fiduciary who commits a breach of contract does not *ipso facto* commit a breach of fiduciary duty.

(B) Breach of contract

By submitting the manuscript for publication, without having first obtained clearance, the respondent committed a clear breach of the express undertaking which he signed when he joined the public service. This was a breach of contract which *prima facie* entitled the Crown to an injunction and damages. The obligation cannot be stigmatised as an unlawful restraint of trade, since the restraint does not exceed what is rendered unlawful by s 1(1) of the Official Secrets Act 1989. This makes it an offence for a member or a former member of the SIS to disclose official information without lawful authority. The offence is committed whether or not the information in question is secret or confidential and whether or not its disclosure would be damaging to the national interest. The respondent's contractual obligation is thus in conformity with the policy which Parliament has adopted in relation to disclosure by members and former members of the SIS.

The Crown has not sought an injunction to prevent publication, and now cannot establish any loss. It is not, therefore, entitled to other than nominal damages.

In the course of the initial hearing, we invited submissions on a second issue which had not previously been considered. The second issue is whether, in the particular circumstances of the present case, the Crown might have a private law claim to restitutionary damages for breach of contract. After giving further consideration to the matter, the Attorney General decided that the Crown did not desire to advance such a claim in this court.

Since the subject is of some importance and we are not convinced that it would not have been open to this court to allow a claim for restitutionary damages for breach of contract in the particular circumstances of the present case, we will express our own views on the subject, even though they are *obiter* and, being without benefit of argument, necessarily tentative.

The general rule is that damages for breach of contract are compensatory, not restitutionary, that is to say, they are measured by the loss to the plaintiff and not by the gain to the defendant. In reality, the doctrine is already subject to exceptions, for the gain (or saving of expense) made by the defendant is sometimes used as the measure of the plaintiff's loss. *Wrotham Park Estates Co Ltd v Parkside Homes Ltd* [1974] 2 All ER 321, and the cases which followed it are examples of this.

If the court is unable to award restitutionary damages for breach of contract, then the law of contract is seriously defective. It means that in many situations the plaintiff is deprived of any effective remedy for breach of contract because of a failure to attach a value to the plaintiff's legitimate interest in having the contract duly performed: see Professor Coote: 'Contract damages, *Ruxley*, and the performance interest' (1997) 56 CLJ 537. In our opinion, the time has come to accept Professor Jones' view (expressed as long ago as 1983 (99 LQR 443, p 452)) that the law is now sufficiently mature to recognise a restitutionary claim for profits made from a breach of contract in appropriate circumstances. The difficult question is not whether restitutionary damages should ever be available for breach of contract, but in what circumstances they should be made available. In *Surrey v Bredero Homes Ltd* [1992] 3 All ER 705, Steyn LJ gave persuasive reasons why such circumstances should remain exceptional.

We do not think that the basis on which damages are awarded should depend on the defendant's moral culpability alone. The fact that his breach of contract is deliberate and cynical is not by itself a good ground for departing from the normal basis on which damages are awarded. It is not only that the line cannot easily be drawn in practice; it is rather that the defendant's motives will normally be irrelevant.

The mere fact that the defendant's breach of his contract with the plaintiff has enabled him to enter into a more profitable contract with someone else should also not be sufficient: *Teacher v Calder* [1899] AC 451 is sound law. But we think that there are at least two situations in which justice requires the award of restitutionary damages where compensatory damages would be inadequate.

The first may be described as the case of skimped performance. This is where the defendant fails to provide the full extent of the services which he has contracted to provide and for which he has charged the plaintiff.

The second case is where the defendant has obtained his profit by doing the very thing which he contracted not to do. In his article, Professor Birks observed [1987] LMCLQ 421, p 434:

> If you promise not to pursue a particular profit making activity and you do pursue it, nothing is more apt than that you should make restitution of your profits.

This covers the present case exactly. The defendant's breach of contract in submitting the book for publication did not merely provide him with an opportunity for profit; nor did his contract with the publishers merely put it out of his power to perform his contractual obligations to the Crown. The connection between the breach and the profit is far more direct. He promised not to disclose official information and he did so profit. He earned the profits by doing the very thing which he had promised not to do.

It appears to us that the general rule that damages for breach of contract are compensatory can safely be maintained without denying the availability of restitutionary damages in exceptional cases.

(2) Public law claims

(A) The Attorney General's role

The nature of the Attorney General's role to bring proceedings in the public interest when an ordinary individual cannot do so, was considered in detail by the House of Lords in *Gouriet v Union of Post Office Workers* [1978] AC 435. That case was not, however, directly concerned with the extent of the Attorney General's powers, the existence of which were not in issue. It was accepted by all the members of the House of Lords that the Attorney General is entitled to invoke the aid of the civil courts in support of the criminal law and that the court has power to grant injunctive relief in an appropriate case in support of the criminal law.

There are situations where the criminal courts are powerless to act. In such circumstances the inherent power of the Attorney General is extremely valuable and should not be artificially confined. As Devlin J said in *AG (on the relation of Hornchurch UDC) v Bastow* [1957] 1 All ER 497, p 501:

> ... the Attorney General is the person who is primarily responsible for the enforcement of the law, he is the first law officer of the Crown and I think that, if he considers it necessary to come into the court by way of a relator action to ask for the assistance of the court in enforcing obedience to a clear provision of the law, the court, although retaining its discretion, ought to be very slow to say that the Attorney General ought to have exhausted other remedies before he came to the court.

However, the power which lies behind the ability of the Attorney General to intervene, is not based on any narrow concept of a statute providing an inadequate remedy or the criminal courts not being able to act in sufficient time. It at least extends to preventing the criminal law being flouted and in consequence being brought into disrepute.

(B) The public interest

In public law, the two significant features of the case are: first, that the respondent is guilty of a serious criminal offence (ie, a breach of the Official Secrets Act) for which he will never be tried and punished, but from which he has derived and, in the absence of a court order, may continue to derive financial benefits; and, secondly, that the plaintiff is the Attorney General, who occupies a unique position of responsibility in public law.

In our judgment, the jurisdiction of the courts, on an application made by the Attorney General, is not limited to granting an injunction restraining the commission or repeated commission of a criminal offence. If, as here, a criminal offence has already been committed, the jurisdiction extends to enforcing public policy with respect to the consequences of the commission of that crime, eg, restraining receipt by the criminal of a further benefit as a result of or in connection with the crime.

(C) Profits of crime – public policy

This is an exceptional case in which the Attorney General is entitled to intervene by instituting civil proceedings, in aid of the criminal law, to uphold the public policy of ensuring that a criminal does not retain profit directly derived from the commission of a crime.

In the legislation providing for court orders to confiscate the proceeds of crime, Parliament recognised the public interest in promoting a policy of preventing a person from retaining property obtained by him as a result of, or in connection with, the commission of a criminal offence. The fact that the statutory machinery cannot be applied in the circumstances of this case, where the defendant has not been and, in all probability, will never be put on trial for his offence, does not detract from force of the policy in the context of the Attorney General's right, as guardian of the public interest, to bring proceedings in the civil courts to enforce that policy.

> For the respondent to receive the balance of the royalties would amount to the law being flouted in a different way. However, the consequence for the reputation of the criminal justice system would be the same. The ordinary member of the public would be shocked if the position was that the courts were powerless to prevent the respondent profiting from his criminal conduct.
>
> **(D) Safeguards against abuse**
>
> The Attorney General, because of his central role in the enforcement of the criminal law, is in a peculiarly appropriate position to judge when to make an application to court for a remedy. Furthermore, even though the Attorney General is in this position, there is a further safeguard in that the court will carefully scrutinise the application to ensure that it is in the interests of justice that the application should be granted.
>
> **(E) Remedy**
>
> In public law proceedings, the Attorney General has standing to seek an injunction and the court has discretion to grant an injunction for the protection of that public right.

In accordance with the general rule, where a fiduciary accepts a bribe in breach of his fiduciary duty, the bribe, including property representing the unauthorised profit, is held upon trust for the persons to whom the duty is owed. On receipt of the bribe, the fiduciary becomes a trustee of the sum for the benefit of the innocent party and is liable to account for this property and any derivative profits. If the bribe is used to purchase other property which decreases in value, the fiduciary is required to account for the difference between the bribe and the undervalue. Alternatively, if the property has increased in value the innocent party is entitled to claim the surplus, for the fiduciary is not entitled to profit from a breach of his duties.

Attorney General for Hong Kong v Reid and Others [1993] 3 WLR 1143, PC (Lords Templeman, Lowry, Goff of Chieveley, Lloyd of Berwick and Sir Thomas Eichlebaum)

The Attorney General for Hong Kong brought an action for an account in respect of bribes received by Mr Reid, the former acting DPP for Hong Kong. The bribes, amounting to NZ$2.5 m were paid to him as inducements to exploit his official position by obstructing the prosecution of certain prisoners. Mr Reid used the bribes in order to purchase three freehold properties in New Zealand valued in excess of NZ$2.4 m. Two of the properties were vested in the joint names of Mr Reid and his wife and the other was conveyed to his solicitor. The Attorney General lodged a caution in respect of each of the properties in order to prevent any dealings pending a full hearing.

The question in issue concerned the status of a fiduciary who received a bribe, in particular, whether such a fiduciary became a mere debtor for the innocent party or alternatively a trustee for the aggrieved party. The defendants mounted an argument claiming that the fiduciary became a debtor for the innocent party and had no equitable interest in the properties, relying on *Lister v Stubbs*. The plaintiff asserted that the decision in *Lister v Stubbs* should not be followed as it was inconsistent with basic equitable principles as illustrated in *Keech v Sandford* (1726) and *Phipps v Boardman* (1967). The fiduciary, on receipt of the bribe, became a constructive trustee of the benefit on behalf of the person injured. Accordingly, the fiduciary became accountable to the plaintiff not only in respect of the bribe but also for any property derived from the bribe (provided that this did not lead to double compensation).

The Privy Council held in favour of the plaintiff. The bribe and representative property acquired by the fiduciary were subject to the claims of the injured party. Since the representative property had decreased in value, the fiduciary was liable to account for the difference between the bribe and the undervalue.

> **Lord Templeman:** A bribe is a gift accepted by a fiduciary as an inducement to him to betray his trust. A secret benefit, which may or may not constitute a bribe, is a benefit which the fiduciary derives from trust property or obtains from knowledge which he acquires in the course of acting as a fiduciary. A fiduciary is not always accountable for a secret benefit but he is undoubtedly accountable for a secret benefit which consists of a bribe. In addition a person who provides the bribe and the fiduciary who accepts the bribe may each be guilty of a criminal offence. In the present case the first respondent was clearly guilty of a criminal offence.
>
> When a bribe is offered and accepted in money or in kind, the money or property constituting the bribe belongs in law to the recipient. Money paid to the false fiduciary belongs to him. The legal estate in freehold property conveyed to the false fiduciary by way of bribe vests in him. Equity, however, which acts *in personam*, insists that it is unconscionable for a fiduciary to obtain and retain a benefit in breach of duty. The provider of a bribe cannot recover it because he committed a criminal offence when he paid the bribe. The false fiduciary who received the bribe in breach of duty must pay and account for the bribe to the person to whom that duty was owed. In the present case, as soon as the first respondent received a bribe in breach of the duties he owed to the Government of Hong Kong, he became a debtor in equity to the Crown for the amount of that bribe. So much is admitted. But if the bribe consists of property which increases in value or if a cash bribe is invested advantageously, the false fiduciary will receive a benefit from his breach of duty unless he is accountable not only for the original amount or value of the bribe but also for the increased value of the property representing the bribe. As soon as the bribe was received it should have been paid or transferred instantly to the person who suffered from the breach of duty. Equity considers as done that which ought to have been done. As soon as the bribe was received, whether in cash or in kind, the false fiduciary held the bribe on a constructive trust for the person injured. Two objections have been raised to this analysis. First, it is said that if the fiduciary is in equity a debtor to the person injured, he cannot also be a trustee of the bribe. But there is no reason why equity should not provide two

remedies, so long as they do not result in double recovery. If the property representing the bribe exceeds the original bribe in value, the fiduciary cannot retain the benefit of the increase in value which he obtained solely as a result of his breach of duty. Secondly, it is said that if the false fiduciary holds property representing the bribe in trust for the person injured, and if the false fiduciary is or becomes insolvent, the unsecured creditors of the false fiduciary will be deprived of their right to share in the proceeds of that property. But the unsecured creditors cannot be in a better position than their debtor. The authorities show that property acquired by a trustee innocently but in breach of trust and the property from time to time representing the same belong in equity to the *cestui que* trust and not to the trustee personally whether he is solvent or insolvent. Property acquired by a trustee as a result of a criminal breach of trust and the property from time to time representing the same must also belong in equity to his *cestui que* trust and not to the trustee whether he is solvent or insolvent.

When a bribe is accepted by a fiduciary in breach of his duty then he holds that bribe in trust for the person to whom the duty was owed. If the property representing the bribe decreases in value the fiduciary must pay the difference between that value and the initial amount of the bribe because he should not have accepted the bribe or incurred the risk of loss. If the property increases in value, the fiduciary is not entitled to any surplus in excess of the initial value of the bribe because he is not allowed by any means to make a profit out of a breach of duty.

This case is of importance because it disposes succinctly of the argument which appears in later cases and which was put forward by counsel in the present case that there is a distinction between a profit which a trustee takes out of a trust and a profit such as a bribe which a trustee receives from a third party. If in law a trustee, who in breach of trust invests trust moneys in his own name, holds the investment as trust property, it is difficult to see why a trustee who in breach of trust receives and invests a bribe in his own name does not hold those investments also as trust property.

It has always been assumed and asserted that the law on the subject of bribes was definitively settled by the decision of the Court of Appeal in *Lister & Co v Stubbs*.[20] In that case the plaintiffs, Lister & Co, employed the defendant, Stubbs, as their servant to purchase goods for the firm. Stubbs, on behalf of the firm, bought goods from Varley & Co and received from Varley & Co bribes amounting to £5,541. The bribes were invested by Stubbs in freehold properties and investments. His masters, the firm Lister & Co, sought and failed to obtain an interlocutory injunction restraining Stubbs from disposing of these assets pending the trial of the action in which they sought, *inter alia*, £5,541 and damages. In the Court of Appeal, the first judgment was given by Cotton LJ, who had been party to the decision in *Metropolitan Bank v Heiron*.[21] He was powerfully supported by the judgment of Lindley LJ and by the equally powerful concurrence of Bowen LJ Cotton LJ said, at p 12, that the bribe could

20 (1890) 45 Ch D 1.

21 (1880) 5 Ex D 319.

not be said to be the money of the plaintiffs. He seemed to be reluctant to grant an interlocutory judgment which would provide security for a debt before that debt had been established. Lindley LJ said, at p 15, that the relationship between the plaintiffs, Lister & Co, as masters and the defendant, Stubbs, as servant who had betrayed his trust and received a bribe:

> ... is that of debtor and creditor; it is not that of trustee and *cestui que* trust. We are asked to hold that it is – which would involve consequences which, I confess, startle me. One consequence, of course, would be that, if Stubbs were to become bankrupt, this property acquired by him with the money paid to him by Messrs Varley would be withdrawn from the mass of his creditors and be handed over bodily to Lister & Co Can that be right? Another consequence would be that, if the appellants are right, Lister & Co could compel Stubbs to account to them, not only for the money with interest, but for all the profits which he might have made by embarking in trade with it. Can that be right?

For the reasons which have already been advanced their Lordships would respectfully answer both these questions in the affirmative. If a trustee mistakenly invests moneys which he ought to pay over to his *cestui que* trust and then becomes bankrupt, the moneys together with any profit which has accrued from the investment are withdrawn from the unsecured creditors as soon as the mistake is discovered. *A fortiori* if a trustee commits a crime by accepting a bribe which he ought to pay over to his *cestui que* trust, the bribe and any profit made therefrom should be withdrawn from the unsecured creditors as soon as the crime is discovered.

The decision in *Lister & Co v Stubbs* is not consistent with the principles that a fiduciary must not be allowed to benefit from his own breach of duty, that the fiduciary should account for the bribe as soon as he receives it and that equity regards as done that which ought to be done. From these principles it would appear to follow that the bribe and the property from time to time representing the bribe are held on a constructive trust for the person injured. A fiduciary remains personally liable for the amount of the bribe if, in the event, the value of the property then recovered by the injured person proved to be less than that amount.

Their Lordships are also much indebted for the fruits of research and the careful discussion of the present topic in the address entitled 'Bribes and secret commissions'[22] delivered by Sir Peter Millett to a meeting of the Society of Public Teachers of Law at Oxford in 1993. The following passage, at p 20, elegantly sums up the views of Sir Peter Millett:

> [The fiduciary] must not place himself in a position where his interest may conflict with his duty. If he has done so, equity insists on treating him as having acted in accordance with his duty; he will not be allowed to say that he preferred his own interest to that of his principal. He must not obtain a profit for himself out of his fiduciary position. If he has done so, equity insists on treating him as having obtained it for his principal; he will

22 [1993] RLR 7.

> not be allowed to say that he obtained it for himself. He must not accept a bribe. If he has done so, equity insists on treating it as a legitimate payment intended for the benefit of the principal; he will not be allowed to say that it was a bribe.

For the reasons indicated their Lordships consider that the three properties so far as they represent bribes accepted by the first respondent are held in trust for the Crown.

A borrower who fraudulently induced a building society to execute a mortgage on a flat was entitled to the surplus proceeds of sale of the flat. This surplus was not held on resulting trust for the building society. Moreover, the building society had no restitutionary remedy against the borrower, whose unjust enrichment was not gained at the expense of the building society. Accordingly, the borrower was not a constructive trustee of the surplus funds for the society. On conviction of the borrower, the Criminal Prosecution Service was entitled to a charging order as against the society.

Halifax Building Society v Thomas and Another [1996] 2 WLR 63, CA

Mr Thomas obtained a 100% mortgage advance from the Halifax Building Society (the society) to finance the purchase of a flat. The purchase was competed in February 1986. In order to obtain the advance, Mr Thomas fraudulently misrepresented himself as Mr Robb. During 1986, Mr Thomas made a number of payments of interest but then defaulted. The society commenced proceedings against Mr Thomas in his assumed name and obtained an order for possession. In 1988, the society learnt from the police of the true identity of the mortgagor. Nevertheless, the society proceeded with the sale of the property. In 1989, the flat was sold and after the society recouped what was due to it under the mortgage, a surplus of £10,504 remained which was placed into a suspense account. Mr Thomas pleaded guilty in respect of criminal proceedings brought against him. A confiscation order in favour of the CPS was made in respect of the funds in the suspense account. The society commenced proceedings for a declaration that it was entitled to the surplus funds. The trial judge held against the society and decided that the CPS stood in the shoes of Mr Thomas and was entitled to the surplus. The society appealed to the Court of Appeal.

The Court of Appeal dismissed the appeal.

Peter Gibson LJ: Mr Waters accepts, as he must, that the surplus does not represent property which the society has lost. Accordingly it cannot rely on the principle of subtractive unjust enrichment, to use the language of Professor Peter Birks QC, in his influential work, *An Introduction to the Law of Restitution* (1985). Instead it relies on the broad principle of restitution for wrongs: Mr Thomas has been enriched at the society's expense, in the sense that he has gained by committing a wrong against the society. Thereby the society seeks a remedy enabling it 'to obtain restitution of a benefit gained by the tortfeasor from a tortious act in circumstances where he has suffered little or no loss':

Goff and Jones, *The Law of Restitution*, 4th edn, 1993, p 715. I accept that the starting point must be Mr Thomas' position before the confiscation order. Indeed the charging order only applied to Mr Thomas' interest in the suspense account. *Prima facie*, that is governed by s 105 of the Law of Property Act 1925, dealing with the application of the proceeds of sale following the exercise by a mortgagee of his power of sale:

> The money which is received by the mortgagee, arising from the sale, after discharge of prior incumbrances to which the sale is not made subject, if any, or after payment into court under this Act of a sum to meet any prior incumbrance, shall be held by him in trust to be applied by him: first, in payment of all costs, charges, and expenses properly incurred by him as incident to the sale or any attempted sale, or otherwise; and secondly, in discharge of the mortgage money, interest, and costs, and other money, if any, due under the mortgage; and the residue of the money so received shall be paid to the person entitled to the mortgaged property, or authorised to give receipts for the proceeds of the sale thereof.

Mr Waters, however, submitted that s 105 does not establish Mr Thomas' entitlement in the present case. He says that, if the surplus is a sum for which Mr Thomas was liable to account to the society, it was money 'due ... under the mortgage' and secured by the mortgage by reason of condition 23 of the society's mortgage conditions. This provides:

> The mortgage shall be security not only for the moneys primarily provided for by it but also for all moneys which may be or become owing by the borrower to the society on any account and at the discretion of the society no property held by the society as security for indebtedness of the borrower shall be released until all moneys owing by the borrower to the society have been paid.

The relationship between the borrower and the bank or building society in respect of any such account is that of debtor and creditor and that is reflected in the words of condition 23: 'moneys ... owing ... on any account.' There is nothing in the mortgage that suggests that the parties ever contemplated that Mr Thomas might incur some liability other than debt to the society. If, for example, he caused damage to the property of the society for which he was held liable in negligence, I would not regard any damages awarded against him as moneys owing on any account to the society within the scope of condition 23. So also with any liability to account for the surplus. In my judgment on the sale of the mortgaged property by the society, in 1989 Mr Thomas became entitled under s 105 to the surplus and the society could not have claimed the surplus on the ground of a further liability to account being established against him in subsequent proceedings.

On the facts of the present case, in my judgment, the fraud is not in itself a sufficient factor to allow the society to require Mr Thomas to account to it.

I would add that, in so far as the society relies on the submission that to allow a fraudster to take a profit derived from his fraud would be offensive to concepts of justice, the House of Lords in *Tinsley v Milligan* [1994] 1 AC 340, although divided in their decision, were unanimous in rejecting the 'public conscience' test as determinative of the extent to which rights created by illegal transactions should be recognised. It is not appropriate to ask whether the allowance of a claim would be an affront to the public conscience. The correct test is whether a claimant to an interest in property must plead or rely on an illegality. If so, he will not be entitled to recover. That question does not arise in the present case where it is the society which is claiming a declaration.

For these reasons I conclude that s 105 required the society to hold the surplus in trust for Mr Thomas, unless a constructive trust operated in its own favour. To that question I now turn.

Mr Waters again relies on the fact that the surplus represents a profit derived from a fraud, which, he submits, justifies allowing the society the benefits of a proprietary claim to the surplus. Again Mr Waters is unable to cite any English authority that lends direct support to this claim. English law has not followed other jurisdictions where the constructive trust has become a remedy for unjust enrichment. As is said in *Snell's Equity*, 29th edn, 1990, p 197:

> In England the constructive trust has in general remained essentially a substantive institution; ownership must not be confused with obligation, nor must the relationship of debtor and creditor be converted into one of trustee and *cestui que* trust.

In considering whether to extend the law of constructive trusts in order to prevent a fraudster benefiting from his wrong, it is also appropriate to bear in mind that Parliament has acted in recent years (notably in Part VI of the Criminal Justice Act 1988) on the footing that without statutory intervention the criminal might keep the benefit of his crime. Moreover, Parliament has given the courts the power in specific circumstances to confiscate the benefit rather than reward the person against whom the crime has been committed. I bear in mind the wise comment of Hoffmann J in *Chief Constable of Leicestershire v M* [1989] 1 WLR 20, p 23:

> The recent and detailed interventions of Parliament in this field suggest that the courts should not indulge in parallel creativity by the extension of general common law principles.

Accordingly, I would reject the argument based on constructive trust. No other argument is put forward by the society for defeating the title of Mr Thomas to the surplus immediately before the confiscation and charging orders made by the CPS or for defeating those orders. For these reasons I would dismiss this appeal.

Occasions when a trustee may be paid: the general rule illustrated in *Williams v Barton* (see above, p 326) is subject to the following four exceptions:

(1) *Authority in the trust instrument*:

The settlor may authorise the trustees to be paid from the trust funds but such power is required to be expressed in the trust instrument. The court will not imply such charging clauses. Professional trustees normally insist on an adequate charging clause before they undertake the duties of trusteeship. It would be prudent for non-professional trustees to insist on the insertion of such clauses even though they may wish to undertake such duties without reward. The reason being to facilitate the appointment of professional trustees should the need ever arise in the future.

However, charging clauses are strictly construed against the trustees in the event of any ambiguity. Furthermore, trustees are not entitled to charge any sums as they wish but may only charge a reasonable amount which would vary with the circumstances of each case.

(2) *Authority of the court*:

The court will only authorise reasonable remuneration for services performed by trustees which are of exceptional benefit to the trust.

See *Boardman v Phipps*,[23] where generous remuneration was awarded by the court for the efforts of the appellants.

Moreover, the court is entitled to increase the amount of the remuneration as laid down in the charging clause, see *Re Duke of Norfolk's Settlement Trusts*.[24]

In *Foster v Spencer*, the court decided that, in the exercise of its inherent jurisdiction, that trustees of a cricket club were entitled to remuneration for past services, but not to future remuneration. In addition, the trustees were entitled to past expenses but not to interest thereon.

Foster and Others v Spencer (1995) *The Times*, 14 June, HC

The plaintiffs had been persuaded, in 1969, to become trustees of a five acre sportsfield at Elmers End, near Beckenham in Kent. The land was purchased in 1921 for £700 which was raised by subscriptions from the members at that time and well wishers. There was no remuneration clause in the trust instrument. The plaintiffs discovered, shortly after appointment, that the club was experiencing a financial crisis. Membership, and consequently income, was declining and there was no capital reserve. For sometime football was played, but that eventually ceased and the only activity which remained centred round the bar in a ramshackle pavilion. At a meeting of contributors in April 1972 unanimous support was given to a proposal to sell the ground for development and to look for another site, but obstacles emerged in that the land was zoned as an open space which would need to be altered and planning permission obtained if a reasonable price was to be obtained from a developer. In addition, there was considerable trouble in evicting gypsy squatters and securing the land against further invasions. The land was finally sold in 1992, the net proceeds amounting to £911,188. The expertise of Mr Foster as a chartered surveyor was particularly valuable in eventually marketing the site. Likewise, the contribution of Mr Sealy as a building contractor and one who lived near the site was substantial. The plaintiffs claimed:

(a) remuneration for their services:

23 [1967] 2 AC 46 (see above, p 321).

24 [1981] 3 All ER 220, CA.

  (i) Mr Foster and Mr Sealy claimed remuneration in bringing about the successful sale; and
  (ii) the other three plaintiffs claimed remuneration in respect of the tasks still to be performed;

(b) reimbursement of their expenses;

(c) interest pursuant to s 35(A) of the Supreme Court Act 1981.

Judge Paul Barker QC decided that:

(a) in the exercise of his inherent jurisdiction, Mr Foster and Mr Sealy were entitled to remuneration for their past services. The decisive factors were:
  (i) there were no funds out of which to pay remuneration at the time of their appointment;
  (ii) the refusal of the claim to remuneration would have resulted in the beneficiaries being unjustly enriched at the expense of the trustees;
  (iii) there was no true appreciation of the extent of the task at the time of appointment. His Lordship concluded that had Mr Foster and Mr Sealy realised what they were in for they would have declined to act unless remunerated in some way;

(b) the quantum of the remuneration, in the absence of guidance from the authorities, was determined at 5% commission on the net proceeds, that is, £45,560 for Mr Foster and a fee of £5,000 per year for the period between 1982 and 1992;

(c) his Lordship refused to allow any amount for future services of the trustees as being unnecessary for the good administration of the trusts;

(d) the trustees were entitled to be reimbursed their expenses under s 30(2) of the Trustee Act 1925;

(e) but his Lordship rejected the plaintiffs' claim to interest on expenses, concluding that he had no jurisdiction to award interest.

(3) *Agreement with all the beneficiaries*:

Where the beneficiaries are all '*sui juris*' and absolutely entitled to the trust property, they may make an agreement with the trustees for the latter to be remunerated. This is an application of the *Saunders v Vautier* rule (see below, p 837).

(4) *The rule in* Cradock v Piper:[25]

The rule is that where a trustee/solicitor acts as a solicitor for himself and his co-trustees, in litigation concerning the trust, then provided the cost of acting for himself and co-trustee is less than or equal to the expense of acting for his co-trustees alone, the solicitor/trustee is entitled to be paid his usual costs. In short, the solicitor/trustee may charge his usual fees for

25 (1850) 1 Mac & G 664.

acting in litigation on behalf of his co-trustees, but is not permitted fees for representing himself.

In this case, a trustee/solicitor who represented his co-trustees and the beneficiaries in proceedings brought by creditors of the testator, was allowed to claim the costs of such representation. The costs of acting for himself were disallowed.

> **Lord Cottenham:** The rule has been supposed to be founded upon the well known principle that a trustee cannot be permitted to make a profit of his office, which he would do, if, being party to a cause as trustee, he were permitted, being also a solicitor, to derive professional profits from acting for himself. The rule is confined to cases in which the business or employment of the solicitor is the proper business of the trustee; but it is no part of the business or employment of a trustee to assist other parties in suits relative to the property. If, therefore, the trustee acts as solicitor for such other parties, such business or employment is not any business or employment of the trustee; and the rule as hitherto laid down does not apply. I am therefore of the opinion that the rule does not extend beyond costs of the trustee, where he acts as solicitor for himself.

This rule is regarded as an anomaly and will not be extended to non-contentious work and to persons other than solicitor/trustees, such as barristers, accountants, etc.

Trustee director's remuneration

The articles of association of a private company may provide that a director must obtain a share qualification within a stated time, that is, in order to advance the interests of the company and shareholders, a person may be appointed a director if he holds the prescribed number of shares. The articles may provide that a director must hold the share qualification 'in his own right'. The requirement will be satisfied even though the shares are held by the individual as a trustee, for as between the company and the trustee, he is the registered holder of the shares. Neither the company nor the court will look behind the share register to identify the beneficial owner.

In *Pulbrook v Richmond Consolidated Mining Co*,[26] Mr P, a director of a company was excluded by his fellow directors from attending directors' meetings. He brought an action against his fellow directors for an injunction to restrain them from wrongfully excluding him from such meetings. Mr P was the registered holder of the relevant number of shares as stated in the company's articles of association, but it was alleged that shortly before his appointment he had executed a charge of his shares as security for a loan. One of the questions in issue was whether Mr P remained qualified as a director.

26 (1878) 9 Ch D 610.

The court held that the clause in the articles of association, 'no person shall be eligible unless he holds in his own right capital of the nominal value of £500', was to be construed by having regard only to the legal ownership of the shares as appears on the register.

> **Sir George Jessel MR:** The company cannot look behind the register as to beneficial interest, but must take the register as conclusive, and cannot inquire, either for this purpose, or indeed for any other, into the trusts affecting the shares. That being so, in my opinion, whether or not there was an absolute trust, or whether Mr Cuthbert was only the mortgagee, is not material; Mr Pulbrook was well elected ...

If the trustee uses the shareholding of the trust in order to secure his appointment as a director, the remuneration or profit received as director may be held as constructive trustee for the trust. In other words, if there is a causal link between the trust and the appointment as a director, the profits received as a director are subject to the trust. This is a question of fact. In *Re Macadam*,[27] under the articles of a company, the trustees of a will had a power to appoint two persons to directorships. The trustees appointed themselves and were liable to account to the trust for the directors' fees received from the company.

> **Cohen J:** Did he acquire the position in respect of which he drew the remuneration by virtue of his position as trustee? In the present case there can be no doubt that the only way in which the plaintiffs became directors was by the exercise of the powers vested in the trustees of the will under article 68 of the articles of association of the company. The principle is one which has always been regarded as of the greatest importance in these courts, and I do not think I ought to do anything to weaken it ... although the remuneration was remuneration for services as director of the company, the opportunity to receive the remuneration was gained as a result of the exercise of a discretion vested in the trustees, and they had put themselves in a position where their interest and duty conflicted. In those circumstances, I do not think that this court can allow them to make a profit out of doing so, and I do not think the liability to account for a profit can be confined to cases where the profit is derived directly from the trust estate ... the root of the matter really is: Did he acquire the position in respect of which he drew the remuneration by virtue of his position as trustee?

It follows that a director who secures his appointment as a director before he acquires the trust shares, is not required to account to the trust for his remuneration as a director. The position remains the same if the trust shares are subsequently registered in his name in order to enable him to continue as a director, see *Re Dover Coalfield Extension*.[28]

In this case, Dover Coalfield Extension Ltd (D Co) held shares in Consolidated Kent Collieries Corporation (K Corp) with whom it conducted

27 [1946] Ch 73.

28 [1908] 1 Ch 65, CA.

business. In order to protect the interests of D Co, a director of D Co, was appointed a director of K Corp. The articles of K Corp, required directors to acquire 1,000 shares within a month. D Co accordingly transferred 1,000 of its shares to the director, which he held on trust for D Co. When D Co was wound up, the liquidator claimed the remuneration which the director received.

The court held that the director was allowed to retain his remuneration. He was appointed a director by an independent board before he had acquired the shares on trust for D Co, even though he could not have continued in office without the shares. In other words, the director did not use his position as a trustee for the purpose of acquiring his directorship for he had been appointed a director before he became a trustee of the shares.

Moreover, a trustee/director will not be accountable to the trust for his remuneration if he secures his appointment as director by the use of shares or votes held in his personal capacity, provided that the use of the trust votes could not prevent his appointment as director. In this event, the trustee would be appointed independently of the trust votes, see *Re Gee*.[29]

In this case, the issued capital of a private company, Gee & Co Ltd, was 5,000 £1 shares. Immediately before his death, Alfred Gee (the testator) was the registered holder of 4,996 shares in Gee & Co. The remaining four shareholders who held one share each were: Miss Gee (the testator's sister); the testator's wife; his daughter; Mrs Hunter; and his son in law, Mr Staples. By his will, the testator appointed his wife, Mrs Hunter and Mr Staples to be his executors and trustees after his death. After the death of the testator and before his will was probated, Mr Staples was appointed managing director of the company by the unanimous agreement of the three executors and Miss Gee, who together constituted all the registered beneficial shareholders at that time. Mr Staples agreed to act as director of the company and received £15,721 as remuneration for the 10 years that he managed the company. The beneficiaries under the will now claimed that Mr Staples was liable to account for the profit.

The court held in favour of Mr Staples. He was not accountable because he was appointed to be a director unanimously by the shareholders for qualities independent of the trust votes. The trust votes were not used to secure his appointment.

> **Harman J:** The principle that a trustee, in the absence of a special contract, can neither make a profit out of his trust, nor be paid for his time and trouble, is an old one ... The difficulty of applying this principle arises where the payment is made not directly out of the trust estate, but by a third party or body, and in particular by a limited company. The modern cases begin with *Re Francis*,[30] from which it appears – though the case is not reported on this point – that Kekewich J declined to allow trustees to retain for their own use remuneration

29 [1948] Ch 284, HC, *per* Harman J.

30 (1905) 92 LT 77.

received by them from a company in which the testator held substantially all the shares. The remuneration was voted at a general meeting, and appears to have been procured by the trustees by the exercise of the voting powers attached to the trust shares which had become registered in their names.

I conclude from this view that a trustee who either uses a power vested in him as such to obtain a benefit (as in *Re Macadam*)[31] or who (as in *Williams v Barton*)[32] procures his co-trustees to give him, or those associated with him, remunerative employment must account for the benefit obtained. Further, it appears to me that a trustee who has the power, by the use of trust votes, to control his own appointment to a remunerative position, and refrains from using them with the result that he is elected to the position of profit, would also be accountable. On the other hand, it appears not to be the law that every man who becomes a trustee holding as such shares in a limited company is made *ipso facto* accountable for remuneration received from that company independently of any use by him of the trust holding, whether by voting or refraining from doing so. For instance, A who holds the majority of the shares in a limited company becomes the trustee of the estate of B, a holder of a minority interest; this cannot, I think, disentitle A to use his own shares to procure his appointment as an officer of the company, nor compel him to disgorge the remuneration he so receives, for he cannot be disentitled to the use of his own voting powers, nor could the use of the trust votes in a contrary sense prevent the majority prevailing.

Many other instances could be given of a similar kind. Of these, *Re Dover Coalfield Extension Ltd*[33] is really one. There the trustees did not earn their fees by virtue of the trust shares, though no doubt the holding of those shares was a qualification necessary for the continued earning of the fees. In so far as Warrington J goes further than this, as he seems to do so by suggesting that remuneration paid by a company could not be a 'profit', it being a mere wage equivalent in value to the work done for it, I feel he goes too far. Certainly, this view was not taken in *Re Macadam*.[34] It would gravely encroach upon the principle which Cohen J, in that case, and Russell J, in *Williams v Barton*,[35] felt to be so important.

I turn now to an examination of the facts in this case to see what (if any) use was made of the trust shares in the appointment of Mr Staples. In my judgment, when the facts are examined, no such use was made. After the death of the testator, only four persons remained on the register of this company, and they alone could attend meetings of it. As I have said before, the meeting of 6 January 1938, was attended by all the corporators. Each of them held one share, and as the resolutions were passed unanimously, they must be supposed to have voted in favour by the use of that share. If the corporators, as I think, held their shares beneficially, they were entitled to vote as they chose.

31 [1946] Ch 73.

32 [1927] 2 Ch 9.

33 [1907] 2 Ch 76.

34 [1946] Ch 73.

35 [1927] 2 Ch 9.

If, on the other hand, they were nominees of the testator, there were still three of them whose votes outweighed the vote of Mr Staples if it was his duty to vote against his own interest. In neither event did the trust shares come into the picture at all.

If this be too narrow a view to take, and it is right for this purpose to look behind the register at the beneficial interests in the shares in the company, then it will be seen that the majority interest belonged to the estate of Robert Gee (the testator's father), and that the persons entitled to have his shares registered in their names, namely, Miss Gee and Mrs Heaton, were in favour of the appointment and the payment of the stipulated remuneration. If, then, the shares in which the testator's estate was interested had all been used against the resolutions, they would still have been carried, and therefore the appointment was not procured by the use of the trust interest vested in the defendant executors or any of them by the will of the testator in which alone the plaintiffs are interested.

Competition

In conformity with the general rule of avoiding a conflict of duty and interest, a trustee, who is required to continue a specialised business in his representative capacity, will not be permitted to start up a similar business in his personal capacity in competition with the trust. An injunction may be obtained restraining the trustee from setting up a competing business.

Re Thomson, Thomson v Allen [1930] 1 Ch 203, HC

In this case, the testator, a yacht broker, by his will appointed three persons to act as his executors and trustees. After his death, the trustees continued to carry on the business. One of the trustees threatened to set up a yacht-broker business in the same town in competition with the trust. On a claim for an injunction to restrain the trustee, the court decided that in view of the specialised nature of such a business, a conflict of duty and interest would have arisen if the trustee was permitted to set up his own competing business. Accordingly, the injunction was granted.

Clauson J: The first thing to ascertain is what is a yacht agent's business, and what effect upon the interests of the beneficiary under the testator's will would result from the executor starting a competing business? For that purpose I am assisted by the statement in paragraph 14 of the defendant's defence, which is in these terms:

> The business of a yacht agent or broker is similar to that of a house agent, ie, the yacht agent receives or solicits the order or permission of yacht owners to place their yachts on his books and, having ascertained by inquiry or advertisement a prospective purchaser of any particular yacht, obtains and submits an offer to the owner and is paid a commission by him if a sale results. The greater part of the yachts for the time being on the market are therefore on the books of all yacht agents and that agent earns a commission on the sale who can first secure a purchaser. Every yacht agent

> consequently carries on a business which competes with that of every other yacht agent. The business of the testator was of the character of those of all other yacht agents in this paragraph described and the testator had no regular or exclusive connection.

Would it or would it not have been a breach of Mr Allen's fiduciary duty between himself and the beneficiaries under the will, if he had started at the time of the commencement of the action a new business yacht agent and had accordingly entered into such a contract as I have described with a yacht owner who might have entered into a similar contract with Mr Thomson's executors which would have enabled Mr Thomson's executors, should they have been the fortunate brokers who were the first to secure a purchaser for the owner of the yacht, to secure a commission?

In order to find the principle I have to apply, I turn to the judgment of Cranworth LC in the House of Lords in the case of *Aberdeen Railway Co v Blaikie Bros*.[36] This case dealt with a fiduciary relation which arose from the fact that the person concerned in the case was the director of a corporate body. 'A corporate body,' says the Lord Chancellor:

> ... can only act by agents, and it is of course the duty of those agents so to act as best to promote the interests of the corporation whose affairs they are conducting. Such agents have duties to discharge of a fiduciary nature towards their principal. And it is a rule of universal application, that no one, having such duties to discharge, shall be allowed to enter into engagements in which he has, or can have, a personal interest conflicting, or which possibly may conflict, with the interests of those whom he is bound to protect. So strictly is this principle adhered to, that no question is allowed to be raised as to the fairness or unfairness of the contract so entered into.

And further:

> The inability to contract depends not on the subject matter of the agreement, but on the fiduciary character of the contracting party, and I cannot entertain a doubt of its being applicable to the case of a party who is acting as manager of the mercantile or trading business for the benefit of others, no less than to that of an agent or trustee employed in selling or letting land.

A little later on he says:

> Mr Blaikie was not only a director, but (if that was necessary) the chairman of the directors. In that character it was his bounden duty to make the best bargains he could for the benefit of the company.

May I translate some portions of this passage into the language which would be appropriate when dealing with this case where the fiduciary relation exists, not because the one party is a director of the other party, but because one party is an executor and trustee who has duties towards a beneficiary under the will of which he is executor and trustee. I find the principle to be this. The rule of universal application is that an executor and trustee having duties to discharge

36 (1854) 1 Macq 461.

> of a fiduciary nature towards the beneficiaries under the will – in this particular case the duty of a fiduciary nature was to carry on the business of the testator to the best advantage of the beneficiaries – he shall not be allowed to enter into the engagement in which he has or can have a personal interest conflicting, or which possibly may conflict, with the interests of those whom he is bound to protect. Now, if Mr Allen had set up this competing business and had entered into such an engagement with a yacht owner as that to which I have referred, would he have been entering into an engagement in which he would have a personal interest conflicting or which possibly might conflict with the interests of those he was bound to protect? Having regard to the special nature of a yacht agent's business, it appears to me clear that I am bound to answer that question by saying that, by starting such a business and entering into such engagements, Mr Allen would have been entering into engagements which would conflict, or certainly possibly might conflict with the interest of the beneficiaries under the will, because he would be obtaining for himself chances of earning a commission which, but for such competition, might be obtained for the beneficiaries under the will. It appears to me, therefore, that, if Mr Allen had set up – he did not, because he was prevented by the injunction granted by the Court of Appeal – a competing business at the time in question, the commencement of the action, he would have been doing something which would have been a breach, as between himself and the beneficiaries, of the fiduciary duties he owed them.

But it ought to be emphasised that the decision appears to be based on the wholly unusual nature of the yacht broking business. Had the business been of a more common nature the injunction may not have been granted. Moreover, a trustee who, at the time of his appointment, was already in business in competition with the trust, would not be required to terminate his business, although this may be a ground for his removal from the trust.

Purchase of trust property

A trustee, without specific authority to the contrary, is not entitled to purchase trust property for his own benefit. The position remains the same even if the purchase appears to be fair. Perhaps the purchase price significantly exceeds the market value of the property. If such purchase takes place, the transaction is treated as voidable, ie, valid until avoided. The objections to such transaction are that the trustee would be both vendor and purchaser and it would be difficult to ascertain whether an unfair advantage had been obtained by the trustees. In addition, the property may become virtually unmarketable since the title may indicate that the property was at one time trust property. Third parties would have notice of this fact and any disputes concerning the trust property may affect their interest.

Wright v Morgan [1926] AC 788, PC

A testator by his will gave his son, Harry Herbert, the option to purchase a plot of land provided that the price was fixed by an independent valuer.

Harry was also a trustee under the will. Harry assigned the option to Douglas Wright, his co-trustee and brother, but who was not authorised to purchase the property. Douglas retired from the trust and purported to exercise the option at a price fixed by the valuers. The beneficiaries under the will brought an action to set aside the sale.

The court decided that the sale ought to be set aside on the ground of a conflict of duty and interest. The position might have been different if Harry had exercised the option and then disposed of the land to Douglas, for in such a case, Douglas would have bought Harry's beneficial interest and not a trust asset.

> **Viscount Dunedin:** The leading question accordingly is whether the option to purchase given by the will to Harry Herbert was assignable and assigned to Douglas to the effect of making him entitled to purchase the trust estate, he himself being a trustee. Technically speaking, he was not a trustee at the time of the purchase of Windermere, but their Lordships have no hesitation in holding with the Court of Appeal that although he had actually resigned, the whole scheme had been arranged by him prior to his resignation, and that in law he must be treated as being a trustee at the time of the will.
>
> Speaking generally, any vested interest is assignable unless there is something in the nature of the interest, or something in the words of the settlement which creates the interest which contradicts the nature of assignability. Their Lordships do not doubt that Harry Herbert's option might have been assigned to a third person. There is nothing in the nature of the interest itself which points to non-assignability, nor are there any words in the will which would seem to forbid assignation. When, however, it is found that the assignation is in favour of the person who is himself a trustee, quite another question arises. The appellant argued that this right to purchase was property in the person of Harry Herbert, who was a *cestui que* trust, and that it is well settled that a trustee may purchase the interest of a *cestui que* trust. In one sense of the word 'property' it is true that this option was the property of Harry Herbert, but the quality of the property was not like the property of land or of a chattel. It was only a right to enter into a contract. If the option had been exercised by Harry Herbert himself, and the property bought, then Harry Herbert might have transferred to a trustee just as well as to any one else. The object of the sale would, in that case, have been no longer trust property. So also if the option had been transferred to a stranger, the resulting contract which would have been its sequel would have been between the trustees and, to use a colloquial expression, an outsider. But as it was, the option transferred to Douglas only gave Douglas a right to ask from the trustees a contract of sale, and that contract of sale was *ex rei necessitate*, a contract between the trustees and himself as a trustee, and that is what the law will not allow. It would be profitless to quote the many cases which have arisen to illustrate the doctrine. They may all be referred to the same root idea, that equity will not allow a person, who is in a position of trust, to carry out a transaction where there is a conflict between his duty and his interest. Accordingly, the real test to be applied to the circumstances is, assuming that Harry Herbert's option was validly assigned, so far as power to assign was concerned, to Douglas, did a

conflict of duty and interest arise which would prevent Douglas from entering into a binding contract with the trustee? It was argued that no such conflict would arise, because by the terms of the will, which was the wish of the testator, the whole conditions of sale are regulated; valuers are to be appointed, and their decision to be accepted as to the price to be payable. There was no possibility of the higgling of the market between vendor and purchaser. Nevertheless, a conflict of duty and interest may arise, although there is no direct association between the two parties as vendor and purchaser.

Directors

Company directors stand in a fiduciary relationship to the company and are subject to the rigours of the trust principle. If a director places himself in a position where his duty to the company conflicts with his personal interest, any benefits obtained as a result is accountable to the company. Thus, any unauthorised profits made by the director which is connected with the company organisation is claimable by the company.

***Regal (Hastings) Ltd v Gulliver* [1942] 1 All ER 378, HL (Viscount Sankey, Lords Russell of Killowen, Macmillan, Wright and Porter)**

In this case, the profit arose through the application by four of the directors of Regal for shares in a subsidiary company which it had been the original intention of the board should be subscribed for by Regal. Regal did not have the requisite money available and the four directors took it on themselves personally to raise the necessary funds, purchase the shares and sold them for a profit. It was found as a fact that all the transactions were *bona fide*. Regal now claimed that the directors were accountable for their profit.

The House of Lords held that the directors were accountable to the company.

> **Lord Russell of Killowen:** The rule of equity which insists on those, who by use of a fiduciary position make a profit, being liable to account for that profit, in no way depends on fraud, or absence of *bona fides*; or upon such questions or considerations as whether the profit would or should otherwise have gone to the plaintiff, or whether the profiteer was under a duty to obtain the source of the profit for the plaintiff, or whether he took a risk or acted as he did for the benefit of the plaintiff, or whether the plaintiff has in fact been damaged or benefited by his action. The liability arises from the mere fact of a profit having, in the stated circumstances, been made. The profiteer, however honest and well-intentioned, cannot escape the risk of being called upon to account.
>
> It now remains to consider whether in acting as directors of Regal they stood in a fiduciary relationship to that company. Directors of a limited company are the creatures of statute and occupy a position peculiar to themselves. In some respects they resemble trustees, in others they do not. In some respect they resemble managing partners, in others they do not. In *Re Forest of Dean Coal*

Mining Co,[37] a director was held not liable for omitting to recover promotion money which had been improperly paid on the formation of the company. He knew of the improper payment, but he was not appointed a director until a later date. It was held that, although a trustee of settled property which included a debt would be liable for neglecting to sue for it, a director of a company was not a trustee of debts due to the company and was not liable. I cite two passages from the judgment of Sir George Jessel, pp 451, 452, he said:

> Directors have sometimes been called trustees, or commercial trustees, and sometimes they have been called managing partners, it does not matter what you call them so long as you understand what their true position is, which is that they are really commercial men managing a trading concern for the benefit of themselves and all other shareholders in it ...

In the result, I am of opinion that the directors standing in a fiduciary relationship to Regal in regard to the exercise of their powers as directors, and having obtained these shares by reason and only by reason of the fact that they were directors of Regal and in the course of the execution of that office, are accountable for the profits which they have made out of them. The equitable rule laid down in *Keech v Sandford* and *Ex p James*, and similar authorities applies to them in full force. It was contended that these cases were distinguishable by reason of the fact that it was impossible for Regal to get the shares owing to lack of funds, and that the directors in taking the shares were really acting as members of the public. I cannot accept this argument. It was impossible for the *cestui que* trust in *Keech v Sandford* to obtain the lease, nevertheless the trustee was accountable. The suggestion that the directors were applying simply as members of the public is a travesty of the facts. They could, had they wished, have protected themselves by resolution (either antecedent or subsequent) of the Regal shareholders in general meeting. In default of such approval, the liability to account must remain. The result is that, in my opinion each of the respondents Bobby, Griffiths, Bassett and Bentley is liable to account for the profit which he made on the sale of his 500 shares in Amalgamated.

In *Belmont Finance Corp v Williams Furniture and Others (No 2)*[38] (see below, p 430), Buckley LJ said:

> A limited company is of course not trustee of its own funds; but in consequence of the fiduciary character of their duties the directors of a limited company are trusted as if they were trustees of those funds of the company which are in their hands or under their control, and if they misapply them they commit a breach of trust.

Similarly, where a fiduciary (director) has obtained sensitive information in his capacity as a fiduciary, he is required to make full disclosure to the company or person to whom he owes such duty. If the director conceals this information and makes a profit as a result of the non disclosure, he is accountable for the profits.

37 (1878) 10 Ch D 450.

38 [1980] 1 All ER 393, CA.

Industrial Development Consultants v Cooley [1972] 1 WLR 443, HC

The defendant was the managing director of the plaintiff company. He was approached by the Chairman of the Eastern Gas Board to work for them, although at the time the plaintiff company was interested in a project for the Gas Board. In his capacity as managing director, he had obtained special knowledge which should have been passed on to the plaintiff company. Concealing this knowledge, he obtained his release from the service of the plaintiff basing his request on alleged ill health. The plaintiff would not have released him had it known the full facts. The plaintiff sued the director claiming that he was a trustee of profits of his new contract on behalf of the plaintiff.

The court held in favour of the plaintiff in view of the conflict of duty and interest in failing to pass on the information to the plaintiff.

> **Roskill J:** A more recent statement of the highest authority will be found in the speech of Lord Upjohn in *Phipps v Boardman*[39] [see above, p 321].
>
> Rules of equity have to be applied to such a great diversity of circumstances that they can be stated only in the most general terms and applied with particular attention to the exact circumstances of each case. The relevant rule for the decision of this case is the fundamental rule of equity that a person in a fiduciary capacity must not make a profit out of his trust which is part of the wider rule that a trustee must not place himself in a position where his duty and his interest may conflict. I should have added that Lord Upjohn's speech was a dissenting speech. I do not, however, detect any difference in principle between the speeches of their Lordships but merely a difference in the application of the facts to principles which were not in dispute. Later, Lord Upjohn stated four propositions as follows, p 127:
>
> (i) the facts and circumstances must be carefully examined to see whether in fact a purported agent and even a confidential agent is in a fiduciary relationship to his principal. It does not necessarily follow that he is in such a position;
>
> (ii) once it is established that there is such a relationship, that relationship must be examined to see what duties are thereby imposed upon the agent, to see what is the scope and ambit of the duties charged upon him;
>
> (iii) having defined the scope of those duties one must see whether he has committed some breach thereof and by placing himself within the scope and ambit of those duties in a position where his duty and interest may possibly conflict. It is only at this stage that any question of accountability arises;
>
> (iv) finally, having established accountability it only goes so far as to render the agent accountable for profits made within the scope and ambit of his duty.

39 [1967] 2 AC 46, pp 123 *et seq*.

I think Mr Brown was right when he said in his reply that that is the basic rule from which all else has been founded. Certainly Viscount Sankey in the *Regal* case, p 137, so stated it and Lord Cranworth's well known statement has been repeated in innumerable cases of the highest authority.

Therefore, the starting point for consideration of the present case is the application of the facts of this case to the propositions stated in *Phipps v Boardman*,[40] bearing in mind, as Lord Upjohn said in the passage I have quoted, that the application of 'this great principle' may be infinitely variable. It is the principle which is important and there is no limit, I venture to think, to the cases to which that principle can be applied, always provided that in applying it, the court does not go outside the well-established limits of the principle.

The first matter that has to be considered is whether or not the defendant was in a fiduciary relationship with his principals, the plaintiffs. Mr Davies argued that he was not because he received this information which was communicated with him privately. With respect, I think this argument is wrong. The defendant had one capacity and one capacity only in which he was carrying on business at that time. That capacity was as managing director of the plaintiffs. Information which came to him while he was managing director and which was of concern to the plaintiffs and was relevant for the plaintiffs to know, was information which it was his duty to pass on to the plaintiffs because between himself and the plaintiffs a fiduciary relationship existed ...

It seems to me plain that throughout the whole of May, June and July 1969 the defendant was in a fiduciary relationship with the plaintiffs. From the time he embarked upon his course of dealing with the Eastern Gas Board, irrespective of anything which he did or he said to Mr Hicks, he embarked upon a deliberate policy and course of conduct which put his personal interest as a potential contracting party with the Eastern Gas Board in direct conflict with his pre-existing and continuing duty as managing director of the plaintiffs. In *Parker v Mackenna*,[41] James LJ said, p 124:

> I do not think it is necessary, but it appears to me very important, that we should concur in laying down again and again the general principle that in this court no agent in the course of his agency, in the matter of his agency, can be allowed to make any profit without the knowledge and consent of his principal; that that rule is an inflexible rule, and must be applied inexorably by this court, which is not entitled, in my judgment, to receive evidence, or suggestion, or argument as to whether the principal did or did not suffer any injury in fact by reason of the dealing of the agent; for the safety of mankind requires that no agent shall be able to put his principal to the danger of such an inquiry as that.

In the nuclear age, that last sentence may perhaps seem something of an exaggeration, but nonetheless, it is eloquent of the strictness with which throughout the last century and indeed in the present century, courts of the highest authority have always applied this rule.

40 [1967] 2 AC 46, p 127, *per* Upjohn LJ.

41 (1874) 10 Ch App 96.

Therefore, I feel impelled to the conclusion that when the defendant embarked on this course of conduct of getting information on 13 June using that information and preparing those documents over the weekend of 14/15 June and sending them off on on 17 June, he was guilty of putting himself into the position in which his duty to his employers, the plaintiffs, and his own private interests conflicted and conflicted grievously. There being the fiduciary relationship I have described, it seems to me plain that it was his duty once he got this information to pass it to his employers and not to guard it for his own personal purposes and profit. He put himself into the position when his duty and his interests conflicted. As Lord Upjohn put it in *Phipps v Boardman*:[42] 'It is only at this stage that any question of accountability arises.'

Does accountability arise? It is said: 'Well, even if there were that conflict of duty and interest, nonetheless, this was a contract with a third party in which the plaintiffs never could have had any interest because they would have never got it.' That argument has been forcefully put before me by Mr Davies.

The remarkable position then arises that if one applies the equitable doctrine upon which the plaintiffs rely to oblige the defendant to account, they will receive a benefit which, on Mr Smetton's evidence at least, it is unlikely they would have got for themselves had the defendant complied with his duty to them. On the other hand, if the defendant is not required to account he will have made a large profit, as a result of having deliberately put himself into a position in which his duty to the plaintiffs who were employing him and his personal interests conflicted. I leave out of account the fact that he dishonestly tricked Mr Hicks into releasing him on 16 June although Mr Brown urged that that was another reason why equity must compel him to disgorge his profit.

In one sense the benefit in this case did not arise because of the defendant's directorship; indeed, the defendant would not have got this work had he remained a director. However, one must as Lord Upjohn pointed out in *Phipps v Boardman*,[43] look at the passages in the speeches in Regal having regard to the facts of that case to which those passages and those statements were directed. I think Mr Brown was right when he said that it is the basic principle which matters. It is an overriding principle of equity that a man must not be allowed to put himself in a position in which his fiduciary duty and his interests conflict ... that there has not previously been a case precisely of this nature with precisely similar facts before the courts is of no import. The facts of this case are, I think, exceptional and I hope unusual. They seem to me plainly to come within this principle.

I think that, although perhaps the expression is not entirely precise, Mr Brown put the point well when he said that what the defendant did in May, June and July was to substitute himself as an individual for the company of which he was managing director and to which he owed a fiduciary duty. It is upon the ground I have stated that I rest my conclusion in this case. Perhaps it is permissible to say I have less reluctance in reaching that conclusion on the application of this basic principle of equity since I know that what happened

42 [1967] 2 AC 46, p 127.

43 *Ibid*, p 125.

> was enabled to happen because a release was obtained by the defendant from a binding contractual obligation by the dishonest and untrue misrepresentations which were made to Mr Hicks on 16 June.
>
> In my judgment, therefore, an order for an account will be issued because the defendant has made and will make his profit as a result of having allowed his interests and his duty to conflict.

Likewise, in *Guinness plc v Saunders and Others*,[44] it was decided that a failure by a director to disclose an unauthorised payment of £5.2 m in connection with the takeover of Distillers plc rendered him a constructive trustee for Guinness. In addition, a *quantum meruit* claim by one of the defendants for reasonable remuneration for services performed, based on an implied contract with the plaintiff, was dismissed.

> **Lord Templeman:** My Lords, the short answer to a *quantum meruit* claim based on an implied contract by Guinness to pay reasonable remuneration for services rendered is that there can be no contract by Guinness to pay special remuneration for the services of a director unless that contract is entered into by the board pursuant to article 91. The short answer to the claim for an equitable allowance is the equitable principle which forbids a trustee to make a profit out of his trust unless the trust instrument, in this case the articles of association of Guinness, so provides. The law cannot and equity will not amend the articles of Guinness. The court is not entitled to usurp the functions conferred on the board by the articles.
>
> Equity forbids a trustee to make a profit out of his trust. The articles of association of Guinness relax the strict rule of equity to the extent of enabling a director to make a profit provided that the board of directors contracts on behalf of Guinness for the payment of special remuneration or decides to award special remuneration. Mr Ward did not obtain a contract or a grant from the board of directors. Equity has no power to relax its own strict rule further than and inconsistently with the express relaxation contained in the articles of association. A shareholder is entitled to compliance with the articles. A director accepts office subject to and with the benefit of the provisions of the articles relating to directors. No one is obliged to accept appointment as a director. No director can be obliged to serve on a committee. A director of Guinness who contemplates or accepts service on a committee or has performed outstanding services for the company as a member of a committee may apply to the board of directors for a contract or an award of special remuneration. A director who does not read the articles or a director who misconstrues the articles is nevertheless bound by the articles. Article 91 provides clearly enough for the authority of the board of directors to be obtained for the payment of special remuneration and the submissions made on behalf of Mr Ward, based on articles 2, 100(D) and 110, are more ingenious than plausible and more legalistic than convincing.
>
> [The other Law Lords who considered this appeal were Lords Keith of Kinkel, Brandon of Oakbrook, Griffith and Goff of Chieveley.]

44 [1990] 2 WLR 324, HL.

Contracts for the sale of land

On the date that a specifically enforceable contract for the sale of land is made, the purchaser becomes the equitable owner of the property. Thus, on the date of the exchange of contracts the vendor becomes a constructive trustee for the purchaser until the date of the completion of the sale, see *Lysaght v Edwards*.[45] Edwards agreed in writing to sell real property to the plaintiff but before completion, Edwards died. By his will, he devised his real property to trustees on trust to sell and invest and invest the proceeds of sale. On a claim by the plaintiff for an order requiring the executors to complete the sale.

The court held in favour of the plaintiff. On the date of the creation of the contract, the equitable title to the property becomes transferred to the purchaser by operation of law.

> **Jessel MR:** The effect of a contract for sale has been settled for more than two centuries. It is that the moment you have a valid contract for sale, in equity, the vendor becomes the trustee for the purchaser of the real estate sold; the beneficial ownership passes to the purchaser of the estate, the vendor retaining a right to the purchase money ...

This rule illustrates the equitable maxim, 'Equity regards as done that which ought to be done'.

Equity will not allow a statute to be used as an engine for fraud

Acts of Parliament are binding on all courts, even a court of equity. However, courts of equity are entitled to adopt a pragmatic approach in considering the validity of claims in equity with an overriding objective to achieve justice. Accordingly, if a strict compliance with a statutory provision (such as the formalities) has the incidental effect of perpetrating a fraud, the court is entitled to suspend such provision. This compromise solution has the effect of preventing unjust enrichment.

Rochefoucauld v Boustead [1897] 1 Ch 196, CA

In this case, the plaintiff was the mortgagor of several estates but found himself in financial difficulty. The defendant purchased the properties from the mortgagee and orally agreed to hold them on trust for the plaintiff subject to the repayment to the defendant of the purchase price and expenses. The defendant sold the estates and later became bankrupt. The plaintiff sued the trustee-in-bankruptcy for an account. The trustee-in-bankruptcy claimed that the oral agreement was not enforceable as the predecessor to s 53(1)(b) of the Law of Property Act 1925 (namely, s 7 of the Statute of Frauds 1677) was not complied with and the plaintiff had no interest in the proceeds of sale.

45 (1876) 2 Ch D 499.

The Court of Appeal held in favour of the plaintiff on the ground that it will not allow s 7 of the Statute of Frauds 1677 to be used as an engine for fraud. It is a fraud for a person to whom land is conveyed on trust, to deny the trust and claim the land as his own. Even if there was insufficient evidence to constitute a memorandum in order to satisfy s 7 of the 1677 Act, parol evidence was admissible to establish that the defendant bought the properties as trustee.

> **Lindley LJ:** We come, therefore, to the conclusion that the plaintiff has proved that the estates in question were conveyed to the defendant on 27 May 1873, upon trust for her, but subject to a charge in his favour in respect of all sums advanced by him in order to obtain the estates from the Dutch company in the first instance, and of all sums advanced by him in order to work them as coffee plantations after he had acquired them.
>
> This conclusion renders it necessary to consider whether the Statute of Frauds affords a defence to the plaintiff's claim. The section relied upon is s 7, which has been judicially interpreted in *Forster v Hale*,[46] and *Smith v Matthews*.[47] According to these authorities, it is necessary to prove by some writing or writings signed by the defendant, not only that the conveyance to him was subject to some trust, but also what that trust was. But it is not necessary that the trust should have been declared by such a writing in the first instance; it is sufficient if the trust can be proved by some writing signed by the defendant, and the date of the writing is immaterial. It is further established by a series of cases, the propriety of which cannot now be questioned, that the Statute of Frauds does not prevent the proof of a fraud; and that it is a fraud on the part of a person to whom land is conveyed as a trustee, and who knows it was so conveyed, to deny the trust and claim the land himself. Consequently, notwithstanding the statute, it is competent for a person claiming land conveyed to another to prove by parol evidence that it was so conveyed upon trust for the claimant, and that the grantee, knowing the facts, is denying the trust and relying upon the form of conveyance and the statute, in order to keep the land himself. This doctrine was not established until some time after the statute was passed. In *Bartlett v Pickersgill*,[48] the trust was proved, and the defendant, who denied it, was tried for perjury and convicted, and yet it was held that the statute prevented the court from affording relief to the plaintiff. But this case cannot be regarded as law at the present day. The case was referred to in *James v Smith*;[49] and was treated as still law by Kekewich J; but his attention does not appear to have been called to *Booth v Turle*,[50] nor to *Davies v Otty (No 2)*,[51] both of which are quite opposed to *Bartlett v Pickersgill*. So is *Haigh v Kaye*.[52] The late Giffard LJ, one of the best lawyers of modern

46 (1798) 3 Ves 696.

47 (1861) 3 DF & J 139.

48 (1960) 1 Eden 515.

49 [1891] 1 Ch 384.

50 (1873) LR 16 Eq 182.

51 (1865) 35 Beav 208.

52 (1872) LR 7 Ch 469.

> times, speaking of *Bartlett v Pickersgill*, said, 'It seems to be inconsistent with all the authorities of this court which proceed on the footing that it will not allow the Statute of Frauds to be made an instrument of fraud': see *Heard v Pilley*.[53] The case not only seems to be, but is, inconsistent with all modern decisions on the subject. See, in addition to those already mentioned, *Lincoln v Wright*,[54] where a conveyance absolute in form was held to be a mortgage only. See also *Re Duke of Marlborough*,[55] in which Stirling J examined the authorities, and held that an assignment absolute in form was subject to a trust for the plaintiff.
>
> The defence, based on the Statute of Frauds, is met by the plaintiff in two ways. First, she says that the documents signed by the defendant prove the existence of the trust alleged; secondly, she says that if those documents do not prove what the trust is with sufficient fullness and precision, the case is one of fraud which lets in other evidence, and that with the aid of other evidence the plaintiff's case is established. In our opinion the plaintiff is correct in this contention. We are by no means satisfied that the letters signed by the defendant do not contain enough to satisfy the Statute of Frauds. Whether this is so or not, the other evidence is admissible in order to prevent the statute from being used in order to commit a fraud; and such other evidence proves the plaintiff's case completely.

Likewise, where property has been obtained by the fraudulent conduct of the defendant, a constructive trust may be imposed on him requiring him to re-transfer the property to the plaintiff or person defrauded. The fraud may take the form of setting up the absolute nature of a conveyance.

This principle was applied in *Bannister v Bannister*,[56] in which the defendant sold a cottage to the plaintiff on the oral understanding that the defendant would be allowed to live rent free in the property for as long as she wished. The purchase price was deflated to take into account this arrangement. The conveyance made no mention of the undertaking. The plaintiff subsequently attempted to evict the defendant in order to sell the property with vacant possession and argued that the conveyance was not obtained fraudulently.

The court held that the plaintiff was bound by the trust obligation to permit the vendor to occupy the premises. The absence of written evidence could not be used to support the plaintiff's case.

> **Scott LJ:** It is, we think, clearly a mistake to suppose that the equitable principle on which a constructive trust is raised against a person who insists on the absolute character of a conveyance to himself for the purpose of defeating a beneficial interest, which, according to the true bargain, was to belong to another, is confined to cases in which the conveyance itself was fraudulently obtained. The fraud which brings the principle into play arises as soon as the

53 (1869) LR 4 Ch 548.

54 (1859) 4 De G & J 16.

55 [1894] 2 Ch 133.

56 [1948] 2 All ER 133, CA.

absolute character of the conveyance is set up for the purpose of defeating the beneficial interest, and that is the fraud to cover which the Statute of Frauds or the corresponding provisions of the Law of Property Act 1925, cannot be called in aid in cases in which no written evidence of the real bargain is available. Nor is it, in our opinion, necessary that the bargain on which the absolute conveyance is made should include any express stipulation that the grantee is in so many words to hold as trustee. It is enough that the bargain should have included a stipulation under which some sufficiently defined beneficial interest in the property was to be taken by another. The above propositions are, we think, clearly borne out by the cases to which we were referred of *Booth v Turle*,[57] *Chattock v Muller*,[58] *Re Duke of Marlborough*,[59] and *Rochefoucauld v Boustead*.[60] We see no distinction in principle between a case in which property is conveyed to a purchaser on terms that a limited beneficial interest in some part of it is to be retained by the vendor as in *Booth v Turle* and a case like the present, in which property is conveyed to a purchaser on terms that a limited beneficial interest in some part of it is to be retained by the vendor. We are, accordingly, of opinion that the third ground of objection to the learned county court judge's conclusion also fails. His finding that there was no fraud in the case cannot be taken as meaning that it was not fraudulent in the plaintiff to insist on the absolute character of the conveyance for the purpose of defeating the beneficial interest which he had agreed the defendant should retain. The conclusion that the plaintiff was fraudulent, in this sense, necessarily follows from the facts found, and, as indicated above, the fact that he may have been innocent of any fraudulent intent in taking the conveyance in absolute form is for this purpose immaterial.

SUPPLEMENTARY READING

Beatson, J and Prentice, D, 'Restitutionary claims by company directors' (1990) 106 LQR 365

Braithwaite, W, 'Directors' liability, constructive trusts and limitation periods' [1980] Conv 200

Gardner, S, 'Two maxims of equity: casenote on *AG for Hong Kong v Reid*' (1995) 54 CLJ 60

Goulding, S, 'Director as constructive trustee: *Guinness plc v Saunders*' [1990] Conv 296

Green, B, 'Restitution for services rendered in breach of trust' (1982) 45 MLR 211

57 (1873) LR 16 Eq 182.

58 (1878) 8 Ch D 177.

59 (1874) 2 Ch D 133.

60 [1897] 1 Ch 196.

Hayton, D, 'Developing the law of trusts for the 21st century' (1990) 106 LQR 87

Hill, J, 'The Settled Land Act 1925: unresolved problems' (1991) 107 LQR 596

Hodkinson, K, 'Casenote on *Re Duke of Norfolk Settlement Trust*' [1982] Conv 231

Hopkins, J, 'Fiduciary duty – receipt of company's property by director' [1990] CLJ 220

Jackson, P, ' Further extensions of the rule in *Keech v Sandford*' (1975) 38 MLR 226

Jackson, P, 'Estate contracts, trusts and registered land' [1983] Conv 64

Jones, A, 'Bribing the DPP: should he profit from abusing his position? *AG for Hong Kong v Reid*' [1994] Conv 156

Jones, G, 'Unjust enrichment and the fiduciary duty of loyalty' (1968) 84 LQR 472

Kenny, P, 'Constructive trust of registered land' (1983) 46 MLR 96

Matthews, P, 'Remuneration for professional trustees' (1995) 9 Tru LI 50

Ockleton, C, 'Keeping it in the family' [1981] CLJ 243

Paling, D, 'The pleadings in *Keech v Sandford*' (1972) 36 Conv 159

Parry, N, 'Remuneration of trustees' [1984] Conv 275

Rider, B, 'The fiduciary and the frying pan' [1978] Conv 114

Shepherd, J, 'Towards a unified concept of fiduciary relationships' (1981) 97 LQR 51

Sparkes, P, 'Beneficial interest or licence for life? *Ungurian v Lesnoff*' [1990] Conv 223

Sullivan, G, 'Going it alone – *Queensland Mines v Hudson*' (1979) 42 MLR 711

Watts, P, 'Bribes and constructive trusts' (1994) 110 LQR 178

Watts, P, 'Unjust enrichment and misdirected funds' (1991) 107 LQR 521

CHAPTER 10

CONSTRUCTIVE TRUSTS: THE FAMILY HOME

PROPRIETARY RIGHTS IN THE FAMILY HOME

This issue concerns the beneficial rights in the family home, probably the most valuable asset belonging to the family. Consider the following example: Mary went to live with Norman. A year later, a house was bought in Norman's name, the purchase money was raised from his savings and by way of a mortgage. Mary gave up her job when a child was born to them. Four years later, when the parties were experiencing financial difficulties, Mary went back to work and used her earnings to contribute towards the housekeeping expenses, the family holidays and to pay for decorations to the house, while Norman continued paying the mortgage instalments. Ten years later, Mary left Norman, taking the child with her. She wishes to claim a beneficial interest in the house on the ground that Norman held the legal title to the house on trust for each of them in equal shares, or some other proportion. Some of the questions that are related to this issue are as follows:

- What principles of trust law are applicable to ascertain the extent of the beneficial interest in the family home?
- When should such interest be valued?
- How may the interest be realised?
- What difference, if any, would it make if the parties were married?

Cooke v Head [1972] 1 WLR 518, CA

In this case, it was decided that the trust principles are applicable to spouses, unmarried couples and any other relationships contracted by the parties.

In this case, the plaintiff, Miss Cooke (C), and Mr Head (H) met in 1962. C became H's mistress. A plot of land was bought and conveyed into H's name. Both parties provided the labour and built a bungalow. C did a great deal of heavy work, including mixing and carting cement. She also contributed some of her earnings towards paying the mortgage instalments. Later, C and H separated and H alone lived in the bungalow, repaying the mortgage instalments. The plaintiff claimed a declaration that the property was jointly owned by the parties.

The Court of Appeal held that the plaintiff was entitled to a one third share in the property on the ground that the parties jointly acquired the property for their joint benefit. In these circumstances, the legal owner holds the property on trust for both of them.

Lord Denning MR: In the light of recent developments, I do not think it is right to approach this case by looking at the money contributions of each and dividing up the beneficial interest according to those contributions. The matter should be looked at more broadly, just as we do in husband and wife cases. We look to see what the equity is worth at the time when the parties separate. We assess the shares as at that time. If the property has been sold, we look at the amount which it has realised, and say how it is to be divided between them. Lord Diplock, in *Gissing v Gissing*,[1] intimated that it is quite legitimate to infer that:

> ... the wife should be entitled to a share which was not to be quantified immediately upon the acquisition of the home but should be left to be determined when the mortgage was repaid or the property disposed of.

Likewise with a mistress.

Mr Dearbergh set out very helpfully the various matters we should take into account in assessing shares. The parties with their earnings and their contributions; the statements made to third parties, such as to Miss Westwood; the method in which they saved, such as the money put into the money box; the method of repaying the mortgage instalments; the amount of the direct cash contributions of each; the amount of the work each had done on the property; the part each had taken in the planning and the design of the house; and the steps by which the transactions were carried out. I quite agree with Mr Dearbergh that all those matters should be taken into account. On them we should decide what the shares should be.

There is a separate point about the £421 which the defendant paid off the mortgage instalments. He paid them after he started living at the bungalow on his own. He has had considerable benefits from it. He has been living there without having to pay any rent. Sometimes, as in *Cracknell v Cracknell*,[2] we consider those payments separately. But in some cases it is preferable to bring them into the final account: and adjust the shares accordingly. That is what was done in the recent case of *Hazell v Hazell*.[3] We should do the same here.

Having discussed it with my brethren, we think that one 12th is far too small, and that the plaintiff's share should be one third of the net proceeds of sale. I would allow the appeal, accordingly.

The principles of resulting and constructive trusts are applicable in this context. These expressions have been used interchangeably by the courts as if they involve the same concepts. The presumption of advancement has outlived its usefulness in view of the social changes in society and would not be adopted readily in these circumstances.

1 [1971] AC 886, p 909.

2 [1971] P 356.

3 [1972] 1 WLR 301.

Pettitt v Pettitt [1970] AC 777, HL

> **Lord Diplock:** The consensus of opinion which gave rise to the presumptions of advancement and resulting trusts in transactions between husbands and wives is to be found in cases relating to the propertied class of the nineteenth century and the first quarter of the twentieth century among whom marriage settlements were common and it was unusual for the wife to contribute by her earnings to the family income. It was not until after World War II that the courts were required to consider the proprietary rights in family assets of a different social class ... It would be an abuse of the legal technique for ascertaining or imputing intention to apply to transactions between the post war generation of married couples, 'presumptions' which are based upon inferences of fact which an entire generation of judges drew as to the most likely intentions of an earlier generation of spouses belonging to the propertied classes of a different social era.

In this case, Mrs Pettitt purchased a cottage with her own money and had the legal title conveyed in her name. Mr Pettitt from time to time redecorated the property expending a total of £725. On a breakdown of the marriage he claimed a proportionate interest in the house (£1,000 *pro rata* value). The House of Lords rejected his claim as his expenditure was not related to the acquisition of the house, in the absence of an agreement or understanding, his expenditure was to be treated as a gift.

A similar decision was reached in *Gissing v Gissing*.[4] Here the parties married in 1935. W, the wife, worked throughout her married life. In 1951, the matrimonial home was purchased by H, the husband, out of his resources and the property was conveyed in his name. W paid £220 for furnishings and laying a lawn. There was no common understanding as to the beneficial interest in the house. On a breakdown of the marriage, the question arose as to the ownership of the house.

The House of Lords held that W was not entitled to an interest for she did not contribute to the purchase price.

The Law Lords in the cases of *Pettitt v Pettitt* and *Gissing v Gissing* reviewed the existing law and decided that settled principles of property law were applicable in this context.

> **Lord Diplock** (in *Pettitt v Pettitt*): In numerous judgments of the Court of Appeal during the last 20 years, this branch of the law of property has undergone considerable development. The cases start with *Re Rogers' Question*[5] and end with *Gissing v Gissing*,[6] a judgment of the Court of Appeal delivered while the present appeal was being heard by your Lordships' House. They manifest a divergence of views among the members of the Court of Appeal as to the origin and extent of the court's powers in dealing with questions of title

4 [1971] AC 886.

5 [1948] 1 All ER 328.

6 [1969] 2 Ch 85.

to property between spouses and as to the principles on which such powers should be exercised; but although some of these cases were commented upon by members of your Lordships' House in *National Provincial Bank Ltd v Hastings Car Mart Ltd*,[7] the present appeal is the first in which your Lordships have had the opportunity as such of examining and, if necessary, correcting the recent developments by the Court of Appeal of this branch of the law. And a very important branch it is. It affects every married couple. We are informed that in the High Court alone there are some 900 applications a year under s 17 of the Married Women's Property Act 1882, and this figure takes no account of applications in the county court, which also has jurisdiction under the section. On a matter of such general social importance the principles applied by the courts in exercising their jurisdiction ought to be clear.

I agree with your Lordships that the section confers no such power upon the court. It is, in my view, a procedural section. It provides a summary and relatively informal forum which can sit in private for the resolution of disputes between husband and wife as to the title to or possession of any property – not limited to 'family assets' as I have defined them. It is available while the husband and wife are living together as well as when the marriage has broken up. The power conferred upon the judge 'to make such order with respect to the property in dispute ... as he shall think fit', gives him a wide discretion as to the enforcement of the proprietary or possessory rights of one spouse to the other or to create new proprietary rights in either spouse.

Where the acquisition or improvement is made as a result of contributions in money or money's worth by both spouses acting in concert the proprietary interests in the family asset resulting from their respective contributions depend upon their common intention as to what those interests should be.

I have used the neutral expression 'acting in concert' because many of the ordinary domestic arrangements between man and wife do not possess the legal characteristics of a contract. So long as they are executory they do not give rise to any chose in action, for neither party intended that non-performance of their mutual promises should be the subject of sanctions in any court (see *Balfour v Balfour*).[8] But this is relevant to non-performance only. If spouses do perform their mutual promises the fact that they could not have been compelled to do so while the promises were executory cannot deprive the acts done by them of all legal consequences upon proprietary rights; for these are within the field of the law of property rather than of the law of contract. It would, in my view, be erroneous to extend the presumption accepted in *Balfour v Balfour* that mutual promises between a man and wife in relation to their domestic arrangements are *prima facie* not intended by either to be legally enforceable to a presumption of a common intention of both spouses that no legal consequences should flow from acts done by them in performance of mutual promises with respect to the acquisition, improvement or addition to real or personal property – for this would be to intend what is impossible in law.

7 [1965] AC 1175.

8 [1919] 2 KB 571.

How, then, does the court ascertain the 'common intention' of spouses as to their respective proprietary interests in a family asset when at the time that it was acquired or improved as a result of contributions in money or money's worth by each of them they failed to formulate it themselves? It may be possible to infer from their conduct that they did in fact form an actual common intention as to their respective proprietary interests and where this is possible the courts would give effect to it. But in the case of transactions between husband and wife relating to family assets their actual common contemplation at the time of its acquisition or improvement probably goes no further than its common use and enjoyment by themselves and their children, and while that use continues their respective proprietary interests in it are of no practical importance to them. They only become of importance if the asset ceases to be used and enjoyed by them in common and they do not think of the possibility of this happening. In many cases, and most of those which come before the courts, the true inference from the evidence is that at the time of its acquisition or improvement the spouses formed no common intention as to their proprietary rights in the family asset. They gave no thought to the subject of proprietary rights at all.

But this does not raise a problem which is peculiar to transactions between husband and wife. It is one with which the courts commonly deal in connection with ordinary contracts and to its solution they apply a familiar legal technique. The common situation in which a court has to decide whether or not a term is to be implied in a contract is when some event has happened for which the parties have made no provision in the contract because at the time it was made neither party foresaw the possibility of that event happening and so never in fact agreed as to what its legal consequences would be upon their respective contractual rights and obligations. Nevertheless the court imputes to the parties a common intention which in fact they never formed and it does so by forming its own opinion as to what would have been the common intention of reasonable men as to the effect of that event upon their contractual rights and obligations if the possibility of the event happening had been present to their minds at the time of entering into the contract. In *Davis Contractors Ltd v Fareham UDC*[9] Viscount Radcliffe analyses this technique as applied to cases of frustration. See also Professor Glanville Williams' analysis of the legal doctrine of implied terms in 'Language and the law'.[10]

In applying the technique to contracts the court starts with the assumption that, *prima facie*, the parties intended that whatever may happen their legal rights and obligations under their contract should be confined to those which they have expressed. Consequentially, the court will not imply a term unless it is of opinion that no reasonable men could have failed to form the common intention to which effect will be given by the term which it implies. But such an assumption, viz, that *prima facie* the parties intended at the time of the transaction to express all the legal consequences as to proprietary rights which would flow from it, whatever might happen in the future, is, for the reasons

9 [1956] AC 696.

10 (1944) 61 LQR 401.

already indicated, inappropriate to transactions between husband and wife in relation to family assets. In most cases they express none and form no actual common intention about proprietary rights in the family asset because neither spouse gave any thought to an event happening, viz, the cesser of their common use and enjoyment of the asset, which alone would give any practical importance to their respective proprietary interests in the asset. Unless it is possible to infer from the conduct of the spouses at the time of their concerted action in relation to acquisition or improvement of the family asset that they did form an actual common intention as to the legal consequences of their acts upon the proprietary rights in the asset the court must impute to them a constructive common intention which is that which in the court's opinion would have been formed by reasonable spouses.

A similar technique is applied in imputing an intention to a person wherever the intention with which an act is done affects its legal consequences and the evidence does not disclose what was the actual intention with which he did it. This situation commonly occurs when the actor is deceased. When the act is of a kind to which this technique has frequently to be applied by the courts the imputed intention may acquire the description of a 'presumption' – but presumptions of this type are not immutable. A presumption of fact is no more than a consensus of judicial opinion disclosed by reported cases as to the most likely inference of fact to be drawn in the absence of any evidence to the contrary, for example, presumptions of legitimacy, of death, or survival and the like. But the most likely inference as to a person's intention in the transactions of his everyday life depends upon the social environment in which he lives and the common habits of thought of those who live in it. The consensus of judicial opinion which gave rise to the presumptions of 'advancement' and 'resulting trust' in transactions between husbands and wives is to be found in cases relating to the propertied classes of the 19th century and the first quarter of the 20th century among whom marriage settlements were common, and it was unusual for the wife to contribute by her earnings to the family income. It was not until after the Second World War that the courts were required to consider the proprietary rights in family assets of a different social class. The advent of legal aid, the wider employment of married women in industry, commerce and the professions and the emergence of property-owning, particularly a real-property-mortgaged-to-a-building-society-owning, democracy has compelled the courts to direct their attention to this during the last 20 years. it would, in my view, be an abuse of the legal technique for ascertaining or imputing intention to apply to transactions between the post-war generation of married couples 'presumptions' which are based upon inferences of fact which an earlier generation of judges drew as to the most likely intentions of earlier generations of spouses belonging to the propertied classes of a different social era.

In imputing to them a common intention as to their respective proprietary rights which as fair and reasonable men and women they presumably would have formed had they given their minds to it at the time of the relevant acquisition or improvement of a family asset, the court, it has been suggested, is exercising in another guise a jurisdiction to do what it considers itself to be fair and reasonable in all the circumstances and this does not differ in result from the jurisdiction which Lord Denning, in *Appleton v Appleton*,[11] considered was expressly conferred on the court by s 17 of the Married Women's Act 1882.

It is true, as Viscount Radcliffe pointed out in *Davis Contractors v Fareham UDC*,[12] that when the court imputes to parties an intention upon a matter to which they in fact gave no thought:

> In their [the parties] place there rises the figure of the fair and reasonable man. And the spokesman of the fair and reasonable man, who represents after all no more than the anthropomorphic conception of justice, is and must be the court itself.

The officious bystander of MacKinnon LJ (see *Shirlaw v Southern Foundries (1926) Ltd*)[13] may pose the question, but the court, not the parties, gives the answer. Nevertheless, there is a significant difference between applying to transactions between husband and wife the general legal technique for imputing intention to the parties and exercising a discretion such as that which Lord Denning suggested was conferred on the court by s 17 of the Married Women's Property Act 1882. In applying the general technique the court is directing its attention to what would have been the common intention of the spouses as fair and reasonable husband and wife at the time of the relevant transaction while they were still happily married and not contemplating its breakdown. The family asset might cease to be needed for the common use and enjoyment of themselves and their children without the marriage breaking down at all. The circumstances of the subsequent breakdown and the conduct of the spouse which contributed to it are irrelevant to this inquiry. If these circumstances are such as to call for an adjustment of the spouses' respective proprietary rights which resulted from their previous transactions the court has jurisdiction to make such adjustments under the Matrimonial Causes Act 1965 (see *Ulrich v Ulrich and Felton*).[14] It has no such jurisdiction under s 17 of the Married Women's Property Act 1882.

In the present case we are concerned not with the acquisition of a matrimonial home on mortgage, but with improvements to a previously acquired matrimonial home. There is no question that at the time that it was acquired the matrimonial home was the wife's property. It was bought not with the help of a mortgage, but with the proceeds of sale of the previous matrimonial home which the wife had inherited from her grandmother. The husband made no contribution to its purchase and the conveyance of it was to the wife alone. The conduct of the parties is consistent only with the sole proprietary interest in it being that of the wife. During the four years that the spouses lived together in their new home the husband in his spare time occupied himself, as many husbands do, in laying out the garden with a lawn and patio, putting up a side wall with a gate, and in various jobs of redecoration and the life in the house itself. He claimed that these leisure activities had enhanced the value of the

11 [1965] 1 WLR 25.

12 [1956] AC 696, p 728.

13 [1939] 2 KB 206, p 227.

14 [1968] 1 WLR 180.

property by £1,000 and that he was entitled to a beneficial interest in it of that amount. The learned registrar declared that the husband had a beneficial interest in the proceeds of sale of the property in the sum of £300. How that sum was arrived at is not wholly clear. It would seem to be the registrar's estimate of the increase in value of the property due to the husband's work. The Court of Appeal with expressed reluctance felt themselves bound by *Appleton v Appleton*[15] to dismiss the wife's appeal from the Registrar's order.

It is common enough nowadays for husbands and wives to decorate and to make improvements in the family home themselves, with no other intention than to indulge in what is now a popular hobby, and to make the home pleasanter for their common use and enjoyment. If the husband likes to occupy his leisure by laying a new lawn in the garden or building a fitted wardrobe in the bedroom while the wife does the shopping, cooks the family dinner or bathes the children, I, for my part, find it quite impossible to impute to them as reasonable husband and wife any common intention that these domestic activities or any of them are to have any effect upon the existing proprietary rights in the family home on which they have undertaken. It is only in the bitterness engendered by the break-up of the marriage that so bizarre a notion would enter their heads.

I agree with the Court of Appeal that the present case cannot be distinguished from that of *Appleton v Appleton*, but in my view *Appleton v Appleton* was wrongly decided, perhaps because the court applied the wrong test laid down in the passage from Lord Denning's judgment which I have already cited and took into account the circumstance in which the marriage in that case broke up. *Button v Button*[16] was, in my view, clearly right. *Jansen v Jansen*[17] falls into a different category. There it was not a case of leisure activities of the spouses. The husband, in agreement with his wife, had abandoned his prospects of paid employment in order to work upon her property which, although the family lived in part of it, had been acquired as a commercial venture to which both were contributing. There were circumstances in that case which, in my view, justified the court in imputing to the spouses a common intention that his work should entitle him to a proprietary interest in the property whose value was enhanced by his full time labours directed to that end.

In *Gissing v Gissing* (for the facts, see above, p 367), the Law Lords reasoned thus:

Lord Pearson: Contributions are not limited to those made directly in part payment of the price of the property or those made at the time when the property is conveyed into the name of one of the spouses. For instance there can be a contribution if by arrangement between the spouses one of them by payment of the household expenses enables the other spouse to pay the mortgage instalments.

15 [1965] 1 WLR 25.

16 [1968] 1 WLR 457.

17 [1965] P 476.

Lord Diplock: Any claim to a beneficial interest in land by a person, whether spouse or stranger, in whom the legal estate in the land is not vested must be based upon the proposition that the person in whom the legal estate is vested holds it as a trustee upon trust to give effect to the beneficial interest of the claimant as *cestui que* trust. The legal principles applicable to the claim are those of the English law of trusts and in particular, in the kind of dispute between the spouses that comes before the courts, the law relating to the creation and operation of 'resulting, implied or constructive trusts'. Where the trust is expressly declared in the instrument by which the legal estate is transferred to the trustee or by a written declaration of trust by the trustee, the court must give effect to it. But to constitute a valid declaration of trust by way of gift of a beneficial interest in land to a *cestui que* trust the declaration is required by s 53(1) of the Law of Property Act 1925, to be evidenced in writing. If it is not in writing it can only take effect as a resulting, implied or constructive trust to which that section has no application.

A resulting, implied or constructive trust – and it is unnecessary for present purposes to distinguish between these three classes of trust – is created by a transaction between the trustee and the *cestui que* trust in connection with the acquisition by the trustee of a legal estate in land, whenever the trustee has so conducted himself that it would be inequitable to allow him to deny to the *cestui que* trust a beneficial interest in the land acquired. And he will be held so to have conducted himself if by his words or conduct he has induced the *cestui que* trust to act to his own detriment in the reasonable belief that by so acting he was acquiring a beneficial interest in the land.

That is why it has been repeatedly said in the context of disputes between the spouses as to their respective beneficial interests in the matrimonial home, that if at the time of its acquisition and transfer of the legal estate into the name of one or other of them an express agreement has been made between them as to the way in which the beneficial interest shall be held, the court will give effect to it – notwithstanding the absence of any written declaration of trust. Strictly speaking this states the principle too widely, for if the agreement did not provide for anything to be done by the spouse in whom the legal estate was not to be vested, it would be merely a voluntary declaration of trust and unenforceable for want of writing. But in express oral agreements contemplated by these dicta it has to be assumed *sub silentio* that they provide for the spouse in whom the legal estate in the matrimonial home is not vested to do something to facilitate its acquisition, by contributing to the purchase price or to the deposit or the mortgage instalments when it is purchased upon mortgage or to make some other material sacrifice by way of contribution to or economy in the general family expenditure. What the court gives effect to is the trust resulting or implied from the common intention expressed in the oral agreement between the spouses that if each acts in the manner provided for in the agreement the beneficial interests in the matrimonial home shall be held as they have agreed.

An express agreement between spouses as to their respective beneficial interests in land conveyed into the name of one of them obviates the need for showing that the conduct of the spouse into whose name the land was conveyed was intended to induce the other spouse to act to his or her detriment upon the faith of the promise of a specified beneficial interest in the land and that the other spouse so acted with the intention of acquiring that beneficial interest. The agreement itself discloses the common intention required to create a resulting, implied or constructive trust.

But the parties to a transaction in connection with the acquisition of land may well have formed a common intention that the beneficial interest in the land shall be vested in them jointly without having used express words to communicate this intention to one another; or their recollections of the words used may be imperfect or conflicting by the time any dispute arises. In such a case – a common one where the parties are spouses whose marriage has broken down – it may be possible to infer their common intention from their conduct.

As in so many branches of English law in which legal rights and obligations depend upon the intentions of the parties to a transaction, the relevant intention of each party is the intention which was reasonably understood by the other party to be manifested by that party's words or conduct notwithstanding that he did not consciously formulate that intention in his own mind or even acted with some different intention which he did not communicate to the other party. On the other hand, he is not bound by inference which the other party draws from his words or conduct. It is in this sense that in the branch of English law relating to constructive, implied or resulting trusts effect is given to the intentions of the parties to a transaction which a reasonable man would draw from their words or conduct and not to any subjective intention or absence of intention which was not made manifest at the time of the transaction itself. It is for the court to determine what those inferences are.

In drawing such an inference, what the spouse said and did which led up to the acquisition of a matrimonial home and what they said and did while the acquisition was being carried through is on a different footing from what they said and did after the acquisition was completed. Unless it is alleged that there was some subsequent fresh agreement, acted upon by the parties, to vary the original beneficial interests created when the matrimonial home was acquired, what they said and did after the acquisition was completed is relevant if it is explicable only upon the basis of their having manifested to one another at the time of the acquisition some particular common intention as to how the beneficial interests should be held. But it would in my view be unreasonably legalistic to treat the relevant transaction involved in the acquisition of a matrimonial home as restricted to the actual conveyance of the fee simple into the name of one or other spouse. Their common intention is more likely to have been concerned with the economic realities of the transaction than with the unfamiliar technicalities of the English law of legal and equitable interests in land. The economic reality which lies behind the conveyance of the fee simple to a purchaser in return for a purchase price the greater part of which is advanced to the purchaser upon a mortgage repayable by instalments over a number of years, is that the new freeholder is purchasing the matrimonial home upon credit and that the purchase price represented by the instalments by which the mortgage is repaid in addition to the initial payment in cash. The conduct of the spouses in relation to the payment of the mortgage instalments may be no less relevant to their common intention as to the beneficial interests in a matrimonial home acquired in this way than their conduct in relation to the repayment of the cash deposit.

Where a matrimonial home has been purchased outright without the aid of an advance on mortgage, it is not difficult to ascertain what part, if any, of the purchase price has been provided by each spouse. If the land is conveyed into the name of a spouse who has not provided the whole of the purchase price, the sum contributed by the other spouse may be explicable as having been intended by both of them either as a gift or as a loan of money to the spouse to whom the land is conveyed or as consideration for a share in the beneficial interest in the land. In a dispute between living spouses the evidence will probably point to one of these explanations as being more probable than the others, but if the rest of the evidence is neutral the *prima facie* inference is that their common intention was the contributing spouse should acquire a share in the beneficial interest in the land in the same proportion as the sum contributed bore to the total purchase price. This *prima facie* inference is more easily rebutted in favour of a gift where the land is conveyed into the name of the wife: but as I understand the speeches in *Pettitt v Pettitt* [see above, p 367] four of the members of your Lordships' House who were parties to that decision took the view that even if the 'presumption of advancement' as between husband and wife still survived today, it could seldom have any decisive part to play in disputes between living spouses in which some evidence would be available in addition to the mere fact that the husband had provided part of the purchase price of the property conveyed into the name of the wife.

Similarly when a matrimonial home is not purchased outright but partly out of moneys advanced on mortgage repayable by instalments, and the land is conveyed into the name of the husband alone, the fact that the wife made a cash contribution to the deposit and legal charges not borrowed on mortgage gives rise, in the absence of evidence which makes some other explanation more probable, to the inference that their common intention that she should share in the beneficial interest in the land conveyed. But it would not be reasonable to infer a common intention as to what her share should be without taking account also of the sources from which the mortgage instalments were provided. If the wife also makes a substantial direct contribution to the mortgage instalments out of her own earnings or unearned income this would be *prima facie* inconsistent with a common intention that her share in the beneficial interest should be determined by the proportion which her original cash contribution bore either to the total amount of the deposit and legal charges or to the full purchase price. The more likely inference is that her contributions to the mortgage instalments were intended by the spouses to have some effect upon her share.

Where there has been an initial contribution by the wife to the cash deposit and legal charges which points to a common intention at the time of the conveyance that she should have a beneficial interest in the land conveyed to her husband, it would be unrealistic to regard the wife's subsequent contributions to the mortgage instalments as without significance unless she pays them directly herself. It may be no more than a matter of convenience which spouse pays particular household accounts, particularly when both are earning, and if the wife goes out to work and devotes part of her earnings or uses her private income to meet joint expenses of the household which would otherwise be met by the husband, so as to enable him to pay the mortgage instalments out of his moneys this would be consistent with and might be corroborative of an original common intention that she should share in the beneficial interest in the matrimonial home and that her payments of other household expenses were intended by both spouses to be treated as including a contribution by the wife to the purchase price of the matrimonial home.

Even where there has been no initial contribution by the wife to the cash deposit and legal charges but she makes a regular and substantial direct contribution to the mortgage instalments it may be reasonable to infer a common intention of the spouses from the outset that she should share in the beneficial interest or to infer a fresh agreement reached after the original conveyance that she should acquire a share. But it is unlikely that the mere fact that the wife made direct contributions to the mortgage instalments would be the only evidence available to assist the court in ascertaining the common intention of the spouses.

Where in any of the circumstances described above contributions, direct or indirect, have been made to the mortgage instalments by the spouse into whose name the matrimonial home has not been conveyed, and the court can infer from their conduct a common intention that the contributing spouse should be entitled to some beneficial interest in the matrimonial home, what effect is to be given to that intention if there is no evidence that they in fact reached any express agreement as to what the respective share of each spouse should be?

I take it to be clear that if the court is satisfied that it was the common intention of both spouses that the contributing wife should have a share in the beneficial interest and that her contributions were made upon this understanding, the court in the exercise of its equitable jurisdiction would not permit the husband in whom the legal estate was vested and who had accepted the benefit of the contributions to take the whole beneficial interest merely because at the time the wife made her contributions there had been no express agreement as to how her share in it was to be quantified.

In such a case the court must first do its best to discover from the conduct of the spouses whether any inference can reasonably be drawn as to the probable common understanding about the amount of the share of the contributing spouse upon which each must have acted in doing what each did, even though that understanding was never expressly stated by one spouse to the other or even consciously formulated in words by either of them independently. It is only if no such inference can be drawn that the court is driven to apply as a rule of law, and not as an inference of fact, the maxim 'equality is equity,' and to hold that the beneficial interest belongs to the spouses in equal shares.

Difficult as they are to solve, however, these problems as to the amount of the share of a spouse in the beneficial interest in a matrimonial home where the legal estate is vested solely in the other spouse, only arise in cases where the court is satisfied by the words or conduct of the beneficial interest was not to belong solely to the spouse in whom the legal estate was vested but was to be shared between them in some proportion or other.

Where the wife has made no initial contribution to the cash deposit and legal charges and no direct contribution to the mortgage instalments nor any adjustment to her contribution to other expenses of the household which it can be inferred was referable to the acquisition of the house, there is in the absence of evidence of an express agreement between the parties no material to justify the court in inferring that it was the common intention of the parties that she should have any beneficial interest in a matrimonial home conveyed into the sole name of the husband, merely because she continued to contribute out of her own earnings or private income to other expenses of the household. For such conduct is no less consistent with a common intention to share the day to day expenses of the household, while each spouse retains a separate interest in capital assets acquired with their own moneys or obtained here to rebut the *prima facie* inference that a purchaser of land who pays the purchase price and takes a conveyance and grants a mortgage in his own name intends to acquire the sole beneficial interest as well as the legal estate: and the difficult question of the quantum of the wife's share does not arise.

On what then is the wife's claim based? In 1951, when the house was purchased, she spent about £190 on buying furniture and a cooker and refrigerator for it. She also paid about £30 for improving the lawn. As to the furniture and household durables are depreciating assets whereas houses have turned out to be appreciating assets it may have been wise to have devoted her savings to acquire an interest in the freehold; but this may not have been so apparent in 1951 as it is now become. The court is not entitled to enter a common intention to its effect from the mere fact that she provided chattels for joint use in the new matrimonial home; and there is nothing else in the conduct of the parties at the time of the purchase or thereafter which supports such an inference. There is no suggestion that a wife's efforts or her earnings made it possible for the husband to raise the initial loan or the mortgage or that her relieving her husband from the expense of buying clothing for herself and for their son was undertaken in order to enable him the better to meet the mortgage instalments or repay the loan. The picture presented by the evidence is one of husband and wife retaining their separate proprietary interests in property whether real or personal purchased with their separate savings and is inconsistent with any common intention at the time of the purchase of the matrimonial home that his wife, who neither then nor subsequently contributed anything to its purchase price or assumed any liability for it, should nevertheless be entitled to a beneficial interest in it.

Both Buckley J and Edmund Davies LJ in his dissenting judgment in the Court of Appeal felt unable on this evidence to draw an inference that there was any common intention that the wife should have a beneficial interest in the house. I think that they were right. Like them I, too, come to the conclusion with regret, because it may well be that had the husband and wife discussed the matter in 1951 when the house was bought he would have been willing for her to have a share in it if she wanted to. But this is speculation, and if such an arrangement had been made between them there might well have also been a difference of the allocation of the household expenses between them in the ensuing years.

> If, as I hold, she has no interest in the matrimonial home in which she is still living, this will no doubt affect her claim for maintenance under the Matrimonial Causes Act, 1965. I would allow the appeal and declare that the sole beneficial interest in the house is vested in the husband.

The parties to the purchase may have the legal title to the property transferred in their joint names, subject to an express trust for sale for themselves as equitable joint tenants or tenants in common, or they may expressly declare the terms of the trust outside the conveyance. Provided that the declaration of trust is evidenced in writing (in compliance with s 53(1)(b) of the Law of Property Act 1925), it shall be conclusive as to the beneficial interests of the parties, in the absence of fraud or mistake.

Goodman v Gallant [1986] 2 WLR 236, CA (Sir Cumming-Bruce, Slade Purchas LJJ)

In 1978, the plaintiff and defendant purchased a house which was conveyed in their joint names 'upon trust to sell ... and until sale upon trust for themselves as joint tenants'. After a dispute arose between the parties, the defendant left the house. The plaintiff gave written notice of severance of the joint tenancy and claimed a declaration to the effect that she was entitled to a three quarters share in the house.

The Court of Appeal held in her favour. In the absence of any claim for rectification or rescission, the express declaration in the conveyance was conclusive as to the intentions of the parties. The notice of severance had the effect of terminating the joint tenancy and substituting a tenancy in common in respect of the beneficial interest.

> **Slade LJ:** Neither the registrar nor Hollis J were invited to go into the evidence. They were invited to deal with a preliminary point of law, raised on behalf of the defendant, which can be simply summarised in two propositions said to be based on a line of previous decisions of this court, namely that:
>
> (1) the declaration contained in the conveyance stating that the plaintiff and the defendant hold the property in trust for themselves as 'joint tenants' is conclusive as to the nature of their respective beneficial interests; and
>
> (2) the inevitable effect of the severance of this beneficial joint tenancy was to leave them entitled to the property or its proceeds of sale in equal shares.
>
> In the present case, therefore, even if the conveyance of the fee simple in the property to the plaintiff and the defendant jointly had contained no express trust for sale and no declaration as to the beneficial interests, a trust for sale would still have arisen through the combined effect of ss 34–36 of the Law of Property Act 1925. However, ss 34–36, while importing a trust for sale in certain cases where it would not otherwise have arisen, are designed merely to simplify the mechanics of conveyancing. They have no effect whatever on the nature and extent of the respective beneficial interests in the proceeds of sale of the several persons interested.

Accordingly, in our judgment, the provisions of clause 2(a) of the conveyance, by which express trusts are declared concerning the beneficial interests in the property or its proceeds of sale, cannot be regarded as otiose. The position is quite the contrary.

In a case where the legal estate in property is conveyed to two or more persons as joint tenants, but neither the conveyance nor any other written document contains any express declaration of trust concerning the beneficial interests in the property (as would be required for an express declaration of this nature by virtue of s 53(1)(b) of the Law of Property Act 1925), the way is open for persons claiming a beneficial interest in it or its proceeds of sale to rely on the doctrine of 'resulting, implied or constructive trusts': see s 53(2) of the Law of Property Act 1925. If, however, the relevant conveyance contains an express declaration of trust which comprehensively declares the beneficial interests in the property or its proceeds of sale, there is no room for the application of the doctrine of resulting implied or constructive trusts unless and until the conveyance is set aside or rectified; until that event the declaration contained in the document speaks for itself.

In *Wilson v Wilson*[18] this court had to consider the case where a matrimonial home had been conveyed into the joint names of the husband and wife and the conveyance contained an express declaration stating that they held the property upon trust for sale and that they would hold the net proceeds of sale and other capital moneys upon trust for themselves as joint tenants. On an application under s 17 of the Married Women's Property Act 1882 to have the rights of the parties in the proceeds of sale in the house determined, the husband claimed the entirety of such proceeds. The wife, however, contended that the effect of the conveyance was to entitle her to one half of the proceeds of sale in any event. This court unanimously upheld this contention. Donovan LJ said, p 607:

> By the conveyance the husband and wife, who were the purchasers thereunder, were to hold the property upon trust to sell the same with power to postpone the sale thereof and to hold the net proceeds of sale and other money applicable as capital and the net rents and profits thereof until sale upon trust for themselves as joint tenants. Thus the entire beneficial interest in the property was declared at the outset. While it was the matrimonial home the spouses owned it as joint tenants. If it should be sold, they were to hold the net proceeds of sale as joint tenants, which I construe as meaning that on a division of these proceeds the division was to be in equal shares.

All the members of the court in *Wilson v Wilson* considered that the court had no power under s 17 of the Married Women's Property Act 1882 to override the clearly defined and formally declared beneficial title of the parties as set out in the conveyance. (Of course, since the decision in *Wilson v Wilson* each spouse now has available the remedy of an application for a property adjustment order: s 24 of the Matrimonial Causes Act 1973.) The facts of *Wilson*

18 [1963] 1 WLR 601.

v Wilson are, so far as we can see, in all material respects indistinguishable from those of the present case ...

Lord Upjohn in *Pettitt v Pettitt*,[19] put the matter thus:

> In the first place, the beneficial ownership of the property in question must depend upon the agreement of the parties determined at the time of its acquisition. If the property in question is land there must be some lease or conveyance which shows how it was acquired. If that document declares not merely in whom the legal title is to vest but in whom the beneficial title is to vest that necessarily concludes the question of title as between the spouses for all time, and in the absence of fraud or mistake at the time of the transaction the parties cannot go behind it at any time thereafter even on death or the break-up of the marriage.

Lord Diplock in *Gissing v Gissing*,[20] reaffirmed the general principle:

> ... where the trust is expressly declared in the instrument by which the legal estate is transferred to the trustee or by a written declaration of trust by the trustee, the court must give effect to it.

However, the reference by Lord Upjohn in *Pettitt v Pettitt* to the possibility of 'fraud or mistake at the time of the transaction' illustrates that there is one (though we think only one) qualification to this principle. The declaration of trust will no longer be binding if the court is satisfied by appropriate evidence either that the relevant document ought to be rectified (as was Buckley J in a case also named *Wilson v Wilson*)[21] or that it ought to be rescinded on the grounds of fraud or mistake.

It seems to us that it is of the very nature of a joint tenancy that, upon a severance, each takes an equal aliquot share according to the number of joint tenants. *Halsbury's Laws of England*, 4th edn,[22] which is headed 'Nature of joint tenants' interests', begins with the words:

> Each joint tenant has an identical interest in the whole land and every part of it. The title of each arises by the same act. The interest of each is the same in extent, nature and duration.

Note 2 to this passage begins:

> Until severance, each has the whole, but upon severance each has an aliquot part (a half or less) according to the number of joint tenants ...

The note then points out that severance can only now take effect in respect of the beneficial interests.

A passage and note in more or less identical terms is to be found in *Halsbury's Laws of England*, 2nd edn.[23] It therefore owes none of its authority to *Wilson v Wilson*.[24] It would no doubt be possible for a trust in terms to provide that the

19 [1970] AC 777, p 813.

20 [1971] AC 886, p 905.

21 [1969] 1 WLR 1470.

22 1982, London: Butterworths, Vol 39, p 349, para 529.

23 1937, London: Butterworths, Vol 27, p 658, para 1140.

24 [1963] 1 WLR 601.

> beneficial interests of two parties should be equivalent to those of joint tenants unless and until severance occurred, but that in the event of severance their interests should be otherwise than in equal shares. In our judgment, however, such an arrangement cannot be spelt out of the relevant wording of the conveyance in the present case, which must be construed according to the traditional sense of a beneficial joint tenancy, with all its incidents, including those relating to the effect of severance.

Where the legal estate in the property is conveyed in the name of one spouse only (say the husband) and the other spouse wishes to claim a beneficial interest, the claimant will be required to establish a contribution to the purchase of the house at the time of the acquisition (which includes the mortgage repayments). In other words, in the absence of an express declaration of trust in writing, the claimant must show that the legal owner holds the legal estate on trust in order to give effect to the interest claimed. Staying at home for the purpose of looking after the house and children without more, would not give the claimant an interest in the house. The reason being that the claimant would have failed to show that he or she has made a contribution to the acquisition of the house.

***Burns v Burns* [1984] 2 WLR 582, CA (Waller, Fox and May LJJ)**

The plaintiff, Mrs Burns lived with the defendant since 1961 for 19 years without being married. She gave up her employment shortly after their first child was born. In 1963, when she was expecting her second child, the defendant bought a house in his sole name for £4,900 of which £4,500 was raised by way of a mortgage. The plaintiff made no direct contributions to the purchase. Until 1975, the plaintiff was unable to take up gainful employment because she performed the duties of bringing up the children. Although the defendant gave her a generous housekeeping allowance and did not ask her to contribute to household expenses, from 1975 she became employed and used her earnings for household expenses and to purchase fixtures and fittings. In 1980, the plaintiff left the defendant and claimed a beneficial interest in the house. The judge decided that the plaintiff did not have an interest in the house. The plaintiff appealed.

The Court of Appeal held that since the plaintiff failed to prove that she had made a contribution, directly or indirectly to the acquisition of the property, she did not have an interest in the property. A common intention that the plaintiff had acquired an interest in the property cannot be imputed to the parties on the basis that the plaintiff lived with the defendant for 19 years, brought up the children and did a fair share of domestic duties. In respect of unmarried couples, the court has no jurisdiction equivalent to the Matrimonial Causes Act 1973 to make an order dividing up the property on the basis of what was fair and reasonable.

> **Fox LJ:** If the plaintiff is to establish that she has a beneficial interest in the property, she must establish that the defendant holds the legal estate upon

trust to give effect to that interest. That follows from *Gissing v Gissing*.[25] For present purposes I think that such a trust could only arise (a) by express declaration or agreement, or (b) by way of a resulting trust where the claimant has directly provided part of the purchase price, or (c) from the common intention of the parties.

In the present case, (a) and (b) can be ruled out. There was no express trust of an interest in the property for the benefit of the plaintiff; and there was no express agreement to create such an interest. And the plaintiff made no direct contribution to the purchase price. Her case, therefore, must depend upon showing a common intention that she should have a beneficial interest in the property. Whether the trust which would arise in such circumstances is described as implied, constructive or resulting does not greatly matter. If the intention is inferred from the fact that some indirect contribution is made to the purchase price, the term 'resulting trust' is probably not inappropriate. Be that as it may, the basis of such a claim, in any case, is that it would be inequitable for the holder of the legal estate to deny the claimant's right to a beneficial interest.

In determining whether such common intention exists it is, normally, the intention of the parties when the property was purchased that is important. As to that I agree with the observations of Griffiths LJ in *Bernard v Josephs*.[26] As I understand it, that does not mean that for the purpose of determining the ultimate shares in the property one looks simply at the factual position as it was at the date of acquisition. It is necessary for the court to consider all the evidence, including the contributions of the parties, down to the date of separation (which in the case of man and mistress will generally, though not always, be the relevant date). Thus the law proceeds on the basis that there is nothing inherently improbable in the parties acting on the understanding that the woman:

> ... should be entitled to a share which was not to be quantified immediately upon the acquisition of the home but should be left to be determined when the mortgage was repaid or the property disposed of, on the basis of what would be fair having regard to the total contributions, direct or indirect, which each spouse had made by that date [see *Gissing v Gissing*].[27]

That approach does not, however, in my view preclude the possibility that while, initially, there was no intention that the claimant should have any interest in the property, circumstances may subsequently arise from which the intention to confer an equitable interest upon the claimant may arise (for example, the discharge of a mortgage or the effecting of capital improvements to the house at his or her expense). Further, subsequent events may throw light on the initial intention.

Looking at the position at the time of the acquisition of the house in 1963, I see nothing at all to indicate any intention by the parties that the plaintiff should have an interest in it ...

25 [1971] AC 886.

26 [1982] Ch 391, p 404.

27 [1971] AC 886, p 909, *per* Lord Diplock.

I come then to the position in the year after the house was purchased. I will deal with them under three heads, namely financial contributions, work on the house and finally housekeeping. There is some overlapping in these categories.

So far as financial contributions are concerned ... The judge's findings as to expenditure by the plaintiff were as follows:

(i) she made gifts of clothing and other things to the defendant and the children;

(ii) she paid for the housekeeping. The defendant allowed her, latterly, £60 per week for housekeeping. It seems to be accepted that the defendant was generous with money and the plaintiff was not kept short as regards housekeeping money;

(iii) she paid the rates. The housekeeping payments made by the defendant were, however, fixed at an amount which took account of this;

(iv) she paid the telephone bills. That was a matter of agreement between her and the defendant because she spent a lot of time on the telephone talking to her friends;

(v) she bought a number of chattels for domestic use: a dishwasher, a washing machine, a tumble dryer and either a drawing room suite or three armchairs and a bed for her separate room. The bed, the dishwasher and the chairs she took with her when she left in 1980;

(vi) she provided some doorknobs and door furnishings of no great value.

None of this expenditure, in my opinion, indicates the existence of the common intention which the plaintiff has to prove. What is needed, I think, is evidence of a payment or payments by the plaintiff which it can be inferred was referable to the acquisition of the house. Lord Denning MR in *Hazell v Hazell*[28] thought that expression, which appears in the speech of Lord Diplock in *Gissing v Gissing* was being overused. He said, quoting from *Falconer v Falconer*,[29] that if there was a substantial financial contribution towards the family expenses that would raise an inference of a trust. I do not think that formulation alters the essence of the matter for present purposes. If there is a substantial contribution by the woman to family expenses, and the house was purchased on a mortgage, her contribution is, indirectly, referable to the acquisition of the house since, in one way or another, it enables the family to pay the mortgage instalments. Thus, a payment could be said to be referable to the acquisition of the house if, for example, the payer either (a) pays part of the purchase price, or (b) contributes regularly to the mortgage instalments, or (c) pays off part of the mortgage, or (d) makes a substantial financial contribution to the family expenses so as to enable the mortgage instalments to be paid.

But if a payment cannot be said to be, in a real sense, referable to the acquisition of the house it is difficult to see how, in such a case as the present, it can base a claim for an interest in the house. Looking at the items which I have listed above, and leaving aside, for the present, the housekeeping which I will deal with separately, none of the items can be said to be referable to the

28 [1972] 1 WLR 301, p 304.

29 [1970] 1 WLR 1333, p 1336.

acquisition of the house. The making of ordinary gifts between members of a family certainly is not. Nor, in the circumstances as found by the judge, are the payments of rates or of the telephone bills. The provision of the door knobs, etc, is of very small consequence. As regards the purchase of chattels for domestic use, the plaintiff must, I think, have regarded at any rate some of these as her own property since she took them away with her when she left. But quite apart from that I do not think that the provision of chattels, by itself, is evidence of any common intention that the plaintiff should have a beneficial interest in the house. In *Gissing v Gissing*,[30] Viscount Dilhorne, after referring to the requirement of a common intention that the wife should have an interest in the house, said, p 900:

> To establish this intention there must be some evidence which points to its existence. It would not, for instance, suffice if the wife just made a mortgage payment while her husband was abroad. Payment for a lawn and provision of some furniture and equipment for the house does not itself point to the conclusion that there was such an intention.

Lord Diplock said, p 910:

> The court is not entitled to infer a common intention ... from the mere fact that she provided chattels for joint use in the new matrimonial home ...

As regard work on the house, in 1971 a fairly substantial improvement was made to the house; the attic was converted into a bedroom with a bathroom *en suite*. That was paid for wholly by the defendant. In 1977 or 1978 the plaintiff decorated the house throughout internally because she wished the house to be wallpapered and not painted. I do not think that carries her case any further. Thus, in *Pettitt v Pettitt*,[31] Lord Diplock said:

> If the husband likes to occupy his leisure by laying a new lawn in the garden or building a fitted wardrobe in the bedroom while the wife does the shopping, cooks the family dinner and bathes the children, I, for my part, find it quite impossible to impute to them as reasonable husband and wife any common intention that these domestic activities or any of them are to have any effect upon the existing proprietary rights in the family home ...

Accordingly, I think that the decoration undertaken by the plaintiff gives no indication of any such common intention as she must assert.

There remains the question of housekeeping and domestic duties. So far as housekeeping expenses are concerned, I do not doubt that (the house being bought in the man's name) if the woman goes out to work in order to provide money for the family expenses, as a result of which she spends her earnings on the housekeeping and the man is thus able to pay the mortgage instalments and other expenses out of his earnings, it can be inferred that there was a common intention that the woman should have an interest in the house – since she will have made an indirect financial contribution to the mortgage instalments. But that is not this case.

30 [1971] AC 886.

31 [1970] AC 777, p 826.

But, one asks, can the fact that the plaintiff performed domestic duties in the house and looked after the children be taken into account? I think it is necessary to keep in mind the nature of the right which is being asserted. The court has no jurisdiction to make such order as it might think fair; the powers conferred by the Matrimonial Causes Act 1973 in relation to the property of married persons do not apply to unmarried couples. The house was bought by the defendant in his own name and, *prima facie*, he is the absolute beneficial owner. If the plaintiff, or anybody else, claims to take it from him, it must be proved the claimant has, by some process of law, acquired an interest in the house. What is asserted here is the creation of a trust arising by common intention of the parties. That common intention may be inferred where there has been a financial contribution, direct or indirect, to the acquisition of the house. But the mere fact that parties live together and do the ordinary domestic tasks is, in my view, no indication at all that they thereby intended to alter the existing property rights of either of them. As to that I refer to the passage from the speech of Lord Diplock in *Pettitt v Pettitt*[32] which I have already mentioned; and also to the observations of Lord Hodson in *Pettitt v Pettitt*[33] and of Lord Reid at p 796. The undertaking of such work is, I think, what Lord Denning MR in *Button v Button*[34] called the sort of things which are done for the benefit of the family without altering the title to property. The assertion that they do alter property rights seems to me to be, in substance, reverting to the idea of the 'family asset' which was rejected by the House of Lords in *Pettitt v Pettitt*. The decision in *Gissing v Gissing*[35] itself is really inconsistent with the contrary view since the parties lived together for ten years after the house was bought. In *Hall v Hall*[36] Lord Denning MR did say:

> It depends on the circumstances and how much she has contributed – not merely in money – but also in keeping up the house; and, if there are children in looking after them.

With respect I do not find support for that in the other authorities and I do not think that it is consistent with principle. I am not clear to what extent the matter was material in *Hall v Hall*. So far as looking after children is concerned, it appears that there were no children: see *per* Dunn LJ, p 382. The case seems to have proceeded on the concession made by the man that the woman was entitled by way of resulting trust to a share in the house. The parties lived together for seven years and it was accepted by the man that they could not have bought the house but for the fact that both were earning: see *per* Lord Denning MR, p 381. The parties, in fact, pooled their resources: see the findings of the judge at p 383. Accordingly, it seems to me that the case may well have been one where the woman, through the pooling of their income, made a contribution, direct or indirect, to the mortgage payments.

32 [1970] AC 777, p 826.

33 *Ibid*, p 811.

34 [1968] 1 WLR 457, p 462.

35 [1971] AC 886.

36 [1982] 3 FLR 379, p 381.

> The result, in my opinion, is that the plaintiff fails to demonstrate the existence of any trust in her favour.

(1) In the absence of an express declaration of an equitable interest (which is required to be in writing), the claimant is required to establish an implied agreement with the legal owner as to beneficial entitlement. The evidence of such agreement may take the form of substantial contributions directly to the purchase of the property, such as the deposit and/or the mortgage repayments. The interest acquired will correspond to the *pro rata* value of the contributions. If the courts cannot ascertain the exact contributions made by each party the best solution may be equal division.

Re Rogers' Question [1948] 1 All ER 328, CA (Lord Greene MR, Asquith and Evershed LJJ)

In this case, the wife, W, paid £100 in cash towards the purchase of a house for £1,000 which was conveyed in the name of her husband, H. W made it clear that this would be the limit of her contribution.

The Court of Appeal held that W acquired a one 10th share in the property.

> **Evershed LJ:** What is the inference proper to be drawn from this evidence? It is clear, and in the circumstances, perhaps not surprising having regard to existing relations, that each party has put forward extreme claims. The husband has alleged that the property was, and was always intended to be, his beneficially, subject only to his obligation to repay the £100 provided by his wife, which, he said, was a loan. That contention the learned judge had rejected. The wife, in the course of her cross-examination, went so far as to suggest that the property is, and was always intended to be, beneficially entirely hers, the husband's obligations and payments as to the mortgage interest, rates, taxes, etc, being entered into or provided as part of the household expenses which it would be his proper function to discharge. It is fair to say that counsel for the wife has not sought to maintain any such extreme claim, and the wife's claim as presented to this court must be taken to be qualified by admitted obligation to indemnify her husband in regard to his mortgage obligation, but this view, too, the learned judge has rejected. In his view, the effect of the evidence of the so called tiff was to support, or, at least not to contradict, in the proportion in which they did, in fact, contribute or (in the case of the husband) make himself liable to contribute. In my judgment he was right. It is more than possible that each went away from the meeting in question with a somewhat different, though vague and certainly never formulated, idea of what its effect had been. It is, at least, clear that, whatever her protests, the wife knew that in spite of them the property would be in her husband's name. Equally it is clear to my mind that the wife was unwilling to make any further contribution to the purchase (though she appears to have been possessed of some £500 which could have been so applied) or to make herself liable, as I understand her cross-examination, for any mortgage which she expected her husband to undertake. In the circumstances, it seems to me wholly unreasonable to suppose that the wife thought she could both have her

cake and eat it, but wholly reasonable to infer, as Roxburgh J (at first instance) inferred, that each intended to contribute to the home in the respective proportions found by the judge.

(2) Moreover, the claimant may acquire an interest in the property by making a substantial indirect contribution to the acquisition of the property (including mortgage repayments). This arrangement may be achieved by an undertaking between the parties to the effect that the claimant agrees to pay the household expenses on condition that the legal owner pays the mortgage instalments. In short, a link between the mortgage payments and the expenses undertaken by the claimant is required to be established and the claimant's expenses are required to be of a substantial nature. This arrangement may take the form of an express agreement, albeit not in writing, following discussions between the parties. An agreement without writing, conveying an interest in land maybe treated as a declaration of trust and is unenforceable by virtue of s 53(1)(b) of the Law of Property Act 1925 (see above, p 57). Frequently, the courts are required to consider whether such agreements may be implied by interpreting the conduct of the parties. Such conduct may form the basis of a constructive or resulting trust which is exempt from s 53(1)(b) by virtue of s 53(2) of the Law of Property Act 1925.

Per Lord Pearson in *Gissing v Gissing* (*obiter*):

> Contributions are not limited to those made directly in part payment of the price of the property or to those made at the time when the property is conveyed into the name of one of the spouses. For instance there can be a contribution if by arrangement between the spouses one of them by payment of the household expenses enables the other to pay the mortgage instalments.

Grant v Edwards [1986] Ch 638, CA

> **Nourse LJ:** Where there has been no written declaration or agreement, nor any direct provision by the plaintiff of part of the purchase price so as to give rise to a resulting trust ... She [the claimant] must establish a common intention between her and the defendant, acted on by her, that she should have a beneficial interest in the property. If she can do that, equity will not allow the defendant to deny that interest and will construct a trust to give effect to it ... In this regard the court has to look at expenditure which is referable to the acquisition of the home.

In this case, the claimant, a woman who lived with the defendant was given a false reason for not having the house put in their joint names. The woman made substantial contributions to the family expenses in the hope of acquiring an interest in the house. The expenses undertaken by the woman enabled the man to keep up the mortgage instalments. The plaintiff claimed an interest in the house.

The Court of Appeal held in her favour and decided that she was entitled to a half share in the property. The plaintiff would not have made the substantial contributions to the housekeeping expenses, which related to the mortgage instalments, unless she had an interest in the house. This was the inevitable inference of the plaintiff's conduct which established a common intention and reliance to her detriment.

> **Nourse LJ:** In most of these cases the fundamental, and invariably the most difficult, question is to decide whether there was the necessary common intention, being something which can only be inferred from the conduct of the parties, almost always from the expenditure incurred by them respectively. In this regard the court has to look for expenditure which is referable to the acquisition of the house: see *per* Fox LJ in *Burns v Burns*.[37] If it is found to have been incurred, such expenditure will perform the twofold function of establishing the common intention and showing that the claimant has acted on it.
>
> There is another and rarer class of case, of which the present may be one, where, although there has been no writing, the parties have orally declared themselves in such a way as to make their common intention plain. Here the court does not have to look for conduct from which the intention can be inferred, but only for conduct which amounts to an acting upon it by the claimant. And although that conduct can undoubtedly be the incurring of expenditure which is referable to the acquisition of the house, it need not necessarily be so. The clearest example of this rarer class of case is *Eves v Eves*.[38]
>
> It seems on the authorities as they stand, that a distinction is to be made between conduct from which the common intention can be inferred on the one hand and conduct which amounts to an acting upon it on the other. There remains this difficult question: what is the quality of conduct required for the latter purpose? The difficulty is caused, I think because although the common intention has been made plain, everything else remains a matter of inference. Let me illustrate it in this way. It would be possible to take the view that the mere moving into the house by the woman amounted to an acting upon the common intention. But that was evidently not the view of the majority in *Eves v Eves*.[39] And the reason for that may be that, in the absence of evidence, the law is not so cynical as to infer that a woman will only go to live with a man to whom she is not married if she understands that she is to have an interest in their home. So what sort of conduct is required? In my judgment it must be conduct on which the woman could not reasonably have been expected to embark unless she was to have an interest in the house. If she was not to have such an interest, she could reasonably be expected to go and live with her lover, but not, for example, to wield a 14 lb sledge hammer in the front garden. In adopting the latter kind of conduct she is seen to act to her detriment on the faith of the common intention.
>
> [After considering the facts as found by the judge, his Lordship continued:]
>
> It is in my view an inevitable inference that the very substantial contribution which the plaintiff made out of her earnings after August 1972 to the

37 [1984] Ch 317, pp 328H–29C.

38 [1975] 1 WLR 1338.

39 *Ibid*.

> housekeeping and to the feeding and to the bringing up of the children enabled the defendant to keep down the instalments payable under both mortgages out of his own income and, moreover, that he could not have done that if he had had to bear the whole of the other expenses as well. For example, in 1973, when he and the plaintiff were earning about £1,200 each, the defendant had to find a total of about £643 between the two mortgages. I do not see how he would have been able to do that had it not been for the plaintiff's very substantial contribution to the other expenses. There is certainly no evidence that there was any money to spare on either side and the natural inference is to the contrary. In this connection, it is interesting to note that when dealing with the moneys in the Leeds Permanent Building Society account the judge said:
>
> > They lived from hand to mouth, as I see it. They put their money in, and when there was some money to spare, they would share it out in this way.
>
> In the circumstances, it seems that it may properly be inferred that the plaintiff did make substantial indirect contributions to the instalments payable under both mortgages. This is a point which seems to have escaped the judge, but I think that there is an explanation for that. He was concentrating, as no doubt were counsel, on the plaintiff's claim that she herself had paid all the instalments under the second mortgage. It seems very likely that the indirect consequences of her very substantial contribution to the other expenses were not fully explored.
>
> Was the conduct of the plaintiff in making substantial indirect contributions to the instalments payable under both mortgages conduct upon which she could not reasonably have been expected to embark unless she was to have an interest in the house? I answer that question in the affirmative. I cannot see upon what other basis she could reasonably have been expected to give the defendant such substantial assistance in paying off mortgages on his house. I therefore conclude that the plaintiff did act to her detriment on the faith of the common intention between her and the defendant that she was to have some sort of proprietary interest in the house.

However, in the same case, Sir Nicolas Browne-Wilkinson VC (as he then was) expressed the approach of the court exclusively in terms of a constructive trust similar to a proprietary estoppel (see above, p 138). The claimant without the legal interest, is required to establish a constructive trust or a proprietary estoppel by showing that it would be inequitable for the legal owner to claim sole beneficial ownership. This requires two matters to be demonstrated:

(a) that there was a common intention that both should have a beneficial interest; and

(b) that the claimant had acted to his or her detriment on the basis of that common intention.

The intention may be established by direct evidence of an express agreement in writing between the parties or an inferred common intention from the conduct of the parties. Direct or indirect substantial financial contributions to the acquisition of the house (including the mortgage instalments) will have this effect. Indeed, contributions may be relevant for four different purposes:

(1) in the absence of direct evidence of intention, as evidence from which the parties' intentions can be inferred;

(2) as corroboration of direct evidence of intention;

(3) to show that the claimant has acted to his or her detriment in reliance on the common intention;

(4) to quantify the extent of the beneficial interest.

Grant v Edwards [1986] Ch 638, CA

Sir Nicolas Browne-Wilkinson VC: In my judgment, there has been a tendency over the years to distort the principles as laid down in the speech of Lord Diplock in *Gissing v Gissing*[40] by concentrating on only part of his reasoning. For present purposes, his speech can be treated as falling into three sections: the first deals with the nature of the substantive right; the second with the proof of the existence of that right; the third with the quantification of that right.

The nature of the substantive right[41]

If the legal estate in the joint home is vested in only one of the parties ('the legal owner') the other party ('the claimant'), in order to establish a beneficial interest, has to establish a constructive trust by showing that it would be inequitable for the legal owner to claim sole beneficial ownership. This requires two matters to be demonstrated: (a) that there was a common intention that both should have a beneficial interest; (b) that the claimant has acted to his or her detriment on the basis of that common intention.

The proof of the common intention

(a) Direct evidence:[42] It is clear that mere agreement between the parties that both are to have beneficial interests is sufficient to prove the necessary common intention. Other passages in the speech point to the admissibility and relevance of other possible forms of direct evidence of such intention.[43]

(b) Inferred common intention:[44] Lord Diplock points out that, even where parties have not used express words to communicate their intention (and therefore there is no direct evidence), the court can infer from their actions an intention that they shall both have an interest in the house. This part of his speech concentrates on the types of evidence from which the courts are most often asked to infer such intention, viz, contributions (direct and indirect) to the deposit, the mortgage instalments or general housekeeping expenses. In this section of the speech, he analyses what types of expenditure are capable of constituting evidence of such common intention: he does not say that if the

40 [1971] AC 886.

41 *Ibid*, pp 905B–05G.

42 *Ibid*, p 905H.

43 *Ibid*, pp 907C–08C.

44 *Ibid*, pp 906A–08D.

intention is proved in some other way such contributions are essential to establish the trust.

The quantification of the right[45]

Once it has been established that the parties had a common intention that both should have a beneficial interest and that the claimant has acted to his detriment, the question may still remain: 'what is the extent of the claimant's beneficial interest?' This last section of Lord Diplock's speech shows that here again the direct and indirect contributions made by the parties to the cost of acquisition may be crucially important.

If this analysis is correct, contributions made by the claimant may be relevant for four different purposes, viz: (1) in the absence of direct evidence of intention, as evidence from which the parties' intentions can be inferred; (2) as corroboration of direct evidence of intention; (3) to show that the claimant has acted to his or her detriment in reliance on the common intention: Lord Diplock's speech does not deal directly with the nature of the detriment to be shown; (4) to quantify the extent of the beneficial interest.

I have sought to analyse Lord Diplock's speech for two reasons. First, it is clear that the necessary common intention can be proved otherwise than by reference to contributions by the claimant to the cost of acquisition. Secondly, the remarks of Lord Diplock as to the contributions made by the claimant must be read in their context.

In cases of this kind the first question must always be whether there is sufficient direct evidence of a common intention that both parties are to have a beneficial interest. Such direct evidence need have nothing to do with the contributions made to the cost of acquisition. Thus, in *Eves v Eves*,[46] the common intention was proved by the fact that the claimant was told that her name would have been on the title deeds but for her being under age.

Again, in *Midland Bank plc v Dobson*[47] this court held that the trial judge was entitled to find the necessary common intention from evidence which he accepted that the parties treated the house as 'our house' and had a 'principle of sharing everything'. Although, as was said in the latter case, the trial judge has to approach such direct evidence with caution, if he does accept such evidence the necessary common intention is proved. One would expect that in a number of cases the court would be able to decide on the direct evidence before it whether there was such a common intention. It is only necessary to have recourse to inferences from other circumstances (such as the way in which the parties contributed, directly or indirectly, to the cost of acquisition) in cases such as *Gissing v Gissing*[48] and *Burns v Burns*[49] where there is no direct evidence of intention.

45 [1971] AC 886, pp 908D–09.

46 [1975] 1 WLR 1338.

47 (1985) unreported, 12 July, Court of Appeal (Civil Division) Transcript No 381 of 1985.

48 [1971] AC 886.

49 [1984] Ch 317.

Applying those principles to the present case, the representation made by the defendant to the plaintiff that the house would have been in the joint names but for the plaintiff's matrimonial disputes is clear direct evidence of a common intention that she was to have an interest in the house: *Eves v Eves*.[50] Such evidence was in my judgment sufficient by itself to establish the common intention: but in any event it is wholly consistent with the contributions made by the plaintiff to the joint household expenses and the fact that the surplus fire insurance moneys were put into a joint account.

But as Lord Diplock's speech in *Gissing v Gissing*[51] and the decision in *Midland Bank plc v Dobson* (unreported) make clear, mere common intention by itself is not enough: the claimant has also to prove that she has acted to her detriment in the reasonable belief by so acting she was acquiring a beneficial interest.

There is little guidance in the authorities on constructive trusts as to what is necessary to prove that the claimant so acted to her detriment. What 'link' has to be shown between the common intention and the actions relied on? Does there have to be positive evidence that the claimant did the acts in conscious reliance on the common intention? Does the court have to be satisfied that she would not have done the acts relied on but for the common intention, for example, would not the claimant have contributed to household expenses out of affection for the legal owner and as part of their joint life together even if she had no interest in the house? Do the acts relied on as a detriment have to be inherently referable to the house, for example, contribution to the purchase or physical labour on the house?

I do not think it is necessary to express any concluded view on these questions in order to decide this case. *Eves v Eves*[52] indicates that there has to be some 'link' between the common intention and the acts relied on as a detriment ... In my judgment where the claimant has made payments which, whether directly or indirectly, have been used to discharge the mortgage instalments, this is a sufficient link between the detriment suffered by the claimant and the common intention. The court can infer that she would not have made such payments were it not for her belief that she had an interest in the house. On this ground therefore I find that the plaintiff has acted to her detriment in reliance on the common intention that she had a beneficial interest in the house and accordingly that she has established such beneficial interest.

I suggest that, in other cases of this kind, useful guidance may in the future be obtained from the principles underlying the law of proprietary estoppel which in my judgment are closely akin to those laid down in *Gissing v Gissing*.[53] In both, the claimant must to the knowledge of the legal owner have acted in the belief that the claimant has or will obtain an interest in the property. In both, the claimant must have acted to his or her detriment in reliance on such belief. In both, equity acts on the conscience of the legal owner to prevent him from acting in an unconscionable manner by defeating the common intention. The

50 [1975] 1 WLR 1338.

51 [1971] AC 886, p 905D.

52 [1975] 1 WLR 1338.

53 [1971] AC 886.

two principles have been developed separately without cross-fertilisation between them: but they rest on the same foundation and have on all other matters reached the same conclusions.

In many cases of the present sort, it is impossible to say whether or not the claimant would have done the acts relied on as a detriment even if she thought she had no interest in the house. Setting up house together, having a baby, making payments to general housekeeping expenses (not strictly necessary to enable the mortgage to be paid) may all be referable to the mutual love and affection of the parties and not specifically referable to the claimant's belief that she has an interest in the house. As at present advised, once it has been shown that there was a common intention that the claimant should have an interest in the house, any act done by her to her detriment relating to the joint lives of the parties is, in my judgment, sufficient detriment to qualify. The acts do not have to be inherently referable to the house: see *Jones (AE) v Jones (FW)*[54] and *Pascoe v Turner*.[55] The holding out to the claimant that she had a beneficial interest in the house is an act of such a nature as to be part of the inducement to her to do the acts relied on. Accordingly, in the absence of evidence to the contrary, the right inference is that the claimant acted in reliance on such holding out and the burden lies on the legal owner to show that she did not do so: see *Greasley v Cooke*.[56]

What then is the extent of the plaintiff's interest? It is clear from *Gissing v Gissing*[57] that, once the common intention and the actions to the claimant's detriment have been proved from direct or other evidence, in fixing the quantum of the claimant's beneficial interest the court can take into account indirect contributions by the plaintiff such as the plaintiff's contributions to joint household expenses: see *Gissing v Gissing*.[58] In my judgment, the passage in Lord Diplock's speech[59] is dealing with a case where there is no evidence of the common intention other than contributions to joint expenditure: in such a case there is insufficient evidence to prove any beneficial interest and the question of the extent of that interest cannot arise.

Where, as in this case, the existence of some beneficial interest in the claimant has been shown, *prima facie* the interest of the claimant will be that which the parties intended: *Gissing v Gissing*.[60] In *Eves v Eves*[61] Brightman LJ plainly felt that a common intention that there should be a joint interest pointed to the beneficial interests being equal. However, he felt able to find a lesser beneficial interest in that case without explaining the legal basis on which he did so. With diffidence, I suggest that the law of proprietary estoppel may again provide useful guidance. If proprietary estoppel is established, the court gives effect to

54 [1977] 1 WLR 438.

55 [1979] 1 WLR 431.

56 [1980] 1 WLR 1306.

57 [1971] AC 886.

58 *Ibid*, pp 909A and D–E.

59 *Ibid*, pp 909G–10A.

60 *Ibid*, p 908G.

61 [1975] 1 WLR 1338, p 1345G.

> it by giving effect to the common intention so far as may fairly be done between the parties. For that purpose, equity is displayed at its most flexible: see *Crabb v Arun District Council*.[62] Identifiable contributions to the purchase of the house will of course be an important factor in many cases. But in other cases, contributions by way of the labour or other unquantifiable actions of the claimant will also be relevant.

In *Midland Bank v Dobson and Dobson*,[63] the Court of Appeal decided that a common intention without evidence of reliance was insufficient to create a constructive trust, and thus a beneficial interest in property. Moreover, in this case, there was no contribution by the claimant, direct or indirect, to the purchase of the property and therefore there was no trust.

Would the claimant's conduct other than by way of a financial contribution, be capable of establishing a common intention between the claimant and the legal owner? The Court of Appeal in *Grant v Edwards* was not opposed to treating such conduct as capable of giving rise to a common intention. The court reviewed the earlier case of *Eves v Eves* and treated it as an illustration of the constructive trust (proprietary estoppel) principle.

Eves v Eves [1975] 1 WLR 1338, CA

In this case, an unmarried couple bought a house which was conveyed in the name of the man (defendant) instead of both parties on the ground that the plaintiff (as suggested by the defendant) was under 21. She bore him two children and did a lot of heavy work in the house and garden before he left her for another woman. The plaintiff applied to ascertain her share of the house. The court decided in her favour and awarded her a quarter share of the house on the ground that the property was acquired and maintained by both parties for their joint benefit.

> **Lord Denning MR:** Although Janet did not make any financial contribution, it seems to me that this property was acquired and maintained by both by their joint efforts with the intention that it should be used for their joint benefit until they were married and thereafter as long as the marriage continued. At any rate, Stuart Eves cannot be heard to say the contrary. He told her that it was to be their home for them and their children. He gained her confidence by telling her that he intended to put it in their joint names (just as married couples often do) but that it was not possible until she was 21. The judge described this as a 'trick' and said that it 'did not do him much credit as a man of honour'. The man never intended to put it in joint names but always determined to have it in his own name. It seems to me that he should be judged by what he told her – by what he led her to believe – and not by his own intent which he kept to himself. Lord Diplock made this clear in *Gissing v Gissing*.[64]

62 [1976] Ch 179.

63 [1985] NLJ 751.

64 [1971] AC 886, p 906.

> It seems to me that this conduct by Mr Eves amounted to a recognition by him that, in all fairness, she was entitled to a share in the house, equivalent in some way to a declaration of trust; not for a particular share, but for such share as was fair in view of all she had done and was doing for him and the children and would thereafter do. By so doing he gained her confidence. She trusted him. She did not make any financial contribution but she contributed in many other ways. She did much work in the house and garden. She looked after him and cared for the children. It is clear that her contribution was such that if she had been a wife she would have had a good claim to have a share in it on a divorce: see *Wachtel v Wachtel*.[65]
>
> In view of his conduct, it would, I think, be most inequitable for him to deny her any share in the house. The law will impute or impose a constructive trust by which he was to hold it in trust for them both. But what would be the shares? I think one half would be too much. I suggest it should be one quarter of the equity. But seeing that she is now remarried, this share would I hope be regarded by her as more in the nature of a provision for the children than for her.

In *Grant v Edwards*, the Court of Appeal interpreted *Eves v Eves* as an illustration of conduct manifesting a common intention between the parties which was relied on by the claimant. Nourse LJ in *Grant v Edwards* made the following observations concerning *Eves v Eves*:

> **Nourse LJ:** First, as Brightman J himself observed, if the work had not been done the common intention would not have been enough. Secondly, if the common intention had not been orally made plain, the work would not have been conduct from which it could be inferred. That, I think, is the effect of the actual decision in *Pettitt v Pettitt*.[66] Thirdly, and on the other hand, the work was conduct which amounted to an acting upon the common intention by the woman. It seems therefore, on the authorities as they stand, that a distinction is to be made between conduct from which the common intention can be inferred on the one hand and conduct which amounts to an acting upon it on the other. There remains this difficult question: what is the quality of conduct required for the latter purpose? The difficulty is caused, I think because although the common intention has been made plain, everything else remains a matter of inference. Let me illustrate it in this way. It would be possible to take the view that the mere moving into the house by the woman amounted to an acting upon the common intention. But that was evidently not the view of the majority in *Eves v Eves*.[67] And the reason for that may be that, in the absence of evidence, the law is not so cynical as to infer that a woman will only go to live with a man to whom she is not married if she understands that she is to have an interest in their home. So what sort of conduct is required? In my judgment it must be conduct on which the woman could not reasonably have been expected to embark unless she was to have an interest in the house. If she was

65 [1973] Fam 72, pp 92–94.

66 [1970] AC 777.

67 [1975] 1 WLR 1338.

> not to have such an interest, she could reasonably be expected to go and live with her lover, but not, for example, to wield a 14 lb sledge hammer in the front garden. In adopting the latter kind of conduct she is seen to act to her detriment on the faith of the common intention.

In *Lloyds Bank plc v Rosset* [1990] 1 All ER 111, the House of Lords (Lords Bridge of Harwich, Griffith, Ackner, Oliver of Aylmerton and Jauncey of Tullichettle) endorsed the approach of the Court of Appeal in *Grant v Edwards*, and laid down two types of evidence which are capable of establishing a beneficial interest. These are:

(1) an agreement, arrangement or understanding reached between the parties concerning the beneficial interest in the property (*Eves v Eves* and *Grant v Edwards* illustrate this proposition); and

(2) reliance on a common intention based on the conduct of the parties which gives rise to a constructive trust, such as direct contributions (including mortgage payments) to the acquisition of the home.

In this case, a semi-derelict farmhouse was conveyed in the name of the husband but the wife spent a great deal of time in the house supervising the work done by builders. She also did some decorating to the house. Unknown to the wife, her husband had taken out an overdraft with the bank. The couple later separated but the wife remained in the house. The husband was unable to repay the overdraft with the result that the bank started proceedings for the sale of the property. The wife resisted the claim on the ground that she was entitled to a beneficial interest in the house under a constructive trust. The trial judge and the Court of Appeal decided that the husband held the property as constructive trustee for wife and himself. The plaintiff appealed.

The House of Lords held in favour of the bank on the ground that the wife had no beneficial interest in the property. There was no understanding between the parties that the property was to be shared beneficially, coupled with detrimental action by the claimant, nor had there been direct contributions to the purchase price. In any event, the court decided that the monetary value of the wife's work was trifling compared with the cost of acquiring the house.

> **Lord Bridge of Harwich** (after considering the facts relied on by the learned judge): I pause to observe that neither a common intention by spouses that a house is to be renovated as a 'joint venture' nor a common intention that the house is to be shared by parents and children as the family home throws any light on their intentions with respect to the beneficial ownership of the property.
>
> It is clear ... that the judge based his inference of a common intention that Mrs Rosset should have a beneficial interest in the property under a constructive trust essentially on what Mrs Rosset did in and about assisting in the renovation of the property between the beginning of November 1982 and the date of completion on 17 December 1982. Yet, by itself, this activity, it seems to

me, could not possibly justify any such inference. It was common ground that Mrs Rosset was extremely anxious that the new matrimonial home should be ready for occupation before Christmas if possible. In these circumstances it would seem the most natural thing in the world for any wife, in the absence of her husband abroad, to spend all the time she could spare and to employ any skills she might have, such as the ability to decorate a room, in doing all she could to accelerate progress of the work quite irrespective of any expectation she might have of enjoying a beneficial interest in the property. The judge's view that some of this work was work 'upon which she could not reasonably have been expected to embark unless she was to have an interest in the house' seems to me, with respect, quite untenable. The impression that the judge may have thought that the share of the equity to which he held Mrs Rosset to be entitled had been 'earned' by her work in connection with the renovation is emphasised by his reference in the concluding sentence of his judgment to the extent to which her 'qualifying contribution' reduced the cost of the renovation.

On any view the monetary value of Mrs Rosset's work expressed as a contribution to a property acquired at a cost exceeding £70,000 must have been so trifling as to be almost *de minimis*. I should myself have had considerable doubt whether Mrs Rosset's contribution to the work of renovation was sufficient to support a claim to a constructive trust in the absence of writing to satisfy the requirements of s 53(1) of the Law of Property Act 1925 even if her husband's intention to make a gift to her of half or any other share in the equity of the property had been clearly established or if he had clearly represented to her that that was what he intended. But here the conversations with her husband on which Mrs Rosset relied, all of which took place before November 1982, were incapable of lending support to the conclusion of a constructive trust in the light of the judge's finding that by that date there had been no decision that she was to have any interest in the property. The finding that the discussions 'did not exclude the possibility' that she should have an interest does not seem to me to add anything of significance.

These considerations lead me to the conclusion that the judge's finding that Mr Rosset held the property as constructive trustee for himself and his wife cannot be supported and it is on this short ground that I would allow the appeal. In the course of the argument your Lordships had the benefit of elaborate submissions as to the test to be applied to determine the circumstances in which the sole legal proprietor of a dwelling house can properly be held to have become a constructive trustee of a share in the beneficial interest in the house for the benefit of the partner with whom he or she has co-habited in the house as their shared home.

The first and fundamental question which must always be resolved is whether, independently of any inference to be drawn from the conduct of the parties in the course of sharing the house as their home and managing their joint affairs, there has at any time prior to acquisition, or exceptionally at some later date, been any agreement, arrangement or understanding reached between them that the property is to be shared beneficially. The finding of an agreement or arrangement to share in this sense can only, I think, be based on evidence of express discussions between the partners, however imperfectly remembered and however imprecise their terms may have been. Once a finding to this effect is made it will only be necessary for the partner asserting a claim to a beneficial interest against the partner entitled to the legal estate to show that he or she has acted to his or her detriment or significantly altered his or her position in reliance on the agreement in order to give rise to a constructive trust or a proprietary estoppel.

In sharp contrast with this situation is the very different one where there is no evidence to support a finding of an agreement or arrangement to share, however reasonable it might have been for the parties to reach such an arrangement if they had applied their minds to the question, and where the court must rely entirely on the conduct of the parties both as the basis from which to infer a common intention to share the property beneficially and as the conduct relied on to give rise to a constructive trust. In this situation direct contributions to the purchase price by the partner who is not the legal owner, whether initially or by payment of mortgage instalments, will readily justify the inference necessary to the creation of a constructive trust. But, as I read the authorities, it is at least extremely doubtful whether anything less will do.

The leading cases in your Lordships' House are *Pettitt v Pettitt*[68] and *Gissing v Gissing*.[69] Both demonstrate situations in the second category to which I have referred and their Lordships discuss at great length the difficulties to which these situations give rise. The effect of these two decisions is very helpfully analysed in the judgment of Lord MacDermott LCJ in *McFarlane v McFarlane*.[70]

Outstanding examples on the other hand of cases giving rise to situations in the first category are *Eves v Eves*[71] and *Grant v Edwards*.[72] In both these cases, where the parties who had co-habited were unmarried, the female partner had been clearly led by the male partner to believe, when they set up home together, that the property would belong to them jointly. In *Eves v Eves* the male partner had told the female partner that the only reason why the property was to be acquired in his name alone was because she was under 21 and that, but for her age, he would have had the house put into their joint names. He admitted in evidence that this was simply an 'excuse.' Similarly in *Grant v Edwards* the female partner was told by the male partner that the only reason for not acquiring the property in joint names was because she was involved in divorce proceedings and that, if the property were acquired jointly, this might operate to her prejudice in those proceedings. As Nourse LJ put it, p 649:

> Just as in *Eves v Eves*, these facts appear to me to raise a clear inference that there was an understanding between the plaintiff and the defendant, or a common intention, that the plaintiff was to have some sort of proprietary interest in the house; otherwise no excuse for not putting her name on to the title would have been needed.

68 [1970] AC 777.

69 [1971] AC 886.

70 [1972] NI 59.

71 [1975] 1 WLR 1338.

72 [1986] Ch 638.

The subsequent conduct of the female partner in each of these cases, which the court rightly held sufficient to give rise to a constructive trust or proprietary estoppel supporting her claim to an interest in the property, fell far short of such conduct as would by itself have supported the claim in the absence of an express representation by the male partner that she was to have such an interest. It is significant to note that the share to which the female partners in *Eves v Eves* and *Grant v Edwards* were held entitled were one quarter and one half respectively. In no sense could these shares have been regarded as proportionate to what the judge in the instant case described as a 'qualifying contribution' in terms of the indirect contributions to the acquisition or enhancement of the value of the houses made by the female partners.

I cannot help thinking that the judge in the instant case would not have fallen into error if he had kept clearly in mind the distinction between the effect of evidence on the one hand which was capable of establishing an express agreement or an express representation that Mrs Rosset was to have an interest in the property and evidence on the other hand of conduct alone as a basis for an inference of the necessary common intention.

Difficulties concerning the *Rosset* analysis

Lord Bridge in *Lloyds Bank v Rosset*, in issuing guidelines as to the relevance of evidence necessary to create proprietary interests in family assets, classified the evidence into two categories:

(a) Evidence of an agreement based on express discussion between the parties:

Lord Bridge: The claimant is required to show that 'there has at any time prior to the acquisition, or exceptionally at some later date, been an agreement, arrangement or understanding between the parties that the property is to be shared beneficially *based on evidence of express discussion between the parties*. The claimant will then be required to establish that he or she acted to his or her detriment in reliance on the agreement in order to give rise to a *constructive trust or proprietary estoppel*;

(b) Evidence of the conduct of the parties based on direct contributions to the purchase of the home:

Lord Bridge: Where there is no evidence to support a finding of an agreement to share and the court must rely entirely on the conduct of the parties in order to infer a common intention to share the property beneficially and as the conduct relied on to give rise to a constructive trust. In this situation *direct contributions* to the purchase price will readily justify the inference necessary to the creation of a *constructive trust*. But it is extremely *doubtful whether anything less will do*.

(1) Express discussion between the parties:

Lord Bridge's first category of evidence suggests that the common intention/agreement may only be established by evidence of express discussion between the parties. This appears to be an unwarranted restriction on the adduction of evidence of an agreement as to a beneficial interest. An agreement or understanding is capable of being inferred by conduct. For the application of this rule, see *Hammond v Mitchell* and *Springette v Defoe* (below, p 401). Glover and Todd, in 'Inferring share of interest in home: *Midland Bank v Cooke*' [1995] 4 Web JCLI, take the view that constructive trusts and proprietary estoppels are separate and alternative ways of acquiring beneficial interests. The explanation of the requirement for express discussion is akin to an express declaration of trust. To be effective, an express declaration of trust must be immediate and attach to an identifiable amount of property. Statements as to future intention are insufficient to amount to declarations of trust, but may be sufficient to found an estoppel. The writers take the view that 'estoppels differ from trusts in that they do not necessarily create full beneficial interests, the position of third parties is different, A's intention can be as to future and indeed, the property need not even be identified'.

(2) Constructive trust/proprietary estoppel:

Lord Bridge equates the constructive trust (first category evidence) with proprietary estoppel. Although proprietary estoppel is to some extent related to a constructive trust, an estoppel operates *inter partes*. Constructive trusts, on the other hand, are capable of enforcement against third parties.

Professor Hayton takes the view that the distinction between common intention constructive trusts and proprietary estoppel is illusory. See 'Equitable rights of co-habitees' [1990] Conv 370.

(3) Constructive/resulting trusts:

The second category of evidence appears to be consistent with a resulting trust, in that the trust is based on direct contributions to the acquisition of the property. However, Lord Bridge equates this trust with a constructive trust. See *Drake v Whipp* (below, p 408).

(4) Indirect financial contributions?

Lord Bridge makes no mention of indirect financial contributions. It could not have been intended from this omission to treat such contributions as irrelevant under the second category of evidence. Indirect contributions to the acquisition of the home were acknowledged in *Gissing v Gissing* and *Burns v Burns*. Such contributions ought to be relevant in determining beneficial interests within both categories of evidence.

(5) It was intended by Lord Bridge that the value of the claimant's interest is to be determined by reference to the two categories of evidence as laid down in *Rosset*. But the courts have adopted a different approach, namely, once an interest has been established under at least one of the categories of evidence, the court has a general discretion to do what it considers just and fair in the circumstances: see *Midland Bank v Cooke*.

The *Rosset* principles were analysed and applied in *Hammond v Mitchell*. The quality of the evidence of an understanding or agreement regarding beneficial entitlement varies significantly with each case.

Hammond v Mitchell [1991] 1 WLR 1127, HC

The parties, Mr Hammond (H) and Miss Mitchell (M) lived together from 1977 to 1988. After the birth of the first of their two children in 1979, the couple moved into a bungalow in Essex, which was bought in H's name with the assistance of a mortgage. H assured M that as he was going through a divorce it would be in their best interests if the house was put in his name. He then told her: 'Don't worry about the future because when we are married it will be half yours anyway ...' In 1980, surrounding land was bought and the bungalow was extended. M assisted H in his business ventures. H purchased a house in Spain and for a short while they lived there but never gave up possession of the Essex house. In 1988, the relationship was terminated and M brought an action claiming a beneficial interest in the properties and other assets.

The court held that in relation to the bungalow there was evidence of an express understanding that M should have a beneficial interest, quantified as one half. But in relation to the Spanish house there was no evidence to justify an intention to share the beneficial interest.

> **Waite J:** Mr Hammond says that virtually all of it is his; Miss Mitchell claims that a substantial part at least of it is hers. Had they been married, the issue of ownership would scarcely have been relevant, because the law these days when dealing with the financial consequences of divorce adopts a forward-looking perspective in which questions of ownership yield to the higher demands of relating the means of both to the needs of each, the first consideration given to the welfare of children. Since this couple did not marry, none of that flexibility is available to them, except a limited power to direct capital provision for their children. In general, their financial rights have to be worked out according to their strict entitlements in equity, a process which is anything but forward-looking and involves, on the contrary, a painfully detailed retrospect.
>
> The template for that analysis has recently been restated by the House of Lords and the Court of Appeal in *Lloyds Bank plc v Rosset*[73] and *Grant v Edwards*.[74] The court first has to ask itself whether there have at any time prior to acquisition of the disputed property, or exceptionally at some later date, been discussions between the parties leading to any agreement, arrangement or understanding reached between them that the property is to be shared beneficially. Any further investigation carried out by the court will vary in depth according to whether the answer to that initial inquiry is 'Yes' or 'No.' If there have been discussions of that kind and the answer is therefore 'Yes', the court then proceeds to examine the subsequent course of dealing between the parties for evidence of conduct detrimental to the party without legal title referable to a reliance upon the arrangement in question. If there have been no

73 [1991] 1 AC 107.

74 [1986] Ch 638.

such discussions and the answer to that initial inquiry is therefore 'No', the investigation of subsequent events has to take the form of an inferential analysis involving a scrutiny of all events potentially capable of throwing evidential light on the question whether, in the absence of express discussion, a presumed intention can be spelt out of the parties' past course of dealing.

... the law requires me in determining beneficial title to apply the principles enunciated in *Lloyds Bank plc v Rosset*[75] and *Grant v Edwards*.[76] It will involve asking this question first: is there any, and if so which, property which has been the subject of some agreement, arrangement or understanding reached between the parties on the basis of express discussion to the effect that such property is to be shared beneficially; and (if there is) has Miss Mitchell shown herself to have acted to her detriment or significantly altered her position in reliance on the agreement so as to give rise to a constructive trust or proprietary estoppel? The answer to that question should, in my judgment, in both its parts be 'Yes'.

In relation to the bungalow there was express discussion which, although not directed with any precision as to proprietary interests, was sufficient to amount to an understanding at least that the bungalow was to be shared beneficially. It will, of course, be a question of fact and degree in every case where A and B acquire Blackacre in A's sole name with a mutual expectation of a shared beneficial interest, and thereafter enlarge it by extension of existing premises or the purchase in A's sole name of an adjoining property Whiteacre, whether B's beneficial interest was intended to extend to the enlarged hereditament. That can only be determined on a review of the whole course of dealing between the parties. I am satisfied in the present case that the parties intended the bungalow, as it became successively enlarged by addition to its own original structure and by the purchase of the adjoining parcels of land and barns, to be subject to the same understanding as governed the original property. Miss Mitchell, by her participation wholeheartedly in what may loosely be called the commercial activities based on the bungalow, not only acted consistently with that view of the situation but also acted to her detriment in that she gave her full support on two occasions to speculative ventures which, had they turned out unfavourably, might have involved the entire bungalow property being sold up to repay the bank an indebtedness to which the house and land were all committed up to the hilt.

There remains the question in relation to the bungalow of what the proportion of Miss Mitchell's beneficial interest should be held to be. This is not an area where the maxim that 'equality is equity' falls to be applied unthinkingly. That is plain from the lesser proportions awarded in both *Grant v Edwards* and in *Eves v Eves*. Nevertheless, when account is taken of the full circumstances of this unusual case, and when Miss Mitchell's contribution as mother/helper/ unpaid assistant and at times financial supporter to the family prosperity generated by Mr Hammond's dealing activities is judged for its proper effect, it

75 [1991] 1 AC 107.

76 [1975] 1 WLR 1338.

> seems right to me that her beneficial interest in the bungalow should be held to be one half.
>
> The next question, arising under the *Lloyds Bank plc v Rosset* formula, is whether there is any property in regard to which an intention to share a beneficial ownership should be imputed to the parties in the absence of any express discussion leading to an agreement or understanding to that effect. Miss Mitchell asserts that there is such a property, namely, the Spanish house. She acknowledges that there was no previous discussion remotely touching upon the terms of its ownership, but her counsel, Miss Gill, claims that when the parties' whole course of dealing is examined (even according to the more rigorous standards which apply when intention has to be inferred from conduct alone) the intention to constitute Mr Hammond a constructive trustee for Miss Mitchell of part of the beneficial interest in the Spanish house becomes manifest. To support that she relies on the cases (both involving married couples and neither of which was cited in *Lloyds Bank v Rosset*) of *Nixon v Nixon*,[77] and *Muetzel v Muetzel*.[78] I reject that submission. Useful at times though her activities may have been in Spain during the fulfilment of the Soriano venture, Miss Mitchell's activities generally fell a long way short of justifying any inference of intended proprietary interest.

If the parties acquire a joint interest in the asset without an express declaration of trust concerning their respective interest, the quantification of their interest is dependent on the proportion of their contributions, ie, the resulting trust solution or the second category of evidence laid down in *Rosset*.

By way of exception, this resulting trust analysis regarding the quantum of interest in the property may be adjusted only if there is evidence of a common intention to share the asset in a different proportion. In order to establish this intention, there is required to be *express discussion* between the parties as to their respective beneficial interests. An uncommunicated intention to share the beneficial interest is insufficient to alter the interest acquired by way of a resulting trust. This was the view put forward by the Court of Appeal in *Springette v Defoe*.

Springette v Defoe [1992] 2 FLR 388, CA

The parties lived as man and wife in a council house. In 1982, they made a formal offer to purchase the house for £14,445 which represented a discount of 41% because the plaintiff, Miss Springette (S), had been a council tenant for 11 years or more. They bought the house jointly with the aid of a mortgage of £12,000. By agreement, they each contributed 50% of the mortgage instalments. The balance of the purchase price was provided by S. The legal title was registered in their joint names but there was no quantification of their interests registered in in Land Registry. During 1985, the relationship between

77 [1969] 1 WLR 1676.

78 [1970] 1 WLR 188.

the parties became strained and the defendant (D) left the home. S claimed that she was entitled to a 75% share of the proceeds of sale of the house as represented by her contribution to the purchase. The learned recorder decided that the beneficial interests were shared equally despite the lack of evidence of any discussion concerning this issue. S appealed to the Court of Appeal.

Held, by the Court of Appeal, allowing the appeal: the interests of the parties were determined by reference to the contributions made. There was no evidence which had the effect of varying the interest acquired by way of a resulting trust because there was no discussion between the parties to that effect. Accordingly, the interests were shared on a 75:25 proportion.

> **Dillon LJ:** In *Walker v Hall* [1984] FLR 126, I expressed the view that it was not open to this court, in the absence of specific evidence of the parties' intentions, to hold that the property there in question belonged beneficially to the two parties in equal shares, notwithstanding their unequal contributions to the purchase price, simply because it was bought to be their family home and they intended – or possibly one should say 'hoped' – that their relationship should last for life. The effect is that, in the absence of an express declaration of the beneficial interests, the court will hold that the joint purchasers hold the property on a resulting trust for themselves in the proportions in which they contributed directly or indirectly to the purchase price, unless there is sufficient specific evidence of their common intention that they should be entitled in other proportions – for example, in equal shares notwithstanding unequal contributions – to rebut the presumption of resulting trust.
>
> There are statements in some more recent authorities which appear at first glance to be expressed more widely.
>
> Thus, in *Stokes v Anderson* [1991] 1 FLR 391, Nourse LJ, in giving the leading judgment with which Lloyd and Ralph Gibson LJJ agreed, said that ' the court must supply the common intention by reference to that which all the material circumstances have shown to be fair'. Nicholls LJ used a similar expression in *Passee v Passee* [1988] 1 FLR 263, where he said:
>
>> They intended, or are to be taken to have intended, that each would be entitled to a share to be determined ... on the basis of what would be fair, having regard to the contributions which in total each had ... made.
>
> The common intention must be founded on evidence such as would support a finding that there is an implied or constructive trust for the parties in proportions to the purchase price. The court does not as yet sit, as under a palm tree, to exercise a general discretion to do what the man in the street, on a general overview of the case, might regard as fair.
>
> But the common intention of the parties must, in my judgment, mean a shared intention communicated between them. It cannot mean an intention which each happened to have in his or her own mind but had never communicated to the other. I find some assistance in this respect in the observation of Lord Bridge of Harwich in *Lloyds Bank plc v Rosset* [1991] AC 107.
>
> [His Lordship then referred to Lord Bridge's judgment and continued:]

> It is not enough to establish a common intention which is sufficient to found an implied or constructive trust of land that each of them happened at the same time to have been thinking on the same lines in his or her uncommunicated thoughts, while neither had any knowledge of the thinking of the other.
>
> Since, therefore, it is clear in the present case that there never was any discussion between the parties about what their respective beneficial interests were to be, they cannot, in my judgment, have had ... any common intention as to the beneficial ownership of the property. I cannot, therefore, support the conclusion of the recorder. The presumption of a resulting trust is not displaced.
>
> **Steyn LJ:** Given that no actual common intention to share the property in equal beneficial shares was established, one is driven back to the equitable principle that the shares are presumed to be in proportion 'to the contributions'. If the matter is approached in this way, it seems to me right in principle that the discount of 41% should be regarded as a direct contribution by the woman to the purchase. That is how Bush J, a most experienced judge, approached the matter in *Marsh v Von Sternberg* [1986] 1 FLR 526. And that is how I consider this court should approach the matter.

In contrast to this decision, the Court of Appeal in *McHardy v Warren* decided that, once the claimant had established an interest in the property, the court will take into account all relevant factors in determining the interest of the parties. The conduct of the parties, irrespective of whether discussions took place or not, may be considered as sufficient to create a common understanding of the respective share of each party. Contributions to the purchase price are factors which are taken into account, but are not decisive as to the quantum of interest acquired by the parties.

McHardy v Warren [1994] 2 FLR 338, CA

The Warren's (W's) purchased their first matrimonial home by a contribution partly financed by Mr W's parents. His parents paid the deposit (£650) on the house as a wedding gift. The house was registered in Mr W's sole name. Two subsequent homes successively purchased by the parties out of the net proceeds of sale of the former homes were likewise put in Mr W's sole name. Mr W then procured a charge on his current home to secure his indebtedness to the plaintiffs, trade creditors. In proceedings to enforce the charge against the Warren's, the plaintiffs claimed that Mrs W was entitled, at best, to an interest equivalent to 8.97% of the value of the house, representing the proportion that 50% of the initial deposit of £650 (the wedding gift) related to the total purchase price of the first home. The learned judge rejected the claim. The Court of Appeal upheld the decision of the trial judge and decided that Mrs W was entitled to an equal share with Mr W, because this represented the intentions of the parties as reflected by their conduct.

> **Dillon LJ:** To my mind it is the irresistible conclusion that where a parent pays the deposit, either directly to the solicitors or to the bride and groom – it matters not which – on the purchase of their first matrimonial home, it is the intention of all three of them that the bride and groom should have *equal interests in the matrimonial home,* not interests measured by reference to the percentage half the deposit there is to the full price, and certainly not an intention that the wife should have no interest at all because the property was put into the sole name of the husband.

Likewise, in *Midland Bank v Cooke*, the Court of Appeal decided that if an intention to share an interest in the matrimonial home has been established by the plaintiff by reference to direct contributions (second category of evidence as established in *Rosset*), the court has the power to quantify the interests of the parties by reference to the express and implied intentions of the parties. The conduct of the parties, which is relevant to ownership of the property may be given effect, even though there may have been no discussion as to the beneficial interests therein.

Midland Bank plc v Cooke and Another [1995] 4 All ER 562, CA

H and W married in 1971 and moved into a house which was purchased for £8,500 and conveyed into H's sole name. The purchase was financed by a mortgage of £6,450. The balance was provided from H's savings and a wedding gift of £1,100 from his parents. In 1978, the mortgage was replaced by a general mortgage in favour of the Midland Bank in order to secure H's business overdraft. In 1979, W signed a form agreeing to postpone any present or future right as against the bank. The property was subsequently transferred into the joint names of H and W. There was no discussion between the parties as to their beneficial interests. In 1987, the bank commenced proceedings against H and W for arrears of payments and possession of the property. W defended on the ground that her signature on the form was procured by H's undue influence to the knowledge of the bank and counterclaimed for a declaration that she was entitled to a 50% share in the house. The judge held that the form was signed under undue influence and that W was entitled to a beneficial interest of 6.74% in the property, equivalent to a half share of the wedding gift of £550 from H's parents, which was contributed to the purchase price of £8,500. W appealed claiming that she was entitled to 50% of the value of the house based on her conduct, the bank cross-appealed on the issue of undue influence.

Held, by the Court of Appeal, allowing W's appeal and dismissing the bank's cross-appeal: applying the principles in *Pettitt v Pettitt, Gissing v Gissing* and *Grant v Edwards,* since W had established an interest in the house through direct contributions, the court was entitled to look at all the circumstances in order to give effect to the true intentions of the parties. Accordingly, the court may attribute to the parties an interest in the property which was different from the resulting trust contributions to the purchase price.

Waite LJ (his Lordship considered the divergent approaches of the Court of Appeal to this question in *Springette v Defoe* and *McHardy v Warren* and observed): I confess that I find the differences of approach in those two cases mystifying. In the one, a strict resulting trust geared to mathematical calculation of the proportion of the purchase price provided by cash contribution is treated as virtually immutable in the absence of express agreement: in the other, a displacement of the cash-related trust by inferred agreement is not only permitted but treated as obligatory. Guidance out of this difficulty is to be found, fortunately, in the passage in the speech of Lord Diplock in *Gissing v Gissing* [1971] AC 886, pp 908–09, where he is dealing with the approach to be adopted by the court when evaluating the proportionate shares of the parties, once it had been established through the direct contributions of the party without legal title, that *some* beneficial interest was intended for both.

[His Lordship referred to Lord Diplock's speech and continued:]

The decision of this court in *Grant v Edwards* [1986] Ch 638 also affords helpful guidance. The context was different, in that the court was there dealing with a legal owner who had made representations to the occupier on which the latter has relied to her detriment so as to introduce equities in the nature of estoppel. Once a beneficial interest had been established by that route, however, the court then proceeded ... to fix the proportions of the beneficial interests on general grounds which were regarded as applying in all cases.

[His Lordship considered the judgments of Nourse LJ and Browne-Wilkinson VC in *Grant v Edwards* and continued:]

The general principle to be derived from *Gissing v Gissing* and *Grant v Edwards* can, in my judgment, be summarised in this way. When the court is proceeding, in cases like the present, where the partner without legal title has successfully asserted an equitable interest through direct contribution, to determine (in the absence of express evidence of intention) what proportions the parties must be assumed to have intended for their beneficial ownership, the duty of the judge is to undertake a survey of the whole course of dealing between the parties relevant to their ownership and occupation of the property and their sharing of its burdens and advantages. That scrutiny will not confine itself to the limited range of acts of direct contribution of the sort that are needed to found a beneficial interest in the first place. It will take into consideration all conduct which throws light on the question what shares were intended. Only if that search proves inconclusive does the court fall back on the maxim 'equality is equity'.

The court is not bound to deal with the matter on the strict basis of the trust resulting from the cash contribution to the purchase price, and is free to attribute to the parties an intention to share the beneficial interest in some different proportions.

Equity has traditionally been a system which matches established principle to the demands of social change. The mass diffusion of home ownership has been one of the most striking social changes of our own time. When people, especially young people, agree to share their lives in joint homes they do so on a basis of mutual trust and in the expectation that their relationship will

> endure. For a couple embarking on a serious relationship, discussion of the terms to apply at parting is almost a contradiction of the shared hopes that have brought them together. There will inevitably be numerous couples, married or unmarried, who have no discussion about ownership and who, perhaps advisedly, make no agreement about it. It would be anomalous, against that background, to create a range of home buyers who were beyond the pale of equity's assistance in formulating a fair presumed basis for the sharing of beneficial title, simply because they had been honest enough to admit that they never gave ownership a thought or reached any agreement about it.
>
> [After referring to the judgments of Dillon and Steyn LJJ in *Springette v Defoe*, his Lordship distinguished that authority, thus:]
>
> ... they are observations which need to be read in the context of the decision relating to the part-pooling of resources by a middle aged couple already established in life, whose house purchasing arrangements were clearly regarded by the court as having the same formality as if they had been the subject of a joint venture or commercial partnership. I cannot, for my part, believe that it was intended in that case to lay down a principle, applicable to all instances, that absence of express agreement precludes inference of presumed agreement. This impression is confirmed by the subsequent participation of Dillon LJ in the decision in the *McHardy* case.
>
> I would therefore hold that positive evidence that the parties neither discussed nor intended any agreement as to the proportions of their beneficial interest does not preclude the court, on general equitable principles, from inferring one.

In *Drake v Whipp* (see below, p 408), Peter Gibson LJ classified the trusts involved in this context into two categories, resulting and constructive trusts. A resulting trust is created by reference to the contributions made by the parties towards the acquisition of the home. The quantum of the beneficial interest is measured by reference to these contributions. The constructive trust, on the other hand, arises by reference to the conduct of the parties. In particular, whether evidence exists of a common understanding between the parties to share the beneficial interest and the claimant relies on such agreement to his or her detriment. The court decided that it is entitled to adopt a 'broad brush' approach in determining the parties' respective shares under the constructive trust. It is entitled to look at the parties' entire course of conduct in evaluating their respective shares. This may involve direct and indirect contributions in money or money's worth and any other evidence of intention of the parties. Accordingly, in the absence of evidence that the claimant intended his or her share to be limited by contributions (resulting trust), the court is entitled to consider the parties' conduct (constructive trust).

Drake v Whipp [1996] 1 FLR 826, CA

Mrs Drake and Mr Whipp purchased a barn for conversion into a dwelling house. Mrs Drake provided 40% of the total purchase price and Mr Whipp provided the remainder. Both parties contributed to the conversion work in labour and financially (although Mr Whipp provided the bulk of the financial resources to effect the conversion). Mrs Drake contributed to the costs of running the house. Mr Whipp formed a new relationship and Mrs Drake brought an action for a declaration of her share in the matrimonial home. The judge decided that Mrs Drake's share stood at 19.4% of the value of the house by way of a resulting trust. This was based on her contributions to the initial purchase and conversion costs.

Held, allowing the appeal, and awarding Mrs Drake a one third share in the property by way of the constructive trust:

> **Peter Gibson LJ:** A potent source of confusion, to my mind, has been suggestions that it matters not whether the terminology used is that of the constructive trust, to which the intention, actual or imputed, of the parties is crucial, or that of the resulting trust, which operates as a presumed intention of the contributing party in the absence of rebutting evidence of actual intention. I, therefore, like Waite LJ in *Midland Bank v Cooke and Another* [1995] 2 FLR 915, p 916, welcome the announcement earlier this year that the Law Commission is to examine the property rights of home sharers (Item 8, Sixth Programme of Law Reform, Law Com No 234).
>
> In the present case the judge has found what was the common intention of the parties as to their beneficial shares, but the only direct evidence in support of that finding was Mr Whipp's evidence as to his own intention. The judge appears to have imputed the like intention to Mrs Drake although there is nothing in her evidence to support it. Further, the judge refused to take into account the contributions of the parties by way of their labour, being unquantified in monetary terms, and similarly Mrs Drake's other contributions to the household were ignored. No doubt this was because he was not invited to consider the matter on the basis of a constructive trust.
>
> In my judgment, the judge's finding on common intention cannot stand in the absence of any evidence that Mrs Drake intended her share to be limited to her direct contributions to the acquisition and conversion costs. I would approach the matter more broadly, looking at the parties' entire course of conduct together. I would take into account not only those direct contributions, but also the fact that Mr Whipp and Mrs Drake together purchased the property with the intention that it should be their home, that they both contributed their labour in 70:30% proportions, that they had a joint account out of which the costs of conversion were met, but that that account was largely fed by his earnings, and that she paid for the food and some other household expenses and took care of the housekeeping for them both. I note that, whilst it was open to Mrs Drake to argue at the trial for a constructive trust and for a 50% share, she opted to rely solely on a resulting trust and a 40.1% share. In all the circumstances I would hold that her fair share should be one third.

Martin Dixon, in 'A case too far' [1997] Conv 66, takes the view that the approach of Waite LJ in *Midland Bank v Cooke* allows quantification on the basis of a presumed, fictitious intention. The parties claiming an interest in the matrimonial home through payments may trigger an interest larger than the actual payments. This is justifiable on the basis that 'the payments are merely evidence of some real common intention which requires the abandonment of the strict resulting trust option'. In addition, the pronouncement by Waite LJ that the parties need not have actually agreed on the extent of the enlarged share, suggests that the court may be tempted to manufacture an agreement as to the quantum of the interest in the home. Indeed, Dixon observes that the court may:

> ... find such an agreement (a 'phantom interest consensus') not only when there is no evidence of the parties' intentions, but even where there is positive evidence that they did not agree.

Moreover, the statutory discretion created by s 37 of the Matrimonial Proceedings and Property Act 1970 could have been used by the claimant to acquire a sizeable share in the property 'without any violence to the principles of resulting and constructive trusts'.

Alison Dunn, in 'Whipping up resulting and constructive trusts' [1997] Conv 467, supports the view adopted by Peter Gibson in *Drake v Whipp*. The distinction between constructive and resulting trusts remains crucial when determining beneficial interests. Where the courts cannot detect a common intention as to beneficial ownership relied on by the claimant to his or her detriment (sufficient to found a constructive trust), 'a resulting trust may be inferred from financial contribution towards the acquisition of the property. But the resulting trust will only apply where there is no finding of a common intention. The two types of trusts therefore involve the judge in examining different aspects of evidence. Further, under the constructive trust, the courts have a discretion to ascertain the extent of the beneficial share of the claimant. The resulting trust, on the other hand, is more formulaic, and the share of the claimant will be in direct proportion to the amount contributed to the acquisition of the property.

In the case of married couples, the same principles as outlined above apply in order to ascertain the interests of the parties in family assets. In addition, under ss 23–25 of the Matrimonial Causes Act 1973 the court is given wide discretionary powers to declare or vary the interests of spouses in family assets on a divorce, decree of nullity or judicial separation. An analysis of these provisions is beyond the scope of this book.

Improvements under s 37 of the Matrimonial Proceedings and Property Act 1970

Under this section, spouses (but not unmarried couples) who contribute in a substantial way in money or money's worth to the improvement of real or personal property in which either or both of them have a beneficial interest, may enjoy a share or an enlarged share in the asset. The court decides whether a contribution is substantial or not by having regard to all the circumstances of the case.

Section 37 provides:

> It is hereby declared that where a husband or wife contributes in money or money's worth to the improvement of real or personal property in which or in the proceeds of sale of which either or both of them has or have a beneficial interest, the husband or wife so contributing shall, if the contribution is of a substantial nature and subject to any agreement between them to the contrary express or implied, be treated as having then acquired by virtue of his or her contribution a share or enlarged share, as the case may be, in that beneficial interest of such an extent as may have been then agreed or, in default of such agreement, as may seem in all the circumstances just to any court before which the question of the existence or extent of the beneficial interest of the husband or wife arises (whether in proceedings between them or in any other proceedings).

DATE OF VALUATION

Having ascertained that the claimant has an interest in the house, the value of that interest is ascertained at the time the property is sold. Accordingly, any increases or decreases in the value of the property are taken into consideration. If a party remains in occupation paying the mortgage, rates and other outgoings, he or she is credited with these expenses. Conversely, the party in occupation is debited with occupation rent for using the premises partly owned by the other. The earlier date of separation, as was laid down in *Hall v Hall*[79] (which may trigger off or prompt a valuation), has been disapproved.

Gordon v Douce [1983] 1 WLR 563, CA

In this case, the plaintiff (female) and defendant (male) co-habited with each other between 1963 and 1980 and had two children. In 1977, a house was bought and conveyed in the sole name of the defendant. In 1980, the defendant left the home but the plaintiff continued to occupy the premises with the children. The defendant conceded that the house should remain the home of the plaintiff and the children and ought not be sold while the children still lived there. The plaintiff claimed a declaration that she was entitled to a half share in the house and an order that the defendant should convey the property in their joint names. The trial judge decided that the plaintiff was entitled to a one quarter share in the house, valued at the time of the separation in 1980 and ordered the defendant to convey the property in their joint names.

On appeal, the court held that there was no hard and fast rule that the interests of unmarried couples are to be valued at the time of the separation.

79 [1982] 3 FLR 379.

Having regard to the reason for the acquisition of the home, the purpose had not come to an end. The plaintiff's share ought to be valued at the time of the sale.

> **Fox LJ:** I now come to the second question, the date at which the shares are to be valued. *Prima facie* if persons are entitled to property in aliquot shares as tenants in common under a trust for sale, the value of their respective shares must be determined at the date when the property is sold, but that may have to give way to circumstances. For example, one of the parties may buy out the other, in which case the value of that party's share may have to be determined at a different date. Thus, in *Bernard v Josephs*,[80] to which I have referred, Lord Denning MR said, p 400:
>
> > After ascertaining the shares, the next problem arises when it is to be turned into money. Usually one of the parties stays in the house, paying the mortgage instalments and the rates and other outgoings. The house also increases in value greatly owing to inflation. None of that alters the shares of the parties in the house itself. But it does mean that when the house is sold – or the one buys the other out – there have to be many adjustments made.
>
> *Bernard v Josephs* was a mistress case in which the judge held that the parties were entitled in equal shares. The relationship broke up in 1976 and the woman left the house. The man stayed in the house and subsequently in 1978 he married. He was still living in the house with his wife at the hearing of the appeal in March 1982. The judge made an order for sale. The Court of Appeal upheld the judge's decision as to the shares of the parties. The court decided that it would be a hardship on Mr Josephs and his new wife if they were compelled to leave the house to enable it to be sold, without an opportunity to buy the plaintiff out. Accordingly the court ordered that the property be sold but the order was not to be enforced if Mr Josephs paid £6,000 to Miss Bernard, the plaintiff, within four months, in return for which she should transfer all her share in the property to him. It is clear that £6,000 was calculated as being the value of Miss Bernard's share at the date of the hearing of the appeal: see the judgment of Griffiths LJ, p 406.
>
> *Hall v Hall*[81] is another example of a case where the valuation of a share may be at a date other than sale. We understand that the short report in that case was read to the judge and I think it must have led him to his conclusion that in a mistress case the valuation should be at the date of the termination of the relationship. I do not think that *Hall v Hall* laid down such a principle. The parties lived together for about seven years. They had both previously been married. There were no children of the relationship. They did not marry and never intended to. The woman (the plaintiff) left in 1978, a year after the house was bought and the man lived with another woman – and another after that. After the plaintiff left she lived with another man and when that relationship ended she lived with yet another. The defendant continued to live in the house

80 [1982] Ch 391.

81 [1982] 3 FLR 379.

after the relationship ended. The judge held that the plaintiff was entitled to one fifth of the equity valued at the date when the relationship ended, to carry 10% interest until realisation.

This court upheld that decision. Lord Denning MR plainly did not proceed on the basis that there was a hard and fast rule that in a mistress case the valuation must be at the date of the termination of the relationship. At p 382 he states that he regards the matter as one for the discretion of the judge. Dunn LJ said, p 385:

> So far as the date for the assessment or valuation of the share is concerned, as Lord Denning MR said in *Cooke v Head*, in the case of a mistress that fell to be assessed at the date of separation. I respectfully agree that, although there may be different considerations when dealing with a resulting trust as between husband and wife, in the case of a mistress the trust comes to an end at the termination of the relationship which gave rise to the trust in the first place.

Lord Denning MR, in *Cooke v Head*,[82] said:

> In the light of recent developments, I do not think it is right to approach this case by looking at the money contributions of each and dividing up the beneficial interest according to those contributions. The matter should be looked at more broadly, just as we do in husband and wife cases. We look to see what the equity is worth at the time when the parties separate. We assess the shares as at that time. If the property has been sold, we look at the amount which it has realised, and say how it is to be divided between them. Lord Diplock in *Gissing v Gissing* intimated that it is quite legitimate to infer that: 'the wife should be entitled to a share which was not to be quantified immediately upon the acquisition of the home but should be left to be determined when the mortgage was repaid or the property disposed of.' Likewise, with a mistress.

That passage suggests to me a flexible rather than a rigid approach to the matter. In my opinion *Hall v Hall* cannot, as a matter of authority, be regarded as establishing a rigid rule that the date of valuation of the shares in cases concerned with mistresses must be the date of separation.

Lord Denning MR thought it was a matter of discretion and there is nothing to suggest that O'Connor LJ, who agreed with the reasons of both the other members of the court, disagreed with it. I agree, however, that in *Hall v Hall*, the court took the view that the trust came to an end at the time of the separation and regarded that as a matter of importance: see Lord Denning MR, p 382 and Dunn LJ, p 385. It was I think primarily upon that basis that the court reached a decision as to the date of valuation.

I see no reason, in the circumstances, why the valuation of the plaintiff's share should be at the date of separation. The plaintiff may make expenditure on the property to enable the children and herself to live there, which will have to be taken into account as between the plaintiff and the defendant at a later date. As

82 [1972] 1 WLR 518, p 521.

> a matter of law it seems to me that there is no rule which would have compelled the judge to decide that valuation must be at the date of separation. If he regarded himself as exercising discretion (and I doubt if he did), I see no reason to suppose that he took into account the very important circumstances that the purpose of the trust had not been determined. In my opinion there was no good reason in the present case for directing the valuation to be at the date of separation.

In *Turton v Turton,* the court used stronger language in doubting the validity of *Hall v Hall.*

Turton v Turton [1987] 3 WLR 622, CA

The defendant and plaintiff lived together as man and wife. In 1972, a house was bought for £8,500 which was conveyed in the joint names of the parties as joint tenants, subject to an express trust for sale for themselves as joint tenants beneficially. The defendant paid £3,000 and the balance of the purchase price was raised by way of a mortgage. The plaintiff made no contributions to the acquisition of the house. The joint tenancy was subsequently severed. It was conceded that the express declaration of trust was definitive of the plaintiff's interest in the house. The parties separated in 1975, but the defendant remained in the house. The plaintiff sought a declaration that she held an equal share in the house and an order for sale. The county court judge made the declaration and ordered that the plaintiff's share be valued in 1975, the date of separation. The plaintiff appealed.

The Court of Appeal held in favour of the plaintiff. The half share interest of the claimant may only be valued on the date of the realisation of the asset.

> **Nourse LJ:** The second and material part of the decision in *Hall v Hall* can best be understood from the judgment of Lord Denning MR:[83]
>
>> The next question is new. At what time should her share be taken to be realised? Should it be taken at the time when she left in 1978? Or should it be taken at the time of the hearing before the court? In the meantime this house has increased in value. At the time she left in 1978 the equity was £15,000-odd. Now it is £24,000-odd. The woman says that her share should be taken as at the date of the hearing. But the judge said it should be one fifth at the time when she left – when the parties separated. Even so, he said that interest should be allowed at 10% over the intervening period. That is a nice point. If it were husband and wife, their relationship was intended to be permanent. The trust should continue during the continuance of that relationship.
>>
>> The trust should not be deemed to be extinguished until the relationship is extinguished. But, in a case of this kind, the relationship comes to an end when the parties separate – whoever orders the other out. This is supported by some observations of this court in *Munday v Robertson*.[84] It

83 [1982] 3 FLR 379, pp 381–82.

84 (1973) unreported, 18 April, Court of Appeal (Civil Division) Transcript No 169 of 1973.

> was pointed out that, in a situation like this, although the house has increased in value, the man has been living in it, keeping up the mortgage payments, keeping it in repair, and the like. Any increase in value is therefore largely due to his efforts in keeping the house going, rather than selling it. In view of the guidance in *Munday v Robertson*, and viewing it in the same way as the judge did, it seems to me that he was quite entitled to treat the trust as extinguished at the time of the separation. He said that he thought it was illogical that the woman should be able to enjoy the benefit of the present value which had been brought about by inflation after she had left what was never a permanent relationship. He went on to make this important observation: 'She gets the benefit of her new set up and I see no reason why she should continue to benefit.' So there it is. She gets the benefit of her new relationship. For all I know, she may be getting the benefit of any inflation in the house in which she now lives. It seems to me that the judge was quite entitled – it would be a matter for his discretion – to treat the trust as being extinguished and the shares to be ascertained as at the date of the separation.

It must always be remembered that the basis on which the court proceeds is a common intention, usually to be inferred from the conduct of the parties, that the claimant is to have a beneficial interest in the house. In the common case where the intention can be inferred only from the respective contributions, either initial or under a mortgage, to the cost of its acquisition it is held that the house belongs to the parties beneficially in proportions corresponding to those contributions. But the effect of *Hall v Hall*[85] as it has now been explained, is to presuppose a completely different intention in the case of an unmarried couple, namely that the original proportions may, at the discretion of the court, be varied by reference to the value of the house if and when they cease to live together.

There are two reasons why that cannot be correct. First, it is impossible to see how, on general principles, such an intention can be inferred or implied. The only fair and reasonable inference is that an interest acquired in circumstances such as these is to be absolute and indefeasible. Second, and perhaps more important, it is of the essence of the principles stated in *Gissing v Gissing*[86] that the court has no discretion in the matter. As Lawton LJ has pointed out in *Walker v Hall*,[87] except in cases to which the Matrimonial Causes Act 1973 applies, the function of the court is not to give an opinion as to what the beneficial interests ought to be, but to make a finding on the evidence as to what they are.

How then did it come about that a different view was taken in *Hall v Hall*?[88] The arguments of counsel are not reported. Lord Denning MR described the question as being a new one. Neither he nor Dunn LJ said or implied anything

85 [1982] 3 FLR 379.

86 [1971] AC 886.

87 [1984] FLR 126, p 135.

88 [1982] 3 FLR 379.

to suggest that it had been argued on behalf of the woman that the question was one which could not arise.

If that had been argued, the question being a new one, I would have expected to find a reference to it. I think that it is possible that the point was never taken. In any event, for the reasons stated, I have to express my respectful opinion that the second part of the decision in *Hall v Hall* is contrary to the principles stated in *Gissing v Gissing*.[89] I am unable to see how it could properly be applied in any other case. I think that it ought no longer to be followed at first instance.

I have so far approached the matter without regard to the express declaration of trust which was contained in the conveyance to the plaintiff and the defendant in the present case. It is obvious that a discretion in the court to quantify the shares of the proceeds of sale by reference to the value of the house at some date other than that on which one or both of them are realised can only operate in derogation of the beneficial interests declared by the conveyance and the subsequent notice of severance.

For these reasons I would allow the appeal.

Kerr LJ: Unless there is some express declaration or agreement to the effect that the parties' respective beneficial shares are to be valued at the time of their separation if and when this should occur, there could never be any sufficient ground for attributing any such intention to them merely by implication from the circumstances. In the result, therefore, the parties' beneficial interests would always have to be regarded in the normal way under a trust for sale, with the effect that they would endure until such time as the property is sold, and that they will then attach to the proceeds of sale. I can see no basis in any event, by the exercise of any discretionary power, for cutting off the effect of the trust at some earlier point in time. The parties' separation will no doubt indicate that the purpose of the implied or constructive trust – to provide a joint home for them both – has failed. But this would merely trigger off a demand for a sale, as in *Bernard v Josephs*.[90] It would not give rise to any discretion, in subsequent proceedings to determine the parties' respective interests, to impose a valuation of these interests retrospectively by reference to the value of the property at that particular time.

REALISATION OF THE ASSET

Section 14 of the Trusts of Land and Appointment of Trustees Act 1996 has enacted a means of resolving disputes concerning trusts of land. The dispute may be between the trustees themselves, or between the trustees and beneficiaries or, indeed, between third parties (such as creditors) and those interested under the trust. Section 14 of the 1996 Act repeals and replaces s 30

89 [1971] AC 836.

90 [1982] Ch 391.

of the Law of Property Act 1925. The section declares that any person interested in the trust property (including the trustees of land), may apply to the court for an order relating to the exercise of the trustees' functions or declaring the extent of the beneficial interests. The application may relate to the exercise of the trustees' powers or duties, such as consultation or obtaining consents. The jurisdiction of the court, as enacted in s 14(a), is sufficiently wide so as to enable the court to authorise the trustees to carry out their duties in a manner which would otherwise constitute a breach of trust, for example, to relieve the trustees of any obligation to obtain the consent of, or to consult, any person. But the court has no power under this section to deal with the appointment and removal of trustees.

The court is directed in s 15 to have regard to a number of factors when deciding an application under s 14. These are:

(a) the intentions of the settlor;

(b) the purposes for which the property subject to the trust is held;

(c) the welfare of any minor who occupies or might reasonably be expected to occupy any land subject to the trust as his home;

(d) the interests of the mortgagee of any beneficiary;

(e) in the case of an application relating to the beneficiary's right to occupy under s 13, the circumstances and wishes of each of the beneficiaries entitled to occupy;

(f) in all other cases, except conveying the land to beneficiaries absolutely entitled, the circumstances and wishes of the adult beneficiaries entitled to possession.

[On an application by the trustee in bankruptcy of a co-owner, see below, pp 418, 422.]

Decisions made under the predecessor to s 14 may afford some guidance as to the interpretation of s 14. The starting point, under the now obsolete s 30 of the Law of Property Act 1925, was to see whether the object or underlying purpose of the trust had been fulfilled, and whether a sale would produce inequitable consequences.

In *Buchanan-Wollaston's Conveyance* [1939] Ch 738, a deed was executed by the co-owners which indicated the purpose of the purchase of the land and they added that the land would not be dealt with except with the unanimous agreement of the trustees. This was sufficient to prevent a sale. In *Jones v Challenger* [1961] 1 QB 176, the house was bought as a matrimonial home, thus, a sale was ordered when the wife divorced her husband.

Before the 1996 Act was passed, the court was required to balance the interests of minors against the interests of the other parties interested in the land. In *Williams v Williams* [1976] Ch 278, the court refused to order a sale when a family home was bought and the wife remained in the home with her four children, despite a divorce from her husband. See also *Re Evers' Trust* (below, p 418), where the Court of Appeal reviewed the leading authorities.

The interests of the mortgagees are required to be balanced as against the interests of minors and co-owners. Under s 30 of the Law of Property Act 1925, the approach adopted by the courts was to regard the interests of the creditors as prevailing over the interests of others, except in 'exceptional circumstances'. In *Re Holliday* [1981] Ch 405, the court deferred a sale of a house for five years when an application for a sale was made at the instance of the trustee in bankruptcy of the husband. The husband became estranged from his wife, who was left to occupy the house with her three children. The husband subsequently became bankrupt. But, in many other cases, the court has ordered a sale at the instance of the trustee in bankruptcy. In *Re Citro* [1991] Ch 142 (see below, p 422), the Court of Appeal stated that the fact that the wife, with young children, is faced with eviction on an application by the husband's trustee in bankruptcy, is not to be considered an 'exceptional circumstance'. This issue is now dealt with under the Insolvency Act 1986 (see below, p 422). In *Abbey National v Moss* [1994] 1 FLR 307, the Court of Appeal decided that no distinction ought to be made in the principles applicable in this context, to a trustee in bankruptcy and a chargee of the land. However, the court decided that the principle in *Citro* is that, since bankruptcy vested the share of the bankrupt's interest in the trustee in bankruptcy, this event has the effect of terminating the co-ownership which was the purpose of the purchase. In *Abbey National v Moss*, Mrs Moss transferred the matrimonial home, following the death of her husband, in the joint names of herself and daughter. The purpose of the transfer was to simplify the transfer arrangements to her daughter on the death of Mrs Moss. Mrs Moss had intended to spend the rest of her life in the house. The daughter forged Mrs Moss' signature and secured a mortgage on the house. The daughter later left the country. On an application by the mortgagees for an order of sale, the court decided that it would be grossly inequitable to order a sale, for Mrs Moss' purpose of living in the house for the rest of her life had not been destroyed, and, in any event, the burden was on the mortgagees to ensure that the mortgage was properly executed by the parties.

Re Evers' Trust [1980] 1 WLR 1327, CA

In this case, Mr Papps and Mrs Evers lived together as man and wife. In April 1978 the parties jointly acquired a cottage for £13,950 which was conveyed in their joint names as trustees for themselves as joint tenants. The purchase price was raised by a mortgage for £10,000, Mrs Evers made a direct contribution of £2,400 and Mr Papps contributed the balance. The cottage was purchased as a family home for the parties and their child as well as Mrs Evers' children from a former marriage. In 1979 the parties separated and Mr Papps applied for an order to sell the cottage under s 30 of the 1925 Act.

The Court of Appeal held, dismissing the application, that the underlying purpose of the trust was to provide a home for the couple and the children and s 30 will not be invoked to defeat this purpose.

Ormrod LJ: The section gives the court a discretion to intervene to deal, *inter alia*, with the situation which arises when the trustees under a trust for sale are unable or unwilling to agree that the property should be sold. In such circumstances, the court can order a sale of the property, and if appropriate impose terms, or it can decline to make an order, leaving the property unsold unless and until the trustees reach agreement or the court makes an order at some future date.

The usual practice in these cases has been to order a sale and a division of the proceeds of sale, thus giving effect to the express purpose of the trust. But the trust for sale has become a very convenient and much used conveyancing technique. Combined with the statutory power in the trustees to postpone the sale, it can be used to meet a variety of situations, in some of which an actual sale is far from the intentions of the parties at the time when the trust for sale comes into existence. So, when asked to exercise its discretionary powers under s 30 to execute the trust, the court must have regard to its underlying purpose. In *Re Buchanan-Wollaston's Conveyance*,[91] four adjoining landowners purchased a plot of land to prevent it being built on and held it on trust for sale. They also covenanted with one another that the land would not be dealt with except with the unanimous agreement of the trustees. Subsequently, one of them wished to sell, but some of the other trustees objected so the plaintiff applied to the court under s 30 for an order of sale. At first instance, Farwell J refused the order, saying:

> The question is this: Will the court assist the plaintiff to do an act which would be directly contrary to his contract with the other parties, since it was plainly the intention of the parties to the said contract that the land should not be sold save with the consent of them all?

His decision was upheld in this court, but on a broader basis. Greene MR said:[92]

> ... it seems to me that the court of equity, when asked to enforce the trust for sale, whether one created by a settlement or a will or one created by the statute, must look into all the circumstances of the case and consider whether or not, at that particular moment and in the particular circumstances when the application is made to it, it is right and proper that such an order shall be made. In considering a question of that kind, in circumstances such as these, the court is bound to look at the contract into which the parties have entered and to ask itself the question whether or not the person applying for execution of the trust for sale is a person whose voice should be allowed to prevail.

Some 20 years later, in *Jones v Challenger*,[93] Devlin LJ reviewed the authorities and affirmed this principle. In *Jones v Challenger* a house had been purchased by a husband and wife jointly as a home. Subsequently the marriage broke down, the wife left and committed adultery and applied to the court for an order for sale of the property, a leasehold with only a few years to run. The husband

91 [1939] Ch 738.

92 *Ibid*.

93 [1961] 1 QB 176.

continued to live in the house as his own; there were no children. In these circumstances the court decided that the house should be sold. Devlin LJ said:

> In the case which we have to consider, the house was acquired as the matrimonial home. That was the purpose of the joint tenancy and, for as long as that purpose was still alive, I think that the right test to be applied would be that in *Re Buchanan-Wollaston*. But with the end of the marriage, that purpose was dissolved and the primacy of the duty to sell was restored.

Had there been children whose home was still in the property, the conclusion in that case might have been different. Later Devlin LJ said: 'The true question is whether it is inequitable for the wife, once the matrimonial home has gone, to want to realise her investment?'

In *Burke v Burke*,[94] however, children were involved. On the husband's application under s 17 the registrar ordered a sale, but postponed it for a year or so as to give the wife, who had custody of the children, an opportunity to find an alternative home for them. This court upheld the registrar's order. The application was actually made under s 17 of the Married Women's Property Act 1882. That section is purely procedural and the principles are the same as under s 30. In giving the leading judgment Buckley LJ took the view that the trust for sale was an immediate binding trust subject to the discretionary power in the court to postpone the execution of the trust for sale, and the court must have regard to all the relevant circumstances of the case and the situation of both beneficial owners. The interests of the children in that case, he thought were:

> ... interests which are only incidentally to be taken into consideration in that sort of way. They are, as I say, proper to be taken into consideration so far as they affect the equities in the matter as between the two persons entitled to the beneficial interests in the property. But it is not, I think, right to treat this case as though the husband was obliged to make provision for his children by agreeing to retain the property unsold. To do so is, as I think, and as was urged on us by counsel for the husband, to confuse with a problem relating to property, considerations which are relevant to maintenance.

He expressed disagreement with an *obiter dictum* of Salmon LJ in the earlier case of *Rawlings v Rawlings*,[95] where he said:

> If there were young children, the position would be different. One of the purposes of the trust would no doubt have been to provide a home for them, and whilst that purpose still existed, a sale would not generally be ordered.

Buckley LJ was plainly anxious to make it clear that the children themselves in such circumstances were not objects of the trust and, therefore, had no beneficial interests in the property, and so were in that sense only 'incidental to

94 [1974] 1 WLR 1063.

95 [1964] P 398.

> the problem, but we do not think that Salmon LJ thought otherwise. The court in *Burke v Burke* was not referred to the *Buchanan-Wollaston* case, so Buckley LJ does not seem to have considered, in so many words, whether or not the primary purpose of the trust, ie, for sale, 'the letter of the trust' in the words of Devlin LJ in *Jones v Challenger*, had been affected by the underlying purpose ... The *dictum* of Salmon LJ appears to be more in line with the judgments of this court in the *Buchanan-Wollaston* case and in *Jones v Challenger*. Moreover, it is now supported by a dictum of Lord Denning MR in *Williams v Williams*:[96] 'The court, in executing the trust, should regard the primary object as being to provide a home and not a sale.'
>
> This approach to the exercise of the discretion given by s 30 has considerable advantages in these 'family' cases. It enables the court to deal with substance (that is reality) rather than form (that is, convenience of conveyancing); it brings the exercise of the discretion under this section, so far as possible into line with the exercise of the discretion given by s 24 of the Matrimonial Causes Act 1973 ...
>
> [After considering the facts of this case, he continued:]
>
> The irresistible inference from these facts is that, as the judge found, the parties purchased this property as a family home for themselves and the three children. It is difficult to imagine that the mother, then wholly responsible for two children and partly for the third, would have invested nearly all her capital in the purchase of this property if it was not to be available to her as a home for the children for the indefinite future. It is inconceivable that the father, when he agreed to this joint venture, could have thought otherwise or contemplated the possibility of an early sale without the consent of the mother. The underlying purpose of the trust was, therefore, to provide a home for all five of them for the indefinite future.

Gordon v Douce [1983] 2 WLR 563, CA

In this case, the Court of Appeal, in considering *inter alia* an application under s 30 of the 1925 Act, adopted the same line of reasoning as laid down in *Re Evers* and refused to follow *Hall v Hall* (see above, p 411).

> **Fox LJ:** This case, however, in my opinion is far removed from *Hall v Hall* on its facts. In this case the relationship between the parties was of much longer duration. There were children and the woman (the plaintiff) is still living in the house with the children. Further, in his evidence the defendant stated that he expected the house 'to be a home for her and the children'. It is not his intention, so I understand, to seek an order for sale while the children are still living in the house. In my opinion, therefore, the purposes of the trust have not come to an end. They are still very much in existence. The expenditure of money by the plaintiff, which was the basis of her entitlement to a share in the property, was therefore for a purpose which has not yet come to an end.

96 [1976] Ch 278.

BANKRUPTCY

If one of the co-habiting partners (co-owners) becomes bankrupt the beneficial interest in the matrimonial home of such partner vests in the trustee in bankruptcy, whose interest is the protection of the creditors. On a petition by the trustee in bankruptcy for an order of sale under s 14 of the Trusts of Land and Appointment of Trustees Act 1996, the court has a general discretion and may consider all the circumstances of the case (including the interests of the family and creditors and the contribution of either party towards the bankruptcy): s 335(A) of the Insolvency Act 1986 (as amended by the Trusts of Land and Appointment of Trustees Act 1996).

Section 335(A)(2) (as amended by the Trusts of Land and Appointment of Trustees Act 1996) provides:

> On ... an application ... the court shall make such order ... under s 14 of the Act of 1996 as it thinks just and reasonable having regard to:
>
> (a) the interests of the bankrupt's creditors;
>
> (b) where the application is made in respect of land which includes a dwelling house which is or has been the house of the bankrupt or the bankrupt's spouse or former spouse:
>
> (i) the conduct of the spouse or former spouse, so far as contributing to the bankruptcy;
>
> (ii) the needs and financial resources of the spouse or former spouse;
>
> (iii) the needs of any children; and
>
> (c) all the circumstances of the case other than the needs of the bankrupt.

If, however, the application is made more than one year after the vesting of the property in the trustee in bankruptcy, the interests of the creditors will prevail, unless there are exceptional circumstances which compel the court to reach a different conclusion: s 335(A)(3) of the Insolvency Act 1986.

Section 335(A)(3) provides:

> Where such an application is made after the end of the period of one year beginning with the first vesting ... of the bankrupt's estate in a trustee, the court shall assume, unless the circumstances of the case are exceptional, that the interests of the bankrupt's creditors outweigh all other considerations.

Re Citro (A Bankrupt) [1991] Ch 142, CA

Two Citro brothers, D and C, ran a garage business. In 1985, they were declared bankrupt. They each had a half share of the beneficial interest in their separate matrimonial homes. The trustees in bankruptcy sought to sell their homes under s 30 of the Law of Property Act 1925. D was judicially separated from his wife, who lived in the house with their three children, the youngest of whom was 12 years old. C lived in his home with his wife. They also had three children, the youngest of whom was 10. Hoffman J made an order for possession and sale, but postponed the order until the youngest child in each case became 16. The trustee in bankruptcy appealed.

Held, allowing the appeal: the Court of Appeal varied the order to the extent that possession and sale were to be postponed for a period not exceeding six months.

> **Nourse LJ:** In a series of bankruptcy decisions relating to matrimonial homes subsequent to *Jones v Challenger* it has been held that the interests of the husband's creditors ought usually to prevail over the interests of the wife and any children and, with one exception, *Re Holliday (A Bankrupt) ex p Trustee of the Property of the Bankrupt v Holliday* [1981] Ch 405, a sale within a short period has invariably been ordered. It has also been assumed that no distinction ought to be made between a case where the property is still being enjoyed as the matrimonial home and one where it is not. That distinction, if it ought to be made, would be of significance on these appeals, which relate to the matrimonial homes of two bankrupt brothers, one of whom is still living there with his wife and the other of whom has been judicially separated and living elsewhere since 1984.
>
> [His Lordship examined the following authorities: *Jones v Challenger* [1961] 1 QB 176; *Re Mayo* [1943] Ch 302; *Re Buchanan-Wollaston's Conveyance* [1939] Ch 738; *Re Solomon* [1967] Ch 573; *Boydell v Gillespie* (1970) 216 EG 1505; *Re Hardy's Trust* (1970) *The Times*, 23 October; *Re Turner* [1974] 1 WLR 1556; *Re Densham* [1975] 1 WLR 1519; *Re Bailey* [1977] 1 WLR 278; *Re Holliday* [1981] Ch 405; *Re Lowrie* [1981] 3 All ER 353 and continued:]
>
> The broad effect of these authorities can be summarised as follows. Where a spouse who has a beneficial interest in the matrimonial home has become bankrupt under debts which cannot be paid without the realisation of that interest, the voice of the creditors will usually prevail over the voice of the other spouse and a sale of the property ordered within a short period. The voice of the other spouse will only prevail in exceptional circumstances. No distinction is to be made between a case where the property is still being enjoyed as the matrimonial home and one where it is not.
>
> What, then, are exceptional circumstances? As the cases show, it is not uncommon for a wife with young children to be faced with eviction in circumstances where the realisation of her beneficial interest will not produce enough to buy a comparable home in the same neighbourhood, or indeed elsewhere. And, if she has to move elsewhere, there may be problems over schooling and so forth. Such circumstances, while engendering a natural sympathy in all who hear of them, cannot be described as exceptional.
>
> I cannot myself see how the circumstances in *Re Holliday* could fairly have been treated as exceptional. I am confirmed in that view by the belief that it would be shared by Balcombe LJ, who, in *Harman v Glencross* [1986] Fam 81, p 95, said that the decision in *Re Holliday* was very much against the run of the recent authorities. I would not myself have regarded it as an exceptional circumstance that the husband had presented his own petition, even 'as a tactical move'. That was not something of the creditors' choosing and could not fairly have been held against them. I do not say that in other cases there might not be other exceptional circumstances. They must be identified if and when they arise.

In the husband and wife cases exemplified by *Jones v Challenger* [1961] 1 QB 176 it is held that neither spouse has a right to demand a sale of the property while the purpose of its enjoyment as a matrimonial home still exists. In order to be so enjoyed, it must be occupied by the spouses jointly. As a matter of property law, the basis of their joint occupation is their joint ownership of the beneficial interest in the home. Although the vesting of one of their interests in a trustee for creditors does not in itself destroy the secondary purpose of the trust, the basis for their joint occupation has gone. It must, I think, be implicit in the principle of *Jones v Challenger* that the secondary purpose can only exist while the spouses are not only joint occupiers of the home but joint owners of it as well.

Did Hoffmann J correctly apply it to the facts which were before him? I respectfully think that he did not. First, for the reasons already stated, the personal circumstances of the two wives and their children, although distressing, are not by themselves exceptional. Secondly, I think that the judge erred in fashioning his orders by reference to those which might have been made in the Family Division in a case where bankruptcy had not supervened. That approach, which tends towards treating the home as a source of provision for the children, was effectively disapproved by the earlier and uncontroversial part of the decision of this court in *Re Holliday*. Thirdly, and perhaps most significantly, he did not ask himself the critical question whether a further postponement of payment of their debts would cause hardship to the creditors. It is only necessary to look at the substantial deficiencies referred to earlier in this judgment in order to see that it would. Since then a further 18 months' interest has accrued and the trustee has incurred the costs of these proceedings as well.

I would allow both appeals by deleting the provisos for postponement from Hoffmann J's orders and substituting short periods of suspension.

SUPPLEMENTARY READING

Cullity, M, 'Joint bank accounts with volunteers' (1969) 84 LQR 530

Ferguson, P, 'Constructive trusts – a note of caution' (1993) 109 LQR 114

Hayton, D, ' Constructive trusts of homes – a bold approach' (1993) 109 LQR 485

Hayton, D, 'Equitable rights of co-habitees' [1990] Conv 370

Lawson, A, 'The things we do for love: detrimental reliance in the family home' [1996] LS 218

Lawson, A, 'Acquiring a beneficial interest in the family home' [1992] Conv 218

Lawson, A, 'Working in a business and ownership of house' [1996] Conv 462

Oldham, M, 'Quantification of beneficial interests in land' (1996) 55 CLJ 194

CHAPTER 11

CONSTRUCTIVE TRUSTS: STRANGERS AS CONSTRUCTIVE TRUSTEES

The general rule is that third parties or persons who have not been appointed trustees (such as agents of trustees, for example, accountants and solicitors) are not constructive trustees if they act in breach of their duties. They may be personally liable in damages for breach of contract or tort and are answerable to their principals, the trustees who appointed them. Provided that the agent acts within the course of his authority and does not receive the trust property for his own benefit and does not have knowledge that he is acting in a manner inconsistent with the terms of the trust, he does not become a constructive trustee. In other words, if the agents of trustees do not become trustees *de son tort*, that is, do not adopt the characteristics of trustees, such as intermeddling with the trust property, they are not constructive trustees, although they may be personally liable if they act negligently.

Lee v Sankey [1872] LR 15 Eq 204, HC

> **Bacon VC:** A mere agent of trustees is answerable only to his principal and not to *cestuis que* trust in respect of trust moneys coming into his hands merely in his character of agent. But it is also not less clearly established that a person receives into his hands trust money, and who deals with them in a manner inconsistent with the performance of the trusts of which he is cognisant, is personally liable for the consequences which may ensue upon his so dealing.

In this case, a firm of solicitors, acting with the authority of two trustees appointed under a will, and with full knowledge of the terms of the will, received the proceeds of sale of trust property and held it pending further instructions as to its investment. The solicitors were induced to transfer part of the proceeds of sale to one of the trustees who dissipated the moneys and died insolvent. The solicitors were held liable in equity on two grounds: first, because the payment to one of two trustees did not discharge them from their duty to account to the principals; and secondly, because they had received the trust property pending instructions on investment and had acted inconsistently with such directions. See, also, *Soar v Ashwell*.[1]

Other examples of agents becoming constructive trustees are *Boardman v Phipps* and *English v Dedham Vale Properties Ltd* (see above, pp 319 *et seq*).

The principle governing the liability of an agent as a constructive trustee was summarised in *Mara v Browne*,[2] thus:

1 [1893] 2 QB 390.

2 [1896] 1 Ch 199.

Smith LJ: If one, not being a trustee and not having the authority from a trustee, takes upon himself to intermeddle with trust matters or to do acts characteristic of the office of trustee, he may therefore make himself a trustee of his own wrong, ie, a trustee *de son tort* or as it is also termed, a constructive trustee.

In this case, a solicitor acting on behalf of the trustees unlawfully invested trust funds on certain mortgages and the trust suffered loss. The court held that the solicitor was not liable as a constructive trustee though he would have been liable in contract for his negligence had the action not become time barred.

Smith LJ (continued): It is said that the facts show that there should be imputed to Hugh Browne the character of a trustee, or, in other words, that he was a trustee *de son tort*, and upon this ground the learned judge has held him liable. It is not contended on behalf of the plaintiffs that Hugh Browne has been guilty of any fraudulent or dishonest conduct to the injury of the *cestuis que* trust, nor, to use Lord Langdale's words in *Fyler v Fyler*,[3] did he, being a solicitor, 'take advantage of his position to acquire a benefit for himself at the hazard, if not to the prejudice, of the trust'; but it was said that he had made himself a constructive trustee, which, so far as I know, is the same thing as a trustee *de son tort*. Now, what constitutes a trustee *de son tort*? It appears to me if one, not being a trustee and not having authority from a trustee, takes upon himself to intermeddle with trust matters or to do acts characteristic of the office of trustee, he may thereby make himself what is called in law a trustee of his own wrong, ie, a trustee *de son tort*, or, as it is also termed, a constructive trustee. Lord Selborne LC dealt with this question in *Barnes v Addy*.[4] He said:

> That responsibility [ie, of a trustee] may no doubt be extended in equity to others who are not properly trustees, if they are found either making themselves trustees *de son tort*, or actually participating in any fraudulent conduct of the trustee to the injury of the *cestui que* trust. But, on the other hand, strangers are not to be made constructive trustees merely because they act as the agent of trustees in transactions within their legal powers, transactions, perhaps of which a court of equity may disapprove, unless those agents receive and become chargeable with some part of the trust property, or unless they assist with knowledge in a dishonest and fraudulent design on the part or the trustees.

And James LJ added:

> I most cordially concur in the general principle with which the Lord Chancellor began his judgment. I have long thought, and more than once expressed my opinion from this seat, that this court has in some cases gone to the very verge of justice in making good to *cestuis que* trust the consequences of the breaches of trust of their trustees at the expense of persons perfectly honest, but who have been, in some more or less degree, injudicious. I do not think it is for the good of *cestuis que* trust, or the good of the world, that those cases should be extended.

3 (1841) 3 Beav 560.

4 [1874] LR 9 Ch 251.

In this, if I may respectfully say so, I entirely agree.

In my judgment it is incorrect to hold that he was acting as trustee *de son tort*; why is this to be assumed? The learned judge came to the conclusion that Arthur Reeves never acted under the deed of January, 1884, and that it was abandoned; but why is it this to be so held? We find Arthur Reeves (a plaintiff) after its execution at once entering upon the business of the trust; and why is it to be assumed and held that he then acted as a trustee in his own wrong rather than as a properly appointed trustee? I can draw no such inference. It is true that in 1890 Hugh Browne ran his pen through the signatures of Mr and Mrs Harold Reeves, lest, as he said, any person should mistake the deed for a living one; but this was many years after it was executed and at a time when it was then required. The learned judge also held that Hugh Browne could not say that he was acting as solicitor for James, for he had treated him as a hostile party. But, with submission, although this was so at one time, the learned judge appears to me to have omitted to notice the part taken by James, as he made good the trust fund, in drawing the cheques in conjunction with Arthur Reeves upon their joint account with the express object that the moneys so obtained should be invested by Hugh Browne for the trust. Upon these questions of fact I find myself differing from the learned judge. In my opinion, between January 1884, and 9 May 1884, it has been proved that Hugh Browne was acting for James and Arthur Reeves in making the investments, that they were the *de facto* trustees, and that he had them as principals, and that in what he did he was not, therefore, a trustee *de son tort*.

Some of the reasons put forward for limiting the liability of the agent as a constructive trustee are that if the principle was otherwise no agent would be prepared to act for the trust, or their services would be more expensive, or they might insist on an indemnity from the trustees. Another powerful reason for restricting the liability of agents concerns the difficult balancing act which agents are sometimes required to make in respect of honouring the contractual obligations to their principals and complying with their broader duty not to participate in a breach of trust.

One of the leading cases in this context is *Barnes v Addy*.[5] In this case, an action was brought against a solicitor and the trustees of a trust settlement. The solicitor advised the settlement trustees against the appointment of a beneficiary as the sole trustee of a part of the trust funds, but nevertheless prepared the necessary documents. The sole trustee misapplied the property and became bankrupt. The court held that the solicitor was not liable for the loss for he did not receive the trust property but acted honestly and within the course of his authority. The settlement trustees were liable. Lord Selbourne laid down the test of liability as follows:

Lord Selbourne: Those who create a trust clothe the trustee with a legal power and control over the trust property, imposing on him a corresponding responsibility. That responsibility may no doubt be extended in equity to

5 [1874] LR 9 Ch App 244.

> others who are not properly trustees, if they are found either making themselves trustees *de son tort*, or actually participating in any fraudulent conduct of the trustee to the injury of the *cestui que* trust ... Strangers are not to be made constructive trustees merely because they act as agents of trustees in transactions within their legal powers, transactions, perhaps, of which a court of equity may disapprove, unless those agents:
>
> (a) receive and become chargeable with some part of the trust property; or
>
> (b) they assist with knowledge in a dishonest or fraudulent design on the part of the trustees.
>
> Those are the principles as it seems to me, which we must bear in mind in dealing with the facts of the case. If those principles were disregarded, I know not how anyone could, in transactions admitting of doubt, as to the view which a court of equity might take of them, safely discharge the office of solicitor, of banker, or of agent of any sort to trustees. But, on the other hand, if persons, dealing honestly as agents, are at liberty to rely on the legal power of the trustees, and are not to have the character of trustees constructively imposed upon them, then the transactions of mankind can safely be carried through; and I apprehend those who create trusts do expressly intend, in the absence of fraud and dishonesty, to exonerate such agents of all classes from the responsibilities which are expressly incumbent, by reason of the fiduciary relation upon the trustees.

The above statement represents an accurate summary of the law concerning the liability of a stranger to the trust as a constructive trustee. The two limbs of liability as stated by Lord Selbourne have been construed by the courts as equivalent to a statutory provision.

The rationale behind the trustee's liability under the first head is based on the premise that the stranger or agent has received the trust property with knowledge of the same, before he acts or fails to act for his own benefit in a manner inconsistent with the trust. Whereas, under the second limb although the stranger does not receive the property for his own benefit, he becomes a constructive trustee by virtue of the mere participation in a fraudulent scheme of the trustees, with knowledge of the fraudulent design. Thus, the basis of liability under the two limbs is dissimilar. Equally, the extent of the knowledge of the stranger under each limb ought to be different. There has been a conflict of judicial views as to the types of knowledge which the stranger is required to possess under each head in order to found liability as a constructive trustee. Within the last two decades there has been renewed judicial interest in this area of the law.

CATEGORIES OF KNOWLEDGE

Peter Gibson J in *Re Baden Delvaux and Lecuit v Société Générale pour Favoriser le Développement de Commerce en France SA* (see below, p 455) enumerated the various kinds of knowledge which are relevant in this context.

> **Peter Gibson J:** What types of knowledge are relevant for the purposes of constructive trusteeship? ... knowledge can comprise anyone of the five different mental states as follows:
>
> (i) actual knowledge;
>
> (ii) wilfully shutting one's eyes to the obvious;
>
> (iii) wilfully and recklessly failing to make such inquiries as an honest and reasonable man would make;
>
> (iv) knowledge of circumstances which would indicate the facts to an honest and reasonable man;
>
> (v) knowledge of circumstances which would put an honest and reasonable man on inquiry.
>
> More accurately, apart from actual knowledge, they are formulations of circumstances which may lead the court to impute knowledge of the facts to the alleged constructive trustee, even though he lacked actual knowledge of those facts.

The real test in every case is whether the stranger conducted himself with such impropriety as to make him accountable as a constructive trustee or at any rate to prevent him relying on lack of actual knowledge as a defence to a claim brought on behalf of the trust.

Agip v Jackson [1990] Ch 265, HC

Note that the Court of Appeal affirmed the decision of the High Court (see below, p 466).

> **Millett J:** The true distinction is between honesty and dishonesty. It is essentially a jury question. If a man does not draw the obvious inferences or make obvious inquiries, the question is: why not? If it is because, however foolishly, he did not suspect wrongdoing or, having suspected it, had his suspicions allayed, however unreasonably, that is one thing. But if he did suspect wrongdoing yet failed to make inquiries because 'he did not want to know' (category ii) or because he regarded it as 'none of his business' (category iii), that is quite another. Such conduct is dishonest and those who are guilty of it cannot complain if, for the purpose of civil liability, they are treated as if they had actual knowledge.

The first three categories of knowledge involve a subjective or partly objective inquiry, whereas, categories (iv) and (v) require a purely objective assessment of the circumstances. Actual knowledge concerns such facts of which the stranger is aware, positively and consciously. Wilfully shutting one's eyes to the obvious is a common law notion involving abstinence from making inquiries because the defendant knows what the result would entail. Similarly, knowledge within category (iii) embraces circumstances when the defendant foresees or suspects the likelihood of a serious risk of loss of the trust property if reasonable inquiries are not made, but is indifferent as to the consequences of failing to make such inquiries. Knowledge within categories (iv) and (v) involve a wholly objective inquiry in that the reasonable man would have made reasonable inquiries or would have been put on inquiry. The court adopts its own standard in fixing an individual with knowledge within categories (iv) and (v). The effect is that the degree of culpability that is required to make a stranger a constructive trustee within the latter two categories borders between fraud and negligence. It is arguable that this test is divorced from dishonesty or want of probity, which ought to be the basis of a constructive trusteeship. In other words, an innocent failure to make reasonable inquiries is distinct from acting dishonestly, or consciously acting with impropriety.

Knowing recipient of trust property

The rationale for liability under this head is that a stranger who knows that a fund is trust property transferred to him in breach of trust, cannot take possession of the property for his own benefit but is subject to the claims of the trust. He is not a *bona fide* transferee of the legal estate for value without notice. Thus, liability may arise where the stranger:

(i) receives trust property knowing that his possession is in breach of trust; or

(ii) receives trust property initially without knowledge that his acquisition is in breach of trust, but subsequently becomes aware of the existence of the trust and acts in a manner inconsistent with the trust.

The contest in this context is based on the assertion of proprietary rights. The trust sues the stranger claiming that it has better title to the property. Equity is entitled to adopt the most strenuous efforts in order to protect the beneficiary's interest under the trust and in the majority of cases has declared that any of the five types of knowledge would be sufficient to make the stranger liable. Thus, actual knowledge, wilful or reckless blindness as well as constructive knowledge on the part of the stranger would make him liable to the trust under the first limb of liability laid down in *Barnes v Addy*.

Belmont Finance Corp v Williams Furniture and Others (No 2) [1980] 1 All ER 393, CA

In this case, Williams Co owned the entire shareholding in City Industrial Ltd which in turn owned all the shares in Belmont. A scheme was arranged whereby Belmont assisted in the unlawful purchase of its own shares in stages as follows: Belmont purchased all the shares in a fourth company called Maximum for £500,000 in cash (a price which was grossly in excess of the value of its assets), Maximum then bought from City the shares it held in Belmont for £489,000. Belmont was subsequently put into receivership – the receiver claimed damages for conspiracy and also sought to recover from City and its directors the £489,000 which City received on the ground that this sum was received by the directors in breach of their fiduciary duty concerning the funds of the company.

The Court of Appeal held in favour of the receiver on the ground that City was liable as a constructive trustee. Liability arose by the receipt of trust moneys and the fact that its directors knew all the circumstances, in particular, the unlawfulness of the transaction, and knew or ought to have known that the sum received from the sale of Belmont's shares was trust money. There was no need to prove fraud.

> **Buckley LJ:** The directors of a limited company are treated as if they were trustees of those funds of the company which are in their hands or under their control, and if they misapply them they commit a breach of trust ... So, if the directors of a company in breach of their fiduciary duties misapply the funds of their company so that they come into the hands of some stranger to the trust who receives them with the knowledge (actual or constructive) of the breach, he cannot conscientiously retain those funds against the company unless he has some better equity. He becomes a constructive trustee of the misapplied funds.

Similarly, in *International Sales and Agencies Ltd v Marcus*,[6] the court decided that, under this head of liability, the stranger will be a constructive trustee if he receives the trust property with knowledge (construed in the widest sense including constructive knowledge) of the breach.

> **Lawson J:** The knowing recipient of trust property for his own purposes will become a constructive trustee of what he receives if either he was in fact aware at the time that his receipt was affected by a breach of trust, or if he deliberately shut his eyes to the real nature of the transfer to him (this could be called imputed notice), or if an ordinary reasonable man in his position and with his attributes ought to have known of the relevant breach. This I equate with constructive notice. Such a position would arise where such a person would have been put on enquiry as to the probability of a breach of trust ...

In this case, the defendant made a personal loan of £30,000 to a major shareholder of the plaintiff company. After the death of the debtor, a friend and director of the plaintiff company repaid the loan with the company's funds to the knowledge of the defendant. The plaintiff sought to make the defendant a constructive trustee of the funds.

The court held in favour of the plaintiff.

Where the plaintiff's interest in the property is seriously disputed by other parties, so that there is a reasonable doubt as to whether the plaintiff has an interest in the property, the defendant who receives the property cannot be made a constructive trustee. He could not really be treated as dealing with the plaintiff's property.

Carl Zeiss Stiftung v Herbert Smith and Co (No 2) [1969] 2 Ch 276, CA

Following the partition of Germany, members of the East German firm of Carl Zeiss fled to the West and founded the West German firm of the same name.

6 [1982] 3 All ER 551.

The East German firm claimed the assets of the West German firm. Solicitors of the West German firm were paid a sum of money for work done for their clients. The East German firm claimed this money from the solicitors contending that they had received the sum knowing that the same belonged to the plaintiff.

The court held in favour of the defendants, for the ownership of the assets of the plaintiff was seriously in dispute on reasonable grounds, the solicitors could have no knowledge that the funds belonged to the claimants. Furthermore, the defendants were under no duty to inquire. In short, the plaintiff had a 'doubtful equity'.

> **Edmund Davies LJ:** It is true that not every situation where probity is lacking gives rise to a constructive trust. Nevertheless, the authorities appear to show that nothing short of it will do. Not even gross negligence will suffice. Thus, in *Williams v Williams*,[7] where a solicitor had acted, as Kay J found, 'with very great negligence towards his client' in dealing with trust property, the judge said, at p 445:
>
> > If it were proved to me upon the evidence that he had wilfully shut his eyes, and was determined not to inquire, then the case would have been very different ... I do not find that anything done by [the solicitor] in the matter was done for his own benefit ... If he had, as I believe had, a *bona fide* conviction that there was no settlement whatever ... I cannot hold that he is affected with such notice as to make him personally liable for the purchase-moneys which passed through his hands as solicitor.
>
> In *In re Blundell*,[8] where solicitors were again absolved in somewhat remarkable circumstances, Stirling J, after reviewing the authorities, said at p 381:
>
> > ... solicitors cannot be made liable as constructive trustees unless they are brought within the doctrine of the court with reference to other strangers, who are not themselves trustees, but are liable in certain cases to be made to account as if they were trustees. What is the general doctrine with reference to constructive trustees of that kind? It is that a stranger to the trust receiving money from the trustee which he knows' – and I stress the word 'knows' – 'to be part of the trust estate is not liable as constructive trustee unless there are facts brought home to him which show that to his knowledge the money is being applied in a manner which is inconsistent with the trust; or (in other words) unless it be made out that he is party either to a fraud, or to a breach of trust on the part of the trustee.
>
> In a further passage, at p 383, the judge added observation of great pertinence to the present case:
>
> > ... to my mind, in order that the solicitor may be debarred from accepting payment out of the trust estate, he must be fixed with notice that at the time when he accepted payment the trustee had been guilty of a breach of

7 (1881) 17 Ch D 437.

8 (1888) 40 Ch D 370.

> trust as would preclude him altogether from resorting to the trust estate for payment of costs, so that in fact the application of the trust estate in payment of costs would be a breach of trust.

The foregoing cases are but two illustrations among many to be found in the reports of that want of probity which, to my way of thinking, is the hall-mark of constructive trust, however created.

The proposition which the plaintiffs' counsel described as fundamental to his case was stated in these terms: that a man who receives property which he knows (or ought to know) is trust property and applies it in a manner which he knows (or ought to know) is inconsistent with the terms of the trust is accountable in a suit by the beneficiaries of the trust. Although the soundness of that proposition was from the beginning accepted without qualification by the defendant solicitors, countless cases were cited to demonstrate its validity. But it turned out that their citation was far from being a sleeveless errand, for it emerged that in not one of those cases was there any room for doubt that a trust already existed. None of them dealt with the fundamental assertion which has here been so strongly contested, and which Pennycuick J summarised by saying that:

> Counsel for the [plaintiffs] contends that [the defendant solicitors] have notice of the trust and if, at the end of the day, the trust is established in the main action, they will be accountable as constructive trustees for all moneys comprised in that trust which they have received from the West German company.

But, as admittedly the West German foundation hold nothing for the plaintiffs under an express trust, and as, even despite the 13 long years that litigation between them has been proceeding, there has been no determination that any trust does exist, Mr Harman has found himself compelled to go further if this appeal is to be put on its feet. He asserts, in effect, that for present purposes claims are the same as facts. More amply stated, he submits that it is sufficient to render the defendant solicitors accountable to the plaintiffs that they have (a) knowledge that the plaintiffs are claiming that the West German foundation holds all their assets in trust for them; (b) knowledge of the nature of the allegations advanced by the plaintiffs which (if established) are said to justify that claim; and (c) knowledge that all sums paid to them by the West German foundation must be and are derived solely and entirely from those assets which are the subject matter of the plaintiffs' claim to be beneficial owners. Such knowledge on the part of the defendant solicitors being established, submits Mr Harman, the preliminary issue raised by this appeal must here and now be determined in favour of the plaintiffs, and it matters not that, as he concedes, the defendant solicitors do not and cannot know for some time to come whether the plaintiffs will succeed in the main action in establishing their claim to a trust. He submits that it is equally immaterial that the plaintiffs accept that the defendant solicitors have throughout acted honestly as solicitors of the West German foundation and received fees, costs and disbursements solely in that capacity and proper in amount.

Like Sachs LJ, I am prepared for present purpose to assume that the plaintiffs will ultimately and at some unknown date succeed in establishing in the main action that the moneys in question are either their own property or are held in trust for them by the West German foundation. Nevertheless, in my judgment, none of the cases cited affords support for the contention that in the present circumstances the defendant solicitors are accountable to the plaintiffs, and it would be supererogation for me to attempt to add to my Lord's analysis of those cases. But so wide is the net spread by the plaintiffs that they even seek to enmesh the defendant solicitors, Dehn & Lauderdale, who incontestably ceased to act for the West German foundation in 1964, three whole years before any allegations of a trust were even hinted at. Only slightly less audaciously, the plaintiffs also claim that the defendant solicitors, Herbert Smith & Co, are accountable for all moneys received by them from the West German foundation with knowledge that they were derived from the assets claimed by the plaintiffs (apparently, in their case also, without regard to whether they were received before or after the vital re-amendment of the statement of claim in the main action in 1967), and that such accountability exists regardless of whether the moneys so received were advanced to cover fees and disbursement already made or were intended to cover those which might arise in the future. The only escape which Mr Harman was prepared to concede might even be conceivably open to the defendant solicitors was that, if they had been advised by experienced counsel the strong probability was that the plaintiffs would fail to establish in the main action that a trust existed, these defendant solicitors might thereby be enabled to avoid liability by invoking s 61 of the Trustee Act 1925.

The observation most helpful to the plaintiffs is possibly that of Fry J, in *Foxton v Manchester and Liverpool District Banking Co*[9] that:

> ... those who know that a fund is a trust fund cannot take possession of that fund for their own private benefit, except at the risk of being liable to refund it in the event of the trust being broken by the payment of the money.

But even there knowledge of the existence of the trust and that the moneys being received are trust moneys was stressed, as opposed to knowledge of a mere claim that a trust exists. Here, in essence, nothing more than the latter is asserted, and it is conceded that the defendant solicitors cannot be expected to conjecture as to its outcome.

Mr Kerr gave the court a helpful distillation of the numerous authorities to which reference has already been made by my Lords. Their effect, he rightly submits, may be thus stated: (A) a solicitor or other agent who receives money from his principal which belongs at law or in equity to a third party is not accountable as a constructive trustee to that third party unless he has been guilty of some wrongful act in relation to that money; (B) to act 'wrongfully' he must be guilty of (i) knowingly participating in a breach of trust by his principal; or (ii) intermeddling with the trust property otherwise than merely as an agent and thereby becomes a trustee *de son tort*; or (iii) receiving or dealing with the money knowing that his principal has no right to pay it over or to instruct him to deal with it in the manner indicated; or (iv) some

9 (1881) 44 LT 406, p 408.

dishonest act relating to the money. These are, indeed, but variants or illustrations of that 'want of probity' to which I have earlier referred.

Do the demands of justice and good conscience bring the present case within any of the foregoing categories? In my judgment, the question is one which demands a negative answer. The law being reluctant to make a mere agent a constructive trustee, as Lord Selborne LC put it in *Barnes v Addy*[10] mere notice of a claim asserted by a third party is insufficient to render the agent guilty of a wrongful act in dealing with property derived from his principal in accordance with the latter's instructions unless the agent knows that the third party's claim is well-founded and that the principal accordingly had no authority to give such instructions. The only possible exception to such exemption arises where the agent is under a duty to inquire into the validity of the third party's claim and, where, although inquiry would have established that it was well-founded, none is instituted. But, as it is conceded by the plaintiffs that the defendant solicitors are under no such duty of inquiry, that further matter does not now call for consideration.

Whatever be the outcome of the main action, in my judgment the foregoing reasons are fatal to the plaintiffs in their present claim, and I therefore do not propose to consider the further objection based upon public policy. On the ground I have stated, I would concur in dismissing the appeal.

Re Montagu's Settlement [1987] Ch 264, HC

Megarry VC reviewed the basis of liability under this head and concluded that 'the constructive trust should not be imposed unless the conscience of the recipient is affected; this depends on knowledge, not "notice"; want of probity includes actual knowledge, shutting one's eyes to the obvious, or wilfully and recklessly failing to make such inquiries as a reasonable and honest man would make; it does not include knowledge of circumstances which would indicate the facts to an honest and reasonable man or would put the latter on enquiry'. Thus, according to Megarry VC, cognisance within the first three categories of knowledge (subjective inquiry) as laid down by Gibson J in *Re Baden Delvaux* is relevant under this head, constructive knowledge including objective recklessness (categories (iv) and (v)) is unsuitable as a test of constructive trusteeship. Similarly, a stranger is not treated as having knowledge of a fact which he has genuinely forgotten.

In this case, the trustees on advice from a firm of solicitors settled chattels in favour of the beneficiary, the 10th Duke, absolutely. The transfer was in breach of trust but as a result of an honest mistake. The Duke disposed of a number of chattels during his lifetime. After his death, the 11th Duke claimed that his predecessor had become a constructive trustee of the chattels and was liable to re-transfer the remaining assets (and traceable proceeds of sale of the disposed chattels) and was also personally liable in respect of the value of any assets disposed of and in respect of which the proceeds were not traceable.

10 [1874] 9 Ch App 244, pp 251–52.

The court held that the Duke (or his estate) was not personally liable as a constructive trustee because he did not have subjective knowledge of the breach but was liable to re-transfer to the settlement trustees undisposed trust assets and traceable proceeds as an innocent volunteer.

> **Megarry VC:** The core of the question (and I put it very broadly) is what suffices to constitute a recipient of trust property a constructive trustee of it. I can leave on one side the equitable doctrine of tracing: if the recipient of trust property still has the property or its traceable proceeds in his possession, he is liable to restore it unless he is a purchaser without notice. But liability as a constructive trustee is wider, and does not depend upon the recipient still having the property or its traceable proceeds. Does it suffice if the recipient had 'notice' that the property he was receiving was trust property, or must he have not merely notice of this, but knowledge, or 'cognisance,' as it has been put?
>
> At the outset, I think that I should refer to *Baden, Delvaux and Lecuit v Société Général pour Favoriser le Développement du Commerce et de l'Industrie en France SA*,[11] a case which, for obvious reasons, I shall call the *Baden* case. That case took 105 days to hear, spread over seven months, and the judgment of Peter Gibson J is over 120 pages long. It was a 'knowing assistance' type of constructive trust, as distinct from the 'knowing receipt or dealing' type which is in issue before me. I use these terms as a convenient shorthand for two of the principal types of constructive trust. Put shortly, under the first of these heads a person becomes liable as a constructive trustee if he knowingly assists in some fraudulent design on the part of a trustee. Under the second head, a person also becomes liable as a constructive trustee if he either receives trust property with knowledge that the transfer is a breach of trust, or else deals with the property in a manner inconsistent with the trust after acquiring occurs under each head; and in the *Baden* case, at p 407, the judge in effect said that 'knowledge' had the same meaning under each head. I pause at that point. In the books and the authorities the word 'notice' is often used in place of the word 'knowledge,' usually without any real explanation of its meaning. This seems to me to be a fertile source of confusion; for whatever meaning the layman may attach to those words, centuries of equity jurisprudence have attached a detailed and technical meaning to the term 'notice,' without doing the same for 'knowledge.' The classification of 'notice' into actual notice, constructive notice and imputed notice has been developed in relation to the doctrine that a *bona fide* purchaser for value of a legal estate takes free from any equitable interests of which he has no notice. I need not discuss this classification beyond saying that I use the term 'imputed notice' as meaning any actual or constructive notice that a solicitor or other agent for the purchaser acquires in the course of the transaction in question, such notice being imputed to the purchaser. Some of the cases describe any constructive notice that a purchaser himself obtains as being 'imputed' to him; but I confine 'imputed' to notice obtained by another which equity imputes to the purchaser.

11 [1983] BCLC 325.

Now, until recently, I do not think there had been any classification. However, in the *Baden* case, at p 407, the judgment sets out five categories of knowledge, or of the circumstances in which the court may treat a person as having knowledge. Counsel in that case were substantially in agreement in treating all five types as being relevant for the purpose of a constructive trust; and the judge agreed with them: p 415. These categories are: (i) actual knowledge; (ii) wilfully shutting one's eyes to the obvious; (iii) wilfully and recklessly failing to make such inquiries as an honest and reasonable man would make; (iv) knowledge of circumstances which would indicate the facts to an honest and reasonable man; and (v) knowledge of circumstances which would put an honest and reasonable man on inquiry. If I pause there, it can be said that these categories of knowledge correspond to two categories of notice: Type (i) corresponds to actual notice, and types (ii), (iii), (iv) and (v) correspond to constructive notice. Nothing, however, is said (at least in terms) about imputed knowledge. This is important, because in the case before me Mr Taylor strongly contended that Mr Lickfold's knowledge must be imputed to the Duke, and that this was of the essence of his case.

It seems to me that one must be very careful about applying to constructive trusts either the accepted concepts of notice or any analogy to them. In determining whether a constructive trust has been created, the fundamental question is whether the conscience of the recipient is bound in such a way as to justify equity in imposing a trust on him. The rules concerning a purchaser without notice seem to me to provide little guidance on this and to be liable to be misleading. First, they are irrelevant unless there is a purchase. A volunteer is bound by an equitable interest even if he has no notice of it; but in many cases of alleged constructive trusts the disposition has been voluntary and not for value, and yet notice or knowledge is plainly relevant. Second, although a purchaser normally employs solicitors, and so questions of imputed notice may arise, it is unusual for a volunteer to employ solicitors when about to receive bounty. Even if he does, he is unlikely to employ them in order to investigate the right of the donor to make the gift or of the trustees or personal representatives to make the distribution; and until this case came before me I had never heard it suggested that a volunteer would be fixed with imputed notice of all that his solicitors would have discovered had he employed solicitors and had instructed them to investigate his right to receive the property. Third, there seems to me to be a fundamental difference between the questions that arise in respect of the doctrine of purchaser without notice and constructive trusts. As I said in my previous judgment:

> The former is concerned with the question whether a person takes property subject to or free from some equity. The latter is concerned with whether or not a person is to have imposed upon him the personal burdens and obligations of trusteeship. I do not see why one of the touchstones for determining the burdens on property should be the same as that for deciding whether to impose a personal obligation on a man. The cold calculus of constructive and imputed notice does not seem to me to be an appropriate instrument for deciding whether a man's conscience is sufficiently affected for it to be right to bind him by the obligations of a constructive trustee.

I can see no reason to resile from that statement, save that to meet possible susceptibilities I would alter 'man' to 'person.' I would only add that there is more to being made a trustee than merely taking property subject to an equity.

Accordingly, although I readily approach the five categories of knowledge set out in the *Baden* case as useful guides, I regard them primarily as aids in determining whether or not the Duke's conscience was affected in such a way as to require him to hold any or all of the chattels that he received on a constructive trust.

There is one further general consideration that I should mention, and that is that 'the court should not be astute to impute knowledge where no actual knowledge exists': see the *Baden* case.[12] This approach goes back at least as far as *Barnes v Addy*.[13] The view of James LJ, at p 256, was that the court had in some cases

> ... gone to the very verge of justice in making good to *cestuis que* trust the consequences of the breaches of trust of their trustees at the expense of persons perfectly honest, but who have been, in some more or less degree, injudicious.

Of the five categories of knowledge set out in the *Baden* case, Mr Chadwick, as well as Mr Taylor, accepted the first three. What was in issue was numbers (iv) and (v), namely, knowledge of circumstances which 'would indicate the facts to an honest and reasonable man' or 'would put an honest and reasonable man on inquiry'. On the view that I take of the present case I do not think that it really matters whether or not categories (iv) and (v) are included, but as the matter has been argued at length, and further questions on it may arise, I think I should say something about it.

First, as I have already indicated, I think that one has to be careful to distinguish the notice that is relevant in the doctrine of purchaser without notice from the knowledge that suffices for the imposition of a constructive trust. This is shown by a short passage in the long judgment of the Court of Appeal in *In re Diplock*.[14] There, it was pointed out that on the facts of that case persons unversed in the law were entitled to assume that the executors were properly administering the estate, and that if those persons received money *bona fide* believing themselves to be entitled to it, 'they should not have imposed upon them the heavy obligations of trusteeship'. The judgment then pointed out:

> ... the principles applicable to such cases are not the same as the principles in regard to notice of defects in title applicable to transfers of land where regular machinery has long since been established for inquiry and investigation.

12 [1983] BCLC 325, p 415, *per* Gibson J.

13 (1874) 9 Ch App 244, pp 251, 252.

14 [1948] Ch 465, pp 478, 479.

To that I may add the obvious point that the provisions about constructive notice in s 199 of the Law of Property Act 1925 apply only to purchasers (as defined in s 205(1)(xxi)) and are not in point in relation to a beneficiary who receives trust property from the trustees. With that, I turn to the cases on constructive knowledge. Mr Taylor relied strongly on *Selangor United Rubber Estates Ltd v Cradock (No 3)*[15] and *Karak Rubber Co Ltd v Burden (No 2)*.[16] Each was a knowing assistance case. In the *Selangor* case, at p 1582, Ungoed-Thomas J, immediately after speaking of tracing property into the hands of a volunteer, said that equity 'will hold a purchaser for value liable as constructive trustee if he had actual or constructive notice that the transfer to him was of trust property in breach of trust...'; and at p 1583 he went on to refer to equitable rights and to say that in general 'it is equitable that a person with actual notice or constructive notice of those rights should be fixed with knowledge of them'. I find this view hard to reconcile with the passage in *In re Diplock*[17] (a case not cited to the judge) which I have just mentioned; and with all respect, it also seems to me to tend to confuse the absence of notice which shields a purchaser from liability under the doctrine of tracing, with the absence of knowledge of the trust which will prevent the imposition of a constructive trust. The judge went on to consider the meaning of 'knowledge' in various judgments, and reached a conclusion that knowledge was not confined to actual knowledge; and with this, as such, Mr Chadwick had no quarrel. But he strongly contended that the cases cited on the extended meaning of 'knowledge' were cases within the 'wilful and reckless' head in the classification in the *Baden* case[18] (ie, type (iii)), and that there was nothing to justify the inclusion of types (iv) and (v). The essential difference, of course, is that types (ii) and (iii) are governed by the words 'wilfully' or 'wilfully and recklessly,' whereas types (iv) and (v) have no such adverbs. Instead, they are cases of carelessness or negligence being tested by what an honest and reasonable man would have realised or would have inquired about, even if the person concerned was, for instance, not at all reasonable. Yet Ungoed-Thomas J in his conclusion, at p 1590, applied the standard of what would have been indicated to an honest and reasonable man, or would have put him on inquiry, and so, I think, included all five of the *Baden* types of knowledge, and not only the first three. In the *Karak* case,[19] Brightman J considered this conclusion. Again *In re Diplock*[20] was not cited, but *Williams v Williams*,[21] another case not cited to Ungoed-Thomas J in the *Selangor* case,[22] was duly examined. Brightman J distinguished that case by pointing out that it was a knowing receipt case, whereas the case before him was a knowing assistance case; and he said, at p 638, that *Williams v Williams* had 'no relevance at all to the case before me'. In

15 [1968] 1 WLR 1555.
16 [1972] 1 WLR 602.
17 [1948] Ch 465.
18 [1983] BCLC 325.
19 [1972] 1 WLR 602.
20 [1948] Ch 465.
21 (1881) 17 Ch D 437.
22 [1968] 1 WLR 1555.

Williams v Williams Kay J had held that the recipient of the trust property, a solicitor, was not liable as a constructive trustee and, at p 445, the judge said that the case would be 'very different' if the recipient had 'wilfully shut his eyes'. He then referred to the 'very great negligence' of the solicitor, *qua* solicitor, in ignoring the trust, though holding that he was not liable as a constructive trustee. I do not see how Kay J could have reached that conclusion if he had thought that knowledge of *Baden* types (iv) and (v) had sufficed; and, of course, what is before me is a case of knowing receipt, like *Williams v Williams* and unlike the *Karak* case.

There is also *In re Blundell*,[23] a case not cited in the *Selangor* case.[24] It was cited but not mentioned in the judgment in the *Karak* case,[25] but like *Williams v Williams*,[26] and *In re Diplock*[27] it does not appear in the *Baden* case:[28] all three, I may say, were duly cited in the *Carl Zeiss* case.[29] In *In re Blundell* Stirling J refused to hold that a solicitor was a constructive trustee of costs that a trustee of property had allowed him to take out of the estate, even though he knew that the trustee was guilty of a breach of trust, 'unless there are facts brought home to him which show that to his knowledge the money is being applied in a manner which is inconsistent with the trust': see p 381. Both *Williams v Williams* and *In re Blundell* figure prominently in the judgments of Sachs and Edmund Davies LJJ in the *Carl Zeiss* case, in support of their conclusion that negligence is not enough and that there must be dishonesty, a conscious impropriety or a lack of probity before liability as a constructive trustee is imposed.

I should also mention certain other cases. *Consul Development Pty Ltd v DPC Estates Pty Ltd*[30] is a case where from the judgments of Barwick CJ and Gibbs and Stephen JJ may be collected a somewhat tentative acceptance of type (iv) knowledge, but not of type (v). *Belmont Finance Corp Ltd v Williams Furniture Ltd*,[31] shows Buckley and Goff LJJ taking the view (though not as a matter of decision) that what is required in a knowing assistance case is actual knowledge, wilful shutting the eyes to dishonesty, or wilful and reckless failure to inquire, but that other forms of constructive notice are not enough; and Orr LJ concurred. Goff LJ at p 275 reaffirmed the view that he had expressed in *Competitive Insurance Co Ltd v Davies Investments Ltd*[32] that 'constructive notice of the s 199 type would not be sufficient'. I do not read the judgments of Buckley and Goff LJJ in *Belmont Finance Corp Ltd v Williams*

23 (1888) 40 Ch D 370.
24 [1968] 1 WLR 1555.
25 [1972] 1 WLR 602.
26 (1881) 17 Ch D 437.
27 [1948] Ch 465.
28 [1983] BCLC 325.
29 [1969] 2 Ch 276.
30 (1975) 132 CLR 373.
31 [1979] Ch 250, pp 267, 275.
32 [1975] 1 WLR 1240.

Furniture Ltd (No 2),[33] as resiling from the views that they had expressed in the earlier stages of the case.

There is a further question that I should consider, and that is forgetfulness. Little was said about this in argument; but in a case in which at one time the true position was known to Mr Lickfold, and possibly to the Duke, I must say something about it. If a person once has clear and distinct knowledge of some fact, is he to be treated as knowing that fact for the rest of his life, even after he has genuinely forgotten all about it? To me, such a question almost answers itself. I suppose that there may be some remarkable beings for whom once known is never forgotten; but apart from them, the generality of mankind probably forgets far more than is remembered. So far as the doctrine of notice is concerned, there is authority, in relation to the rule in *Dearle v Hall*,[34] for saying that the question is whether at the time in question notice previously obtained continues to operate on the mind of the recipient: see *Ipswich Permanent Money Club Ltd v Arthy*.[35] Of course, since 1925 there is a statutory scheme under s 137 of the Law of Property Act 1925 for regulating priority by means of the receipt of written notices; and nothing I say is intended to suggest that such notices might lose their effect if the recipient or anyone else forgets them. But apart from such statutory provisions, it seems to me that a person should not be said to have knowledge of a fact that he once knew if at the time in question he has genuinely forgotten all about it, so that it could not be said to operate on his mind any longer. This is emphasised in relation to constructive trusts in that, in my view, it would be wrong to hold that a person's conscience is affected by something that he does not know about. Even if s 199 of the Law of Property Act 1925 had any application, and notice were in issue, I cannot accept Mr Taylor's contention that the section shows that what a person once knew he is conclusively presumed still to have notice of; for the section is framed in terms of what 'is' within the purchaser's own knowledge, and not 'is or ever has been' within his knowledge.

Of course, the court may be slow to conclude that what was once known has been forgotten; but such a conclusion is likely to be aided if the person has received professional advice which treats the fact forgotten as if it did not exist. The relevance of this is that even if the Duke did once understand the true meaning of clause 14(B), there is nothing to suggest that he still knew it when he received the chattels, especially in the light of what Mr Lickfold had written to him. The fact that he had a copy of the 1923 settlement and could have read clause 14(B) and questioned Mr Lickfold about it does not, in my judgment, show that the Duke at any relevant time had anything that can be called 'knowledge' that the transfer of the chattels to him was a breach of trust or in any way improper. The question must be determined by what knowledge the Duke had at the time of the transfer, and not by his state of knowledge at any previous time.

33 [1980] 1 All ER 393, pp 405, 412.

34 (1828) 3 Russ 1.

35 [1920] 2 Ch 257.

I shall attempt to summarise my conclusions. In doing this, I make no attempt to reconcile all the authorities and *dicta*, for such a task is beyond me; and in this I suspect I am not alone. Some of the difficulty seems to arise from judgments that have been given without all the relevant authorities having been put before the judges. All I need do is to find a path through the wood that will suffice for the determination of the case before me, and to assist those who have to read this judgment:

(1) The equitable doctrine of tracing and the imposition of a constructive trust by reason of the knowing receipt of trust property are governed by different rules and must be kept distinct. Tracing is primarily a means of determining the rights of property, whereas the imposition of a constructive trust creates personal obligations that go beyond mere property rights.

(2) In considering whether a constructive trust has arisen in a case of the knowing receipt of trust property, the basic question is whether the conscience of the recipient is sufficiently affected to justify the imposition of such a trust.

(3) Whether a constructive trust arises in such a case primarily depends on the knowledge of the recipient, and not on notice to him; and for clarity it is desirable to use the word 'knowledge' and avoid the word 'notice' in such cases.

(4) For this purpose, knowledge is not confined to actual knowledge, but includes at least knowledge of types (ii) and (iii) in the *Baden* case,[36] ie, actual knowledge that would have been acquired but for shutting one's eyes to the obvious, or wilfully and recklessly failing to make such inquiries as a reasonable and honest man would make; for in such cases there is a want of probity which justifies imposing a constructive trust.

(5) Whether knowledge of the *Baden* types (iv) and (v) suffices for this purpose is at best doubtful; in my view, it does not, for I cannot see that the carelessness involved will normally amount to a want of probity.

(6) For these purposes, a person is not to be taken to have knowledge of a fact that he once knew but has genuinely forgotten: the test (or a test) is whether the knowledge continues to operate on that person's mind at the time in question.

(7) (a) It is at least doubtful whether there is a general doctrine of 'imputed knowledge' that corresponds to 'imputed notice.'

(b) Even if there is such a doctrine, for the purposes of creating a constructive trust of the 'knowing receipt' type the doctrine will not apply so as to fix a donee or beneficiary with all the knowledge that his solicitor has, at all events if the donee or beneficiary has not employed the solicitor to investigate his right to the bounty, and has done nothing else that can be treated as accepting that the solicitor's knowledge should be treated as his own.

36 [1983] BCLC 325, p 407.

(c) Any such doctrine should be distinguished from the process whereby, under the name 'imputed knowledge', a company is treated as having the knowledge that its directors and secretary have.

(8) Where an alleged constructive trust is based not on 'knowing receipt' but on 'knowing assistance', some at least of these considerations probably apply; but I need not decide anything on that, and I do not do so.

From what I have said, it must be plain that in my judgment the Duke did not become a constructive trustee of any of the chattels. I can see nothing that affected his conscience sufficiently to impose a constructive trust on him: and even if, contrary to my opinion, all of the five *Baden* types of knowledge are in point, instead of only the first three, I do not think that he had any such knowledge. He was a layman, and he accepted and acted on what he was told by his solicitor and was acted on by the trustees and the solicitor to the trustees. Furthermore, as stated in my earlier judgment, the plaintiff himself had executed a deed of appointment of new trustees dated 25 June 1953. This deed contained a full release of the then trustees in respect of all acts and things done or omitted to be done by them; and yet there has been no suggestion that at that time the plaintiff had made any complaint of the massive breaches of trust that the trustees had committed a few years earlier by failing to make the selection of chattels required by clause 14(B) and allowing the Duke to take any chattels he wanted. However, quite apart from this, I would reach the same conclusion. Accordingly, I hold that the Duke never became a constructive trustee of any of the chattels.

Similar views were expressed at first instance by Steyn J in *Barclays Bank v Quincecare Ltd* [1992] 4 All ER 363, and Alliott J in *Lipkin Gorman v Karpnale* [1992] 4 All ER 331.

Likewise, the court (Knox J) in *Cowan de Groot Properties Ltd v Eagle Trust plc* endorsed the decision of Megarry VC in *Re Montagu*. The court decided that a stranger to a trust cannot be made a constructive trustee unless he acts with 'knowledge' (categories (i) to (iii) in the *Baden* case) that his conduct is inconsistent with the trust. The basis of liability under this head, in Knox J's view, is dishonesty, or want of probity. Accordingly, on a counterclaim by the defendant, the court decided that the plaintiff was not a constructive trustee under the 'knowingly receiving' category.

Cowan de Groot Properties Ltd v Eagle Trust plc [1992] 4 All ER 700, CA

E plc agreed to sell three properties for a total of £900,000 to Pinepad Ltd (P Ltd) [a 100% subsidiary of C Ltd] and to grant an option to purchase two other properties to P Ltd. Prior to the completion of the sale E sought to rescind the whole agreement. Shortly thereafter, P purported to exercise the option. In various stages P sold on the three properties to C Ltd. C now brought an action against E, claiming a declaration that the notice exercising the option was valid and effective. E counterclaimed, maintaining that the agreement was defective and that P or C was liable as constructive trustee of the properties and proceeds of sale, on the ground of 'knowing receipt'. It was alleged by E that two of its directors acted fraudulently in bringing about the sale, and that C's managing director (Mr Samuelson) knew of the fraudulent breach. It was alleged that Mr Samuelson knew (subjectively within categories (i) to (iii) of *Baden*'s case) of the undervalue at which the properties were sold. In the alternative, that P Ltd or C Ltd had objective knowledge (categories (iv) and (v) in *Baden*'s case) of the impropriety.

Held, in favour of the plaintiff and rejecting the constructive trust claim. C's managing director did not, on the facts, have subjective knowledge of a fraudulent conduct of E's directors. The duty of directors of a purchasing company was to purchase the property as cheaply as they possibly could. It was reasonable for C's managing director to assume that E was looking for a quick sale and had no time to market the property efficiently. Objective notice was not relevant to found a claim based on the 'knowingly receiving' category of constructive trust.

> **Knox J:** Mr Samuelson did not, in my judgment, have the knowledge in any of the categories (i), (ii) or (iii), of the *Baden* classification, of the facts that constituted the breach of fiduciary duty in the sale at the figure and on the terms on which it was affected. That is fatal to Eagle's claim on the basis of a sale at an undervalue, on the view which I take of the test to be applied to a purchase in a commercial transaction from a company vendor. If, contrary to my view, it is right to have regard to the categories (iv) and (v) of the *Baden* classification, I would still conclude that Mr Samuelson should not be treated as having the requisite knowledge. I have stated my conclusion in terms of the classification of circumstances in *Baden,* principally because that is the way the case was pleaded and argued by the parties. I share the reservations expressed by Millett J in *Agip v Jackson* regarding over refinement in making the distinctions implicit in that classification or a too ready assumption that categories (iv) and (v) are necessarily cases of constructive notice only. In my judgment, it may well be that the underlying broad principle which runs through the authorities regarding commercial transactions is that the court will impute knowledge, on the basis of what a reasonable person would have learnt, to a person who is guilty of commercially unacceptable conduct in the particular context involved.

In *Polly Peck International v Nadir (No 2)* [1992] 4 All ER 769 (see below, p 455), a contrary view was expressed by the Court of Appeal as to the basis of liabilty under the 'knowingly receiving' head. The approach here, which is supported by a wealth of authority, is that liability under this head is restitution based. The rationale for imposing liability on the defendant is based on the premise that he has acquired the plaintiff's property. Dishonesty or want of probity ought not to be the touchstones of liability. The issues in this context are: whether the defendant has acquired the plaintiff's property, and whether he knows that his acquisition was in breach of trust. The reverse situation, which will entitle the defendant to take free of the plaintiff's claim, depends on whether he is a *bona fide* purchaser for value without notice of the breach of trust. Accordingly, 'knowledge' within any of the five categories laid down in *Re Baden* will be sufficient to impose liability on the defendant.

***Polly Peck International plc v Nadir and Others (No 2)* [1992] 4 All ER 769, CA**

The administrators of the plaintiff company (PPI) claimed that N and IBK (a bank controlled by him) had misapplied £142 m of PPI's funds. Part of that money had been transferred by the bank to the London account of the fourth defendant, the Central Bank of the Turkish Republic of Northern Cyprus. The Central Bank exercised the supervisory and regulatory role of a central bank in a sovereign State. The administrators claimed that a scheme whereby PPI's funds were transferred via IBK to Northern Cyprus was, at best, in breach of fiduciary duties owed by N to PPI and, at worst, a dishonest means of diverting PPI's funds for improper purposes. The plaintiffs also contended that either the Central Bank had actual knowledge of the fraudulent scheme or, at best, was put on inquiry as to the impropriety of the scheme. Accordingly, the plaintiffs claimed that the Central Bank was a constructive trustee, a tracing order in respect of some £8.9 m standing to the Central Bank's account at the London clearing bank, and a Mareva injunction against the Central Bank to protect the £8.9 m. The judge granted the injunction subject to the proviso to enable the Central Bank to carry on its banking business in the normal way. The bank appealed against the order.

Held, by the Court of Appeal, allowing the appeal and discharging the order: there was insufficient evidence for finding that the Central Bank had knowledge of the alleged impropriety perpetrated by N and IBK. The tracing claim failed for the same reason.

> **Scott LJ:** Receipt of trust money by a *bona fide* purchaser for value, without notice of the breach of trust, bars any equitable tracing remedy. It follows that actual or constructive knowledge on the part of the Central Bank of the trust character of the funds received from IBK and of the impropriety of the transfers is as much a requirement of the tracing claim as of the constructive trust claim.
>
> There is a general consensus of opinion that, if liability as constructive trustee is sought to be imposed ... on the basis that the defendant has assisted in the misapplication of trust property (knowing assistance), 'something amounting to dishonesty or want of probity on the part of the defendant must be shown' (*per* Vinelott J in *Eagle Trust plc v SBC Securities Ltd*). Vinelott J described as 'settled law' the proposition that 'a stranger cannot be made liable for knowing assistance in a fraudulent breach of trust unless knowledge of the fraudulent design can be impugned to him ...'. I respectfully agree.
>
> Millett J, in the judgment below, treated the present case as one of 'knowing assistance' rather than 'knowing receipt'. In respect of the nine sterling transfers I think that is right. The Central Bank received the funds transferred not in its own right but as banker, and, as banker, credited the funds to IBK in Northern Cyprus. But in respect of the bulk of the transfers the case is, in my opinion, one of 'receipt' rather than 'assistance'. The Central Bank was exchanging Turkish lire for sterling and became entitled to the sterling not as banker for IBK but in its own right.

Liability as constructive trustee in a 'knowing receipt' case does not require that the misapplication of the trust funds should be fraudulent. It does require that the defendant should have knowledge that the funds were trust funds and that they were being misapplied. Actual knowledge obviously will suffice. Mr Potts has submitted that it will suffice if the defendant can be shown to have had knowledge of facts which would have put an honest and reasonable man on inquiry, or at least, if the defendant can be shown to have wilfully and recklessly failed to make such inquiries as an honest and reasonable man would have made (see categories (iii) and (v) of the categories of mental state identified by Peter Gibson in *Baden*'s case). I do not think there is any doubt that, if the latter of the two criteria can be established against the Central Bank, that will suffice. I have some doubts about the sufficiency of the former criterion but do not think that the present appeal is the right occasion for settling the issue. The various categories of mental state identified in *Re Baden*'s case are not rigid categories with clear and precise boundaries. One category may merge imperceptibly into another.

The real question, however, is whether the circumstances in which the transfers were made should have made the Central Bank suspicious of the propriety of what was being done. Millett J thought so. He thought so because of ' the sheer scale of the payments'.

I find myself unimpressed by the 'sheer scale' argument in so far as it is put forward as a ground for contending that the Central Bank ought to have suspected impropriety. Millett J commented that 'these payments were on a scale which was completely unjustified by any legitimate business requirement which Polly Peck or its trading subsidiaries in Northern Cyprus could possibly have had'. With the greatest respect to the judge, I do not think this conclusion is a fair one so far as the Central Bank is concerned ... the constructive trust test, the ' honest and reasonable banker' being put on enquiry (if that is indeed the test), postulates inquiry as to whether or not impropriety is being committed. The test is not satisfied by the inference of no more than curiosity. It is important in this regard to bear in mind that it is common ground, that at the relevant time Mr Nadir was a man of unblemished commercial reputation and integrity. He had achieved quite staggering commercial success over a relatively short period. He loomed in Northern Cyprus like a colossus over the local economy and over the commercial prospects and fortune of the country. Why should the Central Bank have suspected impropriety because of the scale of the funds being transferred into Northern Cyprus? ... The question whether the bank did or did not have an honest belief only arises after the bank has become, or ought to have become, suspicious of possible impropriety. Unless ground had been given for suspicion, no one in the Central Bank would have any relevant belief at all. They would not address their minds to impropriety or to the legitimacy of the purpose for which the funds were being moved.

In the present case the degree of knowledge on the part of the Central Bank that PPI must establish for the purposes of its constructive trust case is, in my judgment, requisite also for the purposes of its equitable tracing claim. It follows that the conclusions I have expressed on the constructive trust claim apply also to the tracing claim.

> Hoffman LJ in *El Ajou v Dollar Land Holdings plc and Another* [see below] said that in order to make the defendant a constructive trustee under the 'knowingly receiving' head, the plaintiff is required to establish the following elements:
>
> > ... first, a disposal of his (plaintiff's) assets in breach of fiduciary duty; secondly, the beneficial receipt by the defendant of assets which are traceable as representing the assets of the plaintiff; and thirdly, knowledge on the part of the defendant that the assets he received are traceable to a breach of fiduciary duty.

In this case, the issue was whether the knowledge of a non-executive director of the defendant company, of a fraudulent dealing with the plaintiff's property, was sufficient to impose liability as a constructive trustee on the defendant company.

El Ajou v Dollar Land Holdings plc and Another [1994] 2 All ER 685, CA

The plaintiff owned substantial funds and securities which were placed under the control of Mr Murad, his investment manager. Mr Murad was bribed in order to invest the plaintiff's money in fraudulent share selling schemes operated by three Canadians. The proceeds of these schemes were ultimately invested in a property company, Dollar Land Holdings plc (DLH), a company unconnected with the three Canadians. Mr Stern, the managing director of DLH was introduced to the Canadians by Mr Ferdman (the chairman and non-executive director of DLH) through his Swiss company, Societe d'Administration et de Financement SA (SAFI). SAFI acted as a fiduciary agent for the Canadians. Mr Stern approached Mr Ferdman for assistance in obtaining finance for DLH's property development project and this led to the introduction to the Canadians. The plaintiff was able to trace his funds through the Canadians into DLH and sought to recover his funds from DLH, on the ground that that company received his funds with knowledge that it represented the proceeds of fraud. Millett J, in the High Court, decided against the plaintiff, on the ground that there was insufficient evidence to establish that the defendant company had knowledge of the fraudulent scheme. The plaintiff appealed.

Held, by the Court of Appeal, reversing the decision of the High Court, that DLH had knowledge of the relevant facts. Mr Ferdman, who played no active part in the management of the company, but performed significant acts on behalf of DLH, was nevertheless the company's 'directing mind and will'. Accordingly, the director's knowledge that assets had been received by the company was sufficient to make the company a constructive trustee on behalf of the plaintiff. The 'directing mind' doctrine is not restricted to directors who make policy decisions on behalf of the company. The nominee director with non-executive responsibility (such as Mr Ferdman) may, in special circumstances, become the company's 'directing mind and will'. Mr Ferdman made all the arrangements for the disbursement of the moneys, and he signed the documents causing the company to become involved in the fraudulent project and subsequently to acquire the assets representing the moneys fraudulently misapplied.

However, on a separate ground, the court decided that Mr Ferdman's knowledge could not be imputed to DLH on agency principles. DLH was under no duty to inquire as to the source of the money and Mr Ferdman was under no duty to inform DLH of the origin of the money.

Knowing assistance in a fraudulent transaction

Under this head of liability, a stranger to a trust becomes a constructive trustee (a form of personal liability) if he knowingly assists in a fraudulent scheme conducted by another (perhaps the settlement trustee). This is the position even though the stranger does not receive the trust property. As was pointed out earlier, the basis of liability here is the stranger's assistance and knowledge of the fraudulent transaction. In short, the stranger acts as an accomplice to the principal fraudulent trustee or party. The stranger acts dishonestly or fraudulently.

According to Peter Gibson J, in *Re Baden Delvaux*, the following four elements are required to be established in order to attach liability to the stranger. They are:

(i) the existence of the trust [or a fiduciary relationship];

(ii) the existence of a dishonest and fraudulent design on the part of the trustees of the trust [or fiduciary];

(iii) the assistance by the stranger in that design; and

(iv) the knowledge of that stranger.

In relation to the first element, the trust need not be a formal trust. It is sufficient that the fiduciary relationship is created between the stranger and another person in respect of the latter's property. A fiduciary is one who is aware that his confidence and judgment is relied on (and this is, in fact, relied on) by another. Thus, bankers, directors and agents stand in a fiduciary relationship to their customers, companies or principals.

With regard to the second element, no distinction is drawn between the words 'fraudulent' and 'dishonest'. They mean the same thing. But the words are to be construed in accordance with principles of equitable relief. Thus, conduct which is morally reprehensible can be said to be dishonest and fraudulent. Accordingly, not every breach of trust will satisfy this requirement, for a breach of trust falling short of dishonesty or fraud would be insufficient to create a constructive trust. Fraud, in this context, involves the taking of a risk which the stranger honestly knows that he has no right to take and which is prejudicial to another's right.

Lord Nicholls in *Royal Brunei Airlines v Tan* (see below, p 472) declared that, in order to decide whether a person is dishonest, the court is required to look at all the circumstances known to the defendant. This would require the court to have regard to the personal attributes of the defendant, such as his experience, intelligence and possible explanations for his actions. The court decided that a dishonest third party who assisted a trustee, or procured him to commit a breach of trust, was liable to the beneficiaries for the resulting loss. It was not necessary to prove, in addition, that the trustee's conduct is dishonest or fraudulent.

The third element involves assistance. This assumes any act (including an omission when there is a duty to act) effected by the stranger which enables the trustee to commit a fraudulent breach of trust. Whether this element is satisfied or not is a question of fact.

To render assistance as an accessory to a dishonest breach of trust, the defendant is required to lend assistance in the knowledge of, or belief in, the existence of the trust, and the knowledge that his or her assistance will facilitate the breach of trust.

Brinks Ltd v Abu-Saleh and Others (No 3) (1995) *The Times*, 23 October, HC

Brinks Ltd suffered a bullion robbery in 1983 when gold and other valuables worth some £26 m were stolen from its warehouse at Heathrow. In order to recover the proceeds, it brought civil proceedings against 57 defendants who had allegedly been involved in the robbery and subsequent laundering operations. One of the defendants was Mrs Elcombe. It was alleged that, between August 1984 and February 1985, she *assisted* her husband, the 12th defendant, in the part he played in laundering part of the proceeds of the stolen gold by carrying approximately £3 m in cash to Mr Parry, one of the convicted robbers, from England to Zurich by car. There were six such trips in total and Mr Elcombe's reward for the journeys was £30,000 plus expenses. The allegations against Mrs Elcombe were, *inter alia*, that Brinks Ltd's funds were stolen with the assistance of a dishonest fiduciary, Mr Black (who was employed as a security guard and generally participated in the planning and execution of the robbery). The plaintiffs had an equity to trace into the proceeds, which were in the nature of trust moneys, and compel the defendants to account to them owing to dishonest assistance in a breach of trust, that is to say:

(a) that Mrs Elcombe knew that the money her husband was carrying represented the proceeds of stolen gold;

(b) that, even if she did not know this fact, she at least believed that he was engaged in a dishonest transaction intended to defeat the claims of the Inland Revenue or of companies in which Mr Parry was interested;

(c) that she provided assistance to her husband by disguising what she knew to be an illegal operation with the apparent innocence of a family holiday or an antique goods buying trip. An important element of the cover intended was to deter the suspicious from regarding the various journeys as other than common place and honest.

Counsel for Mrs Elcombe disputed that his client knew or believed that she was engaged in a dishonest design and assisted her husband in furtherance of Mr Black's breach of trust.

His Lordship found that Mrs Elcombe knew that the purpose of the trips the couple made was to courier money to Zurich at Mr Parry's request. These moneys were in fact the proceeds of gold stolen from Brinks Ltd and Mr Parry knew that to be the case. On the evidence, Mrs Elcombe and her husband believed the money to be derived from Mr Parry's business empire and was the subject of a tax evasion exercise. They were unaware of the true origin of the moneys.

In dismissing the claim, Rimer J decided that:

(i) Mrs Elcombe went on the trips in the capacity of Mr Elcombe's wife. Her presence on such trips did not constitute 'assistance' in furtherance of a breach of trust;

(ii) it was not strictly necessary to decide whether Mrs Elcombe was liable as an accessory to a breach of trust by merely proving that she had provided assistance in the furtherance of a dishonest transaction, regardless of whether she knew that such assistance involved a breach of trust. The Privy Council, in *Royal Brunei Airlines v Tan Ming* [1995] 3 WLR 64, decided the basis on which accessories have been held to be liable for assisting in breaches of trust. The law has not gone so far as to give a beneficiary a remedy against an accessory who dealt with the trustee in ignorance that he was a trustee, or who knew that he was a trustee but had no reason to know or suspect that the transaction in which he was assisting was a breach of trust. The claim based on accessory liability could only be brought against someone who knew of the existence of the trust, or at least of the facts giving rise to the trust, and dishonestly rendered assistance in pursuance of a design intended to defeat the trust.

The fourth element, 'knowledge', has provoked strong judicial disagreement. It is common ground that the stranger must know the three elements as mentioned above. The defendant is required to know that there was a trust in existence (although the details need not be known). He must know of the dishonest and fraudulent design of the trustee and that his act (or omission) will assist in the implementation of such design. The contentious issue involves the extent or scope of the knowledge of the stranger. The authorities are in a state of disarray. On the one hand, there is a series of decisions (the earlier cases) which suggest that any of the five categories of knowledge enumerated by Gibson J in *Re Baden Delvaux* would be sufficient to establish liability on the stranger. (See *Selangor United Rubber Estates Ltd v Cradock (No 3)*,[37] *Karak Rubber Co Ltd v Burden (No 2)*[38] and *Re Baden Delvaux*.)[39] The more recent decisions have established that, since the defendant's conduct is tainted with the fraud of the trustees, he (the defendant) ought not be saddled with liability unless he participated in the breach with knowledge (subjective in categories (i) and (ii), or partly objective knowledge in category (iii)) of the fraudulent design of the trustees (see *Agip (Africa) Ltd v Jackson*;[40] *Eagle Trust plc v SBC Securities Ltd*;[41] *Polly Peck International plc v Nadir and Others (No 2)*;[42] *Cowan de Groot Properties Ltd v Eagle Trust plc*).[43]

Selangor United Rubber Estates Ltd v Cradock (No 3) [1968] 2 All ER 1073, HC

In this case, Mr Cradock offered £188,000 for the plaintiff company which had liquid assets of some £232,500. His offer was accepted. He nominated directors who paid the company's money by several stages into Cradock's account, through the District Bank. Cradock was thereby entitled to fund the original offer. This amounted to an unlawful practice, namely, the company using its money to purchase its own shares. In a claim brought by the company in liquidation, the court held that (in addition to the liability of Cradock and his nominee directors) the District Bank was liable as constructive trustee. The bank did not have subjective knowledge of the fraud, but it was held that it ought to have known (constructive knowledge) of the dishonest design.

Ungoed-Thomas J:

Strangers' liability as constructive trustee

I come now to the question how far a stranger to the trust can become liable as constructive trustee in respect of a breach of the trust.

It is essential at the outset to distinguish two very different kinds of so called constructive trustee:

(i) those who, though not appointed trustees, take on themselves to act as such and to possess and administer trust property for the beneficiaries, such as trustees *de son tort*. Distinguishing features for present purposes are (a) they do not claim to act in their own right but for the beneficiaries, and (b) their assumption to act is not of itself a ground of liability (save in the sense of course of liability to account and for any failure in the duty so assumed), and so their status as trustees precedes the occurrence which may be the subject of claim against them;

37 [1968] 2 All ER 1073.

38 [1972] 1 WLR 602.

39 [1983] BCLC 325.

40 [1992] 4 All ER 385.

41 [1992] 4 All ER 488.

42 [1992] 4 All ER 769.

43 [1992] 4 All ER 700.

(ii) those whom a court of equity will treat as trustees by reason of their action of which complaint is made. Distinguishing features for present purposes are (a) they do not claim to act in their own right but for the beneficiaries, and (b) no trusteeship arises before, but only by reason of, the action complained of.

Until the limitation provisions of the Trustee Act 1925, the first category of constructive trustees could not rely, in defence of claims against them, on statutory limitations or the analogous rules enforced by courts of equity. This was because they acted as trustees for others, and therefore held in right of those others and therefore time was held not to run in their favour against those others; but as the second category of trustees claimed in their own right, time ran in their favour from their obtaining possession. It is largely by reason of this distinction that the first category of constructive trustee is sometimes referred to or included in the authorities under the term 'express trustee' (see *Taylor v Davies*;[44] *Soar v Ashwell*,[45] especially the judgment of Lord Esher MR and Bowen LJ).

It has long been well established that a bank is not a trustee for its customer of the amount to his credit in his bank account (see, for example, *Foley v Hill*[46] and *Burdick v Garrick*).[47] In view of this, and the circumstances in which the constructive trusteeship relied on by the plaintiff company against the defendants is said to arise, the plaintiff company does not rely at all in this case on the establishment of the first category of constructive trusteeship, but exclusively on the second category. The first category is irrelevant to the plaintiff company's case. The cases of *Soar v Ashwell*; *Burdick v Garrick*; *Re Barney, Barney v Barney*;[48] *Mara v Browne*;[49] and *Williams-Ashman v Price and Williams*,[50] to which I was referred, fall within that first category.

Barnes v Addy (1874) contains a formulation of the second category of constructive trusteeship, on which the plaintiff relies.

It is this formulation in *Barnes v Addy*, '... assist with knowledge in a dishonest and fraudulent design on the part of the trustees', that is the basis of the plaintiff company's claim that the defendants are liable as constructive trustees. There are thus three elements: (1) assistance by the stranger; (2) with knowledge; (3) in a dishonest and fraudulent design on the part of the trustees. As appears from the passage quoted, an agent acting for a trustee is a stranger within its meaning in that passage, so that he is not liable as a constructive trustee within the second category, unless he too assist 'with knowledge in a dishonest and fraudulent design on the part of the trustees'.

44 [1920] AC 636.

45 [1891–94] All ER 991.

46 [1843–60] All ER 16.

47 (1870) 5 Ch App 233, *per* Lord Hatherley LC.

48 [1892] 2 Ch 265.

49 [1896] 1 Ch 199.

50 [1942] 1 All ER 310.

What knowledge is required to satisfy the second element? Lord Selborne LC, in *Barnes v Addy*, referred to one of the solicitors, a potential constructive trustee, as having no 'knowledge or suspicion ... of an improper or dishonest design', and says that 'there was nothing to lead him to suppose' that there was any intention to misappropriate; and he says of the other solicitor that 'he never knew nor suspected any dishonest purpose'. These references leave wide open the question what knowledge is required.

It seems to me imperative to grasp and keep constantly in mind that the second category of constructive trusteeship (which is the only category with which we are concerned) is nothing more than a formula for equitable relief. The court of equity says that the defendant shall be liable in equity, as though he were a trustee. He is made liable in equity as trustee by the imposition or construction of the court of equity. This is done because in accordance with equitable principles applied by the court of equity it is equitable that he should be held liable as though he were a trustee. Trusteeship and constructive trusteeship are equitable conceptions.

The court of equity is not administering criminal law but equity. It is equity and not criminal law or even tort or contract that governs whether a person shall be liable in equity as constructive trustee. So, whether a misapplication of company's funds for the purchase of its shares occasions the imposition of liability as constructive trustees, depends not on the statutory provision making it a criminal offence, or on statute or criminal law, or common law conceptions, but on equity and its principles. As mentioned in argument, there are criminal offences nowadays which are not morally reprehensible and are not even blameworthy. Indeed, it appears that nowadays, by the Act of Parliment, a person is made a criminal although he can unquestionably and conclusively prove that he did not even know the facts that establish the crime. If, indeed, this is so, this is crime without guilt. It is to brand such proven innocents as convicted criminals. It may be convenient policing. It is not justice, and it certainly is not equity. On the other hand, there may be actions, dishonest and fraudulent in the eyes of equity, yet not punishable under the criminal law. Equity is not crime and this court is not the Old Bailey; and it is according to 'the plain principles of a court of equity' which this court is, in its administration of equitable relief, that what is 'dishonest and fraudulent' has to be judged. Moreover, the language used by the courts of equity, in the authorities referred to, must be similarly understood in accordance with their equitable principles and conceptions. This may all seem over emphatic emphasis of the obvious; but it is an emphasis that I have found essential if confusion is to be avoided.

Equity is concerned to give effect to equitable interests, though bereft of legal ownership. Thus, it will trace trust property into the hands of a volunteer, where it is not inequitable to do so, and will hold a purchaser for value liable as constructive trustee if he had actual or constructive notice that the transfer to him was of trust property in breach of trust (see the statement in *Snell's Principles of Equity*,[51] which was relied on by the plaintiff company and the

51 Megarry, R and Baker, P (ed), *Snell's Principles of Equity*, 26th edn, 1966, London: Sweet & Maxwell, pp 202, 203.

defendants). Moreover, in conveyancing (apart from the intrusion of statute) actual or constructive notice of equitable rights is enough to fasten a grantee with knowledge of those rights. The governing consideration is to give effect to equitable rights, where it is not inequitable to do so, and when knowledge of the existence of those rights is material to granting equitable relief. In general, at any rate, it is equitable that a person with actual notice or constructive notice of those rights should be fixed with knowledge of them. This is in a context of producing equitable results in a civil action and not in the context of criminal liability. The sort of question to which it is directed is which of two persons should in equity bear the loss; and not whether one of them should be sent to prison. So this seems to me to be the very understandable, and indeed equitable, approach of equity ...

He said that a solicitor having then 'no notice' of any breach of trust was not liable. He also said:

> The knowledge required to hold a stranger liable as constructive trustee in a dishonest and fraudulent design, is knowledge of circumstances which would indicate to an honest, reasonable man that such a design was being committed or would put him on enquiry, which the stranger failed to make, whether it was being committed.

Acts in the circumstances normal in the honest conduct of affairs do not indicate such a misapplication, though compatible with it; and answers to enquiries are *prima facie* to be presumed to be honest, an aspect of the law which I shall deal with more fully later when considering negligence.

I come to the third element, 'dishonest and fraudulent design on the part of the trustees'. I have already indicated my view, for reasons already given, that this must be understood in accordance with equitable principles for equitable relief.

I therefore cannot accept the suggestion that, because an action is not of such a dishonest and fraudulent nature as to amount to some crime, that it is not fraudulent and dishonest in the eyes of equity – or that an intention eventually to restore or give value for property – which it was suggested might provide a good defence to a criminal charge – would of itself make its appropriation and use in the meantime, with its attendant risks and deprivation of the true owner, unobjectionable in equity, and thus make what would otherwise be dishonest and fraudulent free from such objection.

It was suggested for the plaintiff company that 'fraudulent' imports the element of loss into what is dishonest, so that the phrase means dishonest resulting in loss to the claimant. It seems to me unnecessary and, indeed, undesirable to attempt to define 'dishonest and fraudulent design', since a definition *in vacuo*, without the advantage of all the circumstances that might occur in cases that might come before the court, might be to restrict their scope by definition without regard to, and in ignorance of, circumstances which should patently come within them. The words themselves are not terms of art and are not taken from a statute or other document demanding construction. They are used in a judgment as the expression and indication of an equitable principle and not in a document as constituting or demanding verbal application and, therefore, definition.

Re Baden Delvaux and Lecuit v Société Général pour Favoriser le Développement de Commerce en France SA [1983] BCLC 325 , HC

The plaintiff, a liquidator, claimed that the defendant, a bank was liable to account as constructive trustee for over $4 m held in an account designated as a trust account by a trustee, a Bahamian bank (BCB). The trustee instructed the defendant to transfer the funds to a Panamanian bank in an account not designated as a trustee account. The moneys were then dissipated. The defendant had relied on a Bahamian court order apparently releasing the moneys from the trust. The court order had been obtained by fraud and it was alleged that in all the circumstances the defendant ought to have known that the moneys were still trust property.

The court held that the defendant at the time of the transfer did not have knowledge of the existence of the trust or the fraudulent design and was unaware that it was assisting in such a scheme. Accordingly, the defendant was not a constructive trustee. The judge accepted a concession made between counsel for the plaintiff and defendant to the effect that any of the five enumerated categories of knowledge would be sufficient to establish liability as a constructive trustee under either the 'knowing receipt' or 'knowing assistance' head.

> **Peter Gibson J:** It is clear that a stranger to a trust may make himself accountable to the beneficiaries under the trust in certain circumstances. The two main categories of circumstances have been given the convenient labels in *Snell's Principles of Equity*,[52] 'Knowing receipt or dealing' and 'Knowing assistance'. The first category of 'Knowing receipt or dealing' is described, at p 194:
>
>> A person receiving property which is subject to a trust ... becomes a constructive trustee if he falls within either of two heads, namely, (i) that he received trust property with actual or constructive notice that it was trust property and that the transfer to him was a breach of trust; or (ii) that although he received it without notice of the trust, he was not a *bona fide* purchaser for value without notice of the trust, and yet, after he had subsequently acquired notice of the trust, he dealt with the property in a manner inconsistent with the trust.
>
> The quotation in the passage cited from *Snell* is taken from *Barnes v Addy*.[53] In that case, the husband of the life tenant under a trust was appointed sole trustee. He subsequently misappropriated the trust property. The issue for the court was whether the solicitors who had acted in respect of his appointment were liable to make good the misappropriations and the court held that the solicitors could not be made so liable. In referring to 'agents' Lord Selborne LC had in mind professional men who act on instructions from trustees. For, as he went on, after the passage which I have cited, at p 252:

52 28th edn, 1982, London: Sweet & Maxwell, pp 194–95.

53 (1874) LR 9 Ch App 244, p 251, *per* Lord Selborne LC.

> Those are the principles, as it seems to me, which we must bear in mind in dealing with the facts of this case. If those principles were disregarded, I know not how any one could, in transactions admitting of doubt as to the view which a court of equity might take of them, safely discharge the office of solicitor, of banker, or of agent of any sort to trustees.

The 'knowing assistance' category as formulated by Lord Selborne LC appears to be directed to strangers who do not receive trust property and that is how it is described in *Snell.* Mr Price accepts that there are four elements which must be established if a case is to be brought within the category of 'knowing assistance'. They are: (1) the existence of a trust; (2) the existence of a dishonest and fraudulent design on the part of the trustee of the trust; (3) the assistance by the stranger in that design; and (4) the knowledge of the stranger. I would add that whilst it is of course helpful to isolate the relevant constituent elements of the 'knowing assistance' category in this way, it is important not to lose sight of the requirement that, taken together, those elements must leave the court satisfied that the alleged constructive trustee was a party or privy to dishonesty on the part of the trustee.

As to the first element, the trust need not be a formal trust. It is sufficient that there should be a fiduciary relationship between the 'trustee' and the property of another person. If A is placed in possession of or continues to exercise command or control over the property of B while it remains B's property, and A can deal with B's property only for the benefit of B or for purposes authorised by B, A is a trustee of that property for the purposes of constructive trusteeship. Thus directors of a company, in consequence of the fiduciary character of the duties which they owe to the company, are treated as if they were the trustees of the company's property under their control; both the *Selangor* case[54] and the *Karak* case,[55] provide examples of such a trust. Similarly the manager of a company may owe a fiduciary duty to that company in relation to information he acquires in that capacity such as to constitute the manager a trustee within the category of 'knowing assistance: see *Consul Development Pty Ltd v DPC Estates Pty Ltd,*[56] an Australian case in which a stranger was held not liable as constructive trustee within this category because the stranger lacked the requisite knowledge that the manager's design was fraudulent.

The directors of a company owe fiduciary duties to the company not only in relation to the property beneficially owned by the company but also in my judgment in relation to the property of which the company is a trustee. Those duties extend to preventing a misapplication of the trust property, even if the misapplication consists of the wrongful appropriation to the company itself of the trust property. It cannot be in the true interests of the company to steal trust property. In my judgment for the purpose of constructive trusteeship a person beneficially interested in trust property held by a corporate trustee can rely on the fiduciary relationship between the directors and the trustee

54 [1968] 1 WLR 1555.

55 [1972] 1 WLR 602.

56 (1975) 132 CLR 373.

company as well as on the trust affecting the trust property in the hands of the company. Accordingly if Mr Price can satisfy me that the moneys in the hands of BCB were trust moneys held for the Funds and that the directors of BCB were using their position as directors to cause the misappropriation of the trust moneys, I would regard the first element of the *Barnes v Addy*,[57] formulation as satisfied.

As to the second element the relevant design on the part of the trustee must be dishonest and fraudulent. In the *Selangor* case, Ungoed-Thomas J, held that this element must be understood in accordance with equitable principles for equitable relief and that conduct which is morally reprehensible can properly be said to be dishonest and fraudulent for the purposes of that element. But in *Belmont Finance Corp Ltd v Williams Furniture Ltd*[58] the Court of Appeal made clear that it is not sufficient that there should be misfeasance or a breach of trust falling short of dishonesty and fraud. For present purposes there is no distinction to be drawn between the two adjectives 'dishonest' and 'fraudulent:' see the *Belmont* case.[59] It is common ground between the parties that I can take as a relevant description of fraud 'to take a risk to the prejudice of another's rights, which risk is known to be one which there is no right to take': *Regina v Sinclair*.[60] Thus, Mr Leckie did not dispute Mr Price's submission that the director of a company who owes a duty to use the assets of the company in what he honestly believes to be the best interests of the company, is fraudulent if he takes a risk in using the assets which risk no director could honestly believe to be taken in the interests of the company and which is to the prejudice of the rights of others. It is also common ground that while the standard of proof of an allegation of fraud is no higher than a balance of probabilities, the more serious the allegation, the more cogent is the evidence required to overcome the unlikelihood of what is alleged and thus to prove it.

As to the third element it seems to me to be a simple question of fact, whether or not there has been assistance. The payment by a bank on the instructions of fraudulent directors of a company of moneys of the company to another person may be such assistance, as in the *Selangor* case[61] and the *Karak* case.[62] Mr Leckie submitted that there cannot be assistance for the purposes of constructive trusteeship unless that which is done by the stranger inevitably has the consequence that a loss is suffered, and that a mere payment which in itself does not have that consequence is not sufficient. I accept that the assistance must be an act which is part of the fraudulent and dishonest design and must not be of minimal importance.

It is in respect of the fourth element, knowledge, that there has been the greater part of the legal debate, though in the event the area of dispute between Mr

57 (1874) LR 9 Ch App 244.

58 [1979] Ch 250.

59 *Ibid*, p 267.

60 [1968] 1 WLR 1246, p 1249.

61 [1968] 1 WLR 1555.

62 [1972] 1 WLR 602.

Price and Mr Leckie on the principles to be applied was comparatively small. In particular I should make clear that in this case there has been no challenge by Mr Leckie to the correctness of the decisions in the *Selangor* and *Karak* cases.

I start, first, by considering what it is that the alleged constructive trustee must know. I think it clear that he must know the three elements already mentioned. He must know that there was a trust though I do not think it necessary that he should know all the details of the trust: see for example *Foxton v Manchester and Liverpool District Banking Co*.[63] He must know of the dishonest and fraudulent design of the trustee. Again, however, I do not think it need be knowledge of the whole design: that would be an impossibly high requirement in most cases. What is crucial is that the alleged constructive trustee should know that a design having the character of being fraudulent and dishonest was being perpetrated. Further he must know that his act assisted in the implementation of such design. In circumstances such as the present the defendant must be shown to have known that the $4 m was trust property, that the fraudulent and dishonest design extending to the $4 m was being perpetrated by the directors of BCB and that by moving the $4 m to Panama the defendant assisted in the implementation of this design.

Further, the relevant knowledge must be of facts and not of mere claims or allegations. This is established by the decision of the Court of Appeal in *Carl Zeiss Stiftung v Herbert Smith & Co (No 2)*.[64] Although the *Carl Zeiss* case was one relating to the 'knowing receipt or dealing' category of constructive trusteeship I can see no justification for treating the two categories of constructive trusteeship differently on this point. Each category requires knowledge of the trust. It seems to me also that for the 'knowing assistance' category a similar standard must apply to knowledge of the fraud and of the assistance. Again to differentiate between the different matters knowledge of which is requisite would not in my view be justified.

What types of knowledge are relevant for the purposes of constructive trusteeship? Mr Price submits that knowledge can comprise any one of five different mental states which he described as follows: (i) actual knowledge; (ii) wilfully shutting one's eyes to the obvious; (iii) wilfully and recklessly failing to make such inquiries as an honest and reasonable man would make; (iv) knowledge of circumstances which would indicate the facts to an honest and reasonable man; (v) knowledge of circumstances which would put an honest and reasonable man on inquiry. More accurately, apart from actual knowledge they are formulations of the circumstances which may lead the court to impute knowledge of the facts to the alleged constructive trustee even though he lacked actual knowledge of those facts. Thus the court will treat a person as having constructive knowledge of the facts if he wilfully shuts his eyes to the relevant facts which would be obvious if he opened his eyes, such constructive knowledge being usually termed (though by a metaphor of historical inaccuracy) 'Nelsonian knowledge'. Similarly the court may treat a person as having constructive knowledge of the facts – 'type (iv) knowledge' –

63 (1881) 44 LT 406, p 408.

64 [1969] 2 Ch 276.

if he has actual knowledge of circumstances which would indicate the facts to an honest and reasonable man.

Type (iii) knowledge imports in part an objective test in that the inquiries which were wilfully and recklessly omitted must be those which the honest and reasonable man would have made. There are other authorities which support the view that a wholly objective test is appropriate in determining whether knowledge is to be imputed to the alleged constructive trustee. Although the concept of the reasonable man is one of the common law, Megarry J said in *Coco v AN Clark (Engineers) Ltd*,[65] that he saw no reason why that hard worked creature should not labour in equity as well as at law. The *Selangor* case,[66] contains an extensive review by Ungoed-Thomas J of most of the relevant authorities. He reached this conclusion on the principles to be applied, at p 1590:

> The knowledge required to hold a stranger liable as constructive trustee in a dishonest and fraudulent design, is knowledge of circumstances which would indicate to an honest, reasonable man that such a design was being committed or would put him on inquiry, which the stranger failed to make, whether it was being committed.

In the cases before the *Selangor* case no distinction is drawn between type (iv) and type (v) knowledge. But the distinction is drawn in the *Selangor* case and the subsequent cases.

In *Consul Development Pty Ltd v DPC Estates Pty Ltd*,[67] all the judges of the High Court of Australia indicated provisional acceptance of type (iv) knowledge as relevant for a constructive trust. Gibbs J said, at p 398:

> ... it does not seem to me to be necessary to prove that a stranger who participated in a breach of trust or fiduciary duty with knowledge of all the circumstances did so actually knowing that what he was doing was improper. It would not be just that a person who had full knowledge of all the facts could escape liability because his own moral obtuseness prevented him from recognising an impropriety that would have been apparent to an ordinary man.

But three of the four judges indicated that they did not accept that type (v) knowledge was applicable.

In *Feuer Leather Corp v Frank Johnstone & Sons*,[68] it was alleged that leather, the property in which remained in the plaintiff, was sold improperly and in breach of trust by a director of a company, the agent of the plaintiff, to the defendant, and that the defendant received the leather as constructive trustee with notice of the breach of trust by the director of the agent company. Neill J held that the court should apply an objective test and that if by the test notice was given, liability could not be avoided by proof merely of the absence of actual knowledge. Although Neill J went on to deal specifically with Nelsonian

65 [1969] RPC 41, p 48.

66 [1968] 1 WLR 1555.

67 (1975) 132 CLR 373.

68 [1981] Com LR 251.

knowledge, as I read his judgment, he was accepting the applicability of type (iv) knowledge. However he rejected type (v) knowledge as being inapplicable to the commercial transaction which he was considering. It is the relevance of type (v) knowledge that has been the main subject of judicial controversy since the *Selangor* case.[69]

Ungoed-Thomas J reviewed various authorities on this point. In *Barnes v Addy*[70] itself, it is to be noted, there were references in Lord Selborne LC's judgment, at pp 252 and 254, both to the absence of knowledge and to the absence of any suspicion on the part of the alleged constructive trustee. The relevance of suspicion is that it puts, or may put, the person concerned on inquiry. One of the cases cited to Ungoed-Thomas J, as it was to me, was *Berwick-upon-Tweed Corp v Murray*.[71] The question for the court in that case was whether one William Murray, who received a bank deposit note representing moneys misappropriated by a fiduciary, was liable to restore the moneys in circumstances in which he claimed that he had no actual knowledge that the moneys were misappropriated. Lord Cranworth LC said, at p 512: 'But were not the circumstances such as must have forced an honest man to make inquiry?' Lord Cranworth LC then described the circumstances and said: 'It is impossible that suspicions should not have been excited.' He continued, at p 513:

> Perhaps inquiry might not have brought out the truth; but it does not lie in the mouth of William Murray to say this. He made no inquiry, although the circumstances were such as ought to have induced him to do so. ... It is impossible to permit a man who received, by way of security from a defaulting agent, a deposit of money which had been withdrawn from the funds of his principal, to insist in circumstances like these on his ignorance of the truth. I am clearly of opinion, that William Murray must be treated as a person who had notice of the truth.

In a separate judgment in the same case relating to a different point, Lord Cranworth LC, at p 520, referred to William Murray as having received money 'under circumstances which have satisfied me that the latter knew it was the money of the corporation.' It seems to me, as it did to Ungoed-Thomas J, that what Lord Cranworth LC meant by 'knew' was that, by an objective test, the court would impute to him knowledge of the truth.

In *Nelson v Larholt*,[72] Larholt, a turf accountant, had received eight cheques signed by one Potts expressly as an executor. The beneficiaries under the will of which Potts was the executor brought an action against the defendant who contended that he had no notice of Potts' want of authority. Denning J held that the plaintiffs succeeded and in so doing he applied the following test, at p 343:

69 [1968] 1 WLR 1555.

70 (1874) LR 9 Ch App 244.

71 (1857) 7 De GM & G 497.

72 [1948] 1 KB 339.

> But did he have notice of the want of authority? That depends upon what amounts to notice ... He must, I think, be taken to have known what a reasonable man would have known. If, therefore, he knew or is to be taken to have known of the want of authority, as, for instance, if the circumstances were such as to put a reasonable man on inquiry, and he made none, or if he was put off by an answer that would not have satisfied a reasonable man, or, in other words, if he was negligent in not perceiving the want of authority, then he is taken to have notice of it.

Plainly an objective test was applied in that case. Ungoed-Thomas J's formulation of the law applicable to the 'knowing assistance' category of constructive trusteeship was further reviewed in *Karak Rubber Co Ltd v Burden (No 2)*.[73] That formulation was attacked by the defendants in the *Karak* case on the grounds that it was inconsistent with *ratio decidendi* of, and was impliedly overruled by, the decision of the Court of Appeal in *Carl Zeiss Stiftung v Herbert Smith & Co (No 2)*,[74] and that important and decisive cases were not brought to the attention of Ungoed-Thomas J. The *ratio decidendi* of the *Carl Zeiss* case was that knowledge of a doubtful equity was not sufficient to give an alleged constructive trustee knowledge of the trust, and I respectfully agree with Brightman J that the *Selangor* case[75] though expressly referred to in *Carl Zeiss Stiftung v Herbert Smith & Co (No 2)*[76] was not expressly or impliedly overruled. However it is clear that the *obiter* views of Sachs LJ and Edmund Davies LJ cast doubt on the principles stated by Ungoed-Thomas J in the *Selangor* case in relation to knowledge. Sachs LJ[77] was inclined to the view that, even if the circumstances giving rise to type (v) knowledge could be established, the further element of dishonesty had to be proved. But Edmund Davies LJ, whilst also looking for the element of want of probity to be present (in a passage at p 304 to which I have already referred) recognised as a possible exception from the necessity of establishing actual knowledge the case where the agent is under a duty to inquire, but fails to inquire, into the validity of the third party's claim, although inquiry would have established that it was not well founded. In the *Carl Zeiss* case,[78] it was conceded that the solicitors were under no duty of inquiry. Sachs LJ referred to type (v) knowledge by reference to s 199 of the Law of Property Act 1925. So to label knowledge seems to me apt to mislead, as it conjures up the picture of leisurely and detailed inquiries made by conveyancers about title to land and it implies that inquiries are inappropriate in other types of cases. Whether any duty to inquire arises and what sort of inquiry is appropriate must of course depend on the particular facts of each particular case.

73 [1972] 1 WLR 602.

74 [1969] 2 Ch 276.

75 [1968] 1 WLR 1555.

76 [1969] 2 Ch 276.

77 *Ibid*, p 298.

78 *Ibid*.

In the *Karak* case[79] Brightman J was not content simply to accept Ungoed-Thomas J's statement of the law without considering the position afresh and expressing his own opinion thereon. Having reviewed the authorities he reached the conclusion that Ungoed-Thomas J was correct in treating type (iv) and type (v) knowledge as applicable to constructive trusteeship. The *Karak* case was on its facts similar to the *Selangor* case[80] in that it too related to a circular cheque transaction in which a bank participated and which related to the provision by a company of finance to purchase its own shares. It was held that the officers of the bank, though acting honestly, ought to have made inquiries which would have revealed to the bank that the signatories of its customer were misusing their authority and accordingly the bank was held liable both in negligence and as a constructive trustee.

The principles laid down in the *Selangor* and *Karak* cases were applied by Mr John Mills QC sitting as a deputy judge of the Chancery Division in *Rowlandson v National Westminster Bank Ltd*[81] where again a bank was held liable as constructive trustee for failing to make the inquiries which the reasonable banker would have made. But he was not referred to three cases decided after the *Karak* case,[82] in which the question of knowledge in the context of constructive trusteeship arose.

The first case was *Consul Development Pty Ltd v DPC Estates Pty Ltd*[83] to which I have already referred. The second was *Competitive Insurance Co Ltd v Davies Investments Ltd*,[84] in which Goff J distinguished the *Selangor* and *Karak* cases on the ground that they related to the 'knowing assistance' category of constructive trusteeship, whereas the case before him related to the 'knowing, receipt or dealing' category, there being no fraudulent or dishonest design in which there could be participation. But Goff J indicated his approval of the approach of Sachs LJ and Edmund Davies LJ in the *Carl Zeiss* case[85] though he recognised that a liquidator was an agent of a special character with a statutory power to submit questions to the court and as such might be under a duty of inquiry and incur personal liability as a constructive trustee if he wilfully shuts his eyes or neglects his duty to inquire. The third case was the *Belmont* case,[86] and I have already referred to the provisional views of Buckley LJ and Goff LJ that in addition to actual knowledge only Nelsonian knowledge and type (iii) knowledge are relevant.

Because of the judicial controversy to which the *Selangor* and *Karak* cases have given rise and the full citation to me of authorities by counsel on each side I have thought it right to review the authorities even though Mr Price and Mr

79 [1972] 1 WLR 602.
80 [1968] 1 WLR 1555.
81 [1978] 1 WLR 798.
82 [1972] 1 WLR 602.
83 (1975) 132 CLR 373.
84 [1975] 1 WLR 1240.
85 [1969] 2 Ch 276.
86 [1979] Ch 250.

Leckie effectively are at one in accepting that all five types of knowledge are relevant for the purposes of constructive trusteeship and neither has sought to submit that there should be or is any distinction on this point between the 'knowing receipt or dealing' category and the 'knowing assistance' category. I agree with counsel. It is plainly right that a person with Nelsonian knowledge or type (iii) knowledge should be treated as having knowledge for the purpose of constructive trusteeship. It seems to me, as it did to Ungoed-Thomas J and Brightman J, that there is a sufficient line of authorities to justify treating a person with type (iv) or type (v) knowledge as having knowledge for that purpose. It is little short of common sense that a person who actually knows all the circumstances from which the honest and reasonable man would have knowledge of the relevant facts should also be treated as having knowledge of the facts. The dividing line between Nelsonian and type (iv) knowledge may often be difficult to discern. If an objective test is appropriate to let in type (iv) knowledge, it would be illogical not to apply a similar objective test in circumstances where the honest and reasonable man would be put on inquiry (type (v) knowledge).

But in my judgment the court should not be astute to impute knowledge where no actual knowledge exists. In particular, it is only in exceptional circumstances that the court should impute type (v) knowledge to an agent like a bank acting honestly on the instructions of its principal but alleged to have provided knowing assistance in a dishonest and fraudulent design. It is not every inquiry that might be made that the court will treat the agent as having been under a duty to make inquiry even though the omitted inquiry would, if made, have led to the agent having knowledge of the facts. If an explanation is offered, the presumption of honesty is strong and the court will not require the agent to be hypercritical in examining that explanation. Two cases in which banks were held not to be privy to the dishonesty of their customers illustrate the cautious approach of the courts. In the *Selangor* case,[87] as I have indicated, the Bank of Nova Scotia was held not to have been under a duty of inquiry or further inquiry despite its participation in transactions involving the circular movement of cheques. The reason why the bank was not held liable was because the solicitor for the plaintiff company gave as an explanation that the cheques were for internal accounting or bookkeeping reasons. That explanation was not further particularised and was open to criticism, as Ungoed-Thomas J accepted, but it was held that the bank was justified in assuming the explanation to be honest and it did not put the bank on further inquiry. In *John Shaw (Rayners Lane) Ltd v Lloyds Bank Ltd*,[88] a receiver of the plaintiff company under a forged debenture had opened an account with the defendant bank and credited the account with moneys of the plaintiff and then drawn on the account for his own fraudulent purposes. The plaintiff sought to recover from the bank. Hallett J held that the account was the fraudulent receiver's account and the bank was not privy to the receiver's fraud, as despite the existence of some unusual and indeed suspicious

87 [1968] 1 WLR 1555.

88 (1944) 5 LDB 396.

circumstances known to the bank, the bank had no knowledge that the receiver was misappropriating the moneys of the plaintiff. It had consulted and received assurances from the apparent directors appearing on the register, and had also consulted and been reassured by the official receiver as the provisional liquidator of the plaintiff. Although Hallett J held that there was an inquiry which the bank could have made but did not make and which would have revealed the fraud, that is to say an inquiry of the person alleged to be the debenture holder, the bank was nevertheless in all the circumstances not liable in negligence for having failed to make that inquiry.

There are thus limits to what inquiries the banker is under a duty to make. The banker cannot be expected to play the detective.

In considering whether a duty of inquiry arises, the court will have regard to all the circumstances. For a bank a material circumstance is whether the customer's account with the bank is a trust account. It is common ground that a trust account has a special significance.

Mr Price's submissions on making inquiries can be summarised as follows: (a) a duty to inquire only arises if there are such solid grounds for suspicion that the banker cannot safely act without making inquiries; (b) therefore, the banker can be in no better position if inquiries are made and produce unsatisfactory answers than if no inquiries had been made at all; (c) once the duty to inquire has arisen the banker can safely act only if it appears that the result of proper inquiries would have been to dispel in the mind of an honest and reasonable banker the suspicion which initially gave rise to the need for inquiries; (d) it is necessary to ascertain on a balance of probabilities what answers would actually have been given to the inquiries which should have been made, and to decide whether or not those answers would have been acceptable to the honest and reasonable banker in dispelling his initial suspicions; and (e) it is to be presumed against the banker that the answers to any inquiries it ought to have made, but did not make, would have been true although it is open to the banker to prove, if it can, that inquiries would have produced answers acceptable to an honest and reasonable banker.

Again there is a good deal of common ground between the parties. Mr Leckie accepts, indeed stresses, that a mere suspicion is not enough to put the bank on inquiry; something more substantial is required. He further accepts that a bank is under a duty not to act on its customer's instructions not only when the bank knows that the moneys in the customer's account are to be misapplied but also so long as it is under a duty of inquiry. He also agrees that the court must determine what would have been the answers to inquiries which should have been but were not made, and whether those answers would have been acceptable to the honest and reasonable banker. I would add that the like position must obtain in relation to proper inquiries which were made but were not answered and that similarly the court must determine on a balance of probabilities whether answers given or information volunteered would have been acceptable to the honest and reasonable banker or would have put the banker on further inquiry.

The honest and reasonable banker may well have doubts but in all the circumstances be prepared to accept an answer given to an inquiry. A bank with its suspicions not dispelled can always choose to wait and be sued by its customers, but I think it would be going too far to hold that it has a duty to do so once there are no further inquiries it ought to make.

In my judgment therefore, a bank, when put on inquiry, remains under a duty not to comply with its customer's instructions either if it acquires knowledge of the intended misapplication of moneys which it holds or whilst it is pursuing its inquiries it ceases to be under such duty when it receives information, whether in answer to its inquiries or from another source, that the honest and reasonable banker would accept without further inquiry.

I summarise therefore the principles of law that, in my judgment, I must apply in respect of the claim in equity as follows. (1) The plaintiffs must show (a) the existence of a trust affecting the $4 m deposited by BCB with SG; (b) the fraudulent and dishonest design on the part of the directors of BCB who gave instructions to SG to transfer the $4 m to Panama; (c) the assistance by SG in that design; (d) SG's knowledge of (a), (b) and (c). (2) The knowledge must be actual knowledge or knowledge which it would have obtained but for shutting its eyes to the obvious or wilfully and recklessly refraining from making such inquiries as the reasonable banker would have made from the circumstances known to SG or would have obtained from inquiries which the reasonable banker would have made, the onus being on the plaintiffs to establish that SG possessed that knowledge.

The plaintiffs submit that SG knew on 10 May 1973, (i) that the BCB account was a trust account designated as such, that BCB was acting as a trustee or fiduciary and that the funds were the ultimate owners of the moneys in that account; (ii) that there was on foot a dishonest and fraudulent design for misappropriating the moneys of the funds including the $4 m with SG; and (iii) that in permitting the $4 m to be sent to Panama it assisted in that design. They say that SG knew of these matters in the sense that (a) it knew of circumstances which would have indicated the facts to an honest and reasonable banker (type (iv) knowledge); (b) it wilfully shut its eyes to the obvious (Nelsonian knowledge); (c) it wilfully and recklessly failed to make such inquiries as an honest and reasonable banker would have made (type (iii) knowledge); (d) alternatively, it failed to make such inquiries as an honest reasonable banker would have made (type (v) knowledge).

In my judgment the circumstances actually known to SG would not have indicated to the honest and reasonable banker the existence on 10 May of the trust or the existence of the fraudulent design and consequently they would not have indicated that SG by obeying its instructions was assisting in that design. Accordingly, I reject the plaintiff's submissions on type (iv) knowledge. For similar reasons the plaintiffs' submissions that SG wilfully shut its eyes to the obvious must fail. The facts of the trust, the fraud and the assistance were not obvious. Nor in any event can I accept that there was any willfulness on SG's part in failing to recognise the trust, the fraud and the assistance.

In my judgment the reasonable banker would be entitled to assume, and would assume, that the order of a court of competent jurisdiction had been duly obtained and that the agreement which the court had directed to be executed was therefore a proper one.

Agip (Africa) Ltd v Jackson and Others [1991] 3 WLR 116, CA (Fox, Butler-Sloss and Bedlam LJJ)

The plaintiff company brought an action to recover £518,822 from the defendants, who were directors and shareholders of companies formed to 'launder' money in pursuance of a fraudulent scheme. The companies were formed in order to receive funds from Tunisia and pay the same to other companies in a series of transactions. Once the companies had fulfilled their roles, they were liquidated with the defendants acting as liquidators. The defendant, Mr Jackson, a chartered accountant, set up the arrangements to receive and pay out the funds. Another defendant, Mr Griffin was employed to carry out the arrangements. The plaintiff also claimed that a third defendant, Mr Bowers, was vicariously liable for the acts of his partner, Mr Jackson.

The Court of Appeal, affirming the decision of the High Court, decided that the defendants were liable to account as constructive trustees. At best, Messrs Jackson and Griffin were indifferent to the possibility of fraud. They had wilfully or recklessly failed to make inquiries after being put on enquiry.

> **Fox LJ:** I come then to the circumstances in which strangers to the trust relationship (the defendants) may be made liable in equity. The are broadly as follows: (1) knowing receipt of or dealing with the trust property: the judge held that Mr Griffin (the third defendant) did not receive the money at all and that Mr Jackson and Mr Bowers (the first and second defendants) did not receive or apply it for their benefit. Accordingly, he held that none of them could be held liable as constructive trustees on the basis of knowing receipt of the money. There is no cross-appeal as to that; (2) knowing assistance: a person may be liable, even though he does not himself receive the trust property, if he knowingly assists in a fraudulent design on the part of a trustee, including a constructive trustee. Liability under this head is not related to the receipt of trust property by the person sought to be made liable: *Barnes v Addy*.[89]
>
> The degree of knowledge required was described by Ungoed-Thomas J in *Selangor United Rubber Estates Ltd v Cradock (No 3)*[90] as circumstances which would indicate to an honest and reasonable man that such a design was being committed, or would put him on inquiry whether it was being committed. Peter Gibson J, in *Baden, Delvaux and Lecuit v Société Général pour Favoriser le Développement du Commerce et de l'Industrie en France SA*,[91] gave a more expanded description of the circumstances constituting the necessary knowledge under five heads: (i) actual knowledge; (ii) wilfully shutting one's eyes to the obvious; (iii) wilfully and recklessly failing to make such inquiries as an honest and reasonable man would make; (iv) knowledge of any circumstances which would indicate the facts to an honest and reasonable man; (v) knowledge of circumstances which would put an honest and

89 (1874) LR 9 Ch App 244.

90 [1968] 1 WLR 1555, p 1590.

91 [1983] BCLC 325, p 407.

reasonable man on inquiry. I accept that formulation. It is, however, only an explanation of the general principle and is not necessarily comprehensive.

The judge held, and it was not challenged, that Mr Bowers did not participate in the furtherance of the fraud at all; although he was a partner in Jackson & Co, he played no part in the movement of the money and gave no instructions about it. Mr Jackson and Mr Griffin were in quite a different position. Mr Jackson set up the company structures. Mr Jackson and Mr Griffin controlled the movement of the money from the time it reached Baker Oil to the time it was paid out of the account of Jackson & Co in the Isle of Man Bank. On the evidence, and in the absence of evidence from Mr Jackson and Mr Griffin themselves, I agree with the judge that both of them must be regarded as having assisted in the fraud. That, however, by no means concludes the matter. There remains the question of their state of mind. Did they have the necessary degree of knowledge?

The first inquiry is what did they know. As to that: (1) they knew that a very large amount of money was involved: it was $10 m in under two years. It had all come along the same track; (2) they knew the origin of the money and its destination. Its origin was Agip and the destination of most of it was Kinz; (3) Agip was an oil company with operations in Tunisia. Kinz were jewellers in France; (4) there is nothing to suggest that there was any commercial reason why Agip should be paying such sums to Kinz; (5) as the judge said, they must have realised that the only function of the payee companies or of Euro-Arabian was to act as 'cut-outs' in order to conceal the true destination of the moneys from Agip. And the purpose of having two cut-outs instead of one was to bar any connection between Agip and Kinz without reference to the records of Lloyds Bank.

There is also some material documentary evidence. First, there is the letter of 14 August 1984 from Mr Smyth of Knapp-Fishers to Mr Jackson. That contains advice directed to the possibility that 'Agip may be able to establish a cause of action by claiming that the payments were obtained by fraud'.

The letter further states:

> Because of the general principle of banking confidentiality, it would be extremely difficult for the Tunisian Government or Agip to obtain an order requiring Lloyds Bank to disclose banking transactions ...

This shows that the question of fraud was being considered and some anxiety was being felt at the possibility that Agip might obtain access to bank records. The significance of bank records is that they are or may be a signpost to the ultimate destination of the money. Why was concern being felt about what Agip might discover? If there were doubts about fraud they could be set at rest by getting in touch with Agip and disclosing what was known.

It is, of course, possible that Mr Jackson and Mr Griffin were honest men and that there were facts which we do not know which would demonstrate that. But, if so, they could have attended the trial and explained their position in the witness box. They did not do so. One can only infer that they were not prepared to submit their activities to critical examination. In the circumstances I think that the judge rightly came to the conclusion that they must have known they were laundering money, and were consequently helping their clients to make arrangements to conceal some dispositions of money which had such a degree of impropriety that neither they nor their clients could afford to have them disclosed.

Certain excuses, justifications and exculpatory facts were put forward. Thus, it was said that Mr Jackson and Mr Griffin had no cause for suspicion because Jackson & Co took over arrangements already previously in existence and were introduced to the matter by a partner in the very well known accountants, Thornton Baker. I do not find that is of any assistance to the defendants. The respectability of the person making the introduction did not relieve Mr Jackson from obligation to make proper inquiries as to suspicious circumstances coming to his notice then or subsequently. We do not, in fact, know what information was made available to Mr Jackson upon his introduction to the matter. But by August 1984, Jackson & Co cannot have supposed that the matter was clearly free from impropriety. Knapp-Fishers were tendering advice to them about the possibility of fraud. The genesis of the advice of August 1984 requires explanation from Mr Jackson personally and the court has received none. In my opinion, well before the circumstances giving rise to the present case, Mr Jackson and Mr Griffin were put on inquiry. Either they did not inquire at all or, if they did, and the inquiry disclosed innocent activities, they have not disclosed to the court what they learnt.

In the end, it seems to me that the most striking feature in the case is that in August 1984 Mr Jackson and Mr Griffin were being given advice on the possibility that a payment or payments might involve a fraud on Agip. Having got to that point it seems to me that persons acting honestly would have pursued the matter with a view to satisfying themselves that there was no fraud. But there is nothing to show that they did that. They made no inquiries of Agip at all. They let matters continue. In the circumstances, I conclude that Mr Jackson and Mr Griffin are liable as constructive trustees. Mr Bowers is liable for the acts of Mr Jackson, who was his partner, and of Mr Griffin, who was employed by the partnership. Accordingly, I think that the judge came to the right conclusion and I would dismiss the appeal.

Eagle Trust plc v SBC Securities Ltd [1993] 1 WLR 484, HC

The defendant company agreed with the plaintiff company to underwrite the terms of a take over offer. The defendant subsequently arranged to sub-underwrite its liability using a list of sub-underwriters introduced by the plaintiff's chief executive, Mr Ferriday (F). The list included F as underwriting £13.5 m. The defendant was able to discharge its obligation to the plaintiff on payment by F through a number of intermediary companies. It transpired that F had misappropriated the plaintiff's money to fund the payment of £13.5 m to the defendant. The plaintiff sued the defendant claiming that it was a constructive trustee of the funds misappropriated by F, on the ground that the defendant had knowingly participated in a fraudulent breach committed by F. The plaintiff alleged that the defendant should have been aware of the danger that F would have been tempted to discharge his liability by misappropriating the plaintiff's funds, but that the defendant made no inquiries as to the source of F's payments. The defendant applied to have the claim struck out as showing no reasonable cause of action.

The court held in favour of the defendant on the following grounds:

(a) the plaintiff's claim failed to establish that the defendant knew that the moneys were misapplied trust funds. 'Knowledge' for these purposes means that the defendant has (i) actual knowledge of the breach of trust or (ii) wilfully shut its eyes to the obvious or (iii) wilfully and recklessly failed to make inquiries which an honest and reasonable man would have made. But constructive knowledge or purely objective knowledge (within categories (iv) and (v) of Peter Gibson's judgment in *Re Baden Delvaux*) would be insufficient to found liability in these circumstances;

(b) even if the defendant had entertained some suspicion concerning the source of F's funds, further inquiries from F would not necessarily have revealed the misappropriation of the plaintiff's funds;

(c) on the assumption that the alleged facts, as detailed in the plaintiff's claim, are true and that the defendant adduced no evidence, the plaintiff's claim disclosed no cause of action.

> **Vinelott J** (after referring to the principles laid down by the High Court in *Re Baden Delvaux* and the Court of Appeal in *Agip v Jackson*): ... Actual or conscious knowledge gives rise to no difficulty and ... a defendant who wilfully closes his eyes to the obvious or who wilfully and recklessly fails to make such inquiries as an honest and reasonable man would make is disentitled to rely on the lack of actual knowledge.
>
> The rule applies equally in criminal as in civil cases. The explanation is given by Lord Bridge of Harwich in *Westminster City Council v Croyalgrange Ltd*,[92] which concerned a prosecution for knowing or using or causing or permitting the use of premises as a sex establishment without a licence, when he said:
>
>> ... it is perhaps worth remarking, in the hope that it may further allay the anxiety of the council about the enforcement of licensing control of sex establishments, that it is always open to the tribunal of fact, when knowledge on the part of a defendant is required to be proved, to base a finding of knowledge on evidence that the defendant had deliberately shut his eyes to the obvious or refrained from inquiry because he suspected the truth but did not want to have his suspicion confirmed.
>
> Knowledge may also be inferred, at least in civil cases, if the circumstances set out in paragraphs (iv) and (v) of Peter Gibson J's classification in the *Baden* case,[93] are established and if the defendant does not give evidence or offer any explanation of his conduct. If the circumstances are such that an honest and reasonable man would have appreciated that he was assisting in a dishonest breach of trust, the court may infer from the defendant's silence that he either appreciated the fact, or that he wilfully shut his eyes to the obvious, or wilfully

92 [1986] 1 WLR 674, p 684.

93 [1993] 1 WLR 509, pp 575H–76A.

and recklessly failed to make inquiries for fear of what he might learn. Whether in such circumstances a defendant can escape liability on the ground that he acted honestly but failed to draw the obvious inference by reason of his inexperience or because he was unusually or unreasonably trusting, or for some other reason, is a question which I do not need to consider further ... it cannot be relevant in an application to strike out a statement of claim on the ground that it discloses no cause of action.

However, 'notice' is often used in a sense or in contexts where the facts do not support the inference of knowledge. A man may have actual notice of a fact and yet not know it. He may have been supplied in the course of a conveyancing transaction with a document and so have actual notice of its content, but he may not in fact have read it; or he may have read it some time ago and have forgotten its content. Sir Robert Megarry VC observed in *In re Montagu's Settlement Trusts*:[94] 'I suppose that there may be some remarkable beings for whom once known is never forgotten; but apart from them, the generality of mankind probably forgets far more than is remembered.' So also by statute a man may be deemed to have actual notice of a fact which is clearly not within his knowledge. Constructive and imputed notice are most frequently, though not invariably, used in contrast to knowledge – to describe a situation in which a man is treated for some purposes as if he had knowledge of facts which were clearly not known to him. Lord Esher in English and *Scottish Mercantile Investment Co Ltd v Brunton*[95] described the doctrine of constructive notice as 'wholly founded on the assumption that a man does not know the facts'.

Moreover, a man may be affected by constructive notice even if there has been not only no want of probity but no carelessness on his part. He may have imputed to him notice of matters of which his counsel, solicitor or other agent had notice, actual or constructive, in the same transaction in which the question of notice arises: see s 199 of the Law of Property Act 1925, re-enacting s 3(2) of the Conveyancing Act 1882[96] which, in turn, was largely declaratory of the law.

In the field of conveyancing the law has historically set a very high standard; so much so that Maitland observed that:

> ... in reading some of the cases about constructive notice we may be inclined to say that equity demanded not the care of the most prudent father of a family but the care of the most prudent solicitor of a family aided by the skill of the most expert conveyancer [see Maitland's *Equity*].[97]

It is often said that man has constructive notice of matters which he would have discovered if he had made those inquiries which he ought reasonably to have made. But as Lindley LJ pointed out in *Bailey v Barnes*:[98]

94 [1987] Ch 264, p 284.

95 [1892] 2 QB 700, p 708.

96 (1882) 45 and 46 Vict, c 39.

97 2nd edn, 1936, Cambridge: CUP, p 119.

98 [1894] 1 Ch 25, p 35.

> 'Ought' here does not import a duty or obligation; for a purchaser need make no inquiry. The expression 'ought reasonably' must mean ought as matter of prudence, having regard to what is usually done by men of business under similar circumstances.

The phrase 'put on inquiry' suffers from a similar ambiguity. A man may be said to be put on inquiry if he knows of circumstances which point to the probability of fraud. He may then have to satisfy himself that there is an innocent explanation if he is to escape the charge that he wilfully or recklessly abstained from inquiry from fear of what he might have learned. But the phrase 'put on inquiry' may be used to describe the very different situation where a purchaser or his solicitor ought to make further inquiry 'as a matter of prudence, having regard to what is usually done by men of business in similar circumstances'. So, for example, if land contracted to be purchased is in the occupation of some person other than the vendor, the purchaser would in this sense be put on inquiry as to the rights of the occupier and has constructive notice of rights which he would have learned had he made a proper inquiry.

[After reviewing the leading authorities, the learned judge continued:]

It can therefore, in my judgment, now be taken as settled law that, notwithstanding the wider language in which the test of liability as constructive trustee in a 'knowing assistance' case is stated in the *Selangor* case[99] and in the *Karak* case,[100] and, notwithstanding the concession made by counsel and accepted by Peter Gibson J in the *Baden* case ... a stranger cannot be made liable for knowing assistance in a fraudulent breach of trust unless knowledge of the fraudulent design can be imputed to him on one of the grounds I have described. There must have been something amounting to want of probity on his part. Constructive notice is not enough, though, as I have said, knowledge may be inferred in the absence of evidence by the defendant if such knowledge would have been imputed to an honest and reasonable man.

Lord Nicholls' illuminating judgment, in *Royal Brunei Airlines v Tan* (see below, p 472), reviewed the law concerning 'accessory liability'. He opined that the liability of a third party who assisted a trustee to commit a breach of trust is dependent on the state of mind of the third party. Dishonesty on the part of the third party is an essential ingredient of liability, irrespective of the state of mind of the trustee who committed the breach of trust. The trustee will be liable in any event for breach of trust, even if he acted innocently, unless he is relieved by the court or is protected by an exclusion clause in the trust instrument. Dishonesty on the part of the trustee is, however, not a prerequisite in order to attach liability to the dishonest third party.

99 [1968] 1 WLR 1555, p 1590.

100 [1972] 1 WLR 602, p 639.

Royal Brunei Airlines Sdn Bhd v Tan [1995] 3 WLR 64, PC

In 1986, the plaintiff appointed a travel agent, Borneo Leisure Travel Sdn Bhd (BLT), to act in Sabah and Sarawak as its general travel agent for the sale of passenger and cargo transportation. BLT was required to account to the plaintiff for all amounts received from such sales. Thus, BLT became a trustee for the plaintiff of the money. Trust sums received were not paid into a separate account, but were paid into BLT's current account and used for its own purposes. The defendant was BLT's managing director and principal shareholder. He was effectively in charge and in control of BLT. BLT's payments fell into arrears and the plaintiff terminated the agreement. The company later became insolvent. The plaintiff commenced an action against the defendant claiming an account in respect of the unpaid money. The action was based under the second limb of Lord Selborne's *dictum* in *Barnes v Addy* (1874), 'strangers are not to be made constructive trustees merely because they act as the agents of trustees in transactions ... unless they assist with knowledge in a dishonest and fraudulent design on the part of the trustees'. The question in issue was whether the breach of trust which was a prerequisite to liability had to be a dishonest and fraudulent breach of trust by the trustee.

The Privy Council decided in favour of the plaintiff. In equity, a stranger to the trust is liable to make good resulting loss if he dishonestly procured or assisted in a breach of trust or fiduciary obligation. It was not a prerequisite of that liability that, in addition, the trustee or fiduciary acted dishonestly.

> **Lord Nicholls of Birkenhead:** The proper role of equity in commercial transactions is a topical question. Increasingly, plaintiffs have recourse to equity for an effective remedy when the person in default, typically a company, is insolvent.
>
> Plaintiffs seek to obtain relief from others who were involved in the transaction, such as directors of the company, or its bankers, or its legal or other advisers. They seek to fasten fiduciary obligations directly onto the company's officers or agents or advisers, or to have them held personally liable for assisting the company in breaches of trust or fiduciary obligations. Liability as an accessory is not dependent upon receipt of trust property. It arises even though no trust property has reached the hands of the accessory. It is a form of secondary liability in the sense that it only arises where there has been a breach of trust.
>
> The issue on this appeal is whether the breach of trust which is a prerequisite to accessory liability must itself be a dishonest and fraudulent breach of trust by the trustee.
>
> It must be noted at once that there is a difficulty with the approach adopted on this point in the *Belmont* case [1979] Ch 250. Take the simple example of an honest trustee and a dishonest third party. Take a case where a dishonest solicitor persuades a trustee to apply trust property in a way the trustee honestly believes is permissible but which the solicitor knows full well is a clear breach of trust. The solicitor deliberately conceals this from the trustee. In

consequence, the beneficiaries suffer a substantial loss. It cannot be right that in such a case the accessory liability principle would be inapplicable because of the innocence of the trustee. In ordinary parlance, the beneficiaries have been defrauded by the solicitor. If there is to be an accessory liability principle at all, whereby, in appropriate circumstances, beneficiaries may have direct recourse against a third party, the principle must surely be applicable in such a case, just as much as in a case where both the trustee and the third party have been dishonest. Indeed, if anything, the case for liability of the dishonest third party seems stronger where the trustee is innocent, because in such a case the third party alone was dishonest and that was the cause of the subsequent misapplication of the trust property.

The position would be the same if, instead of procuring the breach, the third party dishonestly assisted in the breach. Change the facts slightly. A trustee is proposing to make a payment out of the trust fund to a particular person. He honestly believes he is authorised to do so by the terms of the trust deed. He asks a solicitor to carry through the transaction. The solicitor well knows that the proposed payment would be a plain breach of trust. He also well knows that the trustee mistakenly believes otherwise. Dishonestly, he leaves the trustee under his misapprehension and prepares the necessary documentation. Again, if the accessory principle is not to be artificially constricted, it ought to be applicable in such a case.

These examples suggest that what matters is the state of mind of the third party sought to be made liable, not the state of mind of the trustee. The trustee will be liable in any event for the breach of trust, even if he acted innocently, unless excused by an exemption clause in the trust instrument or relieved by the court. But his state of mind is, essentially, irrelevant to the question whether the third party should be made liable to the beneficiaries for the breach of trust. If the liability of the third party is fault-based, what matters is the nature of his fault, not that of the trustee. In this regard dishonesty on the part of the third party would seem to be a sufficient basis for his liability, irrespective of the state of mind of the trustee who is in breach of trust. It is difficult to see why, if the third party dishonestly assisted in a breach, there should be a further prerequisite to his liability, namely that the trustee also must have been acting dishonestly. The alternative view would mean that a dishonest third party is liable if the trustee is dishonest, but if the trustee did not act dishonestly that of itself would excuse a dishonest third party from liability. That would make no sense.

There has been a tendency to cite and interpret and apply Lord Selborne LC's formulation in *Barnes v Addy* (1874) LR 9 Ch App 244, pp 251–52, as though it were a statute. This has particularly been so with the accessory limb of Lord Selborne LC's apothegm. This approach has been inimical to analysis of the underlying concept. Working within this constraint, the courts have found themselves wrestling with the interpretation of the individual ingredients, especially 'knowingly' but also 'dishonest and fraudulent design on the part of the trustees', without examining the underlying reason why a third party who has received no trust property is being made liable at all. One notable exception is the judgment of Thomas J in *Powell v Thompson* [1991] 1 NZLR 597, pp 610–15. On this point he observed, at p 613:

> Once a breach of trust has been committed, the commission of which has involved a third party, the question which arises is one as between the beneficiary and that third party. If the third party's conduct has been unconscionable, then irrespective of the degree of impropriety in the trustee's conduct, the third party is liable to be held accountable to the beneficiary as if he or she were a trustee.

To resolve this issue, it is necessary to take an overall look at the accessory liability principle. A conclusion cannot be reached on the nature of the breach of trust which may trigger accessory liability without at the same time considering the other ingredients, including, in particular, the state of mind of the third party. It is not necessary, however, to look even more widely and consider the essential ingredients of recipient liability. The issue on this appeal concerns only the accessory liability principle. Different considerations apply to the two heads of liability. Recipient liability is restitution-based; accessory liability is not.

No liability

The starting point for any analysis must be to consider the extreme possibility: that a third party who does not receive trust property ought never to be liable directly to the beneficiaries merely because he assisted the trustee to commit a breach of trust or procured him to do so. This possibility can be dismissed summarily. On this, the position which the law has long adopted is clear and makes good sense. Stated in the simplest terms, a trust is a relationship which exists when one person holds property on behalf of another. If, for his own purposes, a third party deliberately interferes in that relationship by assisting the trustee in depriving the beneficiary of the property held for him by the trustee, the beneficiary should be able to look for recompense to the third party as well as the trustee. Affording the beneficiary a remedy against the third party serves the dual purpose of making good the beneficiary's loss should the trustee lack financial means and imposing a liability which will discourage others from behaving in a similar fashion.

The rationale is not far to seek. Beneficiaries are entitled to expect that those who become trustees will fulfil their obligations. They are also entitled to expect, and this is only a short step further, that those who become trustees will be permitted to fulfil their obligations without deliberate intervention from third parties. They are entitled to expect that third parties will refrain from intentionally intruding in the trustee-beneficiary relationship and thereby hindering a beneficiary from receiving his entitlement in accordance with the terms of the trust instrument. There is here a close analogy with breach of contract. A person who knowingly procures a breach of contract, or knowingly interferes with the due performance of a contract, is liable to the innocent party. The underlying rationale is the same.

Strict liability

The other extreme possibility can also be rejected out of hand. This is the case where a third party deals with a trustee without knowing, or having any reason to suspect, that he is a trustee. Or the case where a third party is aware that he is dealing with a trustee but has no reason to know or suspect that their transaction is inconsistent with the terms of the trust. The law has never gone so far as to give a beneficiary a remedy against a non-recipient third party in such circumstances. Within defined limits, proprietary rights, whether legal or equitable, endure against third parties who were unaware of their existence. But accessory liability is concerned with the liability of a person who has not received any property. His liability is not property-based. His only sin is that he interfered with the due performance by the trustee of the fiduciary obligations undertaken by the trustee. These are personal obligations.

Fault-based liability

Given, then, that in some circumstances a third party may be liable directly to a beneficiary, but given also that the liability is not so strict that there would be liability even when the third party was wholly unaware of the existence of the trust, the next step is to seek to identify the touchstone of liability. By common accord, dishonesty fulfils this role. Whether, in addition, negligence will suffice is an issue on which there has been a well known difference of judicial opinion.

Most, but not all, commentators prefer the test of dishonesty: see, among others, Birks, P, 'Misdirected funds: restitution from the recipient' (1989) LMCLQ 296; Brindle, MJ and Hooley, RJA, 'Does constructive knowledge make a constructive trustee?' (1987) 61 ALJ 281; Harpum, C, 'The stranger as constructive trustee' (1986) 102 LQR 114, p 267; Birks, P, *The Frontiers of Liability*, 1994, Vol 1, p 9; Loughlan, P, 'Liability for assistance in a breach of fiduciary duty' (1989) 9 OJLS 260; Parker, D and Mellows, A, *The Modern Law of Trusts*, 6th edn, 1994, p 253; Pettit, P, *Equity and the Law of Trusts*, 7th edn, 1993, p 172; Sales, P, 'The tort of conspiracy and civil secondary liability' (1990) 49 CLJ 491; *Snell's Equity*, 29th edn, 1990, p 194; and *Underhill's Law of Trusts and Trustees*, 14th edn, 1987, p 355 and noter-up.

Dishonesty

Honesty has a connotation of subjectivity, as distinct from the objectivity of negligence. Honesty, indeed, does have a strong subjective element in that it is a description of a type of conduct assessed in the light of what a person actually knew at the time, as distinct from what a reasonable person would have known or appreciated. Further, honesty and its counterpart dishonesty are mostly concerned with advertent conduct, not inadvertent conduct. Carelessness is not dishonesty. Thus, for the most part, dishonesty is to be equated with conscious impropriety. However, these subjective characteristics of honesty do not mean that individuals are free to set their own standards of honesty in particular circumstances. The standard of what constitutes honest conduct is not subjective. Honesty is not an optional scale, with higher or lower values according to the moral standards of each individual. If a person knowingly appropriates another's property, he will not escape a finding of dishonesty simply because he sees nothing wrong in such behaviour.

In most situations there is little difficulty in identifying how an honest person would behave. Honest people do not intentionally deceive others to their detriment. Honest people do not knowingly take others' property. Unless there is a very good and compelling reason, an honest person does not participate in a transaction if he knows it involves a misapplication of trust assets to the detriment of the beneficiaries. Nor does an honest person in such a case deliberately close his eyes and ears, or deliberately not ask questions, lest he learn something he would rather not know, and then proceed regardless. However, in the situations now under consideration the position is not always so straightforward. This can best be illustrated by considering one particular area: the taking of risks.

Taking risks

All investment involves risk. Imprudence is not dishonesty, although imprudence may be carried recklessly to lengths which call into question the honesty of the person making the decision. This is especially so if the transaction serves another purpose in which that person has an interest of his own.

This type of risk is to be sharply distinguished from the case where a trustee, with or without the benefit of advice, is aware that a particular investment or application of trust property is outside his powers, but nevertheless he decides to proceed in the belief or hope that this will be beneficial to the beneficiaries or, at least, not prejudicial to them. He takes a risk that a clearly unauthorised transaction will not cause loss.

A risk of this nature is for the account of those who take it. If the risk materialises and causes loss, those who knowingly took the risk will be accountable accordingly. This is the type of risk being addressed by Peter Gibson J in the *Baden* case [1993] 1 WLR 509, p 574, when he accepted that fraud includes taking 'a risk to the prejudice of another's rights, which risk is known to be one which there is no right to take'.

Acting in reckless disregard of others' rights or possible rights can be a tell-tale sign of dishonesty. An honest person would have regard to the circumstances known to him, including the nature and importance of the proposed transaction, the nature and importance of his role, the ordinary course of business, the degree of doubt, the practicability of the trustee or the third party proceeding otherwise and the seriousness of the adverse consequences to the beneficiaries. The circumstances will dictate which one or more of the possible courses should be taken by an honest person. He might, for instance, flatly decline to become involved. He might ask further questions. He might seek advice, or insist on further advice being obtained. He might advise the trustee of the risks but then proceed with his role in the transaction. He might do many things. Ultimately, in most cases, an honest person should have little difficulty in knowing whether a proposed transaction, or his participation in it, would offend the normally accepted standards of honest conduct.

Likewise, when called upon to decide whether a person was acting honestly, a court will look at all the circumstances known to the third party at the time. The court will also have regard to personal attributes of the third party, such as his experience and intelligence, and the reason why he acted as he did.

Before leaving cases where there is real doubt, one further point should be noted. To inquire, in such cases, whether a person dishonestly assisted in what is later held to be a breach of trust is to ask a meaningful question, which is capable of being given a meaningful answer. This is not always so if the question is posed in terms of 'knowingly' assisted. Framing the question in the latter form all too often leads one into tortuous convolutions about the 'sort' of knowledge required, when the truth is that 'knowingly' is inapt as a criterion when applied to the gradually darkening spectrum where the differences are of degree and not kind.

Negligence

It is against this background that the question of negligence is to be addressed. This question, it should be remembered, is directed at whether an honest third party who receives no trust property should be liable if he procures or assists in a breach of trust of which he would have become aware had he exercised reasonable diligence. Should he be liable to the beneficiaries for the loss they suffer from the breach of trust?

The majority of persons falling into this category will be the hosts of people who act for trustees in various ways: as advisers, consultants, bankers and agents of many kinds. This category also includes officers and employees of companies in respect of the application of company funds. All these people will be accountable to the trustees for their conduct. For the most part they will owe to the trustees a duty to exercise reasonable skill and care. When that is so, the rights flowing from that duty form part of the trust property. As such, they can be enforced by the beneficiaries in a suitable case if the trustees are unable or unwilling to do so. That being so, it is difficult to identify a compelling reason why, in addition to the duty of skill and care vis à vis the trustees which the third parties have accepted, or which the law has imposed upon them, third parties should also owe a duty of care directly to the beneficiaries.

There remains to be considered the position where third parties are acting for, or dealing with, dishonest trustees. In such cases the trustees would have no claims against the third party. The trustees would suffer no loss by reason of the third party's failure to discover what was going on. The question is whether in this type of situation the third party owes a duty of care to the beneficiaries to, in effect, check that a trustee is not misbehaving. The third party must act honestly. The question is whether that is enough. In agreement with the preponderant view, their Lordships consider that dishonesty is an essential ingredient here. There may be cases where, in the light of the particular facts, a third party will owe a duty of care to the beneficiaries. As a general proposition, however, beneficiaries cannot reasonably expect that all the world dealing with their trustees should owe them a duty to take care lest the trustees are behaving dishonestly.

Unconscionable conduct

Mention, finally, must be made of the suggestion that the test for liability is that of unconscionable conduct. Unconscionable is a word of immediate appeal to an equity lawyer. Equity is rooted historically in the concept of the Lord Chancellor, as the keeper of the Royal Conscience, concerning himself with conduct which was contrary to good conscience. It must be recognised, however, that unconscionable is not a word in everyday use by non-lawyers. If it is to be used in this context, and if it is to be the touchstone for liability as an accessory, it is essential to be clear on what, in this context, unconscionable means. If unconscionable means no more than dishonesty, then dishonesty is the preferable label. If unconscionable means something different, it must be said that it is not clear what that something different is. Either way, therefore, the term is better avoided in this context.

The accessory liability principle

Drawing the threads together, their Lordships' overall conclusion is that dishonesty is a necessary ingredient of accessory liability. It is also a sufficient ingredient. A liability in equity to make good resulting loss attaches to a person who dishonestly procures or assists in a breach of trust or fiduciary obligation. It is not necessary that, in addition, the trustee or fiduciary was acting dishonestly, although this will usually be so where the third party who is assisting him is acting dishonestly. 'Knowingly' is better avoided as a defining ingredient of the principle, and in the context of this principle the *Baden* ... scale of knowledge is best forgotten.

Conclusion

From this statement of the principle it follows that this appeal succeeds. BLT committed a breach of trust by using the money instead of simply deducting its commission and holding the money intact until it paid the airline. The defendant accepted that he knowingly assisted in that breach of trust. In other words, he caused or permitted his company to apply the money in a way he knew was not authorised by the trust of which the company was trustee. Set out in these bald terms, the defendant's conduct was dishonest. By the same token, and for good measure, BLT also acted dishonestly. The defendant was the company, and his state of mind is to be imputed to the company.'

In *Brown v Bennett*, the court decided that a director of a company who was in breach of his managerial duties was not, without more, liable as a constructive trustee under the 'knowing assistance' head.

Brown and Another v Bennett and Others (1998) *The Times*, 3 January, HC

The business of Pinecord Ltd was put into receivership and in February 1991 was purchased from the receiver by three defendants, Maurice and Michael Bennett and Vivian Scott. The purchase was effected through the medium of an off-the-shelf company, Oasis Ltd. The Bennett's and Mr Scott became directors of Oasis. A stock exchange flotation of Oasis followed in June 1995. The plaintiffs' case against the defendants was that the Bennett's became *de facto* directors of Pinecord in February 1988 and shareholders of the company in August 1988. They allegedly followed a course of conduct in their management of Pinecord Ltd which was intended to put the company into financial difficulty in order to enable them to increase their share of its equity. The plaintiffs alleged that the last step in their scheme was to put Pinecord Ltd into receivership with a view to buying the business from the receiver for their benefit. The plaintiffs contended that Oasis had knowingly and dishonestly assisted the defendants so as to become a constructive trustee under the 'knowing assistance' limb of *Barnes v Addy* .

Rattee J decided in favour of the defendants. It was impossible to contend that Oasis had any connection with the defendant directors' alleged breaches of trust. There was insufficient evidence to establish liability on the part of Oasis. His Lordship also decided that where there had been no breach of trust affecting property, but merely a breach of directors' duties in relation to the management of a company's affairs, it would be an unwarranted extension of the *Barnes v Addy* principle to impose liability as constructive trustees on the directors.

Simon Gardner, in 'Knowing assistance and knowing receipt: taking stock' [1996] 112 LQR 56, reviews the authorities imposing liabilty on strangers under the 'knowing assistance' and 'receipt' heads. He comments on the rationale for liability under the knowing assistance head as laid down by Lord Nicholls in *Royal Brunei Airlines v Tan*:

> Lord Nicholls' view appears to be that a liability for knowing assistance involving negligence is either unnecessary or inappropriate. He notes that many potential defendants under the knowing assistance head will be persons and entities such as banks – they may be loosely termed agents – who voluntarily enter into an engagement with the trustees, and consequently owe a duty of care which will normally be in contract but may perhaps, alternatively, be in tort. His Lordship believes that a defendant who has undertaken such a duty of care should be liable under it alone, and not be liable in knowing assistance as well. A defendant who has not undertaken such a duty of care, however, should, according to his Lordship, not find himself placed under such a duty by knowing assistance being allowed to operate in cases of negligence; only in cases of dishonesty.
>
> Lord Nicholls offers an analysis of when a defendant will and will not be under such a negligence liability to the trust in contract or tort. His Lordship's view appears to be that the liability will start out in life as a duty which the agent owes to the trustees, to save them from breaching their trust. It will crystallise, if, failing in this duty, the agent allows the trustees to breach their trust, and thus to incur a loss by way of their own liability for breach. The agent's liability is to make good this loss. Then, says his Lordship, this liability of the agent to the trustees is held by the trustees for the trust. And that is how the agent comes to owe a liability for want of care to the trust. This analysis is in fact a little curious. On the one hand, whilst some agents will owe trustees a duty to save the latter from breach, and must indemnify them if they fail in this, any such duty will, by its nature, be owed to the trustees personally, and not held by them on their trust. This liability thus has no common ground with knowing assistance, which is indeed concerned with the defendant's liability to the trust. On the other hand, such an agent will normally owe the trust itself a duty of care in contract or tort. This is the main effect of an agent being engaged by trustees to provide services for the trust, the trustees in this case certainly holding the benefit of the engagement on the trust. It is this material, therefore, which is comparable with liability for knowing assistance. With the benefit of a duty of care arising thus, however, it should be noted that a defendant who breaks it will be liable to the trust not only where the trustees are innocent, as Lord Nicholls thought, but also where they are fraudulent.

SUPPLEMENTARY READING

Berg, A, 'Accessory liability for breach of trust' (1996) 59 MLR 443

Birks, P, 'Misdirected funds: casenote on *Lipkin Gorman v Karpnale*' (1989) 105 LQR 352

Bryan, M, 'When does a bank receive money?' [1996] JBL 165

Fennell, S, 'Misdirected funds; problems of uncertainty and inconsistency: the bank's liability as a constructive trustee' (1994) 57 MLR 38

Ferris, G, 'The advice of the Privy Council in *Royal Brunei Airlines v Tan*' (1996) 30 Law Teacher 111

Gardner, S, 'Knowing assistance and knowing receipt: taking stock' (1996) 112 LQR 56

Harpum, C, 'Accessory liability for procuring or assisting a breach of trust' (1995) 111 LQR 545

Harpum, C, 'Casenote on *Re Montagu*' (1987) 50 MLR 217

Martin, J, 'Assisting in a breach of trust' (1996) 142 SJ 156

McKendrick, E, 'Restitution, misdirected funds and change of position' (1992) 55 MLR 377

Nolan, R, 'From knowing assistance to dishonest facilitation' (1995) 54 CLJ 505

Speirs, A, 'The destination of an ill-gotten gain: *Halifax Building Society v Thomas*' [1996] Conv 387

Stevens, J, 'Delimiting the scope of accessory liability: *Brinks Ltd v Abu-Saleh (No 3)*' [1996] Conv 447

Watts, P, 'Unjust enrichment and misdirected funds' (1991) 107 LQR 521

CHAPTER 12

SECRET TRUSTS AND MUTUAL WILLS

When a testator dies, his will becomes available for public inspection. Thus, any trust created by his will will be open to public scrutiny. The testator may wish to make provision for some object concealed from the gaze of the public. Originally, the secret objects were mistresses and illegitimate children but the object or objects which the testator may consider to be embarrassing is entirely dependent on his own sentiments.

In order to benefit such objects after his death, the testator may transfer relevant property to an 'acceptable' legatee or devisee under his will subject to the understanding that the legatee or devisee will hold the property upon trust for the intended beneficiary. This is the secret trust device. The essence of a secret trust is an equitable obligation communicated to the intended trustee during the testator's lifetime but which is intended to attach to a gift arising under a will (or exceptionally a transfer created on an intestacy).

Two conditions are required to be satisfied by the testator namely, a transfer of property by will to the legatee or devisee and an understanding between the testator and the trustee that on the latter receiving the property he will hold it on trust for the intended beneficiary.

Section 9 of the Wills Act 1837 (as amended by the Administration of Justice Act 1982) provides:

> No will shall be valid unless:
>
> (a) it is in writing, and signed by the testator, or by some other person in his presence and by his direction; and
>
> (b) it appears that the testator intended by his signature to give effect to the will; and
>
> (c) the signature is made or acknowledged by the testator in the presence of two or more witnesses present at the same time; and
>
> (d) each witness either:
>
> (i) attests and signs the will; or
>
> (ii) acknowledges his signature, in the presence of the testator (but not necessarily in the presence of any other witness), but no form of attestation shall be necessary.

The Chancery Court originally assumed jurisdiction to enforce secret trusts in order to prevent the legatee or devisee fraudulently reneging on his promise, and attempting to take the property beneficially or denying the existence of the promise to the testator. In other words, the court prevented the legatee or devisee setting up s 9 of the Wills Act 1837 (originally s 5 of the Statute of Frauds 1677) as a defence after the death of the testator.

McCormick v Grogan (1869) LR 4 HL 82, HL

> **Lord Hatherley** (*obiter*): ... this doctrine has been established, no doubt, a long time since upon a sound foundation with reference to the jurisdiction of courts of equity to interpose in all cases of fraud.
>
> But this doctrine evidently requires to be carefully restricted within proper limits. It is itself a doctrine which involves a wide departure from the policy which induced the legislature to pass the Statute of Frauds, and it is only in clear cases of fraud that this doctrine has been applied – cases in which the court has been persuaded that there has been a fraudulent inducement held out on the part of the apparent beneficiary in order to lead the testator to confide to him the duty which he so undertook to perform.

A testator, in 1851, had left all his property by a three line will to his friend Mr Grogan. In 1854, the testator was struck down by cholera with only a few hours to live. He sent for Mr Grogan and told him in effect that his will and a letter would be found in his desk. The letter named various intended beneficiaries and the intended gifts to them. The letter concluded with the words:

> I do not wish you to act strictly to the foregoing instructions, but leave it entirely to your own good judgment to do as you think I would if living, and as the parties are deserving.

A disappointed plaintiff whom Mr Grogan thought it right to exclude sued Mr Grogan.

The court held that no trust was created because the testator did not intend to impose a trust on the executor.

The modern basis for enforcing such trusts is simply to give effect to the intention of the testator which has been validly communicated to or acquiesced in by the intended trustee. Once the trustee has acquired the property subject to an undertaking given to the testator, the court will give effect to the arrangement. In so doing the court does not infringe the requirements of s 9 of the 1837 Act but merely compels the legatee or devisee to fulfil his undertaking.

Per Lord Sumner in *Blackwell v Blackwell*:[1]

> The court of equity finds a man in the position of an absolute legal owner of a sum of money, which has been bequeathed to him under a valid will and it declares that, on proof of certain facts relating to the motives of the testator, it will not allow the legal owner to exercise his legal right to do what he wishes with the property. In other words it lets him take what the will gives him and then makes him apply it as the Court of Conscience directs, and it does so in order to give effect to the wishes of the testator, which would not otherwise be effectual.

1 [1929] AC 318 (see below, p 491).

Moreover, it is immaterial that one of the intended beneficiaries under the secret trust witnesses the will. In probate law (and in particular, s 15 of the Wills Act), an attesting witness or spouse who receives an interest under a will loses that interest. The will may be attested by two or more witnesses.

Section 15 of the Wills Act 1837 provides:

> ... if any person shall attest the execution of any will to whom or to whose wife or husband any beneficial devise, legacy, estate, interest, gift, or appointment, of or affecting any real or personal estate ... shall be thereby given or made, such devise, legacy, estate, interest, gift, or appointment shall, so far only as concerns such person attesting the execution of such will, or the wife or husband of such person, or any person claiming under such person or wife or husband, be utterly null and void, and such person so attesting shall be admitted as a witness to prove the execution of such will, or to prove the validity or invalidity thereof, notwithstanding such devise, legacy, estate, interest, gift, or appointment mentioned in such will.

This section was amended by s 1(1) of the Wills Act 1968 which provides:

> For the purposes of s 15 of the Wills Act 1837 ... the attestation of a will by a person to whom or to whose spouse there is given or made any such disposition as is described in that section shall be disregarded if the will is duly executed without his attestation and without that of any other such person.

In short, if there are more than two attesting witnesses and only one of the witnesses or spouses takes an interest under the will, his attestation of the will itself will not deprive him of an interest.

As far as secret trusts are concerned, the interest of the beneficiary under the trust is enjoyed outside (*dehors*) the will and thus outside the Wills Act. The trust is not created in the will but by the separate obligation undertaken by the legatee. The attestation of the will by the secret beneficiary (as opposed to the trustee) does not therefore attract the rigour of s 15 of the 1837 Act.

Re Young [1951] Ch 344, HC

A testator made a bequest to his wife subject to a direction that on her death she would leave the property for the purpose which he had communicated to her. One of the purposes was that she would leave a legacy of £2,000 to the testator's chauffeur, who witnessed the will.

The question in issue was whether the chauffeur had forfeited his interest.

The court held that the trust in his favour was not contained in the will but was created separately from the will.

> **Danckwerts J:** The whole theory of the formation of a secret trust is that the Wills Act 1837 has nothing to do with the matter because the forms required by the Wills Act are entirely disregarded, since the persons do not take by virtue of the gift in the will, but by virtue of the secret trusts imposed upon the beneficiary who does in fact take under the will.

There are two types of secret trusts. A fully secret and a half secret trust.

A fully secret trust is one where the legatee or devisee takes the property beneficially on the face of the will, that is, the existence of the trust as well as its terms are fully concealed by reference to the will.

For example, T, a testator, has bequeathed a legacy of £5,000 to L absolutely. Before his death T communicated the terms of a trust to L who agreed to abide by T's wishes after T's death. When L acquires the property he will be required to hold the property subject to the terms agreed.

A half secret trust is one where the legatee or devisee is named as a trustee on the face of the will but the terms are obviously concealed by the testator, eg, T, a testator, bequeathes a legacy of £5,000 to L 'on trust for purposes communicated to him'. Before executing his will T communicates the purpose of the legacy to L who agrees to carry out T's wishes. L becomes a trustee when he acquires the relevant property.

Although the rules concerning the creation of fully and half secret trusts overlap, there are significant differences in respect of their constitution. Accordingly, it is necessary to distinguish between the two concepts.

FULLY SECRET TRUSTS

Communication and acceptance *inter vivos*

The court draws a distinction between a mere legacy or devise and a legacy or devise subject to a secret trust. The essence of the distinction is that in a legacy subject to a secret trust, the testator has communicated the terms of the trust during his lifetime to the legatee. In this respect, it is immaterial that the communication of the terms is made before or after the execution of the will, provided that it is made before the testator's death.

Indeed, communication of the terms of the trust may even be made constructively by the testator delivering a sealed envelope to the intended trustee, subject to the direction, 'Not to be opened before my death'. This delivery may be treated as communication of the terms (contents) of the trust at the time of delivery even though the addressee becomes aware of the contents of the envelope after the death of the testator. See *Re Keen* (below, p 493).

But, if the legatee only becomes aware of the terms of the trust after the testator's death, he will be entitled to take the property beneficially. Having made no assurances to the testator to hold upon trust he is entitled to retain the legacy beneficially as the will indicates. Section 9 of the Wills Act 1837 may be used by him as a defence.

Wallgrave v Tebbs (1855) 2 K & J 313, HC

A testator, T, bequeathed a legacy of £12,000 to Mr Tebbs and Mr Martin and also devised freehold properties 'unto and to the use of Tebbs and Martin as joint tenants'. T was contemplating whether or not to devote part of the properties to charitable objects. After the will was made, one of his executors, on request from T, prepared a draft letter from the testator to Messrs Tebbs and Martin setting out the charitable objects that T had in mind. The draft letter was not sent to Tebbs and Martin nor did they become aware of it until after the testator's death. In addition, Tebbs and Martin had at no time given an undertaking to carry out T's wishes. The executor brought an action against Tebbs and Martin to have the money and other property applied for charitable purposes. They claimed that no trust was created and that they were entitled to the properties absolutely.

Held in favour of the transferees, the transfers amounted to mere gifts by will not coupled with an obligation to hold upon trust.

> **Wood VC:** I am satisfied that I ought not overstep the clear line which separates 'mere trusts' from 'devises and bequests' ... Where a person, knowing that a testator in making a disposition in his favour intends it to be applied for purposes other than for his own benefit either expressly promises, or by silence implies, that he will carry out the testator's intention into effect, and the property is left to him upon the faith of an undertaking, it is in effect a case of trust and the court will not allow the devisee to set up the Statute of Frauds – or rather the Statute of Wills as a defence. But the question here is totally different. Here there has been no promise or undertaking on the part of the legatee. The latter knew nothing of the testator's intention until after his death. Upon the face of the will, the parties take indisputably for their own benefit.
>
> Lord Sumner in *Blackwell v Blackwell* (see below, p 491) said:
>
> The necessary elements, on which the question turns, are intention, communication and acquiescence. The testator intends his absolute gift to be employed as he and not as the donee desires; he tells the proposed donee of this intention and, either by express promise or by the tacit promise, which is satisfied by acquiescence, the proposed donee encourages him to bequeath the money on the faith that his intentions will be carried out.

If the testator discloses to the legatee the fact that when property is transferred to him, he is required to hold the legacy upon trust, but fails to disclose the terms of the trust before his death, the secret trust will fail but the legatee will hold the property on resulting trust for the estate. In other words, the secret trust fails because there has been a failure to communicate the terms of the trust to the legatee during the lifetime of the testator. But, since the legatee is aware that he is required to hold on trust and acquires the property on the basis of this understanding, he holds the same on resulting trust for the testator.

Re Boyes, Boyes v Carritt (1884) 26 Ch D 531, HC

A testator in a will drawn up by his solicitor (Mr Carritt) gave his residuary estate to Carritt absolutely and appointed him the executor of his will. The testator had previously told Carritt that he wished him (Carritt) to hold the property according to directions which he would communicate by letter and Carritt agreed. Such directions were not given by the testator during his lifetime, but, after his death, two unattested documents, both addressed to Carritt, were found in which the testator stated his wish that Mrs B was entitled to the property under the intended trust. The testator's next of kin sued Carritt claiming a declaration that they (next of kin) were entitled to the property because no valid secret trust was created. Carritt claimed to hold the property as trustee for Mrs B.

The court held that no secret trust was created and the executor held the property for the benefit of the next of kin.

> **Kay J:** No case has ever yet decided that a testator can, by imposing a trust upon the devisee or legatee, the objects of which he does not communicate to him, enable himself to evade the Wills Act by declaring those objects in an unattested paper found after his death. I cannot help regretting that the testator's intention of bounty should fail by reason of an informality of this kind, but in my opinion it would be a serious innovation upon the law relating to testamentary instruments if this were to be established as a trust in her favour.
>
> If the trust was not declared when the will was made, it is essential, in order to make it binding, that it should be communicated to the devisee or legatee in the testator's lifetime and that he should accept that particular trust.

Once the legatee is aware of the terms of the trust, its acceptance may be communicated to the testator expressly or by the silence of the legatee amounting to an acquiescence (Wood VC in *Wallgrave v Tebbs* and Lord Sumner in *Blackwell v Blackwell*, above, p 482 and below, p 492). The obligation is on the legatee to notify his refusal (if he so wishes) to the testator during the lifetime of the testator.

Moss v Cooper (1861) 1 J & H 352, HC

A testator transferred his residuary estate to Gawthorn, Sedman and Owen. At the time of the execution of the will, a memorandum, authorised by the testator, was prepared by Gawthorn to the effect that after the residuary legatees had retained £25 each for their own use the residue was to be divided between named charities. Gawthorn communicated the terms of the memorandum to Sedman and Owen. Sedman told the testator that he would abide by his wishes. Owen did not communicate his assent to the testator. Gawthorn predeceased the testator. The next of kin challenged the validity of the trust.

The court held that a fully secret trust was created and Sedman and Owen held the property upon trust.

> **Wood VC:** If, immediately after making his will (for a bargain before the will is not essential), the testator had invited Gawthorn, Sedman and Owen to his house and had said to them, 'Here is my will, made in this form, because I am told that the property must be put entirely at your disposal; but I want a promise from you to dispose of it in a particular way': and if they, by their silence, led him to believe that they would so apply it, I apprehend it is quite clear that a trust would be created, and that it is altogether immaterial whether the promise is made before or after the execution of the will, that being a revocable instrument.
>
> Here, there are sufficient grounds to infer that Gawthorn, in fact, and to the knowledge or belief of Owen, had authority to make the communication; and, in that case, Owen's silence is a sufficient acceptance of the trust to exclude him from any beneficial enjoyment of the property.

Moreover, on general agency principles, the communication of the terms may be authorised by an agent of the testator. Likewise, express acceptance may be permitted through an agent of the legatee.

For example, T, a testator may appoint X, Y and Z as executors and trustees and authorise X to communicate the terms of the trust to Y and Z.

Thus far, the examples of fully secret trusts are occasions where the trust obligation was accepted *inter vivos* and subsequently the property is transferred by the testator's will to the intended trustees upon trust for the secret objects. But a variation on this principle imposes an obligation on the intended trustee/beneficiary to make a will in favour of a second beneficiary. Thus, the primary donee (and trustee) becomes entitled to an interest for his life and the secondary donee becomes entitled to the relevant property under the will of the primary donee. The approach of the courts is to affirm that the trust is created when the property is acquired by the primary donee but is kept in suspense during his lifetime and attaches to the estate of the trustee on his death. Of course, this principle is subject to the basic rule that the subject matter of the trust is required to be certain.

Re Gardner, Huey v Cunnington (No 1) [1920] 2 Ch 523, CA

A testatrix had given all her estate to her husband for his use and benefit during his life 'knowing that he will carry out my wishes'. Four days later, she signed a memorandum expressing the wish that she described as 'the money I leave to my husband' should on his death be equally divided among certain named beneficiaries. She died in 1919 possessed of personal estate only, and her husband died four days later. After his death, his wife's will and the memorandum were found in his safe, and there was parol evidence that shortly after the execution of the will the testatrix had said in his presence that her property after his death was to be equally divided between the named beneficiaries, and that he assented thereto.

The Court of Appeal held that, after the death of his wife, the husband enjoyed a life interest in the relevant property but was required to transfer the same to the beneficiaries.

Lord Sterndale MR: The obligation upon the husband and his next of kin seems to me to arise from this, that he takes the property in accordance with and upon an undertaking to abide by the wishes of the testatrix, and if he were to dispose of it in any other way he would be committing a breach of trust, or as it has been called in some of the cases a fraud. I do not think it matters which you call it. The breach of trust or the fraud would arise when he attempted to deal with the money contrary to the terms on which he took it.

Ottaway v Norman [1972] Ch 698, HC

A testator, Harry Ottaway, by his will devised his bungalow (with fixtures, fittings and furniture) to his housekeeper, Miss Hodges in fee simple and gave her a legacy of £1,500. It was alleged that Miss Hodges had verbally agreed with the testator to leave by her will the bungalow and fittings, etc, and whatever 'money' was left over at the time of her death to the plaintiffs, Mr and Mrs William Ottaway (the testator's son and daughter in law). By her will, Miss Hodges left all her property to someone else. The plaintiffs sued Mr Norman (Miss Hodges' executor) for a declaration that the relevant parts of Miss Hodges' estate were held upon trust for the plaintiff.

The court held that there was clear evidence that a fully secret trust was created only in respect of the bungalow and fittings, etc, but not in respect of the 'money'. Mr Norman as her executor therefore held the bungalow on trust for Mr and Mrs Ottaway.

Brightman J: It will be convenient to call the person on whom such a trust is imposed the 'primary donee' and the beneficiary under that trust the 'secondary donee'. The essential elements which must be proved to exist are: (i) the intention of the testator to subject the primary donee to an obligation in favour of the secondary donee; (ii) communication of that intention to the primary donee; and (iii) the acceptance of that obligation by the primary donee either expressly or by acquiescence. It is immaterial whether these elements precede or succeed the will of the donor. I am informed that there is no recent reported case where the obligation imposed on the primary donee is an obligation to make a will in favour of the secondary donee as distinct from some form of *inter vivos* transfer. But it does not seem to me that that can really be a distinction which can validly be drawn on behalf of the defendant in the present case.

The basis of the doctrine of a secret trust is the obligation imposed on the conscience of the primary donee and it does not seem to me that there is any materiality in the machinery by which the donor intends that that obligation shall be carried out.

I believe that the suggestion of an express trust was not pursued because certainly Harry Ottaway, and I think also William Ottaway, had complete confidence that Miss Hodges would do what she had been told.

I find as a fact that Harry Ottaway intended that Miss Hodges should be obliged to dispose of the bungalow in favour of the plaintiffs at her death, that he communicated that intention to Miss Hodges and that Miss Hodges accepted the obligation. I find the same facts in relation to the furniture, fixtures and fittings which passed to Miss Hodges under clause4 of Harry Ottaway's will. I am not satisfied that any similar obligation was imposed and accepted as regards any contents of the bungalow which had not devolved on Miss Hodges under clause 4 of Harry Ottaway's will.

I turn to the question of money. First as a matter of fact what did the parties intend should be comprised in Miss Hodges' obligation? All money which Miss Hodges had at her death, including money which she had acquired before Harry's death and money she acquired after his death from all sources? Or, only money acquired under Harry's will? Secondly, if such an obligation existed would it as a matter of law create a valid trust? On the second question I am content to assume for present purposes but without so deciding that if property is given to the primary donee on the understanding that the primary donee will dispose by his will of such assets, if any, as he may have at his command at his death in favour of the secondary donee, a valid trust is created in favour of the secondary donee which is in suspense during the lifetime of the primary donee, but attaches to the estate of the primary donee at the moment of the latter's death. There would seem to be at least some support for this proposition in an Australian case *Birmingham v Renfrew* (1937) 57 CLR 666.

I accept that the parties mentioned money on at least some occasions when they talked about Harry Ottaway's intentions for the future disposition of Ashcroft. I do not, however, find sufficient evidence that it was Harry Ottaway's intention that Miss Hodges should be compelled to leave all her money, from whatever source derived, to the plaintiffs. This would seem to preclude her giving even a small pecuniary legacy to any friend or relative. I do not think it is clear that Harry Ottaway intended to extract any such far-reaching undertaking from Miss Hodges or that she intended to accept such a wide obligation herself.

Therefore, the obligation, if any, is in my view to be confined to money derived under Harry Ottaway's will. If the obligation is confined to money derived under Harry Ottaway's will, the obligation is meaningless and unworkable unless it includes the requirement that she shall keep such money separate and distinct from her own money. I am certain that no such requirement was ever discussed or intended.

There is another difficulty. Does money in this context include only cash or cash and investment, or all moveable property of any description? The evidence is quite inconclusive. In my judgment the plaintiffs' claim succeeds in relation to the bungalow and in relation to the furniture, fixtures and fittings which devolved under clause 4 of Harry Ottaway's will subject, of course, to normal wastage and fair wear and tear, but not to any other assets.

(The explanation by Brightman J of the nature of the trust during the lifetime of the primary donee creates a number of difficulties. In particular, whether the primary donee becomes a tenant for life under the Settled Land Act 1925 with a power of sale over land and, if not, what level of protection is enjoyed by the secondary donees and purchasers of the property in good faith from the primary donee. See *Burgess* (1972) 36 Conv 113 (below, p 490).)

The same principle as stated above applies with equal force where the testator revokes his will on the strength of a promise by the next of kin (trustees) to dispose of the property in a specified manner, in accordance with the intention of the settlor. Likewise, the secret trust principles will extend to occasions where the settlor decides not to make a will on the faith of a promise by his next of kin to dispose of the property in accordance with the settlor's wishes as disclosed to him during the lifetime of the settlor.

McCormick v Grogan (1869) LR 4 HC 82, HL

> **Lord Hatherley LC:** ... if, for example, an heir said to a person who was competent to dispose of his property by will, 'Do not dispose of it by will, I undertake to carry into effect all such wishes as you may communicate to me'. And if the testator, acting on that representation, did not dispose of his property by will, and the heir has kept the property for himself, without carrying those instructions into effect, the court of equity has interposed on the ground of the fraud thus committed by the heir in inducing the testator to die intestate, upon the faith of the heir's representations that he would carry all such wishes as were confided to him into effect.

Sellack v Harris (1708) 5 Vin Ab 521

A father was induced by his heir presumptive (entitled to realty on an intestacy before 1925) not to make a will on the ground that the heir himself would make provision for the mother of the settlor. After the death of his father, the heir refused to make provision as promised.

The court held that the heir was obliged to make the relevant provision for he had induced his father to refrain from making a will.

Robert Burgess, in an article entitled 'Secret trust property' (1972) 36 Conv 113, considers the implications inherent in the decision of *Ottaway v Norman*. His concern was to examine when the secret trust commences and the extent of property capable of being affected by it. For these purposes, he posits four situations:

(1) Where specified property is left by will to X to be applied *inter vivos* in accordance with the terms of the secret trust [the normal secret trust situation].

(2) Where specified property is left by will to X to be left in X's will in accordance with the terms of the secret trust [the *Ottaway v Norman* scenario].

(3) Where specified property is left by will to X and where *all of X's property* is to be left by his will in accordance with the terms of the secret trust [*Re Green*, mutual wills].

(4) Where specified property is left by will to X but where *other property belonging to X* is to be left by his will in accordance with the terms of the secret trust.

Burgess then considers the two issues posed in each of the four situations. The common thread linking the four factual situations is the judgment of Brightman J in *Ottaway v Norman*, who applied a mutual wills solution in deciding when the secret trust is created and the extent of property subject to the trust. Burgess concludes that this innovation is regrettable.

HALF SECRET TRUSTS

As stated earlier, these trusts arise where the legatee or devisee take as trustee on the face of the will but the terms are not specified in the will. Thus, the testator has represented to the public that the transferee under the will takes the property in a representative capacity as trustee for an object whose identity is concealed on the face of the will.

For example, the testator has transferred his property to L, a legatee 'as trustee for purposes communicated to him'.

The following rules are required to be complied with in order to create a valid half secret trust.

(1) It is clearly established that evidence cannot be adduced in order to contradict the terms of the will. The will is considered to be the last testament of the testator and is thus treated as sacrosanct. In accordance with probate rules, the will becomes irrevocable on the death of the testator. The validity of the secret trust is dependent on the will transferring the property to the trustee. To be allowed to contradict the will in order to prove the terms of the secret trust has the potential to perpetrate a fraud. Hence, a rigid principle has been developed by the courts which prohibit the adduction of such contradictory evidence even if this is in accordance with the intention of the testator.

    For example, if the will points to a past communication, evidence may not be adduced which points to a future communication (in any event, such evidence is incapable of being admitted in the first place, see *Blackwell v Blackwell*, below).

    Similarly, if the will refers to the legatee as a trustee, evidence may not be adduced to show that he is intended as a beneficiary (see *Re Rees*, below, p 496).

(2) Where the communication of the terms of the trust is made before or at the time of the execution of the will, evidence may be adduced in order to show the terms of the trust. The adduction of such evidence complements the intention of the testator and the will.

Blackwell v Blackwell [1929] AC 318, HL

A testator by a codicil (alteration of a will executed in accordance with the Wills Act 1837) bequeathed a legacy of £12,000 to five persons 'to apply for the purposes indicated by me to them'. Before the execution of the codicil, the terms of the trust were communicated to the legatees and the trust was accepted by them all. The beneficiaries were the testator's mistress and her illegitimate son. The plaintiff claimed a declaration that no valid trust in favour of the objects had been created on the ground that parol evidence was inadmissible to establish the trust.

The House of Lords held that parol evidence was admissible to establish the terms of a half secret trust in order to prevent the testator's intention being fraudulently avoided.

> **Lord Sumner:** It seems to me that, apart from legislation, the application of the principle of equity in *Fleetwood's Case* (1880) 15 Ch D 594 ... was logical, and was justified by the same considerations as in cases of fraud and absolute gifts. Why should equity forbid an honest trustee to give effect to his promise, made to a deceased testator, and compel him to pay another legatee, about whom it is quite certain that the testator did not mean to make him the object of his bounty? In both cases the testator's wishes are incompletely expressed in his will. Why should equity, over a mere matter of words, give effect to them in one case and frustrate them in the other? No doubt the words 'in trust' prevent the legatee from taking beneficially, whether they have simply been declared in conversation or written in the will, but the fraud, when the trustee, so called in the will, is also the residuary legatee, is the same as when he is only declared a trustee by word of mouth accepted by him.

In other words, the justification for proving the terms of a half secret trust is similar to the rationale for the assumption of jurisdiction by the courts in order to enforce fully secret trusts namely, the prevention of fraud. The fraud which is capable of being committed by a dishonest trustee in the context of a half secret trust is similar to the fraud vis à vis a fully secret trust namely, reneging on the promise made to the testator. The consequences of a fraud intended by a dishonest trustee vary with the type of secret trust. In respect of a half secret trust, the trustee is not entitled to adduce evidence to show that he is beneficially entitled (compare a fully secret trust), but a resulting trust for the benefit of the testator's estate would be set up.

(3) In respect of an intended half secret trust, communication of the terms of the intended trust after the execution of the will but during the testator's lifetime is not admissible (contrast a fully secret trust).

For example, the testator's will transfers property to L 'on trust for purposes to be communicated to him'. If, subsequent to the execution of the will, the testator makes an agreement with L as to the terms of the trust, this agreement will not be admissible to prove the terms of the trust.

The justification given for this prohibition of informal evidence is to prevent an infringement of the provisions of the Wills Act 1837. This is judicially considered to be the case if an unattested document or parol evidence is admitted to prove the terms of the trust when the testator makes provision in his will for a future communication of the terms of the trust.

Lord Sumner (in *Blackwell v Blackwell*): The limits beyond which the rules as to unspecified trusts must not be carried, have often been discussed. A testator cannot reserve to himself a power of making future unwitnessed dispositions by merely naming a trustee and leaving the purposes of the trust to be supplied afterwards, nor can a legatee give testamentary validity to an unexecuted codicil by accepting an indefinite trust, never communicated to him in the testator's lifetime. To hold otherwise would indeed be to enable the testator to 'give the go-by' to the requirements of the Wills Act, because he did not choose to comply with them. It is communication of the purpose to the legatee, coupled with acquiescence or promise on his part, that removes the matter from the provisions of the Wills Act and brings it within the law of trusts.

Re Keen [1937] Ch 236, CA

The same principle was applied in this case. Under clause 5 of the testator's will, a legacy was transferred to two legatees, Hazlehurst and Evershed, 'to be held upon trust and disposed of by them among such persons or charities as may be notified by me to them or either of them during my lifetime'. Prior to the execution of the will, Evershed had been given a sealed envelope subject to the directions, 'Not to be opened before my death'. Evershed considered himself bound to hold the legacy subject to the terms declared in the envelope. The envelope contained the name of the beneficiary under the intended trust. Subsequently, the testator revoked the original will and executed a new will which contained an identical clause 5. No fresh directions were issued to Evershed, who was still prepared to carry out the testator's wishes. After the testator's death, an originating summons was taken out by the executors to determine whether they were required to distribute the property to Evershed and Hazlehurst as trustees for the specified beneficiary or for the residuary estate.

The Court of Appeal held that the trust failed and the property fell into residue on the grounds that:

(a) the delivery of the envelope constituted communication of the terms of the trust at the time of delivery. Since this was made prior to the execution of the will and was inconsistent with the terms of the will, the letter was not admissible;

(b) the provision in the will contained a power to declare trusts in the future. This power was not enforceable and the terms of the intended trust were not admissible.

Lord Wright MR (in deciding that the date of the communication was the date of delivery of the envelope): To take a parallel, a ship which sails under sealed orders is sailing under orders though the exact terms are not ascertained by the captain till later. I note that the case of a trust, put into writing, which is placed in the trustees' hands in a sealed envelope, was hypothetically treated by Kay J [in *Re Boyes*, above, p 486] as possibly constituting a communication in a case of this nature. This, so far as it goes, seems to support my conclusion. The trustees had the means of knowledge available whenever it became necessary and proper to open the envelope. I think Mr Evershed was right in understanding that the giving of the sealed envelope was a notification within clause 5.

There are two main questions: first, how far parol evidence is admissible to define the trust under such a clause as this and secondly, and in particular, how far such evidence, if admissible at all, would be excluded on the ground that it would be inconsistent with the true meaning of clause 5.

It is first necessary to state what, in my opinion, is the true construction of the words of the clause.

These words, in my opinion, can only be considered, as referring to a definition of trusts which have not yet, at the date of the will, been established and which, between that date and the testator's death, may or may not be established ... The words of the clause seem to me to refer only to something future and hypothetical, to something as to which the testator is reserving an option whether to do or not to do it.

In my judgment, clause 5 should be considered as contemplating future dispositions, and as reserving to the testator the power of making such dispositions without a duly attested codicil, simply by notifying them during his lifetime, the principles laid down by Lord Sumner (*Blackwell v Blackwell*) must be fatal to the appellant's claim.

In *Blackwell v Blackwell* [see above, p 491], *Re Fleetwood*,[2] and *Re Huxtable*,[3] the trusts had been specifically declared to some or all of the trustees, at or before the execution of the will, and the language of the will was consistent with that fact. There was, in these cases, no reservation of a future power to change the trusts, in whole or in part. Such a power would involve a power to change a testamentary disposition by an unexecuted codicil, and would violate s 9 of the Wills Act. This was so held in *Re Hetley*.[4]

But there is still a further objection which, in the present case, renders the appellant's claim unenforceable: the trusts which it is sought to establish by parol evidence would be inconsistent with the express terms of the will. That such an objection is fatal appears from the cases already cited, such as *Re Huxtable*. In that case, an undefined trust of money for charitable purposes was declared in the will, as in respect of the whole corpus and, accordingly, evidence was held inadmissible that the charitable trust was limited to the legatee's life, so that he was free to dispose of the corpus after his death. Similarly, in *Johnson v Ball*,[5] the testator by the will left the property to trustees, upon the uses contained in a letter signed 'by them and myself': it was held that that evidence was not admissible to show that, though no such letter was in existence at the date of the will, the testator had made a subsequent declaration of trust; the court held that these trusts could not be enforced.

2 (1880) 15 Ch D 594.

3 [1902] 2 Ch 793.

4 [1902] 2 Ch 866.

5 (1551) 5 De G & Sm 85.

> In the present case, while clause 5 refers solely to a future definition, or to future definitions, of the trust, subsequent to the date of the will, the sealed letter relied on as notifying the trust was communicated before the date of the will. That it was communicated to one trustee only, and not to both, would not, I think, be an objection. But the objection remains that the notification sought to be put in evidence was anterior to the will, and hence not within the language of clause 5, and inadmissible simply on that ground, as being inconsistent with what the will prescribes.

This decision was followed by Pennycuick J in *Re Bateman's Will Trust*.

Re Bateman's Will Trust [1970] 1 WLR 1463, HC

A testator bequeathed £24,000 to his trustees and directed them to pay the income 'to such persons and in such proportions as shall be stated by me in a sealed letter'. After the execution of the will, the testator gave the trustees a sealed envelope written, 'to be opened on my death' which contained the names of the beneficiaries. The residuary beneficiaries brought an action claiming the property.

The court held that the secret trust had failed and the property was held on resulting trust for the residuary beneficiaries.

> **Pennycuick J:** The direction clearly imports that the testator may, in the future after the date of the will, give a sealed letter to his trustees. It is impossible to confine the words to a sealed letter already so given. If that be the true construction of the wording it is not in dispute that the direction is invalid.

It seems that this rule is firmly established by the courts but it is submitted that the reasoning is open to challenge on principle. The enforceability of secret trusts (including half secret trusts) is based on the premise that they exist outside the will. The Wills Act is required to be complied with in order to transfer the property to the trustees, beyond this the formalities under the 1837 Act have nothing to do with the trust. To import the requirement that an attested document is required to be executed if the will points to a future communication but not if the will points to a contemporaneous or past communication seems to confuse the basis for enforcing such trusts. It is submitted that the courts have confused the probate doctrine of incorporation by reference with the enforceability of such trusts. Under the probate doctrine of incorporation by reference it is possible to incorporate in a will a document which is not executed in accordance with the Wills Act provided that the document is in existence on the date of the execution of the will and is specifically referred to in the will. When this principle is complied with the incorporated, unattested document is admitted to probate and the advantage of secrecy, so crucial to secret trusts, is lost. Needless to say that the courts have not openly espoused this principle as the basis for prohibiting evidence of the terms of the agreement between the testator and the trustee posterior to the execution of the will.

(4) The persons named as trustees on the face of the will cannot, in any event, take the property beneficially even if this is in accordance with the intention of the testator. Such named trustees are prohibited from adducing evidence to this effect because to admit such evidence would contradict the terms of the trust. There is no objection in benefiting the trustee by a separate clause in the will.

Re Rees [1950] Ch 204, CA

By his will, a testator appointed his friend H and his solicitor W to be executors and trustees and he devised and bequeathed all his property to 'my trustees absolutely, they well knowing my wishes concerning the same'. The testator told the executors and trustee at the time of making the will that he wished them to make certain payments out of the estate and retain the remainder for their own use. After the payments were made, there was a substantial surplus remaining. The executors claimed that they were entitled to keep the surplus in that there was no secret trust but a conditional gift in their favour.

Held that the surplus funds passed on intestacy. The relevant clause in the will created a half secret trust and the trustees were not entitled to adduce evidence to show that they were entitled beneficially.

> **Sir Raymond Evershed MR:** I agree with the judge that to admit evidence to the effect that the testator informed of the executors – or I will assume both of the executors – that he intended them to take beneficial interests, would be to conflict with the terms of the will as I have construed them; for the inevitable result of admitting that evidence and giving effect to it would be that the will would be regarded not as conferring a trust estate only upon the two trustees, but as giving them a conditional gift which on construction is the thing which, if I am right, it does not do.
>
> In the public interest it is not to be forgotten that Parliament has laid down that *prima facie* a will disposing of the property of a deceased person must follow certain strict forms. The courts have also been very insistent on the importance of the principle that those who assume the office of trustees should not, so far as they fairly can prevent it, allow themselves to be in a position in which their interests and their duties conflict. In the general public interest it seems to me desirable that if a testator wishes his property to go to his solicitor and the solicitor prepares the will, that intention on the part of the testator should appear plainly on the will and should not be arrived at by the more oblique method of what is sometimes called a secret trust.

The same principle was applied in *Re Pugh's Will Trust*.[6]

The testator appointed his solicitor, executor and trustee and left the residue of his estate to the solicitor 'to dispose in accordance with my letters or memoranda I may leave with this my will and otherwise in such manner as he

6 [1967] 1 WLR 1262.

may in his absolute discretion think fit'. The testator died without leaving any letters or memoranda with his will. The solicitor sought a declaration as to whether he was entitled to take the residue beneficially.

The court held that the direction to apply the estate in accordance with the letters and memoranda created a fiduciary obligation on the solicitor. Since the letters, etc, did not exist, the trust had no defined objects and was void. Accordingly, the residuary estate was held on trust for the next of kin.

It must be emphasised that the principle in *Re Rees* is only applicable to half secret trusts. It does not extend to fully secret trusts for in such trusts the intended trustee is not named as a trustee on the face of the will.

ADDITIONS TO SECRET TRUSTS

If a testator wishes to add further property to an intended secret trust, he is required to take the trustees in his confidence and communicate the additional terms of the trust to them. Failure to inform the trustees of the additional property will result in the intended trust failing in respect of the additional property. In the context of a half secret trust, a resulting trust of the extra property will be created.

Re Colin Cooper, Le Neve-Foster v National Provincial Bank [1939] Ch 811, CA

A testator bequeathed the sum of £5,000 to two trustees upon trust for purposes 'already communicated to them'. Shortly before his death he executed a codicil giving the same trustees the sum of £10,000 declaring,'they knowing my wishes regarding that sum'. The testator failed to inform the trustees of this new bequest. On the question of the validity of the trust of the additional bequest, the court held that the gift failed and a resulting trust of the additional £5,000 was created. In respect of £5,000 which the trustees agreed to hold upon trust, a valid secret trust was created.

> **Sir Wilfred Greene MR:** It seems to me that upon the facts of this case it is impossible to say that the acceptance by the trustees of the onus of trusteeship in relation to the first and earlier legacy is something which must be treated as having been repeated in reference to the second legacy or the increased legacy, which ever way one chooses to describe it ... I cannot myself see that the arrangement between the testator and the trustees can be construed as though it had meant '£5,000 or whatever sum I may hereafter choose to bequeath'. That is not what was said and it was not with regard to any sum other than the £5,000 that the consciences of the trustees were burdened.

If, on construction of the will and the circumstances of the case, the court had come to the preliminary conclusion that the intention of the trustees was to hold '£5,000 or whatever sum the testator may from time to time transfer'.

Assuming the testator from time to time increased his bequest to the trustees beyond £5,000. It is arguable that the trustees will be required to hold the final amount bequeathed to them. The trustees, having made a blanket agreement to hold an unlimited amount of property transferred to them would be hard pressed to show that they may, consistently without fraud, hold any additional property on resulting trust. The agreement simply is not restricted to a specific amount or a ceiling.

In principle, the rule in *Re Colin Cooper* ought to be extended to fully secret trusts. Thus, if on the facts, the court decides that the circumstances involve an agreement with the trustees to hold a specific amount of funds, say £5,000 upon trust for the beneficiaries and the testator increases the legacy to £6,000 without informing the trustees. It is open to the court to decide that the extra amount of £1,000 is not subject to the trust. In this event the legatees may take the additional sum beneficially (see *Wallgrave v Tebbs*, above, p 485). Alternatively, if the court considers the circumstances of the agreement and imposes a broad understanding to hold any property transferred to the trustees upon trust for the beneficiaries, then the changes in the amount of funds may be irrelevant.

CONTROVERSIAL ISSUES INVOLVING SECRET TRUSTS

Communication of the terms to some of the trustees

Where a testator leaves property by will to two or more persons apparently beneficially but informs one or some of the apparent legatees or devisees of the terms of the trust, the question has arisen whether the persons who were unaware of the trust are bound to hold upon trust or not. The solution adopted by the courts, which is far from adequate, depends on the status of the co-owners and the time when the communication was made to those who are aware of the trust.

If the informed legatee or devisee was told of the terms of the trust before or at the time of the execution of the will and the multiple owners take as joint tenants, then the uninformed legatee is bound by the terms of the trust communicated to the informed legatee. The reason commonly ascribed to this solution is 'no one is allowed to claim property under a fraud committed by another' (*per* Farwell J in *Re Stead* (see below, p 499)). In other words, the court assumes that the reason why only one person has been informed of the trust is based on a fraud committed by the informed legatee. The testator is assumed to be induced to make his will by the promise of those who have been informed of the trust. Thus, the uninformed legatee ought not to be placed in an advantageous position of profiting from this fraud by being allowed to claim the property (or part thereof) beneficially.

Russell v Jackson (1852) 10 Hare 204, HC

The testator transferred property by his will to joint tenants. Before making the will, he communicated the trust to some but not all of the intended trustees. On the question of the extent of the secret trust. The court held that all the joint tenants were bound by the trust owing to the fraud of the informed beneficiary.

Alternatively, if the promise is made after the execution of the will to one (or some) of the co-owners but not to them all, and the will is left unrevoked, the informed legatee or devisee alone is bound to hold upon the terms of the secret trust. The uninformed co-owners are not bound to hold upon trust and may take the property (or part) beneficially. The status of the co-owners is immaterial. Thus, they may acquire the property as joint tenants or tenants in common. The legatees whose consciences are affected by the terms of the trust are those who made promises to the testator. The justification given for this solution is that the 'gift is not tainted by any fraud in procuring the execution of the will' *per* Farwell J in *Re Stead* (see below).

Tee v Ferris (1856) 2 K & J 357, HC

The testator by his will gave the residue of his estate to Ferris and three other persons as tenants in common. By a contemporaneous memorandum he expressed his confidence that the four persons will hold the property for 'charity objects'. Ferris alone was informed of the trust during the lifetime of the testator. On the question of the validity of the secret trust.

The court held that Ferris alone was bound to hold upon trust. Accordingly, the trust affected one quarter of the estate. The others were each entitled to take a quarter share of the property beneficially.

In *Re Stead*, Farwell J reviewed the authorities and concluded that:

> I am unable to see any difference between a gift made on the faith of an antecedent promise and a gift left unrevoked on the faith of a subsequent promise to carry out the testator's wishes; but apparently a distinction has been made by the various judges who have had to consider the question. I am bound, therefore, to decide in accordance with these authorities.

Re Stead, Witham v Andrew [1900] 1 Ch 237, HC

A testatrix by her will gave her residuary estate to her executrices, Mrs Witham (W) and Mrs Andrews (A) absolutely. Following the death of the testatrix, W alleged that prior to the execution of the will the testatrix had informed her as to the terms of a trust distribution. W further alleged that the testatrix executed her will on the faith of a promise by W to carry out the trust. A claimed that no communication had been made to her during the testatrix's lifetime and that she was entitled to half of the property beneficially.

The court held:

(i) rejecting the evidence of W as to the time of the communication of the terms of the trust to her. A therefore took half of the property beneficially;

(ii) W was nevertheless bound by the terms of the trust communicated to her.

> **Farwell J:** If A induces B either to make, or to leave unrevoked, a will leaving property to A and C as tenants in common, by expressly promising, or tacitly consenting, that he and C will carry out the testator's wishes, and C knows nothing of the matter until after A's death, A is bound, but C is not bound (*Tee v Ferris* (above, p 499)); the reason stated being, that to hold otherwise would enable one beneficiary to deprive the rest of their benefits by setting up a secret trust. If, however, the gift were to A and C as joint tenants, the authorities have established a distinction between those cases in which the will is made on the faith of an antecedent promise by A and those in which the will is left unrevoked on the faith of a subsequent promise. In the former case, the trust binds both A and C (*Russell v Jackson* [see above, p 499]; *Jones v Badley*),[7] the reason stated being that no person can claim an interest under a fraud committed by another; in the latter case A and not C is bound (*Burney v MacDonald*[8] and *Moss v Cooper*),[9] the reason stated being that the gift is not tainted with any fraud in procuring the execution of the will ... I hold that the defendant Mrs Andrews is not bound by any trust.

In conclusion, in respect of a fully secret trust, the authorities on the rule concerning the scope of the liability of multiple trustees where one or some of them has or have been informed of the terms of the trust is at best arbitrary. These cases tend to focus perhaps on the wrong issue. The central issue here ought to be the intention of the testator. If the testator was induced by the promise of A to transfer property to A and B for the benefit of another, and B was unaware of the trust, then A and B ought to be bound for B should not be entitled to profit from the fraud of A. This ought to be the position irrespective of whether A and B are joint tenants or tenants in common. If, on the other hand, the testator would have given the property to B in any event, then there is no justification for subjecting B to the terms of a trust.[10]

In respect of half secret trusts, the consequences concerning a failure to communicate the terms of the trust to all the trustees have been resolved piecemeal by the courts. It is the established practice of the courts that evidence of the terms of the trust is not admissible if made after the execution of the will. In such circumstances, the trustees hold upon resulting trust (see above, p 492). Further, the justification (in the context of a fully secret trust) for imposing a trust on the uninformed trustees in respect of an antecedent communication to some of the trustees who are joint tenants (that is, 'no one is allowed to claim property beneficially under a fraud committed by another' *per* Farwell J in *Re Stead*) has no application to half secret trusts.

7 (1868) LR 3 Ch App 362.

8 (1845) 15 Sim 6.

9 (1861) 1 J & H 352.

10 See Perrins, B, 'Can you keep half a secret?' (1972) 88 LQR 225.

There have been a few occasions when the courts have considered the principle of incomplete communication to all the trustees of an intended half secret trust. The solution adopted by the courts in each case has been restricted to its own facts.

If the will permits communication to one of several trustees such as, 'to all or either of the trustees', the communication to one of the trustees before or at the time of the execution of the will bind all of them.

Per Lord Wright in *Re Keen* (above, p 493):

> ... If the communication was made to one trustee only, and not to both, that would not, I think, be an objection to the secret trust.

Lord Wright did not indicate why he had no objection 'to the secret trust'. It is submitted that possible justifications of Lord Wright's decision are that the adduction of such evidence is consistent with the will and the trusteeship undertaken (as apparent on the face of the will) is a joint office.

If the will declares that the terms of the trust have been communicated to 'all of the trustees', evidence of the communication to one of the trustees is inadmissible in order to bind the conscience of the other trustees. The intended secret trust will fail for uncertainty of objects and a resulting trust will be set up.

***Re Spence* [1949] WN 237, HC**

A testator by his will, dated 11 August 1943, gave his estate to four trustees, A, B, C and D, 'to be dealt with in accordance with my wishes which I have made known to them'. At different times, between January 1941 and August 1943, he obtained promises from B, C and D to dispose of his property in accordance with memoranda to be drawn up at some unspecified future time and to be found among his papers at his death. In January 1943 he sent to A, his solicitor and fourth trustee, an envelope containing three sealed envelopes addressed to A, B and C bearing a statement in the testator's handwriting that they were not to be opened until after his death. Each envelope subsequently turned out to contain a copy of a memorandum by the testator dated 6 and 9 December 1942 setting forth, *inter alia*, a series of dispositions of income and capital of his estate. (Copies of a further memorandum, dated 10 January 1944 and addressed to A, B, C and D, were deposited in the same way with A on 2 February 1944, eight days before the testator died on 10 February 1944.) A, B and C (the surviving trustees) asked the court to decide whether the memoranda dated 6 and 9 December 1942 constituted a valid secret trust or whether there was a resulting trust in favour of the persons entitled to the testator's estate as on total intestacy.

Romer J held that the secret trust failed for uncertainty on the following grounds:

(i) the promises obtained from B, C and D between January 1941 and August 1943 were ineffective as amounting to an irregular dispositive power;

(ii) the delivery of the envelopes to A in January 1943 subject to the directions amounted to a constructive communication of the terms of the trust to A;

(iii) it was not possible to substitute the communication to A for wishes communicated to other trustees (B, C and D) relating to unspecified memoranda to be drawn up in the future.

Classification of secret trusts

The classification of secret trusts is not entirely of academic importance. Express trusts concerning land are required to be 'manifested and proved by some writing' as enacted in s 53(1)(b) of the Law of Property Act 1925 (see above, p 57). On the other hand, constructive trusts in respect of land are exempt from the requirements of writing (see s 53(2) of the Law of Property Act 1925). The question considered here is whether a secret trust is express or constructive.

Half secret trusts

Half secret trusts are treated as express because the existence of the trust is declared on the face of the will, although the objects are not specified in the will. Accordingly, the High Court has decided that a half secret trust is an express trust and if the agreement between the testator and the intended trustee is not evidenced in writing, the purported half secret trust is unenforceable.

Re Baillie (1886) 2 TLR 660, HC

A testator appointed Mrs Fitzgerald his executrix and gave her 'all his real and personal property upon trust to carry out my verbal wishes'. Prior to the execution of the will the testator verbally informed the executrix that she may use the fund to educate and assist the children of the testator's deceased cousin if this was necessary, but subject to her doing so, the property was hers to enjoy beneficially. The trustee claimed to have exhausted the first purpose of the trust and sought to retain the surplus of property beneficially.

The court held that the property was held on resulting trust. The intended secret trust in favour of the trustee failed because:

(a) the trustee was prohibited from adducing evidence that she was entitled beneficially;

(b) the trust of the realty was unenforceable because of failure to comply with s 9 of the Statute of Frauds 1677 (predecessor to s 53(1)(b) of the Law of Property Act 1925).

> **North J:** When an estate is given to a man in the character of a trustee, without anything to indicate that a beneficial interest is intended, then, if the trusts are exhausted there is a resulting trust ... The point raised by counsel for the defendant that the Statute of Frauds applied so far as the realty was concerned was a good one, because the trust was not indicated in writing.

Fully secret trusts

The classification of fully secret trusts has not been positively achieved.

Originally, secret trusts were enforced by the courts in order to prevent the intended trustee committing a fraud. As we have seen, a fully secret trustee takes the property apparently beneficially on the face of the will. It was the practice of the courts, in enforcing such trusts, to prevent the intended trustee setting up s 9 of the Wills Act 1837 as a defence to negate any attempt to take the property beneficially.

Per Lord Westbury in *McCormick v Grogan* (see above, p 482):

> The court of equity has, from a very early period, decided that even an Act of Parliament shall not be used as an instrument of fraud; and if in the machinery of perpetrating a fraud an Act of Parliament intervenes, the court of equity, it is true, does not set aside the Act of Parliament but it fastens on the individual who gets a title under that Act, and imposes upon him a personal obligation, because he applies the Act as an instrument for accomplishing a fraud.

This approach is consistent with the constructive trust jurisdiction. Accordingly, a fully secret trust concerning land may be declared orally.

Alternatively, it is arguable that the trust is express for the testator has declared the trust and transferred the property to the trustees under his will. Thus, the requirements of *Milroy v Lord* are met. Further, the modern basis for enforcing such trusts is to give effect to the intention of the testator, expressed outside the will (see Lord Sumner's judgment in *Blackwell v Blackwell*, above, p 482). If this be the case it is arguable that s 53(1)(b) of the Law of Property Act 1925 is required to be complied with. However, the intended trustee is not entitled to raise the defence of non compliance with the sub section in order to take the property beneficially, for equity would not allow a statute to be used as an engine for fraud.

This issue was not raised in *Ottaway v Norman* (see above, p 488) and remains unresolved.

Proof of the secret trust

The earlier cases were consistent in applying the standard of proof in order to prove the terms of a secret trust, namely 'clear evidence' of the terms of the trust analagous to the standard of proof required for rectification of an instrument. In short, the standard of proof was higher than the ordinary civil standard of a balance of probabilities.

Per Lord Westbury in *McCormick v Grogan* (above, p 482):

> ... it is incumbent on the court to see that a fraud, a *malus animus*, is proved by the clearest and most indisputable evidence.

Per Brightman J in *Ottaway v Norman* (above, p 488):

> ... if a will contains a gift which is in terms absolute, clear evidence is needed before the court will assume that the testator did not mean what he said. It is perhaps analagous to the standard of proof which this court requires before it will rectify a written instrument, for there again a party is saying that neither meant what they have written.

Recently, the court adopted a different approach to the standard of proof of a secret trust. There are two standards of proof in the context of a secret trust. The ordinary civil standard of proof (balance of probabilities) is required to be complied with in a way similar to proving the terms of an ordinary trust. The burden of proof lies on the party seeking to establish the trust. However, if there has been a fraudulent denial of the trust or promise, the standard of proof is higher.

Re Snowden, Smith v Spowage and Others [1979] Ch 528, HC

A testatrix, aged 86, made her will six days before she died. She had no children and her nearest relatives apart from her brother were five nephews and nieces, 13 great-nephews and great-nieces. She left her residuary estate to her brother, Bert (B), absolutely. B died six days after the testatrix, leaving all of his property to his son. Evidence was given by members of a firm of solicitors who had prepared and witnessed the will, that the testatrix wished to be fair to everyone, including her nephews and nieces, and wanted B to look after the division for her. On the question of whether a secret trust was created, the court held that no secret trust was created and B's son took beneficially. B was subject only to a moral obligation to respect the wishes of the testatrix. In the absence of fraud or other special circumstances, the standard of proof that was required to establish a secret trust was merely the ordinary civil standard of proof required to establish an ordinary trust.

> **Megarry VC:** Now it seems perfectly clear that the will was executed by the testatrix on the basis of some arrangement that was made between her and her brother regarding the gift of residue to him. The question is what that arrangement was. In particular, did it impose a trust, or did it amount to a mere moral or family obligation? If it was a trust, what were the terms of that trust?
>
> Although these questions are distinct, they are obviously interrelated to some degree. The more uncertain the terms of the obligation, the more likely it is to be a moral obligation rather than a trust: many a moral obligation is far too indefinite to be enforceable as a trust. As Sir Arthur Hobhouse said in a somewhat different case (*Mussoorie Bank Ltd v Raynor*),[11] uncertainty in the

11 (1882) 7 App Cas 321, p 331.

subject of the gift 'has a reflex action upon the previous words', throwing doubt on the testator's intention, and seeming to show that he would not have intended his words to be imperative words.

I cannot say that there is no evidence from which it could be inferred that a secret trust was created. At the same time, that evidence is far from being overwhelming. One question that arises is thus whether the standard of proof required to establish a secret trust is merely the ordinary civil standard of proof, or whether it is a higher and more cogent standard. If it is the latter, I feel no doubt that the claim that there is a secret trust must fail.

[The learned judge then considered the judgments of Lord Westbury in *McCormick v Grogan* and Brightman J in *Ottaway v Norman* (both above, p 504) and continued:]

On this, I would make four comments. First, the headnote [in the report of the case *Ottaway v Norman*] seems to me to be liable to mislead, since it omits the judge's precautionary word 'perhaps' which preceded 'analogous', and so gives a firmness to the proposition which the judge avoided.

Secondly, the standard for rectification is indeed high, and certainly higher than the ordinary standards. Lord Thurlow's requirements of 'strong irrefragable evidence' (in *Countess Dowager of Shelburne v Earl of Inchiquin*)[12] no longer holds the field, to the relief of those who find in the second word problems both of pronunciation and of meaning. But there is high authority for saying that there must be evidence 'of the clearest and most satisfactory description' (see *Fowler v Fowler*)[13] which will establish the mistake with a 'high degree of conviction' (see *Crane v Hegeman-Harris Co Inc*),[14] and will 'leave no fair and reasonable doubt upon the mind that the deed does not embody the final intention of the parties' (see *Fowler v Fowler*).[15] What is required is 'convincing proof': see *Joscelyne v Nissen*,[16] in delivering the judgment of the Court of Appeal. I feel some uncertainty about the difference between these terms and the 'exceptionally high standard of evidence' which Brightman J rejected; perhaps it lies in the word 'exceptionally'.

Thirdly, I feel some doubt about how far rectification is a fair analogy to secret trusts in this respect. Many cases of rectification do of course involve a party in saying that neither meant what they have written, and requiring that what they have written should be altered. On the other hand, the whole basis of secret trusts, as I understand it, is that they operate outside the will, changing nothing that is written in it, and allowing it to operate according to its tenor, but then fastening a trust on to the property in the hands of the recipient. It is at least possible that very different standards of proof may be appropriate for cases where the words of a formal document have been altered and for cases where there is no such alteration but merely a question whether, when the

12 (1784) 1 Bro CC 338, p 341.

13 (1859) 4 De G & J 250, p 264, *per* Lord Chelmsford LC.

14 [1939] 4 All ER 68, p 71, *per* Greene MR.

15 (1859) 4 De G & J 250, p 264, *per* Lord Chelmsford LC.

16 [1970] 1 All ER 1213, p 1222, *per* Russell LJ.

document has been given effect to, there will be some trust of the property with which it dealt.

Fourthly, I am not sure that it is right to assume that there is a single, uniform standard of proof for all secret trusts. The proposition of Lord Westbury in *McCormick v Grogan* with which Brightman J was pressed in *Ottaway v Norman* was that the jurisdiction in cases of secret trust was – founded altogether on personal fraud. It is a jurisdiction by which a Court of Equity, proceeding on the ground of fraud, converts the party who has committed it into a trustee for the party who is injured by that fraud. Now, being a jurisdiction founded on personal fraud, it is incumbent on the court to see that a fraud, *a malus animus*, is proved by the clearest and most indisputable evidence.'

Of that, it is right to say that the law on the subject has not stood still since 1869, and that it is now clear that secret trusts may be established in cases where there is no possibility of fraud. *McCormick v Grogan* has to be read in the light both of earlier cases that were not cited, and also of subsequent cases, in particular *Blackwell v Blackwell*.[17]

It seems to me that fraud comes into the matter in two ways. First, it provides an historical explanation of the doctrine of secret trusts: the doctrine was evolved as a means of preventing fraud. That, however, does not mean that fraud is an essential ingredient for the application of the doctrine: the reason for the rule is not part of the rule itself. Second, there are some cases within the doctrine where fraud is indeed involved. There are cases where for the legatee to assert that he is a beneficial owner, free from any trust, would be a fraud on his part.

It is to this latter aspect of fraud that it seems to me that Lord Westbury's words are applicable. If a secret trust can be held to exist in a particular case only by holding the legatee guilty of fraud, then no secret trust should be found unless the standard of proof suffices for fraud. On the other hand, if there is no question of fraud, why should so high a standard apply? In such a case, I find it difficult to see why the mere fact that the historical origin of the doctrine lay in the prevention of fraud should impose the high standard of proof for fraud in a case in which no issue of fraud arises. In accordance with the general rule of evidence, the standard of proof should vary with the nature of the issue and its gravity (see *Hornal v Neuberger Products Ltd*).[18]

Now in the present case there is no question of fraud. The will directed the residue to be held in trust for the brother absolutely, and the only question is whether or not the beneficial interest thus given to him has been subjected to a trust, and if so, what that trust is. The trust, if it is one, is plainly one which required the brother to carry it out: it was he who was to distribute the money and see that everything was dealt with properly, and not the trustees of the will. There was thus no attempt to cancel the testamentary trust of residue for the brother and require the trustees of the will to hold the residue on the secret trust instead. Accordingly, I cannot see that rectification provides any real

17 [1929] AC 318.

18 [1956] 3 All ER 970.

> analogy. The question is simply that of the ordinary standard of evidence required to establish a trust.
>
> I therefore hold that in order to establish a secret trust where no question of fraud arises, the standard of proof is the ordinary civil standard of proof that is required to establish an ordinary trust.

The learned judge considered the evidence and decided that the testatrix imposed only a moral obligation on her brother to dispose of the property in accordance with her wishes.

Professor Crane, in commenting on the decision in *Re Snowden* (see [1979] 43 Conv 448), questions whether the rule requiring a higher standard of proof is necessary. Such a rule could be regarded as benefiting unscrupulous trustees. He suggests that it would be preferable to adopt the ordinary civil standard of proof throughout, bearing in mind that the court will have to weigh up the merits of the evidence on both sides.

Trustee predeceasing the testator

In probate law, the general rule (subject to the *per stirpes* rule and a number of other exceptions) is that, if the legatee or devisee predeceases the testator, the legacy or devise lapses and the interest falls into residue, see *Elliott v Davenport*.[19]

In the context of a fully secret trust, if the sole intended trustee predeceases the testator, his interest will lapse and the property which would have been subject to the secret trust will fall into residue. Accordingly, the intended secret trust will fail. Although there is no direct authority which supports this analysis, Cozens Hardy LJ in *Re Maddock* in an *obiter* pronouncement hinted at this conclusion.

***Re Maddock* [1902] 2 Ch 220, CA**

A testatrix by her will left her residuary estate 'absolutely' to X whom she appointed one of her executors. By a subsequent memorandum communicated to X during her lifetime, she directed X to hold part of the residue upon trust for named beneficiaries. There were insufficient assets to pay the debts of the estate. The question in issue was whether the secret beneficiaries took their interests subject to the payment of the debts or not.

The court held that the part of the residuary estate that was bound by the trust must be treated as if it was specifically bequeathed and could not be used to pay the debts.

> **Cozens Hardy LJ:** ... the so called trust does not affect property except by reason of a personal obligation binding the individual devisee or legatee. If he renounces and disclaims, or dies in the lifetime of the testator, the persons

19 (1705) 1 P Wms 83.

> claiming under memorandum can take nothing against the heir at law or next of kin or residuary devisee or legatee.

On the other hand, in the context of a half secret trust, since the trustee takes as trustee on the face of the will it could be argued that the trust ought not fail, provided that the terms of the trust could be established.

Secret beneficiary predeceasing the testator

If the beneficiary under an intended secret trust dies before the testator, on general principles, the trust will fail. The trust is created when the property is transferred to the trustees subject to the trusts of the settlement. The beneficiary's interest may only vest at the time of the creation of the trust. At this point, of course, the beneficiary no longer exists and a trust cannot exist without a beneficiary. But, in *Re Gardner (No 2)*, the court decided that the deceased beneficiary's heirs are entitled to the trust funds.

Re Gardner (No 2) [1923] 2 Ch 230, HC

A testatrix by her will left her estate to her husband absolutely 'knowing that he will carry out my wishes'. During her lifetime she informed her husband of the terms of the trust, namely an equal distribution between her nephews and nieces after his death. The husband died five days after the testatrix and it was discovered that one of the nieces had died before the testatrix but after the communication of the terms to her husband. The question in issue was whether the personal representative of the niece was entitled to a share of the property.

The court held that the personal representative was entitled to succeed on the ground that the trust was created at the time of the *inter vivos* communication by the testatrix.

> **Romer J:** Apart from authority I should, without hesitation, say that in the present case the husband held the corpus of the property upon trust for the two nieces and the nephew, notwithstanding the fact that the niece predeceased the testatrix. The rights of the parties appear to me to be exactly the same as though the husband, after the memorandum had been communicated to him by the testatrix ... had executed a declaration of trust binding himself to hold any property that should come to him upon his wife's partial intestacy upon trust as specified in the memorandum.

It is submitted that this conclusion cannot be supported in trust law or probate law. In trust law, as explained above, the trust may be created at the earliest moment on the death of the testatrix. During the testatrix's lifetime, there could not have been a trust because the trustees would not have acquired the intended trust property. At this time, the intended beneficiaries could only have enjoyed a *spes*. In any event, in probate law a disposition by will takes effect on the death of the testator.

David Hodge, in an article entitled 'Secret trusts: the fraud theory revisited' [1980] Conv 341, examines the theoretical basis for the enforcement of secret trusts. His theory is that the prevention of fraud is the bedrock for enforcing secret trusts. Megarry VC, in *Re Snowden* [1979] 2 All ER 172, formulated the standard of proof needed to establish a secret trust by reference to the existence or non-existence of fraud. In this context, fraud has two meanings, the wider and narrower meaning. The wider view of fraud involves the secret trustee attempting to defeat the wishes of the testator by attempting to renege on the promise made to the testator during the latter's lifetime. Support for this view is to be found in the Court of Appeal's judgments, for example, Scott LJ in *Bannister v Bannister* [1948] 2 All ER 122. The narrower view of fraud is laid down by Lord Westbury in *McCormick v Grogan* (1869) LR 4 HL 82, and is based on the deceitful nature of the secret trustee's conduct considered by reference *to the time he made the undertaking*. Hodge submits that of the two views, the wider view of fraud is preferable, 'for acceptance of the narrower view would not only impose upon a person seeking to establish a secret trust the heavy onus of showing at what point of time the secret trustee decided to resile from his promise, but would also make the validity of the secret trust dependent upon what is in fact an irrelevant consideration'.

On the other hand, Paul Matthews, in 'The true basis of the half secret trust' [1979] Conv 360, subscribes to the view that 'the probate doctrine of incorporation by reference' represents the true basis of half secret trusts. Although there are a variety of objections to such a theory, this doctrine may explain the discrepancy concerning the admissibility of evidence as to the time of the communication of the terms of the trust, see *Blackwell v Blackwell* [1929] AC 318; *Re Keen* [1937] Ch 236.

MUTUAL WILLS

Where two testators desire to make provision for the survivor and other ascertainable beneficiaries and conclude an *inter vivos* agreement to this effect, they may make separate wills (or joint wills) in substantially identical form in each other's favour, perhaps by giving the survivor a life interest in the deceased's estate with remainder to the ultimate beneficiary. Such arrangement attracts the mutual wills doctrine.

The motive of the testators may be to pool their resources together for the benefit of the ultimate beneficiary and to give the survivor a life interest in the property of the first testator to die.

For example, A and B decide that after their death their joint property will be transferred to Cancer Research. They may each make separate wills transferring their property to the named charity. This does not involve mutual wills. Assume, further, that the parties agree that the survivor ought to enjoy a life interest in the deceased's estate and then transfer their joint resources to the specified charity. Each testator makes a will in substantially identical terms transferring his estate to the survivor on the understanding that the *inter vivos* agreement is binding. Each testator's will may spell out the terms of the trust, that is, to the survivor for life with remainder to Cancer Research. Alternatively, each testator may transfer his entire estate to the survivor. When the first testator dies (say A) his will will be probated, a trust will be created and B will enjoy a life interest in accordance with the agreement. When B dies his entire estate (including the property taken under A's will) will be held upon trust for Cancer Research in accordance with the *inter vivos* agreement.

The above represents the intentions of the parties. Whether the intentions will be fulfilled depends on a mixture of rules of contract law, probate law and trust law.

Importance of the agreement

The agreement between the parties acts as the backbone of the trust. Every will is revocable by a testator before his death. If, therefore, the surviving testator revokes his will after the death of the other testator the intended beneficiaries may not have a remedy against the surviving testator, unless they can prove an agreement not to revoke his will.

There must be clear evidence of an agreement, proved on a balance of probabilities, to create irrevocable interests for the beneficiaries. The best evidence of an agreement to create mutual wills would be separate wills (or a joint will) which recites the terms of the agreement made by the parties. But, there is no obligation to include the terms of the agreement in the will. Wherever the terms of the agreement are found, the requirement is whether the agreement creates irrevocable interests.

The fact that the parties have made substantially identical wills on the same date is not by itself proof of an irrevocable agreement although it is a relevant factor to be taken into account along with the other evidence available.

Re Oldham [1925] Ch 75, HC

On 4 January 1907, a husband and wife made substantially identical wills. Each spouse left his or her property to the other absolutely with identical alternatives in the event of the other predeceasing the former. There was no evidence of an agreement that the wills were irrevocable. The husband died in 1914 and the widow received his property under his will. The widow remarried and made a new will which was different from her 1907 will. She died in 1922. The plaintiff, who claimed to be entitled to an interest under the alleged mutual will trust, asserted that the wife's executors held her property on trust for him.

The court held that the dispositions under the wife's second will must be upheld. The court will not presume the existence of a trust on the basis of the simultaneous execution of virtually identical wills.

> **Astbury J:** ... the fact that two wills were made in identical terms does not necessarily connote any agreement beyond that of so making them. There is no evidence that there was an agreement that the trust should in all circumstances be irrevocable. In order to enforce the trust I must be satisfied that its terms are certain and unequivocal and such as in the circumstances I am bound to give effect. What is the evidence of that? Of course it is a strong thing that these two parties came together, agreed to make their wills in identical terms and in fact so made them, but that is not sufficient evidence of an irrevocable interest.

See, also, *Re Goodchild* (below), where the Court of Appeal decided that the execution of identical wills by a married couple did not import the inference that the wills were intended to be mutually binding.

Re Goodchild (Decd), Goodchild and Another v Goodchild [1997] 3 All ER 63, CA

On 11 February 1988, the testator (Dennis) and his first wife (Joan) executed wills in identical form in favour of the survivor of both of them and then to their adult son, Gary. On 14 April 1991, Joan died and Dennis received all of her estate. Dennis married the defendant, Enid, on 16 November 1992 and made a new will leaving his estate to Enid. On 1 January 1993, the testator died. Gary and his wife commenced proceedings against Enid claiming a declaration that Enid held Dennis' estate on trust for Gary and his wife in compliance with the wills executed in February 1988 or, alternatively, an order for reasonable financial provision payable out of Dennis' estate under s 2 of the Inheritance (Provision for Family and Dependants) Act 1975. The judge held that despite the identical nature of the wills of February 1988, there was no clear evidence of an agreement between Dennis and Enid not to revoke the wills. However, Joan's mistaken belief that the terms of the wills were binding imposed a moral obligation on Dennis, which was a special circumstance, exceptional enough to justify the claim under the 1975 Act. The defendant appealed.

The Court of Appeal dismissed the appeal and decided unanimously that an essential ingredient of the doctrine of mutual wills is the existence of a contract between the two testators that both wills are irrevocable and will remain unaltered. There was no evidence of an express agreement between Dennis and Joan and none could be implied on the facts, notwithstanding that the wills were not mutually binding. Joan's understanding of the effect of her will was such as to impose on Dennis a moral obligation to devote to Gary so much of Joan's estate as would have come to him if the mutual wills mechanism was effective.

> **Leggatt LJ:** I am satisfied that for the doctrine to apply there must be a contract at law: see per Morritt J in *In re Dale* [1994] Ch 31, p 38. In reaching this conclusion Morritt J was guided, even if not in strictness bound, by the high authority of Lord Camden LC in *Dufour v Pereira* (1769) 1 Dick 419 (as more fully set out in Hargrave, *Juridical Arguments and Collections,* 1799, Vol 2); Lord Loughborough LC in *Lord Walpole v Lord Orford* (1797) 3 Ves 402; the High Court of Australia in *Birmingham v Renfrew* (1937) 57 CLR 666; and the Privy Council in *Gray v Perpetual Trustee Co Ltd* [1928] AC 391. Delivering the opinion of the Board in the latter case, Viscount Haldane said, at p 400:
>
>> The case before [their Lordships] is one in which the evidence of an agreement, apart from that of making the wills in question, is so lacking that they are unable to come to the conclusion that an agreement to constitute equitable interests has been shown to have been made. As they have already said, the mere fact of making wills mutually is not, at least by the law of England, evidence of such an agreement having been come to. And without such a definite agreement there can no more be a trust in equity than a right to damages at law.
>
> These cases lead unequivocally to the judge's conclusion [1996] 1 WLR 694, p 702:
>
>> ... if a clear agreement can be found, in the wills or elsewhere, that they are to be mutually binding, whether or not that is expressed in language of revocation, the law will give effect to that intention by way of a 'floating trust,' which becomes irrevocable following the death of the first testator and crystallises on the death of the second.
>
> Two wills may be in the same form as each other. Each testator may leave his or her estate to the other with a view to the survivor leaving both estates to their heir. But there is no presumption that a present plan will be immutable in future. A key feature of the concept of mutual wills is the irrevocability of the mutual intentions. Not only must they be binding when made, but the testators must have undertaken, and so must be bound, not to change their intentions after the death of the first testator. The test must always be: suppose that during the lifetime of the surviving testator the intended beneficiary did something which the survivor regarded as unpardonable, would he or she be free not to leave the combined estate to him? The answer must be that the survivor is so entitled unless the testators agreed otherwise when they executed their wills. Hence the need for a clear agreement. Dennis and Joy executed wills in the same terms, save that each left his or her estate to the other. Thus, the survivor was to have both estates. They wanted Gary to inherit the combined estates. But there was no express agreement not to revoke the wills. Nor could any such agreement be implied from the fact that the survivor was in a position to leave both estates to Gary. The fact that each expected that the other would leave them to him is not sufficient to impress the arrangement with a floating trust, binding in equity. A mutual desire that Gary should inherit could not of itself prevent the survivor from resiling from the arrangement. What is required is a mutual intention that both wills should

> remain unaltered and that the survivor should be bound to leave the combined estates to the son. That is what is missing here. The judge found that Joan regarded the arrangement as irrevocable, but that Dennis did not. No mutual intention was proven that the survivor should be bound to leave the joint estate to Gary. That is what they meant to achieve. It could not happen unless they first left their respective estates to the survivor of them. But the fact that each was able to leave the combined estate to Gary does not, without more, mean that both were bound to do so.

The agreement between the two testators to make irrevocable wills operates as a contract between the parties. This contract may be included in a deed, or may be proved by parol evidence, or may exist in the will of each testator. During the lifetime of each testator, if either party withdraws from the agreement and revokes his or her will, the other party to the agreement is entitled to sue the guilty party for breach of contract. The damages recoverable are likely to be nominal since the loss suffered is impossible to quantify (see *Robinson v Ommanney*).[20] If notice of a breach of contract is given to the other party during the lifetime of both parties, the innocent party will be discharged from the agreement and may revoke his will (see *Stone v Hoskins*).[21] It is clear that the ultimate beneficiary under the intended trust, not being privy to the contract has no *locus standi* in the cause of action at this stage.

Section 18(1) of the Wills Act 1837 provides: '... a will shall be revoked by the testator's marriage.' It is arguable that revocation of a will by marriage *per se* will not have the effect of creating a breach of the agreement, entitling the innocent party to claim damages for breach of contract. (See, also, the effect of an annulment of a marriage under s 18(A) of the Wills Act 1937.) A revocation of the will by the subsequent marriage of the second testator to die does not affect the trust created by the mutual wills doctrine: see *Re Goodchild*.

In *Re Marsland*,[22] a husband executed a deed of separation and covenanted in the same deed not to revoke a will previously made. The husband later obtained a divorce and expressed his wishes to remarry. The wife brought an action against him claiming damages for breach of covenant. The court held that remarriage does not have the effect of revoking the contract. To be actionable a revocation of the agreement is required to be intentional.

Moreover, where two testators made mutual wills arrangements, a unilateral alteration of the will by the first testator to die has the effect of terminating the agreement. The second testator to die becomes free to dispose of his or her estate, during his or her lifetime, in whatever way he or she pleases.

20 (1883) 23 Ch D 285.

21 [1905] P 194.

22 [1939] Ch 820.

***Re Hobley (Decd)* (1997) *The Times*, 16 June, HC**

On 4 December 1975, Mr and Mrs Hobley executed mutual wills in favour of each other, whosoever may survive, with substitutionary gifts to common beneficiaries. The house at No 65 Russel Terrace was devised to Mr Blyth and there were 11 pecuniary legatees, eight of whom were entitled to the residue. Some time later, Mr Hobley executed a codicil revoking the devise of No 65 Russel Terrace to Mr Blyth and left it as part of the residuary estate. There was no evidence as to the reason for the change or whether Mrs Hobley knew of or consented to it. Mr Hobley died on 13 January 1980 and Mrs Hobley inherited his entire estate, including No 65 Russel Terrace. On 13 March 1992, Mrs Hobley executed a will which was substantially different from the 1975 will. She died on 23 May 1993. The National Westminster Bank plc was appointed executor of Mrs Hobley's will and commenced the application to the court. The question in issue concerned the effect on the mutual will arrangement of the alteration of Mr Hobley's will. Counsel for the original beneficiaries, relying on *Hong Kong Fir Shipping Co v Kawasaki Kisen Kaisha Ltd* [1962] 2 QB 26, argued that Mr Hobley's codicil did not amount to a fundamental breach of the 1975 agreement so as to discharge Mrs Hobley from the agreement.

The High Court decided that the principles on which the court acted in order to impose a constructive trust, so as to give effect to an agreement to make and not revoke mutual wills, were not precisely the same as applied in the law of contract. The court could not evaluate the significance to the parties of any alteration in the terms of the will of the first testator, nor their subjective intentions. Moreover, it is irrelevant that the alteration did not personally disadvantage the survivor. Accordingly, the unilateral alteration of Mr Hobley's will had the effect of discharging Mrs Hobley from the agreement in 1975. She was, therefore, free to dispose of her estate as she wished.

Creation of the trust

A trust is created by the courts in favour of the beneficiaries and imposed on the survivor, when the first testator dies leaving a will unrevoked complying with the terms of the agreement. If the survivor alters or executes another will as he is entitled to do in accordance with probate rules, this adjusted or new will will be admitted to probate but his personal representatives will hold his property upon trust to perform the agreement.

***Dufour v Pereira* (1769) 1 Dick 419, HL**

This case concerned a joint will made pursuant to an agreement between husband and wife whereby the residuary estate of each of them was to constitute a common fund to be held for the survivor for his or her life with remainders over. On the death of the husband, the wife, who was one of his executors, proved the will.

She took possession of her husband's property and enjoyed the benefit of his residuary estate together with her separate property for many years, but on the death of the wife it was found that her last will disregarded the provisions of the joint will and left her estate to her daughter, the defendant, Mrs Pereira. The plaintiffs were the beneficiaries under the joint will and claimed that the wife's personal estate was held in trust for them.

The court held in favour of the plaintiffs, upholding the mutual will.

> **Lord Camden LC:** Consider how far the mutual will is binding, and whether the accepting of the legacies under it by the survivor is not a confirmation of it. I am of opinion it is. It might have been revoked by both jointly; it might have been revoked separately, provided the party intending it had given notice to the other of such revocation. But I cannot be of the opinion that either of them could, during their joint lives, do it secretly; or that after the death of either, it could be done by the survivor by another will. It is a contract between the parties which cannot be rescinded but by the consent of both. The first that dies carries his part of the contract into execution. Will the court afterwards permit the other to break the contract? Certainly not.
>
> The defendant has taken the benefit of the bequest in her favour by the mutual will; and has proved it as such; she has thereby certainly confirmed it; and therefore I am of opinion, the last will of the wife, so far as it breaks in upon the mutual will, is void. And declare that [the defendant] having proved the mutual will, after her husband's death; and having possessed all his personal estate, and enjoyed the interest thereof during her life, has by those acts bound her assets to make good all her bequests in the said mutual will; and therefore let the necessary accounts be taken.

Re Hagger [1930] 2 Ch 190, HC

A husband and wife made joint wills in 1902 in which it was stated that they agreed to dispose of their property by will and there was to be no alteration or revocation except by agreement. By their will, they gave the whole of their property to the survivor for life and on the death of the survivor to divide the proceeds of sale between nine beneficiaries including Eleanor Palmer. The wife died in 1904 and the husband made another will in 1921 indicating that his property was to be divided between various persons of whom some were not mentioned in the joint will. The husband died in 1928 and Eleanor Palmer died in 1923. Her personal representatives claimed her portion of the estate under the joint will.

The court held that from the time of the wife's death the surviving husband held the property upon trust for those entitled in remainder under the joint will, subject to the husband's life interest.

> **Clauson J:** To my mind, *Dufour v Pereira*[23] decides that where there is a joint will such as this, on the death of the first testator the position as regards that

23 (1769) 1 Dick 419.

> part of the property which belongs to the survivor is that the survivor will be treated in this court as holding the property on trust to apply it so as to carry out the effect of the joint will ... it is clear that Lord Camden (in *Dufour v Pereira*) has decided that if the survivor takes a benefit conferred on him by the joint will he will be treated as a trustee in this court, and he will not be allowed to do anything inconsistent with the provisions of the joint will.
>
> I am bound to hold that from the death of the wife the husband held the property, according to the tenor of the will, subject to the trusts thereby imposed upon it, at all events if he took advantage of the provisions of the will. In my view he did take advantage of those provisions.

Re Cleaver [1981] 1 WLR 939, HC

In October 1967, the testator (H), aged 78, married the testatrix (W), then aged 74. H had three children by a previous marriage. W had no children, but she did have two nieces. H and W both simultaneously made wills in substantially identical terms. H gave each of his three children a legacy of £500, and his residuary estate to W absolutely, subject to her surviving him for one month with gifts over. The testatrix's will was in identical terms, save that in lieu of the legacies of £500 to the testator's children, she gave legacies of £500 to each of her two nieces. H died in 1975, and W duly received the whole of H's net residue. On 23 June 1977, W made her last will, and in this she gave her net residuary estate to M and her husband. No provision was made either for the plaintiffs or for W's two nieces. W died on 30 May 1978. The plaintiffs sought a declaration that W's executors held W's estate on trust to give effect to the mutual will arrangement between H and W.

Held in favour of the plaintiffs.

> **Nourse J:** I would emphasise that the agreement or understanding must be such as to impose on the donee a legally binding obligation to deal with the property in the particular way and that the other two certainties, namely, those as to the subject matter of the trust and the persons intended to benefit under it, are as essential to this species of trust as they are to any other. In spite of an argument by Mr Keenan, who appears for Mr and Mrs Noble, to the contrary, I find it hard to see how there could be any difficulty about the second or third certainties in a case of mutual wills unless it was in the terms of the wills themselves. There, as in this case, the principal difficulty is always whether there was a legally binding obligation or merely what Lord Loughborough LC in *Lord Walpole v Lord Orford* (1797) 3 Ves Jun 402, p 419, described as an honourable engagement.

The constructive trust created by the courts is imposed on the survivor irrespective of whether or not he takes an interest in accordance with the agreement made between the two testators. The reason for this rule is to prevent the survivor committing a fraud on the beneficiaries by attempting to renege on the agreement.

Re Dale (Decd), Proctor v Dale [1993] 3 WLR 652, HC

On 5 September 1988, the father and mother of the plaintiff (daughter) and defendant (son) each made an identical will. Each will contained a clause revoking all former wills and transferring all real and personal property in favour of the plaintiff and defendant in equal shares. The father died on 9 November 1988 without altering his will. Probate of his will was granted to the plaintiff and defendant on 24 August 1990. On 14 July 1990 the mother made a new will revoking her former will and after appointing the defendant to be her executor, modified the terms of her previous will. She bequeathed the sum of £300 to the plaintiff and gave the residue of her estate to her son. The mother died on 30 November 1990 and probate of her will was obtained on 13 June 1992. The value of her net estate was £19,000.

The plaintiff claimed that on her father's death, her mother became bound in equity to give effect to the agreement and dispose of her estate in accordance with the agreement. Thus, the defendant, as executor of his mother's estate, became bound in equity to distribute the estate to the plaintiff and defendant equally. The defendant argued that under the doctrine of mutual wills it was essential that the will of each testator should transfer to the other a direct, personal and financial benefit either absolutely or for life as the consideration for the agreement by each person not to revoke the will. Since this requirement was lacking, the defendant submitted that no trust was created on his father's death and his mother was free to modify her will as she pleased.

The court held in favour of the plaintiff on the ground that the underlying theory of the mutual wills doctrine is the prevention of fraud. It would have been a fraud on the first testator to die (Mr Dale) and the beneficiaries entitled under the agreement (the children equally) to allow the survivor to change the terms of the agreement following the death of the first testator. The fraud remains the same whether the agreement benefits the surviving testatrix or persons other than the surviving testatrix. Accordingly, it is not essential that the surviving testatrix receive a benefit.

> **Morritt J:** There is no doubt that for the doctrine to apply there must be a contract at law. It is apparent from all the cases to which I shall refer later, but in particular from *Gray v Perpetual Trustee Co Ltd*,[24] that it is necessary to establish an agreement to make and not revoke mutual wills, some understanding or arrangement being insufficient – 'without such a definite agreement there can no more be a trust in equity than a right to damages at law' (see *per* Viscount Haldane, at p 400) ... it was submitted, the promise to make and not revoke a mutual will could not constitute a detriment to the first testator because he would be leaving his property in the way that he wished and because he would be able, on giving notice to the second testator, to revoke his will and make another if he changed his mind. Accordingly, it was

24 [1928] AC 391.

argued, consideration for the contract had to take the form of a benefit to the second testator.

I do not accept this submission. It is to be assumed that the first testator and the second testator had agreed to make and not to revoke the mutual wills in question. The performance of that promise by the execution of the will by the first testator is in my judgment sufficient consideration by itself.

[After reviewing the leading authorities the learned judge concluded:]

All the cases show the doctrine applies when the second testator benefits under the will of the first testator. But I am unable to see why it should be any the less a fraud on the first testator if the agreement was that each testator should leave his or her property to particular beneficiaries, for example, their children, rather than to each other. It should be assumed that they had good reason for doing so and in any event that is what the parties bargained for. In each case there is the binding contract. In each case it has been performed by the first testator on the faith of the promise of the second testator and in each case the second testator would have deceived the first testator to the detriment of the first testator if he, the second testator, were permitted to go back on his agreement.

I see no reason why the doctrine should be confined to cases where the second testator benefits when the aim of the principle is to prevent the first testator from being defrauded. A fraud on the first testator will include cases where the second testator benefits, but I see no reason why the principle should be confined to such cases. In my judgment so to hold is consistent with all the authorities, supported by some of them, and is in furtherance of equity's original jurisdiction to intervene in cases of fraud.

Extent of the agreement

It is a question of construction to determine the scope and extent of the property subject to the agreement and thus the trust. If the agreement is expressed to bind the whole of the interest owned by each party, the trust will bind the entire property owned by each party and the surviving testator may be unable to deal with his own property during his lifetime. Each case is determined on its own facts.

Re Green [1951] Ch 148, HC

On 31 August 1940, a husband (H) and wife (W) executed separate mutual wills in identical form. They recited, in effect, that if H's first wife should not survive him, the house in its entirety would be transferred to a specified hospital and the remainder of his estate be divided into two equal parts – one moiety being his personal estate and the other moiety to be disposed of in accordance with the agreement. W died in April 1942 and, under the terms of her will, her residuary estate passed to H absolutely. In April 1945, H remarried and, in December 1946, made a new will whereby after giving certain pecuniary legacies he gave the entire residuary estate to his second wife. H died in 1946. On the question of the validity of the trust, the court held that H's second will operated to transfer only one half of his property, because the other half of his estate was subject to the trusts for named persons on his death. The house was also subject to the trust.

> **Vaisey J:** I think that the testator's moiety was his own personal property to do as he liked with, and, if he chose after his second marriage to make other provisions as regards that moiety, he was at liberty to do so. It is not a very easy point, and it may be that I am not taking the right view when I hold that, as regards his own moiety, the testator was free to do what he liked. Nothing could prevent him revoking the will, which he had done by the act of his second marriage. The only question is over what property any subsequent will operates.
>
> In my view, it can only operate as regards one moiety which was under the testator's control at his death, and, with regard to the other moiety, ie, the moiety which was notionally the property of his first wife, the pre-existing will must take effect, not as a will, but as evidence of a trust which is plainly to be discerned in the two wills, viz, the first will of the testator – which, of course, never became a will in the sense that it was a proved will – and the will of the first wife which was proved and under which the husband took an absolute interest in the residue.
>
> In my judgment, one moiety of the estate must be held on the trusts declared by the first will. The other moiety passes under the provisions contained in the second will subject to this, that, before the moieties are ascertained, the first will is also operative so far as regards the property, 141 Billy Lows Lane, the entirety of which is to pass with the furniture therein to the successors in title, whoever they may be under the National Health Service Act 1946, of the Potters Bar Hospital absolutely.

SUMMARY

Birmingham v Renfrew (1937) 57 CLR 666, HC

> **Dixon J:** It has long been established that a contract between persons to make corresponding wills gives rise to equitable obligations when one acts on the faith of such an agreement and dies leaving his will unrevoked so that the other takes property under its dispositions. It operates to impose upon the survivor an obligation regarded as specifically enforceable. It is true that he cannot be compelled to make and leave unrevoked a testamentary document and if he dies leaving a last will containing provisions inconsistent with his agreement it is nevertheless valid as a testamentary act. But the doctrines of equity attach the obligation to the property. The effect is, I think, that the survivor becomes a constructive trustee and the terms of the trust are those of the will which he undertook would be his last will.
>
> There is a third element which appears to me to be inherent in the nature of such a contract or agreement, although I do not think it has been expressly

considered. The purpose of an arrangement for corresponding wills must often be, as in this case, to enable the survivor during his life to deal as absolute owner with the property passing under the will of the party first dying. That is to say, the object of the transaction is to put the survivor in a position to enjoy for his own benefit the full ownership so that, for instance, he may convert it and expend the proceeds if he chooses. But when he dies he is to bequeath what is left in the manner agreed upon. It is only by the special doctrines of equity that such a floating obligation, suspended, so to speak, during the lifetime of the survivor can descend upon the assets at his death and crystallise into a trust. No doubt gifts and settlements, *inter vivos*, if calculated to defeat the intention of the compact, could not be made by the survivor and his right of disposition, *inter vivos*, is, therefore, not unqualified. But, substantially, the purpose of the arrangement will often be to allow full enjoyment for the survivor's own benefit and advantage upon condition that at his death the residue shall pass as arranged.

SUPPLEMENTARY READING

Andrews, J, 'Creating secret trusts' (1963) 27 Conv 92

Brierly, A, 'Mutual wills – Blackpool illuminations' (1995) 58 MLR 95

Gratton, S, 'Mutual wills and remarriage' [1997] Conv 153

Mitchell, J, 'Some aspects of mutual wills' (1951) 14 MLR 136

Perrins, B, 'Can you keep half a secret?' (1972) 88 LQR 225

Richardson, N, 'Floating trusts and mutual wills' (1996) 10 Tru LI 88

Rickett, C, 'Mutual wills and the law of restitution' (1989) 105 LQR 534

Rickett, C, 'Mutual wills – the New Zealand approach: *Re Newey*' [1996] Conv 136

Stevens, J, 'Avoiding disinheritance' (1996) 146 NLJ 961

Sunnocks, F, 'Close relations of the secret trust' (1988) 138 NLJ 35

Wilde, D, 'Secret and semi-secret trusts: justifying distinctions between the two' [1995] Conv 366

CHAPTER 13

PRIVATE PURPOSE TRUSTS

A purpose trust is designed to promote a purpose as an end in itself, for example, to discover an alphabet of 40 letters, to provide a cup for a yacht race or to provide for the boarding up of certain rooms in a house. The effect is that such intended trusts are void, for the court cannot give effect to a trust which it cannot supervise. There is no beneficiary with a *locus standi* capable of enforcing such trust. In consequence, a resulting trust will be set up in favour of the donor or settlor on the failure of a non-charitable purpose trust. In *Re Astor's Settlement Trust*,[1] Lord Astor purported to create a trust for 'the maintenance of good understanding between nations and the preservation of the independence and integrity of newspapers'. The court held that the trust was void for uncertainty on the grounds that: (1) the means by which the trustees were to attain the stated aims were unspecified; and (2) the absence of a person who was entitled, as of right, to enforce the trust. In other words, a trust creates rights in favour of beneficiaries and imposes correlative duties on the trustees. If there are no persons with the power to enforce such rights, then equally there can be no duties imposed on trustees.

This rule is subject to a number of exceptions to be considered later.

In Re Astor's Settlement Trusts, Astor v Scholfield and Others [1952] Ch D 534, HC

> **Roxburgh J:** The typical case of a trust is one in which the legal owner of property is constrained by a court of equity so to deal with it as to give effect to the equitable rights of another. These equitable rights have been hammered out in the process of litigation in which a claimant on equitable grounds has successfully asserted rights against a legal owner or other person in control of property. *Prima facie*, therefore, a trustee would not be expected to be subject to an equitable obligation unless there was somebody who could enforce a correlative equitable right, and the nature and extent of that obligation would be worked out in proceedings for enforcement. At an early stage, however, the courts were confronted with attempts to create trusts for charitable purposes which there was no equitable owner to enforce. Lord Eldon explained, in *AG v Brown*,[2] how this difficulty was dealt with:
>
>> It is the duty of a court of equity, a main part, originally almost the whole, of its jurisdiction, to administer trusts; to protect not the visible owner, who alone can proceed at law, but the individual equitably, though not legally, entitled. From this principle has arisen the practice of administering the trust of a public charity: persons possessed of funds

1 [1952] Ch 534.

2 (1818) 1 Swan 265.

> appropriated to such purposes are within the general rule: but no one being entitled by an immediate and peculiar interest to prefer a complaint, who is to compel the performance of their obligations, and to enforce their responsibility? It is the duty of the King, as *parens patriae*, to protect property devoted to charitable uses; and that duty is executed by the officer who represents the Crown for all forensic purposes. On this foundation rests the right of the Attorney General in such cases to obtain by information the interposition of a court of equity ...

But if the purposes are not charitable, great difficulties arise both in theory and in practice. In theory because, having regard to the historical origins of equity, it is difficult to visualise the growth of equitable obligations which nobody can enforce, and in practice because it is not possible to contemplate with equanimity the creation of large funds devoted to non-charitable purposes which no court and no department of State can control, or, in the case of maladministration, reform. Moreover ... no officer has ever been constituted to take, in the case of non-charitable purposes, the position held by the Attorney General in connection with charitable purposes, and no case has been found in the reports in which the court has ever directly enforced a non-charitable purpose against a trustee. Indeed where, as in the present case, the only beneficiaries are purposes and at present unascertainable persons, it is difficult to see who could initiate such proceedings. If the purposes are valid trusts, the settlors have retained no beneficial interest and could not initiate them. It was suggested that the trustees might proceed *ex parte* to enforce the trusts against themselves. I doubt that, but at any rate nobody could enforce the trusts against them. This point, in my judgment, is of importance, because in most of the cases which are put forward to [enforce the private purpose trust] the court had indirect means of enforcing the execution of the non-charitable purpose.

These cases I must now consider. First of all, there is a group relating to horses, dogs, graves and monuments, among which I was referred to *Pettingall v Pettingall*;[3] *Mitford v Reynolds*;[4] *In re Dean*;[5] *Pirbright v Salwey*;[6] and *In re Hooper*.[7]

In *Pettingall v Pettingall* a testator made the following bequest by his will:

> Having a favourite black mare, I hereby bequeath, that at my death, £50 per annum be paid for her keep in some park in England or Wales; her shoes to be taken off, and she never to be ridden or put in harness; and that my executor consider himself in honour bound to fulfil my wish, and see that she will be well provided for, and removable at his will. At her death all payment to cease.

It being admitted that a bequest in favour of an animal was valid, two questions were made: first, as to the form of the decree on this point; and secondly, as to the disposition of the surplus not required for the mare. Knight-Bruce VC said:

---

3 (1842) 11 LJ Ch 176.

4 (1848) 16 Sim 105.

5 (1889) 41 Ch D 552.

6 [1896] WN 86.

7 [1932] 1 Ch 38.

> ... that so much of the £50 as would be required to keep the mare comfortably, should be applied by the executor, and that he was entitled to the surplus. He must give full information, whenever required, respecting the mare; and if the mare were not properly attended to, any of the parties interested in the residue might apply to the court. The decree on this point ought to be, that £50 a year should be paid to the executor during the life of the mare, or until further order; he undertaking to maintain her comfortably; with liberty for all parties to apply.

The points which I wish to make are: (1) that it was there admitted that a bequest in favour of an animal was valid; and (2) that there were persons interested in residue who, having regard to the decree made, would have had no difficulty in getting the terms of the 'bequest' enforced.

Mitford v Reynolds related to a sepulchral monument and to horses, and there again there was a remainderman on behalf of charity to see to the enforcement of the directions, and an administration action was on foot.

In *In re Dean* a testator devised his freehold estates, subject to and charged with an annuity of £750, and to a term of 50 years granted to his trustees, to the use of the plaintiff for life, with remainders over; and he gave to his trustees his horses, ponies and hounds; and he charged his said freehold estates with the payment to his trustees, for the term of 50 years, if any of the said horses and hounds should so long live, of an annual sum of £750. And he declared that his trustees should apply the said annual sum in the maintenance of the horses and hounds for the time being living, and in maintaining the stables, kennels and buildings inhabited by the said animals in such condition of repair as his trustees might deem fit; and in consideration of the maintenance of his horses, ponies, and hounds being a charge upon his said estate as aforesaid, he gave all his personal estate not otherwise disposed of the plaintiff absolutely. North J said:

> Then it is said, that there is no *cestui que* trust who can enforce the trust, and that the court will not recognise a trust unless it is capable of being enforced by someone. I do not assent to that view. There is not the least doubt that a man, if he pleases, gives a legacy to trustees, upon trust to apply it in erecting a monument to himself, either in a church or in a churchyard, or even in unconsecrated ground, and I am not aware that such a trust is in any way invalid, although it is difficult to say who would be the *cestui que* trust of the monument. In the same way, I know of nothing to prevent a gift of a sum of money to trustees, upon trust to apply it for the repair of such a monument. In my opinion such a trust would be good, although the testator must be careful to limit the time for which it is to last, because, as it is not a charitable trust, unless it is to come to an end within the limits fixed by the rule against perpetuities, it would be illegal. But a trust to lay out a certain sum in building a monument, and the gift of another sum in trust to apply the same to keeping that monument in repair, say, for 10 years, is, in my opinion, a perfectly good trust, although I do not see who could ask the court to enforce it. If persons beneficially interested in the estate could do so, then the present plaintiff can do so; but, if such persons could not enforce the trust, still it cannot be said that the trust must fail because there is no one who can actively enforce it.

This is the best case in the series from Mr Gray's point of view, because North J did undoubtedly uphold the particular directions, whether or not they could be 'actively enforced'. But putting it at its highest, he merely held that there were certain classes of trusts, of which this was one, in which that objection was not fatal. He did not suggest that it was not generally fatal outside the realms of charity.

In *Pirbright v Salwey* a testator, after expressing his wish to be buried in the enclosure in which his child lay in a certain churchyard, bequeathed to the rector and churchwardens of the parish church £800 Consols, the interest and dividends to be derived therefrom to be applied, so long as the law for the time being permitted, in keeping up the enclosure and decorating the same with flowers. It was held that the gift was valid for at least a period of 21 years from the testator's death, and *semble* that it was not charitable.

In *In re Hooper* a testator bequeathed to his executors and trustees money out of the income of which to provide, so far as they legally could do so, for the care and upkeep of certain graves, a vault and certain monuments. Maugham J said: 'This point is one to my mind of doubt, and I should have felt some difficulty in deciding it if it were not for *Pirbright v Salwey*. That was a decision arrived at by Stirling J, after argument by very eminent counsel. The case does not appear to have attracted much attention in textbooks, but it does not appear to have been commented upon adversely, and I shall follow it.' In this case, and probably also in *Pirbright v Salwey* there was a residuary legatee to bring before the court any failure to comply with the direction. But I think that Maugham J regarded them both as exceptions from general principle.

Last in this group is *In re Thompson*.[8] I have included it in this group because, although it relates to the furtherance of foxhunting and thus moves away from the subject matter of the group and much nearer to the present case, it is expressly founded on *Pettingall v Pettingall*, and it is indeed a most instructive case. The testator bequeathed a legacy of £1,000 to a friend to be applied by him in such manner as he should think fit towards the promotion and furthering of foxhunting, and devised and bequeathed his residuary estate to Trinity Hall in the University of Cambridge. An originating summons was taken out by the executors to determine whether the legacy was valid or failed for want of a definite object or for uncertainty or on other grounds. When counsel, during the course of the argument, observed: 'True, there is no *cestui que* trust who can enforce the application of the legacy, but that is immaterial: *In re Dean*. The object to which the legacy is to be applied is sufficiently defined to be enforced.' Clauson J interposed: 'The college, as residuary legatees, seem to have an interest in the legacy, as, but for the trust for its application, they would be entitled to it.' The procedure adopted by Knight-Bruce VC in *Pettingall v Pettingall*, cited in *Jarman on Wills*,[9] might be followed in this case. And in his judgment he said:

8 [1934] Ch 342.

9 7th edn, London: Sweet & Maxwell, Vol 2, p 877.

> In my judgment the object of the gift has been defined with sufficient clearness and is of a nature to which effect can be given. The proper way for me to deal with the matter will be, not to make, as it is asked by the summons, a general declaration, but following the example of Knight-Bruce VC in *Pettingall v Pettingall*, to order that, upon the defendant Mr Lloyd [the friend] giving an undertaking (which I understand he is willing to give) to apply the legacy when received by him towards the object expressed in the testator's will, the plaintiffs do pay to the defendant Mr Lloyd the legacy of £1,000; and that, in case the legacy should be applied by him otherwise than towards the promotion and furthering of foxhunting, the residuary legatees are to be at liberty to apply.

I understand Clauson J to have held in effect that there was somebody who could enforce the purpose indicated because the college, as residuary legatees, would be entitled to the legacy but for the trust for its application and they could apply to the court to prevent any misapplication or breach of the undertaking given by Mr Lloyd. I infer from what he said that he would not have upheld the validity of this non-charitable purpose if there had been no residuary legatee, and no possibility of making such an order as was made in *Pettingall v Pettingall*.

Lastly, I was referred to *In re Price*[10] where a testatrix by her will gave one half of her residuary estate to the Anthroposophical Society in Great Britain, 'to be used at the discretion of the chairman and executive council of the society for carrying on the teachings of the founder, Dr Rudolf Steiner'. At first sight this case would appear to be a strong card in Mr Gray's hand. The first part of the judgment proceeds upon the footing that the purposes were not charitable. The society was the residuary legatee and there was no room for such an order as was made in *In re Thompson*. There was nobody who could have enforced the carrying out of the purposes. On closer inspection, however, it will be found that this point was not raised in argument or referred to in the judgment, and the decision was based upon *In re Drummond*, which is a different class of case. As the present case cannot, on any view, be assimilated to *In re Drummond*,[11] I need not further consider *In re Price*.

Let me then sum up the position so far. On the one side there are Lord Parker's two propositions with which I began. These were not new, but merely re-echoed what Sir William Grant had said as Master of the Rolls in *Morice v The Bishop of Durham* as long ago as 1804: 'There must be somebody, in whose favour the court can decree performance.' The position was recently restated by Harman J in *In re Wood*: 'A gift on trust must have a *cestui que* trust,' and this seems to be in accord with principle. On the other side is a group of cases relating to horses and dogs, graves and monuments – matters arising under wills and intimately connected with the deceased – in which the courts have found means of escape from these general propositions and also *In re Thompson* and *In re Price* which I have endeavoured to explain. *In re Price* belongs to another field. The rest may, I think, properly be regarded as anamolous and

10 [1943] Ch 422.

11 [1914] 2 Ch 90.

exceptional and in no way destructive of the proposition which traces descent from or through Sir William Grant through Lord Parker to Harman J. Perhaps the late Sir Arthur Underhill was right in suggesting that they may be concessions to human weakness or sentiment.[12] They cannot, in my judgment, of themselves (and no other justification has been suggested to me) justify the conclusion that a court of equity will recognise as an equitable obligation affecting the income of large funds in the hands of trustees a direction to apply it in furtherance of enumerated non-charitable purposes in a manner which no court or department can control or enforce. I hold that the trusts here in question are void on the first of the grounds submitted by Mr Jennings and Mr Buckley.

REASONS FOR FAILURE

There are a number of common reasons why private purpose trusts fail. The list is not exhaustive but pitfalls which a settlor should avoid are: (a) the lack of a beneficiary principle; (b) uncertainty of objects; and (c) the infringement of the perpetuity rule.

Lack of beneficiaries

A trust is mandatory in nature. The courts have always jealously guarded the rights and interests of the beneficiaries under trusts. But, such rights may only be protected if the beneficiary has a *locus standi* to enforce the same. Purposes could not initiate proceedings against the trustees.

Morice v Bishop of Durham (1805) 10 Ves 522, CA

Grant MR: There must be somebody in whose favour the court can decree performance.

On the other hand, with charitable purpose trusts (see below, p 579), the Attorney General is charged with the duty of enforcing public trusts. No public official is required to enforce private trusts.

Uncertainty

As a corollary to the above mentioned rule, it is obvious that the rights of the beneficiaries would be illusory unless the court is capable of ascertaining to whom those rights belong. Thus, as a second ground for the decision in *Re Astor*, the trust failed for uncertainty.

12 See Underhill, A (Sir), *Law of Trusts*, 8th edn, London: Sweet & Maxwell, p 79.

In Re Astor's Settlement Trusts, Astor v Scholfield and Others [1952] Ch D 534, HC

Roxburgh J: The second ground upon which the relevant trusts are challenged is uncertainty. If (contrary to my view) an enumeration of purposes outside the realm of charities can take the place of an enumeration of beneficiaries, the purposes must, in my judgment, be stated in phrases which embody definite concepts and the means by which the trustees are to try to attain them must also be prescribed with a sufficient degree of certainty. The test to be applied is stated by Lord Eldon in *Morice v Bishop of Durham* as follows:

> As it is a maxim, that the execution of a trust shall be under the control of the court, it must be of such a nature, that it can be under that control; so that the administration of it can be reviewed by the court; or, if the trustee dies, the court itself can execute the trust: a trust therefore, which, in case of maladministration could be reformed; and a due administration directed; and then, unless the subject and the objects can be ascertained, upon principles, familiar in other cases, it must be decided, that the court can neither reform mal-administration, nor direct a due administration.

See also *In re Macduff*.[13]

Mr Gray argued that this test was not properly applicable to trusts declared by deed, but I can see no distinction between a will and a deed in this respect.

Applying this test, I find many uncertain phrases in the enumeration of purposes, for example, 'different sections of people in any nation or community' in paragraph 1 of the third schedule, 'constructive policies' in paragraph 2, 'integrity of the press' in paragraph 3, 'combines' in paragraph 5, 'the restoration ... of the independence of ... writers in newspapers' in paragraph 6, and 'benevolent schemes' in paragraph 7. Mr Gray suggested that in view of the unlimited discretion bestowed upon the trustees (subject only to directions from the settlors) the trustees would be justified in excluding from their purview purposes indicated by the settlors but insufficiently defined by them. But I cannot accept this argument. The purposes must be so defined that if the trustees surrendered their discretion, the court could carry out the purposes declared, not a selection of them arrived at by eliminating those that are too uncertain to be carried out. If, for example, I were to eliminate all the purposes except those declared in paragraph 4, but to decree that those declared in paragraph 4 ought to be performed, should I be executing the trusts of this settlement?

But how in any case could I decree in what manner the trusts applicable to income were to be performed? The settlement gives no guidance at all. Mr Hunt suggested that the trustees might apply to the court *ex parte* for a scheme. It is not, I think, a mere coincidence that no case has been found outside the realm of charity in which the court has yet devised a scheme of ways and means for attaining enumerated trust purposes. If it were to assume this (as I think) novel jurisdiction over public but not charitable trusts it would, I believe, necessarily require the assistance of a custodian of the public interest analogous to the Attorney General in charity cases, who would not only help

13 [1896] 2 Ch 451.

to formulate schemes but could be charged with the duty of enforcing them and preventing maladministration. There is no such person. Accordingly, in my judgment, the trust for the application of income during 'the specified period' are also void for uncertainty.

A case which illustrates this principle is *Re Endacott.*[14] A testator transferred his residuary estate to the Devon Parish Council 'for the purpose of providing some useful memorial to myself'. The court held that no out-and-out gift to the council was created but the testator intended to impose an obligation in the nature of a trust on the council which failed for uncertainty of objects.

In re Endacott (Decd), Corpe v Endacott [1960] Ch 232, CA (Lord Evershed MR, Sellers and Harman LJJ)

Lord Evershed MR: I therefore, so far as this case is concerned, conclude (having already stated my view of the meaning of the words) that, though this trust is specific, in the sense that it indicates a purpose capable of expression, yet it is of far too wide and uncertain a nature to qualify within the class of cases cited. It would go far beyond any fair analogy to any of those decisions. I do not wish to take time by much example, particularly because I am not unmindful of having already said that I do not wish to add to the future burden of citation; but merely by way of example, take trusts for the maintenance of memorials, I refer to *In re Hooper*. That was a case where the purpose of the bequest was to provide for the care and upkeep of certain graves, a vault and monuments. Maugham J said:

> This point is one, to my mind, of doubt, and I should have felt some difficulty in deciding it if it were not for *Pirbright v Salwey* (1896) ... That was a decision arrived at by Stirling J after argument by very eminent counsel. The case does not appear to have attracted much attention in textbooks, but it does not appear to have been commented upon adversely, and I shall follow it.

It may be said that other cases in regard to monuments, which were closely on the facts in line, might similarly follow the decision of Stirling J but this case as I construe the purposes of the gift is very different from *In re Hooper*.

In re Drummond[15] is the only other case under this head to which I need refer. That was a case, as will be recalled, where Eve J held valid a gift by will and codicil for the Old Bradfordians Club. He said in a short judgment, that:

> ... there was in his opinion a trust but there was abundant authority for holding that it was not such a trust as would render the legacy void as tending to a perpetuity ... The legacy was not subject to any trust which would prevent the committee of the club from spending it in any manner they might decide for the benefit of the class intended.

In re Drummond was referred to at some little length by Lord Simonds in giving the judgment of the Privy Council in the *Leahy* case;[16] and if I do not misread

14 [1960] Ch 232.

15 [1914] 2 Ch 90.

16 [1959] AC 457.

Lord Simond's judgment he thought that Eve J in treating the *Old Bradfordians Club* case as he did, had somewhat overlooked the ground of the earlier decision to which alone he referred in his judgment in *In re Clarke.*[17] Lord Simonds said:

> He [Eve J] cited only *In re Clarke*, though other cases had been referred to in argument, and he ignored that Byrne J had been able to reach his conclusion in that case just because he regarded the gift as a gift to the individual members of the corps who could together dispose of its assets as they thought fit.

I do not propose to say more about *In re Drummond* save this, that it seems on its facts to be a very widely different case from the present, and I am certainly not prepared to say that *In re Drummond* is an authority which we should use as justifying an acceptance of the validity of this trust, making it (so to speak) a further addition to the anomalous number of cases classified in Morris and Professor Barton Leach's book.

I should, perhaps, not pass from this point without a mention of a recent case (not I think reported but referred to in argument) of *In re Catherall (Decd)* (1958) unreported, decided by Roxburgh J. It was a case in which the testator had made the following disposition, according to the citation in the affidavit of which we have a copy: (1) unto the Vicar and wardens of St John's Church, Great Harwood, £2,500 for a peal of bells and a clock for the tower in memory of my dear parents and devoted sister; (2) unto the Vicar and wardens of Great Harwood Parish Church £1,000 for a suitable memorial, at their discretion, in memory of my dear parents and devoted sister; (3) unto the Vicar and wardens of Great Harwood Parish Church £500 for the upkeep and attention to the family grave. The question arose as to the second of those gifts, namely £1,000 for a suitable memorial. According to the note with which Mr Buckley has provided us, Roxburgh J thought that was valid. He said, according to the note: 'It was argued whether this is a charitable disposition. I have reached no concluded opinion on that.' Then he says: 'Distinctions are very fine,' an observation which may fairly find its place in every judgment on this type of issue:

> I could construe the words as meaning such purpose (of a religious character) as they may think fit, being suitable as a memorial; that is, charitable; or I could construe the words as meaning any purpose suitable as a memorial; that is, non-charitable. But there is another ground on which this trust can be upheld. It is not perpetuitous. I went into these cases in *In re Astor*. Such a trust as this is valid whether charitable or not. Purpose must embody a definite concept, and means to attain it must be described with sufficient certainty. In this case I should have no difficulty in deciding what would be a suitable memorial.

Of course, we do not know much of the facts of that case, but the memorial was to be a 'suitable' memorial in memory of the testator's parents and devoted sister, of whom we know nothing at all. I am not therefore saying that this decision was in any way decided on wrong grounds; but it does seem to

17 [1901] 2 Ch 110.

me, in its context, that in any event the decision could be justified on the ground that in its context the purposes were limited to religious (that is, charitable) purposes.

That brings me then back to the question of construction in relation to the point raised by Mr Buckley, and I have already largely anticipated my answer to it. It is true as Mr Buckley pointed out, that there are several instances in the books of trusts expressed to be for the benefit of the inhabitants of a place or parish which have been held to be valid charitable trusts. They are discussed in a recent case of *Williams' Trustees v IRC*[18] by Lord Simonds; and as regards these cases also, as Lord Simonds observed, there is some ground for saying that they are anomalous. Whether some owe an origin to the strict language of Lord MacNaghten's famous fourth category of charities or not, it is no doubt true to say that that particular formula, 'for the benefit of the inhabitants of A', has been taken on several occasions to be one which inherently has the quality that it is within the intendment of the Statute of Elizabeth, that the benefit indicated is the sort of benefit which would make it a charitable disposition. But the formula is not the same as that here used. It may well be as Mr Buckley observed, that purposes which are useful to the community will also benefit the community; but that, I think, is not the point. The formula is different. What the testator meant was that this council should provide a memorial to himself having the quality that it should be useful, which I take to mean useful rather than (though not necessarily exclusive of) being ornamental. I cannot myself see that the utility is confined to the inhabitants of North Tawton. In the course of the argument a car park was suggested. Whether that is a good illustration, it is not for me to say; but if it were a suitable memorial in other respects, its utility certainly would not be confined to the inhabitants of North Tawton. It would be wrong to treat this formula as being merely synonymous with 'for the benefit of the inhabitants of North Tawton' and so construing it (but, I think, illogically) to give to this formula the inherent quality which would make it a charitable gift. It would be contrary to the tenor of the law, more particularly as it has been recently expounded, and it would be carrying this case beyond any limits which authority justifies.

Those then are my reasons for the conclusion which I stated at the beginning of this judgment, that in my view Danckwerts J rightly decided the case, and I therefore would dismiss the appeal.

Charitable trusts, as we will see later, are subject to a special test for certainty of objects.

Perpetuity rule

English law views with disfavour an obligation to retain property within a group of persons (the family, an unincorporated association, etc) for a period longer than the perpetuity period.

18 [1947] AC 447.

At common law, this period was measured in terms of a life or lives in being plus 21 years. Only human lives may be chosen and not the lives of animals, some of which are noted for their longevity (such as tortoises and elephants). In this respect, an embryonic child (*en ventre sa mère*) constitutes a life in being if this is relevant in measuring the period. A life or lives in being, whether connected with the gift or not, may be chosen expressly by the donor or settlor, or may be implied in the circumstances if the life or lives is or are so related to the gift or settlement that it is capable of being used to measure the date of the vesting of the interest. If no lives are selected or are implied, the perpetuity period at common law is 21 years from the date that the instrument creating the gift took effect (a will takes effect on the date of the death of the testator or testatrix, a deed takes effect on the date of execution).

For example, if S, a settlor, during his lifetime transfers a portfolio of shares to T (1) and T (2) as trustees, on trust contingently for his first child to marry and S has unmarried children, the gift, before the Perpetuities and Accumulations Act 1964, would be void. S would be treated impliedly as the life in being and it was possible that none of his children may marry within 21 years after his death. Thus, the gift may not vest within the perpetuity period. The perpetuity period commences from the date the instrument takes effect and at common law the interest was void if there was any possibility however remote that the gift might vest outside the perpetuity period.

Moreover, the settlor may expressly select a life or lives in being in order to extend the perpetuity period. Any number of lives may be selected. The test is whether the group of lives selected is certain and identifiable to such an extent that it is possible to ascertain the date of death of the last survivor. This test was clearly incapable of being satisfied in *Re Moore*[19] where a testator defined the period as '21 years from the death of the last survivor of all persons who shall be living at my death'. Joyce J decided that the gift was void for uncertainty.

> **Joyce J:** I think this gift is void for uncertainty. It is impossible to ascertain when the last life will be extinguished, and it is, therefore, impossible to say when the period of 21 years will commence. Under these circumstances it is not, I think, necessary for me to consider whether the gift is void as transgressing the rule against perpetuity.

Indeed, the settlor may select lives which have no connection with the trust. It became the practice to select Royal lives such as 'the lineal descendants of Queen Elizabeth II living at my death' with the objective of ascertaining the date of death of the last survivor of such descendants.

In substance, the perpetuity rule not only requires a future interest to vest within the perpetuity period but also stipulates the maximum period of duration in which such interest may be enjoyed following the vesting of the interest.

19 [1901] 1 Ch 936.

On analysis, the rule may be classified into two categories, namely:

(i) the rule against remote vesting; and

(ii) the rule against excessive duration.

The rule against remote vesting

This rule stipulates the maximum period of time in which the vesting of a future interest may be postponed. A future interest (such as a contingent interest) is one which has not vested in the beneficiary. An interest may be vested 'in possession' or 'in interest' and would not be subject to this rule. An interest is vested 'in possession' if the beneficiary has a 'present right of present enjoyment' such as a gift to 'A for life' or a gift to 'A absolutely'. A has an unrestricted right to enjoy the income as it arises or an absolute right to the property respectively. An interest is vested 'in interest' if the beneficiary has a present right to future possession, for example, A for life remainder to B absolutely. B has a present right to the capital which he may sell, exchange or give away as he pleases while A is still alive. B obtains a right to possession when A dies, that is, B obtains the right to the income (in addition to his right to the capital) when A dies. A contingent interest, on the other hand, is not a vested interest while the contingency remains unperformed. A contingent interest is not an immediate right of enjoyment but a future right of enjoyment which may or may not accrue on the fulfilment of a condition, for example, 'to C (who is currently aged 10) if he attains the age of 18' or any other contingency.

The rule at common law was that an interest was void if it was possible to imagine a sequence of events rendering the possibility that the interest might vest outside the perpetuity period.

Before 1964, the common law judges in their enthusiasm to avoid future interests decided absurdly that there was no upper or lower age limit in respect of which a living person was capable of procreation. Thus, it was decided that an octogenarian on the one hand and a toddler at the other extreme were capable of reproducing.

This degree of volatility continued until the passing of the Perpetuities and Accumulations Act 1964. This Act introduced two major reforms to the law, namely, the 'wait and see' rule and the 'statutory life' period. Under the Act, a future interest is no longer void on the ground that it 'might' vest outside the perpetuity period. It is void if, in the circumstances, the interest does not vest within the perpetuity period. In the meantime, the court will 'wait and see' whether or not the gift vests. In addition, the Act introduced a certain and fixed 'statutory life' period, namely, a period not exceeding 80 years. This period may only be adopted by the settlor if he specifically selects this period. In short, the 'statutory life' will not be implied into a settlement. In such a case, the common law period will be adopted.

Rule against excessive duration

Closely related to the above rule is the rule against the inalienability of property. This rule renders void any trust or interest which is required to be enjoyed for longer than the perpetuity period. Charitable trusts are exempt from this principle (see below, p 590). The issue here is not whether the property or interest is, in fact, tied up forever but whether the owner is capable of disposing of the same within the perpetuity period. The question concerns merely the power to dispose, and not the actual disposal, of the capital. Thus, property may be owned perpetually by persons, companies or unincorporated associations, if these bodies are entitled to dispose of the same at any time, but have refrained from exercising the right of disposal.

Re Chardon, Johnston v Davies [1928] Ch 464, HC

In this case, a testator gave a fund to a cemetery company subject to the income being used for the maintenance of two specified graves with a gift over. The court held that the gift was valid for the company was capable of alienating the property.

> **Romer J:** In my opinion that rule does not render invalid a trust to pay the income of a fund to A, his executors, administrators and assigns for twenty-two years. Before I deal with Mr Stamp's point I had better perhaps mention this. It is admitted by Mr Crossman that a trust to pay the income to A, his executors administrators and assigns indefinitely, that is to say for ever, would be a good trust, because it would be equivalent to giving an absolute interest, and so it would, but he says that a trust to pay the income to A for an indefinite period, that is to say until the happening of an event that may never happen, is bad, because that is not equivalent to an absolute interest. While it is true that it is not equivalent to an absolute interest it is very much like, and analogous to, a determinable fee in real estate. Where land was limited to A and his heirs until a certain event should happen, a determinable fee was created, though the question whether since the statute *Quia Emptores* a determinable fee can be created is a matter upon which lawyers are not agreed. But if the determinable fee in real estate can no longer be created it is because of the statute of *Quia Emptores*, and most assuredly the statute of *Quia Emptores* had nothing to do with personal estates. I therefore do not know any reason why a trust to pay the income indefinitely to a certain person his executors, administrators and assigns until a certain event happens should be bad unless it be for the reason advanced by Mr Stamp.
>
> Now Mr Stamp's contention was this. He said, and truly, that there are fundamental differences between real and personal estates, and he said that there is a rule which appears to me, if it be a rule, to be one that is distinct from the rules against inalienability and perpetuity, by virtue of which it is impossible to separate the legal from the equitable interest in personal estate for a longer period than a life in being and 21 years. Now it is agreed that there is no authority for the proposition so stated; indeed, what authority there is is

> against it, because in the case of *In re Gage*,[20] it appears to have been held by Kekewich J that a trust to pay the income to an unborn person for life was a good trust; it certainly did not offend the rule against perpetuities, because the equitable interest vested in a life in being and 21 years, but it was a trust that might last beyond the perpetuity rule. Kekewich J did not seem to find any difficulty in that case in allowing a separation of the legal interest in the fund from the equitable interest in the fund for more than a life in being and 21 years. Mr Stamp says that that is an exception from the rule. But he has not called my attention to any textbook or authority in which the rule itself is stated, and for myself I do not think that any such rule exists. The cemetery company and the persons interested in the legacy, subject to the interest of the cemetery company, could combine tomorrow and dispose of the whole legacy. The trust does not, therefore, offend the rule against inalienability. The interest of the cemetery company is a vested interest; the interest of the residuary legatee, it being agreed on all hands that, subject to the interest of the cemetery company, the legacy falls into residue, are also vested. All the interests therefore created in this £200, legal and equitable, are vested interests and, that being so, the trusts do not offend the rule against perpetuity. I know of no other rule which will enable me to come to the conclusion that this is an invalid gift.

EXCEPTIONS TO THE *ASTOR* PRINCIPLE

There are a number of private purpose trusts which are exceptionally considered to be valid. Despite the objections to the validity of purpose trusts as stated above, a number of anomalous exceptions exist. These trusts are created as concessions to human weakness. However, it must be emphasised that the only concession granted by the courts is that it is unnecessary for the beneficiaries (purposes) to enforce the trust. The other rules applicable to trusts are equally applied to these anomalous trusts. See *Re Endacott* (above, p 528). These trusts are not mandatory in effect but are merely 'directory' in the sense that the trustees are entitled to refuse to carry out the wishes of the settlor and the courts will not force them to do otherwise. At the same time, the courts will not forbid the trustees from carrying out the terms of the trust. These trusts are called, 'hybrid trusts' or 'trusts for imperfect obligations'.

Trusts for the maintenance of animals

Gifts for the maintenance of animals generally are charitable (see below, p 667), but trusts for the maintenance of specific animals, such as pets, are treated as private purpose trusts.

20 [1898] 1 Ch 498.

Pettingall v Pettingall **(1842) 11 LJ Ch 176, HC**

The testator's executor was given a fund to spend £50 per annum for the benefit of the testator's black mare. On her death, any surplus funds were to be taken by the executor. The court held that in view of the willingness of the executor to carry out the testator's wishes, a valid trust in favour of the animal was created. The residuary legatees were entitled to supervise the performance of the trust.

However, this principle was unjustifiably extended by Clauson J in *Re Thompson*.[21] The purpose being the promotion and furtherance of fox hunting.

> **Clauson J:** In my judgment the object of the gift has been defined with sufficient clearness and is of a nature to which effect can be given. The proper way for me to deal with the matter will be, not to make. as it is asked by the summons, a general declaration, but, following the example of Knight-Bruce VC in *Pettingall v Pettingall*, to order that, upon the defendant Mr Lloyd giving an undertaking (which I understand he is willing to give) to apply the legacy when received by him towards the object expressed in the testator's will, the plaintiffs do pay to the defendant Mr Lloyd the legacy of £1,000; and that, in case the legacy should be applied by him otherwise than towards the promotion and furthering of fox hunting, the residuary legatees are to be at liberty to apply.

The courts take judicial notice of the lifetime of the animal and if this does not exceed the perpetuity period the gift may be valid. In *Re Haines*,[22] the testator bequeathed property for the maintenance of specific cats. This gift was valid in view of the lifespan of cats. But, in *Re Dean*,[23] a gift to maintain the testator's horses and hounds for 50 years 'if they should so long live' was held to be valid, despite infringing the perpetuity rule.

Monument cases

A trust for the building of a memorial or monument for an individual is not charitable but may exist as a valid purpose trust if the trustees express a desire to perform the trust.

In *Mussett v Bingle*,[24] a testator bequeathed £300 to his executors to be used to erect a monument to the testator's wife's first husband. The court held that the gift was valid.

Similarly, a gift for the maintenance of a specific grave or particular graves may be valid as a private purpose trust but, additionally, the donor is required to restrict the gift within the perpetuity period, otherwise the gift will be void.

21 [1934] Ch 342.

22 (1952) *The Times*, 7 November.

23 (1889) 41 Ch D 552.

24 [1876] WN 170.

Re Hooper [1932] 1 Ch 38, HC

A bequest was made to trustees on trust to provide 'so far as they can legally do so' for the care and upkeep of specified graves in a churchyard. The perpetuity period was satisfied by the phrase, 'so far as they can legally do so'.

> **Maugham J:** The trustees here have the sum of £1,000 which they have to hold upon trust to 'invest the same and to the intent that so far as they legally can do so and in any manner that they may in their discretion arrange they will out of the annual income thereof' do substantially four things: first, provide for the care and upkeep of the grave and monument in the Torquay cemetery; secondly, for the care and upkeep of a vault and monument there in which lie the remains of the testator's wife and daughter; thirdly, for the care and upkeep of a grave and monument in Shotley churchyard near Ipswich, where the testator's son lies buried; and, fourthly, for the care and upkeep of the tablet in St Matthias' Church at Ilsham to the memories of the testator's wife and children and the window in the same church to the memory of his late father. All those four things have to be done expressly according to an arrangement made in the discretion of the trustees and so far as they legally can do so. I do not think that is distinguishable from the phrase 'so long as the law for the time being permits', and the conclusion at which I arrive, following the decision I have mentioned, is that this trust is valid for a period of 21 years from the testator's death so far as regards the three matters which involve the upkeep of graves or vaults or monuments in the churchyard or in the cemetery. As regards the tablet in St Matthias' Church and the window in the same church there is no question but that that is a good charitable gift, and, therefore, the rule against perpetuities does not apply.
>
> Something has been said with regard to apportionment. To my mind there is no room for a legal apportionment, because it is left to the discretion of the trustees to arrange how much they will out of this income apply during the 21 years to the four objects in question. At the end of the 21 years any part which is not applied for the upkeep of the tablet and the window in St Matthias' Church will, of course, be undisposed of and will fall, unless some other event happens, into residue.

On the other hand, a gift for the maintenance of all the graves in a churchyard may be charitable (see below, p 656).

THE *DENLEY* APPROACH

The approach adopted by the courts is to ascertain whether a gift or trust is intended for the promotion of a purpose *simpliciter* (which is capable of coming within the *Astor* principle) which is void, or alternatively whether the trust is for the benefit of persons who are capable of enforcing the trust. This is a question of construction for the courts to decide. The promotion of virtually all purposes affect persons. The settlor may, in form, create what appears to be a purpose trust but in substance, the trust may be considered to be for the benefit of human beneficiaries.

In this respect, there is a distinction between a form of gift remotely in favour of individuals, to such an extent that those individuals do not have a *locus standi* to enforce the trust. On the other hand, a gift may appear to propagate a purpose which is directly or indirectly for the benefit of individuals. In this event, if the beneficiaries satisfy the test for certainty of objects, the gift may be valid. The courts are required to consider each gift before classification.

Re Denley's Trust Deed [1969] 1 Ch 373, HC

In this case, a plot of land was conveyed to trustees for use, subject to the perpetuity rule, as a sports ground primarily for the benefit of employees of a company and secondarily for the benefit of such other person or persons as the trustees may allow to use the same. The question in issue was whether the trust was void as a purpose trust. The court held that the trust was valid in favour of human beneficiaries.

> **Goff J:** It was decided in *In re Astor's Settlement Trusts*[25] that a trust for a number of non-charitable purposes was not merely unenforceable but void on two grounds; first, that it was not a trust for the benefit of individuals, which I will refer to as 'the beneficiary principle'; and, secondly, for uncertainty.
>
> Mr Mills has argued that the trust in clause 2(c) in the present case is either a trust for the benefit of individuals, in which case he argues that they are an unascertainable class and therefore the trust is void for uncertainty, or that it is a purpose trust, that is, a trust for providing recreation, which he submits is void on the beneficiary principle, or alternatively, that it is something of a hybrid, having the vices of both kinds.
>
> I think there may be a purpose or object trust, the carrying out of which would benefit an individual or individuals, where that benefit is so indirect or intangible or which is otherwise so framed as not to give those persons any *locus standii* to apply to the court to enforce the trust, in which case the beneficiary principle would, as it seems to me, apply to invalidate the trust, quite apart from any question of uncertainty or perpetuity. Such cases can be considered if and when they arise. The present is not, in my judgment, of that character, and it will be seen that clause 2(d) of the trust deed expressly states that, subject to any rules and regulations made by the trustees, the employers of the company shall be entitled to the use and enjoyment of the land. Apart from this possible exception, in my judgment the beneficiary principle of *In re Astor's Settlement Trusts* [see above, p 521], which was approved in *In re Endacott (Decd)*[26] – see particularly by Harman LJ – is confined to purpose or object trusts which are abstract or impersonal. The objection is not that the trust is for a purpose or object *per se*, but that there is no beneficiary or *cestui*

25 [1952] Ch 534.

26 [1960] Ch 232.

que trust. The rule is so expressed in *Lewin on Trusts*,[27] and, in my judgment, with the possible exception I have mentioned, rightly so. In *In re Wood (Decd)*[28] Harman J said:

> There has been an interesting argument on the question of perpetuity, but it seems to me, with all respect to that argument, that there is an earlier obstacle which is fatal to the validity of this bequest, namely, that a gift on trust must have a *cestui que* trust, and there being here no *cestui que* trust the gift must fail.

Again, in *Leahy v Attorney General for New South Wales*,[29] Viscount Simonds, delivering the judgment of the Privy Council, said:

> A gift can be made to persons (including a corporation) but it cannot be made to a purpose or to an object: so also, and these are the important words – 'a trust may be created for the benefit of persons as *cestuis que* trust but not for a purpose or object unless the purpose or object be charitable'. For a purpose or object cannot sue, but, if it be charitable, the Attorney General can sue to enforce it.
>
> Where, then, the trust, though expressed as a purpose, is directly or indirectly for the benefit of an individual or individuals, it seems to me that it is in general outside the mischief of the beneficiary principle. I am fortified in this conclusion by the *dicta* of Lord Evershed MR and Harman LJ in *In re Harpur's Will Trusts*.[30]
>
> I also derive assistance from what was said by North J in *In re Bowes*.[31] That was a bequest of a sum of money upon trust to expend the same in planting trees for shelter on certain settled estates. It happened that there was a father and a son of full age, tenant for life in possession and tenant in tail in remainder respectively; so that, subject to the son disentailing, they were together absolutely entitled, and the actual decision was that they could claim the money, but North J said: 'If it were necessary to uphold it, the trees can be planted upon the whole of it until the fund is exhausted. Therefore, there is nothing illegal in the gift itself' – and later – 'I think there clearly is a valid trust to lay out money for the benefit of the persons entitled to the estate'.
>
> The trust in the present case is limited in point of time so as to avoid any infringement of the rule against perpetuities and, for the reasons I have given, it does not offend against the beneficiary principle; and unless, therefore, it be void for uncertainty, it is a valid trust.
>
> [The learned judge then considered whether the test for certainty of objects was satisfied and decided that the test was satisfied, he continued:]
>
> As it is a private trust and not a charitable one, it is clear that, however it be regarded, the individuals for whose benefit it is designed must be ascertained

27 16th edn, 1964, London: Sweet & Maxwell, p 17.

28 [1949] Ch 498.

29 [1959] AC 457.

30 [1962] Ch 78.

31 [1896] 1 Ch 507.

or capable of ascertainment at any given time: see *IRC v Broadway Cottages Trust*.[32]

It is conceded that 'the employees of the company' in clause 2(c), which must mean for the time being, are so ascertained or ascertainable, but Mr Mills submits that the inclusion in the class of 'such other person or persons (if any) as the trustees may allow' is fatal, and that the qualification 'secondarily' in relation to such persons does not help. In my judgment, however, this is not so. I accept Mr Parker's submission that the provision as to 'other persons' is not a trust but a power operating in partial defeasance of the trust in favour of the employees which it does not therefore make uncertain.

Moreover, as it is a power, it is not necessary that the trustees should know all possible objects in whose favour it is exercisable: see *In re Gulbenkian's Settlements*.[33] Therefore, in my judgment, it is a valid power. If this were a will, a question might arise whether this provision might be open to attack as a delegation of the testamentary power. I do not say that would be so, but in any case it cannot be said of a settlement *inter vivos*.

Another question, perhaps of difficulty, might arise, if the trustees purported to admit not to a given individual or individuals but a class which they failed to specify with certainty, whether in such a case this would import uncertainty into and invalidate the whole trust or would be merely an invalid exercise of the power; but, as that has not in fact occurred, I need not consider it.

There is, however, one other aspect of uncertainty which has caused me some concern; that is, whether this is in its nature a trust which the court can control, for, as Lord Eldon LC said in *Morice v Bishop of Durham*:[34]

> As it is a maxim, that the execution of a trust shall be under the control of the court, it must of such a nature, that it can be under that control; so that the administration of it can be reviewed by the court; or, if the trustee dies, the court itself can execute the trust; a trust therefore, which, in case of maladministration could be reformed; and a due administration directed; and then, unless the subject and objects can be ascertained, upon principles, familiar in other cases, it must be decided, that the court can neither reform maladministration, nor direct a due administration.

The difficulty I have felt is that there may well be times when some of the employees wish to use the sports club for one purpose while others desire to use it at the same time for some other purpose of such nature that the two cannot be carried on together. The trustees could, of course, control this by making rules and regulations under clause 2(d) of the trust deed, but they might not. In any case, the employers would probably agree amongst themselves, but I cannot assume that they would. If there were an *impasse*, the court could not resolve it, because it clearly could not either exercise the trustees' power to make rules or settle a scheme, this being a non-charitable trust: see *In re Astor's Settlement Trusts* [see above, p 521].

32 [1955] Ch 20.

33 [1968] Ch 126.

34 (1805) 10 Ves 522.

In my judgment, however, it would not be right to hold the trust void on this ground. The court can, as it seems to me, execute the trust both negatively by restraining any improper disposition or use of the land, and positively by ordering the trustees to allow the employees and such other persons (if any) as they may admit to use the land for the purpose of a recreation or sports ground. Any difficulty there might be in practice in the beneficial enjoyment of the land by those entitled to use it is, I think, really beside the point. The same kind of problem is equally capable of arising in the case of a trust to permit a number of persons – for example, all the unmarried children of a testator or settlor – to use or occupy a house or to have the use of certain chattels; nor can I assume that in such cases agreement between the parties concerned would be more likely, even if that be a sufficient distinction, yet no one would suggest, I fancy, that such a trust would be void.

In my judgment, therefore, the provisions of clause 2(c) are valid, and it is unnecessary for me to decide whether, if they were void, the gift over in clause 2(j) must also be void in any event, although on the construction of this particular deed I would have thought that would be so.

Mr Mills, however, has submitted that clause 2(j) is inherently defective because it is to operate in three events, two of which – namely, the number of employees subscribing, and the land ceasing to be required or used – are void for uncertainty. Mr Mills has relied on *In re Viscount Exmouth*[35] and particularly where Fry J said, 'Such contingent limitations in the nature of defeasances are, in my view, subject to all the rules which apply to conditions subsequent. One of those rules I understand to be this, that the condition must be clear and certain. That, in my opinion, includes, not only certainty of expression in the creation of the limitation, but also certainty in its operation. It must be such a limitation that, at any given moment of time, it is ascertainable whether the limitation has or has not taken effect'; and again, after referring to *Clavering v Ellison*,[36] where he said: 'No doubt there the want of certainty was rather in the expression used than in the ascertainment of the operation of the limitation. But it is quite plain certainty in the one is as essential as certainty in the other.'

That does not mean, however, that because the provision is one which may give rise to difficulty in applying it to particular facts, or even one which raises questions of construction, it is necessarily void. The provision in *In re Viscount Exmouth*, though certain in expression, yet failed for uncertainty in operation because it propounded a formula which made it impossible to ascertain its operation on any view of the facts for an indefinite period. This was explained by Fry J, where he said:

> In the next place let me inquire whether, in the present instance, it is ascertainable at any given time whether the contingency has or has not happened. Nothing can illustrate better the difficulty in the way of this proviso than the actual circumstances of the case. When the third viscount

35 (1883) 23 Ch D 158.

36 (1859) 7 HL Cas 707.

> died there were living persons, one of whom at least is still living, who were in the entail, some of them before and some of them after the present viscount; that is, their interest would take effect (if at all) some before and some after that of the present Viscount. It follows, therefore, that you cannot, at every given time, tell whether the interests of all the persons named by the testator from the death of the last of whom the 21 years is to commence, have or have not expired. Suppose, for instance, the present Viscount should live to the year 1897, which will be 21 years from 1876, when the third viscount died, and suppose that Henry Edward Pellew should be then living, to whom will the chattels belong? No human being could answer the question.

The classical statement of principle is that of Lord Cranworth in *Clavering v Ellison*:

> I consider that, from the earliest times, one of the cardinal rules on the subject has been this: that where a vested estate is to be defeated by a condition on a contingency that is to happen afterwards, that condition must be such that the court can see from the beginning, precisely and distinctly, upon the happening of what event it was that the preceding vested estate was to determine.

The later authorities show that what the court has to consider is whether the clause in question propounds a 'concept' which is sufficiently clear in expression and operation. That is in part a matter of fair (albeit strict) construction and in part a question whether it can be applied in fact with certainty even if with difficulty.

I must try not to overload this case with citations, but perhaps I may refer to the following: First, I have the speech of Lord Simonds LC in *Bromley v Tryon*,[37] where he said:

> In deference to the argument of learned counsel who sought to illustrate the alleged obscurity of the relevant words by reference to the facts of the present case, I will only add this. It does not follow that because the words of a defeasance clause are sufficiently clear to give the clause validity that there may not be cases in which its application is difficult, and I apprehend that, if there is a real doubt, the court will show the same favour to a vested estate in applying the clause as it does in construing it. But in the present case I did not find in the facts as proved, whether as illustrative of the difficulty of construction or of application, anything which would lead me to a conclusion favourable to the appellants.

Then I would refer to *In re Murray (Decd)*,[38] where Lord Evershed MR accepted the argument of counsel that: 'You are not to observe obscurities in expression, add them together without any real attempt at solving them, and then say that the whole document is too obscure to enable you to determine with sufficient precision how it will operate in practice.'

37 [1952] AC 265.

38 [1955] Ch 69.

Finally, in *In re Neeld (Decd)*,[39] Lord Evershed MR, after referring to *Clavering v Ellison* (1859); *Sifton v Sifton*[40] and *Bromley v Tryon*, summed the matter up as follows:

> It is, however, as I think, clear that the classic formulation of the requirement of construction for divesting clauses such as those with which we are concerned is satisfied if, upon a fair construction of the language used according to its ordinary sense, the court can arrive at a clear conclusion what truly is the obligation which the donor of the estate intends to impose, and what are the event or events which he has in mind as causing a divesting of the estate. It is true also, as Lord Simonds LC observed, that in construing such clauses there would in case of doubt be a tendency to lean in favour of the estate already vested; but, as I have said, it does not, as I think, follow that the language used must be of so exactly precise a character that no question can ever sensibly thereafter arise on the particular facts as they have occurred, whether, according to the terms of the instrument, a divesting has or has not taken place. In other words, I am prepared for my part to accept the argument as it was presented by Mr Lazarus (founded in large degree upon the case above cited of *In re Gape*)[41] that so long as the concept expressed in the will or settlement is clear and can be precisely formulated, then it is no objection to the validity of the clause that on occasion its application may give rise to real difficulty.

I now have to apply this law in this case. Mr Mills submits that in the absence of any provision in the trust deed – and there is none – imposing an obligation to subscribe, or of a contractual obligation, one really cannot see who may fairly be said to be 'subscribing' and in any case one cannot say when a person has ceased to subscribe, and he instances cases of temporary lapse of payment during illness or holiday, or of an employee falling into arrears from any cause, or without cause, and later paying them up. In my judgment, however, the concept of employees 'subscribing', and subscribing at a given rate, is a sufficiently certain concept.

The other limb of clause 2(j) to which exception was taken was 'if the said land shall at any time cease to be required or to be used by the said employees as a sports ground'. Mr Mills submitted that, as a matter of construction, this means required by the employees and he said: 'What does this mean? Would it be all or some, and, if the latter, a majority or a substantial part?' I do not, however, so read it. In my view, this means 'cease to be required as a sports ground' or 'ceased to be used by the employees as a sports ground'. This is consonant with the general tenor of clause 2(j), which is providing a gift over to cover the actual or *de facto* failure of the trust. It covers lack of support; it covers the land ceasing to be required, as, for example, by some better ground being obtained or by the company moving its premises far away or moving anywhere reasonably near at hand and acquiring a new ground there; and it covers the company going out of existence. So construed, both ceasing to be required and

39 [1962] Ch 643.

40 [1938] AC 656.

41 [1952] Ch 743.

ceasing to be used appear to me to be sufficiently certain concepts. Difficulties might arise on this limb as to its operation on the facts, particularly as to user, if there were some, but not many, employees who wished to use it; but that problem has not arisen, and I see no reason to hold the whole clause void because of that possibility.

Having thus decided that the whole trust, including the gift over, is valid, I have now to determine whether, on the facts, an event has happened giving rise to the passing of the property from the employees to the hospital, under clause 2(j). Certainly, that clause is not very well drawn and, though certain, is not in my view easy to construe. The difficulty arises from the fact that there is in parenthesis the words 'subscribing at the rate of two pence per week per man'. The parenthesis follows immediately after the expression 'total number of employees at any given time', but it must qualify the earlier words 'employees subscribing'. It has been suggested, though not seriously pressed in argument, that I ought to construe the whole paragraph as relating only to subscribing men, so that you count the number of such subscribers, and see whether they are 75% of such employees. I do not myself think that is permissible, having regard to the later words, 'or to be used by the said employees', which must, I think, refer to all employees. The choice, therefore, lies between taking the proportion of all employees who subscribe two pence per week, as compared with the total number of employees who subscribe two pence per week, reading 'per man' as 'per person' or 'per head', and taking the proportion of those who in fact subscribe, and in the case of men, those who subscribe at the rate of two pence per week, as compared with the total number of employees. This may produce an extraordinary result if all the men employed by the company subscribed two pence per week and the women did not subscribe anything at all. On the other hand, the parenthesis specifically uses the expression 'men,' whereas the rest of the clause refers to 'employees.' I think, bearing in mind that this is a forfeiture clause and one therefore which ought to be construed strictly and with a leaning in favour of the vested interest, I can and ought to read this as applying only to the event of the number of employees of any kind subscribing, and in the case of men subscribing at the rate of two pence per week, as compared with the total number of employees. There is nowhere in the deed anything apart from this provision which requires anybody to subscribe anything. I think, therefore, I am entitled, in construing this forfeiture clause, to be quite strict and to regard the parenthesis as imposing an obligation only in the case of men. If that be right, it follows on the figures, though by an extraordinarily narrow proportion – I think 0.5 of an employee – that the requisite 75% has so far been obtained.

GIFTS TO UNINCORPORATED ASSOCIATIONS

There is some difficulty in deciding whether a gift to an unincorporated association creates a trust for a purpose which fails for want of a beneficiary to enforce the trust (under the *Astor* principle) or whether the gift will be construed in favour of human beneficiaries, the members of the association.

This involves a question of construction of the circumstances surrounding the gift and the rules of the association.

For example, a gift to the National Anti-Vivisection Society (an unincorporated non-charitable body) may be construed as a gift on trust for the work or purpose of such association and not for the benefit of its members. Accordingly, the gift may be considered void under the *Astor* principle.

Leahy v Attorney General for New South Wales [1959] AC 457, PC

> **Viscount Simonds:** A gift can be made to persons (including a corporation) but it cannot be made to a purpose or to an object: so also, a trust may be created for the benefit of persons as *cestuis que* trust but not for a purpose or object unless the purpose or object be charitable. For a purpose or object cannot sue, but if it be charitable, the Attorney General can sue to enforce it.

An unincorporated association is not a legal person but may take the form of a group of individuals joined together with common aims usually laid down in its constitution. The association was defined in *Conservative and Unionist Central Office v Burrell*.

Conservative and Unionist Central Office v Burrell [1982] 1 WLR 522, CA

> **Lawton LJ:** Two or more persons bound together for one or more common purposes, not being business purposes, by mutual undertakings each having mutual duties and obligations, in an organisation which has rules which identify in whom control of it and its funds rests and on what terms and which can be joined or left at will.

The following solutions have been adopted from time to time by the courts in respect of gifts to unincorporated associations. Although the courts have a wide discretion in construing the intention of the donor or settlor and the function and purpose of the association, the adoption of any of the solutions will vary with the facts of each case:

(i) A settlor may make a gift to an unincorporated association which, on a true construction, is a gift to the members of that association who take as joint tenants free from any contractual fetter. Any member is entitled to sever his share. In these circumstances, the association is used as a label or definition of the class which is intended to take. For instance, a testator may give a legacy to a dining or social club of which he is a member, with the intention of giving an interest which is capable of being severed in favour of each of the members. Such cases are extremely uncommon:

Cocks v Manners (1871) LR 12 Eq 574, HC

The testatrix left part of her estate to the Dominican Convent at Carisbrooke 'payable to the supervisor for the time being'. The court held that the gift was not charitable but was valid in favour of the individual members of the stated community.

(ii) More frequently, the gift to the association may be construed as a gift to the members of the association on the date of the gift, not beneficially, but as an accretion to the funds of the society which is regulated by the contract (evidenced by the rules of the association) made by the members *inter se*. A member who leaves the association by death or resignation, will have no claim to the property, in the absence of any rules to the contrary. This approach was supported in an *obiter* pronouncement by Brightman J in *Re Recher's Will Trust*:

Re Recher's Will Trust [1972] Ch 526, HC

Brightman J: ... it appears to me that the life members, the ordinary members and the associate members of the London Provincial Society were bound together by a contract *inter se*, with the result that the society represented an organisation of individuals bound together by a contract. Now just as two parties to a bi-partite bargain can vary or terminate their contract by mutual assent, so it must follow that the members of the society could, at any moment of time by agreement, authorised by its constitution, vary or terminate their multi-partite contract. There is no private trust or trust for charitable purposes or other trust to hinder the process. The funds of such an association may, of course, be derived not only from the subscriptions of contracting parties but also from donations from non-contracting parties and legacies from persons who have died. In the case of a donation and a legacy which are not accompanied by any words which purport to impose a trust, it seems that the gift takes effect in favour of the existing members of the association not as joint tenants or tenants-in-common so as to entitle each member to an immediate share, but as an accretion to the funds of the organisation.

In this case, a testatrix gave her residuary estate to the 'Anti-Vivisection Society, 76 Victoria Street, London SW1'. The London and Provincial Anti-Vivisection Society had carried on its activities at this address but shortly before the will was made, the society ceased to exist (it was amalgamated with other societies) and it gave up its premises in Victoria Street. The question in issue was whether the gift could be taken by the amalgamated society, or failed and was subject to a resulting trust.

The court held that, on construction of the will, the testator intended to benefit the Society at Victoria Street and not the larger body. Accordingly, the gift failed and a resulting trust was set up.

Brightman J: It will be seen that, until a date shortly before the testatrix made her will, there was in existence an unincorporated society named 'The London and Provincial Anti-Vivisection Society' of 76 Victoria Street, London. When she made her will, there was in existence an unincorporated society named 'The National Anti-Vivisection Society (incorporating the London and Provincial Anti-Vivisection Society)' of 27 Palace Street, London. The legatee named in the will is simply 'The Anti-Vivisection Society, 76 Victoria Street, London SW1'.

As a matter of interpretation, it appears to me clear that clause 7(b)(4) of the will must be construed as if it read 'The London and Provincial Anti-Vivisection Society, 76 Victoria Street, London SW1'. I do not think that sub-paragraph (4) can reasonably be construed as if it read 'The National Anti-Vivisection Society (incorporating the London and Provincial Anti-Vivisection Society), 27 Palace Street, London SW1'.

The substantial question before me, therefore, is whether the Anti-Vivisection company, as the assignee of the National society, is entitled to the share of residue given to the London & Provincial Society. In argument, this question was divided by counsel into two parts, first, whether the gift of a share of residue to the London & Provincial society would have been valid on the hypothesis that the London & Provincial society had continued its separate existence down to the date of the death of the testatrix; secondly, if so, whether the position is changed because the London & Provincial society had no separate existence at the date of the testatrix's death.

The rules do not contain a single expression of a trust except rule 24, stating that the property of the London & Provincial society shall be held by the honorary trustees upon trust to deal with the same as the committee direct.

I accept the third defendant's submission that the gift in clause 7(b)(4) of the will is not a gift to the persons who were the members of the London & Provincial society as the testatrix intended, as soon as the gift fell into possession, that any such member should be entitled, as of right, to demand an aliquot share. Indeed, there is no one joined in these proceedings who would be interested to argue for such a construction, and rightly so. Nor do I think that the gift was intended to take effect in favour of present and future members beneficially.

I turn to the submission that, as a matter of construction, clause 7(b)(4) of the will ought to be read as a gift in trust 'for the purposes of' the London & Provincial society. If so read, it is clear beyond argument that the gift must fail: it is sufficient to cite two sentences from the decision in *Leahy v AG for New South Wales*:[42]

> A gift can be made to persons (including a corporation) but it cannot be made to a purpose or to an object: so also, a trust may be created for the benefit of persons as cestuis que trust but not for a purpose or object unless the purpose or object be charitable. For a purpose or object cannot sue, but, if it be charitable, the Attorney General can sue to enforce it.

It is argued that I am compelled to read clause 7(b)(4) as a gift in trust for the purposes of the London & Provincial society and to decide that it is therefore void. The general proposition relied upon is that where you have a gift to an unidentified institution bearing a name suggesting charitable purposes, particularly if found in the company of a number of gifts to identified charitable institutions, the court may save the unidentified gift by assuming that the testator's bounty is not directed towards the particular institutions

42 [1959] AC 457, p 478.

named by him but is directed towards a purpose. Reference was made to the decisions in *In re Davis*;[43] *In re Knox*[44] and *In re Satterthwaite's Will Trusts*,[45] as examples of this process. The gift to the London & Provincial society accompanied gifts to five other animal societies. The testatrix described all six of the clause 7 beneficiaries as charities, and repeated this description in clause 9. She plainly, it is said, had purposes and not institutions in mind.

I appreciate the force of this argument, but I am not tempted to succumb to it. So far as I am aware, the principle invoked by the third defendant has only been applied by the court to avoid the failure of an unidentified gift. I do not know that it has ever been called into play when it would destroy an identified gift. I can well understand that a court of construction may be disposed to read absent words into a will in order to give what effect it can to an equivocal gift. It would, however, be perverse to read absent words into a will in such a way as to defeat, in the process, the intention of the deceased. As a matter of construction, therefore, I do not read paragraph (4) as a gift in trust for the purposes of the London & Provincial society.

Having reached the conclusion that the gift in question is not a gift to the members of the London & Provincial society at the date of death, as joint tenants or tenants in common, so as to entitle a member as of right to a distributive share, nor an attempted gift to present and future members beneficially, and is not a gift in trust for the purposes of the society, I must now consider how otherwise, if at all, it is capable of taking effect.

As I have already mentioned, the rules of the London & Provincial society do not purport to create any trusts except in so far as the honorary trustees are not beneficial owners of the assets of the society, but are trustees upon trust to deal with such assets according to the directions of the committee.

A trust for non-charitable purposes, as distinct from a trust for individuals, is clearly void because there is no beneficiary. It does not, however, follow that persons cannot band themselves together as an association or society, pay subscriptions and validly devote their funds in pursuit of some lawful non-charitable purpose. An obvious example is a members' social club. But it is not essential that the members should only intend to secure direct personal advantages to themselves. The association may be one in which personal advantages to the members are combined with the pursuit of some outside purpose. Or the association may be one which offers no personal benefit at all to the members, the funds of the association being applied exclusively to the pursuit of some outside purpose. Such an association of persons is bound, I would think, to have some sort of constitution; that is to say, the rights and liabilities of the members of the association will inevitably depend on some form of contract *inter se*, usually evidenced by a set of rules. In the present case it appears to me clear that the life members, the ordinary members and the associate members of the London & Provincial society were bound together by

43 [1902] 1 Ch 876.

44 [1937] Ch 109.

45 [1966] 1 WLR 277.

a contract *inter se*. Any such member was entitled to the rights and subject to the liabilities defined by the rules. If the committee acted contrary to the rules, an individual member would be entitled to take proceedings in the courts to compel observance of the rules or to recover damages for any loss he had suffered as a result of the breach of contract. As and subjecting his money to the disposition and expenditure thereof laid down by the rules. That is to say, the members would be bound to permit, and entitled to require, the honorary trustees and other members of the society to deal with that subscription in accordance with the lawful direction of the committee. Those directions would include the expenditure of that subscription, as part of the general funds of the association. The resultant situation, on analysis, is that the London & Provincial society represented an organisation of individuals bound together by a contract under which their subscriptions became, as it were, mandated towards a certain type of expenditure as adumbrated in rule 1. Just as the two parties to a bi-partite bargain can vary or terminate their contract by mutual assent, so it must follow that the life members, ordinary members and associate members of the London & Provincial society could, at any moment of time, by unanimous agreement (or by majority vote, if the rules so prescribe), vary or terminate their multi-partite contract. There would be no limit to the type of variation or termination to which all might agree. There is no private trust or trust for charitable purposes or other trust to hinder the process. It follows that if all members agreed, they could decide to wind up the London & Provincial society and divide the net asset among themselves beneficially. No one would have any *locus standi* to stop them so doing. The contract is the same as any other contract and concerns only those who are parties to it, that is to say, the members of the society.

The funds of such an association may, of course, be derived not only from the subscription of the contracting parties but also from donations from non-contracting parties and legacies from persons who have died. In the case of a donation which is not accompanied by any words which purport to impose a trust, it seems to me that the gift takes effect in favour of the existing members of the association as an accretion to the funds which are the subject matter of the contract which such members have made *inter se*, and falls to be dealt with in precisely the same way as the funds which the members themselves have subscribed. So, in the case of a legacy. In the absence of words which purport to impose a trust, the legacy is a gift to the members beneficially, not as joint tenants or as tenants in common so as to entitle each member to an immediate distributive share, but as an accretion to the funds which are the subject matter of the contract which the members have made *inter se*.

In my judgment the legacy in the present case to the London & Provincial society ought to be construed as a legacy of that type, that is to say, a legacy to the members beneficially as an accretion to the funds subject to the contract which they had made *inter se*. Of course, the testatrix did not intend the members of the society to divide her bounty between themselves, and doubtless she was ignorant of that remote but theoretical possibility. Her knowledge or absence of knowledge of the true legal analysis of the gift is irrelevant. The legacy is accordingly in my view valid, subject only to the effect of the events of 1 January 1957.

A strong argument has been presented to me against this conclusion and I have been taken through most, if not all, of the cases which are referred to in *Leahy*'s case,[46] as well as later authorities. It has been urged upon me that if the gift is not a purpose gift, there is no half-way house between, on the one hand, a legacy to the members of the London & Provincial society at the date of death, as joint tenants beneficially, or as tenants in common beneficially, and, on the other hand, a trust for members which is void for perpetuity because no individual member acting by himself can ever obtain his share of the legacy. I do not see why the choice should be confined to these two extremes. If the argument were correct it would be difficult, if not impossible, for a person to make a straight forward donation, whether inter vivos or by will, to a club or other non-charitable association which the donor desires to benefit. This conclusion seems to me contrary to common sense.

I do not propose to undertake a lengthy review of the cases. In *In re Clarke*,[47] the well known case dealing with the Corps of Commissionaires, Byrne J said:[48]

> It is, I think, established by authorities that a gift to a perpetual institution not charitable is not necessarily bad. The test, or one test, appears to be, will the legacy when paid be subject to any trust which will prevent the existing members of the association from spending it as they please? If not, the gift is good.

In *In re Ray's Will Trusts*,[49] Clauson J said:

> Another perfectly lawful form of gift would be a gift of a legacy to the controlling officer of a society in his capacity of officer, to be dealt with as he would deal with other funds with which, as such officer of a voluntary society, it would be his duty to deal. Again, that would be a gift which the court will recognise as a good gift, subject only to this point, which sometimes causes difficulty, that if the frame of the gift indicates that the legacy is not to be used at once and immediately for the purposes of the voluntary society, but is to be set aside and invested and the income only to be used, the capital being preserved as an endowment of the voluntary society, the court will not give effect to the gift because it infringes the rule that no gift except a charitable gift is to be a perpetuity, and a gift thus to endow a voluntary society necessarily creates a perpetuity.

There are similar observations in the judgment of Farwell J in *In re Taylor*.[50] I find this passage in *Leahy*'s case:

> For as Lord Tomlin (sitting at first instance in the Chancery Division) said in *In re Ogden*,[51] a gift to a voluntary association of persons for the general purposes of the association is an absolute gift and *prima facie* a good gift.

46 [1959] AC 457.

47 [1901] 2 Ch 110.

48 *Ibid*, p 114.

49 [1936] Ch 520, p 524.

50 [1904] Ch 481.

51 [1933] Ch 678, p 681.

> He was echoing the words of Lord Parker in *Bowman*'s case[52] that a gift to an unincorporated association for the attainment of its purposes 'may ... be upheld as an absolute gift to its members.

Finally, I cite and gratefully adopt the following passage which forms part of the judgment of Cross J in *Neville Estate Ltd v Madden*:[53]

> I turn now, at last, to the legal issue involved. The question of the construction and effect of gift to or in trust for unincorporated associations was recently considered by the Privy Council in *Leahy v AG for New South Wales*.[54] The position, as I understand it, is as follows. Such a gift may take effect in one or other of three quite different ways. In the first place, it may, on its true construction, be a gift to the members of the association at the relevant date as joint tenants, so that any member can sever his share and claim it whether or not he continues to be a member of the association. Secondly, it may be a gift to the existing members not as joint tenants, but subject to their respective contractual rights and liabilities towards one another as members of the association. In such a case a member cannot sever his share. It will accrue to the other members on his death or resignation, even though such members include persons who became members after the gift took effect. if this is the effect of the gift, it will not be open to objection on the score of perpetuity or uncertainty unless there is something in its terms or circumstances or in the rules of the association which precludes the members at any given time from dividing the subject the gift between them on the footing that they are solely entitled to it in equity. Thirdly, the terms or circumstances of the gift or the rules of the association may show that the property in question is not to be at the disposal of the members for the time being, but is to be held in trust for or applied for the purposes of the association as a quasi-corporate entity. In this case the gift will fail unless the association is a charitable body.

In my judgment the London & Provincial society was dissolved on 1 January 1957, and the contract theretofore binding persons together, under the name and according to the rules of the London and Provincial Anti-Vivisection Society, was terminated. The position after 1956 was that all the members of the London & Provincial society lost their rights and shed their obligations under that contract, and some of such persons, namely, the life and ordinary members of the London & Provincial society (or those who wished) automatically acceded to another association of persons who were then bound together by another contract, namely, the National society, and assumed the rights and obligations attaching to members of that association. What I find in the will is a gift to the members of the London & Provincial society as an accretion to the funds subject to the contract between such members. In my judgment, I am not entitled to construe the gift as a gift to the members of a different association as an accretion to the funds subject to a different contract.

---

52 [1917] AC 406, p 442.

53 [1962] Ch 832, p 849.

54 [1959] AC 457.

> At the end of the day, therefore, I feel bound to decide that the share or residue expressed to be given to 'The Anti-Vivisection Society, 76 Victoria Street, London SW1' has failed. This is a conclusion which I reach with reluctance because I cannot help feeling that, if the testatrix had been aware of the facts, she would probably have been content that the share of residue should go to the National society. The will was clearly made under professional advice, although not, I think, the advice of persons now engaged in the matter. I would myself take the view that it is the most elementary duty of a professional adviser in a case such as the present, not only to get the name of the unincorporated association right, but also to confirm that the association is still in existence when the will is made, and not to rely, as presumably this professional adviser relied, on inaccurate information furnished by the client.

The effect of the approach in *Re Recher* is that, if a donor transfers property to the association for its general purposes, the gift may be construed as intended for the benefit of the members of an association to be enjoyed collectively subject to the constitution of the society.

Moreover, a gift to an association for a particular purpose may be construed as a gift to the members of the association for the time being for their own use, where the association exists solely for the benefit of its members. In this respect, the members of the association would be both trustees and beneficiaries.

Re Turkington [1937] 4 All ER 501, HC

In this case, the gift was made in favour of a masonic lodge 'as a fund to build a suitable temple in Stafford'. The members of the lodge were both the trustees and the beneficiaries. The court held that the gift was an absolute one to the members of the lodge for the time being. The purpose stipulated was construed as '... simply an indication by the testator of the purpose for which he would like the money to be expended, without imposing any trust on the beneficiaries'.

> **Luxmoore J:** If the gift had been for the Staffordshire Knot Masonic Lodge, No 726, without anything further, there could have been no question as to its validity: the gift would have been a gift to that body of persons or that society, so that the members for the time being, acting in accordance with their constitution, could deal with the property as they thought fit. It is admitted by Mr Daynes that he could not have attacked the gift if it had been in that form. The attack made on the gift is because of the words that follow: 'as a fund to build a suitable temple in Stafford.' Mr Daynes has argued that that constitutes a binding trust, which limits the purpose for which the money left by the subject-matter of the gift could be used to the building of a suitable temple, and that, even supposing that the temple were built and sold by the lodge under a resolution of its members, even then the trustees for sale would still be impressed with a trust. The whole question is whether this is a trust or whether it is simply an indication by the testator of the purposes for which he would like the money to be expended, without imposing any trust on the beneficiary. It is to be observed that the gift is to the lodge, and that must mean

to the members for the time being. There is no separate trustee of the fund constituted. The beneficial interest in the fund is in the persons who are the trustees – in the body which is said to be the trustee – and, in those circumstances, where one finds the legal and equitable estate equally and co-extensively united in the same person or entity, the equitable interest merges in the legal interest, on the footing that a person cannot be a trustee for himself.

The decision of Farwell J, as he then was, in *Re Selous, Thomson v Selous*,[55] seems to me to lay down the governing principle which is applicable to this case. I therefore hold that this gift is a gift to the masonic lodge for the purpose of the lodge, and that the members of the lodge for the time being are at liberty to deal with it in accordance with their constitution in the ordinary way, in the way they think fit; in other words, they have complete domination over the fund. I think the decision of Byrne J, in *Re Clarke, Clarke v Clarke*,[56] also governs the present case. In that case, the testator had left a sum of money to the committee for the time being of the Corps of Commissionaires in London to aid in the purchase of their barracks, or in any other way beneficial to that corps. Byrne J, in dealing with that case, held that the gift, on the footing that it was a gift to the Corps of Commissionaires, was to aid in the purchase of their barracks and be also dealt with it having regard to the words that followed, but, when he was dealing with the first part of the gift, a gift to aid in the purchase of their barracks what he said was:

> The form of the gift here is: 'to the committee for the time being of the Corps of Commissionaires, to aid in the purchase of their barracks.' Now, it is true enough that 'to aid in the purchase of their barracks' rather points to something that is to last for a considerable time. I do not think I need go into the question of whether the fund for the creation of the barracks is, in fact, itself a charitable fund or not. I think there is considerable room for argument; but it does seem to me that all the members of the society constituted as this one is could, if they so pleased, and unless the building of the barracks be a charity, deal with the funds intended for building or with the buildings just as they please. If it is a charity they could not deal with them as they pleased, but then the gift is perfectly good. If it is not a charity they could deal with them as they please, because there is nothing to prevent all the members of the association joining together to dispose of the funds or of the barracks.

It seems to me that every word of that passage applies to the present case; and in this case I am satisfied that the members for the time being of the Staffordshire Knot Masonic Lodge, No 726, are entitled, under the gift which is made to that lodge, to deal with the fund in the ordinary way in which their constitution allows them to deal with their ordinary property.

(iii) Alternatively, the court may construe a gift to an association as a gift for the benefit of the members of the association, both present and future. In coming to this conclusion, the courts are required to consider the rules of

55 [1901] 1 Ch 921.

56 [1901] 2 Ch 110.

the association, its function, in addition to the intention of the donor. But, if the members of the society (in accordance with its constitution) are incapable of disposing of the assets of the society or are incapable of altering the rules of the association, the gift may fail for infringing the perpetuity rule.

Re Drummond [1914] 2 Ch 90, HC

In this case, a testator transferred his residuary estate to the 'Old Bradfordians Club, London (being a club for old boys of the Bradford Grammar School), to be utilised as the Committee of the Club should think best in the interests of the Club'. On the issue of the validity of the gift, the court held that the gift was valid since the committee was free to spend the capital in any manner it may consider fit. Eve J said that he could not hold that the residuary gift of realty and personalty for the Old Bradfordians Club was a gift to the members individually. There was, in his opinion, a trust and abundant authority for holding that it was not such a trust as would render the legacy void as tending to a perpetuity: see *In re Clarke*.[57] The legacy was not subject to any trust which would prevent the committee of the club from spending it in any manner they might decide for the benefit of the class intended. In his opinion, therefore, there was a valid gift to the club for such purposes as the committee should determine for the benefit of the old boys or members of the club.

However, in *Re Grant's Will Trusts*, a gift for the purposes of the Chertsey Labour Party Headquarters (non charitable unincorporated association) failed because the members of the local association did not control the society's property nor could they change the rules and obtain control, because the rules were subject to the approval of the National Executive Committee. Accordingly, the members of the local labour party did not have the power to liquidate the association and distribute its assets amongst themselves.

Re Grant's Will Trusts [1980] 1 WLR 360, HC

> **Vinelott J:** A convenient starting point is passage in the decision of Cross J in *Neville Estates Ltd v Madden*[58] which is often cited. He said:
>
>> The question of the construction and effect of gifts to or in trust for unincorporated association was recently considered by the Privy Council in *Leahy v AG for New South Wales*.[59] The position, as I understand it, is as follows. Such a gift may take effect in one or other of three quite different ways. In the first place, it may, on its true construction, be a gift to the members of the association at the relevant date as joint tenants, so that any member can sever his share and claim it whether or not he continues to be

57 [1901] 2 Ch 110.

58 [1962] Ch 832, p 849.

59 [1959] AC 457.

> a member of the association. Secondly, it may be a gift to the existing members not as joint tenants, but subject to their respective contractual rights and liabilities towards one another as members of the association. In such a case a member cannot sever his share. It would accrue to the other members on his death or resignation, even though such members include persons who become members after the gift took effect. If this is the effect of the gift, it will not be open to objection on the score of perpetuity or uncertainty unless there is something in its terms or circumstances or in the rules of the association which precludes the members at any given time from dividing the subject of the gift between them on the footing that they are solely entitled to it in equity. Thirdly, the terms or circumstances of the gift or the rules of the association may show that the property in question is not to be at the disposal of the members of the time being, but is to be held in trust for or applied for the purposes of the association as a quasi-corporate entity. In this case the gift will fail unless the association is a charitable body. If the gift is of the second class, ie, one which the members of the association for the time being are entitled to divide among themselves, then, even if the objects of the association are in themselves charitable, the gift would not, I think, be a charitable gift.

This statement (though it may require amplification in the light of subsequent authorities), is still, as I see it, an accurate statement of the law.

In a case in the first category, that is a gift which, on its true construction, is a gift to members of an association who take as joint tenants, any member being able to sever his share, the association is used in effect as a convenient label or definition of the class which is intended to take; but, the class being ascertained, each member takes as joint tenant free from any contractual fetter. So, for instance, a testator might give a legacy or share of residue to a dining or social club of which he had been a member with the intention of giving to each of the other members an interest as joint tenant, capable of being severed, in the subject matter of the gift. Cases within this category are relatively uncommon. A gift to an association will be more frequently found to fall within the second category. There the gift is to members of an association, but the property is given as an accretion to the funds of the association so that the property becomes subject to the contract (normally evidenced by the rules of the association) which govern the rights of the members *inter se*.

Each member is thus in a position to ensure that the subject matter of the gift is applied in accordance with the rules of the association. This category is well illustrated by the decision of Brightman J in *In re Recher's Will Trusts*.[60] There a share of residue was given to 'The Anti-Vivisection Society, 76 Victoria Street, London SW1'. The society in fact ceased to exist, being amalgamated with another society, during the testatrix's lifetime. Brightman J first examined whether the gift would have been valid if the society had continued to exist. He said:[61]

60 [1972] Ch 526.

61 *Ibid*, p 538.

A trust for non-charitable purposes, as distinct from a trust for individuals, is clearly void because there is no beneficiary. It does not, however, follow that persons cannot band themselves together as an association or society, pay subscriptions and validly devote their funds in pursuit of some lawful non-charitable purpose. An obvious example is a members' social club. But it is not essential that the members should only intend to secure direct personal advantages to themselves. The association may be one in which personal advantages to members are combined with the pursuit of some outside purpose. Or the association may be one which offers no personal benefit at all to the members, the funds of this association being applied exclusively to the pursuit of some outside purpose. Such an association of persons is bound, I would think, to have some sort of constitution; that is to say, the rights and liabilities of the members of the association would inevitably depend upon some form of contract *inter se*, usually evidenced by a set of rules. In the present case it appears to be clear that the life members, the ordinary members and the associate members of the London & Provincial society were bound together by a contract *inter se*. Any such member was entitled to the rights and subject to the liabilities defined by the rules. If the committee acted contrary to the rules, an individual member would be entitled to take proceedings in the courts to compel observance of the rules or to recover damages for any loss he had suffered as a result of the breach of contract. As and when a member paid his subscription to the association, he would be subjecting his money to the disposition and expenditure thereof laid down by the rules. That is to say, a member would be bound to permit, and entitled to require, the honorary trustees and other members of the society to deal with that subscription in accordance with the lawful directions of the committee. Those directions would include the expenditure of that subscription in accordance with the lawful directions of the committee. Those directions would include the expenditure of that subscription, as part of the general funds of the association, in furthering the objects of the association. The resultant situation, on analysis, is that the London & Provincial society represented an organisation of individuals bound together by a contract under which their subscriptions became, as it were, mandated towards a certain type of expenditure as adumbrated in rule 1. Just as the two parties to a bi-partite bargain can vary or terminate their contract by mutual assent, so it must follow that the life members, ordinary members and associate members of the London & Provincial society could, at any moment of time, by unanimous agreement (or by majority vote, if the rules so prescribe), vary or terminate their multi-partite contract. There would be no limit to the type of variation or termination to which all might agree. There is no private trust or trust for charitable purposes or other trust to hinder the process. It follows that if all members agreed, they could decide to wind up the London & Provincial society and divide the net assets among themselves beneficially. No one would have any *locus standi* to stop them so doing. The contract is the same as any other contract and concerns only those who are parties to it, that is to say, the members of the society.

> The funds of such an association may, of course, be derived not only from subscription of the contracting parties but also from donations from non-contracting parties and legacies from persons who have died. In the case of a donation which is not accompanied by any words which purport to impose a trust, it seems to me that the gift takes effect in favour of the existing members of the association as an accretion to the funds which are the subject matter of the contract which such members have made *inter se*, and falls to be dealt with in precisely the same way as the funds which the members themselves have subscribed. So, in the case of a legacy. In the absence of words which purport to impose a trust, the legacy is a gift to the members beneficially, not as joint tenants or as tenants in common so as to entitle each members to an immediate distributive share, but as an accretion to the funds which are the subject matter of the contract which the members have made *inter se*.

Two points should be noted. First, as Brightman J pointed out, it is immaterial in considering whether a gift falls within this category that the members of an association have not joined together for a social and recreational purpose, or to secure personal advantage, but in pursuit of some altruistic purpose. The motive which led the testator to make the gift may have been, indeed most frequently will have been, a desire to further that purpose. It may be said that in that sense the gift is made for the furtherance of the purpose. But the testator has chosen as the means of furthering the purpose to make a gift to an association formed for the pursuit of that purpose in the expectation that the subject matter of the gift will be so used, without imposing or attempting to impose any trust or obligation on the members, or the trustees, or the committee of the association. Indeed, there are cases where the gift has been expressed as a gift for the purposes, or one of the purposes, of the association, and nonetheless has been held not to impose any purported trust. Two examples will suffice. In *In re Turkington*,[62] the gift was expressed as a gift to the Staffordshire Knot Masonic Lodge, No 726 as a fund to build a suitable temple in Stafford. Luxmoore J construed the gift as a gift to the members of the lodge and construed the words '... to build a suitable temple in Stafford' as – and I cite from his judgment:[63]

> ... simply an indication by the testator of the purposes for which he would like the money to be expended, without imposing any trust on the beneficiary.

In the recent decision of Oliver J in *In re Lipinski's Will Trusts*,[64] the gift was:

> ... for the Hull Judeans (Maccabi) Association in memory of my late wife, to be used solely in work of constructing new buildings for the association and/or improvements to the said buildings.

Oliver J said:[65]

62 [1937] 4 All ER 501.

63 *Ibid*, p 504.

64 [1976] Ch 235.

65 *Ibid*, p 246.

> If a valid gift may be made to an unincorporated body as a simple accretion to the funds which are the subject matter of the contract which the members have made *inter se* – and *Neville Estate Ltd v Madden* and *In Recher's Will Trusts*[66] show that it may – I do not really see why such a gift, which specifies a purpose which is within the powers of the association and of which the members of the association are beneficiaries, should fail. Why are not the beneficiaries able to enforce the trust or, indeed, in the exercise of their contractual rights, to terminate the trust for their own benefit? Where the donee association is itself the beneficiary of the prescribed purpose, there seems to me to be the strongest argument in common sense for saying that the gift should be construed as an absolute one within the second category the more so where, if the purpose is carried out, the members can by appropriate action vest the resulting property in themselves, for here the trustees and the beneficiaries are the same persons.

As I read his judgment, Oliver J construed the gift as one under which the members of the association could have resolved to use the property for some other purpose, or, indeed, have divided it amongst themselves. He said:[67]

> There is an additional factor. This is a case in which, under the constitution of the association, the members could, by the appropriate majority, alter their constitution so as to provide, if they wished, for the division of the association's assets among themselves.

That leads to the second point. It must, as I see it, be a necessary characteristic of any gift within the second category that the members of the association can by an appropriate majority, if the rules so provide, or acting unanimously if they do not, alter their rules so as to provide that the funds, or part of them, should be applied for some new purpose, or even distributed amongst the members for their own benefit. For the validity of a gift within this category rests essentially upon the fact that the testator has set out to further a purpose by making a gift to the members of an association formed for the furtherance of that purpose in the expectation that although the members at the date when the gift takes effect will be free, by a majority if the rules so provide or acting unanimously if they do not, to dispose of the fund in any way they may think fit, they and any future members of the association will not in fact do so but will employ the property in the furtherance of the purpose of the association and will honour any special condition attached to the gift.

Turning to the third category, the testator may seek to further the purpose by giving a legacy to an association as a quasi-corporate entity, that is, to present and future members indefinitely, or by purporting to impose a trust. In the former case the gift will fail for perpetuity, unless confined within an appropriate period; though if it is so confined and if the members for the time being within the perpetuity period are free to alter the purposes for which the property is to be used and to distribute the income amongst themselves it will not, as I see it, fail upon any other ground. In the latter case, the gift will fail

66 [1972] Ch 526.

67 [1976] Ch 235, p 249.

upon the ground that the court cannot compel the use of the property in furtherance of a stated purpose unless, of course, the purpose is a charitable one.

As Viscount Simonds said in *Leahy v AG for New South Wales*:[68]

> If the words 'for the general purposes of the association' were held to import a trust, the question would have to be asked, what is the trust and who are the beneficiaries? A gift can be made to persons (including a corporation) but it cannot be made to a purpose or to an object: so also, a trust may be created for the benefit of persons as *cestuis que* trust, but not for a purpose or object unless the purpose or object be charitable. For a purpose or object cannot sue, but, if it be charitable, the Attorney General can sue to enforce it. (Upon this point something will be said later.) It is therefore by disregarding the words 'for the general purposes of the association' (which are assumed not to be charitable purposes) and treating the gift as an absolute gift to individuals that it can be sustained.

There are two cases in which, if this analysis is correct, the reason given for the decision, though possibly not the decision itself, are not well founded. First, there is a decision of Eve J in *In re Drummond*,[69] where the testator gave his residuary estate upon trust for the Old Bradfordians' Club, London, and by a codicil directed that the moneys:

> ... should be utilised by the club for such purpose as the committee for the time being might determine, the object and intent of the bequest being to benefit old boys of the Bradford Grammar School residing in London or members of the club, and to enable the committee, if possible, to acquire premises to be used as a clubhouse for the use of members, being old boys of Bradford Grammar School, with power to the committee to make rules and regulations as to residence in or use of the same, and further that it was the object of the bequest that the moneys should be utilised in founding scholarships or otherwise in such manner as the committee for the time being should think best in the interests of the club, or the school.

Eve J held that he could not say that the gift was a gift to the members of the club, but he said:[70]

> There was, in his opinion, a trust, but there was abundant authority for holding it was not such a trust as would render the legacy void as tending to a perpetuity: *In re Clarke*.[71] The legacy was not subject to any trust which would prevent the committee of the club from spending it in any manner they might decide for the benefit of the class intended. In his opinion, therefore, there was a valid gift to the club for such purpose as the committee should determine for the benefit of the old boys or members of the club.

68 [1959] AC 457, p 478.
69 [1914] 2 Ch 90.
70 *Ibid*, p 97.
71 [1901] 2 Ch 110.

The second is *In re Price*,[72] where Cohen J held that a gift of a share of residue to the Anthroposophical Society of Great Britain '... to be used at the discretion of the chairman and executive council of the society for carrying on the teachings of the founder, Dr Rudolf Steiner' was a valid gift. There the only question considered by the judge was whether the gift tended to a perpetuity, and having held that it did not he held the gift was a valid gift, without considering whether it was not void as creating a trust for a non-charitable purpose. It is to be observed that he said:[73] 'Had it been necessary for me to deal with this point, I would have inclined to uphold the gift to the Anthroposophical Society as a valid charitable gift.'

I have also been referred to the recent decision of Goff J in *In re Denley's Trust Deed*.[74] There by clause 2 of a trust deed trustees were given powers of sale over land held by them and were directed to hold the land while unsold during a defined perpetuity period on trust, that:

> ... (c) The same land shall be maintained and used as and for the purpose of a recreation or sports ground primarily for the benefit of the employees of the company and secondarily for the benefit of such other person or persons (if any) as the trustees may allow to use the same with power to the trustees from time to time to make any alterations they shall think proper with regard to the laying out of the ground or the preparation of parts thereof for special purposes or otherwise provided always that the trustees shall not at any time be bound to execute any works in or upon the said land or in or to any buildings erection or works thereon or otherwise to incur any expenses in relation to the said land unless funds shall be provided by the employees of the company or other users of the said land and there shall for the time being be in hand a sum which shall in the opinion of the trustees be available and sufficient to answer the cost of the said works or to meet such expenses.
>
> (d) The trustees shall have power from time to time to make rules and regulations with regard to the times and manner of user of the said land and subject to such rules and regulations as shall from time to time be made by the trustees the employees of the company shall be entitled to the use and enjoyment of the said land.

It was also provided:

> (j) If at any time the number of employees subscribing shall be less than 75% of the total number of employees at any given time (subscribing at the rate of two pence per week per man) or if the said land shall at any time cease to be required or to be used by the said employees as a sports ground or if the company should go into liquidation then the trustees shall notwithstanding anything that shall or may have been done or partly accomplished and subject to repayment to the company of the aforesaid sum of £400 with interest thereon convey the said land to the General Hospital Cheltenham or as it shall direct.

72 [1943] Ch 422.

73 *Ibid*, p 435.

74 [1969] 1 Ch 373.

Goff J, having held that the words 'secondarily for the benefit of such other person or persons if any as the trustees may allow to use the same', conferred on the trustees a power operating in partial defeasance of a trust in favour of the employees, held that the trust deed created a valid trust for the benefit of the employees, the benefit being the right to use the land subject to and in accordance with the rules made by the trustees. That case on a proper analysis, in my judgment, falls altogether outside the categories of gifts to unincorporated associations and purpose trusts. I can see no distinction in principle between a trust to permit a class defined by reference to employment to use and enjoy land in accordance with rules to be made at the discretion of trustees on the one hand, and, on the other hand, a trust to distribute income at the discretion of trustees amongst a class, defined by reference to, for example, relationship to the settlor. In both cases the benefit to be taken by any member of the class can apply to the court to compel the trustees to administer the trust in accordance with its terms. As Goff J pointed out:[75]

> The same kind of problem is equally capable of arising in the case of a trust to permit a number of persons – for example, all the unmarried children of a testator or settlor – to use or occupy a house or to have the use of certain chattels; nor can I assume that in such a case agreement between the parties concerned would be more likely, even if that be a sufficient distinction, yet no one would suggest, I fancy, that such a trust would be void.

Reading the gift in the will in the light of the rules governing the Chertsey and Walton CLP do not control the property, given by subscription or otherwise, to the CLP. The rules which govern the CLP are capable of being altered by an outside body which could direct an alteration under which the general committee of the CLP would be bound to transfer any property for the time being held for the benefit of the CLP to the National Labour Party for national purposes. The members of the Chertsey and Walton CLP could not alter the rules so as to make the property bequeathed by the testator applicable for some purpose other than that provided by the rules; nor could they direct that property to be divided amongst themselves beneficially.

Brightman J observed in *In re Recher's Will Trusts*:[76]

> It would astonish a layman to be told there was a difficulty in his giving a legacy to an unincorporated non-charitable society which he had, or could have, supported without trouble during his lifetime.

It is, in my judgment, impossible, in particular having regard to the gift over to the National Labour Party, to read the gift as a gift to the members of the National Labour Party at the testator's death, with a direction not amounting to a trust, for the National Party to permit it to be used by the Chertsey and Walton CLP for headquarters purposes.

That first ground is of itself conclusive, but there is another ground which reinforces this conclusion. The gift is not in terms a gift to the Chertsey and

75 [1969] 1 Ch 373, p 388.

76 [1972] Ch 526.

Walton CLP, but to the Labour Party property committee, who are to hold the property for the benefit of, that is in trust for, the Chertsey headquarters of the Chertsey and Walton CLP. The fact that a gift is a gift to trustees and not in terms to an unincorporated association, militates against construing it as a gift to the members of the association at the date when the gift takes effect, and against construing the words indicating the purposes for which the property is to be used as expressing the testator's intention or motive in making the gift and not as imposing any trust. This was, indeed, one of the considerations which led the Privy Council in *Leahy*'s case,[77] to hold that the gift '... upon trust for such Order of Nuns of the Catholic Church or the Christian Brothers as my executors and trustees should select would ... have been invalid'.

I am, therefore, compelled to the conclusion that the gift of the testator's estate fails, and that his estate accordingly devolves as on intestacy.

(iv) If a settlor transfers property on trust for an association, it is possible for the court to decide that on construction, the transfer is made on trust for the function or operation of the society and not for its members. If this construction is adopted the court may decide that the trust fails under the *Astor* principle, owing to the intention to promote a purpose. Such a construction would be exceptional. In addition, if the intention of the settlor is to set up an endowment in favour of the beneficiary (that is, the association), the gift may fail on the separate ground of the infringement of the perpetuity rule:

Leahy v Attorney General for New South Wales [1959] AC 457, PC

In this case, a testator devised a plot of land of 730 acres on trust for 'such order of nuns of the Catholic church or the Christian brothers as my trustees shall select'. This transfer was not wholly charitable, as it permitted the trustees to select cloistered nuns. Under Australian law, the trust was capable of being saved as a charitable donation by confining the gift to non-cloistered orders. The trustees, however, wanted to retain the freedom to give to cloistered nuns if possible. The question in issue was whether the trust in its existing form was valid as a non-charitable trust.

The court held that as a non-charitable gift, the trust failed because the testator's intention was clearly to create an endowment for the order of nuns (both present and future) and not for the benefit of individuals.

Viscount Simonds: In law a gift to such a society *simpliciter* (ie, where, to use the words of *Lord Parker in Bowman v Secular Society Ltd*,[78] neither the circumstances of the gift nor the directions given nor the objects expressed impose on the donee the character of a trustee) is nothing else than a gift to its members at the date of the gift as joint tenants or tenants in common. It is for this reason that the prudent conveyancer provides that a receipt by the treasurer or other proper officer of the recipient society for a legacy to the

77 [1959] AC 457.

78 [1917] AC 406, p 437.

society shall be a sufficient discharge to executors. If it were not so, the executors could only get a valid discharge by obtaining a receipt from every member. This must be qualified by saying that by their rules the members might have authorised one of themselves to receive a gift on behalf of them all.

It is in the light of this fundamental proposition that the statements, to which reference has been made, must be examined. What is meant when it is said that a gift is made to the individuals comprising the community and the words are added 'it is given to them for the benefit of the community'? If it is a gift to individuals, each of them is entitled to his distributive share (unless he has previously bound himself by the rules of the society that it shall be devoted to some other purpose). It is difficult to see what it added by the words 'for the benefit of the community'. If they are intended to import a trust, who are the beneficiaries? If the present members are the beneficiaries, the words add nothing and are meaningless. If some other persons or purposes are intended, the conclusion cannot be avoided that the gift is void. For it is uncertain, and beyond doubt tends to a perpetuity.

The question then appears to be whether, even if the gift to a selected Order of Nuns is *prima facie* a gift to the individual members of that Order, there are other considerations arising out of the terms of the will, or the nature of the society, its organisation and rules, or the subject matter of the gift which should lead the court to conclude that, though *prima facie* the gift is an absolute one (absolute both in quality of estate and in freedom from restriction) to individual nuns, yet it is invalid because it is in the nature of an endowment and tends to a perpetuity or for any other reason. This raises a problem which is not easy to solve, as the divergent opinions in the High Court indicate.

The *prima facie* validity of such a gift (by which term their Lordships intend a bequest or devise) is a convenient starting point for the examination of the relevant law. For as Lord Tomlin (sitting at first instance in the Chancery Division) said in *In re Ogden*,[79] a gift to a voluntary association of persons for the general purposes of the association is an absolute gift and *prima facie* a good gift. He was echoing the words of Lord Parker in *Bowman*'s case.[80] that a gift to an unincorporated association for the attainment of its purposes 'may ... be upheld as an absolute gift to its members'. These words must receive careful consideration, for it is to be noted that it is because the gift can be upheld as a gift to the individual members that it is valid, even though it is given for the general purposes of the association. If the words 'for the general purposes of the association' were held to import a trust, the question would have to be asked, what is the trust and who are the beneficiaries? A gift can be made to persons (including a corporation) but it cannot be made to a purpose or to an object: so also, a trust may be created for the benefit of persons as *cestuis que* trust but, if it be charitable, the Attorney General can sue to enforce it. (Upon this point something will be added later.) It is therefore by disregarding the words 'for the general purposes of the association' (which are assumed not to be charitable purposes) and treating the gift as an absolute gift to individuals

79 [1933] Ch 678; 49 TLR 341.

80 [1917] AC 406, p 422.

that it can be sustained. The same conclusion had been reached 50 years before in *Cocks v Manners*[81] where a bequest of a share of residue to the 'Dominican Convent at Carisbrooke (payable to the Superior for the time being)' was held a valid gift to the individual members of that society. In that case no difficulty was created by the addition of words which might suggest that the community as a whole, not its member individually, should be the beneficiary. So also with *In re Smith.*[82] There the bequest was to 'the society or institution known as the "Franciscan Friars of Clevedon County of Somerset" absolutely'. Joyce J had no difficulty in construing this as a gift individually to the small number of persons who had associated themselves together at Clevedon under monastic vows. Greater difficulty must be felt when the gift is in such terms that, though it is clearly not contemplated that the individual members shall divide it amongst themselves, yet it is *prima facie* a gift to the individuals and, there being nothing in the constitution of the society to prohibit it, they can dispose of it as they think fit. Of this type of case *In re Clarke,*[83] may be taken as an example. There the bequest was to the committee for the time being of the Corps of Commissionaires in London to aid in the purchase of their barracks or in any other way beneficial to the Corps. The judge (Byrne J) was able to uphold this as a valid gift on the ground that all the members of the association could join together to dispose of the funds or the barracks. He assumed (however little the testator may have intended it) that the gift was to the individual members in the name of the society or of the committee of the society. This might be regarded as an extreme case had it not been followed by *In re Drummond.*[84] In that case a testator devised and bequeathed his residuary real and personal estate to his trustees upon trust for sale and conversion and to stand possessed of the proceeds upon trust for the Old Bradfordians Club, London (being a club instituted by Bradford Grammar School old boys), the receipt of the treasurer for the time being of the club to be a sufficient discharge to his trustee. By a codicil the testator declared that he desired that the said moneys should be used by the club for such purpose as the committee for the time being might determine, the object and intent of the bequest being to benefit old boys of the Bradford Grammar School residing in London or members of the club and to enable the committee, if possible, to acquire premises to be used as a club house for the use of the members, with various other powers, including the founding of scholarships, as the committee for the time being should think best in the interest of the club of the school. Eve J said that he could not hold, as the result of the will and codicil together, that the residuary gift to the Old Bradfordians Club was a gift to the members individually, but there was in his opinion a trust and there was abundant authority for holding that it was not such a trust as would render the legacy void as tending to a perpetuity. He cited only *In re Clarke,* though other cases had been referred to in argument, and he ignored that Byrne J had been able to reach his conclusion in that case just because he regarded the gift as a gift to

81 (1871) LR 12 Eq 574.

82 [1914] 1 Ch 937; 30 TLR 411.

83 [1901] 2 Ch 110; 17 TLR 479.

84 [1914] 2 Ch 90; 30 TLR 429.

the individual members of the Corps who could together dispose of its assets as they thought fit. The judge added that the legacy was not subject to any trust which would prevent the committee of the club from spending it in any manner they might think fit for the benefit of the class intended. There was therefore a valid gift to the club for such purposes as the committee should determine for the old boys or members of the club. Their Lordships have thought it desirable to state *Drummond*'s case at some length both because it provides an interesting contrast to cases that will be referred to later and was itself an authority relied on by Farwell J in *In re Taylor*[85] and by Cohen J (as he then was) in *In re Price*.[86] In the former case the judge observed that *In re Clarke* showed that a gift to a fund for a voluntary body of persons may be perfectly valid unless the rules governing that fund or the purpose for which the institution was created prevent the members from dealing with it, both capital and income, in any way they please. It does not appear that he was making any distinction between a gift to a voluntary body of persons and a gift to a fund for such a body. Two other cases had in the meantime been decided to which reference may be made. In *In re Prevost*,[87] a testator had devised and bequeathed the whole of his residuary estate to the trustees of the London Library to be held by them upon trust for the general purposes of that institution, including the benefit of the staff. This case, too, came before Eve J, who held that the gift was valid upon the ground that it was a gift to the trustees of the library upon trust to be expended in carrying out the objects of the society according to its rules and that, inasmuch as there was nothing in the terms of the gift or in the rules of the library to prevent the expenditure of the corpus of the property, the gift did not fail for perpetuity. Here there was no question of a gift to an unincorporated society which was to be regarded as a gift to its individual members and capable of being dealt with by them as they should think fit. The judge nevertheless regarded it as falling within the class of case of which *Cocks v Manners*[88] was the leading authority. Nearer to *Cocks v Manners* and nearer too to the present case was *In re Ray's Will Trusts*.[89] In that case a testatrix, who was a nun in a convent, by her will gave all her property to the person who at the time of her death should be or should act as the abbess of the convent. The will was attested by two nuns belonging to the Convent, one of whom was subsequently elected abbess and held that office at the time of the death of the testatrix. The substantial question was whether the gift was invalidated by s 15 of the Wills Act 1837, and it was held not to be so invalidated because the gift was not to the abbess personally but in trust for and as an addition to the funds of the community. As to this Clauson J made the following observations which state the point at issue:

> Another perfectly lawful form of gift would be a gift of a legacy to the controlling officer of a society in his capacity as officer, to be dealt with as he would deal with other funds with which, as such officer of a voluntary

85 [1940] Ch 481; 56 TLR 588.

86 [1943] Ch 422; 59 TLR 367; [1943] 2 All ER 505.

87 [1930] Ch 520; 52 TLR 446.

88 (1871) LR 12 Eq 574.

89 [1936] Ch 520; 52 TLR 446.

> society, it would be his duty to deal. Again that would be a gift which the court will recognise as a good gift, subject only to this point, which sometimes causes difficulty, that if the frame of the gift indicates that the legacy is not to be used at once and immediately for the purposes of the voluntary society, but is to be set aside and invested and the income only to be used, the capital being preserved as an endowment of the voluntary society, the court will not give effect to the gift because it infringes the rule that no gift except a charitable gift is to be a perpetuity, and a gift thus to endow a voluntary society necessarily creates a perpetuity.

The cases that have been referred to (and many others might have been referred to in the courts of Australia, England and Ireland) are all cases in which gifts have been upheld as valid either on the ground that, where a society has been named as legatee, its members could demand that the gift should be dealt with as they should together think fit; or on the ground that a trust had been established (as in *In re Drummond*) which did not create a perpetuity. It will be sufficient to mention one only of the cases in which a different conclusion has been reached, before coming to a recent decision of the House of Lords which must be regarded as of paramount authority. In *Carne v Long*,[90] the testator devised his mansion-house after the death of his wife to the trustees of the Penzance Public Library to hold to them and their successors for ever for the use, benefit, maintenance and support of the said library. It appeared that the library was established and kept on foot by the subscriptions of certain inhabitants of Penzance, that the subscribers were elected by ballot and the library managed by officers chosen from amongst themselves by the subscribers, that the property in the books and everything else belonging to the library was vested in trustees for the subscribers and that it was provided that the institution should not be broken up so long as 10 members remained. It was urged that the gift was to a number or private persons and there were in truth no other beneficiaries. But Campbell LC rejected the plea in words which, often though they have been cited, will bear repetition:

> If the devise had been in favour of the existing members of the society, and they had been at liberty to dispose of the property as they might think fit, then it might, I think, have been a lawful disposition and not tending to a perpetuity. But looking to the language of the rules of this society, it is clear that the library was intended to be a perpetual institution, and the testator must be presumed to have known what the regulations were.

This was perhaps a clear case where both from the terms of the gift and the nature of the society a perpetuity was indicated.

Their Lordships must now turn to the recent case in *In re Macaulay's Estate*,[91] which appears to be reported only in a footnote to *In re Price*. There the gift was to the Folkestone Lodge of the Theosophical Society absolutely for the maintenance and improvement of the Theosophical Lodge at Folkestone. It was assumed that the donee, 'the Lodge,' was a body of persons. The decision of the House of Lords in July 1933, to which both Lord Buckmaster and Lord

90 (1860) 2 De GF & J 75.

91 [1943] Ch 435.

Tomlin were parties, was that the gift was invalid. A portion of Lord Buckmaster's speech may well be quoted. He had previously referred to *In re Drummond* and *Carne v Long*. 'A group of people,' he said:

> ... defined and bound together by rules and called by a distinctive name can be the subject of gift as well as any individual or incorporated body. The real question is what is the actual purpose for which the gift is made. There is no perpetuity if the gift is for the individual members for their own benefit, but that, I think, is clearly not the meaning of this gift. Nor again is there a perpetuity if the society is at liberty in accordance with the terms of the gift to spend both capital and income as they think fit ... If the gift is to be for the endowment of the society to be held as an endowment and the society is according to its form perpetual, the gift is to be for the endowment of the society to be held as an endowment and the society is according to its form perpetual, the gift is bad: but, if the gift is an immediate beneficial legacy, it is good.

In the result he held the gift for the maintenance and improvement of the Theosophical Lodge at Folkestone to be invalid. Their Lordships respectfully doubt whether the passage in Lord Buckmaster's speech in which he suggests the alternative ground of validity, viz, that the society is at liberty in accordance with the terms of the gift to spend both capital and income as they think fit, presents a true alternative. It is only because the society, that is, the individuals constituting it, are the beneficiaries, that they can dispose of the gift. Lord Tomlin came to the same conclusion. He found in the words of the will 'for the maintenance and improvement' a sufficient indication that it was the permanence of the Lodge at Folkestone that the testatrix was seeking to secure and this, he thought, necessarily involved endowment. Therefore, a perpetuity was created. A passage from the judgment of Lord Hanworth MR (which has been obtained form the records) may usefully be cited. He said:

> The problem may be stated in this way. If the gift is in truth to the present members of the society described by their society name so that they have the beneficial use of the property and can, if they please, alienate and put the proceeds in their own pocket, then there is a present gift to individuals which is good: but if the gift is intended for the good not only of the present but of future members so that the present members are in the position of trustees and have no right to appropriate the property or its proceeds for their personal benefit then the gift is invalid. It may be invalid by reason of there being a trust created, or it may be by reason of the terms that the period allowed by the rule against perpetuities would be exceeded.

It is not very clear what is intended by the dichotomy suggested in the last sentence of the citation, but the penultimate sentence goes to the root of the matter. At the risk of repetition their Lordships would point out that, if a gift is made to individuals, whether under their own names or in the name of their society, and the conclusion is reached that they are not intended to take beneficially, then they take as trustees. If so, it must be ascertained who are the beneficiaries. If at the death of the testator the class of beneficiaries is fixed and ascertained or ascertainable within the limit of the rule against perpetuities, all is well. If it is not so fixed and not so ascertainable the trust must fail. Of such a trust no better example could be found than a gift to an Order for the benefit of a community of nuns, once it is established that the community is not confined to living and ascertained persons. A wider question is opened if it appears that the trust is not for persons but for a non-charitable purpose. As has been pointed out, no one can enforce such a trust. What follows? *Ex hypothesi* the trustees are not themselves the beneficiaries yet the trust fund is in their hands, and they may or may not think fit to carry out their testator's wishes. If so, it would seem that the testator has imperfectly exercised his testamentary power; he has delegated it, for the disposal of his property lies with them, not with him. Accordingly, the subject matter of the gift will be undisposed of or fall into the residuary estate as the case may be. Their Lordships do not ignore that from this fundamental rule there has from time to time been a deviation: see, for example, *In re Dean*;[92] *In re Thompson*:[93] and that attempts have been made to explain or justify such cases (see, in particular, *Gray on the Rule against Perpetuities*).[94] But the rule as stated in *Morice v Bishop of Durham*[95] (*per* Sir William Grant MR[96] and *per* Lord Eldon) continues to supply the guiding principle. It may be difficult to reconcile this principle with the decision on *Drummond*'s case, but the judge did treat that case as governed by *Cocks v Manners* and, if so, must have assumed that when the will trustees had got the trust fund in their hands they could be compelled by the members of the Old Bradfordians Club or of the school to apply it as they thought fit. But it is difficult to see how he made such an assumption or arrived at the conclusion that no perpetuity had been created. No similar difficulty arises in regard to the observations of Lord Buckmaster and Lord Tomlin which have already been cited. The effect is the same, whether the gift is to A, B and C or to a society consisting of A, B and C and no others, upon such terms that they can spend both capital and income as they think fit.

It is significant of the fine distinction that are made in these cases that in *In re Price* the judge, to whose attention *In re Macaulay's Estate* had been called, held that a gift of a share of residue to the Anthroposophical Society in Great Britain 'to be used at the discretion of the Chairman and Executive Council of the Society for carrying on the teachings of the founder, Dr Rudolf Steiner', was a valid gift.

Before turning once more and finally to the terms of the present gift, their Lordships must mention the case of *In re Cain (Decd)*.[97] In that case Dean J has made an exhaustive examination of the relevant case law which must prove of great value in similar cases.

It must now be asked, then, whether in the present case there are sufficient indications to displace the *prima facie* conclusion that the gift made by clause 3 of the will is to the individual members of the selected Order of Nuns at the

92 [1889] 41 Ch D 552.

93 [1934] Ch 342.

94 4th edn, 1942, pp 776 *et seq*.

95 (1805) 10 Ves 522.

96 (1804) 9 Ves 399.

97 [1950] VLR 382.

> date of the testator's death so that they can together dispose of it as they think fit. It appears to their Lordships that such indications are ample.
>
> In the first place, it is not altogether irrelevant that the gift is in terms upon trust for a selected Order. It is true that this can in law be regarded as a trust in favour of each and every member of the Order. But at least the form of the gift is not to the members, and it may be questioned whether the testator understood the niceties of the law. In the second place, the members of the selected Order may be numerous, very numerous perhaps, and they may be spread over the world. If the gift is to the individuals it is to all the members who were living at the death of the testator, but only to them. It is not easy to believe that the testator intended an 'immediate beneficial legacy' (to use the words of Lord Buckmaster) to such a body of beneficiaries.
>
> In the third place, the subject matter of the gift cannot be ignored. It appears from the evidence filed in the suit that Elmslea is a grazing property of about 730 acres, with a furnished homestead containing 20 rooms and a number of outbuildings. With the greatest respect to those judges who have taken a different view, their Lordships do not find it possible to regard all the individual members of an Order as intended to become the beneficial owners of such a property. Little or no evidence has been given about the organisation and rules of the several Orders. But it is at least permissible to doubt whether it is a common feature of them, that all their members regard themselves or are to be regarded as having the capacity of (say) the Corps of Commissionaires (see *In re Clarke*) to put an end to their association and distribute its assets. On the contrary, it seems reasonably clear that, however little the testator understood the effect in law of a gift to an unincorporated body of persons by their society name, his intention was to create a trust, not merely for the benefit of the existing members of the selected Order, but for its benefit as a continuing society and for the furtherance of its work.

(v) Moreover, a transfer of property or trust for an association may be construed as a transfer on trust for the current members of the association and not on trust for purposes. In this event, provided that the rules of the association empower the members to liquidate and distribute the assets of the association, the perpetuity rule will not be infringed and the trust will be valid. The position remains the same even though the settlor may specify a purpose for which the fund may be used. Such stipulation may not be sufficient to prevent the members (beneficiaries) disposing of the property in any way they consider appropriate within the rules of the society:

Re Lipinski's Will Trust [1977] 1 All ER 33, HC

In this case, a testator transferred one half of his residuary estate to the Hull Judeans (Maccabi) Association, an unincorporated, non-charitable association, 'in memory of my late wife to be used 'solely' in the work of constructing new buildings for the association and/or improvements to the said buildings'. The question in issue was whether the trust was valid. The court held that the trust was for the benefit of ascertainable beneficiaries (the members at the date of the gift). On construction, the expression 'in memory of my late wife', was not intended as a permanent endowment but merely a tribute which the testator paid to his wife. The stipulation concerning the use of the funds was not intended to reduce the power of the members to dispose of the assets of the association in accordance with the rules of the association. For the same reason, the perpetuity rule was not infringed.

> **Oliver J:** I approach question 1 of the summons, therefore, on the footing that this is a gift to an unincorporated non-charitable association. Such a gift, if it is an absolute and beneficial one, is of course perfectly good: see, for instance, the gift to the Corps of Commissionaires in *Re Clarke*.[98] What I have to consider, however, is the effect of the specification by the testator of the purposes for which the legacy was to be applied. The principles applicable to this type of case were stated by Cross J in *Neville Estates Ltd v Madden*[99] and they are conveniently summarised in *Tudor on Charities*, where it is said:
>
>> In *Neville Estates Ltd v Madden* Cross J expressed the opinion (which is respectfully accepted as correct) that every such gift might, according to the actual words used, be construed in one of three quite different ways: (a) as a gift to the members of the association at the date of the gift as joint tenants so that any member could sever his share and claim it whether or not he continues to be a member; (b) as a gift to the member of the association at the date of the gift not as joint tenants, but subject to their contractual rights and liabilities towards one another as members of the association. In such a case a member cannot sever his share. It will accrue to the other members on his death or resignation, even though such members include persons who become members after the gift took effect. If this is the effect of the gift, it will not be open to objection on the score of perpetuity or uncertainty unless there is something in its terms or circumstances or in the rules of the association which precludes the members at any given time from dividing the subject of the gift between them on the footing that they are solely entitled to it in equity; (c) the terms or circumstances of the gift or the rules of the association may show that the property in question, ie, the subject of the gift – is not to be at the disposal of the members for the time being but is to be held in trust for or applied for the purposes of the association as a quasi-corporate entity. In this case the gift will fail unless the association is a charitable body.
>
> That summary may require, I think, a certain amount of qualification in the light of subsequent authority, but for present purposes I can adopt it as a working guide. Counsel for the next of kin argues that the gift in the present case clearly does not fall within the first category, and that the addition of the specific direction as to its employment by the association prevents it from falling into the second category. This is, therefore, he says, a purpose trust and fails both for that reason and because the purpose is perpetuitous. He relies on

98 [1901] 2 Ch 110.

99 [1961] 3 All ER 769; [1962] Ch 832.

this passage from the judgment of the Board in *Leahy v AG for New South Wales*:[100]

> If the words 'for the general purposes of the association' were held to import a trust, the question would have to be asked, what is the trust and who are the beneficiaries? A gift can be made to persons (including a corporation) but it cannot be made to a purpose or to an object: so also, a trust may be created for the benefit of persons as *cestuis que trustent* but not for a purpose or object unless the purpose or object be charitable. For a purpose or object cannot sue, but, if it be charitable, the Attorney General can sue to enforce it.

Counsel for the next of kin points out, first, that the gift is in memory of the testator's late wife (which, he says, suggests an intention to create a permanent memorial or endowment); secondly, that the gift is solely for a particular purpose (which would militate strongly against any suggestion that the donees could wind up and pocket the money themselves, even though their constitution may enable them to do so); and, thirdly, that the gift contemplates expenditure on 'improvements', which connotes a degree of continuity or permanence. All this, he says, shows that what the testator had in mind was a permanent endowment in memory of his late wife.

For my part, I think that very little turns on the testator's having expressed the gift as being in memory of his late wife. I see nothing in this expression which suggests any intention to create a permanent endowment. It indicates merely, I think, a tribute which the testator wished to pay, and it is not without significance that this selfsame tribute appeared in the earlier will in which he made an absolute and outright gift to the association. The evidential value of this in the context of a construction summons may be open to doubt, and I place no reliance on it. It does, however, seems to me that nothing is to be derived from these words beyond the fact that the testator wished the association to know that his bounty was a tribute to his late wife.

I accept, however, the submission of counsel for the next-of-kin that the designation of the sole purpose of the gift makes it impossible to construe the gift as one falling into the first of Cross J's categories, even if that were otherwise possible. But I am not impressed by the argument that the gift shows an intention of continuity. Counsel prays in aid *Re Macaulay*,[101] which is reported as a note to *Re Price*,[102] where the gift was for the 'maintenance and improvement of the Theosophical Lodge at Folkstone'. The House of Lords held that it failed for perpetuity, the donee being a non-charitable body. But it is clear from the speeches of both Lord Buckmaster and Lord Tomlin that their Lordships derived the intention of continuity from the reference to 'maintenance'. Here it is quite evident that the association was to be free to spend the capital of the legacy. As Lord Buckmaster said in *Re Macaulay*:

100 [1959] 2 All ER 300, p 307; [1959] AC 457, pp 478, 479.

101 [1943] Ch 435.

102 [1943] 2 All ER 505; [1943] Ch 422.

> In the first place it is clear that the mere fact that the beneficiary is an unincorporated society in no way affects the validity of the gift ... The real question is what is the actual purpose for which the gift is made. There is no perpetuity if the gift were for the individual members for their own benefit, but that, I think, is clearly not the meaning of this gift. Nor again is there a perpetuity if the society is at liberty, in accordance with the terms of the gift, to spend both capital and income as they think fit.

Re Price itself is authority for the proposition that a gift to an unincorporated non-charitable association for objects on which the association is at liberty to spend both capital and income will not fail for perpetuity, although the actual conclusion in that case has been criticised, the point that the trust there (the carrying on of the teachings of Rudolf Steiner) was a 'purpose trust' and thus unenforceable on that ground was not argued. It does not seem to me, therefore, that in the present case there is a valid ground for saying that the gift fails for perpetuity.

But that is not the end of the matter. If the gift were to the association *simpliciter*, it would, I think, clearly fall within the second category of Cross J's categories. At first sight, however, there appears to be a difficulty in arguing that the gift is to members of the association subject to their contractual rights *inter se* when there is a specific direction or limitation sought to be imposed on those contractual rights as to the manner in which the subject matter of the gift is to be dealt with. This, says counsel for the next of kin, is a pure 'purpose trust' and is invalid on that ground, quite apart from any question of perpetuity. I am not sure, however, that it is sufficient merely to demonstrate that a trust is a 'purpose' trust. With the greatest deference, I wonder whether the dichotomy postulated in the passage which I have referred to in the judgment of the Board in *Leahy v AG for New South Wales*[103] is not an oversimplification. Indeed, I am not convinced that it was intended as an exhaustive statement or to do more than indicate the broad division of trusts into those where there are ascertainable beneficiaries (whether for particular purposes or not) and trusts where there are none. Indeed, that this is the case, as it seems to me, is to be derived from a later passage[104] of the report, which is in these terms:

> At the risk of repetition, their Lordships would point out that, if a gift is made to individuals, whether under their own names or in the name of their society and the conclusion is reached that they are not intended to take beneficially, then they take as trustees. If so, it must be ascertained who are the beneficiaries. If, at the death of the testator, the class of beneficiaries is fixed and ascertained or ascertainable within the limit of the rule against perpetuities, all is well. If it is not so fixed and not so ascertainable, the trust must fail. Of such a trust, no better example could be found than a gift to an order for the benefit of a community of nuns once it is established that the community is not confined to living and ascertained persons. A wider question is opened if it appears that the trust

103 [1959] 2 All ER 300; [1959] AC 457.

104 *Ibid*, pp 310, 311; p 484.

> is not for persons but for a non-charitable purpose. As has been pointed out, no one can enforce such a trust. What follows? *Ex hypothesi*, the trustees are not themselves the beneficiaries yet the trust fund is in their hands, and they may, or may not, think fit to carry out their testator's wishes. If so, it would seem that the testator has imperfectly exercised his testamentary power; he has delegated it, for the disposal of his property lies with them, not with him. Accordingly, the subject matter of the gift will be undisposed of or fall into the residuary estate as the case may be.

There would seem to me to be, as a matter of common sense, a clear distinction between the case where a purpose is prescribed which is clearly intended for the benefit of ascertained or ascertainable beneficiaries, particularly where those beneficiaries have the power to make the capital their own, and the case where no beneficiary at all is intended (for instance, a memorial to a favourite pet) or where the beneficiaries are unascertainable (as, for instance, in *Re Price*). If a valid gift may be made to an unincorporated body as a simple accretion to the funds which are the subject matter of the contract which the members have made *inter se* and *Neville Estate v Madden*[105] and *Re Recher's Will Trusts*[106] show that it may. I do not really see why such a gift, which specifies a purpose which is within the powers of the unincorporated body and of which the members of that body are the beneficiaries, should fail. Why are not the beneficiaries able to enforce the trust or, indeed, in the exercise of their contractual rights, to terminate the trust for their own benefit? Where the donee body is itself the beneficiary of the prescribed purpose, there seems to me to be the strongest argument in common sense for saying that the gift should be construed as an absolute one within the second category, the more so where, if the purpose is carried out, the members can by appropriate action vest the resulting property in themselves, for here the trustees and the beneficiaries are the same persons.

Is such a distinction as I have suggested borne out by the authorities? The answer is, I think, 'Not in terms', until recently. But the cases appear to me to be at least consistent with this. For instance, *Re Clarke*[107] (the case of the Corps of Commissionaires), *Re Drummond*[108] (the case of the Old Bradfordians) and *Re Taylor*[109] (the case of the Midland Bank Staff Association), in all of which the testator had prescribed purposes for which the gift were to be used, and in all of which the gifts were upheld, were all cases where there were ascertainable beneficiaries; whereas in *Re Wood*[110] and *Leahy v AG for New South Wales* (where the gifts failed) there were none. *Re Price* is perhaps out of line, because there was no ascertained beneficiary and yet Cohen J was prepared to uphold the gift even on the supposition that (contrary to his own conclusion) the purpose was non-charitable. But, as I have mentioned, the point about the trust being a purpose trust was not argued before him.

105 [1961] 3 All ER 769; [1962] Ch 832.
106 [1971] 3 All ER 401; [1972] Ch 526.
107 [1901] 2 Ch 110.
108 [1914] 2 Ch 90; [1914–15] All ER 223.
109 [1940] 2 All ER 637; [1940] Ch 481.
110 [1949] 1 All ER 1100; [1949] Ch 498.

A striking case which seems to be not far from the present is *Re Turkington*,[111] where the gift was to a masonic lodge 'as a fund to build a suitable temple in Stafford'. The members of the lodge being both the trustees and the beneficiaries of the temple, Luxmoore J construed the gift as an absolute one to the members of the lodge for the time being. Directly in point is the more recent decision of Goff J in *Re Denley's Trust Deed*,[112] where the question arose as to the validity of a deed under which land was held by trustees as a sports ground:

> ... primarily for the benefit of the employees of [a particular] company and secondarily for the benefit of such other person or persons ... as the trustees may allow to use the same ...

The latter provision was construed by Goff J as a power and not a trust. The same deed conferred on the employees a right to use and enjoy the land subject to regulations made by the trustees. Goff J held that the rule against enforceability of non-charitable 'purpose or object' trusts was confined to those which were abstract or impersonal in nature where there was no beneficiary or *cestui que* trust. A trust which, though expressed as a purpose, was directly or indirectly for the benefit of an individual or individuals was valid provided that those individuals were ascertainable at any one time and the trust was not otherwise void for uncertainty. Goff J said:

> I think there may be a purpose or object trust, the carrying out of which would benefit an individual or individuals, where that benefit is so indirect or intangible or which is otherwise so framed as not to give those persons any *locus standi* to apply to the court to enforce the trust, in which case the beneficiary principle would, as it seems to me, apply to invalidate the trust, quite apart from any question of uncertainty or perpetuity. Such cases can be considered if and when they arise. The present is not, in my judgment, of that character, and it will be seen that clause 2(d) of the trust deed expressly states that, subject to any rules and regulations made by the trustees, the employees of the company shall be entitled to the use and enjoyment of the land. Apart from this possible exception, in my judgment the beneficiary principle of *Re Astor*,[113] which was approved in *Re Endacott (Decd), Corpe v Endacott*,[114] see particularly by Harman LJ,[115] is confined to purpose or object trusts which are abstract or impersonal. The objection is not that the trust is for a purpose or object *per se*, but that there is no beneficiary or *cestui que* trust. Where, then, the trust, though expressed as a purpose, is directly or indirectly for the benefit of an individual or individuals, it seems to me that it is in general outside the mischief of the beneficiary principle.

I respectfully adopt this, as it seems to me to accord both with authority and with common sense.

111 [1937] 4 All ER 501.

112 [1968] 3 All ER 65, p 67; [1969] 1 Ch 373, p 375.

113 [1952] 1 All ER 1067; [1952] Ch 534.

114 [1959] 3 All ER 562; [1960] Ch 232.

115 *Ibid*, p 570; p 250.

If this is the right principle, then on which side of the line does the present case fall? Counsel for the Attorney General has submitted in the course of his argument in favour of charity that the testator's express purpose 'solely in the work of constructing the new buildings for the Association' referred and could only refer to the youth centre project, which was the only project for the erection of buildings which was under consideration at the material time. If this is right, then the trust must, I think, fail, for it is quite clear that that project as ultimately conceived embraced not only the members of the association, but the whole Jewish community in Hull, and it would be difficult to argue that there was any ascertainable beneficiary. I do not, however, so construe the testator's intention. The evidence is that the testator knew the association's position and that he took a keen interest in it. I infer that he was kept informed of its current plans. The one thing that is quite clear from the minutes is that from 1965 right up to the testator's death there was great uncertainty about what was going to be done. There was a specific project for the purchase of a house in 1965. By early 1966 the youth centre was back in favour. By October 1966 it was being suggested that the association should stay where it was in its rented premises. The meeting of 21 March is, I think, very significant because it shows that it was again thinking in terms of its own exclusive building and that the patrons (of whom the testator was one) would donate the money when it was needed. At the date of the will, the association had rejected the youth centre plans and was contemplating again the purchase of premises of its own; and thereafter interest shifted to the community centre. I am unable to conclude that the testator had any specific building in mind; and, in my judgment, the reference to 'the ... buildings for the Association' means no more than whatever buildings the association may have or may choose to erect or acquire. The reference to improvements reflects, I think, the testator's contemplation that the association might purchase or might, at his death, already have purchased an existing structure which might require improvement or conversion, or even that it might, as had at one time been suggested, expend money in improving the premises which it rented from the Jewish Institute. The association was to have the legacy to spend in this way for the benefit of its members.

I have already said that, in my judgment, no question of perpetuity arises here, and accordingly the case appears to me to be one of the specification of a particular purpose for the benefit of ascertained beneficiaries, the members of the association for the time being. There is an additional factor. This is a case in which, under the constitution of the association, the members could, by the appropriate majority, alter their constitution so as to provide, if they wished, for the division of the association's assets among themselves. This has, I think, a significance. I have considered whether anything turns in this case on the testator's direction that the legacy shall be used 'solely' for one or other of the specified purposes. Counsel for the association has referred me to a number of cases where legacies have been bequeathed for particular purposes and in which the beneficiaries have been held entitled to override the purpose, even though expressed in mandatory terms.

Perhaps the most striking in the present context is the case of *Re Bowes*,[116] where money was directed to be laid out in the planting of trees on a settled estate. That was a 'purpose' trust, but there were ascertainable beneficiaries, the owners for the time being of the estate; and North J held that the persons entitled to the settled estate were entitled to have the money whether or not it was laid out as directed by the testator. He said:

> Then, the sole question is where this money is to go to. Of course, it is a perfectly good legacy. There is nothing illegal in the matter, and the direction to plant might easily be carried out; but it is not necessarily capable of being performed, because the owner of the estate might say he would not have any trees planted upon it at all. If that were the line he took, and he did not contend for anything more than that, the legacy would fail; but he says he does not refuse to have trees planted upon it; he is content that trees should be planted upon some part of it; but the legacy has not failed. If it were necessary to uphold it, the trees can be planted upon the whole of it until the fund is exhausted. Therefore, there is nothing illegal in the gift itself; but the owners of the estate now say 'It is a very disadvantageous way of spending this money; the money is to be spent for our benefit, and that of no one else; it was not intended for any purpose other than our benefit and that of the estate. That is no reason why it should be thrown away by doing what is not for our benefit, instead of being given to us, who want to have the enjoyment of it'. I think their contention is right. I think the fund is devoted to improving the estate, and improving the estate for the benefit of the persons who are absolutely entitled to it.

I can see no reason why the same reasoning should not apply in the present case simply because the beneficiary is an unincorporated non-charitable association. I do not think the fact that the testator has directed the application 'solely' for the specified purpose adds any legal force to the direction. The beneficiaries, the members of the association for the time being, are the persons who could enforce the purpose and they must, as it seems to me, be entitled not to enforce it or, indeed, to vary it.

Thus, it seems to me that whether one treats the gifts as a 'purpose' trust or as an absolute gift with a super added direction or, on the analogy of *Re Turkington* (1937), as a gift where the trustees and the beneficiaries are the same persons, all roads lead to the same conclusion.

In my judgment, the gift is a valid gift, and I will answer question 1 of the summons in sense (a).

THE MANDATE OR AGENCY PRINCIPLE

In some cases, a group of persons may join together in order to promote a common objective, without undertaking mutual duties or obligations, or

116 [1896] 1 Ch 507.

adopting rules which identify where control of the association lies. In these circumstances, the assembly of individuals will not be treated as an unincorporated association and the trust and contract rules mentioned above may not be appropriate to such bodies.

The problem arose in *Conservative and Unionist Central Office v Burrell*.[117] The issue concerned the legal status of the Conservative Party and whether it was liable to corporation tax on its profits (corporation tax is payable by incorporated and unincorporated associations, see ss 6(i); 8(i) and 832 of the Taxes Act 1988). The Court of Appeal decided that the party was not an unincorporated association but an amorphous combination of various elements. The nature of gifts to the party involved an accretion to the funds of the body which were to be dealt with in accordance with its rules, on analogy with *Re Recher*. The legal rights created in favour of donors and contributors exist on the basis of a mandate or agency. A contributor gives funds in effect to the treasurer of the party with a mandate to use the same in a particular way. If the monies were not spent the donor is entitled to demand the return of his monies, except if he agreed that his donation was irrevocable. If the officers within the party spend the funds on unauthorised activities, the donor or contributor retains a *locus standi* to sue for breach of fiduciary obligations based on general principles of agency law. Thus, apart from the fiduciary relationship inherent in the principal agent relationship, there is no trust relationship involved between donors and contributors on the one hand, and treasurer and other officers of the party.

Jean Warburton, in an article entitled 'The holding of property by unincorporated associations' [1985] Conv 318, examines a variety of methods of holding property by unincorporated associations. An unincorporated association, of course, has no separate legal entity. The association cannot own the legal and equitable interests in property. Accordingly, a person or persons must hold property on its behalf. Warburton considers the various methods of retaining such property and comments on the advantages and disadvantages of each method.

She writes:

> It has been said that there are three methods by which property can be held by an unincorporated association. First, property can be held by the members of the association as joint tenants. Secondly, property can be held by the members subject to their contractual rights and liabilities to each other as set out in the rules of the association; and thirdly, it can be held on trust for the purposes of the association. To these methods must be added the holding of property on trust for the members ... [I]t is often not clear which method is being used by an association, either because the rules are silent or because the relevant rule is not properly drafted.

117 [1982] 1 WLR 522.

SUPPLEMENTARY READING

Emery, C, 'Do we need a rule against perpetuities?' (1994) 57 MLR 602

Gravells, N, 'Gifts to unincorporated associations: where there is a will there is a way' (1977) 40 MLR 231

Lovell, P, 'Non-charitable purpose trusts – further reflection' [1970] Conv 77

McKay, L, 'Trusts for purposes' [1973] Conv 420

Rickett, C, 'Unincorporated associations and their dissolution' [1980] CLJ 88

Wilkinson, W, 'Your money or your life or lives in being' (1994) 58 Conv 92

CHAPTER 14

CHARITABLE TRUSTS: PRIVILEGES

A charitable trust is a public trust which is enforceable by the Attorney General on behalf of the Crown. The purpose of the trust is to benefit society as a whole or a sufficiently large section of the community so that it may be considered public. Charitable trusts may be treated as a species of purpose trusts, that is, trusts designed for the benefit of purposes such as the RSPCA; the promotion of cremation, the maintenance of the graves in a churchyard. However, in benefiting or furthering a purpose directly, the trust may result in individuals enjoying indirect benefits, such as the maintenance of schools or places of worship, or, the trust may be designed for the benefit of individuals pure and simple, such as the NSPCC, Oxfam, etc.

Private trusts, on the other hand, seek to benefit defined persons or narrower sections of society than charitable trusts and as we saw, a private purpose trust is void for lack of a person to enforce the trust.

Basically, charitable trusts are subject to the same rules as private trusts but as a result of the public nature of charitable trusts, such trusts enjoy a number of advantages over private trusts in respect of:

(a) certainty of objects;

(b) the perpetuity rule;

(c) the *cy-près* rule; and

(d) fiscal privileges.

Dingle v Turner [1972] AC 601, HL

> **Lord Cross of Chelsea:** In answering the question whether any given trust is a charitable trust the courts – as I see it – cannot avoid having regard to the fiscal privileges accorded to charities. As counsel for the Attorney General remarked in the course of argument the law of charity is bedevilled by the fact that charitable trusts enjoy two quite different sorts of privilege. On the one hand, they enjoy immunity from the laws against perpetuity and uncertainty and though individual potential beneficiaries cannot sue to enforce them, the public interest arising is protected by the Attorney General ... But that is not all. Charities automatically enjoy fiscal privileges which ... have become more and more important ...

CERTAINTY OF OBJECTS

Charitable trusts like private trusts are subject to a test of certainty of objects. We have already examined the tests for certainty of objects in respect of private trusts (fixed trust – *IRC v Broadway Cottages Ltd;* discretionary trusts – *McPhail v Doulton*). A charitable trust is subject to a unique test for certainty of objects, namely, whether the objects are exclusively charitable. In other words, if the trust funds may be used solely for charitable purposes the test will be satisfied. Indeed, it is unnecessary for the settlor or testator to specify the charitable objects which are intended to take the trust property, provided that the trust instrument manifests a clear intention to devote the funds for 'charitable purposes' the test will be satisfied. Thus, a gift 'on trust for charitable purposes' will satisfy this test. The Charity Commissioners and the court have the jurisdiction to establish a scheme for application of the funds (that is, the court will make an order indicating the specific charitable objects which will benefit).

In *Morice v Bishop of Durham,*[1] a fund was given upon trust for such objects of benevolence and liberality as the Bishop of Durham should approve, Sir William Grant in holding the gift to be invalid stated *obiter*:

> That it is a trust, unless it be of a charitable nature, too indefinite to be executed by this court, has not been, and cannot be, denied. There can be no trust, over the exercise of which this court will not assume a control; for an uncontrollable power of disposition would be ownership, and not trust. If there be a clear trust, but for uncertain objects, the property, that is the subject of the trust, is undisposed of; and the benefit of such trust must result to those, to whom the law gives the ownership, in default of disposition by the former owner. But this doctrine does not hold good with regard to trusts for charity. Every other trust must have a definite object. There must be somebody, in whose favour the court can decree performance. But it is now settled, upon authority, which it is too late to controvert, that, where a charitable purpose is expressed, however general, the bequest shall not fail on account of the uncertainty of the object: but the particular mode of application will be directed by the King in some cases, in others by this court.

In *Moggridge v Thackwell,*[2] the testatrix transferred her residuary personalty to a trustee in order to dispose of the same to such charities as he shall think fit. The trustee predeceased the testatrix. The House of Lords held that it was immaterial that the trustee had predeceased the testatrix, on the death of the testatrix the gift had vested for charitable purposes. The court approved a scheme for the disposition of the residuary estate.

---

1 (1804) 9 Ves 399.

2 (1807) 13 Ves 416.

On the other hand, if the trust funds are capable of being devoted for both charitable and non-charitable purposes the gift may be construed as being void as a charity.

***Inland Revenue Commissioners v City of Glasgow Police Athletic Association* [1953] 1 All ER 747, HL (Lords Normand, Morton of Henryton, Reid and Cohen; Lord Oaksey dissenting)**

The question in issue was whether the Police Athletic Association was a charitable body. The House of Lords held that on construction of the objects of the Association the body was not charitable for its primary object was the provision of recreation and sport for its members (non-charitable purposes) although the body had the incidental effect of promoting a charitable purpose namely, improving the efficiency of the Police Force.

> **Lord Normand:** The respondents' contention is that the association falls within the last category of Lord MacNaghten's classification of charities, and that it is established for charitable purposes only. In looking for the purposes for which it is established I begin with the rules. The objects set out in rule 2, to encourage and promote all forms of athletic sports and general pastimes, are not charitable purposes. But it will not do to stop there. The next step is to notice that the members' subscriptions are exclusively spent on their own sports and recreations. The question is what are the purposes for which the association is established, as shown by the rules, its activities and its relation to the police force and the public. And what the respondents must show in the circumstances of this case is that, so viewed objectively, the association is established for a public purpose, and that the private benefits to members are the unsought consequences of the pursuit of the public purpose, and can therefore be disregarded as incidental. That is a view which I cannot take. The private benefits to members are essential. The recreation of the members is an end in itself, and without its attainment the public purposes would never come into view. If the result of establishing the association had been that the members had, instead of being interested, found themselves involved in wearisome and lifeless activities, their efficiency would have suffered, the membership would have fallen off, and there would have been public detriment instead of public benefit. The private advantage of members is a purpose for which the association is established and it therefore cannot be said that this is an association established for a public charitable purpose only.
>
> In principle, therefore, if an association has two purposes, one charitable and the other not, and if the two purposes are such and so related that the non-charitable purpose cannot be regarded as incidental to the other, the association is not a body established for charitable purpose only.

Similarly, where the draftsman of the objects clause uses words such as 'charitable or benevolent purposes', the court may, on construction of the clause, decide that the word 'or' ought to be interpreted disjunctively with the effect that benevolent purposes which are not charitable are capable of taking. Accordingly, the gift will fail as a charity.

See *Chichester Diocesan Fund v Simpson*,[3] where a testator directed his executor to apply the residue of his estate 'for such charitable or benevolent objects' as they may select. The executors assumed that the clause created a valid charitable gift and distributed most of the funds to charitable bodies. The House of Lords held that the clause did not create charitable gifts.

> **Viscount Simon LC:** When, as here, the expression is 'charitable or benevolent', it is impossible to attribute to the word 'benevolent' an equal precision, or to regard the courts as able to decide with accuracy the ambit of the expression. It is not disputed that the words 'charitable' and 'benevolent' do not ordinarily mean the same thing; they overlap in the sense that each of them, as a matter of legal interpretation, covers some common ground, but also something which is not covered by the other. It appears to me that it inevitably follows that the phrase 'charitable or benevolent' occurring in a will must, in its ordinary context, be regarded as too vague to give the certainty necessary before such a provision can be supported or enforced.
>
> Then, is there any special context in this will which would justify a different interpretation? I have listened with much sympathy to the efforts to find one, but it does not seem to me, notwithstanding the opinion of the late Farwell J, that there is any context which might give to the impeached phrase a special meaning. The conjunction 'or' may be sometimes used to join two words whose meaning is the same, but, as the conjunction appears in this will, it seems to me to indicate a variation rather than an identity between the coupled conceptions. Its use is analogous in the present instance to its use in a phrase like 'the House of Lords or the House of Commons', rather than to its use in a phrase like 'the House of Lords or the Upper Chamber'.
>
> I regret that we have to arrive at such a conclusion, but we have no right to set at nought an established principle such as this in the construction of wills, and I, therefore, move the House to dismiss the appeal.

See, also, *AG v National Provincial and Union Bank of England*,[4] where a testator by his will directed his trustees to apply one fifth of his residuary estate 'for such patriotic purposes or objects and such charitable institution or institutions or charitable object or objects in the British Empire' as they should select in their absolute discretion.

The court held that the gift was not a valid charitable donation for the gift was not exclusively for charitable objects.

> **Viscount Cave LC:** It appears to me to be plain that the testator has, as Russell J said, given to his trustees four categories out of which they may select the objects of his benevolence; they may be either patriotic purposes, or patriotic objects, or charitable institutions or charitable objects – they may make a selection of objects from any one or more of those four categories. In short the words are to be read, not conjunctively, but disjunctively.

3 [1944] 2 All ER 60, HL (Viscount Simon LC, Lords Macmillan, Porter and Simonds; Lord Wright dissenting).

4 [1924] AC 262, HL (Viscount Cave, Viscount Haldane, Viscount Finlay, Lords Atkinson, and Sumner).

> It is said that 'patriotic purposes ... in the British Empire' means purposes directed to the public welfare of the British Empire, and so the trust falls within the fourth division of 'trusts for other purposes beneficial to the community, not falling under any of the preceding heads'.
>
> My Lords, it has been pointed out more than once, and particularly by the members of the Court of Appeal in *In re Macduff*,[5] that Lord Macnaghten did not mean that, all trusts for purposes beneficial to the community are charitable, but that there were certain charitable trusts which fell within that category; and accordingly to argue that because a trust is for a purpose beneficial to the community it is therefore a charitable trust is to turn round his sentence and to give it a different meaning. So here it is not enough to say that the trust in question is for public purposes beneficial to the community or for the public welfare; you must also show it to be a charitable trust. My Lords, I am not able to say that this is a charitable trust. The expression 'patriotic purposes' is vague and uncertain. Whether a purpose is patriotic or not is a matter of opinion; it depends to a great extent upon the state of mind of the person who uses the expression. An object which appears to some persons to be patriotic may legitimately appear to others not to fall within that description; and there is no fixed rule by which a court may determine whether a particular purpose is or is not patriotic. Further, it is not difficult to conceive purposes which to most persons would appear patriotic, but which are clearly not charitable within the legal meaning of that term. It seems to me therefore that the expression 'patriotic purposes' is one which cannot be said to bring the trust within the category of a charitable trust.

See, also, *AG of the Bahamas v Royal Trust Co.*

Attorney General of the Bahamas v Royal Trust Co [1986] 1 WLR 1001, PC (Lords Keith of Kinkel, Templeman, Griffiths, Oliver of Aylmerton and Goff of Chieveley)

A testator directed that the residue of his estate be held by trustees 'for any purpose for, and/or connected with the education and welfare of Bahamian children and young people ...'. The question in issue was whether the bequest was valid as a charitable trust.

The court held that the expression 'welfare' was a word of wide import and taken in the context of the expression 'education and welfare' was not restricted to educational prosperity of the objects. The gift was therefore void for charitable purposes.

> **Lord Oliver of Aylmerton:** In the end, however, the question is one of the construction of the particular dispositions of this testator and references to the construction placed upon different expressions in the wills of other testators, whilst perhaps useful as guidelines, are necessarily of limited assistance.
>
> It is true that in the instant case there are two and only two objects specified, so that, to that extent, it is the easier to adopt the conjunctive construction for

5 [1896] 2 Ch 451.

> which Mr Newman contends. But there are a number of formidable difficulties about this, and not least that it is not easy to imagine a purpose connected with the education of a child which is not also a purpose for the child's welfare. Thus, if 'welfare' is to be given any separate meaning at all it must be something different from and wider than mere education, for otherwise the word becomes otiose. Despite Mr Newman's helpful argument, their Lordships have been unable to discern any context from which the inference of subordination can be drawn and that difficulty would remain even if the trustees had been directed simply to apply the income for 'education and welfare'. The difficulty is, however, compounded by the additional and not unimportant words 'for any purposes for and/or connected with', for, if Mr Newman were otherwise able to link the word 'welfare' with the preceding word 'education' in a conjunctive sense, it would then be impossible to find a purpose which was connected with 'welfare' (used in this ancillary sense) which was not also 'connected with' education, so that the reference to 'welfare' would again become otiose. The point is not one which is susceptible of a great deal of elaboration and their Lordships need say no more than that they agree with Blake CJ and the Court of Appeal that the phrase 'education and welfare' in this will inevitably falls to be construed disjunctively. It follows that, for the reasons which were fully explored in the judgments in the courts below, and as is now conceded on the footing of a disjunctive construction, the trusts in paragraph (t) do not constitute valid charitable trusts.

The position would be different if the word 'or' is construed conjunctively or equivalent to the use of the word, 'and' in the phrase, 'charitable and benevolent'.

See *Re Best*.

Re Best [1904] 2 Ch 354, HC

The facts appear in the judgment.

> **Farwell J:** The words here are upon trust for 'such charitable and benevolent institutions' in the city of Birmingham, and so on, as the lord mayor shall determine, and it appears to me that the institutions, the objects of this gift, must be both charitable and benevolent. Having regard to the curiously technical meaning which has been given by the English court to the world 'charitable', I am not surprised that the testator should have desired that the institutions should be not only charitable, but should be also benevolent. There are certainly some which I think it would be difficult to say are benevolent, such as the distribution of the works of Joanna Southcote, although that was held to be charitable. I think the testator here intended that the institutions should be both charitable and benevolent; and I see no reason for reading the conjunction 'and' as 'or'.

In two circumstances, an objects clause which seeks to benefit both charitable and non-charitable purposes will not fail as a charity if:

(i) The non-charitable purpose is construed as being incidental to the main charitable purpose. This involves a question of construction for the courts to evaluate the importance of each class of objects.

In *Re Coxen* [1948] Ch 747, a testator bequeathed £200,000 to the Court of Aldermen of the City of London on trust to pay:

(a) £100 per annum to provide a dinner for the trustees when they met on trust business;

(b) one guinea to each trustee who attended the whole of the meeting; and

(c) the balance of the income for the benefit of orthopaedic hospitals.

The court held that the gifts as a whole were charitable. The principal aim of the trust was stated in (c) above, but purposes (a) and (b), despite being non-charitable, were designed to promote the principal aim.

> **Jenkins J:** I was referred to a number of cases in which the effect of dispositions of this type has been considered, and the result of the authorities appears to be: (a) that where the amount applicable to the non-charitable purpose can be quantified the trusts fail *quoad* that amount but take effect in favour of the charitable purpose as regards the remainder; (b) that where the amount applicable to the non-charitable purpose cannot be quantified the trusts both charitable and non-charitable wholly fail because it cannot in such a case be held that any ascertainable part of the fund or the income thereof is devoted to charity; (c) that there is an exception to the general rule in what are commonly known as the 'Tomb cases', that is to say, cases in which there is a primary trust to apply the income of a fund in perpetuity in the repair of a tomb not in a church, followed by a charitable trust in terms extending only in cases of this particular class being to ignore the invalid trust for the repair of the tomb and treat the whole income as devoted to the charitable purpose; and (d) that there is an exception of a more general character where as a matter of construction the gift to charity is a gift of the entire fund or income subject to the payments thereout required to give effect to the non-charitable purpose, in which case the amount set free by the failure of the non-charitable gift is caught by and passes under the charitable gift. See (for example) *Chapman v Brown;*[6] *In re Birkett;*[7] *In re Taylor;*[8] *In re Porter;*[9] *In re Dalziel;*[10] and *In re Parnell.*[11]
>
> I cannot but think that the court would find means to quantify the income applicable to the invalid trusts rather than divert from purposes admittedly charitable (say) 11 12ths of the income of a fund because a part of such income incapable of exact quantification but incapable also on any reasonable estimate of exceeding (say) one 12th is directed to be held on invalid trusts. On this aspect of the case I think the observations of Sir George Jessel MR in *In re Birkett* are much in point. It seems to me that he clearly would have found no difficulty in ascertaining a figure which the trust for paying guineas for attendances at committee meetings could 'under no conceivable estate' exceed,

6 (1801) 6 Ves 404.

7 (1878) 9 Ch D 576.

8 (1888) 58 LT 538.

9 [1925] Ch 746.

10 [1943] Ch 277.

11 [1944] Ch 107.

in confining any intestacy due to the invalidity of that trust and the dinner trust to the figure of annual income arrived at by adding his estimate for the former to the maximum set by the will for the latter, and in holding that the charitable trust took effect with respect to the remainder of the income.

It remains to consider whether the trusts in question are indeed invalid. In my judgment they are not. It is no doubt perfectly true that a trust simply to provide an annual dinner for the Court of Aldermen of the City of London is not charitable, any more than the trust to provide dinners for the Painters Stainers Company in *In re Barnett*[12] was charitable. It is also no doubt perfectly true that a trust simply to pay periodical guineas to selected aldermen of the City of London is not charitable. But the trusts here in question are of a different character. The annual dinner is to be provided for the Court of Aldermen as trustees of the charitable trust when they meet on the business of the trust, and the guineas are payable only to aldermen who are members of the committee administering the charity when they meet for that purpose, and subject to the express condition that a member in order to qualify for his guinea must be present during the whole of a given committee meeting. The annual dinner and the guinea attendance fees can therefore fairly be regarded as in the nature of remuneration in kind or in cash to the trustees and committee of management for their services in administering the affairs of the trust, and as I have already said the testator no doubt thought that these concrete expressions of his appreciation of the time and trouble involved would be conducive, in the ways mentioned above, to the attainment of his charitable purpose. In other words, his motive and object in providing for the annual dinner and the guinea attendance fees was, I think, clearly to benefit the charity and not the members for the time being of the Court of Aldermen or the members for the time being of the committee appointed by them.

It was suggested on behalf of the testator's brother that a trust for the payment of remuneration in perpetuity to the trustees for the time being of a charitable trust for their time and trouble in acting as such trustees is void as infringing the rule against perpetuities because such a trust involved a gift in perpetuity which is not *per se* charitable. No authority was cited to me for the proposition, which I decline to accept. Such a trust is in my view a charitable trust not because the recipients of the remuneration are objects of charity, but because the provision of the remuneration promotes the efficient management of the trust. The remuneration is in effect an expense of administration. If this were not so, grave difficulties would as it seems to me often arise in the administration of charitable trusts.

(ii) The court is able to apportion the fund and devote the charitable portion of the fund for charitable purposes. An apportionment will be ordered where part only of the fund is payable for charitable purposes and the other part for non-charitable purposes. In the absence of circumstances requiring a different division, the court will apply the maxim 'equality is equity' and order an equal division of the fund.

12 (1908) 24 TLR 788.

In *Salusbury v Denton*,[13] the testator's widow was subject to a duty to dispose, by will, of a fund so as to apply part of it for the benefit of 'a charity school or such other charitable endowment for the benefit of the poor (charitable purpose) ... and to dispose of the remainder among the testator's relatives'. The widow died without making the distribution. The court held that the fund would be divided into two equal parts.

> **Page Wood VC:** In *Down v Worrall*,[14] the testator left part of his residuary personal estate to his trustees to settle it either to or for charitable or pious purposes, at their discretion, or otherwise for the separate benefit of his sister and all or any of her children, in such manner as his trustees should think fit. And there it was held, that a sum which remained at the decease of the surviving trustee, and which had not been applied either to charitable purposes or for the benefit of the testator's sister and their children, was undisposed of, and belonged to the testator's next of kin. Now, whether that case can or cannot be reconciled with all the others on this subject, it is very clearly distinguished from the present: for it is one thing to direct a trustee to give a part of a fund to one set of objects, and the remainder to another, and it is a distinct thing to direct him to give 'either' to one set of objects 'or' to another. *Down v Worrall* was a case of the latter description. There the trustees could give all to either of the objects. This is a case of the former description. Here the trustee was bound to give a part to each. I am therefore of opinion, that even if the case of *Down v Worrall* can be reconciled with the other authorities on this subject, it cannot affect my decision in the case before me. Here there is a plain direction to the widow to give a part to the charitable purposes referred to in the will as she may think fit, and the remainder among the the testator's relatives as she may direct. And the widow having died without exercising that direction, the moiety in question must be divided equally.

See, also, *In re Clark*.

In re Clark, Bracey v Royal National Lifeboat Institution [1923] 2 Ch 407, Ch D

By his will, the testator disposed of his residuary estate as follows:

> I give and bequeath all the residue and remainder of my estate ... to: (a) such institution, society or nursing home ... as assist or provide for persons of moderate means such as clerks, governesses and others who may not be able or eligible to benefit under the National Health Insurance Act Old Age Pensions or other Act of a like character to have either surgical operations performed ... or medical treatment on payment of some moderate contribution; (b) the Royal National Lifeboat Institution; (c) the Lister Institute of Preventive Medicine; (d) and such other funds, charities and institutions as my executors in their absolute discretion shall think fit. And I direct that such residue shall be divided amongst the legatees named in paragraphs (a), (b), (c) and (d) in such shares and proportions as my trustees shall determine.

13 (1857) 3 K & J 529.

14 (1833) 1 My & K 561.

The executors issued a summons to determine whether the gifts within the residuary clause were valid or void.

The court held that the gift within class (d) was void for uncertainty and this one quarter share was taken by the next of kin. Subject to the executors exercising their power of distribution, the fund primarily vested in the objects in equal shares. As the power of distribution became void for uncertainty, the primary gift in favour of the objects in equal shares was allowed to take effect.

> **Romer J:** If therefore in any case the executors cannot refuse to allocate a part of the fund to charitable purposes they must either fix the part to be given to those purposes, or, if they do not exercise their discretion, the court would itself divide the fund between the charitable and the non-charitable objects. The court is therefore able either through the exercise by the executor of his discretion, or by itself dividing the fund, to ascertain the proportion of the fund to be devoted to charitable purposes, and, when once that has been done it appears to me that there is no difficulty in the court giving effect to the trusts affecting the parts so allocated to charitable objects.
>
> The principle of the matter appears to me to be this. Where a fund is directed to be held upon trust for charitable and non-charitable indefinite purposes indiscriminately, the trust fails by reason of the uncertainty as to the non-charitable objects of the trust and the consequent inability of the court to control its administration. Where on the other hand a fund is to be held upon trust for charitable and for non-charitable definite purposes there is no uncertainty as to the non-charitable objects of the trust and the trust is a valid one. In both these cases the question that has to be considered is whether the objects of the trust can or cannot be ascertained by the court. But in a case where a part of a fund is given for charitable purposes and the other part is given for non-charitable purposes, the first question that has to be considered is whether the court can ascertain what are the two parts. In such a case the court finds no difficulty where the non-charitable purposes are definite, as appears from *Salusbury v Denton*, and I cannot see that there is any greater difficulty where the non-charitable purposes are indefinite.
>
> The effect of the residuary gift appears to me to be that the testator has given his residue to the four objects or sets of objects (a), (b), (c) and (d), with power to his executors to determine in what shares and proportions the residue is to be divided between the four. There is no express gift in default of the executors so determining, but the rule of the court in such a case has been laid down as follows, 'If the instrument itself gives the property to a class, but gives a power to A to appoint in what shares and in what manner the members of that class shall take, the property vests, until the power is exercised, in all the members of the class, and they will all take in default of appointment': see *Lambert v Thwaites*.[15]
>
> I therefore arrive at the conclusion that each one of the four objects or sets of objects takes a share in residue, and in accordance with the principle that equality is equity (of which *Salusbury v Denton* is an example) they take it in

15 (1866) LR 2 Eq 151, p 155.

> equal shares. The result is that one-fourth of the residue is held upon trust for the charitable objects specified in heading (a), one fourth each for the Royal National Lifeboat Institution and the Lister Institute of Preventive Medicine and the remaining, one fourth in trust for the persons entitled to the testator's estate as upon an intestacy.

The position is different if the trustees are not under a duty to dispose of, at least, part of the fund for charitable purposes, but may legitimately dispose of the entirety for a non-charitable purpose or purposes. In such a case, there is no power vested in the court to apportion the fund and rescue the intended charitable gift. The entire gift will fail as a charitable donation.

Re Porter [1925] Ch 746, HC

A testator bequeathed a legacy of £10,000 to the trustees of a masonic temple in memory of his son. The income from the fund was required to be used primarily for the maintenance and upkeep of the temple and the balance (if any) to be applied in favour of any masonic charity the trustees should select. The question in issue concerned the validity of the gift.

The court held that the gift was void. The intended gift in favour of the private purpose failed as a trust for imperfect obligations and since there was no duty to transfer a part of the fund for charitable purposes the court had no power to sever the fund and distribute a part for charitable purposes.

> **Eve J:** In my opinion the test to be applied for the solution of this question is whether the gift of the surplus to charity is a gift of the whole income, or a gift of what (if anything) will remain after the void gift has been satisfied. Is the extent or amount of the primary gift sufficiently defined to enable the court to ascertain what was intended to be expended on it? If it is, then although the primary gift fails the corpus is not affected, and the whole income is applicable for charitable purposes, but if on the other hand the first object has not been so defined that the court can fix the amount required for it then the whole must fail, because the whole income might be applied for the first object. Nor do I think it is open to me, as Mr Vaisey suggested, to ascertain how much is required for the void object and to declare the gift of the balance valid. In *In re Birkett*,[16] Sir George Jessel, after stating that the case was a singular illustration of the way in which our law gets altered, proceeds as follows:
>
>> I have no hesitation in saying that, if there were no authorities, I should feel very little difficulty in deciding quite in a different way from that in which I am about to decide. If there were no authorities, I should hold, where there is a gift of money upon trust to apply a portion of the income for a definite purpose, and then to apply the surplus for another purpose, that, if the first purpose were sufficiently defined to enable you to ascertain the amount of the income that would be required for it, and that purpose failed through the gift being invalid, the gift of the surplus would be unaffected beyond the amount so ascertained.

16 (1878) 9 Ch D 576.

Then, as an instance, he says that if a man were to give the income of £10,000 a year in trust in the first place to keep a tombstone in repair, which could not exceed £20, and directed the residue of the £10,000 a year to go to a charity, he should assume that good law and common sense would concur in saying that the £20 gift was void, and that the £9,980 was well given to charity. That is what Mr Vaisey is asking me to do here, to hold that the gift of what is required for the masonic temple is void, but the rest is well given to the charities. But the Master of the Rolls adds:

> If the first object is not so defined that you can reasonably ascertain the amount required, the whole must fail, because you might then apply the whole of the gift to the first object; and therefore, if you could apply the whole of the income properly and fairly to the first object, there would, of course be no ascertainable residue.

Authority for that proposition is to be found in *Chapman v Brown*;[17] *Fisk v AG*;[18] and *In re Taylor*[19] On which side of the line does this particular case fall? The primary purpose of the gift is the maintenance and upkeep of the temple, and the whole income is charged with that trust, and as the expenditure is at the sole discretion of the trustees, they may properly apply the whole. Is the court entitled to control this discretion and to define the limits within which the expenditure ought to be kept? Could it, in fact, ascertain with any certainty whether there would be any surplus or not after providing for this primary object? I do not think it would be possible. The whole income might be properly so applied, and if so there would be no available surplus. It is clear that the testator contemplated that the whole might be required. In my opinion it results from this, that the ultimate gift for the charities is too indefinite and uncertain, and I must hold that the whole gift is void.

PERPETUITY

There are two aspects to the rule against perpetuities (see above, Chapter 13):

(i) the rule against remote vesting (that is, the rule against the vesting of a future interest outside the perpetuity period); and

(ii) the rule against excessive duration.

Charities are not subject to the rule against excessive duration. Indeed, many charities (schools and universities) continue indefinitely and rely heavily on perpetual donations. But charitable gifts like private gifts are subject to the rule against remote vesting, that is, the subject matter of the gift is required to vest in the charity within the perpetuity period.

17 (1801) 6 Ves 404.

18 (1867) 4 Eq 521.

19 (1888) 58 LT 538.

Re Lord Stratheden and Campbell [1894] 3 Ch 265, HC

In this case, an annuity of £100 was bequeathed to the Central London Rangers on the appointment of the next Lieutenant Colonel. Since this appointment might not have been made within the perpetuity period, the condition transgressed the rule and the gift was void. The position would have been different today following the introduction of the principle of 'wait and see' under the Perpetuities and Accumulations Act 1964.

> **Romer J:** If the gift in trust for charity is itself conditional upon a future and uncertain event, it is subject, in our judgment, to the same rules and principles as any other estate depending for its coming into existence upon a condition precedent. If the condition is never fulfilled, the estate never arises; if it is so remote and indefinite as to transgress the limits of time prescribed by the rules of law against perpetuities, the gift fails *ab initio*.
>
> The annuity is not to be paid except on the appointment of the next lieutenant-colonel; and if a lieutenant-colonel is not appointed, the annuity is not to commence or be paid. That being so, it being conditional, can I say that the condition must arise within the time that is prescribed by the rules of law against perpetuities? I am sorry to say I cannot.

But, even with respect to compliance with the perpetuity rule, the courts have introduced a concession for charities, namely, charitable unity. Once a gift has vested in a specific charity, then, subject to any express declarations to the contrary, it vests forever for charitable purposes. Accordingly, a gift which vests in one charity (A) with a gift over in favour of another charity (B) on the occurrence of an event will be valid even if the event occurs outside the perpetuity period. This concessionary rule does not apply to a gift over to a charity after a gift in favour of a non-charity. The normal rules as to vesting applies. Similarly, a gift over from a charity to a non-charity is caught by the rules as to remote vesting.

Re Bowen [1893] 2 Ch 491, HC

A testator who died in 1847 bequeathed a fund to trustees on trust to establish a day school in certain parishes in Wales. He directed that, if the Government established 'a general system of education', the trust shall cease and the surplus shall fall into residue. He appointed his three sisters to be his residuary legatees. Following the Elementary Education Act 1870, the trustees applied to the court to determine whether the legacies had fallen into residue. The court held that the bequest to the residuary legatees was void as infringing the perpetuity rule, consequently the gift was taken by the next of kin.

> **Stirling J:** The sums of £1,700 and £500 are bequeathed to trustees who are obviously selected with a view to the efficient administration of the charitable trusts created by the will, and were not intended by the testator to be charged with any duties as regards any other portion of his property. He directs the trustees named in the will, by means of the funds paid over to them by his

executors, to establish certain schools, 'and to continue the same schools for ever thereafter'. He contemplates a perpetual succession of trustees in whom the execution of the trusts is to be vested. I think that on the true construction of the will there is an immediate disposition in favour of charity in perpetuity, and not for any shorter period. That is followed by a gift over if at any time the Government should establish a general system of education; and under that gift over the residuary legatees take a future interest conditional on an event which need not necessarily occur within perpetuity limits. It follows that the gift over is bad; and, consequently, the summons must be dismissed.

The concessionary rule in respect of charitable unity is capable of abuse by some draftsmen who seek to benefit a non-charitable purpose for a period exceeding the perpetuity period. The technique that has been employed is to provide a fund for a charitable purpose (A) subject to a determining event, to the effect that, if a non-charitable purpose (B) is not fulfilled, a gift over in favour of another charity (C) will take effect. A prudent draftsman would be wise to ensure that no part of the charitable funds is used to promote the private purpose and that the stipulation concerning the non-charitable purpose does not impose an obligation on the trustees.

In Re Tyler [1891] 3 Ch 252, CA

A testator bequeathed £42,000 in stock to the trustees of the London Missionary Society (charity) with a gift over to the Blue Coat School, London (charity) if the Society failed to keep a family vault at Highgate Cemetery in good repair. The Society failed to maintain the vault. The question in issue was whether the gift over took effect. The court held that the gift over to the School took effect for the testator did not impose an obligation on the trustees to maintain the family vault (private purpose).

Lindley LJ: There is no doubt whatever that this condition, in one sense, tends to a perpetuity. The tomb or vault is to be kept in repair, and in repair for ever. There is also no doubt, and I think it is settled, that a gift of that kind cannot be supported as a charitable gift. But, then, this case is said to fall within an exception to the general rule relating to perpetuities. It is common knowledge that the rule as to perpetuities does not apply to property given to charities; and there are reasons why it should not. It is an exception to the general rule.

What is this gift when you come to look at it? It is a gift of £42,000 Russian 5% Stock to the *London Missionary Society*. What for? It is for their charitable purposes. It is a gift to them for the purposes for which they exist. Then there is a gift over to another charity in a given event – that is to say, the non-repair of the testator's vault. It seems to me to fall precisely within the principle on which *Christ's Hospital v Grainger* (1849) 1 Mac & G 460, was decided. A gift to a charity for charitable purposes, with a gift over on an event which may be beyond the ordinary limit of perpetuities to another charity – I cannot see that there is anything illegal in this.

This property is given to the London Missionary Society for their charitable purposes. Then, there is a condition that, if the tomb is not kept in order, the

> fund shall go over to another charity. That appears to me, both on principle and authority, to be valid; and I do not think it is a sufficient answer to say that such a conclusion is an inducement to do that which contravenes the law against perpetuities. There is nothing illegal in keeping up a tomb; on the contrary, it is a very laudable thing to do. It is a rule of law that you shall not tie up property in such a way as to infringe what we know as the law against perpetuities; but there is nothing illegal in what the testator has done here.

Contrast *Re Dalziel*.

Re Dalziel [1943] 2 All ER 656, HC

A testatrix gave the governors of St Bartholomew's Hospital £20,000 'subject to the condition that they shall use the income' for the upkeep and repair of a mausoleum in Highgate Cemetery with a gift over to another charity 'if they failed to do so'. The question in issue was whether the gift over took effect. The court held that the direction concerning the mausoleum created a trust of imperfect obligations which was void for infringing the perpetuity rule. The gift over was also void for infringing the perpetuity rule.

> **Cohen J** (the learned judge considered *Re Tyler* above, and continued): ... the question as to the effect of the imposition of the condition as to the upkeep of the tomb and of the gift over do not really arise; but as it was fully argued and the case may go to a higher court, it is right that I should state shortly the conclusions to which I have come on this point. The portion of the will which contains the condition is as follows:
>
> > I give this legacy upon and subject to the condition that the said Governors of St Bartholomew's Hospital shall use the income to arise from this legacy as far as is necessary for the upkeep of the said mausoleum in Highgate Cemetery and the garden surrounding the same that they shall keep the same in good repair and the inscriptions thereon legible and to rebuild the same when requisite and if they shall fail to carry out this request I give the said sum of £20,000 to [other charities named in the will to be selected by the trustees].
>
> As I construe this part of the clause, it does not merely impose a condition. If this were all it did, Mr Reid's argument, based on a passage in *Jarman on Wills*,[20] that it is a condition subsequent and, being void, the bequest is absolute, might be well founded. On the contrary, I think that it amounts to a direction that the income of the fund shall be applied in the first instance to the purposes therein defined in connection with the tomb. Unless, therefore, I can construe the clause as imposing only a moral obligation, I must find that the trusts, at any rate so far as they relate to the upkeep of the tomb, are bad.
>
> If the gift to charity is residuary upon a void gift, the general rule is that it fails if the court finds that the precedent gift is of unascertainable amount. But the charitable gift is valid if the subject matter needed for the precedent gift can be

20 *Jarman on Wills*, 7th edn, London: Sweet & Maxwell, p 1443.

reduced to certainty by means of an enquiry. The court will not direct an enquiry, and the gift to charity will fail, if it is manifestly impossible to determine the amount needed for the primary gift, or if it is clear that there would be nothing left over after satisfying it. I do not think it can be said here that the subject matter needed for the precedent 'void gift' can be reduced to a certainty by means of the inquiry, and I am fortified in this view by the decision of Eve J, in *Re Porter*.[21]

[The learned judge considered *Re Porter* and continued:]

I think the facts of this case are more like those in *Re Porter* than those in the hypothetical case put by Sir George Jessel, MR, in *Re Birkett*. The obligation as to rebuilding the tomb is not limited to rebuilding out of income, but would require the hospital, if necessary, to have recourse to capital. The void trust might, therefore, involve not only the whole income, but even the corpus. In my judgment, therefore, the gift fails *in toto*, for it is clear that, on the basis of the conclusion to which I have come, the event in which the gift over was to take effect, namely, the breach of an obligation by the hospital, can never occur.

CY-PRÈS DOCTRINE

This rule will be considered in more detail later. The advantage over private trusts is that when a gift vests in a charity then, subject to express provisions to the contrary, the gift vests for charitable purposes. Accordingly, the settlor (and his estate) is excluded from any implied reversionary interests by way of a resulting trust in the event of a failure of the charitable trust. Thus, the *cy-près* doctrine is an alternative to the resulting trust principle.

FISCAL PRIVILEGES

Dingle v Turner [1972] AC 601, HL

Lord Cross of Chelsea: ... charities automatically enjoy fiscal privileges which with the increasing burden of taxation have become more and more important in deciding that such and such a trust is a charitable trust, the court is endowing it with a substantial annual subsidy at the expense of the taxpayer. Indeed, claims for trusts to rank as charities are just as often challenged by the Revenue as by those who would take the fund if the trust was invalid. It is, of course, unfortunate that the recognition of any trust as a valid charitable trust should automatically attract fiscal privileges, for the question whether a trust to further some purpose is so little likely to benefit the public that it ought to be

21 [1925] Ch 746 (see above, p 589).

> declared invalid and the question whether it is likely to confer such great benefits on the public that it should enjoy fiscal immunity are really two quite different questions. The logical solution would be to separate them and to say that only some charities should enjoy fiscal privileges.

A variety of fiscal reliefs are enjoyed by both charitable bodies and members of the public (including companies) who donate funds for charitable purposes.

Tax reliefs available to charities

Under s 505 of the Taxes Act 1988, charities are exempt from income tax and corporation tax in respect of rents, interest, dividends and annual payments provided that the income is applied for charitable purposes only. In respect of income tax deducted at source by the payer, the recipient charity is entitled to recover the tax from the Inland Revenue.

In addition, income tax is not chargeable in respect of profits of a trade carried on by a charity if its profits are applied solely for the purposes of the charity and either the trade is exercised in the course of the actual carrying out of a primary purpose of the charity (for example, an educational charity running a school) or the work in connection with the trade is mainly carried out by beneficiaries of the charity (such as a charity set up to promote concerts arranged and conducted by its members). Where these conditions are not satisfied, it is common for charities to incorporate a company to carry out the work and for the company either to covenant its profits to the main charity or to pay its profits to the main charity by way of dividends. The effect is that the company does not pay corporation tax.

Under s 256 of the Taxation of Chargeable Gains Act 1992 (TCGA), charities do not pay capital gains tax on the disposal of assets, provided that the gain accruing to the charity is applicable and applied for charitable purposes.

Charities are also exempt from stamp duty on conveyances but are required to pay Value Added Tax on goods and services which are bought.

Tax reliefs in respect of donations to charities

A variety of reliefs are available in respect of donations to charities:

Gift aid

Section 25 of the Finance Act 1990 introduced a specific relief, 'gift aid', in respect of single gifts of money to charities. The scheme entitles individuals and companies to make gifts (qualifying donations) which do not exceed the total income of the individual or company for the relevant year. Such sums are paid to the charity after deduction of tax at the basic rate but the charity is entitled to recover from the Revenue the tax deducted. In order to constitute a qualifying donation, the gift to the charity is required to be made by a UK resident individual and also:

(a) the gift constitutes a sum of money not less than £250; and

(b) be subject to no repayment condition; and

(c) must not be a 'covenanted payment to charity (see below); and

(d) must not fall with the 'payroll deduction scheme' (see below, p 597); and

(e) must not be conditional or associated with an arrangement involving the acquisition of property by the charity, otherwise than by way of gift, from the donor or person connected with him.

Similar conditions are required to be satisfied by companies. Donors who are higher rate taxpayers are entitled to deduct the gross sum paid to the charity from their taxable income, and companies are entitled to treat gross payments to charities as charges on income.

Deeds of covenant

Covenanted donations to charities are an effective way for a donor to increase his tax reliefs provided that the deed is capable of lasting for more than three years (hence a four year covenant). The scheme is extended to companies and the effect of such payments is similar to the gift aid scheme above. Thus, higher rate taxpayers are entitled to relief on the gross payments to charities and companies are entitled to treat the payments as charges on income. There is no maximum or minimum sum which qualifies as covenanted payments to charities. A 'covenanted payment to charity' is defined in s 660(3) of the Taxes Act 1988, as 'a payment made under a covenant made otherwise than for consideration in money or money's worth in favour of a body of persons or trust established for charitable purposes only, whereby the like annual payments become payable for a period which may exceed three years and is not capable of earlier termination under any power exercisable without the consent of the persons for the time being entitled to the payments'.

The major difference between a 'covenanted donation to a charity' and 'gift aid' is that the former involves a continuing obligation whereas the latter assumes a single donation of a minimum sum of £250.

Deposit covenants are proving to be increasingly popular. These are deeds whereby the covenantor agrees to pay one quarter of a specified amount over a four year period. The full amount (less the basic rate of tax) is 'deposited' with the charity which releases or withdraws one-quarter of the specified sum per annum for charitable purposes. The Revenue have expressly stated that they will not challenge the legality of such arrangements.

Payroll deduction scheme: s 202 of the Taxes Act 1988

On the assumption that a recognised scheme is run by an employer, an employee is entitled to make tax effective donations to charities of their choice, up to a maximum of £900 during a year of assessment. The employees who wish to participate in the scheme authorise their employers to deduct the relevant sums from their salary, before calculating PAYE tax due, and pay over the sums to an agent approved by the Inland Revenue. The agent then pays the relevant sums to the appropriate charity. The donations by the employees are treated as deductible expenses. Thus, full relief is enjoyed by the donors even in respect of basic rate tax payers.

Relief from capital gains tax:
s 257 of the Taxation of Chargeable Gains Act 1992

A donation of a capital asset to a charity is treated as giving rise to no gain and no loss. Thus, the disposal proceeds are treated as equivalent to the allowable expenditure with the effect that no capital gains tax is payable.

Gifts by businesses to educational establishments:
s 84 of the Taxes Act 1988

Businesses (such as trades, professions, vocations or conducted by companies or unincorporated associations) are entitled to relief in respect of plant and machinery or other equipment (either manufactured, sold or used in the course of its trade) donated to educational establishments.

The business is allowed a deduction in respect of the full cost of producing or acquiring the subject matter of the gift.

Exemption from inheritance tax:
s 23 of the Inheritance Tax Act 1984

Gifts to charities without limit are exempt from inheritance tax.

VARIETIES OF FORMS OF CHARITABLE INSTITUTIONS

Charitable bodies may exist in a variety of forms.

Express trusts

An individual may promote a charitable purpose by donating funds *inter vivos* or by will to trustees on trust to fulfil a charitable objective. The purpose need not be specified by the donor for the test here is whether all the purposes are charitable, for example, a trust will be charitable if the donor disposes of property on trust for 'charitable and benevolent purposes'. It may be necessary for the trustees to draw up a scheme with the charity commissioners or the approval of the court in order to identify the specific charitable purposes which will benefit. It was pointed out earlier that charitable trusts are exempt from the test for certainty of objects applicable to private trusts.

Alternatively, the donor may identify the charitable objectives which he had in mind and if these are contested the courts will decide whether the purposes are indeed charitable.

Corporations

A great deal of charitable activities are conducted through corporations. Such bodies may be incorporated by royal charter such as the 'old' universities or by special statute under which many public institutions, such as hospitals and 'new' universities, have been created. In addition, many charitable bodies have been created under the Companies Act 1985 usually as private companies limited by guarantee. In these circumstances, there is no need for separate trustees, since the corporations are independent persons the property may vest directly in such bodies.

Unincorporated associations

A group of persons my join together in order to promote a charitable purpose. Such an association, unlike a corporation, has no separate existence. The funds are usually held by a committee in order to benefit the charitable purpose. In the absence of such a committee, the funds may be vested in the members of the association on trust for the charitable activity.

SUPPLEMENTARY READING

Gravells, N, 'Public purpose trusts' [1978] Conv 92

Norris, D, 'Charitable covenants: a benefit or not?' [1989] Conv 321

Parry, N, 'Imperfect charitable trust instruments: *AG of Bahamas v Royal Trust Co*' (1987) 131 SJ 1537

Stopforth, D, 'Charitable covenants by individuals' [1986] BTR 101

CHAPTER 15

CHARITABLE TRUSTS: DEFINITION AND PUBLIC BENEFIT

CHARITABLE PURPOSES

There is no statutory or judicial definition of a charity. It has been recognised that a definition of charities would create the undesirable effect of restricting the flexibility which currently exists in permitting the law to keep abreast with the changing needs of society. Most charitable bodies are required, under s 3(2) of the Charities Act 1993, to be registered with the Charity Commissioners. The effect of registration creates a conclusive presumption of charitable status, see s 4(1) of the Charities Act 1993. Section 3(2) enacts: 'There shall be entered in the register every charity not excepted by sub-s (5) below ...'

Section 4(1) provides: 'An institution shall for all purposes other than rectification of the register be conclusively presumed to be or to have been a charity at any time when it is or was on the register of charities.'

Ever since the passing of the Charitable Uses Act 1601 (sometimes referred to as the Statute of Elizabeth I), the courts developed the practice of referring to the preamble for guidance as to charitable purposes. The preamble contained a catalogue of purposes which at that time was regarded as charitable. It was not intended to constitute a definition of charities. The preamble has been expressly preserved by the Charities Act 1960 and s 38(4) endorses the purposes as stated in the preamble as charitable purposes thus: 'a reference to charity within the preamble shall be construed as a reference to charity within the UK law.'

The purposes included in the preamble to the 1601 Act are:

> The relief of aged, impotent and poor people; the maintenance of sick and maimed soldiers and mariners, schools of learning, free schools and scholars of universities; the repair of bridges, ports, havens, causeways, churches, sea banks and highways; the education and preferment of orphans; the relief, stock or maintenance of houses of correction; the marriages of poor maids; the supportation, aid and help of young tradesmen, handicapped men and persons decayed; the relief or redemption of prisoners or captives; and the aid or care of any poor inhabitants concerning the payments of fifteens, setting out of soldiers and other taxes.

Admittedly, the above mentioned purposes were of limited effect, but Lord MacNaghten, in *IRC v Pemsel*, classified charitable purposes within four categories as follows:

> ... charity in its legal sense comprises four principal divisions: trusts for relief of poverty; trusts for the advancement of education; trusts for the advancement of religion; and trusts for other purposes beneficial to the community.

Inland Revenue Commissioners v Pemsel [1891] AC 531, HL

> **Lord MacNaghten:** According to the law of England a technical meaning is attached to the word 'charity', and to the word 'charitable' in such expressions as 'charitable uses', 'charitable trusts', or 'charitable purposes', cannot, I think, be denied. The Court of Chancery has always regarded with peculiar favour those trusts of a public nature which, according to the doctrine of the court derived from the piety of early times, are considered to be charitable. Charitable uses or trusts form a distinct head of equity. Their distinctive position is made the more conspicuous by the circumstance that owing to their nature they are not obnoxious to the rule against perpetuities, while a gift in perpetuity not being a charity is void.
>
> No doubt the popular meaning of the words 'charity' and 'charitable' does not coincide with their legal meaning: and no doubt it is easy enough to collect from the books a few decisions which seem to push the doctrine of the court to the extreme, and to present a contrast between the two meanings in an aspect almost ludicrous. But still it is difficult to fix the point of divergence, and no one as yet has succeeded in defining the popular meaning of the word 'charity'. It would extend to every gift which the donor, with or without reason, might happen to think beneficial for the recipient; and to which he might be moved by the consideration that it was beyond the means of the object of his bounty to procure it for himself. That seems to me much too wide. If I may say so without offence, under conceivable circumstances, it might cover a trip to the Continent, or a box at the opera. 'Charity', in its legal sense, comprises four principal divisions: trusts for the relief of poverty; trusts for the advancement of education; trusts for the advancement of religion; and trusts for other purposes beneficial to the community, not falling under any of the preceding heads. The trusts last referred to are not the less charitable in the eye of the law, because incidentally they benefit the rich as well as the poor, as indeed, every charity that deserves the name must do either directly or indirectly. It seems to me that a person of education, at any rate, if he were speaking as the Act is speaking with reference to endowed charities, would include in the category educational and religious charities, as well as charities for the relief of the poor. Roughly speaking, I think he would exclude the fourth division. Even there it is difficult to draw the line. A layman would probably be amused if he were told that a gift to the Chancellor of the Exchequer for the benefit of the nation was a charity. Many people, I think, would consider a gift for the support of a lifeboat a charitable gift, though its object is not the advancement of religion, or the advancement of education, or the relief of the poor. And even a layman might take the same favourable view of a gratuitous supply of pure water for the benefit of a crowded neighbourhood. But after all, this is rather an academical discussion. If a gentleman of education, without legal training, were asked what is the meaning of 'a trust for charitable purposes', I think he would most probably reply, 'That sounds like a legal phrase. You had better ask a lawyer'.

In *McGovern v AG* (1981) (see below, p 648), Slade J commented on the preamble thus:

> **Slade J:** As a broad proposition, I would thus accept that a trust for the relief of human suffering and distress would *prima facie* be capable of being of a charitable nature, within the spirit and intendment of the preamble to the Statute of Elizabeth, as being what Hoffmann J termed a 'charity of compassion'. It does not, however, follow that a trust established for good compassionate purposes will necessarily qualify as a charity according to English law, any more than it necessarily follows that such a qualification will attach to a trust for the relief of poverty or for the advancement of education or for the advancement of religion. There are other requirements which it must still satisfy if it is to enjoy charitable status.

The approach of the courts is to treat the examples as stated in the preamble as a means of guidance in deciding on the validity of the relevant purpose. Two approaches may be discerned by the courts, namely:

Reasoning by analogy

The approach, here, is to ascertain whether a purpose has some resemblance to an example as stated in the preamble or to an earlier decided case which was considered charitable, for example, the provision of a crematorium was considered charitable by analogy with the repair of churches as stated in the preamble.

Per Lord Wilberforce in *Scottish Burial Reform and Cremation Society v City of Glasgow Corp*:

> What must be regarded is not the wording of the preamble, but the effect of decisions given by the courts as to its scope, decisions which have endeavoured to keep the law as to charities moving according as new social needs arise or old ones become obsolete or satisfied.

The question in issue in this case was whether the disposal of bodies by cremation was a charitable purpose. The House of Lords decided that the purpose was charitable.

***Scottish Burial Reform and Cremation Society v City of Glasgow Corp* [1968] AC 138, HL**

> **Lord Wilberforce:** Was, then the company established for charitable purposes only? I interpret its objects clause as meaning that the company was formed for a general and a particular purpose: the general purpose was to promote methods of disposal of the dead which should be inexpensive and sanitary; the particular purpose (to which the company has in fact confined itself) to promote the method known as cremation. It is this combination of purposes which has to be examined in order to see whether it satisfies the legal test of charitable purposes.
>
> On this subject, the law of England, though no doubt not very satisfactory and in need of rationalisation, is tolerably clear. The purposes in question, to be charitable, must be shown to be for the benefit of the public, or the community, in a sense or manner within the intendment of the preamble to the statute 43

Eliz 1, c 4. The latter requirement does not mean quite what it says; for it is now accepted that what must be regarded is not the wording of the preamble itself, but the effect of decisions given by the court as to its scope, decisions which have endeavoured to keep the law as to charities moving according as new social needs arise or old ones become obsolete or satisfied. Lord MacNaghten's grouping of the heads of recognised charity in *Pemsel*'s case is one that has proved to be of value and there are many problems which it solves. But three things may be said about it, which its author would surely not have denied: first that, since it is a classification of convenience, there may well be purposes which do not fit neatly into one or other of the headings; secondly, that the words used must not be given the force of a statute to be construed: and thirdly, that the law of charity is a moving subject which may well have evolved ever since 1891.

With this in mind, approach may be made to the question whether the provision of facilities for the disposal of human remains, whether, generally, in an inexpensive and sanitary manner, or, particularly, by cremation, can be considered as within the spirit of the statute. Decided cases help us, at any rate, to the point of showing that trusts for the repair or maintenance of burial grounds connected with a church are charitable. This was, if not decided, certainly assumed in *In re Vaughan*[1] as it had been earlier assumed in *AG v Blizard*.[2]

I regard, then, the provision of cremation services as falling naturally, and in their own right, within the spirit of the preamble.

One other point requires mention. The company makes charges for its services to enable it, in the words of the joint agreed minute, to fulfil effectively the objects for which it was formed. These charges, though apparently modest, are not shown to be higher or lower than those levied for other burial services. In my opinion, the fact that cremation is provided for a fee rather than gratuitously does not affect the charitable character of the company's activity, for that does not consist in the fact of providing financial relief but in the provision of services. That the charging for services for the achievement of a purpose which is in itself shown to be charitable does not destroy the charitable element was clearly, and, in my opinion, rightly, decided in *IRC v Falkirk Temperance Cafe Trust*[3] as well as in English authorities.

The spirit and intendment of the preamble

This approach is much wider than the previous approach. The courts decide if the purpose of the organisation is 'within the spirit and intendment' or 'within the equity' of the statute unhindered by the specific purposes as stated in the preamble. In other words, the examples enumerated in the preamble are treated as the context or 'flavour' in respect of which the purpose under

1 (1886) 33 Ch D 187.

2 (1855) 21 Beav 233.

3 [1927] SC 261; 11 TC 353.

scrutiny may be determined. In this respect it has been suggested that purposes beneficial to the community are *prima facie* charitable, unless it is a purpose which could not have been intended by the draftsman of the Statute of Elizabeth, assuming he was aware of the changes in society.

Incorporated Council of Law Reporting v Attorney General [1972] Ch 73, CA

> **Russell LJ:** ... if a purpose is shown to be so beneficial, or of such utility, it is *prima facie* charitable in law, but the courts have left open a line of retreat based on the equity of the statute in case they are faced with a purpose (for example, a political purpose) which could not have been within the contemplation of the statute even if the then legislators had been endowed with the gift of foresight into the circumstances of later centuries.

In this case, the court decided that the Council of Law Reporting was a charitable body on the grounds of advancing education and other purposes beneficial to society. The fact that the reports may be used by members of the legal profession for their 'personal gain' was incidental to the main charitable purposes.

> **Russell LJ:** The council was established for the purpose of recording in a reliably accurate manner the development and application of judge made law and of disseminating the knowledge of that law, its development and judicial application, in a way which is essential to the study of the law. The primary object of the council is, I think, confined to this purpose exclusively and is charitable. The subsidiary objects, such as printing and publishing statutes, the provision of a noting-up service and so forth, are ancillary to this primary object and do not detract from its exclusively charitable character. Indeed, the publication of statues of the realm is itself, I think, a charitable purpose for reasons analogous to those applicable to reporting judicial decisions.
>
> The fact that the council's publications can be regarded as a necessary part of a practising lawyer's equipment does not prevent the council from being established exclusively for charitable purposes. The practising lawyer and the judge must both be lifelong students in that field of scholarship for the study of which the Law Reports provide essential material and a necessary service. The benefit which the council confers upon members of the legal profession in making accurate reports available is that it facilitates the study and ascertainment of the law. It also helps the lawyer to earn his livelihood, but that is incidental to or consequential on the primary scholastic function of advancing and disseminating knowledge of the law, and does not detract from the knowledge of the law, and does not detract from the exclusively charitable character of the council's objects: compare *Royal College of Nursing v St Marylebone Borough Council*.[4]
>
> The service which publication of the Law Reports provides benefits not only those actively engaged in the practice and administration of the law but also those whose business it is to study and teach law academically, and many

4 [1959] 1 WLR 1077.

> others who need to study the law for the purposes of their trades, businesses, professions or affairs. In all these fields, however, the nature of the service is the same: it enables the reader to study, and by study to acquaint himself with and instruct himself in the law of this country. There is nothing here which negatives an exclusively charitable purpose.
>
> Although the objects of the council are commercial in the sense that the council exists to publish and sell its publications, they are unself-regarding. The members are prohibited from deriving any profit from the council's activities, and the council itself, although not debarred from making a profit out of its business, can only apply any such profit in the further pursuit of its objects. The council is consequently not prevented from being a charity by reason of any commercial element in its activities.
>
> I therefore reach the conclusion that the council is a body established 'exclusively for charitable purposes and is entitled to be registered under the Act of 1960'.

PUBLIC BENEFIT REQUIREMENT

It must not be assumed that all public trusts will be treated as charitable (see *Chichester Diocesan Fund v Simpson*, considered above, p 507). The criteria for charitable status are:

(i) the compliance with the public benefit test; and

(ii) the purpose is required to be within the 'spirit and intendment' of the preamble to the Charitable Uses Act 1601.

Public benefit

The public benefit test is used to distinguish a public trust from a private trust. A public trust is required to exist for the benefit of the public (the community) or an appreciable section of society, with the exception of trusts for the relief of poverty. The satisfaction of the test is a question of law for the judge to decide on the evidence submitted to him. The policy which underpins the test was laid down by Lord Simonds in *IRC v Baddeley.*

Inland Revenue Commissioners v Baddeley [1955] AC 572, HL

Lord Simonds held that there is a:

> ... distinction between a form of relief accorded to the whole community yet, by its very nature, advantageous only to a few and a form of relief accorded to a selected few out of a larger number equally willing and able to take advantage of it ... for example, a bridge which is available for all the public may undoubtedly be a charity and it is indifferent how many people use it. But confine its use to a selected number of persons, however numerous and

important; it is then clearly not a charity. It is not of general public utility; for it does not serve the public purpose which its nature qualifies it to serve.

In this case, a trust in favour of Methodists in West Ham and Leyton failed the public element test for the beneficiaries were composed of a class within a class.

Viscount Simonds: While no comprehensive definition of legal charity has been given either by the legislature or in judicial utterance, there is no limit to the number and diversity of the ways in which man will seek to benefit his fellowmen.

In the end, the question is: for what purposes may the trust property be used without trespassing beyond the language of the deed. I find that it may be used for promoting and encouraging all forms of such activities, that is, the provision of facilities for (*inter alia*) social and physical training and recreation, as are calculated to 'contribute to the health and well being of such persons'. My Lords, I do not think it would be possible to use language more comprehensive and more vague. I must dissent from the suggestion that a narrow meaning must be ascribed to the word 'social'; on the contrary, I find in its use confirmation of the impression that the whole provision makes upon me, that its purpose is to establish what is well enough called a community centre in which social intercourse and discreet festivity may go hand in hand with religious observance and instruction. No one will gainsay that this is a worthy object of benevolence, but it is another question whether it is a legal charity, and it appears to me that authority which is binding on your Lordships puts it beyond doubt that it is not. Here we are not concerned to consider whether a particular use to which the trust property may be put is a charitable use: that is a question upon which different minds might well come to different conclusions. On the contrary, we must ask whether the whole range of prescribed facilities or activities (call them what you will) is such as to permit uses which are not charitable: if it is, it is not such as trust as the court can execute and it must fail.

I submit to your Lordships that this trust must fail by reason of its vagueness and generality. The moral, social and physical well being of the community or any part of it is a laudable object of benevolence and philanthropy, but its ambit is far too wide to include only purposes which the law regards as charitable. I need not repeat what I have said in regard to the promotion of religious, social and physical well-being, except to emphasise that to hold the one a valid and the other an invalid trust would be to introduce the sort of refinement which I deplore.

It is, however, in my opinion, particularly important in cases falling within the fourth category to keep firmly in mind the necessity of the element of general public utility, and I would not relax this rule. For here is a slippery slope. In the case under appeal the intended beneficiaries are a class within a class; they are those of the inhabitants of a particular area who are members of a particular church: the area is comparatively large and populous and the members may be numerous. But, if this trust is charitable for them, does it cease to be charitable as the area narrows down and the numbers diminish? Suppose the area is confined to a single street and the beneficiaries to those whose creed

> commands few adherents: or suppose the class is one that is determined not by religious belief but by membership of a particular profession or by pursuit of a particular trade. These were considerations which influenced the House in the recent case of *Oppenheim*. That was a case of an educational trust, but I think that they have even greater weight in the case of trusts which by their nominal classification depend for their validity upon general public utility.
>
> More relevant is the case of *Verge v Somerville*.[5] In that case, in which the issue was as to the validity of a gift 'to the trustees of the Repatriation Fund or other similar fund for the benefit of New South Wales returned soldiers', Lord Wrenbury, delivering the judgment of the Judicial Committee, said:
>
> > ... that, to be a charity, a trust must be for the benefit of the community or of an appreciably important class of the community. The inhabitants of a parish or town or any particular class of such inhabitants, may, for instance, be the objects of such a gift, but private individuals, or a fluctuating body of private individuals, cannot.
>
> Here, my Lords, are two expressions: 'an appreciably important class of the community' and 'any particular class of such inhabitants,' to which in any case it is not easy to give a precise quantitative or qualitative meaning. But I think that in the consideration of them the difficulty has sometimes been increased by failing to observe the distinction, at which I hinted earlier in this opinion, between a form or relief extended to the whole community yet by its very nature advantageous only to the few and a form of relief accorded to a selected few out of a larger number equally willing and able to take advantage of it. Of the former type repatriated New South Wales soldiers would serve as a clear example. To me it would not seem arguable that they did not form an adequate class of the community for the purpose of that particular charity that was being established. It was with this type of case that Lord Wrenbury was dealing, and his words are apt to deal with it. Somewhat different considerations arise if the form, which the purporting charity takes, is something of general utility which is nevertheless made available not to the whole public but only to a selected body of the public an important class of the public it may be. For example, a bridge which is available for all the public may undoubtedly be a charity and it is indifferent how many people use it. But confine its use to a selected number or persons, however numerous and important: it is then clearly not a charity. It is not of general public utility: for it does not serve the public purpose which its nature qualifies it to serve.
>
> Bearing this distinction in mind, though I am well aware that in its application it may often be very difficult to draw the line between public and private purpose, I should in the present case conclude that a trust cannot qualify as a charity within the fourth class in *Income Tax Commissioners v Pemsel*[6] if the beneficiaries are a class of persons not only confined to a particular area but selected from within it by reference to a particular creed.

The public element test will not be satisfied if there is a personal nexus between the donor and the beneficiaries or between the beneficiaries themselves. The nexus may take the form of a 'blood' relationship.

---

5 [1924] AC 496; 40 TLR 279.

6 [1891] AC 531.

In *Re Compton*, the Court of Appeal decided that the test was not satisfied where the gift was on trust for the education of the children of three named relatives.

Re Compton [1945] Ch 123, CA

Lord Greene MR: In the first place it may be laid down as a universal rule that the law recognises no purpose as charitable unless it is of a public character. That is to say, a purpose must, in order to be charitable, be directed to the benefit of the community or a section of the community.

The proposition is true of all charitable gifts and is not confined to the fourth class in Lord MacNaghten's well known statement in *Pemsel*'s case. It does not, of course, mean that every gift that tends to the public benefit is necessarily charitable. What it does mean is that no gift can be charitable in the legal sense unless it is of the necessary public character. When I come to deal with the 'poor relations' cases it will be found that 150 years ago the essential nature of this requirement was perhaps not as clearly appreciated as it is today.

No definition of what is meant by a section of the public had, so far as I am aware, been laid down and I certainly do not propose to be the first to make the attempt to define it. In the case of many charitable gifts it is possible to identify the individuals who are to benefit or who at any given moment constitute the class from which the beneficiaries are to be selected. This circumstance does not, however, deprive the gift of its public character. Thus, if there is a gift to relieve the poor inhabitants of a parish the class to benefit is readily ascertainable. But they do not enjoy the benefit when they receive it by virtue of their character as individuals but by virtue of their membership of the specified class. In such a case the common quality which unites the potential beneficiaries into a class is essentially an impersonal one. It is definable by reference to what each has in common with the others and that is something into which their status as individuals does not enter. Persons claiming to belong to the class do so not because they are AB, CD, and EF, but because they are poor inhabitants of the parish. If in asserting their claim it were necessary for them to establish the fact that they were the individuals AB, CD, and EF, I cannot help thinking that, on principle, the gift ought not to be held to be a charitable gift since the introduction into their qualification of a purely personal element would deprive the gift of its necessary public character. It seems to me that the same principle ought to apply when the claimants, in order to establish their status, have to assert and prove, not that they themselves are AB, CD, and EF, but that they stand in some specified relationship to the individuals AB, CD, and EF, such as that of children or employees. In such a case too, a purely personal element enters into and is an essential part of the qualification which is defined by reference to something, that is, a personal relationship to individuals or an individual which is in its essence non-public. An example of this class of case is to be found in *Re Drummond*. The fact that in cases where a personal element forms an essential part of the qualification the numbers involved may be large does not appear to me to make any difference to the principle to be applied. Once that element is present numbers can make no difference. The gift is in such a case a personal gift. It may, of course fail for uncertainty, but that is neither here nor there. As a personal gift it will be obnoxious to the rule against perpetuities; but it would not have been affected by the Statute of Mortmain. I come to the conclusion, therefore, that on principle a gift under which the beneficiaries are defined by reference to a purely personal relationship to a named *propositus* cannot on principle be a valid charitable gift. And this, I think, must be the case whether the relationship be near or distant, whether it is limited to one generation or is extended to two or three or in perpetuity. The inherent vice of the personal element is present however long the chain and the claimant cannot avoid basing his claim upon it ...

I must now turn to the 'poor relations' cases on the analogy of which Cohen J felt himself constrained against his own view to decide against the appellants. The authorities relied on by the respondents are as follows. In *Isaac v Defriez*[7] the gifts were: (i) a gift of two annuities to the poorest relations of the testator and of his wife; (ii) a gift of income to one poor relation of the testator 'for a portion in the way of marriage and putting him or her out in the world'; and (iii) a similar gift of income to one poor relation of his wife. These gifts were upheld as good charitable gifts but no reasons for the decision appear in the report. This case was followed in *AG v Price*,[8] where the gift was in favour of the testator's 'poor kinsmen and kinswomen and their offspring and issue which shall dwell in the country of Brecon'. Sir William Grant MR, followed *Isaac v Defriez*, saying, at p 374:

> This seems to be just as much in the nature of a charitable bequest as that. It is to have perpetual continuance, in favour of a particular description of poor; and it not like an immediate bequest of a sum to be distributed among poor relations.

In an earlier case *White v White*,[9] Sir William Grant had supported as charitable a gift by a testatrix for the purpose of putting out 'our poor relations' apprentices. By a codicil this gift was confined to two families. Sir William Grant MR appears to have thought that the case was similar to an earlier case of his own where 'a great number of Jews were the objects'; such a gift would no doubt be regarded today as satisfying the well established rule that a good charitable gift must be for the benefit of the public or a section of public, a test which Sir William Grant does not appear to have taken into consideration in *White v White*, or in *AG v Price*. *Bernal v Bernal*[10] was a case in which the only matter decided arose on the construction of a will providing for poor relations who were in fact (as the will was construed) the male descendants of certain named relatives of the testator. It appears from the petition that the gift was established as a charity under a decree of 9 December 1728. What the reasons were for the decision in that behalf does not appear and when the question of construction was raised in 1838, before Lord Cottenham LC, there was no issue

7 (1754) 17 Ves 373.

8 (1810) 17 Ves 371.

9 (1802) 7 Ves 423.

10 (1838) 3 My & Cr 559.

as to the charitable nature of the bequest. In *Brown v Whalley*[11] where the gift was for the relations of the testator 'who might happen to be in want or fall to decay' the charity had similarly been established by a decree of the year 1763. In *Gillam v Taylor*[12] the gift was in favour of such of the lineal descendants of the testator's maternal uncle as they might severally need. This was held to be a good charitable gift on the authority of *Isaac v Defriez* and *AG v Price*. In *AG v Duke of Northumberland*[13] the will as construed by Sir George Jessel MR, was in favour of poor persons generally with a preference for poor persons who were kindred of the testator and in that respect the case was similar to the 'founder kin' cases. But Sir George Jessel in his judgment referred to *Isaac v Defriez* and *AG v Price* and did not cast any doubt upon the correctness of those decisions.

From this review of the authorities it will be seen that they are really all derived from *Isaac v Defriez* and *AG v Price*. We are invited to overrule them. I agree that they are far from satisfactory and the original decisions were given at a time when the public character of a charitable gift had not been as clearly laid down as it has been in more modern authorities. If the question of the validity of gifts of this character had come up for the first time in modern days I think that it would very likely have been decided differently since I should have thought that their purpose was a private family purpose lacking the necessary public character. But it is in my view quite impossible for this court to overrule these cases. Many trusts of this description have been carried on for generations upon the faith that they were charitable and many testators have no doubt been guided by these decisions. The cases must at this date be regarded as good law although they are, perhaps, anomalous.

In these circumstances the question arises whether we ought to extend the analogy of these decisions so as to cover a trust of the kind now in controversy. Taking the view which I do, as already expressed, I do not think that we are bound or ought to do so. There may perhaps be some special quality in gifts for the relief of poverty which places them in a class by themselves. It may, for instance, be that the relief of poverty is to be regarded as in itself so beneficial to the community that the fact that the gift is confined to a specified family can be disregarded: whereas in the case of an educational trust where there is no poverty qualification the funds may at any time be applied for the purpose of educating a member of the family for whose education ample means are already available, thus providing a purely personal benefit and one freed, incidentally, from the burden of income tax. Failing such a ground of distinction, I can only regard the poor relations cases as anomalous and I prefer to let them remain as such rather than to extend the anomaly to a different class of case.

This test was approved and extended to a personal nexus by way of contract in *Oppenheim v Tobacco Securities Trust Co Ltd*.

11 [1866] WN 386.

12 (1873) LR 16 Eq 581.

13 (1877) 7 Ch D 745.

Oppenheim v Tobacco Securities Trust Co Ltd [1951] AC 297, HL (Lords Simonds, Normand, Oaksey and Morton of Henryton; Lord MacDermott dissenting)

Trustees were directed to apply moneys in providing for the education of employees or ex-employees of British American Tobacco or any of its subsidiary companies. The employees numbered 110,000. The court held that in view of the personal nexus between the employees themselves (being employed by the same employer) the public element test was not satisfied.

> **Lord Simonds:** It is a clearly established principle of the law of charity that a trust is not charitable unless it is directed to the public benefit. This is sometimes stated in the proposition that it must benefit the community or a section of the community. Negatively, it is said that a trust is not charitable if it confers only private benefits. In the recent case of *Gilmour v Coats*[14] this principle was reasserted. It is easy to state and has been stated in a variety of ways, the earliest statement that I find being in *Jones v Williams*,[15] in which Lord Hardwicke LC is briefly reported as follows: 'Definition of charity: a gift to a general public use, which extends to the poor as well as to the rich ...' With a single, exception, to which I shall refer, this applies to all charities.
>
> If I may begin at the bottom of the scale, a trust established by a father for the education of his son is not a charity. The public element, as I will call it, is not supplied by the fact that from that son's education all may benefit. At the other end of the scale the establishment of a college or university is beyond doubt a charity. 'Schools of learning and free schools' and 'scholars of universities' are the very words of the preamble to the Statute of Elizabeth. So also the endowment of a college, university or school by the creation of scholarships or bursaries is a charity and none the less because competition may be limited to a particular class of persons.
>
> The difficulty arises where the trust is not for the benefit of any institution either then existing or by the terms of the trust to be brought into existence, but for the benefit of a class of persons at large. Then the question is whether that class of persons can be regarded as such a 'section of the community' as to satisfy the test of public benefit. These words 'section of the community' have no special sanctity, but they conveniently indicate first, that the possible (I emphasise the word 'possible') beneficiaries must not be numerically negligible, and secondly, that the quality which distinguishes them from other members of the community, so that they form by themselves a section of it, must be a quality which does not depend on their relationship to a particular individual. It is for this reason that a trust for the education of members of a family or, as in *In re Compton*,[16] of a number of families cannot be regarded as charitable. A group of persons may be numerous but, if the nexus between them is their personal relationship to a single *propositus* or to several *propositi*,

14 [1949] AC 426.

15 (1767) 2 Amb 651.

16 [1945] Ch 123, p 136.

they are neither the community nor a section of the community for charitable purposes.

I come, then, to the present case where the class of beneficiaries is numerous but the difficulty arises in regard to their common and distinguishing quality. That quality is being children of employees of one or other of a group of companies. I can make no distinction between children of employees and the employees themselves. In both cases the common quality is found in employment by particular employers. The latter of the two cases by which the Court of Appeal held itself to be bound, *In re Hobourn Aero Components Ltd's Air Raid Distress Fund*,[17] is a direct authority for saying that such a common quality does not constitute its possessors a section of the public for charitable purposes. In the former case, *In re Compton*,[18] Lord Greene MR had, by way of illustration, placed members of a family and employees of a particular employer on the same footing, finding neither in common kinship nor in common employment the sort of nexus which is sufficient. My Lords, I am so fully in agreement with what was said by Lord Greene in both cases and by my noble and learned friend, then Morton LJ, in the *Hobourn* case, that I am in danger of repeating without improving upon their words. No one who has been versed for many years in this difficult and very artificial branch of the law can be unaware of its illogicalities, but I join with my noble and learned friend in echoing the observations which he cited from the judgment of Russell LJ, in *In re Grove-Grady*,[19] and I agree with him that the decision in *In re Drummond*[20] 'imposed a very healthy check upon the extension of the legal definition of "charity"'. It appears to me that it would be an extension, for which there is no justification in principle or authority, to regard common employment as a quality which constitutes those employed a section of the community. It must not, I think, be forgotten that charitable institutions enjoy rare and increasing privileges, and that the claim to come within that privileged claim, should be clearly established.

Learned counsel for the appellant sought to fortify his case by pointing to the anomalies that would ensue from the rejection of his argument. For, he said, admittedly those who follow a profession or calling, clergymen, lawyers, colliers, tobacco-workers and so on, are a section of the public; how strange then it would be if, as in the case of railwaymen, those who follow a particular calling are all employed by one employer. Would a trust for the education of railwaymen be charitable, but a trust for the education of men employed on the railways by the Transport Board not be charitable? And what of service of the Crown whether in the civil service or the armed forces? Is there a difference between soldiers and soldiers of the King? My Lords, I am not impressed by this sort of argument and will consider on its merits, if the occasion should arise, the case where the description of the occupation and the employment is in effect the same, where in a word, if you know what a man does, you know

17 [1946] Ch 194.

18 [1945] Ch 123.

19 [1929] 1 Ch 557, p 582.

20 [1914] 2 Ch 90.

who employs him to do it. It is to me a far more cogent argument, as it was to my noble and learned friend in the *Hobourn* case, that if a section of the public is constituted by the personal relation of employment, it is impossible to say that it is not constituted by 1,000 as by 100,000 employees, and, if by 1,000, then by 100, and, if by 100, then by 10. I do not mean merely that there is a difficulty in drawing the line, though that too is significant: I have it also in mind that, though the actual number of employees at any one moment might be small, it might increase to any extent, just as, being large, it might decrease to any extent. If the number of employees is the test of validity, must the court take into account potential increase or decrease, and, if so, as at what date?

Lord MacDermott dissented and expressed the view that although the 'common link' test was of some value, it should not be an overriding consideration as the majority believed.

Lord MacDermott (dissenting): No definition of what constituted a sufficient section of the public for the purpose was applied, for none existed; and the process seems to have been one of reaching a conclusion on a general survey of the circumstances and considerations regarded as relevant rather than of making a single, conclusive test. The investigation left the course of the dividing line between what was and what was not a section of the community unexplored, and was concluded when it had gone far enough to establish to the satisfaction of the court whether or not the trust was public; and the decision as to that was, I think, very often reached by determining whether or not the trust was private.

If it is still permissible to conduct the present inquiry on these broad if imprecise lines, I would hold with the appellant. The numerical strength of the class is considerable on any showing. The employees concerned number over 110,000, and it may reasonably be assumed that the children, who constitute the class in question, are no fewer. The large size of the class is not, of course, decisive but in my view it cannot be left out of account when the problem is approached in this way. Then it must be observed that the *propositi* are not limited to those presently employed. They include former employees (not reckoned in the figure I have given) and are, therefore, a more stable category than would otherwise be the case. And, further, the employees concerned are not limited to those in the service of the 'British American Tobacco Co Ltd or any of its subsidiary or allied companies' – itself a description of great width – but include the employees, in the event of the British American Tobacco Co Ltd being reconstructed or merged on amalgamation, of the reconstructed or amalgamated company or any of its subsidiary companies. No doubt the settlors here had a special interest in the welfare of the class they described, but, apart from the fact that this may serve to explain the particular form of their bounty, I do not think it material to the question in hand. What is material, as I regard the matter, is that they have chosen to benefit a class which is, in fact, substantial in point of size and importance and have done so in a manner which, to my mind, manifests an intention to advance the interests of the class described as a class rather than as a collection or succession of particular individuals.

The test thus propounded focuses upon the common quality which unites those within the class concerned and asks whether that quality is essentially impersonal or essentially personal. If the former, the class will rank as a section of the public and the trust will have the element common to and necessary for all legal charities; but, if the latter, the trust will be private and not charitable. It is ... made clear beyond doubt in *In re Hobourn*, that in the opinion of the Court of Appeal employment by a designated employer must be regarded for this purpose as a personal and not as an impersonal bond of union. In this connection and as illustrating the discriminating character of what I may call 'the *Compton* test' reference should be made to that part of the judgment of the learned Master of the Rolls in *In re Hobourn* in which he speaks of the decision in *Hall v Derby Borough Urban Sanitary Authority*.[21] The passage runs thus:

> That related to a trust for railway servants. It is said that if a trust for railway servants can be a good charity, so too a trust for railway servants in the employment of a particular railway company is a good charity. That is not so. The reason, I think, is that in the one case the trust is for railway servants in general and in the other case it is for employees of a particular company, a fact which limits the potential beneficiaries to a class ascertained on a purely personal basis.

My Lords, I do not quarrel with the result arrived at in the *Compton* and *Hobourn* cases, and I do not doubt that the *Compton* test may often prove of value and lead to a correct determination. But, with the great respect due to those who have formulated this test, I find myself unable to regard it as a criterion of general applicability and conclusiveness. In the first place I see much difficulty in dividing the qualities or attributes, which may serve to bind human beings into classes, into two mutually exclusive groups, the one involving individual status and purely personal, the other disregarding such status and quite impersonal. As a task this seems to me no less baffling and elusive that the problem to which it is directed, namely, the determination of what is and what is not a section of the public for the purposes of this branch of the law. After all, what is more personal than poverty or blindness or ignorance? Yet none would deny that a gift for the education of the children of the poor or blind was charitable; and I doubt if there is any less certainty about the charitable nature of a gift for, say, the education of children who satisfy a specified examining body that they need and would benefit by a course of special instruction designed to remedy their educational defects.

But can any really fundamental distinction, as respects the personal or impersonal nature of the common link, be drawn between those employed, for example, by a particular university and those whom the same university has put in a certain category as the result of individual examination and assessment? Again, if the bond between those employed by a particular railway is purely personal, why should the bond between those who are employed as railway men be so essentially different? Is a distinction to be drawn in this respect between those who are employed in a particular industry before it is nationalised and those who are employed therein after that process

21 (1885) 16 QBD 163.

> has been completed and one employer has taken the place of many? Are miners in the service of the National Coal Board now in one category and miners at a particular pit or of a particular district in another? Is the relationship between those in the service of the Crown to be distinguished from that obtaining between those in the service of some other employer? Or, if not, are the children of, say, soldiers or civil servants to be regarded as not constituting a sufficient section of the public to make a trust for their education charitable?
>
> It was conceded in the course of the argument that, had the present trust been framed so as to provide for the education of the children of those engaged in the tobacco industry in a named county or town, it would have been a good charitable disposition, and that even though the class to be benefited would have been appreciably smaller and no more important than is the class here. That concession follows from what the Court of Appeal has said. But if it is sound and a personal or impersonal relationship remains the universal criterion I think it shows, no less the queries I have just raised in indicating some of the difficulties of the problem, that the *Compton* test is a very arbitrary and artificial rule. This leads me to the second difficulty that I have regarding it. If I understand it aright it necessarily makes the quantum of public benefit a consideration of little moment; the size of the class becomes immaterial and the need of its members and the public advantage of having that need met appear alike to be irrelevant. To my mind these are considerations of some account in the sphere of educational trusts for, as already indicated, I think the educational value and scope of the work actually to be done must have a bearing on the question of public benefit.

More recently, in *Dingle v Turner* (see below, p 627), Lord Cross of Chelsea gave his support for this view.

There is some support (albeit, slender) for the view that if the donor sets up a trust for the benefit of the public or a large section of the public, but expresses a preference (not amounting to an obligation) in favour of specified individuals the gift is capable of satisfying the public element test.

Re Koettgen's Will Trust [1954] Ch 252, HC

In this case, a trust was created for the promotion and furtherance of the commercial education of British born subjects subject to a direction that preference be given to the employees of a company. The court decided, on construction, that the preference was intended as permitting without obliging the trustees to consider distributing the property in favour of the employees.

> **Upjohn J:** In my judgment, it is at the stage when the primary class of eligible persons is ascertained that the question of the public nature of the trust arises and falls to be decided, and it seems to me that the will satisfies that requirement and that the trust is of a sufficiently public nature.
>
> If, when selecting from that primary class the trustees are directed to give a preference to the employees of the company and members of their families, that cannot affect the validity of the primary trust, it being quite uncertain

> whether such persons will exhaust in any year 75% of the trust fund. On the true construction of this will, that is not (as to 75%) primarily a trust for persons connected with John Batt & Co and the class of persons to benefit is not 'confined' to them, and in my judgment the trust contained in clauses 7 and 8 of the will of the testatrix is a valid charitable trust.

This decision has been criticised by Lord Radcliffe in the Privy Council in *Caffoor v Commissioners of Income Tax, Colombo* as being in essence an 'employee trust' and 'had edged very near to being inconsistent with the *Oppenheim* case.

In *Caffoor*'s case, the settlor executed a trust deed transferring property to trustees and directing that the income after the settlor's death be applied by the trustees in their discretion for, *inter alia*, 'the education, instruction or training in England or elsewhere of deserving youths of the Islamic faith'. The recipients of the benefits 'shall be selected from the following classes and in the following order: (i) male descendants of the grantor or any of his brothers and sisters failing whom, youths of the Islamic faith born of Muslim parents ... resident in Ceylon'. The question in issue was whether this gift was charitable.

The Privy Council held that the gift created a family trust and not a charitable trust for the trust lacked the public element necessary to create a charitable trust.

Caffoor v Commissioners of Income Tax, Colombo [1961] AC 584, PC

> **Lord Radcliffe** (after reciting the facts of *Re Koettgen's Will Trust*):[22] It was argued that the trust was one 'primarily for the benefit of the employees ... and their families', and that it was only if there were insufficient employees or members of their families that the public could come in as beneficiaries 'under the trust'. The judge says in his judgment that he did not accept that as the true construction of the clause in question; if he had accepted it, it is evident that he would have rejected the trust as a charitable bequest. The construction that he adopted as correct was that the primary class of beneficiaries consisted of persons without sufficient means to obtain commercial education at their own expense, and that the preference given merely amounted to a duty in the trustees to select employees or members of their families, if available, out of this primary class.
>
> It is not necessary for their Lordships to say whether they would have put the same construction on the will there in question as the judge did, or whether they regard the distinction which he made as ultimately maintainable. The decision edges very near to being inconsistent with *Oppenheim*'s case, but it is sufficient to say that the construction of the gift which was there adopted does not tally with the construction which their Lordships are bound to place upon the trust which is now before them.

22 [1954] Ch 252.

Inland Revenue Commissioners v Educational Grants Association Ltd [1967] 3 WLR 41, CA

The Court of Appeal in this case refused to follow *Re Koettgen* and Pennycuick J (whose decision was affirmed by the Court of Appeal) said:

> I find considerable difficulty in the *Re Koettgen* decision. I should have thought that a trust for the public with reference for a private class comprised in the public might be regarded as a trust for the application of income at the discretion of the trustees between charitable and non-charitable objects.

In this case, the association was established for the advancement of education by *inter alia* making grants to individuals. Its principal source of income consisted of annual sums paid to it by Metal Box Co. About 85% of the association's income during the relevant years was applied to the children of employees of Metal Box Ltd. The question in issue was whether the association was a charitable body.

The court held that the application of the high proportion of the income for the benefit of children connected with Metal Box Ltd was inconsistent with an application for charitable purposes.

> **Lord Denning MR:** A long line of cases show that a trust is for the public benefit if it is for the benefit of the community or a section of the community. The inhabitants of a named place are a section of the community for this purpose: but the employees of a particular company or companies are not. It follows that if a man sets up a trust for the children of the inhabitants of Bournville, it will be held to be for the public benefit. But if he sets up a trust for the children of those employed by Cadburys Ltd at Bournville, it will be held to be for private benefit. In each case the beneficiaries will probably be identical, but in point of law the one trust is charitable and the other is not. There is no logic in it. Lord MacDermott pointed that out in his dissenting speech in *Oppenheim v Tobacco Security Trust Ltd*.[23] Shorn of logic, we can only go by the decided cases. So we come to this: if funds are applied to found a closed scholarship, available only to boys from a particular school, those funds are applied for charitable purposes only. But if funds are applied to found a closed scholarship, available only to boys whose fathers are employed by a particular company, they are not applied for charitable purposes.
>
> Accepting this distinction, albeit illogical, I turn to the present case. The greater part of these funds were applied to advance the education of Metal Box children, that is, the children of employees or former employees of Metal Box. The judge said:
>
>> The inference is inescapable that this part of the association's income – that is, 75% to 85% – has been expended for the benefit of these children by virtue of a private characteristic; that is, their connection with Metal Box. Such an application is not by way of public benefit.

23 [1951] AC 297; [1951] 1 TLR 118; [1951] 1 All ER 31, HL.

> The remaining 15% to 25% was applied for children unconnected with Metal Box and for educational institutions. Those are conceded to be for the public benefit. So we have a case where part of the income was applied for private benefit of Metal Box children (which is not charitable) and the other part for the public benefit (which is charitable). In so far as the income was applied for Metal Box children, it was not applied for charitable purposes and does not qualify for exemption. The commissioners took a different view. They seem to have been influenced by the decision of Upjohn J in *In re Koettgen*'s *Will Trusts*,[24] but that has to be read subject to the doubts thrown out by Lord Radcliffe in *Caffoor v Income Tax Commissioner*.[25] In my opinion we are compelled by *Oppenheim*'s case to hold that the application for Metal Box Children was not charitable.

Similarly, in *IRC v Oldham Training and Enterprise Council*, the court decided that the Oldham Training and Enterprise Council which was set up to promote commerce for the benefit of the public in Oldham was not a charitable entity. The council lacked a public element.

***Inland Revenue Commissioners v Oldham Training and Enterprise Council* (1996) *The Times*, 10 October, HC**

Oldham TEC was incorporated in 1989 as a company limited by guarantee and not having a share capital. Its activities, as authorised by its memorandum of association, were classified under three categories, namely: (i) enterprise services, including information and advice, diagnostic services and business skills training; (ii) business startup services, including a free enterprise training programme for anyone thinking of setting up a new business, and cash payments of up to £2,800 for any individual in lieu of unemployment and social security benefits; and (iii) training, both of the young and re-training of the unemployed. These services were generally provided by private sector firms, universities and colleges. The costs were shared by recipient businesses and Oldham TEC. The question in issue was whether the company was established for charitable purposes within s 506 of the Taxes Act 1988 and exempt from corporation tax. The status of some 80 other training and enterprise councils with identical objects clauses was dependent on this decision. It was submitted on behalf of the council that, on construction of the objects clause, the main purpose of the TEC permitted the application of its funds solely for charitable purposes. Any non-charitable purposes were purely incidental to the main charitable purpose.

The High Court decided in favour of the Revenue on the ground that the objects clause of the company promoted primarily the interests of individuals and other entities engaged in trade, commerce or enterprise, as opposed to a public benefit. Accordingly, the TEC was not a charitable company.

24 [1954] Ch 252; [1954] 2 WLR 166; [1954] 1 All ER 581.

25 [1961] AC 584; [1961] 2 WLR 794, PC.

In essence, the public element test will be satisfied if:

(i) the beneficiaries are not numerically negligible; and

(ii) the beneficiaries have no 'link' in contract or in blood between themselves or with a narrow group of individuals.

Per Lord Simonds in *Oppenheim*'s case:

> To constitute a section of the public, the possible beneficiaries must not be numerically negligible and secondly, the quality which distinguishes them from other members of the community so that they form by themselves a section of it must be a quality which does not depend on their relationship to a particular individual ... A group of persons may be numerous but, if the nexus between them is their personal relationship to a single *propositus* or to several *propositii* they are neither the community nor a section of the community for charitable purposes.

Subject to the absence of a personal nexus between the beneficiaries and/or a limited class of individuals, the issue whether or not the beneficiaries constitute a section of the public in order to satisfy the public element test is a question of degree. There are many decisions which appear to be inconsistent with each other.

In *Gilmour v Coats*, the court decided that a gift to a Carmelite convent which consisted of a community of 20 cloistered nuns, who devoted themselves to prayer and contemplation and engaged in no work outside the convent, did not satisfy the public element test.

Gilmour v Coats and Others [1949] 1 All ER 848, HL (Lords Simonds, du Parcq, Normand, Reid and Morton of Henryton)

> **Lord Simonds:** The nuns take vows of perpetual poverty, chastity and obedience and live under rules which impose and regulate the strict enclosure and observance of silence, which are said to be the conditions of the true and fruitful following of the contemplative life. So, too, their rules prescribe the occupations which are to fill their lives. They must assist devoutly and every day at the celebration of the mass and the recital of the Divine Office and other offices and prayers of the Church, must spend all the time that is not occupied in community duties in prayer or spiritual reading or work in their cells. Further, the rules prescribe practices to further the spirit of humility and particular mortifications, as, for example, a monastic fast lasting from 14 September to Easter, and the prohibition throughout their lives of those aids to comfort which by ordinary women are regarded as necessities rather than luxuries of life.
>
> This, then, is the life which it is the purpose of this community to promote in the women who join it. Is it a charitable purpose and is a trust for its furtherance a charitable trust? The community does not engage in – indeed, it is by its rules debarred from — any exterior work, such as teaching, nursing, or tending the poor, which distinguishes the active branches of the same order. A Catholic woman, it is said, joins such a contemplative order as this to promote

in herself more fully and perfectly the love of God, expressed in as perfect a submission to His will as she can achieve with the help of His Grace, to promote that love in her neighbour and to make reparation to God for the sins of mankind. It is the teaching of the Church that the religious life thus led is, as it is called, 'the state of perfection.' It is this benefit to all the world, arising from the value of their intercessory prayers, that the prioress puts in the forefront of her case in urging the charitable purpose of the trust. Nor is it only on the intercessory value of prayer that the prioress relies for the element of public benefit in the lives of the nuns. I turn then to the question whether, apart from this final consideration, the prioress has established that there is in the trusts which govern this community the element of public benefit which is the necessary condition of legal charity. If now for the first time the necessity for determining that question arose, it might be a more difficult one to answer than it now appears to me to be. But, my Lords, when I consider the law of charity, its origin and the manner of its development, when I find that, though communities such as this have existed over a considerable period and their charitable character has been rarely advocated and never sustained, I do not think that it is possible to open the door and admit them to the house of charity unless there is some novel and compelling reason for doing so.

My Lords, I would speak with all respect and reverence of those who spend their lives in cloistered piety, and in this House of Lords Spiritual and Temporal, which daily commences its proceedings with intercessory prayers, how can I deny that the Divine Being may in His wisdom think fit to answer them? But, my Lords, whether I affirm or deny, whether I believe or disbelieve, what has that to do with the proof which the court demands that a particular purpose satisfies the test of benefit to the community? Here is something which is manifestly not susceptible of proof. But, then it is said, this is a matter not of proof but of belief, for the value of intercessory prayer is a tenet of the Catholic faith, therefore, and, in such prayer there is benefit to the community. But it is just at this 'therefore' that I must pause. It is, no doubt, true that the advancement of religion is, generally speaking, one of the heads of charity, but it does not follow from this that the court must accept as proved whatever a particular church believes. The faithful must embrace their faith believing where they cannot prove: the court can act only on proof. A gift to two or ten or a hundred cloistered nuns in the belief that their prayers will benefit the world at large does not from that belief alone derive validity any more than does the belief of any other donor for any other purpose.

I turn to the second of the alleged elements of public benefit, edification by example, and I think that this argument can be dealt with very shortly. It is, in my opinion, sufficient to say that this is something too vague and intangible to satisfy the prescribed test. The test of public benefit has, I think, been developed in the last two centuries. Today it is beyond doubt that that element must be present. No court would be rash enough to attempt to define precisely or exhaustively what its content must be. But it would assume a burden which it could not discharge if now for the first time it admitted into the category of public benefit something so indirect, remote, imponderable and, I would add, controversial as the benefit which may be derived by others from the example of pious lives. The prioress called in aid the use by Wickens VC of the word 'indirectly' in the passage that I have cited from his judgment in *Cocks v Manners*,[26] but I see no reason to suppose that that learned judge had in mind any such question as your Lordships have to determine.

I must now refer to certain cases on which the prioress relied. They consist of a number of cases in the Irish Courts and *Re Caus*,[27] a decision of Luxmoore J. A consideration of the Irish cases shows that it has there been decided that a bequest for the saying of masses, whether in public or in private, is a good charitable bequest: see, for example, *AG v Hall*[28] and *O'Hanlon v Logue*.[29] In *Re Caus* Luxmoore J came to the same conclusion. I would expressly reserve my opinion on the question whether these decisions should be sustained in this House. So important a matter should not be decided except on a direct consideration of it. It is possible that, particularly in regard to the celebration of masses in public, good reason may be found for supporting a gift for such an object as both a legal and a charitable purpose. It follows, however, from what I have said in the earlier part of this opinion that I am unable to accept the view, which at least in the Irish cases is clearly expressed, that in intercessory prayer and edification that public benefit which is the condition of legal charity is to be found. It is, perhaps, significant that even in Ireland, where in regard to the saying of masses the law has thus been established, there is no consensus of opinion that a gift to a community of contemplative nuns is charitable: see *Munster and Leinster Bank v AG*;[30] *Maguire v AG*;[31] and *Re Keogh*. From the judgment of Black J, in *Munster and Leinster Bank v AG*, I would quote these words[32] which succinctly express my own view:

> There are perhaps few forms of human activity, good in themselves, but solely designed to benefit individuals associated for the purpose of securing that benefit, which may not have some repercussions or consequential effects beneficial to some section of the general community; and unless a further and sweeping inroad is to be made on the rule against perpetuities, the line must be drawn somewhere. *Cocks v Manners* has drawn it.

Of the decision of Luxmoore J, in *Re Caus*, I would only say that his *ratio decidendi* is expressly stated to be, first, that it (ie, a gift for the saying of masses) enables a ritual act to be performed which is recognised by a large proportion of Christian people to be the central act of their religion, and, secondly, that it assists in the endowment of priests whose duty it is to perform the ritual act. The decision, therefore, does not assist the prioress' argument in the present case and I make no further comments on it.

It remains, finally, to deal with an argument which, as I have said, was not presented to the Court of Appeal but appears in the prioress' formal case. It is

26 (1871) LR 12.
27 [1934] Ch 162.
28 [1897] 2 IR 426.
29 [1906] 1 IR 247.
30 [1940] IR 19.
31 [1943] IR 238.
32 [1940] IR 19, p 30.

> that the element of public benefit is supplied by the fact that qualification for admission to membership of the community is not limited to any group of persons but is open to any woman in the wide world who has the necessary vocation. Thus, it is said, just as the endowment of a scholarship open to public competition is a charity, so also a gift to enable any woman (or, presumably, any man) to enter a fuller religious life is a charity. To this argument, which, it must be admitted, as a speciously logical appearance, the first answer is that which I have indicated earlier in this opinion. There is no novelty in the idea that a community of nuns must, if it is to continue, from time to time obtain fresh recruits from the outside world. That is why a perpetuity is involved in a gift for the benefit of such a community. Yet, by direct decision or by way of emphatic example, a community such as this is by them regarded as the very type of religious institution which is not charitable. I know of no consideration applicable to this case which would justify this House in unsettling a rule of law which has been established so long and by such high authority. But that is not the only, nor, indeed, the most cogent, reason why I cannot accede to the prioress' argument. It is a trite saying that the law is life, not logic. But it is, I think, conspicuously true of the law of charity that it has been built up, not logically, but empirically. It would not, therefore, be surprising to find that, while in every category of legal charity some element of public benefit must be present, the court had not adopted the same measure in regard to different categories, but had accepted one standard in regard to those gifts which are alleged to be for the advancement of religion, and it may be yet another in regard to the relief of poverty. I have stressed the empirical development of the law of charity and your Lordships may detect some inconsistency in an attempt to rationalise it. But it appears to me that it would be irrational to the point of absurdity, on the one hand, to deny to a community of contemplative nuns the character of a charitable institution, but, on the other, to accept as a charitable trust a gift which had no other object than to enable it to be maintained in perpetuity by recruitment from the outside world.
>
> Finally, I would say this. I have assumed for the purpose of testing this argument that it is a valid contention that a gift for the advancement of education is necessarily charitable if it is not confined within two narrow limits. But that assumption is itself difficult to justify. It may well be that the generality of the proposition is subject to at least two limitations. The first of them is implicit in the decision of Russell J, in *Re Hummeltenberg*.[33] The second is one that is not in the nature of things likely to occur, but, if it can be imagined that it was made a condition of a gift for the advancement of education that its beneficiaries should lead a cloistered life and communicate to no one, and leave no record of, the fruits of their study, I do not think that the charitable character of the gift could be sustained.

On the other hand, in *Neville Estates v Madden* the members of the Catford Synagogue were treated as an appreciable section of the public and satisfied the public element test because the objects were not numerically negligible and integrated with the rest of society.

---

33 [1923] 1 Ch 237.

Neville Estates Ltd v Madden and Others [1962] 1 Ch 832, HC

Following an appeal by the Catford Synagogue, money was raised to purchase a house. This was achieved and the house was conveyed to trustees by deed which declared that the purchase moneys were the property of the members of the synagogue. Part of the house was used as a synagogue, the other part was used as the minister's residence. Following another appeal other land was bought and conveyed to the trustees on the same terms. The synagogue contracted to sell part of the land to the plaintiff for £10,000. After the contract was signed the synagogue received another offer for £14,300 and wished to accept this offer. The plaintiff brought an action for specific performance. The Charity Commissioners notified the synagogue that they would refuse to consent to the sale to the plaintiff for less than £14,300. The plaintiff commenced proceedings claiming that the consent of the Commissioners was not necessary for the land was not held for charitable purposes.

Held that the purchase moneys following both appeals did not belong to the members beneficially but were held upon trust for the synagogue. The trust was charitable for the purpose of advancing religion and the consent of the Commissioners was a prerequisite to the sale.

> **Cross J:** The question of the construction and effect of gifts to or in trust for unincorporated associations was recently considered by the Privy Council in *Leahy v AG for New South Wales*.[34] The position, as I understand it, is as follows. Such a gift may take effect in one or other of three quite different ways. In the first place, it may, on its true construction, be a gift to the members of the association at the relevant date as joint tenants, so that any members can sever his share and claim it whether or not he continues to be a member of the association. Secondly, it may be a gift to the existing members not as joint tenants, but subject to their respective contractual rights and liabilities towards one another as members of the association. In such a case a member cannot sever his share. It will accrue to the other members on his death or resignation, even though such members include persons who became members after the gift took effect. If this is the effect of the gift, it will not be open to objection on the score of perpetuity or uncertainty unless there is something in its terms or circumstances or in the rules of the association which precludes the members at any given time from dividing the subject of the gift between them on the footing that they are solely entitled to it in equity. Thirdly, the terms or circumstances of the gift or the rules of the association may show that the property in question is not to be at the disposal of the members for the time being, but is to be held in trust for or applied for the purposes of the association as a quasi-corporate entity. In this case the gift will fail unless the association is a charitable body. If the gift is of the second class, that is, one which the members of the association for the time being are entitled to divide among themselves, then, even if the objects of the association are in themselves charitable, the gift would not, I think, be a charitable gift. If, for example, a

34 [1959] AC 457.

number of persons formed themselves into an association with a charitable object – say the relief of poverty in some district – but it was part of the contract between them that, if a majority of the members so desired, the association should be dissolved and its property divided between the members at the date of dissolution, a gift to the association as part of its general funds would not, I conceive, be a charitable gift.

The questions which I have to decide on this branch of the case are, therefore, as I see them, first, whether the members of this synagogue for the time being are legally entitled to divide its property, including the land which is the subject of the contract, between themselves; and, secondly, if they are not so entitled, whether the trusts on which the property of the synagogue is held are charitable.

The chief purposes which a synagogue exists to achieve are the holding of religious services and the giving of religious instruction to the younger members of the congregation. But just as today church activity overflows from the church itself to the parochial hall, with its whist drives, dances and bazaars, so many synagogues today organise social activities among the members. A new clause added to the scheme of the United Synagogue in October 1926, authorised, or purported to authorise, that body to establish, *inter alia*, halls for religious and social purposes, and the Catford Synagogue, as I have said, has erected a communal hall near the synagogue building in which social functions are held. The plaintiffs, fastening on these facts and on the wording of clause 2 of the trust deed, argue that the trust in this case is open to the objections which proved fatal to the trust for the foundation of a community centre which came before the court in *IRC v Baddeley*.[35] But in my judgment there is a great difference between that case and this. Here the social activities are merely ancillary to the strictly religious activities. In the *Baddeley* case, on the other hand, no one sought to argue – indeed it was manifestly impossible to argue that the trust was for the advancement of religion. No doubt it had a religious flavour in that the beneficiaries were confined to Methodists or persons likely to become Methodists, and the premises and the activities in which the beneficiaries were to engage were to be under the control of the leaders of a Methodist mission. Nevertheless the activities in themselves were directed predominantly to the social and not to the religious well being of the beneficiaries.

In my judgment the purposes of the trust with which I am concerned are religious purposed – the social aspect is merely ancillary.

I turn now to the argument that this is a private, not a public trust. In an article which he contributed in 1946 to Vol 62 of the Law Quarterly Review, Professor Newark argued that the courts ought not to concern themselves with the question whether or not a trust for a religious purpose confers a public benefit. Even assuming that such question can be answered at all, judges, he said, are generally ill-equipped to answer them and their endeavours to do so are apt to cause distress to the faithful and amusement to the cynical. I confess that I have considerable sympathy with Professor Newark's views; but the decision of the

35 [1955] AC 572; [1955] 2 WLR 552.

House of Lords in *Gilmour v Coats*[36] has made it clear that a trust for a religious purpose must be shown to have some element of public benefit in order to qualify as a charitable trust. The trust with which I am concerned resembles that in *Gilmour v Coats* in this, that the persons immediately benefited by it are not a section of the public but the members of a private body. All persons of the Jewish faith living in or about Catford might well constitute a section of the public, but the members for the time being of the Catford Synagogue are no more a section of the public than the members for the time being of a Carmelite Priory. The two cases, however, differ from one another in that the members of the Catford Synagogue spend their lives in the world, whereas the members of a Carmelite Priory live secluded from the world. If once one refuses to pay any regard – as the courts refused to pay any regard – to the influence which these nuns living in seclusion might have on the outside world, then it must follow that no public benefit is involved in a trust to support a Carmelite Priory. But the court it, I think, entitled to assume that some benefit accrues to the public from the attendance at places of worship of persons who live in this world and mix with their fellow citizens. As between different religions the law stands neutral, but it assumes that any religion is at least likely to be better than none.

Generally speaking, no doubt, an association which is supported by its members for the purposes of providing benefits for themselves will not be a charity. But I do not think that this principle can apply with full force in the case of trusts for religious purposes. As Lord Simonds pointed out, the law of charity has been built up not logically but empirically, and there is a political background peculiar to religious trusts which may well have influenced the development of the law with regard to them.

In my judgment, this trust with which I am concerned in this case is a charitable trust.

In *Re Lewis*,[37] a gift for the benefit of 10 blind boys and 10 blind girls in Tottenham was charitable. But, in *Williams Trustees v IRC*,[38] a gift in order to create an institute in London, for the promotion of Welsh culture, failed as a charity on the ground that it lacked a public element:

Lord Simonds (in *Williams Trustees v IRC*): My Lords, there are, I think, two propositions which must ever be borne in mind in any case in which the question is whether a trust is charitable. The first is that it is still the general law that a trust is not charitable and entitled to the privileges which charity confers, unless it is within the spirit and intendment of the preamble to the statute of Elizabeth (43 Eliz, c 4), which is expressly preserved by s 13, sub-s (3) of the Mortmain and Charitable Uses Act 1888. The second is that the classification of charity in its legal sense into four principal divisions by Lord MacNaghten in *Income Tax Commissioners v Pemsel*[39] must always be read subject to the

36 [1949] AC 426.

37 [1954] 3 All ER 257.

38 [1947] AC 447, HL.

39 [1891] AC 531, p 583.

qualification appearing in the judgment of Lindley LJ in *In re Macduff*:[40] 'Now Sir Samuel Romilly did not mean, and I am certain Lord MacNaghten did not mean, to say that every object of public general utility must necessarily be a charity. Some may be, and some may not be.' This observation has been expanded by Lord Cave LC in this House in these words:

> Lord MacNaghten did not mean that all trusts for purposes beneficial to the community are charitable, but that there were certain beneficial trusts which fell within that category; and accordingly to argue that because a trust is for a purpose beneficial to the community it is therefore a charitable trust is to turn round his sentence and to give it a different meaning. So here it is not enough to say that the trust in question is for public purposes beneficial to the community or for the public welfare; you must also show it to be a charitable trust.

See *AG v National Provincial & Union Bank of England*.[41] But it is just because the purpose of the trust deed in this case is said to be beneficial to the community or a section of the community and for no other reason that its charitable character is asserted. It is not alleged that the trust is (a) for the benefit of the community, and (b) beneficial in a way which the law regards as charitable. Therefore, as it seems to me, in its mere statement the claim is imperfect and must fail.

If the purposes are not charitable *per se*, the localisation of them will not make them charitable. It is noticeable that Lord Finlay LC expressly overrules a decision or dictum of Lord Romilly to the contrary effect in *Dolan v MacDermot*.[42]

The rule is thus stated by Lord Wrenbury in *Verge v Sommerville*:[43]

> To ascertain whether a gift constitutes a valid charitable trust so as to escape being void on the ground of perpetuity, a first inquiry must be whether it is public – whether it is for the benefit of the community or of an appreciably important class of the community. The inhabitants of a parish or town, or any particular class of such inhabitants, may for instance, be the objects of such a gift, but private individuals, or a fluctuating body of private individuals, cannot.

It is, I think, obvious that this rule, necessary as it is, must often be difficult of application and so the courts have found. Fortunately perhaps, though Lord Wrenbury put it first, the question does not arise at all, if the purpose of the gift whether for the benefit of a class of inhabitants or of a fluctuating body of private individuals is not itself charitable. I may however refer to a recent case in this House which in some aspect resembles the present case. In *Keren Kayemeth Le Jisroel Ltd v IRC*,[44] a company had been formed which had as its main object (to put it shortly) the purchase of land in Palestine, Syria or other

40 [1896] 2 Ch 451, p 466.

41 [1924] AC 262, p 265.

42 (1867) LR 5 Eq 60

43 [1924] AC 650.

44 [1932] AC 650 (see below, p 689).

parts of Turkey in Asia and the peninsula of Sinai for the purpose of settling Jews on such lands. In its memorandum it took numerous other powers which were to be exercised only in such a way as should in the opinion of the company conducive to the attainment of the primary object. No part of the income of the company was distributable among its members. It was urged that the company was established for charitable purposes for numerous reasons, with only one of which I will trouble your Lordships, namely, that it was established for the benefit of the community or of a section of the community, namely, Jews, whether the association was for the benefit of Jews all over the world or of the Jews repatriated in the Promised Land. Lord Tomlin dealing with the argument that I have just mentioned upon the footing that, if benefit to 'a community' could be established the purpose might be charitable, proceeded to examine the problem in that aspect and sought to identify the community. He failed to do so, finding it neither in the community of all Jews throughout the world nor in that of the Jews in the region prescribed for settlement. It is perhaps unnecessary to pursue the matter. Each case must be judged on its own facts and the dividing line is not easily drawn. But the difficulty, of finding the community in the present case, when the definition of 'Welsh people' in the first deed is remembered, would not I think be less than that of finding the community of Jews in *Keren*'s case [1932] AC 650.

The same principle was applied in *IRC v Baddeley* (see above, p 604).

In *McGovern v AG*,[45] Slade J stated that the question whether the public benefit test is satisfied or not is a question of law based on the evidence.

Slade J: The question whether a purpose will or may operate for the public benefit is to be answered by the court forming an opinion on the evidence before it: see *National Anti-Vivisection Society v IRC*,[46] *per* Lord Wright. No doubt in some cases a purpose may be so manifestly beneficial to the public that it would be absurd to call evidence on this point. In many other instances, however, the element of public benefit may be much more debatable. Indeed, in some cases the court will regard this element of being incapable of proof one way of the other and thus will inevitably decline to recognise the trust as being of a charitable nature.

Poverty exception

Trusts for the relief of poverty are charitable even though the beneficiaries are linked *inter se* or with an individual or small group of individuals. In short, trusts for the relief of poverty are not subject to the public element test. The practice of the courts (see *Re Compton*, above, p 607) has always been to exclude such trusts from the public element test. Accordingly, in *Gibson v South American Stores Ltd*[47] and *Dingle v Turner*,[48] the courts reviewed the

45 [1981] 3 All ER 493 (see below, p 648).

46 [1948] AC 31, p 44.

47 [1950] Ch 177.

48 [1972] AC 601.

authorities and decided that gifts in order to relieve poverty amongst employees of a company were charitable.

Dingle v Turner [1972] AC 601, HL (Viscount Dilhorne, Lords MacDermott, Hodson, Simon of Glaisdale and Cross of Chelsea)

A testator by his will transferred property to his trustees and directed them to apply the income '... in paying pensions to poor employees of Dingle Ltd'. At the time of the testator's death, there were 705 full time employees and 189 part time employees. The question in issue was whether the gift was charitable.

The House of Lords held that the gift was charitable. Gifts or trusts for the relief of poverty were not subject to the public element test. Accordingly, the contractual connection between the donor and donees did not invalidate the gift.

> **Lord Cross of Chelsea:** The contentions of the appellant and the respondents may be stated as follows. The appellant says that in the *Oppenheim* case this House decided that in principle a trust ought not to be regarded as charitable if the benefits under it are confined either to the descendants of a named individual or individuals or to the employees of a given individual or company and that though the 'poor relations' cases may have to be left standing as an anomalous exception to the general rule because their validity has been recognised for so long the exception ought not to be extended to 'poor employees' trusts which had not been recognised for long before their status as charitable trusts began to be called in question. The respondents, on the other hand, say, first, that the rule laid down in the *Oppenheim* case with regard to educational trusts ought not to be regarded as a rule applicable in principle to all kinds of charitable trusts, and, secondly, that in any case it is impossible to draw any logical distinction between 'poor relations' trusts and 'poor employees' trusts, and that, as the former cannot be held invalid today after having been recognised as valid for so long, the latter must be regarded as valid also.
>
> The first of the 'poor employees' cases was *In re Gosling*.[49] There the testator sought to establish a fund for 'pensioning off' the old and worn-out clerks of a which he had been a member. It was argued by those interested in contending that the gift was not charitable that there was no public element in it, and that a distinction should be drawn between the relief of poverty among employees of a firm and the relief of poverty among inhabitants of a geographical area. In rejecting that argument Byrne J said, *inter alia*, that it was inconsistent with *AG v Duke of Northumberland*,[50] which was one of the 'poor relations' cases. His judgment continued as follows, at p 301:
>
> > The fact that the section of the public is limited to persons born or residing in a particular parish, district, or county, or belonging to or connected with

49 (1900) 48 WR 300.

50 (1877) 7 Ch D 745.

> any special sect, denomination, guild, institution, firm, name, or family, does not itself render that which would be otherwise charitable void for lack of a sufficient or satisfactory description or take it out of the category of charitable gifts. I therefore hold it to be a good charitable gift.

It is to be observed that he does not confine what he says there to trusts for the relief of poverty as opposed to other forms of charitable trusts. In *In re Drummond*[51] the testator bequeathed some shares in a company, of which he had been a director, to trustees upon trust to pay the income to the directors of the company: 'for the purposes of contribution to the holiday expenses of the workpeople employed in the spinning department of the said company in such manner as a majority of the directors should in their absolute discretion think fit ...'

There were some 500 employees in the department. It was first submitted that this was a trust for the relief of poverty. Eve J rejected that submission but, in doing so, he did not suggest that if he could have held that the workpeople in question were 'poor persons' within the meaning of the Statute of Elizabeth [Charitable Uses Act 1601] the gift would nevertheless have failed on the ground that it was confined to employees of a particular company. Next it was submitted that the gift fell under the last of the four heads of charity set out by Lord MacNaghten in *Income Tax Special Purposes Commissioners v Pemsel*.[52] It was a trust to secure a holiday for a substantial number of the inhabitants of Ilkley who though not poor might in many cases not otherwise be able to get a holiday. Such a trust – it was said – promoted the general well-being of the community; and the beneficiaries could well be considered as constituting a section of the community' for the purpose of the law of charity. Eve J with some regret-rejected that contention saying, at p 97:

> This is not a trust for general public purposes; it is a trust for private individuals, a fluctuating body of private individuals it is true, but still private individuals ...

So Eve J, while not disagreeing with the decision in *In re Gosling* plainly thought that the words of Byrne J which I have quoted though true of poverty cases were not of general application in the law of charity.

Next comes *In re Sir Robert Laidlaw*, a decision of the Court of Appeal given in 1935 but not reported and only brought to light in 1949 [see *Gibson v South American Stores (Gath & Chaves)*].[53] There the testator had bequeathed a legacy of £2,000 upon certain trusts for the relief of poor members or former members of the staff of Whiteaway, Laidlaw & Co Ltd. The judge at first instance [Eve J] having held that the gift failed as not being charitable the Court of Appeal reversed his decision and declared that it was a valid charitable legacy. Unfortunately, neither the reasons given by the judge for holding that the gift failed nor those given by the Court of Appeal for holding that it was charitable

51 [1914] 2 Ch 90.

52 [1891] AC 531, p 583.

53 [1950] Ch 177, p 195.

have been recorded; but the decision of the Court of Appeal was plainly in line with *In re Gosling*.[54]

[His Lordship then considered the following cases (see above, pp 607 *et seq*): *Re Compton; Re Hobourn Aero Components; Oppenheim v Imperial Tobacco Co*; and continued:]

In *In re Cox*[55] a Canadian testator directed his trustees to hold the balance of his residuary estate upon trust to pay its income in perpetuity for charitable purposes only, the persons to benefit directly in pursuance of such charitable purposes being such as were or had been employees of a certain company and/or the dependants of such employees. This disposition raised, of course, a question of construction – namely whether 'charitable purposes' was simply a compendious mode of referring to any purposes a trust to promote which would be charitable provided that the beneficiaries were the public or a section of the public or whether the words meant such purposes only as having regard to the class of beneficiaries named could be the subject of a valid charitable trust. It was only on the latter construction that the question whether *Gibson v South American Stores (Gath & Chaves) Ltd*[56] was rightly decided would arise and in fact both the courts below and the Privy Council held that the former construction was the right one. It is, however, to be observed that the Court of Appeal for Ontario[57] unanimously held that even if the second construction was right the trust would still fail for want of any possible purposes since the 'poor relations' cases formed a class apart and the 'poor employees' cases could not stand with the decision in *Oppenheim*.[58] The Privy Council expressly refrained from expressing any opinion on this point.

In *In re Young (Decd)*,[59] Danckwerts J held that a gift by a testator of his residuary estate to the trustees of the benevolent fund of the Savage Club to be used by them as they should think fit for the assistance of any of his fellow members as might fall on evil days created a valid charitable trust. In so deciding he referred to *Gibson*'s case[60] and said that he could see no distinction in principle between the employees of a limited company and the members of a club.

Finally, we were referred to the Privy Council case of *Davies v Perpetual Trustee Co Ltd*.[61] There a testator who died on 21 January 1897, after giving successive life interests in certain property in Sydney to several life tenants, the last of whom died in 1957, gave the property:

> ... to the Presbyterians the descendants of those settled in the colony hailing from or born in the North of Ireland to be held in trust for the

54 (1900) 48 WR 300.

55 [1955] AC 627.

56 [1950] Ch 177.

57 [1951] OR 205.

58 [1951] AC 297.

59 [1955] 1 WLR 1269.

60 [1950] Ch 177.

61 [1959] AC 439.

> purpose of establishing a college for the education and tuition of their youth in the standards of the Westminster Divines as taught in the Holy Scriptures.

On an originating summons issued in 1918 by the then sole trustee for the determination of certain questions it was held *(inter alia)* by the trial judge and on appeal by the Supreme Court of New South Wales that this devise created a valid charitable trust; but after the death of the last life tenant special leave was given to a representative of the next of kin to appeal to the Privy Council which held the trust to be invalid. The Board held as a matter of construction that a child would only be eligible to be educated at the college if (i) he was descended from a Presbyterian living on 21 January 1897; (ii) that Presbyterian was himself descended from a Presbyterian who had settled in the colony; and (iii) that settler either hailed from or was born in Northern Ireland. After quoting passages from the opinions of Lord Simonds and Lord Normand in *Oppenheim v Tobacco Securities Trust Co Ltd*[62] the Board held that this class of beneficiaries the nexus between whom was simply their personal relationship to several *propositi* was not a section of the public but merely a fluctuating class of private individuals and that though the purposes of the trust – being for the advancement of religion and education – were *prima facie* charitable the trust did not possess the necessary public quality and was invalid.

After this long – but I hope not unduly long – recital of the decided cases I turn to consider the arguments advanced by the appellant in support of the appeal. For this purpose I will assume that the appellant is right in saying that the *Compton* rule[63] ought in principle to apply to all charitable trusts and that the 'poor relations' cases, the 'poor members' cases and the 'poor employees' cases are all anomalous – in the sense that if such cases had come before the courts for the first time after the decision in *In re Compton*[64] the trusts in question would have been held invalid as 'private' trusts.

Even on that assumption – as it seems to me – the appeal must fail. The status of some of the 'poor relations' trusts as valid charitable trusts was recognised more than 200 years ago and a few of those then recognised are still being administered as charities today. In *In re Compton* Lord Greene MR said, at p 139, that it was 'quite impossible' for the Court of Appeal to overrule such old decisions and in *Oppenheim*[65] Lord Simonds in speaking of them remarked, at p 309, on the unwisdom of casting doubt on 'decisions of respectable antiquity in order to introduce a greater harmony into the law of charity as a whole.' Indeed, counsel for the appellant hardly ventured to suggest that we overrule the 'poor relations' cases. His submission was that which was accepted by the Court of Appeal for Ontario in *In re Cox*[66] – namely that while the 'poor relations' cases might have to be left as long standing anomalies there was no good reason for sparing the 'poor employees' cases which only date

62 [1951] AC 297.

63 [1945] Ch 123.

64 *Ibid.*

65 [1951] AC 297.

66 [1951] OR 205.

from *In re Gosling*,[67] and which have been under suspicion ever since the decision in *In re Compton*.[68] But the 'poor members' and the 'poor employees' decisions were a natural development of the 'poor relations' decisions and to draw a distinction between different sorts of 'poverty' trusts would be quite illogical and could certainly not be said to be introducing 'greater harmony' into the law of charity. Moreover, though not as old as the 'poor relations' trusts 'poor employees' trusts have been recognised as charities for many years; there are now a large number of such trusts in existence; and assuming, as one must, that they are properly administered in the sense that benefits under them are only given to people who can fairly be said to be, according to current standards, 'poor persons,' to treat such trusts as charities is not open to any practical objection. So as it seems to me it must be accepted that wherever else it may hold sway the *Compton* rule has no application in the field of trusts for there the dividing line between a charitable trust and a private trust lies where the Court of Appeal drew it in *In re Scarisbrick's Will Trusts*.[69]

Oppenheim[70] was a case of an educational trust and though the majority evidently agreed with the view expressed by the Court of Appeal in the *Hobourn Aero* case[71] that the *Compton* rule[72] was of universal application outside the field of poverty it would no doubt be open to this House without overruling *Oppenheim* to hold that the scope of the rule was more limited. If ever I should be called upon to pronounce on this question – which does not arise in this appeal – I would as at present advised be inclined to draw a distinction between the practical merits of the *Compton* rule and the reasoning by which Lord Greene MR sought to justify it. That relationship has never seemed to me very satisfactory and I have always – if I may say so – felt the force of the criticism to which my noble and learned friend Lord MacDermott subjected it in his dissenting speech in *Oppenheim*. For my part I would prefer to approach the problem on far broader lines. The phrase as 'section of the public' is in truth a vague phrase which mean different things to different people. In the law of charity judges have sought to elucidate its meaning by contrasting it with another phrase: 'a fluctuating body of private individuals'. But I get little help from the supposed contrast for as I see it one and the same aggregate of persons may well be describable both as a section of the public and as a fluctuating body of private individuals. The ratepayers of the Royal Borough of Kensington and Chelsea, for example, certainly constitute a section of the public; but would it be a misuse of language to describe them as a 'fluctuating body of private individuals'? After all, every part of the public is composed of individuals and being susceptible of increase or decrease is fluctuating. So at the end of the day one is left where one started with the bare contrast between 'public' and 'private'. No doubt, some classes are more

67 (1900) 48 WR 300.

68 [1945] Ch 123.

69 [1951] Ch 622.

70 [1951] AC 297.

71 [1946] Ch 194.

72 [1945] Ch 123.

naturally describable as sections of the public than as private classes while other classes, are more naturally describable as private classes than as sections of the public. The blind, for example, can naturally be described as a section of the public; but what they have in common – their blindness – does not join them in such a way that they could be called a private class. On the other hand, the descendants of Mr A Gladstone might more reasonably be described as a 'private class' than as a section of the public, and in the field of common employment the same might well be said of the employees in some fairly small firm. But if one turns to large companies employing many thousands of men and women most of whom are quite unknown to one another and to the directors the answer is by no means so clear. One might say that in such a case the distinction between a section of the public and a private class is not applicable at all or even that the employees in such concerns as ICI or GEC are just as much 'sections of the public' as the residents in some geographical area. In truth the question whether or not the potential beneficiaries of a trust can fairly be said to constitute a section of the public is a question of degree and cannot be by itself decisive of the question whether the trust is a charity. Much must depend on the purpose of the trust. It may well be that, on the one hand, a trust to promote some purpose, *prima facie* charitable, will constitute a charity even though the class of potential beneficiaries might fairly be called a private class and that, on the other hand, a trust to promote another purpose, also *prima facie* charitable, will not constitute a charity even though the class of potential beneficiaries might seem to some people fairly describable as a section of the public. In answering the question whether any given trust is a charitable trust the courts – as I see it – cannot avoid having regard to the fiscal privileges accorded to charities. But, as things are, validity and fiscal immunity march hand in hand and the decisions in the *Compton* and *Oppenheim* cases were pretty obviously influenced by the consideration that if such trust as were there in question were held valid they would enjoy an undeserved fiscal immunity.

To establish a trust for the education of the children of employees in a company in which you are interested is no doubt a meritorious act; but however numerous the employees may be the purpose which you are seeking to achieve is not a public purpose. It is a company purpose and there is no reason why your fellow taxpayers should contribute to a scheme which by providing 'fringe benefits' for your employees will benefit the company by making their conditions of employment more attractive. The temptation to enlist the assistance of the law of charity in private endeavours of this sort is considerable-witness the recent case of the Metal Box scholarships – *IRC v Educational Grants Association Ltd*[73] — and the courts must do what they can to discourage such attempts. In the field of poverty the danger is not so great as in the field of education – for while people are keenly alive to the need to give their children a good education and to the expense of doing so they are generally optimistic enough not to entertain serious fears of falling on evil days much before they fall on them. Consequently the existence of company 'benevolent funds' the income of which is free of tax does not constitute a very

73 [1967] Ch 993.

> attractive 'fringe benefit'. This is a practical justification – though not, of course, the historical explanation – for the special treatment accorded to poverty trusts in charity law. For the same sort of reason a trust to promote some religion among the employees of a company might perhaps safely be held to be charitable provided that it was clear that the benefits were to be purely spiritual. On the other hand, many 'purpose' trusts falling under Lord MacNaghten's fourth head [*Income Tax Special Purposes Commissioners v Pemsel*][74] if confined to a class of employees would clearly be open to the same sort of objection as educational trusts. As I see it, it is on these broad lines rather then for the reasons actually given by Lord Greene MR that the *Compton* rule[75] can be be justified.
>
> My Lords, for the reasons given earlier in this speech I would dismiss this appeal; but as the view was expressed in the *Oppenheim* case[76] that the question of the validity of trusts for poor relations and poor employees ought some day to be considered by this House.

At the same time, the courts have drawn a subtle distinction between private trusts for the relief of poverty and public trusts for the same purpose, for example, a gift for the settlor's poor relations, A, B and C may not be charitable but may exist as a private trust, whereas a gift for the benefit of the settlor's poor relations without identifying them may be charitable. It appears that the distinction between the two types of trusts lies in the degree of precision in which the objects have been identified. The more precise the language used by the settlor in identifying the poor relations, the stronger the risk of failure as a charitable trust. This is a question of degree. In *Re Scarisbrick*, a bequest was made on trust 'for such relations of my said son and daughters as in the opinion of the survivor shall be in needy circumstances'. The court held that the gift was charitable.

Re Scarisbrick [1951] Ch 622, CA

> **Evershed MR:** The 'poor relations' cases may be justified on the basis that the relief of poverty is of so altruistic a character that the public element may necessarily be inferred thereby; or they may be accepted as a hallowed, if illogical, exception. In any case the exception is in favour of trusts for 'poor relations' and not of trusts of a particular type for poor relations. If the latter were the true view, then only those cases would be treated as exceptions to the general rule which, on their facts, were in substance identical with the poor relations cases in the books. Such a conclusion would lead inevitably to fine and irrational distinctions. The exception, in my view, is of 'poor relations' cases generally, that is of persons identified by reference to relationship with particular individuals, and not within a class constituting, in strictness, a section of the community. If poor relations cases are to be qualified in the way suggested, then there will be introduced with poor relations cases a further

74 [1891] AC 531, p 583.

75 [1945] Ch 123.

76 [1951] AC 297.

anomaly, a distinction wholly foreign to all other kinds of charitable disposition. In my opinion it would be wrong for this court so to do. If there must be an anomaly, let it be itself logical and coherent.

In my judgment the appeal should be allowed, and it should be declared that one-half of the testatrix's residue is held upon valid charitable trusts for distribution among poor members of the class of relations of her three children.

Jenkins LJ: The following general propositions may be stated:

(i) it is a general rule that a trust or gift in order to be charitable in the legal sense must be for the benefit of the public or some section of the public: see *In re Compton;*[77] *In re Hobourn Aero Components Ltd's Air Raid Distress Fund;*[78] and *Gilmour v Coats;*[79]

(ii) an aggregate of individuals ascertained by reference to some personal tie (for example, of blood or contract), such as the relations of a particular individual, the members of particular family, the employees of a particular firm, the members of a particular association, does not amount to the public or a section thereof for the purposes of the general rules: see *In re Drummond,*[80] *In re Compton, In re Hobourn Aero Components Ltd's Air Raid Distress Fund,* and *Oppenheim v Tobacco Securities Trust Co Ltd;*

(iii) it follows that according to the general rule above stated a trust or gift under which the beneficiaries or potential beneficiaries are confined to some aggregate of individuals ascertained as above is not legally charitable even though its purposes are such that it would have been legally charitable if the range of potential beneficiaries had extended to the public at large or a section thereof (for example, an educational trust confined as *In re Compton,* to the lawful descendants of three named persons, or, as in *Oppenheim v Tobacco Securities Trust Co Ltd,* to the children of employees or former employees of a particular company);

(iv) there is, however, an exception to the general rule, in that trusts or gifts for the relief of poverty have been held to be charitable even though they are limited in their application to some aggregate of individuals ascertained as above, and are therefore not trusts or gifts for the benefit of the public or a section thereof. This exception operated whether the personal tie is one of blood (as in the numerous so called 'poor relations' cases, to some of which I will presently refer) or of contract (for example, the relief of poverty amongst the members of a particular society, as in *Spiller v Maude,*[81] or amongst employees of a particular company or their dependants, as in *Gibson v South American Stores (Gath & Chaves) Ltd;*[82]

77 [1945] Ch 123.

78 [1946] Ch 194.

79 [1949] AC 426.

80 [1914] 2 Ch 90.

81 (1881) 32 Ch D 158.

82 [1950] Ch 177.

(v) this exception cannot be accounted for by reference to any principle, but is established by a series of authorities of long standing, and must at the present date be accepted as valid, at all events as far as this court is concerned (see *In re Compton*) though doubtless open to review in the House of Lords (as appears from the observation of Lords Simonds and Morton of Henryton in *Oppenheim v Tobacco Securities Trust Co Ltd*).

Applying these general propositions to the present case. I ask myself whether the trust for 'such relations ... as in the opinion of the survivor of the testatrix's son and daughters shall be in needy circumstances for such interests' and 'in such proportions ... as the survivor ... shall by deed or will appoint' is a trust for the relief of poverty. If it is such a trust, then, as, I understand the exception above referred to, it matters not that the potential objects of such trust are confined to relations of the son and daughters. If language means anything, a person in needy circumstances is a person who is poor and as such a proper object of charity, and no one can take under this trust who is poor and as such a proper object of charity, and no one can take under this trust who is not in needy circumstances. I do not think that the effect of the expression 'in needy circumstances' is materially altered by the qualifying words 'in the opinion of the survivor ...'.

'Poverty' is necessarily to some extent a relative matter, a matter of opinion, and it is not to be assumed that the person made the judge of 'needy circumstances' in the present case would have acted otherwise than in accordance with an opinion fairly and honestly formed as to the circumstances, needy or otherwise, of anyone coming into consideration as a potential object of the power. Under a similar trust which did not expressly make the appointor's opinion the test of eligibility, the appointor would in practice have to make the selection according to the best of his or her opinion or judgment. The express reference to the appointor's opinion merely serves to reduce the possibility of dispute as to the eligibility or otherwise of any particular individual on the score of needy circumstances.

It is no doubt true that a gift or trust is not necessarily charitable as being in relief of poverty because the object or objects of it in order to take must be poor. Such a gift or trust may be no more than an ordinary gift to some particular individual or individuals limited to the amount required to relieve his or their necessities if in necessitous circumstances. One can conceive of a testator making a limited provision of this character for a child or children whose conduct in his view had reduced their claims on his bounty to a minimum. A disposition of that sort would obviously not be for the relief of poverty in the charitable sense. The same must be said of gifts to named persons if in needy circumstances, or to a narrow class of near relatives, as for example to such of a testator's statutory next of kin as at his death shall be in needy circumstances.

It is difficult to draw any exact line, but I do not think the trust here in question can fairly be held disqualified as a trust for the relief of poverty in the charitable sense on grounds such as those illustrated above. The class of relations to whom the selective power of appointment here extends is not confined to relations of the testatrix herself but consists of relations of

> testatrix's son and daughters. 'Relations' in this context cannot, in my opinion, be construed as meaning only the statutory next of kin of the son and daughters.
>
> I am accordingly of opinion that as the law now stands the trust in question should be upheld as a valid charitable trust for the relief of poverty.

Similarly, a gift or trust is not necessarily charitable as being for the relief of poverty because the object(s) is (are) identified as being poor. Such a gift or trust may be no more than an ordinary gift to some particular individual or individuals limited to the amount required to relieve his or their necessities in the stated circumstances.

In *Re Segelman*, the testator had selected the members of the class on the basis that the named individuals were persons who might need financial help from time to time. Moreover, the eligible class of beneficiaries was not closed upon the testator's death. It remained open for a further period of 21 years. During that period, issue of the named individuals born after the death of the testator were capable of becoming members of the class. The testator is taken to have intended a gift for the relief of poverty amongst the class of which issue born after the testator's death would become members.

Re Segelman (Decd) [1996] 2 WLR 173, HC

Two months before his death, Mr Segelman, a 92 year old testator, gave instructions to his solicitor to prepare a will for his signature. His solicitors executed a draft will and in clause 11(a) established a trust fund from the residuary estate to be used for the assistance of 'the poor and needy' from a class of persons set out in the second schedule to the will. On his own initiative, the solicitor drafted a proviso to clause 11(a), which provided that, if any of the persons named in the schedule died during the testator's lifetime or within 21 years from his death, 'such issue shall stand in the place of such person and be eligible to benefit' under the trust. Clause 11(b) gave the trustees a discretion to distribute property in favour of 'the poor and needy' from the class named in the schedule, subject to a gift over in favour of charitable institutions and purposes 'in the event of there being no such persons eligible to benefit'. The testator's secretary subsequently provided the solicitor with the list of persons comprising the second schedule. The list contained six named members of the testator's extended family and the 'issue' (unnamed) of five of them. The solicitor failed to appreciate the need to alter the proviso to clause 11(a) in the light of the wording of the second schedule. The will was duly executed.

After the testator's death and the admission of the will to probate, five of the named persons in the schedule commenced proceedings seeking rectification of the will pursuant to s 20(1) of the Administration of Justice Act 1982, by deletion of the proviso to clause 11(a) on the grounds that, in consequence of 'clerical error' and contrary to the intention of the testator, the proviso had the effect of restricting the class of persons constituted in the second schedule, by excluding the issue of the named individuals while their named ancestors were still alive. The executors of the will appealed from a determination of the Inland Revenue, to the effect that, the dispositions within clause 11 were not charitable and, accordingly, not exempt under s 23 of the Inheritance Tax Act 1984. The court consolidated the claims and considered them together. Held:

Chadwick J: ...

(a) the court will order rectification of the will pursuant to s 20(1) of the Administration of Justice Act 1982. On the basis of the evidence of the testator's instructions and the wording of the second schedule to the will it was clear that the testator intended that all the persons identified in the second schedule, including their issue, were entitled to benefit throughout the 21 year period. The proviso to clause 11(a) did not give effect to that intention since, on construction, it operated to restrict the class of persons eligible to benefit by excluding the issue of those individuals while their named ancestors were alive. In the circumstances, the solicitor's failure, through inadvertence, to delete the proviso to clause 11(a) from the draft will is to be regarded as 'clerical error' within s 20(1) of the AJA 1982. Accordingly, the proviso will be deleted;

(b) the gift on discretionary trust for the relief of poor and needy relations of the testator created a valid charitable trust for the relief of poverty;

(c) the gift is treated as charitable and an exempt transfer under s 23(1) of the Inheritance Tax Act 1984.

[After deciding the claim for rectification of the will was successful, continued:]

The second main question raised by the construction summons, is whether clause 11(a) of the will creates a valid charitable gift.

This question must, I think, be answered in conjunction with question 1(H)(1) of the summons: whether the gift in clause 11(b) of the will in favour of 'the poor and needy of the persons set out in the second schedule then living in such proportions as my trustees, may then, in their uncontrolled discretion, determine' creates a valid charitable gift.

Further, it is convenient to determine, in this context, the true meaning and effect of the words in clause 11(b): 'and in the event of there being no such persons eligible to benefit,' which precede the gift over in favour of charitable institutions and charitable purposes. Accordingly, I address these three questions together.

Prima facie, a gift for the benefit of poor and needy persons is a gift for the relief of poverty, and so falls squarely within the first of the four divisions of charity identified by Lord MacNaghten in *Income Tax Special Purposes Commissioners v Pemsel* [1891] AC 531, p 583. Further, a gift for the relief of poverty is no less charitable because those whose poverty is to be relieved are confined to a particular class limited by ties of blood or employment: see *In re Scarisbrick* [1951] Ch 622, pp 648–49; and *Dingle v Turner* [1972] AC 601, pp 622–23.

The position is, therefore, that the court must decide, as a matter of construction, whether (a) the gift is for the relief of poverty amongst poor people of the particular description, or (b) a gift to particular poor persons, the relief of poverty among them being the motive of the gift.

The position, therefore, is that there are at present 26 members of the second schedule class. Of those, 11 are in the third generation of descent from the testator's parents and 10 are in the fourth generation. Their ages are such that it is reasonable to assume that, by the end of the period of 21 years from the testator's death, when the dispositions in clause 11(b) take effect, the second schedule class will be substantially larger. On the other hand, there are at present at least 10 living descendants of the testator's parents who are not members of the second schedule class. It is clear that the testator has made a considered selection of those who are to be the members of the class from amongst the descendants of his parents. He has not included all those descendants, nor all the descendants in any particular line of descent, other than the strips of which his sister Gertrude is the head, nor all those descendants who have been named as pecuniary legatees.

It is clear, also, that the testator has not selected the members of the second schedule class on the basis that they are all poor. The evidence which has been filed on the construction summons by, or on behalf of, members of that class, does not suggest uniform poverty. Rather, it suggests that most members of the class are comfortably off, in the sense that they are able to meet their day-to-day expenses out of income, but not affluent. Like many others in similar circumstances, they need a helping hand from time to time in order to overcome an unforeseen crisis: the failure of a business venture, urgent repairs to a dwelling house or expenses brought on by reason of failing health. Further, the second schedule class includes the issue of named individuals, many of whom are still minors. It is impossible to conclude that the minors have been selected because they are, or are likely to be, poor. No doubt, in common with most of their contemporaries, they will experience relative poverty as students. There will be periods when their income from grants or parental resources fails to cover expenditure on their actual or perceived needs.

But they are not as a class 'poor persons' within any ordinarily accepted meaning of that expression. The conclusion that I draw from the evidence is that the testator selected the members of the second schedule class on the basis that they were persons who might need financial help from time to time in the future – as had been the case, at least in relation to some of them, in the past – and that they were persons who, by reasons of ties of blood or affection, he would wish to help after his death, as he had done from time to time during his lifetime.

Jenkins LJ [in *Re Scarisbrick*] held that the gift was a trust for the relief of poverty in the charitable sense amongst the class of relations described, and that, being a trust for the relief of poverty, it was not disqualified from ranking as a legally charitable trust by the circumstances that it was confined to a class of relations. He went on, at p 655, to formulate the following test, which was later approved by the House of Lords in *Dingle v Turner* [1972] AC 601:

> ... the true question in each case has really been whether the gift was for the relief of poverty amongst a class of persons ... or was merely a gift to individuals, albeit with relief of poverty amongst those individuals as the motive of the gift ...

As Jenkins LJ observed, at p 651, it is difficult to draw any exact line. Wherever the line is to be drawn, it is clear that the present gift is nearer to it than that which the Court of Appeal had to consider in *Re Scarisbrick* [1951] Ch 622. The second schedule class is narrower than a class of relations of every degree on both sides of the family. The question is whether the class is so narrow that the gift must be disqualified as a trust for the relief of poverty in the charitable sense on grounds such as those illustrated by Jenkins LJ in the examples set out at the beginning of the passage to which I have referred. Is this properly to be regarded as a gift to such of a narrow class of near relatives as at the testator's death shall be in needy circumstances?

The basis for disqualification as a charitable gift must be that the restricted nature of the class leads to the conclusion that the gift is really a gift to the individual members of the class. In my view, the gift in clause 11 of the will is not of that character. The gift with which I am concerned has, in common with the gift which the Court of Appeal had to consider in *Re Scarisbrick*, the feature that the class of those eligible to benefit was not closed upon the testator's death. It remained open for a further period of 21 years. During that period issue of the named individuals born after the death of the testator will become members of the class. It is, in my view, impossible to attribute to the testator an intention to make a gift to those after-born issue as such. His intention must be taken to have been the relief of poverty amongst the class of which they would become members.

It follows that I am satisfied that the gift to the poor and needy of the class of persons set out in the second schedule to the will falls on the charitable side of the line, wherever that line has to be drawn. I hold that the gift in clause 11(a) of the will for the assistance of the poor and needy of the class, during the period of 21 years from the death of the testator, is a gift for charitable purposes, and that the gift for distribution among the poor and needy of the class, upon the expiration of that 21 year period, is also a gift for charitable purposes.

SUPPLEMENTARY READING

Atiyah, PS, 'Public benefit in charities' (1958) 21 MLR 138

Bright, S, 'Charity and trusts for the public benefit: time for a rethink' [1981] Conv 28

Cross, G, 'Some recent developments on the law of charity' (1956) 72 LQR 187

Dawson, N, 'Equity is not a computer: *Winkworth v Edward Baron Development Co Ltd*' [1987] Conv 14

Histed, E, 'Rectification of wills – charitable trusts for poor relations – broadening the boundaries: *Re Segelman*' [1996] Conv 379

CHAPTER 16

CHARITABLE TRUSTS: CLASSIFICATION OF CHARITABLE PURPOSES

Lord MacNaghten, in *IRC v Pemsel* (see above, p 599), classified the charitable purposes, as stated in the preamble to the Charitable Uses Act 1601, as follows:

(a) the relief of poverty;

(b) the advancement of education;

(c) the advancement of religion;

(d) other purposes beneficial to the community.

THE RELIEF OF POVERTY

'Poverty' includes destitution but is not interpreted that narrowly to mean destitution. It connotes that the beneficiaries are in straitened circumstances and unable to maintain a modest standard of living (determined objectively).

Re Coulthurst's Will Trust [1951] Ch 661, CA (Lord Evershed MR, Jenkins and Hodson LJJ)

A testator transferred a fund of £20,000 to his trustees and directed that the income be paid to the widows and orphans of deceased officers and ex-officers of Coutts & Co as the trustees may decide the most deserving of such assistance having regard to their financial circumstances. The question in issue was whether the gift was charitable.

The Court of Appeal held that on construction of the terms of the gift the donation was charitable.

> **Evershed MR:** But as was pointed out by Russell J, in *In re Lucas*[1] (quoting from the judgment of Stirling J in *In re Dudgeon*):[2]
>
> > ... it appears to me that the cases cited on behalf of the charity do show this, that it is not absolutely necessary to find poverty expressed in so many words, but that the court will look at the whole gift, and, if it comes to the conclusion that the relief or poverty was meant, will give effect to it although the word 'poverty' is not to be found in it.
>
> It is quite clearly established that poverty does not mean destitution; it is a word of wide and somewhat indefinite import; it may not unfairly be

1 [1922] 2 Ch 52, p 58.

2 (1896) 74 LT 613.

> paraphrased for present purposes as meaning persons who have to 'go short' in the ordinary acceptation of that term, due regard being had to their status in life, and so forth.
>
> The persons selected are persons whose financial circumstances are such that they are not only deserving of assistance, that is to say, wanting help, but, of all such, are those who most want it. I therefore think that this sentence, so far from reversing the tendency which I should have thought emerged from the earlier words, rather emphasised it. The point was made that the use of the phrase 'most deserving' had, in fact, the contrary result. If the persons to benefit were persons who, by reason of their financial circumstance, were deserving of assistance, then it might be said that the standard imposed was an objective one, namely, that they were persons whose financial circumstances left them in want.
>
> The point being short and concerning the interpretation of a few lines of English, I confine myself to saying that I read the relevant words as being an expression of an intention on this testator's part that this money should go to those who had the quality of poverty within the meaning of the Statute of Elizabeth.

In addition, the gift is required to relieve the misery of poverty by providing the basic necessities of human existence – food, shelter and clothing. The expression 'relief' signifies that the beneficiaries have a need attributable to their condition which requires alleviating and which the beneficiaries may find difficulty in alleviating from their own resources. See Gibson J in *Joseph Rowntree Memorial Trust Housing Association Ltd v AG*:[3]

> The word 'relief' implies that the persons in question have a need attributable to their condition ... as poor persons which requires alleviating, and which those persons could not alleviate, or would find difficulty in alleviating themselves from their own resources. The word 'relief' is not synonymous with 'benefit'.

In *Biscoe v Jackson*[4] (see below, p 725), a gift to establish a soup kitchen in Shoreditch was construed as a valid charitable trust for the relief of poverty. Likewise, in *Shaw v Halifax Corp* it was decided that a home for ladies in reduced circumstances was charitable. Similarly, in *Re Clarke*[5], a gift to provide a nursing home for persons of moderate means was charitable.

But, a gift for the 'working classes' does not connote poverty.

3 [1983] 1 All ER 288.

4 (1887) 25 Ch D 460.

5 [1923] 2 Ch 407.

In re Sanders' Will Trusts [1954] 1 Ch 265, Ch D

A testator by his will transferred one third of his residuary estate to his trustees 'to provide or assist in providing dwellings for the working classes and their families resident in the area of Pembroke Dock, Pembridgeshire, Wales'. The question in issue was whether the gift was charitable for the relief of poverty.

Held that the gift was not charitable for the expression 'working classes' was not synonymous with poverty.

> **Harman J:** It has been pointed out recently by Denning LJ when sitting at first instance, in *HE Green & Sons v Minister of Health (No 2)*,[6] that the expression 'working classes' is an anachronism and does not really mean anything in these days. 'Much has been said,' said the judge, 'in this case as to the meaning of 'working classes'. These words, 'working classes', have appeared in a number of Acts for the last 100 years. I have no doubt that in former times it had a meaning which was reasonably well understood. 'Working classes,' 50 years ago, denoted a class which included men working in the fields or the factories, in the docks or the mines, on the railway or the roads, at a weekly wage. The wages of people of that class were lower than those of most of the other members of the community, and they were looked upon as a lower class. That has all now disappeared. The social revolution in the last 50 years has made the words 'working classes' quite inappropriate today. There is no such separate class as the working classes. The bank clerk or the civil servant, the school teacher or the cashier, the tradesman or the clergyman, do not earn wages or salaries higher than the mechanic or the electrician, the fitter of the mine worker, the bricklayer or the dock labourer. Nor is there any social distinction between one or the other. No one of them is of a higher or a lower class. In my opinion the words 'working classes' used in the Acts are quite inappropriate to modern social conditions.

Belcher v Reading Corp [1950] Ch 380, HC

In this case, the court again had to deal with this expression 'the working classes' in a case where certain inhabitants of council houses in Reading sued the Reading Corporation, which had put up the rents of their houses, putting forward various reasons why they should not have their rents raised. That contention was rejected by Romer J, who only in passing glanced at the judgment in *Green*'s case. He said this:

> **Romer J:** As to this, I may say that, in the light of modern conditions, I share the difficulty which Denning LJ felt and expressed in *HE Green & Sons v Minister of Health (No 2)* with regard to who does, and who does not, belong to the working classes; the phrase has a far wider, and far less certain, signification than it used to possess ...
>
> The 'working class', if it means anything, may I suppose, mean persons who occupy council houses; but there are many privately owned houses of that type

6 [1948] 1 KB 34, p 38.

> or standard, and it may be that 'working class' means persons who would occupy such houses if they could get them. I cannot think that the qualification or description of a man as a man who would be anxious to get a council house, if he could, would connote that he was poor. It does not follow at all that poverty is any part of the qualification for getting a house of that type. I do not see that I can infer poverty from the words used.
>
> Finally, in the most recent case, *In re Glyn Will Trusts*,[7] Danckwerts J had to construe the words 'for ... building free cottages for old women of the working classes of the age of 60 years or upwards'. There the expression 'working class' again appears, and he construed it merely as meaning persons who had to work for their living, and he came to the conclusion that an old woman who had worked for her living and was over 60 was a person likely to be in straitened circumstances, and, therefore poor. On that account he held the gift to be a good gift. He also made some observations about aged persons with which I am not concerned here, but the *ratio decidendi* was that out of old age and working class it might be inferred that poverty was a necessary qualification.
>
> What is there here? Nothing of that kind. These are not old persons; they are not widows. They are merely men working in the docks and their families, and, therefore, I cannot infer any element of poverty here.
>
> It follows that this gift of one third of his estate fails because the purpose is not within the Statute of Elizabeth and therefore not charitable.

On the other hand, a gift for the construction of a 'working men's hostel' was construed as charitable under this head, see *Re Niyazi's Will Trust*.

Re Niyazi's Will Trusts [1978] 3 All ER 785, HC

A testator provided his residuary estate valued at £15,000 to be paid to the mayor of Famagusta, Cyprus to be used for the 'construction of or contribution towards the construction of a working men's hostel.' The question in issue was whether the gift was charitable or not.

Held that, on construction of the will and in view of the grave housing shortage in the area, the gift was charitable for the relief of poverty.

> **Megarry VC:** Certain points seem reasonably plain. First, 'poverty' is not confined to destitution, but extends to those who have small means and so have to 'go short'. Secondly, a gift which in terms is not confined to the relief of poverty may by inference be thus confined. In *Re Lucas*,[8] there was a gift of 5 s per week to the oldest respectable inhabitants of a village. As the law then stood, Russell J was unable to hold that a gift merely to the aged was charitable; but he held that the limitation to 5 s a week indicated quite clearly that only those to whom such a sum would be of importance and a benefit were to take, and so the gift was charitable as being for the relief of poverty. I

7 (1950) 66 TLR 510.

8 [1922] 2 Ch 52; [1922] All ER 317.

do not think that it can be said that nothing save the smallness of the benefit can restrict an otherwise unrestricted benefit so as to confine it within the bounds of charity. I think that anything in the terms of the gift which by implication prevents it from going outside those bounds will suffice. In *In re Glyn's Will Trusts*,[9] Danckwerts J held that a trust for building free cottages for old women of the working classes aged 60 or more provided a sufficient context to show an intention to benefit indigent persons, and so was charitable.

I think that the adjectival expression 'working men' plainly has some flavour of 'lower income' about it, just as 'upper class' has some flavour of comfortable means. Of course there are impoverished members of the 'upper' and 'middle' classes, just as there are some 'working men' who are at least of comfortable means, if not affluence: one cannot ignore the impact of such things as football pools. But in construing a will I think that I am concerned with the ordinary or general import of words rather than exceptional cases; and, whatever may be the further meaning of 'working men' or 'working class', I think that by 1967 such phrases had not lost their general connotation of 'lower income'. I may add that nobody has suggested that any difficulty arose from the use of 'working men' as distinct from 'working persons' or 'working women'.

The connotation of 'lower income' is, I think, emphasised by the word 'hostel'. No doubt there are a number of hostels of superior quality; and one day, perhaps, I may even encounter the expression 'luxury hostel'. But without any such laudatory adjective the word 'hostel' has to my mind a strong flavour of a building which provides somewhat modest accommodation for those who have some temporary need for it and are willing to accept accommodation of that standard in order to meet the need. When 'hostel' is prefixed by the expression 'working men's', then the further restriction is introduced of this hostel being intended for those with a relatively low income who work for their living, especially as manual workers. The need, in other words, is to be the need of working men, and not of students or battered wives or anything else. Furthermore, the need will not be the need of the better paid working men who can afford something superior to mere hostel accommodation, but the need of the lower end of the financial scale of working men, who cannot compete for the better accommodation but have to content themselves with the economies and shortcomings of hostel life. It seems to me that the word 'hostel' in this case is significantly different from the word 'dwellings' in *Re Sanders' Will Trusts*,[10] a word which is appropriate to ordinary houses in which the well-to-do may live, as well as the relatively poor.

Has the expression 'working men's hostel' a sufficient connotation of poverty in it to satisfy the requirement of charity? On any footing the case is desperately near the borderline, and I have hesitated in reaching my conclusion. On the whole, however, for the reasons that I have been discussing, I think that the trust is charitable, though by no great margin. This view is in my judgment supported by two further considerations. First, there is the amount of the trust fund, which in 1969 was a little under £15,000. I think

9 [1950] 2 All ER 1150.

10 [1954] 1 All ER 667; [1954] Ch 265; [1954] 2 WLR 487.

one is entitled to assume that a testator has at least some idea of the probable value of his estate. The money is given for the purpose 'of the construction of or as a contribution towards the cost of the construction of a working men's hostel'. £15,000 will not go very far in such project, and it seems improbable that contributions from other sources towards constructing a 'working men's hostel' would enable or encourage the construction of any grandiose building. If financial constraints point towards the erection of what may be called an 'economy hostel', decent but catering for only the more basic requirements, then only the relatively poor would be likely to be occupants. There is at least some analogy here to the 5 s per week in *Re Lucas.* Whether the trust is to give a weekly sum that is small enough to indicate that only those in straitened circumstances are to benefit, or whether it is to give a capital sum for the construction of a building which will be of such a nature that it is likely to accommodate only those who are in straitened circumstances, there will in each case be an implied restriction to poverty.

The other consideration is that of the state of housing in Famagusta. Where the trust is to erect a building in a particular area, I think that it is legitimate, in construing the trust, to have some regard to the physical condition existing in that area. Quite apart from any question of the size of the gift, I think that a trust to erect a hostel in a slum or in an area of acute housing need may have to be construed differently from a trust to erect a hostel in an area of housing affluence or plenty. Where there is a grave housing shortage, it is plain that the poor are likely to suffer more than the prosperous, and that the provision of a 'working men's hostel' is likely to help the poor and not the rich.

In the result, then, I hold that the trust is charitable.

Under this head, it is essential that all the objects fall within the designation 'poor'. If someone who is not poor is able to benefit from the funds, the gift will fail as not being one for the relief of poverty.

In re Gwyon, Public Trustee Attorney General [1930] 1 Ch 255, HC

A testator transferred his residuary estate to his executor upon trust to establish the 'Gwyon's Boys Clothing Foundation'. The details were specified in the will. The income from the fund was required to be used to provide 'knickers' for boys of Farnham aged between 10 and 15, subject to a number of qualifications. No preference was given to boys from poor parents. Indeed, boys maintained by charitable institutions or whose parents were in receipt of poor relief were expressly excluded. The executors applied to the court to consider whether the gift was charitable on the ground of relief of poverty.

Held that the gift was not charitable. There was no element of relief of poverty.

Eve J: None of these conditions necessarily import poverty nor could the recipients be accurately described as a class of aged, impotent or poor persons. The references to the receipt of parochial relief and to the possibility of the last year's garment having been disposed of show, no doubt, that the testator contemplated that candidates might be forthcoming from a class of society

> where incidents of this nature might occur, but although a gift to or for the poor other than those who were in receipt of parochial relief – that is, paupers – would be a good charitable gift, it does not follow that a gift to all and sundry in a particular locality and not expressed to be for the poor ought to be construed as evidencing an intention to relieve poverty merely because the testator is minded to exclude paupers. I think that according to the true construction of these testamentary documents the benevolence of the testator was intended for all eligible boys other than paupers, and I cannot spell out of them any indication which would justify the Foundation Trustees refusing an applicant otherwise eligible on the ground that his material circumstances were of too affluent a character. In these circumstances I cannot hold this trust to be within the description of a legal charitable trust.

THE ADVANCEMENT OF EDUCATION

This classification originates from the preamble to the 1601 Act which refers to, 'the maintenance of schools of learning, free schools and scholars in universities'. Education has been interpreted generously and is not restricted to the classroom mode of disseminating knowledge but requires some element of instruction or supervision. Thus, research is capable of being construed as the provision of education.

Re Hopkin's Will Trust [1964] 3 All ER 46, HC

In this case, money was bequeathed to the Francis Bacon Society to be used to search for the manuscripts of plays commonly ascribed to Shakespeare but believed by the society to have been written by Bacon. The court reviewed the leading authorities and decided that the gift was for the advancement of education. The discovery of such manuscripts would be of the highest value to history and literature.

> **Wilberforce J:** It would seem to me that a bequest for the purpose of search, or research, for the original manuscripts of England's greatest dramatist (whoever he was) would be well within the law's conception of charitable purposes. The discovery of such manuscript, or of one such manuscripts, would be of the highest value to history and to literature. It is objected, against this, that as we already have the text of the plays, from an almost contemporary date, the discovery of a manuscript would add nothing worth while. This I utterly decline to accept. Without any undue exercise of the imagination, it would surely be a reasonable expectation that the revelation of a manuscript would contribute, probably decisively, to a solution of the authorship problem, and this alone is benefit enough. It might also lead to improvements in the text. It might lead to more accurate dating.
>
> I think, therefore, that the word 'education' as used by Harman J, in *Re Shaw* must be used in a wide sense, certainly extending beyond teaching, and that the requirement is that, in order to be charitable, research must either be of educational value to the researcher or must be so directed as to lead to

something which will pass into the store of educational material, or so as to improve the sum of communicable knowledge in an area which education may cover – education in this last context extending to the formation of literary taste and appreciation (compare *Royal Choral Society v IRC*).[11] Whether or not the test is wider than this, it is, as I have stated it, amply wide enough to include the purpose of the gift in this case.

More recently, in *McGovern v AG*,[12] Slade J summarised the principles thus:

Slade J:

(i) A trust for research will ordinarily qualify as a charitable trust if, but only if (a) the subject matter of the proposed research is a useful object of study; and (b) it is contemplated that the knowledge acquired as a result of the research will be disseminated to others; and (c) the trust is for the benefit of the public, or a sufficiently important section of the public.

(ii) In the absence of a contrary context, however, the court will be readily inclined to construe a trust for research as importing subsequent dissemination of the results thereof.

(iii) Furthermore, if a trust for research is to constitute a valid trust for the advancement of education, it is not necessary either (a) that the teacher/pupil relationship should be in contemplation, or (b) that the persons to benefit from the knowledge to be acquired should be persons who are already in the course of receiving 'education' in the conventional sense.

(iv) In any case where the court has to determine whether a bequest for the purposes of research is or is not of a charitable nature, it must pay due regard to any admissible extrinsic evidence which is available to explain the wording of the will in question or the circumstances in which it was made.

McGovern v Attorney General [1981] 3 All ER 493, HC

In this case, Amnesty International, an unincorporated, non-profit making association established a trust and sought registration with the Charity Commissioners. This was refused and the trustees appealed to the court.

The court held that the organisation was not a charitable body because some of its purposes (for example, procuring the abolition of torture or inhuman or degrading treatment) were political and did not comply with the definition of charitable purposes. Admittedly, some of its purposes were charitable such as the promotion of research into the maintenance and observance of human rights. On construction, its main purposes were not exclusively charitable.

11 [1943] 2 All ER 101.

12 [1981] 3 All ER 493.

Slade J:

The requirement of public benefit

Trusts to promote changes in the law of England are generally regarded as being non-charitable for [lacking a public benefit]. Thus, Lord Parker of Waddington said, in *Bowman v Secular Society Ltd*:[13]

> ... a trust for the attainment of political objects has always been held invalid, not because it is illegal, for everyone is at liberty to advocate or promote by any lawful means a change in the law, but because the court has no means of judging whether a proposed change in the law will or will not be for the public benefit, and therefore cannot say that a gift to secure the change is a charitable gift. The same considerations apply when there is a trust for the publication of a book. The court will examine the book, and if its objects be charitable in the legal sense it will give effect to the trust as a good charity: *Thornton v Howe*;[14] but if its objects be political it will refuse to enforce the trust: *De Themmines v De Bonneval*.[15]

In the latter case a gift of some stock in trust to apply the dividends in printing and promoting the circulation of a treatise written in French and Latin, which inculcated the doctrine of absolute supremacy of the Pope in ecclesiastical matters, was held void. As was said in the judgment in that case:[16]

> It is against the policy of the country to encourage, by the establishment of a charity, the publication of any work which asserts the absolute supremacy of the Pope in ecclesiastical matters over the sovereignty of the State.

There is now no doubt whatever that a trust of which a principal object is to alter the law of this country cannot be regarded as charitable. In *National Anti-Vivisection Society v IRC*.[17] As Lord Wright said, at pp 49–50: 'But there is another and essentially different ground on which in my opinion it must fail; that is, because its object is to secure legislation to give legal effect to it.' It is, in my opinion, a political purpose within the meaning of Lord Parker's pronouncement in *Bowman v Secular Society Ltd.*

From the passages from the speeches of Lord Parker and Lord Wright which I have read I extract the principle that the court will not regard as charitable a trust of which a main object is to procure an alteration of the law of the United Kingdom for one or both of two reasons: first, the court will ordinarily have no sufficient means of judging as a matter of evidence whether the proposed change will or will not be for the public benefit. Secondly, even if the evidence suffices to enable it to form a *prima facie* opinion that a change in the law is desirable, it must still decide the case on the principle that the law is right as it stands, since to do otherwise would usurp the functions of the legislature. I interpret the point made by Lord Simonds concerning the position of the

13 [1917] AC 406, p 442.

14 (1862) 31 Beav 14.

15 (1828) 5 Russ 288.

16 *Ibid*, p 292.

17 [1948] AC 31 (see below, p 669).

Attorney General as merely illustrating some of the anomalies and undesirable consequences that might ensue if the courts began to encroach on the functions of the legislature by ascribing charitable status to trusts of which a main object is to procure a change in the law of the United Kingdom, as being for the public benefit.

The point with which I am at present concerned is whether a trust of which the direct and main object is to secure a change in the laws of a foreign country can ever be regarded as charitable under English law. Though I do not think that any authority cited to me precisely covers the point, I have come to the clear conclusion that it cannot.

I accept that the dangers of the court encroaching on the functions of the legislature or of subjecting its political impartiality to question would not be nearly so great as when similar trusts are to be executed in this country. I also accept that on occasions the court will examine and express an opinion upon the quality of a foreign law. Thus, for example, it has declined to enforce or recognise rights conferred or duties imposed by a foreign law, in certain cases where it has considered that, on the particular facts, enforcement or recognition would be contrary to justice or morality. I therefore accept that the particular point made by Mr Tyssen (about the law stultifying itself) has no application in this context. There is no obligation on the court to decide on the principle that any foreign law is *ex hypothesi* right as it stands; it is not obliged for all purposes to blind itself to what it may regard as the injustice of a particular foreign law.

In my judgment, however, there remain overwhelming reasons why such a trust still cannot be regarded as charitable. All the reasoning of Lord Parker of Waddington in *Bowman v Secular Society Ltd*[18] seems to me to apply *a fortiori* in such a case. *A fortiori* the court will have no adequate means of judging whether a proposed change in the law of a foreign country will or will not be for the public benefit. Sir Raymond Evershed MR in *Camille and Henry Dreyfus Foundation Inc v IRC*[19] expressed the *prima facie* view that the community which has to be considered in this context, even in the case of a trust to be executed abroad, is the community of the United Kingdom. Assuming that this is the right test, the court in applying it would still be bound to take account of the probable effects of attempts to procure the proposed legislation, or of its actual enactment, on the inhabitants of the country concerned which would doubtless have a history and social structure quite different from that of the United Kingdom. Whatever might be its view as to the content of the relevant law from the standpoint of an English lawyer, it would, I think, have no satisfactory means of judging such probable effects upon the local community.

Furthermore, before ascribing charitable status to an English trust of which a main object was to secure the alteration of a foreign law, the court would also, I conceive, be bound to consider the consequences for this country as a matter of public policy. In a number of such cases there would arise a substantial *prima facie* risk that such a trust, if enforced could prejudice the relations of this

18 [1917] AC 406.

19 [1954] Ch 672, p 684.

country with the foreign country concerned: compare *Habershon v Vardon*.[20] The court would have no satisfactory means of assessing the extent of such risk, which would not be capable of being readily dealt with by evidence and would be a matter more for political than for legal judgment.

For all these reasons, I conclude that a trust of which a main purpose is to procure a change in the laws of a foreign country is a trust for the attainment of political objects within the spirit of Lord Parker of Waddington's pronouncement and, as such, is non-charitable.

If the crucial test whether a trust is charitable formulated by Lord Simonds in the same case, at p 62 – namely, the competence of the court to control and reform it – is applied, I think one is again driven to the conclusion that trusts of the nature now under discussion, which are to be executed abroad, cannot qualify as charities any more than if they are to be executed in this country. The court, in considering whether particular methods of carrying out or reforming them would be for the public benefit, would be faced with an inescapable dilemma, of which a hypothetical example may be given. It appears from the *Amnesty International Report*, 1978, p 270, that Islamic law sanctions the death penalty for certain well defined offences, namely, murder, adultery and brigandage. Let it be supposed that a trust were created of which the object was to secure the abolition of the death penalty for adultery in those countries where Islamic law applies, and to secure a reprieve for those persons who have been sentenced to death for this offence. The court, when invited to enforce or to reform such a trust, would either have to apply English standards as to public benefit, which would not necessarily be at all appropriate in the local conditions, or would have to attempt to apply local standards, of which it knew little or nothing. An English court would not, it seems to me, be competent either to control or reform a trust of this nature, and it would not be appropriate that it should attempt to do so.

Summary of conclusions relating to trusts for political purposes

Founding them principally on the House of Lords' decisions in the *Bowman* case[21] and the *National Anti-Vivisection Society* case,[22] I therefore summarise my conclusions in relation to trusts for political purposes as follows. (1) Even if it otherwise appears to fall within the spirit and intendment of the preamble to the Statute of Elizabeth, a trust for political purposes falling within the spirit of Lord Parker's pronouncement in *Bowman*'s case can never be regarded as being for the public benefit in the manner which the law regards as charitable. (2) Trusts for political purposes falling within the spirit of this pronouncement include, *inter alia*, trusts of which a direct and principal purpose is either: (i) to further the interests of a particular political party; or (ii) to procure changes in the laws of this country; or (iii) to procure changes in the laws of a foreign country; or (iv) to procure a reversal of government policy or of particular decisions of governmental authorities in this country; or (v) to procure a

20 (1851) 4 De G & Sm 467.

21 [1917] AC 406.

22 [1948] AC 31.

reversal of government policy or of particular decisions of governmental authorities in a foreign country.

This categorisation is not intended to be an exhaustive one, but I think it will suffice for the purposes of this judgment; I would further emphasise that it is directed to trusts of which the purposes are political. As will appear later, the mere fact that trustees may be at liberty to employ political means in furthering the non-political purposes of a trust does not necessarily render it non-charitable.

The requirement that trust purposes must be wholly and exclusively charitable

[The learned judge considered the test for certainty of charitable objects (see above, p 580) and continued:]

I think that two propositions follow in the present case. First, if any one of the main objects of the trusts declared by the trust deed is to be regarded as 'political' in the relevant sense, then, subject to the effect of the proviso to clause 2, the trusts of the trust deed cannot qualify as being charitable. Secondly, however, if all the main objects of the trust are exclusively charitable, the mere fact that the trustees may have incidental powers to employ political means for their furtherance will not deprive them of their charitable status. After this introduction I now turn to examine these trusts themselves.

I do not think that the trust can be construed as being one of which the main purpose is merely to influence public opinion in the country where the imprisonment is taking place. Its very terms suggest the direction of moral pressure or persuasion against governmental authorities.

As Buckley LJ said in *Incorporated Council of Law Reporting for England and Wales v AG*:[23]

> ... in order to determine whether an object, the scope of which has been ascertained by due processes of construction, is a charitable purpose it may be necessary to have regard to evidence to discover the consequences of pursuing that object.

Examples of forms of pressure which would specifically fall within the wording of clause 2B, and were no doubt contemplated by the parties to the trust deed, are to be found in the following extract from the *Amnesty International Handbook*, at p 29:

> Pressure to free prisoners of conscience can mean all of the following: thousands of postcards and letters to the foreign government; distributing leaflets at trade fairs; special appeals signed by prominent individuals; trade union embargoes against goods from the foreign government; continuous international news reports on the human rights violations by the governments concerned.

Expressed in one sentence, the main object of the broadly defined trust contained in clause 2B must in my judgment be regarded as being the procurement of the reversal of the relevant decisions of governments and

23 [1972] Ch 73, p 99.

> governmental authorities in those countries where such authorities have decided to detain 'prisoners of conscience', whether or not in accordance with the local law. The procurement of the reversal of such decisions cannot, I think, be regarded merely as one possible method of giving effect to the purposes of clause 2B, any more than in the *National Anti-Vivisection Society* case[24] the alteration of the law could be regarded as merely one method of giving effect to the purpose of abolishing vivisection. On the construction which I place on clause 2B, it is the principal purpose itself. On this view of the matter, the trust declared by clause 2B cannot in my judgment qualify as a charitable trust. It is a trust for political purposes, within the fifth of the categories listed above.
>
> **Conclusion**
>
> Indisputably, laws do exist both in this country and in many foreign countries which many reasonable persons consider unjust. No less indisputably, laws themselves will from time to time be administered by governmental authorities in a manner which many reasonable persons consider unjust, inhuman or degrading. Amnesty International, in striving to remedy what it considers to be such injustices, is performing a function which many will regard as being of great value to humanity. Fortunately, the laws of this country place very few restrictions on the rights of philanthropic organisations such as this, or of individuals, to strive for the remedy of what they regard as instances of injustice, whether occurring here or abroad. However, for reasons which I think adequately appear from Lord Parker of Waddington's pronouncement in *Bowman*'s case,[25] the elimination of injustice has not as such ever been held to be a trust purpose which qualifies for the privileges afforded to charities by English law. I cannot hold it to be a charitable purpose now.

On the other hand, the mere acquisition of knowledge without dissemination or advancement will not be charitable.

Re Shaw, Public Trustee v Day [1957] 1 All ER 745, HC

In this case, the testator, George Bernard Shaw, bequeathed money to be used to develop a forty letter alphabet and translate his play 'Androcles and the lion' into this alphabet. The court held that the gift was not charitable as it was aimed merely at the increase of knowledge. In addition, the gift was political in the sense of attempting to cause a change in the law.

> **Harman J:** The research and propaganda enjoined by the testator seem to me merely to tend to the increase of public knowledge in a certain respect, namely, the saving of time and money by the use of the proposed alphabet. There is no element of teaching or education combined with this, nor does the propaganda element in the trusts tend to more than to persuade the public that the adoption of the new script would be 'a good thing', and that, in my view, is not education. Therefore I reject this element.
>
> There remains the fourth category.

24 [1948] AC 31.

25 [1917] AC 406.

The testator is convinced, and sets out to convince the world, but the fact that he considers the proposed reform to be beneficial does not make it so any more than the fact that he describes the trust as charitable constrains the court to hold that it is.

A case on a parallel subject, spelling reform, came before Rowlatt J, on an income tax point. That is *Trustees of the Sir GB Hunter (1922) 'C' Trust v IRC*.[26] The headnote reads:

> The trust deed provided that the net income and, after a period of years, the capital, of the trust should be paid or applied to the benefit of the Simplified Spelling Society or in certain circumstances, as to which the trustees had wide discretionary powers, to the benefit of or to promote the formation of any other society or association having similar objects. The objects of the society were to recommend and to further the general use of simpler spellings of English words than those now in use. It engaged in propaganda to influence public opinion in favour of its objects and to gain for them the approval of education authorities. The appellants claimed that the purposes for which the society was established were charitable either as being educational or as being beneficial to the community. Held that the trust was not established for charitable purposes.
>
> The objects of this society or any other society which would benefit under this trust is simply to make spelling more simple. Everyone would agree up to a point that it is probably advantageous. Probably, as you go on, you will get differences of opinion; but, right or wrong, the question is whether that is a charitable object. You have people trying to promote the simplification of spelling, or the simplification of grammar, or the uniformity of pronouncing, or the simplification of dress, or the simplification or reform of any of the conveniences of life. But in my judgment they are nowhere near either of the express categories mentioned by Lord MacNaghten in the well known judgment, *Income Tax Special Purposes Commissioners v Pemsel,* or within the classes of cases which come within the general classes in the Act. I think that this case is hardly arguable.

Such words of such a judge must have great weight with me. It seems to me that the objects of the alphabet trusts are analogous to trusts for political purposes, which advocate a change in the law. Such objects have never been considered charitable.

I, therefore, do not reach the further inquiry whether the benefit is one within the spirit or intendment (as it is called) of the Statute of Elizabeth (43 Eliz, c 4), but, if I had to decide that point, I should hold that it was not.

Gifts which have been upheld as charitable under this head have included trusts for choral singing in London (*Royal Choral Society v IRC*);[27] the diffusion of knowledge of Egyptology and the training of students in Egyptology (*Re*

26 (1929) 14 TC 427.

27 [1943] 2 All ER 101.

British School of Egyptian Archaeology);[28] the encouragement of chess playing by boys or young men resident in the city of Portsmouth (*Re Dupree's Trusts*); the furtherance of the Boy Scout Movement by helping to purchase sites for camping (*Re Webber*); the promotion of the education of the Irish by teaching self-control, elocution, oratory deportment, the arts of personal contact or social intercourse (*Re Shaw's Will Trust*); the publication of law reports which record the development of judge made law (*Incorporated Council of Law Reporting for England and Wales v AG*); the promotion of the works of a famous composer (*Re Delius' Will Trust*)[29] or celebrated writer (*Re Shakespeare Memorial Trust*);[30] the students' union of a university (*Baldry v Feintuck*); the furtherance of the Wilton Park project, that is, a conference centre for discussion of matters of international importance (*Re Koeppler's Will Trust*); the provision of facilities at schools and universities to play association football or other games (*IRC v McMullen*); professional bodies which exist for the promotion of the arts or sciences (*Royal College of Surgeons of England v National Provincial Bank Ltd*).

Evaluation

Before deciding whether the gifts are charitable or not, the courts are required to take into account the usefulness of the gifts to the public. This may be effected by judicial notice of the value of the gift to society. In the event of doubt, the courts may take into account the opinions of experts. The opinions of the donors are inconclusive. In *Re Pinion*, a gift to the National Trust of a studio and contents to be maintained as a collection, failed as a charity. The collection as a whole lacked any artistic merit. The judge could conceive of no useful purpose in 'foisting on the public this mass of junk'.

In re Pinion (Decd), Westminister Bank Ltd v Pinion and Another [1965] 1 Ch 85, CA (Harman, Davies and Russell LJJ)

> **Harman LJ:** Where a museum is concerned and the utility of the gift is brought in question it is, in my opinion, and herein I agree with the judge, essential to know at least something of the quality of the proposed exhibits in order to judge whether they will be conducive to the education of the public. So I think with a public library, such a place if found to be devoted entirely to works of pornography or of a corrupting nature, would not be allowable. Here it is suggested that education in the fine arts is the object. For myself a reading of the will leads me rather to the view that the testator's object was not to educate anyone, but to perpetuate his own name and the repute of his family, hence perhaps the direction that the custodian should be a blood relation of his. However that may be, there is a strong body of evidence here that as a means

28 [1954] 1 All ER 887.

29 [1957] 1 All ER 854.

30 [1923] 2 Ch 389.

of education this collection is worthless. The testator's own paintings, of which there are over 50, are said by competent persons to be in an academic style and 'atrociously bad' and the other picture without exception worthless. Even the so called 'Lely' turns out to be a 20th century copy.

Apart from pictures there is a haphazard assembly – it does not merit the name collection, for no purpose emerges, no time nor style is illustrated – of furniture and objects of so called 'art' about which expert opinion is unanimous that nothing beyond the third rate is to be found. Indeed, one of the experts expresses his surprise that so voracious a collector should not by hazard have picked up even one meritorious object. The most that skillful cross-examination extracted from the expert witnesses was that there were a dozen chairs which might perhaps be acceptable to a minor provincial museum and perhaps another dozen not altogether worthless, but two dozen chairs do not make a museum and they must, to accord with the will, be exhibited stifled by a large number of absolutely worthless pictures and objects.

It was said that this is a matter of taste, and *de gustibus non est disputandum*, but here I agree with the judge that there is an accepted canon of taste on which the court must rely, for it has itself no judicial knowledge of such matters, and the unanimous verdict of the experts is as I have stated. The judge with great hesitation concluded that there was that scintilla of merit which was sufficient to save the rest. I find myself on the other side of the line. I can conceive of no useful object to be served in foisting upon the public this mass of junk. It has neither public utility nor educative value. I would hold that the testator's project ought not to be carried into effect and that his next of kin is entitled to the residue of his estate.

THE ADVANCEMENT OF RELIGION

The preamble to the 1601 Statute refers to 'the repair of churches'. English law steers a neutral course between all forms of religions. 'Religion' is defined in the Oxford Dictionary as a 'recognition on the part of man of some higher unseen power as having control of his destiny and as being entitled to obedience, reverence and worship' or ' a particular system of faith and worship'. There is not a great deal of authority recognising non-Christian religions (although Judaism has been recognised in *Strauss v Goldsmith*[31] and *Neville Estates v Madden*[32] (see above, p 622), but regulations made under the Charities Act 1993 assume that non-Christian religions are charitable. The Goodman Report (1976) declared that account must be taken of all religions whether monotheistic or not. This would include a polytheistic religion such as Hinduism. Buddhism, which does not involve a belief in God is universally regarded as a religion and may be treated as an exception to the rule that a

31 (1837) 8 Sim 614.

32 [1962] Ch 832.

religion involves a faith or spiritual belief in a supreme being. On the other hand, in *Re South Place Ethical Society*,[33] it was decided that the study and dissemination of ethical principles but which did not involve faith in a deity could not constitute religion although the society was charitable on the ground of advancement of education, *per* Dillon J:

> 'Religion,' as I see it, is concerned with man's relations with God and 'ethics' is concerned with man's relation with man. The two are not the same and are not made the same by sincere inquiry into the question: What is God? If reason leads people not to accept Christianity or any known religion, but they do believe in the excellence of qualities such as truth, beauty and love, their beliefs may be to them the equivalent of a religion but viewed objectively they are not religion.

Similarly, a body, such as the Freemason's Society, whose rules demand the highest personal and social standards does not constitute a religion, see *United Grand Lodge of Freemasons in England and Wales v Holborn Borough Council*.[34] With similar effect in principle, a trust to promote atheism or to demonstrate that religious belief is erroneous will not be charitable under this head.

Unlike trusts for the advancement of education, the courts do not evaluate the merit of one religion as opposed to another or indeed the benefit to the public of religious instruction. Provided that the religious gift is not subversive of all morality, the gift will be charitable. In *Thornton v Howe*,[35] a trust was created for the publication of the writings of Joanna Southcote, who believed that she would miraculously conceive and give birth, at an advanced age, to the second Messiah. Although the judge thought that she was 'foolish, deluded and confused', he held that the gift was charitable. Similarly, in *Re Watson*; the court decided that a gift to publish the religious works of Hobbs (which had no intrinsic value) was charitable.

Re Watson (Decd), Hobbs v Smith and Others [1973] 3 All ER 678, HC

> **Plowman J:** There are two questions to consider. The first is, what are the purposes of the trust expressed by the will, and, secondly, whether that trust is a charitable trust. Now as to the first point, the work of God which is referred to in a number of passages in the will which I have read, to quote the will, is 'the work of God as it has been maintained by Mr HG Hobbs and myself since 1942 ... in propagating the truth as given in the Holy Bible'. And I accept counsel for the Attorney General's submission that, on the true construction of the will, read in the light of the evidence of surrounding circumstances, the trust is one for the publication and distribution to the public of the religious works of Mr HG Hobbs. If that is right, to get one point out of the way, that trust will not, in my judgment, fail for impracticability, as counsel for the next

33 [1980] 1 WLR 1565.

34 [1957] 1 WLR 1090.

35 (1862) 31 Beav 14.

of kin suggested on one view of the will that it must. On the second question, whether that trust, namely the trust for the publication and distribution to the public of the religious works of Mr Hobbs, is charitable, counsel for the next of kin submitted that it was not. He submitted that not every religious trust is charitable, that to be charitable there must be an element of public benefit, that whether or not there is a sufficient public benefit is a matter for the court to decide on evidence, irrespective of the opinion of the donor and that there is no sufficient element of public benefit in this case.

Now the result of the cases, including the *Anti-Vivisection* case to which counsel for the next of kin referred, in my judgment, is this. First of all, as Romilly MR said in *Thornton v Howe*, the court does not prefer one religion to another and it does not prefer one sect to another. Secondly, where the purposes in question are of a religious nature – and, in my opinion, they clearly are here – then the court assumes a public benefit unless the contrary is shown. In the *Anti-Vivisection* case, Lord Wright said:

> The test of benefit to the community goes through the whole of Lord MacNaghten's classification [in the *Pemsel* case] though, as regards the first three heads [which of course includes religion], it may be *prima facie* assumed unless the contrary appears.

And Lord Simonds, in his speech, said:

> I would rather say that, when a purpose appears broadly to fall within one of the familiar categories of charity, the court will assume it to be for the benefit of the community and therefore charitable unless the contrary is shown, and further that the court will not be astute in such a case to defeat upon doubtful evidence the avowed benevolent intention of a donor.

And thirdly, that having regard to the fact that the court does not draw a distinction between one religion and another or one sect and another, the only way of disproving a public benefit is to show, in the words of Romilly MR in *Thornton v Howe*, that the doctrines inculcated are – 'adverse to the very foundations of all religion, and that they are subversive of all morality'. and that in my judgment, as I have said already, is clearly not the case here, and I therefore conclude that this case is really on all fours with *Thornton v Howe* and for that reason is a valid charitable trust.

The institution or association is required to promote or advance religion. This was considered by Donovan J in *United Grand Lodge of Freemasons in England and Wales v Holborn Borough Council* (cited above, p 657):

> **Donovan J:** To advance religion means to promote it, to spread its message ever wider among mankind; to take some positive steps to sustain and increase religious belief; and these things are done in a variety of ways which may be comprehensively described as pastoral and missionary. It should include religious instruction, a programme for the persuasion of unbelievers, religious supervision to see that its members remain active and constant in the various religions they may profess.

Religion may be advanced in a variety of ways such as the maintenance of places of worship including the upkeep of churchyards, gifts for the clergy, the provision of an organ or maintenance of a choir, the active spread of religion at home and abroad, although a gift for 'parish work' will be void as including many objects which are not charitable (see *Farley v Westminster Bank*).

Farley and Others v Westminster Bank Ltd and Others, Re Ashton's Estate, Westminster Bank Ltd v Farley [1939] 3 All ER 491, HL (Lords Atkin, Russell of Killowen and Romer)

The facts appear in the judgment of Lord Atkin.

> **Lord Atkin:** The question is, what is the meaning of the words 'the vicar and churchwardens of St Columba's Church, Hoxton (for parish work)'?
>
> Counsel for the appellants in the course of a forcible argument said that that is equivalent to a gift to the vicar and churchwardens of St Columba's Church, Hoxton – it is in fact in Haggerston, but we need not trouble about that – and he says that that would mean a gift to the vicar and churchwardens for the purpose of their spiritual duties as vicar and churchwardens, and that it would be a good charitable bequest – which is perfectly true – if there were no words added. Then he says that the words '(for parish work)' simply mean to express what would be implicit in the words 'the vicar and churchwardens' without the addition of those words in brackets; and, if so, he says, then there is nothing to prevent this gift from being a charitable gift. Alternatively, he says, the words limit their duties in some particular respect which I do not think he found it very easy to define, and which, if he finds it difficult to define, I find it still more difficult to define. In some sense or other, however, he says that the words limit what would be ordinarily understood if one had a gift to the vicar and churchwardens simply.
>
> My Lords, I am entirely unable to accept that construction. I think that the words are quite plainly enlarging words. They are words of definition, it is quite true, but I think that they were used for the very purpose of defining what the testatrix meant as the purpose for which the money was to be applied, and 'parish work' seems to me to be of such vague import as to go far beyond the ordinary meaning of charity, in this case in the sense of being a religious purpose. The expression covers the whole of the ordinary activities of the parish, some of which no doubt fall within the definition of religious purposes, and all of which no doubt are religious from the point of view of the person who is responsible for the spiritual care of the parish, in the sense that they are conducive, perhaps, to the moral and spiritual good of his congregation. However, that, I think, quite plainly is not enough, and the words are so wide that I am afraid that on no construction can they be brought within the limited meaning of 'charitable' as used in the law.

A gift to an officer of the church in his official capacity (the vicar) to be applied in his absolute discretion may be construed as imposing an implied limitation on the transferee's discretion namely, use for ecclesiastical (or official) purposes.

***Re Garrard* [1907] 1 Ch 382, HC**

In this case, a testatrix bequeathed £400 'to the vicar and churchwardens for the time being of Kington, to be applied by them in such manner as they in their sole discretion think fit'.

The court held that on construction, the gift was charitable for the advancement of religion.

> **Joyce J:** The churchwardens are the officers of the parish in ecclesiastical matters, so that a mere gift or legacy to the vicar and churchwardens for the time being of a parish, without more, is a gift or charitable legacy to them for ecclesiastical purposes in the parish. It was suggested that the words in the latter part of the gift were inconsistent with its being a charitable gift, and that they implied that the vicar and churchwardens were to take beneficially. In my opinion there is no contradiction or inconsistency in the will whatever. The words 'to be applied by them in such manner as they shall in their sole discretion think fit', to my mind merely direct that the particular mode of application within the charitable purposes of the legacy is to be settled by those individuals, or rather that there is power given to them to do it, subject always, of course, to the jurisdiction of the court. Therefore, I declare this to be a good charitable legacy for the benefit of the parish of Kington for ecclesiastical purposes.

A gift for the saying of masses in public is charitable for the gift promotes an integral part of religion namely, the saying of prayers. Such prayers, although incapable *per se* of proving beneficial to mankind, is assumed to provide a sufficient element of public benefit. The *prima facie* assumption that is made is that prayers stipulated by a settlor in a will or *inter vivos* instrument is assumed to be said in public.

In *Re Caus*,[36] a testator, a Roman Catholic priest, by his will bequeathed £1,000 'for masses to be said for my soul and the souls of my parents and relatives ... with a reversion to the parish of St Peter's Roman Catholic Church'. On the question of the validity of this gift as a charity.

Held that the gift was charitable for the advancement of religion on the grounds that:

(a) prayers provided a ritual act central to the religion of a large proportion of Christian people; and

(b) the donation assisted in the upkeep of priests whose duties involved performance of the acts.

But, the court failed to draw a distinction between public and private masses and the predominant nexus between the donor and the purpose of the gift.

In *Re Hetherington*, the High Court found support in *Gilmour v Coats* (see above, p 618) which enabled it to limit the effect of *Re Caus*. Accordingly, the

36 [1934] Ch 162.

latter decision is no longer good law to the extent that it condoned the saying of masses in private as a charitable purpose.

Re Hetherington [1989] 2 All ER 129, HC

By her will, a testatrix bequeathed £2,000 to the Roman Catholic Bishop of Westminster for the saying of 'masses of the souls of my husband, parents, sisters and myself'. On the issue of the validity of the gift, the court held that the legacy was donated for the advancement of religion.

> **Browne-Wilkinson J:** In *Gilmour v Coats* comments were made on *In re Caus*, some of them adverse. It is therefore said that the decision in *Gilmour v Coats* has cast doubt on the validity of the decision in *In re Caus*. *In re Caus* has stood now for over 50 years and I would certainly follow it unless it has been undermined by the decision of the House of Lords in *Gilmour v Coats*. In the latter case The House of Lords held that the trusts were not valid charitable trusts since they lacked any element of public benefit. In argument before the House of Lords *In re Caus* was relied upon. Lord Simonds pointed out that the actual grounds for decision in *In re Caus* did not rely on the public benefiting by means of intercessory prayer and example. He reserved the question whether the decision in *In re Caus* was itself right on other grounds. Lord du Parq also reserved the same question. Lord Reid pointed out that there were grounds, other than the alleged public benefit by means of prayer, on which it could be argued that *In re Caus* was rightly decided, but he too expressed no opinion on the point.
>
> In my judgment *Gilmour v Coats* does not impair the validity of the decision in *In re Caus*. Certainly, the judgment of Luxmoore J which suggests that public benefit can be shown from the mere celebration of a religious rite is no longer good law. The same in my judgment is true of Luxmoore J's first ground of decision, if it suggests that the performance in private of a religious ritual act is charitable as being for the public benefit. But in my judgment there is nothing in the House of Lords' decision which impugns Luxmoore J's second ground of decision, namely that the public benefit was to be found in the endowment of the priesthood. Therefore, the decision in *In re Caus* is still good law and I must follow it.
>
> The grounds on which the trust in the present case can be attacked are that there is no express requirement that the Masses for souls which are to be celebrated are to be celebrated in public. The evidence shows that celebration in public is the invariable practice but there is no requirement of Canon law to that effect. Therefore, it is said the money could be applied to saying Masses in private which would not be charitable since there would be no sufficient element of public benefit.
>
> In my judgment the cases establish the following propositions:
>
> (1) A trust for the advancement of education, the relief of poverty or the advancement of religion is *prima facie* charitable and assumed to be for the public benefit. *National Anti-Vivisection Society v IRC*.[37] This assumption of

37 [1948] AC 31, pp 42, 65.

public benefit can be rebutted by showing that in fact the particular trust in question cannot operate so as to confer a legally recognised benefit on the public, as in *Gilmour v Coats*.[38]

(2) The celebration of a religious rite in public does confer a sufficient public benefit because of the edifying and improving effect of such celebration on the members of the public who attend. As Lord Reid said in *Gilmour v Coats*:[39]

A religion can be regarded as beneficial without it being necessary to assume that all its beliefs are true, and a religious service can be regarded as beneficial to all those who attend it without it being necessary to determine the spiritual efficacy of that service or to accept any particular belief about it.

(3) The celebration of a religious rite in private does not contain the necessary element of public benefit since any benefit by prayer or example is incapable of proof in the legal sense, and any element of edification is limited to a private, not public, class of those present at the celebration: see *Gilmour v Coats*; *Yeap Cheah Neo v Ong Cheng Neo*[40] and *Hoare v Hoare*.[41] Where there is a gift for a religious purpose which could be carried out in a way which is beneficial to the public (that is, by public Masses) but could also be carried out in a way which would not have sufficient element of public benefit (that is, by private Masses) the gift is to be construed as a gift to be carried out only by the methods that are charitable, all non-charitable methods being excluded: see *In re White*;[42] and *In re Banfield*.[43]

Applying those principles to the present case, a gift for the saying of Masses is *prima facie* charitable, being for a religious purpose. In practice, those Masses will be celebrated in public which provides a sufficient element of public benefit. The provision of stipends for priests saying the Masses, by relieving the Roman Catholic Church *pro tanto* of the liability to provide such stipends, is a further benefit. The gift is to be construed as a gift for public Masses only on the principle of *In re White*, private Masses not being permissible since it would not be a charitable application of the fund for a religious purpose.

[Declaration made.]

Recently, the court decided that the promotion of faith healing, within limits, was a charitable activity, either for the advancement of religion, or purposes beneficial to the community.

38 [1949] AC 426.

39 *Ibid*, p 459.

40 (1875) LR 6 PC 381.

41 (1886) 56 LT 147.

42 [1893] 2 Ch 41, pp 52–53.

43 [1968] 1 WLR 846.

Funnell v Stewart [1996] 1 WLR 288, HC

Prior to her death, the testatrix had been involved with a small religious and healing movement centred at her home at 139 Hoadswood Road, Hastings. The movement had been operating for at least 30 years. The healing process involved the laying of hands by those with a healing gift and the saying of prayers. The activities of the group fell into two categories: healing sessions and religious services. The spiritual healing sessions were available to the public but only a quarter of the religious services were open to the public.

The testatrix, by her will, left her residuary estate, including the house in Hoadswood Road to Mrs Stewart and Mrs Austen subject to the following declaration, 'and I direct that they shall use the same ... to further the spiritual work carried on by us together ... for so long as the law permits'. The residuary estate was worth £150,000. The executors issued an originating summons against the two trustees and the next of kin, inquiring whether the gift by will created a valid charitable trust or was invalid as being a non-charitable purpose trust.

Counsel representing the next of kin contended that the trust failed as a charitable purpose because the private religious meetings were confined to a narrow group of individuals (working members of the organisation) and thus lacked a 'public benefit', see *Gilmour v Coats* [1949] AC 426. In addition, faith healing was not a charitable activity based on analogy with *Re Hummeltenberg* [1923] 1 Ch 237, where the court decided that a college for the training of mediums was not a charitable purpose.

Counsel for the residuary beneficiaries argued that faith healing had now become recognised as a charitable purpose under the fourth head in *IRC v Pemsel* [1891] AC 531, as being beneficial to the community. He referred to the Report of the Charity Commissioners for England and Wales in 1975 as indicating this. He also submitted that, where the organisation has a religious element, as in the present case, the body is treated as charitable provided that the healing is open to the public. He relied on *Re Watson* (1973) as demonstrating that where the trust is of a religious nature, a different test of public benefit applied. This is presumed to exist unless the contrary is shown.

Judge Hazel Williamson QC accepted the arguments of counsel for the residuary beneficiaries. Her Ladyship decided that a gift to further faith healing was a valid charitable gift for purposes beneficial to the community and also for the advancement of religion. The private element in the religious services was, on the evidence, clearly ancillary to the public faith healing aspect of the group's work and did not disqualify it from being charitable.

Williamson QC:

Clause 6 of the will read:

> Subject to the payment of my just debts funeral and testamentary expenses, I give, devise, bequeath and appoint all the rest of my estate both real and personal wheresoever and whatsoever (including my dwelling

> house known as Hoadswood, 139 Hoadswood Road, Hastings aforesaid) and (subject to clause 5 hereof) the residuary estate of my late mother Lily Maud Clarke over which I have a power of appointment unto and equally between such of the said Mrs Lillian Stewart and Mrs Pamela Austen ...

I should say that that is the lady whom I have described as Mrs Freda Austen:

> ... of 106 Hoadswood Road, Hastings as shall survive me and I direct that they shall use the same together with the investments and other property at present held in the joint names of myself and the said Lillian Stewart (all of which shall together become known as 'The Ruby Rolfe Trust') to further the spiritual work now carried on by us together to the intent that the Ruby Rolfe Trust be continued by them and their successors to carry on such spiritual work for so long as the law permits. I direct that the receipt of the said Lillian Stewart and Pamela Austen or the survivor of them shall be a full and complete discharge to my trustees who shall not in any way be concerned with the application thereof.

By clause 7, Miss Le Cren Clarke further provided:

> I express the following wishes relating to the Ruby Rolfe Trust but so that my trustees shall not in any way be concerned with or responsible for the same, namely: (a) the said Lillian Stewart shall, if possible, continue to reside in my dwelling house known as Hoadswood, aforesaid; (b) the said Lillian Stewart and Pamela Austen shall appoint the said Albert Frederick Smith to be the warden of such house which shall form part of the Ruby Rolfe Trust and of all things pertaining thereto; (c) the said Lillian Stewart and Pamela Austen shall be entitled to invite any person or persons whom they consider to be suitable to join with them in carrying out the spiritual work now carried on by us and by their wills shall provide that the remaining balances of the benefits received by them under clause 6 of this my will shall be left to the person or persons who shall be carrying on the work of the Ruby Rolfe Trust at their respective deaths but if there shall be no such person able and willing to carry on such work then they shall pay or by their wills leave such remaining balances to be divided equally between the National Society for the Prevention of Cruelty to Children and the aforesaid British Deaf Association.

It is these clauses, and in particular clause 6, which have given rise to these proceedings.

The first question which I have to answer is whether the terms of clause 6 are apt to create a gift to the first and second defendants beneficially or upon trust. The question is, therefore, whether the use of the word 'direct' in clause 6 of Miss Le Cren Clarke's will is to be construed as being mandatory or merely precatory. Reading clauses 6 and 7, I have come to the firm conclusion that the direction is mandatory and that clause 6 is apt to create a trust and pass the funds the subject of clause 6 only upon a trust. I note that the will appears to have been professionally drafted, and I contrast the terms of clause 6 with those of clause 7. In my judgment, it is clear that clause 6 directs what is to happen, whereas clause 7 merely expresses wishes, but gives no direction as to how this is to be brought about, if possible.

I turn to the second question, namely, whether the trust is a good charitable trust or whether it is invalid for being a non-charitable purpose trust. The essence of this question involves determining what is being referred to by the testatrix, in clause 6, where she gives the direction to the first and second defendants to use the property to further 'the spiritual work now carried on by us together'. What was the 'spiritual work' to which the testatrix was referring and is it charitable in the sense recognised by law? For the gift to be charitable the purpose of it must be seen to be within one of the four heads of charity listed by Lord MacNaghten in *Income Tax Special Purposes Commissioners v Pemsel* [1891] AC 531, p 583, namely: 'trusts for the relief of poverty; trusts for the advancement of education; trusts for the advancement of religion; and trusts for other purposes beneficial to the community.' The only candidates in this case would seem to be trusts for the advancement of religion and other purposes beneficial to the community. The crucial question is what was meant by 'to further the spiritual work carried on by us'. Viewing the will as a whole, I have the clear impression that the testatrix was regarding the essence of such work as being the faith healing work. First, this is the natural meaning of 'work' as contrasted with 'activity' or with some other word. The word 'work' is outgoing. This flavour is carried over into clause 7(c) of the will. I have also noticed that this usage of the word 'work' has been adopted naturally in the affadivit evidence. The 'work' to which persons are referring carries the connotation of doing something for others, doing good to others outside the movement. As regards the exclusivity point, whilst I recognise the force of Mr Bowles' point, that the testatrix herself would have regarded the private services as an integral part of this general work, in the light of my view of the essence of the work of the group, I find that this private element was clearly ancillary or subsidiary to the public faith healing part of the group's work, which was its predominant function. If one had asked what was the *raison d'être* of this group, it seems to me that the answer that would have been given was clearly the spiritual healing work it did for members of the community. It follows that, in my judgment, the testatrix's gift for the furtherance of this spiritual work is not prevented from being charitable by reason of the inclusion of the possibility that private services, which could clearly not themselves be charitable, might be held as part of such total activity. It is therefore unnecessary for me to consider Mr Henderson's fallback argument based on *In re Hetherington (Decd)* [1990] Ch 1. I have to say, however, that I would not have been prepared to find in favour of charity on this ground if it had been necessary. It seems to me that the position in *In re Hetherington* was that the purpose of the gift was clear. It was given as a gift for the purpose of saying masses for the repose of souls. The possibly vitiating factor was that this clear purpose could have been carried out either in a charitable or in a non-charitable way, namely, either by public or by private religious services, and the court had the choice of directing how, in effect, it was to be done. There was not, therefore, a dual purpose gift. There was a single purpose gift capable of being implemented in two different ways. Here, however, the doubt goes to the very objects of the gift itself, namely, whether the 'work' which is being referred to was itself charitable or was, in fact, including a non-charitable element, and, if so, whether, as a result, the gift was inevitably partly for a non-charitable purpose because the second purpose was private. I do not read *In re Hetherington* as authorising the process of construction to be applied so as to enable one identifiable purpose of a gift, which is clearly present, but is plainly not charitable, simply to be ignored. It appears to me that that is stretching language and the principles of construction too far in pursuit of benignancy. The only question left is, therefore, whether this spiritual healing work itself, in the form of the faith healing part of the group's work, which I find to be the substance of the group's work, is indeed charitable. On this point I have again come to the conclusion that Mr Henderson is right. I accept his argument that it is charitable, and I so hold either on the basis that faith healing has, by the present time (although this would not necessarily have been the case when *In re Hummeltenberg, Beatty v London Spiritualistic Alliance Ltd* [1923] 1 Ch 237 was decided), become a recognised activity of public benefit or, in any event, on the basis that the religious element in the present case, and the religious nature of the faith healing movement in question, renders this work a charitable purpose within which a sufficient element of public benefit is assumed so as to enable the charity to be recognised by law as being such unless there is contrary evidence. There is no such contrary evidence. Accordingly, I find that this is a charitable trust. It follows that it is unnecessary for me to consider the question whether the evidence of actual public benefit in the form of the demonstrable efficaciousness of the healing work of the group is actually required.

OTHER PURPOSES BENEFICIAL TO THE COMMUNITY

The preamble to the 1601 Statute of Elizabeth refers to a list of miscellaneous purposes which are charitable. The approach of the courts to novel purposes capable of being decided under this head has already been mentioned (see above). It does not follow that every purpose which is beneficial to the community will be charitable. Thus, a gift for 'charitable or benevolent purposes' is not charitable (see *Chichester Diocesan Fund v Simpson*). In order to establish that a purpose is charitable under this head, it must be shown that the purpose is beneficial to the community in a way that the law considers charitable, that is, the purpose is within the spirit and intendment of the preamble, *per* Viscount Cave LC in *AG v National Provincial and Union Bank of England*[44] (see above, p 582):

> Lord MacNaghten did not mean that all trusts for purposes beneficial to the community are charitable, but that there are certain beneficial trusts which fall within that category; and accordingly, to argue that because a trust is for a purpose beneficial to the community, it is therefore a charitable trust, is to turn his sentence round and to give it a different meaning ... it is not enough to say that the trust in question is for public purposes beneficial to the community, or for the public welfare; you must also show that it is a charitable trust.

44 [1924] AC 262.

Illustrations of charitable purposes under this head

(i) Animals

A trust which promotes the welfare of animals generally or even a species of animals (as opposed to benefiting specific animals) is a valid charitable trust because it is calculated to promote public morality by checking an inborn tendency in humans towards cruelty. *In re Wedgwood*[45] a trust for the protection and benefit of animals was charitable.

In re Wedgwood, Allen v Wedgwood [1915] 1 Ch 113, CA (Lord Cozens-Hardy MR, Kennedy and Swinfen-Eady LJJ)

A testatrix by her will gave the residue of her estate to the defendant, Cecil Wedgwood on a secret trust. It transpired that Mr Wedgwood had agreed with the testatrix to hold the property upon trust for the protection and benefit of animals.

The Court of Appeal held that a charitable trust was created for the benefit of animals on the ground that the gift promoted public morality by checking an inborn tendency towards cruelty.

> **Lord Cozens-Hardy MR:** The authorities are very numerous. I need only refer to a few. In *University of London v Yarrow*[46] it was held that a trust for the benefit of animals useful to man was good, and there was a clear intimation of opinion that the limitation to domestic animals was not necessary. In *Tatham v Drummond*[47] the establishment of a slaughterhouse for horses was held to be charitable, though the gift failed as it involved the purchase of land. The Society for the Prevention of Cruelty to Animals and a Home for lost dogs are instances in which the doctrine has been extended.
>
> In my opinion it is not possible for us to hold that this trust for the protection of animals is not a good charitable purpose. Apart from authorities which are binding upon us, I should be prepared to support the trust on the ground that it tends to promote public morality by checking the innate tendency to cruelty. In the language of Holmes LJ in *In re Cranston*:[48]
>
>> ... gifts the object of which is to prevent cruelty to animals and to ameliorate the position of the brute creation are charitable ... If it is beneficial to the community to promote virtue and to discourage vice, it must be beneficial to teach the duty of justice and fair treatment to the brute creation, and to repress one of the most revolting kinds of cruelty.

45 [1915] 1 Ch 113, CA.

46 (1857) 1 De G & J 72.

47 (1864) 4 DJ & S 484.

48 [1898] 1 IR 457.

> I desire also to mention the judgment of Chatterton VC in *Armstrong v Reeves*,[49] especially the passage at p 341, where he points out that objects of general mercy to animals of all kinds, whether useful to man or not, are charitable.

Similarly, in *University of London v Yarrow* (1857), a hospital for sick animals was charitable. *In Re Moss*,[50] a home for unwanted or stray cats was charitable.

It is essential to establish that the welfare of the animals provide some benefit to mankind, albeit indirect. Failure to establish such benefit was fatal in *Re Grove-Grady*. An animal sanctuary (game reserve) where all animals were allowed to live free from 'molestation or destruction by man' was not charitable for there were no safeguards against the destruction of the weaker animals by the stronger.

Re Grove-Grady [1929] 1 Ch 557, CA

> **Russell LJ:** It is merely a trust to secure that all animals within the area shall be free from molestation or destruction by man. It is not a trust directed to ensure absence or diminution of pain or cruelty in the destruction of animal life. If this trust is carried out according to its tenor, no animal within the area may be destroyed by man no matter how necessary that destruction may be in the interests of mankind or in the interests of the other denizens of the area or in the interests of the animal itself; and no matter how painlessly such destruction may be brought about. It seems to be impossible to say that the carrying out of such a trust necessarily involves benefit to the public. Consistently with the trust the public could be excluded from entering the area or even looking into it. All that the public need know about the matter would be that one or more areas existed in which all animals were allowed to live free from any risk of being molested or killed by man, though liable to be molested and killed by other denizens of the area. For myself, I feel quite unable to say that any benefit to the community will necessarily result from applying the trust fund to the purposes indicated in the first object.
>
> If then benefit to the community as a necessary result of the execution of the trust is essential, this trust is not charitable. It is well settled that if consistently with the trust the funds may be applied for a purpose not charitable, the trust will fail for perpetuity notwithstanding that the funds might under the trust have been applied for purposes strictly charitable.

Moreover, when the welfare of animals (anti-vivisection) conflicts with the interests of mankind (scientific research), the latter prevails and the animal welfare body will not be charitable. Such an organisation does not promote a public benefit owing to its detrimental effect on medical science and research, see *National Anti-Vivisection Society v IRC*.

49 (1890) 25 LRIR 325.

50 [1949] 1 All ER 495.

***National Anti-Vivisection Society v Inland Revenue Commissioners* [1948] AC 31, HL (Viscount Simon, Lords Wright, Porter, Simonds and Normand)**

The society claimed exemption from income tax on the ground that its purposes (*inter alia*, the total suppression of vivisection) were charitable.

The House of Lords decided that the society's purposes were not charitable for its purposes were detrimental to medical science and research. In addition, one its main objects was political in advocating a change in the law. The House overruled *Re Foveaux*.

> **Lord Simonds:** Here the finding of the commissioners is itself conclusive. 'We are satisfied,' they say, 'that the main object of the society is the total abolition of vivisection ... and (for that purpose) the repeal of the Cruelty to Animals Act 1876, and the substitution of a new enactment prohibiting vivisection altogether'. This is a finding that the main purpose of the society is the compulsory abolition of vivisection by Act of Parliament. What else can it mean? And how else can it be supposed that vivisection is to be abolished? Abolition and suppression are words that connote some form of compulsion. It can only be by Act of Parliament that that element can be supplied.
>
> *Tyssen on Charitable Bequests*, 1st edn, 1898: the passage which is at p 176, is worth repeating at length:
>
>> It is a common practice for a number of individuals amongst us to form an association for the purpose of promoting some change in the law, and it is worth our while to consider the effect of a gift to such an association. It is clear that such an association is not of a charitable nature. However desirable the change may really be, the law could not stultify itself by holding that it was for the public benefit that the law is right as it stands. On the other hand, such a gift could not be held void for illegality.
>
> I would rather say that, when a purpose appears broadly to fall within one of the familiar categories of charity, the court will assume it to be for the benefit of the community and, therefore, charitable, unless the contrary is shown, and further that the court will not be astute in such a case to defeat on doubtful evidence the avowed benevolent intention of a donor. But, my Lords, the next step is one that I cannot take. Where on the evidence before it the court concludes that, however well intentioned the donor, the achievement of his object will be greatly to the public disadvantage, there can be no justification for saying that it is a charitable object. If and so far as there is any judicial decision to the contrary, it must, in my opinion, be regarded as inconsistent with principle and be overruled.
>
> The distinction between a political association and a charitable trust has not been defined and I doubt whether it admits of precise definition. The Attorney General however submitted that any association which included among its objects the passing by Parliment any legislation, unless it were an uncontroversial enabling Act, was to be considered a political association, and must be refused the privileges which the law allows to charities. But no authority was cited which would warrant so extreme a proposition.

The formation of voluntary associations for the furtherance of the improvement of morals is familiar, and such associations are a well recognised sub-division of the fourth of Lord MacNaghten's divisions of charities in *Pemsel's* case.[51] It is also familiar that trusts for preventing cruelty to animals or for improving the conditions of their lives have found a recognised place in that sub-division. Trusts for the benefit of animals are allowed to be charitable because, to quote the language of Swinfen Eady LJ in *In re Wedgwood*:[52]

> ... they tend to promote and encourage kindness towards animals, to discourage cruelty, and to ameliorate the condition of the brute creation, and thus to stimulate humane and generous sentiments in man towards the lower animals, and by these means promote feelings of humanity and morality generally, repress brutality, and thus elevate the human race.

Societies for the amelioration of the condition of animals like other societies for the improvement of human morals do not as a rule limit their activities to one particular method of advancing their cause. Commonly, they hope to make voluntary converts, and they also hope to educate public opinion and so to bring its influence to bear on those who offend against a humane code of conduct towards animals. But they seldom disclaim and frequently avow an intention of inducing Parliament to pass new legislation if a favourable opportunity should arise of furthering their purpose by that means. A society for the prevention of cruelty to animals, for example, may include among its professed purposes amendments of the law dealing with field sports or with the taking of eggs or the like. Yet it would not, in my view, necessarily lose its right to be considered a charity, and if that right were questioned, it would become the duty of the court to decide whether the general purpose of the society was the improvement of morals by various lawful means including new legislation, all such means being subsidiary to the general charitable purpose. If the court answered this question in favour of the society, it would retain its privileges as a charity. But if the decision was that the leading purpose of the society was to promote legislation in order to bring about a change of policy towards field sports or the protection of wild birds it would follow that the society should be classified as an association with political objects and that it would lose its privileges as a charity. The problem is therefore to discover the general purposes of the society and whether they are in the main political or in the main charitable. It is a question of degree of a sort well known to the courts.

I conclude upon this part of the case that a main object of the society is not established for charitable purposes only.

(ii) The relief of the aged and impotent

The preamble to the Statute of Elizabeth 1601 specifically refers to 'the relief of the aged, impotent and poor people'. The words have been construed disjunctively and objects need not qualify on all three grounds.

51 [1891] AC 531, p 583.

52 [1915] 1 Ch 113, p 123.

Joseph Rowntree Memorial Trust Housing Association v Attorney General [1983] 1 All ER 288, HC

> **Peter Gibson J:** The first set of charitable purposes contained in the preamble is 'the relief of aged, impotent and poor people'. Looking at those words, I would have thought that two inferences were tolerably clear. First, the words must be read disjunctively. It would be absurd to require that the aged must be impotent and poor ... Secondly, the gift should relieve aged, impotent and poor people. The word 'relief' implies that the persons in question have a need attributable to their condition as aged, impotent and poor people requires alleviating and which those persons could not alleviate or would find difficulty in alleviating from their own resources.

The plaintiffs housing trust, designed a scheme to build small self-contained dwellings for sale to elderly people on long leases in consideration of a capital payment. The applicants were required to attain the age of 65 if male, and 60 if female, to be able to pay the service charge, to lead an independent life and to be in need of the type of accommodation provided. The Charity Commissioners refused to approve the scheme as charitable in law on the ground that the scheme provided benefits by contract and not by bounty and was merely a commercial enterprise. On appeal by the plaintiffs.

The court held that the scheme was charitable:

(a) the words in the preamble ('relief of aged, impotent and poor people') were to be construed disjunctively;

(b) the purpose of the proposed scheme by the trustees was designed to provide a benefit for old persons in need;

(c) the absence of bounty in the provision of the benefit did not prevent the activity from being considered charitable.

> **Peter Gibson J:** In *In re Lucas*,[53] Russell J was concerned with a bequest to the oldest respectable inhabitants of Gunville of the amount of 5 s per week each. He held that the amount of the gift implied poverty. But he said, at p 55:
>
> > I am not satisfied that the requirement of old age would of itself be sufficient to constitute the gift a good charitable bequest, although there are several *dicta* to that effect in the books. I can find no case, and none has been cited to me, where the decision has been based upon age and nothing but age.
>
> In *In re Glyn (Decd)*,[54] Danckwerts J was faced with a bequest for building cottages for old women of the working classes of the age of 60 years or upwards. He said, at p 511:
>
> > I have not the slightest doubt that this is a good charitable bequest. The preamble to the Statute of Elizabeth refers to the relief of aged, impotent and poor people. The words 'aged, impotent and poor' should be read

53 [1922] 2 Ch 52.

54 [1950] 2 All ER 150n; (1950) 66 TLR 510.

> disjunctively. It had never been suggested that poor people must also be aged to be objects of charity, and there is no reason for holding that aged people must also be poor to come within the meaning of the preamble to the Statute. A trust for the relief of aged persons would be charitable unless it was qualified in some way which would clearly render it not charitable.

He then went on to say that there was a sufficient context to show that the testatrix intended to benefit indigent persons.

In *In re Sanders' Will Trusts*,[55] Harman J said that the *ratio decidendi* of *In re Glyn, decd*,[56] was that 'out of old age and working class it might be inferred that poverty was a necessary qualification'. But I share the views of the editor of *Tudor on Charity*,[57] that that is not not what Danckwerts J said.

In *In re Bradbury (Decd)*,[58] Vaisey J followed *In re Glyn (Decd)* in holding that a bequest to pay sums for the maintenance of an aged person in a nursing home was charitable.

In *In re Robinson (Decd)*,[59] a testator made a gift to the old people over 65 of a specified district to be given as his trustees thought best. Vaisey J held that the words 'aged, impotent and poor' in the preamble should be read disjunctively. He said it was sufficient that a gift should be to the aged, and commented on his decision in *In re Bradbury* that the aged person in a nursing home might be a person not at all in need of any sort of pecuniary assistance.

In *In re Cottam*,[60] a gift to provide flats for persons over 65 to be let at economic rents was said by Danckwerts J to be a trust for the benefit of aged persons and therefore *prima facie* charitable, though he went on to find it was a trust for the aged of small means.

In *In re Lewis (Decd)*[61] there was a gift to 10 blind girls, Tottenham residents if possible, of £100 each, and a similar gift to 10 blind boys. Roxburgh J held that the words 'aged, impotent and poor' in the preamble must be read disjunctively and that the trust was therefore charitable.

In *In re Neal (Decd)*,[62] a testator provided a gift for the founding of a home for old persons. Further directions provided for fees to be charged sufficient to maintain the home with sufficient staff to run it and cover the costs of the trustees. Goff J, in a very briefly reported judgment, said that in order to conclude whether a trust was charitable or not it was not necessary to find in it an element of relief against poverty, but it was sufficient to find an intention to relieve aged persons. The form of the gift and directions were a provision for succouring and supplying such needs of old persons as they had because they were old persons. Therefore, he held it was a charitable bequest.

55 [1954] Ch 265, p 272.

56 [1950] 2 All ER 150n; (1950) 66 TLR 510.

57 6th edn, 1967, London: Sweet & Maxwell, p 61.

58 [1950] 2 All ER 1150n.

59 [1951] Ch 198.

60 [1955] 1 WLR 1299.

61 [1955] Ch 104.

62 (1966) 110 SJ 549.

In *In re Adams (Decd)*,[63] Danckwerts J again referred to the necessity of construing disjunctively the words 'impotent and poor' in the preamble. By parity of reasoning he must be taken to have been of the view that 'aged, impotent and poor' should be read disjunctively, too.

Lastly, in *In re Resch's Will Trusts*,[64] the Privy Council had to consider a gift of income to be applied for the general purposes of a named private hospital. The hospital charged substantial fees but was not run for the profit of individuals. Lord Wilberforce, delivering the judgment of the Board, referred to an objection that had been raised that the private hospital was not carried on for purposes beneficial to the community because it provided only for persons of means, capable of paying the fees required as a condition of admission. He said, at p 542:

> In dealing with this objection, it is necessary first to dispose of a misapprehension. It is not a condition of validity of a trust for the relief of the sick that it should be limited to the poor sick. Whether one regards the charitable character of trusts for the relief of the sick as flowing from the word 'impotent' ('aged, impotent and poor people') in the preamble to 43 Eliz, c 4, or, more broadly, as derived from the conception of benefit to the community, there is no warrant for adding to the condition of sickness that of poverty.

He returned to the question of public benefit and need, at p 544:

> To provide, in response to public need, medical treatment otherwise inaccessible but in its nature expensive, without any profit motive, might well be charitable: on the other hand to limit admission to a nursing home to the rich would not be so. The test is essentially one of public benefit, and indirect as well as direct benefit enters into the account. In the present case, the element of public benefit is strongly present. It is not disputed that a need exists to provide accommodation and medical treatment in conditions of greater privacy and relaxation than would be possible in a general hospital and as a supplement to the facilities of a general hospital. This is what the private hospital does and it does so at, approximately, cost price. The service is needed by all, not only by the well to do. So far as its nature permits it is open to all: the charges are not low, but the evidence shows that it cannot be said that the poor are excluded ...

These authorities convincingly confirm the correctness of the proposition that the relief of the aged does not have to be relief for the aged poor. In other words the phrase 'aged, impotent and poor people' in the preamble must be read disjunctively. The decisions in *In re Glyn (Decd)*; *In re Bradbury (Decd)*; *In re Robinson (Decd)*; *In re Cottam*; and *In re Lewis (Decd)*, give support to the view that it is a sufficient charitable purpose to benefit the aged, or the impotent, without more. But these are all decisions at first instance and with great respect to the judges who decided them they appear to me to pay no regard to the word 'relief.' I have no hesitation in preferring the approach adopted in *In re*

63 [1968] Ch 80, p 93.

64 [1969] 1 AC 514.

Neal (Decd) and *In re Resch's Will Trusts* that there must be a need which is to be relieved by the charitable gift, such need being attributable to the aged or impotent condition of the person to be benefited. My attention was drawn to Picarda, *The Law and Practice Relating to Charities*, 1977, p 79 where a similar approach is adopted by the author.

In any event in the present case, as I have indicated, the plaintiffs do not submit that the proposed schemes are charitable simply because they are for the benefit of the aged. The plaintiffs have identified a particular need for special housing to be provided for the elderly in the ways proposed and it seems to me that on any view of the matter that is a charitable purpose.

The first objection [by the Commissioners] is, as I have stated, that the scheme makes provision for the aged on a contractual basis as a bargain rather than by way of bounty. There are numerous cases where beneficiaries only receive benefits from a charity by way of bargain. *In re Cottam*[65] and *In re Resch's Will Trusts*[66] provide examples. Another class of cases relates to fee-paying schools: see, for example, *Abbey Malvern Wells Ltd v Ministry of Local Government and Planning*.[67] Another example relates to a gift for the provision of homes of rest for lady teachers at a rent: *In re Estlin*.[68] It is of course crucial in all these cases that the services provided by the gift are not provided for the private profit of the individuals providing the services.

If a housing association were a co-operative under which the persons requiring the dwellings provided by the housing association had by the association's constitution contractual rights to the dwellings, that would no doubt not be charitable, but that is quite different from bodies set up like the trust and the association. The applicants for dwellings under the schemes which I am considering would have no right to any dwelling when they apply. The fact that the benefit given to them is in the form of a contract is immaterial to the charitable purpose in making the benefit available. I see nothing in this objection of the Charity Commissioners.

A [further] objection was that the schemes were for the benefit of private individuals and not for a charitable class. I cannot accept that. The schemes are for the benefit of a charitable class. That is to say the aged having certain needs requiring relief therefrom. The fact that, once the association and the trust have selected individuals to benefit from the housing, those individuals are identified private individuals does not seem to me to make the purpose in providing the housing a non-charitable one any more than a trust for the relief of poverty ceases to be a charitable purpose when individual poor recipients of bounty are selected.

[Another] objection was that the schemes were a commercial enterprise capable of producing a profit for the beneficiary. I have already discussed the cases which show that the charging of an economic consideration for a

65 [1955] 1 WLR 1299.

66 [1969] 1 AC 514.

67 [1951] Ch 728.

68 (1903) 89 LT 88.

> charitable service that is provided does not make the purpose in providing the service non-charitable, provided of course that no profits accrue to the provider of the service. It is true that a tenant under the schemes may recover more than he or she has put in, but that is at most incidental to the charitable purpose. It is not a primary objective. The profit – if it be right to call the increased value of the equity a profit as distinct from a mere increase avoiding the effects of inflation, as was intended – is not a profit at the expense of the charity, and indeed it might be thought improper, if there be a profit, that it should accrue to the charity which has provided no capital and not to the tenant which has provided most if not all the capital. Again, I cannot see that this objection defeats the charitable character of the schemes.
>
> [Declaration granted.]

Likewise, in *Re Robinson*,[69] the provision of housing for persons over the age of 65 was charitable.

(iii) Recreational facilities

The promotion of sport *simpliciter* is not charitable as such activity is not within the preamble or spirit and intendment of the preamble, see *Re Nottage*,[70] the provision of a cup annually in order to promote the sport of yacht racing, *IRC v City of Glasgow Police Athletic Association*, sport within the police force (cited above, p 581). But, in appropriate cases, such gifts may be included under the heading, advancement of education. To achieve this status, the sport is required to be provided within a school or as part of the educational curriculum. It is well recognised that adequate recreational activities (physical and mental development) are an integral part of the educational process, see *Re Mariette*,[71] the provision of prizes for sport in a school.

***Inland Revenue Commissioners v McMullen and Others* [1981] AC 1, HL**

By a deed dated 30 October 1972, made between the Football Association and the trustees, the Football Association Youth Trust was established. The main object of the trust was set out in clause 3(a) of the deed as follows:

> ... to organise and provide facilities which will enable and encourage pupils of Schools and Universities in any part of the UK to play football or other games or sports and *thereby* to assist in ensuring that due attention is given to the physical education and development of such pupils as well as to the development and occupation of their minds and with a view to furthering this object ...

69 [1951] Ch 198.

70 [1895] 2 Ch 649.

71 [1915] 2 Ch 284.

The Charity Commissioners registered the trust as a charity, but the Inland Revenue objected and claimed a declaration to de-register the trust. The High Court and the Court of Appeal (by a majority) held in favour of the Revenue. On appeal to the House of Lords.

Held, in favour of of the trustees, on construction of the deed, the trust was charitable for the advancement of education.

> **Lord Hailsham of St Marylebone LC:** The word 'thereby' cannot therefore bear the purely consequential meaning assigned to it by the three judgments appealed from and must bear the controlling and purposive meaning contended for by the appellants and supported by Bridge LJ In short, in the context, the words 'and thereby' bear, and can only bear, a meaning something like 'in such a way as to' and not the meaning attributed to it on behalf of the respondents as reflecting, whether erroneously on the part of the draftsman (as *per* Walton J) or correctly or incorrectly in the mind of the settlor (as *per* Stamp and Orr LJJ) the results automatically effected by the first part of the deed. Moreover, if this were not enough, I find the word 'object' in the singular at the end of the phrase far more consistent with this view than with the other.
>
> On a proper analysis, therefore, I do not find clause 3(a) ambiguous.
>
> In construing trust deeds the intention of which is to set up a charitable trust, and in others too, where it can be claimed that there is an ambiguity, a benignant construction should be given if possible. This was the maxim of the civil law: *semper in dubiis benigniora praeferenda sunt*. There is a similar maxim in English law: *ut res magis valeat quam pereat*. It certainly applies to charities when the question is one of uncertainty (*Weir v Crum-Brown*),[72] and, I think, also where a gift is capable of two constructions one of which would make it void and the other effectual (cf *Bruce v Deer Presbytery*;[73] *Houston v Burns*).[74] In the present case I do not find it necessary to resort to benignancy in order to construe the clause, but had I been in doubt, I would certainly have been prepared to do so.
>
> I do not share the view, implied by Stamp LJ and Orr LJ in the instant case,[75] that the words 'education' and 'educational' bear, or can bear, for the purposes of the law of charity, meanings different from those current in present-day educated English speech. I do not believe that there is such a difference. What has to be remembered, however, is that, as Lord Wilberforce pointed out in *In re Hopkins' Will Trusts*[76] and in *Scottish Burial Reform and Cremation Society Ltd v Glasgow Corp*,[77] especially at p 154, both the legal conception of charity, and within it the educated man's ideas about education, are not static, but moving and changing. Both change with changes in ideas about social values. Both

72 [1908] 1 AC 162, p 167.

73 (1867) LR I Sc & Div 96, p 97.

74 [1918] AC 337, pp 341–42, *per* Lord Finlay LC; and cf, also, *In re Bain* [1930] 1 Ch 224, p 230.

75 [1979] 1 WLR 130, p 139.

76 [1965] Ch 669, p 678.

77 [1968] AC 138.

have evolved with the years. In particular in applying the law to contemporary circumstances it is extremely dangerous to forget that thoughts concerning the scope and width of education differed in the past greatly from those which are now generally accepted.

In saying this I do not in the least wish to cast doubt on *In re Nottage*,[78] which was referred to in both courts below and largely relied on by the respondents here. Strictly speaking *In re Nottage* was not a case about education at all. The issue there was whether the bequest came into the fourth class of charity categorised in Lord MacNaghten's classification of 1891. The mere playing of games or enjoyment of amusement or competition is not *per se* charitable, nor necessarily educational, though they may (or may not) have an educational or beneficial effect if diligently practised. Neither am I deciding in the present case even that a gift for physical education *per se* and not associated with persons of school age or just above would necessarily be a good charitable gift. That is a question which the courts may have to face at some time in the future.

It is, of course, true that no authority exactly in point could be found which is binding on your Lordship in the instant appeal. Nevertheless, I find the first instance case of *In re Mariette*,[79] a decision of Eve J, both stimulating and instructive. Counsel for the respondents properly reminded us that this concerned a bequest effectively tied to a particular institution. Nevertheless, I cannot forbear to quote a phrase from the judgment, always bearing in mind the danger of quoting out of context. Eve J said, at p 288:

> No one of sense could be found to suggest that between those ages [10 to 19] any boy can be properly educated unless at least as much attention is given to the development of his body as is given to the development of his mind.

Apart from the limitation to the particular institution I would think that these words apply as well to the settlor's intention in the instant appeal as to the testator's in *In re Mariette*, and I regard the limitation to the pupils of schools and universities in the instant case as a sufficient association with the provision of formal education to prevent any danger of vagueness in the object of the trust or irresponsibility or capriciousness in application by the trustees. I am far from suggesting that the concept either of education or of physical education even for the young is capable of indefinite extension. On the contrary, I do not think that the courts have as yet explored the extent to which elements of organisation, instruction, or the disciplined inculcation of information, instruction or skill may limit the whole concept of education. I believe that in some ways it will prove more extensive, in others more restrictive than has been thought hitherto. But it is clear at least to me that the decision in *In re Mariette* is not to be read in a sense which confines its application for ever to gifts for annual treats for schoolchildren in a particular locality (another decision of Eve J); to playgrounds for children (*In re Chesters*,[80]

78 [1895] 2 Ch 649.

79 [1915] 2 Ch 284.

80 (1934) unreported, 25 July.

and possibly not educational, but referred to in *IRC v Baddeley*);[81] to children's outing (*In re Ward's Estate*);[82] to a prize for chess to boys and young men resident in the city of Portsmouth (*In re Dupree's Deed Trusts*,[83] a decision of Vaisey J) and for the furthering the Boy Scouts movement by helping to purchase sites for camping, outfits, etc (*In re Webber*,[84] another decision of Vaisey J). In that case, Vaisey J is reported as saying, at p 1501:

> I am bound to say that I am surprised to hear that anyone suggests that the Boy Scouts movement, as distinguished from the Boy Scouts Association, or the Boy Scouts organisation, or any other form of words is other than an educational charity. I should have thought that it was well settled and well understood that the objects of the organisation of Boy Scouts is an education of a very special kind no doubt, but still, none the less, educational.

It is important to remember that in the instant appeal we are dealing with the concept of physical education and development of the young deliberately associated by the settlor with the status of pupilage in schools or universities (of which, according to the evidence, about 95% are within the age group 17 to 22). We are not dealing with adult education physical or otherwise, as to which some consideration may be different.

I reject any idea which would cramp the education of the young within the school or university syllabus. I can find nothing contrary to the law of charity which prevents a donor providing a trust which is designed to improve the balance between the various elements which go into the education of the young.

The provision of recreational facilities in limited circumstances has been regarded as a charitable purpose and many village and town halls are used in part for recreational purposes. The decision of the House of Lords in *IRC v Baddeley* (1955) (above, p 604), created doubts as to whether a number of bodies created for recreational purposes were charitable. The Recreational Charities Act 1958 was passed in order to clarify the law. Section 1(1) of the Act stipulates that the provision of recreational facilities shall be charitable if two criteria are fulfilled, namely; (1) the public benefit test is satisfied; and (2) the facilities are provided in the interests of social welfare.

Section 1 of the Recreational Charities Act 1958 provides:

> (1) Subject to the provisions of this Act, it shall be and be deemed always to have been charitable to provide, or assist in the provision of, facilities for recreation or other leisure-time occupation, if the facilities are provided in the interests of social welfare: Provided that nothing in this section shall be taken to derogate from the principle that a trust or institution to be charitable must be for the public benefit.

81 [1955] AC 572, p 596.

82 (1937) 81 SJ 397.

83 [1945] Ch 16.

84 [1954] 1 WLR 1500.

Section 1(2) of the Act declares that the requirement that the facilities are provided in the interests of social welfare will only be satisfied if:

(a) they are provided with the object of improving the conditions of life of those for whom they are primarily intended; and

(b) either:

  (i) those persons have need for such facilities by reason of their youth, age, infirmity or disablement, poverty or social and economic circumstances; or

  (ii) the facilities are available to the members or female members of the public at large.

Under the Act, the 'social welfare' test will be complied with if two conditions are satisfied as enacted in s 1(2). The first requirement is continuous as stipulated in s 1(2)(a). The second requirement may be satisfied in alternative ways either by proving that the facilities are available to a limited class of objects who have a need for such facilities by virtue of one or more of the factors enumerated within s 1(2)(b)(i) (such as a youth club or an organised outing for orphaned children) or 'the facilities are available to the entire public' (such as a public swimming pool or a public park) or 'female members of the public' (women's institutes, etc).

Section 1(3) of the Act declares that, subject to the provision of social welfare, the Act applies:

> ... in particular to the provision of facilities at village halls, community centres and women's institutes, and to the provision and maintenance of grounds and buildings to be used for purposes of recreation or leisure-time occupation, and extends to the provision of facilities for those purposes by the organising of any activity.

Recently, the House of Lords, in *Guild v IRC*, construed the requirements under s 1(2)(a) liberally and rejected the view that it is necessary to prove that the beneficiaries were deprived of such facilities which are provided in order to alleviate their needs. The test today is whether the facilities are provided with the purpose of improving the conditions of life of the beneficiaries, irrespective of whether the participating members of society are disadvantaged or not. In short, the material issue concerns the nature of the facilities rather than the status of the participants. 'Hyde Park improves the conditions of life for residents in Mayfair and Belgravia as much as those in Pimlico or the Portobello Road, and the village hall may improve the conditions of life for residents for the squire and his family as well as the cottagers.'

Guild v Inland Revenue Commissioners [1992] 2 All ER 10, HL

In this case, a testator by his will disposed of the residue of his estate to the Town Council of North Berwick, '(i) for the use in connection with the Sports Centre in North Berwick; and (ii) some similar purpose in connection with sport'. The Inland Revenue opposed a claim by the executor for exemption from capital transfer tax on the grounds that the gift was not for the promotion of charitable purposes. The House of Lords held in favour of the executor and decided that the gift was charitable under the Recreational Charities Act 1958 and adopting a benignant construction of the second part of the residuary clause, the gift was exclusively in favour of charitable purposes.

> **Lord Keith of Kinkel:** In the course of his argument in relation to the first branch of the bequest counsel for the commissioners accepted that it assisted in the provision of facilities for recreation or other leisure time occupation within the meaning of sub-s (1) of s 1 of the Act, and also that the requirement of public benefit in the proviso to the subsection was satisfied. It was further accepted that the facilities of the sports centre were available to the public at large so that the condition of sub-s (2)(b)(ii) was satisfied.
>
> It was maintained, however, that these facilities were not provided 'in the interests of social welfare' as required by sub-s (1), because they did not meet the condition laid down in sub-s (2)(a), namely, that they should be 'provided with the object of improving the conditions of life for the persons for whom the facilities are primarily intended'. The reason why it was said that this condition was not met was that on a proper construction it involved that the facilities should be provided with the object of meeting a need for such facilities in people who suffered from a position of relative social disadvantage. Reliance was placed on a passage from the judgment of Walton J in *IRC v McMullen*.[85]
>
> He said, at p 675, in relation to the words 'social welfare' in sub-s (1):
>
>> In my view, however, these words in themselves indicate that there is some kind of deprivation – not, of course, by any means necessarily of money – which falls to be alleviated; and I think that this is made even clearer by the terms of sub-s (2)(a).
>>
>> The facilities must be provided with the object of improving the conditions of life for persons for whom the facilities are primarily intended. In other words, they must be to some extent and in some way deprived persons.
>
> When the case went to the Court of Appeal[86] the majority (Stamp and Orr LJJ) affirmed the judgment of Walton J on both points, but Bridge LJ dissented. As regards the Recreational Charities Act 1958 point he said, at pp 142–43:
>
>> I turn therefore to consider whether the object defined by clause 3(a) is charitable under the express terms of s 1 of the Recreational Charities Act 1958. Are the facilities for recreation contemplated in this clause to be 'provided in the interests of social welfare' under s 1(1)? If this phrase stood without further statutory elaboration, I should not hesitate to decide that sporting facilities for persons undergoing any formal process of education are provided in the interests of social welfare. Save in the sense that the interests of social welfare can only be served by the meeting of

85 [1978] 1 WLR 664.

86 [1979] 1 WLR 130.

> some social need, I cannot accept the judge's view that the interests of social welfare can only be served in relation to some 'deprived' class. The judge found this view reinforced by the requirement of sub-s (2)(a) of s 1 that the facilities must be provided 'with the object of improving the conditions of life for the persons for whom the facilities are primarily intended ...'. Here, again, I can see no reason to conclude that only the deprived can have their conditions of life improved. Hyde Park improves the conditions of life for residents in Mayfair and Belgravia as much as for those in Pimlico or the Portobello Road, and the village hall may improve the conditions of life for the squire and his family as well as for the cottagers. The persons for whom the facilities here are primarily intended are pupils of schools and universities, as defined in the trust deed, and these facilities are in my judgment unquestionably to be provided with the object of improving their conditions of life. Accordingly, the ultimate question on which the application of the statute to this trust depends, is whether the requirements of s 1(2)(b)(i) are satisfied on the ground that such pupils as a class have need of facilities for games or sports which will promote their physical education and development by reason either of their youth or of their social and economic circumstances, or both. The overwhelming majority of pupils within the definition of young persons and the tiny minority of mature students can be ignored as *de minimis*. There cannot surely be any doubt that young persons as part of their education do need facilities for organised games and sports both by reason of their youth and by reason of their social and economic circumstances. They cannot provide such facilities for themselves but are dependent on what is provided for them.

In the House of Lords the case was decided against the Crown upon the ground that the trust was one for the advancement of education, opinion being reserved on the point under the Recreational Charities Act 1958.

Reference was also made to the speech of Lord Denning in *National Deposit Friendly Society Trustees v Skegness Urban District Council*,[87] a case concerned with the meaning of 'the advancement of ... social welfare' in s 8(1)(a) of the Rating and Valuation (Miscellaneous Provisions) Act 1955. Lord Denning said:

> A person is commonly said to be engaged in 'social welfare' when he is engaged in doing good for others who are in need – in the sense that he does it, not for personal or private reasons – not because they are relatives or friends of his – but because they are members of the community or of a portion of it who need help ... If a person is engaged in improving the conditions of life of others who are so placed as to be in need, he is engaged in 'social welfare'.

Counsel for the executor, for his part, relied on part of the judgment of Lord MacDermott LCJ in *Commissioner of Valuation for Northern Ireland v Lurgan Borough Council*.[88] A local authority which was owner and occupier of an

87 [1958] 2 All ER 601.

88 [1968] NI 104.

indoor swimming pool claimed exemption from rates in respect of it under s 2 of the Valuation (Ireland) Amendment Act 1854[89] on the ground, *inter alia*, that it was used exclusively for the purposes of a recreational charity under the Act of 1958. A majority of the Court of Appeal held that this ground of exemption was established. Lord MacDermott said, at p 126, having referred to s 1 of the Act:

> Here, I think, there can be no doubt that in the construction, equipment and running of this hereditament the council has provided facilities for recreation. The big question is – have these facilities been provided 'in the interests of social welfare'?
>
> 'Social welfare' is a somewhat vague and uncertain expression. Taken by itself I still incline to the view I expressed in *National Deposit Friendly Society Trustees v Skegness Urban District Council*, that it signifies something more than 'social well being'.
>
> In the present context, however, I do not think it necessary to speculate as to the precise distinction to be drawn between these two expressions as sub-s (2) of s 1, though not exactly a definition, provides in effect, in my opinion, the essential elements which must be present if a state of social well being is to amount to 'social welfare', as that expression is used in the section. These elements are to be drawn from paras (a) and (b) of sub-s (2). By (a) the facilities must be provided with the object of improving the conditions of life for the persons for whom the facilities are primarily intended. To my mind the provision of the hereditament satisfies that requirement. The primary object, even if confined to the phraseology of the preamble to the Baths and Wash-Houses (Ireland) Act 1846,[90] was clearly to improve the conditions of life of the inhabitants of the borough of Lurgan and if, as I have held, this was done in a manner which enured for the benefit of the public at large, para (a) would still be complied with. It is clear from the terms of the case stated that the hereditament was not only provided to improve the conditions of life for those for whom it was primarily intended, but that in fact it has done so. The full use which has been made of the hereditament since its inauguration is, I think, cogent evidence that it has filled a need in the life of the community and has added to the enjoyment of its members.

In this passage Lord MacDermott makes the point that s 1(2) of the Act does not exactly contain a definition but that it does state the essential elements which must be present if the requirement that the facilities should be provided in the interests of social welfare is to be met. It is difficult to envisage a case where, although these essential elements are present, yet the facilities are not provided in the interests of social welfare. Nor do I consider that the reference to social welfare in sub-s (1) can properly be held to colour sub-s (2)(a) to the effect that the persons for whom the facilities are primarily intended must be

89 (1854) 17 and 18 Vict, c 8.

90 (1846) 9 and 10 Vict, c 87.

confined to those persons who suffer from some form of social deprivation. That this is not so seems to me to follow from the alternative conditions expressed in sub-s (2)(b). If it suffices that the facilities are to be available to the members of the public at large, as sub-para (ii) provides, it must necessarily be inferred that the persons for whom the facilities are primarily intended are not to be confined to those who have need of them by reason of one of the forms of social deprivation mentioned in sub-para (i).

The fact is that persons in all walks of life and all kinds of social circumstances may have their conditions of life improved by the provision of recreational facilities of suitable character. The proviso requiring public benefit excludes facilities of an undesirable nature. In my opinion the view expressed by Bridge LJ in *IRC v McMullen* is clearly correct and that of Walton J in the same case is incorrect. Lord MacDermott in the *Lurgan* case plainly did not consider that the category of persons for whom the facilities were primarily intended was subject to any restriction. The observations of Lord Denning in the *Skegness* case are not relevant in the present context. I would therefore reject the argument that the facilities are not provided in the interests of social welfare unless they are provided with the object of improving the conditions of life for persons who suffer from some form of social disadvantage. It suffices if they are provided with the object of improving the conditions of life for members of the community generally.

It remains to consider the point upon which the executor was unsuccessful before the First Division, namely whether or not the second branch of the bequest of residue, referring to 'some similar purpose in connection with sport,' is so widely expressed as to admit of the funds being applied in some manner which falls outside the requirements of s 1 of the Act of 1958. Counsel for the executor invited your Lordships, in construing this part of the bequest, to adopt the benignant approach which has regularly been favoured in the interpretation of trust deeds capable of being regarded as evincing a charitable intention. That approach is appropriate where the language used is susceptible of two constructions one of which would make it void and the other effectual: *IRC v McMullen*.[91]

The matter for decision turns upon the ascertainment of the intention of the testator in using the words he did. The adjective 'similar' connotes that there are points of resemblance between one thing and another. The points of resemblance here with the sports centre cannot be related only to location in North Berwick or to connection with sport. The first of these is plainly to be implied from the fact of the gift being to the town council of North Berwick and the second is expressly stated in the words under construction. So the resemblance to the sports centre which the testator had in mind must be ascertained by reference to some other characteristics possessed by it. The leading characteristics of the sports centre lie in the nature of the facilities which are provided there and the fact that those facilities are available to the public at large. These are the characteristics which enable it to satisfy s 1 of the

91 [1981] AC 1, p 14, *per* Lord Hailsham of St Marylebone LC.

> Act of 1958. Adopting so far as necessary a benignant construction, I infer that the intention of the testator was that any other purpose to which the town council might apply the bequest or any part of it should also display those characteristics. In the result I am of opinion, the first part of the bequest having been found to be charitable within the meaning of s 1 of the Act of 1958, that the same is true of the second part, so that the funds in question qualify for exemption from capital transfer tax.

Miscellaneous examples

Other charitable purposes decided under Lord MacNaghten's fourth heading include the encouragement and advancement of choral singing (*Royal Choral Society v IRC)*; gifts for the promotion of the defence of the United Kingdom (*Re Good*); gifts for the production of better organists and better organ music (*Re Levien*); a gift to provide a local fire brigade (*Re Wokingham Fire Brigade Trusts*); a trust to relieve hardship and suffering by the local people as a result of a disaster (*Re North Devon and West Somerset Relief Fund Trusts*) (but it is imperative that the size of the class of beneficiaries be sufficiently large to satisfy the public element test); the publication and dissemination of law reports (*Incorporated Council for Law Reporting v AG*, cited above, p 603); the promotion of industry, commerce and art (*Crystal Palace Trustees v Minister of Town and Country Planning*); the general improvement of agriculture (*IRC v Yorkshire Agricultural Society*);[92] the promotion of inexpensive and sanitary methods of disposal of the dead, in particular, cremation (*Scottish Burial Reform and Cremation Society Ltd v Glasgow City Corp*);[93] the study and dissemination of ethical principles and the cultivation of a national religious sentiment (*Re South Place Ethical Society*);[94] a gift to the inhabitants of a town or village (*Goodman v Saltash Corp*).[95]

Re Smith [1932] 1 Ch 153, CA

In this case, the Court of Appeal decided that a gift 'unto my country, England' was charitable. The Attorney General was authorised to receive the gift.

> **Lord Hanworth MR:** We have to construe the will, and it is said that a bequest 'unto my country England for own use and benefit absolutely' is so vague as to be void for uncertainty, and that it cannot be held to be a charitable bequest so as to take it out of the rule against perpetuities, and therefore the will is ineffective. It is noticeable that it is an out-and-out gift without any conditions at all, 'unto my country England for own use and benefit absolutely'. The court leans in favour of making the testamentary dispositions of a testator effective if

92 [1928] 1 KB 611.

93 [1968] AC 138.

94 [1980] 1 WLR 1565.

95 [1882] 7 AC 633.

possible within the limitations and in accordance with the principles of law. First of all, on the construction to be placed upon the will there appears to be an entity indicated, namely, England. But is that so vague that it contains no meaning at all? I cannot so interpret the bequest. I think there is an entity, although it would be possible to raise, I will not say doubts, but a criticism that England itself is now joined to Scotland and to Wales and Northern Ireland, and that one uses a different and more comprehensive term when one is speaking of that collocation of countries. At the same time, the word 'England' does connote to many an entity, and I think if a man was asked where he was born he would be content to say, 'I was born in England', without any more specific identification.

I then come to the question: Is a bequest to a country, here England, good? Two questions are somewhat mixed up. One has to consider, at the same time, whether it is good as not being uncertain, and whether it is a charitable gift so as to eliminate any danger from the other rules of law. As far back as *West v Knight*,[96] which was decided in 1669, it was decided that a gift by a testator to the parish of Great Creaton, where he was born, without saying to what use, was good. There were no specific indications of the purposes for which it should be used, and all that was indicated was the parish where the testator was born. It was held that it was good, and that the matter was to be referred to the Master in order to see that the money was disposed of for the benefit of the poor of the parish. That ultimate destination is a matter with which I will deal later on, but the noticeable fact is that the gift to the parish without any specific use was held to be good as a gift to that area, or, rather, of course, for the benefit of those who lived within that area.

Then, in *AG v Mayor, & Co of Carlisle*,[97] a grant from the Crown of certain privileges and property for the defence of and preservation of the peace within the City of Carlisle was held to be a charitable gift. That again was vague in its ultimate terms, but the persons who were to benefit were the particular city – namely, Carlisle.

In *Mitford v Reynolds*,[98] the testator gave the remainder of his property to the Government of Bengal, to be applied:

> ... to charitable, beneficial, and public works, at and in the city of Dacca in Bengal, the intent of such bequest and direction being that the amount shall be applied exclusively for the benefit of the native inhabitants in the manner they and the Government may regard to be most conducive to that end.

It was held that that was good. Lord Lyndhurst LC said:[99]

> If these words ... are to be taken distributively and not conjunctively, and any one of the purposes or of the alternatives would not constitute a valid charitable bequest, the whole disposition will, of course, fail.

96 (1669) 1 Ch Cas 134.

97 (1828) 2 Sim 437.

98 (1848) 1 Ph 185.

99 *Ibid*, p 190.

But it was held there that they were to be taken conjunctively, with the result that the bequest was held to be good. He said ... p 195:

> Now it is argued that this is a void bequest; and that this being a void bequest, and the amount which it will be necessary to expend for the purpose of carrying this design into effect, if it could be paid out of the residue, and the remainder of the residue being to be applied to the charitable objects to which I have already adverted, that if the sum to be applied to this object is uncertain, the balance also must be made uncertain ...

and, therefore, that the whole bequest was void for uncertainty. But he held otherwise, and that the bequest to the Government of Bengal for the purposes of the natives of Dacca was good; another illustration in line with the other cases, where a gift to the inhabitants of an area larger than a parish or a county or a city is also held to be good.

Then comes *Nightingale v Goulburn*[100] where there was a bequest 'to the Queen's Chancellor of the Exchequer for the time being, to be by him appropriated to the benefit and advantage of Great Britain'. That bequest was held to be valid so far as related to the personalty. The question there discussed was whether the bequest given to the benefit and advantage of Great Britain was so wide and vague as to be void. Wigram VC, in his judgment, drew attention to the well known case of *Morice v Bishop of Durham*:[101]

> I do not understand the observation of Sir W Grant, in *Morice v The Bishop of Durham*, as deciding that no general words could be equivalent to the word 'charity'; nor do I think it would be right, with reference to the decided cases, to lay down any such general rule.

Now those cases have all been considered from time to time and held good. In *Goodman v Mayor of Saltash*.[102] Lord Selborne, a master of accurate diction, says: 'A gift subject to a condition or trust for the benefit of the inhabitants of a parish or town, or of any particular class of such inhabitants, is (as I understand the law) a charitable trust: and no charitable trust can be void on the ground of perpetuity,' and he cites some of the cases to which I have already referred. Lord Cairns says:[103]

> It appears to me that there is no difficulty in supposing such a grant, a grant to the corporation before the time of legal memory of a several fishery, a grant by the Crown, with a condition in that grant ... that the free inhabitants of ancient tenements in the borough should enjoy this right, which as a matter of fact the case tells us they have enjoyed from time immemorial. A grant of that kind, it appears to me, would be perfectly legal and perfectly intelligible, and there would be nothing in it which would infringe any principle of law. Such a condition would create that which in the very wide language of our courts is called a charitable, that is

100 (1849) 5 Hare 484.

101 (1804) 9 Ves 399, p 406.

102 (1882) 7 App Cas 633.

103 *Ibid*, p 650.

> to say a public, trust or interest, for the benefit of the free inhabitants of ancient tenements. A trust of that kind would not in any way infringe the law or rule against perpetuities, because we know very well that where you have a trust which, if it were for the benefit of private individuals or a fluctuating body of private individuals, would be void on the ground of perpetuity, yet if it creates a charitable, that is to say a public interest, it will be free form any obnoxiousness to the rule with regard to perpetuities.

It is quite impossible, certainly in this court, to set aside the weighty opinions of two such distinguished lawyers and Lord Chancellors. There seems to be abundant and clear approval of the cases to which I have already referred.

I come to the conclusion that there is a definitive purpose – namely, that the bequest is to be for England. That is good in the same sense that, although general, when the sum bequeathed comes to be used it is to be applied to charitable purposes, as in *AG v Webster*.[104] There is no area or purpose of distribution suggested which is not charitable. Why not then give effect to the plain meaning that it is for the advantage, within the meaning of the rule as to the interpretation of the word 'charitable', of the inhabitants of England?

In my opinion, therefore, the Attorney General succeeds upon his appeal. Under these circumstances the right course is to hand this money over to the person designated under the sign manual by the supreme head of the country for the advantage of the country, England. That supreme head, as Lord Eldon said, being the *parens patriae*, will cause it to be distributed in accordance with the law applicable to charitable moneys.

Political purposes

Political purposes include attempts to change the law and gifts to further the objects of political parties. A trust for political purposes is incapable of subsisting as a charity for the court may not stultify itself by deciding that it is in the public good for the law to be changed, see *National Anti-Vivisection Society v IRC and McGovern v IRC* (above, p 648).

Bowman v Secular Society Ltd [1917] AC 406, HL

In this case, Lord Parker stated the reason behind the general rule thus:

> A trust for the attainment of political objects has always been held invalid, not because it is illegal, for everyone is at liberty to advocate or promote by any lawful means a change in the law, but because the court has no means of judging whether a proposed change in the law will or will not be for the public benefit, and therefore cannot say that a gift to secure the change is a charitable gift.

Accordingly, an educational trust along the lines of the Labour Party failed in *Re Hopkinson*;[105] Similarly, a gift to Amnesty International failed in *McGovern v*

104 (1875) LR 20 Eq 483.
105 [1949] 1 All ER 34.

AG[106] [above, p 648]. Alternatively, a trust may be treated as charitable if its political purpose, on construction, is purely incidental to its main charitable purpose.

A borderline case is *Re Scowcroft*, where the gift for the maintenance of a village club and reading room was construed as charitable, for the advancement of education, even though the reading room was 'to be used for the furtherance of Conservative principles'.

Re Scowcroft [1898] 2 Ch 638, HC

Stirling J: Whether or not a gift for the furtherance of Conservative principles is a good charitable gift is a question upon which I do not think it necessary to express any opinion in this case, because it seems to me that the reading which is suggested is not the true one, but that this is a gift for the furtherance of Conservative principles and religious and mental improvement in combination. It is either a gift for the furtherance of Conservative principles in such a way as to advance religious and mental improvement at the same time, or a gift for the furtherance of religious and mental improvement in accordance with Conservative principles; and in either case the furtherance of religious and mental improvement is, in my judgment, an essential portion of the gift. It is, therefore, a gift in one form or another for religious and mental improvement, no doubt in combination with the advancement of Conservative principles; but that limitation, it appears to me, is not sufficient to prevent it from being a perfectly good charitable gift, as undoubtedly it would be if it were a gift for the furtherance of religious and mental improvement alone. I think that that construction is aided by the direction which follows, which is that the building in question is to be kept free from intoxicants and dancing.

It occurs to me that possibly the whole matter may be viewed in another way, namely, that this is a devise of a building for the public benefit, and that it may be supported on that ground just as the gift of a library or museum would be held to be a good charitable gift. However that may be, I think that all three objects are intended to be advanced simultaneously by this gift, and it seems to me a good charity.

CHARITABLE ACTIVITIES OUTSIDE THE UNITED KINGDOM

A number of British registered charities carry on their activities abroad. There is little judicial authority on the attitude of the courts to such overseas activities. In 1963, the Charity Commissioners issued guidelines on the way they would approach this problem. Their view is that the activities of trusts within the first three heads of Lord MacNaghten's classification (trusts for the relief of poverty, the advancement of education and religion) are charitable

106 [1981] 3 All ER 493.

wherever such operations are conducted. In respect of the fourth head, such purposes would only be charitable if carried on for the benefit (direct or reasonably direct) of the UK community, such as medical research. The Commissioners added that it may be easier to establish this benefit in relation to the commonwealth (although this link has become weaker since this statement was made).

The limited number of authorities in this field seem to make no distinction between activities conducted abroad as opposed to UK activities. In *Keren Kayemeth Le Jisroel Ltd v IRC*, a company was formed with the main object of purchasing land in Palestine, Syria and parts of Turkey for the purpose of settling Jews in such lands. Counsel argued that the company was established for charitable purposes namely, the advancement of religion, the relief of poverty and other purposes beneficial to the community. The court held that the company was not charitable because of the lack of evidence of religion and poverty. In addition, the company was not charitable under the fourth head because of the uncertainty of identifying the community.

Keren Kayemeth Le Jisroel Ltd v Inland Revenue Commissioners [1932] AC 650, HL

> **Lord Tomlin:** We are concerned here only with the language which is employed in this memorandum before us. There is not in it a word which can suggest anything of a religious character. It is quite true that the minds of those who are intimately concerned with the working of this association may be affected by religious motives and religious sentiments in taking the part which they do take in the work which this association performs, but, none the less, the object of the association is not to do something which is in itself religious; it is not, in any sense in which the words, as English words, can be construed, creating a trust for the advancement of religion. It is only when you go subjectively to the minds of those concerned that you are able to introduce any element of the kind at all.
>
> But there is another reason which seems to me disastrous to the appellants' argument on this head, and that is the prescribed region itself, because the whole argument with regard to the religious element is linked up with the return to what they call the Promised Land, and in fact this region is far wider than the Promised Land on any construction of the promise. Even if they are right in the view which they take about an activity to settle Jews in the Promised Land, it seems to me that as soon as you find that the activity is not only to settle Jews in the Promised Land but to settle Jews in lands which are not and never have been part of the Promised Land, you have a combination of objects, religious and non-religious, which cannot be separated, and this combination is fatal to the contention that this association is established for charitable purposes only. In my view, therefore, the first point, that this is a religious charity, necessarily fails.
>
> Then the next point is that, if it is not religious, it is said to be beneficial to the community. I have great difficulty, as indeed counsel for the appellants had, in identifying the community. They suggest some alternatives. First of all, they

> suggest that the community is the community of all the Jews throughout the world. That seems to me to be very difficult. They next suggest that it is the Jews in the prescribed region, but I have great difficulty in seeing why they should be the community, because, although the Jews who are to be settled under the objects no doubt include Jews in the prescribed region, there are also included Jews outside the prescribed region, and whether a settling of Jews from outside the prescribed region – it may or may not be; I do not see any indication one way or the other I think it is extra ordinarily difficult to say that within the meaning of the cases there is really any community to be found in the circumstances before your Lordships' House.
>
> My Lords, that leaves the third point – the poverty point. I confess that this point seems to me very difficult to advance consistently with the argument which has been put before your Lordships on the point that the association is an institution for religious purposes. The two things do not seem to me to be really consistent, but on the merits of the point I confess I am unable to see how, by any straining of the language, this can be limited to poor Jews. Clause 3, sub-clause (1), is 'for the purpose of settling Jews on such land'. It is suggested that there can be got out of the word 'settling' some element which suggests poverty, and reference is made to the case of the repatriation of Australian soldiers: *Verge v Somerville*,[107] where it was said that the word 'repatriating' connoted something suggestive of poverty; but I am unable to find in this word any such element at all.

In *Re Jacobs*,[108] a trust for the planting of a clump of trees in Israel was held to be charitable because soil conservation in arid parts of Israel is of essential importance to the Israeli community. The court relied on *IRC v Yorkshire Agricultural Society*: the promotion of agriculture is a charitable purpose.

Inland Revenue Commissioners v Yorkshire Agricultural Society [1928] 1 KB 611, CA

The Yorkshire Agricultural Society was formed with object of holding an annual meeting for the exhibition of live stock, implements, etc, and the general promotion of agriculture. Special privileges were open to members such as free admission to shows, the use of a reading and writing room on the show grounds, special railway facilities, etc. The society was assessed to income tax on the excess of income over expenditure. The society claimed exemption on the ground that it was a charity. The Special Commissioners for income tax found that the society was a charity. On appeal to the High Court, Rowlatt J reversed this decision. The society appealed against this decision.

Held, by the Court of Appeal, that the society was established for charitable purposes notwithstanding the enjoyment of benefits by its members.

107 [1924] AC 496.

108 (1970) 114 SJ 515.

Atkin LJ: First of all it is said: No, this society was in fact formed for the purpose of giving benefit to its members; it is nothing but a club for the mutual advantage of the members of the club. If that were so I agree that the claim of the society would fail, both because it could not be said that the society was established for a charitable purpose, and because it certainly could not be said that it was established for a charitable purpose only. There can be no doubt that a society formed for the purpose merely of benefiting its own members, though it may be to the public advantage that its members should be benefited by being educated or having their aesthetic tastes improved or whatever the object may be, would not be for a charitable purpose, and if it were a substantial part of the object that it should benefit its members I should think that it would not be established for a charitable purpose only. But, on the other hand, if the benefit given to its members is only given to them with a view of giving encouragement and carrying out the main purpose which is a charitable purpose, then I think the mere fact that the members are benefited in the course of promoting the charitable purpose would not prevent the society being established for charitable purposes only. That I imagine to be this case. You may form a society for the purpose of getting contributions and in order to get contributions you may have to make some reduction to a member, something less than his contribution. That does not, to my mind, prevent the object of the society being still for a charitable purpose. As I said in the course of the argument, in order to get a contribution of 9 d you may have to give your member benefits to the value of 4 d, but you are still 5 d to the good for your charitable purpose, and if you are giving that benefit for the purpose of getting the 5 d and devoting it to charitable purposes, it seems to me your purposes are still what they were – exclusively charitable.

There is plenty of evidence in this case that the operations of the society are general and extend to the promotion of agriculture generally and not merely to the benefit of the members.

The other attack that was made upon the society was this. It was said, this is a voluntary society, there are no rules and by-laws limiting its activities, and therefore at any moment it may devote its funds to a non-charitable purpose. It might, it is said, distribute its funds amongst its members or in relief of its members and that would not be a charitable purpose, and therefore it is to be deemed to be not a society formed for a charitable purpose. I think, with respect, that that is a *non sequitur*. The question you have to consider is whether at the relevant time you are dealing with the income of a society established for charitable purposes only, and in respect of that income also you have to consider whether the income is applied in fact to charitable purposes only. It may be said of every voluntary society that, as it voluntarily came into existence, so it may voluntarily cease to be in existence; as it voluntarily associated so it may voluntarily dissolve. The mere fact that it may dissolve at any time and come to an end seems to me to have nothing to do with this particular problem. As it may dissolve itself, so I think it is fairly plain that it may, if it chooses, reassociate itself for other purposes, either by dissolving itself and forming itself into a society for another purpose, or it may be by adding to its objects, objects which are non-charitable, or by substituting for its objects an object which is non-charitable instead of a charitable object. But if it does so, then it appears to me that the society will cease to be a society established for a charitable purpose, and its funds will presumably not be devoted to charitable purposes only. But until it does do so it appears to me that the question is the same, whether it was established for a charitable purpose and whether it is still operating in that sphere.

In this particular case the society has not changed its constitution, it has not adopted non-charitable purposes, and its investments and income remain quite plainly, to my mind, bound by the obligation to apply them to charitable purposes and to charitable purposes only.

SUPPLEMENTARY READING

Farder, C, 'Too political to be charitable' [1984] Conv 263

Hopkins, J, 'Charity – trusts for the saying of masses' [1989] CLJ 373

Hopkins, J, 'Trusts for the advancement of sport – Recreational Charities Act 1958' [1992] CLJ 429

Nobles, R, 'Politics, public benefit and charity' (1982) 45 MLR 704

Norman, H, 'Sporting charities – social welfare defined: *Guild v IRC*' [1992] Conv 361

Parry, N, 'Trusts for masses – *Re Hetherington*' [1989] Conv 453

Watkin, T, 'Casenote – *Re Koeppler*' [1985] Conv 56

Watkin, T, 'Where there is a will' [1985] Conv 412

CHAPTER 17

CHARITABLE TRUSTS: *CY-PRÈS* DOCTRINE

The expression, *cy-près*, originates from Norman French meaning 'near this'. Over the centuries the expression has been taken to mean 'as nearly as possible'. The *cy-près* doctrine is a principle applicable to gifts for charitable purposes which fail (initially or subsequently) owing to the impossibility or impracticality of giving effect to the donor's intention. Schemes may be approved by the Charity Commissioners and the courts for the application of the funds as nearly as possible to the original purposes as stated by the settlor. When the *cy-près* doctrine is adopted, the donor or his estate is excluded from benefiting by way of a resulting trust.

There are only two conditions to be satisfied for a *cy-près* application namely:

(1) the impossibility or impracticality of carrying out the original charitable purpose or the existence of a surplus of funds after the charitable purpose has been fulfilled; and

(2) the manifestation of a general charitable intention by the donor as opposed to a specific charitable intention.

IMPOSSIBILITY

Prior to the introduction of the Charities Act 1960 (now the Charities Act 1993), the courts approached this question by considering whether the purposes, as stated by the settlor, were capable of being achieved as distinct from merely being undesirable. In *AG v City of London*,[1] trust funds to be used for the advancement and propagation of the Christian religion among the infidels in Virginia were applied *cy-près* when it became clear that there were no longer any infidels in Virginia. Similarly, in *AG v Ironmongers Co*,[2] funds devoted to the redemption of British slaves in Turkey and Barbary were applied *cy-près* when the purpose subsequently became impossible to achieve.

The test of 'impossibility' was construed broadly in *Re Dominion Students' Hall Trust*[3] where a limited company was formed for charitable purposes. The memorandum of association declared its object to maintain a hostel for students 'of European origin' from the overseas dominions of the British

1 (1790) 3 Bro CC 171.

2 (1844) 10 Cl & Fin 908.

3 [1947] 1 Ch 183.

Empire. The company proposed a scheme, for approval by the court, whereby the offensive words 'of European origin' would be deleted so that the company would be better equipped to administer the funds for the benefit of all students from the dominions regardless of racial origin. The court approved the scheme because the retention of the colour bar had the effect of defeating the main object of the charity.

Re Dominion Students' Hall Trust [1947] 1 Ch 183, HC

Evershed J: The purpose of both the petition and the summons is that a restriction which has hitherto been characteristic of the charity, limiting its objects so as to exclude coloured students of the British Empire, should be removed and that the benefits of the charity should be open to all citizens from the Empire without what is commonly known as the 'colour bar'. Having regard to the interest of the Inns of Court in Imperial Students, I have thought it right to be particularly careful to see that I have jurisdiction to authorise the scheme and to sanction the petition. The proposed removal of the 'colour bar' restriction has been put to a substantial number of the subscribers. Owing to the necessities of the case, it has not been possible to put it to all, but those to whom it has been put represent over 75% in value of the subscription and none dissents from what is now proposed.

It is plain that I have to bear in mind the general proposition contained in the headnote to *In re Weir Hospital*,[4] which is to the effect that funds given by a testator for a particular charitable purpose cannot be applied *cy-près* by the court unless it has been shown to be impossible to carry out the testator's intention. True, the present is not a case of a testator and the court is, perhaps, not quite so strictly limited as in the case of a will. It is true, also, that the word 'impossible' should be given a wide significance: see *In re Campden Charities*;[5] *In re Robinson*.[6] It is not necessary to go to the length of saying that the original scheme is absolutely impracticable. Were that so, it would not be possible to establish in the present case that the charity could not be carried on at all if it continued to be so limited as to exclude coloured members of the Empire.

I have, however, to consider the primary intention of the charity. At the time when it came into being, the objects of promoting community of citizenship, culture and tradition among all members of the British Commonwealth of Nations might best have been attained by confining the Hall to members of the Empire of European origin. But times have changed, particularly as a result of the war; and it is said that to retain the condition, so far from furthering the charity's main object, might defeat it and would be liable to antagonize those students, both white and coloured, whose support and goodwill it is the purpose of the charity to sustain. The case, therefore, can be said to fall within the broad description of impossibility illustrated by *In re Campden Charities* and *In re Robinson*.

4 [1910] 2 Ch 124.

5 (1881) 18 Ch D 310.

6 [1923] 2 Ch 332.

On the other hand, the test of impossibility was not satisfied in *Re Weir Hospital*.[7] The testator devised property to be used as the site for a hospital. Expert evidence was admitted to the effect that the site was not suitable for a hospital and a scheme was proposed for the building of a nurses' home instead. The court refused to approve the scheme on the ground that it was not impossible to carry out the testator's wishes but was simply inadvisable.

Re Weir Hospital [1910] 2 Ch 124, CA

> **Cozens-Hardy MR:** Wherever the *cy-près* doctrine has to be applied, it is competent to the court to consider the comparative advantages of various charitable objects and to adopt by the scheme the one which seems most beneficial. But there can be no question of *cy-près* until it is clearly established that the directions of the testator cannot be carried into effect.
>
> It was no part of the Commissioners' duty to consider whether cottage hospitals are or are not desirable at the Hawthorns; the dispensary was already provided for at No 12 Devonshire Road, and a convalescent home was not thought expedient. There remained nothing but the cottage hospital or other medical charity. They have chosen a nurses' home (as to which I will only say that I think it extremely doubtful whether such a home as they proposed is a charity at all), which absorbs only a small sum, and they refuse to set up a cottage hospital partly on the ground that they disapprove of such hospitals and partly because they consider the income is more than sufficient for such a purpose. I am not sure which ground is the more untenable. The first is obviously bad for the reason already given. The second appears to assume that it is wrong to have a large margin on starting such a hospital. In my opinion the reverse is the case. It might be wrong to embark on a scheme which left no margin for contingencies; but the wise man would certainly apportion his expenditure so as to leave some margin, and when I consider the nature of the investments and the amount of margin in this case I see nothing extravagant in its amount. The existence of such a margin does not render the charity named by the testator impossible, but is a guarantee of its success, and I am of opinion that neither the trustees nor the Commissioners have authority to choose their charity so as to leave a surplus to be applied *cy-près*. They are bound to apply the funds in the named charities unless it be impracticable. It is clearly impossible for the Commissioners or trustees to decline to carry out the trusts of a single named lawful charity because they disapproved of it. It is equally clear that if they have the choice of two or more charities they cannot apply a part of the trusts funds towards one of such charities and refuse to apply the balance to the others because they disapprove of them. A case for the *cy-près* application of trust funds cannot be manufactured, but must arise *ex necessitate rei*. I, of course, give the Commissioners and the trustees full credit for desiring to do their best; but it is of great importance that their conduct should be in accordance with law. It is contrary to principle that a testator's wishes should be set aside, and his bounty administered not according to his wishes but according to the view of the Commissioners.

7 [1910] 2 Ch 124.

Section 13 of the Charities Act 1993 (which re-enacts s 13 of the Charities Act 1960), consolidates to some extent and substantially extends the powers of the Charity Commissioners and the courts to apply property *cy-près*. The circumstances when the purposes of the charity will become impractical or impossible are enacted in s 13(1)(a) to (e) of the Charities Act 1993.

Section 13(1)(a) of the Charities Act 1993

> Where the original purposes in whole or in part have been as far as may be fulfilled, or cannot be carried out according the directions given and to the spirit of the gift.

This paragraph gives the court the jurisdiction to decide that the original purposes of the gift have been fulfilled or have become impractical. The only restriction on the discretion of the court is in regard to the construction of the 'spirit of the gift'. This phrase has been interpreted by Pennycuick VC in *Re Lepton's Charity*[8] as meaning 'the basic intention underlying the gift, as ascertained from its terms in the light of admissible evidence'.

Re Lepton's Charity [1972] Ch 276, HL

In this case, a testator who died in 1716 devised specific property to trustees on trust to pay an annual sum of £3 to the Protestant Minister in Pudsey, and the surplus income to the poor and aged people of Pudsey. In 1716, the total income was £5. On the date of the application to the court, that income was £790 per annum. Two questions arose for the determination of the court, namely:

(i) whether on a true construction of the will the minister ought to be paid a fixed sum of £3 or three fifths of the annual income; and

(ii) whether the court would approve a *cy-près* scheme increasing the minister's entitlement to £100 per annum.

The court held that on a construction of the will the minister was not entitled to three fifths of the annual income but only a fixed sum of £3 per annum, but having regard to the spirit of the gift, a *cy-près* scheme would be approved entitling the minister to £100 per annum.

> **Pennycuick VC**: The question raises a narrow but not, to my mind, an easy point. I was referred in the first place to certain authorities setting out the principles upon which, before the enactment of the Charities Act 1960 [now, the Charities Act 1993], the court proceeded in directing the *cy-près* application of any given fund. These authorities were *Philpott v St George's Hospital;*[9] *In re*

8 [1972] Ch 276.

9 (1859) 27 Beav 107.

> *Ashton's Charity*;[10] *In re Campden Charities*,[11] and *In re Weir Hospital*,[12] the two latter cases being in the Court of Appeal.

It is clear from these authorities that the court could not properly direct such application unless it was shown that the particular purpose prescribed by the testator had failed, but there might well be some debatable ground as to what constitutes a failure for this purpose in a particular case; see, in particular, the judgments in the Court of Appeal in the *Campden Charities* and *Weir Hospital* cases.

> **Pennycuick VC:** The occasions for applying property *cy-près* are now set out in s 13 of the Charities Act 1960 [now s 13 of the Charities Act 1993]. It is clear that this section in part restates the principles applied under the existing law, but also extends those principles. The section should be read as a whole, but for the present purpose it will be sufficient to refer specifically only to a few sentences.
>
> [The learned judge then read s 13(1) and continued:]
>
> Sub-section (1)(e)(iii) appears to be no more than a final writing out large of para (a)(ii). The expression 'spirit of the gift' may be an echo of words used in the *Campden Charities* case. It must, I think, be equivalent in meaning to the basic intention underlying the gift, that intention being ascertainable from the terms of the relevant instrument read in the light of admissible evidence.
>
> One must next consider whether in relation to a trust for payment of a fixed annual sum out of the income of a fund to charity A and payment of the residue of that income to charity B the expression 'the original purposes of a charitable gift' in s 13(1) should be construed as referring to the trusts as a whole or must be related severally to the trust for payment of the fixed annual sum and the trust for payment of residuary income. Mr Browne-Wilkinson contends that the former is the correct view. Mr Griffith contends that the latter is the correct view.
>
> It seems to me that the words 'the original purposes of a charitable gift' are apt to apply to the trusts as a whole in such a case. Where a testator or settlor disposes of the entire income of a fund for charitable purposes, it is natural to speak of the disposition as a single charitable gift, albeit the gift is for more than one charitable purpose. Conversely, it would be rather unnatural to speak of the disposition as constituting two or more several charitable gifts each for a single purpose. Nor, I think, is there any reason why one should put this rather artificial construction on the words. The point can, so far as I can see, only arise as a practicale in regard to a trust of the present character. A trust for division of income between charities in aliquot shares would give rise to different considerations, inasmuch as even if one treats it as a single gift the possibility or otherwise of carrying out the trusts of the other share according to the spirit of the gift. The same is true, *mutatis mutandis*, of trusts for charities in succession. But in a trust of the present character there is an obvious inter-

10 (1859) 27 Beav 115.

11 (1880) 18 Ch D 310.

12 [1910] 2 Ch 124.

> relation between the two trusts in that changes in the amount of the income and the value of money may completely distort the relative benefits taken under the respective trusts. The point is familiar in other instances of fixed annuity and residual income.
>
> Once it is accepted that the words 'the original purposes of a charitable gift' bear the meaning which I have put upon them it is to my mind clear that in the circumstances of the present case the original purposes of the gift of Dickroyd cannot be carried out according to the spirit of the gift, or to use the words of para (e)(iii) 'have ceased ... to provide a suitable and effective method of using the property ... regard being had to the spirit of the gift'. The intention underlying the gift was to divide a sum which, according to the values of 1715, was modest but not negligible, in such a manner that the minister took what was then a clear three fifths of it. This intention is plainly defeated when in the conditions of today the minister takes a derisory £3 out of a total of £791.
>
> It is not suggested that sub-s (2) has any significant bearing upon the present question, for it is precisely the condition requiring the failure of the original purposes that sub-s (1)(a)(ii) and sub-s (1)(e)(iii) are concerned to modify.
>
> If, contrary to my view, the words 'the original purposes of a charitable gift' must be read severally in relation to the trust for payment of the fixed annual sum and to the trust for payment of residuary income, I think it is no less clear that paras (a)(ii) and (e)(iii) would have no application. On this footing it would be impossible to maintain in respect of either trust that the original purposes cannot be carried out in the spirit of the gift. The minister is available to receive £3 a year, for what it is worth, and it is conceded by Mr Browne-Wilkinson that there are sufficient poor, aged and necessitous people in Pudsey to absorb £788 a year.

Recently, in *Oldham Borough Council v AG*,[13] the Court of Appeal was required to consider the original purpose of a devise of land to the Oldham Borough Council 'on trust to preserve and manage the same as playing fields known as the 'Clayton Playing Fields' for the benefit of inhabitants of Oldham, Chatterton and Royton'. The Court of Appeal, reversing the decision of the High Court, held that, on construction of the instrument, the original purpose of the devise was not intended to impose an obligation on the council to retain the site in perpetuity, for use only as playing fields for the local community, but to make provision for playing fields for the benefit of the local community. Accordingly, the council was entitled to sell the site to developers and use the proceeds to acquire a new site for playing fields for the local community.

Oldham Borough Council v Attorney General [1993] 2 WLR 224, CA

> **Dillon LJ:** Broadly, the effect (of s 13 of the Charities Act 1960) is that an alteration of the 'original purposes' of a charitable gift can only be authorised by a scheme for the *cy-près* application of the trust property and such a scheme can only be made in the circumstances set out in paras (a) to (e) of s 13(1).

13 [1993] 2 WLR 224.

It follows that if the retention of a particular property is part of the 'original purposes' of a charitable trust, sale of that property would involve an alteration of the original purposes even if the proceeds of the sale were applied in acquiring an alternative property for carrying out the same charitable activities. If so, a sale of the original property could only be ordered as part of a *cy-près* scheme, and then only if circumstances within one or other of paras (a) to (e) are made out. The particular bearing of that in the present case is that the council accepts, and the Attorney General agrees, that the circumstances of this charity do not fall within any of these paragraphs. If, therefore, on a true appreciation of the deed of gift and of s 13, the retention of the existing site is part of the original purposes of the charity, the court cannot authorise any sale.

It is necessary, therefore, to look first at the terms of the deed of gift.

[After considering the terms of the deed Dillon LJ continued:]

I come then to what I regard as the crux of this case, *viz*, the true construction of the words 'original purposes of a charitable gift' in s 13 of the Act of 1960. Do the 'original purposes' include the intention and purpose of the donor that the land given should be used for ever for the purposes of the charity, or are they limited to the purposes of the charity?

Certain of the authorities cited to us can be put on one side. Thus, in *In re JW Laing Trust*,[14] Peter Gibson J said, plainly correctly:

> It cannot be right that any provision, even if only administrative, made applicable by a donor to his gift should be treated as a condition and hence as a purpose.

In that case, however, the provision, which was held to be administrative and was plainly not a 'purpose,' was a provision that the capital was to be wholly distributed within the settlor's lifetime or within 10 years of his death.

Conversely, there are cases where the donor has imposed a condition, as part of the terms of his gift, which limits the main purpose of the charity in a way which, with the passage of time, has come to militate against the achievement of that main purpose. The condition is there part of the purpose, but the court has found itself able on the facts to cut out the condition by way of a *cy-près* scheme under the *cy-près* jurisdiction, on the ground that the subsistence of the condition made the main purpose impossible or impracticable of achievement: see *In re Dominion Students' Hall Trust*,[15] where a condition of a trust for the maintenance of a hostel for male students of the overseas dominions of the British Empire restricted the benefits to dominion students of European origin; and see, also, *In re Robinson, Wright v Tugwell*,[16] where it was a condition of the gift of an endowment for an evangelical church that the preacher should wear a black gown in the pulpit. But unlike those conditions, the intention or purpose in the present case that the actual land given should be used as playing fields is not a condition qualifying the use of that land as playing fields.

14 [1984] Ch 143, p 153.

15 [1947] Ch 183.

16 [1923] 2 Ch 332.

It is necessary, in my judgment, in order to answer the crucial question of the true construction of s 13, to appreciate the legislative purpose of s 13. Pennycuick VC said in *In re Lepton's Charity*[17] that the section 'in part restates the principles applied under the existing law, but also extends those principles'. That section is concerned with the *cy-près* application of charitable funds, but sales of charitable lands have, in so far as they have been dealt with by Parliament, always been dealt with by other sections not concerned with the *cy-près* doctrine.

There are, of course, some cases where the qualities of the property which is the subject matter of the gift are themselves the factors which make the purposes of the gift charitable, for example, where there is a trust to retain for the public benefit a particular house once owned by a particular historical figure or a particular building for its architectural merit or a particular area of land of outstanding natural beauty. In such cases, sale of the house, building or land would necessitate an alteration of the original charitable purposes and, therefore, a *cy-près* scheme because after a sale the proceeds or any property acquired with the proceeds could not possibly be applied for the original charitable purpose. But that is far away from cases such as the present, where the charitable purpose – playing fields for the benefit and enjoyment of the inhabitants of the districts of the original donees, or it might equally be a museum, school or clinic in a particular town – can be carried on on other land.

Accordingly, I would allow this appeal, set aside the declaration made by the judge, and substitute a declaration to the opposite effect.

In *Re Laing Trust*,[18] the court drew a distinction between the 'original purposes' of the trust under s 13 which may be reviewed by the court on a *cy-près* application, and a direction to distribute within a specific period of time, which is treated as an administrative provision outside of s 13. Under the inherent jurisdiction of the court, a scheme may be approved even though the court has no jurisdiction within s 13.

Re Laing Trust [1984] Ch 143, HC

In 1922, a settlor transferred shares to the plaintiff company as trustee to hold for charitable purposes. Both capital and income were to be wholly distributed during the lifetime of the settlor or within 10 years of his death. The settlor died in 1978. By 1982 the capital which was undistributed was worth £24 million. The plaintiff company applied to the court to sanction a scheme dispensing with the obligation to distribute the capital within 10 years of the settlor's death. The court decided that it had no jurisdiction under s 13, as the 'original purposes' of the charitable gift did not include an administrative provision concerning the date of distribution, but in the exercise of its inherent jurisdiction the court would approve the proposed scheme.

17 [1972] Ch 276, p 284F.

18 [1984] Ch 143.

Peter Gibson J: For the court to have jurisdiction to make the order sought by the plaintiff under s 13 two questions must be answered affirmatively: (1) Is the requirement to distribute before the expiration of 10 years from the settlor's death included in the 'the original purposes' of the charitable gift? (2) If so, have the original purposes, in whole or in part, since they were laid down, ceased to provide a suitable and effective method of using the property available by virtue of the gift?

To answer the first question it is necessary to identify the original purposes of the gift. I venture to suggest that, as a matter of ordinary language, those purposes in the present case should be identified as general charitable purposes and nothing further. I would regard it as an abuse of language to describe the requirement as to distribution as a purpose of the gift. Of course, that requirement was one of the provisions which the settlor intended to apply to the gift, but it would, on any natural use of language, be wrong to equate all the express provisions of a gift, which *ex hypothesi* the settlor intended to apply to the gift, with the purposes of a gift. To my mind the purposes of a charitable gift would ordinarily be understood as meaning those charitable objects on which the property given is to be applied. It is not meaningful to talk of the requirement as to distribution being either charitable or non-charitable.

However, as Mr McCall rightly submits, the meaning of 'purposes' in s 13 must be construed in its statutory context. He submits that in the Charities Act 1960 a distinction is recognised between the purposes of a gift and its administration. Thus, in s 46 the word 'trusts' in relation to a charity is defined as meaning the provisions establishing it as a charity and regulating its purposes and administration. He also drew my attention to s 18(1)(a) under which the Charity Commissioners have power to establish a scheme for the administration of a charity, and submitted that such a scheme is to be contrasted with s 13 under which the original purposes of a charitable gift can be altered to allow a *cy-près* application of property the subject of that gift. I accept therefore, that the question I must answer is whether the requirement as to distribution is part of the original purposes or a provision relating to administration.

Both Mr McCall and Mr Picarda advanced a more subtle argument on the following lines: (1) s 13 not merely re-enacted the circumstances in which *cy-près* applications were allowed under the previous law but also extended those circumstances; (2) prior to the Act of 1960 the court had allowed by way of *cy-près* schemes the removal of impracticable conditions attached to charitable gifts; (3) such conditions must be regarded as purposes within the meaning of s 13; (4) the requirement as to distribution is also to be treated as, or as similar to, a condition and so a purpose within s 13. I accept the first and second of these propositions. The first is supported by the remarks of Sir John Pennycuick VC in *In re Lepton's Charity*.[19] The second is illustrated by cases such as *In re Robinson*[20] and *In re Dominion Students' Hall Trust*.[21]

---

19 [1972] Ch 276, p 284.

20 [1923] 2 Ch 332.

21 [1947] Ch 183.

But I have difficulty with the third and fourth propositions. I baulk at the universality of the third. Take the case of *In re Robinson*. The testatrix gave money for the endowment of an evangelical church but imposed 'an abiding condition' that a black gown be worn in the pulpit, a condition held by Lawrence J to be impracticable as defeating the main evangelical intention of the gift. It is not clear from the report whether the money that was given could be used for the provision of black gowns. If it could, then I would accept that the condition might accurately be described as a subsidiary purpose, as indeed the judge, at p 336, appears to describe the condition. But if not, to my mind this case is more accurately described as falling within the class of cases where the main charitable purpose is practicable but a subsidiary purpose or direction is impracticable. I was referred by Mr Picarda to *Tudor on Charities and Mortmain*,[22] where there is a heading 'Subordinate purpose impracticable'. But the text goes on to refer to 'subsidiary purpose or direction'. If a purpose is limited, as I think s 13 requires, to that for which the property comprised in the gift is to be applied and the money given could not be applied in providing a black gown, I do not think that the wearing of a black gown would be a purpose within s 13. But I do not see why the circumstances of *In re Robinson* cannot be fitted within s 13(1)(a)(ii) on the footing that the condition stipulated for is a direction and not an original purpose.

On the other hand, the relevant condition in *In re Dominion Students' Hall Trust*[23] went to defining the class of persons to whom the benefits of the charity were limited, that is to say male students of the overseas dominions of the British Empire of European origin. The requirement that the students be of European origin was removed as tending to defeat the main object of the charity. There is no difficulty in treating that condition as part of the original purposes, or alternatively as a direction and in either event the circumstances of that case would fall within s 13(1)(a)(ii).

In my judgment, therefore, it does not follow that all conditions attached to gifts must be treated as 'purposes' within s 13. It cannot be right that any provision, even if only administrative, made applicable by a donor to his gift should be treated as a condition and hence as a purpose. I confess that from the outset I have found difficulty in accepting that it is meaningful to talk of a *cy-près* application of property that has from the date of the gift been devoted both as to capital and income to charitable purposes generally, albeit subject to a direction as to the timing of the capital distributions. No case remotely like the present had been drawn to my attention. In the result, despite all the arguments that have been ably advanced, I remain unpersuaded that such a gift is capable of being applied *cy-près* and, in particular, I am not persuaded that the requirement as to distribution is a purpose within the meaning of s 13. Rather, it seems to me to fall on the administrative side of the line, going, as it does, to the mechanics of how the property devoted to charitable purposes is to be distributed. Accordingly, I must refuse the application so far as it is based on s 13. That conclusion renders it unnecessary for me to answer the second

22 4th edn, 1906, London: Sweet & Maxwell, pp 202 *et seq*.

23 [1947] Ch 183.

question which had to be answered affirmatively if s 13 were to apply. However, many of the submissions made by counsel on that question are of direct relevance to my consideration of the next question for me to answer, that is to say, whether the court, under its inherent jurisdiction, should direct the removal of the requirement as to distribution. To that question I now turn.

On this question Mr Picarda and Mr McCall submit, and I accept, that the court is not fettered by the particular conditions imposed by s 13(1)(e)(iii), but can, and should, take into account all the circumstances of the charity, including how the charity has been distributing its money, in considering whether it is expedient to regulate the administration of the charity by removing the requirement as to distribution within ten years of the settlor's death.

The evidence before me shows that the settlor throughout his life was a man of strong religious convictions and particularly interested, and personally involved, in the activities of the religious group known as the Christian (or Open) Brethren. That group has never had any central organisation of the group's churches or their missionaries. There are approximately 450 such missionaries. The plaintiff company is now a charity. Although in 1922 it did not hold its property for exclusively charitable purposes, nevertheless it was founded to hold property for missionary purposes and for the transmission of funds for the missionary and other work of the Christian Brethren, and there can be no doubt that it was chosen trustee because of its connections with the Christian Brethren.

For my part, I would have thought that the plaintiff could distribute the capital to any other charitable body or bodies if it thought fit, but that merely serves to emphasise the unimportance of the requirement as to distribution.

In my judgment, the plaintiff has made out a very powerful case for the removal of the requirement as to distribution, which seems to me to be inexpedient in the very altered circumstances of the charity since that requirement was laid down 60 years ago.

Section 13(1)(b) of the Charities Act 1993

Where the original purposes provide a use for part only of the property available by virtue of the gift.

The approval of the court may be granted under this paragraph where a surplus of funds are left over after the original charitable purposes have been carried out. This paragraph merely declares the law that existed before 1960.

Re North Devon and West Somerset Relief Fund [1953] 2 All ER 1032, HC

In this case, following the 1952 floods in North Devon and West Somerset, an appeal was launched 'to contribute to a fund for the relief of all those who have suffered ... We ask the whole country to support this fund'. There was a generous response to this appeal and it was contemplated that a large surplus would remain after providing for all requirements. The questions in issue were whether the collection was charitable and if so, whether the surplus was applicable *cy-près* or was held on resulting trust for the contributors.

The court held that: (i) the purpose of the appeal was to relieve hardship and suffering among the victims of the disaster which was a charitable initiative; (ii) having regard to all the circumstances, the intention of the contributors was to part with their funds out and out. Thus, the surplus fund was applicable *cy-près*.

> **Wynn-Parry J:** The first question which I have to decide on this summons is whether the trusts affecting the funds mentioned in the evidence are valid charitable trusts. I accept, as, indeed, I am bound to do, that in the case such as this where the trust is clearly of a public nature, for the trusts to be good charitable trusts they must be shown not only to be beneficial to the community, or a defined section of the community, but beneficial in the way which the law regards as charitable. For that I need refer to no other authority than the opinion of Lord Simonds in *Williams' Trustees v IRC*.[24]
>
> Before turning to the vital document in this case, I would observe in passing, that in the recent case of *Re Hobourn Aero Components Ltd's Air Raid Distress Fund*, Lord Greene MR, said in the course of his judgment:[25]
>
>> I am not concerned for one moment to dispute the proposition that a fund put up for air raid distress in Coventry generally would be a good charitable gift. I have very little doubt that it would be. But there is all the difference in the world between such a fund and a fund put up by, it may be, a dozen inhabitants of a street, or, it may be, a thousand employees of a firm, to provide for themselves out of moneys subscribed by themselves some kind of immediate relief in case they suffer from an air raid. The Attorney General and Mr Upjohn wish to attribute to the fact that these people were putting up money for their own benefit a very slight importance. To my mind, it is of the greatest importance and is quite conclusive in stamping the character of a private and personal trust upon this fund.
>
> Again, at the end of his judgment Morton LJ said:[26]
>
>> No doubt the provision of relief for air-raid distress is a most excellent object, and I should not myself doubt that a fund for the relief of air raid distress in Coventry was a fund held upon charitable trusts.
>
> Looking at that document as a whole, I extract from it an intention on the part of the authors to apply the money which may be subscribed at their invitation to relieve hardship and suffering which has been experienced both by what are called 'the local people' and others who were within the area at the time of the disaster and to achieve that by the charity of the community. I am unable to dissect this document in such a way as to discover in it, either by looseness of

24 [1947] AC 447 (see above, p 624).

25 [1946] 1 All ER 506.

26 *Ibid*, p 511.

phrasing, and, therefore, by inference, or by express words, any intention to benefit this part of the community in a way which the law would not regard as charitable.

For those reasons, I propose in answer to question (i) of the summons to declare that the trusts affecting the fund are valid charitable trusts.

[On the second question the learned judge continued:]

The nearest case to be found in the reports to the present case is *Re Welsh Hospital (Netley) Fund*.[27] That was a decision of Lawrence J. The facts were that on the outbreak of the war in 1914 a hospital was erected at Netley, and equipped and run during the war, for the benefit of sick and wounded Welsh soldiers by means of large voluntary subscriptions raised in Wales. In 1919 the hospital was closed, the staff disbanded, and the property sold to the War Office, and, after winding-up the affairs of the hospital, there was a surplus of some £9,000. It was held, on the evidence, that there was not a resulting trust of the surplus for the subscribers to the hospital, but a general charitable intention for sick and wounded Welshmen which enabled the court to apply the fund *cy-près*.

The appeal, as the learned judge points out, was an appeal to the inhabitants of Wales for subscriptions to a Welsh hospital. In the course of his judgment, PO Lawrence J says:[28]

> The first question to be determined is whether there is a resulting trust in favour of the subscribers to the fund. Mr Greene has argued on behalf of the subscribers that there is a resulting trust for them, and that the surplus ought to be paid back to the various subscribers. All the other parties to the summons have argued that in the circumstances it must be inferred that there was a general charitable intent and that the court is at liberty to apply the surplus *cy-près*. In my judgment this latter contention is well founded. The fund was created by contributions from various sources and in varying amounts, partly by donations from private individuals of more or less substantial amounts, and partly by the proceeds resulting from concerts and other entertainments given and from collections in streets and at churches made in most of the towns and villages of Wales. So far as regards the contributors to entertainments, street collections, etc, I have no hesitation in holding that they must be taken to have parted with their money out and out. It is inconceivable that any person paying for a concert ticket or placing a coin in a collecting box presented to him in the street should have intended that any part of the money so contributed should be returned to him when the immediate object for which the concert was given or the collection made had come to an end. To draw such an inference would be absurd on the face of it. So far as regards individual subscribers of substantial amounts, the proper inference to be drawn is not quite so plain. In my opinion, however, these subscribers must be taken to have known that they were contributing to a general fund which was

27 [1921] 1 Ch 655.

28 *Ibid*, p 660.

> being raised in the manner I have described, and that their contributions would be aggregated with the proceeds of entertainments, street collections, etc, and would not in any way be earmarked. They must, I think, also be taken to have known that the total funds collected from every source would be applied for the purpose of the charity without discriminating between the moneys derived from any particular source. In these circumstances I am of opinion that the true inference to be drawn is that these subscribers intended to part with their contributions out and out, and that they did not intend that the surplus, if any, of their contributions should be returned to them when the immediate object of the charity should have come to an end. In the result I hold that although all the contributions were in the first instance made for the particular purpose of building, equipping and maintaining the Welsh Hospital at Netley, the main underlying object of the contributors was to provide money for the comfort of sick and wounded Welshmen, and that all the subscribers intended to devote their contributions not only to the particular object, but generally to the benefit of their sick and wounded countrymen.

It appears to me, on careful consideration, that it is impossible to draw a distinction of any substance between the facts of that case and the facts of the present case. It appears to me not in the least decisive that there is a reference in the appeal to persons other than local residents who suffered distress by the disaster. The main underlying object of that appeal was to benefit the people of the district in question. The appeal proceeds in this case, as it did in the case of the Welsh hospital, by emphasising what in the Welsh case was called the immediate object, but which might quite easily in either case have been treated, on a strict construction of the appeal, as the only object. In *Re Welsh Hospital (Netley) Fund*, Lawrence J found no difficulty in drawing the conclusion, for the reasons which he gives, that there was a more extended object than might be said at first sight to appear on the face of the appeal; and when I apply his reasoning to the appeal in question is this case, I feel driven to exactly the same conclusion, namely, that there was a general charitable intent. All the reasons which militated in the mind of Lawrence J, to the conclusion to which he came are present in this case. I, therefore, find it impossible to distinguish that case from this case. In those circumstances, it appears to me to be unnecessary to travel through the rest of the authorities.

Section 13(1)(c) of the Charities Act 1993

> Where the property available by virtue of the gift and other property applicable for similar purposes can be more effectively used in conjunction with property held for common purposes, regard being had to the spirit of the gift.

This provision enables a number of small charities with common purposes to be amalgamated in order to create larger funds.

Re Faraker [1912] 2 Ch 488, CA

A testatrix, who died in 1911, left a legacy to 'Mrs Bailey's Charity, Rotherhithe'. A charity was founded by Mrs Hannah Bayly in 1756 for poor widows in Rotherhithe. In 1905, the charity was consolidated with a number of local charities under a scheme, approved by the Charity Commissioners, for the benefit of the poor in Rotherhithe. The court decided that the legacy was taken by the consolidated charities.

> **Cozens-Hardy MR:** Hannah Bayly's Charity is not extinct, it is not dead, and I go further and say it cannot die. Its objects may be changed, though not otherwise than in accordance with law: they may be changed either by the Court of Chancery in its own jurisdiction over charities or by schemes formed by the Charity Commissioners, to whom Parliament has entrusted that particular duty. Subject to that lawful alteration by competent authority of the objects, Hannah Bayly's Charity is not extinct, it exists just as much as it did when the testatrix died in 1756, as it did when there were changes made in 1814, and as it does today.
>
> Now it is to be remembered, as has been pointed out by Kennedy LJ, that this legacy was not given to Mrs Bayly's Charity for widows; it was simply given to a charity which is identified by name. It was given to an ancient endowed charity, and in my opinion a gift of that kind carries with it the application of it according to the lawful objects of the charity funds for the time being.

Section 13(1)(d) of the Charities Act 1993

> Where the original purposes were laid down by reference to an area which has ceased to be a unit, or by reference to a class of persons or to an area which has ceased to be suitable or practicable, regard being had to the spirit of the gift.

Under this paragraph, the court is entitled to consider that the original class of beneficiaries has become difficult to identify, owing to local government boundary changes, or the class of beneficiaries has dwindled over the years. See *AG v City of London* (1790) (above, p 693) and *Ironmongers Co v AG* (1844) (considered above, p 693).

Peggs and Others v Lamb [1994] 2 WLR 1, HC

In this case, the court considered a *cy-près* scheme under s 13(1)(d) of the Charities Act 1960. Freemen and their widows in the Ancient Borough of Huntingdon were entitled to the income from specific plots of land. In 1992 the number of beneficiaries had dwindled to 15 and the income available for distribution had risen to £550,000. The court decided, under s 13(1)(d), that the original purposes of the gift was to benefit the freemen and widows in the Huntingdon Borough but the class of beneficiaries had dwindled to such an extent that they ceased to be a suitable class for the deployment of the funds (due consideration being paid to the spirit of the gift). Accordingly, a scheme would be approved whereby the class of beneficiaries would be enlarged to include the inhabitants of the borough as a whole.

Morritt J: The issues raised by the amended originating summons may be summarised as follows:

For the freemen it was submitted that the only solution is that suggested in *Tudor on Charities*, at p 113, namely that the particular purpose must be deemed in each case to fall within the spirit and intendment of the preamble to the Charitable Uses Act 1601, whether or not it does so in fact. It was contended that the purposes in this case was the provision of income and general benefits for the freemen and their widows.

I have no hesitation in rejecting the submission for the freemen that the purpose of the trust is merely the provision of income and general benefits for the freemen and their widows. Until the beginning of the 20th century there was no question of the freemen dividing between themselves the whole of the income of the land and of the proceeds of sale of the land. They benefited either from exercising a right to pasture their own cattle or from receipt of the head money if they chose not to. The gross income was used to defray expenses and any balance was carried forward. The exercise of the rights of pasture was controlled by the borough and, in earlier times, limited rights were available for disposal to the poor inhabitants. I do not think that the usage since time immemorial justifies the presumption that the trust existed for the purpose of benefiting the freemen individually, though the provision of such benefits might in suitable circumstances be the way in which the purpose is achieved. There is a difference between the purpose of a trust and the means by which the purpose may be achieved: cf *IRC v McMullen*.[29]

Counsel for the freemen and for the Attorney General knew of no case in which a trust to distribute the income equally amongst a class however large the income or small the class had been held to be charitable. Nor do I. The reason must be that the purpose of such a trust could not come within the spirit and intendment of the preamble.

In the case of the Lammas charity such property has been confined to the Lammas' rights. But this gives rise to no problem because, I was told, there is in the area a well recognised formula by which the value of land is divided between those who are entitled to the Lammas' rights and others interested in the land. In the case of the commons charity it seems to me that the only proper inference is that the whole interest in the land was given for the charitable purposes for the benefit of the freemen even though at the time the only way the charitable purpose could be achieved was by the exercise of grazing rights. This accords with the evidence that there seems to be no instance in which the corporation obtained and retained for itself any benefit from the land, the income from the land or from the proceeds of sale or the income thereof.

In my judgment the income of the land or of the Lammas rights, as the case may be, and of the proceeds of sale of the same is held by the trustees to be

29 [1981] AC 1, p 14.

applied for exclusively charitable purposes for the benefit of qualifying freemen or their widows.

Thus, the question now arises whether a scheme is necessary. For the freemen it was submitted that there was no need for or jurisdiction to order the settlement of a scheme. But this submission was on the basis that the freemen were entitled to divide the annual income between them. In my judgment and for the reasons I have already given that is not so. Moreover, I do not think that the settlement of a scheme would be necessary merely to make plain that the income was to be applied for the original, namely general charitable purposes only amongst the freemen. The declaration of the court should be sufficient. If the trustees wanted a scheme they could always apply to the Charity Commissioners.

The real issue is whether in the circumstances there is jurisdiction to order the settlement of a scheme for the *cy-près* application of the income. This depends on s 13 of the Charities Act 1960.

[The learned judge read out s 13 of the Charities Act 1960, and continued:]

In *In re Lepton's Charity*,[30] Sir John Pennycuick VC construed the phrase 'spirit of the gift' as meaning the basic intention underlying the gift, such intention being ascertainable from the terms of the relevant instrument read in the light of admissible evidence. I do not think that the absence of any founding document precludes the existence of any 'spirit of the gift.' Accordingly such spirit must likewise be inferred. For the freemen it was contended that the spirit of the gift was the benefit of the freemen.

I have concluded that the original purposes were and are general charitable purposes for the benefit of qualifying freemen and their widows. These are presumed to be the purposes laid down in the middle ages. In those days there can be little doubt that the freemen of a borough were a substantial section of the public both numerically and in their social, economic and political importance. As such the class of freemen was then and for several centuries thereafter entirely suitable as a class by reference to which the charitable purposes should be laid down. But I am satisfied that that is no longer so. The effect of the Municipal Corporations Act 1835 was to destroy the political importance of the freemen and thereby to undermine their social and economic importance too. But, of more importance, membership of the class was thereby restricted, in the case of these charities, to those who were the sons of freemen and born in the ancient borough. The inevitable consequence after over 150 years is that the class has dwindled very considerably. There will come a time, if it has not arrived already, when the class of freemen ceases to be a section of the public at all. It is not necessary to decide whether that time has passed so that a case for a scheme can be made out under s 13(1)(e)(ii) of the Act of 1960 because I think it is clear that a sufficient case is made out under para (d).

The original basic intention or spirit of the gift was the benefit of the Borough of Huntingdon. It would, in my judgment, be entirely consistent with that, that in 1993 the class of persons by reference to which the charitable purposes are

30 [1972] Ch 276, p 285.

laid down should be enlarged from the freemen to the inhabitants as a whole. Accordingly I will direct the settlement of a scheme.

Section 13(1)(e) of the Charities Act 1993

Where the original purposes, in whole or in part, have since they were laid down:

(i) been adequately provided for by other reasons; or

(ii) ceased, as being useless or harmful to the community, or, for other reasons, to be in law charitable; or

(iii) ceased in any other way to provide a suitable and effective method of using the property given, regard being had to the spirit of the gift.

Paragraph (e)(i) empowers the court to modify the original purposes as stated by the donor, in view of the charitable purposes being provided for by other bodies such as central and local government, for example. the repair of roads and bridges may not be an appropriate mode of utilising charitable resources.

Paragraph (e)(ii) will rarely be used. It assumes that a purpose was once charitable but owing to changed circumstances the purpose ceases to be charitable, for example, anti-vivisection in the early 19th century was considered a charitable purpose (see *Re Fouveaux*),[31] but with the advance of medical research, anti-vivisection is no longer treated as a charitable purpose. At the time when the anti-vivisection society was removed from the charities' register, its funds could have been applied *cy-près*. Section 13(1)(e)(ii) merely confirms this approach.

Paragraph (e)(iii) enacts a wide ranging provision giving the courts the power to consider whether the original purposes selected by the donor represent an effective method of using the property. In *Re Lepton's Charity* (1972) (cited above, p 696), the court assumed jurisdiction *inter alia*, under s 13(1)(e)(iii), to sanction the scheme.

GENERAL CHARITABLE INTENTION

This is the second condition which is required to be fulfilled before the charitable funds may be applied *cy-près*.

Subsequent failure

But, there is one type of event where the courts have dispensed with the need to prove a general charitable intention. These are cases of 'subsequent failure', that is, occasions when the charitable bodies exist at the appropriate date of

31 [1985] 2 Ch 501.

vesting but which cease to exist subsequently. The appropriate date of vesting varies with the nature of the instrument creating the gift. An *inter vivos* transfer by deed takes effect on the date of the execution of the deed and a transfer by will takes effect on the date of death of the donor. Once the gift vests in the charity, the donor and his heirs are excluded from benefiting on a subsequent liquidation of the charity, irrespective of whether the gift was made subject to a general or specific charitable intention. In *Re Wright*, a testatrix, who died in 1933, gave her residuary estate to trustees on trust for a tenant for life, Mr Webb (who died in 1942) with remainder to found and maintain a convalescent home for 'impecunious gentlewomen'. On the date of the testatrix's death the residuary estate was sufficient to implement her wishes, but at the time of Webb's death, the fund was insufficient to carry out the charitable purpose. It was argued that the appropriate date for deciding whether the charitable purpose was practical or not was on the date of Webb's death. The court rejected this argument and decided that the date for deciding whether the funds were applicable *cy-près* was on the date of vesting, namely, the date of death of the testatrix.

Re Wright [1954] Ch 347, CA

> **Romer LJ:** Once money is effectually dedicated to charity, whether in pursuance of a general or a particular charitable intent, the testator's next-of-kin or residuary legatee are for ever excluded and no question of subsequent lapse, or of anything analogous to lapse, between the date of the testator's death and the time when the money becomes available for actual application to the testator's purpose can affect the matter so far as they are concerned. This conclusion necessarily follows, I think, upon the reasoning in *In re Slevin*.[32]
>
> In *In re Soley*[33] a testator bequeathed money on trust to pay the income thereof to a person for life and, after his death, the fund was given to the Drapers' Company to be applied by them for the benefit of their school at Tottenham, either by founding a scholarship for the encouragement of the scholars in various branches of learning or in such other manner as the masters, Wardens and Court of Assistance in their absolute discretion should think most suited to promote the interests of the college. The gift, accordingly, was for the promotion of a particular charitable purpose. After the testator's death, but during the lifetime of the tenant for life, the college ceased to exist, Byrne J, following *In re Slevin*, held that there had been no lapse of the bequest and directed that it should be applied for charitable purposes *cy-près*. A similar decision was that of Neville J in *In re Geikie*,[34] and indeed the decision of Roxburgh J in *In re Moon*[35] itself proceeded on the same footing. It is true that in all these cases the funds which were in question were to be paid over to other persons or bodies to be applied by them to the designated charitable

32 [1891] 2 Ch 236 (see below, p 712).

33 (1900) 17 TLR 118.

34 (1911) 27 TLR 484.

35 [1948] 1 All ER 300.

> purposes, whereas, in the present case, it is the trustees themselves who were so to apply the residuary trust fund, but in my opinion no difference of principle arises from this; the testatrix's trustees hold the fund impressed with a charitable trust, just as did the third parties in the other cases to whom the gifts were directed to be paid. I am accordingly of opinion that no legitimate distinction exists, either on principle or on authority, between the present case and *In re Moon* and the judge's decision upon this question was right and should be affirmed.
>
> I would only add that, although the question before us is not one of construction, nevertheless a contrary conclusion in the present case would in fact quite clearly defeat the intention of the testatrix. The life interest in residue, which deferred for years the fulfilment of the testatrix's wishes as expressed in her will, arose from the settlement of the probate proceedings and not from any bounty of the testatrix herself. She wanted the charity to be founded immediately upon her death and, but for the change in her testamentary dispositions affected by the compromise, her next of kin could have had no possible claim to the fund. It is, therefore, without reluctance that I have reached the conclusion that the appeal should be dismissed.

The same principle applies where the charity existed at the testator's death but was liquidated before the gift was distributed by the executor. This arose in *In re Slevin*: the testator left money to St Dominic's orphanage in Newcastle. The orphanage existed at the date of the death but closed down soon afterwards, before it received the legacy. The court held that the fund was applied *cy-près*.

In re Slevin [1891] 2 Ch 236, CA

> **Kay LJ:** This case raises a question which seems only to have occurred in two instances in the books, namely, whether a charitable bequest to an institution which comes to an end after the death of the testator, but before the legacy is paid over, fails for the benefit of the residuary legatee, as in the case of a lapse.
>
> Properly speaking, a lapse can only occur by failure of the object in the lifetime to the testator; but it is possible that a will might be so framed as that a subsequent failure of the object of the charitable gift might occasion a resulting trust for the benefit of the testator's estate. We have not been referred to any such case, nor have we found any.
>
> The orphanage did come to an end before the legacy was paid over. In the case of a legacy to an individual, if he survived the testator it could not be argued that the legacy would fall into the residue. Even if the legatee died intestate and without next of kin, still the money was his, and the residuary legatee would have no right whatever against the Crown. So, if the legatee were a corporation which was dissolved after the testator's death, the residuary legatee would have no claim.
>
> Obviously it can make no difference that the legatee ceases to exist immediately after the death of the testator. The same law must be applicable whether it was a day, or month, or year, or, as might well happen, 10 years after; the legacy not having been paid either from delay occasioned by the administration of the estate or owing to part of the estate not having been got in. The legacy became the property of the legatee upon the death of the

testator, though he might not, for some reason, obtain the receipt of it till long after. When once it became the absolute property of the legatee, that is equivalent to saying that it must be provided for; and the residue is only what remains after making such provision. It does not for all purpose cease to be part of the testator's estate until the executors admit assets and appropriate and pay it over; but that is merely for their convenience and that of the estate. The rights as between the particular legatee and the residue are fixed at the testator's death.

In the present case we think that the Attorney General must succeed, not on the ground that there is such a general charitable intention that the fund should be administered *cy-près* even if the charity had failed in the testator's lifetime, but because, as the charity existed at the testator's death, this legacy became the property of that charity, and on its ceasing to exist its property falls to be administered by the Crown, who will apply it, according to custom, for some analogous purpose of charity: *AG v Ironmongers Co*;[36] *Wilson v Barnes*;[37] *Tyseen on Charitable Bequests*.

Recently, in *Re ARMS*, the High Court decided that bequests made to a charitable company, which was in existence on the dates of death of the testators, but subsequently went into liquidation, took effect *prima facie* as gifts beneficially to the company. Unless there was some indication that the gifts took effect as trusts, the testators' estates were excluded from benefiting from a return of the properties. While it is possible that, had the testators known of the company's insolvent liquidation, they may not have wished to donate their properties to it, the court is reluctant to speculate about the testators' intentions in the face of the plain words of the wills. Accordingly, the gifts were taken by the company beneficially and were available for distribution amongst the company's creditors.

In Re ARMS (Multiple Sclerosis Research) Ltd [1997] 1 WLR 877, HC

Several testators made testamentary gifts to a named company which had been incorporated to carry out charitable purposes. The principal objects of the company, as stated in its memorandum of association, were the promotion of research into the cause, cure and prevention of multiple sclerosis and the assistance of its victims. Various gifts by wills were made by deceased testators to the company before it was formally liquidated. The liquidator applied to the court for directions as to how the bequests should be dealt with.

Held that the bequests formed part of the company's assets and were available for distribution among its creditors.

Neuberger J: The application with which I am concerned raises the question of whether certain testamentary gifts to a charitable company, which would otherwise take effect, are rendered ineffective by virtue of the company being wound up by order of the court.

36 (1834) 2 My & K 567; 2 Beav 313.

37 (1886) 38 Ch D 507.

I now turn to the bequest made by Mr HJ Dove. He died on 21 August 1993, after the winding up order. The relevant bequest in his will made on 15 September 1989 was a direction that the residue of his estate be held:

> For the following charities in equal shares absolutely: (1) the Cancer Research Fund of 2 Carlton House Terrace, London; (2) ARMS (Multiple Sclerosis Research) Ltd of 11 Dartmouth Street, London; and I hereby declare that the receipt of the treasurer or other proper officer for the time being of these charities shall be a full and sufficient discharge to my executors.

This gift raises the issue which was of concern to Millett J, namely, whether a gift to a charitable company takes effect according to its terms if the testator dies after the company has gone into compulsory liquidation, but before it has been formally dissolved.

In the present case, at the date of Mr Dove's death, the company was still in existence: indeed, even now it has not been dissolved. Accordingly, Mr Alleyne and the trust contend that Mr Dove has effected a simple 'bequest to a corporate body', namely, the company, which 'takes effect simply as a gift to that body beneficially'. The fact that the body is in liquidation does not alter the fact that it still exists. Furthermore, they contend that there are no circumstances to suggest that the company was intended to take the gift as a trustee.

If, as a matter of construction of the will, the gift is expressed to be for a company then 'unless there are circumstances which show that the recipient is to take the gift as a trustee' (*per* Buckley J in *In re Vernon's Will Trusts (Note)* [1972] Ch 300, p 303) it takes effect so long as the company is in existence at the date of the testator's death.

In general, one has the very strong suspicion that, where a testator makes a will leaving a gift to a company established for charitable purposes, and that company subsequently goes into insolvent liquidation, prior to his death, the testator would not have intended the gift to go to the company. However, in my judgment that is insufficient to justify a departure from the plain words of a will. If, according to their natural tenor, the words of a will provide that a specific gift is to be given to a specific company, then it is not for the court to speculate as to whether the testator would in fact have intended the gift to take effect had he known of a change in the circumstances of the company between the making of his will and his death.

In the case of Mr Dove's will, the use of the word 'charities' in two places in the relevant provision does provide the Attorney General's argument in the particular case with a little assistance. It can be said with some force that the obvious inference is that the testator intended that these bequests be charitable, in the sense that the money be devoted, in one way or another, towards the charitable aims of the company. However, I do not consider that that is sufficient to enable the court to conclude that the gift fails according to its terms, merely because the company is in insolvent liquidation. The description of the company as one of two 'charities' is not inaccurate as a matter of law, because, although it is in insolvent liquidation, it can remain registered with the Charity Commission (although I understand that it is the normal practice of the Charity

> Commissioners to remove a charitable company from the register if it goes into insolvent liquidation). Furthermore, it is hard to contend that the description of the company, even after it has gone into insolvent liquidation, as a 'charity' is inaccurate, bearing in mind that s 63 of the Charities Act 1993 (re-enacting s 30 of the Charities Act 1960) clearly treats a company established for charitable purposes as a charity at all times until it is actually dissolved.
>
> Accordingly, while I have sympathy for the proposition that the testator would not have intended the gift to the company to take effect had he known that the company was in insolvent liquidation at the date of his death, I reject the Attorney General's argument.

However, as a prerequisite to the *Re Wright* solution, it is essential that an absolute and perpetual gift be made to the charity at the time of vesting. If, alternatively, a limited gift (for a number of years) is made to the charity which existed on the date of vesting, but ceases to exist at the time the gift purported to take effect, on construction, the court may decide that a resulting trust in favour of the settlor's estate may take effect in accordance with the settlor's intention.

Re Cooper's Conveyance Trusts [1956] 3 All ER 28, HC

By a deed dated 13 April 1864, a donor conveyed land and buildings to trustees upon trust for the purposes of the Orphan Girls' Home at Kendal and on failure of the trust, for the benefit of specified beneficiaries, 'and upon or for no other trust or purpose whatsoever'. In June 1954, the orphanage was closed. The trustees applied to the court for directions.

Held that:

(i) on a true construction of the trust deed the donor manifested an intention to provide a limited benefit to the charity, namely, so long as the Orphan Girls' Home subsisted;

(ii) the gift over in favour of the specified beneficiaries failed for remoteness of vesting;

(iii) the trust deed manifested a specific charitable intention. Thus, there was no room for the application of the fund *cy-près*.

Accordingly, the property was held on resulting trust for the estate of the donor.

> **Upjohn J:** The question whether the property, ie, the lands and buildings, ought now to be applied on charitable trusts *cy-près* or results to the estate of the donor depends on the true construction of the deed. A number of authorities have been cited to me. They establish clearly the following proposition: Where in terms an absolute and perpetual gift to charity is made with a gift over on cesser which fails for remoteness or for some other reason, the original perpetual gift to charity remains; but, on the other hand, where there is a gift to charity for a limited period then the undisposed of interest reverts to the grantor ...

The general principle is stated in *Tudor on Charities*,[38] where, after referring to the well known passage in the judgment of Parker J, in *Re Wilson, Twentyman v Simpson* ([1913] 1 Ch 314, p 320), the editor continues:

> The importance of the distinction lies in the fact that the *cy-près* principle is confined to property given with a general intention of charity. There is an exception to this rule concerning property given absolutely to an orphanage or to support the home. A meeting was held in December 1953 at which representatives of the Home Office were present, and, as a result, in the circumstances a rule of convenience has grown up that on the subsequent failure of the trust, the fund can be applied *cy-près* irrespective of the donor's intention.

I draw attention to the words 'property given absolutely and perpetually to charity'.

Then I was referred to *Re Slevin, Slevin v Hepburn*,[39] and the more recent case of *Re Wright, Blizard v Lockhart*.[40] Those cases appear to me to establish that if one finds an initial out-and-out or perpetual gift to charity, albeit to a particular charity or to a particular charitable purpose, and that charity or charitable purpose fails after the gift has vested in interest, it is in a sense irrelevant to consider whether there is a general charitable intention. This is because the donor has made initially an out-and-out gift to charity, although to a particular charity or charitable purpose, and has reserved no interest to himself. Thus, in the present case, if there had been no gift over on the failure of the orphanage, it would hardly have been suggested that on the subsequent failure of it there would have been a resulting trust. Where, however, the donor uses language showing an intention that in some circumstances he contemplates a failure of the purpose or indicates that his gift is only to be for a limited time or purpose, then it becomes a question of construction, whether he has made an out-and-out or perpetual gift to charity or not, and that is not inaptly expressed by asking whether he has evinced a general charitable intention.

Accordingly, in my judgment, I think this is a case where the donor intended a gift to charity only for a limited time and for a limited purpose; the time is limited by the time for which the orphanage could be carried on. That period having come to an end, in my judgment, there is an interest in the donor remaining undisposed of; that is held on trust for her estate by way of resulting trust, and I must declare accordingly.

Initial failure

In the event of an initial failure of the charitable institution, it is essential to prove a general charitable intention before the funds are applied *cy-près*. In other words, if, at the time of the vesting of the gift, the charitable body,

38 5th edn, 1929, London: Sweet & Maxwell, p 141.

39 [1891] 2 Ch 236.

40 [1954] 2 All ER 98.

specified by the donor, did not exist, the fund may only be applied *cy-près* on proof of a general charitable intention as opposed to a specific charitable intention.

The intention of the donor is essentially a question of fact. The courts are required to consider all the circumstances in order to determine whether the donor intended to benefit a charitable 'purpose' *simpliciter* identified by reference to a charitable institution (paramount charitable intention), or whether the settlor's intention was to benefit a specific charitable body identified by him.

The court adopted a broad approach to this question in *Re Lysaght*, a testatrix bequeathed £5,000 to the Royal College of Surgeons (trustees) on trust to apply the income in establishing studentships with disqualifications in respect of Jews and Roman Catholics. The college declined to accept the gift but declared that if the religious bar was excised it would be willing to accept the gift. The court decided that in accordance with the paramount charitable intention of the testatrix the religious bar would be deleted. On construction, the court decided that the paramount charitable intention of the testatrix was to make the college a trustee of the fund and since this paramount intention was capable of being defeated if the religious bar was upheld, the court was entitled to delete the offending clause in order to give effect to the paramount intention of the settlor. The judge distinguished a general charitable intention from a specific charitable intention as follows:

Re Lysaght [1966] Ch 191, HC

> **Buckley J**: Let me consider for a moment the meaning of the term 'general charitable intent'. Whether a donor has or has not evinced such an intent is relevant in any case in which the donor has made a charitable gift in terms which cannot be carried out exactly. In such a case the court has to discover whether the donor's true intention can be carried out notwithstanding that it is impracticable to give effect to some part of his particular directions. I take by way of example four imaginary testators. The first bequeaths a fund for charitable purposes generally, the second for the relief of poverty, the third for the relief of poverty in the parish of 'X', the fourth for the relief of a particular class of poor (for example, of a particular faith or of a particular age group) in the parish of 'X'. Each of them couples with his bequest an indication of a particular manner in which the gift should be carried into effect, say, by paying the fares of poor persons travelling by rail from the village of 'X' to the town of 'Y' to obtain medical advice and attention. Between the dates of the wills and of the deaths of the four testators the railway between 'X' and 'Y' is closed, so that it becomes impossible for anyone to travel by rail from the one to the other. In each case the court must consider whether it was an essential part of the testator's intention that his benefaction should be carried into effect in all respects in the particular manner indicated and no other, or whether his true intention was, in the first case to make a gift for charitable purposes without qualification; in the second, to relieve poverty; in the third, to relieve poverty

in the parish of 'X'; and in the fourth, to relieve the poverty of the particular class of persons in the parish of 'X'; the specification of a particular mode of giving effect to such intention being merely an indication of a desire on his part in this respect: see the well known passage in the judgment of Parker J in *In re Wilson*.[41] If on the true construction of any of the wills the latter is the true view, the court will, if it can, carry the testator's true intention into effect in some other way *cy-près* to the impracticable method indicated by the testator. In so doing the court is not departing from the testator's intention but giving effect to his true paramount intention. Such an intention is called a general, charitable intention. It is not general in the sense of being unqualified in any way or as being confined only to some general head of charity. It is general in contrast with the particular charitable intention which would have been shown by any of the four supposed testators who upon the true construction of his will intended to benefit poor people by paying their railway fares when travelling by rail between 'X' and 'Y' to obtain medical advice and attention and in no other way. Such a general intention would not avail if the court could find no practical or legal method of giving effect to it – if, for instance, it could be shown in respect of the bequest of the fourth testator that at the relevant time there was no poor people of the particular class specified in his will to be found in the parish of 'X' and there was no reasonable likelihood of there being any such at any foreseeable time in the future. The question would then arise whether the testator's true intention was restricted to benefiting this particular class of poor people or whether he had some yet more general charitable intent to which the court could give effect.

A general charitable intention, then, may be said to be a paramount intention on the part of a donor to effect some charitable purpose which the court can find a method of putting into operation, notwithstanding that it is impracticable to give effect to some direction by the donor which is not an essential part of his true intention – not, that is to say, part of his paramount intention.

In contrast, a particular charitable intention exists where the donor means his charitable disposition to take effect if, but only if, it can be carried into effect in a particular specified way, for example, in connection with a particular school to be established at a particular place, *In re Wilson*,[42] or by establishing a home in a particular house: *In re Packe*.[43] The alternatives are neatly stated by Younger LJ *In re Willis*:[44]

> The problem which in this case we have to solve is to say by which of two different principles the construction of this gift has to be controlled. The first of these principles is that if a testator has manifested a general intention to give to charity, whether in general terms or to charities of a defined character or quality, the failure of the particular mode in which the charitable intention is to be effectuated shall not imperil the charitable gift.

41 [1913] 1 Ch 314.

42 *Ibid*.

43 [1918] 1 Ch 437.

44 [1921] 1 Ch 44, p 54; 37 TLR 43, CA.

> If the substantial intention is charitable the court will substitute some other mode of carrying it into effect. The other principle which I paraphrase from the judgment of Kay J in *Biscoe v Jackson*[45] is this. If on the proper construction of the will the mode of application is such an essential part of the gift that you cannot distinguish any general purpose of charity but are obliged to say that the prescribed mode of doing the charitable act is the only one the testator intended or at all contemplated, then the court cannot, if that mode fails, apply the money *cy-près*.

In the present case there would be a wide field open to any trustee of the endowment fund for the selection of students who manifestly satisfy the qualification of being neither of the Jewish nor of the Roman Catholic faith. Accordingly, I do not think that this part of the trust is affected by the vice of uncertainty. Nor, in my judgment, is it contrary to public policy, as Mr Balcombe suggests. I accept that racial and religious discrimination is nowadays widely regarded as deplorable in many respects and I am aware that there is a Bill dealing with racial relations at present under consideration by Parliament, but I think that it is going much too far to say that the endowment of a charity, the beneficiaries of which are to be drawn from a particular faith or are to exclude adherents to a particular faith, is contrary to public policy. The testatrix's desire to exclude persons of the Jewish faith or of the Roman Catholic faith from those eligible for the studentship in the present case appears to me to be unamiable, and I would accept Mr Clauson's suggestion that it is undesirable, but it is not, I think, contrary to public policy.

Obviously a trustee will not normally be permitted to modify the terms of his trust on the ground that his own opinions or convictions conflict with them. If his conscience will not allow him to carry out the trust faithfully in accordance with its terms, he must make way for a trustee who can and will do so. But how, if the identity of the trustee selected by the settlor is essential to his intention? If it is of the essence of a trust that the trustees selected by the settlor and no one else shall act as the trustees of it and those trustees cannot or will not undertake the office, the trust must fail: *In re Lawton*[46] and see *Reeve v AG*,[47] and *Tudor on Charities*.[48] I have already reached the conclusion that it is an essential part of the testatrix's intention that the college should be the trustee of the endowment fund. The college is, as I have said, unalterably opposed to accepting the trust if any provision for religious discrimination is an effective part of it.

The impracticability of giving effect to some inessential part of the testatrix's intention cannot, in my judgment, be allowed to defeat her paramount charitable intention.

In *In re Robinson*[49] Lawrence J had to deal with a fund bequeathed many years earlier for the endowment of a church of an evangelical character to which

45 (1887) 35 Ch D 460, p 463, CA.

46 [1936] 3 All ER 378.

47 (1843) 3 Hare 191, p 197.

48 *Op cit*, fn 38, p 128.

49 [1923] 2 Ch 332; 39 TLR 509.

conditions were attached, including what was called an 'abiding' condition that a black gown should be worn in the pulpit unless this should become illegal. The evidence showed that in 1923 the wearing of a black gown in the pulpit, though not illegal, would be detrimental to the teaching and practice of evangelical doctrines and services in the church in question. Lawrence J had to determine whether a scheme could properly be sanctioned dispensing with the observance of this condition. He said:[50]

> The contention on behalf of the petitioner is that the condition as to the wearing of a black gown in the pulpit is impracticable, but that it is subsidiary to the main purpose of the bequest, and that the present case falls within that class of cases when the main charitable purpose is practicable, but a subsidiary purpose is impracticable. If that contention be correct, I am satisfied that the court, on assuming the execution of the charitable trusts declared by the testatrix, has ample jurisdiction to execute those trusts *cy-près* and to sanction a scheme, modifying the trusts by dispensing with the subsidiary purpose, so as to carry out, as nearly as possible, the main charitable intentions of the testatrix. In my judgment, the contention that the condition as to the black gown is subsidiary to the main purpose of the bequest is sound. The dominant charitable intention of the testatrix, as expressed in her will, was to provide a fund towards the endowment of a proposed evangelical church at Bournemouth, the right of patronage and presentation to the living of which should be vested in the trustee of a deed of 24 November 1877. This main purpose can be fully carried into effect apart altogether from the condition as to wearing a black gown in the pulpit, although expressly insisted upon by the testatrix as a condition of her bequest. Consequently, the court, if satisfied that the condition is impracticable, can properly sanction a scheme dispensing with it.

The judge held on the evidence that the effect of insisting upon the condition would be to defeat the main intention of the testatrix. He held that, although compliance with the condition was not impossible in an absolute sense, it was impracticable and ought to be dispensed with.

In that case compliance with the condition in relation to the black gown was not impracticable at the inception of the trust in 1889, but had become so by 1923. In the present case, if the trust is impracticable, this is due to an initial difficulty, not to any change of circumstances. Since *In re Robinson*[51] was decided it has been recognised that different considerations govern the application of the *cy-près* doctrine when impracticability supervenes after a charitable trust has once taken effect from those which apply in cases of initial impracticability. In cases of supervening impracticability it matters not whether the original donor had or had not a general charitable intention (see *In re Wright*).[52] It was not, however, on any such ground as this that the decision *In re Robinson* was based. The passage which I have read from the judgment of

50 [1923] 2 Ch 332, p 336.

51 *Ibid*, p 332.

52 [1954] Ch 347; [1954] 2 WLR 972; [1954] 2 All ER 98.

> Lawrence J makes it clear that he decided as he did because, in his opinion, the testatrix's dominant intention was to endow a church and that the condition as to wearing a black gown was not an essential part of that intention but merely subsidiary.
>
> If I am right in the view that I have formed, that it was an essential part of the testatrix's intention in the present case that the college should be the trustee of the endowment fund, then I think that the reasoning in *In re Robinson* is precisely applicable to the present case.
>
> Accordingly, in my judgment, the court can and should enable the college to carry the trust into effect without any element of religious discrimination.

The court came to a similar conclusion in *Re Woodhams*, a limitation attached to scholarships to two music colleges, restricting applicants to boys from Dr Barnardo's Homes and the Church of England Children's Society Homes, was deleted because the colleges would otherwise have declined the gifts on the ground that the limitation was impractical.

Re Woodhams (Decd) [1981] 1 All ER 202, HC

> **Vinelott J:** It is clear that the testator intended that on the death of Helen Amy Dear a half-share of his residuary estate should be transferred to each of the London College and the old Tonic Sol-fa College and intended that the scholarships which he wanted to provide should be founded and administered by the London College and the old Tonic Sol-fa college and by no one else. Thus each bequest was, in effect, conditional on the London College and the old Tonic Sol-fa College (as the case may be) being willing to accept the bequest as trustee on trust to found a scholarship in accordance with the terms of the will. The willingness of the London College or the old Tonic Sol-fa College to accept the bequest on those terms must, of course, be determined at the date of the testator's death when the bequest first vested in interest and in the light of circumstances and reasonable expectations at that time (see *Re Tacon (Decd)*.[53] The question which I have to decide is whether the fact that each of the London College and the old Tonic Sol-fa College would have refused to accept a reversionary interest in a half share of the residuary estate on terms that they would be bound when the interest fell into possession to found and administer scholarships restricted to absolute orphans from one of the named homes has the consequence that the residuary gifts fail altogether.
>
> A similar question (but without the complication of an intervening life interest) arose in *Re Lysaght (Decd)*.[54] This [judgment] is criticised in *Tudor on Charities*,[55] the editor says:
>
> > It is suggested with diffidence, that this formulation does not accord with the usual understanding of a 'general charitable intention' discussed above. Furthermore, there would seem to be a considerable difficulty, in

53 [1958] 1 All ER 163; [1958] Ch 447.

54 [1965] 2 All ER 888. (The learned judge then considered the facts and judgment of Buckley J in *Re Lysaght* (see above, p 717) and continued.)

55 6th edn, 1967, London: Sweet & Maxwell, pp 247–48.

> view of the detailed provisions in the will, in the way of the construction which was made; and it is respectfully suggested that the learned judge's view of the will was, as a matter of construction, erroneous. Although a 'liberal spirit' may perhaps in some circumstances be commendable, it should not be applied in such a way as to defeat a testator's intention.

That criticism is, I think, ill founded. In a well known passage in *Re Wilson*, Parker J stresses that the jurisdiction of the court to direct a scheme for the carrying out the trust of a charitable gift which has otherwise failed through impracticability is founded on the fact that:

> ... the gift is given for a particular charitable purpose, but it is possible, taking the will as a whole, to say that, notwithstanding the form of the gift, the paramount intention, according to the true construction of the will, is to give the property in the first instance for a general charitable purpose rather than a particular charitable purpose ...

In *Re Crowe (Decd)*[56] a testatrix gave her residuary estate on trust to arrange for:

> ... the creation of a scholarship at the Royal Naval School for Officers' Daughters ... to be used for the best student (such student must be a Naval Officer's daughter in the Spanish and Russian language in memory of my father) ...

Slade J construed the gift as a gift to provide a single scholarship, such scholarship to be awarded in both Spanish and Russian. The school did not teach Russian and was not willing to provide a course at or outside the school. On the construction of the will adopted by Slade J the foundation of a scholarship in Spanish alone, or in Spanish and Russian otherwise than for pupils at the named school, would equally have frustrated the testatrix's intention. No modification was possible which would have made the gift practicable without frustrating her evident intention.

On the other side of the line stands *AG for New South Wales v Perpetual Trustee Co Ltd*.[57] In that case a testatrix whose home was a farming property known as 'Milly Milly' gave it on trust to be used as a training farm for orphan lads in Australia. The farm was too small, the plant was too old-fashioned, and the income would not have sufficed to meet the expenses of the supervisory staff needed. It was held by the majority of the High Court of Australia that the intention that 'Milly Milly' should be the actual place of training was not an essential part of the gift, so that the property could be sold and the proceeds applied for the purpose of training Australian orphan boys in farming without frustrating her intention.

Returning to the residuary gift in the instant case the testator devoted his whole estate to the furtherance of two charitable objects, namely music and the welfare of orphans cared for by Dr Barnardo's or the Church of England Children's Society homes. He pointed out that the gifts over of the legacies settled or purportedly settled by clause 4, paragraphs (b) and (u) of the will were in favour of or with a preference for those bodies. Thus, said counsel, the

56 (1979) unreported, 3 October.

57 (1940) 63 CLR 209.

gifts of the two half shares of the residuary estate are designed to further two ends: first, the activities of the London College and the old Tonic Sol-fa College, and, second, the welfare of orphans brought up in one of Dr Barnardo's or the Church of England Children's Society homes. To delete the requirement that persons to whom scholarships might be awarded should be absolute orphans from one of these homes would be to frustrate the testator's intention as surely as to transfer either bequest so some body other then the London College or the old Tonic Sol-fa College.

I do not take that view, The testator has in clause 7 of his will set out in very considerable and, in view of the modest value of his estate and the indefinite duration of the trust, somewhat excessive detail a scheme for the foundation of scholarship. But as I see it the intention which can be discerned from the bequest is twofold. The testator wanted to further musical education and to do so by means of founding scholarships at colleges with which he had a long and, as is apparent from paragraphs (c) and (d) of clause 4 of the will, a valued connection. He chose absolute orphans from homes run by well-known charities as those most likely to need assistance. But it was not, as I see it, an essential part of this scheme that the scholarships should be so restricted, whatever needs might present themselves in changed circumstances. That being so, that part of the scheme or mode of achieving a charitable purpose can be modified without frustrating his intention.

In my judgment, therefore, the trusts of residue do not fail. At the date of the testator's will the trusts could have been carried into effect by a modification of the trust of each moiety, deleting the restriction to absolute orphans from the named homes. There have been further changes of circumstances as regards the old Tonic Sol-fa College since the testator's death and a more radical scheme may be required, I will therefore refer to the Charity Commissioners the settlement of a scheme.

Form and substance

The classic statement of the distinction between a general charitable intention and a specific charitable intention was issued by Parker J in *Re Wilson*: a testator by will gave his entire property to his three daughters and their children with a gift over in the event of the daughters dying without issue (which in fact happened). The gift over was to provide the salary of a schoolmaster of a school to be built by subscriptions from local residents. The details of the location of the school to be built as well as the duties of the schoolmaster were specified by the testator. There was no prospect of the school being built.

The court held that the testator manifested a specific charitable intention.

Re Wilson [1913] 1 Ch 314, HC

Parker J: For the purposes of this case I think the authorities must be divided into two classes. First of all, we have a class of cases where, in form, the gift is given for a particular charitable purpose, but it is possible, taking the will as a whole, to say that, notwithstanding the form of the gift, the paramount intention, according to the true construction of the will, is to give the property in the first instance for a general charitable purpose rather than a particular charitable purpose, and to graft on to the general gift a direction as to the desire or intentions of the testator as to the manner in which the general gift is to be carried into effect. In that case, though it is impossible to carry out the precise directions, on ordinary principles the gift for the general charitable purpose will remain and be perfectly good, and the court, by virtue of its administrative jurisdiction, can direct a scheme as to how it is to be carried out. In fact the will will be read as though the particular direction had not been in the will at all, but there had been simply a general direction as to the application of the fund for the general charitable purpose in question.

Then there is the second class of cases, where, on the true construction of the will, no such paramount general intention can be inferred, and where the gift, being in form a particular gift, a gift for a particular purpose – and it being impossible to carry out that particular purpose, the whole gift is held to fail. In my opinion, the question whether a particular case falls within one of those classes of cases or within the other is simply a question of the construction of a particular instrument.

It appears to be the fact that there is no reasonable chance of any such school being established at or in the neighbourhood of the place where the testator directs the school to be built, and it is, I think, in substance admitted, on behalf of the Attorney General, that no scheme giving effect to any of these directions is practicable, and that, unless I can construe the gift as a gift for the promotion of higher education in the district, the gift must necessarily be incapable of taking effect.

In my opinion, I am not justified in holding that I can disregard all the particular directions and construe the gift as a general gift for the purposes of promoting higher education. It appears to me that what the testator had in mind is, that he is dissatisfied with the provisions for the education in the district in certain respects, and that he desires that subscriptions shall be collected for the building of a school to teach certain other subjects which have not hitherto been taught, and if those subscriptions are made and a school house and a school are built, then he desires to endow or provide a salary for the schoolmaster subject to certain conditions as to certain scholars being admitted free and otherwise. I think that the whole gift is really in the testator's mind dependent upon it being feasible and possible to carry out these particular directions, and that I am not justified in reading into the will from this gift any such general intention of promoting higher education in the district or neighbourhood of the district as is suggested.

Examples of cases within the first category of circumstances of a general charitable intention, as laid down by Parker J in *Re Wilson* (above), are *Re Lysaght*; *Re Woodhams*; and *Biscoe v Jackson*.[58]

58 (1887) 35 Ch D 460.

In *Biscoe v Jackson*, a legacy for the establishment of a soup kitchen and a cottage hospital in the parish of Shoreditch disclosed, on construction of the will, a general charitable intention to benefit the poor in Shoreditch.

> **Cotton LJ:** Looking at this whole clause, we see an intention on the part of the testator to give £10,000 to the sick and poor of the parish of Shoreditch, pointing out how he desires that to be applied; and that particular mode having failed, as we must for the purposes of this appeal assume to be the case, then the intention to benefit the poor of Shoreditch, being a good charitable object, will have effect given to it according to the general principle laid down long ago by this court, by applying it *cy-près*. If the will had said that the trustees must build the particular building within the parish of Shoreditch there might be some difficulty, but what the testator desires to do is to provide a particular kind of hospital and a soup kitchen for the poor of the parish of Shoreditch. To my mind that shews that he intends not that it is to be located in a particular place, though that would be a proper mode of giving effect to the particular directions contained, if a place in the parish could be found; but that it is for the benefit of the parish, that is of the poor in the parish of Shoreditch.

Within the second category of cases laid down by Parker J in *Re Wilson*, the courts are entitled to draw the inference that the donor has manifested a specific charitable intention if he has described the charitable purpose with precision. Indeed, the clearer the description of the charitable objective which the donor has in mind, the stronger the inference that the intention is specific. Illustrated by *Re Wilson* (above, pp 723–24). Similarly, in *Re Good*,[59] a legacy to provide rest homes in Hull was subject to a detailed scheme as to the types of homes to be provided, the types of inmates to be admitted and the management powers of the trustees. When the scheme proved impracticable because the funds were insufficient, the court decided (Wynn-Parry J) that the testator did not manifest a general charitable intention. Accordingly, the funds resulted to the residuary legatees.

Non-existent charitable bodies

A factor which may influence the judge in deciding the question of the intention of the donor is the fact that the charitable body, selected by the donor has never been in existence. The approach here is that the specification by the donor of a named charitable institution, which never existed, may be construed as a reference to the purpose to which the donor intended to devote his funds and is evidence of a general charitable intention.

Re Harwood [1936] Ch 285, HC

A testatrix bequeathed legacies to: (a) the 'Wisbech Peace Society, Cambridge' (a society which had existed at one time but had ceased to exist before the testatrix's death); and (b) the 'Peace Society of Belfast' (which had never

59 [1950] 2 All ER 653.

existed). The court held that the gift to the Wisbech Peace Society manifested a specific charitable intention for the object of the testatrix's bounty was carefully selected and identified and that portion of the estate was held on resulting trust. But, the legacy to the Belfast Society was applicable *cy-près* because her intention must have been to benefit any charitable society which promoted peace in Belfast.

> **Farwell J:** I do not propose to decide that it can never be possible for the court to hold that there is a general charitable intent in a case where the charity named in the will once existed but ceased to exist before the death. Without deciding that, it is enough for me to say that, where the testator selects as the object of his bounty a particular charity and shows in the will itself some care to identify the particular society which he desires to benefit, the difficulty of finding any general charitable intent in such case if the named society once existed, but ceased to exist before the death of the testator, is very great. Here the testatrix has gone out of her way to identify the object of her bounty. In this particular case she has identified it as being 'the Wisbech Peace Society Cambridge (which is a branch of the London Peace Society)'. Under those circumstances, I do not think it is open to me to hold that there is in this case any such general charitable intent as to allow the application of the *cy-près* doctrine.
>
> Accordingly, in my judgment, the legacy of £200 fails and is undisposed of.
>
> Then there is the gift to the 'Peace Society of Belfast'. The claimant for this legacy is the Belfast Branch of the League of Nations Union. I am quite unable on the evidence to say that that was the society which this lady intended to benefit, and I doubt whether the lady herself knew exactly what society she did mean to benefit. I think she had a desire to benefit any society which was formed for the purpose of promoting peace and was connected with Belfast. Beyond that, I do not think that she had any very clear idea in her mind. That is rather indicated by the pencil note which was found after her death. At any rate I cannot say that by the description, 'the Peace Society of Belfast', the lady meant the Belfast Branch of the League of Nations Union; but there is enough in this case to enable me to say that, although there is no gift to any existing society, the gift does not fail. It is a good charitable gift and must be applied *cy-près*.

A similar approach was adopted by the Court of Appeal in *Re Satterthwaite's Will Trust*. A testatrix, who announced to a bank official that she hated the whole human race and wished to leave her estate to animal charities, made her will in December 1952 and died in 1962 leaving her residuary estate equally to nine animal welfare organisations selected from a telephone directory. Seven of these bodies were animal charities but the remaining two were an anti-vivisection society and the London Animal Hospital. The question in issue concerned the one ninth share bequeathed in favour of the London Animal Hospital. This share was claimed, *inter alia*, by a veterinary surgeon who had carried on his profession under that name from 1943 to July 1952 when, following the Veterinary Surgeons Act 1948, the name was withdrawn from the Register of Animal Hospitals. At all material times, this hospital was private and not charitable. There was no evidence that the testatrix had any knowledge of the surgeon's establishment or that she knew that it was a private hospital.

The court decided that the one ninth share was applicable *cy-près*. The evidence suggested that the testatrix meant to benefit a purpose and not an individual. The other bequests taken as a whole (despite the one ninth share to the anti-vivisection society) showed a general charitable intention to benefit animals.

***Re Satterthwaite's Will Trust* [1966] 1 WLR 277, CA**

> **Harman LJ**: If a particular donee were intended which cannot be identified, no general intent would follow. When one looks at the whole of the residuary bequest, however, it seems plain that each share is intended to go to some object connected with the care or cure of animals. That anti-vivisection has been declared not to be in law a charitable object, *National Anti-Vivisection Society v IRC*,[60] is irrelevant. The society exists to save animals from suffering. The other names make the same sort of suggestion, though it is true that the evidence suggested that the words 'clinic' often indicated a place where the business of animal surgery was carried on rather than a charitable organisation.
>
> The judge has held that there is a general charitable intent sufficient to cause share No (8) to be applied *cy-près*, and it would be inconsistent to come to a different conclusion in the case of share No (4) if, as I have held, the object there too is not identifiable. It follows that a scheme must in this instance also be settled.

Incorporated and unincorporated associations

Another factor, which has found favour with the courts, in deciding the intention of the settlor concerns the distinction between charitable corporations and unincorporated associations. An incorporated association, as distinct from an unincorporated association, has an independent legal existence distinct from its members (see above, p 243).

In *Re Vernon's Will Trust*, Buckley J expressed the view that a gift to a corporate charity is *prima facie* intended to take effect as a beneficial gift to the named body and will lapse if the charity ceases to exist before the testator's death. It will only be possible to apply the funds *cy-près* if the court, on construction, find a general charitable intention. On the other hand, where the gift is to an unincorporated association, the gift *prima facie* takes effect for the purposes of the association. The named unincorporated association is treated as the trustee to carry out the charitable purpose. Accordingly, if the

60 [1947] 2 All ER 217.

association ceases to exist the court is entitled to use its inherent jurisdiction to ensure that the trust will not fail for want of a trustee and may appoint new trustees to continue the charitable purposes. (This *prima facie* rule may be rebutted by evidence which shows that the gift was dependent upon the continued existence of the particular trustees.)

Re Vernon's Will Trust [1972] Ch 300, HC

In this case, a testatrix who made her will in 1937 directed that her residuary estate be divided among several charitable institutions equally, including the Coventry Crippled Children's Guild. The testatrix died in 1960 but, on the date of the execution of the will, an institution was in existence called the 'Coventry and District Crippled Children's Guild'. This institution was incorporated under the Companies Act 1919 and provided orthopaedic clinics and convalescent homes for crippled children. In 1948, the assets of the company were vested in the Minister of Health under the National Health Act 1946. The company was dissolved in 1952 but a clinic and hospital had been founded by the Guild and was in existence at the date of the testatrix's death. However, in 1949 an unincorporated charitable body was formed known as the 'Coventry and District Cripples' Guild'. This association supported cripples but did not carry out any orthopaedic work. The question in issue centred on which institution was entitled to part of the residuary gift.

The court held that the testatrix intended to benefit the institution which existed at the time she made her will in 1937. There was therefore a valid gift to this body for the purpose of its work. Since the body had ceased to exist but its work was still carried on by a hospital and clinic under the control of the Minister of Health the fund was applicable *cy-près*.

> **Buckley J**: Every bequest to an unincorporated charity by name without more must take effect as a gift for a charitable purpose. No individual or aggregate of individuals could claim to take such a bequest beneficially. If the gift is to be permitted to take effect at all, it must be as a bequest for a purpose, ie that charitable purpose which the named charity exists to serve. A bequest which is in terms made for a charitable purpose will not fail for lack of a trustee but will be carried into effect either under the sign manual or by means of a scheme. A bequest to a named unincorporated charity, however, may on its true interpretation show that the testator's intention to make the gift at all was dependent on the named charitable organisation being available at the time when the gift takes effect to serve as the instrument for applying the subject matter of the gift to the charitable purpose for which it is by inference given. If so and the named charity ceases to exist in the lifetime of the testator, the gift fails (*Re Ovey, Broadbent v Barrow*).[61]
>
> A bequest to a corporate body, on the other hand, takes effect simply as a gift to that body beneficially, unless there are circumstances which show that the

61 (1885) 29 Ch D 560.

recipient is to take the gift as a trustee. There is no need in such a case to infer a trust for any particular purpose. The objects to which the corporate body can properly apply its funds may be restricted by its constitution, but this does not necessitate inferring as a matter of construction of the testator's will a direction that the bequest is to be held in trust to be applied for those purposes; the natural construction is that the bequest is made to the corporate body as part of its general funds, that is to say, beneficially and without the imposition of any trust. That the testator's motive in making the bequest may have undoubtedly been to assist the work of the incorporated body would be insufficient to create a trust. It was, I think, with considerations of this kind in mind that Harman J decided *Re Meyers (Decd), London Life Association v St George's Hospital*[62] on the grounds that he did.

I cannot find in the testatrix's will any context indicating that the bequest of one-third of her residue to the incorporated guild ought to be construed as a trust legacy. The pecuniary legacies to two named hospitals do not in my judgment afford such a context; nor does the fact that the other two shares of residue are given to charitable institutions, one of which at any rate, the National Life Boat Institution, is of quite another kind; nor does the reference to the receipt of the treasurer of any such institution; nor do all these circumstances taken together. The bequest was, in my judgment, a simple bequest to the incorporated guild which that body, had it survived the testatrix, would have been entitled to receive as part of its general funds unfettered by any trust imposed by the testatrix as to the purposes for which it should be used. Had the incorporated guild been other than a charitable body, that would be the end of the matter, for the bequest would lapse on account of the dissolution of the incorporated guild in the lifetime of the testatrix.

The guild was, however, incorporated for exclusively charitable purposes, and its memorandum of association was so framed that its funds could never be distributed among its members and that in a winding-up any surplus assets would continue to be applied for objects similar to those of the incorporated guild. Whether and how far it would be right to regard the funds of the incorporated guild as subject to a charitable trust, I do not pause to consider beyond pointing out that any assets which it took over from the unincorporated guild would appear to have been subject to such a trust. Trust or no trust, however, it is true to say that the assets of the incorporated guild were all effectually dedicated to charity. In no circumstances – at least without the intervention of Parliament – could any of those funds have been used otherwise than for charitable purposes of the kind for which the guild existed so long as those purposes remained practicable. Even if those purposes ceased to be practicable, the charity would not cease to exist, although its funds would be applied *cy-près*. Such a charity, considered as a charity and apart from the mechanism provided for the time being and from time to time for holding its property and managing its affairs, could never cease to exist except by exhaustion of all its assets and cessation of its activities. A change merely in its mechanical aspect could not involve the charity ceasing to exist. The principle

62 [1951] 1 All ER 538.

of the decisions in *Re Faraker, Faraker v Durell,*[63] and *Re Lucas (Decd), Sheard v Mello,*[64] is, in my judgment, equally applicable to an incorporated charity of this kind as to a charity constituted by means of a trust. In such cases the law regards the charity, an abstract conception distinct from the institutional mechanism provided for holding and administering the fund of the charity, as the legatee, and so long as the charity as so conceived continues in existence the bequest will not lapse. This result is not a consequence of construing the gift as one made for a charitable purpose to be ascertained by seating oneself in the testator's armchair, for the charity may be entitled notwithstanding that its objects may have been modified or changed in accordance with the law between the date of the will and the testator's death or any later date at which the gift takes effect. It is a consequence of regarding the charity as the legatee in the manner I have stated.

In my judgment, the true view is that the charity which at the date of the testatrix's will was being carried on by the incorporated guild continued in existence down to and after the date of her death in the form of the orthopaedic clinic and hospital which were conducted by the first defendant at 55 Holyhead Road and the Paybody Hospital. The fact that its continued existence after 5 July 1948 may be said to have been precarious, because those with power under the National Health Service Act 1946 to decide such things might at any time have decided to discontinue the use of the properties for orthopaedic purposes and might possibly have done so without transferring the orthopaedic activities theretofore carried on in the clinic and the hospital and continuing them elsewhere, is, in my judgment irrelevant. If on the true view the charity existed at the testatrix's death and so became entitled to the bequest, its subsequently ceasing to exist would not cause the bequest to fail (*Re Slevin, Slevin v Hepburn*).[65]

As in *Re Lucas* the court held that the bequest to the Crippled Children's Home, Lindley Moor, Huddersfield, was on its true construction a gift simply in augmentation of the funds of the charity so described, so in the present case I think the bequest to the 'Coventry Crippled Children's Guild' was on its true construction a gift simply in augmentation of the funds of the incorporated guild; and as in *Re Lucas* the bequest did not fail by reason of the physical home having been closed but took effect in favour of the charity in the new and different form into which it had been transmuted by an order of the charity commissioners, so by parity of reasoning, in my judgment, in the present case the bequest took effect at the death of the testatrix in favour of the charity then being conducted by the first defendant in unbroken continuance of the charity which at the date of the will was being conducted by the incorporated guild.

I accordingly reach the conclusion that the bequest on the one third share of residue with which I am concerned does not take effect in favour of the new guild, and does not fail through lapse or for uncertainty, nor is it undisposed of

63 [1912] 2 Ch 488.

64 [1948] Ch 424.

65 [1891] 2 Ch 236.

> by the will for any other reason but that it took effect as a valid charitable gift in favour of the charity consisting of the orthopaedic clinic at 55 Holyhead Road and the orthopaedic hospital carried on in the building known as the Paybody Hospital which the first defendant was engaged in carrying on when the testatrix died. Accordingly I declare that the gift is a valid charitable gift.

This approach appealed to Goff J in *Re Finger's Will Trust*.

Re Finger's Will Trust [1972] Ch 286, HC

A testatrix, by her will made in 1930 but who died in 1965, transferred her residuary estate on trust in favour of eleven charitable institutions equally. One share was given to the 'National Radium Commission'. No institution by that name existed, although an unincorporated body called the 'Radium Commission' had existed since 1929 but was liquidated in 1947 when the National Health Service was set up. The work previously undertaken by the commission was carried on by the Minister of Health. The court construed the bequest as intended for the Radium Commission. Another share of the bequest was given to the National Council for Maternity and Child Welfare. This was a corporate body which was in existence at the time of the execution of the will but was wound up in 1948. The bulk of the assets was transferred to the National Association for Maternity and Child Welfare, an association similar to the council and which continued the council's activities. The question in issue was whether both shares may be applied *cy-près*.

The court held that the testatrix exhibited a general charitable intention in respect of both gifts. The gift to the unincorporated association (Radium Commission) was construed as intended for the purposes of the commission which was not dependent on the continued existence of the commission. The gift to the incorporated association which ceased to exist on the date of vesting was treated *prima facie* as a gift to the body (see *Re Harwood*) but was still capable of being construed as a general charitable gift since virtually the whole estate was devoted for charitable purposes, the testatrix regarded herself as having no relatives and the council merely had a co-ordinating function.

> **Goff J:** The evidence clearly shows that to all intents and purposes ever since the winding up of the council the association has carried on, and is now carrying on, the work of the council, and indeed this was not seriously disputed.
>
> In these circumstances the first question which arises is whether as a matter of construction the gift of a share of residue to the National Radium Commission was a gift to the corporate body known as the National Radium Trust or to the unincorporated body defined in the charter as the Radium Commission. The words in the will do not describe either body with complete accuracy, but it seems to me that the word 'Commission' has more significance that 'National', particularly as both bodies operated on a national basis. It is also, I think, significant that the commission was in substance the operative body which

organised the supplies. I therefore hold that the first share in question was given to the Radium Commission.

If the matter were *res integra* I would have thought that there would be much to be said for the view that the status of the donee, whether corporate or unincorporated, can make no difference to the question whether as a matter of construction a gift is absolute or on trust for purposes. Certainly drawing such a distinction produces anomalous results. In my judgment, however, on the authorities a distinction between the two is well established, at all events in this court.

[The learned judge referred to Buckley J's judgment in *Re Vernon's Will Trusts* (see above, p 728), and continued:]

As I read the *dictum* in *Re Vernon* Buckley J's view was that in the case of an unincorporated body the gift is *per se* a purpose trust and, provided that the work is still being carried on, will have effect given to it by way of scheme notwithstanding the disappearance of the donee in the lifetime of the testator, unless there is something positive to show that the continued existence of the donee was essential to the gift. Then Buckley J put his *dictum* into practice and decided *Re Morrison, Wakefield v Falmouth*,[66] on that very basis, for there was nothing in that case beyond the bare fact of a gift to a dissolved unincorporated committee. In the case of a corporation, however, *Re Vernon* shows that the position is different as there has to be something positive in the will to create a purpose trust at all.

Accordingly I hold that the bequest to the National Radium Commission being a gift to an unincorporated charity is a purpose trust for the work of the commission which does not fail but is applicable under a scheme, provided (1) there is nothing in the context of the will to show – and I quote from *Re Vernon* – that the testatrix's intention to make the gift at all was dependent on the named charitable organisation being available at the time when the gift took effect to serve as the instrument for applying the subject matter of the gift to the charitable purpose for which it was by inference given; (2) that charitable purpose still survives; but that the gift to the National Council for Maternity and Child Welfare, 117 Piccadilly, London being a gift to a corporate body fails, notwithstanding the work continues, unless there is a context in the will to show that the gift was intended to be on trust for that purpose and not an absolute gift to the corporation.

I take first the National Radium Commission and I find in this will no context whatever to make that body of the essence of the gift.

In my judgment, therefore, this is a valid gift for the purposes of the Radium Commission as specified in article 7 of the supplemental charter of 20 July 1939 and I direct that a scheme be settled for the administration of the gift.

I turn to the other gift and here I can find no context from which to imply a purpose trust. In the present case there are at best three different groups of charities not one; they are not in fact grouped in the order in which they appear in the will, and the particular donees within the respective groups are

66 (1967) 111 SJ 758.

> not all of the same type or character. Further, and worse, two do not fit into any grouping at all, and for what it is worth they come first in the list. In my judgment, therefore, this case is not comparable with *Re Meyers (Decd), London Life Association v St George's Hospital*[67] and I cannot find a context unless I am prepared, which I am not, to say that the mere fact that residue is given to a number of charities, some of which are incorporated and others not, is of itself a sufficient context to fasten a purpose trust on the corporation. In my judgment, therefore, the bequest to the National Council for Maternity and Child Welfare fails.
>
> Finally, I must consider, however whether the share passes on intestacy or whether the will discloses a general charitable intention. Here, of course, I was at once presented with *Re Harwood, Coleman v Innes*,[68] and I feel the force of the argument on behalf of the next-of kin based on that case, although I confess that I have always felt the decision in that case to be rather remarkable. However, Farwell J did not say that it was impossible to find a general charitable intention where there is a gift to an identifiable body which has ceased to exist but only that it would be very difficult.
>
> In the present case the circumstances are very special. First, of course, apart from the life interest given to the mother and two small personal legacies the whole estate is devoted to charity, and that is, I think, somewhat emphasised by the specific dedication to charity in the preface:
>
>> And after payment of the said legacies my trustees shall hold the balance then remaining of my residuary estate upon trust to divide the same in equal shares between the following charitable institutions and funds.
>
> Again, I am, I think, entitled to take into account the nature of the council, which as I have said was mainly, if not exclusively, a co-ordinating body. I cannot believe that this testatrix meant to benefit that organisation and that alone. Finally, I am entitled to place myself in the armchair of the testatrix and I have evidence that she regarded herself as having no relatives.
>
> Taking all these matters into account, in my judgment I can and ought to distinguish *Re Harwood* and find, as I do, a general charitable intention. Accordingly, this share is applicable *cy-près*.

The method by which Goff J was able to distinguish *Re Harwood* was doubted by Megarry VC in *Re Spence*. A testatrix who died in 1972, by her will dated 4 December 1968, bequeathed her residuary estate equally between 'The Blind Home, Scott Street, Keighley' and the 'Old Folks Home at Hillworth Lodge, Keighley, for the benefit of the patients'. The Keighley and District Association for the Blind was the only charity connected with the blind in the Keighley area. It ran a home in Scott Street which was often called 'The Blind Home', 'The Keighley and District Home for the Blind', and 'Keighley Home for the Blind'. A similar home was also run by the Association at Bingley. Hillworth Lodge was built as a workhouse in 1858 and was closed in 1939. In 1948, it

67 [1951] Ch 534.

68 [1936] Ch 285.

became an aged person's home under the National Assistance Act 1948 but was closed down in 1971. Since then the building was used as government offices. The question in issue was whether the testatrix had manifested a general or specific charitable intention.

The court held:

(1) the testatrix intended to benefit the patients at the Blind Home, Scott Street, Keighley and did not intend to augment the funds of the charity which ran the home;

(2) the gift to the 'Old Folk's Home' failed and the fund was not applicable *cy-près*. Applying *Re Harwood* and refusing to follow *Re Finger*: that the testatrix had manifested a specific charitable intention by identifying a particular charitable purpose which on the date of the will was capable of being carried out but was incapable of being fulfilled at the time of death.

Re Spence [1979] Ch 483, HC

Sir Robert Megarry VC: There is therefore the question whether the moiety should go to the charity as an accretion to its endowment, and so be capable of being employed on any part of its activities, or whether it is to be confined to the particular part of the charity's activities that are carried on at the Blind Home in Scott Street, Keighley.

I confess that but for the decision of the Court of Appeal in *In re Lucas*,[69] I should have had little hesitation in resolving this question in the narrower sense, confining the moiety to the particular Blind Home in Scott Street, Keighley.

In re Lucas the testatrix made her will on 12 October 1942, and died on 18 December 1943. The will made gifts to 'the Crippled Children's Home, Lindley Moor, Huddersfield'; and it provided that the receipt of the treasurer or other officer for the time being should be a sufficient discharge. From 1916 there had been an establishment called 'The Huddersfield Home for Crippled Children' at Lindley Moor, governed by the charitable trusts established by a deed dated 29 March 1915, but according to the statement of facts in the report, at p 425, 'On 17 October 1941, this home was closed and a scheme for the future administration of its assets was made by the Charity Commissioners'. Under that scheme the charity thereby created was to be known as 'The Huddersfield Charity for Crippled Children', and the income was to be applied in sending poor crippled children to holiday or convalescent homes.

The question for resolution in *In re Lucas* was thus whether the gift to 'the Crippled Children's Home Lindley Moor Huddersfield' took effect as a gift to 'The Huddersfield Charity for Crippled Children', or whether they were gifts for the upkeep of a particular home for crippled children which had ceased to exist before the will was made, so that they failed.

69 [1948] Ch 424.

At first instance, Roxburgh J held that the latter was the correct view. On appeal, Lord Greene MR delivered the reserved judgment of himself, Somervell LJ and Jenkins J. This reversed the decision below, and held that the gifts were gifts which contributed to the endowment of the charity, and so did not fail.

The main factors in the decision of the Court of Appeal seem to have been that the words used in the will fitted the home that had been closed down no better than the charity which continued in existence, and that the will had omitted to make any specific reference to the upkeep or maintenance of the home which would indicate that the gifts were to be confined to the upkeep of the home. The gifts were accordingly gifts to the charity, and so did not fail. The question for me is whether on the case before me there ought to be a similar result, so that the moiety of residue would go to the Keighley and District Association for the Blind as an addition to its endowment generally, and would not be confined to the Blind Home in Scott Street, Keighley, carried on by the Association.

It seems to me that the case before me is distinguishable from *In re Lucas*, so far as I have correctly understood that case. The testatrix was making provision of the benefit of the patients for the time being at a particular home, namely, the home usually known as the Blind Home at Scott Street, Keighley. She was giving the money not to augment generally the endowment of the charity which runs that home, with the consequence that the money might be used for purposes other than the benefit of the patients at that home, but was giving the money so that it would be used exclusively for the benefit of those patients. The only way in which this can conveniently be done is to give the money to the charity but to confine its use for the benefit of the patients for the time being at the home. That, I think, requires a scheme; but I see no need to direct that a scheme should be settled in chambers. Instead, I think that I can follow the convenient course taken by Goff J in *In re Finger's Will Trusts*.[70] I shall, therefore, order by way of scheme (the Attorney General not objecting) that the moiety be paid to the proper officer of the charity to be held on trust to apply it for the benefit of the patients for the time being of the home known as the Blind Home, Scott Street, Keighley.

I now turn to the other moiety of residue, given by the will to 'the Old Folks Home' at Hillworth Lodge, Keighley for the benefit of the patients.

Now without looking at the authorities, I would have said that this was a fairly plain case of a will which made a gift for a particular purpose in fairly specific terms. The gift was for the benefit of the patients at a particular home, namely, the Old Folks Home at Hillworth Lodge, Keighley. At the date of the will there were patients at that home. When the testatrix died, there was no longer any home there, but offices instead; and so there were no longer any patients there, or any possibility of them. The gift was a gift for a charitable purpose which at the date of the will was capable of accomplishment and at the date of death was not. *Prima facie*, therefore the gift fails unless a general charitable intention has been manifested so that the property can be applied *cy-près*.

70 [1972] Ch 286, p 300.

Mr Mummery's other contention was that the will displayed a sufficient general charitable intention for the moiety to be applied *cy-près*. In doing this he had to contend with *In re Harwood*.[71] This, and cases which apply it, such as *In re Stemson's Will Trusts*,[72] establish that it is very difficult to find a general charitable intention where the testator has selected a particular charity, taking some care to identify it, and the charity then ceases to exist before the testator's death. This contrasts with cases where the charity described in the will has never existed, when it is much easier to find a general charitable intention.

These cases have been concerned with gifts to institutions, rather than gifts for purposes. The case before me, on the other hand, is a gift for a purpose, namely, the benefit of the patients at a particular Old Folks Home. It therefore seems to me that I ought to consider the question, of which little or nothing was said in argument, whether the principle in *In re Harwood*, or a parallel principle, has any application to such case. In other words, is a similar distinction to be made between, on the one hand, a case in which the testator has selected a particular charitable purpose, taking some care to identify it, and before the testator dies that purpose has become impracticable or impossible of accomplishment, and on the other hand, a case where the charitable purpose has never been possible or practicable?

As at present advised I would answer 'Yes' to that question. I do not think that the reasoning of the *In re Harwood* line of case is directed to any feature of institutions as distinct from purposes. Instead, I think the essence of the distinction is in the difference between particularity and generality. If a particular institution or purpose is specified, then it is that institution or purpose, and no other, that is to be the object of the benefaction. It is difficult to envisage a testator as being suffused with a general glow of broad charity when he is labouring, and labouring successfully, to identify some particular specified institution or purpose as the object of his bounty. The specific displaces the general. It is otherwise where the testator has been unable to specify any particular charitable institution or practicable purpose, and so, although his intention of charity can be seen, he has failed to provide any way of giving effect to it. There, the absence of the specific leaves the general undisturbed. It follows that in my view in the case before me, where the testatrix has clearly specified a particular charitable purpose which before her death became impossible to carry out, Mr Mummery has to face that level of great difficulty in demonstrating the existence of a general charitable intention which was indicated by *In re Harwood*.

One way in which Mr Mummery sought to meet that difficulty was by citing *In re Finger's Will Trusts*.[73] There, Goff J distinguished *In re Harwood* and held that the will before him displayed a general charitable intention. He did this on the footing that the circumstances of the case were 'very special'. The gift that failed was a gift to an incorporated charity which had ceased to exist before the testatrix died. The 'very special' circumstances were, first, that apart from a life

71 [1936] Ch 285.

72 [1970] Ch 16.

73 [1972] Ch 286.

interest and two small legacies, the whole estate was devoted to charity, and that this was emphasised by the direction to hold the residue in trust for division 'between the following charitable institutions and funds'. Second, the charitable donee that had ceased to exist was mainly, if not exclusively, a co-ordinated body, and the judge could not believe that the testatrix meant to benefit that body alone. Third, there was evidence that the testatrix regarded herself as having no relatives.

In the case before me neither of these last two circumstances applies, nor have any substitute special circumstances been suggested. As for the first, the will before me gives 17 pecuniary legacies to relations and friends, amounting in all to well over one third of the net estate. Further, in *In re Rymer*,[74] which does not appear to have been cited, the will had prefaced the disputed gift by the words 'I give the following charitable legacies to the following institutions and persons respectively'. These words correspond to the direction which In *In re Finger's Will Trusts* was regarded as providing emphasis, and yet they did not suffice to avoid the conclusion of Chitty J and the Court of Appeal that a gift to an institution which has ceased to exist before the testator's death lapsed and could not be applied *cy-près*. I am not sure that I have been able to appreciate to the full the cogency of the special circumstances that appealed to Goff J; but however that may be, I can see neither those nor any other special circumstances in the present case which would suffice to distinguish *In re Harwood*.

From what I have said it follows that I have been quite unable to extract from the will, construed in its context, any expression of a general charitable intention which would suffice for the moiety to be applied *cy-près*. Instead, in my judgment, the moiety was given for a specific charitable purpose which, though possible when the will was made, became impossible before the testatrix died. The gift of the moiety accordingly fails, and it passes as on intestacy.

In s 14 of the Charities Act 1993 (re-enacting s 14 of the Charities Act 1960), the general rule, as detailed above, is that property given for a specific charitable purpose which fails from the outset cannot be applied *cy-près* if no general charitable intention can be imputed to the donor. Such property will be held on resulting trust for the donor.

By the way of exception to the general rule, s 14 of the Charities Act 1993 enacts that property given for specific charitable purposes which fail shall be applicable *cy-près* as if given for charitable purposes generally. This is the case where the property belongs to a donor who cannot be identified or found after reasonable inquiries and advertisements have been made or who disclaims his right to the property in writing. Section 14 provides as follows:

(1) Property given for specific charitable purposes which fail shall be applicable *cy-près* as if given for charitable purposes generally, where it belong:

74 [1895] 1 Ch 19.

(a) to a donor who after:

(i) the prescribed advertisements and inquiries have been published and made; and

(ii) the prescribed period beginning with the publication of those advertisements has expired,

cannot be identified or cannot be found; or

(b) to a donor who has executed a disclaimer in the prescribed form of his right to have the property returned.

(2) Where the prescribed advertisements and inquiries have been published and made by or on behalf of trustees with respect to any such property, the trustees shall not be liable to any person in respect of the property if no claim by him to be interested in it is received by them before the expiry of the period mentioned in sub-s (1)(a)(ii) above.

(3) For the purposes of this section property shall be conclusively presumed (without any advertisement or inquiry) to belong to donors who cannot be identified, in so far as it consists:

(a) of the proceeds of cash collections made by means of collecting boxes or by other means not adapted for distinguishing one gift from another; or

(b) of the proceeds of any lottery, competition, entertainment, sale or similar money – raising activity, after allowing for property given to provide prizes or articles for sale or otherwise to enable the activity to be undertaken.

(4) The court may by order direct that property not falling within sub-s (3) above shall for the purposes of this section be treated (without any advertisement or inquiry) as belonging to donors who cannot be identified where it appears to the court either:

(a) that it would be unreasonable, having regard to the amounts likely to be returned to the donors, to incur expense with a view to returning the property; or

(b) that it would be unreasonable, having regard to the nature, circumstances and amounts of the gifts, and to the lapse of time since the gifts were made, for the donors to expect the property to be returned.

...

(7) For the purposes of this section, charitable purposes shall be deemed to 'fail' where any difficulty in applying property to those purposes makes that property or the part not applicable *cy-près* available to be returned to the donors.

...

(10) In this section, except in so far as the context otherwise requires, references to a donor include persons claiming through or under the original donor, and references to property given include the property for the time being representing the property originally given or property derived from it.

(11) This section shall apply to property given for charitable purposes, notwithstanding that it was so given before the commencement of this Act.

***Re Henry Wood National Memorial Trusts* (1965) 109 SJ 876, HC**

A nationwide appeal was launched to raise funds to build a concert hall to be named after Sir Henry Wood. One of the purposes as stated in the appeal was 'improving and extending knowledge and appreciation of good music'. The fund raised proved insufficient to build the concert hall. The trustees of the appeal sought directions from the court concerning the surplus. The court decided that notices in *The Times, The Telegraph* and *The Scotsman* newspapers and letters to addresses of donors noted in the appeal records constituted reasonable advertisements and inquiries.

THE CHARITY COMMISSION

The Charity Commission was established in 1853 by the Charitable Trusts Act of that year to provide a simple and inexpensive means of dealing with difficulties encountered by charities. Its constitution is now governed by the Charities Act 1993. There are normally five Charity Commissioners appointed by the Home Secretary, two of whom are required to be lawyers. The Commissioners are subject to the jurisdiction of the High Court in the exercise of its quasi-judicial powers and appeals from their decisions may be made to the High Court.

Charities' register

Under s 3 of the Charities Act 1993, the Charity Commissioners are required to maintain a register of charities which is open to the public. All charities are required to register with the Commissioners, except, exempt charities (specified in Sched 2 to the Charities Act 1993 including the British Museum, the Victoria and Albert Museum and registered Friendly Societies) and excepted charities (including the Boy Scouts and Girl Guides Associations, certain charities connected with the promotion of the efficiency of the armed forces). In addition, religious organisations having places of worship need not register as well as small charities, that is, any charity which has neither: (i) any permanent endowment; nor (ii) the use and occupation of any land and whose income does not in aggregate amount to more than £1,000 per annum (s 3(5)).

The effect of registration under s 4(1) of the Charities Act 1993 is that the organisation is conclusively presumed to be charitable.

Functions of the Charity Commissioners

Section 1(3) of the Charities Act 1993 enacts the general function of the Charity Commissioners shall be 'to promote the effective use of charitable resources by encouraging the development of better methods of administration, by giving charity trustees information or advice on any matter affecting the charity and by investigating and checking abuses'. They are specifically precluded from acting in the administration of charities. The effect is that, although they may advise the charity trustees, they may not intervene directly, unless the conduct of the trustees amount to a breach of their duties.

In their advisory role, the Commissioners' duties cover such matters as advising on the interpretation of trust deeds, making schemes to alter the purposes of charities, encouraging the amalgamation of small charities, appointing new trustees when there is no one with the power to appoint new trustees and advising on the day to day running of charities.

Under s 18 of the Charities Act 1993, the Commissioners are empowered to take action to protect the property of any charity without having to establish that misconduct or maladministration has already occurred. The action which may be taken by the Commissioners, *inter alia*, include the power to suspend any trustee or employee of the charity, to freeze the charity's bank accounts and property, to transfer the charity's property for safekeeping to the official custodian for charities and to appoint a receiver to run the charity's affairs for a period.

Legal proceedings

Section 32 of the Charities Act 1993 empowers the Commissioners to exercise the same powers as are exercisable by the Attorney General in respect of the taking of legal proceedings with reference to charities or to compromise claims with a view to avoiding or ending such proceedings.

Section 33(1) of the Charities Act 1993 lists the persons who may bring proceedings in respect of charitable matters. These are: (i) the charity; (ii) any charity trustees; (iii) any person interested in the charity; (iv) in the case of a local charity, any two or more inhabitants of the area. The sub-section concludes 'but not by any other person'. Thus, no other person may bring proceedings, except the Attorney General in his capacity as *parens patriae*. Owing to the public nature of such trusts the Attorney General is always required to be included as a party to legal proceedings.

Section 33(2) enacts that no such proceedings shall be entertained or proceeded with in any court unless authorised by order of the Commissioners. See *Gaudiya Mission v Brahmachary* (below, p 742).

The expression 'a person interested in the charity' was considered by the court in *Gunning and Others v Buckfast Abbey Trustees and Another*.[75]

The plaintiffs were the fee paying parents of children at a school managed by the first defendants (trustees of property applied in the charitable activities of the monks). The second defendant was the Attorney General. The school was founded by monks in 1967 as a Roman Catholic preparatory school for boys between the ages of eight and 13. The school later opened its doors to girls. The school was charged an internal fee by the monastery for providing the services of the monks. Although the services of the monks were provided free of charge, the parents of children at the school were charged a fee by the trustees. On 15 February 1994, the trustees announced that the school was to be closed at the end of the summer term 1994. The decision was taken by the Abbot with the consent of a committee known as the Abbot's council. The plaintiffs challenged this decision. The issues before the court involved two preliminary questions, namely: (i) whether the plaintiffs possessed a sufficient standing to bring the proceedings; and (ii) whether on a true construction of the trust deed, the consent of the Abbot's council was necessary to close the school. The court was not concerned with the reasons leading to the decision to close the school.

Section 33(1) of the Charities Act 1993 (originally s 28(1) of the Charities Act 1960) provides that:

> Charity proceedings may be taken with reference to a charity either by the charity, or by any of the charity trustees, or by any person interested in the charity ... but not by any other person.

The plaintiffs argued that as parents of pupils at the school, they were persons interested in the charity through the benefit to themselves in having their children educated as they wished. In addition, the plaintiffs had a natural and moral concern for the children's education and a legal obligation that gave them an interest which was materially different from that enjoyed by a member of the public. The plaintiffs also claimed to be subscribers to the charity. They relied on the test laid down by the Court of Appeal in *Re Hampton Fuel Allotment Charity*,[76] a person might, depending on the circumstances, be a person interested if he had an interest in securing the due administration of a charity which was greater than or different from that possessed by ordinary members of the public.

The trustees claimed that the relationship between the parents and the school was one of contract which was renewable annually. This contractual interest was insufficient for the purposes of s 33(1) of the 1993 Act. The trustees relied on the principle laid down by Megarry VC in *Haslemere Estates*

75 (1994) *The Times*, 9 June.

76 [1989] Ch 484, *per* Nicholls LJ.

Ltd v Baker[77] (in considering the equivalent provision under s 28(1) of the Charities Act 1960), he summed up:

> An interest which is adverse to the charity is one thing, an interest in the charity is another. Those who have some good reason for seeking to enforce the trusts of a charity or secure its administration may readily be accepted as having an interest in the charity, whereas those who merely have some claim to the charity, and seek to improve their position at the expense of the charity, will not. The phrase is contemplating those who are on the charity side of the fence ...

On which side of the fence did the plaintiffs stand in the present case?

Mrs Justice Arden held in favour of the plaintiffs on the grounds that:

(i) the plaintiffs' children were beneficiaries of the trust. They could only become pupils as a result of their parents making a contract with the trustees. The mere fact that the plaintiffs had such contract did not mean that they were barred from bringing charity proceedings. They would be so barred if they were seeking to use the charity proceedings to assist them to pursue an adverse claim against the trustees;

(ii) on construction of the trust deed the decision to close the school required the advice but not the consent of the Abbot's council.

In *Gaudiya Mission v Brahmachary*, the Court of Appeal decided that the expression, 'charity', in s 33 of the Charities Act 1993, did not include an institution registered and established under the laws of a foreign jurisdiction. It is impractical for the High Court to seek to extend its supervisory jurisdiction to control an overseas registered charity.

Gaudiya Mission and Others v Brahmachary and Others [1997] 4 All ER 957, CA

The plaintiffs, a registered Indian charity (the Mission), its president and secretary maintained preaching centres and temples in order to advance the doctrines of the Vaishnava faith throughout India and also Cricklewood, North West London. The Mission was not registered in England. Rival factions within the Mission set up a trust under the name, Gaudiya Mission Society Trust (the Society) which was a registered English charity. The defendants were a priest in charge of the charity's London temple and the trustees of the English registered society. The plaintiffs contended that the assets held by the Society belonged to them and that the Society was passing itself off as the Mission. The question in issue was whether the Mission was an institution established for charitable purposes and thereby subject to the control of the High Court under its supervisory jurisdiction. The judge decided that the Mission was within the control of the High Court,

77 [1982] 1 WLR 1109.

consequently, the Attorney General ought to be added as a party to the proceedings. The Attorney General appealed to the Court of Appeal.

Held, allowing the appeal: it was not expressly enacted nor could it be implied that the Charities Act 1993 applied to institutions other than those established for charitable purposes in England and Wales. Charities within England and Wales are required to register with the Charity Commissioners. The implied territorial limits of legislation and the practical considerations of enforceability are decisive factors, which indicate that the Act was never intended to extend to an institution registered abroad. Thus, the Mission was not a charity within the Charities Act 1993, and the Attorney General was not a proper party to be joined.

SUPPLEMENTARY READING

Baxter, C, 'Trustees personal liability and the role of liability insurance' [1996] Conv 12

Luxton, P, 'In pursuit of "purpose" through s 13 of the Charities Act 1960' [1985] Conv 313

Morris, D, 'Broadcast advertising by charities' [1990] Conv 106

Warburton, J, 'Casenote on *Re JW Laing Trust*' [1984] Conv 319

CHAPTER 18

APPOINTMENT, RETIREMENT AND REMOVAL OF TRUSTEES

APPOINTMENT

There are only two occasions when it may be necessary to appoint trustees:

(i) on the creation of a new trust – whether *inter vivos* or by will; and

(ii) during the continuance of an existing trust, either in replacement of a trustee or as an additional trustee.

Creation of a new trust

There are two ways in which a settlor may create an *inter vivos* trust, namely, by way of self-declaration (that is, he declares that he will be a trustee of specific property for the benefit of another or others) or by transferring property to a third party/parties (trustee/trustees) subject to a declaration of trust (see the *Milroy v Lord* rule, above, p 23). In the latter case, it seems clear that if the document purporting to transfer the property to the intended trustee is a nullity no trust is created. This may be the case where the document purporting to transfer the property is improperly executed or where the intended trustees are not identified or are dead or have otherwise ceased to exist. In these circumstances, the property remains vested in the settlor.

On the other hand, if the trust is already completely constituted (that is, the trust property is vested in the trustees subject to the terms of the trust) and circumstances arise where the appointed trustee (or trustees) ceases to exist (for example, death or refusal to act as trustee) the trust will not fail for lack of a trustee. If the trust instrument authorises any person to appoint trustees that power may be utilised. The settlor may have reserved in the instrument the power to appoint trustees. If this is the case, he could then exercise the power to make an appointment not *qua* settlor but as someone entitled to effect an appointment under the instrument. In the absence of such authority, resort may be had to the statutory power enacted in s 36 of the Trustee Act 1925 or ss 19–21 of the Trusts of Land and Appointment of Trustees Act 1996 (see below, pp 748 *et seq*). As a last resort, the court may make an appointment in the exercise of its inherent jurisdiction. In doing so it will apply the maxim, 'Equity will not allow a trust to fail for want of a trustee'.

In the case of a trust declared by the testator's will, a legal transfer of the property is effected automatically in favour of the executor(s) when the latter obtains probate. The executor's functions include the collection of assets belonging to the deceased, settling the deceased's debts and distributing the estate in accordance with the will. If the will declares a trust and obliges the executor to distribute the property accordingly, but no trustees were identified by the testator, or they predecease him or they refuse to act as trustees, the trust will still be valid. The personal representatives will be deemed to be the trustees until replacement trustees are appointed.

Continuance of the trust

When a trust is created (whether *inter vivos* or by will), the trust property (real or personal) vests in all the trustees as joint tenants. The effect is that on the death of a trustee the property devolves on the survivors.

Section 18(1) of the Trustee Act 1925 provides:

> Where a power or trust is given to or imposed on two or more trustees jointly, the same may be exercised or performed by the survivors or survivor of them for the time being.

On the death of the sole or surviving trustee, the property vests in his personal representatives, subject to the trust, until replacement trustees are appointed. Section 18(2) of the Trustee Act 1925 provides:

> Until the appointment of new trustees, the personal representatives or representative for the time being of a sole trustee, or, where there were two or more trustees of the last surviving or continuing trustee, shall be capable of exercising or performing any power or trust which was given to or capable of being exercised by, the sole or last surviving or continuing trustee, or other trustees or trustee for the time being of the trust.

The authority to appoint new trustees may be derived from three sources, namely:

(a) an express power;

(b) a statutory power;

(c) the court.

This hierarchical order of authority to appoint trustees is required to be followed strictly. It is only when there is no person in one group willing to make an appointment can the power be exercised by a person in a different group.

In *Re Higginbottom*,[1] Mary Broadbent became the sole executrix of the sole surviving trustee and entitled to exercise the statutory power to appoint new trustees. Her selection of candidates as trustees was opposed by the majority of the beneficiaries, who petitioned the court to secure the appointment of two other candidates. The court decided that it had no jurisdiction to interfere in the appointment of trustees by Mary, provided that the appointment was made in good faith.

1 [1892] 3 Ch 132.

Express power

The trust instrument may confer the authority to appoint a trustee. This is exceptional for the statutory power to appoint is generally regarded as adequate. The express authority may be general or special. A general authority is one which confers an authority to appoint trustees in any circumstances. If the person named in the instrument is willing to exercise the power, this will be decisive as to the authority to appoint trustees provided that the power is exercised in good faith. Indeed, it is doubtful whether the appointor is entitled to appoint himself for reasons stated by Kay J in *Re Skeat*:[2]

> A man should not be judge in his own case ... and to appoint himself among other people, or excluding them to appoint himself, would certainly be an improper exercise of any power of selection of a fiduciary character.

If the authority is special (that is, exercisable in limited circumstances), it will be strictly construed by the courts (*Re Wheeler and De Rochow*).[3] A marriage settlement gave the husband and wife or the survivor of them, the power to appoint new trustees in specified circumstances, including the occasion when a trustee became 'incapable' to act. One of the trustees became bankrupt. This made him 'unfit' but not incapable of acting as a trustee. The question in issue was whether a new trustee should have been appointed by the husband (as survivor) or by the continuing trustees (under statute).

The court held that the continuing trustees had the power to appoint a new trustee for the occasion entitling the express power to be exercised had not arisen.

Similarly, where two or more persons have the power to appoint new trustees, they are required to exercise the authority jointly, unless there are express provisions to the contrary. It follows that such a joint power cannot be exercised where one of the appointors dies or cannot agree on the candidate to be appointed as trustee. See *Re Harding*.[4]

Statutory power (s 36 of the Trustee Act 1925)

The statutory power to appoint trustees is contained in s 36 of the Trustee Act 1925 (replacing the Trustee Act 1893). The occasions giving rise to the need to appoint trustees are enacted in s 36(1) (replacement trustees) and s 36(6) (additional trustees).

---

2 [1889] 42 Ch 522.

3 [1896] 1 Ch 315.

4 [1923] 1 Ch 182.

Replacement trustees: s 36(1) of the Trustee Act 1925

There are seven circumstances listed in s 36(1) when a replacement trustee may be appointed. These are:

(1) where a trustee is dead. Under s 36(8), this includes the person nominated as trustee under a will but predeceasing the testator;

(2) where a trustee remains outside the UK for a continuous period of 12 months or more. The UK includes England, Wales, Scotland and Northern Ireland but does not include the Channel Islands or the Isle of Man. The motive for remaining outside the UK is irrelevant, this condition will be satisfied even if the trustee remains outside the UK against his will;

(3) where a trustee desires to be discharged from all or any of the trusts or powers reposed in or conferred on him. Thus, a trustee may retire from part only of the trust;

(4) where a trustee refuses to act. This includes the occasion when the trustee disclaims his office. It is advisable that the disclaimer be executed by deed;

(5) where a trustee is unfit to act. Unfitness refers to some defect in the character of the trustee which suggests an element of risk in leaving the property in the hands of the individual, for example, a conviction for an offence involving dishonesty or bankruptcy. See *Re Wheeler and De Rochow* (above, p 747);

(6) where a trustee is incapable of acting. Incapacity refers to some physical or mental inability to adequately administer the trust, but does not include bankruptcy (see *Re Wheeler and De Rochow*). Under s 36(3), a corporation becomes incapable of acting on the date of the dissolution;

(7) where the trustee is an infant, that is, a person under the age of 18. Such a person may become a trustee under an implied trust (resulting or constructive). An infant is incapable of becoming an express trustee.

Persons who may exercise the statutory power

Section 36(1) lists, in order of priority, the persons who are entitled to exercise the statutory power of appointing replacement trustees. These are:

(a) the person or persons nominated in the trust instrument for the purpose of appointing new trustees (see the discussion above, p 747);

(b) the surviving or continuing trustee, if willing to act. This sub-section was enacted to empower a sole retiring trustee to appoint his successor. It enables a 'retiring' or 'refusing' trustee to participate with the surviving trustees in appointing a successor (s 36(8) of the Trustee Act 1925). But there is no obligation on such 'retiring' trustee to concur in making the appointment. An appointment by the remaining trustees would be valid if the retiring trustee did not participate in the appointment. See *Re Coates*.[5]

5 (1886) 34 Ch D 370.

A trustee who is legitimately removed as a trustee is not a 'continuing' or 'refusing' or 'retiring' trustee for the purposes of s 36(8). He is a removed trustee.

Re Stoneham's Settlement Trust [1953] Ch 59, HC

The two trustees of the settlement were X and Y. Y remained out of the UK for a period exceeding 12 months. X executed a deed retiring from the trust and appointed two others in place of Y and himself. Y challenged the validity of the new appointments on the ground that he was entitled to participate in making the appointments. The court rejected his claim and decided that since Y was compulsorily removed from the trust, he was not a 'retiring' or 'refusing' trustee within s 36(8).

> **Danckwerts J:** ... I come to the conclusion quite plainly that a trustee who is removed against his will is not a refusing or retiring trustee, not, at any rate, in the case of a trustee removed because of his absence outside the UK for consecutive periods of more than 12 months.

(c) the personal representatives of the last surviving or continuing trustee. In order to become a surviving or continuing trustee, the property is required to vest in the individual. Accordingly, if all the persons, entitled as trustees under a will predecease the testator, the personal representative of the last to die would not be empowered to appoint new trustees. The personal representative of the testator will become the trustee and, subject to provisions to the contrary, will be entitled to appoint new trustees.

    Section 36(4) provides that the personal representative of the last surviving or continuing trustee, includes those who have proved the will of the testator or the administrator of a person dying intestate.

    Section 36(5) provides that a sole or last surviving executor intending to renounce probate shall have the power of appointment of trustees at any time before renouncing probate.

Additional trustees: s 36(6) of the Trustee Act 1925

Section 36(6) authorises the appointment of additional trustees although no trustee needs to be replaced. Section 36(6) provides:

> Where a sole trustee, other than a trust corporation, is or has been originally appointed to act in a trust, or where, in the case of any trust, there are not more than three trustees (none of them being a trust corporation) either original or substituted and whether appointed by the court or otherwise, then and in any such case:
>
> (a) the person or persons nominated for the purpose of appointing new trustees by the instrument, if any, creating the trust; or
>
> (b) if there is no such person, or no such person able and willing to act, then the trustee or trustees for the time being;

> may, by writing, appoint another person or other persons to be an additional trustee or additional trustees, but it shall not be obligatory to appoint any additional trustee, unless the instrument, if any, creating the trust, or any statutory enactment provides to the contrary, nor shall the number of trustees be increased beyond four by virtue of any appointment.

The sub-section is self-explanatory, but it may be observed that a trust corporation (corporate professional trustee, such as a bank or an insurance company) has the power of two or more individual trustees. No power exists under s 36(6) to increase the number of trustees beyond four.

Direction of the beneficiaries

Sections 19–21 of the Trusts of Land and Appointment of Trustees Act 1996 have invested new powers in the beneficiaries to direct a retirement of trustees and/or appointment of trustees. These provisions relate to trusts of all types of property (whether land or personalty). But the provisions may be excluded in whole or in part by the trust.

Section 19 applies where there is no person nominated under the trust instrument to appoint new trustees, and all the beneficiaries are of full age and capacity and collectively are absolutely entitled to the trust property. The beneficiaries have either one or both of the following rights. A right to direct in writing that one or more of the trustees shall retire from the trust, and/or that a named person or persons be appointed, in writing, as new trustee or trustees. The direction may be by way of substitution for a trustee or trustees directed to retire, or as an additional trustee or trustees.

If a direction to retire is given, the trustee concerned *shall* execute a deed effecting his retirement, if:

(a) reasonable arrangements have been made to protect his rights under the trust;

(b) after retirement, there will be either a trust corporation or at least two persons to act as trustees; and

(c) either a replacement trustee is to be appointed on his retirement or the continuing trustees, by deed, consent to his retirement.

The section contains no provision compelling the trustees (or the personal representative of the last surviving trustee) to act on a direction to appoint a person as a new trustee. On a practical level, the trustee is unlikely to refuse to make the appointment without good reason.

Section 20 of the 1996 Act applies where:

(a) a trustee becomes mentally incapable of exercising his functions as trustee; and

(b) no person entitled to appoint new trustees is willing and able to do so; and

(c) the beneficiaries are of full age and capacity and are collectively entitled to the trust property, then the beneficiaries may give a written direction to the trustee's receiver or his attorney under a registered enduring power or to a person authorised under the Mental Health Act 1983 to appoint a particular person to be a new trustee.

The Act is silent on the consequences of a failure to act on the direction.

Section 21(1) enacts that a direction for the purposes of s 19 or 20 may take one of two forms:

- either a single direction collectively executed by all the beneficiaries; or
- a number of directions, whether solely or jointly with one or more, but not all, of the beneficiaries,

identifying the same person or persons for retirement or appointment.

Section 21(3) declares that the effect of an appointment of a new trustee under s 19 or s 20 is the same as if he were appointed under s 36(7) of the Trustee Act 1925, that is, he shall have the same powers and discretions as if he was appointed under the trust.

Section 36(7) (as amended by the Trusts of Land and Appointment of Trustees Act 1996) enacts that the effect of an appointment under s 36 or under s 19 or s 20 of the Trusts of Land and Appointment of Trustees Act 1996 shall have the same consequences 'as if he had been originally appointed a trustee by the instrument, if any, creating the trust'.

The number of trustees

(a) Realty: s 34 of the Trustee Act 1925 (as amended by the Trusts of Land and Appointment of Trustees Act 1996) provides that where land is held on trust there may not be more than four trustees. If the instrument purports to appoint more than four trustees, only the first four named as trustees will take the property.

    On the other hand, while a sole trustee is not forbidden, s 14(2) of the Trustee Act 1925, enacts that a sole trusteeship (other than a trust corporation) may not give a valid receipt for the proceeds of sale arising under a trust of land or capital money arising under the Settled Land Act 1925.

(b) Personalty: in theory, there is no restriction on the number of persons who may be appointed trustees of personalty.

    In practice, it may be inconvenient and cumbersome having too many trustees. The office of trusteeship requires unanimous approval of all the trustees (charities are treated as an exception). The law does not recognise a 'sleeping' or inactive trustee. A breach may be committed by a 'sleeping' trustee in failing to oppose a decision taken by his colleagues. See *Bahin v Hughes*[6] (below, p 772).

There are rarely more than four trustees and, if the appointment is made under s 36 of the Trustee Act 1925, there will be not more than four trustees.

Alternatively, a sole trustee is most unsatisfactory because of the danger or risks of fraud or misconduct in administering the trust.

Vesting of trust property in trustees

On an appointment of replacement or additional trustees, the trust property is required to be vested in the new trustee or trustees to enable him or them to carry out his or their duties. Trustees hold the property as joint tenants so that the right of survivorship applies.

The vesting of the property in new trustees may be effected in one of two ways, namely:

(1) by a conveyance or transfer effective to vest the property in the transferee. The relevant formalities that are required to be complied with vary with the nature of the property involved. The legal title to unregistered land requires a conveyance, whereas, registered land requires the new owner to be registered as the proprietor. Shares require registration in the share register of the company;

(2) s 40(1) of the Trustee Act 1925, which declares as follows:

   Where by a deed a new trustee is appointed, then:

   (a) if the deed contains a declaration by the appointor to the effect that any estate or interest in any land, or in any chattel, or the right to recover or receive any debt or thing in action, shall vest in the persons who by virtue of the deed become or are the trustees for performing the trust, the deed shall operate without any conveyance or assignment to vest in those persons as joint tenants ...; and

   (b) if the deed ... does not contain such a declaration, it shall, subject to any express provision to the contrary, operate as if it had contained such a declaration by the appointor extending to all the estates, interests and rights with respect to which a declaration could have been made.

Similar provisions are enacted in s 40(2) (as amended by the Trusts of Land and Appointment of Trustees Act 1996) in respect of a retiring trustee.

The effect of ss 40(1) and (2) is to create a short form and inexpensive method of vesting the trust property in the new trustee or trustees. Under s 40(1)(a), if the deed merely declares that the property vests in the new trustee, this would be sufficient without a conveyance, etc. Section 40(1)(b) enacts that if the deed of appointment omits to include a vesting declaration, it will be treated as if it had contained the same.

6 (1886) 31 Ch D 390.

Exceptions

Section 40(4) of the Trustee Act 1925 excludes certain types of properties from the general provisions in s 40(1) and (2). These include:

(i) land held by trustees on a mortgage as security for a loan of trust money;

(ii) leases containing a condition prohibiting dispositions without consent unless the consent has already been obtained;

(iii) stocks and shares.

In these circumstances, the property is required to be transferred in accordance with the appropriate formalities for that type of property.

Appointment by the court

Section 41 enacts the sweeping power of the court to appoint new trustees either as replacement or additional trustees.

Section 41(1) enacts:

> The court may, whenever it is expedient to appoint a new trustee or new trustees, and it is found inexpedient, difficult or impracticable so to do without the assistance of the court, make an order appointing a new trustee or new trustees either in substitution for or in addition to any existing trustee or trustees, or although there is no existing trustee ...

The most popular occasions when the court's discretion may be exercised are where a sole surviving trustee dies intestate or where an appointor is incapable of making an appointment because of infancy or where all the trustees of a testamentary trust predecease the testator or where there is friction between the trustees.

The court will only exercise its power to appoint trustees when all other avenues have been exhausted. Thus, the court will not exercise its power where an express or statutory power can be exercised.

In exercising its discretion under s 41, the court will have regard to the wishes of the settlor, the interests of the beneficiaries and the efficient administration of the trust. In *Re Tempest*,[7] the Court of Appeal issued guidelines concerning appointments of trustees by the court. In this case, a family settlement was created by will. There were two trustees appointed, one of whom predeceased the testator. Those with the power to appoint new trustees were unable to agree as to the appropriate candidate and an application was made for the appointment of Mr Petre (P). One beneficiary opposed this appointment on the ground that P came from a part of the family with whom the testator had quarrelled. The court decided that P was not a suitable person to be appointed a trustee.

7 (1866) 1 Ch App 485.

Turner LJ: The following rules and principles may, I think, safely be laid down as applying to all cases of appointments by the court of new trustees. First, the court will have regard to the wishes of the persons by whom the trust has been created, if expressed in the instrument creating the trust, or clearly to be collected from it ... Another rule which may safely be laid down is this – that the court will not appoint a person to be trustee in opposition to the interests of the beneficiaries ... it is of the essence of the duty of every trustee to hold an even hand between the parties interested under the trust ... A third rule is that the court in appointing a trustee will have regard to the question, whether his appointment will promote or impede the execution of the trust, for the very purpose of the appointment is that the trust may by better carried into execution.

These are the principles by which, in my judgment, we ought to be guided in determining whether Mr Petre ought to be appointed to be a trustee of this will, and, in my opinion, there are substantial objections to his appointment on each of the three grounds to which I have referred.

... there cannot, I think, be any doubt that the court ought not to appoint a trustee whose appointment will impede the due execution of the trust; but, on the other hand, if the continuing or surviving trustee refuses to act with a trustee who may be proposed to be appointed ... I think it would be going too far to say that the court ought, on that ground alone, to refuse to appoint the proposed trustee; for this would be to give the continuing or surviving trustee a veto upon the appointment of the new trustee. In such a case, I think it must be the duty of the court to inquire and ascertain whether the objection of the surviving or continuing trustee is well founded or not, and to act or refuse to act upon it accordingly. If the surviving or continuing trustee has improperly refused to act with the proposed trustee, it must be a ground for removing him from the trust. Upon the facts of this case, however, it seems to me that the objections to the appointment of Mr Petre were and are well founded.

Section 43 of the Trustee Act 1925 enacts that the effect of an appointment by the court will be treated 'as if the appointee had been originally appointed a trustee by the instrument, if any, creating the trust'.

RETIREMENT

A trustee may retire from the trust in one of four ways:

(1) by taking advantage of a power in the trust instrument; or

(2) by taking advantage of a statutory power under:

   (a) s 36(1) of the Trustee Act 1925 when a new trustee is appointed, that is, the trustee is 'desirous of being discharged'; or

   (b) s 39 of the Trustee Act 1925 where no new trustee is appointed; or

(3) by obtaining the consent of all the beneficiaries who are *sui juris* and absolutely entitled to the trust property under the *Saunders v Vautier* principle (see below, p 837); or

(4) by direction from the relevant beneficiaries under s 19 of the Trusts of Land and Appointment of Trustees Act 1996 (see above, p 750); or

(5) by obtaining the authority of the court.

Section 39(1) of the Trustee Act 1925 (as amended by the Trusts of Land and Appointment of Trustees Act 1996) provides:

> Where a trustee is desirous of being discharged from the trust, and after his discharge there will be either a trust corporation or at least two persons to act as trustees to perform the trust, then, if such trustee as aforesaid by deed declares that he is desirous of being discharged from the trust, and if his co-trustees and such other person, if any, as is empowered to appoint trustees, by deed consent to the discharge of the trustee, and to the vesting in the co-trustees alone of the trust property, the trustee desirous of being discharged shall be deemed to have retired from the trust, and shall, by deed, be discharged therefrom under this Act, without any new trustee being appointed in his place.

Unlike a retirement under s 36(1), a trustee is not allowed to retire from part of a trust under s 39. He is required to retire from the trust as a whole or not at all. The procedure for retirement under s 39 is as follows:

(1) at least two individuals will continue to act as trustees or a trust corporation; and

(2) the remaining trustees (or trustee) and other persons empowered to appoint trustees consent to the retirement by deed; and

(3) the retiring trustee makes such a declaration by deed.

It should be noted that a retiring trustee remains liable for breaches of trust committed whilst he was a trustee. He is absolved from liability in respect of subsequent breaches, unless he retired in order to facilitate a breach of trust. See *Head v Gould*[8] (below, p 885).

Retirement under a court order

Generally speaking, the court will not discharge a trustee under its statutory jurisdiction under s 41 unless it appoints a replacement trustee. However, the court has an inherent jurisdiction to discharge a trustee without replacement, in accordance with its responsibility to administer the trust. This will be the position when s 39 is not applicable because the appropriate consent cannot be obtained.

8 [1898] 1 Ch 250.

REMOVAL OF TRUSTEES

A trustee may be removed from office in one the four ways:

(1) by virtue of a power contained in the trust instrument. This is highly unusual, but if such power exists the court is required to construe the instrument to ascertain whether the circumstances have arisen which give rise to the exercise of the power;

(2) under s 36 of the Trustee Act 1925. This involves the removal of and appointment of a replacement trustee in circumstances laid down in s 36(1) (see above, p 748);

(3) in the circumstances specified in ss 19 to 21 of the Trusts of Land and Appointment of Trustees Act 1996;

(4) under a court order under s 41 of the Trustee Act 1925 or the inherent jurisdiction of the court.

Court order

Under s 41 of the Trustee Act 1925, the court has the jurisdiction to remove an existing trustee and appoint a replacement trustee (see above, p 753).

Under its inherent jurisdiction to secure the proper administration of the trust, the court has the power to remove a trustee without appointing a replacement trustee. In *Letterstedt v Broers*, the Privy Council declared that the court had a general duty to ensure that the trusts were properly executed and their main guide was the welfare of the beneficiaries. Accordingly, friction and hostility between the trustees and the beneficiaries which is likely to prejudice the proper administration of the trust may be a ground for the removal of trustees.

Letterstedt v Broers (1884) 9 AC 371, HL

In this case, a beneficiary, under a trust created by will, made allegations of misconduct against a trustee concerning the administration of the trust. The court decided that, notwithstanding the allegations were not substantiated, the court would exercise its jurisdiction to remove the trustees.

> **Lord Blackburn:** ... the whole case has been argued here, and, as far as their Lordships can perceive, in the court below, as depending on the principles which should guide an English court of equity when called upon to remove old trustees and substitute new ones. It is not disputed that there is a jurisdiction 'in cases requiring such a remedy' as is said in Story's *Equity Jurisprudence*, s 1287, but there is very little to be found to guide us in saying what are the cases requiring such a remedy; so little that their Lordships are compelled to have recourse to general principles.
>
> Story says, s 1289:

> But in cases of positive misconduct, courts of equity have no difficulty in interposing to remove trustees who have abused their trust; it is not indeed every mistake or neglect of duty, or inaccuracy of conduct of trustees, which will induce courts of equity to adopt such a course. But the acts or omissions must be such as to endanger the trust property or to show a want of honesty, or a want of proper capacity to execute the duties, or a want of reasonable fidelity.
>
> It seems to their Lordships that the jurisdiction which a court of equity has no difficulty in exercising under the circumstances indicated by Story is merely ancillary to its principal duty, to see that the trusts are properly executed. This duty is constantly being performed by the substitution of new trustees in the place of original trustees for a variety of reasons in non-contentious cases. And therefore, though it should appear that the charges of misconduct were either not made out, or were greatly exaggerated, so that the trustee was justified in resisting them, and the court might consider that in awarding costs, yet if satisfied that the continuance of the trustee would prevent the trusts being properly executed, the trustee might be removed. It must always be borne in mind that trustees exist for the benefit of those to whom the creator of the trust has given the trust estate.
>
> ... if it appears clear that the continuance of the trustee would be detrimental to the execution of the trusts, even if for no other reason than that human infirmity would prevent those beneficially interested, or those who act for them, from working in harmony with the trustee ... the trustee is always advised by his own counsel to resign, and does so. If, without any reasonable ground, he refused to do so, it seems that the court might think it proper to remove him.
>
> It is quite true that friction or hostility between trustees and the immediate possessor of the trust estate is not of itself a reason for the removal of the trustees. But where the hostility is grounded on the mode in which the trust has been administered, where it has been caused wholly or partially by substantial overcharges against the trust estate, it is certainly not to be disregarded.
>
> Looking, therefore, at the whole circumstances of this very peculiar case, the complete change of position, the unfortunate hostility that has arisen, and the difficult and delicate duties that may yet have to be performed, their Lordships can come to no other conclusion than that it is necessary, for the welfare of the beneficiaries, that the Board should no longer be trustees

The guiding principles were also considered by the court in *Re Wrightson*.[9] The trustees admitted a breach of trust in connection with an advance of a part of the trust funds upon mortgage. The question in issue was whether one of the trustees should be removed. A substantial proportion of the beneficiaries opposed his removal but others supported it. The court decided that, having regard to all the circumstances, it would not make an order for the removal of the trustee. The test was whether the trust property could safely be left in the

9 [1908] 1 Ch 789.

hands of the trustee. Important factors to be taken into consideration were a substantial number of the beneficiaries wished the trustee to continue, a change of trustees would involve expense and the court foresaw that there was unlikely to be any future breaches of trust.

> **Warrington J:** Is it necessary here, having regard to the welfare of the beneficiaries and for the protection of this trust to remove the trustee? At the present moment nothing remains for the trustees to do except to wind up the estate; the testator's widow is dead; the whole of the estate is divisible amongst a number of persons who are *sui juris* ... having regard to the fact that the court has now the power of seeing that the trust is properly executed, to the fact that a large proportion of the beneficiaries do not require the trustees to be removed, and further to the extra expense and loss to the trust estate which must be occasioned by the change of trustees, I think it would not be for the welfare of the beneficiaries generally, or for the protection of the trust estate, that these trustees should be removed.

In *Moore v McGlynn*,[10] it was decided that a trustee who, started up a business in competition with the trust, was placed in such a position of conflict with the trust that his removal was justified.

SUPPLEMENTARY READING

Hopkins, N, 'The Trusts of Land and Appointment of Trustees Act 1996' [1996] Conv 411

Jones, G, 'Delegation by trustees – a reappraisal' (1959) 22 MLR 381

Kenny, A, 'Living up to expectations' (1996) 146 NLJ 348

Parry, N, 'Remuneration of trustees' [1984] Conv 275

10 (1894) 1 IR 74.

CHAPTER 19

DUTIES AND POWERS OF TRUSTEES

The office of a trustee or fiduciary reflects a variety of onerous duties on the trustee or fiduciary. Far from receiving gratitude from the beneficiaries, the trustees may be subject to claims by beneficiaries for breaches of trust. See *Williams v Barton* (above, p 326). In performing their duties, the trustees are required to act honestly, diligently and in the best interests of the beneficiaries. Thus, the trustees are not entitled to show favour to a beneficiary or group of beneficiaries but are required to act impartially and in the best interests of all the beneficiaries.

In *Lloyds Bank plc v Duker*,[1] the court refused an application by a residuary beneficiary to her share (46 80ths or 574 shares) of the residuary estate of 999 shares. This would have entitled her to a majority holding which would have exceeded the value of the rest of the shares subject to the trust. Instead, the court ordered all the shares to be sold and the proceeds divided between the beneficiaries in accordance with the will.

> **Mowbray QC:** ... the general rule stated in *Snell's Principles of Equity*[2] is as follows:
>
> > The general rule is that in the absence of some good reason to the contrary a person who is indefeasibly entitled to a share in divisible personalty is entitled to have his share transferred to him, even if the property is held on trust for sale with power to postpone sale and the transfer would diminish the value of the other shares.
>
> For that proposition *Snell's Principles of Equity*, and Mr Harrod, cite *In re Marshall*;[3] *In re Sandeman's Will Trusts*[4] and *In re Weiner (Decd)*.[5] Those authorities all concerned the case where only one out of several aliquot parts of an estate had become distributable. I am assuming that the same rule applies in a case like the present where all are immediately distributable. Nevertheless, as Snell indicates, the rule is not without exceptions. The general rule requiring a distribution was applied in the first three authorities I have mentioned, but in *In re Marshall*,[6] Cozens-Hardy MR recognised that it could be excluded by 'special circumstances', and in *In re Sandeman's Will Trusts*,[7] Clauson J said the

1 [1987] 3 All ER 193.

2 Baker, P and Langan, P, *Snell's Principles of Equity*, 28th edn, 1982, London: Sweet & Maxwell, p 233.

3 [1914] 1 Ch 192.

4 [1937] 1 All ER 368.

5 [1956] 1 WLR 579.

6 [1914] 1 Ch 192, pp 199, 200.

7 [1937] 1 All ER 368, p 371.

court would not order a transfer if there was some good ground to the contrary and he said, at p 373:

> I can conceive that there might be circumstances – they would have to be very special – which would justify the court in refusing to give effect to the plaintiff's rights ...

The plaintiff there was the beneficiary whose aliquot part had become distributable. Likewise in *In re Weiner (Decd)*[8] Harman J recognised that special circumstances could justify him in holding up the shares.

Are the circumstances in the present case such as to require the bank to sell all 999 shares, rather than distributing 574 of them to Mr Duker? To answer this question, I need to see what kind of circumstances would exclude his normal right to have this aliquot part of the shares distributed to him. Clauson J ruefully said in *In re Sandeman's Will Trusts*:[9] 'The court has, I think, been rather careful never to define in precise terms exactly.'

The first three decisions I have named do not, as decisions, throw any light on the question whether the discrepancy between share numbers and values is to be considered a sufficiently special circumstance to exclude the general rule. The reason is that there was no such discrepancy in those cases. In all of them, beneficiaries immediately entitled called for transfers of their aliquot parts of a block of shares held in residue by the trustees, and this was ordered. In *In re Marshall*[10] the block only formed about a sixth of the issued shares in a public company with some 360 shareholders. It was not suggested (and could not have been) that shares in the part of the block to be distributed were worth more per share than the shares retained. The block of shares in *In re Sandeman's Will Trusts*[11] was a controlling interest which carried 1,018 out of the 1,927 votes which would be cast at general meetings of a private company. Half the estate was distributable, and half the holding was ordered to be distributed. Nothing at all seems to have been said about differential share values, and naturally enough, because the half distributed would have had just the same value per share as the half retained. In the third case, *In re Weiner (Decd)*,[12] the block in the estate was 75% of the shares in a private company and 45% of this was ordered to be distributed. Again, the shares in such a holding could not have been worth more per share than the shares in the 55% of the block that remained with the trustees.

I accept *In re Sandeman's Will Trusts*[13] and *In re Weiner (Decd)*[14] as authorities which ought to be followed at first instance that the general rule is not excluded by the fact that the distribution breaks up a controlling interest, and so reduces the value of the whole. I assume that is correct, and if that were the

8 [1956] 1 WLR 579, p 584.
9 [1937] 1 All ER 368, p 372.
10 [1914] 1 Ch 192.
11 [1937] 1 All ER 368.
12 [1956] 1 WLR 579.
13 [1937] 1 All ER 368.
14 [1956] 1 WLR 579.

> only reason for ordering a sale of the 999 shares as a whole in the present case, the decisions in *In re Sandeman's Will Trusts* and *In re Weiner (Decd)* would be against it. But it is not the only reason for a sale in the present case, as I see it. The operative reason is that, if the shares were transferred out in the one 80th fractions, Mr Duker would get a greater value per share than the other beneficiaries and so would get more than his 46 80ths of the total value received by the beneficiaries as a body.
>
> I can, though, get some help from another general principle. I mean the principle that trustees are bound to hold an even hand among their beneficiaries, and not favour one as against another, stated for instance in *Snell's Principles of Equity*.[15] Of course Mr Duker must have a larger part than the other beneficiaries. But if he takes 46 80ths of the shares he will be favoured beyond what Mr Smith intended, because his shares will each be worth more than the others. The trustees' duty to hold an even hand seems to indicate that they should sell all 999 shares instead. Mr Romer pointed out that it is this duty which imposes a trust for sale under the first branch of the rule in *Howe v Earl of Dartmouth*.[16]
>
> In all the circumstances, to prevent the unfairness which would result from a transfer of 574 of the shares to Mr Duker, and to ensure that he takes 48/80ths of the residuary estate measured by value, I consider that the bank should not transfer any of the shares to him, but should sell all 999 on the general market, Mr Duker being left free to become a buyer.

The effect, therefore, is that the trustees are required to take steps to avoid placing themselves in a position where their duties may conflict with their personal interests. If there is a conflict of the trustees' duties and interest, the trustees are required to hand over any unauthorised benefit to the beneficiaries (see above, pp 314 *et seq*). Thus, it is imperative that the trustees do not deviate from the terms of the trust without the authority of the beneficiaries or the court.

The standard of care and skill

Throughout the administration of the trust, the trustees are required to exhibit an objective standard of skill as would be expected from an ordinary prudent man of business. In the case of a power of investment, the duty would be exercised so as to yield the best return for all the beneficiaries, judged in relation to the risks inherent in the investments and the prospects of the yield of income and capital appreciation. The classical statement of the rule was laid down by Lord Watson in *Learoyd v Whiteley*:[17]

15 *Op cit*, fn 2, p 225.

16 (1802) 7 Ves Jun 137a.

17 (1887) 12 AC 727.

> ... As a general rule the law requires of a trustee no higher degree of diligence in the execution of his office than a man of ordinary prudence would exercise in the management of his own private affairs. Yet he is not allowed the same discretion in investing the moneys of the trust as if he were a person *sui juris* dealing with his own estate. Businessmen of prudence may, and frequently do, select investments which are more or less of a speculative character but it is the duty of a trustee to confine himself to the class of investments which are permitted by the trust and likewise to avoid all investments of that class which are attended with hazard. As long as he acts in the honest observance of these limitations the general rule already stated will apply.

The courts will have regard to all the circumstances of each case in order to ascertain whether the trustees' conduct fell below the standard imposed on such persons.

In considering the investment policy of the trust, the trustees are required to put on one side their own personal interests and views. They may have strongly held social or political views. They may be firmly opposed to any investments in companies connected with alcohol, tobacco, armaments or many other things. In the conduct of their own affairs, trustees are free to abstain from making any such investments. However, in performance of their fiduciary duties, if investments of the morally reprehensible type would be more beneficial to the beneficiaries than other investments, the trustees must not refrain from making the investments by reason of the views that they hold. Trustees may even act dishonourably (though not illegally) if the interests of their beneficiaries require it, as in *Buttle v Saunders*.[18] Here, trustees for sale had struck a bargain for the sale of the trust property but had not bound themselves by a legally binding contract, the court held that they were under a duty to consider and explore a better offer received by them and were not required to accept the lesser offer because they felt morally bound. Similarly, in *Cowan v Scargill and Others*,[19] the defendants were trustees of the Mineworkers Pension Scheme who raised an objection to a new investment plan of trust funds, on the grounds that the proposed strategy involved investments overseas in competing forms of energy. The court decided that the plan would yield the best return for the beneficiaries and refused the application.

Cowan v Scargill and Others [1984] 3 WLR 501, HC

> **Megarry VC:** I turn to the law. The starting point is the duty of trustees to exercise their powers in the best interests of the present and future beneficiaries of the trust, holding the scales impartially between different classes of beneficiaries. This duty of the trustees towards their beneficiaries is paramount. They must, of course, obey the law; but subject to that, they must

18 [1950] 2 All ER 193.

19 [1984] 3 WLR 501.

put the interests of their beneficiaries first. When the purpose of the trust is to provide financial benefits for the beneficiaries, as is usually the case, the best interests of the beneficiaries are normally their best financial interests. In the case of a power of investment, as in the present case, the power must be exercised so as to yield the best return for the beneficiaries, judged in relation to the risks of the investments in question; and the prospects of the yield of income and capital appreciation both have to be considered in judging the return from the investment.

The legal memorandum that the union obtained from their solicitors is generally in accord with these views. In considering the possibility of investment for 'socially beneficial reasons which may result in lower returns to the fund', the memorandum states that 'the trustees' only concern is to ensure that the return is the maximum possible consistent with security; and then it refers to the need for diversification. However, it continues by saying:

> Trustees cannot be criticised for failing to make a particular investment for social or political reasons, such as in South African stock for example, but may be held liable for investing in assets which yield a poor return or for disinvesting in stock at inappropriate times for non-financial criteria.

This last sentence must be considered in the light of subsequent passages in the memorandum which indicate that the sale of South African securities by trustees might be justified on the ground of doubts about political stability in South Africa and the long term financial soundness of its economy, whereas trustees could not properly support motions at a company meeting dealing with pay levels in South Africa, work accidents, pollution control, employment conditions for minorities, military contracting and consumer protection. The assertion that trustees could not be criticised for failing to make a particular investment for social or political reasons is one that I would not accept in its full width. If the investment in fact made is equally beneficial to the beneficiaries, then criticism would be difficult to sustain in practice, whatever the position in theory. But if the investment in fact made is less beneficial, then both in theory and in practice the trustees would normally be open to criticism.

This leads me to the second point, which is a corollary of the first. In considering what investments to make trustees must put on one side their own personal interests and views. Trustees may have strongly held social or political views. They may be firmly opposed to any investment in South Africa or other countries, or they may object to any form of investment in companies concerned with alcohol, tobacco, armaments or many other things. In the conduct of their own affairs, of course, they are free to abstain from making any such investments. Yet under a trust, if investments of this type would be more beneficial to the beneficiaries than other investments, the trustees must not refrain from making the investments by reason of the views that they hold. Trustees may even have to act dishonourably (though not illegally) if the interests of their beneficiaries require it. Thus, where trustees for sale had struck a bargain for the sale of trust property but had not bound themselves by a legally enforceable contract, they were held to be under a duty to consider and explore a better offer that they received, and not to carry through the bargain to which they felt in honour bound (*Buttle v Saunders*).[20] In other words, the duty of trustees to their beneficiaries may include a duty to 'gazump,' however honourable the trustees. As Wynn-Parry J said at p 195, trustees 'have an overriding duty to obtain the best price which they can for their beneficiaries'. In applying this to an official receiver in *In re Wyvern Developments Ltd*,[21] Templeman J said that he 'must do his best by his creditors and contributories. He is in a fiduciary capacity and cannot make moral gestures, nor can the court authorise him to do so'. In the words of Sir James Wigram VC in *Balls v Strutt*:[22]

> It is a principle in this court, that a trustee shall not be permitted to use the powers which the trust may confer upon him at law, except for the legitimate purposes of his trust ...

Powers must be exercised fairly and honestly for the purposes for which they are given and not so as to accomplish any ulterior purpose, whether for the benefit of the trustees or otherwise: see *Duke of Portland v Topham*,[23] a case on a power of appointment that must apply *a fortiori* to a power given to trustees as such.

Thirdly, by way of caveat I should say that I am not asserting that the benefit of the beneficiaries which a trustee must make his paramount concern inevitably and solely means their financial benefit, even if the only object of the trust is to provide financial benefits. Thus, if the only actual or potential beneficiaries of a trust are all adults with very strict views on moral and social matters, condemning all forms of alcohol, tobacco and popular entertainment, as well as armaments, I can well understand that it might not be for the 'benefit' of such beneficiaries to know that they are obtaining rather larger financial returns under the trust by reason of investments in those activities than they would have received if the trustees had invested the trust funds in other investments. The beneficiaries might well consider that it was far better to receive less than to receive more money from what they consider to be evil and tainted sources. 'Benefit' is a word with a very wide meaning, and there are circumstances in which arrangements which work to the financial disadvantage of a beneficiary may yet be for his benefit: see, for example, *In re T's Settlement Trusts*[24] and *In re CL*.[25] But I would emphasise that such cases are likely to be very rare, and in any case I think that under a trust for the provision of financial benefits the burden would rest, and rest heavy, on him who asserts that it is for the benefit of the beneficiaries as a whole to receive less by reason of the exclusion of some of the possibly more profitable forms of investment. Plainly the present case is not one of this rare type of cases. Subject to such matters, under a trust for the provision of financial benefits, the

---

20 [1950] 2 All ER 193.

21 [1974] 1 WLR 1097, p 1106.

22 (1841) 1 Hare 146, p 149.

23 (1864) 11 HL Cas 32.

24 [1964] Ch 158.

25 [1969] 1 Ch 587.

paramount duty of the trustees is to provide the greatest financial benefits for the present and future beneficiaries.

Fourthly, the standard required of a trustee in exercising his powers of investment is that he must:

> ... take such care as an ordinary prudent man would take if he were minded to make an investment for the benefit of other people for whom he felt morally bound to provide ...

Per Lindley LJ in *In re Whiteley*.[26] That duty includes the duty to seek advice on matters which the trustee does not understand, such as the making of investments, and on receiving that advice to act with the same degree of prudence. This requirement is not discharged merely by showing that the trustee has acted in good faith and with sincerity. Honesty and sincerity are not the same as prudence and reasonableness. Some of the most sincere people are the most unreasonable; and Mr Scargill told me that he had met quite a few of them. Accordingly, although a trustee who takes advice on investments is not bound to accept and act on that advice, he is not entitled to reject it merely because he sincerely disagrees with it, unless in addition to being sincere he is acting as an ordinary prudent man would act.

Fifthly, trustees have a duty to consider the need for diversification of investments. By s 6(1) of the Trustee Investments Act 1961:

> In the exercise of his powers of investment a trustee shall have regard:
>
> (a) to the need for diversification of investments of the trust, in so far as is appropriate to the circumstances of the trust;
>
> (b) to the suitability to the trust of investments of the description of investment proposed and of the investment proposed as an investment of that description.

The reference to the 'circumstances of the trust' plainly includes matters such as the size of the trust funds: the degree of diversification that is practicable and desirable for a large fund may plainly be impracticable or undesirable (or both) in the case of a small fund.

I can see no reason for holding that different principles apply to pension fund trusts from those which apply to other trusts. Of course, there are many provisions in pension schemes which are not to be found in private trusts, and to these the general law of trusts will be subordinated. But subject to that, I think that the trusts of pension funds are subject to the same rules as other trusts.

Trustees must do the best they can for the benefit of their beneficiaries, and not merely avoid harming them. I find it impossible to see how it will assist trustees to do the best they can for their beneficiaries by prohibiting a wide range of investments that are authorised by the terms of the trust. Whatever the position today, nobody can say that conditions tomorrow cannot possibly make it advantageous to invest in one of the prohibited investments. It is the duty of trustees, in the interests of their beneficiaries, to take advantage of the

26 (1886) 33 Ch D 347, p 355; see also pp 350, 358; and see *Learoyd v Whiteley* (1887) 12 App Cas 727.

> full range of investments authorised by the terms of the trust, instead of resolving to narrow that range.
>
> Accordingly, on the case as a whole, in my judgment the plaintiffs are right and the defendants are wrong.

Where the investment policy of the trust incorporates the requirement that the trustees take into consideration non financial considerations, the trustees have the difficult task of balancing such non-financial considerations with the most profitable, authorised return.

Harries and Others v Church Commissioners for England [1992] 1 WLR 1241, HC

In this case, the court considered the extent of this balancing process that is required to be conducted by the trustees. The Church Commissioners for England, a charitable body corporate, were trustees owning assets worth £2.6 billion upon trust for the advancement of religion. The investment policy of the Commissioners, as set out in their annual report, declared that their primary aim in the management of the assets was to produce the best return and, in so doing, they would take proper account of social, ethical and environmental issues. The plaintiffs instituted proceedings against the Commissioners claiming a declaration that the defendants were guided too rigorously by purely financial considerations and, while not ignoring moral factors, gave insufficient weight to ethical considerations, for example, the plaintiffs alleged that investments in an additional 24% of UK companies which traded with South Africa ought to have been withheld. The defendant's view was that while they took ethical considerations into account the restricted investment policy proposed by the plaintiffs was not sufficiently balanced to be adopted.

Nicholls VC decided in favour of the defendants on the ground that there was no evidence that the Commissioners failed to take into account proper ethical considerations in adopting a balanced portfolio of investments.

> **Nicholls VC**: Broadly speaking, property held by charity trustees falls into two categories. First, there is property held by trustees for what may be called functional purposes. The National Trust owns historic houses and open spaces. The Salvation Army owns hostels for the destitute. And many charities need office accommodation in which to carry out essential administrative work. Secondly, there is property held by trustees for the purpose of generating money, whether from income or capital growth, with which to further the work of the trust. In other words, property held by trustees as an investment. Where property is so held, *prima facie*, the purposes of the trust will be best served by the trustees seeking to obtain therefrom the maximum return, whether by way of income or capital growth, which is consistent with commercial prudence. That is the starting point for all charity trustees when considering the exercise of their investment powers. Most charities need money; and the more of it there is available, the more the trustees can seek to accomplish.

In most cases this *prima facie* position will govern the trustees' conduct. In most cases the best interests of the charity require that the trustees' choice of investments should be made solely on the basis of well established investment criteria, having taken expert advice where appropriate and having due regard to such matters as the need to diversify, the need to balance income against capital growth, and the need to balance risk against return.

In a minority of cases the position will not be so straightforward. There will be some cases, I suspect comparatively rare, when the objects of the charity are such that investments of a particular type would conflict with the aims of the charity. Much cited examples are those of cancer research companies and tobacco shares, trustees of temperance charities and brewery and distillery shares, and trustees of charities of the Society of Friends and shares in companies engaged in production of armaments. If, as would be likely in those examples, trustees were satisfied that investing in a company engaged in a particular type of business would conflict with the very objects their charity is seeking to achieve, they should not so invest. Carried to its logical conclusion the trustees should take this course even if it would be likely to result in significant financial detriment to the charity. The logical conclusion, whilst sound as a matter of legal analysis, is unlikely to arise in practice. It is not easy to think of an instance where in practice the exclusion for this reason of one or more companies or sectors from the whole range of investments open to trustees would be likely to leave them without an adequately wide range of investments from which to choose a properly diversified portfolio.

There will also be some cases, again I suspect comparatively rare, when trustees' holdings of particular investments might hamper a charity's work either by making potential recipients of aid unwilling to be helped because of the source of the charity's money, or by alienating some of those who support the charity financially. In these cases the trustees will need to balance the difficulties they would encounter, or likely financial loss they would sustain, if they were to hold the investments against the risk of financial detriment if those investments were excluded from their portfolio. The greater the risk of financial detriment, the more certain the trustees should be of countervailing disadvantages to the charity before they incur that risk. Another circumstance where trustees would be entitled, or even required, to take into account non-financial criteria would be where the trust deed so provides.

No doubt there will be other cases where trustees are justified in departing from what should always be their starting point. The instances I have given are not comprehensive. But I must emphasise that of their very nature, and by definition, investments are held by trustees to aid the work of the charity in a particular way: by generating money. That is the purpose for which they are held. That is their *raison d'être*. Trustees cannot properly use assets held as an investment for other, viz, non-investment, purposes. To the extent that they do they are not properly exercising their powers of investment. This is not to say that trustees who own land may not act as responsible landlords or those who own shares may not act as responsible shareholders. They may. The law is not so cynical as to require trustees to behave in a fashion which would bring them or their charity into disrepute (although their consciences must not be too

> tender: see *Buttle v Saunders*).[27] On the other hand, trustees must act prudently. They must not use property held by them for investment purposes as a means for making moral statements at the expense of the charity of which they are trustees. Those who wish may do so with their own property, but that is not a proper function of trustees with trust assets held as an investment.
>
> I should mention one other particular situation. There will be instances today when those who support or benefit from a charity take widely different views on a particular type of investment, some saying that on moral grounds it conflicts with the aims of the charity, others saying the opposite. One example is the holding of arms industry shares by a religious charity. There is a real difficulty here. To many questions raising moral issues there are no certain answers. On moral questions widely differing views are held by well-meaning, responsible people. This is not always so. But frequently, when questions of the morality of conduct are being canvassed, there is no identifiable yardstick which can be applied to a set of facts so as to yield one answer which can be seen to be 'right' and the other 'wrong'. If that situation confronts trustees of a charity, the law does not require them to find an answer to the unanswerable. Trustees may, if they wish, accommodate the views of those who consider that on moral grounds a particular investment would be in conflict with the objects of the charity, so long as the trustees are satisfied that course would not involve a risk of significant financial detriment. But when they are not so satisfied trustees should not make investment decisions on the basis of preferring one view of whether on moral grounds an investment conflicts with the objects of the charity over another. This is so even when one view is more widely supported than the other.
>
> The evidence does show that the commissioners have declined to adopt financially disadvantageous policies advocated by, among others, the Bishop of Oxford. I add only this. In bringing these proceedings the Bishop of Oxford and his colleagues are actuated by the highest moral concern. But, as I have sought to show, the approach they wish the commissioners to adopt to investment decisions would involve a departure by the commissioners from their legal obligations. Whether such a departure would or would not be desirable is, of course, not an issue in these proceedings. That is a matter to be pursued, if at all, elsewhere than in this court.

On the other hand, in *Ward v Ward*,[28] the House of Lords decided that a trustee had acted reasonably in not suing a debtor (who was also a beneficiary) for the repayment of a loan, for this could have resulted in his (the debtor's) financial ruin and would have put his children (who were also beneficiaries) in precarious circumstances.

In an action for breach of trust, the plaintiff is required to establish that the trust has suffered a loss which is attributable to the conduct or omission of the trustees. If the trustees' conduct or omission fell below the required standard

27 [1950] 2 All ER 193.

28 (1843) 2 HL Cas 777.

imposed on trustees, he becomes personally liable whether he acted in good faith or not. *In Re Lucking's Will Trust*,[29] a trustee-director of a company was liable to the trust when he allowed the managing director and friend to appropriate £15,000 of the company funds through the delivery of blank cheques to the managing director which were signed by the trustee.

> **Cross J:** ... trustees holding a controlling interest ought to ensure so far as they can that they have such information as to the progress of the company's affairs as directors would have. If they sit back and allow the company to be run by the minority shareholder and receive no more information than shareholders are entitled to, they do so at their risk if things go wrong.

With regard to professional trustees such as banks and insurance companies, the standard of care imposed on such bodies is higher than the degree of diligence expected from a non-professional trustee. The professional trustee is required to administer the trust with such a degree of expertise as would be expected from a specialist in trust administration. This objective standard is applied by the courts after due consideration of the facts of each case.

Bartlett v Barclays Bank [1980] Ch 515, HC

> **Brightman J:** ... trust corporations, including the bank, hold themselves out as possessing a superior ability for the conduct of trust business ... a trust corporation holds itself out in its advertising literature as being above ordinary mortals. With a specialist staff of trained trust officers and managers, with ready access to financial information and professional advice, dealing with and solving trust problems day after day, the trust corporation holds itself out, and rightly, as capable of providing an expertise which it would be unrealistic to expect and unjust to demand from the ordinary prudent man or woman who accepts, probably unpaid and sometimes reluctantly from a sense of family duty, the burdens of trusteeship.

In this case, the trust estate was the majority shareholder in a property company and the trustee was a professional trust company. The board of directors, for good commercial reasons, decided to restructure the investment portfolio and invest in land development. The trustee did not actively participate in the company's deliberations nor was it provided with regular information concerning the company's activities but was content to rely on the annual balance sheet and profit and loss account. One of the schemes pursued by the company proved to be disastrous. In an action brought against the trustee the court held that the trustee was liable for it (the trust corporation) had not acted reasonably in the administration of the trust.

On the other hand, the plaintiff failed in her action in *Nestle v National Westminster Bank*,[30] on the ground that she failed to prove positively that the defendant's action or inaction resulted in a loss to the trust. The plaintiff was

29 [1968] 1 WLR 866.

30 [1993] 1 WLR 1260.

the remainderman under a trust created by her grandfather at a time when the property was worth £50,000. In 1986, the plaintiff became absolutely entitled to the trust property which was then worth £269,203. During the trust period, the cost of living index had multiplied by a factor of 20. Had the trust fund increased at the same rate, it would have been worth £1 m. It was apparent that the real value of the fund was reduced during the trust period. The plaintiff claimed that the trustees had mismanaged the investments without adducing evidence to this effect, but sought to rely on a presumption of a loss to the trust as a result of the actions of the trustees. The Court of Appeal held in favour of the defendant on the ground that the plaintiff failed to prove that the trustees made decisions which reasonable trustees would not have made or failed to make decisions which reasonable trustees would have made.

Nestle v National Westminster Bank [1993] 1 WLR 1260, CA

Dillon LJ: The starting point must, in my judgment, be that, as the plaintiff is claiming compensation, the onus is on her to prove that she has suffered loss because from 1922 to 1960 the equities in the annuity fund were not diversified: see *Hotson v East Berkshire Area Health Authority*[31] and *Wilsher v Essex Area Health Authority*.[32] In some cases, it is sufficient to prove loss of a chance because in such cases, as in *Chaplin v Hicks*,[33] the outcome, if the plaintiff had not lost the chance, can never be proved. But in the present case, if the annuity fund had been invested wholly in fixed interest securities, it would have been relatively easy to prove, even though the event never happened, that the annuity fund would have been worth much more if a substantial part had been invested in equities. Consequently, fair compensation could have been assessed.

Equally, it would have been possible, even though more difficult and much more expensive, to prove, if it be the fact, that the equities in the annuity fund would have performed even better if diversified than they did as concentrated in bank and insurance shares. But the plaintiff has not provided any such proof. She has not even provided any material which would enable the court to assess the strength of, or value, the chance which she claims she has lost. Therefore her claim for compensation or damages in respect of the investment of the annuity fund from 1922 to 1960 must, in my judgment, fail.

Staughton LJ: The misunderstanding of the investment clause and the failure to conduct periodic reviews do not by themselves, whether separately or together, afford the plaintiff a remedy. They were symptoms of incompetence or idleness – not on the part of National Westminster Bank but of their predecessors; they were not, without more, breaches of trust. The plaintiff must show that, through one or other or both of those causes, the trustees made decisions which they should not have made or failed to make decisions which they should have made. If that were proved, and if at first sight loss

31 [1987] AC 750.

32 [1988] AC 1074.

33 [1911] 2 KB 786.

resulted, it would be appropriate to order an inquiry as to the loss suffered by the trust fund.

It may be difficult to discharge that burden, and particularly to show that decisions were not taken when they should have been. But that does not absolve a plaintiff from discharging it, and I cannot find that it was discharged in this case.

That brings me to what I regard as the substance of the case, the failure to invest a higher proportion of the trust fund in ordinary shares. Here one must take care to avoid two errors. First, the trustees' performance must not be judged with hindsight: after the event even a fool is wise, as a poet said nearly 3,000 years ago. Secondly (unless this is the same point), one must bear in mind that investment philosophy was very different in the early years of this trust from what it became later. Inflation was non-existent, overall, from 1921 to 1938. It occurred in modest degree during the war years, and became a more persistent phenomenon from 1947 onwards. Equities were regarded as risky during the 1920s and 1930s, and yielded a higher return then gilt-edged securities. It was only in 1959 that the so called reverse yield gap occurred.

During the period from 1922 until the death of Mrs Barbara Nestle in 1960, the proportion of ordinary shares in the trust fund as a whole varied between 46 and 82%. Until 1951 it never rose above 57%; there was then quite a sharp rise until 1960, not caused by any change in investment policy but presumably by a general rise in the value of ordinary shares (183%, according to the index, between 1950 and 1960).

In my judgment the trustees are not shown to have failed in their duties at any time up to 1959 in this respect. I cannot say that, in the light of investment conditions then prevailing, they were in breach of trust by not holding a higher proportion of ordinary shares. I see no reason to believe that equities bought in 1959 with the proceeds of the house and contents would have remained exempt from the trustees' general policy, of according some preference to income from tax-exempt gilts, and maintaining roughly speaking proportions of 50:50 overall. So I do not find that there is a *prima facie* case of loss to the trust from the 1959 transaction.

I would dismiss the appeal.

Unanimity

Subject to provisions to the contrary in the trust instrument, trustees are required to act unanimously. The settlor has given all of his trustees the responsibility to act on behalf of the trust. The acts and decisions of some of the trustees (even a majority of trustees) are not binding on others. Thus, once a trust decision is made, the trustees become jointly and severally liable to the beneficiaries in the event of a breach of trust. There is no such thing as an 'active' or 'passive' trustee. Each becomes liable as a representative of the trust. The main issue in this context is, whether a trustee who disagrees with the decision or views of his co-trustee ought to hold firm and make an application to the court or succumb to the views of his co-trustees. This would vary with the circumstances of each case.

Bahin v Hughes (1886) 31 Ch D 390, CA (Cotton, Bowen and Fry LJJ)

In this case, three trustees, A (Eliza Hughes), B (Mrs Burden) and Mrs C (Mrs Edwards) held property on trust for Mrs Bahin for life with remainder to her children. A invested the funds in unauthorised investments and a loss occurred. Mrs C had died before proceedings had commenced. Mrs Bahin sued A, B and Mr C (Mrs C's husband) for breach of trust. B and Mr C claimed an indemnity from A on the ground that A was an 'active' trustee. The court held that they were all liable. An indemnity would only be available if A was the solicitor to the trust or had obtained a personal gain from the breach.

> **Cotton LJ:** On going into the authorities, there are very few cases in which one trustee, who has been guilty with a co-trustee of breach of trust and held answerable, has successfully sought indemnity as against his co-trustee. *Lockhart v Reilly*[34] and *Thompson v Finch*[35] are the only cases which appear to be reported. Now, in *Lockhart v Reilly* it appears from the report of the case in the Law Journal that the trustee by whom the loss was sustained had been not only trustee, but had been and was a solicitor, and acting as solicitor for himself and his co-trustee, and it was on his advice that Lockhart had relied in making the investment which gave rise to the action of the *cestui que* trust. The Lord Chancellor (Lord Cranworth) refers to the fact that he was a solicitor, and makes the remark:
>
>> The whole thing was trusted to him. He was the solicitor, and, independently of the consideration that one cannot help seeing it was done with a view of favouring his own family, yet if that had not been so, the co-trustee leaves it with the solicitor-trustee, by whose negligence (I use no harsher word) all this evil, in a great degree, has arisen.
>
> Therefore, the Lord Chancellor, in giving his decision, relies upon the fact of the trustee being a solicitor. In *Thompson v Finch* a right was conceded to prove against the estate of the deceased trustee for the full loss sustained; but it appears that in this case also he was a solicitor, and that he really took this money to himself, for he mixed it with his own money, and invested it on a mortgage, and therefore it was held that the trustee was entitled to indemnity from the estate of the co-trustee, who was a solicitor. This was affirmed in the Court of Appeal; and the Court of Appeal took so strong a view of the conduct of the solicitor that both of the judges concurred in thinking that he ought to be called on to show cause why he should not be struck off the rolls. Of course, where one trustee has got the money into his own hands, and made use of it, he will be liable to his co-trustee to give him an indemnity. Now I think it wrong to lay down any limitation of the circumstances under which one trustee would be held liable to the other for indemnity, both having been held liable to the *cestui que* trust; but so far as cases have gone at present, relief has

34 (1856) 25 LJ Ch 697.

35 (1856) LJ Ch 681.

only been granted against a trustee who has himself got the benefit of the breach of trust, or between whom and his co-trustees there has existed a relation which will justify the court in treating him as solely liable for the breach of trust ...

Miss Hughes was the active trustee and Mr Edwards did nothing, and in my opinion it would be laying down a wrong rule to hold that where one trustee acts honestly, though erroneously, the other trustee is to be held entitled to indemnity who by doing nothing neglects his duty more than the acting trustee. That Miss Hughes made an improper investment is true, but she acted honestly, and intended to the best she could, and believed that the property was sufficient security for the money, although she made no inquiries about their being leasehold houses. In my opinion the money was lost just as much by the default of Mr Edwards as by the innocent though erroneous action of his co-trustee, Miss Hughes. All the trustees were in the wrong, and every one is equally liable to indemnify the beneficiaries.

Fry LJ: It appears to me that on the first point arising in this appeal there is no case at all. The law of England, which has long existed, is that the husband is responsible for the breaches of trust of his wife. Upon the second point, I also agree with my brother Lord Justice Cotton. This part of the appeal is based upon the same notion that one trustee is liable to indemnify his co-trustee against loss or injury from his acts, but I cannot think that such liability exists, for if it did exist the books would be full of authorities bearing upon the point, and the courts would be crowded with litigation on the subject. It is well known that the authorities are extremely few, and the authorities which do exist do not favour the appellant's contention. It has been pointed out by Lord Justice Cotton that in each of the two cases cited the trustee who was held to be secondarily liable, and who had a right of indemnity, had been misled by his co-trustee, who was the solicitor to the trust, and had been proved to have been guilty of negligence in his duty as such solicitor. In my judgment the courts ought to be very jealous of raising any such implied liability as is insisted on, because if such existed it would act as an opiate upon the consciences of the trustees; so that instead of the *cestui que* trust having the benefit of several acting trustees, each trustee would be looking to the other or others for a right of indemnity, and so neglect the performance of his duties. Such a doctrine would be against the policy of the court in relation to trusts.

In the present case, in my judgment, the loss which has happened is the result of the combination of the action of Miss Hughes with the inaction of Mr Edwards. If Miss Hughes has made a mistake, it was through simple ignorance and want of knowledge, and if on the other hand Mr Edwards had used all the diligence which he ought to have done, I doubt whether any loss would have been incurred. The money might have been recovered before the property went down in value. I think, therefore, that it is not possible for Mr Edwards to obtain any relief, and I concur with my brethren that this appeal must be dismissed with costs.

A claim by one trustee against his co-trustee is now subject to the Civil Liability (Contribution) Act 1978 (see below, pp 884 *et seq*). Briefly, a trustee who is sued for breach of trust may claim a contribution from his co-trustee.

The court has a discretion to make a contribution order if such 'is just and equitable having regard to the extent of the [co-trustee's] responsibility for the damage in question'.

Duty to act personally

Generally speaking, a trustee is appointed by a settlor because of his personal qualities. He may possess a number of attributes which appeal to the settlor – such as honesty and integrity, reliability and business skill. It is expected that the trustee will act personally in the execution of his duties. The general rule is *delegatus non potest delegare.*

However, in the contemporary commercial climate the functions and needs for the proper administration of a trust have become increasingly complex, requiring specialised skill and knowledge. Accordingly, it is unrealistic to expect trustees to act personally in all matters relating to the trust. Trustees are entitled to appoint agents to perform acts in respect of the trust.

Section 23(1) of the Trustee Act 1925 lays down the general rule thus:

> Trustees or personal representatives may, instead of acting personally, employ and pay an agent. Whether a solicitor, banker, stockbroker or other person, to transact any business or do any act required to be transacted or done in the execution of the trust, or the administration of the testator's or intestate's estate, including the receipt and payment of money, and should be entitled to be allowed and paid all charges and expenses so incurred, and shall not be responsible for the default of any such agent if employed in good faith.

Thus, trustees may appoint agents in order to transact trust business even if the trustees themselves could have properly conducted the transaction. Of course, the trustees are required to exercise care in making the appointment and are entitled to pay the agent for his services.

Fry v Tapson (1884) 28 Ch D 268, HC

In this case, trustees employed a solicitor to effect a mortgage in respect of trust property and directed the solicitor to appoint a surveyor to value the property. The surveyor appointed had no local experience and stood to gain £75 commission if the mortgage went through. The property proved insufficient security for the loan and loss resulted to the trust. In an action for breach of trust in failing to exercise care in appointing an agent, the court held that the trustees were liable and further observed that the solicitor acted outside the course of his authority.

> **Kay J:** No prudent man reading Mr Kerr's report of 1875 would have put the value of the property as a security for trust money higher than £7,000, and to lend £5,000 upon it was obviously rashly to disregard the ordinary rule. But the most incautious act was to employ Mr Kerr to value for the mortgagees, and to accept his report as a sufficient evidence of value.

> He was a London surveyor, not shown to have any of that local knowledge which was so important in this case, and his employment was inexpedient for that reason ... But then it has been argued, supposing his valuation to be excessive, and that it was improper to act upon any valuation by him, the trustees employed competent solicitors, who instructed Mr Kerr, and that this completely absolves them. And I have been pressed with the authority of *Speight v Gaunt*[36] and other cases as deciding this question in their favour.
>
> *Speight v Gaunt* did not lay down any new rule, but only illustrated a very old one, viz, that trustees acting according to the ordinary course of business, and employing agents as a prudent man of business would do on his own behalf, are not liable for the default of an agent so employed. But an obvious limitation of that rule is that the agent must not be employed out of the ordinary scope of his business. If a trustee employs an agent to do that which is not the ordinary business of such an agent, and he performs that unusual duty improperly, and loss is thereby occasioned, the trustee would not be exonerated.
>
> Suppose in *Speight v Gaunt* the trustee had exercised no discretion as to the choice of a broker, but had left that to his solicitors, who had employed a man known to them to be untrustworthy, would the trustee have been exonerated? In my opinion clearly not, because he would have delegated to his solicitors that which was not properly the business of the solicitors, but a matter as to which his own judgment should have been exercised.
>
> Now, is it part of the ordinary business of a solicitor to choose a valuer for trustees intending to invest trust money on mortgage? To take Lord Hardwicke's words in *Ex p Belchier*,[37] is that a case 'where trustees act by other hands, either from necessity or conformable to the common usage of mankind'? I should suppose not. But the matter is not left in any doubt. Some eminent solicitors have been called on behalf of the defendants, and they all agree that this is not the solicitor's business, but that if asked to name a valuer, the ordinary course is to submit a name or names to the trustees and to tell them everything which the solicitor knows to guide their choice, but to leave the choice to them ...

But, s 23(1) declares that the trustee 'shall not be responsible for the default of such agent if employed in good faith'. Furthermore, s 30(1) of the Trustee Act 1925 enacts that the trustee is answerable for his own acts, receipts, neglects or defaults and not for those of other persons 'unless the same happens through his own wilful default'. The question in issue is, to what extent may a trustee be liable for the acts of an agent if the latter was appointed in good faith? In other words, what is meant by the phrase 'wilful default'?'

In the leading case *Re Vickery*,[38] the expression was described as involving 'a consciousness of negligence or breach of duty or recklessness'. In this case,

36 (1883) 9 AC 1.

37 (1754) Amb 218.

38 [1931] 1 Ch 572.

the defendant, an executor appointed a solicitor to wind up an estate. Subsequently, a beneficiary told the defendant that the solicitor had twice been suspended from practice. This was true but he was put back on the register. The beneficiary asked the executor to appoint another solicitor but this request was refused. The solicitor ultimately absconded with moneys belonging to the estate. In an action brought against the executor, Maugham J held that the agent was appointed validly in good faith and the defendant was not liable for wilful default because he did not act with the intention to commit a breach nor did he act recklessly in the sense of not caring whether his act constituted a breach or not.

Although the *Vickery* test has been subjected to severe criticism, in *Re Lucking* (cited above, p 769), Cross J decided that the trustee retains his duty of care and may be liable for breach of trust if he does not act like a prudent man of business in supervising the actions of the agent.

Re Lucking's Will Trusts [1968] 1 WLR 866, HC

> **Cross J**: Counsel relied on the decision in *Re Vickery*. Maugham J held that s 23 of the Trustee Act 1925 empowered the executor to employ the solicitor for the purpose in question in the first instance and that as s 30 of the Act provides, *inter alia*, that a trustee shall not be liable for the defaults of any person with whom any trust money or securities may be distributed unless the resulting loss happens through his own wilful default. The executor in the case before him would only be liable if he was guilty of wilful default. I see no reason whatever to think that Maugham J would have considered that a person employed by a trustee to manage a business owned by the trust was a person with whom trust money or securities were deposited within the meaning of s 30. In support of the proposition that directors are only liable for 'wilful default' counsel referred to the *City Equitable* case,[39] but there one of the company's articles provided that directors should only be liable for 'wilful default'. Romer J made it clear in his judgment that but for that article he would have held some of the directors liable in some matters for negligence falling short of 'wilful default'. In my view, 'wilful default' does not enter into the picture in this case at all. The conduct of the defendant trustees is, I think, to be judged by the standard applied in *Speight v Gaunt*,[40] namely, that a trustee is only bound to conduct the business of the trust in such a way as an ordinary prudent man would conduct a business of his own.

Under s 30(2) of the Trustee Act, a trustee is entitled to claim a refund from the trust property for expenses incurred in relation to the trust (see below, p 828).

Other examples of occasions when agents may be appointed under statutory power are:

39 [1925] Ch 407.

40 (1883) 9 AC 1.

- *Section 23(2) of the Trustee Act 1925*: trustees or personal representatives are given the power to appoint agents to deal with property situated abroad.
- *Section 23(3) of the Trustee Act 1925*: a trustee may appoint a solicitor or banker to be his agent in order to receive and give a discharge for any trust moneys.
- *Section 25 of the Trustee Act 1925*: empowers a trustee to delegate by a power of attorney all his powers and discretions for a period not exceeding twelve months.
- *Section 25(1) of the Trustee Act 1925* provides that:

  > ... notwithstanding any rule of law or equity to the contrary, a trustee may, by power of attorney, delegate for a period not exceeding 12 months the execution or exercise of all or any of the trusts, powers and discretions vested in him as trustee either alone or jointly with any other person or persons.

  The trustees delegating their powers within s 25(1) of the 1925 Act retain liability for the acts and omissions of their agent. Thus, the breaches of duties committed by the agent appointed under s 25(1) are attributable to the delegating trustee (contrast s 23 of the Trustee Act 1925 above, p 774).
- *Section 25(5) of the Trustee Act 1925* provides:

  > The donor of a power of attorney given under this section shall be liable for the acts and defaults of the donee in the same manner as if they were the acts or defaults of the donor.

Delegation under the Trusts of Land and Appointment of Trustees Act 1996

Section 9 of the 1996 Act enacts that trustees of land may delegate any of their 'powers in relation to the land' to adult beneficiaries who are currently entitled to 'interests in possession'. The trustees' powers in respect of land and an interest in possession require some elucidation.

The 'powers of trustees in respect of land' are enacted in s 6 of the 1996 Act, which states that these powers are equivalent to 'all the powers of an absolute owner', in accordance with the rules of law and equity. This includes the power to transfer land included in the trust to an adult beneficiary or beneficiaries who are solely entitled, whether or not they have requested it (s 6(2)). This may effectively terminate the trust. If the land is conveyed to more than one beneficiary, the beneficiaries will, in turn, become trustees of a trust of land. The trustees' powers include the power to purchase land as an investment, or as a home for a beneficiary, or for any other reason (s 6(4)). The trustees have the power to reinvest the proceeds of sale of land or other assets in which the proceeds have been invested, in purchasing the legal estate in other land (ss 6(3) and 17(3)).

In exercising their powers, the trustees are required to have regard to the rights of the beneficiaries and are obliged to observe any rules of law and equity. Thus, the trustees may not favour or prejudice the interest of any beneficiary when exercising their powers. The trustees have a general duty to consult, so far as is practicable, adult beneficiaries with interests in possession, and give effect to their wishes (or of the majority of them, according to their combined interests), insofar as this is consistent with the general interest of the trust (s 11(1)). The latter duty is excluded in respect of a power under s 6(2) to convey the trust land to an adult beneficiary absolutely entitled.

The powers included in s 6 relate only to a trust of land and not to any personal property, for example, s 6 is applicable to freehold land (but not shares) held by T1 and T2 upon trust for A for life, remainder to B and C equally. These powers enacted in s 6 may be amended or excluded by the settlement, or made subject to obtaining the consent of any person (s 8). Thus, the settlor may prevent any dealing with the land (although this could be challenged under s 14). In the case of charitable trusts, the trustees' powers may not be amended or excluded, but they may be made subject to obtaining consent.

An 'interest in possession in land' as distinct from 'an interest in remainder', on general principles, involves a present right to present possession of the land or a right to the income from the land, for example, the interest in land of a life tenant, as opposed to the interest of the remainderman. It follows that the interest of an object under a discretionary trust is not a vested interest and certainly not an interest in possession. Emphasis is placed on the expression, 'right'. A beneficiary has a right in possession if he is entitled to demand the property subject to the right. If the trustees are entitled to decide whether or not to pay the sum over to the beneficiary, the beneficiary does not have a right to possess, see *Re Pilkington* (below). But, there is no reason why the settlor cannot expressly include the relevant powers of the trustees in respect of land, or some of these powers, in the trust instrument.

Delegation of the powers of trustees under s 9 of the 1996 Act is by power of attorney (which cannot be an enduring power of attorney). All the trustees, jointly, are required to join in the delegation, which may be for an indefinite or fixed time. The trustees are not liable for the acts of the delegate, unless they did not exercise reasonable care in deciding to delegate their powers to a beneficiary or beneficiaries (s 9(8)). Thus, if the trustees failed to exercise reasonable care in deciding to delegate their powers, they will be jointly and severally liable for any act or default of the delegate-beneficiary. But, assuming reasonable care had been taken by the trustees of land in deciding to delegate their powers, there is no duty on the part of the trustees, imposed by the 1996 Act, to supervise the delegate. The delegate is liable for his acts as if he were the trustee, but he is not a trustee in any other sense. The effect is that the delegate, 'pseudo-trustee', cannot, in turn, delegate his functions and his receipt of capital money will not discharge the purchaser (s 9(7)).

Revocation

A power of attorney (through which the delegation is required to be made) is required to be executed by all the trustees jointly. Unless the power of attorney is stated to be irrevocable and is to secure a mortgage or similar security, it may be revoked by any one trustee. It may also be revoked by the appointment of a new trustee (s 9(3)). The delegation is also revoked in respect of a delegate who ceases to be beneficially entitled to an interest in possession under the trust. Likewise, in respect of a delegation to a number of beneficiaries, if one or more ceases to be entitled beneficially to an interest in possession, the delegation is revoked in respect of each of the delegates whose interest ceases, but the delegation remains valid with respect to the remaining beneficiaries. The position remains the same whether the powers are exercisable jointly or separately (s 9(5)).

Protection of purchasers from delegate

In respect of land, where a person deals with the delegate in good faith in the belief that the trustees were entitled to delegate to that person, it is presumed that the trustees were entitled to delegate to that person, unless the purchaser had knowledge at the time of the transaction that the trustees were not entitled to delegate to that person (s 9(2)). 'Knowledge,' for these purposes, has not been defined in the legislation, but it is submitted that, since we are concerned here with a proprietary interest, any type of cognisance will suffice for these purposes, even constructive knowledge.

Where further transactions have taken place in relation to a relevant plot of land since the first transaction by the delegate, a subsequent purchaser in good faith is entitled to rely on a statutory declaration made by the first or subsequent purchasers, before, or within three months after, completion of the most recent purchase. Under s 9, such transaction is treated as giving rise to a 'conclusive presumption'. The declaration is required to state that the first or subsequent purchaser dealt in good faith and without notice that the trustees were not entitled to make the delegation.

Exclusion clauses

On analogy with the law of contract, exclusion clauses which are validly inserted in trust instruments may have the effect of limiting the liability of trustees. Much depends on the wording of such clauses. *Prima facie*, any ambiguities inherent in such clauses are construed against the trustees. Such clauses are not, without more, void on public policy grounds. Moreover, provided the clause does not purport to exclude the basic minimum duties of the trustees, it may not be construed as being void for repugnancy to the trust. Some of the minimum duties which may not be excluded are the duties of honesty, good faith and acting for the benefit of the beneficiaries.

Armitage v Nurse and Others [1997] 3 WLR 1046, CA

By a settlement made on 11 October 1984, the income from a farm was held by trustees upon trust to accumulate until the plaintiff, Paula (then aged 17), attained the age of 25. Thereafter, the trustees were required to pay the income to Paula until she attained the age of 40. On attaining that age, Paula became entitled to the capital, subject to gifts over in the event of her death under that age. Clause 15 of the settlement (which was properly incorporated) exempted the trustees from liability for any loss or damage to the income or capital of the fund 'unless such loss or damage shall be caused by his [their] own *actual fraud*'. The plaintiff brought an action against the trustees alleging breaches of trust committed by them. The tenor of the claim involved a deliberate or reckless course of conduct on the part of the trustees to disregard the interests of Paula and subordinate them to the interests of family members who were not objects of the trust. The judge decided that the defendants were absolved from liability by virtue of clause 15 and that the claim was not statute-barred. The judge also decided that the trustees would be deprived of 20% of their costs and they were barred from recovering their costs from the trust fund.

The plaintiff appealed to the Court of Appeal to set aside the judge's declaration regarding clause 15 and the defendants cross-appealed from the judge's order as to costs.

Held, dismissing the plaintiff's appeal and allowing the trustees' cross-appeal, by the Court of Appeal, that:

- on analogy with the law of contract, it was open to the parties to a settlement to exclude or restrict their liability for breach of trust;
- on construction of the clause the expression, 'actual fraud' will be given its literal meaning. 'Actual fraud' involves an intention on the part of the trustee to pursue a course of action, either knowing that it is contrary to the interests of the beneficiaries or being recklessly indifferent whether it is contrary to their interests or not. The word,'actual', was deliberately selected by the settlor and was clearly distinguishable from 'constructive or equitable fraud'. In *Derry v Peek* (1889) 14 App Cas 337, the House of Lords established that nothing short of a fraudulent intention in the strict sense will suffice for a case of deceit or fraud. This requires proof of dishonesty. Clause 15 of the settlement validly excluded 'constructive or equitable fraud'. This expression connotes some dealing by a fiduciary involving a risk that the fiduciary may have exploited his position to his own advantage. Examples include breach of fiduciary duties, undue influence, abuse of confidence, unconscionable bargains, the self dealing rule and making unauthorised profits with the aid of trust property. The word, 'fraud', does not mean deceit or dishonesty but connotes an abuse of the fiduciary's position. This concept is distinct from actual fraud. Indeed, the trustees' actionable liability was restricted to conduct leading to a breach of trust which was committed with a dishonest intention;

- certain types of conduct on the part of trustees which amounted to equitable fraud may not necessarily have been excluded by clause 15. As an illustration, a sale of Paula's trust property to one of the trustees would have been liable to be set aside. Clause 15 would not have capable of protecting the purchasing trustee because Paula's claim in these circumstances would not be dependent on 'loss or damage' to the trust. The purchasing trustee could have obtained nothing more than a defeasible title. But, the clause may be sufficient to protect the other trustees, provided that they acted in good faith;
- the trustees' conduct is not dishonest if they act in breach of trust but in good faith and in the honest belief that they were acting in the interest of the beneficiaries. The trustees may commit a breach of trust which is deliberate or intentional but may not necessarily amount to a fraudulent breach. The trustees may consciously act beyond their powers (for example, an investment which they know to be unauthorised) but, if this is done in good faith and in the honest belief that they are acting in the interests of the beneficiaries, their conduct may not be fraudulent;
- the exclusion clause was not repugnant to the trust or contrary to public policy;
- the plaintiff was allowed to examine the trust documents and investigate the trustees' management;
- s 21(1)(a) of the Limitation Act 1980 was limited to cases of fraudulent breaches of trust without a time limit. This was not evident on the facts of this case;
- the general limitation period for actions for breach of trust is six years from the date that the breach occurred: see s 21(3) of the Limitation Act 1980. However, a cause of action does not accrue in favour of a beneficiary entitled to a future interest in the trust property until the interest falls into possession, see the proviso to s 21(3) of the Limitation Act 1980. Under the settlement, prior to Paula attaining the age of 25, the trustees were under a duty to accumulate the income subject to a power to pay the same to Paula. Thus, Paula did not have a present right to the capital or income. She had merely a right to require the trustees to consider from time to time whether to accumulate the income or apply it for her benefit. Accordingly, she did not have an interest in possession. Paula enjoyed a future interest until she attained the age of 25. Consequently, her claim was not statute-barred;
- the trustees were entitled to a lien on the trust fund for the costs of successfully defending an action for breach of trust. Thus, there was no basis for the judge's order depriving them of this entitlement. Accordingly, the trustees were entitled to recover their costs from the trust fund.

Millett LJ: The main questions which arise in this appeal are concerned with the true construction of a trustee exemption clause in a settlement and the legitimate scope of such clauses in English law.

The expression, 'actual fraud', in clause 15 is not used to describe the common tort of deceit. As the judge appreciated, it simply means dishonesty. I accept the formulation put forward by Mr Hill on behalf of the respondents which (as I have slightly modified it) is that it:

> ... connotes, at the minimum, an intention on the part of the trustee to pursue a particular course of action, either knowing that it is contrary to the interests of the beneficiaries or being recklessly indifferent whether it is contrary to their interests or not.

The permitted scope of trustee exemption clauses

It is submitted on behalf of Paula that a trustee exemption clause which purports to exclude all liability except for actual fraud is void, either for repugnancy or as contrary to public policy. There is some academic support for the submission (notably an article by Professor Matthews, 'The efficacy of trustee exemption clauses in English law' [1989] Conv 42 and *Hanbury and Martin's Modern Equity,* 14th edn, 1993, pp 473–74) that liability for gross negligence cannot be excluded, but this is not the view taken in *Underhill and Hayton's Law of Trusts and Trustees,* 15th edn, 1995, pp 560–61 (where it appears to be taken only because the editor confusingly uses the term 'gross negligence' to mean reckless indifference to the interests of the beneficiaries). In its consultation paper, *Fiduciary Duties and Regulatory Rules: A Summary,* 1992, Law Com No 124, London: HMSO, para 3.3.41, the Law Commission states:

> Beyond this, trustees and fiduciaries cannot exempt themselves from liability for fraud, bad faith and wilful default. It is not, however, clear whether the prohibition on exclusion of liability for 'fraud' in this context only prohibits the exclusion of common law fraud or extends to the much broader doctrine of equitable fraud. It is also not altogether clear whether the prohibition on the exclusion of liability for 'wilful default' also prohibits exclusion of liability for gross negligence although we incline to the view that it does.

This passage calls for two comments. First, the expression 'wilful default' is used in the cases in two senses. A trustee is said to be accountable on the footing of wilful default when he is accountable not only for money which he has in fact received, but also for money which he could, with reasonable diligence, have received. It is sufficient that the trustee has been guilty of want of ordinary prudence: see, for example, *In re Chapman, Cocks v Chapman* [1896] 2 Ch 763. In the context of a trustee exclusion clause, however, such as s 30 of the Trustee Act 1925, it means a deliberate breach of trust: *In re Vickery, Vickery v Stephens* [1931] 1 Ch 572. The decision has been criticised but it is in line with earlier authority: see *Lewis v Great Western Railway Co* (1877) 3 QBD 195; *In re Trusts of Leeds City Brewery Ltd's Debenture Stock Trust Deed, Leeds City Brewery Ltd v Platts (Note)* [1925] Ch 532 and *In re City Equitable Fire Insurance Co Ltd* [1925] Ch 407. Nothing less than conscious and wilful misconduct is sufficient. The trustee must be:

> ... conscious that, in doing the act which is complained of or in omitting to do the act which it is said he ought to have done, he is committing a breach of his duty, or is recklessly careless whether it is a breach of his duty or not [see *In re Vickery*];

A trustee who is guilty of such conduct either consciously takes a risk that loss will result, or is recklessly indifferent whether it will or not. If the risk eventuates he is personally liable. But if he consciously takes the risk in good faith and with the best intentions, honestly believing that the risk is one which ought to be taken in the interests of the beneficiaries, there is no reason why he should not be protected by an exemption clause which excludes liability for wilful default.

Secondly, the Law Commission was considering the position of fiduciaries as well as trustees, and in such a context, it is sensible to consider the exclusion of liability for so called equitable fraud. But it makes no sense in the present context. The nature of equitable fraud may be collected from the speech of Viscount Haldane LC, in *Nocton v Lord Ashburton* [1914] AC 932, p 953, and *Snell's Equity*, 29th edn, 1990, pp 550–51. It covers breach of fiduciary duty, undue influence, abuse of confidence, unconscionable bargains and frauds on powers. With the sole exception of the last, which is a technical doctrine in which the word 'fraud' merely connotes excess of *vires*, it involves some dealing by the fiduciary with his principal and the risk that the fiduciary may have exploited his position to his own advantage. In *Earl of Aylesford v Morris* (1873) LR 8 Ch App 484, pp 490–91, Lord Selborne LC said: 'Fraud does not here mean deceit or circumvention; it means an unconscientious use of the power arising out of these circumstances and conditions ...' A trustee exemption clause, such as clause 15 of the settlement does not purport to exclude the liability of the fiduciary in such cases. Suppose, for example, that one of the respondents had purchased Paula's land at a proper price from his fellow trustees. The sale would be liable to be set aside. Clause 15 would not prevent this. This is not because the purchasing trustee would have been guilty of equitable fraud, but because by claiming to recover the trust property (or even equitable compensation) Paula would not be suing in respect of any 'loss or damage' to the trust. Her right to recover the land would not depend on proof of loss or damage. Her claim would succeed even if the sale was at an undervalue; the purchasing trustee could never obtain more than a defeasible title from such transaction. But clause 15 would be effective to exempt his fellow trustees from liability for making good any loss which the sale had occasioned to the trust estate, so long as they had acted in good faith and in what they honestly believed was Paula's interests.

It is a bold submission that a clause taken from one standard precedent book and to the same effect as a clause found in another, included in a settlement drawn by chancery counsel and approved by counsel acting for an infant settlor and by the court on her behalf, should be so repugnant to the trusts or contrary to public policy that it is liable to be set aside at her suit. But the submission has been made and we must consider it. In my judgment it is without foundation.

> I accept the submission made on behalf of Paula that there is an irreducible core of obligations owed by the trustees to the beneficiaries and enforceable by them which is fundamental to the concept of a trust. If the beneficiaries have no rights enforceable against the trustees there are no trusts. But I do not accept the further submission that these core obligations include the duties of skill and care, prudence and diligence. The duty of the trustees to perform the trusts honestly and in good faith for the benefit of the beneficiaries is the minimum necessary to give substance to the trusts, but in my opinion it is sufficient.
>
> It is, of course, far too late to suggest that the exclusion in a contract of liability for ordinary negligence or want of care is contrary to public policy. What is true of a contract must be equally true of a settlement.

Paul Matthews, in an article entitled 'The efficacy of trustee exemption clauses in English law' (1989) Conv 42, subscribes to the view that a trustee exemption clause may effectively exclude liability (vis à vis beneficiaries) in relation to want of ordinary prudence, but may not do so for fraud, intentional wrongdoing or gross negligence.

Mr Matthews summarises the position in English law as follows:

(1) It is unclear whether s 30(1) of the Trustee Act 1925 goes so far as to protect a trustee against liability for want of ordinary prudence: it does if *Re Vickery* (1931) is correct.

(2) It is not free from doubt whether an exemption clause may confer protection greater than that contained in s 30.

(3) It is clear that neither liability for fraud nor intentional wrongdoing nor duties leading to such liability can be validly excluded, nor powers to commit acts otherwise giving rise to such liability validly included.

(4) It is very likely that neither liability for gross negligence nor duties leading to such liability can be validly excluded, nor powers to commit acts otherwise giving rise to such liability validly included (Scots law and American law are clear on this point, and may even go further).

(5) It is arguable that any otherwise effective exemption clause is, in cases of professional trustees appointed by the settlor, subject to the provisions of the Unfair Contract Terms Act 1977 and, in particular, to the test of 'reasonableness'.

(6) It will not be easy for a professional trustee to demonstrate the 'reasonableness' of his exemption clause, should he be called to do so.

(7) An otherwise enforceable exemption clause may still fail to have effect, if imposed in breach of fiduciary duty or through undue influence.

(8) In any event, such exemption clauses are always construed strictly against trustees.

William Goodhart, in 'Trustee exemption clauses and the Unfair Contract Terms Act 1977' [1980] Conv 333, has argued that UCTA is capable of applying to trustee exemption clauses. Assuming that the clause is incorporated under a contract of 'business liability', which Goodhart suggests would apply to corporations and 'professional' trustees, there are a number of limitations envisaged. The Act has no application to trustees appointed by the court under s 41 of the Trustee Act 1925. In addition, the exemption clause is required to satisfy the test of 'reasonableness' referred to in s 2(3) of UCTA 1977. Goodhart submits that, in the ordinary case, the trustee will be hard pressed to persuade the court that an exemption clause is reasonable. Trustees are adequately protected by s 30 of the Trustee Act 1925 and s 61 of the Trustee Act 1925 affords them some measure of relief.

John Stannard, in an article entitled 'Wilful default' [1979] Conv 345, examines the development of the interpretation placed on the expression 'wilful default', as used in s 30 of the Trustee Act 1925. Initially, there were two interpretations of the expression:

(a) the orthodox view, namely:

> ... consciousness that in doing the act which is complained of, or in omitting to do the act which it is said he ought to have done, he is committing a breach of his duty, or is recklessly careless whether it is a breach of his duty or not ...;

(b) the technical view originally applied by courts of equity included some degree of neglect.

The equitable jurisdiction connected with the interpretation of wilful default was, in respect of (a), an account, and (b), an indemnity clause. In an action for an account owing to the wilful default of the defendant, the latter was required to account not only in respect of the profits actually made but also in relation to notional profits, that is,profits that he would have made but for his wilful default. The approach adopted by the courts was insular, in that failure on the part of the defendant to discharge a number of duties made him liable for 'wilful default'. Whereas, with respect to trustee indemnity clauses 'wilful default' includes negligence, that is, a failure to act as a prudent man of business would act. In other words, a trustee is not liable for the acts and defaults of agents unless he (trustee) failed to act as a prudent man of business with regard to the activities of the agent, see *Speight v Gaunt*. Stannard examines another group of cases which he calls 'contract cases'. Prior to 1925, he contends, 'the meaning of 'wilful default' depended on its context, but the inclination was probably to treat the expression in a contract as denoting deliberate misconduct.

In *City Equitable Fire Insurance* [1925] Ch 407 (a company law case), Romer J, at first instance, interpreted 'wilful default' in the contract sense. He decided that not all breaches, including negligent breaches, amounted to wilful default. The defendant is required to be conscious of the commission of the breaches alleged. The Court of Appeal affirmed the reasoning of Romer J. Stannard remarks, 'the decision cannot be criticised. But in failing to recognise the technical meaning of "wilful default" the court went sadly astray'. In *Re Vickery*, Maugham J adopted the definition given by Romer J in *Re City Equitable*, in the context of trustees employing agents.

Stannard concludes thus:

> ... 'wilful default' is used in two senses. Its technical definition would be something on the lines of 'failure to do what is reasonable' and would involve no intentional misconduct. What is reasonable will depend on the circumstances – the liability of a trustee for his agents is not the same as that of a mortgagee in possession, or an executor. But the liabilities of these parties are well settled by law and should not be tinkered with by any slavish adherence to the words 'wilful default'. This technical meaning applies in the trustee indemnity clause and in the account on the footing of wilful default.

Gerard McCormack, in 'The liability of trustees for gross negligence' [1998] Conv 100, examines the English and Scottish authorities on trustee exemption clauses, referred to by Millett LJ in *Armitage v Nurse*. These are *Wilkins v Hogg* (1861) 31 LJ Ch 41; *Knox v Mackinnon* (1888) 13 App Cas 753; *Pass v Dundas* (1880) 43 LT 665; *Rae v Meek* (1889) 14 App Cas 558; and *Clarke v Clarke's Trustees* [1925] SC 693. Millett LJ, in *Armitage v Nurse*, referred to these authorities as decisions on the true construction of the particular clauses which were in common form at the time. McCormack questions the correctness of Millett LJ's interpretation of these cases and responds thus:

> It may be straining things a little to say that the judicial hostility to clauses exempting trustees from liability for gross negligence manifested therein reflects simply a principle of construction.

McCormack concludes with the following suggestions:

(1) the *contra proferentem* principle of construction ought to be adopted in construing ambiguous exemption clauses. He states:

> The party proferring the clause is purporting to relieve himself from general legal liabilities that would otherwise apply and on this basis alone the clause should be accorded a narrow construction;

(2) trustee exemption clauses ought to be treated differently from contractual exemption clauses, because trustees are fiduciaries. He states:

> The trustee is placed under an obligation to safeguard the interests of trust beneficiaries. That is the essence of trusteeship. Clauses in a trust instrument which permit the trustee to engage in subjective wrongdoing to the detriment of the beneficiaries are at variance with the key concept of trusteeship and cannot be recognised because of this;

(3) Parliament ought to enact legislation in order to control trustee exemption clauses. McCormack writes:

> Perhaps the clearest path out of the thicket is to follow the lines suggested by Millett LJ in *Armitage v Nurse* and to advocate an extension of the legislative solution. Precisely what sort of legislative solution is envisaged? Should one adopt the approach found in s 33 of the Pensions Act 1995, which subjects all clauses excluding liability for negligent investment decisions to an invalidating taint? A less draconian solution would be to subject trustee exemption clauses to a requirement of reasonableness. It is submitted that this is the best approach.

Duty to provide accounts and information

Owing to the nature of the fiduciary relationship of trustees, a duty is imposed on them to keep proper accounts for the trust. In pursuance of this objective, the trustees may employ an agent (an accountant) to draw up the trust accounts. The beneficiaries are entitled to inspect the accounts but if they need copies they are required to pay for these from their own resources. Where there is a succession of beneficial interests, the accounts should differentiate between income and capital. The income beneficiaries would be entitled to inspect the 'full accounts'. The remainderman is only entitled to information relating to the 'capital accounts'.

There is no general requirement that the accounts be audited annually but, by virtue of s 22(4) of the Trustee Act 1925, the trustees in their discretion may have the accounts examined by an independent auditor every three years and may pay the costs out of income or capital.

In addition, the beneficiaries are entitled to be informed about matters concerning the trust. In order to have such information at hand a prudent trustee would maintain a trust diary in which decisions and other relevant facts are recorded. Documents created in the course of the administration of the trust are trust documents and are *prima facie* the property of the beneficiaries and available for inspection. Indeed, trust documents were described by Salmon LJ in *Re Marquess of Londonderry's Settlement*[41] as possessing the following characteristics:

(i) they are documents in the possession of the trustees as trustees;

(ii) they contain information about the trust, which the beneficiaries are entitled to know;

(iii) the beneficiaries have a proprietary interest in the documents, and, accordingly, are entitled to see them.

The difficulty faced by trustees concern the circumstances when they have a discretion and are not required to give reasons for their decisions but *bona fide* record these reasons in a trust document. An aggrieved beneficiary may be entitled to challenge the decisions of the trustees by resorting to his right to inspect the documents. If the grounds for trustees' decisions are known, the court will consider them. In the above case the court adopted an approach which to some extent preserved the confidential nature of the trustees' discretion.

Re Marquess of Londonderry's Settlement [1965] Ch 918, CA

In this case, an object under a discretionary trust was dissatisfied with the manner in which trustees exercised their discretions. She sought to obtain

41 [1965] Ch 918.

copies of the agenda and minutes of meetings, correspondence between trustees and between the trustees and solicitors in connection with the administration of the trust. The trustees were reluctant to allow her to see the documents for this would have revealed the reasons for their decisions which they claimed were confidential. The trustees applied to the court for a declaration as to which, if any of the following documents they were bound to disclose:

(a) the minutes of trust meetings;

(b) agendas and other documents prepared for the purpose of such meetings;

(c) correspondence concerning the administration of the trust between:

  (i) the trustees and other fiduciaries (called appointors, that is, named persons who were required to consent to an appointment in special circumstances);

  (ii) the trustees and the solicitors; and

  (iii) the trustees and the beneficiaries.

The court held in favour of the trustees. Their right to exercise their discretion in confidence prevailed over the beneficiary's right to inspect, for the disclosure of such documents had the potential to cause 'family strife'. Indeed, the court went so far as to say that if trust documents contain confidential information which ought not to be disclosed, the relevant portions of the documents may be covered up. On the facts, the correspondence between the trustees were not trust documents and were not available for inspection.

> **Harman LJ:** The court is really required here to resolve two principles that come into conflict, or at least apparent conflict. The first is that ... trustees exercising a discretionary power are not bound to disclose to the beneficiaries the reasons actuating them in coming to a decision. This is a long standing principle and rests largely, I think, on the view that nobody could be called upon to accept a trusteeship involving the exercise of a discretion unless, in the absence of bad faith, he were not liable to have his motives or his reasons called in question either by the beneficiaries or by the court. To this there is added a rider, namely, that if trustees do give reasons, their soundness can be considered by the court ...
>
> It would seem on the face of it that there is no reason why this principle should be confined to decisions orally arrived at and should not extend to a case, like the present, where, owing to the complexity of the trust and the large sums involved, the trustees, who act subject to the consent of another body called the appointors, have brought into existence various written documents, including, in particular, agenda for and minutes of their meetings from time to time held in order to consider distributions made of the fund and its income. It is here that the conflicting principle is said to emerge. All these documents, it is argued, came into existence for the purpose of the trust and are in the possession of the trustees as such and are, therefore, trust documents, the property of the beneficiaries, and as such open to them to inspect ...

Apart from this, the defendant relied on certain observations in *O'Rourke v Darbishire*.[42] The decision was that the plaintiff was not entitled to the production of what were called the 'trust documents', and I find Lord Parmoor making this observation:

> A *cestui que* trust, in an action against his trustees, is generally entitled to the production for inspection of all documents relating to the affairs of the trust. It is not material for the present purpose whether this right is to be regarded as a paramount proprietary right in the *cestui que* trust or as a right to be enforced under the law of discovery.

Lord Wrenbury says:

> If the plaintiff is right in saying that he is a beneficiary, and if the documents are documents belonging to the executors as executors, he has a right to access to the documents which he desires to inspect upon what has been called in the judgments in this case a proprietary right. The beneficiary is entitled to see all the trust documents because they are trust documents and because he is a beneficiary. They are in a sense his own. Action or no action, he is entitled to access to them. This has nothing to do with discovery. The right to discovery is a right to see someone else's documents. A proprietary right is a right to access to documents which are your own. No question of professional privilege arises in such a case. Documents containing professional advice taken by the executors as trustees contain advice taken by trustees for their *cestuis que* trust, and the beneficiaries are entitled to see them because they are beneficiaries.

General observations of this sort give very little guidance, for first they beg the question what are trust documents, and secondly their Lordships were not considering the point here that papers are asked for which bear on the question of the exercise of the trustees' discretion. In my judgment category (a) ... viz, the minutes of the meetings of the trustees ...; and part of (b) viz, agenda prepared for trustees' meetings, are, in the absence of an action impugning the trustees' good faith, documents which a beneficiary cannot claim the right to inspect. If the defendant is allowed to examine these, she will know at once the very matters which the trustees are not bound to disclose to her, namely, their motives and reasons. Trustees who wish to preserve their rights in this respect must either commit nothing to paper or destroy everything from meeting to meeting. Indeed, if the defendant be right, I doubt if the last course is open, for she must succeed, if at all, on the ground that the papers belong to her, and if so, the trustees have no right to destroy them.

I would hold that even if documents of this type ought properly to be described as trust documents, they are protected for the special reason which protects the trustees' deliberations on a discretionary matter from disclosure. If necessary, I hold that this principle overrides the ordinary rule. This is, in my judgment, no less in the true interest of the beneficiary than of the trustees. Again, if one of the trustees commits to paper his suggestions and circulates them among his co-trustees; or if inquiries are made in writing as to the

42 [1920] AC 581.

> circumstances of a member of the class; I decline to hold that such documents are trust documents, the property of the beneficiaries ... On the other hand, if the solicitor advising the trustees commits to paper an *aide memoire* summarising the state of the fund or of the family and reminding the trustees of past distributions and future possibilities, I think that must be a document which any beneficiary must be at liberty to inspect. It seems to me, therefore, that category (b) embraces documents on both sides of the line.
>
> As to (c), I cannot think that communications passing between individual trustees and appointors are documents in which beneficiaries have a proprietary right. On the other hand, as to category (ii), in general the letters of the trustees' solicitors to the trustees do seem to me to be trust documents in which the beneficiaries have a property. As to category (iii) I do not think letters to or from an individual beneficiary ought to be open to inspection by another beneficiary.

Duty to distribute to the right beneficiaries

It is an elementary principle of trust law that the trustees are required to distribute the trust property (income and/or capital) to the beneficiaries properly entitled to receive the same. Failure to distribute to the correct beneficiary subjects the trustees to liability for breach of trust, although in appropriate cases they may apply to the court for relief under s 61 of the Trustee Act 1925. Thus, in *Eaves v Hickson* (1861) 30 Beav 136, trustees were liable to make good sums wrongly paid to a beneficiary in reliance on a forged marriage certificate. Likewise, in *Re Hulkes* (1886) 33 Ch D 552, the trustees were liable for sums paid to the wrong beneficiaries based on an honest, but incorrect, construction of the trust instrument.

Where the trustee makes an overpayment of income or instalment of capital, he may recover the amount of the overpayment by adjusting the payments subsequently made to the same beneficiary. Where the payment is made to a person who is not entitled to receive the sum, the trustee has the right to recover the amount based on a quasi-contractual claim of money paid under a mistake of fact. Such claim will not succeed if the mistake was one of law. See *Re Diplock* [1947] Ch 716 (below, p 932). In *Woolwich Building Society v IRC (No 2)* [1992] 3 All ER 737, the House of Lords decided that, money paid by a member of the public to a public authority in the form of taxes paid, pursuant to an *ultra vires* demand by the authority, is *prima facie* recoverable by the member of the public as of right. An aggrieved beneficiary may, in addition to his right to sue the trustee, trace his property in the hands of the wrongly paid person (see below, p 900).

Where the trustees have a reasonable doubt as to the validity of claims of the beneficiaries, they may apply to the court for directions, and will be protected, provided that they act in accordance with those directions. The court has the power to make a '*Benjamin* order' (derived from the case, *Re*

Benjamin [1902] 1 Ch 723), authorising the distribution of the trust property without identifying all the beneficiaries and creditors. In addition, where the trustees cannot identify all the beneficiaries, they are entitled to pay the trust funds into court as a last resort, see *Re Gillingham Bus Disaster Fund* [1959] Ch 62 (see above, p 241). Where there is no good reason for a payment into court, the trustees may personally have to pay the costs of such an application.

Under s 27 of the Trustee Act 1925 (see below), a simplified form of distribution is allowed and, at the same time, the trustees or personal representatives are given protection from claims for breach of trust. The section permits the trustees (or personal representatives) to advertise for beneficiaries in an appropriate newspaper or gazette, and after the expiration of a period of time, not being less than two months, they are entitled to distribute the property to the beneficiaries of whom the trustees are aware. If the trustees comply with the requirements of s 27, they will not be liable for breach of trust at the instance of beneficiaries, of whom the trustees were unaware. However, the ignored beneficiaries are entitled to trace their property in the hands of the recipient. Finally, the section is incapable of being excluded or modified by the trust instrument.

Section 27 of the Trustee Act 1925 (as amended by the Trusts of Land and Appointment of Trustees Act 1996) provides:

> (1) With a view to the conveyance to or distribution among the persons entitled to any real or personal property, the trustees of a settlement, trustees of land, trustees for sale of personal property or personal representatives, may give notice by advertisement in the Gazette, and in a newspaper circulating in the district in which the land is situated, and such other like notices, including notices elsewhere than in England and Wales, as would, in any special case, have been directed by a court of competent jurisdiction in an action for administration, of their intention to make such conveyance or distribution as aforesaid, and requiring any person interested to send to the trustees or personal representatives within the time, not being less than two months, fixed in the notice or, where more than one notice is given, in the last of the notices, particulars of his claim in respect of the property or any part thereof to which the notice relates.
>
> (2) At the expiration of the time fixed by the notice, the trustees or personal representatives may convey or distribute the property or any part thereof to which the notice relates, to or among the persons entitled thereto, have regard only to claims, whether formal or not, of which the trustees or personal representatives then had notice and shall not, as respects the property so conveyed or distributed, be liable to any person of whose claim the trustees or personal representatives have not had notice at the time of conveyance or distribution; but nothing in this section:
>
> (a) prejudices the right of any person to follow the property, or any property representing the same, into the hands of any person, other than a purchaser, who may have received it; or

(b) frees the trustees or personal representatives from any obligation to make searches or obtain official certificates of search similar to those which an intending purchaser would be advised to make or obtain.

(3) This section applies notwithstanding anything to the contrary in the will or other instrument, if any, creating the trust.

Powers of investment

Trustees have an obligation to maintain the real value of trust funds and may need to consider investing the trust property. An 'investment' for these purposes refers to property which will produce an income yield, see *Re Wragg*.[43] So far, the courts have considered that the purchase of property for the purpose of pure capital appreciation without producing income will not constitute an investment, for example, a painting or land which does not produce rents. In *Re Power*,[44] the court decided that a power to invest in the purchase of freehold property did not authorise the purchase of a freehold house for the occupation of the beneficiary.

The trustees are required to consider the investment policy of the trust with the standard of care expected from an ordinary prudent man of business (see above, p 761). The powers of investment may exist in the trust instrument or may be implied by statute or the court may enlarge the power of the trustees.

Express power

A prudent settlor will include a wide investment clause in the trust instrument in order to give the trustees the maximum flexibility in the selection of investments. The modern approach of the courts is to construe investment clauses liberally.

In *Re Harari's Settlement*,[45] the issue concerned the effect of a clause in the trust instrument, to make such 'investments as the trustees may think fit'. The court decided that the words will be given their ordinary meaning without any restriction.

> **Jenkins J:** The question turns primarily on the meaning to be attached to the words 'in or upon such investments as to them may seem fit'. *Prima facie* those words mean what they say – that the trustees are not to be limited in any way by any statutory range of investments, but can invest in any investment which they may select as seeming to them a fit one for the money subject to the trusts of the settlement.

43 [1918–19] All ER 233.

44 [1947] Ch 572.

45 [1949] 1 All ER 430.

> It seems to me that I am left free to construe this settlement according to what I consider to be the natural and proper meaning of the words used in their context, and, so construing the words 'in or upon such investments as to them may seem fit', I see no justification for implying any restriction. I think the trustees have power, under the plain meaning of these words, to invest in any investments which they honestly think are desirable investments ... To hold otherwise would really be to read words into the settlement which are not there.
>
> The real ground, however, for my decision is the plain and ordinary meaning of the words 'in or upon such investments as to them may seem fit'. Having found nothing in the authorities to constrain me to construe those words otherwise than in accordance with their plain meaning, that is the meaning I propose to place on them.

Moreover, the settlor may authorise the trustees to purchase a dwelling house for the benefit of a beneficiary, thus overcoming the limitation that existed in *Re Power*. In addition, the settlor may impose an obligation on the trustees to invest exclusively in shares in a specified company or in any other specific investments. In such a case, the trustees will have no choice but to comply with the directions of the settlor.

Statutory power under the Trustee Investments Act 1961

Prior to this Act, the range of authorised trust investments was limited to 'fixed interest' investments which may be bought at the Post Office (referred to as the 'Statutory List' under s 1 of the Trustee Act 1925) and mortgages of land.

These investments took no account of inflation or the depreciation of sterling. What was needed was the authority to invest in stocks and shares which would give the trust a share in the company and compensation for the reduction in the value of sterling. This was to some extent effected by the Trustee Investments Act 1961 (TIA).

The structure of the Act is that it replaces the old 'Statutory List'. The new list of authorised investments is set out in the First Schedule to the Act comprising a threefold division of categories of investments namely, Pts I and II 'narrow range' investments and Pt III 'wider range' investments.

The investments detailed in Pt I 'narrow range' include Defence Bonds, National Savings Certificates and may be described as 'small savings' investments. Generally, these may be bought at the Post Office and there is no obligation on the trustees to seek advice before investing. The capital value of these investments do not fluctuate. Part II narrow range investments by and large correspond with the old Statutory List and include debentures in UK companies which comply with a number of conditions, fixed interest investments issued by local or public companies. Units of a gilt unit trust scheme were added to the list of investments by SI 1994/1908. The trustees are required to seek written advice (s 6(5)) from a person whom the trustees reasonably believe to be qualified to give it by reason of his ability and experience (s 6(4) of the TIA 1961 'proper advice is the advice of a person who is reasonably believed by the trustee to be qualified by his ability in and practical experience of financial matters; and such advice may be given by a person notwithstanding that he gives it in the course of his employment as an officer or servant'). The wider range investments created by Pt III of the First Schedule to the Act, include unit trusts and shares in certain UK companies and shares in building societies. Trustees are required to obtain and consider advice from suitable persons (see above, p 765) before making these investments: s 6(2) of the TIA 1961:

> Before exercising any power ... to invest in a manner specified in Pt II or III of the First Schedule or s 3(2) of this Act, a trustee shall obtain and consider proper advice on the question whether the investment is satisfactory ...

having regard to the need for diversification of the investments and the suitability to the trust of the relevant investments.

An authorised investment in shares and debentures in UK companies is required to satisfy the following conditions laid down in para (3) of Pt IV of the First Schedule, namely:

(1) the shares are required to be quoted on the stock exchange;

(2) the shares are required to be fully paid up or issued on terms that they will be fully paid up within nine months from the date of issue;

(3) the company has a total issued and paid up share capital of at least £1 m;

(4) the company is required to have paid a dividend in each of the preceding five years on all of its shares.

Division of the fund: s 2(1) of the Trustee Investments Act 1981

The scheme of the Act requires the trustees who wish to invest in wider range investments to value the fund and divide it into two unequal parts (three quarters and one quarter) (SI 1996/845) the narrower range and wider range parts. The Trustee Investment (Division of Trust Fund) Order 1996, which came into force on 11 May 1996, states:

> ... any division of the trust fund made in pursuance of s 2(1) of [The Trustee Investment Act 1961] shall be made so that the value of the wider range part at the time of the division bears to the then value of the narrower range part the proportion of three to one.

A valuation in writing from a person reasonably believed by the trustees to be qualified to make it, shall be conclusive evidence of the relevant fact: s 5(1) of the TIA 1961:

> If ... a trustee obtains, from a person reasonably believed by the trustee to be qualified to make it, a valuation in writing of any property, the valuation shall

> be conclusive in determining whether the division of the trust fund ... or any transfer or apportionment of property ... has been made'.

The division of the fund is permanent and the two parts are kept distinct. Three quarters of the fund may be invested entirely in wider range investments (Pt III of the First Schedule) or partly in wider range and partly in narrower range investments, that is, after the division of the fund there is no obligation on the trustees to invest the wider range part of the fund entirely in wider range investments, provided that a portion of the fund is so used. The remainder of the fund may only be invested in narrower range investments. Moreover, if property is transferred from either part of the fund to the other part, a 'compensating transfer' in the opposite direction is required to be made. Thus, if property from the narrower range part of the fund is transferred to the wider range part, a compensating transfer to the narrower range part is required to be made as soon as possible.

Section 2(1) provides:

> A trustee shall not have power ... to make or retain any wider-range investment unless the trust fund has been divided into two parts (the narrower-range part and the wider-range part), the parts being ... three quarters and one quarter in value at the time of the division ... and no property shall be transferred from one part of the fund to the other unless either:
>
> (a) the transfer is authorised ...; or
>
> (b) a compensating transfer is made at the same time.
>
> 'Compensating transfer' means a transfer in the opposite direction of property of equal value.

Accruals

If property accrues to the trustees as owners of property comprised in either part of the fund, it shall be treated as belonging to that fund, for example, a bonus issue of shares will belong to the fund which comprised the shares.

Withdrawals

Generally speaking, s 2(4) provides that a withdrawal of funds in the exercise of any power or duty of the trustees may be made from either part of the fund in the discretion of the trustees. This provision has the effect of abrogating the '75:25' rule but was inserted in the Act in order to give the trustees a greater latitude in performing their powers.

For example, if £500 is invested in narrower range investments and £1,500 in wider range investments and £600 is required to be paid by the trustees to a beneficiary by way of an advancement (under s 32 of the Trustee Act 1925, see below, pp 814 *et seq*), the trustees are at liberty to withdraw the amount from either part of the fund or three quarters and one quarter from each part without a compensating transfer.

However, if the trustees wish to withdraw funds in order to form a separate trust, the withdrawal may be made at the trustees' discretion, but the division of the fund of the new trust need not be on a '75:25' basis (assuming the trustees of the new trust wish to invest in wider range investments) but may be effected in the form of one of the following alternative modes:

(a) 75:25; or

(b) the same proportion to each other as the two corresponding parts of the original fund bore at the time of the appropriation, for example, 85:15; or

(c) in some intermediate proportion, for example, 80:20 (see s 4(3)).

Special range investments

Section 3(1) declares ,if property is acquired as a result of additional powers conferred on the trustees by the trust investment or the court, such property will comprise a 'special range' part of the fund. If the trustees wish to dispose of special range property without further investment in special range assets, the proceeds are required to be divided equally between the wider range and narrower range investments. Accordingly, the '50:50' rule is maintained.

Special duty of diversification

In addition to the general duty of care imposed on trustees (see above, p 761), the Act imposes a special duty on the trustees to have regard to the need for securing 'diversification' of the investments and to consider the suitability to the trust of the investments proposed (s 6(1)). The satisfactory performance of this duty will vary with the facts of each case.

Section 6(1) provides:

> In the exercise of his powers of investment a trustee shall have regard:
>
> (a) to the need for diversification of investments of the trust, in so far as is appropriate to the circumstances of the trust.

Mortgages of land

Under s 8 of the Trustee Act 1925, which consolidated previous statutory provisions, trustees are authorised to lend trust moneys by way of a mortgage provided that the following conditions are satisfied:

(a) The trustees are required to act on a report as to the value of the property made out by a person whom they reasonably believe to be an able practical surveyor or valuer instructed and employed independently of any owner of the property.

There is a conflict of authority as to whether the valuer is required, in fact, to be employed independently of the owner of the property or whether the trustees' reasonable belief of independent employment is sufficient. In *Re Walker*,[46] it was suggested that the valuer is required to be employed independently of the owner but, in *Re Solomon*,[47] it was suggested that a reasonable belief held by the trustees was sufficient.

(b) The amount of the loan does not exceed two thirds of the value of the property as stated in the report. This is the upper limit. It is generally advisable to lend less in order to leave a margin in the event of the property depreciating excessively. If the loan exceeds the upper limit but is otherwise proper in the circumstances, the trustees may be liable for breach of trust in respect of the excess amount, see s 9 of the Trustee Act 1925 (which replaced s 8 of the Trustee Act 1893) and *Shaw v Cates*.

Shaw v Cates [1909] 1 Ch 389, HC

In this case, trustees invested £4,400 on a mortgage of a property. The valuer, who was introduced by the mortgagor and was also the latter's rent collector, made an inaccurate report in respect of the value of the properties. The trustees advanced two thirds of the stated value of two out of four properties. The mortgagor defaulted on repayments of interest. The plaintiff beneficiaries brought an action against the trustees who denied negligence and claimed relief.

The court held that the trustees were in breach of trust.

> **Parker J:** The principle involved seems to be that within the limits of what is often called the 'two thirds' rule a prudent man may, as to the amount which can properly be advanced on any proposed security ... rely on expert advice obtained with certain precautions, it being of course assumed that in giving the advice the expert will consider all the circumstances of the case, including the nature of the property, and will not advise a larger advance than under all the circumstances can be prudently made.
>
> It is as true now as it was before the Act that the maximum sum which a prudent man can be advised to lend upon a mortgage depends on the nature of the property and upon all the circumstances of the case. If the property is liable to deteriorate or is specially subject to fluctuations in value, or depends for its value on circumstances the continual existence of which is precarious, a prudent man will now, as much as before the Act, require a larger margin for his protection than he would in the case of property attended by no such disadvantages, and an expert who does his duty will take this into consideration ...

46 (1890) 62 LT 449.

47 [1912] 1 Ch 261.

I have come to the conclusion that, under the circumstances which I have shortly stated, Mr Barton's report is not such a report as was contemplated by the Act. To advise an advance of two thirds of the value of four properties is not the same thing as advising an advance of two thirds of the value of any one or more of the properties apart from the others or other. This is more especially the case where one of the properties is not at the date of the report an income-bearing property. As I have already pointed out, the amount of income which a property is producing is material in considering what amount can properly be advanced therein ...

In my opinion the advance which was actually made was not the advance which Mr Barton advised, and his report, therefore, cannot be relied on as within s 8 of the Trustee Act 1893. Again, I do not think that Mr Barton was in fact instructed and employed independently of the mortgagor. He was suggested by the mortgagor, instructed by the mortgagor's solicitors, referred to the mortgagor both as to his fee and as to the properties he was to value, and was accompanied by the mortgagor when he made his survey. I am not suggesting that he was consciously influenced by the mortgagor or that he acted otherwise than honestly in the matter, but I do not think that he in fact fulfilled the conditions mentioned in the section as to his instructions and employment. If, according to the true meaning of the section, the belief of the trustees is the material point, I am unable to hold that the trustees did reasonably believe that Mr Barton was instructed and employed independently of the mortgagor. They left the instructions to be given by Beckingsale & Co, who were also the mortgagor's solicitors, and after ascertaining that Mr Barton was a competent person took no further trouble in the matter ...

If, apart from s 8 of the Trustee Act 1893, I ask myself whether in the matter of this mortgage the trustees acted reasonably and took all the precautions which a prudent man acting in his own affairs might be expected to have taken, I can only answer the question in the negative. In leaving Mr Barton to be instructed by their solicitors, whom they knew to be acting for the mortgagor, in taking no means to see that he was properly instructed or that he was instructed and employed independently of the mortgagor, in not themselves considering the surveyor's report when made, but leaving it to their solicitors to decide whether the report might be acted on, in making an advance not advised in the report to two-thirds of the value of two only of the properties mentioned in the report, notwithstanding that one of the properties consisted of unfinished houses – in all this it seems to me that they failed to act as a prudent man might reasonably be expected to act in the management of his own affairs.

Considering all the facts of this case, I have come to the conclusion that the largest sum for which the property could be considered a good security in 1897 is £3,400; and therefore, under s 9 of the Act, the trustees' liability is confined to making good the excess of the sum actually advanced over this amount and with interest.

Section 9(1) of the Trustee Act 1925 provides:

Where a trustee improperly advances trust money on a mortgage security which would at the time of the investment be a proper investment in all respects for a smaller sum than is actually advanced thereon, the security shall be deemed an authorised investment for the smaller sum, and the trustee shall only be liable to make good the sum advanced in excess thereof with interest.

(c) The loan is made on the advice of the surveyor or valuer expressed in the report.

Subject to the above conditions, a loan secured on the mortgage of land is an authorised investment under the Trustee Investments Act 1961 falling within the narrower range investments requiring advice (Pt II of Sched 1), if made on a mortgage of freehold land in the UK or a leasehold which has more than 60 years to run. It is generally advisable to invest in 'first legal mortgages' in order to gain the maximum security for the benefit of the beneficiaries.

Purchase of land

The Trustee Investments Act 1961 does not treat the purchase of land as an authorised investment but, under the Settled Land Act 1925, trust moneys may be invested in freehold land or leasehold property with not less than 60 years to run. In any event, the settlor may authorise the purchase of land in the trust instrument.

Moreover, under s 6 of the Trusts of Land and Appointment of Trustees Act 1996, trustees of land have the 'powers of an absolute owner'. This includes the power to buy a legal estate in land as an investment for the trust, or for occupation by any beneficiary (including the right to impose conditions on such beneficiaries) or for any other reason (s 6(4)). Where the land is leasehold, the restriction under the Settled Land Act 1925, with respect to leases with at least 60 years unexpired, will not apply. The trustees may sell all the land subject to the trust and purchase further land with the proceeds of sale (s 17). The trustees of land have unlimited powers to mortgage or lease the land, though not to make a gift of the property or a sale at an undervalue (for such action will involve a loss to the trust, but may be lawful if all the beneficiaries, being of full age and capacity, agreed). The trustees will be in breach of trust if they enter into a dealing for less than full market value. The trustees may convey the land to adult beneficiaries absolutely entitled, irrespective of whether they agree or not. These powers of the trustees may be excluded or varied by the trust deed.

In exercising the above powers, the trustees of land are required, under the Trusts of Land and Appointment of Trustees Act 1996, to have regard to the rights of the beneficiaries and any rule of law or equity or statute. The trustees are required to consult the beneficiaries entitled to possession and give effect to the wishes of the majority, measured by reference to the value of their interest (if consistent with the general interests of the trust). Moreover, the trust deed may impose an obligation on the trustees to obtain the consent of any person prior to a dealing. Failure to do so may not necessarily invalidate the transaction, but will give rise to liability for breach of trust, unless the court dispenses with the need to obtain consent by an order under s 14.

The right of beneficiaries to occupy land

Section 12 of the Trusts of Land and Appointment of Trustees Act 1996 confers on a beneficiary entitled to an interest in possession under a trust of land the right to occupy the land. The right to occupy exists where the purposes of the trust include making the land available for occupation by him personally or by beneficiaries of whom he is one, or the terms of the trust make the land available for occupation by him. But, the right to occupy does not apply where the land is not available or is unsuitable for occupation by the beneficiary. Section 13 of the Act allows the trustees to impose reasonable conditions on a beneficiary who is allowed to occupy the land (for example, to pay rates and outgoings or an occupation rent, or to restrict the use of land).

Where a number of beneficiaries are entitled to occupy land under s 12, the trustees are empowered under s 13 to exclude or restrict, on reasonable grounds, the right of some of the beneficiaries to occupy. Moreover, the trustees are entitled to impose reasonable conditions on an occupying beneficiary and, if appropriate, to compensate a beneficiary whose right of occupation has been excluded or restricted. In exercising their s 13 powers, the trustees are required to have regard to the settlor's intentions, the purposes of the trust, and the wishes of the beneficiaries entitled to possession. In addition, the trustees are required to act reasonably when dealing with the claims of competing beneficiaries. The s 12 power cannot be used to evict an existing occupier (whether or not he is a beneficiary), without his consent or a court order.

Enlargement of investment powers

Trustees are entitled to apply to the court under s 57 of the Trustee Act 1925 or under the Variation of Trusts Act 1958 (see below, p 846), in order to widen their investment powers. After some initial uneasiness (see *Re Kolb's Will Trusts*),[48] the approach of the courts has been encouraging in granting its approval in order to update the investment policy of trusts beyond the scope of the Trustee Investments Act 1961. In *Mason v Farbrother*,[49] the court approved a scheme to widen the investment powers of trustees of the employees of the Co-operative Society's pension fund owing to the effects of inflation and the size of the funds (some £127 m).

48 [1962] Ch 531.

49 [1983] 2 All ER 1078.

> **Blackett-Ord VC:** I have indicated that after 1959 a great many applications were made by trustees of trusts under the Variation of Trusts Act 1958 to obtain wider investment powers, but Parliament then passed the 1961 Act extending investment powers of trustees and in two later cases, namely, *Re Cooper's Settlement*,[50] and *Re Kolb's Will Trust*,[51] Buckley J and Cross J respectively expressed the view that in the light of such recent expression of the views of Parliament, it would not be right for the courts to continue to extend investment clauses with the enthusiasm with which they had done up to date; and for many years few applications, if any, were made.
>
> But the rule was not an absolute one; it was said to apply in the absence of special circumstances, and the special circumstances in the present case are manifest: in a word, inflation since 1961. And also of course the fact that the trust is an unusual one in that it is not a private or family trust but a pension fund with perhaps something of a public element.
>
> In my judgment there is no reason why in a proper case an application such as the present one should not be acceded to under s 57 of the Trustee Act 1925. And it seems to me on the evidence that it is (in the words of the section) 'expedient' that the application should succeed.

In *Trustees of the British Museum v AG*,[52] the trustees' powers were enlarged to include a power to invest abroad. The judge enumerated a number of factors to be taken into account, such as the standing of the trustees, the size of the fund, the object of the trust, the effectiveness of provisions for advice and exercising control over investment decisions.

This approach was followed in *Steel v Wellcome Custodian Trustee*[53] (see below, p 840). The trustees of the Wellcome Trust, a group of charitable trusts with combined assets worth £3,200 m, were entitled to have their powers of investment enlarged.

Duty to convert

A duty to convert trust assets may arise from the express terms of the trust instrument or by statute. Under s 3 of the Trusts of Land and Appointment of Trustees Act 1996, the doctrine of conversion is abolished in respect of a trust of land. In short, where land is held by trustees subject to a trust for sale, the land is not treated as personal property. Irrespective of the source of the duty, the trustees are required to comply with the duty. In this section we are concerned with the creation of the duty by the courts.

As a corollary to the duty of impartiality imposed on the trustees (see above, p 759), where there is a conflict of beneficial interests under the trust,

50 [1962] Ch 826.

51 [1962] Ch 531.

52 [1984] 1 All ER 337.

53 [1988] 1 WLR 167.

equity presumes that the trustees will hold a balance between them. This is in accordance with the presumed intention of the testator.

For example, if a testator by will bequeaths the residue of his estate upon trust for A for life with remainder to B absolutely. Let us assume that the residue estate consists of a car, a computer and paintings. If these assets are retained in their original state, A would derive the greater enjoyment of the depreciating assets (car and computer) which may become virtually worthless at the time of A's death. On the other hand, A may derive no income from the paintings and if these are appreciating assets B will derive a disproportionate benefit from the capital. The courts presume that this could not have been the testator's intention. The trustees are required to sell the assets and invest the proceeds into authorised investments but, in the interim period, to apportion the income and pay part of it to the life tenant and capitalise the balance.

Where the trust assets consist of residuary personalty bequeathed under a will and the assets are of a wasting, hazardous, reversionary or unauthorised character, and the beneficiaries enjoy their interests in succession, the trustees are required to convert the trust property into authorised investments in accordance with the rule in *Howe v Lord Dartmouth*.[54] Under the residuary clause in his will, a testator transferred bank stock and annuities to beneficiaries in succession which the trustees converted and reinvested. The question in issue was whether the trustees were in breach of trust. The court held that the conversion was quite proper in the circumstances.

> **Lord Eldon LC:** ... unless the testator directs the mode so that it is to continue as it was, the court understands that it shall be put in such a state, that the others may enjoy it after the decease of the first; and the thing is quite equal.

Hinves v Hinves (1844) 3 Hare 609, HC

> **Wigram VC** (explained the rule thus): ... where personal estate is given in terms amounting to a general residuary bequest to be enjoyed by persons in succession, the interpretation the court puts upon the bequest is that the persons indicated are to enjoy the same thing in succession; and, in order to effectuate that intention, the court as a general rule converts into permanent investments so much of the personalty as is of a wasting or perishable nature at the death of the testator, and also reversionary interests. The rule did not originally ascribe to testators the intention to effect such conversions, except in so far as a testator may be supposed to intend that which the law will do, but the court, finding the intention of the testator to be that the objects of his bounty shall take successive interests in one and the same thing, converts the property, as the only means of giving effect to that intention.

54 (1802) 7 Ves 137.

Exclusion: the rule in *Howe v Lord Dartmouth*, that is, an implied duty to convert, does not operate if the testator has manifested a contrary intention. Such contrary intention may be express, as with an express duty to convert (see *Alcock v Sloper*),[55] or may be implied, with respect to a discretion to convert (*Re Sewell's Estate*),[56] or a direction that the property is to be enjoyed *in specie* (see *McDonald v Irvine*).[57]

The rule is not applicable to *inter vivos* settlements on the basis that the settlor intended the specific assets settled to be enjoyed by the beneficiaries (see *Re Straubenzee*).[58] For a similar reason, the rule does not extend to settlements of land. It is believed that the testator intended the land to be enjoyed *in specie*. See *Re Woodhouse*.[59] It is unclear whether short leaseholds (that is, with less than 60 years to run) are still within the rule since 1925. Long leaseholds are authorised investments under s 73(1)(ix) of the Settled Land Act 1925.

Equitable apportionments

Rule in Howe v Lord Dartmouth

Having converted the assets into authorised investments, one of the features of the rule in *Howe v Lord Dartmouth* is that the life tenant is entitled to receive income at the rate of 4% per annum (less income tax) from the date of death to the date of conversion. The value on which the 4% is to be calculated depends on whether the trustees are given the power to postpone conversion of the investment or not. The position is as follows:

(a) where the trustees have no power to postpone conversion, the 4% is based on the value of the investment at the end of the executor's year (one year from the date of death) or the proceeds of sale, if earlier. See *Re Fawcett*;[60]

(b) where the trustees are given a power to postpone the conversion, the 4% is based on the value of the investment at the date of death. See *Re Parry*.[61]

Where there is insufficient income to pay the 4%, the shortfall may be made good out of the sale proceeds of unauthorised investments or out of the income from unauthorised investments.

55 (1833) 2 My & K 699.

56 (1870) 11 Eq 80.

57 (1878) 8 Ch D 101.

58 [1901] 2 Ch 779.

59 [1941] Ch 332.

60 [1940] Ch 402.

61 [1947] Ch 23.

Rule in Re Earl of Chesterfield's Trusts

This rule applies where there are different interests in a trust which includes a non-income producing asset such as a reversion or a life policy. The proceeds of the non-income producing asset are apportioned between the life tenant and the remainderman. The remainderman receives a sum which, if invested at compound interest at the date of death at 4% per annum (less income tax), would produce the proceeds of sale. The balance is paid over to the life tenant.

Rule in Allhusen v Whittell

Where the residue of an estate is left to a life tenant, the assumption is that the life tenant is to be entitled to income on the 'pure residue' only. Where there is a delay in paying debts, inheritance tax, legacies and other liabilities, the life tenant's income is augmented. But for the rule, the longer the delay in settling debts the larger the gain to the life tenant. The effect of the rule is to charge the life tenant with interest on the sums used to pay debts and other liabilities in order to maintain equality between the beneficiaries. As the various expenses are paid, they should be apportioned between income and capital. The amount charged to capital should be such capital sum which, if invested at the date of death, would amount exactly to the sum paid. The balance is charged to income. The rate of interest to be used in this calculation is the average rate of interest received during the year.

Rule in Re Atkinson

This rule applies where one of the assets of an estate consists of a loan on mortgage and the security is insufficient to repay the principal and interest in full. The proceeds of sale are apportioned between the life tenant and remainderman in the proportion which the arrears bear to the amount due in respect of principal. In short, the proceeds of sale are abated *pro rata* between the life tenant and the remainderman as follows:

(a) the amount due to the remainderman is the principal outstanding plus any interest due to the date of death minus any rent received as mortgagee in possession;

(b) the amount due to the life tenant is the income due from the date of death to the date of realisation minus any rent received as mortgages in possession or, where a foreclosure order is obtained, the income due to the date of the foreclosure order minus any rent received as mortgagee in possession. Rent received after foreclosure belongs to the life tenant in lieu of interest.

Rent received as mortgagee in possession is to be applied as follows:

(a) interest to the date of death (remainderman);

(b) interest from the date of death to realisation or foreclosure order (life tenant);

(c) repayment of capital (remainderman).

Powers of maintenance and advancement

Let us suppose that one of the beneficiaries under a trust is an infant (person under the age of 18). The settlor, for personal reasons, may not wish to transfer an immediate interest to the child but may postpone the enjoyment of his interest subject to a contingency, such as attaining the age of majority or qualifying as an accountant.

For example, a fund is transferred to trustees on trust for A provided that he attains the age of 18. A is 14 years old and in need of funds for his education. Since A does not have a vested interest in the income or capital but merely a contingent interest, the trustees, *prima facie*, are not entitled to pay A any part of the income and capital.

Prior to the fulfilment of the contingency, circumstances may arise which indicate the need for the beneficiary to have access to part of the fund. It would be senseless to treat the beneficiary as entitled to a fortune in the future but in the meantime to be deprived of any access to his potential fortune. In this regard it might be possible for the trustees to pay some or all of the income to or on behalf of an infant beneficiary until his interest becomes vested in possession or fails before achieving the relevant event (power of maintenance) or to pay part of the capital for the benefit of the beneficiary whether or not he is an infant, pending the vesting or failure of his interest (power of advancement).

Maintenance payments are expenditure incurred out of the income of a fund for routine recurring purposes such as food, clothing, rent and education.

Advancements are payments out of capital to cover major non recurring capital expenses such as the purchase of a business or a home.

Maintenance

A power of maintenance is a discretion granted to the trustees to pay or apply income for the benefit of an infant beneficiary at a time prior to the beneficiary acquiring a right to the income or capital of the trust.

The issues that are required to be considered by the trustees are:

(a) whether they have a power to maintain an infant beneficiary;

(b) whether there is any income available for maintenance;

(c) whether the trustees are prepared to exercise their discretion to maintain the beneficiary.

Power to maintain

Express power

A settlor may expressly include a power of maintenance in the trust instrument. Most professionally drafted settlements will include this power. If this is the case the trustees' duties will be encapsulated in the clause.

Inherent power

The court has an inherent power to authorise the trustees to maintain beneficiaries. The underlying unexpressed intention of the settlor must have been consistent with the maintenance payments in favour of the infant beneficiary or beneficiaries.

Statutory power

Section 31 of the Trustee Act 1925 authorises the trustees in their discretion, to pay the whole or part of the income from the trust to the parent or guardian of an infant beneficiary, or otherwise apply the relevant amount towards the maintenance, education or benefit of the infant beneficiary, during his infancy or until his interest fails.

Section 31(1) Trustee Act 1925 provides:

> Where any property is held by trustees in trust for any person for any interest whatsoever, whether vested or contingent, then, subject to any prior interests or charges affecting that property:
>
> (i) during the infancy of any such person, if his interest so long continues, the trustees may, at their sole discretion, pay to his parent or guardian, if any, or otherwise apply for or towards his maintenance, education or benefit, the whole or such part, if any, of the income of that property as may, in all the circumstances, be reasonable, whether or not there is:
>
> (a) any other fund applicable to the same purpose; or
>
> (b) any person bound by law to provide for his maintenance or education.

But this statutory power may be modified or excluded by the settlor in the trust instrument. See s 69(2) of the 1925 Act.

Section 69(2) of the Trustee Act 1925 provides:

> The powers conferred by this Act on trustees are in addition to the powers conferred by the instrument, if any, creating the trust, but those powers, unless otherwise stated, apply if and so far only as a contrary intention is not expressed in the instrument, if any, creating the trust, and have effect subject to the terms of that instrument.

An exclusion of the power may be express or implied in the settlement. Section 31 was intended to be implied into every settlement subject to any contrary intention expressed by the terms of the instrument. A contrary intention will be established if the settlor has specifically disposed of the income, for example, a payment of the income to another or has directed an accumulation of income.

Indeed, the settlor may impliedly exclude s 31, even though the clause in the settlement that has this effect is void. In *Re Erskine's Settlement Trust*,[62] the clause directing the accumulation of income (which expressed a contrary intention) was void for infringing the perpetuity rule.

Re Delamere's Settlement Trust [1984] 1 WLR 813, CA

In this case, the trustees of a settlement executed a revocable deed of appointment in 1971 whereby the income from trust funds was to be held upon trust for six infant beneficiaries 'in equal shares absolutely'. The income was not distributed and, in 1980, the trustees executed a further deed revoking the trusts of the 1971 appointment and appointed new trusts in respect of that capital and its future interest. The trustees applied to the court to determine whether the accumulated income was vested in the beneficiaries between 1971 and 1980.

The Court of Appeal held (reversing the decision of Goulding J), on construction of the 1971 appointment, that the beneficiaries had acquired indefeasible interests in the income during the relevant period. In so far as the terms of the appointment were inconsistent with s 31 of the 1925 Act, the Act was excluded. Accordingly s 31(2) was excluded but not s 31(1).

> **Slade LJ:** ... it is indisputable that each of the six appointees has a vested interest in his share of income accruing under the 1971 appointment before that appointment is revoked, and that any exercise of such powers cannot divest him of income which has already accrued: see *In re Master's Settlement*.[63] [The learned judge then considered whether the word 'absolutely' as used in the 1971 deed of appointment had a restricted interpretation.] To place a restricted interpretation on the word 'absolutely' on this account would be to confine the ambit of the word to less than its natural meaning and to base one's conclusion on mere speculation as to the intention of the parties to the 1971 appointment.
>
> Furthermore, it would involve reaching a conclusion which rendered the word 'absolutely' superfluous since, as appears from *In re Master's Settlement*,[64] even in the absence of the word 'absolutely', an exercise of the trustees' power of revocation could not have affected the destination of income which had already accrued. Nevertheless, the court is, in my opinion, entitled to deduce the intention of the trustees in making the 1971 appointment only from the

62 [1971] 1 WLR 162.

63 [1911] 1 Ch 321.

64 *Ibid*.

words which they, or their draftsman, chose to employ. Furthermore, as I have said, due weight must be given to every word which they chose to employ.

Accordingly, I conclude that the force of the word in this context must be to express the intention that the appointees' respective interests in income accruing during the subsistence of the appointment should not be defeasible in any circumstances whatsoever – in other words, as Mr Walker put it, they should keep it 'come what may'. I might add that this is the clear force of the word as used in s 31(2)(i) and s 31(4) of the Trustee Act 1925 itself.

I accept, that, for reasons which I have already given, the very wording of s 31(2) itself shows that it is capable of applying, even though there may be an apparent inconsistency between the provisions of that sub-section and the provisions of the relevant trust instrument. I also accept that it cannot be safely assumed that, in using the phraseology which he did, the draftsman of the 1971 appointment specifically had in mind the provisions of s 31(2) or s 69(2) of the Trustee Act 1925 at all. Nevertheless, he for his part accepted that in the end the relevant test must be the test in *IRC v Bernstein*.[65]

When the *Bernstein* test is translated to the facts of the present case the relevant question must, in my opinion, be this: have the appointees shown that the application of s 31(2)(i) and (ii) of the Trustee Act 1925 would be inconsistent with the purport of the 1971 appointment? For my part I am satisfied that they have shown that the application of those paragraphs, which would have the effect of defeating the interest of an infant appointee in the accumulations made in respect of his interest if he were to die before attaining 18 or marrying, would be wholly inconsistent with the purport of this particular instrument. It follows that while there is no reason why s 31(1) should not apply to the 1971 appointment, s 31(2)(i) and (ii) must be deemed to have been excluded.

Waller LJ: Section 31 of the Trustee Act 1925 was enacted in order both to simplify the task of the draftsman of a trust instrument and to fill gaps which he might unwittingly leave in the disposal of the trust income. And in the absence of a contrary intention in the trust instrument s 31(2) provided in effect that income of a beneficiary up to the age of 18, which was not applied for his maintenance, should be accumulated as part of the trust fund so that if he died unmarried before the age of 18 the accumulated income would form part of the trust fund and not vest in his personal representatives. By contrast s 31(4) provided that in the case of a vested annuity accumulations made during his infancy should belong to him or his personal representatives 'absolutely'. There are no doubt good reasons for making this distinction in the absence of a contrary intention but the difference between the two sub-sections does emphasise the necessity of examining the wording of the trust instrument carefully. In this case the deed of appointment is commendably brief in form and I agree with Slade LJ that this circumstance indicates that every word is included for a purpose. Even in the absence of the word 'absolutely' the effect of the 1971 appointment would have been to give the grandchildren a title to all accrued income defeasible only if he or she died before the age of 18 unmarried. Without the word 'absolutely', however, the construction

65 [1961] Ch 399.

> contended for by the seventh defendant would have taken effect and the income would have been held by the trustees in accordance with the provisions of s 31(2). One has to ask therefore why the word 'absolutely' was included.
>
> In my opinion there are two features of the deed of appointment which make it clear that the deed must be construed as having been intended to vary the provisions of s 31(2). These two features are that the deed was expressed to be a settlement of income and that it was expressed to be on trust for the grandchildren in equal shares 'absolutely'. In my opinion that combination leads to the conclusion that the deed was intended to ensure that the income vested in the appointee as and when it became due and in so far as it was not used for maintenance of the appointee was held by the trustees absolutely and indefeasibly for the appointee.

Availability of income

The issue here is whether the income of the trust is available to maintain the infant beneficiary. The effect of complex rules of case law, s 175 of the Law of Property Act 1925 and s 31(3) of the Trustee Act 1925 is that a vested interest carries the intermediate income unless someone else is entitled to it or the income is required to be accumulated.

Section 175 of the Law of Property Act 1925 provides:

> A contingent or future specific devise or bequest of property, whether real or personal, and a contingent residuary devise of freehold land, and a specific or residuary devise of freehold land to trustees upon trust for persons whose interests are contingent or executory shall, subject to the statutory provisions relating to accumulations, carry the intermediate income of that property from the death of the testator, except so far as such income, or any part thereof, may be otherwise expressly disposed of.

Section 31(3) of the 1925 Act provides:

> This section applies in the case of a contingent interest only if the limitation or trust carries the intermediate income of the property, but it applies to a future or contingent legacy by the parent of, or a person standing *in loco parentis* to the legatee, if and for such period as, under the general law, the legacy carries interest for the maintenance of the legatee, and in any such case the rate of interest shall (if the income available is sufficient, and subject to any rules of court to the contrary) be 5% per annum.

Thus, if A, an adult, is entitled to the income for life with remainder to B an infant, absolutely. The income will not be available to maintain B. This is because the income is expressly payable to another beneficiary, namely A. Another way of expressing the same point is to recognise that the settlor by paying the income to A has expressed a contrary intention in the trust instrument, that is, the power to maintain B during infancy has been excluded.

Re McGeorge [1963] Ch 544, HC

In this case, a testator by his will devised land to his daughter, Helen. By clause 4 of the will, he declared that the gift shall not take effect 'until after the death of my wife, should she survive me'. This gift was subject to gifts over if Helen did not survive the widow. Helen survived the testator and claimed the income under s 31(1)(ii) of the 1925 Act.

Cross J held that the income was required to be accumulated on the following grounds:

(i) the devise to Helen was a future specific devise within s 175 of the Law of Property Act and thus carried the intermediate income, subject to defeasance if Helen died before the widow;

(ii) Helen was not entitled to be maintained from the income because:

   (a) the will expressed a contrary intention by deferring Helen's interest until the widow's death; and

   (b) Helen did not have a contingent but a vested interest in the land (albeit not in possession but in interest) which was outside s 31(1)(ii). This sub-section applied to those without a vested interest in property.

> **Cross J:** It has long been established that a gift of residuary personalty to a legatee in being on a contingency or to an unborn person at birth carried the intermediate income so far as the law would allow it to be accumulated, but that rule had been held, for reasons depending on the old land law, not to apply to gifts of real property, and it was apparently never applied to specific dispositions of personalty. Section 175 of the Law of Property Act 1925 was plainly intended to extend the rule to residuary devises and to specific gifts whether of realty or of personalty. It is now established, at all events so far as courts of first instance are concerned, that the old rule does not apply to residuary bequests whether vested or contingent which are expressly deferred to a future date which must come sooner or later (see *Re Oliver*,[66] *Re Gillett's Will Trusts*[67] and *Re Geering*).[68] There is a good reason for this distinction. If a testator gives property to X contingently on his attaining the age of thirty it is reasonable to assume, in the absence of a direction to the contrary, that the testator would wish X, if he attains thirty, to have the income produced by the property between the testator's death and the happening of the contingency. If, on the other hand, he gives property to X for any sort of interest after the death of A, it is reasonable to assume that he does not wish X to have the income accruing during A's lifetime unless he directs that he is to have it. This distinction between an immediate gift on a contingency and a gift which is expressly deferred was not drawn until after the Law of Property Act 1925 was passed. There were statements in textbooks and even in judgments to the effect that the rule applied to deferred as well as to contingent gifts of residuary

66 [1947] 2 All ER 162.

67 [1950] Ch 102.

68 [1964] Ch 136.

personalty. The legislature, when it extended this rule to residuary devises and specific gifts, must, I think have adopted this erroneous view of the law. I would have liked, if I could, to construe the reference to 'future specific devises' and 'executory interest' in s 175(1) of the Act of 1925 in such a way as to make it consistent with the recent cases on the scope of the old rule applicable to residuary bequests. To do that, however, would be to rectify the Act, not to construe it, and I see no escape from the conclusion that whereas before 1926 a specific gift or a residuary devise which was not vested in possession did not *prima facie* carry intermediate income at all, now such a gift may carry intermediate income in circumstances in which a residuary bequest would not carry it.

It was argued in this case that the fact that the will contained a residuary gift constituted an express disposition of the income of the land in question which prevented the section from applying. I am afraid that I cannot accept this submission. I have little doubt that the testator expected the income of the land to form part of the income of residue during his widow's lifetime, but he has made no express disposition of it. I agree with what was said in this connection by Eve J in *Re Raine*.[69] As the devise is not vested indefeasibly in the daughter but is subject to defeasance during the mother's lifetime the intermediate income which the gift carries by virtue of s 175 ought *prima facie* to be accumulated to see who eventually becomes entitled to it. It was, however, submitted by counsel for the daughter that she could claim payment of it under s 31(1) of the Trustee Act 1925.

[The learned judge summarised the sub-section, and continued:]

There are, as I see it, two answers to the daughter's claim. The first – and narrower – answer is that her interest in the income of the devised land is a vested interest. It is a future interest liable to be divested but it is not contingent. Therefore s 31(1) does not apply to it. The second – and wider – answer is that the whole framework of s 31 shows that it is inapplicable to a future gift of this sort and that a will containing such a gift expresses a contrary intention within s 69(2) which prevents the sub-section from applying. By deferring the enjoyment of the devise until after the widow's death the testator has expressed the intention that the daughter shall not have the immediate income. It is true that as he has not expressly disposed of it in any other way, s 175 of the Law of Property Act 1925 defeats that intention to the extent of making the future devise carry the income, so that the daughter will get it eventually, if she survives her mother or dies before her leaving no children to take by substitution. Even if, however, the words of s 31(1) of the Trustee Act 1925 fitted the case, there would be no warrant for defeating the testator's intention still further by reading s 31(1) into the will and thus giving the daughter an interest in possession in the income during her mother's lifetime. In the result, the income ... must be accumulated.

Contingent interests created *inter vivos* or by will carry the intermediate income (save insofar as the settlor or testator has otherwise disposed of the

69 [1929] 1 Ch 716.

income). A contingent pecuniary legacy does not carry the income except where the gift was made by the infant's father or a person standing *in loco parentis*, and the contingency is attaining the age of majority and no other fund is set aside for the maintenance of the legatee.

Exercise of power during infancy

Subject to the above, the trustees have a discretion which they are required to exercise responsibly and as objectively as ordinary prudent men of business. Thus, trustees who applied the income automatically to the infant's father without consciously exercising their discretion, were liable to the beneficiaries for breach of trust when the father used the sums for his own benefit. In *Wilson v Turner*,[70] a trust settlement was created for Mrs Wilson for life with remainder to her children. The trustees were given express power to pay the income for the maintenance, education or benefit of any infant children. The wife died leaving a nine year old son who was maintained by his father. The trustees, without exercising their discretion, paid the father the income as it arose as though the property belonged to him. Such property was dissipated and after his death an action was brought requiring repayment to the trust. The court held that the trustees were liable to repay the income for the benefit of the son.

Under the proviso to s 31(1) of the Trustee Act 1925, the trustees are required to take a number of factors into account such as the age and requirements of the infant and whether other income is applicable for the same purpose and generally all the surrounding circumstances. The exercise of the power will vary with the facts of each case.

The proviso to s 31(1) declares:

> Provided that, in deciding whether the whole or any part of the income of the property is during the minority to be paid or applied for the purposes aforesaid, the trustees shall have regard to the age of the infant and his requirements and generally to the circumstances of the case, and in particular to what other income, if any, is applicable for the same purposes; and where trustees have notice that the income of more than one fund is applicable for those purposes, then, so far as practicable, unless the entire income of the funds is paid or applied as aforesaid or the court otherwise directs, a proportionate part only of the income of each fund shall be so paid or applied.

Accumulations

Alternatively, the trustees may accumulate the income instead of maintaining the infant with the fund. Such accumulations (or capitalised income) will

70 (1883) 22 Ch 521.

produce further income if invested in authorised investments. The additional income as well as accumulations of income become available for maintenance of the infant beneficiary in the future, should the need arise (proviso to s 31(2)).

Proviso to s 31(2) provides:

> But the trustees may, at any time during the infancy of such person if his interest so long continues, apply those accumulations, or any part thereof, as if they were income arising in the then current year.

If, in accordance with the express terms of the trust instrument, the beneficiary attains a vested interest in the income on attaining the age of majority (18) or marries under that age, he becomes entitled to the accumulated income (s 31(2)(i)(a)).

Section 31(2) provides:

> During the infancy of any such person, if his interest so long continues, the trustees shall accumulate all the residue of that income in the way of compound interest by investing the same and the resulting income thereof from time to time in authorised investments, and shall hold those accumulations as follows:
>
> (i) If such person:
>
> (a) attains the age of 18 years, or marries under that age, and his interest in such income during his infancy or until his marriage is a vested interest; or
>
> (b) on attaining the age of 18 years or on marriage under that age becomes entitled to the property from which such income arose in fee simple, absolute or determinable, or absolutely, or for an entailed interest;
>
> the trustees shall hold the accumulations in trust for such person absolutely, but without prejudice to any provision with respect thereto contained in any settlement by him made under any statutory powers during his infancy, and so that the receipt of such person after marriage, and though still an infant, shall be a good discharge; and
>
> (ii) In any other case the trustees shall, notwithstanding that such person had a vested interest in such income, hold the accumulations as an accretion to the capital of the property from which such accumulations arose, and as one fund with such capital for all purposes, and so that, if such property is settled land, such accumulations shall be held upon the same trusts as if the same were capital money arising therefrom.

For example, 'On trust for A for life provided that he attains the age of 18': on attaining the age of majority, A becomes entitled to the accumulated income. He also becomes entitled to future income (s 31(2)(i)(a)).

Where the beneficiary acquires a vested interest in capital on attaining the age of majority or earlier marriage, he also becomes entitled to the accumulated income (s 31(2)(i)(b)).

For example, 'Shares are held on trust for A provided that he attains the age of 18'. On attaining the age of majority, A becomes entitled to the accumulated dividends from the shares in addition to the capital.

Attaining the age of majority

If the beneficiary attains the age of majority without attaining a vested interest under the terms of the trust, the trustees are required to pay the income to the beneficiary until he acquires a vested interest or dies or his interest fails (s 31(1)(ii)). The payment includes accumulated income. Accordingly, a beneficiary acquires a vested interest in the income of the trust by statute on attaining the age of majority even though under the trust he does not enjoy a vested interest.

Section 31(1)(ii) provides:

> If such person on attaining the age of 18 years has not a vested interest in such income, the trustees shall thenceforth pay the income of that property and of any accretion thereto under sub-s (2) of this section to him, until he either attains a vested interest therein or dies, or until failure of his interest.

For example, 'On trust for A provided he attains the age of 25': on attaining the age of 18, the beneficiary becomes entitled to an interest in possession.

However, this provision is subject to any contrary intention stipulated by the settlor. Such contrary intention may be manifested by the settlor directing the income to be accumulated beyond the age of majority.

In *Re Turner's Will Trust*,[71] a testator gave a share of his residuary estate on trust for such of the children of his late son, Charles, as shall attain the age of 28 years. The will contained an express power of maintenance of such children as shall attain the age of 21 years and included instructions to the trustees to accumulate the surplus. Two of the testator's grandchildren attained the age of 28 but a third, Geoffrey, died having attained the age of 24. His share of the income had been accumulated. The question in issue was whether estate duty was payable on his death. The court held that no duty was payable because he did not have a vested interest in income under s 31(1)(ii). A contrary intention was manifested as evidenced by a direction to accumulate the income.

Power of advancement

An advancement is a payment from the capital funds of a trust to or on behalf of a beneficiary in respect of some long term commitment such as the purchase of a house or establishment of a business. A potential beneficiary

71 [1937] Ch 15.

may be in need of capital from the trust fund prior to the beneficiary becoming entitled as of right to the capital from the fund. In such a case, the trustees may be entitled to accelerate the enjoyment of his interest by an advance payment of capital to the beneficiary.

For example, S transfers £50,000 to T(1) and T(2) on trust for B contingently on attaining the age of 25. Assuming that while B is only 14 years old, a legitimate need for capital arises. But for special provisions to the contrary, the trustees would be prevented from making an advancement to B on the grounds that the contingency entitling B to the capital has not taken place and in any event B, as a minor, is incapable of giving a valid receipt for the payment of capital. If, on the other hand, the trustees validly exercise their power of advancement, capital may be released in favour of B before the satisfaction of the contingency and B will be prevented from claiming the capital a second time.

Authority to advance

The authority to exercise a power of advancement may originate from a variety of sources such as the trust instrument, the inherent jurisdiction of the courts or statutory power. These would be considered in turn.

Trust instrument

A settlor may be prompted to include an express power of advancement in the trust instrument perhaps in order to widen or vary the statutory power which would otherwise be excluded in the instrument. The trustees are required to obey the express provision, the purport of which will vary with the circumstances of each case.

Inherent jurisdiction

Under the inherent jurisdiction of the court, an order may be made authorising an infant's property to be transferred so that capital may be applied for his advancement or benefit.

Statutory power

Section 32 of the Trustee Act 1925, creates a statutory power of advancement which is not limited to minors but invests the trustees with a discretion to distribute capital in favour of any beneficiary who may become entitled to the whole or part of the capital in the future.

Section 32 of the Trustee Act 1925 provides:

(1) Trustees may at any time or times pay or apply any capital money subject to a trust, for the advancement or benefit, in such manner as they may, in

> their absolute discretion, think fit, of any person entitled to the capital of the trust property or of any share thereof, whether absolutely or contingently on his attaining any specified age or on the occurrence of any other event, or subject to a gift over on his death under any specified age or on the occurrence of any other event, and whether in possession or in remainder or reversion, and such payment or application may be made notwithstanding that the interest of such person is liable to be defeated by the exercise of a power of appointment or revocation, or to be diminished by the increase of the class to which he belongs:
>
> Provided that:
>
> (a) the money so paid or applied for the advancement or benefit of any person shall not exceed altogether in amount one half of the presumptive or vested share or interest of that person in the trust property; and
>
> (b) if that person is or becomes absolutely and indefeasibly entitled to a share in the trust property the money so paid or applied shall be brought into account as part of such share; and
>
> (c) no such payment or application shall be made so as to prejudice any person entitled to any prior life or other interest, whether vested or contingent, in the money paid or applied unless such person is in existence and of full age and consents in writing to such payment or application.
>
> (2) This section applies only where the trust property consists of money or securities or of property held upon trust for sale ...

However, this statutory power may be excluded expressly or impliedly by the settlor. An implied exclusion involves any power of advancement which is inconsistent with the statutory power such as an express power which exceeds the statutory maximum amount which may be used to advance the beneficiaries. In *IRC v Bernstein*,[72] the Court of Appeal decided that a direction to accumulate income during the lifetime of the settlor expressed a contrary intention to exclude s 32 of the 1925 Act. The direction was indicative of the intention of the settlor to build up a large capital sum and to prohibit the advancement of capital.

Advancement or benefit

Under s 32, the trustees are entitled to pay or apply capital in their discretion for the 'advancement or benefit' of a beneficiary. The expression has been considered widely by the courts and 'benefit' has been interpreted as extending the wide ambit of 'advancement'.

72 [1961] Ch 399.

***Pilkington v Inland Revenue Commissioners* [1964] AC 612, HL**

> **Viscount Radcliffe:** The word 'advancement' itself meant ... the establishment in life of the beneficiary who was the object of the power or at any rate some step that would contribute to the furtherance of his establishment ... Typical instances of expenditure for such purposes under the social conditions of the nineteenth century were an apprenticeship or the purchase of a commission in the Army or of an interest in a business. In the case of a girl there could be an advancement on marriage ... such words as 'or otherwise for his or her benefit' were often added to the word 'advancement'. It was always recognised that these added words were 'large words' ... The expression means any use of the money which will improve the material situation of the beneficiary.

Thus, the phrase includes the use of money not only for the immediate personal benefit of the beneficiary but also an indirect 'benefit'. In *Re Clore's Settlement*,[73] a wealthy beneficiary under a trust who had a future interest in capital, felt morally obliged to make charitable donations. The court decided that he was entitled to request the trustees to make advancements to charities selected by him.

Similarly, the power may be exercised with the intention of benefiting the object under a trust by making a loan to the beneficiary's husband to facilitate him to set up a business in England in order to keep the family together. See *Re Kershaw*.[74]

Property subject to s 32 of the Trustee Act 1925

Under s 32(2), the power to advance is available in respect of 'money or securities or property held on trust for sale', provided that such property is not treated as land. The settlor may expressly extend the power that exists under the section by manifesting such an intention in the trust instrument.

Status of the beneficiaries under s 32 of the Trustee Act 1925

The widest form of definition of the types of beneficiaries who may benefit under s 32 is adopted by the section, thus:

> ... any person entitled to the capital of the trust property or any share thereof, whether absolutely or contingently on his attaining any specified age or on the occurrence of any other event, or subject to a gift over on his death under any specified age or on the occurrence of any other event, and whether in possession or in remainder or reversion ... and notwithstanding that the interest of such person is liable to be defeated by the exercise of a power of appointment or revocation, or to be diminished by the increase of the class to which he belongs.

73 [1966] 2 All ER 272.

74 (1868) LR 6 Eq 322.

Scope of s 32 of the Trustee Act 1925

The policy of s 32 is to invest trustees with a discretion to appoint up to one-half of the presumptive share of the capital of the beneficiary for his advancement or benefit.

The value of the presumptive share of the beneficiary is measured on the date of the advancement. If the ceiling concerning the statutory power of advancement has been reached (that is, one quarter of the presumptive share of capital) the statutory power of advancement would be exhausted even if the value of the capital increases subsequently, see *Marquess of Abergavenny v Ram*.

Marquess of Abergavenny v Ram [1981] 2 All ER 643, HC

By the Marquess of Abergavenny's Estate Act 1946, a trust was created in favour of the plaintiff for life with remainder in favour of other beneficiaries. The trustees were expressly given a wide discretionary power to pay 'any part or parts not exceeding in all one half in value of the settled fund of which he becomes tenant for life in possession'. In 1965, the trustees exercised their power to its full extent in favour of the plaintiff. Since then, the money value of the retained half share of the fund had considerably appreciated. The question in issue was whether the trustees were entitled to make further advancements based on the appreciation in the value of the trust property.

Held that, since the plaintiffs received the maximum amount of property as stated in the trust deed, the trustees had no power to make further payments to him.

> **Goulding J:** I think myself that the reason why there is no direct authority on the question is because the answer has always seemed plain. Any layman, and any lawyer I think ... would feel that where there is a power to make successive payments to a person up to a limit of a certain fraction of a fund and at a certain date, he, the beneficiary, has received assets then fully reaching the prescribed limit, thereafter no further exercise of the power is possible. All that the settlor authorised has been done. It would be to my mind strange and unexpected if the object of the power as such retained an interest or possibility of interest in the fund still in settlement, so that he could require accounts from the trustees and demand reconsideration of his position whenever there should be an appreciation of assets.

However, the settlor may increase the ceiling of sums which may be advanced but this may only be done expressly.

The sum (or sums) advanced is (or are) credited to the prospective share of the beneficiary (or beneficiaries), so that if a beneficiary becomes absolutely entitled to a share as of right, the sum advanced is taken into account (s 32(1)(b)).

For example, shares worth £100,000 are held on trust for B provided that he attains the age of 25. B is currently 22 years of age. The trustees advance up to £50,000 to him. When B attains the relevant age and acquires a vested and indefeasible interest in the capital, the sum advanced is brought into account.

Prior interests

If a beneficiary is entitled to a prior interest (life interest), whether vested or contingent, the consent in writing of such beneficiary is required to be obtained prior to the exercise of the power of advancement. The reason being that an advancement reduces the income available to other beneficiaries (s 32(1)(c)).

For example, gift to A for life remainder to B absolutely. A's consent in writing is required before B receives any part of the capital by way of an advancement.

Resettlement

In *Pilkington v IRC*,[75] the question arose as to whether a 'resettlement' of part of the capital of a beneficiary by way of an advancement would be a proper exercise of the discretion of the trustees.

For example, assuming property is held by T1 and T2 on trust for A for life, remainder to B absolutely. The trustee (with the consent of A in writing) for fiscal purposes propose to advance one quarter of the capital to T3 and T4) on 'protective' trust for B. Would the exercise be valid?

Two objections are capable of being levelled against such exercise namely:

(a) the resettlement or sub-trust is capable of infringing the rule prohibiting the trustees from delegating their discretions. The House of Lords in *Pilkington v IRC* rejected this objection on the ground that the real issue is one of authority. The rule is not that the trustees cannot delegate their powers *per se* but the trustees cannot delegate their discretions without authority. If, therefore, the trustees possess the authority to delegate their discretions, then provided that the exercise of their power to delegate is *bona fide* and in accordance with their duty of care the delegation is valid;

(b) the resettlement or sub-trust is subject to the rule against perpetuities. The exercise of the power of advancement under the 'head' settlement is analogous to the exercise of a special power of appointment. Accordingly, the perpetuity period is measured by reference to the 'head' settlement. In other words, the perpetuity rule will be construed as if the resettlement was a term of and read into the 'head' settlement. Before the Perpetuities

75 [1964] AC 612.

and Accumulations Act 1964, the resettlement was capable of being invalidated on the basis of the possibility of not vesting within the perpetuity period. This point was accepted by the House of Lords in *Pilkington v IRC*. Under the Perpetuities and Accumulations Act 1964, the court will 'wait and see' whether or not the property subject to the resettled trust will vest within the relevant period.

Pilkington v Inland Revenue Commissioners (1868) LR 6 Eq 322, HL

In *Pilkington v IRC*, the testator, William, bequeathed the income of his residuary estate on protective trusts for his nephews and nieces. The will authorised the principal beneficiaries to consent to the trustees exercising their power of advancement without causing a forfeiture. The capital was required to be held on trust for the children of the beneficiaries in such shares as the beneficiaries may appoint and in default of appointment in equal shares. Richard, one of the testator's nephews, had three children, one of whom was Penelope, a two year old. The trustees proposed (subject to Richard's consent) to advance up to one half of Penelope's expectant share on a new trust for Penelope's benefit. The purpose of the intended advancement was to save estate duty on Richard's death. Under the proposed new trust, Penelope would become entitled to capital at the age of 30, but was entitled to be maintained from the income. The trustees sought directions from the court.

The House of Lords held:

(1) that the exercise of the power was within s 32 of the Trustee Act for the benefit of Penelope, even though the exercise amounted to a re- settlement; but

(2) the proposed exercise would be void for infringing the perpetuity rule as the gift in favour of Penelope was capable of vesting beyond the period of 21 years from the death of Richard.

> **Viscount Radcliffe:** I have not been able to find in the words of s 32 anything which in terms or by implication restricts the width of the manner or purpose of advancement. It is true that, if this settlement is made, Miss Penelope's children, who are not objects of the power, are given a possible interest in the event of her dying under thirty leaving surviving issue. But if the disposition itself, by which I mean the whole provision made, is for her benefit, it is no objection to the exercise of the power that other persons benefit incidentally as a result of the exercise. Thus, a man's creditors may in certain cases get the most immediate advantage from an advancement made for the purpose of paying them off, as in *Lowther v Bentinck*;[76] and a power to raise money for the advancement of a wife may cover a payment made direct to her husband in order to set him up in business (*Re Kershaw's Trusts*).[77] The exercise will not be bad, therefore, on this ground.

76 (1874) LR 19 Eq 166.

77 (1868) LR 6 Eq 322.

Nor in my opinion will it be bad merely because the moneys are to be tied up in the proposed settlement. If it could be said that the payment or application permitted by s 32 cannot take the form of a settlement in any form but must somehow pass direct into or through the hands of the object of the power, I could appreciate the principle upon which the Commissioners' objection was founded. But can that principle be asserted? Anyone can see, I think, that there can be circumstances in which, while it is very desirable that some money should be raised at once for the benefit of an owner of an expectant or contingent interest, it would be very undesirable that the money should not be secured to him under some arrangement that will prevent him having the absolute disposition of it. I find it very difficult to think that there is something at the back of s 32 which makes such an advancement impossible. Certainly neither Danckwerts J nor the members of the Court of Appeal in this case took the view. Both Lord Evershed MR and Upjohn LJ explicitly accept the possibility of a settlement being made in exercise of a power of advancement. Farwell J authorised one in *Re Halsted's Will Trusts*,[78] a case in which the trustees had left their discretion to the court. The trustees should raise the money and 'have' it 'settled', he said. So, too, Harman J in *Re Ropner's Settlement Trusts*[79] authorised the settlement of an advance provided for an infant, saying that the child could not 'consent or request the trustees to make the advance, but the transfer of a part of his contingent share to the trustees of a settlement for him must advance his interest and thus be for his benefit ...'. All this must be wrong in principle if a power of advancement cannot cover an application of the moneys by way of settlement.

It is not as if anyone were contending for a principle that a power of advancement cannot be exercised 'over the head' of a beneficiary, that is, unless he actually asks for the money to be raised and consents to its application. From some points of view that might be a satisfactory limitation, and no doubt it is the way in which an advancement takes place in the great majority of cases. But, if application and consent were necessary requisites of advancement, that would cut out the possibility of making any advancement for the benefit of a person under age, at any rate without the institution of court proceedings and formal representation of the infant: and it would mean, moreover, that the trustees of an adult could not in any circumstances insist on raising money to pay his debts, however much the operation might be to his benefit, unless he agreed to that course. Counsel for the Commissioners did not contend before us that the power of advancement was inherently limited in this way: and I do not think that such a limitation would accord with the general understanding. Indeed its 'paternal' nature is well shown by the fact that it is often treated as being peculiarly for the assistance of an infant.

The Commissioners' objections seem to be concentrated upon such propositions as that the proposed transaction is 'nothing less than a resettlement' and that a power of advancement cannot be used so as to alter or vary the trusts created by the settlement from which it is derived. Such a

78 [1937] 2 All ER 570.

79 [1956] 1 WLR 902.

transaction, they say, amounts to using the power of advancement as a way of appointing or declaring new trusts different from those of the settlement. The reason why I do not find that these propositions have any compulsive effect upon my mind is that they seem to me merely vivid ways of describing the substantial effect of that which is proposed to be done and they do not in themselves amount to convincing arguments against doing it. Of course, whenever money is raised for advancement on terms that it is to be settled on the beneficiary, the money only passes from one settlement to be caught up in the other. It is therefore the same thing as a resettlement. But, unless one is to say that such moneys can never be applied by way of settlement, an argument which, as I have shown, has few supporters and is contrary to authority, it merely describes the inevitable effect of such an advancement to say that it is nothing less than a resettlement. Similarly, if it is part of the trusts and powers created by one settlement that the trustees of it should have power to raise money and make it available for a beneficiary upon new trusts approved by them, then they are in substance given power to free the money from one trust and to subject it to another. So be it: but, unless they cannot require a settlement of it at all, the transaction they carry out is the same thing in effect as an appointment of new trusts.

In the same way I am unconvinced by the argument that the trustees would be improperly delegating their trust by allowing the money raised to pass over to new trustees under a settlement conferring new powers on the latter. In fact I think that the whole issue of delegation is here beside the mark. The law is not that trustees cannot delegate: it is that trustees cannot delegate unless they have authority to do so. If the power of advancement which they possess is so read as to allow them to raise money for the purpose of having it settled, then they do have the necessary authority to let the money pass out of the old settlement into the new trusts. No question of delegation of their powers or trusts arises.

I have not yet referred to the ground which was taken by the Court of Appeal as their reason for saying that the proposed settlement was not permissible. To put it shortly, they held that the statutory power of advancement could not be exercised unless the benefit to be conferred was 'personal to the person concerned, in the sense of being related to his or her own real or personal needs'. Or, to use other words of the learned Master of the Rolls, the exercise of the power 'must be an exercise done to meet the circumstances as they present themselves in regard to a person within the scope of the section, whose circumstances call for that to be done which the trustees think fit to do'. Upjohn LJ expressed himself in virtually the same terms.

My Lords, I differ with reluctance from the views of judges so learned and experienced in matters of this sort: but I do not find it possible to import such restrictions into the words of the statutory power which itself does not contain them. First, the suggested qualification, that the considerations or circumstances must be 'personal' to the beneficiary, seems to me uncontrollably vague as a guide to general administration. What distinguishes a personal need from any other need to which the trustees in their discretion

> think it right to attend in the beneficiary's interest? And, if the advantage of preserving the funds of a beneficiary from the incidence of death duty is not an advantage personal to that beneficiary, I do not see what is. Death duty is a present risk that attaches to the settled property in which Miss Penelope has her expectant interest, and even accepting the validity of the supposed limitation, I would not have supposed that there was anything either impersonal or unduly remote in the advantage to be conferred upon her of some exemption from that risk. I do not think, therefore, that I can support the interpretation of the power of advancement that has commended itself to the Court of Appeal, and, with great respect, I think that the judgments really amount to little more than a decision that in the opinion of the members of that court this was not a case in which there was any occasion to exercise the power. That would be a proper answer from a court to which trustees had referred their discretion with a request for its directions; but it does not really solve any question where, as here, they retain their discretion and merely ask whether it is impossible for them to exercise it.
>
> To conclude, therefore, on this issue, I am of opinion that there is no maintainable reasons for introducing into the statutory power of advancement a qualification that would exclude the exercise in the case now before us ... It is quite true, as the Commissioners have pointed out, that you might have really extravagant cases of resettlements being forced on beneficiaries in the name of advancement, even a few months before an absolute vesting in possession would have destroyed the power. I have tried to give due weight to such possibilities, but when all is said I do not think that they ought to compel us to introduce a limitation of which no one, with all respect, can produce a satisfactory definition. First, I do not believe that it is wise to try to cut down an admittedly wide and discretionary power, enacted for general use, through fear of its being abused in certain hypothetical instances. And moreover, as regards this fear, I think that it must be remembered that we are speaking of a power intended to be in the hands of trustees chosen by a settlor because of his confidence in their discretion and good sense and subject to the external check that no exercise can take place without the consent of a prior life tenant; and that there does remain at all times a residual power in the court to restrain or correct any purported exercise that can be shown to be merely wanton or capricious and not to be attributable to a genuine discretion. I think, therefore, that, although extravagant possibilities exist, they may be more menacing in argument than in real life.

Trustees' duties

The trustees are required to exercise their power of advancement in a fiduciary manner. The exercise will not be *bona fide* and will be void if the trustees advance funds to a beneficiary on condition that the sum is used to repay a loan made by one of the trustees (see *Molyneux v Fletcher*).[80] Moreover,

80 [1898] 1 QB 648.

the trustees may transfer the capital to the beneficiary directly if they reasonably believe that he may be trusted with the money. If the trustees specify a particular purpose which they reasonably believe the beneficiary is capable of fulfilling, they (trustees) may pay the fund over to him. But the trustees are under an obligation to ensure that the beneficiary, recipient of the fund, expends the sum for the specific purpose.

***Re Pauling's Settlement Trust* [1964] Ch 303, CA**

> **Willmer LJ:** What they [the trustees] cannot do is prescribe a particular purpose and then raise and pay the money over to the advancee leaving him or her entirely free, legally and morally, to apply it for that purpose or to spend it in any way he or she chooses without any responsibility on the trustees even to inquire as to its application.

In this case, the trustees of a marriage settlement held property upon trust for a wife for life with remainder to the children of the marriage. The trustees were given a power to advance up to half of the children's presumptive share to the children. The trustees made advances notionally to the children but the money was used for the benefit of the family generally. The family lived beyond their means. The trustees believed that they were exercising their power validly by paying the sums to the children and leaving them to do what they wished with the sums. A claim was brought against the trustees for breach of trust. The Court of Appeal held that the trustees were liable in that they had improperly exercised their discretion.

Powers of sale

Trustees as controllers of property are required to manage the trust on behalf of the beneficiaries. Accordingly, trustees may have a power of sale. The source of this power may vary with the circumstances of each case. Thus, trustees may be given express authority in the trust instrument to sell the trust assets or the power may be implied or the power may originate by statute. The precise source of the power is required to be identified.

Trust instrument

Whether the instrument authorises the trustees to sell the property is a question of fact. Many professionally drafted trust instruments will include such a clause subject to qualifications or not. Assuming the trustees have such authority, they are still required to exercise the requisite standard of skill and prudence in the exercise of such power.

Implied power

In exceptional circumstances, the court may impose a duty on the trustees to sell trust property and apply the proceeds in a particular manner (see *Howe v Lord Dartmouth*,[81] in respect of residuary personal property).

Statutory power

The power of sale may be created by statute. There are many statutory sources imposing a power of sale on trustees. The following are mentioned by way of illustration:

Section 16 of the Trustee Act 1925

> Where trustees are authorised by the trust instrument, creating the trust or by law to pay or apply capital money subject to the trust for any purpose or in any manner, they shall have and shall be deemed always to have had power to raise the money required by sale, conversion, calling in, or mortgage of all or any part of the trust property for the time being in possession.

Section 1(1) of the Trustee Investments Act 1961

> A trustee may invest any property in his hands, whether at the time in a state of investment or not, in any manner specified in Pt I or II of the First Schedule to this Act ... in any manner specified in Pt III of that Schedule, and may also from time to time vary any such investments.

Section 38 of the Settled Land Act 1925

> A tenant for life:
>
> (i) May sell the settled land, or any part thereof, or any easement, right or privilege of any kind over or in relation to the land; and
>
> (ii) ... [repealed]
>
> (iii) may make an exchange of the settled land, or any part thereof, or of any easement, right, or privilege of any kind ... including an exchange in consideration of money paid for equality of exchange.

It should be noted here that the person with the power of sale is not the trustees of the settlement *qua* trustees but the tenant for life who is treated as the 'statutory owner'.

Section 67(1) of the Settled Land Act 1925

> Where personal chattels are settled so as to devolve with settled land, or to devolve therewith as nearly as may be in accordance with the law or practice in force at the date of the settlement, or are settled together with land, or upon trusts declared by reference to the trusts affecting land, a tenant for life of the land may sell the chattels or any of them.

81 (1802) 7 Ves 137.

Section 130(5) of the Law of Property Act 1925

> Where personal chattels are settled without reference to settled land on trusts creating entailed interests therein, the trustees, with the consent of the usufructuary (beneficiary with a limited interest in the property) for the time being if of full age, may sell the chattels or any of them, and the net proceeds of any such sale shall be held in trust for and shall go to the same persons successively ...

Section 6 of the Trusts of Land and Appointment of Trustees Act 1996

Under s 6 of the 1996 Act, the trustees of land have all the 'powers of an absolute owner' in respect of the land. This includes a power to sell the land subject to the trust. In exercising this power, the trustees are required to have regard to the rights of the beneficiaries and any rules of law or equity or statutory provisions. The trust of land may require the consent of any person to any dealing with the land. Moreover, any power of the trustees, including the sale of the land, may be excluded or restricted by the trust deed.

In exceptional circumstances where the trustees have no power of sale within any of the above sources, they may apply to the court under s 57 of the Trustee Act 1925 (see below, p 839).

A power of sale is required to be exercised with the same degree of diligence and care as would be exercised by a prudent man in the conduct of his affairs (see Trustee's standard of care, above, p 761).

The mode of effecting the sale is stipulated in s 12 of the Trustee Act 1925 (as amended by the Trusts of Land and Appointment of Trustees Act 1996) which provides:

> (1) Where a trustee has a duty or power to sell property, he may sell or concur with any other person in selling all or any part of the property ... either together or in lots, by public auction or by private contract, subject to any such conditions respecting title or evidence of title or other matter as the trustee thinks fit, with power to vary any contract for sale, and to buy in at any auction, or to rescind any contract for sale and to re-sell, without being answerable for any loss.
>
> (2) A duty or power to sell or dispose of land includes a duty or power to sell or dispose of part thereof, whether the division is horizontal, vertical, or made in any other way.
>
> (3) This section does not enable an express power to sell settled land to be exercised where the power is not vested in the tenant for life or statutory owner.

In order to protect both trustees and third party purchasers who have acted *bona fide* and prudently, s 13 of the Trustee Act 1925 provides:

> (1) No sale made by a trustee shall be impeached by any beneficiary upon the ground that any of the conditions subject to which the sale was made may have been unnecessarily depreciatory, unless it also appears that the consideration for the sale was thereby rendered inadequate.

(2) No sale made by a trustee shall, after the execution of the conveyance, be impeached as against the purchaser upon the ground that any of the conditions subject to which the sale was made may have been unnecessarily depreciatory, unless it appears that the purchaser was acting in collusion with the trustee at the time when the contract for sale was made.

(3) No purchaser, upon any sale made by a trustee, shall be at liberty to make any objection against the title upon any of the grounds aforesaid.

Power to partition land under a trust of land

Section 7 of the Trusts of Land and Appointment of Trustees 1996, which repeals s 28 of the Law of Property Act 1925, confers on trustees of land the power to partition the land, or part of it, among adult beneficiaries who are absolutely entitled in undivided shares, subject to their consent. If an infant is absolutely entitled to a share, partition may still take place, but the trustees will hold his share on trust for him. This may end the co-ownership of the whole or part of the land subject to the trust. This section may be excluded or varied by the settlement, except in the case of trusts for ecclesiastical, public or charitable trusts.

The trust settlement may require the trustees to obtain the consent of any person before exercising any of their powers as trustees of land. If the consent of more than two persons are required, and have not been obtained, the purchaser is protected if, at least, two consents are obtained (s 10). But, this is without prejudice to the liability of the trustees for breach of trust. In the case of land held on ecclesiastical, charitable or public purposes, the purchaser is required to ensure that all necessary consents have been obtained. The consent of an infant is not required, but in such a case the trustees are duty bound to obtain the consent of the person with parental responsibility for the infant or his guardian.

Power to give receipts

In order to protect third party purchasers of trust property from the trustees, s 14 of the Trustee Act 1925 provides:

(1) The receipt in writing of a trustee for any money, securities, or other personal property or effects payable, transferable, or deliverable to him under any trust or power shall be a sufficient discharge to the person paying, transferring, or delivering the same and shall effectually exonerate him from seeing to the application or being answerable for any loss or misapplication thereof.

(2) This section does not, except where the trustee is a trust corporation, enable a sole trustee to give a valid receipt for:

(a) the proceeds of sale or other capital money arising under a ... trust of land;

(b) capital money arising under the Settled Land Act 1925.

(3) This section applies notwithstanding anything to the contrary in the instrument, if any, creating the trust.

In addition, it ought to be mentioned that, subject to provisions to the contrary in the trust instrument, transactions involving the trust are the joint actions of the trustees. Accordingly, only a joint receipt by all the trustees is capable of binding the trust (see above).

Power to claim reimbursement

Trustees as managers or representatives of the trust property are entitled to claim a refund or reimbursement from the trust funds for expenses properly incurred in the administration of the trust. Prior to the introduction of s 30(2) of the Trustee Act 1925 (see below), it was decided that trustees' right of reimbursement was equivalent to a lien or first charge on the trust assets in respect of expenses properly incurred in the administration of the trust. This right of reimbursement takes priority over the claims of beneficiaries and third parties.

In *Stott v Milne*,[82] the defendant trustees brought proceedings against third parties in connection with the trust using their own resources. The trustees recouped their expenses from part of the income. The plaintiff beneficiary (life tenant) was unaware of such proceedings and brought an action claiming repayment of the income by the trustees.

The Court of Appeal held, reversing the decision of the High Court, that the trustees were entitled to retain part of the income.

> **Lord Selborne LC:** I feel no doubt that the trustees acted *bona fide* and reasonably in bringing the actions. The property was peculiarly circumstanced, it was not large, but was available for building purposes, and anything done by tenants or neighbours which would give any other persons rights over it might cause a material depreciation in its value. The trustees therefore had an anxious duty to perform.
>
> The right of trustees to indemnity against all costs and expenses properly incurred by them in the execution of the trust is a first charge on all the trust property, both income and *corpus*. The trustees, therefore, had a right to retain the costs out of the income until provision could be made for raising them out of the corpus. I am of opinion that their costs of this action ought to be raised and paid out of the estate in the same way as the costs of the former actions.

The position today is enacted in s 30(2) of the Trustee Act 1925.

Section 30(2) of the Trustee Act 1925 provides:

82 (1884) 25 Ch D 710.

> A trustee may reimburse himself or pay or discharge out of the trust premises all expenses incurred in or about the execution of the trusts or powers.

In *Armitage v Nurse*, Millett LJ considered the rights of the trustees to a lien on the trust fund for their costs of litigation.

Armitage v Nurse [1997] 3 WLR 1046, CA

> **Millett LJ:**
>
> **Costs**
>
> Trustees are entitled to a lien on the trust fund for the costs of successfully defending themselves against an action for breach of trust. That was the position in *In re Spurling's Will Trusts* [1966] 1 WLR 920, as it was in *Walters v Woolbridge* (1878) 7 Ch D 504, which it followed. But on what principle can one justify their right to recoup themselves out of the trust fund for the costs of unsuccessfully defending themselves against such action? It offends all sense of justice. The respondents rely on *Turner v Hancock*, (1882) 20 Ch D 303 and submit that that was just such a case; but I do not think that it was. The action was an action for an account. On taking the accounts it was found that a sum was due from the trustee and not to him as he contended. It was, therefore, a case in which the trustee was unsuccessful; but it was not a case in which he was found to be guilty of misconduct or breach of trust. In the course of his judgment Sir George Jessel MR said, at p 305:
>
>> These rights ... can only be lost or curtailed by such inequitable conduct on the part of a mortgagee or trustee as may amount to a violation or culpable neglect of his duty under the contract ... It is not the course of the court in modern times to discourage persons from becoming trustees by inflicting costs upon them if they have done their duty, or even if they have committed an innocent breach of trust.
>
> In the present case, the judge deprived the respondents of 20% of their costs because they had put forward arguments on which they had been unsuccessful. That was a proper exercise of his discretion. But he also deprived them of their right to recoup themselves out of the trust fund to the extent of the 20%, on the ground that the claim was a hostile claim against them personally for breach of trust. In my opinion, that was not a sufficient ground for denying them their contractual rights.

It must be stressed that this right of recovery exists only in respect of expenses reasonably incurred. If, therefore, trustees incurred unreasonable expenses they have no right to recover their loss from the trust assets.

Holding and Management Ltd v Property Holding and Investment Trust plc and Others [1989] 1 WLR 1313, CA

The plaintiff, a trustee company, were maintenance trustees of a block of flats. The plaintiff proposed a programme of works which was opposed by the tenants. The plaintiff applied to the court for directions as to whether the scheme was within its powers. A compromise arrangement was reached between the parties during the course of the hearing. On the question of costs, the Court of Appeal ruled that the trustees were not entitled to a refund as they had acted unreasonably and could not be said to have represented the interests of the beneficiaries.

> **Nicholls LJ:** To be entitled to an indemnity the costs and expenses in question must have been properly incurred by the trustee. This is axiomatic. In the present case the plaintiff did not bring proceedings to protect the maintenance fund for the benefit of the beneficiaries. The beneficiaries of that fund, as I have sought to indicate, are the tenants plus the landlord. The proceedings were brought against the tenants to establish whether they were obliged to engage the fund to be applied for their benefit beyond what they and the landlord wished. I do not think that costs so incurred were properly incurred.

Under s 30(2) of the Trustee Act 1925, trustees are entitled to recover from the trust fund the costs and expenses properly incurred in respect of legal proceedings conducted in the interests of the trust. A prudent trustee will seek a *Beddoe* order (that is, leave from the court to bring or defend an action) before entering into legal proceedings on behalf of the trust. The effect of the order is to protect him against the *cestui que* trust and entitle him to be reimbursed the costs of litigation from the trust fund, irrespective of the result of the litigation in the main proceedings. A trustee who omits to take the precaution of obtaining leave from the court, but nevertheless becomes involved in trust litigation, runs the risk of not recovering his expenses if the court decides that litigation was unnecessary. Alternatively, if the trustees omit to apply for a *Beddoe* order (derived from the case *Re Beddoe* [1893] 1 Ch 547), they are still entitled to be reimbursed their costs if the action is considered to have been properly brought or defended on behalf of the trust.

Lightman J in *Alsop Wilkinson v Neary* (see below, p 831) decided that the trustees might be involved in three types of disputes:

(a) a 'trust dispute', namely, a dispute concerning the terms of the trust. This may be friendly, that is, involving the construction of the trust instrument, or hostile, that is, a challenge as to the validity of the trust;

(b) a 'beneficiaries dispute', namely, when one or more beneficiaries question the propriety of any action taken or omitted by the trustees;

(c) a 'third party dispute', namely, proceedings involving a stranger to the trust in respect of rights or liabilities under the trust.

This analysis, of course, does not determine whether the trustees' involvement in the action is necessary. This will depend on the nature and extent of the claim. Lightman J criticised Kekewich J's decision in *Ideal Bedding Company v Holland* [1907] 2 Ch 157, where the plaintiffs obtained an order against the trustees declaring the settlement void as against the plaintiffs and other creditors. The question arose whether one of the trustees who had defended the action ought to have his costs paid out of the trust estate. Kekewich J decided that the trustees had a duty to defend the action brought against the trust. Lightman J in the *Alsop* case felt that the trustees ought to have remained neutral in such proceedings.

Alsop Wilkinson v Neary and Others [1996] 1 WLR 1220, HC

The plaintiff applied by summons for an order under s 423 of the Insolvency Act 1986 to set aside a trust. The beneficiaries under the trust threatened proceedings for breach of trust if the trustees failed to defend the action. In the same proceedings, the applicants, trustees, sought leave from the court to determine whether they ought to defend the action (the *Beddoe* application).

Lightman J declined to grant leave to the trustees to defend the action. The dispute was between rival claimants to a beneficial interest in the subject matter of the trust. In such circumstances the trustees are duty bound to remain neutral and offer to submit to the court's directions, leaving the rival claimants to fight their battle. Moreover, the *Beddoe* application ought to be brought in proceedings separate from the main action: first, because it would involve disclosure of the trustees' case and other confidential information to the other parties to the main action and, secondly, to ensure that all the relevant parties to the application were before the court.

Lightman J:

A Background

Trustees may be involved in three kinds of dispute:

(1) The first (which I shall call 'a trust dispute') is a dispute as to the trusts on which they hold the subject matter of the settlement. This may be 'friendly' litigation involving, for example, the true construction of the trust instrument or some other question arising in the course of the administration of the trust; or 'hostile' litigation, for example, a challenge in whole or in part to the validity of the settlement by the settlor, on grounds of undue influence, or by a trustee in bankruptcy or a defrauded creditor of the settlor, in which case the claim is that the trustees hold the trust funds as trustees for the settlor, the trustee in bankruptcy or creditor in place of or in addition to the beneficiaries specified in the settlement. The line between friendly and hostile litigation, which is relevant as to the incidence of costs, is not always easy to draw: see *In re Buckton, Buckton v Buckton* [1907] 2 Ch 406.

(2) The second (which I shall call 'a beneficiaries dispute') is a dispute with one or more of the beneficiaries as to the propriety of any action which the trustees have taken or omitted to take or may or may not take in the future. This may take the form of proceedings by a beneficiary alleging breach of trust by the trustees and seeking removal of the trustees, and/or damages for breach of trust.

(3) The third (which I shall call 'a third party dispute') is a dispute with persons, otherwise than in the capacity of beneficiaries, in respect of rights and liabilities, for example, in contract or tort assumed by the trustees, as such, in the course of administration of the trust.

Trustees (express and constructive) are entitled to an indemnity against all costs, expenses and liabilities properly incurred in administering the trust and have a lien on the trust assets to secure such indemnity. Trustees have a duty to protect and preserve the trust estate for the benefit of the beneficiaries and accordingly to represent the trust in a third party dispute. Accordingly, their right to an indemnity and lien extends in the case of a third party dispute to the costs of proceedings properly brought or defended for the benefit of the trust estate. Views may vary whether proceedings are properly brought or defended, and to avoid the risk of a challenge to their entitlement to the indemnity (a beneficiary dispute), trustees are well advised to seek court authorisation before they sue or defend. The right to an indemnity and lien will ordinarily extend to the costs of such an application. The form of application is a separate action to which all the beneficiaries are parties (either in person or by a representative defendant). With the benefit of their views, the judge, thereupon exercising his discretion, determines what course the interests of justice require to be taken in the proceedings: see *In re Evans (Decd)* [1986] 1 WLR 101, considered by Hoffmann LJ in *McDonald v Horn* [1995] ICR 685. So long as the trustees make full disclosure of the strengths and weaknesses of their case, if the trustees act as authorised by the court, their entitlement to an indemnity and lien is secure.

A beneficiaries dispute is regarded as ordinary hostile litigation in which costs follow the event and do not come out of the trust estate: see *per* Hoffmann LJ in *McDonald v Horn* [1995] ICR 685, p 696.

The role of trustees in case of a trust dispute was considered by Kekewich J in two cases. Miss Proudman cited and relied on these cases as authority for the proposition that in cases of a challenge to the validity of the trusts (in particular, by a trustee in bankruptcy), the trustee is under a duty to defend to protect the existing beneficiaries and whatever the outcome is entitled to his costs out of the trust fund.

In *Merry v Pownall* [1895] 1 Ch 306 a settlor's trustee in bankruptcy brought proceedings against the trustees to set aside a limitation over in the settlement on the bankruptcy of the settlor. At the suggestion of the trustees, the beneficiaries were joined as defendants. The trustees in their defence and in argument submitted to act as the court directed. The beneficiaries disputed the claim. The action succeeded. Kekewich J held that the trustees, who had acted as very little more than stakeholders and in no wise acted wrongly in suggesting the joinder of the beneficiaries, were entitled to their costs out of the trust fund. In no wise does this case support Miss Proudman's proposition.

In *Ideal Bedding Co Ltd v Holland* [1907] 2 Ch 157, the plaintiffs, who were judgment creditors, obtained against the trustees of a settlement, an order declaring the settlement void as against the plaintiffs and other creditors under the statute 13 Eliz, c 5 on the ground that it 'delayed, hindered and defrauded' the plaintiffs and other creditors. The question arose whether one of the trustees who had defended the action ought to have his costs out of the trust estate. Kekewich J held that the trustee had had a duty to defend the trust as he did and that in his discretion he should have his costs.

I do not think that the view expressed by Kekewich J in the *Ideal Bedding* case, that in the case of a trust dispute (as was the dispute in that case), a trustee has a duty to defend the trust, is correct or in accordance with modern authority. In a case where the dispute is between rival claimants to a beneficial interest in the subject matter of the trust, rather, the duty of the trustee is to remain neutral and (in the absence of any court direction to the contrary and substantially, as happened in *Merry's Case* [1898] 1 Ch 306) offer to submit to the court's directions leaving it to the rivals to fight their battles. If this stance is adopted, in respect of the costs necessarily and properly incurred, for example, in serving a defence agreeing to submit to the courts direction and in making discovery, the trustees will be entitled to an indemnity and lien. If the trustees do actively defend the trust and succeed, for example, in challenging a claim by the settlor to set aside for undue influence, they may be entitled to their costs out of the trust, for they have preserved the interests of the beneficiaries under the trust: consider *In re Holden ex p Official Receiver* (1887) 20 QBD 43. But if they fail, then, in particular, in the case of hostile litigation, although in an exceptional case the court may consider that the trustees should have their costs (see *Bullock v Lloyds Bank Ltd* [1955] 1 Ch 317), ordinarily, the trustees will not be entitled to any indemnity, for they have incurred expenditure and liabilities in an unsuccessful effort to prefer one class of beneficiaries, for example, the express beneficiaries specified in the trust instrument, over another, for example, the trustees in bankruptcy or creditors, and so have acted unreasonably and otherwise than for the benefit of the trust estate: consider RSC Ord 62 r 6; and see *National Anti-Vivisection Society v Duddington* (1989) *The Times*, 23 November; and *Snell's Equity*, 29th edn, 1990, p 258.

B Present applications

***Beddoe* application**

The trustees have sought by means of a summons, in this action, to obtain directions whether or not to defend the action. Master Gower held that this course was not appropriate and I agree.

The attempted *Beddoe* application is, I think, fundamentally flawed on at least two grounds. The first is that the application must be made in separate proceedings. This is for good reason. The purpose of the application is to inform the judge as to the strengths and weaknesses of the trustees' case and the course to be taken, for example, in respect of a possible compromise. It would be quite inappropriate for all this to be revealed to the court which has to try the case or the other parties to the litigation. On the other hand, as a matter of principle, each of the parties to the action itself is entitled to know everything that is communicated to the court in that action: see *Smith v Croft* [1986] 1 WLR 580, p 588.

The second is that the necessary parties are not before the court. The parties to the action and the necessary parties to a *Beddoe* application are not the same: in particular, the settlor's wife and their issue are not represented. The justification for the protection afforded to trustees by *Beddoe* order is that the beneficiaries are given the opportunity to make representations to the court before the order is made. (In the case where there are unresolved disputes as to the identity of the beneficiaries, for example, because of a trust dispute, then all possible claimants should be joined). An order should not be made in proceedings which are so constituted that beneficiaries are precluded from being heard. It is nothing to the point, as suggested by Miss Proudman, that it is obvious what the representations of such beneficiaries would have been and that they may be thought incapable of affecting the decision.

The matter has not been argued whether the *Beddoe* application should be the courts of the forum of administration, that is, Jersey, rather than of England, and I do not have to consider that question.

I therefore take the view that the application for directions must be refused.

SUPPLEMENTARY READING

Bartlett, R, 'The Law Reform Committee's trust investment recommendations' [1992] Conv 425

Beatson, J, 'Restitution of taxes, levies and other imports: defining the extent of the *Woolwich* principle' (1993) 109 LQR 401

Clements, L, 'The changing face of trusts: the Trusts of Land and Appointment of Trustees Act 1996' (1998) 61 MLR 56

Ham, R, 'Third party liability of trustees – contract, tort and tax' (1996) 10 Tru LI 45

Jaconelli, J, 'Decision taking by private and charitable trustees' [1991] Conv 30

Kenny, A, 'Are a bank trustee's fees performance related? *Nestle v National Westminster Bank*' [1993] Conv 63

Kenny, A, 'Living up to expectations' (1996) 146 NLJ 348

Lee, N, 'Absolutely entitled – a new meaning?' [1978] Conv 456

Luxton, P, 'Ethical investments in hard times' (1992) 55 MLR 587

Matthews, P, ' Trusts of flawed assets: the liability of trustees' (1998) 4 T & T 6

McCormack, G, 'Liability of trustees for gross negligence' [1998] Conv 100

Megarry, R, 'The ambit of a trustee's duty of disclosure' (1965) 81 LQR 192

Lord Nicholls of Birkenhead, 'Trustees and their broader community: where duty, morality and ethics converge' (1995) 9 Tru LI 71

Nobles, R, 'The exercise of trustees' discretion under a pension scheme' [1992] JBL 261

O'Hagan, P, 'Trustees' duty to disclose' (1995) 145 NLJ 1414

Paling, D, 'The trustees' duty of skill and care' (1973) 37 Conv 48

Pearce, P and Samuels, A, 'Trustees and beneficiaries and investment politics' [1985] Conv 52

Riddall, J, '*Re Ransome* Revisited or First The Good Nuns' (1979) 43 Conv 423

Russell, M, 'Apportioning windfalls' (1998) 142 SJ 284

Samuels, A, 'Disclosure of trust documents' (1965) 28 MLR 220

Shindler, G, 'Casenote – *Bartlett v Barclays Bank Trust Co Ltd*' [1980] Conv 155

Virgo, G, 'Restitution of overpaid tax – justice at the expense of certainty' [1993] CLJ 31

Watt, G, 'Escaping s 8(1) provisions in "new style" trusts of land' [1997] Conv 263

CHAPTER 20

VARIATION OF TRUSTS

Trustees are required to administer the trust in accordance with its terms. They have a primary duty to obey the instructions as detailed by the settlor or implied by law. Any deviation from the terms of the trust is a breach, making them personally liable, irrespective of how well intentioned the trustees may have been. But, circumstances may have arisen, since the setting up of the trust, which indicate that the trust may be more advantageously administered if the terms were altered.

For example, the investment powers of the trustees may prove to be extremely limited and obsolete or the impact of a potential liability to taxation may have the effect of depreciating the trust assets if no action is taken. A partitioning of the trust property between the life tenant and remainderman may have the effect of avoiding inheritance tax if the life tenant survives for seven years or more. Whereas, if no action is taken the entire capital suffers inheritance tax on the death of the life tenant and a second time on the death of the remainder.

In these circumstances, the trustees are in need of some mechanism whereby authority may be conferred on them to depart from or vary the terms of the trust. Such authority may be conferred in a variety of ways.

In *Saunders v Vautier*,[1] it was held that, where the beneficiaries are of full age and of sound mind and are absolutely entitled to the trust property, they may deal with the equitable interest in any way they wish. They may sell, exchange or gift away their interest. As a corollary to this rule such beneficiaries acting in unison are entitled to terminate the trust. Equally, such beneficiaries acting in concert are entitled to empower the trustees to perform such acts as they (the beneficiaries) consider appropriate. In short, the beneficiaries, collectively, are entitled to rewrite the terms of the trust.

Saunders v Vautier (1841) Cr & Ph 240, CA

In this case, stock was bequeathed upon trust to accumulate the dividends until Vautier (V) attained the age of 25. At this age, the trustees were required to transfer the capital and accumulated income to V. V attained the age of majority (21) and claimed the fund at this age. The question in issue was whether the trustees were required to transfer the fund to V.

1 (1841) Cr & Ph 240.

Held that, since the fund had vested in V, the sole beneficiary, subject to the enjoyment being postponed and he was of full age, he was entitled to terminate the trust.

> **Lord Langdale MR:** I think that principle has been repeatedly acted upon; and where a legacy is directed to accumulate for a certain period, or where the payment is postponed the legatee, if he has an absolute indefeasible interest in the legacy, is not bound to wait until the expiration of that period, but may require payment the moment he is competent to give a valid discharge.

But, where minors or persons under a disability or persons unborn are beneficiaries (or potential beneficiaries), there cannot be a departure from the terms of the trust without the court's approval.

The courts draw a distinction between:

(a) a variation concerning the management and administration of trusts; and

(b) a variation of the beneficial interests under the trusts.

Management and administration

Inherent jurisdiction of the court

The court has an inherent jurisdiction to depart from the terms of a trust in the case of an 'emergency', that is, an occasion when no provision was made in the trust instrument and the event could not have been foreseen by the settlor. This power is very narrow and arises in order to 'salvage' the trust property such as effecting essential repairs to buildings.

The power was exercised in *Re New*[2] which was described as the 'high water mark' of the emergency jurisdiction.

Re New [1901] 2 Ch 534, CA

In this case, the trust property consisted of shares in a company divided in £100 units. The court approved a scheme of capital reconstruction on behalf of minors and unborn persons by splitting the shares into smaller units so that they could be more easily realised. Romer LJ, in giving the judgment of the court, summarised the court's jurisdiction thus:

> **Romer LJ:** In the management of a trust it not infrequently happens that some peculiar state of circumstances arises for which provision is not expressly made by the trust instrument, and which renders it most desirable, and it may be even essential, for the benefit of the estate and in the interests of all the *cestuis que* trust, that certain acts should be done by the trustees which in ordinary circumstances they have no power to do. In a case of this kind, which

2 [1901] 2 Ch 534.

> may reasonably be supposed to be one not foreseen or anticipated by the author of the trust, where the trustees are embarrassed by the emergency that has arisen and the duty cast on them to do what is best for the estate, and the consent of all the beneficiaries cannot be obtained by reason of some of them not being *sui juris* or in existence, then it may be right for the court, to sanction on behalf of all concerned such acts on behalf of the trustees. The jurisdiction is one to be exercised with great caution, and the court will take care not to strain its powers ... it need scarcely be said that the court will not be justified in sanctioning every act desired by trustees and beneficiaries merely because it may appear beneficial to the estate; and certainly the court will not be disposed to sanction transactions of a speculative or risky character.

In *Re Tollemache*,[3] the court refused to sanction a scheme authorising the mortgage of the life tenant's beneficial interest in order to increase her income. There was no emergency.

Section 57 of the Trustee Act 1925

The section is drafted in fairly wide terms and empowers the court to confer the authority on the trustees to perform functions whenever it is expedient to do so.

Section 57 provides:

> (1) ... where in the management or administration of any property ... any sale, lease, mortgage, surrender, release or other disposition or any purchase, investment, acquisition, expenditure or other transaction is in the opinion of the court expedient, but the same can not be effected by reason of the absence of any power ... the court may by order confer on the trustees, either generally or in any particular instance the necessary power ...
>
> (2) The court may from time to time, rescind or vary any order made under this section, or may make any new or further order.
>
> (3) An application to the court ... may be made by the trustees, or by any of them, or by any person beneficially interested under the trust.
>
> (4) This section does not apply to trustees of a settlement for the purposes of the Settled Land Act 1925.

The policy of s 57 is to secure that the trust property is managed as advantageously as possible in the interests of the beneficiaries and to authorise specific dealings with the trust property outside the scope of the inherent jurisdiction of the court. It may not be possible to establish an emergency or that the settlor could not reasonably have foreseen the circumstances which have arisen. In these circumstances, the court may sanction the scheme presented for its approval. See Lord Evershed MR in *Re Downshire's Settled Estates*[4] (below, p 844).

3 [1903] 1 Ch 955.

4 [1953] Ch 218.

However, there are a number of limitations within s 57. First, the scheme proposed by the trustees is required to be for the benefit of the trust as a whole and not only for an individual beneficiary. In *Re Craven's Estate (No 2)*,[5] the court refused to sanction a scheme authorising an advancement to a beneficiary for the purpose of becoming a Lloyd's underwriter. The scheme would not have been expedient for the trust as a whole. Second, additional powers may only be conferred on the trustees with regards to the 'management or administration' of the trust. No power exists under s 57 to alter the beneficial interest or to re-write the trust administration clause as opposed to merely authorising specific dispositions or transactions. This distinction is one of degree. See *Re Coates' Trusts*[6] and *Re Byng's Will Trusts*.[7]

Under this provision, the courts have sanctioned schemes for the partition of land: *Re Thomas*;[8] a sale of land where the necessary consent could not be obtained: *Re Beale's Settlement Trust*;[9] the sale of a reversionary interest which the trustees had no power to sell until it fell into possession: *Re Heyworth's Contingent Reversionary Interest*;[10] blending two charitable trusts into one: *Re Shipwrecked Fishermen's and Mariners' Benevolent Fund*;[11] the extension of investment powers of pension fund trustees: *Mason v Farbrother*[12] (see above, p 800); a power to invest abroad: *Trustees of the British Museum v AG*;[13] a power to invest as if the trustees were beneficial owners, subject to certain guidelines: *Steel v Wellcome Custodian Trustee*.[14]

In *Steel v Wellcome Custodian Trustees*, the plaintiffs were professional trustees of a charitable fund established in 1932 by the will of the philanthropist, Sir Henry Solomon Wellcome. The trustees were bequeathed the entire share capital in Wellcome Ltd (W) with limited powers of investment. In 1956, the powers of investment were extended by order of the court so as to allow investment in UK and US fixed interest stocks and equities, but the use of the extended powers was limited to two thirds of the value of the assets. The plaintiffs applied to the court for approval in order to extend their powers of investment to acquire any property whatever as if they were beneficial owners of the fund, save that they were required to observe certain guidelines in choosing investments. The court granted the approval sought by the plaintiff.

---

5 [1937] Ch 431.
6 [1959] 1 WLR 375.
7 *Ibid*.
8 [1939] 1 Ch 194.
9 [1932] 2 Ch 15.
10 [1956] Ch 364.
11 [1959] Ch 220.
12 [1983] 2 All ER 1078.
13 [1984] 1 All ER 337.
14 [1988] 1 WLR 167.

Hoffman J: In *Trustees of the British Museum v AG*,[15] Sir Robert Megarry VC decided that the Act of 1961 was now sufficiently in the past to cease casting any shadow over the court's jurisdiction to mould investment clauses in accordance with what appeared to satisfy the prudence principle at the present time and in the particular circumstances of the case. Sir Robert Megarry VC,[16] drew attention to several features of the case which are also present in the application before me. First, there was general evidence of changes in investment practice over the previous 20 years. Inflation had caused a general movement away from long term investment in fixed interest securities and into equities and property. The abandonment of exchange control and fixed parities had made it possible and desirable to invest in the securities of various foreign countries and to hedge against currency losses. Small companies with specialist markets had grown faster than old established giants in sunset industries. New financial investments such as Eurobonds had been created. Evidence to much the same effect, updated to 1987, was contained in the affidavits before me.

Secondly, the Vice Chancellor drew attention to the relatively large size of the fund, which had a value of between £5 m and £6 m. The fund with which I am concerned is about 600 times as big. Thirdly, he was impressed by the expert advice available to the trustees from Lazard Securities Ltd and two distinguished unpaid investment advisers, as well as the eminent character of the trustees themselves. In this case the trustees propose to engage four professional fund managers each to manage a part of the fund, as well as a specialist firm to monitor and report on their performance.

It seems to me clear that the powers conferred by the will of 1932 and augmented by the order of Upjohn J are hopelessly out of date. The only reason why the present application was not forced on the trustees at a much earlier date is because, until the Wellcome plc flotation, only a relatively tiny part of the value of the fund was subject to those investment powers. The requirement that a third of the fund must be in fixed interest securities is unnecessarily restrictive and the provision for determining the proportions from time to time is both administratively cumbersome and a penalty on success. The prohibition against investing in equities not quoted on the London or New York stock exchanges has prevented the trustees from participating in the boom in Pacific Basin shares, while the need for a five year dividend record means that they cannot buy shares in privatised industries. The Attorney General therefore accepts that the investment powers must be recast.

The most important difference between the scheme in this case and that approved in the British Museum case is that the latter scheme contained a requirement that part of the fund should be invested in narrower range securities and some restrictions upon the kind of securities authorised for the rest of the fund. The present scheme has no division of the fund and no restriction upon the nature of the investments.

15 [1984] 1 WLR 418.

16 *Ibid*, pp 422–23.

I therefore think that if I were to insist in this case on a specific provision which Sir Robert Megarry VC in the *British Museum* case thought appropriate for a different fund in 1983, I would be failing to apply the general principle on which he acted, namely that the court should judge each application on its merits.

Having regard therefore to the size of this fund, the eminence of the trustees, the provisions of the scheme for obtaining and acting on advice and the quality of advice available, as well as the special circumstances pertaining to the large holding in the shares of a single company, I am willing to approve the present scheme without any restriction on the kind of assets in which all or any of the fund may be invested.'

Variation of beneficial interest

The court has the jurisdiction to approve schemes which go beyond an alteration of the management powers of trustees and effect arrangements which vary the beneficial interest under a trust.

Section 53 of the Trustee Act 1925

Where an infant is beneficially entitled to real or personal property and the property does not produce income which may be used for the infant's maintenance, education or benefit, the court may adopt a proposal authorising a 'conveyance' of the infant's interest with a view to the application of the capital or income for the maintenance, education or benefit of the infant.

The section may not be used simply to terminate a settlement without making some new trust provision for the infant. In *Re Meux*,[17] the plaintiff was a life tenant of a trust fund and his infant son was entitled to a contingent reversionary interest. The court sanctioned a scheme on behalf of the infant whereby a person was appointed to convey the infant's interest to the plaintiff in consideration of a purchase price which was paid to the trustees for the benefit of the infant.

Section 64 of the Settled Land Act 1925

Settled land is excluded from s 57 of the Trustee Act 1925 because of the separate provision enacted for such property.

Section 64 provides:

(1) Any transaction affecting or concerning the settled land, or any part thereof, or any other land (not being a transaction otherwise authorised by this Act, or by the settlement) which in the opinion of the court would be

17 [1958] Ch 154.

for the benefit of the settled land, or any part thereof, or the persons interested under the settlement, may, under an order of the court, be effected by a tenant for life, if it is one which could have been validly effected by an absolute owner.

(2) In this section 'transaction' includes any sale, exchange, assurance, grant, lease, surrender, reconveyance, release, reservation, or other disposition, and any purchase or other acquisition, and any covenant, contract or option and any application of capital money, and any compromise or other dealing or arrangement; and 'effected' has the meaning appropriate to the particular transaction; and the references to land include references to restrictions and burdens affecting land.

The jurisdiction of the courts under s 64 is much wider than the jurisdiction under s 57 (above, p 839). Section 64 not only entitles the court to sanction schemes connected with the management and administration of the trust but also the alteration of beneficial interests under the settlement. Moreover, s 64 by implication extends to land held upon trust for sale for s 28(1) of the Law of Property Act 1925 confers upon trustees of land held upon trust for sale all the powers which the Settled Land Act confers upon the tenant for life of settled land. See *Re Simmons*.[18] A protected life tenant, who had a general power of appointment exercisable by will or codicil, wanted to dispose of capital. The High Court approved a scheme whereby some capital was to be transferred to her in return for releasing her general power of appointment over part of the fund.

Section 28(1) of the Law of Property Act 1925 provides:

Trustees for sale shall, in relation to land or to manorial incidents and to the proceeds of sale, have all the powers of a tenant for life and the trustees of a settlement under the Settled Land Act 1925, including in relation to the land the powers of management conferred by that Act during a minority; and (subject to any express trust to the contrary) all capital money arising under the said powers shall, unless paid or applied for any purpose authorised by the Settled Land Act 1925, be applicable in the same manner as if the money represented proceeds of sale arising under the trust for sale.

The limitation within s 64 requires the scheme or transaction to be beneficial to the settled land itself or for the benefit of any person interested under the settlement. Thus, variations of beneficial interests and transactions designed to reduce fiscal liability have been sanctioned by the courts.

Peter Gibson J in *Raikes v Lygon*[19] pointed out that s 64(1) of the Settled Land Act 1925 created five prerequisites for the approval of a scheme. These are as follows:

(i) a 'transaction' as defined in sub-s (2) of s 64 of the 1925 Act;

(ii) affecting or concerning the settled land or any part thereof;

18 [1956] Ch 125.

19 [1988] 1 All ER 884.

(iii) not being a transaction otherwise authorised by the 1925 Act or the settlement;

(iv) in the opinion of the court would be for the benefit of:

 (a) the settled land or any part of it; or

 (b) the persons interested under the settlement; and

(v) being one which could have been effected by an absolute owner.

In this case, the High Court authorised the transfer of trust property to a maintenance fund. The transaction was regarded as fiscally advantageous but otherwise an unauthorised investment.

In *Re White-Popham Settled Estates*,[20] the Court of Appeal approved an arrangement whereby the debts of the life tenant were repaid out of capital because on the facts this arrangement was for the benefit of all the beneficiaries. The capital was to be repaid by an insurance policy on the life of the life tenant of which all the premiums except the first were to be charged to the income of the trust fund.

In *Re Downshire's Settled Estates*,[21] the Court of Appeal approved a scheme designed to avoid estate duty. Under the scheme, the tenant for life of settled land proposed to surrender his protected life interest in £700,000 of capital money and settled land worth £400,000 in favour of the remainderman. Provision would be made for any possible future beneficiaries under the protective trust by means of insurance policies. The transaction 'affected or concerned' the settled land indirectly.

Recently, the High Court assumed jurisdiction under s 64 to permit the trustees of a settled estate, which could in the future devolve to a financially irresponsible heir, to prepare a scheme for the proper running of the estate. This is the position notwithstanding the heir was of full age and capacity and did not consent to the proposed scheme.

Hambro and Others v The Duke of Marlborough and Others [1994] 3 WLR 341, HC

By an Act of Parliament in 1704, Queen Anne gave the manor of Woodstock and surrounding lands to the first Duke of Marlborough in fee simple as a reward for his services, particularly his victory at Blenheim. By a further Act of Parliament in 1706 it was provided that, in the event of the failure of his male issue, which occurred, the titles of the first duke would pass to his daughters and their male issue in tail male severally in succession, with remainders over. This Act prohibited any duke from undertaking any activity which would hinder, bar or disinherit a successor from possessing and

20 [1936] 2 All ER 1486.

21 [1953] Ch 218.

enjoying the land ('the entrenching provision'). The effect of these Acts and a series of 19th century decisions is that the duke for the time being is an ordinary tenant in tail, notwithstanding his inability to bar the entailed interest. Under s 20(1)(i) of the Settled Land Act 1925, each successive duke has the powers of a tenant for life. The first defendant (the 11th duke) currently the tenant in tail in possession and the trustees of the settlement (the plaintiffs) became very concerned about the future of the estate. In particular, the irresponsible disposition of the second defendant, the Marquis of Blandford, (the eldest son of the duke and heir apparent) led the plaintiffs and the duke to conclude, reluctantly, that the marquis was not capable of managing the estate. The plaintiffs prepared a scheme for the proper running of the estate in the future. Under the scheme, a new settlement was to be created whereby the estate would be subject to a trust for sale and the trust fund was to be held to pay the income to the duke for life and, subject thereto, on protective trust for the marquis for his life and, subject thereto, as to both income and capital on the trusts of the existing settlement. The effect of the scheme, if approved, would affect the marquis in a material way in that he would be deprived of the benefits to be derived from being a tenant for life, with the right to live in and manage Blenheim Palace. The marquis opposed the scheme. The issue before the court was not concerned with the merits of approving the scheme or not, but with whether the court has the jurisdiction to approve the scheme under s 64 of the Settled Land Act 1925.

The trustees contended that the court has the jurisdiction to approve the scheme without the consent of the marquis and in alteration of his beneficial interests. The marquis submitted that s 64 of the 1925 Act does not authorise the beneficial interests of a person who is *sui juris* to be varied without his consent though it may be used to alter the interests of infant, unborn or unascertained beneficiaries as part of the transaction to be sanctioned by the court. In particular, it was submitted that the word 'transaction' does not cover the unilateral act of imposing on the estate a trust for sale (thereby freeing it and the trustees from the Settled Land Act 1925) and that the concluding words in sub-s (1) 'if it is one which could have been validly effected by an absolute owner' does not cover the case of one person disposing of the property of another. In addition, the entrenching section of the 1706 Act prohibits the alteration of beneficial interests proposed by the scheme.

Morritt J held in favour of the trustees on the following grounds:

(1) on construction, the expression, 'transaction' was a word of wide import. The proposed new settlement or conveyance was a 'transaction' within s 64(2) of the 1925 Act as it amounted to a transfer of property which was an 'assurance ... or other disposition';

(2) as far as jurisdiction is concerned, a transaction approved under s 64 of 1925 Act may vary the beneficial interest of an ascertained beneficiary of

full age and capacity provided such variation is for the benefit of the settled land or of all the beneficiaries under the settlement;

(3) the proposed conveyance was inconsistent with the entrenched section of the 1706 Act and amounted to a 'hindrance' under this Act. However, s 20(1)(i) of the Settled Land Act 1925 (which repealed and re-enacted s 58(1)(i) of the Settled Land Act 1882) confers the powers of a tenant for life on a tenant in tail. These powers include powers of sale. The effect, therefore, was that the 1882 Act overrode the entrenching provision.

Compromise

The court has the jurisdiction to approve compromise arrangements governing the rights of beneficiaries including infants and unborn persons under trusts. Before the House of Lords decision in *Chapman v Chapman*,[22] there was some doubt as to whether the jurisdiction exists if there is not a genuine dispute between the beneficiaries. The House of Lords in *Chapman v Chapman* clarified the meaning of the expression 'compromise', by deciding that its jurisdiction concerned cases of genuine disputes about the existence of rights. In this case, the trustees applied for leave to execute a scheme releasing certain properties from the trust in order to avoid estate duty. Some of the interests were enjoyed by infants and may be enjoyed by unborn persons so that any re-arrangement of interests required the consent of the court. The House of Lords held that the scheme would not be approved because the court had no jurisdiction to sanction a re-arrangement of beneficial interests on behalf of infants and unborn persons where there was no real dispute.

The Variation of Trusts Act 1958

The Variation of Trusts Act 1958 was passed in order to reverse the decision of the House of Lords in *Chapman v Chapman* and to introduce sweeping changes in the law. The jurisdiction of the courts was extended in order to approve variations of trusts (in respect of both administrative matters and beneficial interests) on behalf of infants, unborn persons and others. The court is entitled to sanction 'any arrangement varying or revoking all or any trusts or enlarging the powers of the trustees of managing or administering any of the property subject to the trusts'.

The court in its discretion may make an order approving a scheme provided that the following four conditions are satisfied:

(1) property, whether real or personal, is held on trust; and

(2) the trust was created by will or *inter vivos* settlement or other disposition; and

22 [1954] AC 429.

(3) the beneficiary (or beneficiaries) actual or potential falls within at least one of the four categories as enumerated in s 1(1) of the Act, namely:

(a) any person having directly or indirectly, an interest, whether vested or contingent under the trusts, who by reason of infancy or other incapacity is incapable of assenting; or

(b) any person (whether ascertained or not) who may become entitled, directly or indirectly, to an interest at a future date or on the happening of a future event, a person of any specified description or a member of any specified class of persons, but not including any person who would be of that description or a member of that class if the said date had fallen or the said event had happened at the date of the application to the court; or

(c) any person unborn; or

(d) any person in respect of any discretionary interest of his under protective trusts where the interest of the principal beneficiary has not failed or determined.

(4) Provided that, with the exception of para (d) above, the arrangement was carried out for the benefit of that person.

The court is entitled 'to vary or revoke all or any of the trusts or enlarge the powers of the trustees of managing or administering any of the property subject to the trusts'.

The purpose of the Act is to permit the court to approve arrangements on behalf of beneficiaries who cannot give their consent by virtue of infancy or other incapacity or because their identity is unascertained such as a future spouse. It follows, therefore, that the court has no jurisdiction to approve arrangements on behalf of beneficiaries who are *sui juris*, adult and ascertained. Thus, the consent of all adult ascertained beneficiaries must be obtained before the court grants its approval to a scheme.

For example, T1 and T2 hold property on trust for A (adult) for life, remainder to B (an infant) for life with remainder to C (adult) absolutely. A scheme of equal division is proposed. The court may approve the scheme on behalf of B (the infant) but not in respect of A and C. Their consent is required to be obtained.

The only exception to the above rule is to be found in s 1(1)(d) of the Act namely the court may consent on behalf of an adult 'beneficiary' who may become entitled to an interest on the failure of the principal beneficiary's interest under a protective trust.

For example, trustees hold property on protective trust for M for life. A scheme is submitted for the approval of the court to grant M's wife, W, a one fifth share of the capital. The court may approve the arrangement on behalf of W, but M is required to consent to the scheme.

The nature of the jurisdiction of the court under the Variation of Trusts Act 1958 was described by Lord Reid in *Re Holmden's Settlement Trusts* [1968] AC 685, thus:

Lord Reid: Under the Variation of Trusts Act 1958, the court does not itself amend or vary the trusts of the original settlement. The beneficiaries are not bound by variations because the court has made the variation. Each beneficiary is bound because he has consented to the variation. If he was not of full age when the arrangement was made, he is bound because the court was authorised by the Act of 1958 to approve of it on his behalf and did so by making an order. If he was of full age and did not in fact consent, he is not affected by the order of the court and he is not bound. So the arrangement must be regarded as an arrangement made by the beneficiaries themselves. The court merely acted on behalf of or as representing those beneficiaries who were not in a position to give their own consent and approval.

Section 1(1)(b) of the Variation of Trusts Act 1958

Generally, the court may consent on behalf of potential beneficiaries who have a contingent interest in the trust (see s 1(1)(b)). But, the proviso to s 1(1)(b) prevents the court from approving on behalf of adult beneficiaries who stand only one step removed from entitlement under the trust. It was the intention of Parliament that such persons should be allowed to consent for themselves.

For example, trustees hold property on trust for A for life with an ultimate remainder for his next of kin. A is a widower with one son, B (adult). A scheme is proposed in order to divide the fund equally between A and B. In such a case, B is required to consent to the arrangement under the proviso to s 1(1)(b), on the ground that B is only one step removed (namely, the death of A) from acquiring a vested interest.

Re Suffert's Settlement [1961] Ch 1, HC

Under a settlement, B, was granted a protected life interest with a power to appoint the capital and income on trust for their children. The settlement provided that, if B had no children, the property was to be transferred to anyone in respect of whom B may appoint (that is, a general power) with a gift over in default of appointment in favour of B's statutory next of kin. B was 61 years of age, unmarried and without issue. She had three first cousins (next of kin) all of whom had attained the age of majority. B and one of her cousins sought to vary the settlement. The other two cousins had not consented and were not joined as parties. The court was asked to approve the arrangement on behalf of any unborn or unascertained persons and the two adult cousins.

The court held that it had jurisdiction to approve on behalf of unborn and unascertained persons but could not approve on behalf of the two cousins. Their consent was required.

Buckley J: What the sub-section required was that the applicant should be treated as having died at the date of the issue of the summons, to find out who in that event would have been her statutory next of kin, and any persons who are within that class are persons whose interest the section provides that the

> court cannot bind. It is impossible to say who are the statutory next of kin of somebody who is alive, but it is not impossible to say who are the persons who would fill that description on the hypothesis that the *propositus* is already dead.

Knocker v Youle [1986] 1 WLR 934, HC

Under a settlement created in 1937, property was settled on trust for the settlor's daughter for life and on her death (her share including accumulated income) was to be held on trust for such persons as she may appoint by her will. In default of appointment, the property was to be acquired by the settlor's son upon a similar trust. It was provided in the trust instrument that in the event of the trusts failing the property was to be held on trust for the settlor's wife for life and subject thereto for the settlor's four married sisters or their children *per stirpes*. The settlor's wife and sisters were all dead. There were numerous children from the four sisters. The settlor's daughter and son sought a variation of the trust under s 1(1)(b) of the 1958 Act which would have affected the children from the settlor's four sisters.

The court held that it had no jurisdiction in the circumstances. Section 1(1)(b) of the Act was not applicable to a person who had an interest under the trust. The children of the settlor's four sisters had a contingent interest under the trust, however remote thus depriving the court of jurisdiction.

> **Warner J:** It is not strictly accurate to describe the cousins as persons 'who may become entitled ... to an interest under the trusts'. There is no doubt of course that they are members of a 'specified class'. Each of them is, however, entitled now to an interest under the trusts, albeit a contingent one (in the case of those who are under 21, a doubly contingent one) and albeit also that it is an interest that is defeasible on the exercise of the general testamentary powers of appointment vested in Mrs Youle and Mr Knocker. Nonetheless, it is properly described in legal language as and is used in its technical, legal sense. Otherwise, the words 'whether vested or contingent' in s 1(1)(a) would be out of place. It seems to me, however, that a person who has an actual interest directly conferred upon him or her by a settlement, albeit a remote interest, cannot properly be described as one who 'may become' entitled to an interest.

Variation or resettlement?

Although the Act gives the court a wide discretion to approve a scheme varying the terms of a trust, there appears to be a limitation on this discretion. The courts have adopted the policy of not 'rewriting' the trust. Accordingly, a distinction is drawn between a 'variation' and a 'resettlement'. A 'variation' retains the basic fundamental purpose of the trust but alters some important characteristic of the trust, whereas, a 'resettlement' destroys the foundation or substance of the original design or purpose of the trust. Whether a scheme amounts to a variation or a resettlement will vary with the facts of each case.

Re Ball's Settlement **[1968] 1 WLR 899, HC**

A settlement conferred a life interest on the settlor with remainder subject to a power of appointment in favour of his sons and grandchildren. In default of appointment, the fund was to be divided between the two sons of the settlor or their issue *per stirpes* (that is, the son's issue if either predeceased the settlor). A scheme was proposed for approval by the court whereby the original settlement would be revoked and replaced by new provisions in which the fund would be split into two equal portions each held on trust for each of the sons for life and subject thereto, for such of each son's children equally as were born before 1 October 1977.

The court decided to approve the scheme.

> **Megarry J:** The test is if the arrangement changes the whole substratum of the trust, then it may well be that it cannot be regarded merely as varying that trust. But if an arrangement, while leaving the substratum, effectuates the purpose of the original trusts by other means, it may still be possible to regard that arrangement as merely varying the original trusts, even though the means employed are wholly different and even though the form is completely changed ... In this case, it seems to me that the substratum of the original trust remains. True, the settlor's life interest disappears; but the remaining trusts are still in essence trusts of half the fund for each of the two named sons and their families ... The differences between the old and new provisions lie in detail rather than substance.

Settlor's intention

In exercising its discretion whether to approve an arrangement or not, the function of the court is to determine, by reference to all the circumstances, whether the arrangement as a whole is beneficial to the stipulated class of beneficiaries. Under the proviso to s 1(1) of the Variation of Trusts Act 1958, the court is prohibited from approving a scheme, unless it is designed for the *benefit* of the classes of persons within s 1(1)(a), (b) or (c) of the 1958 Act. The court acts on behalf of the specified classes of persons and, in appropriate cases, supplies consent for persons incapable of consenting. The requirement of benefit to the relevant classes of persons is mandatory.

On the other hand, the court may or may not approve a scheme under the 1958 Act, irrespective of whether the arrangement is or is not for the benefit of persons classified within s 1(1)(d) of the Act. In short, benefit is not a requirement, under the Act, for this category of persons. See *Re Steed* (below, p 851).

Although the 1958 Act makes no mention of the settlor or testator, rules of court have been made requiring the joinder of the settlor, if living, as a defendant to an application under the Act.

RSC Ord 93 r 6(2) provides:

> In addition to any other persons who are necessary and proper defendants to the originating summons by which an application under the said s 1 is made, the settlor and any other person who provided property for the purposes of the trust to which the application relates must, if still alive and not the plaintiff, be made a defendant unless the court for some special reason otherwise directs.

However, in the context of deciding whether to approve an arrangement or not, the intention of the settlor or testator is only a factor (if relevant) to be taken into consideration by the court. But the settlor's or testator's intention is certainly not an overriding factor, nor even a weighty consideration in determining how the discretion of the court is to be exercised. The role of the court is not to act as a representative of the settlor or testator in varying the trusts.

Re Steed's Will Trust [1960] Ch 407, CA

A testator devised a farm to trustees on protective trust for his housekeeper, Gladys, for life and after her death for such persons as she may by deed or will appoint, and in default of appointment on trust for her next of kin. The will declared the testator's 'wish that she shall have the use and enjoyment of the capital value if she needs it during her life and if and when the property is sold the trustees may apply the proceeds to or for her benefit provided that they shall consider the necessity for retaining sufficient capital to prevent her from being without adequate means at any time during her life'. Gladys exercised the power of appointment in her favour. The farm was let to her brother but he failed to pay any rent. The trustees decided to sell the farm but Gladys opposed the sale and brought a summons under the Variation of Trusts Act 1958, asking the court to approve an arrangement under which the trustees will hold the property on trust for herself absolutely.

The court held that, having regard to all the circumstances, including the intention of the settlor, the scheme would not be approved.

> **Lord Evershed:** The court must, in performing its duty under the Variation of Trusts Act 1958, regard the proposal in the light of the purpose of the trust as shown by the evidence of the will or settlement itself and any other relevant evidence available ... It was part of the testator's scheme, made manifest in the will, that it was his intention and desire that this trust should be available for Gladys so that she would have proper provision made for her throughout her life, and would not be exposed to the risk that she might, if she had been handed the money, part with it in favour of another individual about whom the testator felt apprehension, which apprehension is plainly shared by the trustees.

In *Re Remnant's Settlement Trust* [1970] Ch 560 (see below, p 858), the High Court decided on the special facts of that case that a forfeiture clause, promoting a religious bar, would be deleted from a trust, despite defeating the intention of the settlor. The settlor's wishes were regarded as warranting serious consideration, but were not conclusive. In any event, *Re Steed* was not considered in *Re Remnant.*

In *Goulding v James*, Mummery LJ reviewed *Re Steed* and decided that the latter case did not lay down 'any rule, principle or guideline of general application on the importance of the intentions and wishes of the settlor or testator to applications to approve arrangements under the 1958 Act'. In other words, the settlor's wishes coincided with, but were not a cause for, the court's refusal to vary the trust.

Goulding v James [1997] 2 All ER 239, CA

> **Mummery LJ:**
>
> (7) A close examination of the facts and reasoning in *Re Steed's Will Trusts* reveals two significant features of that case: (a) The applicant in that case, unlike Mrs Jane Goulding [who had a life interest under the settlement], had only a protected life interest, held on protective trusts in s 33 of the Trustee Act 1925. (b) Very different considerations affected the court's discretion in *Re Steed's Will Trusts*. The court was asked to approve the arrangement proposed by the protected life tenant on behalf of the person or persons specified in s 1(1)(d) of the 1958 Act ... The proviso as regards benefit does not apply to that paragraph, so that the court may approve an arrangement, the carrying out of which would not be for the benefit of that person. The court may consider whether or not there is benefit as a discretionary factor, but lack of benefit for such a person is no barrier to the approval of the court.
>
> [In *Re Steed's Will Trust*] the Court of Appeal was satisfied that the testator's purpose, evidenced in the will, was still justified at the time of the application to vary. That was a view shared by the trustees, who opposed the application by the protected life tenant. In those circumstances there was an overwhelming reason for the continuation of the protective trusts and in the continuance of the interest of the para (d) class of person. That explained and justified the court's refusal to approve. The court in that case was not engaged in the exercise demanded in this case of deciding whether a mandatory benefit, bargained on behalf of a specified class, is outweighed by some other countervailing discretionary factor, such as the purpose of the trust or the intention of the testatrix in making it.

The court decided that, in the exercise of its discretion, it would approve a scheme of variation of a trust, despite the contradiction of the clear intention of a testatrix concerning adult, ascertained beneficiaries.

Goulding and Another v James and Another [1997] 2 All ER 239, CA

The testatrix (Mrs Froud) made a will in 1992 and, *inter alia*, left her estate equally to her daughter (June) and son in law (Kenneth). In 1994, the testatrix revoked her will and executed a new will under which she gave a life interest in her residuary estate to June with remainder to her grandson, Marcus, provided that he attained the age of 40. This contingent remainder interest was subject to gifts over in favour of any of Marcus' children who were alive at the time of Marcus' death. One effect of this new will was that June did not have an interest in the capital of the trust. The testatrix died in December 1994. June and Marcus (who had no children) applied to the court for the approval of a scheme under s 1(1)(c) of the Variation of Trusts Act 1958. Under the proposed variation, the will trust would be varied from the date of the testatrix's death in order to transfer 90% of the residuary estate to June and Marcus equally. The remaining 10% of the estate would be invested in a fund for the benefit of any children of Marcus.

The plaintiffs adduced actuarial evidence to the effect that the proposed scheme was capable of being eight times more beneficial to Marcus' unborn children than the existing arrangement. The defendants, trustees of the testatrix's will trusts, did not oppose the plaintiffs' proposals, but felt obliged to put a number of relevant issues before the court. These were that the testatrix made it abundantly clear to her solicitors and accountants that she did not want her daughter to have an interest in the capital of her estate. She also felt that Marcus would, with time, adopt a more financially responsible attitude to life. The proposed scheme was contrary to the views expressed by the testatrix. The trial judge decided against the scheme: in his discretion, he felt that he was not entitled to disregard the clear views of the testatrix. The plaintiffs appealed, contending that there was no statutory requirement that the views of the testatrix ought to be conclusive and, while her views may not be ignored, very little weight ought to be attached to them. The court's discretion was restricted to the benefit of the potential beneficiaries within s 1(1)(c) of the 1958 Act, namely, the unborn children of Marcus. The evidence was clearly in favour of such objects. Moreover, the rule in *Saunders v Vautier* [1835–42] All ER 58 entitled beneficiaries, who are *sui juris* and absolutely entitled, to put an end to the trust, even if this had the effect of disappointing the settlor.

The Court of Appeal reversed the decision of the trial judge and approved the scheme of variation. The testatrix's views concerning the adult beneficiaries were irrelevant in deciding whether the court may exercise its jurisdiction under s 1(1)(c) of the Variation of Trusts Act 1958. The court's discretion is exercisable with regard to all the relevant considerations in the statutory context. The flaw in the trial judge's reasoning was that he allowed extrinsic evidence of the testatrix's intention to outweigh the benefit to the class of adult, consenting beneficiaries. The court also issued a caution to trustees and their advisers to take special care in considering the relevance, quality and cogency of extrinsic evidence of the settlor's or testator's intentions and wishes in making applications under the 1958 Act. The purposes being to avoid the risk of irrelevant evidence being admitted and to reduce the costs of such applications.

Mummery LJ: I leave consideration of the evidence with this comment. Trustees and those advising them should, before filing extrinsic evidence of a testator's or settlor's intentions, wishes and motives in relation to an application under the 1958 Act, take particular care to consider its relevance, quality and cogency. If in doubt, trustees can outline the nature of such evidence to the court and seek directions as to whether more detailed evidence should be filed. Unless special care is taken with such evidence there is a risk that irrelevant, and possibly inflammatory, collateral issues will be raised, thereby adding unnecessarily to the costs of the case.

In my judgment, the legal position is as follows:

(1) The court has a discretion whether or not to approve a proposed arrangement.

(2) That discretion is fettered by only one express restriction. The proviso to s 1 prohibits the court from approving an arrangement which is not for the benefit of the classes referred to in (a), (b) or (c). The approval of this arrangement is not prevented by that proviso, since it is plainly the case that it is greatly for the benefit of the class specified in s 1(1)(c).

(3) It does not follow from the fact of benefit to unborns that the arrangement must be approved. In *Re Van Gruisen's Will Trusts, Bagger v Dean* [1964] 1 WLR 449, p 450, Ungoed-Thomas J said:

   It is shown that, actuarially, the provisions for the infants and unborn persons are more beneficial for them under the arrangement than under the present trusts of the will. That, however, does not conclude the case. The court is not merely concerned with this actuarial calculation, even assuming that it satisfies the statutory requirement that the arrangement must be for the benefit of the infants and unborn persons. The court is also concerned whether the arrangement as a whole, in all the circumstances, is such that it is proper to approve it. The court's concern involves, *inter alia*, a practical and business-like consideration of the arrangement, including the total amounts of the advantages which the various parties obtain, and their bargaining strength.

(4) That overall discretion described by Ungoed-Thomas J is to be exercised with regard to all relevant factors properly considered in the statutory context. The context is that the court is empowered to approve an arrangement 'on behalf of' the members of the specified class. As Lord Denning MR said in *Re Weston's Settlements* [1969] 1 Ch 223, p 245, 'in exercising its discretion, the function of the court is to protect those who cannot protect themselves'.

In relation to the members of the specified class who cannot act for themselves, the court is almost in the position of a 'statutory attorney', a striking expression used by Mr Goulding QC in his illuminating submissions to the Court of Appeal in *Re Weston's Settlement*. The court is not in the position of a statutory attorney for the settlor or for the adult beneficiaries and the court is not, as was made clear in *Re Holmden's Settlement*, in the position of a statutory settlor.

(5) Viewed in that context, an important factor in this case is that Mrs June Goulding and Mr Marcus Goulding are *sui juris* and Mrs Froud's intentions and wishes related to their beneficial interests under the testamentary trusts rather than to the contingent interests of her unborn

great grandchildren whom the court is concerned to protect. Mrs Froud's contrary non-testamentary wishes could not inhibit Mrs June Goulding's proprietary rights, as a person beneficially entitled to the life interest in residue.

(6) In these circumstances, the critical question is: what relevance, if any, can Mrs Froud's intentions and wishes with regard to the interests in residue taken under the will by her daughter and grandson and with regard to the exclusion of her son in law from direct or indirect benefit, have to the exercise of the court's jurisdiction on behalf of unborn great-grandchildren of Mrs Froud?

(7) [The judge reviewed the principle in *Re Steed's Will Trusts*, distinguishing that case, and continued:] ...

(8) The fact that the rules of court require a living settlor to be joined as a party to proceedings under the 1958 Act does not mean that the court attaches any overbearing or special significance to the wishes of the settlor. The court has a discretion to approve an arrangement under the Act, even though the settlement or will may make it crystal clear that the settlor or testator does not want any departure from any of the strict terms of the trust.

In *Re Remnant's Settlement Trusts, Hooper v Wenhasten* [1970] Ch 560, the forfeiture provision plainly expressed a strongly held wish on the part of the testator as to who should not benefit under his will. The court nevertheless approved an arrangement deleting that forfeiture provision and thereby defeated the testator's clear intentions. The court did so because Pennycuick J was of the view that it was for the benefit of all concerned to delete that provision; he was satisfied that the arrangement was a fair and proper one.

It may also be worthy of note that in *Re Weston's Settlement*, it was the settlor himself who applied for the approval of an arrangement for the export of his trust to Jersey, where he had gone to live. But he was unable to persuade either Stamp J or the Court of Appeal to approve the arrangement. They held that it was not for the benefit of the specified class and refused to approve it.

To sum up, the flaw in the judge's refusal to approve the arrangement is that, in reliance on the supposed scope of the decision in *Re Steed's Will Trusts*, he allowed extrinsic evidence of the subjective wishes of Mrs Froud as regards her daughter, son in law and grandson to outweigh considerations of objective and substantial benefit to the class on whose behalf the court is empowered to act. If the judge had adopted the correct approach to the exercise of his discretion, he could only have come to the conclusion that the intentions and wishes of Mrs Froud, expressed externally to her will in relation to the adult beneficiaries and an adult non-beneficiary, had little, if any, relevance or weight to the issue of approval on behalf of the future unborn great-grandchildren, whose interest in residue was multiplied five-fold under the proposed arrangement.

Benefit (proviso to s 1(1))

The scheme of variation is required to display some benefit for the persons as stated in s 1(1)(a)–(c) of the Variation of Trusts Act 1958. No such requirement exists for persons in category (d) of s 1(1) of the Act. The statute does not list the factors which the court is required to take into account in deciding the issue. It seems that all the circumstances are required to be considered and the court must weigh up the possible advantages against the disadvantages of adopting a scheme of variation of the trust and decide accordingly. A wide variety of factors have been prominent in either approving or rejecting schemes of variations.

(a) Tax avoidance

The majority of applications have been made with a view to reducing the tax which would otherwise have been payable if the variation was not made.

For example, if property was settled on trust for A for life with remainder to B absolutely. Inheritance tax would be payable on the entire estate on A's death and a second time on B's death. If the settlement was varied so that the fund is divided between A and B equally, inheritance tax would only be payable on half of the trust fund on the death of each of the beneficiaries.

The courts are required to be satisfied that the scheme as a whole is advantageous to the objects. It follows that the court will not approve a scheme if the overall effect is detrimental to the objects even though there may be financial rewards inherent in the scheme. Tax avoidance is merely one factor to be taken into account by the courts.

***Re Weston's Settlement* [1969] 1 Ch 223, CA**

The settlor created two settlements in 1964 for the benefit of his two sons. A total of 500,000 shares was transferred to the trustees. In 1965, capital gains tax was introduced. The shares rose in value and at the time of hearing the tax due on a disposal of the shares was £163,000. The settlor lived in England until 1967. He made three short visits to Jersey in 1967 and then purchased a house there in August 1967 in which he intended to live. An application was made to the court under the Variation of Trusts Act 1958, in November 1967, to appoint two trustees in Jersey as trustees of the two English settlements. In addition, the plaintiff sought the court's sanction to 'export' the trust to Jersey on identical terms. The motive was to save capital gains tax and estate duty.

The Court of Appeal decided that the scheme would not be approved because it would have been morally and socially detrimental to the beneficiaries despite being financially advantageous.

> **Lord Denning:** The court should not consider merely the financial benefit to the infants and unborn children but also their educational and social benefit. There are many things in life more worthwhile than money. One of these things is to be brought up in this our England, which is still the envy of less happier lands. I do not believe it is for the benefit of children to be uprooted from England and transported to another country simply to avoid tax. I should

> imagine that even if they had stayed in this country they would have had a very considerable fortune at their disposal even after paying tax. The only thing that Jersey can do for them is to give them a greater fortune. Many a child has been ruined by being given too much. The avoidance of tax may be lawful, but it is not yet a virtue. The children may well change their minds and come back to this country to enjoy their untaxed gains. Are they to be wanderers over the face of the earth moving from this country to that according to where they can best avoid tax? Children are like trees, they grow stronger with firm roots.

On the other hand, where the applicants have a long standing connection with the foreign country concerned in the proposed scheme, the court may grant its approval, see *Re Windeatt's Will Trust*[23] in this case. The settlor who was domiciled in England created a trust for the benefit of his children who had lived in Jersey for 19 years prior to the application to transfer the trust to Jersey. The court approved the scheme because the beneficiaries were permanently resident in Jersey.

(b) Moral benefit

The court may have regard to evidence which establishes the financial instability of infant beneficiaries and may adopt a scheme which has the effect of postponing the vesting of such beneficiary's interest in capital.

***Re T's Settlement* [1964] Ch 158, HC**

An infant was entitled absolutely to a quarter of a trust fund on attaining the age of 21 years (age of majority at this time) and a further quarter on the death of her mother. Eighteen days before she reached the age of majority, her mother asked the court to approve a transfer to new trustees of the infant's share to be held either:

(i) on protective trust for her for life; or

(ii) to postpone the vesting of capital until she reached the age of 25, but in the meantime the property would be held on protective trust.

The court accepted that the infant was alarmingly immature and irresponsible in respect of financial matters.

The court held that:

(a) the protective trust for life would have amounted to a 'resettlement' of property which was outside the jurisdiction of the court and in any event would not be beneficial to the child; but

(b) the postponement of the capital until a later date and the interim protective trust was approved.

23 [1969] 1 WLR 692.

> **Wilberforce J:** ... it appears to me to be a definite benefit for this infant for a period during which it is to be hoped that independence may bring her to maturity and responsibility to be protected against creditors ... And this is the kind of benefit which seems to be within the spirit of the Act.

In *Re Holt*,[24] the court approved *Re T's Settlement* but postponed the vesting of an infant's benefit without evidence of financial immaturity.

Re Holt's Settlement [1969] 1 Ch 100, HC

Personal property was settled on Mrs Wilson for life with remainder to such of her children as would reach the age of 21 years and if more than one, in equal shares. She wanted to surrender her life interest in half of the income for the benefit of the children (in order to reduce the impact of income tax on her husband and her) and to rearrange the trusts so that the interest of the children would vest at the age of 30 years.

The court sanctioned the scheme, for on the whole it was for the benefit of the children.

> **Megarry J:** It seems to me that the arrangement proposed is for the benefit of each of the beneficiaries contemplated by s 1(1) of the 1958 Act. The financial detriment to the children is that the absolute vesting of their interests will be postponed from age 21 to 30. As against this, they will obtain very substantial financial benefits, both in the acceleration of their interests in a moiety of the trust fund and in the savings of estate duty ... it is also most important that young children should be reasonably advanced in a career and settled in life before they are in receipt of an income sufficient to make them independent of the need to work. The word 'benefit' in the proviso to s 1(1) is plainly not confined to financial benefit, but may extend to moral and social benefit as is shown in *Re T's Settlement*.

(c) Avoidance of family dissension

The court may approve an arrangement if its effect would be to prevent real or potential conflict within a family. In this respect, although the intention of the settlor carries a great deal of weight, it is not conclusive.

Re Remnant's Settlement Trust [1970] Ch 560, HC

A trust gave contingent interests to the children of two sisters, 'Dawn' and 'Merrial', and contained a forfeiture clause if they practised Roman Catholicism or married or lived with a Roman Catholic. The children of Dawn were Protestants, whereas the children of Merrial were Roman Catholics. The sisters sought the court's approval of a scheme which deleted the forfeiture clause.

---

24 [1969] 1 Ch 100.

The court gave its approval in order to prevent family conflict. Although Dawn's children did not benefit financially from the deletion of the clause, the court decided that, on the whole, they would be better off, for the religious bar could have deterred them from selecting a spouse.

> **Pennycuick J:** Obviously a forfeiture provision of this kind might well cause very serious dissension between the families of two sisters ... I am entitled to take a broad view of what is meant by 'benefit', and so taking it, I think this arrangement can fairly be said to be for their 'benefit' ... It remains to be considered whether the arrangement is a fair and proper one. As far as I can see, there is no reason for saying otherwise, except that the arrangement defeats this testator's intention. That is a serious but by no means conclusive consideration. I have reached the clear conclusion that these forfeiture provisions are undesirable in the circumstances of this case and that an arrangement involving their deletion is a fair and proper one.

SUPPLEMENTARY READING

Cooke, E, 'What to do with an unbarrable entail – *Hambro v The Duke of Marlborough*' [1994] Conv 492

Cotterell, R, 'The requirement of "benefit" under the Variation of Trusts Act 1958' (1971) 34 MLR 96

Evans, D, 'The variation of trusts act in practice' (1963) 27 Conv 6

Harris, J, 'Ten years of variation of trusts' (1969) 33 Conv 113 and 183

Hayes, M, 'Breaking and varying trusts painlessly' (1998) 4 MLR 17

Luxton, P, 'An unascertainable problem in variation of trusts' (1986) 136 NLJ 1057

Riddall, J, 'Does it or doesn't it? Contingent interests and Variation of Trusts Act 1958' [1987] Conv 144

CHAPTER 21

BREACH OF TRUST

A trustee is liable for a breach of trust if he fails to perform his duties either by omitting to do any act which he ought to do, or doing an act which he ought not to do. Such duties may be created by the settlor in the trust instrument (such as the duty to distribute both income and capital) or may be imposed generally, in accordance with trust law (for example, duties of care and impartiality). A breach of trust may range from a fraudulent disposal of trust property, to an innocent dereliction of duties by investing trust monies in unauthorised investments. The beneficiary is required to establish a causal connection between the breach of trust and the loss suffered, either directly or indirectly by the trust. Indeed, even if the trust suffers no loss, the beneficiary is entitled to claim any profit accruing to the trustees as a result of a breach.

Measure of liability

Trustees' liability for breach of trust is based on principles of restitution to the trust estate. The trustee in default is required to restore the trust property, or its equivalent, to the trust estate. In respect of a breach of trust claim, the basic right of the beneficiary is to have the trust duly administered in accordance with the trust instrument and the general law. In respect of a monetary claim, the equitable rules of compensation are based on the restoration to the trust fund of property that ought to be there. Thus, the trustees responsible for the breach are required to pay, to the trust estate, assets or compensation for loss suffered by the trust as a result of their breach. In this respect, the common law rules of remoteness of damage and causation are not applied strictly, but there still has to be some causal link between the breach of trust and loss to the estate. Once the trust fund is 'reconstituted', the defaulting trustee becomes a bare trustee for the plaintiff and will have no answer to a claim by the plaintiff for the payment over of the moneys in the 'reconstituted' fund.

Bartlett v Barclays Bank Trust Co Ltd (No 2) [1980] 2 All ER 92, HC

> **Brightman J:** The obligation of a trustee who is held liable for breach of trust is fundamentally different from the obligation of a contractual or tortious wrongdoer. The trustee's obligation is to restore to the trust estate the assets of which he has deprived it.

If the trust property cannot be restored to the trust, compensation may be payable to the trust in order to maintain the value of the trust assets. The trust is required to be compensated fully for any loss caused by the breach. The extent of this liability is not restricted by the strict common law principles governing remoteness of damage in actions in tort or breach of contract. Once a breach of trust has been committed, the trustees become liable to place the trust estate in the same position as it would have been if no breach had been committed. Although liability is not unlimited, the time of assessment of the loss is at the time of the trial. In *Caffrey v Darby* (1801) 6 Ves 488, trustees, owing to their negligence, failed to recover possession of part of the trust assets and, later still, the assets became lost. The trustees argued that the subsequent loss was not attributable to their neglect. The court rejected this argument and decided that once the trustees had committed a breach of trust, they were responsible for compensating the estate in respect of the resulting loss. The judge said:

> ... if they have already been guilty of negligence, they must be responsible for any loss, in any way, to that property, for whatever may be the immediate cause, the property would not have been in a situation to sustain that loss if it had not been for their negligence. If the loss had happened by fire, lightning, or any other accident, that would not be an excuse for them if guilty of previous negligence.

At common law, there are two principles which are fundamental to the award of damages:

(1) the breach must cause the loss claimed by the plaintiff; and

(2) the plaintiff must be put in the same position as he would have been, had he not suffered a breach.

In equity, although the starting point to a compensation claim is different, the award of damages is, to a large extent, governed by the same two principles. The strict test of foreseeability is not a concern in assessing compensation, but it is essential that the losses claimed are the losses which are caused by the breach:

> In both systems the defendant is not responsible for damage not caused by his wrong or to pay more compensation than the loss suffered by the plaintiff. Under both systems liability is fault-based. The defendant is only liable for the consequences of the legal wrong he has done to the plaintiff and to make good the damage caused by such wrong. The detailed rules of equity as to causation and the quantification of loss differ, at least ostensibly, from those applicable at common law. [*Per* Lord Browne-Wilkinson in *Target Holdings v Redferns* (see below, p 863).]

But, if at the time of the action the trust is at an end, so that the trustees hold the trust property as *bare* trustees, the beneficiary has the right to have the trust assets retained by the trustees until they have fully accounted for the assets to him, for example, a trust for A for life with remainder to B absolutely, after A's death, B becomes absolutely entitled to the trust property. If the trustees commit a breach of trust, there is no reason for compensating the breach by way of compensation to the trust fund as opposed to the beneficiary himself. The beneficiary's right, in these circumstances, is no longer to have the trust duly administered, for he is the sole owner of the trust estate. The measure of compensation is the difference between what the beneficiary would have received and what he had in fact received.

A trustee who wrongly pays away trust money, like a trustee who makes an unauthorised investment, commits a breach of trust and comes under an immediate duty to remedy such breach. If immediate proceedings are brought, the court will make an immediate order requiring restoration to the trust fund and will order a sale of the unauthorised investments and payment of compensation for any loss suffered. But the fact that there is an accrued cause of action as soon as the breach is committed does not mean that the quantum of the compensation payable is ultimately fixed as at the date when the breach occurred. The quantum is fixed at the date of judgment, according to circumstances which would put the beneficiary back into the position he would have been in, but for the breach. The plaintiff's actual loss is assessed with the full benefit of hindsight. In *Target Holdings v Redferns*, the court rejected the claim of the plaintiffs that the loss is to be measured at the time of the breach. This would have entitled the plaintiffs to obtain compensation of an amount which exceeded its loss and would not have reflected the basic principles of equitable compensation.

***Target Holdings Ltd v Redferns and Another* [1995] 3 All ER 785, HL**

A company, Crowngate Ltd (C Ltd), agreed to purchase a property for £775,000 and then approached the plaintiffs, Target Holdings Ltd (T Ltd), mortgagees, for a loan of £1.525 m to be secured by way of a mortgage on the property. The purchase price of the property was stated as £2 m, having been valued negligently by a firm of estate agents. T Ltd were not informed that the property was not being purchased for £775,000. A scheme was arranged by C Ltd to obtain a mortgage for £1.525 m from T Ltd in order to purchase a property for £775,000. C Ltd instructed one of the defendants, a firm of solicitors, to incorporate another company, Panther Ltd (P Ltd) in order to purchase the property from the vendors for £775,000. P Ltd would sell the property to Kohli Ltd (K Ltd, owned by C Ltd) for £1.25 m and K Ltd would sell the property to C Ltd for £2 m. The defendants, solicitors, acted for the three companies and the plaintiffs. T Ltd approved the loan and paid the defendants £1.525 m. Prior to the completion of the sale, the defendants (solicitors) notified the plaintiffs that the sale of the property and mortgage charge had been completed. Some days later C Ltd arranged for £775,000 to be paid to the vendor of the property and the various transfers and the plaintiffs' charge were completed. C Ltd became insolvent and the plaintiffs repossessed the property. The property was sold for £500,000. The plaintiffs brought an action against the defendants, solicitors and the valuer. The firm of solicitors conceded that it acted in breach of trust by paying out the mortgage funds to the three companies without authority, but that it was not liable to compensate T Ltd for the loss suffered because its breach did not cause the loss sustained by the company.

The House of Lords reversed the decision of the Court of Appeal and decided in favour of the defendant. The loss suffered by the plaintiffs was not attributable to the defendant but was wholly caused by the fraud of third parties. T Ltd advanced the same amount of money, obtained the same security and received the same amount on the realisation of that security, with or without the breach of trust committed by Redferns.

> **Lord Browne-Wilkinson:** My Lords, this appeal raises a novel point on the liability of a trustee who commits a breach of trust to compensate beneficiaries for such breach. Is the trustee liable to compensate the beneficiary not only for losses caused by the breach but also for losses which the beneficiary would, in any event, have suffered even if there had been no such breach?
>
> Before considering the technical issues of law which arise, it is appropriate to look at the case more generally. Target allege, and it is probably the case, that they were defrauded by third parties (Mr Kohli and Mr Musafir and possibly their associates) to advance money on the security of the property. If there had been no breach by Redferns of their instructions and the transaction had gone through, Target would have suffered a loss in round figures of £1.2 m (that is, £1.7 m advanced less £500,000 recovered on the realisation of the security). Such loss would have been wholly caused by the fraud of the third parties. The breach of trust committed by Redferns left Target in exactly the same position as it would have been if there had been no such breach: Target advanced the same amount of money, obtained the same security and received the same amount on the realisation of that security. In any ordinary use of words, the breach of trust by Redferns cannot be said to have caused the actual loss ultimately suffered by Target unless it can be shown that, but for the breach of trust, the transaction would not have gone through.
>
> At common law, there are two principles fundamental to the award of damages. First, that the defendant's wrongful act must cause the damage complained of. Second, that the plaintiff is to be put 'in the same position as he would have been in if he had not sustained the wrong for which he is now getting his compensation or reparation': *Livingstone v Rawyards Coal Co* (1880) 5 App Cas 25, p 39, *per* Lord Blackburn. Although, as will appear, in many ways equity approaches liability for making good a breach of trust from a different starting point, in my judgment those two principles are applicable as much in equity as at common law. Under both systems liability is fault-based: the defendant is only liable for the consequences of the legal wrong he has done to the plaintiff and to make good the damage caused by such wrong. He is not responsible for damage not caused by his wrong or to pay by way of compensation more than the loss suffered from such wrong. The detailed rules of equity as to causation and the quantification of loss differ, at least ostensibly, from those applicable at common law. But the principles underlying both systems are the same. On the assumptions that had to be made in the present case until the factual issues are resolved (that is, that the transaction would

have gone through even if there had been no breach of trust), the result reached by the Court of Appeal does not accord with those principles. Redferns as trustees have been held liable to compensate Target for a loss caused otherwise than by the breach of trust. I approach the consideration of the relevant rules of equity with a strong predisposition against such a conclusion.

The considerations urged before your Lordships, although presented as a single argument leading to the conclusion that the views of the majority in the Court of Appeal are correct, on analysis comprise two separate lines of reasoning, viz: (a) an argument developed by Mr Patten (but not reflected in the reasons of the Court of Appeal), that Target is now (ie, at the date of judgment) entitled to have the 'trust fund' restored by an order that Redferns reconstitute the trust fund by paying back into client account the moneys paid away in breach of trust. Once the trust fund is so reconstituted, Redferns as bare trustee for Target will have no answer to a claim by Target for the payment over of the moneys in the reconstituted 'trust fund'. Therefore, Mr Patten says, it is proper now to order payment direct to Target of the whole sum improperly paid away, less the sum which Target has received on the sale of property; and (b) the argument accepted by the majority of the Court of Appeal that, because immediately after the moneys were paid away by Redferns in breach of trust, there was an immediate right to have the 'trust fund' reconstituted, there was then an immediate loss to the trust fund for which loss Redferns are now liable to compensate Target direct.

The critical distinction between the two arguments is that argument (a) depends upon Target being entitled now to an order for restitution to the trust fund, whereas argument (b) quantifies the compensation payable to Target as beneficiary by reference to a right to restitution to the trust fund at an earlier date and is not dependent upon Target having any right to have the client account reconstituted now.

The basic right of a beneficiary is to have the trust duly administered in accordance with the provisions of the trust instrument, if any, and the general law. Thus, in relation to a traditional trust, where the fund is held in trust for a number of beneficiaries having different, usually successive, equitable interests (for example, A for life with remainder to B), the right of each beneficiary is to have the whole fund vested in the trustees so as to be available to satisfy his equitable interest when, and if, it falls into possession. Accordingly, in the case of a breach of such a trust involving the wrongful paying away of trust assets, the liability of the trustee is to restore to the trust fund, often called 'the trust estate', what ought to have been there.

The equitable rules of compensation for breach of trust have been largely developed in relation to such traditional trusts, where the only way in which all the beneficiaries' rights can be protected, is to restore to the trust fund what ought to be there. In such a case the basic rule is that a trustee in breach of trust must restore or pay to the trust estate either the assets which have been lost to the estate by reason of the breach, or compensation for such loss. Courts of equity did not award damages but, acting *in personam*, ordered the defaulting trustee to restore the trust estate: see *Nocton v Ashburton (Lord)* [1914] AC 932, pp 952, 958, *per* Viscount Haldane LC. If specific restitution of the trust property is not possible, then the liability of the trustee is to pay sufficient compensation to the trust estate to put it back to what it would have been had the breach not been committed: *Caffrey v Darby* (1801) 6 Ves 488; *Clough v Bond* (1838) 3 M & C 490. Even if the immediate cause of the loss is the dishonesty or failure of a third party, the trustee is liable to make good that loss to the trust estate if, but for the breach, such loss would not have occurred: see Underhill and Hayton, *Law of Trusts and Trustees*, 14th edn, 1987, pp 734–36; *In re Dawson (Decd); Union Fidelity Trustee Co Ltd v Perpetual Trustee Co Ltd* [1966] 2 NSWR 211; *Bartlett v Barclays Bank Trust Co Ltd (Nos 1 and 2)* [1980] Ch 515. Thus, the common law rules of remoteness of damage and causation do not apply. However, there does have to be some causal connection between the breach of trust and the loss to the trust estate for which compensation is recoverable, viz, the fact that the loss would not have occurred but for the breach: see also *In re Miller's Deed Trusts* (1978) 75 LSG 454; *Nestlé v National Westminster Bank plc* [1993] 1 WLR 1260.

Hitherto, I have been considering the rights of beneficiaries under traditional trusts where the trusts are still subsisting and therefore the right of each beneficiary, and his only right, is to have the trust fund reconstituted as it should be. But what if at the time of the action claiming compensation for breach of trust those trusts have come to an end? Take as an example again the trust for A for life with remainder to B. During A's lifetime B's only right is to have the trust duly administered and, in the event of a breach, to have the trust fund restored. After A's death, B becomes absolutely entitled. He, of course, has the right to have the trust assets retained by the trustees until they have fully accounted for them to him. But if the trustees commit a breach of trust, there is no reason for compensating the breach of trust by way of an order for restitution and compensation to the trust fund as opposed to the beneficiary himself. The beneficiary's right is no longer simply to have the trust duly administered: he is, in equity, the sole owner of the trust estate. Nor, for the same reason, is restitution to the trust fund necessary to protect other beneficiaries. Therefore, although I do not wholly rule out the possibility that even in those circumstances an order to reconstitute the fund may be appropriate, in the ordinary case, where a beneficiary becomes absolutely entitled to the trust fund, the court orders, not restitution to the trust estate, but the payment of compensation directly to the beneficiary. The measure of such compensation is the same, that is, the difference between what the beneficiary has in fact received and the amount he would have received but for the breach of trust.

Thus, in *Bartlett v Barclays Bank Trust Co Ltd (Nos 1 and 2)* [1980] Ch 515 by the date of judgment some of the shares settled by the trust deed had become absolutely vested in possession: see p 543A. The compensation for breach of trust, though quantified by reference to what the fund would have been but for the breach of trust, was payable directly to the persons who were absolutely entitled to their shares of the trust fund: see p 544. Accordingly, in traditional trusts for persons by way of succession, in my judgment, once those trusts have been exhausted and the fund has become absolutely vested in possession, the beneficiary is not normally entitled to have the exhausted trust reconstituted. His right is to be compensated for the loss he has suffered by reason of the breach.

I turn then to the two arguments urged before your Lordships.

Argument (a)

Even if the equitable rules developed in relation to traditional trusts were directly applicable to such a case as this, as I have sought to show, a beneficiary becoming absolutely entitled to a trust fund has no automatic right to have the fund reconstituted in all circumstances. Thus, even applying the strict rules so developed in relation to traditional trusts, it seems to me very doubtful whether Target is now entitled to have the trust fund reconstituted. But in my judgment it is in any event wrong to lift wholesale the detailed rules developed in the context of traditional trusts and then seek to apply them to trusts of quite a different kind. In the modern world the trust has become a valuable device in commercial and financial dealings. The fundamental principles of equity apply as much to such trusts as they do to the traditional trusts in relation to which those principles were originally formulated. But in my judgment it is important, if the trust is not to be rendered commercially useless, to distinguish between the basic principles of trust law and those specialist rules developed in relation to traditional trusts which are applicable only to such trusts and the rationale of which has no application to trusts of quite a different kind.

This case is concerned with a trust which has at all times been a bare trust. Bare trusts arise in a number of different contexts: for example, by the ultimate vesting of the property under a traditional trust, nominee shareholdings and, as in the present case, as but one incident of a wider commercial transaction involving agency. In the case of moneys paid to a solicitor by a client, as part of a conveyancing transaction, the purpose of that transaction is to achieve the commercial objective of the client, be it the acquisition of property or the lending of money on security. The depositing of money with the solicitor is but one aspect of the arrangements between the parties, such arrangements being for the most part contractual. Thus, the circumstances under which the solicitor can part with money from client account are regulated by the instructions given by the client: they are not part of the trusts on which the property is held. I do not intend to cast any doubt on the fact that moneys held by solicitors on client account are trust moneys or that the basic equitable principles apply to any breach of such trust by solicitors. But the basic equitable principle applicable to breach of trust is that the beneficiary is entitled to be compensated for any loss he would not have suffered but for the breach. I have no doubt that, until the underlying commercial transaction has been completed, the solicitor can be required to restore to client account moneys wrongly paid away. But to import into such trust an obligation to restore the trust fund once the transaction has been completed would be entirely artificial. The obligation to reconstitute the trust fund applicable in the case of traditional trusts reflects the fact that no one beneficiary is entitled to the trust property and the need to compensate all beneficiaries for the breach. That rationale has no application to a case such as the present. To impose such an obligation in order to enable the beneficiary solely entitled (that is, the client) to recover from the solicitor more than the client has in fact lost, flies in the face of common sense and is in direct conflict with the basic principles of equitable compensation. In my judgment, once a conveyancing transaction has been completed, the client has no right to have the solicitor's client account reconstituted as a 'trust fund'.

Argument (b)

The key point in the reasoning of the Court of Appeal is that where moneys are paid away to a stranger in breach of trust, an immediate loss is suffered by the trust estate: as a result, subsequent events reducing that loss are irrelevant. They drew a distinction between the case in which the breach of trust consisted of some failure in the administration of the trust and the case where a trustee has actually paid away trust moneys to a stranger. There is no doubt that in the former case, one waits to see what loss is in fact suffered by reason of the breach, that is, the restitution or compensation payable is assessed at the date of trial, not of breach. However, the Court of Appeal considered that where the breach consisted of paying away the trust moneys to a stranger, it made no sense to wait: it seemed to Peter Gibson LJ [1994] 1 WLR 1089, pp 1103G–H, obvious that in such a case 'there is an immediate loss placing the trustee under an immediate duty to restore the moneys to the trust fund'. The majority of the Court of Appeal therefore considered that subsequent events which diminished the loss in fact suffered were irrelevant, save for imposing on the compensated beneficiary an obligation to give credit for any benefit he subsequently received. In effect, in the view of the Court of Appeal, one 'stops the clock' at the date the moneys are paid away: events which occur between the date of breach and the date of trial are irrelevant in assessing the loss suffered by reason of the breach.

A trustee who wrongly pays away trust money, like a trustee who makes an unauthorised investment, commits a breach of trust and comes under an immediate duty to remedy such breach. If immediate proceedings are brought, the court will make an immediate order requiring restoration to the trust fund of the assets wrongly distributed or, in the case of an unauthorised investment, will order the sale of the unauthorised investment and the payment of compensation for any loss suffered. But the fact that there is an accrued cause of action as soon as the breach is committed does not, in my judgment, mean that the quantum of the compensation payable is ultimately fixed as at the date when the breach occurred. The quantum is fixed at the date of judgment at which date, according to the circumstances then pertaining, the compensation is assessed at the figure then necessary to put the trust estate or the beneficiary back into the position it would have been in had there been no breach. I can see no justification for 'stopping the clock' immediately in some cases but not in others: to do so may, as in this case, lead to compensating the trust estate or the beneficiary for a loss which, on the facts known at trial, it has never suffered.

[His Lordship considered the decisions of *Re Dawson (Decd)* [1966] 2 NSWR 211 and *Canson Enterprises Ltd v Boughton & Co* (1991) 85 DLR 129, and continued:]

The equitable compensation for breach of trust has to be assessed as at the date of judgment and not at an earlier date. Equitable compensation for breach of trust is designed to achieve exactly what the word compensation suggests: to make good a loss in fact suffered by the beneficiaries and which, using hindsight and common sense, can be seen to have been caused by the breach.

The Court of Appeal relied on two authorities in support of the 'stop the clock' approach: *Alliance & Leicester Building Society v Edgestop Ltd* (1991) unreported, 18 January (Hoffmann J), was another case of mortgage fraud very similar to the present. The plaintiff building society had paid moneys to solicitors in circumstances similar to the present case and the solicitors had wrongly paid them away in breach of their instructions. The building society obtained orders for interim payment against the solicitors on the grounds that they were liable for breach of trust. The case however is distinguishable because of one crucial difference, viz, the judge found that if the building society had known the true facts it would not have made the advance, that is, one of the facts that has to be assumed to the contrary in the present case. In that case, therefore, at the date of judgment, a certain loss had been demonstrated in that the breach of trust had caused the building society to enter into a transaction in which they would not have participated had there been no breach of trust.

In *Bishopsgate Investment Management Ltd v Maxwell (No 2)* [1994] 1 All ER 261, the plaintiff company was a trustee of a pension fund. It brought proceedings for breach of fiduciary duty against a director who had improperly transferred to a stranger shares held by the plaintiff company as such trustee. The Court of Appeal held that the judge had properly given summary judgment for an assessment of damages for breach of fiduciary duty and ordered an interim payment of £500,000. In that case, apart from one possibility, there was no doubt the shares were irretrievably lost and that the value of the shares so lost was in excess of £500,000. The only possibility of reducing that loss was that the plaintiff might have a claim to recover the shares from the transferee on the grounds that the transferee had notice of the impropriety. In the context of the claim for an interim payment, Hoffmann LJ said, at p 267:

> Secondly, [counsel] says it does not follow that the company's loss would be the full value of the shares. It might be able to get something back from Credit Suisse. But the company held the shares as trustee for the pension fund and its liability as trustee was to restore the fund. *Prima facie*, therefore, its loss was its liability to make good the value of the shares. Credit Suisse appears to have taken the shares on the basis that they were registered in the name of Robert Maxwell Group plc and claim to be *bona fide* pledgees. I do not think that the judge was required to speculate on the possibility that the company might be able to defeat this plea. It has no duty to engage in doubtful litigation for the purpose of minimising the loss for which Mr Ian Maxwell is liable. In my judgment, therefore, the judge was acting within his discretion in deciding that £500,000 was a reasonable proportion of the damages which the company was likely to recover.

In my judgment, these remarks provide no basis for holding that final judgment can be given when, on the facts known at the date of judgment, the plaintiff has eventually suffered no loss. First, Hoffmann LJ was only considering the amount of the interim payment: the order for final judgment was for damages to be assessed. Secondly, it is sound law that a plaintiff is not required to engage in hazardous litigation in order to mitigate his loss. The only way in which the plaintiff company's loss could be less than the value of the shares wrongly transferred was if such hazardous litigation should be successfully pursued to judgment. It did not lie in the mouth of the wrongdoing director to seek to reduce the quantum of his liability by relying on the plaintiff company to take steps it was under no legal duty to take. The position is wholly different in the instant case where, on the facts to be assumed, it is demonstrated that no loss has in fact been incurred by reason of the breach of trust.

Mr Patten (for Target) relied on *Nant-y-glo and Blaina Ironworks Co v Grave* (1878) 12 Ch D 738, as showing that a trustee can be held liable to recoup to the trust fund the value of shares at the highest value between the date of breach and the date of judgment. In my view, that case has no relevance. The claim there was not for breach of trust but for account of profits made by a fiduciary (a company director) from shares which he had improperly received in breach of his duty. The amount recoverable in an action claiming an account of profits is dependent upon the profit made by the fiduciary, not the loss suffered by the beneficiary.

Mr Patten also relied on *Jaffray v Marshall* [1993] 1 WLR 1285, where the principles applicable in an action for an account of profits were, to my mind, wrongly applied to a claim for compensation for breach of trust. In my judgment, that case was wrongly decided not only because the wrong principle was applied but also because the judge awarded compensation by assessing the quantum on an assumption (viz, that the house in question would have been sold at a particular date) when he found as a fact that such sale would not have taken place even if there had been no breach of trust.

For these reasons I reach the conclusion that, on the facts which must currently be assumed, Target has not demonstrated that it is entitled to any compensation for breach of trust. Assuming that moneys would have been forthcoming from some other source to complete the purchase from Mirage if the moneys had not been wrongly provided by Redferns in breach of trust, Target obtained exactly what it would have obtained had no breach occurred, that is, a valid security for the sum advanced. Therefore, on the assumption made, Target has suffered no compensatable loss.

In an action based on constructive fraud, the aggrieved party is required to establish a causal connection between the breach of fiduciary duties and the loss. A claim for equitable compensation based on constructive fraud (that is, an abuse or breach of a fiduciary relationship, see *Nocton v Ashburton (Lord)* [1914] AC 932), as distinct from deceit or actual fraud, is not dependent on proof of dishonesty or deception. The equitable remedies available for breach of fiduciary duties are more varied as opposed to the common law remedy of damages for fraud or deceit. Equitable remedies include rescission, where restitution is possible; accounting for profits and benefits acquired in breach of duties; and payment of compensation to put the aggrieved party in a pecuniarily similar position as he was in before the breach. The measure of compensation may not always be the same as damages. In considering equitable compensation in respect of breach of fiduciary obligation, foreseeability and remoteness of damage are, in general, irrelevant. The focus of attention is restitution. But it is still necessary to address the question of causation.

Swindle and Others v Harrison and Others [1997] 4 All ER 705, CA

Mrs Harrison owned a house known as 13 Warwick Place, Leamington Spa, where she lived. In June 1991, she mortgaged the house to the National Home Loans Corp (NHL) in order to finance, in part, the purchase of a hotel, Aylesford Hotel. This mortgage raised £180,000. The plaintiff's firm of solicitors, Alsters, were instructed to act on behalf of Mrs Harrison. A further £100,000 was proposed to be raised by a loan from Banks' Brewery. In July 1991, contracts for the purchase of Aylesford for £220,000 were exchanged. A non-refundable deposit of £44,000 was paid on exchange. Completion was fixed for 5 August 1991. Time was of the essence. Access to the hotel was given to Mrs Harrison in order to carry out alterations and repairs. The brewery loan had failed to materialise, an issue which the plaintiff and his firm had known before Mrs Harrison. It was necessary to raise over £70,000 in order to complete the purchase. Alsters negotiated a postponement of the completion date on 8 August 1991. Efforts to raise the balance of the purchase price proved unsuccessful. On 7 August 1991, Alsters offered a bridging loan to Mrs Harrison for £75,000 secured by a first charge on Aylesford. The rate of interest was 2.5% above base rate. Alsters borrowed this sum from the Royal Bank of Scotland at base rate. Mrs Harrison was required to pay the arrangement fee of £1,000. Mrs Harrison was unaware that the firm would make a profit of £625 on this fee. Mrs Harrison was advised by Alsters of her right to take independent legal advice, but there was no time for this to be done. Completion took place on 8 August 1991. Aylesford Hotel failed. NHL obtained a possession order on 15 December 1992 on 13 Warwick Place. The plaintiffs started proceedings for possession of Aylesford. The defendants counterclaimed, on the ground that the plaintiffs were in breach of their fiduciary obligations and were liable to pay the defendants equitable compensation. The judge decided in favour of the plaintiffs and dismissed the counterclaim The defendants appealed.

The Court of Appeal, dismissed the appeal and decided that:

(a) there is no doubt that the solicitor/client relationship is a confidential relationship. Accordingly, Mr Swindle, the defendant's solicitor, was a fiduciary. The firm made an unauthorised 'profit' from its client as a result of this relationship. The profit was part of the arrangement fee as well as the differential in the rate of interest payable on the loan. These material facts were not disclosed to Mrs Harrison. These omissions evidently amounted to breaches of the fiduciary relationship. Mrs Harrison would have been entitled to recover the unauthorised profit made by the firm from the bridging loan;

(b) the particulars of the breaches in respect of the bridging loan were that the plaintiffs failed to disclose to Mrs Harrison:
   - the split of the arrangement fee with the bank;
   - the differential in the rate of interest which they were charging Mrs Harrison; and
   - information that the brewery were unlikely to make the loan;

(c) however, Mrs Harrison's claim was drafted in order to recover compensation for the alleged 'loss' that she suffered. But the 'loss' suffered by Mrs Harrison, namely, her home and a substantial debt to NHL, did not flow from the plaintiffs' breach of fiduciary duties. Mrs Harrison would have accepted the bridging loan and completed the purchase of the hotel, even if full disclosure had been made. Since she would have lost the value of the equity in her home in any event, her claim was not sustainable.

Mummery LJ: The decision of the House of Lords in *Nocton v Ashburton* [1914] AC 932, is the seminal case. It is possible to extract from the speeches the following principles relevant to this appeal: (1) a solicitor stands in a fiduciary relationship with his client; (2) a solicitor who enters into a financial transaction with his client is under a fiduciary duty, when advising his client, to make full disclosure of all relevant facts known to him; (3) liability for breach of fiduciary duty is not dependent on proof of deceit or negligence. Equity imposes duties in special relationships above and beyond the minimal legal duties to be honest and to be careful. Fiduciary duties rest on the idea of trust and of conduct offensive to conscience; (4) the equitable remedies available for breach of fiduciary duty are 'more elastic' than the sanction of damages attached to common law fraud and negligence. (Remedies include rescission where *restitutio in integrum* is possible; replacement of property improperly acquired from the person to whom the duty is owed; accounting for profits and benefits acquired in breach of duty). Payment of compensation may be ordered to put the plaintiff 'in as good a position pecuniarily as that to which he was in before the injury'. The measure 'may not always be the same as in an action for deceit or for negligence'. It is instructive to examine the remedy granted by the House of Lords in *Nocton v Ashburton*. The claim against the solicitor alleged fraud. The trial judge found that fraud was not proved and dismissed the action. The Court of Appeal, in what Lord Haldane LC described as a 'rash proceeding' reversed the judge, found fraud and directed an inquiry as to what damage, if any, had been sustained by the plaintiff *'by reason of'* the defendant's wrongdoing, as identified in the terms of the inquiry. Although the House of Lords held that the Court of Appeal were wrong to reverse the judge, they upheld the order for an inquiry as to damages on the basis that the defendant, though not fraudulent, was liable to pay compensation for breach of fiduciary duty. The terms of that inquiry made it clear that a causal link had to be established between the defendant's wrongdoing and the loss suffered by the plaintiff.

On applying the relevant principles to the facts of this case, I conclude that the recorder was right to reject Mrs Harrison's claim for substantial equitable compensation for breach of fiduciary duty by Alsters. I would dismiss the appeal on that point.

Extent of liability and causation

A wrongdoer is only liable for the consequences of his being wrong and not for all the consequences of a course of action. In the present case, there was no fiduciary duty on Alsters to abstain from lending money to Mrs Harrison in all circumstances or to prevent her from completing the purchase of Aylesford Hotel in accordance with the contract of purchase. Alsters' duty was to make full disclosure of material facts relevant to the bridging loan to enable her to make a fully informed decision about it. They were in breach of that duty; but, as found by the judge, the probabilities are that Mrs Harrison would still have entered into the bridging loan, even if that breach of duty had not occurred, because she was intent on completing the purchase of the Aylesford Hotel, whatever independent legal advice she received. The loss which she suffered did not flow from that breach of fiduciary duty. It flowed from her own decision to take the risk involved in mortgaging her own home to finance her son's restaurant business at the hotel. Alsters were not under a duty to decline to act for Mrs Harrison on the purchase or to stop her from going ahead with the purchase, if that is what she wanted to do.

In brief, the loss of the equity in 13 Warwick Place was not a result of Alsters' breach of fiduciary duty in relation to the bridging loan which enabled Mrs Harrison to complete the contract for the acquisition of the Aylesford Hotel. It would be contrary to common sense and fairness to put on Alsters the whole risk of the purchase transaction on the basis that they had failed to make full disclosure in a related loan transaction, when disclosure would not have affected the client's decision to proceed with the purchase. Mrs Harrison's position would have been the same even if there had been no breach of duty.

Hobhouse LJ (in *Swindle v Harrison*): Breach of fiduciary duty is not to be equated with common law deceit. It simply gives rise to a personal equity which is to be recognised by a court having chancery jurisdiction so as to lead to a grant of an equitable remedy. It does not, itself, give rise to a right to damages. It relates to the transaction between the fiduciary and the person to whom he owes the duty. The remedy is essentially restitutionary in its character. The fiduciary may be restrained from enforcing the transaction. It may be rescinded. Accounts and restitution may be ordered. But, if the plaintiff seeks to recover common law damages, he must discharge the same burden of proof as would be required by a court applying the common law.

Once there has been a breach of a fiduciary duty in relation to a transaction, the fiduciary is not allowed to enforce that transaction. Equity does not allow him to benefit from the improper transaction and can require him to rescind the transaction and make restitution (*Armstrong v Jackson* [1917] 2 KB 822). It is no answer for the fiduciary to say that the other party would still have entered into the transaction had he made full disclosure. One can see the same reasoning being adopted in relation to the doctrine of *uberrimae fidei* (for example, s 17 of the Marine Insurance Act 1906); the transaction is voidable. The principle is not a principle relating to the recovery of damages, nor does it give rise to common law rights. It is, essentially, a principle which precludes the fiduciary from enforcing his common law rights. It will thus be seen that this principle cannot be used to enable a claimant to recover common law damages without establishing a causal connection between the relevant loss and the relevant wrong (see *Bristol and West Building Society v May, May & Merrimans (A Firm)* [1996] 2 All ER 801).

The following examples illustrate the principles that are applied by the courts:

(1) Where the trustees make an unauthorised investment, they are liable for any loss incurred on the sale of the unauthorised assets. The position remains the same even if the sale is ordered by the courts and, but for the order of sale within a specified time, the investments would have produced a profit had they been retained for a longer period. The loss is measured by deducting the proceeds of sale of the unauthorised investment (accruing to the trust) from the amount improperly invested.

Knott v Cottee (1852) 16 Beav 77, CA

In this case, a testator who died in 1844 directed his trustee to invest in government stocks and land in England and Wales. In 1845 and 1846, the executor-trustee invested part of the estate in Exchequer bills which in 1846 were ordered into court and sold at a loss. In 1848, the court declared that the investment was improper. If, however, the investment had been retained, its realisation at the time of the declaration in 1848 would have resulted in a profit.

The court held that the trustee was liable to compensate the estate for the difference in the value of the assets between 1848 and the sale proceeds in 1846.

> **Romilly MR:** The case must either be treated as if these investments had not been made, or had been made for his own benefit out of his own monies, and that he had at the same time retained monies of the testator in his hands.

(2) Where the trustees, in breach of their duties, fail to dispose of unauthorised investments and improperly retain the assets, they will be liable for the difference between the current value of the assets and the value at the time when they should have been sold.

In *Fry v Fry*,[1] a testator who died in March 1834 directed his trustees to sell a house 'as soon as convenient after his death ... for the most money that could be normally obtained'. In April 1836, the trustees advertised the house for £1,000. In 1837, they refused an offer of £900. A railway was built near the property in 1843 which caused it to depreciate in value. The property remained unsold in 1856, by which time both the original trustees had died. The court held that their estates were liable for the

1 (1859) 28 LJ Ch 591.

difference between £900 and the sum receivable for the house when it was eventually sold.

(3) Where the trustees retain an authorised investment they will not be liable for breach of trust unless their conduct falls short of the ordinary prudence required of trustees. See *Re Chapman*.[2] Under s 6 of the Trustee Investment Act 1961 (see above, p 794), the trustees, from time to time, are required to obtain and consider advice on whether the retention of the investment is satisfactory, having regard to the need for diversification and suitability of the investment.

(4) Where the trustees improperly sell authorised investments and re-invest the proceeds in unauthorised investments, they will be liable to replace the authorised investments if these have risen in value, or the proceeds of sale of the authorised investments.

In *Re Massingberd's Settlement*,[3] the trustees of a settlement had power to invest in Government securities. In 1875, they sold consols (authorised investments) and re-invested in unauthorised mortgages. The mortgages were called in and the whole of the money invested was recovered. At this time the consols had risen in value. In an action for an account, the court held that the trustees were required to replace the stock sold or its money equivalent.

(5) Where the trustees are directed by the settlor to invest in an identified or specific investment (for example, shares in British Telecom plc) and the trustees fail to acquire the stipulated investments, they will be required to purchase the same at the proper time. If the specified investments have fallen in value, the trustees may be ordered to pay compensation to the trust, equivalent to the difference between the values of the investments at the time the investments should have been made, and the value of the investments at the time of the judgment.

On the other hand, where the trustees retain a discretion to invest in a specified range of investments and they fail to invest, they are chargeable with the trust fund itself and not with the amount of one or other of the investments which might have been purchased. In short, there is no one specific investment which may be used to measure the loss suffered by the trust (see *Shepherd v Mouls*).[4]

(6) Where the trustees, in breach of trust, make a profit in one transaction and a loss in another separate venture, they are not allowed to set off the loss incurred in one scheme against the profit made in a different transaction. However, a set off is allowed when the profit and loss are made as part of

---

2 [1896] 2 Ch 763.

3 (1890) 63 LT 296.

4 (1845) 4 Hare 500.

one transaction. This may occur if the trustees adopt a consistent commercial strategy in respect of two or more business ventures with varying success.

Bartlett v Barclays Bank Trust Co (No 2) [1980] Ch 515, HC

In this case, the trust estate consisted of a majority shareholding in a property company and the trustees were a professional trust company. For a number of years, the property company maintained traditional investments and these were sufficient to maintain large dividends. As a result of inflation, the board resolved to restructure the investment portfolio into land developments. The new investments, known as the 'Old Bailey' project and the 'Guildford' project, were not completely successful and resulted in a loss to the trust. The court found that the new investments were in breach of trust and, *inter alia*, the trustees attempted to set off a loss made in the 'Old Bailey' project against a gain made in the 'Guildford' scheme. The court allowed the set off as the mixed fortunes originated from the same transaction.

> **Brightman J:** The general rule as stated in all the textbooks, with some reservations, is that where a trustee is liable in respect of distinct breaches of trust, one of which has resulted in a loss and the other a gain, he is not entitled to set off the gain against the loss unless they arise in the same transaction. The relevant cases are not, however, altogether easy to reconcile. All are centenarians and none is quite like the present. The 'Guildford' development stemmed from exactly the same policy and exemplified the same folly as the 'Old Bailey' project. Part of the profit was in fact used to finance the 'Old Bailey' disaster. By sheer luck the gamble paid off handsomely on capital account. I think it would be unjust to deprive the bank of this element of salvage in the course of assessing the cost of the shipwreck. My order will therefore reflect the bank's right to an appropriate set off.

(7) The principles of restitution which govern the computation of the loss to the trust, are concerned with the gross loss suffered by the estate. The tax position of the beneficiaries is irrelevant in the assessment of the loss to the estate. Accordingly, compensation to the trust will not be reduced by an equivalent amount of tax which the beneficiaries would have paid, had the trustees not committed a breach of trust (see *BTC v Gourley*).[5]

Bartlett v Barclays Bank Trust Co Ltd (No 2) [1980] Ch 515, HC

> **Brightman J:** I have reached the conclusion that tax ought not to be taken into account ... but I do not feel that the established principles on which equitable relief is granted enable me to apply the *Gourley* principles to this case.

(8) Interest: as a general rule, the court is entitled to award simple interest under s 35A of the Supreme Court Act 1981 on monetary sums payable by the trustees. There is no consistent view as to the rate of interest. In recent

5 [1956] AC 185.

years some courts have taken the view that the rate of interest is 1% above the minimum lending rate: see *Belmont Finance Corporation v Williams Furniture Ltd (No 2)* [1980] 1 All ER 393. Other courts have suggested that the appropriate rate is that allowed from time to time on the court's short term investment account: see *Bartlett v Barclays Bank (No 2)* [1980] 2 WLR 448.

The court has a discretion to award compound interest against the trustees. The purpose of such an order is not designed to punish the trustees, but to require them to disgorge the benefit of the use of the trust funds. The principle here stems from the policy of preventing the trustees profiting from their breach. The Law Lords in the *Westdeutsche* case (see below, p 878) considered that the jurisdiction to award compound interest originated exclusively in equity. In the absence of fraud, this jurisdiction is exercised against a defendant who is a trustee or otherwise stands in a fiduciary position, and makes an unauthorised profit or is assumed to have made an unauthorised profit. The majority of the Law Lords decided that, since the defendant did not owe fiduciary duties to the bank in relation to the payment made in June 1987, compound interest would not be awarded. To award compound interest in the circumstances of this case would be tantamount to the courts usurping the function of Parliament. However, simple interest would be awarded on the balance of the fund remaining outstanding, calculated from the date of the original payment by the bank to the local authority.

The two dissenting Law Lords, Lords Goff and Woolf, adopted a more robust view concerning the award of compound interest. They took the view that since the council had the use of the bank's money, which it would otherwise have had to borrow at compound interest, it had, to that extent, profited from the use of the bank's money. Moreover, if the bank had not advanced the money to the council, it would have employed the money in its business. The award of compound interest should be based on the principle of promoting justice or to prevent unjust enrichment. If the defendant has wrongfully profited, or may be presumed to have so profited from having the use of the plaintiff's money, justice demands that the sum be repayable with compound interest. This would be the position irrespective of whether the plaintiff's claim arises *in personam* or *in rem*.

The court decided unanimously that the facts of the case did not reveal a resulting trust in favour of the bank. The circumstances of the transfer of money under the agreement did not fit any of the recognisable categories of resulting trust. Moreover, the parties had entered into a commercial transaction which proved to be void. The plaintiff bank ought not to be given any additional benefits which flow from a proprietary claim, such as priority over the defendant's creditors in the event of insolvency. After all, the bank had entered into a commercial transaction, just like the defendant's other creditors who had contracted with it. The bank's claim to restitution at common law arose from the fact that the payment made by the bank to the council was effected under a purported contract which, unknown to both parties, was *ultra vires* and void *ab initio*. Accordingly, no consideration had been given for the making of the payment.

***Westdeutsche Landesbank Girozentrale v Islington Borough Council* [1996] 2 All ER 961, HL**

On 16 June 1987, an interest rate swap agreement was made between the council and the bank. The arrangement was intended to run for 10 years, starting on 18 June 1987. The interest sums were to be calculated on a notional principal sum of £25 m. The bank was the fixed rate payer at a rate of 7.5% per annum and the council was the floating rate payer at the domestic London Interbank Offered Rate (LIBOR). In addition, on 18 June 1987, the bank made an 'upfront payment' of £2.5 m to the council. The council made four payments totalling approximately £1.35 m. Further to the decision in *Hazell v Hammersmith and Fulham BC* [1992] 2 AC 1 (where the House of Lords decided that such arrangements were *ultra vires* and void), the council discontinued making payments to the bank. The bank brought an action against the local authority, claiming repayments of approximately £1.15 m, representing the difference between the initial lump sum payment and the payments made by the local authority, with interest as from 18 June 1987. The judge decided that the bank was entitled to recover the principal sum plus compound interest awarded as from April 1990. The Court of Appeal dismissed the local authority's appeal but allowed a cross-appeal from the bank to award compound interest as from June 1987. The local authority conceded that it was personally liable to repay the balance of the capital, but appealed to the House of Lords against the award of compound interest.

Held:

(i) by a majority of 3:2, the court allowed the appeal by the local authority concerning the award of compound interest. The court has no jurisdiction to award compound interest on these facts. Accordingly, only simple interest was payable under s 35A of the Supreme Court Act 1981, as from the date of the accrual of the cause of action, namely, 18 June 1987;

(ii) the House unanimously considered, *obiter*, that the right to recover the balance of the capital of £1.15 m was not based on the notion of a trust, but a personal action at law on the ground of a total failure of consideration.

> **Lord Browne-Wilkinson:** My Lords, in the last decade many local authorities entered into interest rate swap agreements with banks and other finance houses. In *Hazell v Hammersmith and Fulham BC* [1992] 2 AC 1, your Lordships held that such contracts were *ultra vires* local authorities and therefore void. Your Lordships left open the question whether payments made pursuant to such swap agreements were recoverable or not. The action which is the subject matter of this appeal is one of a number in which the court has had to consider the extent to which moneys paid under such an agreement are recoverable.

An interest rate swap agreement is an agreement between two parties, by which each agrees to pay the other on a specified date or dates, an amount calculated by reference to the interest which would have accrued over a given period, on a notional principal sum. The rate of interest payable by each party (on the same notional sum) is different. One rate of interest is usually fixed and does not change (and the payer is called 'the fixed rate payer'); the other rate is a variable or floating rate based on a fluctuating interest rate such as the six month London Interbank Offered Rate ('LIBOR') and the payer is known as 'the floating rate payer'. Normally, the parties do not make the actual payments they have contracted for, but the party owing the higher amount pays to the other party the difference between the two amounts.

The local authority now accepts that it is personally liable to repay the balance to the bank. The local authority appeals to your Lordships only against the award of compound interest. But, as will appear, notwithstanding the narrow scope of the appeal, it raises profound questions for decision by your Lordships.

Compound interest in equity

In the absence of fraud, courts of equity have never awarded compound interest, except against a trustee or other person owing fiduciary duties, who is accountable for profits made from his position. Equity awarded simple interest at a time when courts of law had no right under common law or statute to award any interest. The award of compound interest was restricted to cases where the award was in lieu of an account of profits improperly made by the trustee. We were not referred to any case where compound interest had been awarded in the absence of fiduciary accountability for a profit. The principle is clearly stated by Lord Hatherley LC in *Burdick v Garrick* (1870) LR 5 Ch App 233, p 241:

> ... the court does not proceed against an accounting party by way of punishing him for making use of the plaintiff's money by directing rests, or payment of compound interest, but proceeds upon this principle: either that he has made, or has put himself into such a position as that he is to be presumed to have made 5%, or compound interest, as the case may be.

The principle was more fully stated by Buckley LJ *in Wallersteiner v Moir (No 2)* [1975] QB 373, p 397:

> Where a trustee has retained trust money in his own hands, he will be accountable for the profit which he has made or which he is assumed to have made from the use of the money.

In *AG v Alford* (1855) De GM & G 843, p 851, Lord Cranworth LC said:

> What the court ought to do, I think, is to charge him only with the interest which he has received, or which it is justly entitled to say he ought to have received, or which it is so fairly to be presumed that he did receive that he is estopped from saying that he did not receive it.

This is an application of the doctrine that the court will not allow a trustee to make any profit from his trust. The defaulting trustee is normally charged with simple interest only, but if it is established that he has used the money in trade, he may be charged compound interest ... The justification for charging compound interest normally lies in the fact that profits earned in trade would be likely to be used as working capital for earning further profits. Precisely similar equitable principles apply to an agent who has retained moneys of his principal in his hands and used them for his own purposes: *Burdick v Garrick*.

These authorities establish that, in the absence of fraud, equity only awards compound (as opposed to simple) interest against a defendant who is a trustee or otherwise in a fiduciary position, by way of recouping from such a defendant an improper profit made by him. It is unnecessary to decide whether in such a case compound interest can only be paid where the defendant has used trust moneys in his own trade or (as I tend to think) extends to all cases where a fiduciary has improperly profited from his trust. Unless the local authority owed fiduciary duties to the bank in relation to the upfront payment, compound interest cannot be awarded.

Although the actual question in issue on the appeal is a narrow one, on the arguments presented, it is necessary to consider fundamental principles of trust law. Does the recipient of money under a contract subsequently found to be void for mistake or as being *ultra vires* hold the moneys received on trust even where he had no knowledge at any relevant time that the contract was void? If he does hold on trust, such trust must arise at the date of receipt or, at the latest, at the date the legal title of the payer is extinguished by mixing moneys in a bank account: in the present case, it does not matter at which of those dates the legal title was extinguished. If there is a trust, two consequences follow: (a) the recipient will be personally liable, regardless of fault, for any subsequent payment away of the moneys to third parties, even though, at the date of such payment, the 'trustee' was still ignorant of the existence of any trust: see Burrows, A, 'Swaps and the friction between common law and equity' [1995] RLR 15; (b) as from the date of the establishment of the trust (ie, receipt or mixing of the moneys by the 'trustee') the original payer will have an equitable proprietary interest in the moneys, so long as they are traceable into whomsoever's hands they come, other than a purchaser, for value of the legal interest without notice. Therefore, although in the present case the only question directly in issue is the personal liability of the local authority as a trustee, it is not possible to hold the local authority liable without imposing a trust which, in other cases will create property rights affecting third parties, because moneys received under a void contract are 'trust property'.

The relevant principles of trust law

(i) Equity operates on the conscience of the owner of the legal interest. In the case of a trust, the conscience of the legal owner requires him to carry out the purposes for which the property was vested in him (express or implied trust) or which the law imposes on him by reason of his unconscionable conduct (constructive trust).

(ii) Since the equitable jurisdiction to enforce trusts depends upon the conscience of the holder of the legal interest being affected, he cannot be a trustee of the property if and so long as he is ignorant of the facts alleged to affect his conscience, that is, until he is aware that he is intended to hold the property for the benefit of others in the case of an express or implied trust, or, in the case of a constructive trust, of the factors which are alleged to affect his conscience.

(iii) In order to establish a trust, there must be identifiable trust property. The only apparent exception to this rule is a constructive trust imposed on a person who dishonestly assists in a breach of trust who may come under fiduciary duties even if he does not receive identifiable trust property.

(iv) Once a trust is established, as from the date of its establishment, the beneficiary has, in equity, a proprietary interest in the trust property, which proprietary interest will be enforceable in equity against any subsequent holder of the property (whether the original property or substituted property into which it can be traced), other than a purchaser for value of the legal interest without notice.

These propositions are fundamental to the law of trusts and, I would have thought, uncontroversial.

Those basic principles are inconsistent with the case being advanced by the bank. The latest time at which there was any possibility of identifying the 'trust property' was the date on which the moneys in the mixed bank account of the local authority ceased to be traceable when the local authority's account went into overdraft in June 1987. At that date, the local authority had no knowledge of the invalidity of the contract but regarded the moneys as its own to spend as it thought fit. There was, therefore, never a time at which both (a) there was defined trust property, and (b) the conscience of the local authority in relation to such defined trust property was affected. The basic requirements of a trust were never satisfied.

Resulting trust

Under existing law a resulting trust arises in two sets of circumstances: (a) where A makes a voluntary payment to B or pays (wholly or in part) for the purchase of property which is vested either in B alone or in the joint names of A and B, there is a presumption that A did not intend to make a gift to B: the money or property is held on trust for A (if he is the sole provider of the money) or, in the case of a joint purchase by A and B, in shares proportionate to their contributions. It is important to stress that this is only a presumption, which presumption is easily rebutted either by the counter-presumption of advancement or by direct evidence of A's intention to make an outright transfer: see Underhill and Hayton, *Law of Trusts and Trustees*, [14th edn, 1987,] pp 317 *et seq*; *Vandervell v IRC* [1967] 2 AC 291, pp 312 *et seq*; *In re Vandervell's Trusts (No 2)* [1974] Ch 269, pp 288 *et seq*; (b) where A transfers property to B on express trusts, but the trusts declared do not exhaust the whole beneficial interest: *ibid* and *Quistclose Investments Ltd v Rolls Razor Ltd (In Liquidation)* [1970] AC 567. Both types of resulting trust are traditionally regarded as examples of trusts giving effect to the common intention of the parties. A resulting trust is not imposed by law against the intentions of the trustee (as is a constructive trust) but gives effect to his presumed intention. Megarry J in *In re Vandervell's Trusts (No 2)* suggests that a resulting trust of type (b) does not depend on intention but operates automatically. I am not convinced that this is right. If the settlor has expressly, or by necessary implication, abandoned any beneficial interest in the trust property, there is, in my view, no resulting trust: the undisposed-of equitable interest vests in the Crown as *bona vacantia*: see *In re West Sussex Constabulary's Widows, Children and Benevolent (1930) Fund Trusts* [1971] Ch 1.

Applying these conventional principles of resulting trust to the present case, the bank's claim must fail. There was no transfer of money to the local authority on express trusts: therefore a resulting trust of type (b), above could not arise. As to type (a), above, any presumption of resulting trust is rebutted since it is demonstrated that the bank paid, and the local authority received, the upfront payment with the intention that the moneys so paid should become the absolute property of the local authority.

[His Lordship reviewed the decision of *Sinclair v Brougham* [1914] AC 398, and continued:]

As has been pointed out frequently over the 80 years since it was decided, *Sinclair v Brougham* is a bewildering authority: no single *ratio decidendi* can be detected; all the reasoning is open to serious objection; it was only intended to deal with cases where there were no trade creditors in competition and the reasoning is incapable of application where there are such creditors. In my view the decision as to rights *in rem* in *Sinclair v Brougham* should also be overruled. Although the case is one where property rights are involved, such overruling should not in practice disturb long settled titles. However, your Lordships should not be taken to be casting any doubt on the principles of tracing as established in *In re Diplock*.

If *Sinclair v Brougham*, in both its aspects, is overruled the law can be established in accordance with principle and commercial common sense: a claimant for restitution of moneys paid under an *ultra vires*, and therefore void, contract has a personal action at law to recover the moneys paid as on a total failure of consideration; he will not have an equitable proprietary claim which gives him either rights against third parties or priority in an insolvency; nor will he have a personal claim in equity, since the recipient is not a trustee.

[His Lordship expressed his views on the decision of Goulding J in *Chase Manhattan Bank NA v Israel-British Bank (London) Ltd* [1981] Ch 105 and continued:]

However, although I do not accept the reasoning of Goulding J, *Chase Manhattan* may well have been rightly decided. The defendant bank knew of the mistake made by the paying bank within two days of the receipt of the moneys: see p 115A. The judge treated this fact as irrelevant (p 114F) but in my judgment it may well provide a proper foundation for the decision. Although the mere receipt of the moneys, in ignorance of the mistake, gives rise to no trust, the retention of the moneys after the recipient bank learned of the mistake may well have given rise to a constructive trust: see *Snell's Equity*, 29th edn, 1990, p 193; Pettit, *Equity and the Law of Trusts*, 7th edn, 1993, p 168; *Metall und Rohstoff AG v Donaldson Lufkin & Jenrette Inc* [1990] 1 QB 391, pp 473–74.

Restitution and equitable rights

Although the resulting trust is an unsuitable basis for developing proprietary restitutionary remedies, the remedial constructive trust, if introduced into English law, may provide a more satisfactory road forward. The court, by way of remedy, might impose a constructive trust on a defendant who knowingly retains property of which the plaintiff has been unjustly deprived. Since the remedy can be tailored to the circumstances of the particular case, innocent third parties would not be prejudiced and restitutionary defences, such as change of position, are capable of being given effect. However, whether English law should follow the United States and Canada by adopting the remedial constructive trust will have to be decided in some future case when the point is directly in issue.

The date from which interest is payable

I fully appreciate the strength of the moral claim of the bank in this case to receive full restitution, including compound interest. But I am unable to accept that it would be right in the circumstances of this case for your Lordships to develop the law in the manner proposed. I take this view for two reasons.

First, Parliament has twice since 1934 considered what interest should be awarded on claims at common law. Both s 3(1) of the [Supreme Court] Act of 1934 and its successor, s 35A of the [Supreme Court] Act of 1981, make it clear that the Act does not authorise the award of compound interest. However, both Acts equally make it clear that they do not impinge on the award of interest in equity. At the time those Acts were passed, and indeed at all times down to the present day, equity has only awarded compound interest in the limited circumstances which I have mentioned. In my judgment, your Lordships would be usurping the function of Parliament if, by expanding the equitable rules for the award of compound interest, this House were now to hold that the court exercising its equitable jurisdiction in aid of the common law can award compound interest which the statutes have expressly not authorised the court to award in exercise of its common law jurisdiction.

Secondly, the arguments relied upon by my noble and learned friends were not advanced by the bank at the hearing. The local authority would have a legitimate ground to feel aggrieved if the case were decided against them on a point which they had had no opportunity to address. Moreover, in my view it would be imprudent to introduce such an important change in the law without this House first having heard full argument upon it.

For these reasons, which are in substance the same as those advanced by my noble and learned friend, Lord Lloyd of Berwick, I am unable to agree with the views of Lord Goff of Chieveley and Lord Woolf.

David Capper, 'Compensation for breach of trust' [1997] Conv 14, in reviewing the decision in *Target Holdings Ltd v Redferns*, comments:

The specific test applied in *Target* was whether the loss would have happened 'but for' the breach. There seems to be no need to enquire whether the breach is a predominant cause or to compare its importance to other operative causes. But where the loss would have occurred regardless of the breach, the causation requirement is not satisfied.

Their Lordships' decision that there can be no liability for breach of trust absent causation is to be welcomed. It resolves a difficult problem on which there was no authority and little expression of view from commentators. The contrary view would be an affront to common sense and productive of much

> injustice ... the approach to calculating equitable compensation is to look back to the breach and see if the loss can be traced to it. This contrasts with contract and tort where one looks forward from the acceptance of contractual risks or the breach of duty and asks whether the loss occurring was foreseeable.

Contribution and indemnity between trustees

Trustees are under a duty to act jointly and unanimously. In principle, each trustee has an equal role and standing in the administration of the trust. Accordingly, if a breach of trust has occurred each trustee is equally liable or the trustees are collectively liable to the beneficiary. Thus, the liability of the trustees is joint and several. The innocent beneficiary may sue one or more or all of the trustees.

If a successful action is brought against one trustee, he has a right of contribution against his co-trustees, with the effect that each trustee will contribute equally to the damages awarded in favour of the plaintiff, unless the court decides otherwise. The position today is that the right of contribution is governed by the Civil Liability (Contribution) Act 1978. The court has a discretion concerning the amount of the contribution which may be recoverable from any other person liable in respect of the same damage. The discretion is enacted in s 2 of the Act, thus:

> ... the amount of contribution shall be such as may be found by the court to be just and equitable having regard to the extent of that person's responsibility for the damage in question.

The Act does not apply to an indemnity which is governed entirely by case law. There are three circumstances when a trustee is required to indemnify his co-trustees in respect of their liability to the beneficiaries:

(a) Where one trustee has fraudulently obtained a benefit from a breach of trust. Such a claim for indemnity failed in *Bahin v Hughes*.[6] A testator bequeathed a legacy of £2,000 to his three daughters, Miss Hughes, Mrs Edwards and Mrs Burden on specified trusts. Miss Hughes did all the administration of the trust. The trust money was invested in unauthorised investments resulting in a loss. Miss Hughes and Mrs Burden (in whose name the money was entered) selected the investment and by letter told Mrs Edwards who failed to give her consent. The trustees were liable to the beneficiaries for breach of trust. Mr Edwards (whose wife had died) claimed that Miss Hughes, as an active trustee, ought to indemnify him against his late wife's liability. The court decided that the defendants were jointly and severally liable to replace the £2,000 and Edwards had no right of indemnity against Miss Hughes.

6 (1886) 31 Ch D 390.

Bahin v Hughes (1886) 31 Ch D 390, CA

Cotton LJ: ... where one trustee has got the money into his own hands, and made use of it, he will be liable to his co-trustee to give him an indemnity ... relief has only been granted against a trustee who has himself got the benefit of the breach of trust, or between whom and his co-trustees there has existed a relation which will justify the court in treating him solely liable for the breach of trust ... Miss Hughes was the active trustee and Mr Edwards did nothing, and in my opinion it would be laying down a wrong rule that where one trustee acts honestly, though erroneously, the other trustee is to be held entitled to an indemnity who by doing nothing neglects his duty more than the acting trustee ... In my opinion the money was lost just as much by the default of Mr Edwards as by the innocent though erroneous action of his co-trustee, Miss Hughes.

(b) Where the breach of trust was committed on the advice of a solicitor-trustee. The requirements here, in addition to a breach of trust, are:

(1) a co-trustee is a solicitor; and

(2) the breach of trust was committed in respect of his advice; and

(3) the co-trustees had relied solely on his advice and did not exercise an independent judgment.

In *Re Partington*,[7] Mrs Partington and Mr Allen, a solicitor, were trustees who were liable for a breach of trust. The trust fund was invested in an improper mortgage which resulted in a loss. Mr Allen had assured Mrs Partington that he would find a good investment on behalf of the trust. He failed in his duties to verify statements by the borrower, he failed to give proper instructions to the valuers and he did not give sufficient information to Mrs Partington to enable her to exercise an independent judgment.

The court held that Mrs Partington was entitled to claim an indemnity from Mr Allen.

In *Head v Gould*,[8] the claim for an indemnity against a solicitor-trustee failed because the co-trustee actively encouraged the solicitor-trustee to commit the breach of trust. The mere fact that the co-trustee is a solicitor is insufficient to establish the claim.

Head v Gould [1898] 2 Ch 250, HC

Kekewich J: I do not think that a man is bound to indemnify his co-trustee against any loss merely because he was a solicitor, when that co-trustee was an active participator in the breach of trust complained of, and is not proved to have participated merely in consequence of the advice and control of the solicitor.

7 (1887) 57 LT 654.

8 [1898] 2 Ch 250.

(c) The rule in *Chillingworth v Chambers*.[9] This rule is that where a trustee is also a beneficiary (whether he receives a benefit or not is immaterial) and the trustees are liable for breach of trust, the beneficiary/trustee is required to indemnify his co-trustee to the extent of his beneficial interest. If the loss exceeds the beneficial interest, the trustees will share the surplus loss equally insofar as it exceeds the beneficial interest.

Defences to an action for breach of trust

In pursuance of an action against trustees for breach of trust, there are a number of defences which the trustees are entitled to raise. These are:

Knowledge and consent of the beneficiaries

A beneficiary who has freely consented to or concurred in a breach of trust is not entitled to renege on his promise and sue the trustees.

In order to be prevented from bringing an action against the trustees, the beneficiary is required to be of full age and sound mind, with full knowledge of all the relevant facts and to exercise an independent judgment. The burden of proof will be on the trustees to establish these elements.

In *Nail v Punter*,[10] the husband of a life tenant under a trust encouraged the trustees to pay him money from the trust fund in breach of trust. The life tenant commenced proceedings against the trustees, but died shortly afterwards. The husband became a beneficiary and continued the action against the trustees for breach of trust. The court held that the action could not succeed because the husband was a party to the breach.

The trustees are required to prove that the consent was not obtained as a result of undue influence. In *Re Pauling's Settlement Trust*[11] (see above, p 824), the trustees claimed that the children were not entitled to bring an action because they had consented to the advancements.

The court rejected this argument and decided that the consent was not freely obtained from the children because they were under the influence of their parents who benefited from the advancements. The statement of the principle by Wilberforce J was approved by the Court of Appeal.

> **Wilberforce J:** The court has to consider all the circumstances in which the concurrence of the beneficiary was given with a view to seeing whether it is fair and equitable that, having given his concurrence, he should afterwards turn around and see the trustees ... subject to this, it is not necessary that he

9 [1896] 1 Ch 385.

10 (1832) 5 Sim 555.

11 [1964] Ch 303.

> should know that what he is concurring in is a breach of trust, provided that he fully understands what he is concurring in, and ... it is not necessary that he should himself have directly benefited by the breach of trust.

Impounding the interest of a beneficiary

In the above section, the beneficiary who concurs or acquiesces in a breach of trust will not be allowed to bring an action against the trustees. But, this principle does not prevent other beneficiaries from bringing an action against the trustees. In these circumstances, the court has a power to impound the interest of the beneficiary who instigated the breach.

Under the inherent jurisdiction of the court, a beneficiary who instigated the breach of trust may be required to indemnify the trustees. The rule was extended in s 62 of the Trustee Act 1925, which declares:

> Where a trustee commits a breach of trust at the instigation or request or with the consent in writing of a beneficiary, the court may if it thinks fit make such order as the court seems just for impounding all or any part of the interest of the beneficiary in the trust estate by way of indemnity to the trustee or persons claiming through him.

It is clear from the section that the court has a discretion which it will not exercise if the beneficiary was not aware of the full facts. Section 62 is applicable irrespective of an intention, on the part of the beneficiary, to receive a personal benefit or not. The beneficiary's consent is required to be in writing.

Relief under s 61 of the Trustee Act 1925

Section 61 of the Trustee Act 1925, provides:

> If it appears to the court that a trustee ... is or may be personally liable for any breach of trust ... but has acted honestly and reasonably, and ought fairly to be excused for the breach of trust and for omitting to obtain the directions of the court in the matter in which he committed such breach, then the court may relieve him either wholly or partly from personal liability for the same.

This section re-enacted, with slight modifications, s 3 of the Judicial Trustees Act 1896.

The section provides three main ingredients for granting relief, namely:

(a) the trustee acted honestly; and

(b) the trustee acted reasonably; and

(c) the trustee ought fairly to be excused in respect of the breach and omitting to obtain directions of the court.

These ingredients are cumulative and the trustee has the burden of proof.

The expression, 'honestly', means that the trustee acted in good faith. This is a question of fact. The word 'reasonably' indicates that the trustee acted prudently. If these two criteria are satisfied, the court has a discretion whether to excuse the trustee or not. The test in exercising the discretion is to have regard to both the interests of the trustees and the beneficiaries and deciding whether the breach of trust ought to be forgiven in whole or in part. In the absence of special circumstances, a trustee who has acted honestly and reasonably, ought to be relieved.

Perrins v Bellamy [1899] 1 Ch 797, HC

In this case, the trustees of a settlement were erroneously advised by their solicitor that they had a power of sale. They sold the leaseholds comprised in the settlement, thereby diminishing the income of the plaintiff, the tenant for life. The plaintiff brought an action against the trustees for breach of trust. The trustees claimed relief under the predecessor to s 61 of the Trustee Act 1925.

The court granted relief.

> **Kekewich J:** I venture, however, to think that, in general and in the absence of special circumstances, a trustee who has acted 'reasonably' ought to be relieved, and it is not incumbent on the court to consider whether he ought 'fairly' to be excused, unless there is evidence of a special character showing that the provisions of the section ought not to be applied in his favour.

But, each case is decided on its own facts. A factor which is capable of influencing the court is whether the trustee is an expert, professional trustee or not.

In *National Trustee Co of Australia Ltd v General Finance Co*,[12] the court refused relief to professional trustees who had acted honestly and reasonably and on the advice of a solicitor in committing a breach of trust.

A similar view was echoed by Brightman J in *Bartlett v Barclays Bank* (1980) (see above, p 876). The professional trustee company was refused relief under s 61 of the Trustee Act 1925 because they acted unreasonably in failing to keep abreast or informed of the changes in the activities of the investment company.

> **Brightman J:** A trust corporation holds itself out in its advertising literature as being above ordinary mortals. With a specialist staff of trained trust officers and managers, with ready access to financial information and professional advice, dealing with and solving trust problems day after day, the trust corporation holds itself out, and rightly, as capable of providing an expertise which it would be unrealistic to expect and unjust to demand from the ordinary prudent man or woman who accepts, probably unpaid and sometimes reluctantly from a sense of family duty, the burden of trusteeship. Just as, under the law of contract, a professional person possessed a particular skill is liable for breach of contract if he neglects to use the skill and experience which he professes, so I think that a professional corporate trustee is liable for breach of trust if loss is caused to the trust fund, because it neglects to exercise the special care and skill which it professes to have.

12 [1905] AC 373.

Other factors that have been taken into account by the courts are the status of the adviser to the trust and the size of the trust estate. It has been suggested that nothing less than the advice of a Queen's Counsel should be taken by the trustees in respect of a large estate. Other considerations that are relevant include whether the breach of trust originated from a complicated rule of law, and whether the trustees acted on an erroneous belief that the beneficiaries had consented.

Limitation and laches

The limitation periods concern the time limits during which a beneficiary is entitled to pursue a cause of action in respect of trust property. The remarks of Kekewich J in *Re Timmins*[13] refer to the rationale concerning an earlier limitation statute.

> **Kekewich J:** The intention of the statute was to give a trustee the benefit of the lapse of time when, although he had done something legally or technically wrong, he had done nothing morally wrong or dishonest, but it was not intended to protect him where, if he pleaded the statute, he would come off with something he ought not to have, ie, money of the trust received by him and converted to his own use.

Six year limitation period

Under s 21(3) of the Limitation Act 1980, the general rule concerning the limitation period for actions for breach of trust is six years from the date on which the cause of action accrued. A cause of action does not accrue in respect of future interests (remainders and reversions) until the interest falls into possession. Thus, a life tenant under a trust is required to bring an action within six years of the breach of trust but a remainderman has up to six years from the death of the life tenant before his cause of action becomes time-barred. In addition, time does not begin to run against a beneficiary suffering from a disability (infancy or mental incapacity) at the time of the breach until the disability ends. For these purposes a trustee includes a personal representative and no distinction is drawn between express, implied or constructive trustees.

Section 21(3) provides:

> Subject to the preceding provisions of this section, an action by a beneficiary to recover trust property or in respect of any breach of trust, not being an action for which a period of limitation is prescribed by any other provision of this Act, shall not be brought after the expiration of six years from the date on which the right of action accrued.

13 [1902] 1 Ch 176.

> For the purposes of this sub-section, the right of action shall not be treated as having accrued to any beneficiary entitled to a future interest in the trust property until the interest falls into possession.

In *Armitage v Nurse*, Millett LJ considered s 21 of the Limitation Act 1980 and said:

Armitage v Nurse [1997] 3 WLR 1046, CA

> **Millett LJ:**
>
> **Limitation**
>
> [His Lordship referred to s 21 of the Limitation Act 1980, and continued:]
>
> Two questions have been argued. The first is whether s 21(1)(a) is limited to cases of fraud or fraudulent breach of trust property so called, that is to say to cases involving dishonesty. The judge held that it is. In my judgment, he was plainly right. I have explained the meaning of the word 'fraud' in a trustee exemption clause, and there is no reason to ascribe a different meaning to the word where it appears in s 21(1)(a) of the Limitation Act 1980.
>
> The second question is whether Paula had a present interest while she was under the age of 25 or whether she had only a future interest which fell into possession when she attained that age. The judge held that she had merely a future interest. In my judgment, he was right. Until Paula attained 25 the trustees held the trust fund upon trust to accumulate the income with power instead to pay it to Paula or to apply it for her benefit. She had no present right to capital or income but only the right to require the trustees to consider from time to time whether to accumulate the income or to exercise their power to pay or apply it for her benefit. That, in my judgment, is not an interest in possession.
>
> The rationale of s 21(3) of the Limitation Act 1980 appears to me to be not that a beneficiary with a future interest has not the means of discovery, but that he should not be compelled to litigate (at considerable personal expense) in respect of an injury to an interest which he may never live to enjoy.

Exceptions to the six year rule

Under s 21(1), where a beneficiary brings an action in respect of any fraud by the trustee or to recover trust property or the proceeds of sale from trust property (that is, actions *in rem* (see below, p 900)), the limitation period fixed shall not apply. A transferee from a trustee is in the same position as the trustee unless he is a *bona fide* transferee of the legal estate for value without notice.

Section 21(1) provides:

> No period of limitation prescribed by this Act shall apply to an action by a beneficiary under a trust, being an action:
>
> (a) in respect of any fraud or fraudulent breach of trust to which the trustee was a party or privy; or

(b) to recover from the trustee trust property or the proceeds of trust property in the possession of the trustee, or previously received by the trustee and converted to his use.

Section 21(2) provides:

> Where a trustee who is also a beneficiary under the trust receives or retains trust property or its proceeds as his share on a distribution of trust property under the trust, his liability in any action brought by virtue of sub-s (1)(b) above to recover that property or its proceeds after the expiration of the period of limitation prescribed by this Act for bringing an action to recover trust property shall be limited to the excess over his proper share.
>
> This sub-section only applies if the trustee acted honestly and reasonably in making the distribution.

Where the right of action has been concealed by fraud or where the action is for relief from the consequences of a mistake, time does not begin to run until the plaintiff discovers the fraud or mistake or ought with reasonable diligence to have discovered it (s 32).

Section 32(1) provides:

> ... where in the case of any action for which a period of limitation is prescribed by this Act, either:
>
> (a) the action is based upon the fraud of the defendant; or
>
> (b) any fact relevant to the plaintiff's right of action has been deliberately concealed from him by the defendant (defined in s 32(2)); or
>
> (c) the action is for relief from the consequences of a mistake,
>
> the period of limitation shall not begin to run until the plaintiff has discovered the fraud, concealment or mistake (as the case may be) or could with reasonable diligence have discovered it.
>
> References in this sub-section to the defendant include references to the defendant's agent and to any person through whom the defendant claims and his agent.

Under s 22, the limitation period in respect of any claim to the estate of a deceased person must be brought within a period of 12 years.

Section 22 provides:

> Subject to s 21(1) and (2) of this Act:
>
> (a) no action in respect of any claim to the personal estate of a deceased person or to any share or interest in any such estate (whether under a will or on intestacy) shall be brought after the expiration of 12 years from the date on which the right to receive the share or interest accrued; and
>
> (b) no action to recover arrears of interest in respect of any legacy, or damages in respect of such arrears, shall be brought after the expiration of six years from the date on which the interest became due.

Furthermore, the limitation periods mentioned above do not apply to an action for an account brought by the Attorney General against a charitable trust, because charitable trusts do not have beneficiaries in a way similar to private trusts. See *AG v Cocke*.[14]

In addition, where a cause of action in negligence is statute-barred, an alternative claim in equity for breach of a fiduciary duty arising out of the same subject matter will not be subject to the Limitation Act 1980.

***Kershaw v Whelan (No 2)* (1997) *The Times*, 10 February, HC**

The plaintiff, suffering from severe physical disabilities, was aged 18 when his father died intestate in 1979. His father left £45,000 on discretionary trust in favour of the plaintiff, his stepmother and his sister. The trustees distributed nearly £40,000 to the stepmother and the balance to the two children. The plaintiff was unhappy with the distribution and suspected that the defendant, a solicitor acting for the plaintiff's stepmother, improperly influenced the trustees. It transpired that, in June 1979, the defendant wrote a letter to the trustees detailing false or highly misleading information concerning the plaintiff. In the letter, the defendant also suggested that the stepmother should benefit from the fund to the exclusion of the plaintiff. The defendant deliberately concealed the existence of this letter until 1983. The plaintiff commenced an action in March 1991 claiming under two heads, namely, the common law action of negligence or, alternatively, breach of fiduciary duty. It was conceded that time started to run from 1983, so that the common law claim was statute-barred. The plaintiff contended that the alternative claim in equity was not statute-barred. The defendant submitted that although the six year limitation period did not *prima facie* apply to the claim in equity, the limitation period ought to apply by analogy for, 'equity follows the law'.

Mrs Ebsworth J rejected the argument put forward by the defendant and decided that no limitation period was applicable to the plaintiff's claim in equity. The plaintiff's claim had to be construed to ascertain whether the defence of laches and acquiescence was made out: see *Nelson v Rye* [1996] 2 All ER 186, below, p 894. Her Ladyship was required to balance the long delay which was due to the deliberate concealment by the defendant, against the possibility that a real injustice had been committed to the plaintiff through the unconscionable conduct of the defendant.

Laches

Where no period of limitation has been specified under the Act (see s 21(1)), the doctrine of laches will apply to equitable claims. Section 36(2) of the Limitation Act 1980 enacts that 'nothing in the Act shall affect any equitable jurisdiction to refuse relief on the grounds of acquiescence or otherwise'.

14 [1988] Ch 414.

The doctrine of laches consists of a substantial lapse of time coupled with the existence of circumstances which make it inequitable to enforce the claim of the plaintiff. The doctrine is summarised in the maxim, 'equity aids the vigilant and not the indolent'. The rationale behind the doctrine was stated by Lord Camden LC.

Smith v Clay **(1767) 3 Bro CC 639, HL**

> **Lord Camden LC:** A court of equity has always refused its aid to stale demands, where a party has slept upon his rights and acquiesced for a great length of time. Nothing can call forth this court into activity, but conscience, good faith and reasonable diligence; where these are wanting, the court is passive and does nothing.

It may be treated as inequitable to enforce the plaintiff's claim where the delay has led the defendant to change his position to his detriment in the reasonable belief that the plaintiff's claim has been abandoned, or the delay has led to the loss of evidence which might assist the defence or if the claim is to a business (for the plaintiff should not be allowed to wait and see if it prospers).

The jurisdiction of the court in respect of laches was summarised by Lord Selborne in *Lindsay Petroleum Co v Hurd*:[15]

> Now the doctrine of laches in courts of equity is not an arbitrary or technical doctrine. Where it could be practically unjust to give a remedy either because the party has, by his conduct, done that which might fairly be regarded as equivalent to a waiver of it or where by his conduct the neglect he has, though perhaps not waiving that remedy, yet put the other party in a situation in which it would not be reasonable to place him if the remedy were afterwards to be asserted, in either of these cases lapse of time and delay are most material.

The applicability of the equitable doctrines of laches and acquiescence depend on the facts of each case. Unreasonable delay by the plaintiff, substantial prejudice and manifest injustice to the defendant, are significant factors to be taken into consideration by the court. In order to raise a successful defence, the defendant is required to establish the following three elements:

(1) that there has been unreasonable delay in bringing the action by the plaintiff;

(2) that there has been consequent substantial prejudice or detriment to the defendant;

(3) the balance of justice requires the plaintiff's claim to be withheld.

15 (1874) LR 5 PC 221.

Nelson v Rye [1996] 2 All ER 186, HC

The plaintiff, William Nelson, a musician, retained the defendant as his manager pursuant to an oral agreement. From August 1980, Mr Rye ran the plaintiff's business affairs. The relationship between them deteriorated. On 2 October 1990, Mr Rye wrote to Mr Nelson terminating the relationship. In December 1991, Mr Nelson sued the defendant claiming, *inter alia*, an account. Prior to the trial, Master Dyson ordered an account in respect of all moneys received by the defendant on behalf of Mr Nelson. Mr Nelson complained that the account was deficient, but on the figures disclosed, Mr Rye owed Mr Nelson £280,000. The defendant claimed that Mr Nelson owed him £64,000. At the trial of the outstanding claims, the defendant raised two defences in respect of the duty to account concerning the period prior to December 1985: (i) the claim was outside the statutory limitation period for contractual causes of action; (ii) the plaintiff was prevented from bringing an action owing to the equitable doctrine of laches and acquiescence. The plaintiff responded by asserting that his cause of action was not contractual but was based on breach of a fiduciary duty or, alternatively, a claim arose in trust and, accordingly, no limitation period applied.

The High Court held the following:

(a) the defendant was under a duty to account to the plaintiff and failed to do so. While not every breach of a fiduciary relationship gave rise to a constructive trust, the facts in the present case created such a trust. The defendant received the plaintiff's income which became trust property. After proper deductions by the defendant, the balance remaining was also trust property. The plaintiff's action was in respect of the recovery of such property. No limitation period was applicable in respect of the cause of action;

(b) the defences of laches and acquiescence were made out in respect of the plaintiff's claim for an account in respect of the period prior to December 1985. The court decided that, on the facts, Mr Nelson was not interested in receiving a financial analysis of his situation by Mr Rye. He knew or suspected that a financial appraisal of his situation would merely confirm that he was living beyond his means. In his Lordship's view, Mr Nelson showed a wilful refusal to involve himself in his financial affairs. There was unreasonable delay in commencing the proceedings. On the question of whether Mr Rye suffered substantial prejudice, the evidence demonstrated this to be the case. A number of documents, such as invoices, receipts and vouchers, no longer existed. Mr Rye's evidence was that from time to time, when he wanted space he destroyed old documents, that is, documents more than six years old. Furthermore, his recollection of events beyond six years was, inevitably, poor. In the circumstances, the judge decided that Mr Rye would suffer substantial prejudice if he was required to account for the period beyond six years, that is, prior to December 1985. In addition the facts indicated that it would be unreasonable and unjust to allow Mr Nelson to assert his right to an account against Mr Rye for the period prior to December 1985.

Laddie J: The statutes [the Limitation Act 1980 and its predeccessors] have imposed essentially arbitrary time limits on certain defined causes of action. It does not matter in such cases whether the plaintiff is to blame for not keeping within the time limit, nor is it relevant that in some cases it will be thought unfair that the defendant is allowed off the hook. The defendant is entitled to play possum in the hope that the plaintiff will make a mistake and fail to commence proceedings before the statutory time limit is breached. If the limitation period is exceeded then the defendant is entitled to call down the guillotine on the plaintiff's action unless a statutory exception exists, such as the extension of time provided by s 32 of the Act of 1980 in cases where there is fraud or concealment.

Furthermore, the arbitrary time limits imposed by statute vary from cause of action to cause of action. For example, an action for breach of contract must be commenced within six years, an action upon a specialty must be commenced within 12 years and an action in respect of personal injuries must be commenced, in many cases, within three years. What, then, if one set of facts gives rise to two or more potential causes of action with different limitation periods? For example, it may well be that the breakdown of a relationship which arises out of a contract gives rise to alternative causes of action for breach of contract, negligence and breach of trust. No doubt the injured party cannot use the alternatives so as to receive duplicate or triplicate relief (see *United Australia Ltd v Barclays Bank Ltd* [1941] AC 1; *AG for Hong Kong v Reid* [1994] 1 AC 324), but that does not mean that he cannot sue under all of the heads simultaneously. Each cause of action may have its own strengths and weaknesses, so that, say, the plaintiff may succeed in his cause of action based in negligence but fail in his action for breach of contract, or vice versa. In particular, where a limitation period exists and can be invoked in relation to one cause of action, it is *nihil ad rem* that no, or a different, limitation period applies to an alternative cause of action which has been or could have been pleaded by the plaintiff.

Historically, actions by beneficiaries against trustees for misappropriation of trust property have been excluded from the imposition of such arbitrary time limits. The courts and the legislature have treated trustees as bearing a special responsibility to the trust property and the beneficiary's interest in it. The beneficiary's right to complain of breach of trust has been treated as persisting indefinitely unless, of course, in all the circumstances it would be inequitable to allow him to enforce his rights. There is nothing to which my attention has been drawn which suggests that the Act of 1980 effected a significant change in this area.

With those considerations in mind it is possible to address the arguments advanced by the parties to this action.

In my view, s 23 of the Act does not have the meaning for which Mr Oppenheim contends. The section simply confirms that the limitation period which applies to a particular cause of action applies equally to the relief by way of account which flows from it. For example, in this case, certain claims for copyright infringement arise. Section 96(2) of the Copyright, Designs and Patents Act 1988 entitles a copyright owner to seek relief by way of an account where infringement is proved. The effect of s 21 of the Act of 1980 is that the limitation period for the account is the same as that for the claim for infringement. I do not accept that s 21 has the effect of circumventing and rendering nugatory the provisions of s 23. The former is concerned with whether or not there is a limitation period for actions for breach of trust, whereas the latter is only concerned with the limitation period to be applied to a form of relief which may be ordered in favour of a successful plaintiff.

Since that is so, what limitation period, if any, applies to the cause of action in this case? As I have indicated above, where a limitation period exists and can be invoked in relation to one cause of action, it is *nihil ad rem* that no, or a different, limitation period applies to an alternative cause of action which has been or could have been pleaded by the plaintiff. If the cause of action here is one for breach of fiduciary duty or breach of trust, it does not avail Mr Rye to argue that the relationship arose out of a contract and that the relationship between him and Mr Nelson can be treated as one between debtor and creditor. If Mr Nelson had chosen to sue for breach of contract alone, then the limitation period for contractual claims would have applied. He has not done so. If Mr Oppenheim's argument on this were right, the provisions of s 21(1) would be virtually valueless because, in most cases of breach of trust, the trustee would be able to argue that he could have been sued for breach of contract.

I accept Mr Anderson's basic premise that the Act of 1980 only imposes limitation periods on those actions it specifically identifies. A cause of action for which the Act, or other legislation, makes no limitation provision is not subject to a limitation period. Actions for breach of fiduciary duty are not expressly covered. It follows that, *prima facie*, no limitation applies to them. However, if this were all, s 21 would serve little purpose. As far as I can see, in all cases of breach of trust covered by the section it would be possible to say that there had been a breach of fiduciary duty. Although, as I have held, no limitation period applies to actions for breach of fiduciary duty *simpliciter* and s 21(1) provides that no limitation period applies in respect of many actions for breach of trust, some actions for breach of trust are the subject of limitation periods: see s 21(3). If those were treated as actions for breach of fiduciary duty, the limitation would be sidestepped.

The fallacy, it appears to me, is to treat breach of fiduciary duty and breach of trust as different causes of action. In a case where, because of the existence of a fiduciary duty, a constructive trust comes into existence, breach of trust and breach of fiduciary duty are the same cause of action. Similarly, where an express trust has been created, breach of that trust and breach of fiduciary duty are also the same cause of action. It is, therefore, not possible to sidestep the limitation provisions of s 21(3) by referring to the action as one for breach of fiduciary duty.

Since I accept Mr Oppenheim's argument that not all breaches of fiduciary duty give rise to constructive trusts, the following propositions appear to follow: (1) an action for breach of fiduciary duty *simpliciter* is outside the provisions of the Limitation Act 1980 and therefore is not subject to a period of limitation: see *AG v Cocke* [1988] Ch 414; (2) where breach of fiduciary duty gives rise to a constructive trust, the provisions of s 21 of the Act determine whether there is a limitation period and its duration; (3) an action for breach of an express trust is, in like manner, subject to the limitation provisions of s 21; (4) in neither case (2) nor (3) is it possible to avoid any limitation period imposed by the Act by treating the case as one of breach of fiduciary duty.

There is no dispute between the parties that Mr Rye owed Mr Nelson a fiduciary duty. He was obliged to account to Mr Nelson annually. He did not. There has been a breach of that duty and, *prima facie*, no limitation period applies.

The equitable defence

For Mr Nelson it was argued that, to succeed on this issue, Mr Rye must show: (a) that there was an express or implied representation by the plaintiff that he intended not to compel performance *in specie* by the defendant of the obligation in question; (b) that the plaintiff was aware, or ought to have been aware, of the possibility that the defendant would act to his prejudice in reliance on the representation; and (c) that, in consequence of that representation, it becomes unjust to grant the equitable relief sought as the defendant has been prejudiced by reliance on it (in the sense of being in a 'substantially worse position' than he would otherwise have been). For these propositions Mr Anderson relied on *Spry on Equitable Remedies*, 4th edn, 1990, London: Sweet & Maxwell, pp 236–38. In relation to laches, he said that in order to raise a *prima facie* case, a defendant must establish two facts: (a) that there has been unreasonable delay by the plaintiff; and (b) that there has been consequent substantial prejudice or detriment to the defendant which justifies the refusal of the equitable relief sought. He said that mere delay *per se* is not sufficient. A defendant must show a causal link between the delay and the prejudice/detriment: see *Lindsay Petroleum Co v Hurd* (1874) LR 5 PC 221, pp 239–40; *Lazard Bros & Co v Fairfield Properties Co (Mayfair) Ltd* (1977) *The Times*, 12 October; and *Spry*, 4th edn, pp 227–28. At least at one stage in his argument, Mr Anderson suggested that the defendant needs to prove that the prejudice was substantially caused by the delay.

It can be misleading to approach the equitable defences of laches and acquiescence as if they consisted of a series of precisely defined hurdles over each of which a litigant must struggle before the defence is made out. In *Lindsay Petroleum Co v Hurd* (1874) LR 5 PC 221, pp 239–40, the Privy Council stated:

> Now the doctrine of laches in courts of equity is not an arbitrary or a technical doctrine. Where it would be practically unjust to give a remedy, either because the party has, by his conduct, done that which might fairly be regarded as equivalent to a waiver of it, or where by his conduct and neglect he has, though perhaps not waiving that remedy, yet put the other party in a situation in which it would not be reasonable to place him if the remedy were afterwards to be asserted, in either of these cases, lapse of time and delay are most material. But in every case, if an argument against

> relief, which otherwise would be just, is founded upon mere delay, that delay, of course, not amounting to a bar by any statute of limitations, the validity of that defence must be tried upon principles substantially equitable. Two circumstances, always important in such cases, are the length of the delay and the nature of the acts done during the interval, which might affect either party and cause a balance of justice or injustice in taking the one course or the other, so far as relates to the remedy.

In *Erlanger v New Sombrero Phosphate Co* (1878) 3 App Cas 1218, pp 1279–80, after quoting this passage, Lord Blackburn went on to say:

> I have looked in vain for any authority which gives a more distinct and definite rule that this; and I think, from the nature of the inquiry, it must always be a question of more or less, depending on the degree of diligence which might reasonably be required, and the degree of change which has occurred, whether the balance of justice or injustice is in favour of granting the remedy or withholding it. The determination of such a question must largely depend on the turn of mind of those who have to decide, and must therefore be subject to uncertainty; but that, I think, is inherent in the nature of the inquiry.

So, here, these defences are not technical or arbitrary. The courts have indicated over the years some of the factors which must be taken into consideration in deciding whether the defence runs. Those factors include the period of the delay, the extent to which the defendant's position has been prejudiced by the delay and the extent to which that prejudice was caused by the actions of the plaintiff. I accept that mere delay alone will almost never suffice, but the court has to look at all the circumstances, including in particular those factors set out above, and then decide whether the balance of justice or injustice is in favour of granting the remedy or withholding it. If substantial prejudice will be suffered by the defendant, it is not necessary for the defendant to prove that it was caused by the delay. On the other hand, the plaintiff's knowledge that the delay will cause such prejudice is a factor to be taken into account. With these considerations in mind, I turn to the facts.

[His Lordship reviewed the facts and continued:] In my view there was a wilful refusal by Mr Nelson to involve himself in his financial affairs. He deliberately ignored advice both from Mr Rye and Mr Thomas to get round the table to see how the figures worked out. I find as a fact that he declined to attend two meetings with Mr Rye and Mr Thomas for no good reason. He was happy to drive his Rolls Royce, live in a mansion and take far more out of Happytronics than could be justified on the basis of its receipts, but he did not want to know the details of how the sums added up – or failed to add up. He rejected all advice. He was not interested in the account as between him and Mr Rye. He knew or suspected that working out any of the figures would merely confirm that he was living beyond his means. This was something which he preferred to ignore. He would leave his manager and Mr Thomas to sort out the problems. His only concerns arose when Mr Rye sought to put a brake on his wages. I accept that then he would demand to know why he could not have more and, from time to time, asked to see the figures. But this was simply part and parcel of trying to place the blame for his financial problems on others and, in particular, Mr Rye. During the 10 years of the relationship, Mr Nelson did not want an account and that was apparent to Mr Rye. He wanted to complain about lack of funds but he was not interested in any explanation which would support Mr Rye's constant warning that he was living beyond his means. In particular, he did not want to see it in black and white. Mr Thomas told Mr Rye that he wanted a meeting between the three of them so that he, Mr Thomas, could explain to Mr Nelson that he could not continue to draw 'vast amounts out of the company when it does not have the funds'. Even if Mr Nelson was not aware of the contents of this particular communication between Mr Thomas and Mr Rye, he was aware that this was the message he would be given if there was a meeting, and it was not one he was prepared to listen to. He was quite content to convince himself that he was too busy to meet to discuss the problems. I have little doubt that, had Mr Rye not terminated the relationship in 1990, Mr Nelson would have continued to refuse to look at any accounting material. As far as Mr Rye is concerned, I find that he wanted and tried to explain the accounts to Mr Nelson. It was in his interests to do so.

I have come to the conclusion that there was unreasonable delay in commencing these proceedings.

I turn to consider whether Mr Rye has suffered prejudice as a result of that delay. Mr Oppenheim relied on two matters. First, he says that documents relevant to the account which did exist in the past now no longer exist. Secondly, he says that it is inevitable that matters more than six years ago will be poorly remembered. In other words, Mr Rye's ability to give evidence has been prejudiced by the delay. I will consider each of these in turn, but, before doing so, I should mention one matter. Mr Nelson raised before the master certain objections to the account given by Mr Rye. In particular, although Mr Nelson accepts that Mr Rye was entitled to deduct legitimate expenses, a very large number of expenses claimed have been challenged on the basis that vouchers do not exist to support them. Mr Nelson is therefore seeking to have excluded from the account some or all of these expenses. Mr Anderson confirmed before me that Mr Nelson intends to continue to attack the account rendered on behalf of Mr Rye on this basis.

As far as the vouchers are concerned, Mr Rye's evidence was that from time to time when he wanted space he would clear out of storage and destroy old documents. In particular, invoices and receipts and the like would fall within the category of documents eligible for disposal. He said that he would not deliberately dispose of any vouchers less than six years old. This space-making exercise was not regular nor was it consistent. The result is that very many, but not all, vouchers which were more than six years old have gone. Under cross-examination, Mr Rye said that as soon as he received the letter from Mr Nelson's solicitors shortly after 21 December 1990 he stopped this deliberate destruction practice, at least in relation to Mr Nelson's affairs. It is apparent that Mr Rye's document retention practices within the six year period are less than perfect. Even comparatively recent documents can no longer be found.

> I turn now to the second part of Mr Oppenheim's argument on prejudice, namely, that the passage of time will make it more difficult for his client to give reliable evidence in relation to the first half of the 1980s. Whenever there is delay, the party being sued can claim that the passage of time will make it more difficult for him to present evidence in support of his case. Mr Rye is particularly anxious that he will find it impossible to recall the minutiae of what expenses, including many very small ones, were incurred on what date and for what purpose. The court should bear in mind that a party may be inclined to understate his powers of recall when it is in his interests to do so. Nevertheless, I am satisfied that Mr Rye's fears are justified. We are not here considering major events in Mr Rye's life but the comparative trivia of the day to day movement of funds in a small business. During the existence of his managerial relationship with Mr Nelson, Mr Rye had every reason to believe that Mr Nelson was not in the slightest bit interested in raking through the minutiae of what expenses were paid on his behalf. Indeed, I accept Mr Rye's evidence that Mr Nelson made it clear to him that his primary duty was to pass money to Mr Nelson and, that if that involved deferring or declining payment to others, so be it.
>
> I have considered all of the above matters. In my view Mr Rye will suffer substantial prejudice for both of the reasons advanced by Mr Oppenheim and this is a case where it would be unreasonable and unjust to allow Mr Nelson to assert his right to an account against Mr Rye in the period prior to 24 December 1985. The defence of laches or acquiescence is made out.

Proprietary remedies (tracing or the claims *in rem*)

The plaintiff beneficiary who suffers a loss as a result of a breach of trust is entitled to claim restitution of the trust estate in an action for an account against the wrongdoers, trustees. Such an action is a claim against the trustees and is referred to as a claim *in personam*, that is, the claim is against the trustees personally who are required to satisfy the claim from their personal assets. Provided that the trustees are solvent and have sufficient assets to satisfy the claim of the innocent beneficiary the plaintiff will not be out of pocket. But if the trustees are insolvent the plaintiff's claim will rank with the claims of the trustees' other unsecured creditors. This may result in the order of the court remaining unsatisfied. An alternative remedy available to the beneficiary is to 'trace' the trust assets in the hands of the trustees or third parties, not being *bona fide* transferees of the legal estate for value without notice, and recover such property or obtain a charging order in priority over the trustees' creditors. This is known as a proprietary remedy or a claim *in rem* or a tracing order.

A 'tracing order' is a remedy whereby the claimant establishes and protects his title to assets in the hands of another. The remedy is 'proprietary' in the sense that the order is attached to specific property under the control of another or may take the form of a charging order thereby treating the claimant as a secured creditor. The remedies at common law and equity are mainly 'personal' in the sense that they are remedies which force the defendant to do or refrain from doing something in order to compensate the plaintiff for the wrong suffered. But the proprietary remedy exists as a right to proceed against a particular asset in the hands of the defendant.

In *Boscawen v Bajwa* [1996] 1 WLR 328, Millett LJ commented on the process of tracing as follows:

> Equity lawyers habitually use the expressions 'the tracing claim' and 'the tracing remedy' to describe the proprietary claim and the proprietary remedy which equity makes available to the beneficial owner who seeks to recover his property *in specie* from those into whose hands it has come. Tracing properly so called, however, is neither a claim nor a remedy but a process. Moreover, it is not confined to the case where the plaintiff seeks a proprietary remedy; it is equally necessary where he seeks a personal remedy against the knowing recipient or knowing assistant. It is the process by which the plaintiff traces what has happened to his property, identifies the persons who have handled or received it, and justifies his claim that the money which they handled or received (and, if necessary, which they still retain) can properly be regarded as representing his property. He needs to do this because his claim is based on the retention by him of a beneficial interest in the property which the defendant handled or received. Unless he can prove this he cannot (in the traditional language of equity) raise an equity against the defendant or (in the modern language of restitution) show that the defendant's unjust enrichment was at his expense.
>
> In such a case, the defendant will either challenge the plaintiff's claim that the property in question represents his property (that is, he will challenge the validity of the tracing exercise) or he will raise a priority dispute (for example, by claiming to be a *bona fide* purchaser without notice). If all else fails, he will raise the defence of innocent change of position. This was not a defence which was recognised in England before 1991 but it was widely accepted throughout the common law world. In *Lipkin Gorman v Karpnale Ltd* [1991] 2 AC 548, the House of Lords acknowledged it to be part of English law also. The introduction of this defence not only provides the court with a means of doing justice in future, but allows a re-examination of many decisions of the past in which the absence of the defence may have led judges to distort basic principles in order to avoid injustice to the defendant.
>
> If the plaintiff succeeds in tracing his property, whether in its original or in some changed form, into the hands of the defendant, and overcomes any defences which are put forward on the defendant's behalf, he is entitled to a remedy. The remedy will be fashioned to the circumstances. The plaintiff will generally be entitled to a personal remedy; if he seeks a proprietary remedy he must usually prove that the property to which he lays claim is still in the ownership of the defendant. If he succeeds in doing this the court will treat the defendant as holding the property on a constructive trust for the plaintiff and will order the defendant to transfer it *in specie*, to the plaintiff. But this is only one of the proprietary remedies which are available to a court of equity. If the plaintiff's money has been applied by the defendant, for example, not in the

> acquisition of a landed property but in its improvement, then the court may treat the land as charged with the payment to the plaintiff of a sum representing the amount by which the value of the defendant's land has been enhanced by the use of the plaintiff's money. And if the plaintiff's money has been used to discharge a mortgage on the defendant's land, then the court may achieve a similar result by treating the land as subject to a charge by way of subrogation in favour of the plaintiff.

A personal claim for 'money had and received', on the other hand, is distinct from a proprietary claim. Such personal claim is based on the notion that the defendant, without authority, has received the plaintiff's money. It is immaterial whether or not the defendant has retained the plaintiff's money. The plaintiff's claim is complete when the defendant receives the money, subject to the defence of change of position. But this personal action will be of no benefit to the plaintiff if the defendant becomes bankrupt. The claim is essentially a quasi-contractual remedy based on the principle of reversing the unjust enrichment of the defendant at the expense of the plaintiff. With this rationale in mind, Nourse LJ, in *FC Jones v Jones* [1996] 3 WLR 703 (see below, p 905), decided that the plaintiff is entitled to recover any profit made by the defendant through the use of the funds.

Advantages of the proprietary remedy over personal remedies

The proprietary remedy has a number of advantages over the personal remedy, namely:

(a) the plaintiff's claim is not dependent on the solvency of the defendant. Indeed, the plaintiff's claim is based on an assertion of ownership of the asset in question;

(b) the plaintiff may be able to take advantage of increases in the value of the property in appropriate cases;

(c) on a proprietary claim, interest accrues from the date the property was acquired by the defendant, while claims *in personam* carry interest only from the date of the judgment.

Tracing at common law

To a limited extent, the right to trace exists at common law. The approach here is that provided the claimant's property is 'identifiable' the process of tracing may continue through any number of transformations. The form in which the property exists is irrelevant provided that the plaintiff shows a direct connection between his property in its original form and the property in its altered form in the hands of the defendant.

The main restriction in the common law right to trace is that the property ceased to be 'identifiable' when it became comprised in a mixed fund or when the asset ceases to be wholly owned by the claimant.

In *Taylor v Plumer*,[16] the defendant, Sir Thomas Plumer (later Master of the Rolls) had given money to Walsh, his stockbroker, in order to purchase Exchequer bills. Walsh without authority purchased American investments and bullion and attempted to abscond to America. There was a dramatic chase by the defendant's attorney and a police officer caught up with Walsh at Falmouth where he was waiting for a boat bound for Lisbon. Walsh handed the property over to the defendant's agents and was later adjudicated bankrupt. His assignee in bankruptcy claimed to recover the property from the defendant. The court held in favour of the defendant for the property had belonged to him.

> **Lord Ellenborough CJ:** It makes no difference in reason or in law into what other form, different from the original, the change may have been made ... for the product of or substitute for the original thing still follows the nature of the thing itself, as long as it can be ascertained to be such and the right only ceases when the means of ascertainment fail which is the case when the subject is turned into money and mixed and compounded in a general mass of the same description.

Lipkin Gorman (A Firm) v Karpnale Ltd [1991] 3 WLR 10, HL

> **Lord Goff:** It is well established that a legal owner is entitled to trace his property into its product, provided that the latter is indeed identifiable as the product of his property ... Of course, 'tracing' or 'following' property into its product involves a decision by the owner of the original property to assert his title to the product in place of his original property ... the bank was the debtor and the solicitors were its creditors. Such a debt constitutes a chose in action, which is a species of property; and since the debt was enforceable at common law, the chose in action was legal property belonging to the solicitors at common law. There is in my opinion no reason why the solicitors should not be able to trace their property at common law in that chose in action, or in any part of it, into its product, ie, cash drawn by loss from their client account at the bank. Such a claim is consistent with their assertion that the money so obtained by loss was their property at common law.

In this case, Mr Cass, a partner in the plaintiff's firm of solicitors, was a compulsive gambler, unbeknown to the other partners. He drew cheques on the firm's client account by making out cheques for cash and sending the firm's cashier to cash them. He withdrew a total of £323,222 from the account. From this amount, £100,313 was replaced, accounted for or recovered. The balance of £222,909 represented money which Cass stole from the firm and was irrecoverable from him. Cass used the relevant funds at the gaming tables

16 (1815) 3 M & S 562.

of the Playboy Club, owned by the defendant. It was conceded that the club was still in possession of £154,695 which was derived from the firm's account. On one occasion, Cass procured a banker's draft for £3,735 drawn in favour of the firm which was paid for by a cheque drawn on the firm's account. He endorsed the draft on behalf of the firm (without authority) and proferred it to the club for 'chips' which Cass used for gambling. Within the club, 'chips' were treated as the currency and Cass would redeem these for money whenever he chose to do so. The 'chips' were worthless outside the casino and at all times remained the property of the club. Cass was convicted of theft. The club at all times had acted in good faith and had no knowledge that Cass was using unauthorised funds.

The questions in issue were first, whether the plaintiff was entitled to maintain an action against the defendant in quasi-contract for money had and received and, secondly, whether the defendant was entitled to retain the proceeds of the draft of £3,735.

The House of Lords held as follows:

(i) the club, as the recipient in good faith of stolen money, was under an obligation to pay the equivalent to the plaintiff. The club had provided no valuable consideration to Cass and had been unjustly enriched at the expense of the plaintiff;

(ii) the 'purchase' and use of 'chips' were convenient mechanisms for facilitating gambling. Gamblers did not make separate contracts to 'purchase' or acquire 'chips'. The property in the 'chips' remained in the club. No valuable consideration was provided by the club in exchanging cash for 'chips' or vice versa;

(iii) each bet placed by a gambler and accepted by the club created a separate contract, which was void by virtue of s 18 of the Gaming Act 1845. The club was under no legal obligation to honour bets. If it paid out funds in respect of winning bets, these payments were construed as gifts. Equally, gamblers who lost bets were treated as making gifts of their stakes to the club. Accordingly, the club did not provide any valuable consideration, despite running the risk of voluntarily paying out sums in respect of winning bets;

(iv) the firm of solicitors was entitled to recover the amount as stated in the banker's draft (£3,735). The club did not become a holder in due course under s 29(1) of the Bills of Exchange Act 1882. The draft was made payable to the firm and the unauthorised indorsement by Cass, in favour of the club, was done on behalf of the firm of solicitors.

In *Lipkin Gorman*, although the plaintiff had not sought a tracing order (proprietary claim), Lord Goff of Chieveley considered that such a claim may have had a reasonable chance of success. The relationship of banker and customer (debtor and creditor) created a chose in action in favour of the plaintiff. The customer is entitled to trace his property (chose) in its unconverted form or in its substituted form, such as the cash drawn by Cass from the client's account. Since the club had conceded that it had retained some of the solicitor's cash, namely, £154,695, the firm would have been entitled at common law to trace this sum into the hands of the defendant (see *Taylor v Plumer*).

Had Cass mixed his money with the firm's property, the right to trace would have been governed by equitable rules. The plaintiff would be entitled to trace their property in the hands of Cass, who would be considered a constructive trustee. The firm would then have a first charge on the mixed fund in the hands of Cass. See *Re Hallett's Estate* (below, p 912). The onus would be on Cass to establish the amount of the mixed fund which belongs to him. See Ungoed-Thomas J in *Re Tilley*. The firm of solicitors would then be entitled to trace their property in the hands of the club, an innocent volunteer, and effect a charge ranking in *'pari passu'*. See *Sinclair v Brougham*.

The common law right to trace property belonging to the plaintiff extends to profits accruing to such property. The justification for allowing the plaintiff to claim the profits made by the defendant lies in restitution, to prevent the defendant being unjustly enriched at the expense of the plaintiff, see Millett LJ's judgment in *FC Jones v Jones* (below). However, Nourse LJ, in the same decision, extended the basis of the claim for money had and received to include the recovery of profits made by the defendant's use of the plaintiff's money. The justification here is based on the defendant's conscience.

***Trustee of the Property of FC Jones and Sons (A Firm) v Jones* [1996] 3 WLR 703, CA**

In 1984, the partners of FC Jones and Sons, potato growers, committed an act of bankruptcy and in due course were adjudicated bankrupt. Following the act of bankruptcy but, before the adjudication the defendant, the wife of one of the partners paid in £11,700 of partnership money to the account of commodity brokers. The defendant subsequently dealt in potato futures which proved to be a success. She received cheques totalling £50,760 from the brokers and paid these sums into an account she had opened with R Raphael and Sons plc. The Official Receiver informed Raphaels of his claim to the money, thereupon, the defendant demanded the release of it. On an interpleader summons, the sum was ordered to be paid into court. The defendant conceded to the trustee's claim to the original £11,700, but argued that their claim could not extend to the profits generated by the original sum. The trial judge held in favour of the plaintiff on the ground that the defendant had received the money in a fiduciary capacity and was a constructive trustee of the money, including the profit element. The defendant appealed to the Court of Appeal.

Held, by the Court of Appeal, dismissing the appeal, but deciding the case on different grounds. The defendant had clearly not received the money as a fiduciary and was not a constructive trustee. She had no title to the money at law or in equity but was merely in possession of it. This was due to the bankruptcy doctrine of relation back. The effect of this doctrine was to vest the legal title in the trustee in bankruptcy. The trustee's claim to trace the money was not made in equity. There was no mixture of the funds and, as such, the trustee was required to bring his claim at common law. He was entitled to trace his funds (including the profits) by applying common law principles because the money and profits belonged to him at law.

> **Millett LJ:** It is, however, in my view plain that the defendant did not receive the money in a fiduciary capacity and that she did not become a constructive trustee. The deputy judge's conclusion presupposes that A, who in this case is the bankrupt, had a legal title to transfer. In the present case, however, the bankrupt had been divested of all title by statute. Mr FWJ Jones had no title at all at law or in equity to the money in the joint account at Midland Bank, and could confer no title on the defendant. While, however, I accept the submissions of counsel for the defendant that she did not become a constructive trustee, I do not accept the proposition that the trustee in bankruptcy is unable to recover the profits which the defendant made by the use of his money unless she can be shown to have received it in one or other of the two capacities mentioned; nor do I consider it necessary for him to invoke the assistance of equity in order to maintain his claim. In short, I do not accept the main submission of counsel that the only action at law which was available to the trustee was an action against the defendant for money had and received.
>
> It is, in my view, unhelpful to categorise the payment of the £11,700 to the defendant as either 'void' or 'voidable.' Neither term is strictly accurate. In order to see why this is so it is necessary to consider the effect of the doctrine of relation back under the old bankruptcy law. I recently had occasion to examine this in detail in *In re Dennis (A Bankrupt)* [1996] Ch 80. I said, at p 104:
>
>> It is clear from the authorities that the relation back of the trustee's title did not merely make the title of the debtor himself, or any person claiming through the debtor, defeasible in the event of adjudication. If the debtor was adjudicated bankrupt, then, as from the date of the act of bankruptcy, neither the debtor nor any such person claiming under him who could not bring himself within the protective provisions of the Bankruptcy Acts, had any title at all; as from that date title was vested in the trustee. The position of the debtor and persons who claimed under him during the intermediate period was extremely curious. They did not possess a defeasible title, but either an indefeasible title if the act of bankruptcy was not followed by adjudication or no title at all if it was. Outside the law of bankruptcy no similar ambulatory title was known to the law.
>
> Accordingly, as from the date of the act of bankruptcy the money in the bankrupts' joint account at Midland Bank belonged to the trustee. The account holders had no title to it at law or in equity. The cheques which they drew in favour of the defendant were not 'void' or 'voidable' but, in the events which happened, they were incapable of passing any legal or equitable title. They were not, however, without legal effect, for the bank honoured them. The result was to affect the identity of the debtor but not the creditor and to put the

defendant in possession of funds to which she had no title. A debt formally owed by Midland Bank, apparently to Mr FWJ Jones and Mr AC Jones, but in reality, to their trustee, ultimately became a debt owed by Raphaels, apparently to the defendant, but in reality to the trustee.

What is the result? If the cheques had passed the legal title to the defendant but not the beneficial ownership, she would have received the money as constructive trustee and be liable to a proprietary restitutionary claim in equity (sometimes, though inaccurately, described as a tracing claim). The defendant would have been obliged, not merely to account for the £11,700 which she had received, but to hand over the £11,700 *in specie* to the trustee. Her position would have been no different from that of an express trustee who held the money in trust for the trustee; or from that of Mr Reid in *AG for Hong Kong v Reid* [1994] 1 AC 324, whose liability to account for the profits which he made from investing a bribe was based on his obligation to pay it over to his principal as soon as he received it. The existence of any such obligation has been disputed by commentators, but no one disputes that, if the obligation exists, it carries with it the duty to pay over or account for any profits made by the use of the money.

But the defendant was not a constructive trustee. She had no legal title to the money. She had no title to it at all. She was merely in possession; that is to say, in a position to deal with it even though it did not belong to her.

The defendant had no title at all, at law or in equity. If she became bankrupt, the money would not vest in her trustee. But this would not be because it was trust property; it would be because it was not her property at all. If she made a profit, how could she have any claim to the profit made by the use of someone else's money? In my judgment she could not. If she were to retain the profit made by the use of the trustee's money, then, in the language of the modern law of restitution, she would be unjustly enriched at the expense of the trustee. If she were a constructive trustee of the money, a court of equity, as a court of conscience, would say that it was unconscionable for her to lay claim to the profit made by the use of her beneficiary's money. It would, however, be a mistake to suppose that the common law courts disregarded considerations of conscience. Lord Mansfield CJ, who did much to develop the early law of restitution at common law, founded it firmly on the basis of good conscience and unjust enrichment. It would, in my judgment, be absurd if a person with no title at all were in a stronger position to resist a proprietary claim by the true owner than one with a bare legal title. In the present case equity has no role to play. The trustee must bring his claim at common law. It follows that, if he has to trace his money, he must rely on common law tracing rules, and that he has no proprietary remedy. But it does not follow that he has no proprietary claim. His claim is exclusively proprietary. He claims the money because it belongs to him at law or represents profits made by the use of money which belonged to him at law.

Counsel for the defendant acknowledges that the trustee can successfully trace his money into her account at Raphaels, for his concession in respect of the £11,700 acknowledges this. I do not understand how his concession that the trustee is entitled to £11,700 of the money in court is reconcilable with his submission that the only cause of action available to the trustee is an action for money had and received.

I say this for two reasons. In the first place, the trustee has never brought such an action, and any such action would now be long out of time. In the second place, in an action for money had and received, it would be irrelevant what the defendant had done with the money after she received it. Her liability would be based on her receipt of the money, and she would be personally liable to a money judgment for £11,700. But, while the trustee would be entitled to a money judgment for that sum, he would not be entitled to any particular sum of £11,700, such as the money in court *in specie*.

But in my judgment, the concession that the trustee can trace the money at common law is rightly made. There are no factual difficulties of the kind which proved fatal in this court to the common law claim in *Agip (Africa) Ltd v Jackson* [1991] Ch 547. It is not necessary to trace the passage of the money through the clearing system or the London potato futures market. The money which the defendant paid into her account with the commodity brokers represented the proceeds of cheques which she received from her husband. Those cheques represented money in the bankrupts' joint account at Midland Bank which belonged to the trustee.

In *Lipkin Gorman v Karpnale Ltd* [1991] 2 AC 548, p 573, Lord Goff of Chieveley held that the plaintiffs could trace or follow their 'property into its product' for this 'involves a decision by the owner of the original property to assert his title to the product in place of his original property'. In that case, the original property was the plaintiffs' chose in action, a debt owed by the bank to the plaintiffs. Lord Goff held, at p 574, that the plaintiffs could 'trace their property at common law in that chose in action, or in any part of it, into its product, ie, cash drawn by Cass from their client account at the bank'.

Accordingly, the trustee can follow the money in the joint account at Midland Bank, which had been vested by statute in him, into the proceeds of the three cheques which the defendant received from her husband. The trustee does not need to follow the money from one recipient to another, or follow it through the clearing system; he can follow the cheques as they pass from hand to hand. It is sufficient for him to be able to trace the money into the cheques and the cheques into their proceeds.

In *Agip (Africa) Ltd v Jackson* [1990] Ch 265, p 285, I said that the ability of the common law to trace an asset into a changed form in the same hands was established in *Taylor v Plumer* (1815) 3 M & S 562. Lord Ellenborough CJ in that case had said, at p 575:

> ... the product of or substitute for the original thing still follows the nature of the thing itself, as long as it can be ascertained to be such, and the right only ceases when the means of ascertainment fail, which is the case when the subject is turned into money, and mixed and confounded in a general mass of the same description.

In this it appears that I fell into a common error, for it has since been convincingly demonstrated that, although *Taylor v Plumer* was decided by a

> common law court, the court was in fact applying the rules of equity: see Lionel Smith, 'Tracing in *Taylor v Plumer*: equity in the court of King's Bench' [1995] LMCLQ 240.
>
> But this is no reason for concluding that the common law does not recognise claims to substitute assets or their products. Such claims were upheld by this court in *Banque Belge pour l'Etranger v Hambrouck* [1921] 1 KB 321 and by the House of Lords in *Lipkin Gorman v Karpnale Ltd* [1991] 2 AC 548.
>
> There is no merit in having distinct and differing tracing rules at law and in equity, given that tracing is neither a right nor a remedy, but merely the process by which the plaintiff establishes what has happened to his property, and makes good his claim that the assets which he claims can properly be regarded as representing his property. The fact that there are different tracing rules at law and in equity is unfortunate though probably inevitable, but unnecessary differences should not be created where they are not required by the different nature of legal and equitable doctrines and remedies. There is, in my view, even less merit in the present rule which precludes the invocation of the equitable tracing rules to support a common law claim; until that rule is swept away, unnecessary obstacles to the development of a rational and coherent law of restitution will remain.
>
> Given that the trustee can trace his money at Midland Bank into the money in the defendant's account with the commodity brokers, can he successfully assert a claim to that part of the money which represents the profit made by the use of his money? I have no doubt that, in the particular circumstances of this case, he can. There is no need to trace through the dealings on the London potato futures market.
>
> Given, then, that the trustee has established his legal claim to the £11,700 and the profits earned by the use of his money, and has located the money, first, in the defendant's account with the commodity brokers and, later, in the defendant's account at Raphaels, I am satisfied that the common law has adequate remedies to enable him to recover his property. He did not need to sue the defendant; and he did not do so. He was entitled to bring an action for debt against Raphaels and obtain an order for payment. When he threatened to do so, Raphaels interpleaded, and the issue between the trustee and the defendant was which of them could give a good receipt to Raphaels. That depended upon which of them had the legal title to the chose in action. The money now being in court, the court can grant an appropriate declaration and make an order for payment.
>
> In my judgment the trustee was entitled at law to the money in the joint account of the bankrupts at Midland Bank, which had vested in him by statute. He was, similarly, entitled to the balance of the money in the defendant's account with the commodity brokers, and the fact that it included profits made by the use of that money is immaterial. He was similarly entitled to the money in the defendant's account at Raphaels and able to give them a good receipt for the money. The defendant never had any interest, legal or equitable, in any of those moneys.

Beldam LJ 's judgment was similar to Millett LJ's.

Nourse LJ: I also agree that the appeal must be dismissed. I recognise that our decision goes further than that of the House of Lords in *Lipkin Gorman v Karpnale Ltd* [1991] 2 AC 548, in that it holds that the action for money had and received entitles the legal owner to trace his property into its product, not only in the sense of property for which it is exchanged, but also in the sense of property representing the original and the profit made by the defendant's use of it.

Millett LJ has explained how that extension is justified on the particular facts of this case. But there is, I think, a broader justification to be found in the seminal judgment of Lord Mansfield CJ in *Clarke v Shee and Johnson* (1774) 1 Cowp 197, pp 199–200, where he said of the action for money had and received:

> This is a liberal action in the nature of a bill in equity; and if, under the circumstances of the case, it appears that the defendant cannot in conscience retain what is the subject matter of it, the plaintiff may well support this action.

In my view the defendant cannot in conscience retain the profit any more than the original £11,700. She had no title to the original. She could not have made the profit without her use of it. She cannot, by making a profit through the use of money to which she had no title, acquire some better title to the profit.

Chu, W and Todd, P, in 'Profits recoverable in common law tracing claim: *FC Jones v Jones*' [1996] 5 Web JCLI, after examining Millett and Nourse LJJ's views, conclude:

At first Millett LJ's view is limited to the unusual situation where the money is not mixed with any of the recipient's own, but closer examination shows that he is merely removing an anomaly. Had the money become mixed, legal title would have passed to Mrs Jones, and she would have been liable as a constructive trustee. Clearly, there is no reason why she should be better off merely because the money never became mixed. It is, however, more difficult to justify the result where the recipient's conscience is unaffected, since, in that event, the outcome will depend on whether or not the money is mixed.

Nourse LJ's view is far more radical than that of Millett LJ, but seems to confuse personal and proprietary claims. It is also unclear when the broad brush principles derived from Lord Mansfield CJ's judgment will apply. It is therefore to be hoped that the views of Millett LJ, rather than those of Nourse LJ, will be developed in future cases.

Box v Barclays Bank plc [1998] 1 All ER 108, HC

In *Box v Barclays Bank plc* (see above, p 328), Ferris J reviewed the principles laid down in the *Lipkin Gorman* case and said:

Ferris J: A number of points arise from this decision [*Lipkin Gorman*'s case]. First, a claim made on the basis upheld in that case is exclusively a common law claim. It is essential, therefore, that the plaintiff shall be able to show that the property which has come into the hands of the defendant is, or represents, by the application of common law rules of tracing, property to which the plaintiff had a legal title. It will not suffice for the plaintiff to claim that he had an equitable title to the property, or that he can trace his property into that

> which has come into the hands of the defendant by the application of equitable rules of tracing. Secondly, although the right to recover depends upon the plaintiff showing the requisite proprietary interest at the outset of the transaction, that right will not be defeated by showing that the defendant no longer has the plaintiff's property (unless he has parted with it in circumstances enabling him to take advantage of the defence of change of position) or that he has mixed it with other property in such a way that it can no longer be identified. Thirdly, the defendant must have received the plaintiff's property for its own benefit. Fourthly, it will be a defence if the defendant can show that it was a *bona fide* purchaser for value.
>
> Where the plaintiffs' claim [in *Box v Barclays Bank plc*] based on a common law right to recover money had and received breaks down, is, in my judgment, that the plaintiffs cannot show that what came in to Sylcon's No 1 account was their money at the time when it reached that account. This can be illustrated by reference to the first deposit made by Mrs Jacobs. This was the cash sum of £10,000 which Mrs Jacobs withdrew from her building society account. There is no doubt that Mrs Jacobs had a legal title to this cash. But she then paid it over to Mr Reuben who received it on behalf of Sylcon on the terms of what I have held to be a contractual deposit. The cash then became Sylcon's property. Mrs Jacobs obtained in return for it contractual rights against Sylcon. No doubt these rights constituted a legal, not an equitable, chose in action vested in the Mrs Jacobs, but it was not this item of property which reached the hands of the bank. What the bank received was the cash. But when the bank received it the cash was Sylcon's property, not Mrs Jacobs'. The facts of her case are thus distinguishable in a vital respect from those of *Lipkin Gorman*, where, on the facts, the House of Lords accepted that the solicitors had a legal right to the cash which Cass paid to the gambling club at the time when it was paid over.

Tracing in equity

Equity had developed a more realistic approach to tracing as opposed to the common law. Equity had conceived the notion that once property was identifiable, recognition of the claimant's right could be given by attaching the order:

(i) to specific property; or

(ii) by charging the asset for the amount of the claim.

Unmixed fund

Equity followed the common law and declared that where the trust property has been transformed into property of a different form by the trustees and has been kept separate and distinct from the trustees' resources, the beneficiary may take the proceeds. If the proceeds of sale have been used to acquire further property, the beneficiary may elect:

(i) to take the property which has been acquired wholly with the trust property; or

(ii) to charge the property for the amount belonging to the trust.

Re Hallett's Estate (1880) 13 Ch D 696, CA

Sir George Jessel MR: The modern doctrine of equity as regards property disposed of by persons in a fiduciary position is a very clear and well established doctrine. There is no distinction between a rightful or wrongful disposition of the property so far as the right of the beneficial owner to follow the 'proceeds'. You can take the proceeds of sale if you can identify them. But it very often happens that you cannot identify the proceeds. The proceeds may have been invested together with money belonging to the person standing in a fiduciary position, in a purchase. He may have bought land with it. In that case, according to the now well established doctrine of equity, the beneficial owner has a right to elect either to take the property purchased, or to hold it as security for the amount of the purchase money, or, as we generally express it, he is entitled at his election either to take the property or to have a charge on the property for the amount of the trust money ...

See, also, *Banque Belge pour l'Etranger v Hambrouck.*[17]

Banque Belge pour l'Etranger v Hambrouck [1921] 1 KB 321, CA

Hambrouck was an accounts clerk at the Pelabon works. By fraud, he procured more than £6,000 by drawing cheques on his employer's bank account at Banque Belge. Hambrouck paid the cheques into his own account at Farrow's bank. Hambrouck voluntarily paid various sums to his Belgian mistress, Mlle Spanoghe, and she in turn paid sums into the Twickenham branch of her bank, the London Joint City and Midland Bank. After Hambrouck was convicted and sentenced for fraud, Banquc Belge sought restitution of some £315 which remained in Mlle Spanoghe's account. The bank paid that sum into court. The judge awarded restitution and Mlle Spanoghe appealed.

Held, by the Court of Appeal, dismissing the appeal, the fund was traceable into the account.

Atkin LJ: If the question be the right of the plaintiffs in equity to follow their property, I apprehend that no difficulty arises. The case of *Re Hallett's Estate* makes it plain that the court will investigate a banking account into which another person's money has been wrongfully paid, and will impute all drawings out of the account in the first instance to the wrongdoer's own moneys, leaving the plaintiff's money intact so far as it remains in the account at all. There can be no difficulty in this case in following every change of form of the money in question, whether in the hands of Hambrouck or of the appellant, and it appears to me that the plaintiffs were entitled to a specific order for the return of the money in question.

17 [1921] 1 KB 321, CA.

> The question whether they are entitled to a common law judgment for money had and received may involve other considerations. If, following the principles laid down in *Re Hallett*, it can be ascertained either that the money in the bank, or the commodity which it has bought, is 'the product of, or substitute for, the original thing', then it still follows 'the nature of the thing itself'. On these principles, it would follow that, as the money paid into the bank can be identified as the product of the original money, the plaintiffs have the common law right to claim it, and can sue for money had and received. In the present case less difficulty than usual is experienced in tracing the descent of the money, for substantially no other money has ever been mixed with the proceeds of the fraud.

Mixed fund

Where the trustee or fiduciary has mixed his funds with that of the beneficiary or has purchased further property with the mixed fund, the beneficiary loses his right to elect to take the property acquired. The reason being that the property would not have been bought with the beneficiary's money pure and simple but with the mixed fund. However, in the exercise of the exclusive jurisdiction of equity, the beneficiary would be entitled to have the property charged for the amount of the trust money.

Re Hallett's Estate (1880) 13 Ch D 696, CA

> **Sir George Jessel MR:** But where the trustee has mixed the money with his own the beneficiary can no longer elect to take the property, because it is no longer bought with the trust money but with a mixed fund. He is, however, still entitled to a charge on the property purchased for the amount of the trust money laid out in the purchase ... That is the modern doctrine of equity ...

In this case, Mr Hallett was a solicitor and a trustee of his own marriage settlement in favour of his wife for life and subject thereto for himself for life with remainder to the issue of the marriage. He paid the trust monies into his bank account. As a solicitor he acted on behalf of Mrs Cotterill and paid a sum of money received on her behalf into his account. He made various payments into and out of the account. At the time of his death the account had sufficient funds to meet the claims of the trust and Mrs Cotterill but not, in addition, the claims of the general creditors.

The personal representatives of Hallett sued to ascertain whether or not the trustees and Mrs Cotterill (collectively) had priority in satisfaction of their claim over the general creditors.

The Court of Appeal held that the trustees and Mrs Cotterill had priority and were entitled to a charge on the bank account.

The personal representatives had argued that the amounts withdrawn from the account were primarily trust monies so that the balance remaining in the account belonged to the personal representatives. This argument was rejected by the Court of Appeal on the ground that an individual who controls funds belonging to an innocent person which have been mixed with his own and withdraws part of the fund which is dissipated, is assumed to have withdrawn his own funds before depleting the innocent person's balance in the account.

> **Sir George Jessel MR:** Where a man does an act which may be rightfully performed, he cannot say that that act was intentionally and in fact done wrongly. When we come to apply that principle to the case of a trustee who has blended trust monies with his own, it seems to me perfectly plain that he cannot be heard to say that he took away the trust money when he had a right to take away his own money. The simplest case put is the mingling of trust monies in a bag with money of the trustee's own. Suppose he had 100 sovereigns in a bag and he adds to them another 100 sovereigns of his own, so that they are co-mingled in such a way that they cannot be distinguished and the next day he draws out for his own purposes £100, is it tolerable for anybody to allege that what he drew out was the first £100 of trust monies and that he misappropriated it and left his own £100 in the bag? It is obvious he must have taken away that which he had a right to take away, his own £100.

Similarly, if the trustee uses trust money to improve the asset of someone else, such as an innocent third party, *prima facie*, the beneficiaries will be entitled to a charge over the asset in order to recover their funds. This is not a transaction that attracts the notion of a constructive trust, for the trustee has no beneficial interest in the asset. The application of this charge is subject to the limitation of not producing unfairness to the innocent third party: see Lord Greene MR in *Re Diplock* [1948] Ch 465 (see below, p 932). Thus, where a trustee misappropriated trust funds in order to continue to pay premiums on an insurance policy on his life but held for the benefit of innocent third parties, the trust beneficiaries did not become equitable part owners of the policy proceeds, but were entitled to recover the sums expended on the premiums plus interest.

Foskett v McKeown and Others [1997] 3 All ER 392, CA

Messrs Murphy and Deasy held sums totalling £2.7 m as trustees for various investors in an Algarve property development scheme. Although land in the Algarve was purchased the land was never developed. The funds of the investors, which existed in two accounts, were dissipated. In November 1986, which was prior to the Algarve land development scheme, Mr Murphy effected a whole life insurance policy in the sum of £1 m. A premium of £10,220 was payable annually throughout Mr Murphy's life. The first two annual premiums (November 1986 and 1987) were paid out of Mr Murphy's funds. The source of the third premium (November 1988) was unclear, but it was conceded that the fourth and fifth premiums (November 1989 and 1990) were paid out of the investors' funds. Mr Murphy committed suicide in March 1991. The insurance company duly paid the proceeds to the trustees of the policy. At the time the policy was issued, Mr Murphy's estate was not excluded from any beneficial interest under the policy, but after 16 March

1989, Mr Murphy's estate was excluded from all beneficial interest under the policy. Moreover, Mr Murphy was, from the inception of the policy until his death, a trustee of the policy. Mr Foskett, the plaintiff, sued as a representative of the investors. Mrs McKeown and another, the defendants, were the surviving trustees of the policy.

The plaintiffs claimed that a trust was created in their favour when Mr Murphy received their money in pursuance of the Algarve land development scheme. In fraudulent breach of trust, Mr Murphy used their money to pay the 1989 and 1990 (and in part the 1988) premiums. These payments gave them an equitable proprietary interest in the policy and its proceeds. Accordingly, they claimed a *pro rata* share of the proceeds of the policy. Alternatively, they contended that they were entitled to an equitable charge upon the policy and its proceeds to ensure the repayment of the premiums.

The defendants contended that although the investors' money could be traced into the premiums, it could not be traced into the policy proceeds. The policy conferred a contractual right to payment of £1 m on the death of Mr Murphy. This contractual right was acquired when the contract was made and the first premium was paid. Mr Murphy financed all the premiums from his own funds, save for the 1989 and 1990 premiums. Since the premiums paid after the inception of the policy had not contributed to the creation of the contractual right, those persons whose money was used to pay the premiums could not claim an interest in the proceeds.

Laddie J decided in favour of the plaintiffs on the basis that the investors were entitled to a *pro rata* share of the proceeds of the policy. He treated the policy and its proceeds as if they had been assets standing in the name of Mr Murphy beneficially. On this basis, the judge decided that the plaintiffs were entitled to 53.46% share of the proceeds. He arrived at this percentage by calculating the contribution which the payments out of the plaintiffs' trust funds had made to the investment value of the policy at the date of the death of Mr Murphy. The defendants appealed to the Court of Appeal.

Held, allowing the appeal by a majority: that the plaintiffs were entitled to a charge over the proceeds of the policy in order to recover such of their money as could be traced into the premiums, together with interest thereon. They were not entitled to a *pro rata* share in the proceeds, since the beneficiaries under the policy were innocent of any part in the breach of trust, and the benefit which accrued to them from the use of the investors' money consisted merely of the keeping on foot of the policy (*contra* the dissenting view of Morritt LJ). No question of resulting or constructive trust arose, for payment of the premiums did not make the investors part owners in equity of the policy.

> **Scott VC:** What was the benefit acquired by Mr Murphy out of his use of the purchasers' money to pay the 1988 premium that equity would regard as held upon trust for the purchasers? As I have already observed, equity will use the

> means of a constructive trust in order, *inter alia*, to hold a trustee accountable to his beneficiaries for a benefit that the trustee has obtained by a wrongful use of trust money. In a case, however, in which it is unclear that any benefit has been obtained, it is not easy to see why a constructive trust should be imposed. If a trustee used trust money to improve or maintain his house, the beneficiaries would, in my view, be entitled to a charge on the house to recover their money. But unless it appeared that the improvements had increased the value of the house there would be no basis for a claim to a pro rata share in the house and no reason for the imposition of a constructive trust. There would, in such a case, be no benefit acquired by the use of the trust money for which the trustee would be accountable. Similar reasoning applies, in my opinion, in the present case. If the purchasers' money was used to pay the 1988 premium, they became entitled to a charge over the policy to recover their money.
>
> I am satisfied that on the facts of this case that ... the purchasers are entitled to the restitutionary remedy of a charge over the proceeds of the policy in order to recover such of their money as can be traced into the premiums, with interest thereon.
>
> **Hobhouse LJ:** In the present case, the policy already existed and was on foot. The doctrine of tracing does not extend to following value into a previously acquired asset (see *Bishopsgate Investment Management Ltd v Homan* [1995] 1 All ER 347.
>
> The equitable rights of the plaintiffs are as equitable chargees for the purposes of securing their right to the reimbursement of their money and the reinstatement of their trust funds. Their money was used: in equity they are entitled to have it back with interest. Their trust funds were misapplied: they are entitled to have the trust funds reinstated with interest. This is the nature of their right against an innocent third party and it does not extend any further.

The rule in *Re Hallett's Estate* seems to be that, if a trustee or fiduciary mixes trust monies with his own:

(a) the beneficiary is entitled, in the first place, to a charge on the amalgam of the fund in order to satisfy his claim;

(b) if the trustee or fiduciary withdraws monies for his own purposes, he is deemed to draw out his own monies, so that the beneficiary may claim the balance of the fund as against the trustee's general creditors.

Assets purchased

Since the beneficiaries are entitled to trace their property (including a charge) into a mixed fund, it follows that that right (to trace) may extend to property (assets) acquired with the mixed fund. Accordingly, if a part of the fund is used to purchase an asset which is identifiable and the remainder of the fund has been exhausted (the right to trace against the fund becoming otiose), the beneficiary may claim to trace against the asset acquired by the trustees.

In short, from the point of view of the beneficiary, the trustee and his successors in title are prevented from denying the interest deemed to be acquired with the mixed fund.

Re Oatway [1903] 2 Ch 356, HC

In this case, O, a trustee paid trust monies of £3,000 into his private bank account containing his own monies. He later purchased shares in Oceana Ltd for £2,137. After this drawing out, there was still more in the account than the amount of trust monies paid in. O paid further sums into the account but his subsequent drawings for his own purposes exhausted the entire amount standing to his credit. The shares were later sold for £2,474. O died insolvent. The beneficiaries claimed that the proceeds of sale of the shares represented their monies. The personal representatives claimed that, as O had sufficient monies in his account to satisfy the claim of the beneficiaries at the time of the purchase of the shares, that purchase was met by the trustee's own funds.

The court held in favour of the beneficiaries.

> **Joyce J:** It is clear that when any of the money drawn out has been invested and the investment remains in the name or under the control of the trustee, the balance having been dissipated by him, he cannot maintain that the investment which remains represents his own money and that what was spent and can no longer be recovered was the money belonging to the trust. In other words, when private money of the trustee and that which he held in a fiduciary capacity have been mixed in the same banking account from which various payments have been made, then, in order to determine to whom any remaining balance or any investment paid for out of the account ought to be deemed to belong, the trustee must be debited with all the sums that have been withdrawn and applied to his own use so as to be no longer recoverable, and the trust money in like manner debited with any sums taken out and duly invested in the names of the proper trustees. The personal representatives have contended that the trustees were entitled to withdraw from the account and rightly applied the fund for his own purposes; and accordingly the shares belong to his estate. To this I answer that he never was entitled to withdraw the £2,137 from the account or, at all events, that he could not be entitled to take that sum from the account and hold it or the investments made therewith, freed from the charge in favour of the trust, unless and until the trust money paid into the account had been first restored and the trust fund reinstated by due investment of the money in the joint names of the proper trustees, which was never done.

Scope of the charge

After some hesitation, it appears that a beneficiary who has a right to trace into an asset bought by the trustees, would be permitted to claim any increase in the asset purchased. It makes no difference whether the asset was bought with an unmixed or a mixed fund. No difficulty arises if the asset was bought with an unmixed fund for the claimant is the sole owner of such asset. But, the difficulty surrounds the claim to any increase in the value of the asset bought with a mixed fund. One argument which has been put forward is that the charge on the asset ought to be limited to the amount of the trust monies and no more, for the claimant is only seeking to recover his money and not claiming the asset bought with his funds. Supporters of this view refer to Jessel MR's judgment in *Re Hallett's Estate* as advancing this argument. However, Ungoed-Thomas J in *Re Tilley's Will Trust*,[18] distinguished the statement by Jessel MR in *Re Hallett* on the ground that the judge was not considering the question of the 'proportion' of the property that would have been subject to the charge, but was only considering whether the charge existed or not. Furthermore, Ungoed-Thomas J declared *obiter* that the beneficiary's charge on the asset would be in respect of a proportionate part of the increase in value, for otherwise, the trustee (and his successors in title who ought to be in no better position) may profit from the breach of trust.

Re Tilley's Will Trust [1967] Ch 1179, HC

In this case, a testator who died in 1932 left property to his widow, as sole trustee, on trust to her for life, remainder to Charles and Mabel (his children by a former marriage) in equal shares. The trust properties were realised between 1933 and 1952 for a total of £2,237 (trust moneys). This amount was paid into the widow's bank account and was blended with her own moneys. Until 1951, the widow's bank account was at various times substantially overdrawn (in 1945, she had an overdraft of £23,536). Investments were purchased by the widow financed by overdraft facilities at the bank. From 1951, her account was sufficiently in credit from her own personal contributions, that is, without regard to any trust monies. In 1959, the widow died with an estate valued at £94,000. Mabel had predeceased the widow and her administrators sued the widow's personal representatives claiming that Mabel's estate was entitled to one half of the proportion of the profits made by the widow, that is, on the assumption that the widow's personal representative failed to show that Mrs Tilley's investments were made out of her personal monies the claimant was entitled to a *pro rata* amount of the profits from the investments. The court held that the trust monies were not used to purchase the investments made by Mrs Tilley (the trustee) but were used only to reduce her overdraft which was the source of the purchase monies. In short, there was a *causa sine qua non* between the trust monies and the investments, but the trust monies were not the *causa causans* of the profit.

> **Ungoed-Thomas J:** ... it seems to me, on a proper appraisal of all the facts of this case, that Mrs Tilley's breach halted at the mixing of the funds in her bank account. Although properties bought out of those funds would, like the bank

18 [1967] Ch 1179.

account itself (at any rate if the monies in the bank account were inadequate) be charged with repayment of the trust monies which then would stand in the same position as the bank account, yet the trust monies were not invested in properties at all but merely went in reduction of Mrs Tilley's overdraft which was in reality the source of the purchase monies. The plaintiff's claim therefore failed and he was entitled to no more than repayment of half of £2,237 ...

[However, Ungoed-Thomas J considered *obiter* the scope of the charge on the assets bought, had the claimant been entitled to trace into the investments and reasoned thus:]

In *Re Hallett* the claim was against a bank balance of mixed fiduciary and personal funds, and it is in the context of such a claim that it was held that the person in a fiduciary character drawing out money from the bank account must be taken to have drawn out his own money in preference to the trust money, so that the claim of the beneficiaries prevailed against the balance of the account.

Re Oatway was the converse of the decision in *Re Hallett*. In that case the claim was not against the balance left in the bank of such mixed monies, but against the proceeds of sale of shares which the trustee had purchased with monies which, as in *Re Hallett*, he had drawn from the bank account. But unlike the situation in *Re Hallett*, his later drawings had exhausted the account so that it was useless to proceed against the account. It was held that the beneficiary was entitled to the proceeds of sale of the shares which were more than their purchase price but less than the trust monies paid into the account. Further, *Re Oatway* did not raise the question whether the beneficiary is entitled to any profit made out of the purchase of property by the trustee out of a fund consisting of his personal monies which he mixed with the trust monies and so the judgment was not directed to, and did not deal with that question ... Lord Parker in *Sinclair v Brougham* had considered *Re Hallett* but he did not address his mind to the question of whether the beneficiary could claim a proportion of the property corresponding to his own contribution to the purchase. In *Snell's Principles of Equity*, the law is thus stated:

> Where the trustee purchases shares with part of a mixed fund and then dissipates the balance, the beneficiary's charge binds the shares; for although the trustee is presumed to have bought the shares out of his own money, the charge attaches to the entire fund and could be discharged only be restoring the trust monies. Where the property purchased has increased in value, the charge will not be merely for the amount of the trust monies but for a proportionate part of increased value.

Lowest intermediate balance

The rule in *Re Hallett's Estate* (vis à vis the 'balance' in a blended bank account) is to the effect that withdrawals from a mixed fund are deemed to take the order of the trustee's monies before the beneficiary's funds. Accordingly, if the funds in the account fall below the amount of the trust funds originally paid in, that part of the trust fund (the depreciation) is presumed to have been spent. The right to trace into the balance held in the bank account will be depreciated to the extent of the lowest balance in the account. The lowest intermediate balance is presumed to be the trust property. Subsequent payments in are not *prima facie* treated as repayments to the trust fund in order to repair the breach unless the trustee earmarks such repayments as having that effect.

Roscoe v Winder [1915] 1 Ch 62, HC

In this case, in accordance with an agreement for the sale of the goodwill of a business, the purchaser, Wigham, had agreed to collect the debt and pay it over to the company. He collected the debt (£623, 8 s, 5 d) and paid £455, 18 s, 1 d into his personal bank account. The remainder of the debt was unaccounted for. He drew out funds which were dissipated until the credit balance in his account was only £25, 18 s. Later, he paid in more of his own monies and died leaving a balance in the account of £358, 5 s, 5 d.

The question in issue was the extent to which the plaintiff could claim a charge under the rule in *Re Hallett's Estate*. It was held that, although Wigham had held the money as trustee, the charge was limited to £25, 18 s – the lowest intermediate balance subsequent to the appropriation.

> **Sargant J:** It appears that after the payment in by the debtor of a portion of the book debts which he had received, the balance at the bank was reduced by his drawings to a sum of £25, 18 s. So that, although the ultimate balance at the debtor's death was about £358, there had been an intermediate balance of only £25, 18 s. The result of that seems to me to be that the trust monies cannot possibly be traced into this common fund which was standing to the debtor's credit at his death to an extent of more than £25, 18 s because although *prima facie* under the second rule in *Re Hallett* any drawings out by the debtor ought to be attributed to the private monies which he had at the bank and not to the trust monies, yet, when the drawings out had revealed such an amount that the whole of his private money part had been exhausted, it necessarily followed that the rest of the drawings must have been against trust monies. Counsel for the plaintiff contended that the account ought to be treated as a whole and the balance from time to time standing to the credit of that account was subject to one continual charge or trust ... you must for the purpose of tracing put your finger on some definite fund which either remains in its original state or can be found in another shape. That is tracing and tracing seems to be excluded except as to £25, 18 s.
>
> Certainly, after having heard *Re Hallett's Estate* stated over and over again, I should have thought that the general view of that decision was that it only applied to such an amount of the balance ultimately standing to the credit of the trustee as did not exceed the lowest balance of the account during the intervening period.

***Bishopsgate Investment Management Ltd v Homan* [1994] 3 WLR 1270, CA**

BIM Ltd was trustee of certain assets of pension schemes, held on trust for the benefit of employees and ex-employees of Maxwell Communication Corporation plc (MCC). MCC fraudulently paid these assets into its overdrawn account. The liquidator of BIM claimed to be entitled to an equitable charge in priority to all of the other unsecured creditors of MCC. The judge refused to make the order. The plaintiff appealed. The Court of Appeal dismissed the appeal on the ground that equitable tracing did not extend to tracing through an overdrawn account, whether overdrawn at the time the money was paid into the account or subsequently. The court applied the principle in *Roscoe v Winder* and distinguished the *Space Investments* case.

> **Dillon LJ:** [Counsel for BIM] claims (as it has been explained to us) to be entitled to an equitable charge as security for its claims against MCC: (i) over any moneys standing to the credit at the time of the appointment of the administrators of MCC of any banking account maintained by MCC into which any moneys of BIM or the proceeds of any assets of BIM misappropriated from it were paid; and (ii) over any assets acquired out of any such bank account, whether or not in credit as at the date such assets were acquired.
>
> So far as (i) is concerned, the point is that the National Westminster Bank account into which the misappropriated BIM trust moneys were paid, happened to be in credit when the administrators were appointed. BIM therefore claims a lien on that credit balance in the National Westminister Bank account for the amount of the misappropriated trust moneys. It is difficult to suppose, however, in the circumstances of Robert Maxwell's last days – and I know no evidence – that Robert Maxwell intended to make good the misappropriation of the BIM pension moneys by the cryptic expedient of arranging to put MCC's account with National Westminster Bank into credit – but without repaying the credit balance this created to BIM. But in the absence of clear evidence of intention to make good the depredations on BIM, it is not possible to assume that the credit balance has been clothed with a trust in favour of BIM and its beneficiaries: see *James Roscoe (Bolton) Ltd v Winder* [1915] 1 Ch 62. As to (ii), this seems to be going back to the original wide interpretation of what Lord Templeman said in the *Space Investments* case [1986] 1 WLR 1072 and applying it to an overdrawn account because the misappropriated moneys that went into the account were trust moneys and thus different from other moneys that may have gone into that account. But the moneys in the *Space Investments* case were also trust moneys, and so, if argument (ii) is valid in the present case, it would also have been valid, as a matter of law, in the *Space Investments* case. But that was rejected in *In re Goldcorp Exchange Ltd* [1994] 3 WLR 199, because equitable tracing, though devised for the protection of trust moneys misapplied, cannot be pursued through an overdrawn and therefore non-existent fund. Acceptance of argument (ii) would, in my judgment, require the rejection of *In re Diplock* [1948] Ch 465, which is binding on us, and of Lord Mustill's explanation of Lord Templeman's statement in the *Space Investments* case in *In re Goldcorp Exchange Ltd* [1994] 3 WLR 199, p 222.

> It is not open to us to say that because the moneys were trust moneys the fact that they were paid into an overdrawn account or have otherwise been dissipated presents no difficulty to raising an equitable charge on assets of MCC for their amount in favour of BIM. The difficulty Lord Mustill referred to is not displaced.

This decision was approved and applied by the Privy Council in *Re Goldcorp Exchange Ltd*.

Re Goldcorp Exchange Ltd [1994] 3 WLR 199, PC

Goldcorp Exchange Ltd (the company), a dealer in gold and other precious metals, was put into receivership by the Bank of New Zealand under the terms of a debenture issued by the company. The company in its promotional literature had made excessive claims and attracted a great deal of interest from members of the public. Amongst its assets was a stock of gold, platinum and silver bullion. This stock was insufficient to satisfy the claims of members of the public who had purchased precious metals for future delivery. The debts secured by the debentures and floating charges were in excess of the entire assets of the company, so that if the secured interest of the bank was satisfied in preference to the claims of the purchasers, the latter was entitled to nothing. The private investors asserted proprietary claims in respect of the bullion. They were classified into three categories. The first and largest category comprised those customers who were referred to as 'non-allocated claimants'. These were customers who had purchased bullion for future delivery. The second category of claimant was Mr Liggett who purchased specific gold coins from the company and agreed to buy a further 1,000 coins on a non-allocated basis and to store all the coins with the company. The company subsequently acquired a substantial quantity of gold coins, but not expressly for him. The third category of claimants consisted of those who had made contracts for the purchase of bullion from Walker & Hall Commodities Ltd (W Ltd) before the business of that company was acquired by Goldcorp Ltd. The receivers applied to the court for directions concerning the disposal. The High Court rejected the claims of the first two categories of claimants but allowed the claims of W Ltd's customers. The Court of Appeal of New Zealand allowed the appeals of the first and second categories of claimants, on the ground that these claimants had retained beneficial interests in the purchase moneys paid under the contracts of sale. Such interests entitled the claimants to trace into the general assets of the company in priority to the bank's charges. The Court of Appeal also declared that customers of W Ltd were in the same position. The receivers and bank appealed to the Privy Council.

Allowing the appeal, the Privy Council decided the following:

(a) the first and second category of claimants had contracted to purchase unascertained goods in which no property passed to them in law or in equity immediately on making the purchases;

(b) the collateral promises made in the company's brochures and its employees did not constitute declarations of trust by the company in favour of the customers;

(c) the company did not become a fiduciary towards its customers;

(d) the company did not become a trustee of the purchase monies for each customer and, as such, was entitled to spend such sums as it wished;

(e) the bullion belonging to W Ltd's claimants comprised the lowest balance thereof held by the company at any time.

> **Lord Mustill:** It followed that when the company absorbed the hitherto separated bullion into its own trading stock upon the acquisition of Walker & Hall's business, and thereafter drew upon the mixed stock, it wrongfully dealt with goods which were not its own.
>
> Thus far, the decision of Thorp J was favourable to the Walker & Hall claimants. There remained, however, the question of relief. Here, the judge applied conventional principles of tracing and concluded that the proprietary recoveries of the Walker & Hall claimants and those in a similar position could not exceed the lowest balance of metal held by the company between the accrual of their rights and the commencement of the receivership: see *James Roscoe (Bolton) Ltd v Winder* [1915] 1 Ch 62 and the passages from Ford and Lee's *Principles of the Law of Trusts*, 2nd edn, 1990, p 738–68, paras 1716–30, and Goff, R and Jones, G, *The Law of Restitution*, 3rd edn, 1986, p 74, cited by the judge.
>
> On the facts found by the judge, the company as bailee held bullion belonging to the individual Walker & Hall claimants, intermingled the bullion of all such claimants, mixed that bullion with bullion belonging to the company, withdrew bullion from the mixed fund and then purchased more bullion, which was added to the mixed fund, without the intention of replacing the bullion of the Walker & Hall claimants. In these circumstances, the bullion belonging to the Walker & Hall claimants which became held by the company's receivers consisted of bullion equal to the lowest balance of metal held by the company at any time: see *James Roscoe (Bolton) Ltd v Winder* ...
>
> The Walker & Hall claimants now seek to go further and ask the court to impose an equitable lien on all the property of the company at the date of the receivership to recover the value of their bullion unlawfully misappropriated by the company. Such a lien was considered by the Board in *Space Investments Ltd v Canadian Imperial Bank of Commerce Trust Co (Bahamas) Ltd* [1986] 1 WLR 1072. In that case the Board held that beneficiaries could not claim trust moneys lawfully deposited by a bank trustee with itself as banker in priority to other depositors and unsecured creditors. But Lord Templeman considered the position which would arise if a bank trustee unlawfully borrowed trust moneys. He said, at p 1074:
>
>> A bank in fact uses all deposit moneys for the general purposes of the bank. Whether a bank trustee lawfully receives deposits or wrongly treats trust money as on deposit from trusts, all the moneys are in fact dealt with and expended by the bank for the general purposes of the bank. In these circumstances, it is impossible for the beneficiaries interested in trust

> money misappropriated from their trust to trace their money to any particular asset belonging to the trustee bank. But equity allows the beneficiaries, or a new trustee appointed in place of an insolvent bank trustee, to protect the interests of the beneficiaries, to trace the trust money to all the assets of the bank and to recover the trust money by the exercise of an equitable charge over all the assets of the bank.

These observations were criticised by Professor Goode in his 'Mary Oliver Memorial Address' (1987) 103 LQR 433, pp 445–47, as being inconsistent with the observations of the Court of Appeal in *In re Diplock* [1948] Ch 465, p 521, where it was said:

> The equitable remedies presuppose the continued existence of the money either as a separate fund or as part of a mixed fund or as latent in property acquired by means of such a fund. If, on the facts of any individual case, such continued existence is not established, equity is as helpless as the common law itself. If the fund, mixed or unmixed, is spent upon a dinner, equity, which dealt only in specific relief and not in damages, could do nothing. If the case was one which at common law involved breach of contract the common law could, of course, award damages but specific relief would be out of the question. It is, therefore, a necessary matter for consideration in each case where it is sought to trace money in equity, whether it has such a continued existence, actual or notional, as will enable equity to grant specific relief.

In the case of a bank which employs all borrowed moneys as a mixed fund for the purpose of lending out money or making investments, any trust money unlawfully borrowed by a bank trustee may be said to be latent in the property acquired by the bank and the court may impose an equitable lien on that property for the recovery of the trust money.

The imposition of such an equitable lien for the purpose of recovering trust money was more favourably regarded by Professor Peter Birks in *An Introduction to the Law of Restitution*, 1989, pp 377 *et seq*, and by Goff and Jones, *The Law of Restitution*, 4th edn, 1993, especially at pp 73–75.

The law relating to the creation and tracing of equitable proprietary interests is still in a state of development. In *AG for Hong Kong v Reid* [1994] AC 324, the Board decided that money received by an agent as a bribe was held in trust for the principal who is entitled to trace and recover property representing the bribe. In *Lord Napier and Ettrick v Hunter* [1993] AC 713, pp 738–39, the House of Lords held that payment of damages in respect of an insured loss created an equitable charge in favour of the subrogated insurers so long only as the damages were traceable as an identifiable fund. When the scope and ambit of these decisions and the observations of the Board in the *Space Investments* case fall to be considered, it will be necessary for the history and foundations in principle of the creation and tracing of equitable proprietary interests to be the subject of close examination and full argument and for attention to be paid to the works of Paciocco (1989) 68 Can Bar Rev 315, Maddaugh and McCamus, *The Law of Restitution*, 1990, Sherwin, EL ... 'Constructive trusts in bankruptcy' (1989) Ill UL Rev 297, p 335, and other commentators dealing with equitable

> interests in tracing and referring to concepts such as the position of 'involuntary creditors' and tracing to 'swollen assets'.
>
> In the present case it is not necessary or appropriate to consider the scope and ambit of the observations in the *Space Investments* case [1986] 1 WLR 1072 or their application to trustees other than bank trustees, because all members of this Board are agreed that it would be inequitable to impose a lien in favour of the Walker & Hall claimants. Those claimants received the same certificates and trusted the company in a manner no different from other bullion customers. There is no evidence that the debenture holders and the unsecured creditors at the date of the receivership benefited directly or indirectly from the breaches of trust committed by the company or that Walker & Hall bullion continued to exist as a fund latent in property vested in the receivers.
>
> In these circumstances, the Walker & Hall claimants must be restored to the remedies granted to them by the trial judge.

The logical effect of this rule is that, *prima facie*, if the mixed account is left without funds after the appropriation by the trustee, the plaintiff will not be entitled to a charge under *Re Hallett*. This is the position whether subsequent funds are paid in or not.

Conversely, if the trustees, after the appropriation, deliberately earmark a repayment or purchase as belonging to the trust, the beneficiaries will be entitled to trace into that fund or asset. See *Robertson v Morrice*,[19] where, a trustee, who held stock subject to a trust and additionally similar stock of his own, mixed both sets of properties and treated them as one holding. He sold parts of the mixed stock from time to time so that shortly before his death the amount left was less than what he should have been holding on trust. On his deathbed, he instructed the clerk to buy more stock of a similar nature in order to replace that which he had misappropriated from the trust. This was done by the clerk. The beneficiaries claimed to be entitled to the stock as trust property.

It was held that the entire portfolio of stock was subject to the trust on the following grounds:

(i) the balance of the original mixed holding was subject to the charge that attached on the mixing;

(ii) the newly acquired holding was trust property owing to the declaration by the trustee that such purchase was designed to replace the trust property.

Rule in *Clayton's Case*

The rule in *Clayton's Case* is a rule of banking law and one of convenience which had been adopted in the early part of the nineteenth century to ascertain the respective interests in a bank account of two innocent parties

19 (1845) 4 LTOS 430.

inter se. Where a trustee mixes trust funds subsisting in an active current bank account belonging to two beneficiaries, the amount of the balance in the account is determined by attributing withdrawals in the order of sums paid in to the account. First in, first out (FIFO).

The rule is applied as between beneficiaries (or innocent parties) *inter se* in order to:

(a) ascertain ownership of the balance of the fund; and

(b) ascertain ownership of specific items bought from funds withdrawn from the account.

The basis of the rule lies in the fact that as between the beneficiaries (or innocent parties) the 'equities are equal', that is, there is no need to give one beneficiary any special treatment over the other. But it is worth noting that as between the trustee and beneficiary, the rule in *Re Hallett* and not *Clayton* applies. The wrongdoer may never take advantage of the FIFO rule.

Clayton's Case, Devaynes v Noble (1816) 1 Mer 529, CA

In this case, Mr Clayton, a customer at a bank, had a balance of £1,713 in his favour at the time of the death of Devaynes, a partner in a bank. Clayton drew out more than £1,713 (thus creating an overdraft) and then paid in further sums totalling more than the overdraft. Later, the firm of bankers went bankrupt. Clayton sought to recover from Devaynes' estate. It was held that the sums withdrawn by Clayton, after Devaynes died, must have been appropriated to the earlier debt of £1,713 so that Devaynes' estate was free from liability. The sums which Clayton subsequently paid in constituted a 'new debt' for which the surviving partners alone were liable.

> **Grant MR:** This is a case of a banking account, where all the sums paid in form one blended fund, the parts of which have no longer any distinct existence. Neither banker nor customer ever thinks of saying, this draft is to be placed to the account of the £500 paid in on Monday, and this other to the account of the £500 paid in on Tuesday. There is a fund of £1,000 to draw upon, and that is enough. In such a case, there is no room for any other appropriation than that which arises from the order in which the receipts and payments take place and are carried into the account. Presumably, it is the sum first paid in, that is first drawn out. It is the first item on the debit side of the account that is discharged, or reduced, by the first item on the credit side. The appropriation is made by the very act of setting the two items against each other. Upon that principle, all accounts current are settled, and particularly cash accounts.

The rule in *Clayton's Case*, as originally formulated, was a rule in banking law applicable in determining ownership of funds in an account. However, the rule has been extended to ascertain the interests of:

(a) beneficiaries *inter se* under two or more separate trusts; and

(b) competing claimants or beneficiaries under the same trust.

In *Re Stenning*,[20] the court considered the application of the rule in *Clayton's Case* in an *obiter* pronouncement. In this case, a solicitor paid monies belonging to a number of clients into his personal bank account. This money included £448, 18 s, 6 d due to Mrs Smith. There was often more than this amount in the account, but there was often less than the total of the clients' monies paid in. On a claim made by Mrs Smith alleging that she was a beneficiary under a trust, the court held that no trust had been created on the facts, but only a loan was made by agreement. But, if £448, 18 s, 6 d had been trust moneys, *Clayton's Case* would have applied as between Mrs Smith and the other clients.

One criticism that has been levelled against the rule in *Clayton's Case* is that it lacks justice as between claimants of equal standing. The rule exists as a rough and ready solution the outcome to which depends on a matter of chance, that is, the application of the rule depends on the precise time when money from two trusts (or monies from the same trust but belonging to two or more beneficiaries) was paid into a current account. A more equitable solution would have been to allow the two groups of beneficiaries to share the balance in the account, rateably, in proportion to the sums originally placed in the account from the two trusts, that is, the beneficiaries ought to be entitled to an order ranking in *pari passu*.

The House of Lords adopted this equitable solution in respect of the claims of two innocent parties *inter se* to a fund, not being a current account, which had been mixed by a fiduciary. See *Sinclair v Brougham*.

Sinclair v Brougham [1914] AC 398, HL

The litigation arose when the Birkbeck Building Society, having borrowing power, established and developed, in addition to the legitimate business of a building society, a banking business which was admittedly *ultra vires*. In connection with this banking business, customers deposited sums of money. In 1911, the society was wound up. The assets were claimed *inter alia* by the ordinary shareholders and the depositors. Each group claimed priority over the other. The House of Lords held that the two classes of claimants were entitled to the assets rateably following the rule in *Re Hallett*, that is, an order was made entitling both groups of claimants to a charge ranking in *pari passu* according to the proportion of their respective contribution.

> **Lord Sumner:** My Lords, I agree that the principle on which *Hallett's* case is founded justifies an order allowing the appellants to follow the assets, not merely to the verge of actual identification, but even somewhat further in a case like the present, where after a process of exclusion only two classes or groups of persons, having equal claims, are left in and all superior classes have been eliminated. Tracing in a sense it is not, for we know that the money

20 [1895] 2 Ch 433.

> coming from A went into one security and that coming from B into another and that the two securities did not probably depreciate exactly in the same percentage and we know further that no one will ever know anymore. Still I think this well within the 'tracing' equity, and that among persons making up these two groups the principle of rateable division of the assets is sound ...

Re Hallett extended in *Sinclair v Brougham*

The litigation in *Re Hallett* was between persons of unequal standing, namely, the innocent claimant and the wrongdoer (or successor). The wrongdoer is prevented from denying the interest acquired by the innocent claimant to the mixed fund.

Whereas, the litigation in *Sinclair v Brougham* was between two groups of innocent claimants (of equal standing) whose monies had been represented in assets available for distribution. Accordingly, the House of Lords extended the principle in *Re Hallett* in concluding that the claimants were entitled to the assets rateably.

Re Diplock [1948] Ch 465, CA

> **Lord Greene MR** (analysing the *Sinclair v Brougham* decision): Each of the two classes of contributors claimed priority over the other. Until the case reached the House of Lords, the possibility that they might rank *pari passu* does not appear to have been considered ... The House of Lords held that on the principle on which *Hallett's* case was founded, the two classes shared rateably. In one respect, no doubt, this application of the principle is an extension of it since, although the right of individuals to trace their own money (if they could) was preserved in the order of the House, the order provided for tracing the aggregate contributions of the two classes as classes ... the extension of the principle in *Sinclair v Brougham* was the obvious and, indeed on the facts, the only practical method of securing a first distribution of the assets ...

Similarly, in *Barlow Clowes v Vaughan*, the Court of Appeal favoured the *pari passu* charge where the claimants were investors in a common fund, as opposed to the 'rough and ready' solution in *Clayton's Case*.

Barlow Clowes International Ltd (In Liquidation) and Others v Vaughan and Others [1992] 4 All ER 22, CA

The companies promoted and managed certain investment plans in gilt-edged stock. Funds had been misapplied and the companies went into liquidation and receivers were appointed. At the time of the collapse the companies had a total liability of £115 m owed to around 11,000 investors. The amount available was far less than the amount of the investors' claims. The moneys and assets available for distribution to investors were contributed by three classes of claimants, namely:

(i) moneys paid by investors for investments in gilts which were acquired by the companies;

(ii) moneys in bank accounts awaiting investment in gilts at the time the receivers were appointed;

(iii) the net proceeds of sale of additional assets, including a yacht, *Boukephalos*.

The receivers brought proceedings for directions as to the basis on which the assets and moneys ought to be distributed. The judge (Peter Gibson J) decided that the distribution should be made in accordance with the rule in *Clayton's Case* ('first in, first out'). Thus, the investors were to be paid in the reverse order to that in which they had made deposits, so that later investors were more likely to be repaid. The second defendant appealed.

The Court of Appeal reversed the decision of the judge. Where the rule in *Clayton* is impractical, or may cause injustice, or is contrary to the intention of the investors, the court is entitled to refuse to apply it, provided that an alternative method of distribution is available. *Clayton*'s rule was considered to be time consuming and expensive. In addition, the rule would cause injustice, because a relatively small number of investors would become entitled to most of the fund and the rule was, in any event, not applicable to tracing claims. An alternative method, known as the 'rolling charge' was rejected by the court. This solution regards a mixture of funds from different sources as a 'blend or cocktail'. The effect is that a withdrawal is treated as a depletion of an interest in the account in the same proportion as the interest bears to each other immediately before the withdrawal is made. Thus, losses are borne proportionately, but later payments in the account are unaffected by earlier withdrawals. The court rejected this solution as complex, expensive and impractical. The moneys and assets were intended to form a common investment pool and the claimants ranked in *pari passu*. Thus, they were entitled to a charge on the common investment pool shared rateably, in proportion to their contributions, in accordance with the principle in *Sinclair v Brougham*.

> **Dillon LJ:** My conclusion is, however, that what was envisaged was some form of common fund in which all investors would in some way participate. I attach particular importance to the factor of the 'expected' as well as the 'guaranteed' rate of interest, and therefore differ, with all respect, on this point from the conclusion of Peter Gibson J.
>
> It follows, in my judgment, that the gilt-edged investments actually acquired by BCI, which are part of the additional assets, were lawful investments of investors' moneys as part of a common fund, and not allocated, under the arrangements, to individual investors. It would, consequently, be contrary to the intention of the original arrangements to trace through under *Clayton's Case* the moneys actually applied in the purchase of these gilts so as to allocate them to individual investors. The proceeds of sale of the gilts should be allocated pro rata to all investors, like the moneys to the credit of the bank accounts specified in schedule B to the order of Peter Gibson J.

The question is then, in relation to the balances in the bank accounts specified in schedule A to the judge's order: which were moneys contributed by investors for investment, which had not been invested by the time BCI went into liquidation and the receivers were appointed, whether these moneys became part of the common funds as soon as they were received into the bank accounts of BCI from the investors?

There are attractions in the view that if moneys are paid for investment in a common fund of gilt-edged investments they only become part of the common fund when invested in gilts, and are, in the meantime, held on resulting trust for the payers. On the other hand, the terms of application, in general, expressly authorise the placing of any uninvested funds with any bank, etc, on such terms as BCI thinks fit, whether bearing interest or not.

What troubles me at this stage, on the particular facts of the present case, is the contrast between the large amounts held in the accounts specified in schedule A to the judge's order and the much smaller amount of the gilts, abovementioned, which came into the control of the receivers. There is also the consideration of the very large amounts of investors' moneys which have been lost to the investors without ever having been invested as envisaged in the documents relating to the portfolios. In one sense, it is unreal to treat the moneys in the bank accounts in schedule A as the uninvested part of a common investment fund. But the question posed by Lord Halsbury LC in *Mecca* [1897] AC 286, p 290 ['... the circumstances of a case may afford ground for inferring that transactions of the parties were not so intended as to come under the rule in *Clayton*'], must, I apprehend, be answered by considering the nature of the transaction as the investors intended it to be at the outset, when they paid their moneys to BCI, not the very different circumstances of the actual outcome, of which, when they contributed, they knew nothing. Therefore, after considerable hesitation, I conclude that the moneys in the bank accounts in schedule A ought to be treated, for the purposes of distribution, as the uninvested part of the common investment fund.

As for the proceeds of sale of the yacht, *Boukephalos*, on the material before this court the yacht was never an authorised investment for funds paid to BCI for investment in gilt-edged securities, and its purchase was a misapplication of trust moneys. Nonetheless, the moneys applied in the purchase of the yacht were part of the the common investment fund – for the same reasons as the moneys in the accounts specified in schedule A to the judge's order. Accordingly, the proceeds of the yacht must also be treated as part of the common fund.

I would allow this appeal and set aside the order of the judge and I would declare that the rule in *Clayton's Case* is not to be applied on the distribution of the moneys in the bank accounts specified in schedules A and B to the judge's order or of the proceeds of sale of the additional assets. Instead, these were held on trust for all unpaid investors *pari passu* rateably, in proportion to the amounts due to them.

Woolf LJ: The approach, in summary, which I would adopt to resolving the issues raised by this appeal are as follows:

(i) While the rule in *Clayton's Case* is, *prima facie*, available to determine the interests of investors in a fund into which their investments have been paid, the use of the rule is a matter of convenience and if its application in particular circumstances would be impracticable or result in injustice between the investors it will not be applied if there is a preferable alternative.

(ii) Here, the rule will not be applied because this would be contrary to either the express or inferred or presumed intention of the investors. If the investments were required by the terms of the investment contract to be paid into a common pool, this indicates that the investors did not intend to apply the rule. If the investments were intended to be separately invested, as a result of the investments being collectively misapplied by BCI, a common pool of the investments was created. Because of their shared misfortune, the investors will be presumed to have intended the rule not to apply.

(iii) As the rule is inapplicable, the approach which should be adopted by the court depends on which of the possible alternative solutions is the most satisfactory in the circumstances. If the North American solution [rolling charge] is practical, this would probably have advantages over the *pari passu* solution. However, the complications of applying the North American solution in this case make the third solution the most satisfactory.

(iv) It must, however, be remembered that any solution depends on the ability to trace and if the fund had been exhausted (that is, the account became overdrawn) the investors whose moneys were in the fund prior to the fund being exhausted will not be able to claim against moneys which were subsequently paid into the fund.

Their claims will be limited to following, if this is possible, any of the moneys paid out of the fund into other assets before it was exhausted.

For these reasons I would allow the appeal and substitute the orders proposed by Dillon J.

Leggatt LJ: All the moneys which were provided by the investors were treated by BCI as a common pool to which they could have resort for their own purposes. Since all the investors have equitable charges, and their equities are equal, and they presumably intended their money to be dealt with collectively, they should share rateably what is left in the pool, as did the claimants in *Sinclair v Brougham.*

Innocent volunteers

In *Sinclair v Brougham*, the mixing of the funds of the two innocent claimants was effected by a fiduciary, namely, the directors of the building society. This was consistent with the *Hallett* principle.

But, a controversial issue was whether the tracing remedy would be available to a claimant when the mixing was effected by an innocent volunteer and not by the fiduciary. The Court of Appeal, in *Re Diplock*, enunciated (*obiter*) that the remedy would be available.

For example, trustees hold property on trust for A for life, remainder to B absolutely. The trustees, without authority, distribute £2,000 of the trust income to remainderman, B, who pays the same into a bank account containing £3,000 of his personal monies. The trust is later terminated (see *Saunders v Vautier* (above, p 837)) and B becomes bankrupt. A may be entitled to a charge on B's bank account ranking in *pari passu*.

Re Diplock [1948] Ch 465, CA

> **Greene MR:** Where an innocent volunteer (as distinct from a purchaser for value without notice) mixes 'money' of his own with 'money' which in equity belongs to another person, or is found in possession of such a mixture, although that other person cannot claim a charge on the mass superior to the claim of the volunteer ... it appears to us to be wrong to treat the principle which underlies *Hallett*'s case as coming into operation only where the person who does the mixing is not only in a fiduciary position but is also a party to the tracing action. If he is a party to the action he is, of course, precluded from setting up a case inconsistent with the obligations of his fiduciary position. But supposing he is not a party? The result cannot surely depend on what equity would or would not have allowed him to say if he had been a party.

In *Re Diplock*, Caleb Diplock, by his will, directed his executors to apply the residue of his estate 'for such charitable institutions or other charitable or benevolent objects in England as they may select in their absolute discretion'. The executors assumed that the will created a valid charitable trust and distributed £203,000 among 139 different charities before the validity of the distribution was challenged by the next of kin. In the earlier litigation in *Chichester Diocesan Fund v Simpson*[21] (above, p 236), the House of Lords decided that the clause in Caleb Diplock's will failed to create a charitable trust for uncertainty of charitable objects. The next of kin sued the executors and charities. The claim against the executors was eventually compromised. But, the claimants persisted in their action against the wrongly paid charities on two grounds, namely:

(i) claims *in personam* against the recipient institutions (see *Ministry of Health v Simpson*,[22] affirming the decision of the Court of Appeal); and

(ii) claims *in rem* against the assets held by the institutions.

It was held by the Court of Appeal that the action *in rem* would not succeed because the next of kin's moneys were no longer identifiable and, in any event, the charge ranking in *pari passu* would have inflicted an injustice on the institutions in causing the institutions to sell such assets.

21 [1944] AC 341.

22 [1951] AC 251.

Limitations

The Court of Appeal, in *Re Diplock*, enunciated the limits surrounding the right to trace:

(i) the equitable remedy does not affect rights obtained by a *bona fide* transferee of the legal estate for value without notice. All equitable claims are extinguished against such persons;

(ii) tracing will not be permitted if the result will produce inequity for, 'he who comes to equity must do equity'. Accordingly, if an innocent volunteer spends money improving his land, there can be no declaration of charge for the method of enforcing the charge would be by way of sale, thus forcing the volunteer to convert his property.

In English law, there is no general recognition of the defence of change of position in the context of restitutionary claims. The usual approach adopted by the courts is based on estoppel, which has limitations that makes it unsuitable to restituionary claims. The estoppel is based upon a representation by the plaintiff, whether express or implied, that the defendant is entitled to treat the money as his own. The mere payment of money under a mistake, cannot, by itself, constitute a representation which will estop the payer from asserting his right to receive his payment.

The defence of change of position has been recognised throughout the common law world. It has gained statutory recognition in the United States of America. Section 142 of the Restatement of the Law on Restitution states:

> (1) The right of a person to restitution from another, because of a benefit received, is terminated or diminished if, after the receipt of the benefit, circumstances have so changed that it would be inequitable to require the other to make full restitution.
>
> (2) Change of circumstances may be a defence or a partial defence if the conduct of the recipient was not tortious and he was no more at fault for his receipt, retention or dealing with the subject matter than was the claimant.
>
> (3) Change of circumstances is not a defence if:
>
> (a) the conduct of the recipient in obtaining, retaining or dealing with the subject matter was tortious; or
>
> (b) the change occurred after the recipient had knowledge of the facts entitling the other to restitution, and had an opportunity to make restitution.

In New Zealand, see s 94B of the Judicature Act 1908; in Western Australia, see s 24 of the Western Australia Law Reform (Property, Perpetuities and Succession) Act 1962 and s 65(B) of the Western Australia Trustee Act 1962. In addition, the defence has been judicially recognised by the Supreme Court of Canada. See *Rural Municipality of Storthooks v Mobil Oil of Canada Ltd* (1975) 55 DLR (3ed) 1.

In the *Lipkin Gorman* case, Lord Goff of Chieveley advocated that a general defence of change of position ought to be adopted in the UK. The defence ought to be developed on a case by case basis. It would be available to an innocent volunteer who, after receiving the claimant's money, has altered his position to such an extent that, having regard to all the circumstances, it would be inequitable to require him to make full restitution to the claimant. The defence ought not to be available to a defendant who has changed his position in bad faith, that is, a defendant who spends the plaintiff's money after knowledge of facts entitling the plaintiff to restitution. Similarly, the defence should not be available to a wrongdoer. In any event, the mere fact that the defendant has spent the money in whole or in part, in the ordinary course of things, does not, of itself, render it inequitable that he should be called upon to repay the claimant. But, if the defendant has spent the plaintiff's money on a venture which would not have been undertaken but for the gift, such conduct would be capable of being construed as a change of position. In the *Lipkin Gorman,* case the defence was not available to the club, for it did not provide consideration for the bets placed by Cass and had agreed that it had retained £154,695 of the plaintiff's money.

> **Lord Goff** (in *Lipkin Gorman (A Firm) v Karpnale*):[23] Whether change of position is, or should be, recognised as a defence to claims in restitution is a subject which has been much debated in the books. It is, however, a matter on which there is a remarkable unanimity of view, the consensus being to the effect that such a defence should be recognised in English law. I myself am under no doubt that this is right ... At present I do not wish to state the principle any less broadly than this: that the defence is available to a person whose position has so changed that it would be inequitable in all the circumstances to require him to make restitution or alternatively to make restitution in full.

(iii) The right to trace is extinguished if the claimant's property is no longer identifiable, for example, the trust moneys have been spent on a dinner or a cruise or in paying off a loan.

Re Diplock [1948] Ch 465, CA

> **Greene MR:** The equitable remedies presuppose the continued existence of the money either as a separate fund or as part of a mixed fund or as latent in property acquired by means of such a fund. If, on the facts of any individual case, such continued existence is not established, equity is as helpless as the common law itself ...

(iv) It is essential that the claimant proves that the property was held by another on his behalf in a fiduciary or quasi fiduciary capacity in order to attract the jurisdiction of equity. This fiduciary need not be the person who mixes the funds or the assets. The mixture may be effected by an innocent volunteer as in *Re Diplock.*

23 [1991] 3 WLR 10.

In *Agip (Africa) Ltd v Jackson and Others*,[24] the Court of Appeal decided that the plaintiff company was entitled to trace in equity a fraudulent payment of £518,822, which was received by the defendants.

> **Fox LJ:** ... in the present case, there is no difficulty about the mechanics of tracing in equity. The money can be traced through the various bank accounts to Baker Oil and onwards. It is, however, a prerequisite to the operation of the remedy in equity that there must be a fiduciary relationship which calls the equitable jurisdiction into being. There is no difficulty about that in the present case since Mr Zdiri must have been in a fiduciary relationship with Agip. He was the chief accountant of Agip and was entrusted with the signed drafts or orders ...

In *Chase Manhattan Bank v Israel-British Bank*,[25] the court decided that a payment of funds, by mistake, from the plaintiff bank to the defendant bank affected the conscience of the latter to such an extent that the defendant bank became subject to a fiduciary duty to repay the fund to the plaintiff.

In *Boscawen v Bajwa*, Millett LJ clarified the relationship between 'tracing' and 'subrogation'. The issue concerned the rights of a bank (Abbey National) to be subrogated to the rights of the mortgagee. The bank's fund intended for its customer for the purchase of property, through an error of judgment on the part of the purchaser's solicitor, was released, prematurely, to the vendor. This fund was then used to discharge the vendor's mortgage. The intended purchase by Abbey's customer fell through and the vendor became bankrupt.

Boscawen and Others v Bajwa and Others, Abbey National plc v Boscawen and Others [1995] All ER 769, CA

At all material times, the property was registered in the name of Mr Bajwa. In 1989, he charged the property to the Halifax Building Society and the charge was duly registered. In 1990, Mr Bajwa exchanged contracts for the sale of the property for £165,000. The balance of the purchase price payable on completion was £140,000. The intended purchasers had obtained a mortgage offer from Abbey National for £140,000, which was to be secured by a first legal charge on the property. On 9 August 1990, Abbey National sent £140,000 by telegraphic transfer to the purchaser's solicitors, Dave and Co, who were acting as solicitors for both the purchaser and Abbey National. Dave and Co received the sum from Abbey National on terms which obliged them to use the amount for completion of the purchase or return it if, for any reason, completion did not take place. On 16 August, following discussions between Hill Lawson (Mr Bajwa's solicitors) and Dave and Co, Dave and Co issued instructions to their bank for the transmission of £137,405 to Hill Lawson. Dave and Co sent a cheque to Hill Lawson for £2,595 in respect of the balance

24 [1991] Ch 547.

25 [1979] 3 All ER 1025.

of the purchase moneys. On 23 August 1990, Hill Lawson remitted £140,000 to the Halifax by telegraphic transfer. In October 1990, Dave and Co ceased to exist and Mr Dave, the sole equity partner, was made the subject of a bankruptcy order. The sale fell through and the purchasers never acquired the legal title to the property. The plaintiffs were judgment creditors of Mr Bajwa and had obtained a charging order on the property. They commenced proceedings against Mr Bajwa and Abbey National for enforcement of the charging order. An order for the sale of the property was made and the property was sold for £105,311. Abbey National counterclaimed, claiming an interest in the proceeds of sale.

The judge held that £137,405 of Abbey National's money could be traced into the payment to Halifax which was used to discharge Halifax's legal charge. Abbey National was entitled to a charge on the property by way of subrogation to the rights of the Halifax Building Society. The plaintiffs appealed on the grounds that Abbey National's tracing claim failed because its (Abbey National's) money was used to pay off a debt and no traceable assets were received in exchange for Abbey National's money. In addition, the judge erred by invoking the doctrine of subrogation, which had the effect of giving Abbey National an interest in priority over the plaintiff's charging order.

Held, dismissing the appeal on the following grounds:

(i) it was a prerequisite of the right to trace in equity that there was a fiduciary relationship which attracted the equitable jurisdiction, see *Agip (Africa) Ltd v Jackson* [1991] Ch 547. That requirement was satisfied in the present case by the fact that from the first moment of its receipt by Dave and Co, the £140,000 was money held in trust for Abbey National;

(ii) Abbey National had not intended to be an unsecured creditor of anyone. It had intended to retain the beneficial interest in its money, unless and until that interest was replaced by a first legal mortgage on the property. Abbey National's equitable right to subrogation arose from the conduct of the parties at the moment that the building society's charge was discharged in whole or in part with its (Abbey National's) money.

Millett LJ: Equity lawyers habitually use the expressions 'the tracing claim' and 'the tracing remedy' to describe the proprietary claim and the proprietary remedy which equity makes available to the beneficial owner who seeks to recover his property *in specie* from those into whose hands it has come. Tracing properly so called, however, is neither a claim nor a remedy but a process. Moreover, it is not confined to the case where the plaintiff seeks a proprietary remedy; it is equally necessary where he seeks a personal remedy against the knowing recipient or knowing assistant. It is the process by which the plaintiff traces what has happened to his property, identifies the persons who have handled or received it, and justifies his claim that the money which they handled or received (and, if necessary, which they still retain) can properly be regarded as representing his property. He needs to do this because his claim is based on the retention by him of a beneficial interest in the property which the defendant handled or received. Unless he can prove this he cannot (in the traditional language of equity) raise an equity against the defendant or (in the modern language of restitution) show that the defendant's unjust enrichment was at his expense.

If the plaintiff succeeds in tracing his property, whether in its original or in some changed form, into the hands of the defendant, and overcomes any defences which are put forward on the defendant's behalf, he is entitled to a remedy. The remedy will be fashioned to the circumstances. The plaintiff will generally be entitled to a personal remedy; if he seeks a proprietary remedy he must usually prove that the property to which he lays claim is still in the ownership of the defendant. If he succeeds in doing this, the court will treat the defendant as holding the property on a constructive trust for the plaintiff and will order the defendant to transfer it, *in specie*, to the plaintiff. But this is only one of the proprietary remedies which are available to a court of equity. If the plaintiff's money has been applied by the defendant, for example, not in the acquisition of a landed property, but in its improvement, then the court may treat the land as charged with the payment to the plaintiff of a sum representing the amount by which the value of the defendant's land has been enhanced by the use of the plaintiff's money. And if the plaintiff's money has been used to discharge a mortgage on the defendant's land, then the court may achieve a similar result by treating the land as subject to a charge by way of subrogation in favour of the plaintiff.

Subrogation, therefore, is a remedy, not a cause of action: see Goff and Jones, *Law of Restitution*, 4th edn, 1993, pp 589 *et seq*; *Orakpo v Manson Investments Ltd* [1978] AC 95, p 104, *per* Lord Diplock; and *In re TH Knitwear (Wholesale) Ltd* [1988] Ch 275, p 284. It is available in a wide variety of different factual situations in which it is required in order to reverse the defendant's unjust enrichment. Equity lawyers speak of a right of subrogation, or of an equity of subrogation, but this merely reflects the fact that it is not a remedy which the court has a general discretion to impose whenever it thinks it just to do so. The equity arises from the conduct of the parties on well settled principles and in defined circumstances, which make it unconscionable for the defendant to deny the proprietary interest claimed by the plaintiff. A constructive trust arises in the same way. Once the equity is established, the court satisfies it by declaring that the property in question is subject to a charge, by way of subrogation in the one case, or a constructive trust in the other.

It is still a prerequisite of the right to trace in equity that there must be a fiduciary relationship which calls the equitable jurisdiction into being: see *Agip (Africa) Ltd v Jackson* [1991] Ch 547, p 566, *per* Fox LJ. That requirement is satisfied in the present case by the fact that, from the first moment of its receipt by Dave and Co in their general client account, the £140,000 was trust money held in trust for the Abbey National.

> **Subrogation**
>
> In the present case, the payment was made by Hill Lawson, and it is their intention which matters. As fiduciaries, they could not be heard to say that they had paid out their principal's money otherwise than for the benefit of their principal. Accordingly, their intention must be taken to have been to keep the Halifax's charge alive for the benefit of the Abbey National pending completion. In my judgment, this is sufficient to bring the doctrine of subrogation into play.
>
> The application of the doctrine in the present case does not create the problem which confronted Oliver J in *Paul v Speirway Ltd* [1976] Ch 220. The Abbey National did not intend to be an unsecured creditor of anyone. It intended to retain the beneficial interest in its money unless and until that interest was replaced by a first legal mortgage on the property. The factual context in which the claim to subrogation arises is a novel one which does not appear to have arisen before, but the justice of its claim cannot be denied. The Abbey National's beneficial interest in the money can no longer be restored to it. If it is subrogated to the Halifax's charge its position will not be improved, nor will Mr Bajwa's position be adversely affected. Both parties will be restored as nearly as may be to the positions which they were respectively intended to occupy.

Subrogation is the process whereby the claimant (A) steps in the shoes of another (B) and thereby claims as against the defendant (C), the rights and remedies to which the other (B) is entitled. For example, if the A Co Ltd insures B's car under a comprehensive insurance policy and C, another motorist, negligently causes damage to B's car, the A Co may compensate B for the damage, but is entitled to bring proceedings against C (albeit in B's name). The underlying basis of subrogation is the reversal of unjust enrichment. The remedy is available in a wide variety of different circumstances. Some of these are contracts of guarantee, contracts of indemnity insurance and the trust relationship. In the *Banque Financière* case, the House of Lords decided that as a restitutionary remedy, subrogation is dependent on the following four principles:

(a) whether the defendant would be enriched; and

(b) whether the enrichment was at the expense of the claimant; and

(c) whether the enrichment would be unjust; and

(d) whether there are any policy reasons for denying the remedy.

Banque Financière de la Cite v Parc (Battersea) Ltd and Others [1998] 2 WLR 475, HL

Parc was a company registered in the UK, owning land for development in Battersea. Omnicorp Overseas Ltd (OOL) was registered in the British Virgin Islands. They belonged to the Omni Group, based in Switzerland, where the ultimate holding company, Omni Holding AG, was incorporated. The principal officers of Holding were its founder and principal shareholder, Mr Rey and its chief financial officer, Mr Herzig. Parc acquired the Battersea property in 1988 with the aid of a £30 m bridging loan from Royal Trust Bank (Switzerland) (RTB), secured by a first charge. Additional finance was obtained from OOL in return for a second charge. The RTB loan was partially repaid in 1989, but £20 m was extended until 28 September 1990. Parc was unable to refinance its borrowing on the London market and turned to Mr Herzig for help. He approached Banque Financière (BFC), which had previously lent to the Omni Group. On 14 September 1990, it agreed, in principle, to advance DM30 m for two months. A difficulty was that a further loan to a member of the Omni Group would have had to be reported to the Swiss banking authorities. To avoid this, BFC agreed to make the loan to Mr Herzig personally, on the basis that he would pass it on to Parc. In return Parc would issue him with a promissory note which he would assign to BFC as security. The principal security was to be the pledge of 35,000 bearer shares in Holding, which BFC valued at DM40 m and BFC required an undertaking from the Omni Group to postpone any claims by the group for repayment of loans until full repayment of the loan of DM30 m to Mr Herzig was made (a postponement letter). Completion took place on 28 September 1990, when Mr Herzig handed over the pledged shares and postponement letter and BFC paid DM30 m to RTB for the account of Parc. On 1 October 1990, Parc issued a promissory note for the relevant sum and Mr Herzig assigned the note to BFC.

Mr Herzig defaulted on repayment of the loan. In April 1991, the Omni Group collapsed. Parc was insolvent. BFC obtained a judgment order for £12 m against Parc, representing the sum due on the note with interest. BFC had realised some of the pledged shares before they became worthless. Parc still owned the Battersea land. BFC brought a claim against Parc and OOL contending that, by reason of the letter of postponement and its utilisation to obtain the refinancing package, the rights of BFC took priority over the rights of OOL (in short, BFC stepped into the shoes of RTB and was claiming a first charge on the assets of the defendants). Parc and OOL had been unaware of the letter of postponement, and contended that the debt owed to OOL took priority over the debt owed to BFC.

The House of Lords held in favour of the plaintiffs, BFC, on the following grounds:

(a) there was no difficulty in tracing the plaintiff's money into the discharge of the debt owed to RTB;

(b) there was no conceptual difficulty about the plaintiffs and RTB appearing to share the same security. The plaintiffs were not seeking to obtain priority over RTB's security, but relied on it only for the purpose of obtaining priority over OOL;

(c) RTB's security was 'kept alive' for the benefit of the plaintiffs, to prevent OOL from being unjustly enriched at the plaintiffs' expense. The plaintiffs' money was used to pay off RTB's charge, thus, the plaintiffs did not obtain rights for which they had not bargained;

(d) the plaintiffs were entitled to be treated, as against OOL, as if they had the benefit of RTB's charge.

Lord Hoffman: It is a mistake to regard the availability of subrogation as a remedy to prevent unjust enrichment as turning entirely upon the question of intention, whether common or unilateral. Such an analysis has inevitably to be propped up by presumptions which can verge upon fictions more appropriate to a less developed legal system than we now have. I would venture to suggest that the reason why intention has played so prominent a part in the earlier cases is because of the influence of cases on contractual subrogation. But I think it should be recognised that one is here concerned with a restitutionary remedy.

In this case, I think that, in the absence of subrogation, OOL would be enriched at BFC's expense and that, *prima facie*, such enrichment would be unjust. The bank advanced the DM30 m upon the mistaken assumption that it was obtaining a postponement letter which would be effective to give it priority over any intra-group indebtedness. It would not otherwise have done so. On the construction of the letter adopted by Robert Walker J (at first instance), namely that Holdings was purporting to contract on behalf of all companies in the Omni Group, the payment was made under a mistake as to Holdings' authority. On the construction adopted by the Court of Appeal, the mistake was as to the power of Holdings to ensure that other group companies would postpone their claims. For my part, I prefer the construction adopted by the judge. But I do not think that, for present purposes, it matters which view one takes. In either case, BFC failed to obtain that priority over intra-group indebtedness which was an essential part of the transaction under which it paid money. It may have attached more importance to the pledge of the shares but the provision of the postponement letter was a condition of completion. The result of the transaction is that BFC's DM30 m has been used to reduce the debt secured by RTB's first charge and that this reduction will, by reason of OOL's second charge, enure wholly to the latter's advantage.

[His Lordship examined and rejected the grounds on which the Court of Appeal decided that the enrichment of OOL would not be unjust, and continued:]

In my view, the phrase, 'keeping the charge alive' needs to be handled with some care. In a case in which the whole of the secured debt is repaid, the charge is not kept alive at all. It is discharged and ceases to exist. In a case like the present, in which part of the secured debt is repaid, the charge remains alive only to secure the remainder of the debt for the benefit of the original chargee. Nothing can affect his rights and there is no question of competition between him and the party claiming subrogation.

It follows that subrogation as against OOL, which is all that BFC claims in the action, would not give it greater rights than it bargained for. All that would happen is that OOL would be prevented from being able to enrich itself to the extent that BFC's money paid off the RTB charge. This is fully within the scope of the equitable remedy.

Millett, PJ, in 'Tracing the proceeds of fraud' [1991] 107 LQR 71, submits that the requirement for a breach of trust or some other fiduciary obligation in order to initiate the tracing process in equity is indefensible and should be discarded. He declares:

> The doctrine can be reconsidered only by the House of Lords. It assumes that tracing is a product of equity's exclusive rather than its auxiliary jurisdiction; but it is far from clear that this is so. It has been suggested (Jacobs, *Law of Trusts in Australia*, 4th edn, 1977, p 570) that it rests upon a misreading of the decision of the House of Lords in *Sinclair v Brougham* [see above, p 927], a case which, it has been justly observed, 'is largely what one chooses to make of it'.
>
> The requirement is, in fact, less restrictive of equity's ability to intervene than is often supposed. In the first place, it is not necessary that the fund to be traced should have been the subject of fiduciary obligations before it got into the wrong hands; it is sufficient that the payment to the defendant itself gave rise to a fiduciary relationship: *Chase Manhattan Bank NA v Israel-British Bank Ltd* [see above, p 935].
>
> In the second place, the requirement is readily satisfied in most cases of commercial fraud, since the embezzlement of a company's funds almost inevitably involves a breach of fiduciary duty on the part of one of the company's employees or agents. The question has been asked: 'What sort of fiduciary is relevant for tracing purposes and why?' An answer was suggested in *Agip (Africa) Ltd v Jackson* [1990] Ch 265, p 290. He need not be a director or a signatory on the company's bank account. It is sufficient that he was a person whose fiduciary position gave him control of the company's funds or provided him with the opportunity to misdirect them.
>
> The only situation, in practice, in which it may be impossible to invoke the assistance of equity is where the money has been stolen by a thief. In England, at least, it would be heretical to regard a thief as a fiduciary or a simple theft as giving rise to a constructive trust ... There is no reason, in principle, why equity should not intervene in such a case on the basis of a resulting trust. Theft does not deprive the true owner of his legal title; *a fortiori*, it does not deprive him of his equitable title. It has never been a requirement of the equitable tracing claim that the legal and equitable titles should be divided. The requirement that the loss must have arisen from a breach of fiduciary duty is difficult to understand and impossible to defend.

Box v Barclays Bank plc [1998] 1 All ER 108, HC

In *Box v Barclays Bank plc* (above, p 328), Ferris J considered the plaintiffs' claim to trace in equity and reasoned thus:

> **Ferris J:** Mr Browne-Wilkinson (counsel for the plaintiffs) argued that, even if the plaintiff cannot succeed in a common law claim for money had and received, they can trace their money in equity into Sylcon's No 1 account and are entitled to recover it from the bank unless the bank is able to show that it had no knowledge of the plaintiffs' rights. He referred me to the succinct statement of Millett J in *Agip (Africa) Ltd v Jackson* [1990] Ch 265, p 290:

> The tracing claim in equity gives rise to a proprietary remedy which depends on the continued existence of the trust property in the hands of the defendant. Unless he is a *bona fide* purchaser for value without notice, he must restore the trust property to its rightful owner if he still has it. But even a volunteer who has received trust property cannot be made subject to a personal liability to account for it as a constructive trustee, if he has parted with it without having previously acquired some knowledge of the existence of the trust.

The bank cannot, he contended, claim that it has parted with the plaintiffs' property because, in accordance with the rule in *Re Hallett's Estate* [1880] 13 Ch D 696, it is to be deemed to have used its own money, not the plaintiffs' in making whatever payments have been made and debited to Sylcon's account.

This argument cannot prevail in the light of my earlier conclusion that the relationship between the plaintiffs and Sylcon was purely contractual, not that of trustee and beneficiary. Equitable tracing is only available where there is an equity to trace, which requires that there must be an initial fiduciary relationship between the person claiming to trace and the party who is said to have misapplied that person's money (see *Snell's Equity*, 29th edn, 1991, London: Sweet & Maxwell, p 302 and *Agip*, p 290 [above, p 466]).

That, by itself, is a complete answer to the claim to trace in equity. But there is another equally complete answer, namely, that it is impossible to trace in equity through an overdrawn account (see *Re Goldcrop Exchange Ltd* [1995] AC 74, pp 104–05; the *Westdeutsche* case [1996] AC 669, p 105G–H; and – most explicitly – *Bishopsgate Investment Management Ltd v Homan* [1995] Ch 211, particularly pp 220F–20H and 222D–22F). It is not necessary in these circumstances to consider whether or not the bank had notice of the plaintiffs' rights. There were no relevant rights for the bank to have notice of.

SUPPLEMENTARY READING

Andrews, N, 'Tracing and subrogation' (1996) 55 CLJ 199

Beatson, J and Prentice, D, 'Restitutionary claims by company directors' (1990) 106 LQR 365

Birks, P, 'Proprietary restitution: an intelligible approach' (1995) 9 Tru LI 43

Birks, P, 'Tracing misused – *Bank Tejarat v Hong Kong and Shanghai Banking Corp*' (1995) 9 Tru LI 91

Birks, P, 'Tracing, subrogation and change of position' (1996) 9 Tru LI 124

Chambers, R, 'Tracing, trusts and liens' (1997) 11 Tru LI 86

Goldsworth, J and Andre, R, ' Exculpation: a trustee's last hope' (1997) 3 T & T 22

Goode, R, 'The right to trace and its impact on commercial transactions' (1976) 92 LQR 360 and 528

Ham, R, 'Trustees' liability' (1995) 9 Tru LI 21

Hayton, D, 'Rights of creditors against trustees and trust funds' (1997) 11 Tru LI 58

Jones, A, 'Identification of improperly appropriated trust money – mixing and *Maxwell*' [1996] Conv 129

Jones, G, '*Ultra vires* swaps: the common law and equitable fall out' (1996) 55 CLJ 432

Kenny, A, 'Living up to expectations' (1996) 146 NLJ 348

Maudsley, R, 'Proprietary remedies for the recovery of money' (1959) 75 LQR 234

McBride, N, 'Trustees' exemption clauses' (1998) 57 CLJ 33

Mitchell, C, 'Subrogation, tracing and the *Quistclose* principle' [1995] LMCLQ 45

Oakley, AJ, 'Proprietary claims and their priority in insolvency' (1995) 54 CLJ 377

Oliver, P, 'The extent of equitable tracing' (1995) 9 Tru LI 78

Panesar, S, ' Actual fraud and gross negligence: the scope of trustee exemption clauses' (1998) 19 BLR 8

Rickett, C, 'Equitable compensation: the Giant stirs' (1996) 112 LQR 521

Sealy, L, 'Contract to sell unascertained goods – no passing of property, no equitable or restitutionary relief' (1994) 53 CLJ 443

Smith, L, 'Tracing into the payment of a debt' (1995) 54 CLJ 290

Ulph, J, 'Harmony in the law: hitting the target? *Target Holdings v Redferns*' (1995) 9 Tru LI 86

CHAPTER 22

THE TAXATION OF TRUSTS

When a trust is validly created, there are three parties who become potentially liable to pay the tax: namely, the settlor, trustees and beneficiaries. The liability of each is mutually exclusive, that is, when the settlor of a trust becomes liable to income tax, the trust itself (trustees and beneficiaries) is exempt from liability to income tax and, similarly, when the trustees become liable to income tax, the beneficiaries and the settlor are not liable.

INCOME TAX

Income tax is chargeable on individuals. Each individual is entitled to claim personal reliefs against his income and may become liable to lower, basic and higher rates of income tax on his taxable income. Trustees, on the other hand, are regarded as a single, continuing body of persons distinct from the persons who are appointed trustees. Accordingly, they are treated as a separate taxable entity and the death or retirement of trustees has little or no tax consequences. Since trustees are not individuals, they are not liable to higher rate tax nor are they entitled to tax reliefs. Trustees are liable to basic rate tax and, sometimes, the additional rate tax.

There are no special income tax provisions which make trustees liable to income tax whenever a trust is in existence. The basic rule is that the person in receipt of the income (or entitlement to the income) is liable to pay income tax. This may be the trustees or the beneficiaries. Thus, prior to the exercise of their discretion under a discretionary trust, the trustees are liable to pay income tax on the income because no object can be said to be entitled to the income. On the other hand, if the beneficiary is absolutely entitled to the income from the trust fund, then he is liable to income tax irrespective of whether the income is paid to him or not. The general rule is illustrated by *Williams v Singer*.[1] The trustees authorised a third party, under mandate, to pay the dividends from shares directly to the beneficiary who was resident and domiciled outside the UK. The Revenue assessed the trustees to income tax but the court held that the chargeable person was the beneficiary.

> **Viscount Cave:** The fact is that if the Income Tax Acts are examined, it will be found that the person charged with the tax is neither the trustee nor the beneficiary as such, but the person in actual receipt and control of the income

1 [1921] 1 AC 65.

> which it is sought to reach. The object of the Acts is to secure for the State a proportion of the profits chargeable, and this end is attained by the simple and effective expedient of taxing the profits where they are found. If the beneficiary receives it he is liable to be assessed on them. If the trustee receives and controls them, he is so liable.

When the trustees are liable to income tax, they are assessable under the income tax Schedule and Case appropriate to the source of income, for example, trustees carrying on a trade are assessed under Schedule D, Case I; rental income from unfurnished dwellings are assessable under Schedule A.

Subject to provisions to the contrary, no management expenses (that is, the expenses of managing the trust as opposed to the expenses of managing the trust property) are deductible by the trustees from the income liable to income tax. In *Aikin v McDonald's Trustees*,[2] trustees were assessed to tax under Schedule D, Case V on the gross income received from trust properties abroad. They claimed to be entitled to deduct management expenses but the court rejected their claim.

> **Lord McLaren:** The management of the trustees is really of private and domestic use. I think it is plain enough that the only kind of deductions allowed is expenditure incurred in earning profits and no deduction ... is allowable for expenditure incurred in managing profits which have been already earned and reduced into money.

Additional rate of tax for discretionary and accumulation trusts

An additional rate of tax payable by trustees was introduced in 1973 in order to penalise trustees who fail to distribute the income from discretionary and accumulation trusts. The rate of tax is 10% or such other rate as Parliament may determine (see s 832(1) of the Income and Corporation Taxes Act 1988 (ICTA)). Under s 686 of the ICTA 1988, the additional rate of tax does not apply to the income which is treated as belonging to the settlor or income arising under charitable trusts or any person other than the trustees. The 'income utilised in defraying the expenses of trustees which are properly chargeable to income' (that is, management expenses) are deductible from the trust income before the additional rate liability arises. These are treated as expenses which, under the general law, would be chargeable to income. Thus, in *Carver v Duncan*,[3] annual premiums on endowment assurance policies effected in order to meet future capital liabilities were not deductible from the gross trust income.

By virtue of s 687, where under a discretionary trust the trustees make a payment which is treated as the income of the beneficiary the payment is

2 (1894) 3 TC 306.

3 [1985] STC 356.

treated as a net amount equivalent to a gross sum from which basic and additional rates of tax had been deducted and such tax is assessable on the trustees. The tax assessable under s 687 may be set off against the tax assessed under s 686. Thus, if the basic and additional rates of tax have remained unchanged between accrual to the discretionary trustees and distribution to the objects, no further tax is payable by the trustees. Where the rates have increased, the trustees will be liable to pay the amount of the increase.

From the beneficiary's point of view, any income tax paid by the trustees under ss 686 and 687 is treated as tax paid by the beneficiary. Accordingly, he is entitled to credit the trustees' liability against his own liability for higher rate tax and is liable to tax on any surplus income. If the beneficiary is not a tax payer (because his reliefs are equivalent to or exceed his income) he is entitled to reclaim the tax paid on his behalf. If the trustees make a distribution out of capital and this is treated as a capital receipt of the beneficiary, the payment will not be charged to income tax. In *Stevenson v Wishart*,[4] discretionary trust distributions were made out of capital to meet the medical and nursing expenses of the beneficiary. The court held that these payments were outside the additional rate charge.

Beneficiary's income

The beneficiary under a trust is liable to income tax on income received from the trustees during a year of assessment or in respect of income to which he has become entitled as of right. In some cases (for example, s 687), the income is required to be 'grossed up' at the basic and additional rates of tax.

The basic rule is that the beneficiary is liable to income tax on the income accruing to the trustees, if he is beneficially entitled as of right to the income as it arises, whether or not he receives the income. In *Baker v Archer-Shee*,[5] a tenant for life claimed that because she did not receive the income that had arisen under a trust, she was not liable to income tax. The court rejected this argument and decided that she was liable to income tax.

Similarly, where the trustees provide benefits in kind to the beneficiaries which are convertible into money the beneficiary is assessable on the value of the benefits received. In *Lord Tollemache v IRC*,[6] the beneficiary was assessed on the annual value of a mansion which the trustees allowed the beneficiary to occupy.

Under s 31 of the Trustee Act 1925 (see above, p 806), the beneficiary is not liable to income tax when income under a trust is accumulated during his

4 [1987] 2 All ER 428.

5 [1927] AC 844.

6 [1926] All ER 568.

infancy prior to enjoying a vested interest in possession. In *Stanley v IRC*,[7] the Revenue assessed the beneficiary (a minor) to surtax in respect of income to which he was entitled contingently on attaining the age of majority. During minority, the income was accumulated. The court held that the beneficiary was not liable to tax. However, subject to any contrary intention manifested by the trust instrument, on attaining the age of majority a beneficiary under a trust attains a vested interest in the income under s 31 of the Trustee Act 1925. Thus, it is immaterial whether or not the trustees pay him the income. Such a beneficiary would be the appropriate chargeable person (*IRC v Hamilton-Russell's Executors*).[8]

Where the trustees in their discretion make payments to a beneficiary from accumulated income at a time when the beneficiary does not have a vested interest in the income, the payments are treated as capital (or more precisely as capitalised income) and not liable to income tax (see *IRC v Blackwell Minor's Trustees*).[9]

Anti-avoidance provisions

A large number of anti-avoidance provisions have been enacted in Pt XV of the ICTA 1988, as amended (ss 660–85), with the object of preventing a settlor alienating his income in order to avoid income tax. These provisions are extremely complex and beyond the scope of this book.

The statutory provisions when they operate have two consequences:

(i) in some cases, they treat the settlement income as belonging to the settlor for 'all' purposes of income tax (see ss 660–82 of the ICTA 1988). The settlement is thus rendered ineffective for income tax purposes because the settlor is treated as though he did not alienate the income subject to the settlement. In addition, the provisions deny the beneficiary the right to claim a repayment of basic rate income tax;

(ii) in other cases, the provisions treat the income as the settlor's only for the purpose of excess liability, for example, higher rate income tax (see ss 683–85). The effect is that the income is retransferred to the settlor for the purpose of the higher rate tax, but the beneficiary has the right to reclaim the basic rate of tax.

To avoid the provisions of Pt XV of the ICTA 1988, a settlement is required to be created for any individual, other than the infant and unmarried child of the settlor, provided that there is no discretionary power to benefit the settlor or his spouse, and the entire settled income is distributed and the payment of the income under the settlement is capable of exceeding six years. Alternatively,

7 [1944] 1 All ER 230.

8 [1943] 1 All ER 474.

9 (1925) 10 TC 235.

the same result may be achieved by irrevocable covenanted payments to charities which are capable of exceeding three years.

CAPITAL GAINS TAX

Capital gains tax was introduced by the Finance Act 1965 which had been repealed and replaced by the Capital Gains Tax Act 1979. This Act was also repealed and replaced by the Taxation of Chargeable Gains Act 1992 (TCGA).

Capital gains tax is charged on the chargeable gains accruing to a person (other than a company) on the disposal of an asset during a year of assessment (s 1 of the TCGA 1992).

A chargeable gain means any capital gain accruing to a taxpayer on the disposal of an asset after 6 April 1982 as reduced by reliefs and allowances. Generally speaking, a chargeable gain is the difference between the consideration in money or money's worth, received or deemed to have been received, on a disposal of the asset, reduced by the cost of acquisition (including incidental expenses of acquisition and disposal and expenditure on the improvement of the asset which is reflected in the asset on the date of disposal) and indexation allowance on the cost of acquisition and improvement expenditure.

The taxable gain is added to the chargeable person's income for the relevant year of assessment and is subject to income tax at the individual's marginal rate of tax. Thus, an individual's highest rate of tax for the year of assessment ending 1999 is 40%. Trustees are not individuals but are treated as a single and continuing body of persons distinct from the persons who from time to time may be trustees. The trustees' highest rate of income tax for the year ending 1999 is 33% (that is, basic rate of 23% + additional rate of 10%). Since capital gains will not be chargeable to the additional rate tax, it follows that the highest rate of tax chargeable on trustees, in respect of capital gains made during a year of assessment, will be 23%. In addition, trustees are entitled to 50% of the annual exemption available to individuals (1998–99 – 50% of £6,800 = £3,400) in respect of gains accruing to the trust.

No capital gains tax is charged on death (but inheritance tax is chargeable). On a person's death, the assets of which a deceased was competent to dispose are deemed to be acquired by his personal representatives for a consideration equal to their market value on the date of death (s 65 of the TCGA 1992). Thus, the personal representatives acquire a new acquisition cost (base value) for the assets. Furthermore, when the personal representatives distribute the assets to those entitled under the will or on intestacy, these 'legatees' are treated as acquiring the assets on the date and for the value at which the personal representatives acquired the assets.

In the context of the trust, there are three separate occasions when a disposal may be effected, namely:

(i) the creation of a settlement;

(ii) disposals, actual and notional, by the trustees during the continuance of the settlement;

(iii) disposals by the beneficiaries.

Creation of the settlement

On the creation of a settlement (whether revocable or not and irrespective of whether or not the settlor is a beneficiary or one of the trustees), a disposal is effected by the settlor (s 70 of the TCGA 1992). A settlement or settled property is defined as any property held in trust (s 68 of the TCGA 1992) with the exception of 'property held by a person as nominee for another or as trustee for another person absolutely entitled as against the trustee or where a person would be so entitled but for being an infant or other person under disability' (s 60 of the TCGA 1992). Thus, property held on trust by bare trustees or trustees who would be bare trustees but for the beneficiaries being infants or under a disability, will be treated as unsettled property (see *Tomlinson v Glyn's Executors*).[10] In addition, property held on trust for two or more persons who are or would be jointly entitled is unsettled. The expression 'jointly' includes the interests of both joint tenants and tenants in common but does not include the interests in property enjoyed in succession (see *Kidson v McDonald*;[11] *Stephenson v Barclays Bank*[12] and *Booth v Ellard*).[13]

Disposals by trustees

In addition to actual disposals (for example, sales) by the trustees, the Act provides a number of occasions when a deemed disposal will take place.

Section 71 of the TCGA 1992 provides that when a person becomes absolutely entitled to any settled property (including the situation when the beneficiary would so become but for being an infant or person under disability) as against the trustees, all the assets to which he becomes so entitled will be treated as disposed of and reacquired by the trustees at their market value. Insofar as s 71 applies, the property will be treated as unsettled. This is known as an 'exit' charge.

10 [1970] 1 Ch 112.

11 [1975] 2 WLR 566.

12 [1975] 1 WLR 882.

13 [1980] 3 All ER 569.

For example, T1 and T2, the trustees hold shares on trust for A until he attains the age of 25 or marries. When A attains the age of 25, the property becomes unsettled and there is a disposal by the trustees at market value.

It is irrelevant that the person becoming absolutely entitled to the property does not become beneficially entitled but becomes entitled to the property in a representative capacity. Thus, if trust property is resettled under a new settlement, the trustees of the 'new' settlement will become absolutely entitled as against the trustees of the 'old' settlement thereby triggering off a liability to capital gains tax under s 71. On the other hand, the creation of a sub-trust, which is not distinctive or separate from the original trust, is treated as part of the original trust as both sets of trustees are treated as a single body and no disposal is effected under s 71.

A settlement may be treated as separate from another if some identifiable property is subjected to trusts which are separate and distinct from the original trust. It has been suggested that the distinctive feature of the 'new' trust is such that 'no one will ever again need to refer to the original settlement except to confirm that it has ceased to exist', *per* Brightman J in *Hoare Trustees v Gardiner*.[14] This new trust may be created by the exercise of a power of appointment or advancement (under s 32 of the Trustee Act 1925) or a variation of beneficial interests under the Variation of Trusts Act 1958 or under the *Saunders v Vautier* rule.

It is a difficult question to decide whether a new trust or a sub-trust has been created. See *Roome v Edwards*;[15] *Swires v Renton*;[16] and *Bond v Pickford*.[17]

Death of the life tenant

In accordance with the policy that death does not trigger a liability to capital gains tax, s 73 enacts that the termination of a life interest in possession as a result of the death of the life tenant gives rise to a deemed disposal and reacquisition at market value but no capital gains tax is chargeable. Thus, if the property becomes unsettled by virtue of the death of the life tenant, a new capital gains tax base at market value will be adopted but there is no liability to capital gains tax.

For example, if trustees, T1 and T2 hold shares on trust for A for life with remainder to B absolutely. When A dies, there is an uplift in the capital gains base at market value but no liability to capital gains tax.

14 [1978] 1 All ER 991.

15 [1981] 1 All ER 736.

16 [1991] STC 490.

17 [1983] STC 517.

A similar rule applies if the settlement continues by virtue of the death of the life tenant. No capital gains tax is chargeable. If the property reverts to the settlor on the death of the life tenant, a possible uplift in the acquisition cost was considered too generous, instead the disposal and acquisition is treated as though neither a gain nor a loss accrues to the trustees. In short, the notional disposal proceeds are equivalent to the amount of the allowable expenditure incurred.

Disposal of beneficial interests

Section 76 of the TCGA 1992 enacts that no chargeable gain accrues on the disposal by a beneficiary of an interest under a settlement.

For example, trustees hold property on trust for A for life, remainder to B absolutely. If A disposes of his interest under the trust to C so that the latter enjoys the interest for so long as A is alive, no liability to capital gains tax arises.

Proviso to s 76(1) of the Trusts and Capital Gains Act 1992

The proviso declares that if the interest was acquired for money or money's worth (including an interest derived from such person), an actual or deemed disposal by such person will be chargeable to capital gains tax.

INHERITANCE TAX

Inheritance tax (IHT) was introduced by the Inheritance Tax Act (IHTA) 1984 as a replacement for capital transfer tax. Inheritance tax is designed to tax transfers of wealth which occur on death and certain *inter vivos* transfers including transfers of value made within seven years of the transferor's death (known as potentially exempt transfers). IHT is charged on individuals including trustees and executors but does not apply to transfers by companies.

Section 4 of the IHTA 1984 provides that on the death of an individual a deemed transfer of value occurs immediately before his death in respect of property of which the deceased was beneficially entitled immediately before his death. Subject to exemptions and reliefs, this transfer is aggregated with property transferred by the deceased within seven years prior to his death. The rate of tax on death is 40% which is double the lifetime rate.

Section 1 of the Act charges tax on the value transferred by a chargeable transfer. Section 3 defines a chargeable transfer as any disposition or transfer of value which reduces the estate of the transferor. The expression 'disposition' is not defined in the Act. But, this is an ordinary English expression and covers all forms of transfers or alienation of property including gifts, settlements, exchanges and sales and has been extended to include an omission to exercise a right except accidental or non-deliberate omission. A disposition is not a transfer of value if the transaction entered into is commercial and is not intended to confer a gratuitous benefit.

In addition, where a transferor disposes of property by way of a gift and, at the same time or subsequently, he retains an interest or possession or enjoyment in the property, the transfer may be treated as a nullity. If the donor retains an interest immediately before his death, the property may be included in his estate even though the transfer was made more than seven years before his death (see s 102 of the Finance Act 1986). If the reservation of the benefit ceases during his (donor's) lifetime, he is treated as making a potentially exempt transfer at that time.

Potentially exempt transfers (PETs)

A potentially exempt transfer is defined in s 3(A) of the IHTA 1984 as a lifetime disposition by an individual which becomes comprised in the estate of the transferee or increases the estate of the transferee or constitutes a gift into an accumulation and maintenance trust or trust for disabled persons.

The effect of a PET is that provided the transferor outlives the transfer by more than seven years, the PET becomes an exempt transfer and no inheritance tax is payable on such transfers of value. If, however, the transferor dies within seven years of the transfer, the transfer of value enters the transferor's cumulative total of chargeable transfers at the value when the transfer was made and the tax payable on the deceased's estate may need to be recalculated. In the interim period, it is assumed that the transfer will prove to be exempt.

Settlements with an interest in possession are treated as PETs. Accordingly, the *inter vivos* creation of such settlements qualify as PETs. Likewise, the *inter vivos* termination of the interest in possession may also constitute a PET provided that the settlement continues with an interest in possession.

For example, a settlor, S, creates a trust in favour of X for life or until marriage, remainder to Y for life, remainder to Z absolutely. The creation of the trust *inter vivos* constitutes a PET on the part of the settlor. If X's life interest is terminated *inter vivos* (by surrender or marriage) so that Y's life interest is activated, X will be treated as making a PET in favour of Y.

Settlements without an interest in possession (such as discretionary trusts) are not PETs. Accordingly, the transfer into such settlements are chargeable in the hands of the settlor.

Inheritance tax in respect of settled property

Following the creation of a settlement, the trustees' liability to IHT varies with the nature of the settlement in existence. There are the following three main types of settlements dealt with by the Act:

(i) settlements with an interest in possession;

(ii) settlements without an interest in possession;

(iii) settlements which are given special treatment such as accumulation and maintenance trusts.

A 'settlement' is defined in s 43(2) of the IHTA 1984 as any disposition of property whereby the property is:

(a) held in trust for persons in succession or subject to a contingency; or

(b) held by trustees on trust to accumulate the income or with the power to make payments out of the income at the discretion of the trustees; or

(c) charged with the payment of any annuity or other periodical payment for life or other limited or terminable period.

This definition is not as wide as the definition of a 'settlement' for income tax purposes.

Section 43(2)(a) covers life and contingent interests, for example, on trust for A for life, remainder to B absolutely. Likewise, a gift on trust for A absolutely provided that he attains the age of 25. But concurrent interests for persons of full age and sound mind are outside of s 43(2)(a), for example, on trust for A and B equally (this is also unsettled property for capital gains tax, see above).

Section 43(2)(b) applies to accumulation or discretionary trusts.

Section 43(2)(c) includes annuities and periodical payments charged on property as well as leases for lives or a period ascertainable by reference to death.

Settlor

Section 44(1) of the IHTA 1984 adopts the widest possible definition of a settlor including any person by whom the settlement was made directly or indirectly and includes any person who has provided funds directly or indirectly for the purpose of, or in connection with, the settlement or has made a reciprocal arrangement with another person to make the settlement. This follows the income tax definition of the settlor and is wide enough to include one or more settlors in relation to a settlement.

Trustee

Section 45 of the IHTA 1984 adopts the ordinary meaning of this term. In addition to persons named as trustees, the term includes any person in whom the settled property or its management is vested.

Settlements with an interest in possession

Subject to a number of exceptions, s 52 of the IHTA 1984 imposes a charge to inheritance tax on the trustees when an interest in possession is terminated.

There is no statutory definition of an 'interest in possession' and its meaning is to be discerned by having regard to general principles of property law. An interest in possession subsists if the beneficiary has a present right to present possession of property, for example, a vested life interest. On the other hand, a present or future right to future possession is not enjoyed as an interest in possession, for example, a remainder or reversionary interest or a contingent interest. The objects under a discretionary trust do not have an interest in the property (prior to the exercise of the discretion) but merely a 'hope' of acquiring an interest. See *Gartside v IRC* (1968) (above, p 198).

In 1976, the Board of Inland Revenue published a Statement of Practice concerning their understanding of an interest in possession. The statement is to the effect that an individual has an interest in possession if he has an immediate entitlement to the income produced as it arises but if the interest is subject to a power of defeasance after it arises (such as a power to accumulate or to withhold the income) this negatives the existence of an interest in possession. This Practice Statement was unsuccessfully challenged in the House of Lords in *Re Pilkington, Pearson v IRC*.[18] By a settlement dated November 1964, capital and income were transferred to trustees for the benefit of the settlor's three daughters in equal shares. The settlement also provided the trustees with an overriding power to appoint the whole or part of the fund to the same objects or to accumulate so much of the income as the trustees think fit. On 20 March 1976, the trustees appointed a sum of £16,000 (part of the capital) to one of the objects, Fiona. The Revenue contended that capital transfer tax (now inheritance tax) was payable for, prior to the appointment, Fiona did not enjoy an interest in possession because the trustees were under a duty to consider whether the income should be paid to the objects in equal shares or be accumulated. The appointment gave Fiona an interest in possession (which she never had). The court held in favour of the Revenue; the presence of the overriding power to accumulate the income prevented a present right of present enjoyment arising.

18 [1980] 2 All ER 479.

Viscount Dilhorne: The sisters never secured an interest in possession for they never acquired the right to enjoyment of anything. Their enjoyment of any income from the trust fund depended on the trustees' decision as to the accumulation of income. They would only have a right to any income from the trust fund if the trustees decided it should not be accumulated or if they failed to agree that it should be or if they delayed a decision on this matter for so long that a decision then to accumulate and withhold income from the sisters would have been unreasonable.

Extent of the beneficiary's entitlement (chargeable slice)

The rules for determining the value of a beneficial interest in possession in settled property are enacted in ss 49 and 50 of the IHTA 1984.

Under s 49, a person beneficially entitled to an interest in settled property is regarded as beneficially entitled to the property (capital) in which the interest subsists, that is, the underlying assets. In short, the settled property or capital is treated as part of the beneficiary's estate.

For example, if a plot of land, Blackacre, is held on trust for A for life, remainder to B absolutely. A is treated as beneficially entitled to Blackacre (for IHT purposes) and not merely a life interest in it.

Under s 50, where the beneficiary is entitled to an interest in part of the income, the chargeable interest is treated as subsisting in an appropriate portion of the property or capital.

For example, if the income from Blackacre is held on trust for A, B and C equally. Each of them is entitled to a one third share of the capital.

Since a transfer of value is defined in terms of a reduction in the value of the transferor's estate, it follows that the creation of such a settlement will not be a chargeable event *inter vivos* if the settlor retains a life interest in the entire income from the trust because the settlor's estate has not been reduced. A similar principle applies if the settlor's spouse is the life tenant.

If the beneficiary is entitled to a specified amount of the income (annuity) rather than a proportion of the trust income, his interest will be equated with such part of the settled property that produces the quantified amount, that is, the annuity. This will be calculated by reference to the income yield from the property.

For example, if Blackacre is settled on trust to pay the income to A for life subject to an annuity of £100 per annum payable to B for life with remainder to C absolutely. Assuming Blackacre produces income of £1,000 per annum B will be entitled to one 10th of Blackacre and A is entitled to nine 10ths of Blackacre.

If the beneficiary is entitled to the use and enjoyment of the property together with others, he will be treated as having an interest equal to the proportion which the annual value of his interest bears to the aggregate of the annual values of all the beneficiaries including himself.

Chargeable events: ss 51–53 of the Inheritance Tax Act 1984

The events that are treated as dispositions by a person beneficially entitled to an interest in possession are stated in ss 51 to 53.

The beneficiary's circumstances determine the rate of IHT payable and whether any reliefs or exemptions are available. The value transferred is added to the beneficiary's cumulative total of chargeable transfers to ascertain the amount of tax payable and to determine his liability on subsequent transfers.

In effect, there is one clear occasion when IHT becomes payable: on the death of a person beneficially entitled to an interest in possession on settled property. The settled property (or part) is treated as forming part of his estate. The trustees settle the inheritance tax payable by reference to the deceased life tenant's rates and circumstances.

Subject to special anti-avoidance provisions, the *inter vivos* termination of a beneficial interest in possession will be a PET within s 3(A) of the IHTA 1984. The termination of such an interest may take the form of a gift, sale or exchange of the interest in possession. The effect is that inheritance tax is payable in the event of the life tenant dying within seven years of the termination.

A charge to inheritance tax arises when a transaction is entered into between the trustees on the one hand and any beneficiary or potential beneficiary or persons connected therewith on the other hand, which results in a depreciation of the value of the property, for example, where the trustees grant an unsecured free loan to the beneficiary which is not repayable on demand or a lease or sale of the trust property is made in favour of the beneficiary at an undervalue. The value of the depreciation of the trust property will be the value transferred.

Exceptions

The basic charging provisions take effect subject to the following exceptions:

(a) reverter to the settlor or the spouse of the settlor – inheritance tax is not chargeable on the termination of an interest in possession if the settled property then reverts to the settlor in his lifetime. The rationale behind this provision is that the settlor or spouse is merely resuming his former position. This exception does not apply if the settlor or spouse had acquired the reversionary interest for money or money's worth;

(b) dispositions for the maintenance of the family – where a disposition of an interest in possession is effected in order to maintain the disponer's family (children and dependant relatives), the termination of the interest will not be treated as the coming to an end of an interest;

(c) protective trust – the determination of the principal beneficiary's interest in property which is subject to a protective trust is not a chargeable event;

(d) order under the Inheritance (Provision for Family and Dependants) Act 1975 – an order under this Act terminating an interest in possession gives rise to no charge;

(e) trustees' remuneration – no charge to inheritance tax arises on the termination of an interest in possession paid to the trustees as reasonable remuneration;

(f) dispositions of reversionary interests – a reversionary interest, subject to two exceptions, is treated as excluded property. Accordingly, a disposition of a reversionary interest does not give rise to a charge to inheritance tax.

    A reversionary interest is defined in s 47 of the IHTA 1984 'as a future interest under a settlement, whether vested or contingent, including an interest expectant on the termination of an interest in possession'. A contingent or remainder interest are reversionary interests. Equally, a contingent life interest in remainder is a reversionary interest, for example, a gift on trust to A for life, remainder to B for life if he should survive A with remainder to C absolutely. B and C are entitled to reversionary interests.

    The rationale for exempting reversionary interests from the charge is that, since a life tenant in possession is treated as the beneficial owner of the whole (or part) of the capital, an element of double taxation would have arisen if a disposition of the reversionary interest in the same property was also chargeable. The Revenue is prepared to wait and tax the disposition by the life tenant.

    The two exceptions when reversionary interests will not be treated as excluded property are:

    (1) where the interest was acquired for money or money's worth; and

    (2) where the interest is expectant on the determination of a lease treated as settled property;

(g) charities – tax is not charged if the property is held on trust for charitable purposes on the termination of an interest in possession;

(h) variations and disclaimers – dispositions of the deceased may be altered, following death, by means of an instrument in writing of variation or disclaimer within two years following death. Such variation or disclaimer may be effected without incurring a second charge to inheritance tax. The variation or disclaimer is treated as having been made by the deceased immediately before death.

Settlements without an interest in possession (discretionary trusts)

There are special charges to inheritance tax in respect of settlements without an interest in possession, other than certain privileged trusts, the main ones being accumulation and maintenance trusts, protective trusts, trusts for disabled persons and charities.

The policy behind such charges is that such trusts offer an attractive vehicle for the avoidance of tax.

The philosophy for taxing such trusts is totally different from interests in possession trusts. Instead of attributing the fund to one of the beneficiaries, it is the settlement itself which is the taxable entity for inheritance tax purposes. Accordingly, the trustees are required to keep a record of chargeable transfers made but the settlement is taxed at the lifetime rates as it never dies.

Methods of charges

There are three modes of assessment in respect of discretionary trusts:

(1) the creation of the settlement;

(2) the periodic charge;

(3) the exit charge.

(1) Creation of the discretionary trust

This constitutes an immediately chargeable transfer for inheritance tax purposes. Such trusts are not PETs. If the settlement is created *inter vivos*, grossing up may exist unless inheritance tax is paid out of the fund. The effect is that the creation of such settlement increases the settlor's cumulative total by the value of the property settled.

If the settlor dies within seven years after the creation of such settlement, inheritance tax on the discretionary trust will be recalculated for PETs made by the settlor within seven years before his death will enter the settlor's cumulative total.

(2) Periodic charges: s 64 of the Inheritance Tax Act 1984

The principal charge to inheritance tax on settlements without an interest in possession occurs immediately before a 10 year anniversary. The value of property subject to such charge is the value of the relevant property in the settlement at that time. 'Relevant property' means the property which was settled (other than excluded property) in which no qualifying interest in possession subsists, with the exception of property settled on privileged trusts.

The 10 year anniversary is the 10th anniversary of the date on which the settlement commenced and subsequent anniversaries at 10 yearly intervals. But, no date before 1 April 1983 counts as a 10 year anniversary.

(3) Exit charges: s 65 of the Inheritance Tax Act 1984

A charge is imposed on trustees whenever settled property ceases to be relevant property.

The effect is that an exit charge arises whenever property ceases to be subject to a trust without an interest in possession, for example, trustees distribute capital to an object of a discretionary trust or create a sub-trust with an interest in possession.

In addition, a charge is imposed if the trustees make a disposition as a result of which the value of the relevant property is reduced, that is, a depreciatory transaction.

But, the exit charge does not apply in respect of:

(a) a payment of costs and expenses (so far as they are fairly attributable to relevant property); or

(b) a payment which is or will be income of any person for income tax purposes.

Accumulation and maintenance trusts: s 71 of the Inheritance Tax Act 1984

An accumulation and maintenance trust is, in effect, a trust without an interest in possession but which is given favourable treatment by the IHT regime.

The advantages enjoyed by such trusts are:

(a) the creation constitutes a PET;

(b) no inheritance tax is charged when a beneficiary becomes beneficially entitled to the settled property even becoming entitled to an interest in possession. Thus, there is no exit charge;

(c) the periodic charge is not applicable.

The effect is that once such a trust is created there is no inheritance tax liability.

An accumulation and maintenance trust is defined in s 71(1) and (2) and requires compliance with three conditions:

Condition 1

> One or more of the beneficiaries will, on or before attaining a specified age not exceeding 25, become entitled to an interest in possession in the settled property or part of it.

The requirement here is that a beneficiary has the potential of becoming entitled to an interest in possession within an upper age limit of 25.

Under s 31 of the Trustee Act, an infant beneficiary under a trust may obtain an interest in possession on attaining the age of majority, subject to any contrary intention (see above, p 806). If the beneficiary dies before attaining the specified age, such death is not treated as a chargeable occasion.

Condition 2

> No interest in possession subsists and the income is to be accumulated so far as it is not applied for the maintenance, education or benefit of such a person.

The requirement here is the non-existence of an interest in possession subsisting in the trust property. As soon as such an interest is enjoyed, the settlement ceases to be an accumulation and maintenance trust. As was pointed out earlier, under s 31 of the Trustee Act 1925, subject to any contrary intention, a beneficiary on attaining the age of 18 acquires a vested interest in possession. The settlement falls outside of s 71 but this does not give rise to a chargeable occasion.

The payment of the income to a beneficiary before he obtains a vested interest does not deprive the trust from being an accumulation and maintenance trust. In short, such payments have no effect for inheritance tax purposes. The payment will not attract the exit charge.

Condition 3

> Either:
>
> (a) not more than 25 years have elapsed since the commencement of the settlement; or
>
> (b) the beneficiaries are the children or grandchildren of a common grandparent, including widows and widowers of grandchildren.

Generally, once an accumulation and maintenance trust is set up, inheritance tax will rarely be payable. Exceptionally, an 'exit' charge may arise when:

(1) depreciatory transactions are entered into by trustees which reduce the value of the fund; or

(2) property is advanced for the benefit of a non-beneficiary; or

(3) property is resettled on trusts which are not accumulation and maintenance trusts.

Other trusts enjoying privileged treatment

Property leaving temporary charitable trusts:
s 70 of the Inheritance Tax Act 1984

When settled property is held temporarily for charitable purposes only, it will be subject to inheritance tax when it ceases to be held for charitable purposes and where trustees effect depreciatory transactions.

Protective trusts:
s 88 of the Inheritance Tax Act 1984

For the definition of a protective trust, see above, p 215. When the forfeiture event occurs, the principal beneficiary (life tenant) is deemed to continue to have an interest in possession for inheritance tax purposes. The effect is that the inheritance tax rules for interests in possession continue in respect of the trust even though, under trust law, a discretionary trust is created following the forfeiting event.

Trusts for the benefit of mentally or physically disabled persons:
s 89 of the Inheritance Tax Act 1984

If the disabled person creates such trust for his own benefit, the disposition is treated as an exempt transfer. If other settlors create such trusts, the transfer is treated as a PET. A payment out of the trust fund for the benefit of the disabled person is not a taxable distribution for it is exempt. If the payment is made to a person other than a disabled person, the trustees are treated has having made a PET. Accordingly, if the disabled person survives for seven years or more following the payment, the transfer is exempt.

SUPPLEMENTARY READING

Kirkbride, J, '*Fitzwilliam v IRC* – another success for the tax avoidance industry' [1994] Conv 67

Murphy, W, 'Fiona's fragile possession – *Pearson v IRC*' (1980) 43 MLR 712

INDEX